INTELLIGENCE AND NATIONAL SECURITY

The Secret World of Spies

An Anthology

Second Edition

Edited with Introductions by

Loch K. Johnson
University of Georgia
School of Public and International Affairs

James J. Wirtz
Naval Postgraduate School

New York   Oxford
OXFORD UNIVERSITY PRESS
2008

Oxford University Press, Inc., publishes works that further Oxford University's
objective of excellence in research, scholarship, and education.

Oxford   New York
Auckland   Cape Town   Dar es Salaam   Hong Kong   Karachi
Kuala Lumpur   Madrid   Melbourne   Mexico City   Nairobi
New Delhi   Shanghai   Taipei   Toronto

With offices in
Argentina   Austria   Brazil   Chile   Czech Republic   France   Greece
Guatemala   Hungary   Italy   Japan   Poland   Portugal   Singapore
South Korea   Switzerland   Thailand   Turkey   Ukraine   Vietnam

Published by Oxford University Press, Inc.
198 Madison Avenue, New York, New York 10016
http://www.oup.com

Oxford is a registered trademark of Oxford University Press

ISBN 978-0-19-533247-6

Printing number: 9 8 7 6 5 4 3 2

Printed in the United States of America
on acid-free paper

This book is dedicated to the memory of
Michael Handel, Naval War College,
and to H. Bradford Westerfield,
Yale University Professor Emeritus,
early leaders in the field of intelligence studies.

About This Book

The **Second Edition** of *Intelligence and National Security: The Secret World of Spies (An Anthology)* provides a comprehensive set of readings in the field of intelligence studies. Loch K. Johnson and James J. Wirtz's anthology, now in its second edition, spans a wide range of topics, from how the United States gathers and interprets information collected around the world to comparisons of the American intelligence system with the secret agencies of other nations. The readings are written by renowned experts, and each article is prefaced by a brief, framing introduction written by the editors.

The text addresses a wide range of material including: the meaning of strategic intelligence; methods of intelligence collection; intelligence analysis; the danger of intelligence politicization; relationships between intelligence officers and the policymakers they serve; covert action; counterintelligence; accountability and civil liberties; the implications of the major intelligence failures in 2001 and 2002 regarding, respectively, the terrorist attacks against the United States and the faulty estimates about weapons of mass destruction in Iraq; and intelligence as practiced in other nations.

This edition also contains valuable pedagogical features, including: 38 articles on intelligence by leading experts; 10 thorough, chapter-length introductory essays by Johnson and Wirtz, which serve as "road maps" for the reader; brief synopses of each article; author profiles; charts and figures on intelligence organization and leadership; discussion questions following each chapter; and a select bibliography. ✦

Contents

PART I. INTELLIGENCE IN THE UNITED STATES: AN INTRODUCTION

PART II. INTELLIGENCE COLLECTION

*New in the Second Edition.

the difficult task facing the Russian government as it creates new intelligence organizations from the remnants of the KGB.

Bruneau describes an issue that is often overlooked in the literature on transitions to democracy: the reform of intelligence organizations and their role in fledgling democracies.

A British investigation into intelligence failures regarding Iraqi WMD estimates produced several recommendations for reform, outlined here.

About the Editors

Loch K. Johnson is Regents Professor of Political Science at the University of Georgia, senior editor of the international journal *Intelligence and National Security*, and author of several books on U.S. American foreign policy and national security, including most recently *Seven Sins of American Foreign Policy* (Longman, 2007). He has won the Certificate of Distinction from the National Intelligence Study Center; the *Studies in Intelligence* Award from the Center for the Study of Intelligence; and the V.O. Key Prize from the Southern Political Science Association. He has served as secretary of the American Political Science Association and president of the International Studies Association, South. Johnson was special assistant to the chair of the Senate Select Committee on Intelligence in 1975–76; staff director of the House Subcommittee on Intelligence Oversight in 1977–79; and special assistant to Les Aspin, chair of the Aspin-Brown Commission on Intelligence, in 1995.

Born in Auckland, New Zealand, Professor Johnson received his Ph.D. in political science from the University of California, Riverside. At the University of Georgia, he has won the Josiah Meigs Prize, the university's highest teaching honor, as well as the Owens Award, its highest research honor. He also led the founding of the new School of Public and International Affairs at the University in 2001. Professor Johnson has been a Visiting Fellow at Oxford University (2003) and at Yale University (2005).

James J. Wirtz is professor in the Department of National Security Affairs, Naval Postgraduate School, Monterey, California. He is the author of *The Tet Offensive: Intelligence Failure in War* (Cornell University Press, 1991, 1994) and has co-edited several books, including *Strategic Denial and Deception* (Transaction, 2002) and *Balance of Power: Theory and Practice in the 21st Century* (Stanford, 2004). He is section chair of the Intelligence Studies Section of the International Studies Association and the President of the International Security and Arms Control Section of the American Political Science Association. He is general editor of the book series *Initiatives in Strategic Studies: Issues and Policies*, published by Palgrave MacMillan.

A native of New Jersey, Professor Wirtz earned his degrees in Political Science from Columbia University (M.Phil. 1987, Ph.D. 1989), and the University of Delaware (M.A. 1983, B.A. 1980). He was a John M. Olin Fellow at the Center for International Affairs, Harvard University, and a Visiting Professor at the Center for International Security and Cooperation, Stanford University. ✦

About the Contributors

Matthew M. Aid is managing director in the Washington, D.C., office of Citigate Global Intelligence and Security and co-editor of *Secrets of Signals Intelligence During the Cold War and Beyond* (2001).

James A. Barry served as deputy director of the CIA's Center for the Study of Intelligence.

Richard K. Betts is Leo A. Shifrin Professor of War and Peace Studies in the Department of Political Science at Columbia University and author of *Soldiers, Statesmen, and Cold War Crises* (1991).

Robert D. Blackwill served as Special Assistant to the President and Senior Director for European and Soviet Affairs on the National Security Council staff from 1989–90 and, more recently, as adviser to President George W. Bush on Iraq.

Thomas C. Bruneau, formerly of McGill University, teaches in the Department of National Security Affairs at the Naval Postgraduate School, Monterey, California, and is former director of the school's Center for Civil-Military Relations.

Conrad Burns, a third-term Republican U.S. senator from Montana, is a senior member of the Defense Appropriations Subcommittee and a former Marine.

William E. Burrows has written about aviation and space flight for more than three decades, with the *New York Times*, the *Washington Post*, and other newspapers, and has written as well for *Foreign Affairs* and the *New York Times Magazine*.

Frank Church, Democrat of Idaho, led the 1975–76 Senate inquiry into allegations of CIA abuses and served as chairman of the Senate Foreign Relations Committee.

Jack Davis, a former CIA analyst, is currently with the CIA's Sherman Kent Center.

Alan Dershowitz is Felix Frankfurter Professor of Law at Harvard University and author most recently of *Preemption: A Knife That Cuts Both Ways*.

John M. Diamond covers national security, foreign policy, and intelligence issues for the Washington Bureau of the *Chicago Tribune*, and from 1989 to 1999 he reported on national security matters in Washington for the Associated Press.

John J. Donohue is Leighton Homer Surbeck Professor of Law at Yale University.

Shlomo Gazit is a retired major general in the Israeli army and author of *Intelligence Estimates and the Decision Maker* (1988).

E. Drexel Godfrey, Jr., served in the Intelligence Directorate of the CIA from 1957 to 1970, as well as the CIA's director of current intelligence and subsequently as director of the Masters of Public Administration Program at Rutgers University in Newark.

Glenn Hastedt received his Ph.D. in political science from Indiana University, is chair of the Justice Studies Department at James Madison University, and is the author of *American Foreign Policy: Past, Present, Future,* 6th ed. (Prentice Hall).

Richard Helms served as Director of Central Intelligence in the United States from 1966 to 1973.

Michael Herman is a leading British intelligence scholar and author of *Intelligence Power in Peace and War* (2001).

Frederick P. Hitz, inspector general of the CIA from 1990 to 1998, is a lecturer in public and international affairs at Princeton University and lecturer at the University of Virginia School of Law.

Peter Jackson is Senior Lecturer in International Politics in the Department of International Politics at the University of Wales, Aberystwyth, co-editor of the international journal *Intelligence and National Security*, and author of *France and the Nazi Menace: Intelligence and Policy-Making, 1933–1939* (2000).

Ephraim Kahana is a senior research associate in the National Security Center at the University of Haifa and a faculty member in the Political Science Department in the Western Galilee College.

Mark M. Lowenthal, author of *Intelligence: From Secrets to Policy*, 3rd ed. (2006), has served as deputy assistant secretary for functional analysis in the State Department's Bureau of Intelligence Research, as staff director of the House Permanent Select Committee on Intelligence, and assistant director of Central Intelligence for analysis and production.

Frederic F. Manget is with the Office of Legal Affairs at the CIA.

Phyllis Provost McNeil is a former CIA intelligence officer, U.S. Naval officer, and director of the Federal Executive Programs at the Kennedy School of Government, Harvard University, who served on the staff of the Aspin-Brown Commission in 1995–96 and wrote the intelligence history section of its final report.

Kevin A. O'Brien is a former research associate with the Canadian Institute of Strategic Studies and is currently a senior analyst for RAND Europe.

Robert W. Pringle, a former CIA specialist on Soviet and Russian affairs, is currently an adjunct professor with the Patterson School of Diplomacy at the University of Kentucky.

Harry Howe Ransom is professor emeritus in political science at Vanderbilt University and the author of numerous studies on the U.S. intelligence community.

Patrick R. Riley is the *nom de plume* of a former officer in the CIA's Directorate of Operations, with a specialization in Aegean and Eastern Mediterranean affairs.

David B. Rivkin, Jr., is a partner in the Washington, D.C., office of Baker-Hostetler, and has served in legal and policy positions in the Reagan and George H. W. Bush Administrations.

Dakota Rudesill is a recent graduate of Yale University School of Law and severed in the U.S. Senate as a national security aide from 1995 to 2003.

Richard L. Russell is professor at the Near East-South Asia Center for Strategic Studies, the National Defense University, and is a former political-military analyst with the CIA, where he specialized in security issues in the Middle East and Europe.

Len Scott is Professor of International Politics at the University of Wales, Aberystwyth, where he is Director of the Centre for Intelligence and International Security Studies, and co-editor of *Understanding Intelligence in the Twenty-first Century: Journeys in Shadows* (2004).

Daniel Snow received an M.B.A. degree from the Marriott School of Management at Brigham Young University and has published on economic espionage.

Robert D. Steele is president of Open Sources, Inc., of Oakton, Virginia, and has served as an intelligence officer with the CIA and in the Marine Corps.

Stan A. Taylor, a professor of political science at Brigham Young University, has served as a staff member of the Senate Select Committee on Intelligence (1976–79) and has co-authored *America the Vincible: U.S. Foreign Policy for the Twenty-First Century* (1994).

Gregory F. Treverton served on the staff of the Church Committee and as vice chairman of the National Intelligence Council, and is currently with RAND in Santa Monica, California School of Law.

Stephen A. Vaden is a student at the Yale University School of Law.

Frederick L. Wettering is a retired CIA operations officer who managed clandestine operations in Europe and Africa for more than three decades, as well as a senior director for Africa for the National Security Council (1981–84) and the CIA's National Intelligence Officer for Africa from 1985 to 1987.

Amy B. Zegart is Associate Professor of Public Policy at the School of Public Affairs at the University of California, Los Angeles. ✦

Preface and Acknowledgments

As the references at the end of this anthology indicate, several fine texts on intelligence have been published in the past few years. Missing, though, has been a set of readings to accompany them. We have tried to fill that gap with this collection of outstanding articles on intelligence. To help orient those who use this book, we have added essays of our own to introduce each set of readings. Selecting the pieces for this anthology proved difficult, because space limitations forced us to exclude many first-rate articles. We believe, however, that the articles included in this volume will provide the reader with a good introduction to the breadth of this fascinating and relatively new field of scholarly inquiry.

We have a number of people to thank for helping us prepare this book. Most of all, we would like to express our appreciation to the authors and publishers whose work we reprint for allowing us to assemble their research in this format. We would also like to thank the Freedom House and the U.S. Senate for allowing us to draw on our earlier writings for them in the preparation of a couple of the introductory essays in this volume.

Finally, we want to acknowledge our debt to Claude Teweles of Roxbury Publishing Company for encouraging and supporting the first and second editions of this project; to Jim Ballinger, Scott Carter, and Kimmie Calvert-Lehman of Roxbury for production assistance; to Jackie Estrada for copyediting; to Rebecca Eversole and Scott Oney for proofreading; to William J. Daugherty (Armstrong Atlantic State University), Allen Dupont (Young Harris College), Bruce Farcau (Valencia Community College), Gardel Feurtado (The Citadel), George C. Fidas (The George Washington University), Glenn Hastedt (James Madison University), Ann Marie Kinnell (University of Southern Mississippi), Ken Kitts (Marion University), David Lorenzo (Virginia Wesleyan College), Pete Peterson (University of San Diego), Edward Schatz (Southern Illinois University), J. David Singer (University of Michigan), Stephen Sloan (University of Oklahoma), Frank J. Smist, Jr. (Rockhurst University), John D. Stempel (University of Kentucky), and Michael Turner (Alliant International University) for their guidance on article selection; to Leena S. Johnson for editorial suggestions; and to Lawrence J. Lamanna, Ph.D. candidate in International Affairs at the University of Georgia, for his research assistance. ◆

Part I

Intelligence in the United States: An Introduction

Hamlet: ". . . we defy augury. There is a special providence in the fall of a sparrow. If it be now, 'tis not to come—if it be not to come, it will be now—if it be not now, yet it will come—the readiness is all . . ."

—*Shakespeare*, Hamlet, *5.2.217–219*

Americans have mixed attitudes when it comes to intelligence and intelligence agencies. Some are fascinated with the image of the secret agent, spy, or covert operator who moves easily across international boundaries, uses the latest high-tech gadgetry, frequents only the trendiest resorts, and spends his or her time with glamorous members of the opposite sex. Intelligence professionals happily cultivate this image. A Central Intelligence Agency (CIA) identification card and a well-crafted story about secret operations has gotten more than one Agency mail clerk off the hook for speeding in some country village. Some see intelligence agencies as rogue elephants, giant bureaucracies beyond public scrutiny or the control of elected officials. From this perspective, intelligence agencies are threats to democratic institutions because they can be hijacked by conspiratorially minded politicians to undertake some nefarious scheme.

Given that public accountability is central to democracy, some wonder whether intelligence organizations that undertake secret operations, deal with secret information, and produce restricted reports are compatible with government based on democratic principles. Others never think at all about intelligence organizations or prefer to believe that intelligence agencies possess unlimited information about all significant threats to national security. Every so often, however, a tragic event shatters the complacency of this third group, which of course includes its share of government officials, leading to much recrimination and a hunt for those responsible for the latest intelligence failure.

Today we live in the Information Age, in a world undergoing an information revolution. The Internet and desktop computers allow millions of people to access and manipulate unlimited amounts of data and to transmit information to a global audience at virtually no cost. This type of capability was available only to large government organizations (for example, the CIA) just a few short decades ago. As the Al Qaeda terrorist attacks against the United States in September 2001 demonstrate, we also live in an age when intelligence, the ability to make sense out of this endless stream of data, is at a premium. The information revolution is affecting everyone, including intelligence analysts and the way they gather, analyze, and disseminate intelligence reports and estimates. But the full impact of the Information Age on intelligence agencies remains a matter of debate. With more state and nonstate actors acquiring the communications, transportation, and weaponry needed to influence world events, intelligence agencies face the challenge of trying to stay ahead of these actors before they can wreak havoc on U.S. interests. The Information Age has actually placed even greater pressure on the U.S. intelligence community to sift through this torrent of information to detect new threats to the United States and its interests.

Defining Intelligence

So what exactly is intelligence? Scores of definitions are available. Some are simple; Thomas F. Troy, for instance, defines intelligence as "knowledge of the enemy" (Troy 1991–92, 433). And some definitions, like the one offered by *The Economist*, are a bit more convoluted. According this respected periodical, intelligence is

> the painstaking collection and analysis of fact, the exercise of judgment, and clear and quick presentation. It is not simply what serious journalists would do if they had time; it is something more rigorous, continuous, and above all operational . . . that is to say related to something that somebody wants to do or may be forced to do. (quoted in Troy 1991–92, 442)

Many definitions of intelligence begin with Sherman Kent's description of the concept. Kent, an early theorist and practitioner of intelligence, defined it as *knowledge,* as *organization,* and as an *activity.* This definition allowed him to describe the way intelligence services collect and analyze information, the finished intelligence product that agencies provide to policymakers, and the way intelligence services are organized (Kent 1949). Mark Lowenthal, a contemporary intelligence theorist and practitioner, borrowed a page from Kent's work when he devised this succinct description of the three facets of intelligence:

> Intelligence as process: Intelligence can be thought of as the means by which certain types of information are required and requested, collected, analyzed, and disseminated, and as the way in which certain types of covert action are conceived and conducted.

> Intelligence as product: Intelligence can be thought of as the product of these processes, that is, as the analyses and intelligence operations themselves.

> Intelligence as organization: Intelligence can be thought of as the units that carry out its various functions. (Lowenthal 2006, 9)

We have added a twist to Lowenthal's definition by adding the word *strategic* to the term *intelligence* to suggest that the readings we have collected focus on issues of great importance, the stuff of national policy debate. *Strategic intelligence* contributes to the processes, products, and organizations used by senior officials to create and implement national foreign and defense policies. Strategic intelligence thus provides warning of immediate threats to vital national security interests and assesses long-term trends of interest to senior government officials. Strategic intelligence is of political importance because it can shape the course and conduct of U.S. policy.

Interdisciplinary Approach

In the essays that follow, our contributors address intelligence in the three ways described by Kent and Lowenthal. Sometimes they address intelligence as a process: Parts II and III, for example, address key facets of the "intelligence cycle," a commonly accepted way to divide the process of producing intelligence. Sometimes they write about intelligence as a product. References abound, for instance, to finished intelligence (research reports and analysis) and current intelligence (daily news summaries such as the *National Intelligence Daily*). The contributors also discuss the impact of organization on intelligence—that is, the way the structure of national intelligence and the relationship between and within intelligence organizations shapes intelligence processes and products.

Three academic disciplines have focused on the study of intelligence, and essays from each of these schools are contained in this volume. *Political scientists* are primarily interested in intelligence as a process. Drawing on the fields of psychology, organizational theory, security studies, and international relations, they explore the challenges inherent in developing accurate and timely estimates of current and future events. *Historians* provide compelling accounts of intelligence failures, explaining how the road to surprise, paved with what in hindsight appears to be clear indications of trouble, was missed or misinterpreted by analysts or ignored by policymakers. *Scholars of public policy* focus on the management and oversight of secret organizations in a democratic setting. They are particularly interested in striking a balance between the need for secrecy in intelligence matters to preserve and enhance national security and the need for citizens in a democracy to know about the activities of their government.

Because each of these schools borrows freely from the others, they generally use the same concepts, terminology, and history in their research. Their work also is cumulative in the sense that it incorporates earlier findings and reflects points of consensus in the literature on intelligence. The essays we have chosen suggest that despite different approaches and formal training, those writing about intelligence are forming a distinct and relatively coherent field of scholarly endeavor, a true interdisciplinary approach to the study of intelligence.

The essays we have selected reflect the way scholars organize their research in the field of intelligence studies. Part I offers an overview of the evolution of the U.S. intelligence community, as well as a look at the current literature on intelligence and a wide-ranging conversation on key intelligence issues. Parts II and III contain readings that address critical functions of the intelligence cycle (collection and analysis), which inevitably leads to a discussion of intelligence failures and surprise. Parts IV and V deal with intelligence dissemination (another critical aspect of the intelligence cycle), the general relationship between the intelligence community and policymakers and intelligence politicization, and the deliberate or inadvertent corruption of intelligence estimates. Parts VI and VII discuss the paramilitary (covert action) and security (counterintelligence) operations conducted by the U.S. intelligence community, activities of increasing importance to policymakers in the aftermath of the September 11 terrorist attacks on the Pentagon and the World Trade Center. The essays in Part VIII probe into the issue of intelligence oversight and the problems that arise when secret organizations are maintained in a democracy. Part IX looks at the circumstances surrounding the major intelligence failures associated with the terrorist attacks of 9/11 in the United States, along with the faulty intelligence analysis in 2002 that concluded Iraq probably possessed weapons of mass destruction. Finally, Part X offers a brief look at intelligence organizations in other countries.

The U.S. Intelligence Community

Although some intelligence agents live in foreign capitals, work the diplomatic cocktail circuit, undertake daring operations, and are known to most of the world by an assumed name, most intelligence managers and analysts spend their careers at a desk, becoming experts on a few subjects. Their job is to scrutinize and make sense of the deluge of information provided by national collection systems—everything from agent reports to pictures taken by spy satellites. Some analysts work with information collected from people who know or have access to sensitive information. This human source intelligence is known as *humint*. The Central Intelligence Agency and the Defense Humint Service, which is part of the Defense Intelligence Agency, are the organizations within the U.S. intelligence community that collect the majority of humint. Analysts also work with signals intelligence (*sigint*), which is information obtained from intercepted communications, radar emissions, or data transmissions. The National Security Agency is the primary collector of sigint. Imagery (*imint*) is information gath-

ered chiefly by the National Geospatial-Intelligence Agency, through the use of spy satellites and reconnaissance aircraft. Imint sometimes offers real-time electro-optical, radar, or infrared images of specific areas of interest. Measurement and signature intelligence (*masint*) consists of data that describe distinctive physical characteristics of a specific event, such as measuring the contents of a rocket plume or the size of a nuclear explosion. The Defense Intelligence Agency and the armed forces collect masint. Analysts also participate in the interagency process, the way mid-level officials from across the U.S. government make and implement policy. They are members of specific expert communities who have a professional or academic interest in a given area of study. Most intelligence work has little to do with physical exertion and everything to do with mental activity.

Once information is collected, it is disseminated to a variety of organizations to produce "all-source" finished intelligence. These analyses are at the heart of the "data fusion process" because they are intended to combine all relevant information to provide a coherent and accurate depiction of the topic at hand. All-source analyses of long-term interest are generally referred to as "intelligence estimates," although the intelligence community also provides all-source intelligence on topics of immediate concern.

Three civilian organizations provide the majority of strategic all-source intelligence estimates to national policymakers. The National Intelligence Council (NIC) consists of about 20 National Intelligence Officers who are experts on specific issues or regions. Working for the Director of Central Intelligence, they supervise the production of major intelligence reports, often referred to as National Intelligence Estimates (NIEs). The National Foreign Intelligence Board, which is made up of senior representatives drawn from across the intelligence community, approves the estimates produced by the NIC, thereby generating a "community-wide" position on a particular subject. The Directorate of Intelligence (DI) is where the majority of all-source analysis is conducted within the CIA. Organized into offices that cover geographic regions and specific political, military, or economic issues, analysts produce current intelligence and undertake long-term research efforts, such as NIEs. The third organization that produces all-source intelligence is the State Department's Bureau of Intelligence and Research (INR). It is organized into bureaus covering regional and issue areas, and its analysts supply finished intelligence to the Secretary of State and other Department of State officials. It produces the *Morning Summary*, which is provided daily to the Secretary of State.

The Department of Defense also maintains a vast network of organizations that produce finished intelligence, which deals mostly with foreign militaries. The DIA provides finished intelligence on military issues to the Secretary of Defense, the Office of the Secretary of Defense, and the Joint Chiefs of Staff. Additionally, each of the military services maintains specialized intelligence capabilities. The U.S. Army runs the National Ground Intelligence Center. It produces all-source analysis on foreign armies and security forces. The Intelligence Center of the Office of Naval Intelligence gathers information about foreign surface ships, submarines, and undersea weapons and monitors the capabilities of foreign sensor systems and ocean surveillance systems. The National Air Intelligence Center is the Air Force's analytical organization that monitors foreign air forces and space programs. The Marine Corps Intelligence Activity provides finished intelligence to guide acquisition decisions for the Marines and to plan military operations. Each of the unified commands (such as the U.S. Central Command, or CENTCOM) runs a Joint Intelligence Center that produces intelligence directly related to military activities in the unified command's area of responsibility.

Other government departments and agencies operate specialized intelligence bureaus. The Department of Energy's Office of Intelligence, for instance, collects open-source information and produces classified and unclassified estimates dealing with foreign energy and technology programs. The DOE is especially concerned with monitoring international programs that could lead to the further proliferation of nuclear weapons. The Treasury Depart-

ment also maintains a small intelligence bureau that monitors international economic, financial, and security affairs.

Domestic counterintelligence activities are primarily the responsibility of the Federal Bureau of Investigation's National Security Division. The FBI investigates and monitors foreign efforts to spy against the U.S. government and industry. It also conducts operations against hostile intelligence services operating within the United States. Recently, the bureau has been under pressure to place less emphasis on investigating terrorist activities within the United States with an eye toward criminal prosecution and to take more direct action to capture or interdict terrorists before they can strike.

The Readings

In our first essay, an appendix to the Aspin-Brown Commission's report on the roles and missions of the U.S. intelligence community, Phyllis Provost McNeil offers a quick overview of the evolution of the U.S. intelligence community. She places the history of the intelligence community in the context of U.S. diplomatic history, demonstrating how the community evolved to meet the changing role and status of the United States in world politics. The second essay, Len Scott and Peter Jackson's "The Study of Intelligence in Theory and Practice," defines the term *intelligence* and provides a sense of who is writing on what within the field of intelligence studies. The third reading, a conversation with the former Director of Central Intelligence Richard Helms, presents one important official's views on a range of intelligence issues. ✦

1

The Evolution of the U.S. Intelligence Community—An Historical Overview

Phyllis Provost McNeil

Written by an Aspin-Brown Commission staff member, this piece demonstrates that a long history of failures, successes, reforms, scandals, and a host of colorful characters have shaped the cultures of the U.S. intelligence organizations.

The function of intelligence as an activity of the U.S. Government is often regarded as a product of the Cold War. Indeed, much of what is known today as the Intelligence Community was created and developed during the Cold War period. But intelligence has been a function of the Government since the founding of the Republic. While it has had various incarnations over time, intelligence has historically played a key role in providing support to U.S. military forces and in shaping the policies of the United States toward other countries.

The Early Years of the Republic

During the Revolutionary War, General George Washington was an avid user of intelligence as well as a consummate practitioner of the intelligence craft. Records show that shortly after taking command of the Continental Army in 1775, Washington paid an unidentified agent to live in Boston and surreptitiously report by use of "secret correspondence" on the movements of British forces. Indeed, Washington recruited and ran a number of agents, set up spy rings, devised secret methods of reporting, analyzed the raw intelligence gathered by his agents, and mounted an extensive campaign to deceive the British armies. Historians cite these activities as having played a major role in the victory at Yorktown and in the ability of the Continental Army

to evade the British during the winters at Valley Forge.

In a letter to one of his officers written in 1777, Washington wrote that secrecy was key to the success of intelligence activities:

> The necessity of procuring good intelligence is apparent and need not be further urged—All that remains for me to add is, that you keep the whole matter as secret as possible. For upon Secrecy, success depends in most Enterprises of the kind, & for want of it, they are generally defeated, however, well planned . . . . [letter to Colonel Elias Dayton, 26 July 1777]

Washington was not the only one to recognize the importance of intelligence to the colonials' cause. In November of 1775, the Continental Congress created the Committee of Secret Correspondence to gather foreign intelligence from people in England, Ireland, and elsewhere on the European continent to help in the prosecution of the war.

Washington's keen interest in intelligence carried over to his presidency. In the first State of the Union address in January 1790, Washington asked the Congress for funds to finance intelligence operations. In July of that year the Congress responded by establishing the Contingent Fund of Foreign Intercourse (also known as the Secret Service Fund) and authorizing $40,000 for this purpose. Within three years, the fund had grown to $1 million, about 12 percent of the Government's budget at the time. While the Congress required the President to certify the amounts spent, it also allowed him to conceal the purposes and recipients of the funds. (In 1846, this latter provision was challenged by the House of Representatives, but President Polk, citing national security grounds of protection of sources, refused to turn over more specific information on the use of the Fund to the Congress.) Judging by the paucity of the historical record, interest in intelligence as a tool of the Executive appears to have waned in succeeding Administrations, although occasional lapses in performance sometimes produced controversy. During the War of 1812, for example, military intelligence failed to discover that British troops were advancing on Washington until they were 16 miles from the Capital. The Secretary of War had refused to believe that the British would invade Washington, and military intelligence reported from this perspective.

Intelligence regained prominence during the Civil War. Both the Union and Confederate leadership valued intelligence information, established their own spy networks, and often railed at the press for providing intelligence to the other side. The Confederate forces established the Signal and Secret Service Bureau with the primary charter of obtaining northern newspapers. On the Union side, the Departments of the Navy, State, and War each maintained an intelligence service. Union code-breakers decoded Confederate messages and learned that the plates for Confederate currency were being manufactured in New York. In June of 1861, the first electronic transmission of information was sent from an aerial reconnaissance platform—in this case, a balloon—directly to President Lincoln on the ground. Two months later, Union forces established a Balloon Corps. Although disbanded after two years, it succeeded in detecting a large concentration of Confederate troops preparing to attack at Fair Oaks, Virginia.

In 1863, the first professional intelligence organization was established by the Union forces, the Bureau of Military Intelligence. Headed by the Commander of the Army of the Potomac, General Joseph Hooker, the Bureau prepared evaluations of the Confederate Army's strength and activities based on sources that included infiltrations of the Confederacy's War and Navy Departments. It was considered the best run intelligence operation of the Civil War. Yet, Hooker's ineffective use of intelligence (reportedly he was inundated with information) was largely responsible for the Confederate victory at Chancellorsville. Similarly, it has been suggested that Lee's defeat at Gettysburg was partially attributable to his lack of intelligence on the strength and deployment of Union forces.

The Bureau of Military Intelligence was disestablished at the end of the war. A byproduct of its dissolution was the Secret Service, established in 1865 to combat counterfeiting.

A Peacetime Role for Intelligence

Prior to the 1880s, intelligence activities were devoted almost exclusively to support of military operations, either to support deployed forces or to obtain information on the views or participation of other countries in a particular conflict. In March 1882, however, the first permanent intelligence organization—the Office of Naval Intelligence—was created within the Department of the Navy to collect intelligence on foreign navies in peace-time and in war. Three years later, a similar organization—the Military Intelligence Division—was created within the Army to collect foreign and domestic military data for the War Department and the Army.

The Administration of Theodore Roosevelt saw perhaps the most active use of intelligence for foreign policy purposes by any President until that time. Historians note that Roosevelt used intelligence operatives to incite a revolution in Panama to justify annexing the Panama Canal. In 1907, the President also relied on intelligence that showed

the military build-up of the Japanese as justification to launch the worldwide cruise of the "Great White Fleet" as a display of U.S. naval force.

For the most part, however, the early part of the twentieth century was marked not by an expanded use of intelligence for foreign policy purposes, but by an expansion of domestic intelligence capabilities. The Justice Department's Bureau of Investigation (the forerunner of the FBI) was established in 1908 out of concern that Secret Service agents were spying on members of Congress. By 1916, the Bureau had grown from 34 agents focusing primarily on banking issues to 300 agents with an expanded charter that included internal security, Mexican border smuggling activities, neutrality violations in the Mexican revolution, and Central American unrest. After war broke out in Europe, but before the United States joined the Allied cause, the Bureau turned its attention to activities of German and British nationals within our borders.

World War I

At the time the United States entered the war, it lacked a coordinated intelligence effort. As a champion of open diplomacy, President Woodrow Wilson had disdained the use of spies and was generally suspicious of intelligence. His views on the subject appeared to change, however, as a result of a close association developed with the British intelligence chief in Washington.

In fact, British intelligence played a major role in bringing the United States into World War I. Public revelations of German intelligence attempts to prevent U.S. industry and the financial sector from assisting Great Britain greatly angered the American public. Subsequently, British intelligence presented Wilson with the decryption of German diplomatic and naval traffic showing a German effort to entice the Mexican government into joining Germany against the United States in return for Texas, Arizona, and New Mexico if Germany won the war. Later declassified and disclosed to the public, this intercepted communication, known as the "Zimmerman Telegram," infuriated Wilson and added support to his address before a joint session of Congress in 1917 urging that the U.S. declare war on Germany.

In June of 1917, the first U.S. signals intelligence agency was formed within the Army. Known as "MI-8," the agency was charged with decoding military communications and providing codes for use by the U.S. military. In 1919, at the end of the war, the agency was transferred to the State Department. Known as the "Black Chamber," it focused on diplomatic rather than military communications. In 1921, the Black Chamber celebrated perhaps its most significant success by decrypting certain Japanese diplomatic traffic. The intelligence gained from this feat was used to support U.S. negotiators at a Washington conference on naval disarmament. Yet, despite such successes, President Hoover decided that the State Department's interception of diplomatic cables and correspondence could not be tolerated. Apparently agreeing with the alleged, yet oft-quoted statement of his Secretary of State, Henry Stimson, that "Gentlemen do not read each other's mail," Hoover returned the agency to a military orientation under the Army Signal Corps.

Other intelligence entities remained in existence after the end of WWI but saw their resources cut substantially. An exception to this general trend was the Justice Department's Bureau of Investigation, which saw a marked expansion of its mission and workforce. In 1924, J. Edgar Hoover was named director of the Bureau [renamed the Federal Bureau of Investigation (FBI) in 1935]. The FBI's charter was broadened particularly in the years leading to World War II, when concerns for U.S. internal security were mounting in the face of German aggression in Europe. The FBI was made responsible for investigating espionage, counterespionage, sabotage, and violations of the neutrality laws. It was also during this period that the first effort was made to coordinate the activities of the various intelligence elements of the Government. An Interdepartmental Intelligence Coordinating Committee was created for this purpose, but because the Committee lacked a permanent chair and participating agencies were reluctant to share information, it had limited impact.

World War II and Its Aftermath

The years immediately before the United States entered World War II saw American interest in developments in Europe and the Pacific intensify dramatically, prompting both formal and informal efforts to gather and analyze information. President Franklin Roosevelt relied heavily on American and British friends traveling abroad to provide him with intelligence on the intentions of other leaders. One such friend was William J. Donovan, an aficionado of intelligence and a veteran of World War I, whom Roosevelt sent to Europe in 1940 to gather information on the stability of Britain and again in the spring of 1941 to gather information on Italian Dictator Mussolini, among other matters. Upon his return, Donovan lobbied hard for the creation of a centralized, civilian intelligence apparatus to complement that of the military.

In July 1941, in response to Donovan's urging, Roosevelt appointed Donovan as Coordinator of Information (COI) to form a non-military intelligence organization. The Coordinator of Information was to "collect and analyze all information and data which may bear upon the national security" for the President and those he designated. The Coordinator was given the authority, "with the approval of the President," to request data from other agencies and departments, but was specifically admonished not to interfere with the duties and responsibilities of the President's military and naval advisers. FBI Director J. Edgar Hoover, fearing a loss of authority to the new Coordinator, secured the President's commitment that the Bureau's primacy in South America would not change.

Borrowing heavily from the British intelligence model, Donovan created a special staff to pull together and analyze all national security information and empaneled an eight-member review board, drawn from academia, to review analysis and test its conclusions. In concert with the Librarian of Congress, COI Donovan organized the Division of Special Information at the Library, to work with Donovan's analytical staff and to coordinate scholarship within the Library and in academia. In theory, the Division was to provide unclassified information to Donovan's staff, who would combine it with classified information to produce an analysis that would be reviewed by the special board before presentation to the President. Although in practice the process did not operate precisely as planned, the concept of centralized analysis was established.

The surprise attack on Pearl Harbor by the Japanese on December 7, 1941, brought America into the war and revealed a significant failure on the part of the U.S. intelligence apparatus. As subsequent investigations found, intelligence had been handled in a casual, uncoordinated manner, and there had been insufficient attention to certain collection requirements. The lack of coordination among agencies, principally the Army and the Navy, resulted in a failure to provide timely dissemination of relevant information to key decisionmakers. Moreover, intelligence analysts had grossly underestimated Japanese capabilities and intentions, revealing a tendency to misunderstand Japanese actions by looking at them with American cultural biases. After the war, the resolve of America's leaders "never again" to permit another Pearl Harbor largely prompted the establishment of a centralized intelligence structure.

America's entrance into World War II created an immediate need for intelligence to support the warfighter. While the Army and the Navy maintained their own intelligence capabilities, none were prepared to provide the kind of support needed.[1] To bolster this effort, the Office of Strategic Services (OSS) was created in June 1942, under the recently established Joint Chiefs of Staff to succeed the Coordinator of Information. William Donovan remained in charge of the reorganized unit. In addition to assuming the analytical role of its predecessor, the OSS was chartered to carry out clandestine operations against the Axis powers on a worldwide scale. It was not, however, readily accepted by the Joint Chiefs of Staff (JCS), who remained skeptical of the value of OSS activities, and the new unit faced strong competition from the FBI and the Army's intelligence organization.

Usually glamorized as the dashing operations arm of the U.S. Army (with its well-known espionage exploits with the Resistance in Europe), the OSS' contribution to intelligence production has gone largely unnoticed. It was, however, one of the seven major intelligence producers and was an important training ground for a generation of intelligence analysts, as well as operatives. Decidedly different than the British system, the OSS established the tradition of putting analysts and operatives in the same organization. The difficulties, however, that the OSS had in establishing itself within the JCS structure reaffirmed Donovan's belief that the peacetime successor to the OSS should be a civilian organization directly responsible to the President. In 1944, Donovan started campaigning for this model.

In the meantime, substantial intelligence capabilities were created in the military services to support the war effort. Army intelligence operations were supervised by the Military Intelligence Division of the Army General Staff. Its operating arm, the Military Intelligence Service (MIS), was created in 1942 and carried out collection activities around the world, including agent operations, signals interception, and photo reconnaissance. MIS also provided intelligence analysis to U.S. and allied commands. At the same time, intelligence elements were assigned directly to operating forces in the field. These intelligence units collected and analyzed tactical signals intelligence, interpreted photos, and performed ground reconnaissance missions. Aerial reconnaissance missions were run by the Army Air Corps. To provide counterintelligence support, including the debriefing of prisoners and defectors, the Army Counterintelligence Corps was established in 1942 with both domestic and overseas missions.

Army signals intelligence analysts succeeded in breaking and exploiting the code systems used by the Imperial Japanese Army, producing intelligence which many believe shortened the war in the Pacific. In England, after the U.S. joined the war, Army teams participated in the work begun by the Polish and continued by the British to decode German military communications encrypted with the Enigma cipher machines. The intelligence produced by this effort, codenamed "ULTRA," gave the Allies unparalleled insight into the workings of the German military and shortened the war in Europe.

Within three days of the devastating and embarrassing attack on Pearl Harbor, the Navy's Combat Intelligence Unit at Pearl Harbor was busy trying to crack the Japanese Fleet code, JN25. By April 1942, enough information was known to allow the American Pacific Fleet to deal the first blow without visual sighting of the Japanese Fleet at the Battle of Coral Sea. By May 1942, Navy cryptanalysts succeeded in cracking the Japanese code. This significant naval intelligence capability, on par with the British and Polish decryption of the German code, allowed the Americans to defeat the Japanese at the Battle of Midway and to countermeasure the Japanese during the rest of the war in the Pacific.

Also in the Pacific theater, an Allied Translator and Interpreter Section, composed of 2,000 American Nisei soldiers, interrogated Japanese prisoners and exploited captured documents. Since the OSS did not operate in the South Pacific Theater, special human source intelligence capabilities were established, using Australian and Philippine guerrilla forces as well as a special Army long-distance reconnaissance team known as the Alamo Scouts.

Similarly, the Marine Corps developed and deployed the Navajo Code Talker Program in May 1942. By 1945, operating in both theaters of the War, 400 Native American Navajo members of the Corps were encoding, transmitting, and decoding English messages in the complex language of the Navajo Indians. The Code Talkers have been credited with playing a significant role in the Marine Corps victory on Iwo Jima. So successful was this method of encryption and communication that it was employed in the Korean and Vietnam conflicts.

Toward the end of the war, the Administration was left to decide what to do with these intelligence capabilities. A vigorous and heated debate ensued between those who favored the Donovan idea of an independent, civilian intelligence organization reporting directly to the President and those who favored retention and control of intelligence by the military. The State Department, among others, weighed in heavily against the Donovan approach.

In September 1945, while the debate continued, President Truman, acting on a recommendation from his Budget Director, abolished the OSS by Executive Order and divided its functions between the War and State Departments. State received the research and analysis function, combining it with the existing analytical office to form the Interim Research and Intelligence Service (IRIS). The War Department formed the Strategic Services Unit (SSU) out of the clandestine side of the OSS. President Truman had unrealized hopes that the State Department would take over the coordination of intelligence for the Government.

At about the time the OSS was being disbanded, a study commissioned by Navy Secretary James Forrestal and chaired by private businessman Ferdinand Eberstadt was published. While the report dealt principally with the issue of military unification, it also recommended coordination of the intelligence function through the establishment of a National Security Council (NSC) and a Central Intelligence Agency (CIA). The NSC would coordinate the civilian and military national security policy for the President. The CIA, under the auspices of the NSC, would serve "to coordinate national security intelligence." While the military generally supported the recommendation calling for centralized coordination of "national security" intelligence, it was unwilling to give up its own collection programs and analytical capabilities.

The Central Intelligence Group

While the recommendations of the Eberstadt study were to influence significantly the content of what eventually became the National Security Act of 1947, they were not immediately implemented. However, President Truman decided to settle the question of whether there should be a centralized civilian intelligence organization.

Reflecting his dissatisfaction with what he perceived to be the haphazard nature of intelligence collection, his desire to have one authoritative source for intelligence advice, and, above all, his desire to avoid another Pearl Harbor, President Truman issued an executive directive on 22 January 1946 establishing a National Intelligence Authority, a Central Intelligence Group (CIG) "under the direction of a Director of Central Intelligence" (DCI), and an Intelligence Advisory Board. The latter body comprised civilian and military heads of intelligence agencies who were to advise the DCI. The National Intelligence Authority, comprising the Secretaries of War, State, Navy, and the President's personal representative, was charged with planning, developing, and coordinating the intelligence effort. Finally, the CIG (a small interdepartmental group—not an independent agency) was responsible for coordinating, planning, evaluating, and disseminating intelligence and overtly collected information. Funding and staffing of the CIG were provided by other departments and agencies which retained control over their own intelligence efforts.

The first DCI, Rear Admiral Sidney Souers (who wrote the intelligence section of the Eberstadt study), reluctantly accepted the appointment and stayed in the position only six months. Under his tenure, the CIG played a limited analytical role due to Souers' reluctance to challenge the analytical

product of the State Department's IRIS. But the IRIS was soon decimated by congressional budget cutting, and most of its positions were dispersed throughout the Department and to other agencies. In all, 600 positions were transferred from the IRIS to the National Intelligence Authority, the CIG, and the military services. This left the Department with a skeleton analytic group, thus limiting its mission to providing intelligence support only to the policymakers within the Department of State.[2]

The second DCI, Lieutenant General Hoyt Vandenberg, proved more aggressive than his predecessor, gaining authority for the CIG to hire personnel and acquire its own administrative support, as well as expanding clandestine collection, research and analysis, and the overall size of the organization. At the behest of the President, the first national estimate, on Soviet intentions and capabilities, was produced in 1946 during Vandenberg's tenure.

At the time Vandenberg became DCI, in June of 1946, legislation was being drafted in the Congress and in concert with the Truman Administration to provide for the unification of the military establishment under a Secretary of Defense. Inasmuch as the CIG would need an annual appropriation to continue in existence, Vandenberg saw an opportunity to incorporate legislative language creating an independent central intelligence agency with several features modeled on the existing charter of the CIG. Within a month of assuming the duties of DCI, Vandenberg submitted a proposal describing this new entity, with the support of the Truman Administration, which consisted basically of the pertinent language from the 1946 presidential directive and language that had been previously published in the Federal Register.

The National Security Act of 1947

In the ensuing congressional debate on the Vandenberg proposal, several issues emerged about the role of the DCI.

One was whether the DCI should be a civilian or military officer. Some argued that if the DCI were an active duty military officer, he would be subject to the control of his parent service. On the other hand, the military was recognized as the principal consumer of intelligence and controlled most of the resources devoted to it. The legislation ultimately provided that the President could appoint either a civilian or a military officer as the DCI, but if a military officer were appointed, he would be removed from the control of his parent service.

Another issue was whether the DCI should be a member of the National Security Council that was being established by the bill as the White House focal point for national security matters. Navy

Secretary James Forrestal argued strongly against this proposal saying that the Council would be too large to accomplish its business and that the new DCI would have ready access without formal membership. His argument was persuasive and the DCI's proposed membership on the NSC was dropped.

A third issue was the relationship of the DCI to other agencies, in particular, the FBI. The draft proposal provided that the new Central Intelligence Agency would serve as the focal point within the Government where intelligence would be gathered and evaluated. As such, the CIA would necessarily require access to information collected by other agencies. The military agreed to this coordinating role for the CIA so long as the military was able to maintain its own collection and analytical capabilities to support military operations. The FBI, however, insisted on limiting the CIA's access to FBI files only if written notice was given first and only if access was "essential to the national security."

On July 27, 1947, President Truman signed into law the National Security Act of 1947, creating a postwar national security framework. A National Security Council was created to coordinate national security policy. The Act created the position of Secretary of Defense and unified the separate military departments (the Army, the Navy, and the newly-created Air Force) under this position. The Act also established the Joint Chiefs of Staff to serve as the principal military advisers to the President and the Secretary of Defense. Finally, a Central Intelligence Agency was established with the Director of Central Intelligence as its head. At the time of its creation, the CIA was the only agency charged with a "national" intelligence mission.

The statutory language regarding the authorities and functions of the new Central Intelligence Agency was left intentionally vague. In part this reflected the bureaucratic sensitivities involved in specifying in the law the DCI's roles and missions in regard to other agencies, and, in part, the desire to avoid wording that other governments might find offensive. Thus, there was no mention of "espionage" or "spying" in the statute, nor was there any wording to suggest that covert actions (i.e., secret operations to influence political conditions in other countries) were part of the new agency's charter. Rather, the CIA was authorized to perform "services of common concern" to other intelligence agencies as may be determined by the National Security Council and to perform "such other functions and duties related to intelligence affecting the national security as the National Security Council may from time-to-time direct." (The NSC did, in fact, issue directives in 1947 and 1948, providing specific authority for CIA's operational and analytical functions.)

The 1947 Act also included an express prohibition on the CIA's having any "police, subpoena, law-enforcement powers, or internal security functions," reflecting the congressional and public desire to ensure that they were not creating a U.S. "Gestapo" and to preserve the FBI's primacy in domestic matters. The law also made the DCI responsible for "protecting intelligence sources and methods from unauthorized disclosure."

The Early Years of the CIA

The early years of the CIA appear to have been difficult ones as the Agency attempted to establish itself within the Government, amid growing concern about Communist gains in Eastern Europe and Soviet expansionism.

Rear Admiral Roscoe Hillenkoetter was DCI at the time the CIA was created. He organized the Agency into two principal divisions: one dealing with intelligence operations and the other with analysis. The analytical arm, in response to policy-maker interest, prepared and disseminated short-term intelligence pieces. DCI Hillenkoetter found it difficult, however, to force other agencies to participate in the development of longer papers despite the language of the 1947 Act. The emphasis on producing short-term pieces, on the other hand, was often seen as intruding on the role of other producers such as the State Department, the military departments, and the FBI. There was also conflict on the operational side. The Government considered initiating psychological warfare operations overseas to counter Soviet expansionism, but the NSC preferred that the State Department, rather than the CIA, be responsible for them. It was only when the Secretary of State vigorously objected to this role for the Department that it was assigned to the CIA.

In January 1948, less than a year after the CIA was created, the National Security Council, exercising its oversight role under its Executive Secretary Sidney Souers,[3] asked three private citizens to examine comprehensively CIA's "structure, administration, activities, and interagency relations." Allen Dulles, William Jackson and Matthias Correa, three New York lawyers with experience in intelligence, submitted their highly critical report in January 1949. Although the NSC found the criticism of DCI Hillenkoetter and the CIA "too sweeping," it nevertheless accepted the report's basic findings: CIA was not coordinating intelligence activities in the Government; the correlation and evaluation functions were not well organized, and other members of the fledgling Intelligence Community were not fully included in the estimates process; and the DCI lacked sufficient day-to-day contact with the work of CIA. The Dulles-Jackson-Correa report called upon the DCI to exert "forthright leadership," and to actively use existing coordination bodies, such as the Intelligence Advisory Committee ((IAC) comprising the leaders of the military and civilian intelligence agencies. For example, the report urged that the final coordination of intelligence estimates be done through IAC, to establish estimates as "the most authoritative statement[s] available to policymakers."

The Dulles-Jackson-Correa report also made the point that coordination and planning could only be effective with a strong DCI and CIA. It therefore recommended that the DCI reorganize his office to include on his immediate staff the heads of CIA's main components. The report also stated that the CIA would benefit from civilian leadership and recommended that if another military DCI was appointed, he should resign his military commission "to free him from all service ties and from rotations that would preclude the continuity needed for good intelligence work."[4]

Also during 1948, the Congress established "The Commission on Organization of the Executive Branch of the Government." Chaired by former President Herbert Hoover, the Commission established a sub-group to look at national security organizations, including CIA. This group, headed by New York businessman Ferdinand Eberstadt,[5] concluded that the basic organizational arrangements for national security were sound, but there were problems in carrying out the function. The CIA was specifically criticized for not being properly organized to assimilate all information concerning scientific developments abroad, to estimate the significance of these developments, and to give direction to collectors. Concern was also expressed that the CIA was not being given access to all available information within the Government. The fear that other countries might develop nuclear weapons led the Eberstadt group, with some urgency, to state:

> Failure properly to appraise the extent of scientific developments in enemy countries may have more immediate and catastrophic consequences than failure in any other field of intelligence.

In its November 1948 report, the Hoover Commission called for "vigorous efforts" to improve CIA's internal structure and the quality of its product, especially in scientific and medical intelligence. A senior-level "evaluation board or section" within CIA was proposed to work solely on intelligence evaluations. Finally, the Commission urged positive efforts to foster "relations of mutual confidence" between CIA and its consumers.[6]

Lieutenant General Walter Bedell Smith, who succeeded Hillenkoetter as DCI soon after the outbreak of the Korean War, took the initial steps to implement the recommendations of the Hoover and the Dulles-Jackson-Correa reports. Among his first steps was to recruit Allen Dulles, an OSS veteran, as Deputy Director for Plans, and to establish a Board of National Estimates chaired by William Langer of Harvard University.

In 1949, Congress enacted additional legislation for the CIA providing its Director with certain administrative authorities necessary for the conduct of clandestine intelligence activities that were not available to government agencies generally. In particular, the new law permitted the DCI to expend appropriated funds for procuring goods and services to carry out the Agency's functions without having to comply with the cumbersome procurement rules applicable to other government agencies. It also permitted the Agency to expend appropriated funds based solely on a voucher signed by the DCI.

1950s and 1960s: The Development of the Intelligence Community

The decades of the 1950s and 1960s saw an expansion and an intensification of the Cold War as well as an expansion in the size and responsibilities of U.S. intelligence agencies to cope with its challenges.

The 1950s

Acting on the recommendations of a commission of senior officials headed by George Brownell, President Truman, by classified memorandum, established the National Security Agency (NSA) in October 1952 in recognition of the need for a single entity to be responsible for the signals intelligence mission of the United States. Placed within the Department of Defense, NSA assumed the responsibilities of the former Armed Forces Security Agency as well as the signals intelligence responsibilities of the CIA and other military elements. In 1958, the National Security Council issued directives that detailed NSA's mission and authority under the Secretary of Defense.

CIA meanwhile made important strides. Its analytical efforts during the Korean War established the Agency as a key player in the defense and foreign policy areas. On the operational side, the National Security Council reissued its 1948 directive on covert action to achieve peacetime foreign policy objectives in 1955, reemphasizing that implementation responsibility was with the CIA. In 1954, President Eisenhower approved the concept of a high-flying reconnaissance aircraft to fly above the Soviet air defense systems. Due largely to CIA's special procurement authorities and ability to carry out the mission in secret, the President established the effort as a joint CIA-Air Force program. The ability of the program to develop and field the U-2 (by 1955) earlier than planned and below the original cost estimate was a clear success for the participants. Before the end of the decade photos provided by the U-2 figured prominently in defense planning.

In 1954, Congress once again sought to examine the organization and efficiency of the Executive Branch and revived "The Commission on Organization of the Executive Branch of the Government." With former President Hoover again at the helm, the "Second Hoover Commission" formed a subgroup headed by General Mark Clark to study the agencies of the Intelligence Community.[7]

The Clark task force recommended that the CIA be reorganized internally to focus better on its primary missions, and that the DCI appoint a "Chief of Staff" or executive officer to run the day-to-day operations.[8] It also called for a permanent "watchdog" commission to oversee the CIA, comprising members of the House and Senate and distinguished private citizens appointed by the President.[9] A year later, in 1956, President Eisenhower established the Presidential Board of Consultants on Foreign Intelligence Activities (later renamed the President's Foreign Intelligence Advisory Board by President Kennedy). Shortly after it was formed, the Board issued a critical review of the DCI's management of the Intelligence Community. Later, in 1957, on the Board's recommendation, President Eisenhower established the United States Intelligence Board as the single forum for all intelligence chiefs to provide advice to the DCI on intelligence activities.

In 1957, spurred by the Soviet launch of Sputnik, the CIA and the Air Force began planning for the first photo reconnaissance satellite. Publicly referred to as "the Discoverer Weather System" and recently declassified as "CORONA," the system was successfully operational by 1962.

The 1960s

The decade of the 1960s was marked by significant technological advances, further expansion of the Intelligence Community, and the first tentative efforts of a DCI to exert control over it. But, as far as the public was concerned, it started with the notable failure of the CIA at the Bay of Pigs. An invasion of Cuban expatriates, trained by the CIA, launched an invasion of Cuba in the spring of 1961 with the intent of ousting the Castro regime. Without U.S. military assistance, the invasion crumbled. The reputation of the Agency suffered significantly.

In August of the same year, Secretary of Defense McNamara created the Defense Intelligence Agency (DIA) to consolidate and to coordinate the production of intelligence analysis by each of the military services and to serve as the principal source of intelligence support to the Secretary and his staff, as well as to the Joint Chiefs of Staff and the unified commands. DIA opened a new production center in 1963, but the military departments continued to maintain their own analytical capabilities. In 1965, DIA was given responsibility for administering the newly-created Defense Attache system, consisting of uniformed military personnel serving in embassies and collecting, by overt means, information useful to the military.

In the meantime, there were substantial advances in U.S. technical collection capabilities. Photographs taken by the U-2 were a large factor in the successful resolution of the Cuban missile crisis in 1962. The first photo reconnaissance satellite was launched the same year. The first high altitude, high speed reconnaissance aircraft, the SR-71, was built and tested by the CIA a short while later. While these technical collection efforts had been ongoing for several years in both CIA and the Air Force, they were formally consolidated, pursuant to a national security directive, in 1961 within the National Reconnaissance Office (NRO).

While the fact of its existence remained classified, the NRO was designated a separate operating agency of the Department of Defense, reporting to the Secretary of Defense albeit with the DCI retaining a role in selecting key personnel as well as substantial control over the budget, requirements, and priorities of the organization. Using the special procurement authorities of the DCI, the NRO was able expeditiously to procure and to operate satellite collection systems for the Intelligence Community.

In addition to the NSA, DIA, and NRO, each of the military services maintained substantial intelligence organizations, both at the departmental level and at the tactical level. These organizations typically collected information and provided analysis regarding the weapons systems, tactics, and capabilities of foreign counterpart forces. This information and analysis were used to support the weapons acquisition process in each service, to support force development and contingency planning, and were incorporated into training programs.

The growth of intelligence efforts within the Department of Defense served to accentuate the relative lack of the DCI's role over the rest of the Community. In July 1961, the President's Foreign Intelligence Advisory Board proposed to the President that the DCI be separated from the CIA and head-up an Office of Coordination in the White House. President Kennedy did not endorse the recommendation but in January 1962 issued a letter to his new DCI John McCone stating:

> As head of the Central Intelligence Agency, while you will continue to have overall responsibility for the Agency, I shall expect you to delegate to your principal deputy, as you may deem neces-

sary, so much of the detailed operation of the Agency as may be required to permit you to carry out your primary task as Director of Central Intelligence.

In 1963, DCI McCone established a National Intelligence Programs Evaluation Staff to review and evaluate Community programs and cost–effectiveness. Later in the decade, DCI Helms set up a National Intelligence Resources Board to review all community programs and budgets, and to referee community disputes.[10]

But the burgeoning U.S. military involvement in the Vietnam War, the efforts to block Communist expansion in Laos and to deal with conflicts in the Middle East (notably the Arab-Israeli Six-Day War of 1967), effectively precluded serious efforts by the DCIs to assert greater control over the Intelligence Community.

The 1970s: The Decade of Turmoil and Reform

The decade of the 1970s began with serious efforts to institute DCI control over the Intelligence Community, but they were eventually undermined by a series of sensational disclosures in the media, followed by unprecedented investigations of the Intelligence Community within the Executive Branch and by the Congress. During the latter half of the decade, new reforms were adopted and new oversight mechanisms put into place. While the intelligence functions of the Government continued, Congress began to take a much more active role in determining their cost and overseeing their execution.

In December 1970, President Nixon directed Deputy Director of the Office of Management and Budget James Schlesinger to recommend how the organizational structure of the Intelligence Community should be changed to bring about greater efficiency and effectiveness. The Schlesinger report, completed in March 1971, found, among other things, that intelligence functions were fragmented and disorganized; collection activities were unnecessarily competitive and redundant; intelligence suffered from unplanned and unguided growth; intelligence activities were too costly; and, because analytical products were provided on such a broad range of topics, they often suffered in quality. The report called for basic reform of the management structure with a strong DCI who could bring intelligence costs under control and improve analytic quality and responsiveness. Among other things, the study recommended that the DCI put together a consolidated budget for the Intelligence Community and oversee its execution.

Following-up on the recommendations in November 1971, President Nixon issued a directive calling for improvement in the intelligence product and for more efficient use of resources. The DCI was made responsible for "planning, reviewing, and evaluating all intelligence programs and activities and in the production of national intelligence." The Nixon directive reconstituted the United States Intelligence Board to assist the DCI, and set up the Intelligence Committee[11] of the NSC to coordinate and to review intelligence activities. It also established an Intelligence Resources Advisory Committee, comprising representatives from the State and Defense Departments and OMB, to advise the DCI on the consolidated intelligence budget. In March 1972, DCI Helms created a special "Intelligence Community Staff" to assist him in the daily execution of his Community responsibilities.

None of these changes had a substantial impact at the time, however, because the Government became largely preoccupied with the Watergate affair in 1973 and 1974. There was only tangential involvement by the CIA in Watergate primarily through the activities of former employees, and in the preparation of a psychological profile of Daniel Ellsberg.[12] The press, however, motivated to some extent by the distrust generated by Watergate, increasingly began to report critically on intelligence activities. Press articles covered allegations of collection efforts undertaken against U.S. citizens during the Vietnam era, attempts to assassinate foreign leaders or destabilize communist regimes, and efforts to raise the remains of a Soviet submarine off the floor of the Pacific.

In December 1974, in reaction to reports of CIA's support to the non-Communist resistance forces in Angola, Congress passed an amendment to the Foreign Assistance Act, known as the "Hughes-Ryan amendment," which for the first time required that the President report any covert CIA operations in a foreign country (other than for intelligence collection) to the relevant congressional committees (which, at that time, included the armed services committees, foreign relations committees, and appropriations committees in each house of Congress).

The various media revelations also led to official investigations in both the Executive branch and the Congress:

A. The Rockefeller Commission

The Commission on CIA Activities Within the United States, chaired by Vice President Rockefeller, was created by President Ford on 4 January 1975, to determine whether CIA employees had engaged in illegal activities in the United States. The inquiry was later expanded to include the CIA's foreign intelligence charter and to make suggestions for operational guidelines. In June 1975, the Commission issued its report which, among other things, confirmed the existence of a CIA domestic mail opening operation; found that in the late 1960s and early 1970s the Agency had kept files on 300,000 U.S. citizens and organizations relating to domestic dissident activities; found that President Nixon tried to use CIA records for political ends; and concluded that the CIA had no involvement in President Kennedy's assassination. The Commission also found "that the great majority of the CIA's domestic activities comply with its statutory authority." In looking to the future, the Commission called for a joint congressional oversight committee and a stronger executive oversight mechanism; consideration by the Congress to disclose "to some extent" CIA's budget; and appointment of two confirmed deputy directors, one to manage the CIA and one to advise the DCI on military matters. The Commission further recommended that the DCI serve no more than 10 years.

B. The Church Committee

Twenty-three days after the Rockefeller Commission was empaneled, the Senate announced its own investigatory body, the Committee to Study Government Operations with Respect to Intelligence Activities (also known as the Church Committee after its Chairman). Handling one of the largest investigations ever undertaken by the Senate, the Church Committee was charged with looking at CIA domestic activities; covert activity abroad, including alleged assassinations of foreign leaders; alleged abuses by the Internal Revenue Service and the FBI; alleged domestic spying by the military; and the alleged interceptions of the conversations of U.S. citizens by the National Security Agency. The Committee's inquiry lasted for almost a year, resulting in a six-volume report, released in April 1976. The Committee recommended, among other things, that the President consider separating the DCI from the CIA; that the authorities of the DCI over elements of the Intelligence Community be enhanced; that statutory charters be established for CIA, DIA, and NSA; that the National Foreign Intelligence Budget be published; and that clandestine support to repressive regimes that disregarded human rights be prohibited by law. The Committee lauded several reforms (including a ban on assassination) already implemented by President Ford.

C. The Pike Committee

The House counterpart to the Church Committee was the Select Committee on Intelligence to Investigate Allegations of Illegal or Improper Activities of Federal Intelligence Agencies. Impanelled in February 1975, the committee was also known by the name of its Chairman, Congressman Otis Pike. The Pike Committee's report was voted down by the House in January 1976, and was never officially issued. Portions, however, were leaked to a New York newspaper, the *Village Voice*.

D. The Murphy Commission

In June 1975, around the time that the Rockefeller Commission was completing its inquiry into intelligence improprieties, another congressional commission, the Commission on the Organization of the Government for the Conduct of Foreign Policy, was culminating a three-year study which included an examination of the organization and performance of the Intelligence Community. Headed by veteran diplomat Robert Murphy,[13] the Commission recommended that the DCI be given greater status in the White House and the Intelligence Community; that the DCI delegate his responsibility for running the CIA to a deputy; that the DCI occupy an office geographically closer to the White House to better enable him to carry out his role as presidential adviser; and that the CIA change its name to the Foreign Intelligence Agency.[14] The Commission also recommended that covert action should be employed only where it is clearly essential to vital U.S. purposes and only after a careful process of high level review. It further urged that the NSC's Committee on Intelligence be actively used as the principal forum to resolve the differing perspectives of intelligence consumers and producers, and "should meet frequently for that purpose."

Reform and Oversight

Even as the Church and Pike Committees were continuing their investigations, the Executive branch undertook extensive efforts to bring about reform.[15]

In the summer of 1975, President Ford ordered the implementation of 20 of the 30 recommendations of the Rockefeller Commission, to include measures to provide improved internal supervision of CIA activities; additional restrictions on CIA's domestic activities; a ban on mail openings; and an end to wiretaps, abuse of tax information, and the testing of drugs on unsuspecting persons. Ford did not agree to public disclosure of the intelligence budget, however, nor did he readily agree to a separate congressional oversight committee.

President Ford issued the first Executive Order on intelligence on 18 February 1976 (E.O. 11905),[16] before either the Church or Pike investigating committees had reported. For the first time, a description of the Intelligence Community and the authorities and responsibilities of the DCI and the heads of other intelligence agencies, were specified in a public presidential document. The order also set up a Committee on Foreign Intelligence as part of the National Security Council, chaired by the DCI and reporting directly to the President, as the focal point for policy and resource allocation on intelligence.[17] A number of restrictions on intelligence agencies were also instituted, including a ban on assassinations as an instrument of U.S. policy. To monitor compliance with the Order, a new Intelligence Oversight Board was established within the Executive Office of the President.

Both congressional investigating committees recommended in their final reports that permanent follow-on committees be created to provide oversight of the intelligence function and to consider further legislative actions as might be necessary.

The Senate acted first in May 1976, creating the Select Committee on Intelligence. The House followed suit a little over a year later, creating the Permanent Select Committee on Intelligence. Both committees were made responsible for authorizing expenditures for intelligence activities (although the Senate was limited to "national" intelligence, whereas the House mandate included both "national" and "tactical" intelligence activities), and for conducting necessary oversight. The resolutions creating both committees recognized that they would be kept "fully and currently informed" of intelligence activities under their purview. Both committees were added to the list of those to receive notice of covert actions under the Hughes-Ryan amendment. The Senate committee also was given responsibility for handling the confirmation proceedings when the DCI and the Deputy DCI were nominated by the President.

While efforts were made in succeeding months to let emotions over intelligence activities subside and to establish more "normal" relationships between the Legislative and Executive branches, the hiatus was relatively short-lived. In 1977, the Senate Committee reexamined the question whether the aggregate intelligence budget should be released publicly. This issue would continue to be debated for the next two decades. The statement of newly-appointed DCI Turner that he had no problem with the release of this figure aroused protests from those who believed disclosure could assist hostile intelligence services in deciphering U.S. intelligence activity.

In August 1977, DCI Turner prompted a more substantial controversy by announcing his intention to reduce the CIA's Directorate of Operations by 800 people. The first reductions occurred on 31 October 1977 (called the "Halloween Massacre" within CIA) when 200 officers were fired. Critics of the DCI charged that he was destroying the CIA's human source collection capability in favor of technical collection programs run by the Department of Defense. (Some in Defense, on the other hand, perceived Turner as attempting to take over those programs.)

On 24 January 1978, President Carter issued a new Executive Order on intelligence which reaffirmed the DCI's Community-wide authority over priorities, tasking, and the budget; contained additional restrictions on collection techniques, participation in domestic activities, and human experimentation; and reiterated the ban on assassinations. Intelligence agencies were specifically required to promulgate procedures to govern the collection of information on U.S. citizens and persons admitted to the U.S. for permanent residence.

Notwithstanding the new presidential order, both congressional committees proceeded to consider bills in 1978 which would have dramatically overhauled the Intelligence Community. Following the suggestions of the Church Committee as well as incorporating various aspects of the Executive branch reforms, the Senate committee developed a comprehensive bill entitled the "National Intelligence Reorganization and Reform Act of 1978." The bill called for the creation of a "Director of National Intelligence" with broader powers than the DCI to serve as head of the Intelligence Community. The Director of National Intelligence would have retained leadership of CIA[18] with the authority to delegate this responsibility to a Deputy or Assistant Director at the President's discretion. The bill also contained a long list of restricted or banned activities, provided specific missions and functions for each element of the Intelligence Community, stipulated rigorous review and notification procedures for covert action and clandestine collection, and instituted numerous requirements for reporting to Congress.

While the Carter Administration initially supported the attempt to draft "charter" legislation, it ultimately withdrew its support in the face of growing concern that the intelligence function would be hamstrung by having too much detailed regulation in statute. After extended negotiations with the two intelligence committees, the Administration agreed to a measure limited to establishing the ground rules for congressional oversight. The Intelligence Oversight Act of 1980 provided that the heads of intelligence agencies would keep the oversight committees "fully and currently informed" of their activities including "any significant anticipated intelligence activity." Detailed ground rules were established for reporting covert actions to the Congress, in return for the number of congressional committees receiving notice of covert actions being limited to the two oversight committees.

Congress also passed, with the support of the Carter Administration, the Foreign Intelligence

Surveillance Act of 1978, providing for a special court order procedure to authorize electronic surveillance for intelligence purposes, activities that had previously been conducted based upon a claim of constitutional authority of the President.

Finally, in response to continued criticism from the congressional committees over the usefulness of national intelligence estimates, a new mechanism for the development of estimates was established. DCI Colby, in 1973, had established the National Intelligence Officer system in lieu of the Board of Estimates. He had appointed the first six NIOs in an effort to make intelligence more responsive to policymaking. By the end of the decade, DCI Turner formed the NIOs into the National Intelligence Council. Reporting to the DCI, the Council comprised a Chairman and eight National Intelligence Officers, who were considered the senior analysts of the Intelligence Community within their respective areas of expertise. As such, they would supervise the preparation of estimates, ensure quality control, and present the results of their work to policymakers as required.

1980s: A Decade of Growth and Scandal

The beginning of the decade saw the election of a new President, Ronald Reagan, who had made the revitalization of intelligence part of his campaign. Intelligence budgets were increased, and new personnel were hired. The vast majority of rules and guidelines adopted during the Ford and Carter Administrations remained in place. However, by the middle of the decade, the U.S. experienced a series of spy scandals, and the first serious breach of the oversight arrangements with the Congress. While the organization of the Intelligence Community remained stable during the decade, it was a period of burgeoning growth and activity.

During the 1980 presidential election, intelligence became a targeted campaign issue. The Republican Party platform contained a plank asserting that the Democrats had impaired the efficiency of the Intelligence Community and had underestimated the Soviet's military strength. President Reagan came into office promising to improve intelligence capabilities by upgrading technical systems and strengthening counterintelligence.

To make good on these promises, Reagan appointed William Casey, a veteran of the OSS, as DCI, and announced that the DCI, for the first time, would hold cabinet rank. With this presidential mandate, Casey sought and received higher budgets for intelligence and instituted an unprecedented period of personnel growth across the Intelligence Community.

On 4 December 1981, almost a year into his Administration, President Reagan issued his Executive Order on intelligence (E.O. 12333). It generally reaffirmed the functions of intelligence agencies (as outlined in the previous order) and continued most of the previous restrictions, but it set a more positive tone than its predecessor, and gave the CIA greater latitude to gather foreign intelligence within the United States and to provide assistance to law enforcement. The Executive Order also provided a new NSC structure for reviewing intelligence activities, including covert actions.[19]

Meanwhile, the congressional intelligence committees demonstrated a willingness to provide legislative authority sought by the Intelligence Community. In 1980, the Classified Information Procedures Act was passed to protect classified information used in criminal trials. In 1982, following the public revelation of the names of certain CIA officers that appeared to result in the murder of one officer, the Congress passed a new law making it a crime to reveal the names of covert intelligence personnel. In October 1984, Congress exempted certain operational files of the CIA from disclosure under the Freedom of Information Act. However, legislative proposals offered in 1984 calling for a fixed term for the DCI and Deputy DCI and requiring that they be career intelligence officers, were not passed.

The 1986 Goldwater-Nichols Act, which reorganized the Department of Defense and shifted authority from the military departments to the Joint Chiefs and theater commands, also had an impact on intelligence. The Defense Intelligence Agency and Defense Mapping Agency were specifically designated as combat support agencies, and the Secretary of Defense, in consultation with the DCI, was directed to establish policies and procedures to assist the National Security Agency in fulfilling its combat support functions. The Act also required that the President submit annually to Congress a report on U.S. national security strategy, including an assessment of the adequacy of the intelligence capability to carry out the strategy.

1985: The Year of the Spy

Beginning in 1985, the Intelligence Community experienced an unprecedented rash of spy cases that led to numerous recommendations for change.

The defection of former CIA officer Edward Lee Howard in the spring of 1985 was followed by the arrests of John A. Walker, Jr. and Jerry A. Whitworth, Navy personnel with access to highly sensitive information; CIA employees, Sharon Scranage and Larry Wu-Tai Chin; former NSA employee, Ronald W. Pelton; FBI agent, Richard

Miller; and an employee of Naval intelligence, Jonathan J. Pollard. The Walker-Whitworth, Pelton, and Howard cases dealt especially serious blows to U.S. intelligence. As the year drew to a close, a Marine guard at the U.S. Embassy in Moscow confessed to having passed information to the Soviets and was charged with allowing Soviet personnel to enter the chancery building. It was further disclosed that the U.S. had determined its new chancery in Moscow had been thoroughly bugged during its construction. Coming in close succession, these disclosures shocked the public and the Congress.

Various efforts were taken within the Executive branch to identify and correct shortcomings in counterintelligence and security. The Secretary of Defense commissioned a special inquiry into Defense policy and practice. The Secretary of State commissioned a review of embassy security, including the vulnerability of U.S. diplomatic establishments to electronic penetration. The CIA undertook an internal review of counterintelligence and its procedures for handling defectors.

The congressional intelligence committees also investigated these problems and prepared lengthy reports recommending change. In 1988, the Senate committee asked a group of distinguished private citizens, led by New York businessman Eli Jacobs, to review the progress that had been made in counterintelligence and to provide recommendations for further improvements. Their report was provided in 1989, but did not result in any legislation being enacted at the time. This was due in part to the fall of the Berlin Wall, and dramatic changes taking place in the Soviet Union, which lessened the intensity of focusing on problems with spies.

The Iran-Contra Affair and Its Aftermath

In November 1986, Congress learned that representatives of the Reagan Administration, contrary to the announced policies of the Government, had sold arms to the Government of Iran in return for its assistance in securing the release of U.S. hostages held in Lebanon. Initiated by members of the NSC staff, the operation was accomplished with the assistance of some officers of the CIA and the Defense Department pursuant to a retroactive covert action "finding" signed by President Reagan in January 1986, which had never been reported to the Congress. It was also disclosed that the NSC staff members involved in the sales had overcharged the Iranians for the weapons and had used the proceeds to support the anti-Communist rebels, the "Contras," in Nicaragua at a time when such assistance was prohibited by law. The veracity of public statements made by the President and other senior officials with knowledge of the episode appeared in doubt. CIA and other intelligence agencies were quickly drawn into the controversy, which collectively became known as the Iran-Contra affair.

A special prosecutor was appointed to look into possible criminal activity, and investigations ensued in both the Executive branch and the Congress. In December 1986, the President commissioned a Special Review Board, chaired by former Senator John Tower. Three months later, the Tower Board found that the Iran and Contra operations were conducted outside of regularly established channels and that intelligence oversight requirements had been ignored. The Board also faulted President Reagan's management style. While not recommending organizational changes *per se*, the Board urged that a better set of guidelines be developed for approving and reporting covert action. The Board also recommended that Congress consider merging the two intelligence committees into a single joint committee.

In early 1987, the House and Senate formed separate investigating committees, but later agreed to form a Joint Committee for purposes of interviewing witnesses and holding hearings. After months of intense public hearings, a majority of the Committee issued a lengthy account of its work in the fall of 1987. It recommended, among other things, that a statutory Inspector General be created at the CIA and that the legal requirements for reporting covert actions to the congressional oversight committees be tightened.

Lawrence Walsh, the special prosecutor appointed in January 1987, carried on his investigation of the Iran-Contra affair for almost seven years, and brought criminal prosecutions against the key NSC figures involved, some CIA employees, and a former Secretary of Defense. President Bush later issued pardons to six of those charged.

Legislation creating a statutory Inspector General for the CIA was enacted in 1989. Although the Inspector General reported to the DCI, he could be removed only by the President. Among other things, the law required that the Inspector General submit semi-annual reports to the congressional intelligence committees, summarizing problems that had been identified and corrective actions taken.

Legislative efforts to tighten the covert action reporting requirements did not succeed for several more years. In 1988, with the election of President George Bush, a former DCI, Congress received assurances that the experience of Iran-Contra would not be repeated and that appropriate consultations would occur on future covert actions. These assurances did not put the matter to rest as far as the committees were concerned, but did serve to dampen congressional fervor to legislate precise time requirements for reporting.

1990–1995: The End of the Cold War and Retrenchment

The three years following the election of President Bush saw profound changes in the world that had enormous impacts on the Intelligence Community. In the fall of 1989, the Berlin Wall came down and Germany began the process of reunification. The Communist regimes of Eastern Europe gave way to democratic rule. In August 1990, Iraq invaded Kuwait. Shortly thereafter, the Soviet Union began to break apart with many former Soviet Republics declaring independence. In early 1991, the U.S. together with NATO allies (and the agreement of the Soviet Union) invaded Kuwait to oust the occupying Iraqi forces with a fearsome display of modern weaponry. Later in the year, Communist rule ended in Russia.

Some began to question whether an intelligence capability was needed any longer; others urged significant retrenchment. Leaders within the Intelligence Community began streamlining their agencies and reorienting toward new missions, with a greater focus on transnational threats. Congress pushed them along by proposing a new Intelligence Community structure, and mandating across-the-board reductions in personnel.

The period ended with a shocking new spy case at the CIA and renewed calls for reform.

The Gulf War

The Gulf War of 1991, brief though it was, had profound repercussions for U.S. intelligence. Never had so much information been conveyed so quickly from intelligence systems to warfighters with such devastating effect. The accuracy of U.S. precision guided weapons astounded the world. The war also highlighted the need for the United States to expand its own efforts to link intelligence systems with combat systems and to train military personnel to use these systems effectively. The U.S. recognized that the future of warfare was apt to be battles fought at a distance between opposing forces, placing a premium on the availability of intelligence on the nature and disposition of hostile forces.

Yet the Gulf War also demonstrated problems with intelligence. Initially, the Intelligence Community was not well prepared to support military operations in this locale, but given time in the fall and winter of 1990 to put together a capability, the job was done. The Joint Intelligence Center was established during the war with representation from the key intelligence agencies and provided a model of providing crisis support to military operations. Indeed, a permanent National Military Joint Intelligence Center was established shortly after the conflict at the Pentagon and later at all unified commands. Still, the war illuminated problems in disseminating imagery to the field as well as the limitations of U.S. human intelligence capabilities. In addition, a substantial problem arose with competing CIA and military assessments of the damage caused by allied bombing.

The Gates Task Forces

In 1991, after a wrenching confirmation process which provided the first public examination of the analytical process at the CIA, DCI Robert Gates undertook a comprehensive reexamination of the post-Cold War Intelligence Community. The recommendations of 14 separate task forces produced significant change: analysis would be made more responsive to decisionmakers; a formalized requirements process would be established for human source intelligence collection; new offices were created at the CIA to coordinate the use of publicly available ("open source") information and to improve CIA support to the military. The staff of the DCI, which supported him in his Community role, was strengthened. And, after much negotiating about which entities to include, a new Central Imagery Office, under the joint control of the DCI and the Secretary of Defense, was established to coordinate imagery collection and to establish uniform standards for the interpretation and dissemination of imagery to the field.

Boren-McCurdy Legislation

While the Gates task forces were at work, legislation was introduced by the respective Chairmen of the Senate and House intelligence committees to restructure the Intelligence Community. The bills called for the creation of a Director of National Intelligence with authority over the intelligence budget as well as authority to transfer personnel temporarily from one intelligence agency to another. The DNI would continue to establish requirements and priorities for intelligence collection and serve as the President's intelligence adviser. In this regard, the analytical element of the CIA would be transferred under the control of the DNI, leaving the remainder of the CIA to be administered by a separate agency director. The legislation also proposed a National Imagery Agency to coordinate imagery tasking, collection, processing, and dissemination.

Given the actions taken by DCI Gates to implement the results of his task forces, however, the committees did not push for enactment of their alternative proposals. Instead they opted to codify and to clarify the existing statutory framework that had been largely unchanged since 1947. The Intelligence Organization Act of 1992 (enacted as part of the Intelligence Authorization Act for 1993) for the first time defined the Intelligence Community by law, enunciated the three roles of the DCI, set forth the authorities and responsibilities of the DCI in relation to other elements of the Intelligence Community, and articulated the responsibilities of the Secretary of Defense for the execution of national intelligence programs. Among other things, the Secretary was required to consult with the DCI prior to appointing the Directors of the NSA, the NRO,[20] and the DIA.

Congress continued to debate whether the intelligence budget should be declassified. In 1991 and 1992, Congress passed non-binding "Sense of Congress" resolutions urging the President to make public the aggregate funding for intelligence. President Bush declined to do so, as did President Clinton in 1993.

The Vice President's National Performance Review

In 1993, as part of the Clinton Administration's overall effort to "reinvent" government, a team from the Vice President's National Performance Review looked at the Intelligence Community and suggested that several actions be taken to consolidate activities and build a sense of Community in order to be more efficient and to better serve customers. The review found that the Community was too often drawn apart by the competition for new programs and budget allocations and recommended rotational assignments among agencies as a means of promoting a broader, more collegial perspective. The review's recommendation that the Intelligence Oversight Board be merged into the President's Foreign Intelligence Advisory Board was accomplished by Executive Order in September 1993.

The Ames Spy Case

In February 1994, Aldrich H. Ames, a CIA employee with almost 30 years' experience in operations, was charged with spying for the Soviet Union since at least 1985. During this period, he was alleged to have disclosed virtually all of the CIA's active Soviet agents, many of whom were later executed or imprisoned. In May, Ames and his wife pled guilty and were sent to prison.

The ensuing investigations by the CIA Inspector General and by the congressional intelligence committees reported that Ames had exhibited serious personal problems and a penchant for exorbitant spending which should have brought him under security scrutiny. The investigations also highlighted problems in coordinating counterintelligence cases between the FBI and the CIA. Notwithstanding the seriousness of Ames' disclosures and the numerous shortcomings on the part of CIA officers, DCI Woolsey meted out what were perceived as relatively mild disciplinary measures. The confidence of the public and the Congress in the CIA appeared considerably eroded.

In the fall of 1994, new legislation was enacted to improve counterintelligence and security practices across the Intelligence Community, and, in particular, to improve the coordination between the FBI and CIA. In addition, the President created a new bureaucratic framework for handling counterintelligence matters, to include the placement of FBI counterintelligence specialists within the CIA.

The Creation of a New Commission

Even before the Ames case provided the immediate impetus, the congressional intelligence committees anticipated that the Executive branch would conduct a comprehensive review of the Intelligence Community. When this failed to materialize, the Senate committee, and, in particular, its Vice Chairman, Senator John Warner, developed legislation to establish a commission to study the roles and capabilities of intelligence agencies in the post-Cold War era, and to make recommendations for change. The legislation was approved in October 1994, as part of the Intelligence Authorization Act for 1995.

Questions for Further Discussion

1. Which do you think was a more important factor leading to the establishment of the CIA: the Pearl Harbor attack in 1941 or the rising threat of the Soviet Union? Why?

2. When did the CIA become a "key player" in the government, according to the author?

3. What do you think were the most important reforms advocated by the Church Committee in 1975–76?

4. Why is the author reluctant to have a Director of National Intelligence (DNI) separated from the CIA? Do you agree or disagree?

Endnotes

1. Former Secretary of State Dean Rusk recalled the 1941 state of the U.S.'s intelligence effort in testimony before a Senate subcommittee: "When I was assigned to G-2 in 1941, well over a year after the war had started in Europe, I was asked to take charge of a new section that had been organized to cover everything from Afghanistan right through southern Asia, southeast Asia, Australia, and the Pacific. Because we had no intelligence organization that had been giving attention to that area up to that time, the materials avail-

able to me when I reported for duty consisted of a tourist handbook on India and Ceylon, a 1924 military attache's report from London on the Indian Army, and a drawer full of clippings from the *New York Times* that had gathered since World War One. That was literally the resources of the G-2 on that vast part of the world a year after the war in Europe started."

2. In 1957, this group was renamed the Bureau of Intelligence and Research.

3. The same Sidney Souers who had been appointed the first DCI by President Truman in January 1946. Souers served as Executive Secretary of the NSC from 1947 to 1950.

4. Although NSC 50 was issued to implement the report's recommendations, DCI Hillenkoetter did not take follow-up action on its numerous recommendations.

5. The same person who proposed the creation of the National Security Council and the CIA in a 1945 report to Navy Secretary Forrestal.

6. The depth and importance of this problem was revealed when President Truman announced that the Soviets had detonated a nuclear device in September 1949. The CIA's only coordinated estimate on the urgent question of when the Soviets would have a nuclear weapon gave three incorrect predictions: 1958, 1955 and 1950–1953, and none of the predictions was accepted by all departments.

7. In its 1955 report, the Second Hoover Commission recognized for the first time the existence of an "intelligence community" within the Government, naming the NSC, CIA, NSA, FBI, Department of State, Army, Navy, Air Force, and the Atomic Energy Commission as its members.

8. Allen Dulles, who had been elevated to DCI in 1953, did not appoint a Chief of Staff, due to his active interest in the operation of the CIA. Instead, he appointed General Lucien Truscott as his deputy to resolve jurisdictional disputes between CIA and the military services, in an attempt to increase his community coordination capabilities.

9. In 1956, the House and Senate Armed Services Committees, and the Senate Appropriations Committee established intelligence subcommittees, and the House Appropriations Committee formed a "special group" under its chairman.

10. The United States Intelligence Board, previously established in the 1950s to serve as the DCI's primary advisory body, was used unevenly by DCIs depending on their interests in Community management.

11. The Intelligence Committee, chaired by the National Security Advisor, consisted of the Attorney General, the Under Secretary of State, the Deputy Secretary of Defense, the Chairman of the Joint Chiefs of Staff, and the DCI.

12. CIA officials refused the White House request that the CIA be used to cover-up the Watergate affair.

13. In 1976, Murphy was appointed by President Ford as the first chairman of the newly-formed Intelligence Oversight Board, and as a member of PFIAB.

14. The principal author of these conclusions was reportedly William Casey, later to become DCI.

15. It should also be noted that DCI Colby appointed a study group within CIA, headed by James Taylor, which issued an internal report in October 1975: "American Intelligence: A Framework for the Future." The Taylor study asserted that intelligence needed to become more efficient and effective, and more compatible with our democracy. The study suggested refining the current intelligence system and focused on the role of the DCI, including the relationship with the Secretary of Defense and the Intelligence Community, arguing that the DCI needed more influence over both substantive judgments and resource management. The report noted that the DCI's responsibilities, but not his authorities, had grown considerably since 1947. The study recommended separating the DCI from CIA (which would be run by its own director), and appropriating funds to the DCI who would allocate them to program managers.

16. This order and succeeding orders issued by President Carter (E.O. 12036, 1978) and President Reagan (E.O. 12333, 1981) listed the following members of the Intelligence Community: CIA, NSA, DIA, DOD reconnaissance offices, INR/State, intelligence elements of Army, Navy, Air Force, Marines, FBI, Treasury, and DOE (then known as the Energy Research & Development Administration). Staff elements of the DCI were added in the Carter and Reagan orders.

17. The other members of the CFI were the Deputy Secretary of Defense for Intelligence and the Deputy Assistant to the President for National Security Affairs. The CFI reported directly to the NSC.

18. Those who thought the DNI must retain a direct management role over the CIA argued that separating the DNI from the CIA would deprive the Director of a strong institutional base and would subject him to more pressure from the policymakers.

19. Neither President Bush nor President Clinton issued executive orders on intelligence that supersede E.O. 12333. It remains in effect.

20. In 1992, as the legislation was under consideration, the President declassified the fact of the NRO's existence. ✦

Phyllis Provost McNeil, Aspin-Brown Commission, "The Evolution of the U.S. Intelligence Community—An Historical Perspective," Preparing for the 21st Century: An Appraisal of U.S. Intelligence, Appendix A, *Report of the Commission on the Roles and Capabilities of the United States Intelligence Community* (March 1, 1996).

2

The Study of Intelligence in Theory and Practice

Len Scott and Peter Jackson

Professors Scott and Jackson explore the definitional problems in the study of intelligence and provide a perspective on the state of the scholarly literature in this field.

The first few years of the twenty-first century have witnessed a transformation in the role of secret intelligence in international politics. Intelligence and security issues are now more prominent than ever in Western political discourse as well as the wider public consciousness. Public expectations of intelligence have never been greater, and these demands include much greater disclosure of hitherto secret knowledge. Much of this can be attributed to the shock of the terrorist attacks of September 2001. These events drove home the vulnerability of Western societies and the importance of reliable intelligence on terrorist threats. But debates over the role of intelligence in the build-up to the Second Gulf War have played an equally important role in transforming the profile of the 'secret world' in Western society. As Christopher Andrew points out in his contribution to this collection 'In the space of only a year, the threats posed by Osama bin Laden and Saddam Hussein had succeeded in transforming British government policy on the public use of intelligence'.[1] The relationship between political leaders and their intelligence advisors came under unprecedented public scrutiny in both Britain and the United States. Both Prime Minister Tony Blair and President George W. Bush were widely charged with purposefully distorting intelligence information in order to justify their decision to make war on Iraq in April 2003. The need for a better understanding of both the nature of the intelligence process and its importance to national and international security policy has never been more apparent.

Understanding Intelligence in the Twenty-First Century draws upon the views of academics, journalists and former practitioners to consider the nature of intelligence and its evolving role in domestic and international politics. It also examines the development of intelligence as an area of academic study and assesses its emerging contribution to the study of international relations. It aims to explore the way the subject is studied, for what purpose and with what consequences.

It is nearly five decades since intelligence first emerged as a subject of serious academic study with the publication of Sherman Kent's *Strategic Intelligence for American World Policy*.[2] It is some 20 years since two eminent British historians invoked Sir Alexander Cadogan's description of intelligence as the missing dimension of international affairs.[3] The development of intelligence studies as a sub-field of international relations has continued to gather momentum ever since. Initially the terrain of political scientists, the role of intelligence in domestic and international politics now attracts the attention of an ever larger number of historians. The subject is firmly established in centres of teaching and research in both Europe and North America. As a result, the study of international security has been increasingly influenced by a better understanding of the role of intelligence in policy making—although Christopher Andrew maintains that intelligence 'is still denied its proper place in studies of the Cold War'.[4] And, as Andrew argues persuasively . . . the specific and potentially crucial subject of signal intelligence remains almost wholly neglected in Cold War historiography.[5]

The rapid growth of intelligence as a focus of academic enquiry will surely continue. Recent progress in archival disclosure, accelerated by the end of the Cold War and by changing attitudes towards official secrecy and towards the work of the security and intelligence services, has further facilitated research, understanding and debate.[6] Newly released documents, along with a range of other sources, provide an opportunity to reconsider long-standing assumptions about the motives of policy makers and the institutional character of foreign and security policy making. The events of September 11 and the war on Iraq have focused attention on all aspects of the subject. In light of these developments, the time seems right to take stock of what has been accomplished in this relatively new area of scholarly enquiry, to reflect upon the various methodological approaches used by scholars as well as the epistemological assumptions that underpin research and writing about intelligence.

Scope and Focus: What Is Intelligence? How Do We Study It?

Popular perceptions and general understanding of the nature of intelligence and its role in international relations leaves much to be desired. A starting point is the question: what is intelligence? The way intelligence is defined necessarily conditions approaches to research and writing about the subject. Sherman Kent's classic characterisations of intelligence cover 'the three separate and distinct things that intelligence devotees usually mean when they use the word'; these are: knowledge, the type of organisation that produces that knowledge and the activities pursued by that organisation.[7] In most contemporary analyses, intelligence is understood as the process of gathering, analysing and making use of information. Yet beyond such basic definitions are divergent conceptions of exactly what intelligence is and what it is for. This is perhaps because, as James Der Derian has observed, intelligence is the 'least understood and most "undertheorized" area of international relations'.[8] David Kahn, one of the most eminent scholars in the field, similarly laments that '[n]one of the definitions [of intelligence] that I have seen work'.[9] A brief survey of various approaches to the study of intelligence illuminates the difficulties inherent in any search for an inclusive definition.

Many observers tend to understand intelligence primarily as a tool of foreign and defence policy making. Others focus on its role in domestic security. Still others concentrate on the role intelligence services have played as mechanisms of state oppression.[10] One interesting divergence of views pertains to the basic character of intelligence. Michael Herman (a former practitioner) treats it as a form of state power in its own right and this conceptualisation is at the heart of the analysis in his influential study *Intelligence Power in Peace and War*.[11] John Ferris (an historian) proffers a different view, judging that 'Intelligence is not a form of power but a means to guide its use, whether as a combat multiplier, or by helping one to understand one's environment and options, and thus how to apply force or leverage, and against whom.'[12] Whichever formulation one adopts and whatever the quality of intelligence on offer, it is the judgement of political leaders and their grasp of the value and limitations of intelligence that is most crucial.[13]

So how do we define intelligence work? Should we make a distinction between 'secret' and 'open source' information? Does the internet change how we evaluate 'open source' information? What distinguishes the intelligence process from the information gathering activities of other government agencies? Michael Herman has offered a solution to this problem by identifying 'government intelligence' as 'the specialised organizations that have that name, and what they do and produce'.[14] This distinction can become problematic, however, when it comes to analyzing the impact of intelligence on decision making. Assessments drafted by intelligence agencies are usually based on a combination of 'secret' and 'open' source information. And a substantial percentage of the information from open sources is quite often drawn from material acquired and processed by other government departments, the popular media and even work that has been contracted out to non-government agencies. Since all of these areas cannot reasonably be defined as intelligence activity, this suggests that the essence of intelligence lies at the level of analysis or assessment.[15] The problem is that assessments are only one element in the decision-making process, and the illumination that they provide may only complement information provided by other government agencies or other sources of information at the level of decision. It therefore remains difficult to make confident judgements about exactly what intelligence is and precisely how it influences decision making. Should scholars accept this level of imprecision as inevitable? Or, conversely, should we continue to strive to come up with a definition of intelligence that resolves this uncertainty?

A good illustration of the difficulties inherent in defining intelligence is the controversial question of secret intervention in other societies (most commonly referred to as 'covert action'). Scholars have frequently ignored covert action in their analyses of intelligence. As Elizabeth Anderson has argued: 'the specific subject of covert action as an element of intelligence has suffered a deficiency of serious study'. She further observes that

> while academics have developed different theoretical concepts to explain other instruments of international relations—for example, weapons, trade and diplomacy—the separation of covert action from 'traditional' foreign policy instruments means that these same concepts have not been applied to covert action.[16]

There is a clear need to locate 'covert action' within the study of international relations in general and within intelligence in particular. This may also pose an interesting challenge for theorists of intelligence because considering covert action as intelligence work means that intelligence might be better understood as a tool *for the execution* of policy as well as a tool *to inform* policy. Since September 11 the political context, both national and international, has changed. Amid widespread calls for intelligence reform in the United States there are those who argue for a radical new conceptualisation of the role of intelligence in national security policy. . . . Charles Cogan, a former senior officer in the American Central Intelligence Agency (CIA), advocates, *inter alia*, a change in the orientation of US intelligence from gathering information to hunting the United States' adversaries. Such a transformation may require a new conceptual architecture for intelligence reflecting its changed role in the exercise of US military power.

There is also substantial, if rarely articulated, divergence in approaches to studying intelligence. Scholars tend to approach the subject from three relatively distinct perspectives, in the pursuit of relatively distinct objectives. The first approach, favoured among international historians in particular, but also characteristic of theoretical approaches that seek to explain the relationship between organisational structure and policy making, conceives of the study of intelligence primarily as a means of acquiring new information in order to explain specific decisions made by policy makers in both peace and war. Close attention is paid by these scholars to the process of intelligence collection, to the origin and nature of individual sources of intelligence, and to the precise use that is made of intelligence as it travels up the chain of decision. A thorough understanding of the organisational structure of government machinery, and of the place of intelligence within this machinery, is crucial to this approach. This literature overlaps with journalistic endeavours that focus on particular cases of espionage and biographies of individual officials and agents.

A second approach strives to establish general models that can explain success and failure in the intelligence process. Characteristic of political science approaches to the discipline, it focuses almost exclusively on the levels of analysis and decision. Decisive importance is attributed by adherents of this approach to structural and cognitive obstacles to the effective use of intelligence in the policy process. The aim is to identify and analyse the personal, political and institutional biases that characterise intelligence organisations and affect their performance in the decision-making process. The emphasis is on the role of preconceptions and underlying assumptions in conditioning the way intelligence is analysed and used. The result has been a range of insights into the nature of perception and misperception, the difficulty in preventing surprise, and the politicisation of the intelligence process.[17] Both of the first two conceptual approaches focus primarily on intelligence as a tool of foreign and defence policy making.

A third approach focuses instead on the political function of intelligence as a means of state control.

The past decade, in particular, has seen the appearance of a range of historical and political science literature on this subject. If the Gestapo has long been a subject of historical study, recently released archival material has enabled scholars to study the role of state security services in political and social life in the USSR and Eastern bloc states after 1945. This has provided a stimulus for a new wave of scholarship on state control since 1789. Historians are now working on a wide range of topics from the role of British and French intelligence services in maintaining imperial control overseas to the activities of security services such as MI5 or the FBI and their impact on political culture in Britain and the United States.[18] Many of the scholars engaged in this research would not consider themselves as contributing to 'intelligence studies'. Their focus is instead the use of intelligence sources to understand better the role of ideology and state power in political, social and cultural life. Yet there are strong arguments for embracing this scholarship under a broader definition of 'intelligence studies' and no reason to remain confined by disciplinary boundaries that are porous and arbitrary. One area of contemporary social science that has clear relevance to intelligence studies is the concept of surveillance. The potential of this area of enquiry is demonstrated . . . by Gary Marx in his analysis of the new forms of surveillance in both official and private contexts. Marx explores an 'empirical, analytic and moral ecology' of surveillance and demonstrates how the evolution of information technology poses serious challenges to existing conceptions of individual liberty and security.[19]

The best writing about intelligence incorporates all three of the above approaches in different ways. But there are nearly always differences in emphasis even in the seminal works that have been crucial in pushing research forward. At the heart of these divergences, arguably, is disagreement concerning the extent to which political assumptions and political culture shape the intelligence process at all levels. Few would deny that the process of identifying threats is inextricably bound up with political choices and assumptions. The same is true for the gathering, assessment and dissemination of information on these threats. Yet how we understand political processes and political culture is crucial. Scholars vary in the importance that they attribute to political culture and to ideology. Christopher Andrew, for example, argues . . . that, 'For the conceptual framework of intelligence studies to advance further, it is essential to make a clearer distinction than is usually made at present between the roles of intelligence communities in authoritarian and democratic regimes'.[20] It is interesting to note, for example, that the first two lines of enquiry tend to pay less attention to the importance of ideological assumptions in the business of gathering, analysing and using intelligence than does the third.

One notable area where differing approaches converge is research into the role of Soviet and other Communist intelligence organisations, whose study has been facilitated by (some) declassification in former communist states. One especially fascinating area that has begun to be illuminated is nuclear threat perception. It now seems clear that in the early 1960s and in the 1980s Soviet authorities became genuinely concerned about the prospect of imminent US nuclear attack.[21] The role of Soviet intelligence in generating these perceptions was crucial and study of this issue offers fertile ground for exploring the role of cognitive, bureaucratic and ideological obstacles to the effective assessment of intelligence. Moreover, such revelations have cast new light on the nature of the Cold War in general and the danger of inadvertent nuclear war in particular.

Another crucial set of questions concerns the methodological and epistemological assumptions underpinning the way the subject is studied. There has been insufficient consideration of these issues on either side of the Atlantic. Richard Aldrich has cautioned against interpreting the official records of the Public Record Office 'as an analogue of reality'.[22] He has argued persuasively that British archives are a highly manipulated source of evidence for historians. The British government's success in controlling knowledge of its wartime achievements in signals intelligence and strategic deception is a good example of official policy shaping the parameters of historical enquiry. There are almost certainly other such cases that have yet to come to light. One does not need to embrace a conspiratorial view of contemporary politics to appreciate the ramifications of this state practice for the generation of knowledge. These questions are especially important to consider in light of criticisms of studies of Soviet security and intelligence services that have been based on partial and controlled access to Soviet records.[23] When advancing such criticisms, we are obliged to consider whether recent archive-based histories of British or US intelligence are based on a more comprehensive and reliable sample of the documentary record.

And what of other sources, in particular oral testimony and interviews? Many journalists have written authoritative and well-researched accounts of intelligence-related issues, which rely on extensive contacts with officialdom.[24] Are these accounts more or less reliable than those based on the written archival record? Are they more or less prone to manipulation? And what of memoirs? And spy fiction? In his essay on 'Fiction, Faction and Intelligence'

Nigel West demonstrates that behind the supposedly impenetrable veil of British official secrecy, many former intelligence officers have written accounts (factual, fictional and factional) of their experiences. While this material cannot take the place of greater transparency and oversight, it does provide an interesting perspective on how various former members of the secret services choose to represent the world of intelligence to the wider public. The extent to which British intelligence memoirs and spy fiction can function as propaganda for the secret services remains an open question. While this material must be used with care, it should not be ignored by scholars of British intelligence. There are areas, such as the role of women in espionage/intelligence and the perspective of gender where so far the study of the subject has often been dependent on such sources.[25]

Questions about the manipulation of intelligence have been underlined by September 11 and by allegations that the British government 'sexed up' intelligence to mislead the public about Iraqi Weapons of Mass Destruction (WMD). It was through the media that details of al-Qaeda operations and plans were made known to Western populations. For the student of intelligence—as for the practitioner—the provenance and credibility of the source remains central to understanding. Yet where the dissemination of knowledge accords with discernable agendas, how we deal with the problem of knowledge is crucial. Claims made about contacts between Mohammed Atta and Iraqi intelligence officers in Prague have now been shown to be false. Yet they were of potential importance in helping prepare the public and political ground for an attack on Iraq. The same is true of claims about Iraqi attempts to acquire uranium from Niger. Whether the claim about al-Qaeda represents misinformation or disinformation, it underlines the fact that we learn of some events because those in control of relevant information wish us to learn of them, and what we learn may inform broader political perceptions. Michael Smith's paper . . . is a reminder of the tension between disclosing intelligence and risking sources, and how different leaders in different political cultures view their options and responsibilities differently.[26] These issues are of central importance to any attempt to establish the methodological foundations necessary for the effective study of intelligence.

Intelligence and the Study of International Relations

A further objective . . . is to assess both the influence and importance of intelligence studies in broader debates concerning the history and theory of international relations. Intelligence has attracted limited interest from scholars of political philosophy and International Relations (IR) theory. Tsun Tsu is much quoted for the importance he attaches to military intelligence, but later thinkers on war were less interested and less impressed. Von Clausewitz held that knowledge of 'the enemy and his country' was 'the foundation of all our ideas and actions'.[27] Yet much of the knowledge or 'information' obtained in war is 'false' and 'by far the greatest part is of a doubtful character'. How the information was acquired and processed did not detain Clausewitz, who looked to officers with a 'certain power of discrimination' to guide their analysis.

Clausewitz's omissions are shared by many political and international theorists, including classical realists and contemporary neo-realists. Machiavelli, for example, demonstrates understanding of, and enthusiasm for, what the twentieth century would come to know as strategic deception: 'Though fraud in other activities be detestable, in the management of war it is laudable and glorious, and he who overcomes an enemy by fraud is as much to be praised as he who does so by force.' Yet elsewhere in the Discourses, when reflecting on conspiracy, he shows no understanding of the opportunities for espionage and counter-espionage in dealing with the conspiracies of coup plotters.[28] On the other hand, Toni Erskine makes clear in her essay . . . that Thomas Hobbes, writing in the seventeenth century, understood the potential importance and value of espionage.[29]

Writing in 1994 Michael Fry and Miles Hochstein observed that, while intelligence studies had developed into an identifiable intellectual community, there was a noticeable 'failure to integrate intelligence studies, even in a primitive way, into the mainstream of research in international relations'.[30] In Britain the academic study of intelligence has developed overwhelmingly within international history, and thus reflects the methodological predisposition towards archive-based research characteristic of this sub-discipline. Common methodological cause between British and US historians has not prevented robust and fruitful exchanges and debates on the subject.[31] In North America, however, political scientists have played at least as prominent a role as historians in the study of intelligence in international relations. Their contributions have provided students of intelligence with a range of theoretical reflections on the nature of intelligence and its role in decision making. But interest in intelligence within the political science community has been confined mainly to those scholars working on theories of decision making. Intelligence is all but absent, conversely, in the work of most international relations theorists, and does not figure in key IR theory debates between realist, liberal institutionalist, constructivist and postmodernist approaches. It is interesting to note that, while there exists an implicit (and sometimes explicit) assumption that the study of intelligence falls within the realist camp, contemporary neo-realist writers have largely ignored intelligence in their reflections. The literature on US covert action for example, is ignored by leading neo-realist theorist, Stephen Krasner, in his analysis of the systematic violations of sovereignty in world politics. Although he advances trenchant arguments about the 'organised hypocrisy' of international discourse on sovereignty, he does not explore the potential role of intelligence as a source of both evidence and theoretical insight.[32]

The neglect of intelligence is apparent in other areas of international relations. Although one prominent item on the post-Cold War agenda was the role of intelligence in support of the United Nations and its agencies, the role of intelligence has not engaged the attention of those writing about humanitarian intervention, even though it is clear that intelligence has various roles to play, not least in providing evidence in war crimes tribunals. The role of intelligence services in promoting (or retarding) human rights is an area particularly worthy of exploration. Similarly, in debates about the democratic peace (whether democracies are less likely to engage in military operations against other democracies), attempts at regime change by clandestine means are an important dimension illuminated by the history of US covert action in various democracies (Chile, Italy, Iran and so forth). How far the events of September 11 and the war on Iraq may help change academic attitudes and research agendas in these areas remains to be seen.

If international relations theory has shown limited interest in intelligence, to what extent have students of intelligence engaged with international relations theory? It seems clear that different theoretical perspectives are beginning to permeate the sub-field of intelligence. The journal *Intelligence and National Security* has carried important theoretical contributions which reward Fry and Hochstein's optimistic assertions that international relations and intelligence studies can fruitfully search for common ground. One notable example is Andrew Rathmell's essay on the potential importance of post-modern theorizing to the practice of intelligence.[33] Rathmell argues that intelligence services must make radical changes in terms of both conceptual approach and organizational structure to adapt to the social, cultural and technological conditions of the twenty-first century. He posits that existing state-based intelligence agencies are products of modernity, but that the political and economic conditions of the modern era are disappearing. Capital intensive modes of mass production in highly urbanised nation-states are giving way, in the age of the world-wide web and digital technology, to 'knowledge intensive, dispersed globalized systems'. The end result is what Rathmell calls the 'fragmentation' of threat. What is needed, he argues, are different conceptual approaches to understanding the nature of security threats and radical changes in the way intelligence agencies collect and process knowledge on these threats. Obvious questions arise about how these new approaches might be implemented in practical terms. What is also necessary is greater awareness of the political role of the analyst in the construction of threats and threat assessments for makers of security policy of all kinds.[34]

The need to engage constructively with postmodernist thinking on security will surely increase, and this includes identifying areas where postmodernists themselves need to reflect further on existing approaches. The history of intelligence before the onset of the Cold War, for example, is often neglected. One resulting misconception is that open sources have only recently risen to prominence. The reality is that open sources have nearly always provided the majority of information for intelligence services during peacetime. It is also misleading to describe the emergence of 'globalised' threats as a 'post-modern' phenomenon. Imperial intelligence services faced such challenges throughout the nineteenth and twentieth centuries. Information technology has changed many aspects of intelligence work, but the intellectual challenges of dealing with security problems across immense spaces and over different cultures are by no means exclusively 'postmodern'. This is admirably demonstrated by the fascinating recent work of Martin Thomas.[35] It is also the case that the threat from non-state actors did not arrive with the end of the Cold War, as the history of the Anarchists and the Fenians well testifies.

An important argument made by Rathmell is that intelligence communities must become less hierarchical and more based on the concept of information 'networks' with a greater focus on 'open' sources of information. Here, the challenges identified by Rathmell and others have stimulated rather different diagnoses and prognoses. Writing before September 11, and from a very different ontological perspective, Bruce Berkowitz also argues the case for breaking down 'hierarchies and stovepipes' that restrict information flows within the intelligence community.[36] Berkowitz's article is notable for his analysis of the litany of what he terms US intelligence failures. The pressure to reform structure and

culture in the US intelligence community is strengthened, and in some cases even driven, by advances in information technology. These trends and pressures are critically examined by John Ferris in his article. . . . Where post-modernism rejects the notion of an absolute truth, the epistemological goal of those who proselytise the revolution in information warfare is perfect battlefield knowledge. Ferris casts doubt on their various assumptions and moreover reminds us that concerns with hierarchies and structures are crucial in communications security and counter-intelligence. He rightly observes that web-based nets within the US intelligence community are the 'richest treasure ever for espionage' and a grave potential vulnerability.[37]

Other theoretical innovations may well have something to offer. Recent constructivist theorising about the importance of identity and political culture in shaping both elite and public perceptions of international politics is a case in point. Its focus on identity as a central factor in the process of threat identification has obvious relevance to the study of security and intelligence. The same is true with the emphasis on cultural–institutional contexts of security policy. Intelligence services certainly have their own institutional cultures and a focus on the rules and norms which govern intelligence work in different national contexts has much to offer intelligence studies.[38] Reluctance to engage with this and other currents in international relations theory will not help efforts to expand the conceptual parameters of intelligence studies. In addition, a reluctance to engage with different strains of social theory may also comply with the intentions of those who seek to configure and inform public understanding of intelligence through the control of information. The way we choose to study the subject informs our analysis and our conclusions. As Aldrich warns, taking the archive as analogue of reality is a methodological and epistemological trap that can inadvertently legitimise activities that merit a much more critical approach.

Speaking 'Truth Unto Power' or 'Power Unto Truth'?

Much of the study of intelligence concerns the relationship between power and knowledge, or rather the relationship between certain kinds of power and certain kinds of knowledge. A sophisticated exponent of this view has been Michael Herman, writing on the basis of 25 years' experience at Government Communications Headquarters (GCHQ) and the Cabinet Office. Herman has received wide acclaim for his expositions of the process of intelligence and has been described as 'an historian and philosopher of intelligence'.[39] Although an advocate of broadening the scope of the subject, Herman's primary aim is to promote greater public understanding of intelligence. Yet, it is also undeniable that, in engaging with critical issues about the practice of the intelligence process, Herman seeks to legitimise that process. The same goals of education and legitimisation may also be ascribed to other intelligence mandarins who have written about intelligence after their retirement, notably Sir Percy Cradock, former Chairman of the Joint Intelligence Committee (JIC).[40] The work of both Herman and Cradock epitomizes the prevalent self-image of the intelligence mandarin as providing objective, 'policy-free' analysis to decision makers. Sir Percy Cradock's characterisation of the JIC and its staff as 'having an eye always to the future and to British interests, and free from the political pressures likely to afflict their ministerial masters' reflects the self-image of the intelligence community as guardian of the national interest against transient and feckless politicians.

The role of the intelligence official in the British context is therefore represented as 'speaking truth unto power'. This self-image, so central to the identity of the public servant, has been the cornerstone of both the structure and the culture of British intelligence. It is represented as the fundamental safeguard against the politicisation of intelligence, which is often alleged to be a defining characteristic of autocratic and totalitarian regimes. Clearly this image of an independent and apolitical intelligence community has been called into serious question by the 'Iraq Dossier' affair.

In the summer of 2003 the British government and intelligence community became embroiled in one of the most serious political controversies in recent memory amid charges that intelligence on Iraqi weapons of mass destruction was politicised in order to bolster support for the government's bellicose posture towards the regime of Saddam Hussein. The publication of an intelligence dossier, written by the chair of the JIC, John Scarlett, included both Joint Intelligence Committee assessments and raw human intelligence obtained by the Secret Intelligence Service (SIS). The aim was to strengthen support both at home and abroad for war with Iraq. It was claimed in the dossier that 'The Iraqi military are able to deploy [chemical and biological] weapons within 45 minutes of a decision to do so'.[41] When introducing the dossier in the House of Commons, Prime Minister Tony Blair explained that it concluded

> that Iraq has chemical and biological weapons, that Saddam has continued to produce them, that he has existing and active military plans for the use of chemical and biological weapons,

which could be activated within 45 minutes, including against his own Shia population, and that he is actively trying to acquire nuclear weapons capability.[42]

In this instance, intelligence was clearly employed to gain public support for government policy rather than as a guide for policy makers. Intelligence information was selected and presented in such a way as to emphasise the need to deal forcefully with the Iraqi regime. As Michael Handel observed nearly two decades ago, the closer the relationship between intelligence assessment and policy making, the greater the likelihood that the whole process will become politicised.[43] Indeed, a former Chairman of the JIC, Sir Rodric Braithwaite, has criticised his successors with the observation that JIC members went 'beyond assessment to become part of the process of making and advocating policy. That inevitably undermined their objectivity'.[44] At the same time, contemporary concern with use of intelligence should not obscure the fundamental reality that intelligence informs but rarely drives policy: Joint Intelligence Committees propose and Prime Ministers dispose. Another serious indictment of the Blair government policy concerns its commitment to counter-proliferation. If the Iraqi state possessed WMD, the destruction of that state means that ownership and control of these weapons are dispersed. These events could hasten the nightmare scenario of terrorist use of WMD against centres of population.

As Christopher Andrew points out . . . the publication of Joint Intelligence Committee assessments is unprecedented. It is unlikely to remain so rare, however. Changes in the international system will likely make the public use of intelligence common practice. The decline of the Westphalian principle of non-intervention in the affairs of other states, along with the effects of September 11 and the 'war on terror', has led to the emergence of the doctrine of 'pre-emptive self defence' in the United States. This has introduced an important new dimension to the role of intelligence in international relations which students and practitioners have yet fully to comprehend. In this context it will be essential to establish the existence of a threat before public opinion in order to provide legitimacy for pre-emptive interventions. Despite the political problems created by the public use of intelligence to justify the invasion of Iraq, intelligence will remain central to debates about future pre-emptive action. Pressure on governments to disclose secret intelligence will lead to pressure on intelligence services to meet public needs. This was almost certainly the case in the months leading up to the Second Gulf War. It is a trend that will surely grow as long as the doctrine of pre-emptive intervention holds sway in Western foreign policy.

All this means that we need to evaluate critically this image of the intelligence official as apolitical interpreter of the real world for political decision makers. The dangers of not doing so are clear. The case of government deception over the role of British intelligence during the Second World War is just one example of the state's willingness to intervene in an effort to shape the conceptual horizons of intellectual enquiry. An uncritical acceptance of official or semi-official representations of the intelligence process as singularly free of ideological assumptions and political biases leaves the intelligence scholar open to the familiar charge that she or he is merely legitimising and perpetuating the ideology of the state. These issues are of central concern for all scholars interested in the relationship between power and knowledge. Again it seems clear that intelligence studies and international relations theory would both benefit from greater engagement with one another.

The idea of speaking truth unto power also has clear relevance to debates over the proper relationship between government and academia.[45] Among academics, notions and theories of truth and power are more explicitly contested. Claims of objectivity run counter to concern with developing multiple rather than unitary narratives of the past. This, of course, is the very antithesis of Whitehall's immaculate conception of a Joint Intelligence Committee. At the same time, official practice and academic study exercise an undeniable attraction to one another. But there are obstacles in the way of sustained engagement between the government and the academy. Intelligence is probably the field of academic enquiry over which the British government has been most anxious to exert control. Despite a recent trend toward more openness, particularly on the part of the British Security Service (MI5), access to archival material remains tightly regulated, though the National Archives (formerly the British Public Record Office) and the Lord Chancellor's Advisory Council on Public Records have endeavoured to engage British historians in the development of declassification policy. Yet it should be noted that, although the Freedom of Information Act (FOIA) will be fully enacted in January 2005, the intelligence agencies are specifically exempt from its provisions.[46]

In the United States the relationship between academics and government has always been much more porous. Since the formation of the first centralised US intelligence agency, the Office of Strategic Services, during the Second World War, academics have played a prominent role in the evolution of US intelligence policy. The study of intelligence is often informed by quasi-official links, and the CIA has been keen to promote the academic study of the subject. Both the National Security Agency and the CIA each employ their own team of full-time professionally trained historians. Each has also invited 'scholars in residence' to spend extended periods working within the agencies. Such links have at times generated debate about the proper limits and intellectual integrity of such endeavours.[47]

But the overall benefits of these relationships are widely acknowledged. In Britain it has long been difficult to discern any comparable relationship. A greater distance has generally been maintained between 'academics' and 'practitioners'. And, as Wolfgang Krieger demonstrates . . . , the situation in Germany, as elsewhere in Europe, shows even less engagement.[48] There have been important exceptions to this general trend, most notably the scholars who were given privileged access to official records in order to write the official histories of the Second World War. Another notable exception is Christopher Andrew, whose collaborations with KGB defectors Oleg Gordievsky and Vasili Mitrokhin have illuminated KGB activities as well as British (and particularly SIS) successes in the espionage war. But it is only recently that a culture of greater openness has led to greater engagement between Britain's intelligence community and its universities. A good illustration of this trend was the willingness of Sir Stephen Lander, then Director-General of MI5, to attend academic meetings and conferences on the study of intelligence over the past few years. Further evidence of greater openness, at least on the part of the Security Service, is MI5's recent appointment of an academic historian, Christopher Andrew, to write its centenary history. Yet there are those who would argue that this kind of engagement is not without costs. For some academics the Ivory Tower should remain a sanctuary from the compromises of officialdom and provide a panorama (or, a *camera obscura*) on the world outside. For others, academics are there to tell the world about the world. Yet, while many academics aspire to policy relevance, intelligence is one area where officialdom may remain sceptical about the value of engagement with the academy.

Dark Sides of Moons

Reflecting on the work of the JIC, Sir Percy Cradock has observed that 'it has a predilection for threats rather than opportunities, for the dark side of the moon'.[49] Certainly the issues of strategic surprise and of intelligence failure have loomed large in the evolution of the study of intelligence. This is unlikely to change significantly. Providing warning against surprise is central to both official and public perceptions of the fundamental role of intelligence services. The events of September 11, 2001 have clearly reinforced this trend. Desmond Ball has described September 11 as 'the worst intelligence failure by the US intelligence community since Pearl Harbor'.[50] Yet such judgements also raise questions about the meaning we give to the term intelligence failure as well as to how we explain and assign responsibility for what happened. Historians and political scientists will continue to study Pearl Harbor, the Tet offensive, the Yom Kippur War, Argentina's seizure of the Falklands/Malvinas, Iraq's invasion of Kuwait, and, of course, the terrorist attacks on the World Trade Center and the Pentagon. But they will also need to revisit from time to time the conceptual foundations of their studies.

Recent developments in the study of security in international politics have attempted to broaden predominant conceptions of security to provide a more sophisticated understanding of the problem of instability in international society. The study of intelligence, with its focus on the identification and interpretation of threat, and on the architecture of threat perception, has much to offer and much to gain from greater engagement with new approaches to security. Contemporary intelligence agendas (both official and academic) range from economic security to environment to health to organised crime, as well as to more traditional areas of arms transfers, proliferation of WMD, and UN peace keeping and peace enforcing. Changes in world politics since the end of the Cold War have created greater awareness of the importance of these issues. The fact that the CIA has primary responsibility for the HIV/AIDS threat suggests that official thinking in Washington has responded to these trends in ways that have not always been acknowledged. Intelligence communities must pay closer attention to the many dimensions of global insecurity, not least so that policy makers can better understand the need to alleviate social and economic conditions that are one source of disaffected recruits for extremist groups. In short, the practice of intelligence will change and adapt to new political problems facing world politics, as well as to more long-standing concerns with injustices that lie at the heart of much global instability. The same is true of the study of intelligence. . . .

The role of threat perception in the policy process is bound to remain a central concern in the study of intelligence. The same is true of the relationship between 'producers' and 'consumers'. But it is important to remember that many intelligence services do more than just collect and process information. Many internal security agencies in democratic as well as non-democratic states possess pow-

ers of arrest and thus function as tools of state power. Indeed the Gestapo, the KGB and the Stasi are only the most notorious examples of the potential threat to individual freedom posed by domestic security and intelligence services. Yet another controversial and problematic area of intelligence activity is that of secret intervention in the affairs of other states (and non-state actors). As noted above, the case of 'covert action' provides an interesting perspective on the role of intelligence and intelligence services in the exercise of power. Over the past half-century, covert action has often undermined the legitimacy of Western intelligence services both domestically and internationally. A fundamental question is therefore: to what extent and in what ways should covert action be considered a function of intelligence and intelligence services. One answer is provided by Sherman Kent in his arguably tautological observation that intelligence is what intelligence services do. A variation on this might be to say that intelligence knowledge is power, and other exercises of power by intelligence services fall within the same ambit. A rather different view would be to suggest that secrecy, rather than power or knowledge, is the unifying theme of intelligence discourse. This is the line of argument pursued by Len Scott . . . ; a more radical perspective on secrecy is proffered by Robert A. Goldberg who argues that secrecy plays a crucial and perfidious role in sustaining conspiracy theories.[51]

The distinction between gathering intelligence and intervening in the internal affairs of other states, and thus the distinction between intelligence as a guide to policy rather than a tool of policy, can be misleading. This is particularly true in the realm of human intelligence, where the idea of an agent of influence, for example, challenges a simple distinction between gathering knowledge and taking action. It is interesting to compare the British and US literature on covert action. In the United States there has been long-standing awareness of the subject that has generated both public and scholarly debates. More recently, systematic declassification of files dealing with covert action has made a significant contribution to understanding the origins and dynamics of the Cold War. The declassification of CIA records has more clearly revealed the scope and scale of operations from Cuba to Chile to Indonesia to Guatemala. Indeed, in the view of some scholars, the history of covert action compels revision of the historical and political accounts of the Cold War, and fatally weakens the view that the US policy was simply concerned with containment.[52] These issues have not received the attention they deserve in the study of British intelligence so far. Although recently published studies by Richard Aldrich and Stephen Dorril have illuminated a great deal, British covert action in both Cold War and post-imperial contexts is an area that requires further study. Here the endeavours of senior intelligence mandarins to divert the focus to the sanitised and cerebral contexts of Whitehall analysis may reflect a conscious (or unconscious) attempt to divert attention away from the more dramatic and controversial question of covert action. It may be that such activities are marginal to the primary missions of the British intelligence services. Yet the fact is that this question remains shrouded in uncertainty.

Intelligence and Ethics

One contribution of the (largely US) study of covert action has been to bring together ethics and intelligence studies. There is a significant literature which has been largely ignored by scholars working on the role of intelligence in policy making.[53] The ethical and legal dimensions of intelligence are rarely analysed, particularly in historical accounts—although in the United States ethical issues have frequently been explored within debates over intelligence accountability. The need for an explicit concern with moral issues has been identified by Michael Herman, who has begun to explore ethical dimensions of intelligence in a broader sense.[54] Herman has argued that intelligence requires 'a similar ethical foundation' to the use of armed force. An equally telling and compelling observation is his view that 'Ethics should be recognized as a factor in intelligence decisions, just as in anything else'.[55] Such a view compels attention not least given its provenance. This is not an entirely new concern. Abram Shulsky has also contended that an ethical case for conducting intelligence operations can be found in Tsun Tsu as early as the fifth century BC.[56]

In his famous essay on 'The Profession and Vocation of Politics', Max Weber observes that 'No ethics in the world can get round the fact that the achievement of "good" ends is in many cases tied to the necessity of employing morally suspect or at least morally dangerous means'.[57] This dilemma is a central concern for all those interested in the role of intelligence in politics. To what ends should the 'morally suspect' means of intelligence be put? For whose 'good ends' should these means be employed? To whom, or to what, should they be ultimately responsible? Can their responsibilities ever be to the universal or will they always be to the particular? The crux of the issue, according to Weber, is a crucial dilemma of politics: that the interests of particular communities or polities will not always be compatible with the wider interests of humanity. Weber rejects the universalist assumptions of the 'ethics of principled conviction' for their disregard

of the consequences of political choice. He argues instead that the first responsibility of those involved in politics must be to their own community.[58] These questions are addressed by both Michael Herman and Toni Erskine. . . . Michael Herman reflects further on the ethical justifications for intelligence and explores the opportunities for doing so in the wake of September 11.[59] In her contribution, Toni Erskine locates emerging ethical reflections on intelligence gathering within the traditional frameworks of realist, consequentialist and deontological traditions.[60] Such an approach offers new vistas for potential research and has obvious relevance to efforts to combine intelligence and security concerns with an 'ethical foreign policy'.

Hitherto ethics has remained an under-explored area in intelligence studies. A former permanent secretary at the Ministry of Defence, Sir Michael Quinlan, who played a key role in British thinking about the morality of nuclear deterrence and was also responsible for an official overview of British intelligence in the post-Cold War era, has remarked upon the lack of a conceptual structure for studying the morality of espionage. Quinlan has lamented the absence of a doctrine for what he terms 'Just Espionage'.[61] On the other hand, Quinlan fascinatingly refers to ethical problems as a 'cost' of intelligence. The tension between these two positions suggests that intelligence may often be situated at the fault-line between the theory and practice of international politics. In any case, this is a fascinating and important aspect of intelligence that bears further reflection and research.

Ethics are not only relevant at the level of high-policy. The ethical ethos of an intelligence organisation is of great importance to understanding it as an institution. Studying that ethos remains a significant methodological hurdle. How intelligence services and intelligence officers view their responsibilities to their agents and to others, for example, is a potentially fascinating question. How far intelligence agencies will go to protect their sources is an ethical and operational matter that has surfaced for example in accounts and allegations concerning British security activities in Northern Ireland. The codes of conduct—both written and unwritten—of intelligence services provide one potential avenue for exploring the ethical constraints and dilemmas involved in human intelligence gathering as (to a lesser extent) do the ethical views of the individual agents. This is an aspect on which there has been little systematic study, though memoirs and other accounts of operations, including authoritative accounts by journalists, provide vignettes and insights.[62]

Debate about a range of ethical issues concerning the conduct of intelligence in war extends to legal questions about whether prisoners should be taken and how they should be treated. In the United States and elsewhere there has been serious public discussion about the use of torture in extracting information from terrorist suspects, reflecting the dramatic impact of events on public debate. US debates about the use of assassination as an instrument of statecraft have been rekindled.[63] Ethics seems destined to be ever more closely entwined with public debate and discourse concerning intelligence. Yet public perceptions of what intelligence is and what it does owe as much to fictional representations as to public debate in the 'real' world of international politics.

Popular Culture and Intelligence

At least since the aftermath of the Franco-Prussian war in 1871, popular culture has often played an important role in shaping both official and public attitudes towards intelligence. Michael Miller has demonstrated the way fears of foreign espionage and national insecurity gripped the French imagination during this period. The Dreyfus Affair, which had such grievous consequences for French intelligence, unfolded in an atmosphere of spy mania over the machinations of an imaginary army of German spies in France controlled by the notorious spymaster Wilhelm Stieber. The fact that there was no army of spies and that Stieber was a police chief rather than a master of espionage, did not matter. Through to the outbreak of war in 1914 spy mania was created and sustained by memories of France's defeat in 1871 and by a spy literature which played on national anxieties about France's vulnerability to foreign espionage.[64] The British public demonstrated a similar appetite for espionage stories and invasion scares, of which some of the most widely read were produced by William Le Queux. It was in the context of a wave of greatly exaggerated official and popular concern over the threat of foreign espionage that a British security service was established in 1909.[65]

Fictional representations of international politics as a struggle for survival between national intelligence services thus played an important role in the evolution of both French and British intelligence before the First World War. Between the two World Wars, spy adventures stories, and even spy films, became a permanent fixture of Western popular culture. This trend continued through the Cold War era. Graham Greene, John Le Carré, Ian Fleming and Tom Clancy are only the most prominent of several generations of novelists who used intelligence as both medium and metaphor when interpreting the era of superpower rivalry for the reading public. For most of the twentieth century, representations of intelligence in popular culture were far and away the most influential factors shaping public attitudes and perceptions. Yet, with a few notable exceptions, scholars have been reluctant to reflect upon the implications of this in their analyses of the relationship between intelligence and politics. Once again, there is potentially interesting work being done in the cognate field of cultural history which could enrich the study of intelligence. Cultural historians, especially those interested in Cold War popular and political culture, have begun to pay careful attention to the role of film and fiction in shaping both elite and popular attitudes towards international politics. The intersection between this work and the study of intelligence has not received the attention it deserves.

Jeremy Black provides an interesting perspective on the issue of popular culture in his exploration of the geopolitics of James Bond. Of particular interest is his analysis of the way Anglo-American relations are represented in the Bond genre.[66] Fictional representations of intelligence form the basis of much public understanding. As Nigel West observes, no less an authority than former SIS Chief, Sir Colin McColl, considered Bond 'the best recruiting sergeant the service ever had'[67]—perhaps the converse view of intelligence critic Philip Knightley who complained that the 'fictional glorification of spies enables the real ones to go on playing their sordid games'.[68] A more perplexing if intriguing relationship between reality and fiction is illustrated by the occasion recounted by Jeremy Black when the Soviet Politburo issued instructions to the KGB to acquire the gadgetry displayed in the latest Bond film.

Fiction provides a range of ethical representations of intelligence.[69] Jeremy Black observes that 'the world of Bond is not characterized by ambiguity . . . there is good (including good rogues . . .) and bad'.[70] Other representations convey a very different moral reality. One of Le Carré's characters, Connie Sachs, characterizes Cold War espionage as 'half angels fighting half devils'.[71] This can be read as Le Carré's own perspective on intelligence and intelligence work. It stands in contrast to the self-image of Western intelligence officers proffered by a former senior member of the Secret Intelligence Service: 'honesty inside the service, however much deception might be practiced outside it, and never descend to the other side's methods'.[72] Fiction also illustrates specific ethical problems and dilemmas. How far an intelligence organisation is prepared to risk or sacrifice its own 'side' in pursuit of a 'higher' objective is a popular theme, well illustrated in Le Carré's *The Spy Who Came in From the Cold*.[73]

Other representations of intelligence go further in this regard. In the 1975 film *Three Days of the*

Condor, for example, the CIA assassinates its own officers to protect its designs for global control of oil resources. The film illustrates various themes commonly found in conspiracy theories, not least that intelligence services are malign, all-powerful and all-pervasive. This manner of representing the ethics of intelligence services is very common in both literature and in film. A more recent example is the 2002 film version of Robert Ludlum's *The Bourne Identity*—which depicts the CIA as both omnipotent and utterly immoral.[74] The extent to which these types of cultural representations are influenced by public disclosure of intelligence activities would be an interesting avenue for further research.

Fictional conspiracy theories frequently accord with the genuine kind in giving meaning to events. As Robert Goldberg argues in his essay . . . :

> Despite their weaknesses, conspiracy theories offer much to believers. If slippery in their logic and often careless of facts and assumptions, they order the random and make consistent the paradoxical. In the face of national crisis and human failure, conspiracy theorists rush to find purpose in tragedy and clarity in ambiguity. They also respond to the traumatized who cry for vengeance and demand the identities of those responsible. Conspiracy thinking thus becomes an antidote to powerlessness.[75]

Some of these observations resonate with James Der Derian's analysis of Hollywood's representation of conspiracy when he writes of:

> the conspiratorial aesthetic, which produces and is sustained by the tension between fear and desire. The world system might, on the face of it, be speeding out of control, yet we cling to metaphysical faith and find perverse pleasure in cinematic confirmation that somewhere under the table, in the highest corporate or government office, someone is pulling the strings or at the very least is willing with the best technology, fastest speed and longest reach to intervene secretly, if sinisterly, when necessary. It then makes sense to find in coeval events, synchronicities, even odd accidents, the intellectual evidence and psychological comfort of the hidden hand.[76]

Yet, merely because there are individual or collective psychological needs in a hidden hand does not mean that hidden hands do not exist. One reason why there are conspiracy theories is because there are conspiracies. Indeed the history of covert action is the history of conspiracy. While it would be simplistic to suggest that the former begat the latter, covert action is nevertheless the sturdy twin of conspiracy theory. The suggestion, for example, that the British state undertakes the murder of its citizens for political purposes is a familiar trope in popular representations of intelligence activity. The suggestion that Hilda Murrell, an elderly anti-nu-

clear protester, was killed by the security service in an operation against nuclear protesters gained surprising currency. MI5's website currently proclaims that 'We do not kill people or arrange their assassination'.[77] Yet it is now clear that there was collusion between British officials and loyalist paramilitaries in murders and other crimes in Northern Ireland.[78] As Sir John Stevens has commented: 'the unlawful involvement of agents in murder implies that the security forces sanction killings'.[79]

Fictional representation thrives on the plausibly implausible. Had the events of September 11 been crafted by a script writer, they may well have been dismissed as incredible and fanciful (even if they would have gained attention for transgressing Hollywood's devotion to happy endings). In the aforementioned *Three Days of the Condor*, the CIA analyses books to check, whether they depict actual CIA operations. After September 11 there are indications of new-found interest in how fiction writers conceptualise and represent threat. Conspiracy and conspiracy theory will remain inextricably linked with intelligence in popular perception and cultural representation. Disentangling the two remains an essential part of the enterprise. Michael Smith's defence of Prime Minister Churchill's use of intelligence on Nazi atrocities in the Soviet Union is a good illustration of how this can be done.[80] The issue of how far fiction corresponds to reality is linked to questions concerning the way we perceive and construct reality. Le Carré's novels are widely accepted as authentic depictions of the techniques and tradecraft of espionage—though his representation of the ethics of the service provoked anger from within.[81] More recently, the film *U-571* was criticised for depicting the seizure of the German naval Enigma by US rather than by British forces.[82] There is of course a long tradition of changing or manipulating historical 'events' for dramatic effect. But to what extent do such fictional representations actually shape popular attitudes? This is a question that awaits systematic exploration. How far fictional representations are *intended* to frame popular understandings has received rather more attention—particularly in the recent boom of studies of the cultural history of the Cold War.[83] The events of September 11 and the 'war on terror' have given these questions a new saliency and urgency. How Hollywood will now depict intelligence services and how it will represent the US government will be issues to watch carefully.

A Final 'Missing Dimension': National and International Intelligence Co-operation

One other relatively neglected aspect in the study of intelligence is cooperation between different intelligence services at both the national and international levels. At the national level, efficient co-operation between secret services is crucial to the effective exploitation of intelligence. The importance of a rational system of inter-service co-ordination was highlighted, once again, by the events of September 11, 2001. Insufficient co-operation between various US security and intelligence services is consistently cited as a central factor in the failure to prevent the successful attacks on the World Trade Center and the Pentagon. The 858-page Congressional Report on these events published in July 2003 severely criticised both the CIA and the FBI for failing to develop an effective system for sharing intelligence on terrorist activity inside the United States with one another and with other departments concerned with national security.[84] Yet, despite the valuable start made by pioneers, this is a field that has not received systematic study by either political scientists or historians.[85] A comparative study, examining different national approaches to solving this problem, would be particularly valuable and policy relevant.

The question of intelligence co-operation at the international level has received more attention, particularly from historians. The origins, development and functioning of Anglo-American 'intelligence alliance' since 1940 have been the subject of relatively intense study from a range of perspectives.[86] Important research has also been done on such diverse subjects as intelligence sharing between the West and the Soviet Union during the Second World War, on intelligence collaboration within the Soviet bloc during the Cold War and between Soviet and Cuban intelligence, and between Western intelligence and former Nazi intelligence officers.[87] We also have a very useful collection of essays on the subject of 'Knowing One's Friends' that provides fascinating insights into the ambiguous role of intelligence between friendly states.[88]

Michael Herman and Richard Aldrich have both provided useful reflections on the nature of international intelligence co-operation.[89] This will assist the growing number of scholars now researching the potential role of intelligence in international organisations such as NATO, the European Union or the United Nations.[90] Important work has also been undertaken on the role of intelligence in international police work. The changing parameters of intelligence collaboration after September 11, and increased public awareness of this co-operation, suggest that this will be an area of great potential growth in the field. When a British arms dealer was arrested in August 2003 attempting to sell a surface-to-air missile to FBI agents posing as terrorists, news of the role of SIS and MI5 was immediately made public, illustrating changing attitudes towards disclosure as well as in practice.[91] One ne-

glected aspect identified by Len Scott . . . is the role of intelligence services in conducting clandestine diplomatic activities with adversaries, both states and non-states.[92]

All of this augurs well for opening new avenues for students of intelligence and security in contemporary international relations. Yet the research trends outlined above remain disparate. There are still few monographs or collections of essays devoted to the specific question of co-operation and collaboration between national intelligence services. Nor has sufficient research and reflection been given to the delicate relationship between intelligence and political relations between states. The successful prosecution of the present 'war on terror' depends largely on the ability of national intelligence services to collaborate with one another effectively in rooting out international terrorist cells. The relationship between politics and intelligence has never been more important. There is a clear need for more systematic study of this area.

Conclusion

The publication in 1946 of the lengthy and detailed Congressional Report on the Pearl Harbor attack provided the primary raw material for one of the founding texts in the intelligence studies canon.[93] Roberta Wohlstetter's marriage of communications theory with detailed historical research in *Pearl Harbor: Warning and Decision* demonstrated the rich potential of an interdisciplinary approach to the study of intelligence and policy making.[94] Whether or not the recently published Congressional Report on the surprise attacks of September 11 produces another seminal text, the events of the past three years are bound to have profound implications for the study of intelligence.

Michael Herman has argued that, 'Governments' and people's views of intelligence will be permanently affected by the events of September 11'.[95] While this is debatable, it is undeniable that intelligence occupies a more prominent place in the public sphere than ever before. Quite apart from the publication of secret intelligence on Iraq, debates about the practice of intelligence now take place on a scale and at a level that would have been inconceivable three years ago. Issues such as the relative importance of human intelligence as against 'technical assets', the importance of international intelligence collaboration and the cognitive obstacles to effective analysis and warning have all been debated. As Wesley Wark is surely right to argue: 'Learning to live with an open-ended "war on terrorism" will mean learning to live with intelligence.'. . . These developments will doubtless provide both challenges and opportunities to scholars interested in the study of intelligence.

Should the terror attacks in New York and Washington force us to rethink the subject we are studying? Will they change the nature and conduct of intelligence operations forever? If so, how will this affect the study of intelligence and its role in world politics? These are questions that bear further reflection in any exercise aimed at establishing a future agenda for intelligence studies. The evidence so far suggests that, while the role of intelligence in international politics has certainly evolved, and scholars will have to adjust to its evolution, the changes may not be as revolutionary as they at first appeared. As in other areas of world politics, the immovable object of change confronts the irresistible force of continuity.

It is true that there was no Pearl Harbor precedent for the debates about the ethical restraints on intelligence activity. Nor was there much public discussion of the need for trans-national intelligence co-operation. These differences reflect changes that have taken place in world politics since the Second World War. International norms have evolved and now place greater limitations on the exercise of power than those that existed during and after the Second World War. Globalisation, and in particular advances in information technology, have thrown up new challenges that require new solutions. But there are nonetheless remarkable parallels between debates over Pearl Harbor and the aftermath of September 11. In both instances, predictably, the overwhelming focus was on learning lessons and prescribing policies. Many of the themes are very similar: the inability to conduct effective espionage against a racially or culturally 'alien' adversary; the failure to organise and co-ordinate inter-service intelligence collection and analysis; the lack of resources for both gathering, translating and analysing intelligence and, finally, the failure of political leaders to understand the value and limitations of intelligence. The surprise attack on United States territory in December 1941 killed over 2,000 people and precipitated the United States' entry into war in Europe and Asia. Pearl Harbor portended a transformation in the US role in world politics, and indeed in world politics itself. The surprise attack on United States territory on September 11, 2001 killed a similar number of people (though these were not military personnel and included many hundreds of non-Americans). It too precipitated US wars—in Afghanistan and Iraq. How far it has transformed world politics will remain open to debate. The context in which intelligence is conducted and studied continues to change. This collection will hopefully provide some guidance and illumination along the dimly lit pathways that lie ahead.

Questions for Further Discussion

1. Why has the study of intelligence been a peripheral topic for most academics who write about international affairs and national security?

2. What do you think are the greatest barriers to research in the field of intelligence studies?

3. Where would you say are the largest gaps in scholarly knowledge about intelligence?

4. Why did the field of intelligence studies begin to come into its own after the mid-1970s?

Endnotes

1. Christopher Andrew, 'Intelligence, International Relations and "Under-theorisation"', *Intelligence and National Security*, Volume 19, Number 2, June 2004, pp. 170-184 (15).
2. Sherman Kent, *Strategic Intelligence for American World Policy* (Princeton, NJ: Princeton University Press 1949).
3. Christopher Andrew and David Dilks (eds.), *The Missing Dimension: Governments and Intelligence Communities in the Twentieth Century* (Urbana, IL: University of Illinois Press 1984).
4. Christopher Andrew, 'Intelligence in the Cold War: Lessons and Learning', in Harold Shukman (ed.), *Agents for Change: Intelligence Services in the 21st Century* (London: St Ermin's Press 2000), pp. 1–2.
5. Andrew, 'Intelligence, International Relations', pp. 29–41. For recent research on signals intelligence, see Matthew Aid and Cees Wiebes (eds.), *Secrets of Signals Intelligence during the Cold War and Beyond*, Special Issue of *Intelligence and National Security*, 16/1 (2001).
6. An important recent development in the evolution of more liberal classification and declassification policies in the United States is the implementation of Executive Order 12958 'Classified National Security Information' in April 1995, although the significance of this has been contested. The Blair government has been largely unsuccessful in its attempts to establish a similar regime in Britain. For an interesting perspective on US attitudes towards government secrecy see the report of the 'Commission on Protecting and Reducing Government Secrecy' established in Washington in 1995: *Secrecy: Report of the Commission on Protecting and Reducing Government Secrecy* (Washington, DC: Government Printing Office 1997); and Daniel Moynihan, *Secrecy* (New Haven, CT: Yale University Press 1998). On the British side see David Vincent, *The Culture of Secrecy* (Oxford: Oxford University Press 1998).
7. Kent, *Strategic Intelligence*, p. ix.
8. James Der Derian, *Antidiplomacy: Spies, Terror, Speed and War* (Oxford: Blackwell 1992); see also Michael Fry and Miles Hochstein, 'Epistemic Communities: Intelligence Studies and International Relations' in Wesley K. Wark (ed.), *Espionage: Past, Present, Future?* (London: Frank Cass 1994), pp. 14–28 (also published as a Special Issue of *Intelligence and National Security*, 8/3 (1993)).
9. David Kahn, 'An Historical Theory of Intelligence', *Intelligence and National Security*, 16/3 (2002), p. 79. For

a thoughtful comparative analysis of the concept of intelligence in different national contexts see Philip H. J. Davies, 'Ideas of Intelligence: Divergent National Concepts and Institutions', *Harvard International Review* (Autumn 2002), pp. 62–6. For an earlier valuable collection of essays dealing with these issues see Kenneth G. Robertson (ed.), *British and American Approaches to Intelligence* (Basingstoke: Macmillan 1987).

10. Examples of the last approach include Richard Thurlow, *The Secret State: British Internal Security in the Twentieth Century* (Oxford: Blackwell 1994), Amy Knight, *Beria: Stalin's First Lieutenant* (Princeton, NJ: Princeton University Press 1993), Robert Gellately, *The Gestapo and German Society: Enforcing Racial Policy 1933–1945* (Oxford: Oxford University Press 1990).

11. Michael Herman, *Intelligence Power in Peace and War* (Cambridge: Cambridge University Press 1996).

12. John Ferris, 'Intelligence' in R. Boyce and J. Maiolo (eds.), *The Origins of World War Two: The Debate Continues* (Basingstoke: Palgrave 2003), p. 308.

13. For an excellent analysis of US presidents and their use of intelligence see Christopher Andrew, *For the President's Eyes Only: Secret Intelligence and the American Presidency From Washington to Bush* (London: HarperCollins 1995).

14. Michael Herman, 'Diplomacy and Intelligence', *Diplomacy & Statecraft*, 9/2 (1998), pp. 1–2.

15. For discussion see Herman, *Intelligence Power* and Abram Shulsky, *Silent Warfare: Understanding the World of Intelligence* (London: Brassey's US 1993).

16. Elizabeth Anderson, 'The Security Dilemma and Covert Action: The Truman Years', *International Journal of Intelligence and CounterIntelligence*, 11/4 (1998/99), p. 404.

17. See, for example, Michael I. Handel, *The Diplomacy of Surprise* (Cambridge, MA: Center for International Affairs, Harvard University 1980), idem, 'Intelligence and Military Operations' in idem (ed.), *Intelligence and Military Operations* (London: Frank Cass 1990), pp. 1–95; Richard Betts, 'Analysis, War and Decision: Why Intelligence Failures are Inevitable', *World Politics*, 31/1 (1978), pp. 961–88; and Robert Jervis, 'Intelligence and Foreign Policy', *International Security*, 2/3 (1986/87), pp. 141–61.

18. See Martin Thomas, 'French Intelligence Gathering and the Syrian Mandate, 1920–1940', *Middle Eastern Studies*, 38/2 (2002) and his forthcoming, *Intelligence and Empire: Security Services and Colonial Control in North Africa and the Middle East, 1919–1940* (Berkeley, CA: University of California Press, forthcoming). See also Richard J. Popplewell, *Intelligence and Imperial Defence: British Intelligence and the Defence of the Indian Empire, 1904–1924* (London: Frank Cass 1995).

19. See Gary Marx, 'Some Concepts That May Be Useful in Understanding the Myriad Forms and Contexts of Surveillance', *Intelligence and National Security*, pp. 78–98. For an authoritative overview of the concepts and context of surveillance in social and political theory see Christopher Dandeker, *Surveillance, Power and Modernity* (Oxford: Polity Press in association with Blackwell 1990).

20. Andrew, 'Intelligence, International Relations', p. 34.

21. See in particular Aleksandr Fursenko and Timothy Naftali, *'One Hell of a Gamble': Khrushchev, Castro, Kennedy and the Cuban Missile Crisis 1958–1964* (London: John Murray 1997); Christopher Andrew and Oleg Gordievsky, *KGB: The Inside Story* (London: Hodder & Stoughton 1990); and Benjamin B. Fischer, *A Cold War Conundrum: The 1983 Soviet War Scare* (Washington, DC: Central Intelligence Agency, Center for the Study of Intelligence 1997).

22. Richard Aldrich, *The Hidden Hand: Britain, America and Cold War Secret Intelligence* (London: John Murray 2001), p. 6. On this important methodological issue see also idem, *Intelligence and the War Against Japan* (Cambridge: Cambridge University Press 2000), pp. 385–7, and P. Jackson, 'The Politics of Secret Service in War, Cold War and Imperial Retreat', *Contemporary British History*, 14/4 (2003), pp. 423–31.

23. See Sheila Kerr, 'KGB Sources on the Cambridge Network of Soviet Agents: True or False', *Intelligence and National Security*, 11/3 (1996), pp. 561–85, and 'Oleg Tsarev's Synthetic KGB Gems', *International Journal of Intelligence and Counter-Intelligence*, 14/1 (2001), pp. 89–116; see Nigel West's rejoinder, 'No Dust on KGB Jewels', *International Journal of Intelligence and CounterIntelligence*, 14/4 (2001–2002), pp. 589–92.

24. See for example, Mark Urban, *UK Eyes Alpha: The Inside Story of British Intelligence* (London: Faber & Faber 1996) and Michael Smith, *New Cloak, Old Dagger: How Britain's Spies Came in From the Cold* (London: Victor Gollancz 1996). The pre-eminent figure in combining recently released archival material with the fruits of personal disclosure and oral testimony is undoubtedly Peter Hennessy; see his *The Secret State: Whitehall and the Cold War* (London: Allen Lane Penguin Press 2002).

25. For recent examples of writing on women, gender and intelligence see Sandra C. Taylor, 'Long-Haired Women, Short-Haired Spies: Gender, Espionage, and America's War on Vietnam', *Intelligence and National Security*, 13/2 (1998), pp. 61–70 and Tammy M. Proctor, *Female Intelligence: Women and Espionage in the First World War* (New York and London: New York University Press 2003); see also the journal, *Minerva: Women and War* published by Taylor & Francis. We are grateful to Jenny Mathers for this information.

26. Michael Smith, 'Bletchley Park and the Holocaust', *Intelligence and National Security* 19 (Summer 2004), pp. 111–21.

27. Carl von Clausewitz, *On War* (ed. by Anatol Rapoport, New York: Pelican 1968), p. 162. For analysis of Clausewitz on intelligence see John Ferris and Michael I. Handel, 'Clausewitz, Intelligence, Uncertainty and the Art of Command in Military Operations', *Intelligence and National Security*, 10/1 (1995), pp. 1–58.

28. John Plamenatz (ed.), *Machiavelli, The Prince, Selections From the Discourses and Other Writings* (London: Fontana/Collins 1975), pp. 252–71.

29. Toni Erskine, " 'As Rays of Light to the Human Soul"? Moral Agents and Intelligence Gathering', *Intelligence and National Security*, 10/1 (1995), pp. 195–215.

30. Fry and Hochstein, 'Epistemic Communities', p. 14.

31. See in particular the reflections of John Lewis Gaddis, 'Intelligence, Espionage, and Cold War Origins', *Diplomatic History*, 13 (Spring 1989), pp. 191–212, and D. Cameron Watt, 'Intelligence and the Historian: A Comment on John Gaddis's "Intelligence, Espionage, and Cold War Origins" ', ibid., 14 (Spring 1990), pp. 199–204.

32. Stephen D. Krasner, 'Rethinking the Sovereign State Model', in Michael Cox, Tim Dunne and Ken Booth (eds.), *Empires, Systems and State: Great Transformations in International Politics* (Cambridge: Cambridge University Press 2001). We are grateful to Tim Dunne for drawing our attention to this.

33. Andrew Rathmell, 'Towards Postmodern Intelligence', *Intelligence and National Security*, 17/3 (2002), pp. 87–

104. See also the work of James Der Derian who has written extensively on aspects of intelligence from a post-modern perspective. See, for example, his *Antidiplomacy*.

34. This is a central focus of the interesting and important work being done in France by scholars such as Didier Bigo and others, whose work is most often published in the journal *Cultures et Conflits*.

35. See Thomas, 'French Intelligence Gathering' and *Intelligence and Empire*.

36. Bruce Berkowitz, 'Better Ways to Fix US Intelligence', *Orbis* (Fall 2001), pp. 615–17.

37. John Ferris, 'Netcentric Warfare, C4ISR and Information Operations: Towards a Revolution in Military Intelligence?', *Intelligence and National Security*, 10/1 (1995), p. 64.

38. For constructivist approaches to IR see, for example, the essays in Peter J. Katzenstein (ed.), *The Culture of National Security* (New York: Columbia University Press 1996), and Alexander Wendt, *Social Theory of International Politics* (Cambridge: Cambridge University Press 1999).

39. Hennessy, *Secret State*, p. xiii. See also Lawrence Freedman, 'Powerful Intelligence', *Intelligence and National Security*, 12/2 (1997), pp. 198–202.

40. Percy Cradock, *Know Your Enemy: How the Joint Intelligence Committee Saw the World* (London: John Murray 2002).

41. *Iraq's Weapons of Mass Destruction: The Assessment of the British Government* (London: The Stationery Office, 24 September 2002), p. 17.

42. *Hansard, HC deb.* Vol. 390, Col. 3, 24 September 2002.

43. Michael Handel, 'The Politics of Intelligence', in idem, *War, Strategy and Intelligence* (London: Frank Cass 1987), pp. 187–228.

44. Richard Norton-Taylor, 'Intelligence Heads Under Fire', *The Guardian*, 6 December 2003.

45. See William Wallace, 'Truth and Power, Monks and Technocrats: Theory and Practice in International Relations', *Review of International Studies*, 22/3 (1996), pp. 301–21 and replies: Ken Booth, 'A Reply to Wallace', *Review of International Studies*, 23/3 (1997), pp. 371–7 and Steve Smith, 'Power and Truth: A Reply to William Wallace', *Review of International Studies*, 23/4 (1997), pp. 507–16.

46. We are grateful to Stephen Twigge for this information.

47. For scrutiny of the relationship between US academia and US intelligence see Robin Winks, *Cloak and Gown: Scholars in the Secret War* (New York: William Morrow 1987).

48. Wolfgang Krieger, 'German Intelligence History: A Field in Search of Scholars', *Intelligence and National Security* 19 (Summer 2004), pp. 42–53.

49. Cradock, *Know Your Enemy*, p. 4.

50. Desmond Ball, 'Desperately Seeking Bin Laden: The Intelligence Dimension of the War Against Terrorism', in Ken Booth and Tim Booth (eds.), *Worlds in Collision: Terror and the Future of Global Order: Intelligence and National Security* 19 (Summer 2004), (Basingstoke: Palgrave Macmillan 2002), p. 60.

51. Len Scott, 'Secret Intelligence, Covert Action and Clandestine Diplomacy', *Intelligence and National Security* 19 (Summer 2004), pp. 162–79; Robert A. Goldberg, " 'Who Profited From the Crime?" Intelligence Failure, Conspiracy Theories and the Case of September 11', *Intelligence and National Security* 19 (Summer 2004), pp. 99–110.

52. Sara-Jane Corkem, 'History, Historians and the Naming of Foreign Policy: A Postmodern Reflection on American Strategic Thinking During the Truman Administration', *Intelligence and National Security*, 16/3 (2001), pp. 146–63.

53. See for example, John Barry, 'Covert Action Can Be Just', *Orbis* (Summer 1993), pp. 375–90; Charles Beitz, 'Covert Intervention as a Moral Problem', *Ethics and International Affairs*, 3 (1989), pp. 45–60; William Colby, 'Public Policy, Secret Action', *Ethics and International Affairs*, 3 (1989) pp. 61–71; Gregory Treverton, 'Covert Action and Open Society', *Foreign Affairs*, 65/5 (Summer 1987), pp. 995–1014; idem, *Covert Action: The Limits of Intervention in the Postwar World* (New York: Basic Books 1987), idem, 'Imposing a Standard: Covert Action and American Democracy', *Ethics and International Affairs*, 3 (1989), pp. 27–43.

54. Michael Herman, 'Modern Intelligence Services: Have They a Place in Ethical Foreign Policies?', in Shukman, *Agents for Change*, pp. 287–311.

55. Cited in Herman, 'Modern Intelligence Services', ibid., pp. 305 and 308 respectively.

56. Shulsky, *Silent Warfare*, p. 187.

57. Max Weber, 'The Profession and Vocation of Politics', in *Political Writings* (Cambridge: Cambridge University Press 1994), p. 360.

58. Ibid., pp. 357–69.

59. See Herman, 'Ethics and Intelligence after September 11', pp. 180–94.

60. Erskine, 'Rays of Light to the Soul'.

61. Michael Quinlan, 'The Future of Covert Intelligence', in Shukman, *Agents for Change*, pp. 67–8. Michael Herman also embraces the Just War notion of proportionality as a criterion for determining what is acceptable in covert collection. Herman, 'Modern Intelligence Services', p. 308.

62. See Mark Urban, *Big Boys' Rules: The SAS and the Secret Struggle Against the IRA* (London: Faber & Faber 1992), Peter Taylor, *The Provos: The IRA and Sinn Fein* (London: Bloomsbury 1997), and idem, *Brits: The War Against the IRA* (London: Bloomsbury 2001).

63. See Jeffrey Richelson, 'When Kindness Fails: Assassination as a National Security Option', *International Journal of Intelligence and CounterIntelligence*, 15/2 (2002), pp. 243–74.

64. See Michael Miller, *Shanghai on the Metro: Spies, Intrigue and the French* (Berkeley, CA: University of California Press 1994), pp. 21–36.

65. On this question see Christopher Andrew, *Secret Service: The Making of the British Intelligence Community* (London: Sceptre 1991) pp. 67–137 and Nicholas P. Hiley, 'The Failure of British Espionage Against Germany, 1907–1914', *Historical Journal*, 26/2 (1983), pp. 866–81.

66. J. Black, 'The Geopolitics of James Bond,' *Intelligence and National Security*, Volume 19, Number 2, June 2004, pp. 290–303 (14).

67. N. West, 'Fiction, Faction and Intelligence', *Intelligence and National Security*, 19 (Summer 2004), pp. 122–34.

68. Wesley K. Wark (ed.), *Spy Fiction, Spy Films and Real Intelligence* (London: Frank Cass 1991), p. 9.

69. For discussion see J. J. Macintosh, 'Ethics and Spy Fiction' in ibid., pp. 161–84.

70. Black, 'Geopolitics of James Bond', p. 144.

71. J. Patrick Dobel, 'The Honourable Spymaster: John Le Carré and the Character of Espionage', *Administration and Society*, 20/2 (August 1988), p. 192. We are grateful

to Hugh Burroughs for drawing our attention to this source.

72. Shukman, *Agents for Change*, discussion of the 'The Future of Covert Action', pp. 91–2.
73. Le Carré, *The Spy Who Came in From the Cold* (London: Victor Gollancz 1963). For discussion of these themes see Jeffrey Richelson, 'The IPCRESS File: the Great Game in Film and Fiction, 1953–2002', *International Journal of Intelligence and CounterIntelligence*, 16/3 (2003), pp. 462–98.
74. *Three Days of the Condor* (Paramount Pictures 1975); *The Bourne Identity* (Universal Pictures 2002).
75. Robert A. Goldberg, 'Who Profited from the Crime? Intelligence Failure, Conspiracy Theories and the Case of September 11', *Intelligence and National Security*, 19 (Summer 2004), pp. 99–110.
76. James Der Derian, 'The CIA, Hollywood, and Sovereign Conspiracies', *Queen's Quarterly*, 10/2 (1993), p. 343.
77. <http://www.mi5.gov.uk/output/Page119.html#3>.
78. Stevens Enquiry, *Overview and Recommendations*, 17 April 2003, para. 4.8, <www.met.police.uk/index/index.htm>.
79. Ibid., para. 4.8. The collusion identified by Commissioner Stevens was by the Army and the RUC, and not by MI5 (or SIS).
80. Smith, 'Bletchley Park and the Holocaust'.
81. See Tom Bower, *The Perfect English Spy: Sir Dick White and the Secret War, 1935–1990* (London: Heinemann 1995), p. 275 for the views of Sir Dick White, former Chief of SIS and Director-General of MI5, on Le Carré.
82. See <www.home.us.net/*encore/Enigma/moviereview.html>. For explanatory discussion of the historical reality see <www.history.navy.mil/faqs/faq97-1.htm>. We are grateful to Gerald Hughes for drawing our attention to these sources.
83. See, for example, Frances Stonor Saunders, *Who Paid the Piper? The CIA and the Cultural Cold War* (London: Granta Books 1999), Scott Lucas, *Freedom's War: The US Crusade Against the Soviet Union, 1945–1956* (Manchester: Manchester University Press 1999) and Giles Scott-Smith and Hans Krabbendam (eds.), *The Cultural Cold War in Western Europe 1945–1960* Special Issue of *Intelligence and National Security*, 18/2 (2003).
84. *Report of the Joint Inquiry Into the Terrorist Attacks of September 11, 2001—by the House Permanent Select Committee on Intelligence and the Senate Select Committee on Intelligence*, <www.gpoaccess.gov/serialset/creports/911.html>.
85. See, for example, the reflections in Bradford Westerfield, 'America and the World of Intelligence Liaison', *Intelligence and National Security*, 11/2 (1996), pp.

523–60, Herman, *Intelligence Power*, pp. 100–112, 165–83, and *Intelligence Services in the Information Age: Theory and Practice* (London: Frank Cass 2001).
86. See, among others, Jeffrey Richelson and Desmond Ball, *The Ties That Bind: Intelligence Cooperation Between the UK–USA Countries* (Boston, MA: Allen & Unwin 1985); Christopher Andrew, 'The Making of the Anglo-American SIGINT Alliance', in Hayden Peake and Samuel Halpern (eds.), *In the Name of Intelligence: Essays in Honor of Walter Pforzheimer* (Washington, DC: NIBC Press 1994); Aldrich, *Hidden Hand*; idem, 'British Intelligence and the Anglo-American "Special Relationship" during the Cold War', *Review of International Studies*, 24/3 (1998), pp. 331–51; David Stafford and Rhodri Jeffreys-Jones (eds.), 'American–British–Canadian Intelligence Relations 1939–2000', Special Issue of *Intelligence and National Security*, 15/2 (2000); Stephen Twigge and Len Scott, *Planning Armageddon: Britain, the United States and the Command of Western Nuclear Forces* (Amsterdam: Routledge 2000).
87. Bradley Smith, *Sharing Secrets with Stalin: How the Allies Traded Intelligence, 1941–1945* (Lawrence, KS: University Press of Kansas 1996); Paul Maddrell, 'Operation Matchbox', forthcoming in Jennifer Siegel and Peter Jackson (eds.), *Intelligence and Statecraft* (Westport, CT: Greenwood Press 2004); Fursenko and Naftali, 'One Hell of a Gamble'.
88. Martin Alexander (ed.), *Knowing One's Friends* (London: Frank Cass 1998).
89. Herman, *Intelligence Power*, pp. 200–219, Aldrich, 'British Intelligence and the Anglo-American "Special Relationship" '.
90. An excellent example of such an approach is the important recent monograph by Cees Wiebes, *Intelligence and the War in Bosnia, 1992–1995* (Munster: Lit Verlag 2003).
91. 'Briton arrested in "terror missile" sting', <www.news.bbc.co.uk/1/hi/world/americas/3146025.stm>, 13 August 2003.
92. Scott, 'Secret Intelligence'.
93. *Hearings Before the Joint Committee on the Investigation of the Pearl Harbor Attack, 79th Congress* 39 vols. (Washington, DC: United States Government Printing Office 1946).
94. Roberta Wohlstetter, *Pearl Harbor: Warning and Decision* (Palo Alto, CA: Stanford University Press 1962).
95. Herman, *Intelligence Services*, p. 228. ✦

Reprinted with permission from Len Scott and Peter Jackson, "The Study of Intelligence in Theory and Practice," *Intelligence and National Security* 19 (Summer 2004), pp. 139–169.

3

A Conversation With Richard Helms, a Director of Central Intelligence

Loch K. Johnson

Professor Johnson, on the faculty of the School of Public and International Affairs at the University of Georgia, covers a range of intelligence issues in a conversation with the popular Director of Central Intelligence (DCI), Richard Helms (1966–73).

On 23 October 2002, Richard McGarrah Helms, who led the Central Intelligence Agency from 30 June 1966, to 2 February 1973, succumbed to multiple myeloma at the age of 89. Before his death he completed his memoirs, published in the spring of 2003.

Helms is widely regarded as one of the most memorable of the 18 individuals to hold the office of Director of Central Intelligence (DCI) since its creation in 1947. Helms's nearly seven-year tenure made him the second longest serving DCI (after Allan Dulles) at the pinnacle of the American 'intelligence community.'[1] Often thought of as the 'professional's professional',[2] Helms was the first DCI to come up through the ranks of the CIA, reaching the top by way of the action-oriented (as opposed to the analytic) field component of the Agency: the Operations Directorate (DO). The DO is the home of the case officers who run spies abroad, as well as the Covert Action Staff that attempts secretly to manipulate events in other lands through the use of clandestine propaganda, political and economic operations, and paramilitary wars—even assassination plots against foreign leaders who have become an aggravation (until such activities were restricted to wartime situations by executive order in 1976).

Helms was a strong proponent of espionage—stealing information overseas to augment what the United States knew about the world from open sources—but he was lukewarm toward most large-scale covert actions, even though he ran his fair share of covert actions, large and small, during his tenure as DCI. He felt that the outcome of large clandestine operations was difficult to predict and could lead to unintended consequences, as with the Bay of Pigs fiasco in 1961, which he opposed.

Born on 30 March 1913, in St Davids, Pennsylvania, Helms lived chiefly in South Orange, New Jersey, as a youth, but broke free from these prosaic bonds for two years of high schooling in Switzerland. During this time he became conversant in French and German—useful skills for a future intelligence officer as war in Europe began to simmer again. He received a Bachelor of Arts degree in 1935 from Williams College in the forested hills of northwestern Massachusetts, a small and highly selective liberal arts college where he managed to impress faculty and peers alike with his leadership and academic abilities. Upon graduation, he entered the field of journalism, traveling in Europe and writing about the Nazis as they began to grab power in Germany. He and a few other reporters managed to meet with Der Führer briefly at a rally in Nuremberg in 1936.

After the Japanese attack against Pearl Harbor, the US Naval Reserve commissioned Helms, but his language training soon landed him in America's premier wartime intelligence organization: the Office of Strategic Services (OSS). After the war, like many OSS alumni, he made a natural segue into the Operations Directorate (then called the Directorate for Plans or the Clandestine Services) of the newly established Central Intelligence Agency.

By the early 1950s, he had risen to the position of deputy to the head of the Directorate for Plans. During this period (in 1955), he supervised the digging of a 500-meter tunnel from West Berlin to East Berlin, from which US intelligence was able to tap the main Soviet telephone links from Moscow to East Berlin. This operation was eventually discovered by the Soviets and used for disinformation against the West; but Helms's superiors at the CIA were sufficiently impressed by the operation at the time to boost him further up the Agency's career ladder, next as head of the Directorate for Plans (1962), then as Deputy Director of Central Intelligence or DDCI (1965), and finally as DCI (1966).

During the Kennedy administration, the White House drew Helms into its efforts to rid the Western hemisphere of Fidel Castro's influence by driving him from power or, if necessary, killing him. Though not directly responsible for the Bay of Pigs, Helms was high enough in the Operations Directorate to know what was going on. When the presidential axe fell on those in charge after the disaster (notably the Deputy Director of Plans, Richard E.

Bissell), Helms managed to escape culpability. When murder of the Cuban leader became the next objective, however, Helms found himself right in the middle of the planning, including the hiring of the mafia to help carry out the execution. All of the plots, from exploding cigars to poison pills, failed (Castro was elusive and well guarded by KGB-trained security forces); but when they come to public light in 1975 during the Church Committee investigations, Helms found himself on the hot seat.

He got himself into trouble with congressional investigators for other reasons, too. Most importantly, the most extensive phase of illegal CIA domestic spying occurred on his watch. As a part of this dark chapter in the CIA's history, Helms had signed a document known as the Huston Plan that permitted extensive use of America's intelligence agencies for domestic spying against Vietnam War dissenters.

He was also 'up to his scuppers' (to use one of his favorite phrases) with the Senate Foreign Relations Committee for misleading it about the extent of CIA involvement in efforts to overthrow Salvadore Allende, the President of Chile. Helms was less than forthright about the extent of the CIA's covert actions in Chile. Subsequently, the Committee discovered that indeed the CIA had been deeply involved in such operations.

Years later, in 1977, he admitted in a court of law that he had misled the Committee. He defended himself on grounds that he had a sworn obligation to keep the nation's secrets.[3] This argument ignored the fact that he could have demanded that the Committee go into closed session to discuss such matters; or he could have told the Committee members he simply was unable at his paygrade to address their highly sensitive questions under any conditions, referring them to the White House for further guidance about the role of the executive branch in Chile. Instead, Helms prevaricated.

Unimpressed by his arguments that by virtue of his oath to protect intelligence sources and methods he was unable to respond to the senators, the court convicted Helms on two misdemeanor counts. The federal judge fined him $2,000, but suspended his sentence. Outside the courtroom, Helms declared that he would wear his conviction 'like a badge of honor'. At a reunion with former CIA colleagues, the hat was passed on Helms's behalf, quickly raising $2,000 to cover his fine.

In 1975, Helms drew fire from the Church Committee for supposedly 'cooking' or politicizing intelligence to suit the policy needs of the Nixon administration—an allegation he staunchly denied. Whatever the truth of that particular charge, Helms while DCI seemed to have done his best to guard against the spinning of the intelligence product on the Vietnam war to suit President Lyndon B. Johnson's political agenda. The CIA told the Johnson administration that its war in Vietnam was going badly and likely to fail—good advice, ignored.

During the Helms years—the middle of the Cold War—the CIA continued to carry out a subterranean struggle against the Soviet Union and other communist powers through espionage and covert actions, chalking up propaganda successes against these adversaries, managing to pull off a few deep penetrations of their intelligence services, and enjoying some operational victories here and there (along with a good many failures) in its efforts to resist Moscow's control over third world countries. Then came the Watergate scandal and President Richard M. Nixon's attempt to drag the CIA into that muck, steadfastly resisted by Helms. The DCI's relationship with the President, never close, went into a rapid downward spiral and Helms, seeing the handwriting on the wall, stepped down from the DCI position. The President granted his request that he be sent to Iran in March as the US Ambassador. Helms served in Iran from March 1973 until December 1976, leaving a year before the country became engulfed in revolution. Upon returning to Washington, he started a private consulting practice that specialized in matters of the Middle East.

On 12 December 1990, I spent an hour with Helms in his office in downtown Washington DC, reflecting back on his career. The name of his international consulting firm, Safeer, Inc., came from an Anglicized version of the Arabic and Persian word 'safir' ['ambassador'], which Helms decided to spell with a double 'e' to make it easier for Americans to pronounce. Tall, fit and distinguished looking at 77, he wore a freshly starched, buttoned-down white shirt, a gray suit with a subdued tie and a gold tie clasp, accentuated with a natty white handkerchief in his lapel pocket. He sat with his glasses in one hand on his lap, his legs crossed casually at the knee, with an elbow resting on the chair top.

In appearance, he had not changed much since 1975 when I was a young staff aide on the Church Committee taking a deposition from him regarding his knowledge of CIA domestic spying. On that occasion, he was weary from a 24-hour plane ride from Tehran. In response to my interrogatories about the Huston spy plan, he provided a string of 'I don't recall. . . . I don't remember. . . . I don't knows', except when I asked him about his relations with the Director of the FBI, J. Edgar Hoover. Then his eyes brightened at the opportunity to malign an old rival and he explained the Director's shortcomings at length, settling back into his 'I don't remembers' when I returned to his own role in intelligence controversies. As I later noted in a history of the Church

Committee, 'Whatever was hidden in the abyss of his memory refused to come out.'[4]

As I sat in his office 15 years later, he seemed vaguely aware that I had been on the Church Committee, but not that I had been Church's special assistant during that 'Year of Intelligence' (or 'The Intelligence Wars', as some embittered intelligence officers remember the investigations). I did not remind him, for fear of spoiling the interview right from the start. I only hoped for a better memory than he seemed to have in 1975 regarding the charges of abuse leveled against him. My first questions were about his views on legislative oversight of intelligence, which I anticipated might be a sore issue.

Intelligence Oversight

Johnson: What do you think of this experiment in intelligence oversight that we have had, which started in 1975–76?

Helms: It's definitely here to stay. Whether it got started for a good reason or a bad reason, it now has its own constituency in the Senate and the House and, as usually happens in those situations, they don't like to give up this constituency. Some of the senators and congressmen feel that they have made a genuine contribution to a better understanding of intelligence, better control over covert operations, and so forth.

I would think that the downside of the oversight process is the number of man-hours that it takes out of high officials of the agencies, testifying before various committees, subcommittees, staffers, and Lord knows what. In fact, I was aghast when I heard the number of hours in a year that somebody from the Agency [the CIA] is talking to senators, congressmen, or their staffers. I wonder if, in a rational world, this couldn't be cut down.

Johnson: Is this one reason why you favor a Joint [Intelligence] Committee?

Helms: That's one reason I favor a Joint Committee. The other reason is that it cuts down on the number of people involved in the secrets of this process. As you well know, the more people who have information, the better chance it has of getting out.

Johnson: What do you make of the counter-argument that one committee would be too easy to co-opt; that when you have two oversight committees [one in the House of Representatives and one in the Senate], you reduce the chances of that happening?

Helms: That question of co-option has never seemed to me to be very realistic. Let's use an analogy. In the days before the seventies, committee chairmen in both the Senate and the House were very powerful. That all broke down in the sixties and seventies—probably in the seventies; I don't

think it happened so much in the sixties. In these earlier days, every senator and every congressman on a committee felt just the opposite: they weren't co-opted. They were too tough. So, that [co-optation thesis] doesn't impress me as an argument.

Johnson: It's not that easy to co-opt a Richard Russell, for example?[5]

Helms: You could no more co-opt him than you could fly to the moon. He was a man who, in his fairness about these things, nevertheless had opinions, stated them, and was very hard to get off them. So, I don't think it's a very good argument.

Johnson: Do you believe there was too little congressional interest in intelligence matters before 1975?

Helms: I didn't ever find there was too little interest. What gave the impression that the Senate wasn't serious about its oversight responsibilities after Senator Russell died [in 1971] and Senator [John] Stennis [Democrat, Mississippi] took over really went to an entirely different matter, and that was the animosity that existed—the hostility that existed—between Senator Stennis and Senator [Stuart] Symington [Democrat, Missouri]. When Senator Stennis refused to make Senator Symington the chairman of the Preparedness Subcommittee (which Stennis had chaired before and which Symington thought he was entitled to), Symington went over to the Foreign Relations Committee and got Senator [and Chairman J. William] Fulbright [Democrat, Arkansas] to give him a comparable subcommittee. So Symington was on both Committees.

But Stennis did not like having meetings on the Agency when Symington was present. The net result of this was that, even though Senator [Henry] Jackson [Democrat, Washington] attempted to broker between them—he even suggested to Stennis that Stennis set up a small subcommittee to hear the Agency's problems more frequently, and so forth, in order to avoid this kind of a get-together—Senator Stennis declined and didn't do it. So, this was really not the Agency's fault. If the Senate sort of backed up on its responsibilities, it was because of this animosity between two senators.

The House went right along all during this period, without any hiccups at all. They had regular [executive session or closed] hearings; and the budget process in the House Appropriations Subcommittee was very thorough and very good. Mr [George] Mahon [Democrat, Texas] and his predecessors wanted to keep [these meetings] private. They held the meetings in secrecy in the basement of the Capital building, where no one knew they were taking place. They had one staffer who did the work and sat in on the meetings. But they had very thorough hearings, and went through the entire budget with the greatest of care.

Johnson: And probably no leaks?

Helms: There were no leaks. The record indicates—as far as the Agency was concerned—that the committees and subcommittees in both the Senate and the House for years were absolutely impeccable; they never leaked anything.

Johnson: What about today: do you think there is too much access to sensitive intelligence information by the Congress? Have we gone too far?

Helms: Well, I don't know how to judge that, Dr Johnson, because I'm not in touch any more. I've been out of the Agency now 13 years or more.

Johnson: Maybe I can phrase it this way: what do you think of the argument that, because of the sensitivity of 'sources and methods', Congress shouldn't be given access to sensitive intelligence information from the intelligence community? Is that a good argument?

Helms: Well, it is a good argument. It is an argument that had great validity before the end of the Cold War. Now the question is whether there isn't more leakage out of the foreign relations committees and the armed services committee than there is out of the intelligence committees; in other words, Congress is a sieve.

Johnson: Some people argue that the sources-and-methods argument is bogus, because Congress doesn't want to know any sources and really doesn't want to know the details of methods either.

Helms: Well, unfortunately, that sentence means different things to different people. It was originally put in there in the early days at the request of the military, because they didn't want any civilians in the CIA mucking around with their particular operations, or analyses, or whatever the case might be. It really wasn't to protect things from the public, or from the Congress, or from anything else. At least, I believe that is what the legislative history shows. You might talk to Larry Huston [a former CIA legal counsel], or one of those fellows who were involved in those matters back in the days when the Agency was being set up; they could tell you much more precisely what was involved in that.

Johnson: What do you make of this concept of prior notification on covert actions to the two Intelligence Committees? Do you prefer a delayed, 48-hour reporting requirement? Where do you stand on that debate?

Helms: Certainly before the end of the Cold War I would have taken the line that the Agency should have had more [time] than a 48-hour notification. [During the Iranian hostage crisis in 1979], some hostages were in the Canadian Embassy and the Canadians were going to get them out. [The CIA's assistance to the Canadians in helping the hostages get out of Iran] was certainly a covert operation of a sort and should have been notified to the Congress; but the [Carter] administration was scared to death that it might leak. Someone in a cheerful mood might have said, 'Great Scott, we're going to get those hostages back!' And next thing you know, it might have been in the papers.

My arguments, I realize, fall on deaf ears with those senators, because [they think] they're just as solid as anybody else: 'Don't worry about it; just come up and tell us—the chairman and the deputy chairman—everything will be all right, you don't need to worry.' Well, I was raised in the wrong tradition. My service in intelligence came during World War II, when secrets were really important to keep and everybody agreed they were important to keep. I've felt that way all the way along. That's the way the Russians do it, the British do it, almost everyone else does it; but we have our own American ways and I assume that the Senate is going to win out in the end and get some kind of a notification [requirement] like 48-hours.[6] You asked me my opinion: I'm just opposed to it.

Johnson: So you would prefer no prior notice. When would you report, if at all on these matters?

Helms: I wouldn't mind prior notice in most cases. I'm not extreme about this; I just think that, once in a while, there are those situations where it shouldn't be required. The devil of these things is that as soon as they write this stuff into law, then somebody—if they break it—is 'above the law' and that big argument starts all over again: 'What right has this guy got to do that?' This is what's tough about it. This is what that whole Iran-*contra* argument was about. What was it: the Boland Amendment [to restrict covert actions in Nicaragua during the 1980s]?[7] Lord, if there's anything that would tear up a man's . . . I was going to say, his soul . . . tear up a man's disposition, it is to deal with a messy thing like that.

Johnson: It went through seven different incarnations.

Helms: Exactly.

Johnson: What do you make of the idea that we need a rewriting of the 1947 National Security Act and a full-blown, detailed legislative charter for intelligence?

Helms: Don't rewrite anything. Once you start rewriting things in the Congress, you don't know where they are going to go. I would be very much against rewriting anything; leave it the way it is.

Intelligence Funding

Johnson: Are there monies available to the CIA other than those funds appropriated into law?

Helms: When I was there, there were certainly no [such] monies. Anything over and above the appropriations [that is, profits earned by the CIA's business fronts] went back to the Treasury, because we did make some money sometimes from cover organizations [proprietaries]. But we were absolutely religious about returning that money.

Johnson: Do 'detailees' [intelligence officers loaned to other agencies or departments] stay on the CIA payroll while they are on, say, the White House staff?

Helms: It depends. During my tenure, the ones assigned to the White House were certainly paid for by the CIA; the White House never paid for anything. All those telephone operators and communicators and various people down there, over time, have always been paid for by the agency to whom they report. The White House never has enough money.

Johnson: Some people say this is a scheme by the CIA to infiltrate the White House and have its way there.

Helms: It was never any such thing. It was a direct request by the White House to send down these various people. And it was a pain in the neck, because it obviously meant you didn't have access to those people—and you were paying them.

Intelligence Collection

Johnson: Looking at collection for a moment, what is the usefulness of Humint [human intelligence]? What if we eliminated Humint; would it be a big deal?

Helms: You would eliminate most of the information that comes into the United States government. This idea that photographic satellites, satellites that pick up electronic emissions, satellites that provide communications, and all the rest of it—all those technical things—they're Jim-dandy when it comes to photographing missile installations, listening to missile firings, checking on telemetry, looking at the number of tanks being produced in certain factories—in other words, bean-counting mostly. Great. But once you eliminate the issue of bean-counting, what good do those pictures do you? They're nice to have, in a situation like now in the Persian Gulf. You can count the tanks and so forth the Iraqis are putting in there. It's a wonderful device. But it doesn't tell you what's inside [Iraqi leader Saddam] Hussein's head; it doesn't tell you what he is going to do. It doesn't give you the price of oil; it doesn't give you the price of gold; it doesn't tell you what the wheat production is going to be within a given place. Even though you photograph [something] and can make some assessments from the photographs, that isn't the final word that you want.

In short, the end of the Cold War means that there's going to be more emphasis on human intelligence than there was before.

Johnson: Do you believe that we have had too much collection? Do we get overwhelmed by the technical collection?

Helms: I wouldn't be surprised. I've been out of the Agency for so long that I can't tell you what . . .

Johnson: What about when you were there? Did you feel sometimes that you were drowning in technical information?

Helms: The big takeoff came after I left, because I was very much involved in building the photographic satellite systems, which now just brings in the stuff endlessly.

Experience as Ambassador in Iran

Johnson: You were Ambassador in Iran for about four years . . .

Helms: Three-and-three-quarters.

Johnson: . . . and the Shah came tumbling down. The obvious question: What sense did you have that this might occur?

Helms: I left Iran physically just before New Year's, 1976–77. The Shah fell in '79—February. The riots that led to his downfall started in '78. So there was an entire year before this trouble developed and, at the time I left, I don't know of a single soul that would have predicted that the Shah would fall.

Johnson: Is it true that maybe we were too easy with the Shah, in going along with his insistence that the CIA reduce its activities inside his country?

Helms: He never asked that we reduce our activities. This is one of these myths—phony stories—that got going, that we had some agreement with him that we wouldn't do this, we wouldn't do that. That's absolutely untrue. The Shah was most helpful to us. We had two listening posts in Iran that were very well-situated geographically for picking up emissions from the missile-launching fields [in the Soviet Union]. The relations with his intelligence service [SAVAC] weren't very good, but at least we had some access there. Obviously, he—no more than anyone else—didn't like us roaming around and reporting on his country; but he could not stop us, and he didn't try to stop it. And once in a while when it came up, he would say to me, 'Do you know, that's kind of embarrassing to have you trying to recruit' this man or that man or something. But then [the matter] was dropped. So, I assure you, that's a canard.

Johnson: Do you feel that when you were Ambassador the CIA collection and reporting was effective and good in Iran?

Helms: Well, it was a mixed bag. The Embassy had some good officers; the Agency had some good officers. You see, quite honestly, I've never been able to understand why so many people have had the feeling that the Shah's falling was a failure of intelligence. It seemed to me it was a failure of *policy*. From the day in January 1978, when the riots started, it was quite clear to anybody who could read a newspaper that there was trouble with the people in Iran. Now, when this went on every 40 days or so throughout the year, and with changes in the government—prime ministers going and coming and so forth—anybody judging the policy relationships with Iran would have seen, I think, that something was going sour.

Now that doesn't necessarily mean that they would have come to the conclusion that the Shah was going to fall, or that anybody was going to come to that conclusion; but the fact remains that [the White House] might have adjusted the policy, rather that having President [Jimmy] Carter going and practically falling in the Shah's arms and asking him to involve himself in more human rights and so forth. And the Shah involved himself in more human rights—and the heavens start to fall in.

So, if you look back at the record, you will find that the historians or political scientists who used to roam around Iran—like James Bill and Marvin Zonas and Nickey Keddie and the rest of them— were all predicting that the Socialists were going to take over: the Social Democrats. In other words, the nationalist party. They completely missed the points about the Mullahs. And they admit this; Bill has told me this.

Johnson: Had the CIA picked up on that point?

Helms: The CIA didn't pick up on the Mullahs either. I don't think anybody picked up on the Mullahs. But getting back to my original point: nobody that I have ever come across predicted a 'shoot the Shah', as the French call it, which I think is rather dramatic. There was even an assertion at one time that an Israeli who was serving at that time in Tehran was predicting that the Shah was going to fall. This is not true. As a matter of fact, the Director General of the Israeli Foreign Office came to see me one day in Washington (after I had retired) and said, 'I think you have probably been bothered by this assertion that we knew about the fall of the Shah. I visited Iran in the summer of 1978 and I had a talk with our people there and what they were saying was that "The Shah *might* fall some day".'

Intelligence Analysis

Johnson: Some people argue that analysts really need to be nuisances; they need to bring to the attention of policymakers annoying facts, reports, and so on. Is that the way you view it?

Helms: I don't have any trouble with that. I don't have trouble with any type of analytic approach to these problems. But what you are trying to say here is that if analysts did their job better, policymakers would do their job better, and this has not been my experience. Policymakers get certain ideas in their heads, and they find these analytic notations as irritants.

Presidents and DCIs

Helms: If you want to get on to the question of the DCI's role, there is a disagreement between people like [former DCI] John McCone and me, or [former DCI] William Casey and me, on this particular point. My view was that the DCI should be the man who called things the way he saw them, the purpose of this being to give the president one man in his administration who was not trying to formulate a policy, carry out a policy, or defend a policy. In other words, this was the man who attempted to keep the game honest. When you sit around the table and the Secretary of State is propounding this and defending this, and the Secretary of Defense is defending this and propounding that, the President has the right to hear somebody who says, 'Now, listen, this isn't my understanding of the facts' or 'That isn't the way it worked.' This in the Johnson administration was the way I did it, and this is the way Johnson wanted it.

Johnson: Without any policy axes to grind?

Helms: That's right. He didn't want me messing in the policy. He just wanted to know: Is the bombing doing well? Are we getting along with this, are we getting along with that? And I was the guy who was bringing the bad news.

Johnson: What was the result of that, after a while?

Helms: The result was the Johnson just pursued his own policy; but that's his right, and that's what we elected the man to do. We didn't elect the DCI to make the policy; we elected that fellow to make the policy. But at least when the bombing wasn't working, we told him so; when this wasn't working, we told him so, etc., etc. And presidents get mad about this. But presidents are usually better than their secretaries of State and Defense, who feel that they've got to carry out the president's wishes and that if they're not really in there extra strong, they're not really doing right by their patron. The McCone view and the Casey view was that the DCI should wear two hats: first, on the facts, and, second, to help with policy—we ought to do this, or we ought to do that, or we ought to do the other thing. I could talk about this at greater length; but there is a difference about what the function of the DCI is.

Johnson: What about the notion of access? You can have the best intelligence in the world, but if you don't have access to the Oval Office to give it to the president . . .

Helms: There is no sense in being DCI unless you have access.

Johnson: But isn't it true that access has been uneven over the years? Some have had better than others?

Helms: Well, I suppose so; but I don't know of any DCI who has said that he couldn't get to see the president if he wanted to, or couldn't get a memorandum to him if he wanted to. And presidents work differently; they don't all work the same way. Johnson liked the written paper. He didn't want people coming in and talking at him; he wanted to do the talking. He was that kind of personality. But he would read your memorandum, and absorb it and know what it said.

Johnson: How did you know that he had?

Helms: He would react to it. Nixon didn't like being talked at either, very much; but he would read the written paper, and there was never any question about being able to see him if I needed to. Nixon didn't like to see people. You know, all these stories you used to hear about [Bob] Haldeman being the gatekeeper,[8] keeping people out of the Oval Office, and wasn't it terrible and so forth? Nixon was *telling* him to keep them out. He would say, 'Bob, *don't* let that fellow in here. I have work to do. I don't need to talk to that man.' So, you mustn't be taken in by all the writing that you might read about how I did that for the president, and this for the president, and so forth; presidents tell these guys what they want done, and they're pretty set in their ways and they want to run [the White House] the way they want to run it. They didn't get elected to president to run it the way [Professor] Joe Nye or somebody at Harvard wants them to run it.

Johnson: But you felt that whenever you had an important piece of information, you could get in?

Helms: I had no trouble at all.

Covert Action

Johnson: Switching to covert action: How useful do you find covert action?

Helms: Covert action is just like anything else: good, bad, and indifferent.

Johnson: When I read the Thomas Powers book,[9] which is about you in large part, I get the impression that you were skeptical about a large number of covert actions.

Helms: The operations I was concerned about were the big ones. There was one in Indonesia one time that I thought was kind of cockamamie. It was just the ones that we weren't big enough, or had enough people, to handle. And the structure that you have to put in, in order to carry out a covert action, is so delicate that if the thing gets above a certain size it's unmanageable and isn't covert any more. It's like this Nicaraguan thing: overt-covert-covert-overt![10] What the hell is it?

But I was not against the war in Laos [1962–68], where I felt the Agency, with a relatively few people, could do a hell of a lot of good work. And we really won that war, you know. When you look at the record, it wasn't won in the victory sense, because when Saigon collapsed that obviously released all of those North Vietnamese troops and the war was over. But, up to that time, we had kept viable an anti-communist government in Laos. In other words, we did what the President asked us to do, and we achieved the objective that he asked us to achieve; and I don't know what more you can do. It's largely a question of size.

Counterintelligence

Johnson: Was the CIA ever penetrated? [Former DCI] Bedell Smith said that he acted in his own mind as though it were, just to play it safe.

Helms: I don't know what he meant by that, because that doesn't make too much sense. I've never had any evidence, or seen any evidence, or been told any evidence of what I would regard as a successful penetration of the Agency. Now, if there's been one, somebody's got to tell me what it was. I realize that a guy's been picked up here, a little Chinese man who did translations and so forth; there's been a contract fellow picked up who was alleged to have been working for the Czechs.[11] There's been various things like that over time. But the years when I was there, up until February 1973, I've never seen nor been told any evidence that led me to believe that the Agency had been penetrated—despite all the Angleton talk, all the jibber-jabber from [Soviet defectors] Golitsin and Nosenko and various other people.[12] You've got to show me the guy and demonstrate to me what he was doing; otherwise, I still feel that we were okay.

There's no argument about the sensitivity and the nightmare here. Any Director who knows anything about the business has constantly on his mind, subliminally anyway, the worry that he will wake up some morning and be told that one of the officers down there [at the CIA] has been on the KGB payroll for God knows how long. So I was very conscious of this; but I was also conscious of the fact that it is very easy to have witch hunts in an organization, so I did my very best to keep a balance. But I know of no penetrations. I don't think it was penetrated up to 1973. What came afterwards [when Helms left the Agency], I don't know.

Johnson: Was Nosenko treated poorly, and was Angleton responsible for this?

Helms: No . . . well, let me put it this way: [Former DCI] Stansfield Turner, for reasons that are unknown to me, claims that Angleton was involved in this. Angleton was not involved in this, directly. I mean Angleton had his role, but actually the Nosenko case was handled by the [CIA's] Security Office. And it was handled that way because Nosenko was in the United States. We needed US apparatus—structure—to handle him, to house him, to do all the rest of those things. So I gave it to the Security Office to handle. He was not well treated, because they were trying to get a confession out of him. There isn't any argument about this.

If I had it to do over again, I don't know whether I would have done it any differently. There are two or three things about this that I want to make absolutely clear. One, we did go to the Department of Justice with our problem. I did talk to [Nicholas deB.] Katzenbach, who was the Deputy Attorney General. I did get his clearance to try and hold on to this fella and see if we could get some kind of information out of him to establish his *bona fides.* We've never in history before had a situation in which a Russian agent, from a country that was almost at war with us—and a President who's just been shot, killed in office, and the feeling in this country about how he was killed and particularly about President Kennedy—and then in walks this man who says that the Russians had absolutely nothing to with it.

[FBI Director] J. Edger Hoover believed him, and then you have this terrible problem of the Agency's responsibility for asserting that the man is *bona fide.* That was the role the Agency had [in 1964]. I personally went—with [then DCI] Mr McCone's approval—to see Chief Justice [Earl] Warren, when the Warren Commission was sitting, and told him what the problem was. I laid it out, so that the Warren Commission Report didn't simply use the FBI material, and that it would be said that the Agency went along. What went on after that God only knows, but it was rough. I don't think we'd ever have done anything like that again. We wouldn't have done it in those circumstances if it had not involved the assassination of a President.

The Office of Inspector General at the CIA

Johnson: During your tenure as DCI, was the Office of the Inspector General (IG) within the CIA worth anything at all?

Helms: Yeah, sure, the IG did the job that I wanted the IG to do: to go through the Agency, look at the various elements, come up with reports of what was going on. I think it was just fine.

Johnson: It simply wasn't low-level, innocuous material the IG was getting?

Helms: If you're an IG and you go digging into things, you can always find something the matter—in any organization. And they did. But then the judgment that has to be made by the superiors is: Do you pay attention to it? Do you think it's serious? Is it necessary to revamp? Should we do it different? And there were always recommendations, some which were accepted and some which were not accepted. I never liked an IG who liked his job, because any IG who likes his job likes to punish people.

So when the Senate decided [in 1990] they were going to have their own sort of IG in there,[13] this to me was not only to laugh at, but—more important from the standpoint of the morale of the Agency and so forth—kind of a finger that I didn't think was particularly pretty. I don't know what they know [in the Senate] that is so superior. If the Cold War had not been over pretty much by this time, I think there would have been more of a stink raised. But, anyway, that is over and done with now and no sense in tossing around spilled milk.

The DCI and the Intelligence Community

Johnson: Does the DCI tend to be biased in favor of the CIA within the intelligence community? You've heard this argument before.

Helms: Oh, I've heard it over and over again—used to be accused of it. At least at the time I was in the Agency, I found no evidence of this. I found no specific thing that I could put my finger on and say, 'Yes, that showed a bias in favor of the civilians versus the military' or what have you. I think most of [the DCIs] were terribly conscientious in trying to accommodate all the disparate views. And it's not easy, because you have the Air Force with one point of view, the Defense Department with another, the State Department with a third . . . and trying to get a consensus about an [intelligence] estimate is hard work in those circumstances.[14]

I know that I was accused in the [Church Committee] hearings [in 1975] of having waffled about certain estimates, because I was threatened by the Secretary of Defense. That was total nonsense. One of the problems that I now see with respect to the Office of National Estimates as it existed at that time—this has now all been changed for the better or the worst—but one of the problems was that those fellows [senior CIA analysts] got the impression they were the only people in the world who understood these things and really had to be supported. That was a lot of baloney.

Anyway, I never felt that I was swayed by pressure. I felt sometimes that I was swayed by argument. Also at other times I felt: well, can we support this assertion that [the National Intelligence Officers, NIOs] have brought forth: that this is not going to happen or that is not going to happen? When I didn't feel that we could, I took [the statement] out. After all, it was my estimate.

Helms's Relations With Congress

Johnson: What about this notion that you didn't always give the martini straight up to the Congress? That you weren't always entirely candid with them in hearings?

Helms: You mean in my testimony?

Johnson: Yes.

Helms: Untrue. Totally untrue. The trouble that I got into later was over testimony before the [Senate] Foreign Relations Committee, not before the [intelligence] oversight committee. To the best of my knowledge, I never told an untruth to one of the appropriately appointed oversight committees.

Johnson: What about the Senate Foreign Relations Committee; what happened in that instance?

Helms: Well, it was rather a protracted issue. When I went up for confirmation in a public hearing, I was asked a question by Senator Symington and I gave him what I would refer to as a convoluted answer, because—from him being on the [intelligence] oversight committee—I assumed that he knew the answer to the question he was asking. It was a puffball question, and I thought he meant it as a puffball question; and I gave him a puffball answer. Later I was brought back to testify further about certain matters, particularly Watergate; and then there were some Subcommittee hearings chaired by Senator Church.

Johnson: On Multinational Corporations.

Helms: . . . and that was not my oversight committee. [The senators] had no secrecy inhibitions on them. We had some things going in Chile, where the people could have been arrested, or shot, or whatever the case was. I didn't lie, in point of fact; I just didn't tell them everything in that case.

A Self-Critique

Johnson: When you look back over your career as DCI, what do you think your most important contributions were? Certainly the satellite development would be one.

Helms: That certainly was one thing. I also inherited and brought on to finish the so-called 'Ox Cart' [the U-2 program]—or what is known in the Air Force as the SR-71. I was credited by [then DCI] Allen Dulles earlier with something I was pleased to

hear. He autographed a photograph to me, saying that he took great pleasure in my contribution to the establishment of a professional intelligence service. And I certainly worked on that the whole time I was there: getting it settled in Washington and helping with all the things that had to be done to get it established.

I was particularly pleased when I was Director with the estimates we had on the June war of 1967 [in the Middle East between Arabs and Israelis] and how accurate the analysts were about the outcome of that war. Vietnam was messy: sometimes we were good, sometimes we were bad. We didn't call them all right, that's for sure—particularly about the goods that went in through Sihanoukville.[15] I think that's enough; after all, there's no sense in going around saying I was responsible for this, that, and the other thing. I think that I had the respect of the Congress; the last year I was Director, we got every dollar of money we asked for.

Johnson: What about shortcomings, things you might want to do over?

Helms: I'm sure there are, Dr Johnson, but right now I don't have them in the forefront of my mind. The Sihanoukville thing I mentioned. Certainly if I had that to do over again I would have brought someone in to help out a little more with the model—the economic model—which was used to try and estimate how many goods came through and what their contribution was, because we really blew that. And there are some others I'm sure we blew; but, after all, that's in the nature of life.

You know, in the last three months I've never—in all my years in Washington—been asked so many times by so many people, in exactly the same words, the same question, which is: What is going to happen in the Persian Gulf? Obviously, I don't know what is going to happen in the Persian Gulf; but I quote that malapropism from Yogi Bera—you remember, the famous Yankee catcher, who said a lot of strange things like 'It's not over 'til it's over.' But the one I like best is: 'Predictions are very difficult to make—especially about the future.'

Cooperating With the Church and Pike Committees

Johnson: When William Colby was DCI [1973–75] and working with the Church and the Pike Committees, did he sell the ranch? Did he go too far?

Helms: I thought so, but I have done my level best to avoid any public arguments with Bill Colby or Stansfield Turner, for the simple reason that I think it is demeaning to have these public spats between former directors of Central Intelligence, just as it is among presidents of the United States or secretaries of state. I mean, it just gives the public a very sour impression: what kind of a place is that Washington—these guys are always squabbling with each other. They have certainly not taken me on, and I have certainly not taken them on.

But I think that Bill Colby went overboard when he decided that he knew all about the Constitution and that he was going to send all that material up to those Committees. I frankly thought that what he should have done is gone to the President [Gerald R. Ford] and made him either make the decision to relinquish classified documents to the Congress or force the issue up to the Supreme Court and get it to decide whether he had to turn over the papers. Period.

Economic Intelligence

Johnson: Is the CIA helping industry by gathering economic intelligence and sharing it with our companies? Is that a good thing to be doing?

Helms: I don't know. The British have been doing it for years; but whether you can 'make that dog hunt', as President Johnson use to say, in this country, I don't know. Whether you can get that by the Congress—even an informal opinion—I just don't know. The Congress, with the Foreign Corrupt Practices Act and various other things, has made it hard for Americans in business to work overseas. Whether you can get anything like this, it would probably take sort of a real depression or a real serious disaster of some kind to wake those fellas up to the fact that the United States is not isolated, that we can't have ice cream with our cookies, and all the rest of it. But I think that as the competition from the Japanese, the European Community, and other people intensifies, there's going to be pressure for something like that.

Managing the CIA

Johnson: Frank Carlucci said that he felt like he was a man on one side of a wall, pulling a lot of levers when he was Deputy Director of the CIA, and he walked around to look at the other side of the wall and they weren't connected to anything.[16] That was his way of saying that he never felt in control when he was at the Agency.

Helms: Control of what?

Johnson: Of the day to day management, and what the various offices were doing. The notion is that the CIA is a very difficult organization to come into at the top and manage.

Helms: Look, I would agree with that. My advantage, if there was one, was that I grew up with the organization. I knew where all the plumbing was. I knew who did what. So I would raise the telephone and talk to someone in the bowels of the Agency—through all the hierarchy and so forth—because I wanted the answer to a certain question and I knew that was the fella who dealt with it. So, I had a distinct advantage in this respect; and all the fellas knew that I had grown up with them, and they knew there was no sense in bullshitting me about this, that, or the other thing. So, I did have an advantage there. I could see to it that when I issued an order, something got done about it.

Johnson: It seemed to me that when you're selecting a DCI, someone like you is perfect in many ways; but then when you look at [DCI William J.] Casey, there's a certain characteristic of his tenure that was useful, too, namely, his close ties to the president [Ronald Reagan]. I'm wondering what the perfect model for the DCI is: Someone from the inside? A political person with good ties to the president?

Helms: This issue is the one I was discussing with you earlier, about what your role [as DCI] with the president is. Casey was a policy man; he had his own foreign policy. He and George Schultz [Secretary of State in the Reagan administration] had the daggers drawn. I mean, somebody will write a book some day, I suppose, about the Casey foreign policy and the Schultz foreign policy. I just didn't see the role [of the DCI] that way. You can well answer me by saying, 'Well, after all, these are Big League fellas and they didn't see any reason why they couldn't do both these things perfectly well.' I just don't think that in this large town, with all the people that are in the government, that it's too expensive to have one man who worries about the facts. That's what the DCI is supposed to do in foreign affairs.

Johnson: I ask a lot of people about who their favorite DCI is. Your name frequently comes up. So does McCone's. Intelligence officers may not have liked his policymaking, but they did like his management skills.

Helms: Well, McCone came in there with no prior experience and he managed the Agency very well, so I can only say it can be done.

Johnson: Thank you, Mr Helms.

Helms: Thank you. Good to see you.

Questions for Further Discussion

1. How would you evaluate Mr. Helms's record of service as DCI?

2. Do you agree with his comments on intelligence oversight?

3. Did Mr. Helms have any other way of responding to congressional questioning than to evade the key question about covert action in Chile?

4. Do you think the nation's intelligence chiefs should come from within the intelligence community or from outside? Should they be civilians or military personnel? Is it all right if they have held elective office and have a strong party identification?

Endnotes

1. For a full biography, see Thomas Powers, *The Man Who Kept the Secrets: Richard Helms and the CIA* (NY, Simon & Schuster 1979). For a review of the Helms memoir, see Loch K. Johnson, 'Pucher Up', *Washington Monthly* 35 (June 2003) pp. 53–4.
2. Roy Jonkers, 'In Memoriam', Electronic Newsletter, Association of Former Intelligence Officers (26 Oct. 2002).
3. See the case study by Mark Lilla, entitled 'The Two Oaths of Richard Helms', Kennedy School of Government, Harvard University (Cambridge, MA: 1983).
4. Loch K. Johnson, *Season of Inquiry: The Senate Intelligence Investigation* (Lexington: The UP of Kentucky 1985) p. 83.
5. Senator Richard Bevard Russell (Democrat, Georgia), highly regarded in the Senate for his knowledge of national security affairs, headed small intelligence oversight panels on the Armed Services and Appropriations Committees during the 1960s and 1970s.
6. The language of the Intelligence Authorization Act of 1991 (Public Law 102-88) ended up with a requirement that the President report on covert actions to the Intelligence Committees 'as soon as possible after such approval and before the initiation of the covert action', except in extraordinary circumstances. In extraordinary conditions, the President is expected to notify at least the top leaders of Congress; if not, he is required to explain to the Intelligence Committees 'in a timely fashion' why he failed to provide prior notice even to the congressional leadership.
7. Named after the chief sponsor, Edward P. Boland (Democrat, Massachusetts), then Chairman of the House Permanent Select Committee on Intelligence.
8. H. R. 'Bob' Haldeman was Chief of Staff in the Nixon administration.
9. See note 1 *supra*.
10. This is a reference to the covert actions in Nicaragua carried out during the Reagan administration and widely covered in the media.
11. Larry Wu-Tai Chin spied for the People's Republic of China while working for the CIA, committing suicide when he was discovered in 1985; and in 1984 a naturalized American, Karl Koecher, was arrested for spying for his native Czechoslovakia during the time he did contract translation work for the CIA (1973–77).
12. James J. Angleton served as Chief of CIA Counterintelligence from 1954 to 1974; Major Anatoli Golitsin defected from the KGB in 1962 (though he had worked for the CIA secretly for many years before); Yuri Nosenko, another KGB defector, came to the CIA in 1964 to offer his services against the USSR. The reliability of both men was questioned by some American counterintelligence officers, and accepted by others; in Angleton's case, he trusted Golitsin but not Nosenko, whom he viewed as a false defector. See Tom Mangold, *Cold Warrior* (NY: Simon & Schuster 1991). Ironically, at the time of this interview with Helms, CIA officer Aldrich H. 'Rick' Ames was stealing secrets right and left for the Soviets from the heart of the Operations Directorate. His treachery, which began in the mid-1980s, would not be discovered until 1994.
13. Title VIII of the Intelligence Authorization Act of 1990 (Public Law 101-193) created an new Office of Inspector General for the CIA, whose incumbent had to be confirmed by the Senate and was expected to report to the Senate periodically.
14. In American intelligence, an estimate is 'a statement of what is going to happen in any country, in any area, in any given situation, and as far as possible into the future' [Lyman Kirkpatrick, *Military Review* (May 1961) p. 20], cited by Harry Howe Ransom, *The Intelligence Establishment* (Cambridge, MA: Harvard UP 1960) p.14. In its most formal form, a National Intelligence Estimate (NIE) attempts to assess the current situation in some part of the world and often makes a prediction about future developments [see Loch K. Johnson, *America's Secret Power* (NY: Oxford UP 1989), pp. 92–94].
15. Cambodian elites had profited in the 1960s from shipping weapons and other supplies from the port of Sihanoukville to the Vietcong and North Vietnamese troops located near the Vietnam border. See Stanley Karnow, *Vietnam: A History* (NY: Viking 1983) p. 604.
16. Carlucci served as Deputy Director of Central Intelligence during the Carter administration. This observation is drawn from Admiral Stansfield Turner, *Secrecy and Democracy: The CIA in Transition* (Boston: Houghton Mifflin 1985) p. 185. ✦

Reprinted with permission from Loch K. Johnson, "Spymaster Richard Helms," *Intelligence and National Security* 18 (Autumn 2003), pp. 24–44.

Part II

Intelligence Collection

Hamlet: "If thou art privy to thy country's fate
Which happily foreknowing may avoid
O, speak!"

—*Shakespeare*, Hamlet, *1.1.134–136*

Professional intelligence officers often think of their primary mission of information collection and analysis in terms of an "intelligence cycle" (see Figure II.1). The CIA defines the cycle as "the process by which information is acquired, converted into intelligence, and made available to policymakers" (CIA 1983, 17). The first phase in the cycle is planning and direction—that is, the identification of what kinds of information need to be collected ("requirements"), which agencies will do the collecting, and what means ("tradecraft" or modus operandi) will be used. These are questions for senior management, and the top senior manager in the U.S. intelligence community is the Director of Central Intelligence (DCI), whose office is located at CIA Headquarters in Virginia.

Once these decisions about planning and direction are made—and they are driven chiefly by a sense of threats to the United States—the collection of information begins by way of machines (surveillance satellites, for example) and human agents. Then the acquired information is processed. This processing step can involve the translation of materials into English if originally in a foreign tongue or, say, the enlargement of photographs taken by satellite or U-2 cameras. Once the material is in a format an analyst can work with, the job is to make sense of the information, bringing insight to "raw" data—what we mean by *analysis* (or what the British call

assessment). Finally, the evaluated information must be disseminated in a timely manner to policy officials in the White House and elsewhere. It must be accurate and relevant to the current issues of the day, as well as free of bias.

The purpose of the intelligence cycle is to provide policymakers with useful knowledge to assist them in weighing decision options. As the CIA puts it, "Intelligence is knowledge and foreknowledge of the world around us—the prelude to Presidential decision and action" (CIA 1983, 17). The seemingly simple sweep of the cycle, as depicted in Figure II.1, is in fact a complicated series of interactions among, on the one hand, intelligence officers and their

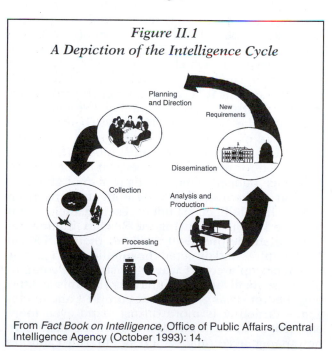

*Figure II.1
A Depiction of the Intelligence Cycle*

Planning and Direction

New Requirements

Dissemination

Collection

Analysis and Production

Processing

From *Fact Book on Intelligence*, Office of Public Affairs, Central Intelligence Agency (October 1993): 14.

organizations (the producers of information) and, on the other hand, policymakers (the consumers of information). As information moves from aerial surveillance platforms or agents ("assets") in the field back to the CIA and other intelligence agencies in the United States and then on to policy councils, many things can go wrong. As discussed in the articles of this part of the book, the collection phase alone is replete with challenges, beginning with decisions about which nations or groups the United States wishes to target for gathering information.

Targeting

From the vantage point of an astronaut in space, the world may seem small, and it is indeed becoming smaller, in a sense, as advancing technology brings about a decrease in communications and travel time between continents. Yet from the vantage point of an intelligence agency, the world remains vast, with nearly 200 sovereign nations and a wide galaxy of groups, factions, and cells spread across the globe—a fragmentation greatly accentuated by the end of the Cold War and the splintering of the bipolar world of that era. No nation—not even one with the affluence enjoyed by the United States—can hope for perfect transparency into all these nations and factions. Priorities must be set. So nations and groups with intelligence organizations engage in "threat assessment" calculations, establishing a list of places and people that are especially threatening or that present an opportunity to advance the national interests. These targets are ranked from high to low priority—say, from the high of the Al Qaeda terrorist organization to the low of Japanese fishing boats off America's shores suspected of harvesting illegal quotas of salmon. This assessment—which can lead to heated debate among policymakers and intelligence managers—is important, for it becomes a blueprint for spending priorities with respect to intelligence collection.

During the Cold War (1945–1991), the United States had one preeminent intelligence target: the Soviet Union and its communist allies. This target accounted for upward of 70 percent of the U.S. intelligence budget (which tends to run at about 10 percent of the overall defense budget in any given year). The intelligence budget reached a high point of some $30 billion during the Reagan Administration, when the president declared the U.S.S.R. an "evil empire" and directed the intelligence agencies to ratchet up a covert war against global communism (especially in Nicaragua and Afghanistan). Today, the world has grown more complex, and intelligence targeting is more diffuse—and even more expensive: more than $44 billion, according to newspaper accounts. As President Bill Clinton's

first DCI, R. James Woolsey, observed, the Soviet dragon had been slain, but "we live now in a jungle filled with a bewildering variety of poisonous snakes" (Woolsey 1993).

Throughout the Clinton years, Target No. 1 was not a single nation or group but a more generic global threat: the proliferation of weapons of mass destruction (WMD), or so-called NBC weapons (nuclear, biological, chemical) that could destroy thousands—even millions—of people in a brief interlude of horror. The events of September 11, 2001 had a profound effect on reassessing America's threat status, as the perpetrators of the catastrophic attacks against New York City and the Pentagon catapulted their organization, Al Qaeda (and its patron, the Taliban regime in Afghanistan), to Intelligence Priority No. 1. Stunning events of violence can quickly change America's sense of threat, leading to a rapid reorientation of intelligence resources toward new requirements and "tasking."

Often such events seem to come out of the blue, as with the Japanese attack against Pearl Harbor or the September 11 attacks—although in both of these instances there were early warnings that were missed, ignored, or lost in the labyrinths of the intelligence bureaucracy. Sometimes the failure to anticipate danger is not so much related to mistakes in intelligence collection as it is to the inability or unwillingness of policymakers to take action on the information they have been provided. In 1995, the CIA warned the Clinton Administration of "aerial terrorism" in which airplanes might be used by terrorists to destroy skyscrapers in the United States or abroad, but policymakers did little to enhance airport security (Johnson 2002).

As they examine collected information, intelligence officials and policymakers can also suffer a failure of imagination as to what it means. "The danger is not that we shall read the signals and indicators with too little skill," Thomas C. Schelling (1962) noted, looking back at the Pearl Harbor attack. "The danger," he continued, "is in a poverty of expectations—a routine obsession with a few dangers that may be familiar rather than likely"—in sum, a "great national failure to anticipate."

Rwanda provides a memorable example of how unanticipated disasters can leap quickly from the bottom to the top of America's international threat-assessment priorities. In 1993, a genocidal civil war suddenly erupted in this African nation. "When I became Secretary of Defense [in 1993], I served several months without ever giving Rwanda a thought," recalled Les Aspin of the Clinton Administration. "Then for several weeks, that's all I thought about. After that, it fell abruptly off the screen again and I never again thought about Rwanda" (quoted in Johnson 2002, 20). The list of "shooting stars" or "flavors of the month," as intelligence professionals sometimes refer to these sudden crises, has included such places in recent decades as Grenada, Panama, Yugoslavia, and Somalia. All too often, the United States has had inadequate information about these locations, having focused its intelligence resources on more obvious threats from "rogue nations" such as North Korea and Iraq.

Types of Intelligence

Substantive Intelligence

Policymakers and intelligence professionals must decide, too, what substantive types of intelligence should be collected: military, political, economic, or cultural. Respectively, *military intelligence* might involve a concentration on the worldwide flow of weapons of mass destruction or, more narrowly, on the efficiencies of North Korean missile fuel. *Political intelligence* can run the gamut from gathering information on presidential candidates in a French national election to sorting out the plethora of party factions in the Russian *duma*. For *economic intelligence*, U.S. officials may want to have information on the likely strategies of the Organization of Petroleum Exporting Countries (OPEC) or on the degree to which Afghanistan in the wake of the Taliban regime has a chance of building a viable economic infrastructure. Regarding *cultural intelligence*, officials may want to know the extent to which high vodka consumption is ravaging Russian society, or the destabilizing effects of the AIDS epidemic on the leadership in countries (such as Zaire) that are heavily afflicted by this global pandemic.

From among these choices, the military dimension has been in the forefront of considerations about the funding of intelligence collection. In the United States, about 85 percent of the intelligence dollar is spent on the military intelligence agencies (although these agencies do collect some information relevant to the other substantive areas). Critics of intelligence collection in the United States have complained that the tasking is tilted too much toward Support to Military Operations (SMO, in Pentagonese)—especially protecting the war fighter in the foxhole or at sea, or the pilot in the cockpit of a fighter plane—at the expense of Support to Diplomatic Operations (SDO), that is, gathering "diplomatic intelligence" (political, economic, and cultural information) that might help prevent the outbreak of war in the first place.

"The traditional idea of intelligence is the spy who provides the enemy's war plans," noted a CIA memorandum written during the Cold War. Yet, as the memo correctly argued, despite the pressures toward SMO:

> . . . intelligence is concerned not only with war plans, but with all the external concerns of our government. It must deal with the pricing debates of OPEC and the size of this year's Soviet crop. . . . It is concerned with Soviet strength along the Sino-Soviet boarder, with the intricacies of Chinese politics, with the water supply in the Middle East, with the quality of Soviet computers and its impact on our own export controls, with the narcotics trade in Southeast Asia, even with the struggle for control of Portuguese Timor. (Senior CIA analyst, declassified by the Church Committee, 1975a)

Current and Research Intelligence

Officials must decide as well whether they seek information about what happened yesterday and what is likely to happen today and tomorrow (*current intelligence*), such as answers to the questions, "Where is Osama bin Laden?" "Where will Al Qaeda strike next?" or information of a deeper kind that provides a longer perspective and more nuanced understanding of world affairs (*research intelligence*, addressing such questions as, "How has Al Qaeda been able to attract so many young recruits to its anti-American cause?" "To what extent will Muslim extremists rally in Iraq to drive out U.S. troops?"). Most officials desire current intelligence, and they want precision—not vague warnings about a possible attack somewhere, sometime. This kind of information can be hard to obtain and can often be wrong. Research intelligence poses its own set of difficulties inherent to any deep probe into a topic, including the costs of time and money required to carry out the research. Further, research intelligence is often unread by busy policymakers who shun lengthy, footnoted tomes. Yet in-depth intelligence is vital for a more meaningful understanding of world events. Unfortunately, though, it is being given short shrift, as increasingly resources are directed toward current intelligence, anticipating and trying to answer questions that flare up in the daily in-boxes of harried policymakers.

Secrets and Mysteries

An added dimension of intelligence collection is the distinction made by intelligence professionals between secrets and mysteries. *Secrets* are empirical facts that, with luck and perseverance, the United States might be able to acquire—steal, if necessary—such as information about the number of Chinese nuclear submarines, their range, and the location of their docking sites. *Mysteries* are the more imponderable questions faced by intelligence officers and policymakers, such as the likely longevity of the current Chinese leadership, or whether democracy will take root in Iraq in the aftermath of the U.S. invasion to overthrow the regime of dictator Saddam Hussein. No one really knows the answers to mysteries; their importance, though, warrants grappling with possible outcomes regardless, and a well-trained analyst can often come up with helpful insights for policymakers to consider as they contemplate the future. The collection phase of the intelligence cycle concentrates on unearthing secrets, leaving the sifting of tea leaves about mysteries to analysts steeped in the history and culture of foreign lands.

Collection Methods

After deciding what kinds of information are required to assist foreign policy decision making, officials ask the intelligence agencies to gather the desired data. Here we enter the domain of the "ints"—that is, the various intelligence methods used for collecting information around the world (Berkowitz and Goodman 2000; Lowenthal 2003; Shulsky and Schmitt 1993).

Osint

The most mundane of the ints, though in some ways the most important, is simply tapping into public sources of information—open-source intelligence, or *osint*. Authorities report that about 80 percent of all the information found in intelligence reports during the Cold War was based on data acquired by traditional library research, such as digging through Soviet and Chinese newspapers. Today the osint figure is even higher, approaching 95 percent, as Russian, Chinese, and other formerly closed societies have become more open, as the Internet takes on importance as a wellspring of information, and as television and radio stations (along with periodicals and newspapers) proliferate around the globe. Ironically, in spite of these burgeoning open sources, intelligence analysts often eschew publicly available data in favor of the more titillating and exotic information that comes to their desks from overseas clandestine sources—even though they are trained to search open sources first, then turn to clandestine sources to fill in the missing pieces of the puzzle.

On the clandestine side of intelligence collection, the ints (as introduced in the Introduction to Part I) include imint, sigint, masint, and, last but not least, humint. These acronyms, widely used by intelligence professionals, stand for imagery intelligence, signals intelligence, measurement and signals intelligence, and human intelligence.

Imint

Imagery refers to photography, the snapshots taken by reconnaissance airplanes such as the U-2 or unmanned drones such as the Predator, as well as by surveillance satellites that revolve around the earth at altitudes ranging from a few hundred miles to over 200,000 miles in deep space (either in polar orbit, sweeping around the earth, or geosynchronous orbit, hovering over a particular country or region). Today, the photographs from satellites do not even have to be developed; they are sent digitally to U.S. ground stations and fed quickly to policymakers and warriors who need the information in as close to real time as possible. The picture resolution is impressive, capable of distinguishing a football from a jackrabbit.

Imint is much sought and appreciated by policymakers when it can display irrefutable evidence about an adversary's hostile actions against the United States, as when the U.S. ambassador to the United Nations, Adlai E. Stevenson, was able during the 1962 Cuban missile crisis to convince American and world opinion of Soviet provocation in the Western Hemisphere by laying on the table clear U-2 photos of Russian missiles in Cuba. More recently, in 2003 Secretary of State Colin Powell used satellite photographs to argue the U.S. case that Iraq still possessed chemical weapons capabilities and had permitted the establishment of a terrorist training camp within its nation—although in this instance (unlike Cuba) confirmation of the intelligence reports proved elusive.

Imagery is hardly a panacea, even though it attracts the lion's share of the U.S. intelligence budget. (Just the launching of a Greyhound-bus-sized intelligence satellite can cost $1 billion.) For starters, half the world is covered with clouds at any moment and, naturally, darkness is a hindrance as well (although the United States has made great strides in developing cameras that can overcome these obstacles to some extent). More difficult to deal with has been the tidal wave of images flowing back to the United States, cloudy weather and nocturnal conditions notwithstanding—some 400 images a day. A shortage of photo interpreters means that only a small fraction of these pictures are carefully studied.

Further, adversaries have grown skilled at hiding their activities, as demonstrated by the surprise nuclear tests in India during 1994 (Johnson 2001). Indian officials had determined exactly when U.S. satellite cameras would be passing over their nuclear testing facility near Pokharan in the Rajasthan Desert. In synchrony with these flights (every three days), Indian nuclear scientists camouflaged their activities. Ironically, U.S. officials had explicitly informed the Indian government about the timing of U.S. satellite coverage for South Asia, in hopes of impressing on them the futility of trying to conceal test activity. Even without this unintended assistance, though, the Indians could have calculated the cycles for themselves, as even amateur astronomers can track the orbits of spy satellites.

The Indians also adroitly used deception techniques to fool intelligence photo interpreters. For instance, ground cables normally moved into place for a nuclear test were nowhere to be seen in U.S. satellite photographs of the site; the Indians had devised less-visible ignition techniques. The Indians also stepped up activities at their far-removed missile testing site, in an attempt to draw the attention of spy cameras away from the nuclear testing site.

In 2002, when U.S. troops first entered eastern Afghanistan's rugged Shah-i-Kot Valley as part of Operation Anaconda in search of Al Qaeda terrorists and their Taliban hosts, the military command had at its disposal the best imint platforms available: satellites, reconnaissance airplanes, Predator drones. Nonetheless, "despite these high-tech systems, the intelligence estimate failed to accurately portray the enemy's size, location, principal weapons and course of action," notes *New York Times* reporter Sean Naylor (2003, A13).

Imint has other liabilities. Satellite and U-2 cameras are unable to see through roofs into buildings or basements where chemical and biological weapons may be manufactured. Even large-scale nuclear weapons programs can be hidden from the prying cameras, as the North Koreans have managed to demonstrate by locating their nuclear weapons operations in deep underground caverns. Moreover, while the spy cameras can provide some idea of an adversary's military capabilities, they have nothing to say about the intentions of these adversaries.

Sigint

To supplement imagery, nations also rely on the gathering of signals intelligence, especially the electronic communications that travel between telephones and personal computers. At the United Nations in 2003, Secretary Powell also played the transcripts of confidential telephone conversations between Iraqi officials to demonstrate further that they were trying to deceive U.N. inspectors and world public opinion. Once again, though, we run into the problem of information overload, as a firehose of sigint transcripts from around the world overwhelms the ability of U.S. translators and analysts to keep up with the torrent. According to a recent estimate (Millis 1998), only about 10 percent of all sigint transcripts are examined by analysts. An intercepted September 10, 2001 telephone conversation between Al Qaeda terrorists indicating that a

major attack would occur against the United States the next day ("Tomorrow is zero hour") was not translated until September 12, the day after the attacks.

In addition, adversaries have learned to use deception against sigint just as they do against imint. Reportedly, in 2002 Bin Laden handed his cell phone to his bodyguard and had him travel away from where the Al Qaeda leader was heading in his escape from Afghanistan, thereby drawing U.S. intelligence officers in the wrong direction. People tell lies over the telephone, too; intercepts cannot be taken at face value but rather are sometimes a source of disinformation. Further, the current switch in technologies from airwave transmissions of telephone conversations to underground optic fibers ("light pipes") has significantly complicated the science of intercepting telephone conversations. Still, sigint has had its moments of success and is highly valued by policymakers, as when intercepted communications in an African nation recently saved the lives of a U.S. ambassador and his family on their way to a local airport by tipping them off to a planned ambush by an indigenous rebel faction. The ambassador altered his travel route, and he and his family escaped the trap.

Masint

Weapons systems, such as ballistic missiles and nuclear warheads, give off emissions as they are being tested, and factories produce gases and waste products. Measurement and signatures intelligence can provide information about these and other forms of weapons systems and can add significantly to America's understanding of an adversary's military preparedness. Or they can reveal what is being made inside a factory: normal pharmaceuticals or lethal chemical or biological substances.

Humint

The oldest form of spying (and some say the world's second oldest profession) is the use of human intelligence—the cloak and dagger agents of James Bond fame. These spies are not Americans but rather local assets recruited by U.S. intelligence officers, who then serve as their "case officers." To avoid the kinds of concealment and deception against imint and sigint as practiced by the Indians and the North Koreans, the United States would like to have an asset inside the Indian test bunkers or within the North Korean caverns. A well-placed asset might also be able to ascertain whether a suspicious factory is making aspirin or serin (a chemical nerve agent)—a distinction that distant satellites and U-2s are unable to make. Particularly helpful in today's world would be having an asset in attendance at Al Qaeda strategy sessions in a cave somewhere in the mountains of northern Pakistan, perhaps sitting on the dirt floor next to Bin Laden himself. Afterward the spy could secretly transmit, by using rapid electronic communications from a palm-held computer to a satellite and down to his CIA case officer in Kabul, the plans for the next Al Qaeda operations in the jihad against the United States.

These wishes are difficult to fulfill, since access to North Korean caverns or Al Qaeda strategy sessions in the rugged mountains of Afghanistan is, to say the least, difficult. North Korea has sophisticated security systems, and Al Qaeda painstakingly vets its recruits—especially those given proximity to Bin Laden. Beyond questions of access, spies can be highly unreliable. Sometimes they fabricate reports just to justify their stipend from the CIA. Of 200 asset reports on missile sightings in Cuba during the crisis of 1962, only six proved accurate (Powers 1979, 447). Sobering, too, is the fact that all of America's assets in Cuba and in East Germany during the Cold War turned out to be double agents, loyal not to their CIA case officers but to their own communist governments.

Spies are often the most venal individuals in a society, with dubious histories of human rights abuses—perhaps even with criminal records as murderers. Though sometimes necessary for America's security, assets are unlikely to be boy scouts or nuns (as realists like to chide those squeamish about the business of espionage). The employment of unsavory characters by the United States raises serious ethical questions, however, about the extent to which the United States should be in alliance with drug dealers, liars, thieves, and assassins— even if they can occasionally provide useful information.

Despite the controversies and drawbacks associated with the use of human assets, the United States has had some notable humint successes. Prior to the missile crisis, for example, the Soviet military intelligence officer Col. Oleg Vladimirovich Penkoski provided valuable information about Soviet military bases and missile sites. These data, including drawings of missile bases in the U.S.S.R., helped CIA analysts discern the presence of Soviet ballistic missiles in Cuba.

All-Source Fusion

None of these collection methods is perfect. At best, each may provide some pieces for the puzzle that the intelligence agencies have been asked to solve. The objective is to use them all and hope for a synergism among them—an "all-source fusion," in intelligence lingo—that will provide policymakers with a more comprehensive understanding of the world and especially of our adversaries. As the United States has become more sophisticated in its techint capabilities, the nation's collection successes have continued to improve, and the country is generally regarded as the most effective gatherer of intelligence in the world—even in the face of a rising ability of nations and groups to evade surveillance, and despite the striking failure of the intelligence agencies to warn the American people of the September 11 attacks.

The weakest link in the collection chain has been humint, and, in the aftermath of the 9/11 tragedy and the mistakes about WMDs in Iraq in 2002, the United States is now engaged in a crash program to improve this part of the equation by hiring new case officers, assets, analysts, managers, and translators who understand the language and culture of places like Afghanistan, Iraq, and Pakistan, a part of the world largely ignored throughout most of the Cold War. Another weakness has been the lack of adequate sharing of information among the intelligence agencies and with policy officials—a defect that will require significant organizational and cultural changes throughout the government, further complicated by the creation in 2003 of a poorly defined Department of Homeland Security that has been plagued in its early days with management and organizational confusion.

The Readings

The articles that follow provide a sense of some of the challenges faced by intelligence collectors. Patrick R. Riley, a former case officer in the CIA's Operations Directorate, addresses the question of whether his Agency can any longer succeed in its primary mission: the collection of intelligence. He is especially concerned about the flood of information requests from policy officials, which threaten to overwhelm the collection capacities of the CIA and (by implication) the other intelligence agencies. "The central mission of the CIA was, and remains today," he points out,

> to obtain, perhaps to steal, information that policymakers (e.g., the President, Secretary of State, Secretary of Defense) truly must have to make their most important national security decisions, and which cannot be obtained in any other way. This means a short list of requirements of the very highest priority.

For Riley (a pseudonym), the key to success lies in the ability of policymakers to define "a coherent, and limited, set of intelligence interests and objectives in order for Langley [home place of the CIA] to regain its bearings." How likely this is to happen is another matter, for every policymaker has different information needs, and the lists of requirements continue to grow in a world that is now far more complex than it was during the bipolar Cold War era.

In the next selection, John M. Diamond worries, too, about a related problem that has emerged in the domain of imagery collection (and, in fact, every other "int"): a deluge of information gathered by satellites without a concomitant ability for analysts on the ground to make sense of it all. Diamond refers to this phenomenon as "information glut concurrent with knowledge scarcity." In his discussion of additional imagery problems, Diamond notes two trends. First, to lower the expense of imagery collection and the vulnerability of large satellites to attack, the United States is turning toward the use of small satellites in place of an exclusive reliance on a few large satellites. Second, the intelligence community is trying to encourage policymakers to define their imagery requirements more sharply, rather than relying on imagery analysts to perform this task by guessing what those requirements may be. This sounds sensible in theory, but in practice busy policymakers have often been unable to find or take the time necessary to define their intelligence needs with precision.

William E. Burrows provides a sense of America's use of surveillance satellites—machines that provide, in his words, "instant intelligence." The article captures the difficulties in developing space intelligence "platforms" that can serve the global information needs of the United States. Especially difficult is sifting through the deluge of data that the satellite cameras and listening devices are able to obtain.

The fourth selection, written by Matthew M. Aid, asks whether the National Security Agency—America's premier signal intelligence agency and the largest of the nation's intelligence collectors—is accomplishing its mission in the post–Cold War era. He finds that the NSA was actually able to improve its sigint capabilities during the 1990s. Still, the Agency is not without its problems. Foremost, according to Aid, is a lack of analysts and information technology specialists. Past directors of the NSA have frequently complained that their biggest headaches are threefold: processing, processing, and processing. This dilemma continues, and Aid notes that new information processing technologies are critical to the ongoing success of sigint. The Agency also faces difficult challenges in its bumpy relationships with sigint consumers in Washington, D.C. Moreover, Aid criticizes the NSA's internal management, with its bloated bureaucracy, disorderly financial accounts, and pronounced opaqueness that make accountability difficult to maintain. Few would dispute the importance of the sigint mission; the issue is how to go about improving the NSA's performance of that mission.

In the fifth selection, Richard Russell paints a picture of how difficult it is to gather intelligence against Iraq, a nation little understood by the United States in the early 1990s—and even now. The article illustrates, as well, the problem of extracting good analysis from an incomplete set of data points. ✦

4

CIA and Its Discontents

Patrick R. Riley

A former Directorate of Operations case officer explores whether the CIA can cope with all the intelligence requirements placed on it since the end of the Cold War. He calls for a more discriminating list of targets for intelligence collection.

Public criticism of the Central Intelligence Agency has taken a new twist. Unlike many of the older approaches, this one does not paint the CIA as a menacing threat to liberal democracy. It does not claim the agency is out of control, or that it roams the world committing nefarious acts of sabotage, subversion, and assassination. No, sabotage and subversion are pursuits far too virile to find a place in this new portrait of the CIA. The fearsome rogue elephant of the Watergate era has been replaced by a weasel, and a stupid weasel at that.

The new criticism attempts to make the case, not so much that the CIA is doing things it should not, but rather that it has become incapable of doing the things it should. The agency is described as decrepit. A bureaucratic version of Gresham's Law is allegedly doing its work at Langley, as mediocre officers displace the sterling in positions of leadership. Dishonesty is said to be commonplace. Careers are being built on exaggerated accomplishments, if not out and out fabrications. And the unkindest cut of all: the CIA's intelligence product—its raison d'être—is awful. As much good information on Mu'ammar al-Qadhafi can supposedly be gleaned by reading the open press or State Department telegrams as can be obtained from the CIA's clandestine intelligence reports. And this should not be surprising, according to the new criticism, since the bulk of the agency's product—when it is of any value at all—is said to consist mainly of recycled, and thinly disguised, newspaper pieces.

Strains of this new approach are encountered all over, from the editorial pages of the prestige press to off-handed remarks by pundits on the Sunday morning chat shows. A good example is a recent cover story in the *Atlantic Monthly*, written by a former CIA officer using the alias Edward G. Shirley.[1]

The new criticism, admittedly, is not wholly without merit. But it is terribly one-sided, and the nuggets of reality it contains are contaminated with large doses of exaggeration and seriously flawed analysis.

A more balanced look at the CIA is warranted.

Four Theses

The CIA is a big place. Most of its employees have no direct involvement in the complex profession of developing and safely managing spies against foreign governments, terrorist organizations, and drug cartels. A plurality work for the Directorate of Administration, whose job is to keep the agency's bureaucratic gears oiled. Then there is the Directorate of Science and Technology, where the concern is with satellites and such. A third sector is the Directorate of Intelligence, the people who combine all-source intelligence information into the finished product for Washington policymakers.

But when most people talk about the CIA, they are talking about the Directorate of Operations (DO). The DO is also known as the Clandestine Service, a title which better suggests those skills and responsibilities that distinguish the DO from the rest of the CIA, and the CIA from the rest of the federal government. The DO does the spying, runs the agents, plans and executes the operations, and takes the human risks inherent in the theft of another government's secrets.

So what exactly is the complaint against the CIA and, in particular, the DO? What 95 theses are the latter-day Martin Luther's nailing to the church door at Langley? For the sake of manageability, the figurative 95 can be narrowed down to four.

(1) The bureaucracy is bad. It is stifling. The agency has become too large, too cumbersome. It is not well managed and good people are leaving.

(2) The CIA's intelligence product is inadequate.

(3) An 'English only' mentality predominates, as the value of substantive area knowledge—e.g., foreign languages, cultural and historical familiarity—is ignored, or at least downplayed.

(4) Promotions in the DO are based more on the numbers game—How many agents did you recruit?—than on merit.

Bureaucratic Problems?

The broadest, most general area of criticism, and the one containing the most truth, refers to the agency bureaucracy. Part of the problem is simply that the CIA has been around for over a half century and, not surprisingly, arteriosclerosis is setting in as it ages. It is fatter and slower than it used to be, more likely to cling to the status quo. In short, the CIA is facing the same challenges all large, middle-aged organizations face—it needs to be smaller, leaner, and faster.

But there is also a bureaucratic malaise in the agency today that cannot be blamed on age. The roots of the malady go back to the end of the cold war, an event which has had two harmful (albeit indirect) effects on the CIA.[2]

The first is disorientation and drift. Part of the source of this disorientation lies at Langley, but most comes from the other side of the Potomac, from the larger U.S. foreign policy establishment. The CIA should get its direction from the top levels of the Executive branch, but that direction has been weak and vacillating since the fall of the Soviet Union. The fight against the USSR gave the CIA's mission a primary focus and unity—a standard by which resources were prioritized and operational risks weighed and evaluated—precisely because it provided the same focus and unity for top level U.S. policymakers, the agency's customer base. But today, that purpose and direction at the top have dimmed.

In other words, can the CIA have clarity about what it should be doing when the official foreign policy establishment is confused about what it wants? Where should the agency's searchlight be trained? Is Russia still a threat to U.S. national security? If so, in which areas? Militarily? Economic espionage? Regional stability? What about China?

The intelligence requirements being handed down by policymakers today are many, while vision, direction, and leadership among those same policymakers is in short supply. There are requirements on the global economy, U.S. competitiveness, nuclear proliferation, human rights, and arms trafficking. The DO is expected to do counternarcotics and counterterrorism (e.g., penetrate drug syndicates and terrorist networks), alongside the traditional counterintelligence.

Demands are being made for environmental and ecological intelligence—the list is long, ill-defined, and constantly shifting. The only possible outcome is flux and uncertainty in the CIA.

But most of all, this proliferation of intelligence requirements springs from a fundamental misunderstanding of the CIA's central mission. Because that mission never was the USSR, or the Warsaw Pact, or even the Communist threat, it should not be described in those terms. The central mission of the CIA was, and remains to this day, to obtain, perhaps steal, information that policymakers (e.g., the President, Secretary of State, Secretary of Defense) truly must have to make their most important national security decisions, and which cannot be obtained in any other way. This means a short list of requirements of the very highest priority.

Besides having a crushing effect on morale—and some good officers are indeed resigning—this national foreign policy fog is fueling the growth of the agency's bureaucracy. The strategy within the organization today is to have lots of people doing many things on many fronts, rather than a focused few going against top priority targets. Of course, this is the case because there are no top priorities, just sundry demands. The CIA needs clear priorities, and these must come from the national leadership.

The second harmful effect, an excessive aversion to risk, really applies only to the DO, not to the other three Directorates. Here is the story behind it.

There were abuses within the Directorate of Operations during the cold war. Their extent has been exaggerated in some quarters, but they happened. For a long time they lay hidden, frozen in the cold war tundra. Then the Soviet Bloc fell, and stories surfaced of offenses long forgotten.

The DO took it on its collective chin for these rediscovered abuses, and DO officers became obsessed with avoiding the sorts of things that had brought much wrath down on their heads.[3] The solution was to make the system more "open" and, inevitably, more bureaucratic. New regulations were introduced. Checks, double checks, and triple checks were added. The authority to make decisions was moved up the hierarchy, and consultations came to involve more and more people. This occurred around 1995–1996, and the top posts at the agency were filled by well-meaning people (some having come over from senior positions at the Department of Defense) who, unfortunately, had a weak grasp of the profession of espionage. They brought practices and instituted reforms that were better suited to larger, more conventional government organizations.

The agency's personnel system is a good example of this bureaucratic growth. In the cold war years, an officer would be posted abroad after fulfilling two or three objective criteria (e.g., training, desk work), but then it would quickly come down to what the Chief of Station (COS) thought of him/her. Or an officer would land a job on a headquarters desk based, once again, on a few objective standards, but with much depending on the branch or division chiefs personal perceptions. Though perhaps unfair at times, this method certainly reduced the red tape.

But the changes of the mid-1990s remade the personnel system into a safe place lined with soft, bureaucratic cotton. All jobs were advertised—not just within the DO, but throughout the agency— regardless of operational security. So, if a station needed someone with a specific language capability to translate transcripts from telephone taps against a particular foreign embassy, that information was put in a job notice and circulated around the agency. Besides fueling bureaucratic growth, such job advertising constituted a breach of compartmentation that would have been unthinkable during the cold war.

The position of Chief of Station is another quandary. In the past, the COS was a powerful counterweight to the bureaucracy. As the senior agency officer in a foreign country, the COS had great authority. Unless there was an overwhelming reason not to, headquarters deferred to the COS on practically everything of substance related to U.S. intelligence activities in the country in which he was posted. Today things have changed. While still retaining considerable latitude, the COS is no longer as free of institutional shackles as in the cold war era. The DO has gained a bit more protection from the occasional COS cowboy, but it has done so by weakening an office that traditionally was a formidable enemy of groupthink and bureaucratic management-by-consensus.

Possible Remedies

Only the national political leadership can solve the first problem: inconsistency, drift, and uncertainty. Policymakers must define a coherent, and limited, set of intelligence interests and objectives in order for Langley to regain its bearings. And recognizing that the Clandestine Service should be the collector of last resort, these should be objectives of truly the highest importance.

A solution to the second problem, institutional risk aversion, also involves the national leadership. In this case, a sense of balance and proportion in dealing with possible abuses at the CIA must be recovered. Everyone wants to prevent nightmarish offenses, but nothing is more useless than a clandestine service afraid to take risks, one that is constantly looking over its collective shoulder and fretting about whether this decision or that operation might be misinterpreted somewhere down the road. Of course, if the collection objectives are confined to questions of only the highest importance to policymakers (as they should be), then the risk calculus becomes somewhat easier.

Internal reforms must be done carefully and with an eye toward all possible consequences. For instance, in recent years the need to downsize was addressed through early departures and incentive retirement packages. Unfortunately, as is so often the case, many of those who took advantage of the programs were often the people who should have been encouraged to stay—that is, the talented and the energetic.

Yet, the agency's prospects in this area are probably brighter today than they have been in some time. George Tenet, Director of Central Intelligence (DCI) since 1997, and his Deputy Director of Operations (DDO), Jack Downing, understand and appreciate the intelligence profession. They have begun to roll back the bureaucratic excesses of the recent past, e.g., by redesigning the promotion system to reduce management layers.[4] Tenet is also helping to shape a sharper and clearer national vision of U.S. intelligence interests and priorities. As an article in the *Washington Post* recently put it:

> . . . shifting foreign policy interests of presidents—"the flavor of the month," one source said Tenet called it—had seen temporary surges and then retreats in clandestine activities in certain areas of the world.

> To replace this uneven approach, Tenet said his human intelligence emphasis would be a "sustained commitment" to recruitment, training and retention of personnel to enable the agency to operate on hard targets around the world.[5]

Though the CIA is not out of the woods yet, it is now, at least, being led by people who know the terrain.

Inadequate Intelligence?

When discussing the CIA's intelligence product, the reference here is to the secretly acquired intelligence of the Director of Operations.[6] With rare exceptions, human intelligence, (HUMINT) comes from agents—from spies—as opposed to, for example, overhead photography. The DO takes HUMINT and puts it out in intelligence reports.

The key thing to remember about a DO intelligence report is that it is provisional. It is fragmentary, intended to be only one piece of the puzzle. Across every report is a warning that the information is raw, minimally evaluated, and not intended to be used as a firm answer to anybody's questions about anything. It is caveat emptor, and everyone in the Intelligence Community knows it. How could the situation be different? By its very nature, HUMINT is dicey stuff. It becomes useful only in the hands and mind of a trained analyst (either in the agency's own DI, or in another analytical shop elsewhere in the Intelligence Community) who can evaluate it, judge its accuracy, and put it in context.

When a critic calls DO intelligence reporting mediocre, the question to ask is: Compared to what? The first, and most obvious, place to search for intelligence reporting to which the DO's product can be compared is the world's other intelligence services.

But a problem develops immediately. Intelligence reports are secret. Since outsiders do not have access to them, how can anything be known about the quality of intelligence reports produced by other countries? They don't just give them to the United States, do they?

As it turns out, they do. Intelligence services around the world have liaisons with one another, and through these liaisons reporting is shared.

Intelligence liaisons vary widely in closeness and mutual trust, and the closer the relationship (generally speaking), the higher the quality of the intelligence exchanged. And even in the closest of liaisons, neither side gives the other everything—the assumption should always be that the best is being withheld. So, comparing DO reporting to that received from liaison services cannot be done thoughtlessly, nor by the inexperienced.

Nevertheless, after looking at thousands of reports, year in and year out, a satisfactory view of how other services' work stacks up against the DO's is possible. And the verdict? The DO's reporting is as good as any, and far better than most.[7]

For instance, one well-known European service is widely acknowledged as top flight. Taken as a totality, its reports are good, pretty much on the same plane as those of the DO—no worse, but certainly no better. On one occasion, this service might have a spy in a position that the DO does not, in which case its intelligence will be more useful. At other times, the DO has the uniquely positioned spy, and hence the superior intelligence. In fact, the reporting from the DO and this service are remarkably similar. This is not surprising, given the cozy bond between the two countries. Of course, because of the greater breadth of DO activities worldwide (not to mention its far larger budget), the total tonnage of good DO reports is more than that from its sister service across the pond. And this other service readily acknowledges that the CIA's input to its national security deliberations is invaluable. But overall, each service is about as good as the other when it comes to the intelligence it produces.

Another service has a well-deserved reputation as being among the world's best intelligence collectors against Middle Eastern targets. This service is far more focused than the DO—its targets are few, whereas the DO's interests span the globe. And, as can be expected, this service is good against that short list. In a handful of small, dark corners it even sheds light unavailable from the DO's sources. But the remarkable thing is, even given that service's relatively small basket of targets, its intelligence is no better overall than that of the DO against the same targets. And when shifting into the larger world— even the larger Arab and North African world—the quality of intelligence from the DO quickly outstrips anything produced by this elite service.

The same could be said about other services. Some produce intelligence against esoteric targets comparable in quality to what would be received from the DO, but generally the DO's product is superior. And, after these few other services, the competition falls off dramatically. From there on out, the quality of the DO's reporting swamps everything else in the First and Third Worlds.

As for the intelligence produced by the Communist regimes, not much from either the dead (the former Soviet bloc) or the living dead (North Korea, Communist China, and the rest) deserves to be put in the CIA's league. Of course, the Soviets and their East European satellites did have some remarkable successes, but the CIA still outstripped them overall. Even the Aldrich Ames affair, as terrible as that was, would have been far worse for the West had the KGB officers handling Ames been anywhere near as competent and professional as the typical CIA officer. Instead of directing Ames to obtain the strategic national intelligence to which he had access, the KGB used him only as a counterintelligence agent. They asked him about CIA spies within the USSR, but not for information on larger U.S. policies and intentions. That was just stupid of the KGB; no CIA officer would have squandered such an opportunity.

And the overall high quality of DO reporting should not be a surprise. Every piece of HUMINT that the DO disseminates is reviewed beforehand. When an agent provides information the case officer believes to be intelligence, the officer first discusses it with his/her supervisor, normally the COS, and with the intelligence officer, if the station is large enough to warrant a DO officer fully dedicated to analysis. Station officers will then informally present the information to their embassy colleagues from the State Department to solicit their views on its worth and veracity. If all has gone well, the intelligence is put into a report. That report is cabled to headquarters, with "info" copies sent to any station in the world that might have some light to throw on its contents. These stations are required to reply; their comments must include a recommendation about whether the report merits dissemination to other departments and agencies of the U.S. government.

After the other stations respond, intelligence officers at headquarters begin an even more intensive review of the information. Analysts in the Directorate of Intelligence—the analytical, think tank side of the Langley house—are commonly consulted; and the DO has its own expert resources to draw on internally. These reviewers can insert their own comments (clearly marked as such) into the text of the report.

If the report survives the review process, it is disseminated to the Intelligence Community. If not, it goes into a burn bag—it is ND'd (nondisseminated). A surprisingly large number of reports sent to headquarters every day are ND'd, particularly when the review process that has already taken place in the field is considered.[8]

Upgrading Performance

Does this mean that there are no problems with Directorate of Operations reporting, no areas for improvement?

Not at all. For instance, the tendency is for station officers to look at a marginal piece of intelligence they have collected and say, "Let's go ahead and send this in to headquarters. It's of little value, but it might help some analyst somewhere make sense of something." This line of reasoning is seductive. After all, the station already has the information, and the desire not to "waste" it can be strong. But it's a bad habit to develop.

And there is the time-honored "perceptions" trap. It goes like this. The CIA station may have an agent in the host country's foreign ministry. The agent gives the station a foreign ministry document containing details about opposition groups in, perhaps, Iraq. The information in the document, although true, is already known. But instead of putting it in the burn bag (where it really belongs), the station submits it to headquarters, not as intelligence on opposition groups in Iraq, but as intelligence on the foreign ministry's perceptions about opposition groups in Iraq. Now, there is nothing dishonest about this, and the information submitted may in fact be valuable. (To take an example from recent headlines, would it not have been important for Washington to know the perceptions of the Pakistani Foreign Ministry on the state of Indian nuclear delivery systems, even if the U.S. already knew everything about those systems?) But over time the perceptions trap can dilute the general quality of DO intelligence.

These and other lapses are the exception, but they should not happen at all. The DO can do better, as the vast majority of CIA officers will agree.

There is also a problem in the DO of relinquishing longstanding, outdated requirements against the 'internal target'—that is, the government of the country in which an overseas station is located. It's a difficult thing to do. After all, situations in which such reporting would be valuable are always apparent, and the agents to provide it are already tested and in place. But the need for such reporting must be looked at critically, and the list of internal requirements should be carefully pared down to the essential few—or eliminated entirely, if appropriate. (DCI Tenet and DDO Downing are currently making solid progress in this area, as they try to refocus national intelligence priorities on matters truly important.)

A word or two must be said about the recent Jeremiah Report. At the request of DCI Tenet, Admiral David Jeremiah, the former vice chairman of the Joint Chiefs of Staff, conducted an investigation into the failure of American intelligence to give any advance warning to policy makers about the 11 May 1998 Indian nuclear test.[9]

Jeremiah's investigation was completed, and his report issued, by early June. While the report contained many important observations, as well as practical suggestions for reform, some of the most interesting comments were on the problem of what Harvard professor Richard Pipes has called "mirror-imaging."[10] This is the tendency, quite common among Americans, to view and interpret a foreign country's words and actions through one's own cultural optic, rather than from the perspective of the foreigners themselves. In this particular case, Jeremiah found that U.S. intelligence analysts (and policymakers, too) assumed that India's Bharatiya Janata Party would not conduct a nuclear test, basically because the United States would not have conducted such a test—to do so would be "irrational," counterproductive, needlessly provocative toward the Pakistanis, and so on. Unfortunately, Indian nationalists evidently do not see the world in the same light an American intelligence analyst does.

The problem of mirror-imaging is real, and it is no doubt partly to blame for the "Indian Bomb" fiasco. Jeremiah was correct in insisting that the issue must be addressed. But mirror-imaging is a problem found largely among analysts (in the Directorate of Intelligence and elsewhere in the Intelligence Community), and not all that much in the Clandestine Service. DO officers spend half or more of their careers abroad, dealing intimately with foreign cultures. They quickly learn that the ways of Uzbekistan are not necessarily the same as those of New Hampshire.

A final note on DO reporting. Some of today's critics claim that DO officers overseas routinely poach from the State Department, that they use their diplomatic cover jobs to steal information that is, or should be, reported through normal State channels. This criticism has little merit.

Without doubt, sources being developed and managed by DO officers will sometimes report on matters that technically fall within the purview of the genuine diplomats (e.g., the content of interesting cocktail party conversation, or talk on the street). But that is normally because the diplomats simply are not reporting the information, for any number of reasons.[11] And even when this sort of State-like material is submitted by the agency station, it almost always goes as an "ops intel"—that is, a normal staff cable which is passed informally to the DI analysts back at headquarters—and not as an actual DO intelligence report.

English Only?

According to critics, knowledge of foreign cultures, including languages, history, and politics, is not taken seriously in the DO, or at least not as seriously as it should be.

At one level, this charge is simply false. No serious person within the DO believes that language ability, cultural knowledge, and political and geographical expertise is unimportant. No Chief of Station, given the choice between an officer who speaks the country's language and one who does not, will pick the latter over the former—all other skills being relatively equal. Over the long haul, officers with strong language skills and area knowledge do better than those without. Coveted assignments are easier to get, and successful tours more likely, for officers who excel in foreign languages and the associated cultural familiarity. On another level, of course, matters are not as clear-cut.

A DO case officer is not an academic. While languages and area expertise are high on the list of tools that make for a good performer, a case officer needs more—a talent for the recruitment and handling of agents being an obvious example. The case officer must be able to convince the agent to do something manifestly not in the agent's enlightened self-interest, that is, spy against his own country. Then during moments of doubt—and if the agent has half a brain, there will be many such moments—the officer must be reassuring, but at the same time controlling and directing. He must be able to crank up the agent's courage tight enough to accomplish the mission, and yet still keep him fearful enough to strictly follow the security plan the case officer has given him. These are vital talents for a case officer, and they have nothing to do with whether he/she has done postgraduate work in Altaic languages.

Does the ability to converse fluently in the agent's native tongue (and other cultural familiarities) help in recruitment and handling, the sine qua non of case officering? Unquestionably so, which is why these skills are prized in the DO. Still, there is some truth to the adage that a good recruiter can recruit anywhere. The ability to talk fast, to think on one's feet, to project an aura of trustworthiness, to judge and intuitively measure very basic human motives and responses—these can, in some cases, stand on their own. But the simple fact is that certain officers with excellent agent recruiting and handling skills will do better in their careers than officers who may have stronger language abilities, but are weaker in the people department.

It is also helpful here to recall the problems of bureaucracy. The lack of clear direction and focus among the CIA's top-level customers, combined with budget cuts, means the DO is trying to do more with less, and one of the areas that has suffered has undoubtedly been language/culture instruction. So, when the DO finds itself suddenly required to put scores of people on the ground somewhere (e.g., in support of American forces in a UN operation), some will doubtless be inadequately trained in local politics and language.

Promotions: A Numbers Game?

In large organizations there are many evaluative systems, not only the promotion system, that require ranking, and ranking means quantification.

When awarding promotions to its case officers, the most common element which the DO quantifies is recruited agents. Of course, the number of recruitments is only one criterion against which a case officer is evaluated for promotion (others are more subjective), but it is an important one.

Critics contend that this quantification process has gotten out of hand. Sheer numbers of recruitments are what matter, they allege, with quality playing second fiddle to quantity. Case officers are said to take "recruitment tours" in countries where getting local officials onto the agency payroll is relatively easy. These tours give officers the numbers they need to move up the DO's promotional ladder, with the actual intelligence value of the recruitments only a minor consideration. Are these charges true or false? Once again, the reality is complicated.

The number of recruitments a case officer makes does carry considerable weight when it comes to promotion. It has to. Agent recruitment is the lifeblood of the DO, the vitality of the agency, the thing that makes the CIA different from the State Department or the Carnegie Foundation. The DO's stable of agents must be constantly replenished—targets change; agents die, or lose access, or quit, or are demoted; governments leave office and are replaced by new ones; and so on. If an officer in the Clandestine Service wants to move up, he must understand this lifeblood, understand agent recruitment. He must know first hand what it takes, what it feels like, what the techniques are, where the problems lie, what it looks like when it's going right, how to tell when it's going wrong. And that comes only with experience, with the recruiting of agents—all things being equal (and, of course, they never are), the more recruitments, the better.

But the quality of the recruitments does count.[12] To help get an officer promoted, recruitments must (1) be against countries that policymakers care about, and (2) the agents recruited must be in positions that matter. Granting the occasional egregious counterexample (of which nobody is proud), case officers do not move up the ranks by recruiting nothing but safehouse keepers.

And when a putatively important recruitment is made, the individual is evaluated under an intense and critical light. For example, in the mid-1980s, I did a tour on a headquarters desk in the Latin America Division (LA). The station I supported had just recruited an important asset, a penetration of one of the region's Marxist guerilla groups. The group was supported by the Soviet Union through its Cuban proxy, and was wreaking havoc in a country friendly to the United States—friendly by Cold War standards, anyway. There had never been a penetration of this particular band of insurgents before. The COS was justifiably proud, headquarters was excited about the intelligence possibilities, and the case officer who recruited the agent thought he had struck gold. Stellar careers are made of such recruitments. Kudos were extended all around.

The agent began producing HUMINT. The reports carried a warning that the source was untested—standard procedure—but they were nonetheless eagerly received within the Intelligence Community.

Then the LA Reports and Requirements staff discovered a disturbing pattern. The agent's reporting was detailed and plausible, but it was usually about events that had already occurred—a bridge on a river that was blown up last month, leaflets distributed in a village the week before. Was the agent simply embellishing on things he had heard in the street, or read in the press? No, said the COS and the case officer, this agent was the genuine article. But the troublesome pattern in the intelligence continued.

Headquarters formulated test questions and cabled them out to the station—again, standard procedure. The questions were about the future, and they required predictions concerning the guerillas' plans and intentions. The agent answered the questions. Time went by. Some of his predictions were on target, and he had plausible excuses for those that were not. The COS and the case officer were satisfied, as were many at headquarters. This agent's reporting was heady stuff, and it was going over big in the Intelligence Community. But suspicions continued and criticism intensified. Finally, the COS agreed to allow a case officer from headquarters to come out and interrogate the agent. The interrogation lasted several days, with short breaks for food and sleep. Finally, caught in a skillfully spun web of questions and counter-questions, the agent broke and admitted he had lied about everything. LA Division issued burn notices on every report the agent had provided, probably 30 or 40 in all.

That's an example of how the system is designed to function. Recruitments are scrutinized and questions asked. Although all cases in the DO are tightly compartmented, even the most sensitive and restricted are reviewed by multiple officers up and down the chain of command. Marginal or even worthless agents do slip by, but overall the vetting system works.[13]

Admittedly, promotions do not come quickly in the DO, thereby causing some dissatisfaction. But, when all is said and done, the most cogent observation I ever heard about the nature of promotion systems came from a colleague with whom I served overseas. He was a former Marine Corps officer who reached the senior ranks before jumping to an equally successful second career in the CIA. One day while we were talking about promotions in the DO, I asked him if he thought they were doled out fairly. He smiled, leaned back in his chair with his hands behind his head, and replied, "Ask whether the Navy's promotion system is fair, and all the admirals will assure you it is."

Still the Best

The criticism directed at the Central Intelligence Agency in recent times carries the most truth when its target is the bureaucracy. The post-cold war drift in U.S. foreign policy has caused an identity crisis at Langley, and the reactions to rediscovered cold war abuses have left the DO skittish and defensive. Both factors have contributed to bureaucratic growth, erosion of morale, and even the resignations of some fine officers. But there is also good news, as the Tenet/Downing regime now moves to address these problems and help senior policymakers restore a clear, limited set of U.S. national intelligence interests. The recent decision to recruit widely for a greatly enhanced case officer corps could, and should, significantly enhance the agency's overseas capabilities.[14]

The CIA is the world's premier intelligence organization, and nothing has happened over the past decade to change that fact. Contrary to what its latest critics claim, the agency is not on the ropes, its people are not incompetent, and radical surgery is not in order. What is needed is clear national direction on foreign intelligence priorities, coupled with a cool, deliberate, and balanced approach to the problem of abuse prevention within the Clandestine Service. Once these are firmly in place, the Agency can quietly get on with the moderate reforms and adjustments that any organization needs after 50 years of honorable service.

Questions for Further Discussion

1. With sixteen separate agencies, has the U.S. intelligence bureaucracy grown too large? Where could consolidations be made?

2. What is meant by the phrase "mirror-imaging"? Can you think of some possible examples of mirror-imaging today?

3. In what sense is agent recruitment "a numbers game"? Should there be a different approach to acquiring "assets" abroad?

4. What should be America's national foreign intelligence priorities today? How about domestic intelligence priorities?

Endnotes

1. Edward G. Shirley, "Can't Anybody Here Play This Game?," *Atlantic Monthly*, February 1998, Vol. 281, No. 2, pp. 45–61.
2. Throughout this section on the bureaucracy, I draw heavily on a recent conversation I had with a former senior DO official.
3. Punishments may not have been as severe nor as widespread as some critics think they should have been, but they nonetheless had considerable effect within the DO.
4. "A Low Profile for CIA Chief; Behind the Scenes, Tenet Gains Growing Respect," *Washington Post*, 13 January 1998.
5. "CIA Chief Cited Loss of Agency's Capabilities; Remarks Preceded Indian Bomb Tests," *Washington Post*, 25 May 1998.
6. Sometimes when people use the word "intelligence" they are referring not to the raw intelligence from the DO, but to finished intelligence. Finished intelligence comes from the Directorate of Intelligence (DI)—the overt side of the house—and is largely analysis, prediction, and estimation. Of all the information that goes into finished intelligence, only a small part is obtained by the DO through its spies. Most comes from a variety of open sources, pretty much the same ones used by academics and think tanks. For those who are interested, there is an extensive literature on the value of the DI's finished intelligence. One good place to start is an article by Richard Pipes, "What to Do About the CIA," *Commentary*, March 1995, Vol. 99, Issue 3.
7. Some readers will have a problem with this. I am basically saying, "I've seen lots of raw production from many intelligence services, and you haven't. In fact, you haven't seen any of it—you *can't* see it. But believe me, the DO's is the best of the lot. Take my word for it." While this is admittedly not an argument likely to win over the skeptics, there is plenty of general corroboration available in the overt literature. For instance, Loch K. Johnson's *America's Secret Power: The CIA in a Democratic Society* (New York: Oxford University Press, 1989) contains much criticism of the agency, but still gives the intelligence product generally high marks, e.g. on page 256: "The Agency has served the nation well, from high competence in the monitoring of Soviet weapons to sound appraisals of global economic trends."
8. Regarding bureaucracy, does the outlined quality control process for intelligence reports not seem rather bureaucratic? Maybe so. Still, it's worth noting that the process is designed to be more akin to peer review than to running some bureaucratic gauntlet. And there are all sorts of little loopholes scattered here and there to keep the bureaucracy at bay. For instance, if the station believes a report is urgent or its value is beyond reasonable dispute, it can always send the report in as a "direct dissem," thus bypassing the whole review process and getting the information out to the Intelligence Community within minutes. Of course, this puts considerable responsibility on the station, responsibility which in these days of organizational timidity many officers may be reluctant to exercise. But this is not so much a criticism of the intelligence quality control process, as it is just one more reason for understanding and correcting the problem of institutional risk aversion discussed earlier.
9. Tim Weiner, "C.I.A. Study Details Failures; Scouring of System Is Urged," *New York Times*, 3 June 1998, p. A1.
10. Pipes, op. cit.
11. For example, the political opinions of the ambassador might make it difficult for a State Department officer to put certain observations into embassy traffic.
12. Certainly, some case officers have moved up into the senior ranks on a string of awful recruitments, just as there are chiefs of surgery in major university hospitals who shouldn't be allowed to even write a prescription for allergy pills. I fully admit there are exceptions to these generalizations.
13. At its best evaluation is a technical discussion among colleagues, not a bureaucratic exercise. But, as in the case of quality control for intelligence reporting, this is an area where bureaucratic creep is a real danger in a spy organization loath to take chances—the problem of risk aversion, once again.
14. James Risen, "Getting Back to Basics, C.I.A. Is Hiring More Spies," *New York Times*, 27 June 1998, p. A9. ✦

Reprinted with permission from Patrick R. Riley, "CIA and Its Discontents," *International Journal of Intelligence and Counterintelligence* 11 (Fall 1998): 255–269.

5

Re-examining Problems and Prospects in U.S. Imagery Intelligence

John M. Diamond

Journalist John M. Diamond points to a perennial problem of intelligence collection: how to acquire useful knowledge from the glut of information gathered by spy machines and human agents. In this article, he focuses on how to cope with the flood of photographs (or images) that pour back to the United States from surveillance satellites.

Four years ago Georgetown University's *National Security Studies Quarterly* published my article on the problems and prospects for United States space-based imagery intelligence.[1] Many developments then only emerging in imagery intelligence are now well along the way, either in research, development or actual implementation. Other issues barely visible then, or originally overlooked, have since emerged.

The National Reconnaissance Office (NRO) has been aggressively pushing development technologies for a lighter, less expensive suite of imagery satellites. The NRO, National Imagery and Mapping Agency (NIMA), and military services are working on new systems for faster dissemination and exploitation of space imagery intelligence. Adversary skills at denial and deception of the U.S. system have emerged and grown. And commercial involvement in space imagery has begun to challenge the exclusive hold on space imagery of classified national systems. Indeed, commercial space imagery now supplements and supports national systems. Budgetary limitations on space-based intelligence continue to crimp research and development in ways unfamiliar to those who grew up in the Cold War intelligence community, when progress at any cost was the watchword. The difficulties of collecting information on sub-national targets such as ter-

rorist groups or potential weapons proliferators are as great as predicted in the mid-1990s. The emergence of unmanned aerial vehicles has challenged space-based platforms for missions too dangerous for manned aircraft. And warfighters continue to press for more instantaneous and direct access to space intelligence for battlefield use, cutting U.S.-based analysts out of the loop.

The imagery intelligence community has also become more open about what it does. The Clinton administration declassified thousands of spy satellite images from the Cold War, revealing capabilities and targets of interest in the Soviet Union. Public release of current space imagery, though limited, occurs fairly regularly, most recently during the 1999 Kosovo conflict and in connection with alleged Iraqi violation of the international trade embargo.[2] The NRO became determined to operate more like a business, adopting "customer-oriented" language, declassifying some of its contractor relationships, and announcing satellite launches.

Amid these bureaucratic developments, a number of incidents have pointed up weaknesses and vulnerabilities in the spy satellite system. They include the year 2000 shutdown of the ground-based receiving system for the imagery satellites; the disclosure of previous, non-Y2K-related imagery system shutdowns; NATO's bombing of the Chinese embassy in Belgrade; the destruction of a pharmaceutical plant in Khartoum, Sudan; North Korea's launch of a multi-stage missile; and the failure to predict India's 1998 nuclear test. Not all of these incidents occurred solely due to faults in imagery intelligence, but all pointed up vulnerabilities.

In integrating these trends and developments several key points became evident:

1. The U.S. space imagery community has yet to clearly lay out a path forward that is unanimously supported within the intelligence community and by congressional overseers.

2. The current space imagery intelligence architecture has yet to demonstrate an ability to contribute decisively in one of the nation's most important national security areas: terrorism and weapons proliferation.

3. The primary mission of imagery intelligence is trending away from the national strategic mission of the Cold War and toward a real-time battlefield information role. That role can be fully exploited only if U.S. intelligence makes significant strides in speeding the processing of usable imagery to warfighters.

4. Despite a major transformation of the major national security challenges facing the United States, the imagery intelligence system in use

today is essentially the same as that used during the Cold War.

5. Among sophisticated adversaries, development of the skills involved in denying and deceiving observation from space appears to be outpacing advancements in satellite intelligence collection.

Any open-source examination of imagery intelligence has its built-in limitations revolving around denied access to the vast store of classified information on the topic. While much information remains cloaked in the black world of classification, a growing body of information on imagery intelligence is available and will become vital to those in and out of government debating the strategically and financially important decisions that lie ahead for the intelligence community and the government as a whole.

Redefining, Redesigning

Four decades after a capsule containing grainy photographs of a Soviet air base became the first object recovered from space, the U.S. imagery intelligence system, an apparatus as vast and costly as the National Aeronautics and Space Administration's (NASA), is moving toward a critical stage in its history.[3] Where the military has dramatically redesigned itself since the end of the Cold War, the spy satellite architecture deployed today remains largely unchanged from that used over the Soviet Union. Though the system components have improved, the United States still relies on a handful of heavy, which is to say expensive, satellites to produce imagery intelligence of unmatched quality but limited breadth. The same system used to monitor a well-catalogued array of fixed targets in Soviet territory—sites inaccessible through any other means—must now cover a much broader universe of threats, harder to find and often mobile, but also accessible to land-based spies.

Demands on imagery intelligence have increased since the end of the Cold War even as technical capability appears to have plateaued. Where once the resources available to the imagery intelligence community were all but unlimited, they are now sharply constrained and likely to decline. Resolving the conflict between the increasing demand for imagery and declining resources requires fundamental changes in the imagery intelligence architecture. To find a cost-effective solution, planners are turning away from the past approach of loading ever-increasing imagery capability onto ever-costlier platforms. Their energies and resources are being turned to the neglected area of information processing and management. And a suite of lighter, less expensive satellites is being developed.

Because of their ability to spot troop concentrations, satellites can provide early warning of possible or impending military aggression. Early on in their history, satellites were vital for enabling the U.S. Air Force to select bombing targets in the Soviet Union, and in the gradual shift from the "city-busting" approach to nuclear war to the targeting of military assets. Satellites can yield information about economic health by monitoring crop production. By scanning smokestack emissions, analysts can make educated guesses about the kind of manufacturing going on behind factory walls.[4] Despite their enormous cost, satellites can rightly be credited with saving the United States substantial sums of money on more than one occasion by clearly identifying what the Soviets did not have and thus enabling policymakers to fend off military requests for more. The non-existent bomber and missile gaps of the late 1950s and early 1960s are two prime examples of this.[5]

Imagery intelligence can also serve as a powerful diplomatic tool. The now familiar image of a U.S. ambassador to the United Nations marching into the Security Council to display reconnaissance photographs of some foreign outrage is but one of the more visible demonstrations of its power. After Iraq invaded Kuwait in August 1990, satellite imagery showing Iraqi troop concentrations near the Saudi border helped U.S. officials convince King Fahd to approve the massive U.S. and allied troop deployment to the Persian Gulf.[6]

Satellite intelligence, in addition to its ability to provide long-term threat assessments and early warning of enemy action, can also be used to plan and coordinate offensive military operations, as was done in the Persian Gulf War when Coalition forces advanced into Kuwait and Iraq. As Vipin Gupta, a specialist in satellite remote sensing and arms control at the Lawrence Livermore National Laboratory, noted:

> The same set of images required for threat assessment can be used to search for weaknesses in an adversary's defenses, identify targets for destruction, and plan the composition of forces for the occupation of conquered territory. Satellite remote sensing can provide the attacker with the reconnaissance element of air superiority before the initiation of an offensive.[7]

The reliance of U.S. combat forces on spy satellites for at least part of their tactical intelligence has grown to the point where deployment scenarios are eclipsing strategic scenarios in the imagery intelligence world.[8] The National Reconnaissance Office has laid out an ambitious plan that goes far beyond what it made available to warfighters during the Cold War. At that time, satellite imagery products were almost a bonus, an extra for commanders, while the bulk of the imagery and analysis went to national, long-term policymakers. The change in mindset was laid out in a 1998 speech by NRO Director Keith Hall:

> During the NRO's period of cover and secrecy, the Military Services developed ways to exploit NRO systems via TENCAP—Tactical Exploitation of National Capabilities. In these programs, the NRO would give a few selected military folks briefings on NRO systems, then ask them to quietly figure out how to support real-time military operations with NRO data. Today, we're turning that type of approach on its head. Today's military wants global surveillance-like capabilities, not reconnaissance, and that means capabilities in space.[9]

The concept of surveillance, of course, carries with it connotations of real-time information flow, of instantaneous, or near instantaneous, information flow from the sensor to the shooter. Reconnaissance, on the other hand, is information gathering for near-term future planning. For the NRO, surveillance means new collection, collation, and transmission technologies. For the National Imagery and Mapping Agency, it means faster imagery management. In unclassified NIMA briefings slides presented in late October 1999, Air Force Lt. Gen. James C. King, NIMA's director, said the agency now measures its imagery analysis and forwarding timelines in days and months, and is moving toward technologies that will compress that timeline into minutes and hours.[10]

The new, operations-oriented thinking of imagery providers shows up not only in how imagery is processed, but in what is collected. NIMA's national information priorities include terrain information to help program guided weapons, data on population, vegetation, boundaries, surface drainage and transportation links. The key elements of information superiority, as defined by NIMA, are almost exclusively related to military operations, including such items as assured flow of information, information warfare capabilities, situation awareness, and "dominant battlespace awareness."[11]

Imagery intelligence specialists are involving warfighters in research and development, a clear shift from Cold War-era ways of doing business. As NRO Director Hall said in 1998, gone is the time "when the NRO built systems for intelligence purposes, and then looked for military applications for those systems."[12]

Some of this research and development has been taking place not in laboratories, but in the field. In 1997, the Defense Advanced Research Projects Agency (DARPA) fielded a Bosnia Communications and Control Augmentation System, or BC2A. It used high bandwidth, direct broadcast technology to support Operation Joint Endeavor with imagery, maps, and other operational information piped at the Secret/NATO level of classification to 29 locations in the theater.

DARPA is well along on three "advanced concept technology demonstrators" in the imagery intelligence field. The Semiautomated Imagery Processing program involves computerized algorithms that can automatically screen imagery in search of targets, reducing the volume of pictures that require human analysis. "These cue isolated targets and force structures and allow analysts to exploit high-resolution imagery in a tiny fraction of the time it takes now," DARPA's director, Larry Lynn, told lawmakers in 1997. Second, a Battlefield Awareness and Data Dissemination program is an information-handling apparatus that fuses satellite, unmanned aerial vehicle, and reconnaissance aircraft imagery into tailored information packages for use by field commanders. The program is designed to give commanders an ability to easily assemble a comprehensive picture of the battlefield. Third, a Countercamouflage, Concealment, and Deception program involves improvements in foliage-penetrating radar. This real-time collection system will be mounted on aircraft.[13]

In Kosovo, the National Imagery and Mapping Agency field-tested a new "NIMA in a box" product. The program involved sending a portable computer loaded with relevant NIMA imagery to the theater for use by search-and-rescue crews. In one instance, crews aboard an Air Force EC-130E, flying Airborne Command and Control Center, were able to speed helicopter rescue crews to the location of a downed F-16 pilot in enemy territory.[14]

The instantaneity of the search-and-rescue application of imagery intelligence points to a growing trend on the demand-side of imagery intelligence: users want imagery immediately, without a raft of analysis to go with it. "We need direct downlink. We need direct access to that data. We do not need that data sent back through various methods and dissemination means to be exploited somewhere back in CONUS (Continental United States) and then have that answer being sent forward," said Col. Darrell Lance, director of the Army Space Program Office. "I need pixels . . . I don't need reports." Lance said the Future Imagery Architecture being contemplated by NIMA involves too much processing and time, with NIMA insisting on retaining full control of the data until a finished intelligence product is delivered to the warfighter. That will take too long, Lance warned. Significantly, that "too long" in his definition is about 90 minutes. A direct downlink into the theater would cut the waiting time to about 19 minutes. With an increasing array of long-range missiles and ordnance in its arsenal, Lance said, the Army needs "detailed knowledge of what's out there that we're going to shoot at."[15]

During the Cold War, the concern was whether the Soviet Union would build ICBM launchers at night and camouflage the construction during the day; whether mobile ICBMs could be moved by night and obscured in shelters by day; whether Soviet bombers would be able to fly to Arctic staging bases in preparation for an attack on the United States, all under cloud cover; and whether spare Soviet SS-17 and SS-18 missiles could be moved to cold-launch ICBM silos at night. These were not idle fears, as it turned out. The Soviets, after developing a solid understanding of the U.S. satellite collecting regime, turned to camouflage and night activity as a way of avoiding detection. They even developed a word for such sleight-of-hand: *maskirovka*.[16] During the Persian Gulf War and the "Great Scud Hunt," Iraqi forces used similar tactics. Aided by 50 percent cloud cover, they kept their mobile missile launchers out of the sights of Coalition aircraft.[17]

The new Lacrosse radar-imagery satellite did not completely solve this problem. Its through-the-weather imaging lacked the breadth needed to detect small enemy unit movements accurately. Nor was the system fast enough to get timely information to battlefield commanders, especially once they were on the move. Navy Capt. Robert Brown, a senior Defense Intelligence Agency official during the Gulf War, said that had Iraq moved its armor and other mechanized units around as it did with the Scuds, the United States would have had much greater difficulty developing an accurate estimate of enemy strength. This points up a two-headed problem that imagery intelligence has with mobility: moving enemy forces are tougher to detect and track; moving friendly forces are tougher to keep informed.

In the decade since the Gulf War, the intelligence community has worked toward a space-based capability for tracking moving targets, a system called the Moving Target Indication, or MTI.[18]

Fully 22 percent of the budgets of the agencies that make up the National Intelligence Community goes to the National Reconnaissance Office, the agency that manages the acquisition, launch, and guidance of spy satellites. That figure excludes assets at the Central Intelligence Agency (CIA), Defense Intelligence Agency, Central Imagery Office, service intelligence commands, and the National Imagery and Mapping Agency devoted to satellite intelligence processing.[19] Two-thirds of the NRO budget, or about $4.1 billion, goes to procurement and research and development through such companies as Rockwell International, Lockheed Martin, TRW, and Itek Optical Systems.[20]

Watching the Bottom Line

The days are long gone when the intelligence community could count on an unlimited budget. In the mid-1980s, the NRO, with the momentum of the Reagan administration's defense budgets behind it, developed an array of new designs, systems, concepts, and even prototype hardware that intelligence experts viewed as potentially revolutionary. By the mid-1990s, with the Cold War over, Congress lost interest and cancelled at least half a dozen of these concepts. The problem was that the imagery intelligence community's "customers," which is to say, the White House, Pentagon, State Department, and field commanders, preferred a continuation of existing capabilities to the risk involved in launching new collection ventures. In 1996, a blue-ribbon panel of government and industry experts warned that "the not-yet-understood information superiority imperative of the next century will require, in addition to the continuation of expected service to today's customers, a revolutionary path to an entirely new innovative architecture."[21]

In 1996, then-CIA Director John Deutch argued for a more warfighter-oriented imagery community able to function on a "demand-pull" basis, meaning that consumers get what they want, when they want it. The Pentagon, after all, is largely paying for the equipment:

> When we buy a new satellite system or acquire an enhanced capability it usually is to meet a predominant military need and it usually is paid for largely from the defense budget. This effectively trades off additional military platforms for more intelligence. Therefore, the key judgment in the decision is whether the military capability to perform a mission is better achieved by buying additional intelligence or more platforms.[22]

Since then pressure on imagery intelligence budgets has only grown. Congress has repeatedly criticized the intelligence community for devoting too much of its money to collection and not enough to analysis and dissemination. Critical attention to budgetary practices at both NRO and NIMA have added to the pressure. And, for the first time, there have been indications from the oversight committees in Congress of new doubts about the cost-effectiveness of space imagery collection systems.

The House Intelligence Committee, in report language accompanying the fiscal 1999 intelligence authorization bill, said the intelligence community was moving too slowly on its recommendation to move to a larger constellation of smaller, less expensive satellites. The committee said the Director of Central Intelligence could no longer rely on the recommendations of major program managers, but would have to develop his own team capable of evaluating the cost-effectiveness of collection programs. And the committee established an 11-member commission to perform a top-to-bottom review of the National Reconnaissance Office. Members of Congress, as opposed to committees, use blunter language in expressing their views. Rep. Jerry Lewis (Rep., California), a member of the House Intelligence Committee and chairman of the House Appropriations Defense Subcommittee, said in November 1999 that the multi-billion dollar Future Imagery Architecture program, "has the potential of being the biggest white elephant in U.S. intelligence history."[23]

Constrained financially while faced with expanding collection challenges, the NRO response has been to look to the rapidly expanding commercial sector to relieve some of the pressure on classified national systems. Director Hall referred to it as "the thundering herd of commercial satellites."[24] The Senate Intelligence Committee reported in 1998 that planned private-sector launches could provide up to six U.S.-owned commercial satellites capable of providing "medium-resolution imagery requirements"—meaning resolutions down to one meter—prior to the launch of the first in what is billed as a new constellation of government-owned imagery satellites.[25]

The NRO views commercial satellites as freeing up higher-capability government systems to concentrate on the most difficult intelligence targets. With this freedom will come new challenges, however, most grappling particularly with the increasingly open availability of space imagery, once the sole purview of the intelligence community. In short, U.S. intelligence will have the information, but will it have the information advantage? The Pentagon is in the early stages of developing strategies to preserve its information exclusivity long associated with the spy satellite system, including asserting "shutter control" over U.S.-owned commercial satellites to keep them from capturing imagery that might be compromising to U.S. forces, for example. At the other end of the spectrum, the Pentagon is working on anti-satellite weapons that could blind enemy, or even commercial, imagery satellites.[26]

But wider access to space imagery is here to stay. It has appeared prominently in four areas, all involving the new Ikonos satellite managed by Space Imaging, the Arlington, Virginia, firm that is operating a one-meter resolution imagery satellite for commercial purposes. Since January 2000, the firm, working for a variety of media, academic and government clients, has provided imagery—later made public—of a North Korean missile complex; a suspected mass grave site in Bosnia; Iranian weapons installations on an island in the Strait of Hormuz disputed between Iran and the United Arab Emirates; and Pakistani nuclear research and weapons facilities. In each case, the public was allowed almost immediate access to imagery of denied sites of national security interest in a way that, only a few months before, would have been the sole purview of the classified intelligence community.[27]

Gaps Persist

Despite the post-Cold War focus on proliferation and chemical and biological weapons, the United States has a long way to go to adequately detect and monitor such activities. Testifying before the House Intelligence Committee, Herbert Lee Buchanan III, director of the Pentagon's Advanced Research Projects Agency, said, "Down at the lower level, many of the sensors that we now think are going to be crucial for determining national policies don't even yet exist. For instance, our ability to sense and detect manufacturing, testing and even use of chemical and biological weapons is very, very limited." Missile fields, nuclear submarines, and laser weapons, hard as they are at times to detect, are susceptible to detailed and repeated observation from space, Buchanan said. In contrast, he continued, chemical and biological weapons can be developed and tested with no telltale industrial-scale signs.

This problem showed up in the failure to predict India's nuclear weapons test in 1998, and in the intelligence community's apparent lapses in connection with the Sudanese drug manufacturing plant bombed in connection with the suspected activities of Osama bin Laden, the reputed mastermind of the bombings of the U.S. embassies in Kenya and Tanzania. Human intelligence was required to go in and get a soil sample from the plant grounds pointing to suspected biological weapons activity. Satellite coverage of the plant was apparently unable to confirm what publicly available records showed: that the facility was a legitimate drug manufacturer. U.S. intelligence has closely followed missile developments in North Korea, using spy satellites in particular to monitor missile testing. But these systems failed to provide the CIA with any warning of North Korea's 1998 test of a three-stage Taepo-Dong I space-launch vehicle. Though billed as a non-military satellite launch, the three-stage rocket suggests that North Korea may be fast approaching the time when it will have an intercontinental missile capability.[28]

Similarly, satellite imagery failed to show analysts that a suspected Yugoslav military procurement complex in Belgrade was, in fact, the Chinese embassy compound. The far-flung nature of these targets underscores a problem identified by Admiral David Jeremiah, who headed a panel that studied the India case: "We are no longer looking at Russia and China as sort of the key places—we now have to be able to look at almost anywhere in the world."[29]

As imagery satellite technology becomes more widely available to nations, evasion and obscuration techniques have grown more widespread and sophisticated. These include camouflage, concealment, decoys, use of tunnels, foliage and natural cloud cover, and the timing of activities to coincide with periods when satellites are out of range.[30] Iraq used these techniques in the Persian Gulf War not only to hide Scud missiles and some of country's most threatening weapons-of-mass-destruction programs but also to hide Saddam Hussein himself. A House Armed Services Committee study reported that information gleaned from defectors and other sources after the war indicate that the United States was unaware of more than half of all the major nuclear weapons installations in Iraq. The five-and-a-half months Saddam had to prepare for combat with the Coalition probably enabled him to reshuffle important laboratories and individual scientists and to place facilities behind even deeper cover. The committee criticized the intelligence community for its work on Iraq before the war, noting that in July 1990 the Defense Intelligence Agency had 42 people in Washington devoted to prisoner of war/missing in action (POW-MIA) issues compared to only two assigned to Iraq. Nevertheless, satellite assets had long targeted Iraq. The famous "baby formula" plant was watched by satellite intelligence for more than eight years. Throughout that time, the intelligence community could do no better than identify the plant as a potential biological weapons site.[31] David Kay, a senior inspector with the International Atomic Energy Agency (IAEA) who toured Iraqi facilities after the war, described the approach:

Iraq understood the deception advantage of hiding a clandestine program in plain sight. Its major declared nuclear research center at Al Tuwaitha was also the initial center of Iraq's clandestine nuclear program. Al Tuwaitha was visited every six months by IAEA safeguard inspectors who announced, at the conclusion of such visits, that there was no sign of diversions of nuclear material. The inspectors gave a clean bill of health to the facility.[32]

Needless to say, if inspectors on the ground have difficulty uncovering a hidden activity, the problem confronting spy satellites is daunting indeed. Kay said the Iraqis exhibited an accurate understanding of the limitations facing U.S. technical collection assets. Concealment techniques included the construction of buildings within buildings, as the IAEA discovered at Al Tuwaitha, deliberately making buildings designed for the same purposes look different; concealing water and power lines leading into buildings; hiding the value of a target by omitting security fences and guard facilities; burying key facilities underground; moving equipment at night; and controlling the emissions from facilities.[33]

The limitations of satellite collection against countries suspected of developing weapons of mass destruction were underscored during the eighteen months that the United Nations Special Commission inspectors were barred from Iraq, beginning in the fall of 1998. Defense Department spokesman Kenneth Bacon made clear that the Pentagon is watching, but is limited in what it can see. "We do know that they have rebuilt buildings," Bacon said of the Iraqis. "We don't know what goes on in those buildings."[34]

Denial and deception techniques continue to improve to the point where the CIA is now warning policymakers that it may not be able to spot new developments in weapons-of-mass-destruction technology among countries of concern and known proliferators. "More than ever, we risk substantial surprise," CIA Director George Tenet told lawmakers in February 2000. "First and most important, proliferators are showing greater proficiency in the use of denial and deception."[35] In a sure sign that the problem has the attention of senior managers, the intelligence community now has an abbreviation for the practice of evading technical collection: C3D2, which stands for cover, concealment, camouflage, denial, and deception. Defense Intelligence Agency chief Vice Admiral Thomas R. Wilson predicted that "advances in satellite warning capabilities, the growing availability of camouflage, concealment, deception and obscurant materials, advanced technology for and experience with building underground facilities, and the growing use of fiber optics and encryption, will increase the C3D2 challenge." Wilson also warned that by the year 2015 adversaries will be employing a variety of techniques lumped by the intelligence community under the heading, "denial, deception and signal jamming." These will be aimed at the U.S. space support system, which will include communications relay satellites needed to beam imagery and other forms of satellite-based intelligence to ground stations. Electronic warfare, jamming, and improvements in the already advanced science of space-object tracking will be among the tools employed.[36]

The concealment problem shows that the challenges facing imagery intelligence are not limited to new types of "asymmetric" security threats ill-suited to observation from space. Indeed, the kinds of activities in Iraq and other adversary states that the intelligence community is looking for are similar to those the spy satellite system was quite successful in pinpointing in the Soviet Union during much of the Cold War. William Schneider Jr., an adjunct fellow at the Hudson Institute, says that vast underground facilities constructed by Iran and North Korea, among other nations, have become a routine means of protecting missile and weapons of mass destruction programs from detection.

Thus, much of the R&D work that was visible to U.S. observation during the Soviet period could now be carried out in underground facilities shielded from view, and perhaps pre-emptive attack,

Schneider testified.[37]

In the case of India's nuclear tests, a number of factors, including a shortage of analysts and a lack of human intelligence sources, contributed to the failure. And in the final hours before the test, imagery intelligence did pick up indications of an impending blast. India deliberately chose May because sandstorms are routine in the test region at that time of year. The storms not only made it difficult to see activity from above, they also covered up tire tracks, always a useful indicator of major recent activity at a test site. And high temperatures at the site helped reduce the effectiveness of heat-sensing satellite systems. In addition, through a variety of means, India was able to track the pass-over times of the U.S. spy satellites, and plan highly visible activity accordingly to evade detection. The test itself occurred in the middle of a five-hour fly-over gap; not for another 2.5 hours was the United States able to examine the scene through imagery collected by a cloud-piercing Lacrosse radar-imagery satellite.[38]

The completeness of India's coup was made clear after the test blast when the U.S. intelligence community belatedly assigned more than a dozen intelligence analysts to examine the imagery of the India test site that had been collected earlier and gave them ten days to look it over. Even then, the indications of a test were sketchy at best.[39]

Veteran intelligence analyst Allen Thomson had predicted the problem three years earlier when he described the activities of amateur satellite-watchers who make sport of spotting and tracking satellite orbits, including those of intelligence platforms, and posting the orbital parameters on the Internet. A nation such as India, with military attaches around the world, could easily do its own tracking, or simply dial up the parameters conveniently made public by these amateur space-watchers. "The presumption that reconnaissance satellites can operate covertly is obsolete," Thomson said flatly.[40] Moreover, the task of satellite spotters, whether amateur or professional, is made easier by the small number of imagery platforms. The United States is widely believed to have five close-look satellites in orbit, three advanced KH-11s and two Lacrosse radar imagers.

"The Cold War inventory of satellites is nearly gone," NRO Director Hall warned lawmakers. "We must have your continued solid support for our future programs to minimize the risk of outages and gaps in coverage."[41]

Disclosing Deficiencies

Over the next two decades, the NRO hopes to acquire the ability to provide "near continuous, all-weather, day/night imaging" with the ability to follow moving targets. But as yet there is no indication that such a system is even close to being fielded.[42]

Congressional analysis often provides the clearest window into the internal weaknesses of the intelligence community. The House Intelligence Committee, in 1998, for example, directed the CIA director to produce a comprehensive plan for "storing and archiving all imagery—both U.S. reconnaissance, and, to the extent necessary, commercially-procured imagery." Perhaps the most revealing aspect of this directive, aside from its daunting scope, was the implication that no such plan was either already in place or in the works.[43]

Given what NIMA predicts will be "staggering projected volumes of new (imagery) information," the imagery architecture now in the planning phase poses a problem that intelligence professionals refer to as "information glut concurrent with knowledge scarcity."[44]

That a handful of satellites, possibly as few as two or three high-resolution satellites in orbit at a time, can produce an unmanageable volume of intelligence points to another problem that the intelligence community faces: the heavy dependence on a few assets for the bulk of national technical collection. The occasional launch failure, a faulty main mirror, a wobbly orbit, or a strike by an enemy's anti-satellite weapon could, and in some cases has, substantially degraded imagery intelligence. The Aspin/Brown Commission study summed up the problem:

The current U.S. capability in space is vulnerable to the failure of any single system. There are a relatively small number of large and expensive systems deployed, and the failure of one causes a substantial reduction in overall capability. This structure has evolved, in part, from the need to make maximum use of each satellite platform and to reduce the cost of separate launches.[45]

The Brown Commission's warning came to fruition in an unusually public way on 31 December 1999 at 7 p.m. EST when a computer glitch in the system that processes incoming coded digital signals from the nation's five imagery satellites failed. The timing was pegged to midnight Greenwich Mean Time, or "Zulu"—the benchmark time for most major military systems—and it stemmed from the Year 2000 changeover. For several hours that night, information processors at Area 58, the main satellite imagery receiving station at Fort Belvoir, Virginia, were getting untranslatable garble from all five satellites. For a time, technicians had to manually key in data to develop usable images. Eventually spy satellite imagery was re-routed through a NASA processing center in New Mexico. The spy satellites, the two Lacrosse radar-imaging satellites of the 6100 series, and three advanced KH-11s, serial numbers 2104, 2105, and 2106, continued to orbit and collect information normally. The difficulty, the Pentagon's most significant Y2K-related failure, was on the ground.[46]

Technicians traced the problem to a varied collection of computers, some of them dating back to the 1970s, in the NRO's ground processing center at Area 58. Some of the computers were believed to be 1970s-era Digital Equipment Corporation PDP-11 computers. Others are of newer vintage, with the NRO having updated the ground processing center to keep up with newer space platforms. Deputy Defense Secretary John Hamre said NRO technicians had worked hard on the Y2K problem but decided not to conduct a complete "end-to-end" test of the ground processing station computers because it would have required a temporary shut-down of the spy satellite receiving system. In other words, the NRO opted to take the risk of a real-world shut-down in order to avoid having to experience a controlled test shut-down.[47]

Subsequent media reports indicated that the shut-down had been more serious than the Pentagon initially reported. The official line was that the shut-down lasted only a few hours before some imagery was being recovered and that technicians gradually restored full recovery of imagery by the end of the New Year's weekend. But media reports indicated that statements by Hamre and others claiming that most of the essential imagery intelligence was captured glossed over the fact that technicians had to drastically reduce the recoverable imagery to only top-priority targets. National Security Council officials reported that, in some instances, no imagery for major regions of the globe was produced over the three-day weekend. The Pentagon's rejoinder to these reports provided little reassurance. Pentagon spokesman Kenneth Bacon inadvertently acknowledged past system shutdowns when he insisted that the Y2K glitch was not out of the ordinary: "There are various weather and other events that can affect our systems, and this was well within the type of temporary interruption that we experience on a fairly regular basis." Given that the Pentagon had never previously acknowledged any type of spy satellite system shutdown, what was billed as a routine explanation was, in fact, an extraordinary disclosure.[48]

Amid the disclosures about the Y2K glitch, additional reporting provided new details into some of the past shutdowns in the imagery satellite system. Four days earlier, a problem in an electronic switch used to distribute imagery intelligence to customers failed, causing outages of 12 hours or more that affected the transfer of imagery to South Korea and to the U.S. Central Command headquarters in Tampa, Florida. And on 30 December 1999, officials scrambled to restore a downlink from one of the Lacrosse satellites.[49]

Improving the System

The imagery intelligence community is moving in two directions. First, to address the cost problem, as well as some of the vulnerabilities of the current satellite architecture, the community is moving in the direction of a "small satellite" system in which more proliferate but lower cost platforms would be orbited. Second, the community is trying to revamp its information processing toward a "demand pull" system. Whereas during the Cold War, imagery analysts largely determined the tasking of satellites to build an ever-increasing body of knowledge about the Soviet Union, now the user community, particularly the military, will play the lead role in determining imagery assignments.

A House Intelligence Committee study noted that the NRO's initial response to the cost concerns raised by a 1992 panel was to reduce the number of aircraft in orbit and load still more capability on new platforms. The result was that costs leveled out, but at still higher levels. According to the NRO, "We have roughly doubled our costs per spacecraft, as well as increasing our vulnerability to denial and deception."[50] The availability of heavy-lift Titan IV launchers represented a disincentive to reduce bus weight by building equipment out of the latest lightweight materials. Perhaps seeking to provide such an incentive, the study also recommended that NRO funding levels be reduced.[51]

Interestingly, a senior Air Force officer involved in military space matters described a few years ago how the exigencies of putting payloads into space actually creates an incentive to *increase* satellite weight. The military costs its satellite missions in terms of dollars per pound of payload. If a rocket capable of carrying 30,000 pounds into space is loaded with a 20,000-pound payload, the cost per pound is higher than if the payload weighs another 10,000 pounds. Thus the Air Force seeks to "optimize" its payloads to match the lift capability of its rockets. On a launch-by-launch basis, spending money on exotic, lightweight materials to minimize the weight of a payload doesn't pay off. He explained that it is easier and cheaper, under this construct, to build a more powerful rocket that will carry the heavier payload than to engineer lighter payloads.[52]

The Air Force, an enthusiastic backer of the small satellite concept, has noted the need for new technology development to bring the idea to fruition. The Air Force envisions a constellation of low-flying SAR-based satellites with one-meter resolution. The Air Force plan would give up some resolution in favor of more frequent revisits—four times a day normally, every hour during conflict. It will require investment in materials, sensors, satellite stabilization techniques, and light boosters in a package capable of launch-on-demand. The Air Force plan envisions research into "large aperture inflatable optics" designed to tackle the thorny problem of heavy weight in optical systems. Another area of research would focus on developing a geosynchronous satellite that would produce "long-dwell" imagery—a system that so far exists only in simulation. Ever mindful of the antisatellite weaponry that might be brought to bear, the Air Force plan would include low-cost decoys, a countermeasure that would be prohibitively expensive under today's system architecture.[53] Moving far beyond the *IC21* vision, the Air Force proposes a constellation of 10 to 20 satellites that would cost $25 million each with a lifetime of six months to a year. Much of the resolution lost by flying small satellites could be made up by computer-based optical enhancement. Under this scheme, the Air Force would "trade mass for megaflops" by using flexible, lightweight materials for the primary mirror—a Mylar-coated umbrella structure, for example, or a small compensating lens to go with a non-rigid primary mirror. A key to this solution will be continued development of algorithms such as the phase diverse spectral imaging method to produce high resolution from imperfect optical equipment.[54]

Astronomers are using "adaptive optics" in ground-based telescopes that can adjust a mirror's shape to cancel out atmospheric distortion of light from space. The *New York Times* reported in 1997 that the new technologies

> include powerful computers, new telescope mounts, better observatory designs, feedback systems that squelch the distortive twinkling of stars . . . special glass mixtures that resist deformation while undergoing temperature changes and much more.[55]

The techniques for eliminating atmospheric distortion of space images bound for earth are little different from those used to eliminate earth images bound for space. The technological thrust supported by all parties appears to be toward a substantial improvement in processing. Imagery processing experts are seeking automation, preferably onboard automation, that would do as much of the tedious work of combing images for as much important intelligence as possible before the pictures go to the light tables of human analysts. This potentially expensive technology, though it may prove beyond the reach of the NRO's budget, is seen as increasingly important to coping with the existing information overload.[56]

The *IC21* staff study concluded that, even when time is of the essence, as in military operations, human involvement will always be a part of imagery interpretation. Improvement lies in developing "soft copy exploitation" workstations that allow for quick retrieval from imagery archives with no loss of quality. Key technologies include greater screen brightness, flat screens with high resolution, and stereoscopic screens that do not require special viewing goggles. More important, the study found that the community must produce automated analysis devices with a low false alarm rate—that is, equipment that can flag to human analysts new developments visible in the latest images of a frequently photographed target without bringing forward insignificant developments. The NRO has developed processes for aligning images and using computers to scan for changes such as new roads, missile sites, and even troop concentrations. Such screening will be essential if the NRO's new "direct broadcast" capability, used to distribute imagery to mobile forces worldwide, can provide more than raw imagery data.[57]

One of the intelligence success stories of the Persian Gulf War was in the area of information screening and management. Aware that once the ground war started little time would be available to task platforms and collect and analyze imagery, CENTCOM devised a "key reads" system in which the needed information on enemy troop dispositions in certain locations and at certain times was identified and tasked ahead of time. Both airborne and national assets were used to meet this key reads request, providing General Norman Schwarzkopf with enough information to make the "go/no go" decision two hours before commencing the assault. With the lessons of the Persian Gulf War in mind, the Pentagon in 1996 awarded Northrop Grumman Corporation a $15 million contract to develop the Common Imagery Processor, a device intended to process raw infrared, electro-optical, and SAR imagery into useful battlefield intelligence.[58]

Areas of recent NRO focus include: shockless stage separation mechanisms to spare future satellites of the added weight needed to protect ultra-precision optics from the shock of entry into orbit; lightweight and highly accurate star-tracking devices to provide satellites autonomous position-fixing ability in low-earth orbit; expanded data-recording capacity; advanced lightweight batteries; and more efficient solar arrays. All of these were part of the NRO's Space Technology Experiment Satellite, or STEX, launched in October 1998 from Vandenberg Air Force Base.[59]

Thus, while imagery intelligence specialists talk of the potential for revolutionary transformation of their specialty, a look at some of the technical priorities indicates that any revolutionary change is likely to come from an accumulation of incremental improvements in an array of satellite components.

Questions for Further Discussion

1. Against what kinds of intelligence targets do you think "imagery" is most useful? Least useful?

2. Who are the major customers for "imint"?

3. Do you agree with the "demand-pull" approach to intelligence dissemination?

4. Which do you think are likely to be more useful: large or small satellites? What mix would you suggest and why?

Endnotes

1. John M. Diamond, "Problems and Prospects in U.S. Imagery Intelligence," *National Security Studies Quarterly,* Spring 1997.
2. See transcript of the U.S. State Department Briefing, James Rubin, spokesman, 29 February 2000, at http://www.secretary.state.gov/.
3. For a history of the Corona program see Kevin D. Ruffner, ed., *CORONA: America's First Satellite Program* (Washington, D.C.: Central Intelligence Agency, 1995).
4. Ronald Kessler, *Inside the CIA: Revealing the Secrets of the World's Most Powerful Spy Agency* (New York: Pocket Books, 1992) p. 85.
5. William E. Burrows, *Deep Black: Space Espionage and National Security* (New York: Random House, 1986) pp. 80–81.
6. Jeffrey Richelson, "The Future of Space Reconnaissance," *Scientific American,* Vol. 264, No. 1, January 1991, p. 41.
7. Vipin Gupta, "New Satellite Images for Sale: The Opportunities and Risks Ahead," 28 December 1994, retrieved from Internet at http://www.llnl.gov/cst, see section on "Offensive Military Application of High-Resolution Imaging." Gupta, a specialist in satellite remote sensing and arms control, is a post-doctoral fellow at the Center for Security and Technology Studies, Lawrence Livermore National Laboratory.
8. Allen Thomson, "Satellite Vulnerability: A Post-Cold War Issue?", *Space Policy,* February 1995, Vol. II, No. 1, p. 19.
9. National Reconnaissance Office Director Keith Hall, Remarks to the National Space Symposium, Colorado Springs, Colo., 9 April 1998, located at www.nro.mil/speeches/nss-498.html.
10. Air Force Lt. Gen. James C. King, "NIMA: Guaranteeing the Information Edge," 27 October 1999, briefing slides presented to AFCEA Fall Intelligence Symposium, hereinafter, "King briefing slides."
11. King briefing slides.
12. Statement of Keith R. Hall, director, National Reconnaissance Office, to the U.S. Senate Armed Services Committee, 11 March 1998, found at www.nro.mil/speeches/Sfrfinal.html.
13. Prepared remarks by Larry Lynn, director, Defense Advanced Research Projects Agency, "Investing in High-Payoff Technology Concepts," presented to the U.S. Senate Armed Services Acquisition and Technology Subcommittee, 11 March 1997, found at www.defenselink.mil:80/speeches/1997/tl 9970311-lynn.html.
14. Senior Airman Angela Furry, 31st Air Expeditionary Wing Public Affairs, "Nima-in-a-Box Debuts During Operation Allied Force," *Air Force News,* 9 June 1999, found at www.af.mil/news/Jun1999/n19990609-991144.html.
15. Erin Q. Winograd, "Space Official Says Army Must Have Direct Access to National Assets," *Inside the Army,* 22 November 1999, Vol. 11, No. 46.
16. See Bruce G. Blair and Garry D. Brewer, "Verifying Salt Agreements," in Potter, ed., *Verification and SALT,* 11. See Robert Butterworth, Chapter 2, Essay I in Roy Godson, ed., *Intelligence Requirements for the 1990s: Collection Analysis, Counterintelligence, Covert Action* (Lexington, Mass.: Lexington Books, 1987) p. 35. Bruce D. Berkowitz and Allan Goodman, *Strategic Intelligence for American National Security* (Princeton, N.J.: Princeton University Press, 1989), pp. 76–77, 199. Victor Suvorov, *Inside the Soviet Army* (New York: Macmillan, 1983) p. 106.
17. Jeffrey T. Richelson, *The U.S. Intelligence Community,* 3rd ed., (Boulder, Colo.: Westview Press, 1995) p. 157.
18. NRO Director Keith Hall, Remarks to the National Network of Electro-Optical Manufacturing Technologies Conference, 9 February 1998.
19. Federation of American Scientists (FAS), http://www.fas.org/irp/agency/budgetl.htm; author's interview with John Pike, FAS director, 24 October 1996.
20. National Reconnaissance Office fact sheet, 2 October 1996, p. 6.
21. Jeremiah Panel, unclassified version of Report to the Director, National Reconnaissance Office, "Defining the Future of the NRO for the 21st Century," Final Report, Executive Summary, 26 August 1996, p. 16.
22. John Deutch, Director of Central Intelligence, speech, "The Future of the National Reconnaissance Pro-

gram," ARPATech '96 18th Science and Technology Symposium, Atlanta, 22 May 1996, p. 4.

23. Intelligence Authorization Act for Fiscal Year 1999, Committee Report, 5 May 1998; Richard Lardner, "Congress Creates Independent Panel to Review Spy Satellite Office," *Inside Missile Defense*, Vol. 5, No. 23, 17 November 1999.

24. NRO Director Keith Hall, Remarks to the National Network of Electro-Optical Manufacturing Technologies Conference, 9 February 1998, found at www.nro.mil/speeches/Hall9802.html.

25. U.S. Senate Intelligence Committee, Report accompanying annual intelligence authorization bill, 7 May 1998, Report 105–185.

26. Ron Laurenzo, "NRO Chief Sees Industry Helping Out With Satellite Spy Duties," *Defense Week*, 7 February 2000, Vol. 21, No. 6, p. 3; Robert Wright, "Private Eyes," *The New York Times Magazine*, 5 September 1999, p. 50; Pamela Hess, "Low-Power Chemical Laser Backed Up Army's Troubled MIRACL Test Shot," *Inside the Air Force*, 24 October 1997. A set of NIMA briefing charts presented at an intelligence symposium 27 October 1999, lists the NRO's loss of its "collection monopoly" as a "ponderable" question, suggesting the intelligence community is only beginning to consider the implications of wide access to space-based imagery.

27. Author's interview with Mark Brender, director, Washington operations, Space Imaging, 14 March 2000.

28. Statement for the record of Robert D. Walpole, National Intelligence Officer for Strategic and Nuclear Programs, CIA, to the Senate Subcommittee on International Security, Proliferation and Federal Services, 9 February 2000.

29. News conference of Admiral David Jeremiah, 2 June 1998, found at www.fas.org/irp/cia/product/jeremiah .html. CIA Director George Tenet, speaking to the House Intelligence Committee on 22 July 1999, regarding the China embassy bombing incident, said, "Satellite imagery of the target provided no indication that the building was an embassy—no flags, no seals, no clear markings." The remark may have inadvertently hinted at the level of accuracy achievable by U.S. space imagery systems.

30. Gupta, "New Satellite Images for Sale." See section on "Responses to Overhead Observation," p. 39.

31. House Armed Services Committee, Subcommittee on Oversight and Investigations, House of Representatives, *Intelligence Successes and Failures in Operations Desert Shield/Storm*, 103rd Congress, 1st Session (Washington, D.C.: House Armed Services Committee, 1993), 16 August 1993, pp. 35–37.

32. David Kay, "Denial and Deception: The Lessons of Iraq," in Godson, et al., *U.S. Intelligence at the Crossroads*, p. 119.

33. Ibid., p. 120.

34. Defense Department news briefing, 1 February 2000, 1:38 p.m. The Pentagon, Kenneth Bacon, Defense Department spokesman, briefer.

35. Statement of George J. Tenet, Director of Central Intelligence, before the Senate Select Committee on Intelligence, 2 February 2000.

36. Statement of Vice Admiral Thomas R. Wilson, Director, Defense Intelligence Agency, Senate Select Committee on Intelligence, 2 February 2000.

37. Statement of William Schneider Jr., Adjunct Fellow, Hudson Institute, before the Subcommittee on International Security, Proliferation, and Federal Services, U.S. Senate Armed Services Committee, 9 February 2000.

38. Douglas Waller, "Why the Sky Spies Missed the Desert Blast," *Time*, 25 May 1998, Vol. 151, No. 20. See also, memo from Allen Thomson, former CIA analyst, "India Evaded Spysats?" 18 May 1998, found on Federation of American Scientists Website at <www.fas.org/irp/news/1998/05/980518-at.htm>.

39. Adm. David Jeremiah, assigned to head up an intelligence review of the India test incident, said, "When you do that retrospectively you can begin to piece together things that might have brought you to the conclusion that something might be going on." See transcript of Jeremiah news conference on the Federation of American Scientists Website, www.fas.org/irp/cia/product/jeremiah.html.

40. Allen Thomson, "Satellite Vulnerability: A Post-Cold War Issue?" *Space Policy*, February 1995, Vol. II, No. 1, p. 19. See also, Vernon Loeb, "Hobbyists Track Down Spies in Sky: Glowing Satellites Are Not So Covert," *The Washington Post*, 20 February 1999, p. 1.

41. Statement of Keith R. Hall, Director, National Reconnaissance Office, U.S. Senate Armed Services Strategic Force Subcommittee, 11 March 1998, found at www.nro.mil/speeches/Sfrfinal.html.

42. Ron Laurenzo, "NRO Chief Sees Industry Helping Out With Satellite Spy Duties," *Defense Week*, 1 February 2000, Vol. 21, No. 6, p. 8.

43. House Intelligence Committee, Report accompanying the Intelligence Authorization Act for fiscal 1999, 5 May 1998.

44. Unclassified briefing slides presented by Air Force Lt. General James C. King, Director, National Imagery and Mapping Agency, to the AFCEA Fall Intelligence Symposium, 27 October 1999.

45. The Commission on Roles and Capabilities of the United States Intelligence Community, known as the Brown Commission after its chairman, former Defense Secretary Harold Brown, reported percentage breakdowns among the various branches of the intelligence community. See *Preparing for the 21st Century: An Appraisal of U.S. Intelligence*, hereinafter, Brown Commission Report (Washington, D.C.: U.S. Government Printing Office, 1995), p. 117.

46. Department of Defense news briefing, 1 January 2000, 12 noon EST, The Pentagon, Deputy Defense Secretary John Hamre, briefer. Available at DoD Website, www.defenselink.mil/. Hamre did not provide any detail on which satellite system was affected by the Y2K problem, but a number of media outlets, citing unnamed Pentagon sources, determined that the imagery satellites were involved. See also, "Spy Satellites Had Y2K Glitch," by Pamela Hess, United Press International, 1 January 2000.

47. Joseph C. Anseimo, "Y2K Knocks Out NRO Imagery," *Aviation Week & Space Technology*, 10 January 2000, p. 27. See also. Department of Defense news briefing, 4 January 2000, 1:46 p.m. EST, The Pentagon, Deputy Defense Secretary John Hamre, briefer. Available at DoD Website, <www.defenselink.mil/>.

48. John Diamond, "Satellites on the Blink for Days," *Chicago Tribune*, 13 January 2000, p. 1, and John Diamond, "Pentagon Defends Reliability of Satellites," *Chicago Tribune*, 14 January 2000, p. 1. See also. Department of Defense Briefing, 13 January 2000, 1:32 p.m. EST, The Pentagon, Kenneth Bacon, DoD spokesman, briefer. Available at DoD Website <www.defenselink.mil/>.

49. Richard Lardner, "Pre-Y2K Problems Undercut Operation of U.S. Satellite Imagery Network," *Inside the Pentagon*, 13 January, 2000, Vol. 16, No. 2, p. 1.

50. Permanent Select Committee on Intelligence, House of Representatives, 104th Congress Staff Study, *IC21: Intelligence Community in the 21st Century*, herein after IC21 Staff Study, (Washington, D.C.: U.S. Government Printing Office, 1996) p. 107.

51. Ibid., p. 118.

52. Author's interview with Air Force Col. Richard W. McKinney, system Program Director, Evolved Expendable Launch Vehicle Program, Los Angeles Air Force Base, 20 December 1996.

53. United States Air Force (USAF), *New World Vistas: Air and Space Power for the 21st Century* (Washington, D.C.: United States Air Force, 1996), Space Applications Volume, pp. 30–31, 43.

54. USAF, *New World Vistas*, Sensors Volume, pp. 65, 117. See also, Godson, et al., *Intelligence at the Crossroads*, p. 103.

55. Malcolm W. Browne, "New Vistas Open for Earthbound Astronomers," *New York Times*, 11 February 1997, p. C1.

56. Testimony of Herbert Lee Buchanan III, Director, Defense Sciences Office, Advanced Research Projects Agency, before the Permanent Select Committee on Intelligence, Staff Study, p. 87.

57. *IC21* Staff Study, pp. 133–135; see also Jeffrey K. Harris, Director, National Reconnaissance Office, speech, "The Future of Space Intelligence Reconnaissance & Surveillance," Rochester Institute of Technology, Center for Imaging Science Industrial Associates, Meeting, 23 October 1995, retrieved from NRO Internet site, http://www.nro.odci.gov/ritsp.htm, p. 4.

58. House Armed Services Committee, *Intelligence Successes and Failures in Operations Desert Shield/Storm*, p. 16. Colin Clark, "Pentagon Awards Imagery Processor Work," *Defense Week*, 4 November 1996, p. 5.

59. NRO Press Release, "Space Technology Experiment Satellite Completes Mission," 18 June 1999, found at www.nro.mil/PressReleases/prs-rel31.html.

Bibliography

Altmann, Jurgen, Henry van der Graaf, Patricia M. Lewis, and Peter Marki, eds., *Verification at Vienna: Monitoring Reductions of Conventional Forces* (Philadelphia: Gordon and Breach Science Publishers, 1992).

Berkowitz, Bruce D., and Allan E. Goodman, *Strategic Intelligence for American National Security* (Princeton, N.J.: Princeton University Press, 1989).

Burrows, William E., *Deep Black: Space Espionage and National Security* (New York: Random House, 1986).

Friedman, Col. Richard S., Bill Gunston, David Hobbs, Lt. Col. David Miller, Doug Richardson, and Max Walmer, *Advanced Technology Warfare* (New York: Harmony Books, 1985).

Godson, Roy, ed., *Intelligence Requirements for the 1990s: Collection, Analysis, Counterintelligence, Covert Action* (Lexington, Mass: Lexington Books, 1987).

Godson, Roy, Ernest R. May, and Gary Schmitt, eds., *U.S. Intelligence at the Crossroads* (London: Brassey's, 1995).

Jasani, Bhupendra, *Outer Space—Battlefield of the Future?* (New York: William Morrow, 1987).

Jasani, Bhupendra, and Frank Barnaby, eds., *Verification Technologies: The Case for Surveillance by Consent* (Leamington Spa: Berg Publishers Ltd., 1984).

Jasani, Bhupendra, and Toshibomi Sakata, eds., *Satellites for Arms Control and Crisis Monitoring* (Oxford: Oxford University Press, 1987).

Kessler, Ronald. *Inside the CIA: Revealing the Secrets of the World's Most Powerful Spy Agency* (New York: Pocket Books, 1992).

Mazarr, Michael J., Don M. Snider, and James A. Blackwell Jr., *Desert Storm: The Gulf War and What We Learned* (Boulder, Colo.: Westview Press, 1994).

Potter, William C., *Verification and SALT: The Challenge of Strategic Deception* (Boulder, Colo.: Westview Press, 1980).

Richelson, Jeffrey T., *America's Secret Eyes in Space: The U.S. Keyhole Spy Satellite Program* (New York: Harper & Row, 1990).

Richelson, Jeffrey T., *The U.S. Intelligence Community*, Third Edition (Boulder, Colo.: Westview Press, 1995).

Ruffner, Kevin D., ed., *CORONA: America's First Satellite Program.* (Washington, D.C.: Central Intelligence Agency, 1995).

Suvorov, Victor, *Inside the Soviet Army* (New York: Macmillan, 1983).

United States Air Force. *New World Vistas: Air and Space Power for the 21st Century* (Washington, D.C.: USAF, 1996). ✦

Reprinted with permission from John M. Diamond, "Re-examining Problems and Prospects in U.S. Imagery Intelligence," *International Journal of Intelligence and Counterintelligence* 14 (Spring 2001): 1–24.

6

Satellite Surveillance

William E. Burrows

A journalist who writes widely on aviation and space flight, Burrows provides a look at America's early ventures in spying from space.

Jimmy Carter's first full day as president of the United States—January 21, 1977—was deliriously hectic and peppered with controversy, as contemporary news accounts and the handful of memoirs written by those who were close to him indicate.

Newspapers throughout the country gave substantial space on their front pages to the fact that, in his first major act as president, the Navy engineer turned politician granted a pardon to almost all of the ten thousand or so young men who had evaded service in Vietnam. The document that accomplished this, a historically important one whose specter had fired deep emotions during the campaign the previous autumn, was signed in the early hours that Friday and was then reported, along with attendant expressions of praise by pro-amnesty groups and equal doses of wrath by the veterans' lobby, on television that evening and in the morning papers the next day. The White House press corps played up the amnesty angle, but it also laced its record of the day's events by noting that several celebrations took place in the mansion to honor the new president's friends and fellow Georgians, as well as members of the Democratic National Committee, state campaign managers, representatives of labor, business, and the entertainment industry, and those who had acted as hosts and hostesses during the inaugural festivities. The day was punctuated by the parties, the first film (moving or still) or on tape, from which they could be digitally manipulated to highlight particular features or characteristics. It was therefore possible to have photographs of, say, the occupied U.S. embassy in Teheran, taken from a spot in the sky that the Ayatollah Khomeini's young militants could not even see, much less attack, on the desk of the president within an hour of their having been requested.

Since transporting the large apparatus used at Fort Belvoir to turn the KH-11's data into pictures was obviously out of the question, Knoche decided to select several images of no particular importance that were representative of the KH-11's capability, have them printed, and simply carry them to the White House. His first inclination was to try to get the pictures to Carter on the day they came in, but he quickly decided that interrupting the jubilation, or "merry-making," as he put it, might have been considered intrusive and therefore would probably not have been welcome. Accordingly, the excited CIA officer made an appointment to see the president at three-fifteen the following afternoon.

Knoche and Admiral Daniel J. Murphy, a senior CIA official who was responsible for coordinating the work of all the nation's foreign intelligence organizations, arrived at the White House the next day with what Knoche has recalled was a "handful" of photographs, each of which was black-and-white and measured about six inches square. Both men were ushered into the Map Room on the second floor, where they met Carter and Zbigniew Brzezinski, the Columbia University professor of international relations who had become his national security adviser.

Knoche spread the photographs on the map table, a large ornate one that was planted solidly in the center of the room. Although Carter had never seen KH-11 imagery, he had been told of the satellite's existence as part of the presidential transition process a few weeks earlier, when George Bush and others at Langley had spent the better part of a day briefing him on the world situation. The CIA's view of the world and how that view was to be shaped in years to come, Carter had been told, would depend to a significant extent on the new spacecraft. They had then told the president-elect about the KH-11 in some detail.

At twenty minutes past three on the afternoon of his first full day as president of the United States, Jimmy Carter looked down and studied the photographs that Knoche had just spread on the map table: detailed photographs that had been taken from space the previous morning when the first KH-11 had been pronounced operational. After scrutinizing the pictures for a few moments, Carter looked up at Knoche, grinned, and then laughed appreciatively. He congratulated the two CIA men on the apparent excellence of their system and then asked Knoche to send over some more samples for the following day's National Security Council meeting, his first as president. "Of course," Jimmy Carter said as he turned to Brzezinski, "this will also be of value in our arms control work." The KH-11 had made its White House debut, and on that hopeful note the meeting in the Map Room came to an end.

* * *

When the KH-11 came on-line that January 1977, it joined two other imaging spacecraft, the KH-8 and KH-9, which were the last in the line of distinct close-look and area-surveillance platforms. Together, the three would bear the burden of the nation's space-borne reconnaissance for another decade.

The refinement of close-look and area-surveillance spacecraft before the advent of the KH-11 had been driven by three factors.

First, there was the persistent fear that however capable U.S. orbital reconnaissance was, it lagged behind the opposition's ability to conceal, confuse, and confound. The technical collectors, and especially those in the Air Force, tended to be less gratified by what they could see than frustrated and apprehensive by what they were convinced was eluding them. The seeming absence of something did not so much mean that it wasn't there, in the view of the men of Air Force intelligence and their superiors, as that it most likely was diabolically hidden. Someone had even claimed during the missile gap that a church tower in the Ukraine clothed an ICBM. Russia was the land of Grigori Potemkin, after all, and he had been a master of guile. Russia was a place where chess, a game of subterfuge and cunning (not to mention sacrifice) amounted to a national pastime. The Russians had even institutionalized deception, concealment and distortion, and given it a name: *maskirovka*. And this evil talent was most worrisome where ballistic missiles, or at least the ballistic missiles that could not be located, were concerned. But although the Air Force never said so, the phantom Soviet missiles had at least two salutary effects: they helped make the case in Congress for more strategic nuclear weapons, and they were used to try to convince the executive branch that more and better space reconnaissance systems were needed to improve the search process.

There was also the pressing matter of technical intelligence collection, which was vital to the three armed services as well as to the CIA. Although technical intelligence involved targeting to the extent that radars had to be measured for jamming to allow the bombers to get through, and silos and other structures had to be gauged so that appropriate kilotonnage could be used against them, there were much wider concerns. The armed services wanted to know what their counterparts had in the way of equipment so that an effective response could be mounted against them if necessary. The Army thought it imperative to know not only how many heavy tanks the Warsaw Pact had, for example, but what those tanks' operational characteristics were and what it would take to stop them. Similarly, Tactical Air Command generals needed intelligence regarding the MiG fighters and Sukhoi interceptors and fighter-bombers with which their pilots might have to tangle, and high-resolution photographs of such planes, even parked on tarmacs, would reveal a great deal about them to the aeronautical engineer-photo interpreters who studied them at the DIA, the CIA, and in Air Force intelligence.

Finally there was the brand-new realm of arms control, which primarily concerned the State Department (with the CIA acting as its first-line intelligence-gatherer). Arms control requirements amounted to an amalgamation of counting and analyzing technical intelligence—of determining, in other words, which equipment came under the terms of the various treaties, what that equipment could do, and how much of it there was.

The most celebrated example of controversy involving interpretation in arms control had to do with the U.S.S.R.'s Tu-26 bomber, code-named Backfire by NATO, and its relation to the SALT II negotiations, which in part set a limit on the number of heavy bombers each side could have. But was the swept-wing twin-engine bomber a heavy one? The question was more than esoteric because "heavy" is military shorthand for a bomber with intercontinental range, meaning one that could carry bombs or cruise missiles to an enemy country. Before and during the SALT II debate, both the CIA and the DIA scrutinized the same satellite photographs and tried to determine whether the plane constituted a real threat to the continental United States by studying the Tu-26's shape, fuel capacity and consumption rate at various speed and altitude combinations, in-air refueling capability (or lack of it), weapons-carrying capacity, and other factors.

What sort of pictures were required to make such a determination? The analysts needed high-resolution stereo verticals and obliques so they could use photogrammetric equipment to calculate the bomber's precise size. They also needed infrared photographs that would show how much fuel was in the Backfire's wings by contrasting the cooler surfaces of the wings (inside which the cold jet fuel was stored) with the relatively warmer sections. Accurate fuel-load measurements could be made with such data.

After all of the calculations had been tossed into the respective hoppers at the DIA and the CIA, the airmen concluded that the Tu-26 could in certain circumstances make round-trip bombing missions against the United States. In order to do that, they would have to take off from bases in the Arctic, refuel in midair, and fly at high altitude to conserve fuel. "All Backfire aircraft apparently are either equipped for or actually carry air refueling probes," one Air Force general told the Senate Foreign

Relations Committee at the SALT II ratification hearings in November 1979. But the CIA took a less threatened view of the Soviet bombers, apparently because its analysts were not convinced that the Tu-26s had midair refueling capability and, anyway, the tanker aircraft needed to refuel them were in extremely short supply. (It is also quite likely that the agency disputed the feasibility of Tu-26s making a high-altitude attack which would have been suicidal in the face of the Distant Early Warning radar network spread across Canada and Greenland; bombing doctrine since the early 1960s has called for low-level attack to avoid radar detection.) In the end, the DIA recalculated and lowered its estimate, though it didn't get around to doing so until the fifth year of the Reagan presidency.

Far from being mutually exclusive, these technical collection requirements were in most cases complementary and together drove a single space reconnaissance system that became increasingly sophisticated during the sixties and seventies, particularly with regard to the specialized sensors carried on the satellites and the increasing use of Digital Image Processing (DIP) to extract information beyond the range of the human eye.

* * *

The third-generation area-surveillance and close-look satellites were called the KH-7 and KH-8, respectively. Whatever else the two satellites may have accomplished (and in the case of the KH-8, it was considerable), they were notable for being the first reconnaissance platforms to carry infrared and multispectral scanners. Resolution of the infrared scanners, in particular, was by most accounts poor to terrible (and nil through cloud cover), but the effort marked the beginning of the move toward effective night imagery for reconnaissance satellites that would only be achieved with the launch of a spacecraft called the KH-12 some two decades later.

The infrared capability, which had been around since World War II, allowed film or silicon receptors to register heat the way a standard camera's film registers visible light. And like a camera, an infrared sensor is able to register even minute differences in the temperatures of the objects it scans, thereby producing an image that can define several objects at once according to their differing temperatures. High-altitude aircraft photos taken of air bases at night had by then revealed planes, fuel trucks, buildings, and sometimes even people because of the heat they radiated relative to their surroundings. Infrared color film, which is also known as false color film, records objects according to the heat they radiate and depicts them in colors that have nothing to do with those in the visible part of the electromagnetic spectrum. Infrared film there-

fore shows healthy vegetation as red, while dying or dead vegetation shows as pink or blue. It therefore generally does no good to paint an object green or toss a camouflage net over it in order to make it appear like grass or foliage from the air or from space.[1] Infrared imagery can even be used to record the past by depicting shadows. Airplanes, for example, cast shadows on the concrete aprons where they are parked even in hazy weather. Hours after the plane has departed, its shadow silhouette, which is cooler than the surrounding area, remains visible to the infrared sensor. Although this capability was realized in aerial reconnaissance, and in fact was widely used in Vietnam, it was an unachieved goal in space reconnaissance until the advent of the third-generation reconnaissance satellites.

Multispectral scanning (MSS), which was developed by Itek, a Massachusetts firm that manufactures lenses and cameras for both air- and spaceborne reconnaissance, involves the use of separate lenses to shoot the same scene in several pictures, each in a different part of the visible and infrared electromagnetic spectrum. This allows the wavelengths of the various substances—their characteristic radiation—to be screened, sorted out, and analyzed. Plywood painted green might look like grass in a standard color photograph shot from high altitude, but MSS imagery would show it to be what it was: a coat of paint. By the same token, MSS would differentiate between aluminum, steel, and titanium so that analysts could determine the composition of Soviet aircraft, which, in turn, would have a bearing on their performance.

Like infrared imaging, multispectral scanning did not produce high-resolution intelligence data, however. In the case of the KH-7, a low-resolution area surveillance craft, this was in part due to the use of radio-link transmission, but it also had to do with the inherent limits of resolution in the MSS itself. MSS was therefore supplemented on the KH-7 and KH-8 series of reconnaissance satellites by thematic mapping cameras. The thematic mappers had three times the resolving power of multispectral scanners. They used a movable mirror that could be made to drop onto the focal plane of the satellite's telescope and direct the image from the earth to a group of sensors that registered electromagnetic energy in seven bands: blue, green, red, near-infrared, first mid-infrared, second mid-infrared, and far-infrared. The resulting picture was then converted into digital numbers that quantified the intensity of the light in each band resulting in a single picture that was made of as many as three hundred million digits, which, taken together, constituted a richly detailed portrait of the chemical elements of whatever had been imaged.

The first of twenty-nine successfully launched KH-7s lifted off at Vandenberg on August 9, 1966, on top of a Long Tank Thrust-Augmented Thor and went into an elliptical orbit of 120 by 178 miles with a near-polar inclination of slightly more than 100 degrees. Besides carrying infrared and multispectral scanners, the first KH-7 took to orbit an improved four-and-a-half-foot-wide unfurlable antenna designed to help improve the still-poor resolution of the Air Force's radio-link imaging system.

The KH-8, a direct descendant of the CIA's Discoverer and KH-6 close-look programs, was designed for use on the special occasions when extremely close examination of a target had to be made even at the cost of having the satellite decay relatively quickly. At about sixty-six hundred pounds, Keyhole 8 was so heavy that it had to be sent up on top of a two-stage liquid-fueled Titan 3B, a modified ICBM that towered a dizzying eleven stories above its launch pad and developed more than a half million pounds of thrust. And like so many of its predecessors, the satellite itself was a specially adapted version of the tried and true Agena-D.

The first KH-8 blasted off from Vandenberg on July 29, 1966, beating the first KH-7 into space by twelve days. The third-generation close-look platform had a telescopic system that could produce standard photographs with resolutions of six inches, in addition to the poorer-quality infrared imagery, MSS, and thematic mapping. That first KH-8, with the restartable Aerojet engine, was ordered into a low 98- by 155-mile orbit two days after launch. Not surprisingly, the multimillion-dollar spacecraft turned into a fireball and disintegrated a week later because of the severe atmospheric friction. The lifetime of the KH-8 series increased as their launches continued into the mid-1980s, however, apparently because their orbits were made more elliptical.

The spacecraft were typically sent up under special circumstances, either because an area-surveillance platform had spotted something that was thought to require close inspection, or because some other intelligence source had performed that job. A KH-8 was launched on January 21, 1982, for example, with orbital characteristics that took it over the frontier shared by Libya, Chad, and the Sudan at a time when Qaddafi's troops were thought to be massing for an attack on either of those countries and when Soviet Tu-22 Blinder bombers were being flown for possible air support.[2]

As was the case with the two previous close-look satellite series, the KH-8s were programmed to eject film pods as they sped past the Arctic so that they could be snatched over the Pacific near the Ha-waiian Islands. There were at least two, and possibly four, "buckets" on each of the KH-8s. More than fifty-two of the satellites were launched through 1985 to photograph specific developments in Libya, Poland, Nicaragua, and Afghanistan, to name only four of the low-orbiter's target countries.[3]

One event that was satellite-covered, almost undoubtedly by a KH-8 because of the extremely high resolution pictures that were required, was the massive series of explosions that took place in mid-May 1984 at the ammunition depot at Severomorsk. At least one in a group of tremendous detonations was so big that it was at first thought to be nuclear. The explosions blew out the roofs and walls of several ammunition-storage buildings and bunkers, strewing a variety of intact weapons, including missiles, mines, and torpedoes (and possibly cruise missiles) throughout the area. This presented an irresistible photo opportunity to the technical intelligence collectors, but one that demanded extremely high resolution imagery so that the weapons could be scrutinized in great detail. Dipping as low as 69 miles, a KH-8 can take photographs with a resolution of between three and four inches. Typical missions of the KH-8, which was Byeman code-named Gambit, had fifty- to eighty-day durations by 1980 because of extensive maneuvering into more elliptical orbits, with parameters averaging 77 by 215 miles.

However good U.S. reconnaissance satellites had become by the end of the 1960s, they had problems that irked their users. The area-surveillance platforms sent their imagery down relatively quickly, but it was not of very high quality. The close-look types, which took fine pictures, were still dropping them out of orbit on parachutes, a time-consuming and chancy operation. What was needed was a single satellite that could produce uniformly high-quality area-surveillance and close-look imagery and get it down as the event being watched was happening. But this was a dream of such technical sophistication that it could not be realized for several more years.

Meanwhile, the nation's fourth-generation area-surveillance satellite, the KH-9, appeared, representing a compromise of sorts, but definitely a step in the right direction. The new spacecraft was itself a partial substitute for another of the extremely ambitious programs conceptualized by the Air Force in the 1960s. This one was called the Manned Orbiting Laboratory, or MOL, and it was supposed to be able to accomplish a formidable variety of tasks, including inspecting satellites in space, testing the accuracy of an orbital bombardment system, commanding and controlling military operations during all-out war, testing the effects of month-long missions on astronauts, and performing both imaging and ELINT reconnaissance.

The MOL, a cylinder having about thirty-four cubic yards of work space, was to be lifted to orbit by a thrust-augmented Titan 3C. Once in low orbit, it was to be joined by two astronauts in a Gemini capsule who would dock, climb inside, and perform the various experiments in addition to operating the reconnaissance apparatus. They were then to return to earth in their capsule, leaving the laboratory to await a replacement crew.

The MOL's potential as a fine reconnaissance platform was not wasted on Langley, which decided early that it had enormous potential as a kind of very high flying SR-71, and that in such a role it properly belonged under the operational mantle of Central Intelligence, notwithstanding the fact that it was an Air Force project. The Air Force reacted to the CIA's overture with customary belligerence and the rhubarb that followed was only settled by Lyndon Johnson himself, who insisted that the MOL be a space asset of common concern when he approved it in 1965. Whatever its other roles, the orbiting "laboratory's" chief mission was to be reconnaissance. Having a manned platform in orbit was attractive to the technical intelligence community because the human eye could compensate for the motion of a spacecraft relative to the earth better than machines could, at least at that point. A crewman would therefore take the required imagery. The MOL's main camera was to have a lens measuring six feet across that would have a theoretical resolution of four inches and an actual resolution, allowing for atmospheric distortion, of nine inches. In the end, however, the MOL succumbed to cost overruns (it was to consume $1.6 billion), interest in other kinds of manned space projects, and political considerations (the CIA, suddenly fretting that Russians would use an ABM to attack the manned spy platform as they had attacked Powers, finally had the MOL killed). But for their part, the KH-7s, KH-8s, and ferrets had proved to be effective enough so that they largely preempted the MOL's reconnaissance role anyway. The space laboratory was scratched in 1969.

Where reconnaissance was concerned, the MOL had a backup. Lockheed was working on a project called Program 612, which it had contracted for with the National Reconnaissance Office at about the time Johnson approved the MOL. Evidently, the NRO had decided to take the precaution of developing an alternate space reconnaissance system in case something happened to the manned platform. And Program 612 was in fact far enough along even in 1967 that the Air Force was able to contract with Martin Marietta for a suitably powerful new booster: the Titan 3D. The fact that the Air Force

contracted for the new booster two years before the MOL was killed further suggests that the project had been going sour for some time.

By 1968 design work on the fourth-generation U.S. reconnaissance satellite had progressed substantially. That year its code number was arbitrarily changed to 467, possibly so that it would be easily confused with DSP-647, the missile early warning system. It was also given the designation KH-9 and the Byeman code name Hexagon. Unofficially, however, the new platform would come to be known as Big Bird.

It is unlikely that any reconnaissance system has ever been more aptly named than Big Bird. The NRO wanted an unprecedented array of sensors in the KH-9, which was intended to be primarily an area-surveillance spacecraft but was nonetheless to have close-look capability as well.

Big Bird's heart was a Perkin-Elmer Cassegrain telescope having a "folded" focal length of twenty feet and a concave primary mirror that was more than six feet in diameter. The primary mirror, a giant perfectly curved, highly polished version of the sort found in many bathrooms, would direct the image it picked up to a smaller, secondary mirror that faced it some eight feet away. The image reflected off the primary mirror would strike the secondary mirror and would in turn be sent through a hole in the center of the primary mirror, behind which was the focal plane, where the earth's images picked up by the primary mirror would come into sharp focus. The telescope was said to be folded because use of the two large mirrors doubled the system's focal length in a relatively small space.

The sharply focused image that struck the focal plane would in turn be directed to any of the satellite's specialized sensors by the use of a series of small mirrors and prisms set around the focal plane. Big Bird's controllers at Sunnyvale would therefore be able to obtain infrared imagery, for example, by tilting the appropriate mirror in the area of the focal plane so that it directed the incoming image to the infrared sensor. The same would be true for the multispectral scanner, thematic mapper, and other sensors, such as a photomultiplier that would excite photons to make a picture taken on a clear night useful for analytical purposes. For standard photographs, the image would be split and overlapped by another mirror to give it a three-dimensional effect. It would then hit thin, highly sensitive low-grain film that wound around a series of spools leading to between four and six capsules that were to be ejected from orbit in the same way as those that had been carried by the Discoverers, KH-6s, and KH-8s. Resolution would be about a foot, and possibly a bit better than that.

And that wasn't all. Big Bird would carry a second large imaging system, this one a double-lens area-surveillance camera made by Kodak. One of the lenses would be used for relatively high (for area surveillance) resolution pictures, perhaps on the order of about three feet, while the other captured the broad, wide-field, low-resolution imagery whose collection constituted the KH-9's primary mission. The Kodak camera would have its own infrared and multispectral scanning systems. The resulting imagery was not to be dropped in buckets, however, but scanned by a television camera that would tape-record it for transmission either to a relay satellite or directly to New Boston, New Hampshire, Vandenberg, Oahu, Kodiak Island, Guam, or the British Seychelles.

Not counting some SIGINT equipment and related antennas, plus the guidance system, ground control receivers, transmitters, and other standard hardware, plus provision for three or four of the small ferret subsatellites, that was the total load except for fuel. Hexagon was going to need to carry a lot of fuel in order to maneuver in orbit. Two kinds of maneuvers, horizontal and vertical, would be mission-related, while a third maneuvering "situation" would arise only in the event that one of the satellites appeared to be coming under attack by an opponent in a closing orbit. Mission-related maneuvering would be used to put the KH-9's sensors within reach of targets that might otherwise go uncovered, and also to raise it periodically to prolong its life. In addition, the satellite's engine would have to be started for a short time every seven to ten days to stave off for as long as possible the decaying effect of atmospheric drag.

The spacecraft that started as an NRO concept and basic design specification and then progressed to Lockheed's drawing boards, to the company's machine shop and fabrication facility at Sunnyvale, and to the assembly area—where the Perkin-Elmer telescope, Kodak camera, and other sensors were precisely mated to computers, radio receivers, large folding antennas, paddle-type solar collectors, the guidance system, engine, and other components for an eventual launch at Vandenberg—was nothing short of a colossus by reconnaissance satellite standards. The engineers had taken the reliable Agena and then widened and lengthened it until it was ten feet across and fifty feet long and weighed about thirty thousand pounds (twenty thousand of it being the sensors and related hardware). Big Bird was as big as the MOL itself was supposed to have been, and that was as big as a Greyhound bus.

Early on the evening of June 15, 1971, a Titan 3D spewing flame from all three exhaust nozzles and developing almost three million pounds of thrust lifted the first KH-9 to a moderately elliptical orbit of 114 by 186 miles Its inclination was 96.4 degrees. This orbit allowed the spacecraft to circle the earth once every eighty-nine minutes passing over every spot on its ground track once in daylight and once at night during each twenty-four hour period. During its fifty-two-day lifetime, the first of the Big Birds proved out its sensing, guidance, communication, and propulsion systems, made test transmissions, and was extensively calibrated, as is done to all reconnaissance satellites.[4] It also returned imagery taken over denied territory. The newest of the nation's space assets was directed out of orbit on August 6 and incinerated on its way down.

There were three launches in 1972. The first KH-9 to go up that year did so on January 20 carrying one of the 130-pound ferrets which was then rebooted to its own 293- by 340-mile orbit. That second KH-9 had a lifetime of only forty days, but it also had the distinction of being the last of those committed mainly to operational testing.

Since the SALT I interim strategic arms treaty was signed in Moscow on May 28, the third Big Bird, which went up on July 7, was assigned the task of helping to provide national technical means of verification that the agreement's terms were being honored, in addition to its collateral intelligence-gathering chores. It had seemed prudent to continue launching KH-7s while Big Bird's wrinkles were being ironed out, so four of the older area-surveillance spacecraft were sent up while the initial two KH-9s were being tested, thereby providing overlapping, redundant coverage. With the July 7 launch, however, the NRO decided that the new system was fully operational. The KH-7s were therefore phased out, with the last of them going into orbit three days before SALT I was signed. The third and last Big Bird to be launched in 1972 went up on October 10 carrying yet another passenger, this one going into an 882- by 911-mile-high orbit that would keep it up for about ten thousand years. The little hitchhiker had all the earmarks of a radar-sniffer. It was clear at that point that Big Birds were going to carry quite a bit of freight to orbits other than their own.

The Soviet missile test program received special attention from KH-8s and KH-9s during 1972 and 1973. Tests of the then experimental SS-16, -17, -18, and -19 ICBMs were closely monitored. Satellite intelligence, as well as data from the various ground stations and tracking ships, showed that by early 1974 the SS-16 remained in an early developmental stage, the SS-17 was encountering serious technical problems, and the SS-18 and SS-19 programs were moving along quite smoothly. In January 1974, in fact, the SS-19 made its long-range flight test debut before a veritable audience of Washington's intelligence-gathering platforms on land, at sea, and in space. Preparations for the launch were undoubt-edly photographed by a KH-9 that had gone up the previous November 10. And far above that particular Big Bird, unsuspected by the Russians, the first of the Rhyolites listened quietly in the starry blackness to the beat of the SS-19's pumps and the working of its gyros and other systems as transmitted in a stream of uncoded telemetry.

Nor were ICBMs the only long-range Soviet missile that aroused Washington's curiosity. Both the technical intelligence collectors and NASA were keenly interested in the Russians' enigmatic G-1, a mysterious monster booster that seemed to have been developed to get cosmonauts on the moon. Its engines, which were thought to date back to 1963, delivered 4.75 million pounds of thrust, or enough to put 155 tons into low orbit, 63 tons on the moon, and up to 27 tons on Venus. KH-7s and KH-8s had first spotted G-1 test facilities under construction at Tyuratam in the summer of 1966. By early June 1969 the massive rocket had been ready for a series of full-blown rehearsals prior to an actual test launch or, perhaps, even for the real thing. KH-8 imagery taken over Tyuratam on June 3 showed that the awesome booster, which towered 360 feet above its pad, was being serviced.

But pictures of the same spot taken only eleven days later revealed evidence of a massive explosion and fire that left charred and twisted debris scattered over a wide area. The pad itself was left unusable. As reconstructed by the interpreters, the G-1's first stage had been filled with fuel, its second stage had been nearly topped off, and its third, or uppermost, stage had just started filling when a large leak developed in the second stage. Fuel had then gushed over the side of the second stage and had flowed down the length of the booster until the entire launch pad had become a pool of propellant. Then a fire had started near the base of the seventy-seven-foot-wide first stage, enveloping it and the second stage and causing the fuel tanks in both to rupture. It was plain to those who studied the KH-8's high-resolution photographs that the ensuing explosion had blown the G-1 apart and destroyed much of its pad.

A second G-1 did make it off the ground in August 1971, but it literally shook itself to pieces at an altitude of only seven and a half miles, probably because of a first-stage malfunction. A third, and final, attempt to get the G-1 into space was made on November 24, 1972. Less than two minutes after liftoff, however, some new catastrophe struck, and the giant rocket had to be destroyed in flight by its ground controllers. Although no other G-1 launches are known to have been tried, satellite reconnaissance in the summer of 1974 showed that the G-1's test stand was being modified and the pad de-stroyed five years earlier was being rebuilt. This indicates that the G-1 or a successor may still be under development, perhaps for use in lifting pieces of a prefabricated space station to orbit or for sending a very heavy probe out into the galaxy.

Big Birds continued going up throughout the 1970s and well into the 1980s, initially three a year and then, beginning in 1974, on an average of two a year as their orbital lifetimes increased steadily from 52 to 275 days. And as their time in orbit increased, so did their intelligence yield.

KH-9s spotted the development of a phased array radar at the Sary Shagan ABM test center and closely monitored submarine construction under the huge canvas shrouds at Severomorsk. During the summer of 1974, a KH-9 discovered that the Russians were trying to conceal construction of what appeared to be new missile silos. That winter, another of the spacecraft recorded the first deployment of SS-18s. In the following months, KH-9s inventoried ten SS-17s, an equal number of SS-18s, and fifty SS-19s, all of them deployed. Big Birds also participated in the discovery and subsequent monitoring of an important new ballistic missile being tested: the mobile SS-20 IRBM.

In July 1976, one of the Perkin-Elmer telescopes, which could spot individuals from the KH-9's mean perigee of 103 miles, recorded the fact that the Russians were beginning to modify the six hundred IRBMs pointed at NATO countries and China with Multiple Independently Targeted Reentry Vehicles, or MIRVs. That same telescope, mounted in the twelfth KH-9, also counted forty SS-17s, more than fifty SS-18s, and one hundred forty SS-19s in their hardened silos. Such precise inventories would produce national intelligence estimates that were a far cry from those of the fifties and sixties that could only refer to "from 100 to several hundred bombers," and so forth. The KH-8s and KH-9s were replacing uncertainties about the Soviet and Chinese weapons programs with data banks and files full of hard information. Coverage by the mid-1970s had gotten to be very good.

But from the point of view of some in the intelligence community, George Keegan among them, it was by no means good enough. Jeffrey Richelson, an assistant professor of government at The American University and a leading authority on intelligence, particularly on technical collection, has calculated that 365-days-a-year PHOTINT coverage began only in 1977. There were only 158 days of coverage in 1971, when the first Big Bird went up, and although coverage climbed to the low 300s during 1973 through 1975, it dropped to only 248 days in 1976. This, of course, meant that there was no coverage for 117 days that year.

Such lapses made George Keegan's flesh crawl. It was hard enough trying to figure out what the opposition was up to when you were watching it, Keegan reflected, but it was obviously impossible when you weren't watching it at all, and he profoundly hated that. Maybe nothing important was happening during periods of noncoverage. But maybe something important *was* going on, yet remained unnoticed, because there weren't enough imaging platforms to carry the whole PHOTINT load. And the reason the number of KH-8s and KH-9s was thinning out, the chief of Air Force intelligence knew, was that fantastic sums were being diverted from production of the two existing systems to finance the CIA's pet imaging satellite project. And ironically, that project was the conceptual descendant of the Air Force's own SAMOS, a system the CIA had denigrated and tried to kill since its inception. Meanwhile, the Air Force now found itself championing the KH-8 and the KH-9, both of which were the sort of bucket-droppers that had developed from Discoverer—a CIA project—against the better judgment of the Air Force.

Langley's hot new project had its genesis in the Six-Day War of 1967, which demonstrated a need for faster technical intelligence collection than was possible with either of the film-return satellites. Although film could go from orbit to NPIC in four or five days under ideal conditions, three or four weeks was more often the case because of the intricate logistics involved and the vagaries of weather. In the case of the Israeli attack on Egypt, this meant that a whole war could be fought and concluded before a single photograph showed up in Washington, leaving the National Command Authority virtually blind. That wouldn't do. In addition, film-return spacecraft were the prisoners of their buckets. When the last ejectable capsule and its spool of exposed film had been kicked out of orbit, a KH-8 was utterly useless, and a KH-9 nearly so.

Accordingly, study panels analyzing PHOTINT requirements for the NRO after the Six-Day War shaped specifications for a fifth-generation imaging satellite, code-named KH-X, that would have a significant advantage over other imaging satellites: it would take pictures electronically and transmit them in near-real time, or virtually as events occurred. But the money to develop KH-X would in part come out of the Gambit and Hexagon programs, thereby cutting into an actual coverage of the U.S.S.R. at a time when several ballistic missile systems were being tested and deployed. In such circumstances, curtailing operations in order to pursue research and development—and particularly R and D on a such a far-out, high-risk system as the KH-X—seemed to George J. Keegan to smack of a level of folly that was almost treasonous.

* * *

Early in 1972, the National Reconnaissance Office selected TRW to develop the KH-X, thereby awarding a contract for an imaging satellite to a company other than Lockheed for the first time. The project was immediately dubbed Program 1010, and later it was assigned the Keyhole number 11 and, as noted, the Byeman name Kennan.[5]

Those who once dreamed that SAMOS's radio-link resolution would someday be the equal of the standard photographs that come out of the bucket-droppers have seen their vision come true. Semiofficial statements, "backgrounders," and leaks to the trade press have it that the KH-11's electro-optical resolution is inferior to that of the bucket-droppers that used standard film. While that was true at the outset of the KH-11 program, it no longer is. By 1984 the resolution of the KH-11's electro-optical system was every bit as good as that of its bucket-dropping immediate predecessor, the KH-9.

The KH-11 owes its real-time capability and high resolution to the charge-coupled device, or CCD, which was invented at the Bell Telephone Laboratories in New Jersey in 1970 and today is in widespread use in hundreds of civilian and military programs, including medical imaging, plasma physics, astronomy (both the Galileo spacecraft and the space telescope use them), and home video cameras. The CCD is a technical work of art: a simple, easily produced, extremely sensitive radiation collector whose scientific elegance and practical versatility are revolutionizing high-speed imaging. And most CCDs are smaller than a postage stamp.

Basically, a CCD collects radiated particles of energy, including those in the visible part of the light spectrum, by capturing them in an array of tiny receptors, or picture elements, called pixels, which automatically measure their intensity and then send them on their way in orderly rows until they are electronically stacked up to form a kind of mosaic. A standard CCD manufactured by Texas Instruments for use in the Space Telescope measures eight hundred by eight hundred pixels, for a total of 640,000, yet it is less than half an inch square.

The analogy most often used to explain the working of CCDs is that of buckets collecting rain in a field. Each of the 640,000 buckets, all arranged in neat rows to form a square, represents a pixel. The rain, heavy in some places and light in others, is the equivalent of incident radiation (photons, electrons, neutrons, or protons, for example). Since different amounts of rain are coming down on the various parts of the field, the buckets catch varying amounts of water and therefore fill to different levels. As the buckets catch the water they move in vertical rows, called channels, toward a conveyor belt —a line transport register—which in turn carries them, a line at a time, off to the side where each of the eight hundred buckets in each line is simultaneously measured for its water content. If the amount of water in each bucket represents a different color or tone—say, black, white, and several shades of gray—then the entire string of eight hundred would take on the appearance of a line that is dark in some spots and lighter in others. Eight hundred pieces of precisely quantified information, constituting a line in a picture, would have been created. No sooner has the last of the eight hundred buckets moved off the conveyor than a second line gets on, and it, too, is measured. Then a third line follows, and so on, until all eight hundred lines of eight hundred buckets have been measured for their water content, or tonality. The net effect would be a highly detailed "picture" composed of 640,000 dots of varying tone. But the process is instantaneous and continuous, so that the picture moves.

A CCD collects photons and other particles of radiated energy instead of water, but the principle is roughly the same, except that the pixels themselves do not move. The photons that strike the pixels generate charges that move along from one pixel to the next along a series of horizontal "gates." As a result, the CCD acts as a kind of tiny, extremely precise light meter that captures radiated energy emissions across the visible and invisible bands of the spectrum so that they can be amplified and turned into pictures. A charge-coupled device, then, is an electronic tabula rasa that continuously registers whichever photons strike it, automatically moving the resulting photo-generated charges along, down the channels and through the gates, in an endlessly flowing procession. Unlike the standard cameras in its predecessors, the KH-11's CCDs do not "stop the action." Rather, they keep recording it as fast as it happens, in real time. The fact that the imagery can take up to an hour and a half to reach Fort Belvoir has to do with delays in the transmission process, not with the CCDs. Like a television camera, a charge-coupled device cannot be overwhelmed by the frequency of the particles hitting it.

No reconnaissance satellite system remains static. Just as the first SR-71s and other intelligence-gathering aircraft have been steadily modified through the years with state-of-the-art electronic systems to keep them operating optimally, so, too, are spacecraft like the KH-11. Two satellites in the same series may have different modifications, depending upon varying operational needs.

The KH-11's imaging system consists of four essential parts: a powerful mirror telescope, an infrared scanner, a separate sensor electronics package containing a photomultiplier tube, thematic mapper, multispectral scanner and appropriate mirrors and prisms, and an array of CCDs linked to each other to form a mosaic. As usual, the telescope brings in all the radiated energy within its field of view at great magnification. That energy can then be directed to any of the sensors, depending upon tasking requirements, so that it is broken down according to whichever part of the electromagnetic spectral band is wanted for analysis. Night preparations for a missile launch at Plesetsk, for example, might call for the use of the infrared scanner. The telescope would draw in all the radiated energy coming from the scene, but routing the image to the infrared scanner would automatically filter out energy on all wavelengths but infrared. The infrared imagery would pass through the scanner and register on the CCD array to form a moving infrared picture, which would then be amplified, digitized, encrypted, and transmitted up to one of the SDS spacecraft or another type for downlinking to Fort Belvoir.

But infrared imaging is not the only way the KH-11 "sees" at night. It can also use its photomultiplier to take advantage of existing light, even at night, for clear imaging. Photomultipliers used in combination with CCDs are employed all the time in astronomy to count photons, even at levels so low that they come in at a rate of only about one a minute (by comparison, an automobile's headlight generates many trillions of photons a second). Given the fact that KH-11s pass over or near their targets in a matter of a minute or so, such pervasive darkness would make it impossible to pick up imagery with a photomultiplier. But near total darkness is not a problem on earth.

"It's never going to be pitch-black because there's sky glow, which is significant," James R. Janesick, an authority on CCDs at the Jet Propulsion Laboratory, has noted. "There's got to be some sort of energy out there. If you don't have energy, you're not going to see anything. But it's to the point now where a photomultiplier system would work at any time because there's enough light. If you've got the moon, you know, it's incredibly light. But the universe has its own light source," Janesick added. "When you go out at night [with no moon], you can still see around because there's light coming from the galaxy." A photomultiplier used with an infrared scanner can provide fine imagery of objects such as darkened buildings from the KH-11's operational altitude on even the darkest nights. And the resulting real-time pictures, like those taken in broad daylight, are three-dimensional. Similar imagery has been collected on the Viking missions to Mars when scientists wanted to use the three-dimensional effect to study the planet's canyons. The resulting imagery was "spectacular," Janesick recalled.

However efficient the KH-11's charge-coupled devices are (and they are a hundred times more efficient than standard film cameras at collecting visible light), they are only as good as the telescope in front of them. And the indications are that that is very good indeed. Since the Air Force donated six 1.8-meter (71-inch) mirrors to the University of Arizona and Harvard's Smithsonian Observatory several years ago, it can be inferred that the KH-11's primary mirror is wider than that, though not so wide as the Space Telescope's, which measures 94.5 inches across. The KH-11's primary mirror is therefore most likely on the order of two meters, or roughly six and a half feet, wide. Its secondary mirror would therefore be about a foot in diameter, a size that would narrow the image coming off the primary mirror and sharply focus it. And the telescope itself is almost undoubtedly plugged into a two-position zoom lens, giving it both area-surveillance and close-look capability.

There has also been some speculation that the KH-11's primary mirror is a so-called rubber type whose thin, highly polished surface can be continuously computer-adjusted to compensate for atmospheric distortion when the zoom lens is in its close-look mode (distortion is less important when large tracts are under surveillance). Light travels up to the satellite along wave fronts that are theoretically straight but in fact bend in many directions because of the effects of thermal currents and pollution in the lower atmosphere. Active optics, as the corrective system is called, compensates for the distortion by relying on computers to detect curved light waves hitting the mirror and then adjusting for them—flattening them out—by making extremely subtle changes in the shape of the mirror itself (which is why it is called a "rubber" mirror, even though it is metallic).

One way to do this is by using a shearing interferometer to look at the whole wave front in order to spot slope errors so that they can be automatically corrected. "If you're looking at a point source [of light], then its non-flatness is a measure of what's wrong with it, and if you can detect the non-flatness, you can correct it out'" according to Dr. Jerry Nelson, a professor of astronomy at the Lawrence Berkeley Laboratory in San Francisco. Nelson designs ten-meter aperture optical and infrared telescopes.

How clearly, then, can the KH-11 see? The resolution of the satellite's main telescopic imaging system is one of Washington's most closely guarded secrets. Yet it is easily calculated by anyone with a knowledge of optical science and just as easily confirmed through the use of political science. The results in both instances are surprisingly close, and

show that the popular analogy about reading license plates is in fact correct.

Nelson calculated in a matter of seconds that the theoretical limit of the resolution of the system described here (and which he thought was an entirely reasonable one for a reconnaissance satellite like the KH-11) is two inches in the visible light part of the spectrum, including night imaging with the photomultiplier, and somewhat more than that for the invisible bands.

This calculation is borne out by the terms of the SALT II agreement, which not only limits each side to the development of only one new ICBM, but stipulates that ICBMs existing at the time the treaty came into effect could not be altered in length, diameter, launch weight, or throw weight (the size of their payloads) by more than 5 percent.

As is the case with all of the other terms of the agreement, the 5 percent proviso is subject to monitoring and verification by national technical means—in this instance, by imaging satellites. Prior to signing the agreement, in other words, Arthur Lundahl or someone else from NPIC assured the State Department negotiators that U.S. spaceborne imaging platforms could produce pictures that would show whether changes of more than 5 percent were being made on Soviet ICBMs. This would have to apply to the smallest of the Kremlin's long-range missiles as well as to the largest. The smallest Soviet ICBM at the time SALT II was concluded was the SS-11, a three-stage MIRV'd missile that was sixty-four feet long and six feet in diameter. Five percent of six feet is 3.6 inches. That is how good resolution in the visible light spectrum has to be to enable the United States to spot a widening of the SS-11 by 5 percent or more. This closely matches Nelson's calculation, the more so because his theoretical limit would be unattainable much of the time owing to some atmospheric effects that even active optics might not be able to cope with. And, as noted, the KH-11's electro-optical imaging system using CCDs has caught up with the finest of the film cameras where resolution is concerned.

* * *

The second of the KH-11's—5502—went up on June 14, 1978, and functioned for 1,166 days. No. 5503, which was orbited on February 7, 1980, had a lifetime of 993 days, despite a malfunction that reportedly reduced coverage of the early stages of the Iran-Iraq war. A fourth KH-11 was sent up on September 3, 1981, and a fifth on November 17, 1982. No. 5504 remained in orbit for a record 1,175 days. A fifth KH-11 was sent up on November 17, 1982, and functioned for 987 days. A sixth, sent up in 1984, was still in orbit at this writing. No. 5507, which had been intended to replace one of its aging predecessors, was lost on August 28,1985, when its Titan 34D booster had a partial power failure just short of two minutes after lift-off.

The KH-11's real-time reconnaissance exploits appear to be formidable. The satellite is supposed to have disproved reports that the Russians had built a new chemical and biological warfare manufacturing facility by returning pictures that showed the place to be an arms storage depot. It was a KH-11 that was used to locate the Americans being held hostage inside the U.S. embassy in Teheran in April 1980 and also to provide data on the route that the ill-fated Delta Force rescue team was supposed to use.[6] A year later a KH-11 reportedly photographed the space shuttle Columbia on its inaugural flight so that an accurate damage assessment could be made after several of the spacecraft's protective heat-shield tiles broke off during launch. This indicates that the satellite's imaging apparatus can be used to look in directions other than down, a handy capability for use in checking out the opposition's low-orbiting satellites, both reconnaissance and otherwise.

The single KH-11 operating in April 1986 was evidently worked overtime.[7] Its imagery was used to plan the air attack on Libya that took place on the fifteenth and then to provide intelligence on damage assessment following the raid. Less than two weeks later the satellite sent down imagery showing that the explosion at the nuclear reactor at Chernobyl had blown off most of the reactor building's roof, that the large graphite moderator was burning, and even that a soccer game was in progress in a field adjacent to the stricken plant after the accident.

The KH-11 has capabilities that are thought to be so good that on at least one occasion it received credit where none was due. It was widely assumed during and immediately after the Falkland Islands war between Argentina and Great Britain in the spring of 1982 that intelligence was gathered for Washington and London by one or both of the KH-11s in orbit at the time. One detailed study even went so far as to analyze KH-11 ground tracks and orbital maneuvering during the war to show that the satellites, working in conjunction with a Big Bird and with the Navy's White Cloud ocean surveillance satellites, gathered intelligence on the military activities taking place below. The analysis is compelling But it is wrong. Weather conditions during the conflict precluded KH-11 coverage. Although the satellite's imagery through haze or partial cloud cover can be enhanced by Digital Image Processing, it does not function through the kind of thick blanket that hung over much of the South Atlantic during that conflict.

For all its accomplishments, the vast majority of which concern the relatively small day-to-day intelligence triumphs that go unrecorded, the KH-11 is not without its faults. As noted, its development and production were so expensive that other systems had to be curtailed. This resulted in the sort of lapses in coverage that angered George Keegan. "The volume of coverage began to steadily decrease" as funds were diverted to the KH-11, according to another highly knowledgeable source, to the point where "by the mid-seventies, it really began to pinch. For months at a time, or even up to a year or more, there were lapses in wide-area coverage, and that's how the erection of the large ABM radar [at Abalakova] in Siberia went undetected."

Jeffrey Richelson has shown that with the exception of fifteen days in 1981, there has been continuous imaging satellite coverage since 1977. But by "coverage," the American University professor meant time in orbit, not necessarily time during which the sensors were working. The indication, in fact, is that through mid-1983 imaging sensors were not turned on as much as they ought to have been as a cost-saving strategy. At about that time, however the effects of the Reagan administration's doubling the NRO s budget began to alleviate the problem.

And there were restrictions on the ground as well, some of which remain. "A great deal of collected data is not being analyzed because of manpower shortages," a former high-ranking intelligence official has complained. "They gave up manpower in 1971 and afterward in order to buy more systems," the foremost of which was the KH-11 itself. Ironically, then, the KH-11 also forced reductions in the ranks of the very people who were supposed to cope with the enormous amount of data it was designed to produce.

But even at full strength the people on the ground are easily swamped by all the data that come down from space when the satellites are operating at full strength. This leads to what is perhaps the central paradox of the new space reconnaissance. Partly closed down, the system can miss an event that may be of considerable importance. Unbridled real-time reconnaissance, on the other hand, can bury its interpreters under more intelligence than they can assimilate.

"The information coming down from these things is just going to choke you," said Jerry Nelson, who is well acquainted with the remote sensing satellites that are the KH-11's civilian counterparts. "It gets awful real fast. You can't buy big enough computers to process it. You can't buy enough programmers to write the codes or to look at the results to interpret them. At some point you just get saturated," the physicist added, "and that defeats your whole purpose."

Questions for Further Discussion

1. In what sense was the KH-11 satellite an important breakthrough?

2. To what extent is effective arms control dependent on reliable imagery? How reliable is "verification" through imint?

3. How valuable are surveillance satellites in the war against terrorism?

4. To what extent is the annual intelligence budget driven by "techint" demands?

Endnotes

1. Typically, there is an exception. The Israelis have developed a lightweight, reversible camouflage netting that reflects light on a chlorophyll green wavelength similar to natural vegetation.

2. That particular KH-8 had a most unusual life. After its first orbits, which were quite elliptical at 88 by 233 miles, it bounded to a higher and more circular orbit of 330 by 415 miles, which is well out of photographic range and more indicative of a ferret mission. Twenty-four hours after launch the Agena-D's engine was turned on twice, raising it to an orbit of 346 by 403 miles. Then, on January 29, its perigee was moved up slightly to 364 miles. It was moved yet again in the following days until it reached its final orbit of 389 by 403 miles—nearly circular. On March 21 the spacecraft released three smaller satellites into orbits similar to its own and then loosed yet another on May 3. The satellite was ordered out of orbit twenty days later and was incinerated reentering the atmosphere. The four sub-satellites may have been ferrets or ocean surveillance types, which go up in fours. Whatever the mission, that sort of maneuvering gives an indication of how versatile reconnaissance satellites had become.

3. Primary close-look targets as set by COMIREX almost invariably came with a list of secondary targets that would be imaged in the same mission in an effort to make each as cost-effective as possible.

4. Imaging satellites are routinely calibrated, or fine-tuned, by photographing targets in the United States or elsewhere whose dimensions and other characteristics, including energy emissions, are precisely known. This gives a clear indication of how to judge the quality of the intelligence they send back from operational missions.

5. There was a satellite assigned to Keyhole number 10, though it was never built because the KH-11 made it obsolete. The MOL was the KH-10.

6. Sometime after the failed rescue attempt, purported copies of KH-11 imagery of the embassy compound and a sports stadium that was supposed to be used as a landing area for the evacuation of the hostages were distributed in Teheran, together with various maps of the city and lists of code words. The documents were painstakingly pieced together from U.S. files marked "Secret" that had been shredded immediately before U.S. personnel evacuated the embassy, according to Iran. Even as photocopied several times, the overhead pictures show considerable detail.

7. Standard procedure called for the use of two KH-11s at all times, one working in the morning light, the other in the afternoon for maximum shadow effect. ✦

7

The Time of Troubles: The U.S. National Security Agency in the Twenty-First Century

Matthew M. Aid

America's largest intelligence organization, the National Security Agency, is beset with a variety of bureaucratic problems, according to this expert on signals intelligence. Matthew M. Aid recommends improvements in management and outreach, as well as technological remedies, to put this important agency back in order.

> Anything we see is a State secret. Also if it's an illusion it's a State secret. Even if it doesn't work and never will, it's a State secret. And if it's a lie from top to bottom, then it's the hottest State secret of the lot.
>
> —*John Le Carré*, The Russia House
> *(1989)*

On 6 December 1999, the *New Yorker* magazine carried a lengthy article by prize-winning investigative reporter Seymour M. Hersh, which revealed that America's largest intelligence organization, the National Security Agency (NSA), is currently suffering from a multitude of serious problems which are impairing its ability to generate the kind of quality information that it had produced throughout the Cold War.[1] The Hersh article prompted other news reports, almost all of which painted a bleak picture of the Agency's current health and a poor prognosis for NSA's future.

The question then becomes, as one newspaper article put it, 'Is the National Security Agency doing its job—or stumbling through a midlife crisis?'[2] This article seeks to determine if NSA is, in fact, in a state of crisis by reviewing what has occurred at NSA during the last decade, the Agency's current Sigint collection, processing and reporting capabilities, the impact of technology on NSA's capacity to perform its mission, and the Agency's future prospects.

The Importance of Sigint Today

Given the intense secrecy surrounding even the most mundane aspects of the NSA's activities, it is extremely difficult for an outsider to accurately evaluate the current importance of this agency to the US foreign intelligence effort. No agency of the US intelligence community has been able to better insulate itself from public scrutiny, and because of the complexity of the technology involved in its work, American journalists and academics have generally tended to shy away from examining NSA's inner workings.[3]

Despite these obstacles, it is possible to sketch some of NSA's work from recently declassified documents, newspaper reports, and interviews with former and current NSA officials. An examination of the public record revealed a curious contradiction. The somber portrait that has been painted in recent months in the American press about NSA's current state of health runs contrary to a larger body of documentation which shows that the Agency remains one of the most productive members of the US intelligence community.

It should be noted that NSA is not a single stand-alone entity. Rather, NSA sits atop an empire called the United States Sigint System (USSS), which consists of several American intelligence organizations that conduct the US government's national Sigint mission. The USSS is comprised of the National Security Agency; which has operational control over the three so-called Service Cryptologic Elements (SCEs), consisting of the cryptologic elements of the US Army Intelligence and Security Command (INSCOM), the Naval Security Group Command (NAVSECGRU), and the Air Intelligence Agency (AIA); as well as the thousands of Sigint personnel assigned to the US military's various unified and specified commands. NSA also exercises operational control over the joint CIA-NSA Sigint organization called the Special Collection Service (SCS), which currently operates covert listening posts located in several dozen American diplomatic establishments around the world.[4]

The power of NSA extends well beyond the confines of the USSS. NSA works closely with the CIA's

Sigint organization, the Office of Technical Collection (OTC), which was formed in August 1993 from the merger of the old Office of Sigint Operations (OSO) with the CIA's Office of Special Projects (OSP). A small unit comprised of only a few hundred personnel, OTC not only manages the CIA's Sigint collection operations, both overt and covert, but also managed and conducted clandestine operations overseas that obtained foreign cryptographic systems by surreptitious means, such as embassy break-ins and subborning code clerks.[5] Since September 1997, the head of OTC has been James L. Runyan, a 30-year NSA veteran seconded to the CIA.[6] NSA is also deeply involved in the operations of the National Reconnaissance Office (NRO), the US intelligence agency which develops, builds, and operates America's reconnaissance satellites. According to declassified documents, over 13 percent of NRO's workforce (or 300 men and women) are NSA employees, most of whom work within the NRO's Sigint Directorate, which operates the fleet of Sigint satellites in orbit over the Earth.[7]

Despite its huge workforce and budget, some analysts believe that NSA produces today on a dollar-for-dollar basis more 'bang for the buck' than any other intelligence source, with perhaps the exception of NRO's spy satellites.[8] In 1995, NSA Director Vice Admiral John M. 'Mike' McConnell said that

> There is not a single event that the US worries about in a foreign policy or foreign military context that NSA does not make a very direct contribution to.[9]

In 1998, John Millis, the late staff director of the House Intelligence Committee, characterized Sigint as 'the INT of choice of the policy maker and the military commander.'[10] According to one estimate contained in a 1 June 1998 article in *US News & World Report*, 80 percent of all 'useful intelligence' being collected by the US intelligence community was coming from Sigint, although this figure is impossible to verify and seems excessively high.[11]

On the battlefields of the 1990s, Sigint probably was clearly one of the most important sources of intelligence information available to American combat commanders.[12] NSA played a vital role during Operations 'Desert Shield/Storm' in 1990–91, collecting much of the intelligence information that allowed Allied warplanes to destroy the Iraqi national command and control infrastructure and air defense network early in the war. Sigint also played an important role in enabling Allied forces to win the Battle of Khafji in January 1991.[13] Since the end of Operation 'Desert Storm,' a wide variety of American Sigint collection systems, including Air Force RC-135 'Rivet Joint' and Navy EP-3E 'Aries' Sigint aircraft, have continued to closely monitor Saddam Hussein's regime in Iraq as part of Operation 'Southern Watch,' the ongoing military operation which enforces compliance with the United Nations' mandated no-fly zones over southern Iraq.[14]

Sigint successfully monitored Haitian and Cuban military activities during Operation 'Uphold Democracy,' the 1994 operation which ousted the military junta ruling Haiti.[15] NSA was an important source of intelligence information during the war in Bosnia from 1991 to 1996.[16] And by all accounts, NSA performed well during the 1999 conflict in Kosovo.[17]

Sigint provided White House, Pentagon and State Department officials and intelligence analysts with important information about foreign political, economic and military developments, as well as details of the intelligence operations, scientific and technical developments, weapons systems capabilities, and nuclear and chemical weapons development activities of foreign countries.[18]

In 1990, Sigint detected Pakistani military forces moving to a higher state of alert as tensions with neighboring India over the province of Kashmir escalated.[19] On 24 February 1996, NSA intercepted the communications of two Cuban MiG-29 fighters as they shot down two unarmed Cessna aircraft flown by Cuban-Americans over international waters off Cuba, killing four of the crew members.[20]

Sigint helped the US government block attempts by foreign countries to violate UN imposed sanctions on Iraq.[21] Between 1996 and 1998, NSA and the CIA operated a covert Sigint system inside Iraq to help UN weapons inspectors locate and destroy weapons of mass destruction that the Iraqi government was trying to hide.[22]

Sigint helped the US government thwart planned deliveries of equipment by Russia and China to Iran, Pakistan and North Korea that could have been used to manufacture nuclear and chemical weapons. For example, in February 1998 NSA intercepts reportedly revealed that Russia's foreign intelligence service, the SVR, had facilitated the sale of Russian missile technology to Iran.[23] Sigint and other intelligence sources revealed that beginning in November 1992, Pakistan had received from China 30 nuclear-capable CSS-6 ballistic missiles.[24] Sigint also proved to be an important means for tracing the flow of ballistic missile technology from China to North Korea during the 1990s.[25]

And Sigint provided State Department officials with unusually detailed insights into war crimes committed in Bosnia during the mid-1990s.[26] In January 1999, NSA radio intercepts revealed that high-ranking Yugoslavian government officials had ordered an attack on the village of Racak in Kosovo, which resulted in the massacre of 45 unarmed ethnic Albanian civilians.[27]

By all appearances, NSA's consumers seemed to be happy with the product that they were receiving during the 1990s. In a speech to NSA staff members at Fort Meade on 1 May 1991, President George H. W. Bush stated that '[S]ignals intelligence is a prime factor in the decisionmaking process by which we chart the course of this nation's foreign affairs.'[28] In May 1994, Defense Secretary William Perry said in a speech that

> I don't make a significant decision without taking into account the products from this agency . . . NSA's work will be a critical factor in our ability to deal with this particularly complex and particularly uncertain world.[29]

In 1996, a presidential review panel stated in its final report that 'NSA's contributions continue to be cited by national policymakers and deployed military forces alike for being of immense value.'[30] In March 1997, NSA received the Joint Meritorious Unit Award from Secretary of Defense William S. Cohen for its work during the period 1 June 1991 to 1 June 1995. The award citation stated, in part, that

> During this period, the Agency's constant vigilance and outstanding intelligence support in response to international conflicts, crises, and countless time-sensitive situations requiring decision-maker attention was unparalleled.[31]

All of this raises the question: Is what is described above in any way consistent with an intelligence organization that today is reportedly in a state of crisis? Even one of the loudest critic of NSA, the House Intelligence Committee, reported only four years ago that 'NSA is an extremely successful organization,' adding that 'The Sigint system performs well.'[32]

What has happened in the last four years to change so many minds? The only way to reconcile the two sides of the story and discover the truth is to examine what has happened to NSA in the last ten years.

NSA and the Peace Dividend

In the fall of 1989, the East German regime collapsed and the Berlin Wall came crashing down. On 9 November 1989, the East German government allowed its people for the first time to freely leave the country, and by 1 June 1990 the Berlin Wall had ceased to exist and all crossing points between East and West Berlin had been opened. In the next two years, the Warsaw Pact was dissolved. East and West Germany were united into a single country on 1 October 1990, and the Soviet Union disintegrated into 16 separate countries. The Cold War was over, and NSA's main target for almost 45 years had vanished almost overnight, forcing the Agency to adapt in order to survive in the post-Cold War era.

As far as many inside the US government and Congress were concerned, the end of the Cold War meant that there was no longer a need for 'all those spies.' Congress demanded a 'peace dividend,' so the Washington budget-cutters began to trim the size of the US intelligence community. Between 1991 and 1996, the intelligence community's budget was reduced by 19 percent, from approximately $34.5 billion to slightly more than $27 billion, according to press accounts.[33]

NSA's budget took a harder hit than the rest of the intelligence community, in part because the White House, the CIA and Congress emphasized cuts in the US intelligence community's expensive technical collection assets.[34] Between 1990 and 1995, NSA's budget was cut by 35 percent, falling from about $5.2 billion in 1990 to $3.47 billion in Fiscal Year 1995. A report issued by a presidential commission in March 1996 indicated that NSA's Fiscal Year 1996 budget had risen slightly to about $3.7 billion, which accounted for roughly 15 percent of the entire US intelligence budget.[35]

Accompanying these deep budget cuts were substantial reductions in the number of men and women spying for America. In 1991, Congress ordered that the number of personnel employed by the US intelligence community be cut by 17.5 percent by the end of 1999. The CIA and Defense Departments later agreed to expand these personnel reductions to 22.5 percent. As a result, between 1991 and 1998, the US intelligence community's manpower was cut by more than 20 percent, meaning that 20,559 men and women were either given early retirement or laid off.[36]

NSA's staff cuts during this period were also more severe than the other agencies comprising the intelligence community. The expectation in 1992 was that the size of NSA's workforce would be reduced by 17.5 percent between 1992 and 1997, which was in line with the above-mentioned congressional plan.[37] But by 1996, the US Sigint system had lost one-third of its personnel, falling from 75,000 military and civilian personnel in 1990 to slightly more than 50,000 military and civilian personnel by 1996.[38] NSA, which was the largest component of the USSS, lost about one-third of its personnel, with its manpower levels falling from about 56,000 personnel in 1990 (26,000 civilians and 30,000 military personnel) to approximately 38,000 by 1996 (20,000 civilians and 18,000 military personnel).[39]

NSA was able to slash its budget and manpower in large part by making deep cuts in the size of its Sigint collection network. Between 1990 and 1998, NSA closed 20 of its 40 listening posts, most of which were large HF intercept stations situated around the periphery of the Soviet Union, and the size of its military Sigint intercept force was slashed by one-third from 21,000 to 14,000 personnel.[40] NSA also trimmed the size of its civilian staff, most of whom worked at NSA headquarters at Fort Meade, by almost 7,000 men and women between 1990 and 1998.[41]

A Poor State of Affairs: The Internal Management of NSA

Carefully hidden from public view were a host of internal problems which continue to bedevil NSA today.

The first problem was that classified financial audits and internal reviews of the Agency conducted in the early 1990s found that NSA possessed one of the largest, multi-layered bureaucracies in the entire US intelligence community, which was impeding the effective management of the Agency.[42] Upon becoming the director of NSA in 1992, Vice Admiral McConnell found widespread duplication of effort, inefficiency, and a huge number of personnel carried on NSA's payroll who had 'little involvement in actually accomplishing the Agency's mission.'[43]

The bureaucratic inefficiency of NSA manifested itself in various ways. For example, an internal study in the early 1990s found that NSA's logistics office needed ten days to get a box of paperclips to someone inside the Agency from the time it was ordered; NSA's telecommunications and computer services office took four months to install a desktop computer from the time an employee requested the system; and the Agency's contracting office required over six months to award a contract after it had received all proposals and tender offers from contractors. In one NSA directorate, on average it took 13 days to send a letter, measured from the time the letter was drafted to the time it was actually mailed, due to all of the reviews, endorsements and approvals that the letter had to go through before it could be sent.[44]

This situation had developed because historically there has been very little internal or external oversight of the Agency's operations, especially during the so-called 'Go-Go 1980s.' A 1991 audit by the Defense Department's Inspector General revealed that 'NSA did not have sufficient oversight mechanisms to ensure the Agency efficiently accomplished its mission.'[45] A 1991 House Intelligence Committee report found 'very limited internal oversight of Agency [NSA] programs,' as well as no supervision of the Agency by either the Department of Defense Inspector General's office or the congressional watchdog agency, the General Accounting

Office (GAO).[46] In December 1995, former CIA Director John M. Deutsch reportedly intervened with key members of Congress to prevent the GAO from auditing a particularly troubled NSA project.[47] A 1996 Department of Defense Inspector General report on NSA also found that the Agency still was lacking adequate internal management oversight or controls.[48]

Then there were questionable decisions made in the mid-1990s about how to spend NSA's shrinking budget. For example, despite the fact that the Agency's budget and personnel were cut by one-third between 1990 and 1996, somehow the cost of paying for NSA's civilian personnel rose by a whopping 26 percent during the same years. According to a 1996 report, 40 percent of NSA's $3.7 billion FY 1996 budget went to pay the salaries and benefits of the Agency's civilian workforce.[49] Part of the increased personnel costs were attributable to a reported 29 percent pay increase in 1993 for NSA's senior managers, which occurred at the same time that the Agency was letting thousands of its employees go.[50]

This naturally left a limited amount of money for the actual conduct of NSA's operations. During the mid-1990s, a furious battle raged between NSA's Sigint and Information Security (INFOSEC) directorates over who got the lion's share of what remained of NSA's budget. The apparent loser in this battle was NSA's 4,000-person Technology and Systems Directorate, which ran the Agency's information technology infrastructure and managed its research and development program. Faced with a financial pinch, NSA chose to cut spending on infrastructure and research and development in order to keep the core Sigint and INFOSEC missions up and running.[51]

It should therefore come as no surprise that NSA has had a less than stellar record managing its finances over the last decade. In 1994, an investigation by the Defense Department found that NSA had wasted almost $7.0 million dollars on two communications security programs called 'Blacker' and 'Cane Ware.'[52] In 1994, NSA asked Congress for $250 million to fund the purchase of a new supercomputer system to be used against advanced foreign encryption systems. When pressed to justify the need for the new computer system, NSA reportedly refused to provide Congress with information about how many computers it had, how they were being used, and took months to finally develop a plan for the use of the requested computer system.[53]

In the late 1990s, NSA spent millions of dollars on a project called 'Light Core,' which was an upgrade of the Agency's data network. Civilian contractors working for the Agency told NSA officials that the upgrade would not work, but the Agency went ahead with the project anyway. According to press reports, 'Today the system requires frequent technological band-aids' to keep it up and running, all of which is costing NSA millions of dollars.[54]

A 1996 audit of NSA by the Defense Department's Inspector General (IG) found glaring management and accounting deficiencies. For instance, the IG report revealed that in 1991 and 1992 alone, NSA lost $82 million worth of equipment, which it wrote off on its financial statements rather than determine what had become of the material.[55]

Two years later, a still-classified August 1998 DOD Inspector General report, entitled *Fiscal Year 1997 Financial Statements for the National Security Agency,* found that NSA still could not track what it paid for, suffered from 'material' weaknesses in its accounting system, and that the Agency had not corrected the financial problems identified in the above-mentioned 1996 IG audit which it had told the Pentagon had been fixed.[56] In 1998, the House Intelligence Committee discovered that NSA had not spent any money on programs for attacking new communications technologies that Congress had previously approved. Moreover, NSA officials were not able to provide the committee with an accurate accounting of how the funds had been spent.[57]

Where Have All the People Gone?

The second significant problem that escaped public attention until years later was that during the 1990s NSA lost many of its best employees. As noted above, NSA lost almost 7,000 of its civilian employees between 1990 and 1998.[58] But many of those employees taking early retirements in the early 1990s were some of the Agency's most experienced senior managers, analysts and technical personnel, most of whom had served with the Agency for more than 20 years. Lost with these men and women was much of the Agency's institutional knowledge. Then many of the Agency's middle-level managers left NSA in the late 1990s for better paying jobs in the private sector.[59]

As if this was not bad enough, NSA also lost many of its best technical personnel during the 1990s, especially in the engineering, computer science and information technology fields, most of whom left for better paying jobs in the private sector.[60] NSA also lost a large number of skilled personnel who worked in the non-technical fields, such as hundreds of highly-trained linguists.[61] Former NSA officials point out that despite repeated requests, Congress did not make more money available for pay raises or retention incentives in order to help NSA keep its skilled personnel.[62]

To make matters worse, throughout the 1990s NSA experienced considerable difficulty in recruiting new personnel with the right skill sets to replace the losses. This was because of a government-wide hiring and wage freeze in effect for most of the 1990s, and a lack of financial incentives needed to attract young potential recruits possessing the requisite technical skills that NSA needed, particularly in the computer science and information technology fields.[63]

The result was that by 1996, NSA was experiencing 'a particularly severe problem with the size, age, skills and make-up of its workforce.'[64] NSA's current director, Air Force Lieutenant General Michael V. Hayden, has recently admitted that NSA's staff today is largely comprised of two groups: the first consists of a large group of older senior managers who are fast nearing retirement age, and a very young group of less experienced employees who are increasingly comprised of military personnel on rotational duty with the Agency. Apparently there is little in between these two groups because of high personnel attrition rates during the late 1990s.[65] NSA's consumers began to complain that the younger NSA civilian analysts and managers that they had to deal with were inexperienced and knew less about their customers' needs than their predecessors who were let go or resigned in the early 1990s.[66]

In recent years NSA has resorted to desperate measures to try to keep as many of its remaining managers and technicians 'in the fold.' Between 1996 and 1998, 500 NSA personnel were 'retired,' and were moved immediately onto the payrolls of some of the Agency's largest civilian contractors, where they continued to do the same job as when they worked at NSA. Not eligible to participate in this 'Soft Landing' program are Agency computer scientists, linguists, mathematicians, and engineers, who NSA obviously wanted to keep. This meant that the only NSA personnel eligible to participate in the program were support personnel. NSA claimed that 'Soft Landing' saved the government about $25 million. Yet given how NSA has managed its finances it the past, this would seem to be a dubious claim.[67]

The Quest for Global Access: NSA's Sigint Collection Effort

Ironically, the one area that has recently been highlighted as NSA's biggest current trouble spot— its Sigint collection capabilities—is probably the one area where NSA is not really experiencing any significant problems at present.

It is true that NSA's Sigint collection environment has changed dramatically in the last decade. As of 1989, the year that the Berlin Wall fell, more than 50 percent of NSA's Sigint collection and processing assets were still dedicated to intelligence coverage of the Soviet Union. By early 1999, it is believed that Sigint coverage of the countries that formerly comprised the Soviet Union had dropped to less than 20 percent of NSA's intercept and processing resources.[68]

Today, the Agency's target list is much larger and more complicated. Since the breakup of the Soviet Union in the early 1990s, NSA's attention has been shifted to other targets. One of the most important of its priorities is expanded Sigint coverage of international economic matters, including international trade negotiations and economic summits, bribery attempts by foreign governments and companies competing with American companies for international business, and money transfers by international banks.

NSA has moved in a significant way into the war against drugs, with the Agency expanding its cooperation with the CIA and the Drug Enforcement Agency (DEA) in ongoing intelligence gathering operations aimed at rooting out and destroying international drug rings, particularly in Latin America.

And NSA's intelligence coverage of international terrorism and the sources of their financing has been expanded and refined, especially since the 1993 bombing of the World Trade Center in New York City.[69]

Then there are substantive problems that the Agency has had to face because of the still-ongoing technological revolution in the telecommunications field. Congressional documents and recent press reports about NSA's travails have made much of these obstacles, in some cases making it sound as if NSA has suffered the technological equivalent of the attack on Pearl Harbor. For example, the late staff director of the House Intelligence Committee stated that 'technology has become the enemy of NSA.'[70] Even NSA's Director, General Hayden, told an interviewer in 1999 that 'Technology has now become a two-edged sword. . . . On the dark days, it has become the enemy.'[71]

From a technological perspective, things were much simpler for NSA 50 years ago. When the Agency was created in 1952, there were only 5,000 computers in the entire world, and no fax machines or cellular telephones. By the late 1990s, there were more than 180 million personal computers, 14 million fax machines and 40 million cellular telephones in use around the world.[72] Other new telecommunications technologies that have become more widely used in the last decade include the Internet, digital signals technology, fibre-optic cables, high speed modems, and powerful commercially-produced encryption systems.[73] Complicating NSA's task even further is the migration of many communications systems in the developed world to wireless networks, such as Local Area Networks (LANs) and Wide Area Networks (WANs).[74]

The technological revolution is also changing the face of communications on the world's battlefields. NSA has found in the last decade that some foreign military forces, particularly in Europe, have begun using new telecommunications technologies, such as spread spectrum links, laser point-to-point communications, fast frequency-hopping technology, tactical satellite communications, increased useage of millimeter wave communications systems, data compression techniques, burst transmitters, imbedded decoy signals, increased signal directionality, encryption at all levels, and greater use of low-probability of intercept communications systems, such as walkie-talkies and even cellular telephones. All of these relatively new technologies are making NSA's Sigint collection mission in support of US military operations overseas more difficult than they were ten years ago.[75]

Then there is the problem of how to deal with the vastly increased volume of communications traffic now coursing through the airwaves. The new telecommunications systems on the market today, such as personal computers and related communications software, cellular telephones and fax machines, are faster, more flexible and most importantly, cheaper to buy. Costs have fallen to the point that it is now cheaper to send an e-mail message than to send a letter. This has led to exponential growth in the volume of digital information being transmitted around the world in the last decade. From NSA's perspective, this has meant that as the volume of communications traffic has increased, it has become increasingly difficult to find the few nuggets of intelligence gold amid all the material it is picking up every day.[76]

A small but increasing amount of international communications traffic has been moved in the last decade from the airwaves to landlines, such as buried fibre-optic cables, which NSA theoretically cannot intercept. It should come as no surprise that NSA and its allies have invested hundreds of millions of dollars since the late 1980s trying to come up with technical means to get at traffic passing through fibre-optic cables. As of the mid-1990s, the American and British scientists and engineers had not reportedly made any headway with this problem other than to physically tap the cables.[77]

But the most significant technological threat that NSA now faces is how to deal with the rapidly proliferating number of powerful commercially-produced encryption systems available on the open market, many of which are difficult (but not impossible) for NSA to solve through conventional cryptanalytic means. For example, in recent years a new generation of 128-bit encryption systems have been developed by private companies in the US and elsewhere that offer a degree of encryption protection for commercial users that is several tens of thousands of times greater than the previously available 40-bit and 56-bit encryption systems.

By the early 1990s, these cryptographic systems were small enough to be placed on computer chips, which meant that even laptop computers could carry the most sophisticated communications protection available.

Some have suggested that these new systems are resistant to NSA's 'brute force' method of attacking foreign cipher systems with the Agency's huge inventory of supercomputers, although this is hotly disputed by cryptographers in the private sector. Regardless of the merits of each side's argument, these cryptographic systems are now widely available, easy to use and relatively inexpensive, with the price for these systems coming down as the technology improves. Efforts by NSA during the 1990s to curb the development and export of strong commercial encryption technologies have met with fierce resistance from members of Congress, privacy advocates, and most of the American computer software industry.[78]

But in recent interviews, former NSA officials stated that the recent pessimistic commentary has distorted NSA's current Sigint collection predicament.[79] Most of these former officials agree with an assessment contained in a 1996 House Intelligence Committee report, which stated that the technical challenges facing NSA are 'daunting.' But the officials added that many of the obstacles described above can or already have been overcome.[80] Moreover, internal NSA documents make clear that NSA and its allies are currently enjoying, from a collection perspective, a 'golden age' because of the recent movement of previously unobtainable communications traffic to the airwaves where the Agency's intercept operators can now get it.[81]

US intelligence sources point out that the new telecommunications technologies, such as the Internet and digital communications, are almost exclusively being used in the US and other developed countries since they are the only nations who can afford them. For example, as of 1992 there were 18 million cellular phone users worldwide, of whom 10 million were in the US, 5 million in Europe, and 1.5 million in Japan. This meant that there were only 1.5 million cellular telephone users outside of the developed world.[82] One former NSA official stated that 'Things are much more low-tech once you get outside of Western Europe and Japan.'[83]

This also means that most of the usage of high-grade encryption technology has also been limited to the US, and to a much lesser degree in Europe and Japan, because this is where the vast majority of the world's Internet and cellular phone users are located.[84]

Finally, American intelligence officials point out that the worldwide use of buried fibre-optic cable is actually quite small outside of submarine cables (most of which touch land in the US or Great Britain) and within developed countries.[85]

More importantly, the vast majority of international communications traffic continues to flow through communications satellites, which NSA and its allies can intercept. The communications satellites operated by the International Telecommunications Satellite Organization (Intelsat) carry two-thirds of all the world's international telephone calls, almost all international television broadcasts, as well as most of the world's international telex, digital computer data, video teleconferencing, e-mail, and fax traffic.[86]

To deal with the dramatic shifts in national intelligence requirements and the growth of new telecommunications technologies, NSA drastically reengineered its Sigint collection network beginning in the early 1990s.[87] By the late 1990s, NSA's Sigint collection system had become smaller but more capable and flexible than the old Cold War architecture. NSA's new Sigint collection system consists of a mixture of Sigint satellites, large listening posts, a growing number of covert listening posts in American embassies, as well as a sizeable number of mobile airborne, surface ship and submarine reconnaissance platforms dedicated for Sigint collection.[88]

A new generation of Sigint satellites were put into orbit by NSA and the NRO during the 1990s that were significantly more capable than their predecessors. Between 1994 and 1998, four new communications intelligence (Comint) satellites were put into geosynchronous orbit over the Earth to replace the older 'Vortex/Mercury' satellites that had been in orbit since the late 1970s and early 1980s.[89] These huge satellites were far more capable than their predecessors. They could intercept not only VHF radio signals and UHF microwave telephone circuits, but also huge volumes of digital and analog computer data, facsimile traffic, computer-to-computer modem transmissions, and cellular telephone calls.[90] In addition, between 1994 and 1997 three new Sigint satellites, called 'Trumpet,' were launched into elliptical Molniya orbits around the Earth. These satellites were designed to monitor radio traffic and electronic emissions coming from military targets.[91] And finally, four constellations of the new 'Advanced Parcae' ocean surveillance satellite were placed into orbit on 8 June 1990, 7 November 1991, 12 May 1996 and 22 May 1999.[92]

The ground-based command, control and communications infrastructure for these Sigint satellites has become impressively large over the last 30 years. NSA and the CIA operate four large Mission Ground Stations to control the Sigint satellites, located at Menwith Hill Station in England, Bad Aibling Station in Germany, Buckley Air National Guard Base in Colorado, and Pine Gap in Australia.[93] Day-to-day management of the various Sigint satellite systems is handled by an NSA unit called the Overhead Collection Management Center (OCMC), which is responsible for tasking the satellites currently in orbit from its operations center at Fort Meade.[94]

The US Navy operates three 'Classic Wizard' stations on Diego Garcia in the Indian Ocean, Guam, and Winter Harbor, Maine, to process information received from its constellations of 'Advanced Parcae' ocean surveillance satellites.[95] Operational control of the Parcae ocean surveillance satellites is handled by a joint NSA-Naval Security Group Command unit called that Program Operations Coordination Group (POCG), which is also located at NSA headquarters at Fort Meade.[96]

In 1998 the NRO announced that is was developing a new and larger Sigint satellite system which will combine the functions of all three existing Sigint satellites now in orbit. The new satellite, which is expected to be launched in 2002–2003, would 'improve Sigint performance and avoid costs by consolidating systems, utilizing new satellite and data processing technologies.' NSA will also be able to reduce the number of Mission Ground Stations needed to process information from this satellite as part of what NSA refers to as the Integrated Overhead Sigint Architecture.[97]

Three multi-service Regional Sigint Operations Centers (RSOCs) were activated in the mid-1990s at the Medina Annex outside San Antonio, Texas; Fort Gordon, Georgia; and Kunia, Hawaii, each consisting of over 1,000 military and civilian personnel. The Medina RSOC performs Sigint collection in Latin America, the Caribbean, and along the Atlantic littoral of Africa for the US Southern Command (SOUTHCOM) and the US Central Command (CENTCOM). The Fort Gordon RSOC provides Sigint support to the US European Command (EUCOM) and US Central Command in Europe, North Africa, the Middle East, the Near East, and the Persian Gulf. The Kunia RSOC is responsible for Sigint coverage throughout Asia on behalf of the US Pacific Command (PACOM). The RSOCs replaced many of NSA's overseas listening posts that had been closed since 1990. Each RSOC receives their intercepts from national and tactical Sigint collection assets in their overseas regions of responsibility, such as ground-based Remote Operating

Facilities, Sigint-equipped U-2 aircraft, and ships equipped with remote-controlled intercept receivers. The intercepts are relayed in realtime via satellite communications links to the RSOCs, where they are processed, analyzed and reported.[98]

In the late 1980s, NSA began expanding the size and capabilities of its network of six satellite communications (Satcom) intercept stations around the world in order to handle the increased volume of telecommunications traffic passing through the new generation of satellites operated by the International Satellite Organization (Intelsat). The six NSA Satcom intercept stations are located at Sugar Grove, West Virginia; Yakima, Washington; Sabana Seca, Puerto Rico; Menwith Hill Station in England; Bad Aibling Station in Germany; and Misawa Air Base in Japan. These stations work in tandem with four Satcom intercept stations operated by NSA's UKUSA partners, located at Morwenstow, England; Leitrim, Canada; Kojarena, Australia; and Waihopai, New Zealand.[99]

The capabilities of this network of Satcom intercept stations is impressive. As of 1998, these stations reportedly intercepted approximately 100 million messages a month that were being relayed through the 19 Intelsat satellites and four Inmarsat maritime communications satellites then in orbit over the Earth, such as regular telephone calls, digital cellular telephone traffic, fax transmissions, e-mail messages, bank wire transfers, computer transmissions, teleconferencing and video conferencing signals. The NSA Satcom intercept stations are also now capable of intercepting data, voice and video signals passing through so-called Very Small Aperture Terminals (VSAT), which are small commercial satellite systems that use small 30-foot satellite dishes.[100]

The joint NSA-CIA Special Collection Service (SCS), which operates covert listening posts inside American diplomatic establishments abroad, has continued to grow in size and importance during the 1990s. Today the SCS controls approximately 45 covert listening posts in overseas American diplomatic establishments, which intercept military, political, police and economic radio traffic.[101] NSA has its own covert Sigint collection unit, the Office of Unconventional Programs, which engages in unconventional Sigint collection operations against foreign targets that cannot be accessed by more traditional means.[102]

Then there are the multitude of mobile Sigint collection platforms operating around the world on behalf of NSA. Today, the three military services fly 81 dedicated Sigint collection aircraft, and there are an additional 38 aircraft that are configured or can be converted for Sigint collection on short notice.[103] The US Navy currently operates 61 ships that are equipped with Sigint collection suites.[104] Finally, US Navy submarine reconnaissance missions, including Sigint collection, are now being conducted by 51 *Los Angeles*-class nuclear attack submarines and a few remaining *Sturgeon*-class attack submarines.

All of these Sigint systems together give NSA comprehensive coverage of the full range of radio signals and electronic emitters operating today. These Sigint collection assets are capable of not only intercepting traditional HP, VHP, and UHF radio signals, but also the new high-tech telecommunications systems, such as digital, satellite, cellular telephone and data communications traffic, and even low probability of intercept (LPI) radio emissions, that is, walkie-talkie radio traffic.[105]

NSA's Sigint efforts are greatly assisted by the CIA and the FBI, which intensified their efforts during the 1990s to surreptitiously obtain foreign cryptographic materials. A 1996 report by the House Intelligence Committee stated: 'Arguably, a clandestine service's greatest contribution to intelligence is the compromising of codes. The proliferation of sophisticated cryptographic systems ensures the growing importance of this role of the [CIA] Clandestine Service.'[106] A 1997 congressional report stated that 'adding enormously to the value of clandestine Humint is its contribution to clandestine technical operations and in compromising foreign cryptographic materials.'[107]

Clearly getting to communications traffic is not one of the major problems currently facing NSA. If anything, the Agency's access to global communications has been significantly expanded and improved during the 1990s. Moreover, the dramatic increase in worldwide of communications traffic means that there is more for NSA to get, if it can find the means to process and exploit these new veins of information.[108]

This is not to say that there are not problems in NSA Sigint collection program. Because of the worldwide explosion in communications traffic volumes, NSA must now intercept significantly more in order to continue to produce the same amount of intelligence as it did ten years ago. This means that NSA must maintain a much broader array of intercept capabilities than it did at the height of the Cold War, which of course means a higher pricetag in order to maintain this capability.[109]

Many of NSA's 'vacuum cleaner' collection systems are, however, extremely expensive and not particularly productive. In December 1992, former NSA director Admiral William O. Studeman described a collection system which on average produced only one reportable intelligence item from one million intercept inputs.[110] And because of NSA's problems processing the intercepts that it is

getting now, which is described in greater detail below, many high-ranking NSA officials believe that the addition of more collection systems would only exacerbate NSA's current problems.[111]

Finally, one longstanding problem is that there is a great deal of duplication of effort within the NSA collection effort, in large part because the Agency does not have the internal management controls or oversight systems in place to make sure that the same targets were being copied by multiple sensors.[112]

Boys Versus Toys: The State of the Sigint Infrastructure

As one can see above, NSA's biggest problem is *not* its ability to collect intelligence. In reality, the Agency's biggest problem is the continuing decline of its Sigint processing, analysis and reporting infrastructure.

As it has done since the early 1970s, NSA spent the majority of its Sigint budget during the 1990s on building new and very expensive Sigint collection systems.[113] The capabilities of these new Sigint collection systems that came online in the 1990s were impressive. As of 1995, NSA was capable of intercepting the equivalent of the entire collection of the US Library of Congress (1 quadrillion bits of information) every three hours.[114] The problem was that NSA spent comparatively little on the equipment and personnel needed to take these intercepts and turn them into finished intelligence. As one NSA insider put it, NSA was 'buying all these new toys, but they don't have the people to use them.'[115] Agency insiders have pointed out in recent interviews that Congress bears much of the blame for this situation. Until 1997, both of the congressional intelligence committees pushed NSA to spend more money on new collection systems and technologies, but they did not provide the Agency with the money needed for requested infrastructure improvements.[116]

What happened next was inevitable. The new high-tech collection systems produced such a massive volume of intercepts that NSA's analysts and their computers at Ft. Meade were quickly swamped. As time went by, an increasing number of the intercepts went unread, and NSA's Sigint production fell dramatically.[117] By one estimate, by the mid-1990s NSA was only processing approximately 1 percent of the intercepts that were reaching Ft Meade, down from a reported 20 percent in the late 1980s.[118] NSA's current director, General Hayden, has admitted that NSA is collecting far more data than it processes, and that the Agency processes more data than it actually reports to its consumers in Washington and elsewhere.[119] In 1998, Congressman Porter J. Goss, chairman of the House Intelligence Committee, chastized NSA and the other members of the intelligence community for allowing this to happen, stating that 'Expending resources to collect intelligence that is not being analyzed is simply a waste of money.'[120]

The consequences of NSA's resource allocation decisions made a decade ago go even deeper. As senior American intelligence officials have recently pointed out, NSA is today producing less intelligence than it was a decade ago.[121] A former White House official was quoted as saying of NSA that 'They're spending more money and working harder and getting less and less information out of sources.'[122] One recent press report even indicated that the amount of Sigint information appearing in the daily intelligence summary sent to the President of the United States, the President's Daily Brief (PDB), has declined by almost 20 percent since 1989.[123]

Solutions to this massive conundrum have not been easy to come by. NSA has sought to deal with the problem by attempting to further automate the Sigint processing task, with a bevy of new computers being added to try to help NSA's analysts cope with the growing volume of intercepts. According to publicly available information, NSA today owns at least 26 supercomputers with a combined computing power of 5,516.83 gigaflops, making the Agency the largest supercomputer operator in the world.[124] In 1993, a powerful new computer system called 'Normalizer' was purchased for the specific purpose of processing, storing and distributing time-sensitive intelligence information.[125]

But this effort has been extremely expensive and fraught with problems. For four days during the week of 23 January 2000, the main Sigint processing computer at NSA failed, reportedly because of a 'software anomaly.' The result was an intelligence blackout, with no intelligence reports coming out of Ft Meade for more than 72 hours.[126]

Another facet of the Sigint processing problem is that although NSA owns and operates the largest computer and telecommunications system in the federal government, these resources have not been particularly well managed. NSA has in its inventory today dozens of computer and communications systems that are not interoperable with other systems operated by the Agency.[127]

Furthermore, NSA has not yet fielded a telecommunications network that can adequately handle the vast amount of data that moves every day between NSA headquarters, its intercept units, and its consumers. During the 1999 military operations in Kosovo, NSA had to reduce to a minimum the transmission of all routine communications traffic on its communications system in order to make room for the Sigint information being sent from Ft Meade to US and Allied forces operating in Kosovo.[128]

NSA is also experiencing increased difficulty reporting Sigint information in a timely manner. Today, NSA's intelligence consumers are demanding that NSA get its information to them in near realtime. This means that NSA has had to speed up the processing of information in order to meet this requirement. However, this has severely strained NSA's already tightly-stretched Sigint processing capabilities, and forced NSA to cut back on the amount of material that it processes and analyzes in order to meet its customers short-term needs.[129]

Most informed observers of NSA have concluded that more technology is not the panacea for what ails NSA. Several past and present NSA officials have stated that what the Agency desperately needs is more personnel to read what the computers process.[130] But NSA's senior management has been curiously reluctant to ask Congress for money to hire more analysts because, according to former NSA officials, personnel is not a 'sexy' budget line item on Capitol Hill.[131] James Bamford, author of the *Puzzle Palace*, has written that 'It has always been far easier for the NSA to persuade Congress to provide more money for a sexy new piece of technology, like a satellite with the ability to vacuum 50 percent more phone calls from the ether, than for 200 more analysts to sift through the mountains of information.'[132]

NSA's director, General Hayden, has recently confirmed this assessment, telling an interviewer that 'Technology alone is not the solution to the data processing problem. . . . The agency needs to add more analysts and linguists to its staff.' But General Hayden has noted that hiring these highly qualified men and women in the midst of a booming economy is an extremely difficult proposition given that NSA is competing for the same people that private industry wants.[133] If NSA fails to recruit a new corps of young and talented information technology specialists, one could suggest that all else is for naught. As former NSA director General Kenneth A. Minihan put it, 'If we don't win the talent war, it doesn't matter if we invest in the infrastructure.'[134]

The Unhappy Customers

Not surprisingly, the people who are the most unhappy with the turn in events at NSA are its clients inside the US government. An October 1999 NSA management study found that NSA's cavalier attitude towards its customers had 'created a perception among customers that NSA places higher value on its tradecraft than it does on outcomes for the nation.' One NSA customer was quoted in the report as saying 'I sometimes think you give us the party line rather than the real scoop on how you spend your money. And you don't want guidance from the community.'[135]

Another study conducted in the spring of 1995 revealed that there was widespread consensus among NSA's Sigint consumers that recurring turf battles among military and civilian factions within NSA's Operations Directorate had unnecessarily created bureaucratic obstacles to the free flow of intelligence information to the Agency's consumers.[136] Many of NSA's customers in the government complained that the National Sigint Requirements Systems (NSRS), the system by which consumers around the world tasked NSA, was obsolete and unresponsive to NSA's customer needs.[137]

There is also evidence that NSA's relationship with the Defense Department has also deteriorated somewhat in recent years. For example, in 1997 Pentagon officials complained that NSA still was reluctant to give the military the intelligence information that they needed to do their job because of concerns about compromising the security of the Agency's sources. This led one Pentagon official to charge that 'long-entrenched civilian NSA employees are still fighting the Cold War and are more worried about maintaining security than improving tactical warfighting capabilities.'[138]

Interviews with current and former officials of the US Army and Air Force cryptologic organizations confirm that there exists today considerable unhappiness within the military services about their diminished role in the national Sigint effort. One former high-ranking Army intelligence official stated that in recent years, the US Army Intelligence and Security Command (INSCOM) has lost many of its strategic Sigint missions to NSA, and that there exists today a widespread feeling within the military that NSA is ignoring their needs.[139] A former Navy cryptologist has publicly stated that the role of the US Navy's cryptologic organization, the Naval Security Group Command, has been 'reduced by NSA to a backwater effort.'[140]

The Push for Modernization at NSA

On 15 November 1999, NSA Director General Hayden launched a major reform program at NSA that he called the '100 Days of Change.' The program was prompted by a scathing report that he received in October 1999, which described 'an agency mired in bureaucratic conflict, suffering from poor leadership and losing touch with the government clients it serves.' The report's principal recommendation called for scrapping NSA's entire senior lead-

ership team so as to better deal with the multitude of other problems that NSA faces.[141] General Hayden's commitment to the reform program appears to be sincere. In December 1999, he told reporters from *Newsweek* that 'the agency has got to make some changes because by standing still, we are going to fall behind very quickly.'[142]

General Hayden's reform plan appears to have been partly crafted by his predecessor, US Air Force Lieutenant General Kenneth Minihan. In March 1997, General Minihan told his staff that NSA had to 'accelerate the effort to decrease our internal bureaucracies, flatten our organization, and establish a flexible, responsive, decentralized structure suited for an environment that will be highly unpredictable and will demand continuous innovation.'[143] To effect these changes, General Minihan believed that the Agency's internal culture would have to be radically changed. The only problem, Minihan wrote, was that 'Deep cultural changes require crisis felt by all levels of the organization.'[144] The only problem was that there was no crisis around which General Minihan could mobilize support within NSA for change, and his plan was derailed by NSA's senior civilian officials.[145]

Apparently General Hayden has learned from the mistakes made by his predecessors. Not only has General Hayden adopted almost all of General Minihan's reform plan, but he has also apparently created an environment conducive to getting the money that he needs to implement his plan. Suddenly, recent congressional and press reports about NSA have almost uniformly used words that are synonymous with 'crisis' to describe NSA's current condition. For example, in October 1998 the late staff director of the House Intelligence Committee, John Millis, said that 'Signals intelligence is in a crisis.'[146] The House Intelligence Committee, in its February 1999 annual report to Congress, concluded that 'NSA is in serious trouble.'[147] An October 1999 study of the Agency's management stated that 'NSA has been in a leadership crisis for the better part of a decade.'[148] Given this sort of strong language, it is hard to see how the Clinton administration or congress could deny any 'reasonable' funding request from NSA.

The real challenge that General Hayden and his supporters face is that every one of his predecessors who tried to effect major change at NSA had to fight a continuous, uphill battle against the Agency's powerful and deeply entrenched bureaucracy.[149] NSA's former senior civilian, Barbara A. McNamara, the Agency's Deputy Director from October 1997 to July 2000, came under intense fire from reformers within NSA and outside observers, with one reporter describing her as 'Among the most caustic defenders of the agency's old ways.'[150]

But unlike his predecessors, Hayden has some important allies on Capitol Hill who firmly support his plan for drastic changes at NSA. In May 1998, the House Intelligence Committee issued a report which stated that 'very large changes in the National Security Agency's culture and method of operations need to take place.' The committee's report concluded that 'NSA will not meet its Unified Cryptologic Architecture (UCA) goals without tackling head-on some very fundamental internal obstacles,' specifically 'the stultifying effect that the bureaucracy of such a large organization can have.'[151]

In February 1999, the Senate Intelligence Committee reported that NSA's Sigint mission 'must be dramatically rejuvenated.' The committee found that declining budgets and obsolete equipment were impeding NSA's ability to maintain a technical edge over its opponents, and recommended a massive modernization of NSA's Sigint effort, greater emphasis on and more money for advanced research and development, the revitalization and NSA's recruiting and hiring program, and a complete revamping of NSA's organizational structure, including a recommendation that NSA outsource many of its administrative and support functions.[152]

Beginning in November 1999, General Hayden began enacting some of the changes that he wanted. In the first 50 days of the '100 Days of Change' program, General Hayden junked the three management committees which heretofore had run NSA—the Senior Agency Leadership Team (SALT), the Critical Issues Group (CIG), and the Corporate Management Review Group (CMRG)—and replaced them with a single committee called the Executive Leadership Team (ELT). The membership on the ELT was to consist solely of the director, the Agency's deputy director, and the heads of the operations, technology and systems, and information systems security directorates. He brought in a new chief financial officer, Beverly L. Wright, formerly the chief financial officer of the investment banking firm of Legg Mason Wood Walker, Inc., to reform NSA's financial and accounting practices. He also appointed Air Force Major General Tiiu Kera as the new Deputy Chief of the long-dormant Central Security Service, with a mandate to improve NSA's relationship with the Pentagon and the military services.[153]

In a further development, NSA's Deputy Director, Barbara McNamara, stepped down from her position in July 2000 to become NSA's liaison officer in London. Ms McNamara's departure from her post, NSA insiders believe, will go a long way towards allowing General Hayden to implement his reform and modernization plans.[154]

But as usual, NSA officials have made it clear that their reform and modernization programs cannot be accomplished without a massive infusion of money, and Congress seems inclined to give NSA what it wants. Not coincidentally, congressional concern about NSA began at about the same time that NSA began to quietly push on Capitol Hill for more money to fund modernization of the Agency. In the fall of 1998 Congress quietly approved a whopping 10 percent increase in the size of NSA's Fiscal Year 1999 budget. This brought NSA's annual budget over the $4 billion mark for the first time since the end of the Cold War.[155] In late 1999, Congress also approved a reported $200 million increase in NSA's FY 2000 budget.[156] This year (Fiscal Year 2001), NSA is expected once again to ask for a substantial increase in the size of its budget so that it can triple the size of its recruiting effort and double the size of its research and development program. It remains to be seen whether NSA can recruit the people it wants in the midst of a robust economy.[157]

Conclusions

Some of the reports concerning NSA's purported problems would appear to have missed their mark. No one disputes that the Sigint product coming out of Ft Meade remains one of the most important intelligence sources available to the US intelligence community. But statements that have appeared in the American press that NSA was solely responsible for some of the US intelligence community's recent intelligence failures, such as failing to detect India and Pakistan's 1998 nuclear tests, are factually incorrect.

Furthermore, NSA's Sigint collection capabilities have actually improved considerably during the last decade, and evidence suggests that the technological obstacles that have been often cited in press reports as contributing to NSA's current problems (i.e., strong encryption and fibre-optic cables) have not yet begun to be widely used outside of the developed countries in Western Europe and East Asia.

NSA's most pressing problem is an area which unfortunately has received little public attention in recent months, specifically the deterioration of the Agency's Sigint processing, analysis and reporting capabilities. As detailed above, NSA currently does not have the computer power or the personnel to process, translate or read even a fraction of the ever increasing volume of communications traffic that it intercepts. It is clear that NSA must recruit substantial numbers of analysts and information technology specialists in the near future, and invest money in acquiring new processing technologies in order to begin to address this problem. And until this happens, it would seem prudent to recommend that NSA cut back its spending on new collection systems and instead use this money to restore the Agency's Sigint processing and analytic infrastructure to a semblance of health.

The Agency must also take immediate steps to shore up its strained relations with its customers inside the US government and the armed forces in order to restore confidence in NSA's intelligence product. Moreover, given the transient and oftentimes fickle nature of politics, NSA must realize that it cannot depend solely on a few allies in the US Congress for its continued survival.

Equally important, but more difficult to empirically quantify, is how to effectively deal with NSA's internal management problems, such as how to trim the Agency's large bureaucracy, eliminate duplication of effort and waste, put NSA's financial accounts in order, and break down the Agency's cultural opposition to outside oversight of its operations. Given that NSA has not passed a single outside financial audit, it would seem unreasonable for Congress to increase the size of NSA's budget without ensuring that NSA takes steps to bring about a greater level of transparency as to how it spends its money.

And finally, it is time that NSA adopt a policy of greater openness about what it does and how it does it. One obvious way to do this is to declassify documents which detail the Agency's significant accomplishments since the end of World War II. Former NSA director Vice Admiral McConnell put it best when he told the Agency in 1994 that 'In these changing times we, as an Agency, must take advantage of appropriate opportunities to give today's customer base (which includes the general public) a clear understanding of why we are relevant.[158] Many outside observers agree with these sentiments, believing that this would go a long way towards reestablishing a semblance of confidence and trust in NSA amongst an increasingly skeptical NSA customer base and the general public.

Questions for Further Discussion

1. What are the advantages and disadvantages of relying on "sigint" for intelligence about U.S. adversaries?

2. What are the major problems faced by the NSA today?

3. Would it be useful to consolidate into one organization the three major technical agencies: NRO, NSA, and NGA, or some combination of these three?

4. Are you concerned about the possibility that NSA's "big ear" could be turned against citizens of the United States, at the order of a president or DNI? Should the president be allowed to conduct warrantless wiretaps? Under what circumstances?

Endnotes

1. Seymour M. Hersh, 'The Intelligence Gap: How the Digital Age Left Our Spies Out in the Cold,' *New Yorker*, 6 Dec. 1999, p. 58ff.
2. Neal Thompson, 'Putting NSA Under Scrutiny,' *Baltimore Sun*, 18 Oct. 1998, p. 1C.
3. A more detailed discussion of these matters is contained in Matthew M. Aid, 'Not So Anonymous: Parting the Veil of Secrecy About the National Security Agency,' in Athan G. Theoharis (ed.) *A Culture of Secrecy: The Government Versus the People's Right to Know* (Lawrence: UP of Kansas 1998) pp. 65–67.
4. USSID 1, Sigint *Operating Policy*, 29 June 1987, p. 1, NSA FOIA; USSID 4, Sigint *Support to Military Commanders*, 1 July 1974, pp. 1–2, NSA FOIA; USSID 18, *Limitations and Procedures in Signals Intelligence Operations of the USSS*, 20 Oct. 1968, p. 7, NSA FOIA; Memo for the Special Assistant, Office of the Secretary of Defense, *NSA Transition Briefing Book*, 9 Dec. 1980, p. 1; NSGTP 69304-B, *Naval Cryptology in National Security*, 1985, p. 59, COMNAVSECGRU FOIA; 'NSA/CSS Future Day—the Services Perspective,' *National Security Agency Newsletter*, Oct. 1996, p. 2; Tom Bowman and Scott Shane, 'Espionage from the Frontlines,' *Baltimore Sun*, 8 Dec. 1995, pp. 1A, 20A.
5. Central Intelligence Agency, OPAI 93-00092, *A Consumer's Guide to Intelligence*, Sept. 1993, p. 12; National Performance Review, *Accompanying Report of the National Performance Review: The Intelligence Community*, Sept. 1993, p. 36.
6. CIA Biographical Data Sheet, James L. Runyan, via Dr. Jeffrey T. Richelson; NSAN, Nov. 1997, p. 6.
7. Jeffrey T. Richelson, 'Out of the Black: The Disclosure and Declassification of the National Reconnaissance Office,' *International Journal of Intelligence and Counterintelligence*, Spring 1998, p. 12; Organization Chart, National Reconnaissance Office, 2 Oct. 1996. The author is grateful to Dr. Jeffrey T. Richelson for making a copy of this document available.
8. David A. Fulghum, 'Sigint Aircraft May Face Obsolescence in Five Years,' *Aviation Week & Space Technology*, 21 Oct. 1996, p. 54.
9. Norman Polmar and Thomas B. Allen, *Spy Book* (NY: Random House 1997) p. 402.
10. 'Address at the CIRA Luncheon, 5 Oct. 1998; John Millis' Speech,' *CIRA Newsletter*, Winter 1998/1999, p. 6.
11. Bruce B. Auster, 'What's Really Gone Wrong With the CIA,' *US News & World Report*, 1 June 1998. See also Walter Pincus, 'CIA Chief Cited Loss of Agency's Capabilities,' *Washington Post*, 25 May 1998, p. A4.
12. Alfred Monteiro, Jr., 'Mustering the Force: Cryptologic Support to Military Operations,' *Defense Intelligence Journal* 4/2 (Fall 1995) p. 70; Maj. Paul Ackeriey, 'Team AIA,' *Spokesman*, Jan. 1995, p. 4.
13. Vice Admiral Michael McConnell letter to Senator Sam Nunn, 28 April 1992, p. 6, via Jeffrey T. Richelson; Mark Urban, *UK Eyes Alpha* (London: Faber 1996) pp. 159, 169–170; Brig. Gen. Robert H. Scales, *USA, Cer-*

tain Victory: The US Army in the Gulf War (Washington, DC: Brassey's 1994), pp. 189–190; Michael R. Gordon and Bernard E. Trainor, *The Generals' War* (Boston: Little, Brown 1995) pp. 285–287.

14. For RC-135 missions and other USAP Sigint operations against Iraq, see Air Intelligence Agency, *History of the Air Intelligence Agency: 1 January–31 December 1994*, Vol. I, Appendix C, AIA FOIA; *World Air Power Journal* 21 (Summer 1995) p. 13; 'AFIC Crew Takes Gen. Jerome F. O'Malley Award,' *Spokesman*, Aug. 1993, p. 9; 1st Lt. John Henry, 'Duty in the Desert,' *Spokesman*, March 1995, p. 18; 'RC-135 takes to the sky.' *Spokesman*, April 1995, p. 7. For Navy airborne Sigint missions against Iraq, see *Command History Fleet Air Reconnaissance Squadron One for CY 1992*, Enclosure 1, p. 3; *Command History Fleet Air Reconnaissance Squadron One for CY 1993*, Enclosure 1, p. 4; *Command History Fleet Air Reconnaissance Squadron Six. for CY 1994*, Enclosure 1, p. 4; *Command History Fleet Air Reconnaissance Squadron Six for CY 1995*, Enclosure 1, pp. 3–4; *Command History Fleet Air Reconnaissance Squadron Six for CY 1996*, Enclosure 1, pp. 3–4, all Naval Aviation History Branch, Naval Historical Center, Washington DC.

15. Air Intelligence Agency, *History of the Air Intelligence Agency: 1 January–31 December 1994*, Vol . 1, pp. 30–31, AIA FOIA; 'Interest in ARL Grows After Aircraft's Uphold Democracy Performance,' *Inside the Army*, 13 March 1995, p. 9; Wayne P. Gagner, 'Army Electronic Warfare Gears for Contingency Operations,' *Signals*, Oct. 1996, p. 35; David A. Fulghum, 'Communications Intercepts Pace EP-3s,' *Aviation Week & Space Technology*, 5 May 1997, pp. 53–54; David A. Fulghum, 'Navy Spying Masked by Patrol Aircraft,' *Aviation Week & Space Technology*, 8 March 1999, pp. 32–33.

16. Urban, UK Eyes Alpha (note 13) p. 217; Rick Atkinson, 'GIs Signal Bosnians: Yes, We're Listening,' *Washington Post*, 18 March 1996, p. A14; Walter Pincus, 'US Sought Other Bosnia Arms Sources,' *Washington Post*, 26 April 1996, p. A15; Charles Lane and Thorn Shanker, 'Bosnia: What the CIA Didn't Tell Us,' *New York Review of Books*, 9 May 1996, p. 11.

17. Robert K. Ackerman, 'Security Agency Transitions From Backer to Participant,' *Signal*, Oct. 1999, p. 23; Eric Schmitt, 'Hundreds of Yugoslav Troops Said to Desert,' *New York Times*, 20 May 1999, p. A15; 1st Lt Kevin Gulick, '26th Intelligence Group: An Integral Part of European Operations,' *Spokesman*, Aug. 1999, http://www.aia.af.mil/commo...pages/pa/cyber spokesman/august/cover.htm.

18. Kenneth W. Dam and Herbert S. Lin (eds.), *Cryptography's Role in Securing the Information Society* (Washington DC: National Academy Press 1996) p. 97.

19. Seymour M. Hersh, 'On the Nuclear Edge,' *The New Yorker*, 29 March 1993, p. 65.

20. John M. Goshko, 'Transcripts Show Joking Cuban Pilots,' *Washington Post*, 28 Feb. 1996, pp. A1, A15; Barbara Crossette, 'US Says Cubans Knew They Fired on Civilian Planes,' *New York Times*, 28 Feb. 1996, p. 1.

21. 'Sanction Busting,' *Newsweek*, 31 Dec. 1990, p. 4. See also Director of Central Intelligence, *Annual Report on Intelligence Community Activities*, 22 Aug. 1997, at http://www.fas.org.

22. Colum Lynch, 'US Used UN to Spy on Iraq, Aides Say,' *Boston Globe*, 6 Jan. 1999, p. A1; Barton Gellman, 'Annan Suspicious of UNSCOM Probe,' *Washington Post*, 6 Jan. 1999, pp. A1, A22; Bruce W. Nelan, 'Bugging Saddam,' *Time*, 18 Jan. 1999; Seymour M. Hersh, 'Saddam's Best Friend,' *New Yorker*, 5 April

1999, pp. 32, 35; David Wise, 'Fall Guy,' *Washingtonian*, July 1999, pp. 42–3.

23. Bill Gertz, *Betrayal* (Washington DC: Regency 1999) pp. 184–6.

24. R. Jeffrey Smith and David B. Ottaway, 'Spy Photos Suggest China Missile Trade; Pressure Builds for Sanctions Builds Over Evidence Pakistan Has M-11s,' *Washington Post*, 3 July 1995, p. A1; Gertz (note 23) p. 268.

25. Bill Gertz, 'China Breaks Vow, Sends N. Korea Missile Materials,' *Washington Times*, 6 Jan. 2000, p. A16.

26. Confidential interviews with State Department officials; Regarding war crimes in Bosnia, see Roy Gutman, 'Federal Army Tied to Bosnia War Crimes/Serb Leaders "Death Camp" Link,' *Newsday*, 1 Nov. 1995, p. A4; Charles Lane and Thom Shanker, 'Bosnia: What the CIA Didn't Tell Us,' *New York Review of Books*, 9 May 1996, pp. 12–13.

27. R. Jeffrey Smith, 'Serbs Tried to Cover Up Massacre,' *Washington Post*, 28 Jan. 1999, pp. A1, A24; Jeffrey Fleishman, 'Yugoslav Official Tied to Bid to Hide Massacre,' *Philadelphia Inquirer*, 28 Jan. 1999, p. 1.

28. *Remarks at a Presentation Ceremony for the National Security Agency Worldwide Awards in Fort Meade, Maryland, May 1, 1991*, http://csdl.tamu.edu/bushlibrary/papers/1991/9105010.html.

29. 'Honoring the Best of the Best,' *NSA Newsletter*, July 1994, p. 3.

30. Commission on the Roles and Capabilities of the United States Intelligence Community, *Preparing for the 21st Century: An Appraisal of US Intelligence* (Washington DC: GPO, 1, March 1996) p. 125.

31. 'NSA Earns JMUA,' *NSA Newsletter*, July 1997, p. 6.

32. US House of Representatives, Permanent Select Committee on Intelligence, *IC21: Intelligence Community in the 21st Century*, 104th Congress, 1996, pp. 37, 120.

33. For 19 percent cut in the intelligence budget, see US Senate, Permanent Select Committee on Intelligence, Report 104–258, *Report Authorizing Appropriations for Fiscal Year 1997 for the Intelligence Activities of the United States Government*, 104th Congress, 2nd Session, 30 April 1996, p. 3; US House of Representatives, Permanent Select Committee on Intelligence, Report 104–578, *Intelligence Authorization Act for Fiscal Year 1997*, 104th Congress, 2nd Session, 15 May 1996, p. 8. For $34.5 billion figure, see 'Spying Cost US $26 billion in Fiscal '97,' *Washington Times*, 16 Oct. 1997.

34. Memorandum, Studeman to All NSA Employees, *Farewell*, 8 April 1992, NSA FOIA.

35. The $5 billion 1990 NSA budget is from Michael Wines, 'Washington Is Tired of Supporting All Those Spies,' *New York Times*, 4 Nov. 1990, p. E5; and Neil Munro, 'The Puzzle Palace in Post-Cold War Pieces,' *Washington Technology*, 11 Aug. 1994, p. 14. For the 35 percent cut in NSA's budget, see Warren P. Strobel, 'The Sound of Silence?,' *US News & World Report*, 14 Feb. 2000. For FY 1995 budget, see Tony Capaccio and Eric Rosenberg, 'Deutsch Approves $27 billion for Pentagon Spy Budgets,' *Defense Week*, 29 Aug. 1994, pp. 1, 13. For FY 1996 budget, see R. Jeffrey Smith, 'Making Connections With Dots To Decipher US Spy Spending,' *Washington Post*, 12 March 1996, p. A11.

36. US Senate, Permanent Select Committee on Intelligence, Report 104–258 (note 33); US House of Representatives, Report 104-578 (note 33). Charles Allen, 'Intelligence Community Overview for Japanese Visitors from the Public Security Investigation Agency,' 22 June 1998, located at http://cryptome.org/cia-ico.htm.

37. Memo for the NSA/CSS Representative Defense, *NSA Transition Book for the Department of Defense*, 9 Dec. 1992, p. 22.

38. For the 75,000 NSA personnel figure in 1989–1990, see Declaration of Dr. Richard W. Gronet, Director of Policy, National Security Agency, June 14, 1989, p. 5, in CIV. No. HM87-1564, *Ray Lindsey v. National Security Agency/Central Security Service*, US District Court for the District of Maryland, Baltimore, Maryland. The 50,000 figure was calculated as follows: as of 1995 the total number of military cryptologic personnel stood at 27,366 officers and enlisted men (US Army: 11,022; US Navy: 6,697; US Air Force: 8,533; US Marine Corps: 1,114; Total: 27,366), for which see 16 Nov. 1994 National Military Intelligence Association (NMIA) Briefing. The author is grateful to Dr. Jeffrey T. Richelson for this information. If one adds these personnel to the 20,000+ NSA civilians, plus the NRO, SCS, CIA and civilian contractor personnel performing Sigint missions, one comes up with a total manpower figure of slightly more than 50,000 men and women working in the USSS.

39. Authors estimates based on confidential interviews. For 38,000 strength figure, see Commission on the Roles and Capabilities of the United States Intelligence Community, *Preparing for the 21st Century: An Appraisal of US Intelligence* (Washington DC: GPO: 1996) pp. 96, 132; Jeffrey Smith (note 35).

40. Jeffrey Richelson, 'Cold War's Wake Transforms Signals Intelligence,' *Defense Week*, J24 July 1995, pp. 6–7; Hersh (note 1) p. 60. Remarks by Adm. William O. Studeman, Acting Director of Central Intelligence, at Marquette University, 20 April 1995 located at www.fas.org/inp/cia/productdci_speech_42095.html.

41. Strobel (note 35).

42. Memo for the NSA/CSS Representative Defense (note 37) p. 13, NSA POIA; Dept. of Defense, Office of the Inspector General, Report No. 96-03, *Final Report on the Verification Inspection of the National Security Agency*, 13 Feb. 1996, p. 2, DOD FOIA; Memo (note 34); 'NSA Plans for the Future,' *NSAN*, Jan. 1993, p. 4.

43. Ibid.

44. Robert L. Prestel, 'TQM at NSA,' *American Intelligence Journal* (Spring/Summer 1994) p. 44.

45. Dept. of Defense (note 42).

46. US House of Representatives, Permanent Select Committee on Intelligence, Report No. 101-1008, *Report by the Permanent Select Committee on Intelligence*, 101st Congress, 2nd Session, 2 Jan. 1991, p. 9.

47. Tom Bowman and Scott Shane, 'Congress has Tough Time Performing Watchdog Role,' *Baltimore Sun*, 15 Dec. 1995, p. 23A.

48. Dept. of Defense (note 42).

49. This works out to an average cost of $75,000 for each of NSA's approximately 20,000 civilian employees, which if correct, suggests that NSA's staff must rank as the best paid in the entire federal government! Commission on the Roles and Capabilities of the United States Intelligence Community, *Preparing for the 21st Century: An Appraisal of US Intelligence* (Washington DC: GPO, 1 March 1996) p. 125.

50. 'Let Them Eat Cake!,' *NSA Newsletter*, June 1993, p. 15.

51. US House of Representatives, Permanent Select Committee on Intelligence, *IC21: Intelligence Community in the 21st Century*, 104th Congress, (Washington DC: GPO, 1996) pp. 120–121. For the size of the Technology and Systems Directorate, see Rodney B. Sorkin Biographical Data Sheet, NSA FOIA. For cuts in infrastructure and research spending, see Commission on

the Roles and Capabilities of the United States Intelligence Community (note 49) p. 125.

52. Bowman and Shane (note 41).

53. Walter Pincus, 'Military Espionage Cuts Eyed,' *Washington Post*, 17 March 1995, p. A6.

54. Strobel (note 35).

55. Dept. of Defense (note 42) p. 3ff.

56. Colin Clark, 'Audit Finds NSA Finances in Jumble,' *Defense Week*, 10 Aug. 1998, p. 2.

57. Walter Pincus, 'Panel Ties NSA Funds to Changes at Agency,' *Washington Post*, 7 May 1998, p. A21.

58. Dept. of Defense (note 42) p. 6; Scott Wilson, 'NSA's Quest for Diversity Called Threat,' *Baltimore Sun*, 6 July 1997; Strobel (note 35).

59. Wilson (note 58) pp. 1A, 19A; Richard Lardner, "The Secret's Out,' *Government Executive*, Aug. 1998.

60. Wilson (note 58) pp. 1A, 19A; Lardner (note 59); Hersh (note 1) pp. 64, 73.

61. Confidential interview.

62. Confidential interview.

63. Wilson (note 58) pp. 1A, 19A; Lardner (note 59) Aug. 1998.

64. US House of Representatives, Permanent Select Committee on Intelligence, Report 104–578, *Intelligence Authorization Act for Fiscal Year 1997*, 104th Congress, 2nd Session, 15 May 1996, p. 8.

65. Robert K. Ackerman, 'Security Agency Transitions From Backer to Participant,' *Signal*, Oct. 1999, p. 23.

66. Monteiro (note 12) pp. 75–6; General Accounting Office, NSIAD-96-6, *Personnel Practices at CIA, NSA and DIA Compared With Those of Other Agencies*, March 1996, p. 5.

67. Richard Lardner, 'Soft Landing Effort Praised, Criticized: NSA, Industry Partnership Gives Agency Room to Move Under Personnel Ceilings,' *Defense Information and Electronics Report*, 21 Aug. 1998, p. 2; Vernon Loeb, 'Finding the Secret to Downsizing? NSA Moves Workers to Private Sector,' *Washington Post*, 29 Sept. 1998, p. A15.

68. H.D.S. Greenway and Paul Quinn-Judge, 'CIA Chief Voices Final Hopes and Fears,' *Boston Globe*, 15 Jan. 1993, p. B17; Confidential interviews.

69. Major General Gary O'Shaughnessy, USAF, 'Command Enters New Era,' *Spokesman*, Sept. 1990, p. 1; William M. Carley, 'As Cold War Fades, Some Nations' Spies Seek Industrial Secrets,' *Wall Street Journal*, 17 June 1991, p. A1, A5; David E. Sanger and Tim Weiner, 'Emerging Role for the CIA: Economic Spy,' *New York Times*, 15 Oct. 1995, pp. 1, 12; Paul Blustein and Mary Jordan, 'US Eavesdropped on Talks, Sources Say,' *Washington Post*, 17 Oct. 1995, p. B1; Scott Shane and Tom Bowman, 'America's Fortress of Spies,' *Baltimore Sun*, 3 Dec. 1995, p. 12A; Tom Bowman and Scott Shane, 'Battling High-Tech Warriors,' *Baltimore Sun*, 15 Dec. 1995, p. 22A.

70. 'Address at the CIRA Luncheon,' 5 Oct. 1998; John Millis' Speech, *CIRA Newsletter*, Winter 1998/1999, p. 6.

71. Bob Brewin, Daniel Verton, and William Matthews, 'NSA Playing IT Catch-Up,' *Federal Computer Week*, 6 Dec. 1999.

72. Lt. Gen. Kenneth A. Minihan, *Maths and National Security—A Perfect Match for the 21st Century*, Address to the Joint Meetings of the American Mathematical Society and the Mathematical Association of America, 9 Jan. 1998, Baltimore, Maryland; Dana Roscoe, 'NSA Hosts Special Partnership Breakfast,' *NSAN*, Jan. 2000, p. 4.

73. Central Intelligence Agency, 'Selected Foreign Trends in Telecommunications Technology, 1993,' in Bruce Schneier and David Banisar, *The Electronic Privacy Papers: Documents on the Battle for Privacy in the Age of Surveillance* (NY: Wiley 1997) pp. 596–607; US Army, *The United States Army Modernization Plan*, Jan. 1993, Vol. II, Annex I Intelligence/Electronic Warfare, p. 1–7; Whitfield Diffie and Susan Landau, *Privacy on the Line: The Politics of Wiretapping and Encryption* (Cambridge: MIT Press 1999) pp. 97–9; Gregory Vistica and Evan Thomas, 'Hard of Hearing,' *Newsweek*, 13 Dec. 1999.

74. Central Intelligence Agency, 'Selected Foreign Trends in Telecommunications Technology,' 1993, in Schneier and Banisar (note 73) p. 602; Ackerman (note 17) p. 23.

75. US Army (note 73); Dept. of Defense, *FY96 Electronic Warfare Plan*, April 1995, p. 2, DoD FOIA; Mark Hewish and Joris Janssen Lok, 'The Intelligent War: Signals Intelligence Demands Adaptable Systems,' *Jane's International Defense Review*, Dec. 1997, p. 28.

76. Ackerman (note 17) p. 23; Gregory Vistica and Evan Thomas, 'Hard of Hearing,' *Newsweek*, 13 Dec. 1999; Jeffrey T. Richelson, 'Desperately Seeking Signals,' *Bulletin of Atomic Scientists*, March/April 2000, pp. 47–51.

77. US Senate, Committee on Armed Services, *Department of Defense Authorization for Appropriations for Fiscal Year 1994 and The Future Years Defense Program*, 103rd Congress, First Session (Washington DC: GPO, 1993) p. 449; Urban (note 13) pp. 245–9.

78. An excellent compilation of documents relating to this issue can be found in Schneier and Banisar (note 73). See also US House of Representatives, Committee on the Judiciary, Written Statement to the House Committee on the Judiciary, Subcommittee on Courts and Intellectual Property: Hearing on H.695 'SAFE Act,' by William P. Crowell, Deputy Director, National Security Agency, 20 March 1997, pp. 9–11; Kenneth W. Dam and Herbert S. Lin, *Cryptography's Role in Securing the Information Society* (Washington DC: National Academy Press 1996) pp. 101–2; Diffie and Landau (note 73) (1999) pp. 99–101; John Markoff, 'US Export Ban Hurting Makers of New Devices to Code Messages,' *New York Times*, 19 Nov. 1990, pp. A1, D6; Neil Munro, 'The Puzzle Palace in Post-Cold War Pieces,' *Washington Technology*, 11 Aug. 1994, p. 14; Marcia Smith, *Encryption Technology: Congressional Issues* (Washington, DC: Congressional Research Service, 18 Feb. 1997) pp. 1–3.

79. Confidential interviews.

80. US House of Representatives (note 51) p. 121.

81. Confidential interviews. See also Diffie and Landau (note 73) p. 94.

82. Central Intelligence Agency, *Selected Foreign Trends in Telecommunications Technology*, 1993, in Schneier and Banisar (note 73) p. 596.

83. Confidential interview.

84. Confidential interviews. There is an unconfirmed report that terrorist leader Osama bin Laden has used encrypted cellular telephones made in Europe, for which see Gregory Vistica and Evan Thomas, 'Hard of Hearing,' *Newsweek*, 13 Dec. 1999.

85. Confidential interviews.

86. Brochure, International Telecommunications Satellite Organization *INTELSAT: The Global Telecommunications Cooperative*, 1985.

87. Memo for the NSA/CSS Representative Defense, *NSA Transition Book for the Department of Defense*, 9 Dec. 1992, Top Secret Edition, p. 19, NSA FOIA.

88. Lt. Gen. Claudia J. Kennedy, USA, 'Staying Ahead of the Threat and the Technology Curve,' *Army*, Oct. 1999, p. 152; Robert K. Ackerman, 'Security Agency Transitions From Backer to Participant,' *Signal*, Oct. 1999, p. 23.

89. The new geosynchronous Sigint satellites were launched on 25 Aug. 1994, 14 May 1995, 24 April 1996 and 8 May 1998. Jeffrey T. Richelson, *The US Intelligence Community*, 4th ed. (Boulder, CO: Westview Press 1999) p. 189; Jonathan McDowell, 'U.S. Reconnaissance Satellite Programs, Part 2: Beyond Imaging,' *Quest* 4/4 p. 43; Richelson (note 1) p. 1; 'New Blueprint for US Sigint,' *Intelligence Newsletter*, 26 Oct. 1995, p. 1; Jeffrey T. Richelson, 'Despite Management/Budget Woes, NRO Launches Continue,' *Defense Week*, 12 Aug. 1996, p. 16.

90. Confidential interview.

91. The launch dates of the 'Trumpet' Sigint satellites were 3 May 1994, 10 July 1995 and 7 Nov. 1997. Richelson, *U.S. Intelligence Community* (note 89) p. 189; Richelson (note 40) p. 1; Tom Bowman and Scott Shane, 'Battling High-Tech Warriors,' *Baltimore Sun*, 15 Dec. 1995, p. 22A; McDowell (note 89); Richelson 'Despite Management/Budget Woes' (note 89).

92. Richelson, *U.S. Intelligence Community* (note 89) p. 187; Dwayne A. Day, 'A Review of Recent American Military Space Operations,' *Journal of the British Interplanetary Society*, Dec. 1993, pp. 462–3; Walter Pincus, 'Military Espionage Cuts Eyed,' *Washington Post*, 17 March 1995, p. A6; Craig Covault, 'Titan Succeeds in NRO Flight,' *Aviation Week & Space Technology*, 31 May 1999, pp. 34–5; Bruce A. Smith, 'In Orbit,' ibid., 5 July 1999, p. 5.

93. Richelson, *U.S. Intelligence Community* (note 89) p. 190.

94. Confidential interviews.

95. CINCPACFLT Instruction S3251.1D, *Classic Wizard Reporting System*, 23 Sept. 1991, CNCPACFLT FOIA; Richelson, *U.S. Intelligence Community* (note 89) p. 14.

96. Headquarters Naval Security Group Command, 1987, *Command History*, p. 7, COMNAVSECGRU FOIA; HQNSGINST C5450.2D, *Naval Security Group Command Headquarters Organizational Manual*, 17 Sept. 1986, pp. G50-8–G50-9, COMNAVSEC GRU FOIA.

97. Richelson, *U.S. Intelligence Community* (note 89) p. 189; R. Jeffrey Smith, 'As Woolsey Struggles, CIA Suffers,' *Washington Post*, 10 May 1994, p. A7; 'New Blueprint for US Sigint,' *Intelligence Newsletter*, 26 Oct. 1995, p. 1; Confidential interviews.

98. Air Intelligence Agency, *History of the Air Intelligence Agency: 1 January–31 December 1994*, Vol. I, pp. 14, 37, AIA FOIA; Draft, FM 34–37, *Regional Signal Intelligence Operations Brigade*, http://www.fasdir/anny/fm34-37_97/7-chap.htm; Defense Airborne Reconnaissance Office (DARO), *Unmanned Aerial Vehicles (UAV) Program Plan*, April 1994, pp. 11–16; Richelson, *U.S. Intelligence Community* (note 89) pp. 197–8; Lt. Gen. Ira C. Owens, USA, 'Army Intelligence in Transition,' *American Intelligence Journal* (Autumn/Winter 1993/94) p. 18; *Spokesman*, Sept. 1993, 'Commander's Column,' p. 1; 1st Lt Tamara Cinnamo, 'Medina RSOC Stands Up,' *Spokesman*, Oct. 1993, p. 5; TSgt Gabriel Marshall, 'Road to Information Dominance,' *Spokesman*, Dec. 1995, p. 7.

99. Richelson, *U.S. Intelligence Community* (note 89) p. 200; Duncan Campbell, 'They've Got It Taped,' *New Statesman*, 12 Aug. 1998, European Parliament, Scientific and Technological Options Assessment (STOA), *Development of Surveillance Technology and Risk of Abuse of Economic Information*, April 1999, pp. 10–11; Richelson (note 76) pp. 47–51.

100. Nicky Hager, *Secret Power* (Nelson, AZ: Craig Potton 1996) p. 29; Claudio Gatti, 'License to Spy,' *Milan Il Mondo*, 20 March 1998, pp. 10–16, in FBIS-WEU-98-076; Elmar Gusseinov, 'Scandalous Echelon,' *Izvestia*, 25 Sept. 1998, at http://www.jya.com.

101. Air Intelligence Agency (note 98) p. 39, AIA FOIA; Richelson, *U.S. Intelligence Community* (note 89) p. 201; Tom Bowman and Scott Shane, 'Espionage From the Frontlines,' *Baltimore Sun*, 8 Dec. 1995, p. 20A.

102. Dept. of Defense, Office of Public Affairs, *Release No. 520-99: DOD Distinguished Civilian Service Awards Presented*, 4 Nov. 1999.

103. The US Air Force's 55th Strategic Reconnaissance Wing at Offutt Air Force Base, Nebraska flies 16 RC-135V/W 'Rivet Joint' Sigint aircraft, 2 RC-135U 'Combat Sent' ELINT collection aircraft, and 3 RC-135S 'Cobra Ball' missile monitoring aircraft. The 9th Strategic Reconnaissance Wing at Beale AFB, California flies 32 U-2R/S high-altitude reconnaissance aircraft that can be configured with a wide range of Sigint sensors depending on mission requirements. The US Navy possesses 12 EP-3 'Aries' Sigint aircraft, while the US Army flies 48 'Guardrail' Sigint aircraft and 6 Airborne Reconnaissance Low (ARL) aircraft that collect both imagery and Sigint.

104. The Navy has 13 destroyers equipped with the 'Classic Outboard' Sigint suite; and 27 *Ticonderoga*-class cruisers, 11 *Arleigh Burke*-class destroyers, 5 helicopter carriers, and 6 *Wasp*-class amphibious command ships which carry the 'Combat DF' Sigint collection system. *Cryptologic Systems Group*, http://css.rgesvc.com/LHD-7/volume2/35.htm; PMW 163 Programs, *Combat DF*, http://jmios.spawar.navy.mil/programs/program-detail.cfm; *Cryptologic Technician Training Series, Module 8—Fleet Operations—Electronic Warfare*, 1987, pp. 3–33, 3–35; Robert Holzer and Neil Munro, 'Navy Eyes Eavesdropping System,' *Defense News*, 25 Nov. 1991, p. 12; Norman Friedman, *The Naval Institute Guide to World Naval Weapons Systems, 1991/1992* (Annapolis, MD: Naval Inst. Press 1991), p. 532; and 'Duty Stations,' located at http://www.bupers.navy.mil/codes/pers2/N132D8/ctr.

105. *Signals Intelligence* (Sigint) *Umbrella Study*, Appendix B, *Hierarchy of Sigint Functions, Processes, and Tasks*, undated.

106. US House of Representatives (note 51) p. 189.

107. US House of Representatives, Permanent Select Committee on Intelligence, Report 104-578, *Intelligence Authorization Act for Fiscal Year 1998*, 105th Congress, 1st Session, 18 June 1997, p. 18.

108. Lt. Gen. Ken Minihan, USAF, *NSA/CSS Position Report*, 9 Nov. 1998, p. 6, NSA FOIA.

109. Confidential interviews.

110. Remarks by Admiral William O. Studeman, Deputy Director of Central Intelligence, at the Symposium on 'National Security and National Competitiveness: Open Source Solutions,' 1 Dec. 1992, p. 8, McLean, Virginia.

111. Ackerman (note 17) p. 23.

112. Dept. of Defense (note 42) pp. 19–20; Walter Pincus, 'Panel Ties NSA Funds to Changes at Agency,' *Washington Post*, 1 May 1998, p. A21.

113. Neal Thompson, 'Putting NSA Under Scrutiny,' *Baltimore Sun*, 18 Oct. 1998, p. 1C; Walter Pincus, 'NSA System Crash Raises Hill Worries,' *Washington Post*, 2 Feb. 2000, p. A19.

114. Scott Shane and Tom Bowman, 'America's Fortress of Spies,' *Baltimore Sun*, 3 Dec. 1995, p. 12A.

115. Neal Thompson, 'Putting NSA Under Scrutiny,' *Baltimore Sun*, 18 Oct. 1998, p. 1C; Walter Pincus, 'NSA System Crash Raises Hill Worries,' *Washington Post*, 1 Feb. 2000, p. A19.

116. Confidential interviews. See also US House of Representatives (note 51) p. 121.

117. James Bamford, 'Our Best Spies Are in Space,' *New York Times*, 20 Aug. 1998, p. A23; Bob Brewin, Daniel Verton, and William Matthews, 'NSA Playing IT Catch-Up,' *Federal Computer Week*, 6 Dec. 1999; Hersh (note 1) p. 64; David Ignatius, 'Where We Can't Snoop,' *Washington Post*, 17 April 2000, p. A21.

118. Loch K. Johnson, *Secret Agencies: US Intelligence in a Hostile World* (New Haven, CT: Yale UP 1996) p. 21; Robert D. Steele, *Improving National Intelligence Support to Marine Corps Operational Forces: Forty Specific Recommendations*, 3 Sept. 1991, p. 5, located at http://www.oss.net/Papers/reform.

119. Ackerman (note 17) p. 23.

120. Walter Pincus, 'Intelligence Community Faulted by House Panel,' *Washington Post*, 19 June 1997, p. A19.

121. Walter Pincus, 'CIA Chief Cited Loss of Agency's Capabilities,' *Washington Post*, 25 May 1998, p. A4.

122. Brewin, Verton and Matthews (note 117).

123. Hersh (note 1) p. 60.

124. Gunter Ahrendt's *List of the World's Most Powerful Computing Sites*, 1 Jan. 1999.

125. *Government Executive*, Dec. 1994, p. 24.

126. John McWethy, 'Major Failure: NSA Confirms Serious Computer Problem,' 29 Jan. 2000, *ABCNEWS.com*, located at http://abcnews.go.com/sectionsus/DailyNews/nsa-000129.html; Walter Pincus, 'NSA System Inoperative for Four Days,' *Washington Post*, 30 Jan. 2000, p. A2; Walter Pincus, 'NSA System Crash Raises Hill Worries,' *Washington Post*, 2 Feb. 2000, p. A19; Laura Sullivan, 'Computer Failure at NSA Irks Intelligence Panels,' *Baltimore Sun*, 2 Feb. 2000, p. 9A.

127. It was not until 1997 that NSA created the position of Chief Information Officer (CIO), who is responsible for planning and integrating the Agency's vast computer and telecommunications resources. 'The Agency's CIO,' *NSA Newsletter*, July 1998, p. 2.

128. For NSA owning the largest communications system in the federal government, see 'Prestigious Roger W. Jones Award Presented,' *NSA Newsletter*, Dec. 1994, p. 3. For network problems, see Ackerman (note 17).

129. Ibid.

130. Confidential interviews.

131. Confidential interview.

132. Bamford (note 117).

133. Ackerman (note 17).

134. Ibid. p. 24.

135. Brewin, Verton and Matthews (note 117).

136. Monteiro (note 12) p. 75.

137. Memo, COMNAVSECGRU Assistant Chief of Staff for Strategic Plans, Policy and Readiness to Command Historian, *1996 History Report for N3/N5*, 31 Jan. 1997, p. 4, COMNAVSECGRU FOIA; Monteiro (note 12) p. 74.

138. David A. Fulghum, 'Computer Combat Rules Frustrate the Pentagon,' *Aviation Week & Space Technology*, 15 Sept. 1997, p. 68.

139. Confidential interviews.

140. Michael S. Loescher, 'Navy Cryptology Is Broken,' *Proceedings*, Feb. 2000, p. 112.

141. Brewin, Verton, and Matthews (note 117).

142. Gregory Vistica and Evan Thomas, 'Hard of Hearing,' *Newsweek*, 13 Dec. 1999.

143. 'DIRNSA's Desk,' *NSA Newsletter*, March 1997, p. 3.

144. 'Ask DIRNSA,' *NSA Newsletter*, April 1998, p. 11.

145. Confidential interview.

146. 'Address at the CIRA Luncheon, 5 Oct. 1998; John Millis' Speech' (note 10) p. 6.

147. US House of Representatives, Permanent Select Committee on Intelligence, Report 106-130, Part 1, *Intelligence Authorization Act for Fiscal Year 2000*, 106th Congress, 1st Session, 7 May 1999, p. 12.

148. Bob Brewin, Daniel Verton, and William Matthews, 'NSA Playing IT Catch-Up,' *Federal Computer Week*, 6 Dec. 1999.

149. James Risen, 'A Top-Secret Agency Comes Under Scrutiny and May Have to Adjust,' *New York Times*, 5 Dec. 1999; Hersh (note 1) p. 62; Strobel (note 35).

150. Hersh (note 1) p. 62; Richard Lardner, 'NSA Deputy Director Under Fire as Hayden Pushes Reforms at Agency,' *Inside the Air Force*, 10 Dec. 1999; Strobel (note 35).

151. US House of Representatives, Permanent Select Committee on Intelligence, Report 105–8, *Intelligence Authorization Act for Fiscal Year 1999*, 105th Congress, 2nd Session, 5 May 1998, pp. 9–11; Walter Pincus, 'Panel Ties NSA Funds to Changes at Agency,' *Washington Post*, 1 May 1998, p. A21.

152. US Senate, Select Committee on Intelligence, Report 106-3, *Special Report: Committee Activities*, 106th Congress, 1st Session, 3 Feb. 1999, pp. 33–4.

153. Brewin, Verton and Matthews (note 117); Hersh (note 1) p. 76; Richard Lardner, 'NSA Director Aims for Control of Sigint Agency's Budgeting Process,' *Inside the Air Force*, 10 Dec. 1999; Richard Lardner, 'NSA Deputy Director Under Fire as Hayden Pushes Reforms at Agency,' ibid.; 'DIRNSA's Desk,' *NSA Newsletter*, Jan. 2000, p. 3.

154. 'NSA Deputy Chief to Quit,' *Intelligence Newsletter*, #375, 3 Feb. 2000.

155. Richard Lardner, 'New National Security Agency Director Sure to Face Major Challenges,' *Inside the Pentagon*, 5 Nov. 1998; Tabassum Zakaria, 'Top Secret US Spy Agency Shapes Up for a New World,' *Baltimore Sun*, 14 Dec. 1999.

156. Hersh (note 1) p. 76.

157. Zakaria (note 155).

158. 'A Message From the Director,' *Communicator* 2/41, 24 Oct. 1994, p. 1. ✦

Reprinted with permission from Matthew M. Aid, "The Time of Troubles: The U.S. National Security Agency in the Twenty-First Century," *Intelligence and National Security* 15 (Autumn 2000), pp. 1–32.

8

CIA's Strategic Intelligence in Iraq

Richard L. Russell

In this report on the Central Intelligence Agency's performance prior to and during the first Gulf War (1990–91), Russell gives analysts high marks for offering accurate estimates regarding Iraqi intentions and capabilities, as well as on the performance of U.S. forces in battle. Despite this laudable record, however, several controversies about the adequacy and accuracy of Agency collection emerged during the war, as key military and policy decisions hinged on the thoroughness of intelligence collection efforts.

> The CIA was the only agency to dissent: on the eve of the ground war, it was still telling the President that we were grossly exaggerating the damage inflicted on the Iraqis. If we'd waited to convince the CIA, we'd still be in Saudi Arabia.
>
> —*H. Norman Schwarzkopf,* It Doesn't Take a Hero

> War is the realm of uncertainty; three quarters of the factors on which action in war is based are wrapped in a fog of greater or lesser uncertainty.
>
> —*Carl von Clausewitz,* On War

The role of strategic intelligence in the foreign policy decision-making process at the highest echelons of government remains a neglected field of study. Much of the scholarly literature on intelligence is written from the perspective of intelligence officers, while significantly less is written from the perspective of policy makers. As Robert Gates observes,

> A search of presidential memoirs and those of principal assistants over the past 30 years or so turns up remarkably little discussion or perspective on the role played by directors of central intelligence [DCIs] or intelligence information in presidential decision making on foreign affairs,

while

> in intelligence memoir literature, although one can read a great deal about covert operations and technical achievements, one finds little on the role of intelligence in presidential decision making.[1]

The study of intelligence from the policy maker's perspective would potentially yield a more robust understanding of the strengths and weaknesses of strategic intelligence and focus attention on areas where intelligence collection and analysis need improvement. The need for improving strategic intelligence performance was painfully made clear to Americans by the tragic events of September 11, 2001, in which their intelligence community failed to detect the Osama bin Laden-orchestrated conspiracy that killed several thousand civilians on American soil.

In the United States, the principal intelligence entity responsible for providing strategic intelligence to the president is the Central Intelligence Agency (CIA). Despite media-inflated public perceptions, strategic intelligence generally plays only a modest role in the day-to-day affairs of statecraft. Michael Herman correctly points out,

> Those in CIA who produce the President's Daily Brief [PDB] and the National Intelligence Daily [NID] do not expect them to lead regularly to immediate action, any more than newspapers expect to change the world with every issue. Of all the contents of daily and weekly high-level intelligence summaries only a minute proportion feed directly into decisions.[2]

Herman notes that "the role of most intelligence is not driving decisions in any short term, specific way, but contributing to decision-takers' general enlightenment; intelligence producers are in the business of educating their masters."[3]

Strategic Intelligence and the Senior Bush Administration

The impact of strategic intelligence on the American policy-making process reached an apex with President George Herbert Walker Bush. During his administration, the United States had its first commander-in-chief who had previously served as a DCI. Few, if any, presidents had had Bush's grasp of the power—and limitations—of intelligence before occupying the Oval Office. The president who probably comes closest to Bush with prior intelligence experience was Dwight Eisenhower who, as commander of Allied forces in Europe during World

War II, had relied heavily on intelligence, particularly intercepted German communications, to inform strategy. As Christopher Andrew observes, Bush's

> experience as DCI was to give him a clearer grasp than perhaps any previous president of what it was reasonable to expect from an intelligence estimate.[4]

Ironically, Bush had accepted his appointment as DCI by President Gerald Ford with significant reservations. From his post in Beijing as chief of the U.S. Liaison Office, Bush in November 1975 telegraphed President Ford and Secretary of State Henry Kissinger his acceptance of the nomination as DCI out of a sense of duty. Bush remarked in the cable: "I do not have politics out of my system entirely and I see this as the total end of any political future."[5]

Bush proved to be less than prophetic on this score, but, as president, he personally paid close attention to intelligence and sought to integrate it into the policy-making process. Bush held a daily national security briefing at which CIA briefed him on the latest world developments. In attendance at these briefings were the President, his national security adviser Brent Scowcroft or his deputy Robert Gates—himself a former high-level CIA official and later to be DCI—his chief of staff, and once or twice per week DCI William Webster. The CIA briefer would present the PDB, a printed book, with a rundown of important intelligence reports and analyses. Bush read the PDB in the presence of the CIA briefer and Scowcroft or Gates in order to task the briefer to provide more information or have his National Security Council (NSC) staff lieutenants field policy-related questions as they emerged in the course of discussion of the intelligence briefings.[6]

The Bush administration is a particularly lucrative case for the study of the role of strategic intelligence in statecraft for several additional reasons. Most notably, the United States under Bush's leadership waged a major war in the Persian Gulf. CIA influenced the decision-making process to a degree well beyond that exercised in peacetime, because of insatiable policy-maker appetite for intelligence on Iraq and the region given the high risks to American national interests. In addition, many of the key policy makers who received a daily flood of intelligence during the war have published accounts of their time in office, which give outsiders invaluable insight into the policy-making process and can be mined for evidence of the impact of strategic intelligence on decision making. Finally, many military accounts of the war by scholars, journalists, and military officers are windows through which to view how policy makers and military commanders used intelligence during the Gulf crisis.

This article serves several purposes. First, it attempts to help fill a major gap in intelligence literature on the role of strategic intelligence in informing statecraft. Strategic intelligence in this article refers to the use of information—whether clandestinely or publicly acquired—that is synthesized into analysis and read by the senior-most policy makers charged with setting the objectives of grand strategy and ensuring that military force is exercised for purposes of achieving national interests.[7] Strategic intelligence is a tool to help ensure that civilian authorities control military means for achieving political objectives, as Clausewitz sagely wrote of war. Second, the article traces the uses and limitations of strategic intelligence in major dimensions of the Gulf War to include the warning and waging of war. The article concludes with an assessment or balance sheet of the strengths and weaknesses of strategic intelligence during the Gulf crisis. It draws insights from this case study to inform the future evolution of American intelligence and its support of statecraft, particularly in situations where policy makers face dilemmas posed by the use of armed force.

Warning of Invasion

American intelligence effectively tracked the physical build-up of Iraqi forces across the border from Kuwait in mid-July 1990. Details of the President's Daily Brief in the run-up to Iraq's invasion of Kuwait have not been publicly disclosed. Nevertheless, information from the National Intelligence Daily, CIA's current intelligence publication that received a wider dissemination among policy officials than the more tightly controlled PDB, has made its way into the public domain. The NID warned on 24 July that "Iraq now has ample forces and supplies available for military operations inside Kuwait" and during that day doubts grew as to whether Saddam Hussein was bluffing.[8] DCI Webster traveled to the White House on 24 July and briefed Bush on satellite imagery showing the movement of two Republican Guard divisions from garrisons in central Iraq to positions near the Kuwait border.[9] The NID on 25 July published an article "Iraq-Kuwait: Is Iraq Bluffing?" which stated that unless Kuwait meets Iraq's oil production demands—the ostensible Iraqi reason for military posturing along the border—Baghdad will step up pressure on Kuwait. The NID article, however, lacked specific intelligence on Saddam's intentions.[10] Working-level analysts at CIA—primarily in the Directorate of Intelligence's Office of Imagery Analysis (OIA) and Near

East and South Asia Analysis (NESA)—were the authors of analyses published in the NID.

One high-level intelligence official on the National Intelligence Council (NIC), charged with advising the DCI, was more forward leaning than the analytic judgments published in the NID. The National Intelligence Officer (NIO) for Warning Charles Allen on 25 July issued a "warning of war" memorandum in which he stressed that Iraq had nearly achieved the capability to launch a corps-sized operation of sufficient mass to occupy much of Kuwait. The memo judged that the chances of a military operation of some sort at better than 60 percent.[11] Allen on 26 July visited NSC's senior director for the Middle East Richard Haass and briefed him with satellite imagery that showed the magnitude of Iraq's military build-up near Kuwait.[12] Allen on 1 August personally informed Haass that an Iraqi attack against Kuwait was imminent. Haass, in turn, informed Scowcroft, but the White House refrained from moving to a crisis mode.[13] Other analytic voices coming from the NIC may have significantly softened the alarm of Allen's warnings in the ears of key Bush administration policy makers. The NIO for the Near East and South Asia—more directly responsible for analysis of Iraq than Allen as the NIO for Warning—wrote in a 31 July memorandum that Iraqi military action, such as seizing the Rumaila oil field straddled on the border or Kuwait islands, was likely unless Kuwait made oil concessions. The NIO for the Near East and South Asia judged, however, that a major attack to seize most or all of Kuwait was unlikely.[14]

While strategic intelligence performed well in detecting and tracking the buildup of Iraqi military hardware along the border with Kuwait, there was a dearth of human source reporting on Saddam's intentions. Such reporting was needed to give a weight of evidence to competing analytic judgments between the NIOs and the working-level CIA analysts. Although a critical mass of intelligence led CIA to conclude by the afternoon of 1 August that an Iraqi invasion was imminent, the magnitude of Iraqi invasion plans was not anticipated by working-level analysts.[15] Deputy Director for Central Intelligence Richard Kerr—briefed the mainstream analytic assessment to a Deputies Committee meeting of key policy makers chaired by Undersecretary of State Robert Kimmit late in the day on 1 August. Kimmit and other participants recall that Kerr emphasized the limited land grab Iraqi option, not a massive invasion of Kuwait.[16] Other accounts stressed that Kerr emphatically told the Deputies Committee meeting that the "Iraqis were ready to move."[17]

And move they did. Iraqi forces began their invasion of Kuwait at 0100 on the morning of 2 August. The invasion was led by two Republican Guard armored divisions, the Hammurabi and the Medina, and eventually included about 140,000 troops and 1,800 tanks. The armored divisions moved rapidly to Kuwait City, while Iraqi Special Force commandos attacked the city in advance of the armored divisions. Commandos loaded on helicopters seized key positions throughout Kuwait, including Bubyian and Warba Islands in the northern Gulf. On 3 August, a Republican Guard mechanized division secured Kuwait's border with Saudi Arabia. The 16,000-man Kuwait Army was overwhelmed. Iraqi forces fully occupied Kuwait in about twelve hours.[18]

Despite CIA's intelligence warning in the week before the invasion, Iraq's behavior had defied the Agency's earlier assessments of the regime. CIA judged in a 1989 National Intelligence estimate, "Iraq: Foreign Policy of a Major Regional Power," published under NIC auspices, that Baghdad after its bloody eight-year war with Iran needed time to rest, recuperate, and rebuild both its conventional and unconventional military power before undertaking another major war.[19] As Michael Gordon and Bernard Trainor point out, CIA and intelligence community analysts suffered from "mirror imaging" in which they projected their own American values to the Iraqis. They assumed that because the United States had needed time to rest and rebuild after its major wars, the Iraqis would have to do the same.[20]

Iraq's situation was fundamentally different than that of the United States, however. Saddam had a large standing military and no doubt feared that demobilization would let loose unemployed and weapons-trained young men into the streets who would pose a risk to his regime. Saddam, moreover, preferred to launch a war against a minor power rather than suffer humiliation from the burden of debt that he acquired to the Gulf states during his war with Iran. Paul Wolfowitz, undersecretary of defense for policy during the Gulf War, also faulted the intelligence community for not warning the policy community about the changing character of Saddam's public statements in early 1990. He has suggested,

> Somebody should have catalogued his increasingly belligerent rhetoric, compared and contrasted his statements to prior formulations, and laid out one or more plausible explanations for the change.[21]

In defense of CIA analysis though, its assessment on the eve of Iraq's invasion that Saddam would likely launch a military campaign to seize a limited piece of Kuwaiti territory was forward leaning at the time. Many of the most astute observers of Middle East politics, including Arab heads of state intimately familiar with Saddam Hussein such as King

Hussein of Jordan and President Hosni Mubarak of Egypt, were predicting that Iraq was militarily posturing to politically pressure the Kuwaitis over oil production levels. King Hussein even assured President Bush in a 31 July phone conversation that the crisis between Iraq and Kuwait would be resolved without fighting. The king told Bush, "On the Iraqi side, they send their best regards and highest esteem to you, sir."[22]

A major shortcoming in warning of the Gulf war was the lack of human intelligence to help decipher Saddam's political intentions. As Norman Schwarzkopf observed after the war, "our human intelligence was poor."[23] Civilian policy makers shared his assessment of human intelligence during the war. As Secretary of State James Baker characterized the situation, "U.S. intelligence assets on the ground were virtually nonexistent."[24] He judged that "there wasn't much intelligence on what was going on inside Iraq."[25]

Judging the Danger of Wider War

Notwithstanding CIA human intelligence shortcomings in warning of war, CIA's analysis was effective in gauging the magnitude of Iraq's invasion and potential repercussions on the international political landscape. At the first meeting of the NSC convened on 2 August to discuss the crisis, the tone of participants was that of accepting Iraq's invasion as a *fait accompli.*[26] CIA analysis delivered in the following NSC meeting on 3 August appears to have influenced the discussion of participants to a more assertive American policy stance. DCI Webster told the President and NSC officials that Saddam was consolidating his hold on Kuwait, and intelligence showed that he would not pull out despite Saddam's public pledges to do so in a couple of days. Webster warned that Saddam would control the second- and third-largest proven oil reserves with the fourth-largest army in the world, Kuwaiti financial assets, access to the Gulf, and the ability to devote money to a military buildup. Webster also noted that there was no apparent internal rival to Saddam's rule, and his ambition was to increase his power.[27] The NSC participants also discussed CIA analysis that argued that

> the invasion posed a threat to the current world order and that the long-run impact on the world economy could be devastating. Saddam was bent on turning Iraq into an Arab superpower—a balance to the United States, the Soviet Union, and Japan.[28]

As General Colin Powell, then chairman of the Joint Chiefs of Staff, recalled, Webster "gave us a bleak status report," which prompted Scowcroft to declare that "We've got to make a response and accommodating Saddam is not an option."[29]

Strategic intelligence painted a dismal picture of the threat to Saudi Arabia posed by the Iraqi military behemoth in Kuwait. Saudi forces were no match for the Iraqis, and CIA estimated that Iraqi forces could reach Riyadh—located about 275 miles south of Kuwait—in three days.[30] In the 5 August NSC meeting, Webster reported that CIA was uncertain about Saddam's intentions and that it would be difficult to provide warning of an attack on Saudi Arabia. Webster remarked, moreover, that Iraqi forces were massing on the Kuwait-Saudi border, and reinforcements were on the way giving Iraq more forces in the area than were needed solely for occupying Kuwait.[31] The minutes of the 5 August NSC meeting indicate that CIA analysts were more concerned about the potential for Iraqi offensive operations into Saudi Arabia than their Defense Intelligence Agency (DIA) counterparts.[32] By Schwarzkopf's account, it was not until mid-September that intelligence showed that Iraqi forces were moving to a defensive posture in Kuwait as Republican Guard divisions pulled back from the Saudi border and were replaced by tens of thousands of infantry digging trenches and building barricades, preparing for a long siege.[33]

The debate over whether Saddam ever had designs on Saudi Arabia continues today. The Gulf War Air Power Survey (GWAPS) concluded in retrospect that it was unlikely that Iraq had intended to invade Saudi Arabia immediately after seizing Kuwait, because Iraqi forces assumed a defensive posture to hold Kuwait rather than to prepare for further land advances.[34] Nevertheless, over the medium to longer runs, had Iraq been allowed to consolidate control over Kuwait and had the United States not intervened on the ground to defend Saudi Arabia, the Kingdom would have been an attractive target of opportunity for Saddam's forces. Saudi forces standing alone would have collapsed in the face of a massive Iraqi air and ground campaign much as the Kuwaiti military had.

Assessing Measures Short of War

In the aftermath of the Iraqi invasion, many in the United States, particularly those in the halls of Congress, were looking for American policy options short of waging war against Iraq. Many viewed economic sanctions as the best policy option to avoid the direct engagement of American troops in war overseas.

CIA analysis of international sanctions against Iraq became entangled in the policy debates taking place between the White House and Capitol Hill.[35] Webster in early August approved the dissemination of CIA's weekly reports on the effectiveness of international sanctions against Iraq to the President, Departments of State and Defense, as well as the Senate Select Committee on Intelligence and the House Permanent Select Committee on Intelligence. In general, CIA analysts judged that in the short to medium terms, sanctions seemed unlikely to force Saddam out of Kuwait.[36] Webster passed along this analytic judgment when he testified to Congress in December 1990 and said that economic sanctions had little prospect for forcing Saddam to withdraw his forces from Kuwait. Webster later reiterated this assessment in a 10 January letter to Congressman Les Aspin. He wrote that

> Our judgment remains that, even if the sanctions continue to be enforced for another six to twelve months, economic hardship alone is unlikely to compel Saddam Hussein to retreat from Kuwait or cause regime-threatening popular discontent in Iraq . . . . He [Saddam] probably continues to believe that Iraq can endure sanctions longer than the international coalition will hold and hopes that avoiding war will buy him time to negotiate a settlement more favorable to him.[37]

To a Congress eager to seek economic sanctions as a way of escaping the hard issues raised by the prospect of sending American forces to the region, CIA's bleak analytic assessment of their efficacy was not welcome news. To his credit, Webster refused to submit to the congressional browbeating intended to force him to change the Agency's assessment.

The congressional and public discourse over the wisdom of sanctions was moot, because President Bush had already determined that war probably would be necessary. After an 11 October White House meeting, Bush and his top advisers had concluded that military action, not economic sanctions, would almost certainly be needed to evict Iraq's military from Kuwait. The President also had accepted the view of Chairman Colin Powell that airpower alone was unlikely to achieve the task.[38] Historical hindsight and the eleven-year experience with the United Nations' failure to use international sanctions to compel Saddam to alter course—particularly in regard to fully disclosing the scope of his weapons of mass destruction programs—shows that CIA's judgment that sanctions would not significantly change Saddam's political behavior was accurate.

Gauging Conventional and Unconventional Military Capabilities

Intelligence estimates of Iraqi conventional military power stressed the mass of Iraqi ground forces coupled with their battlefield experience fighting the eight-year war with Iran. U.S. intelligence as-

sessed that beyond the Republican Guard divisions and eight to ten regular army divisions, the quality of Iraqi divisions significantly decreased.[39] American intelligence was effective in identifying the locations of these less capable regular Iraqi army units along the Kuwaiti border as well as those of the more capable Republican Guard units, which backed-up frontline forces in a strategic reserve in northern Kuwait and southern Iraq. CIA in late 1990 assessed that Iraq would defend in place, try to force the coalition into a war of attrition on the ground, and attempt to create a stalemate that would undermine American political resolve.[40] From Saddam's perspective, the strategy had proved its worth in Iraq's war against Iran. He probably judged that the United States, with its purported fear of casualties, would be even more vulnerable to the strategy than Iran had been.

The Agency correctly anticipated the impact of Iraq's Air Force on the course of battle. CIA in October 1990 assessed that

> The Iraqi Air Force would not be effective because it would either be neutralized quickly by Coalition air action or it would be withheld from action in hardened shelters. Within a few days, Iraqi air defenses would be limited to AAA [anti-aircraft artillery] and hand-held and surviving light SAMs [surface-to-air missiles].[41]

The course of battle clearly showed CIA analysis to be on the mark, although it had not anticipated that many Iraqi pilots would flee with their aircrafts to Iran rather than face coalition pilots in air-to-air combat.

CIA analysis paid close attention to Iraq's unconventional weapons capabilities that Baghdad worked assiduously to hide from the world. CIA had tracked the development of Iraqi chemical weapons in the course of Baghdad's war with Teheran. CIA estimated before the war that Saddam's chemical stock-pile was more than a thousand tons and included artillery rounds, bombs, and caches possibly moved into Kuwait. In fall 1990, CIA assessed that Iraq would use those stocks in the event of war with the coalition.[42] These estimates had an impact on American policy makers. As Powell recalls,

> We knew from CIA estimates that the Iraqis had at least a thousand tons of chemical agents. We knew that Saddam had used both mustard and nerve gases in his war against Iran. We knew that he had used gases on Iraq's rebellious Kurdish minority in1988, killing or injuring four thousand Kurds.[43]

CIA's grasp of Iraq's biological warfare program, however, was sketchy at best. In October 1990, American intelligence warned that "Iraq's biological weapons capability was sufficiently sophisticated to cause coalition casualties within four hours after the weapons were used."[44]

American intelligence had closely watched the growth of Iraq's ballistic missile capabilities, some of which were demonstrated in the missile exchanges between Baghdad and Teheran during the "war of the cities" in their eight-year struggle. Shortly before the war with the coalition, intelligence estimated that Iraq's inventory of Scud missiles was about 300–700, but it was uncertain as to how many were Soviet-supplied Scud-Bs and how many were longer-range Iraqi modified variants.[45] American intelligence also had identified twenty-eight concrete launch pads for the Scuds in western Iraq, while it estimated that Iraq had thirty-six mobile launchers, both Soviet-supplied and Iraqi manufactured.[46]

Intelligence estimates on Iraq's nuclear weapons program were less confident than on its ballistic missile programs and grew more conservative and alarmist as the eve of the coalition ground war approached. Before Iraq's invasion of Kuwait, intelligence judged that Iraq would not acquire nuclear weapons for five to ten years. In July 1990, Israel shared with Secretary of Defense Richard Cheney evidence that Iraqi work on high-speed centrifuges needed to enrich uranium for nuclear weapons was progressing fast, which in turn instigated a new American intelligence estimate. A special estimate prepared for President Bush in fall 1990 concluded that it would take Iraq six months to a year and probably longer to acquire a nuclear weapon.[47]

Postwar revelations made largely by United Nations weapons inspections teams gave a truer picture of the scope of Iraq's weapons of mass destruction programs. Despite the air campaign against Iraq's chemical weapons facilities, UN inspectors discovered about 150,000 chemical munitions that survived the war.[48] American intelligence, moreover, failed to detect prior to the war that Iraq had more than seventy chemical warheads for its Scud missiles.[49] UN inspectors helped to lift the shroud of secrecy surrounding the massive Iraqi nuclear weapons program. In January 1992, Iraq admitted having a uranium enrichment program to produce nuclear weapons. Baghdad had bought the components for as many as 10,000 centrifuges for the large-scale production of fissile material. Had Iraq's efforts not been interrupted by the war, Baghdad could have produced enough uranium for four bombs per year.[50] The GWAPS assessed that Iraq's nuclear weapons program was fiscally unconstrained, closer to fielding a nuclear weapon, and less vulnerable to destruction by precision bombing than U.S. intelligence realized before the war. The target list on 16 January contained two nuclear-related targets, but after the war, UN inspectors un-

covered more than twenty sites involved in the nuclear weapons program, sixteen of which were described as "main facilities."[51]

Controversy in War

In the midst of the air campaign against Iraq, major analytic disputes erupted between CIA civilian analysts and their uniformed counterparts in the Pentagon and in Schwarzkopf's Central Command (CENTCOM) staff. The initial conflict occurred over the battle damage assessment (BDA) of CENTCOM's efforts to destroy Iraqi ballistic missiles and their mobile launchers. The political pressure on Schwarzkopf to stop Iraqi missile attacks against Israel and Saudi Arabia was intense and caused him to divert substantial military resources against the problem and away from his primary concern to prepare the theater for a ground campaign to evict Iraqi troops from Kuwait. The second controversy between CIA and CENTCOM emerged over the BDA of Iraqi ground forces, which for Schwarzkopf was a barometer for determining the kick-off of the ground campaign.

A major rift in analysis emerged during the war between CIA and CENTCOM intelligence analysts over the BDA of Iraqi Scuds and mobile launchers. During the air war in January 1991, Schwarzkopf told a television interviewer that 30 fixed Scud sites had been destroyed and that his forces may have destroyed as many as 16 of about 20 suspected mobile launchers. Behind the scenes though, CIA heatedly contested Schwarzkopf's BDA of the Iraqi missiles and launchers. CIA analysts argued that there was no confirmation that any mobile launcher had been destroyed.[52]

The military continued to dispute CIA's analysis of the issue well after the war. Coalition aircrews reported destroying about 80 mobile launchers, while special operations forces claimed about 20 more, according to the GWAPS. Most of these reports stemmed from attacks against decoys or vehicles and equipment such as tanker trucks, which from a distance resembled Scud mobile launchers.[53] The GWAPS concluded after painstaking research that

> there is no indisputable proof that Scud mobile launchers—as opposed to high-fidelity decoys, trucks, or other objects with Scud-like signatures—were destroyed by fixed-wing aircraft.[54]

That judgment vindicates CIA's wartime analysis—largely conducted by its Office of Imagery Analysis—and belies the critical appraisals of CIA analysis made by Schwarzkopf and other senior commanders.

The controversy over the BDA of Iraqi ground forces had its origins in Schwarzkopf's determination that the transition from the air campaign to a ground war would occur at the point at which Iraqi ground forces had suffered a 50 percent attrition. By his own admission, the figure was solely a benchmark and not a "hard and fast rule" for gauging how much Iraqi combat power had been eroded by the air campaign. Schwarzkopf in his autobiography acknowledged that the 50 percent attrition of Iraqi order of battle was an arbitrary figure:

> Pulling a number out of the air, I said I'd need 50 percent of the Iraqi occupying forces destroyed before launching whatever ground offensive we might eventually plan.[55]

Nevertheless, Schwarzkopf reinforced the importance of this 50 percent figure in deliberations with his civilian policy masters, who were eager to achieve that mark and to kick off the ground war. As with many things though, the devil of this BDA benchmark was in the details. As the GWAPS points out, no one really knew what would constitute a measurable 50 percent attrition of Iraqi combat effectiveness. CENTCOM staffers merely applied the indicators to measurable military equipment such as tanks, armored personnel carriers, and artillery in the Kuwaiti theater of operations.[56]

CENTCOM was assessing in February 1991 that the air campaign was close to achieving the 50 percent attrition benchmark, but CIA analysts were substantially more conservative in their BDA of Iraqi ground forces. CENTCOM, for example, estimated in mid-February that it had destroyed about 1,700 Iraqi tanks or nearly 40 percent of Iraqi armor in the theater. CIA analysts, however, by examining satellite photography for blown tank turrets and shattered hulls could only confirm about one-third destroyed.[57]

CIA brought the discrepancy in BDA to the President's attention. In a PDB memorandum, it reported that CIA was unable to confirm all of CENTCOM's reported damage to Iraqi forces. CIA informally sent the PDB memorandum to Schwarzkopf who went into a rage, because he was about to make the decision to launch the ground attack. He viewed CIA as cynically hedging its bets and providing itself with an alibi in the event that the Iraqis inflicted heavy casualties on U.S. forces.[58]

President Bush asked Scowcroft to investigate the BDA dispute. On 21 February, Webster along with his NIO for conventional forces, retired Army General David Armstrong, met with Powell, Secretary of Defense Richard Cheney, and a CENTCOM representative. Armstrong argued that aside from the dispute over the numbers of tanks destroyed, CIA was not interested in usurping Schwarzkopf's command prerogatives. Armstrong reiterated that regardless of the tank tally, Iraq's army was "highly degraded."[59] Despite CIA's argument, Scowcroft realized that rejecting CENTCOM's BDA would signal a devastating loss of confidence in the military. He saw no political alternative but to side with CENTCOM in the dispute. Subsequently, Powell announced that CIA was not to conduct and report BDA, which set the precedent for the loss of that responsibility long after the Gulf War.[60]

Notwithstanding policy-maker difference to CENTCOM's BDA, postwar analysis showed CIA analysis to be superior. The House Armed Services Committee concluded that Schwarzkopf's BDA on Iraqi tanks was exaggerated by perhaps as much as 134 percent. For example, postwar analysis confirmed that 166 tanks from three Republican Guard divisions were destroyed, while CENTCOM had estimated during the war that 388 had been destroyed.[61] As had been the case in the BDA of ballistic missiles, CENTCOM's overestimation of the BDA of Iraqi ground forces was in large measure due to an overreliance on pilot reports to estimate destroyed Iraqi equipment. Pilots fly high, fast, and in hostile territory under enemy fire and have only fleeting moments to see bomb impacts. They have too small an opportunity to assess damage fairly. In contrast, satellite imagery taken after the battlefield dust has had a chance to settle is a more consistently accurate means of gauging BDA.

Drawing a Balance Sheet and Future Lessons

Before addressing the specifics of strategic intelligence performance during the Gulf War, a broad characterization of the quality of the intelligence picture at the disposal of Iraqi and American policy makers and military commanders is in order. The Iraqis, for their part, lacked an accurate strategic intelligence picture of the theater. They were blind as to the coalition force deployments that made possible the operational concept for nearly enveloping Iraqi forces in the Kuwaiti theater in the ground campaign. In marked contrast, the American intelligence community provided its consumers one of the broadest and clearest pictures of an adversary that any American president and high command has ever had in the nation's history. The United States, by Schwarzkopf's own admission during the war, had managed to identify Iraqi units "practically down to the battalion level."[62] The House Armed Services Committee concluded that American intelligence had an excellent handle on the units, locations, and equipment of Iraqi forces.[63]

That performance is hard to reconcile with the disparaging postwar assessments of CIA's performance made by Schwarzkopf and other CENTCOM commanders. One wonders what General George Patton would have given to have had a comparable picture of opposing German forces in Europe during World War II. These criticisms, moreover, neglect the fact that CIA is not designed to be a "combat support agency." CIA's charter has been to provide strategic-level intelligence primarily to civilian policy makers and not tactical intelligence to battlefield commanders. While military commanders are prone to fault CIA for perceived shortcomings, they appear reticent to fault their own military service intelligence shops and DIA whose charters are to provide tactical combat support to field commanders. Accordingly, DIA and military intelligence manpower for conducting tactical military analysis dwarfs that of CIA. The House Armed Services Committee noted that at the height of the Gulf War, about one-third of DIA's several thousand employees were assisting the war effort, a number that exceeds CIA's total analytic workforce.[64]

These observations aside, what does a balance sheet of American strategic intelligence during the Gulf War look like? On the plus side, CIA's analysis gave warning of war days before Iraq's invasion of Kuwait. CIA analysis gauged fairly well the threat posed to Saudi Arabia by a potential follow-on Iraqi attack, an assessment that probably had a major influence on the Bush administration's decision to counter and reverse Iraq's military land grab. CIA accurately assessed the dim prospects for international economic sanctions compelling Saddam to withdraw his forces from Kuwait. The international sanctions that have been on Iraq since the Gulf War have yet to compel Saddam to comply with UN demands, and it is doubtful that sanctions would have forced him to vacate Kuwait without war.

In hindsight, CIA analysts—in many cases imagery analysts—scored high marks for making accurate BDA of ballistic missile capabilities and the attrition of Iraqi ground forces even though their analysis is much maligned in the common wisdom of the lessons of the war perpetuated by military commanders. A small group of CIA imagery analysts stood alone in informing civilian policy makers that, contrary to Schwarzkopf's extravagant claims, CENTCOM had not destroyed a single Scud missile or launcher during the war. CIA's BDA, which caused substantial controversy toward the eve of the ground war, was proved with postwar analysis to be much closer to ground truth than CENTCOM's inflated BDA of Iraqi forces.

Strategic intelligence in the Gulf War has a fair number of entries in the debit side of the balance sheet. The greatest weakness of CIA's performance was its lack of human assets inside the Iraqi regime able to report on Saddam's plans and intentions. As Christopher Andrew points out,

Though a limited number of agents had been recruited in Iraqi diplomatic and trade missions abroad, none seems to have had access to Saddam's thinking or to his inner circle.[65]

The lack of human intelligence contributed to an inadequate assessment of the magnitude of Iraq's ballistic missile and weapons of mass destruction capabilities. The House Armed Services Committee judged that the intelligence community had a good estimate of Iraqi chemical weapons, while it was hard to assess the performance on the biological warfare program because the UN had extracted very little information from the Iraqis on that issue. A debate also continues as to how many ballistic missiles and mobile launchers Iraq could have preserved during the war. Strategic intelligence performed badly against Iraq's nuclear weapons program. The House Armed Services Committee report assessed that American intelligence was unaware of more than 50 percent of all major nuclear weapons installations in Iraq.[66] To fill in the intelligence gaps created by poor human intelligence, moreover, CIA analysts resorted to mirror imaging, which led analysts to judge that Iraq would only go for a limited land grab against Kuwait instead of an all-out occupation.

The poor human intelligence performance is not a lone incident in CIA's history. CIA has traditionally performed poorly in human operations against the United States's most ardent adversaries. In evaluating the performance of human intelligence one should point out the distinction that many intelligence professionals and scholars make between secrets and mysteries. Secrets are facts that can be stolen by human intelligence collectors. Mysteries, on the other hand, are projections of the future that are less vulnerable to human collection and tend to be the bailiwick of analysis.[67] As Gates reflects on CIA's human intelligence operations for gaining access to the intentions of our adversaries during the cold war,

We were duped by double agents in Cuba and East Germany. We were penetrated with devastating effect at least once—Aldrich Ames—by the Soviets, and suffered other counterintelligence and security failures. We never recruited a spy who gave us unique political information from inside the Kremlin, and we too often failed to penetrate the inner circle of Soviet surrogate leaders.[68]

CIA has done a better job of human operations against lesser nation-state threats and at stealing technical secrets, but has failed too often in the human intelligence game against the intentions of the most formidable risks to American security. With the benefits of time, hindsight, and independent review, the lack of robust human intelligence sources is likely to be found as one of the prime root causes of the intelligence failure witnessed on 11 September 2001 in New York and Washington.

In the post-cold war age, American security has a narrower margin for error because of technological advances that allow nation-states as well as nonstate actors to project force farther and weapons of mass destruction that allow them to strike with more devastating effects. In this environment, the United States needs to rectify the substantial shortcomings in human intelligence collection operations if it is to successfully deal with issues of war and peace in the future. CIA must reform and make qualitative improvements in its human intelligence operations to increase the odds that American policy makers and military commanders will have access to the thoughts and intentions of their adversaries. Even if the intentions of U.S. adversaries prove elusive and remain hidden, a critical task for human intelligence is to illuminate the policy pressures at play on foreign leaders and to help analysts narrow the range of ambiguity for American policy makers. Substantially improved human intelligence capabilities will help ensure that in the event of a future war with Iraq or any other adversary armed with ballistic missiles and weapons of mass destruction (WMD) the United States has the strategic intelligence needed to target WMD assets before these weapons are used against American troops and citizens.

A Gulf War legacy that must be redressed is the removal of a civilian check of military BDA in wartime. The civil-military intelligence controversies that emerged during the Gulf War were reminiscent of arguments during the Vietnam War, in which civilian CIA analysts were more objective than the politically and operationally tainted analyses coming from DIA and military intelligence services. Since the Gulf War, CIA has been relieved of any responsibility for BDA, and its once impressive imagery analytic capabilities have been stripped from the Agency and moved to the National Imagery and Mapping Agency, a designated combat support agency controlled by the Pentagon. To ensure that accurate and objective strategic intelligence reaches senior civilian policy makers, CIA needs to resume its exercise of independent imagery analysis and again be charged with critical reviews of military intelligence analyses in peace and war to avoid future policy debacles like those suffered—although increasingly forgotten—during the Vietnam conflict. The absence of an independent civilian analytic check on military intelligence threatens American civilian control of the military instrument for political purpose.

Questions for Further Discussion

1. To what extent was U.S. intelligence accurate in its support of the first U.S. war against Iraq in the early 1990s?

2. Why can battle damage assessments (BDA) lead to bureaucratic conflicts inside the U.S. government?

3. What was the CIA's most serious deficiency in its intelligence reporting on Iraq, and why?

4. Why is the oversight of military intelligence viewed as a major issue by the author?

Endnotes

1. Robert M. Gates, "An Opportunity Unfulfilled: The Use and Perceptions of Intelligence at the White House," *Washington Quarterly* 12 (Winter 1989): 35.
2. Michael Herman, *Intelligence Power in Peace and War* (Cambridge, UK: Cambridge University Press, 1999), 143.
3. Ibid., 144.
4. Christopher Andrew, *For the President's Eyes Only: Secret Intelligence and the American Presidency from Washington to Bush* (New York: HarperPerennial, 1995), 504.
5. "Telegram from George Bush to the President through Secretary Kissinger," 2 November 1975, George Bush Personal Papers, Subject File—China, Pre-CIA, Classified [1975–1977], George Bush Presidential Library.
6. George Bush and Brent Scowcroft, *A World Transformed* (New York: Vintage Books, 1999), 30.
7. For treatments of strategic intelligence, see Adda B. Bozeman, *Strategic Intelligence and Statecraft* (Washington, DC: Brassey's Inc., 1992); and Sherman Kent, *Strategic Intelligence for American World Policy* (Princeton: Princeton University Press, 1951).
8. Lawrence Freedman and Efraim Karsh, *The Gulf Conflict, 1990–1991: Diplomacy and War in the New World Order* (Princeton: Princeton University Press, 1993), 50.
9. U.S. News & World Report, *Triumph Without Victory: The History of the Persian Gulf War* (New York: Times Books, 1993), 21.
10. Ibid., 31–32.
11. Charles E. Allen, "Warning and Iraq's Invasion of Kuwait: A Retrospective Look," *Defense Intelligence Journal* 7 (no. 2, 1998): 40.
12. Michael R. Gordon and Bernard E. Trainor, *The Generals' War: The Inside Story of the Conflict in the Gulf* (New York: Little, Brown and Company, 1995), 16.
13. Ibid., 5–6.
14. Ibid., 25.
15. Freedman and Karsh, *Gulf Conflict*, 73.
16. Gordon and Trainor, *Generals' War*, 28.
17. U.S. News & World Report, *Triumph Without Victory*, 33, 18.
18. Freedman and Karsh, *Gulf Conflict*, 67.
19. Gordon and Trainor, *Generals' War*, 9.
20. Ibid., 11.
21. Jack Davis, "Paul Wolfowitz on Intelligence-Policy Relations," *Studies in Intelligence* 39 (no. 1, 1995): 7.
22. Memorandum of Telephone Conversation, "Telephone Conversation with King Hussein," 31 July 1990,

OA/ID CF01043, Richard N. Haass Files, Working Files-Iraq, National Security Council, George Bush Presidential Library.

23. H. Norman Schwarzkopf and Peter Petre, *It Doesn't Take a Hero* (New York: Bantam Books, 1992), 319.

24. James A. Baker III with Thomas M. DeFrank, *The Politics of Diplomacy: Revolution War and Peace, 1989–1992* (New York: G.P. Putnam's Sons, 1995), 7.

25. Ibid., 267–268.

26. Bush and Scowcroft, *World Transformed*, 317.

27. Ibid., 322–323. The oil-related estimates in Webster's brief probably originated in an analytic paper on world oil reserves prepared by economists in CIA's Office of Resource, Technology, and Trade. See U.S. News & World Report, *Triumph Without Victory*, 65. For a first-hand account of the NSC meeting, see Memorandum for Brent Scowcroft, "Minutes from NSC Meeting, 3 August 1990, on Persian Gulf," OA/ID CF01518, Richard N. Haass Files, Working Files—Iraq, National Security Council, George Bush Presidential Library.

28. Bob Woodward, *The Commanders* (New York: Simon & Schuster, 1991), 237.

29. Colin L. Powell with Joseph E. Persico, *My American Journey* (New York: Random House 1995), 463–64.

30. Freedman and Karsh, *Gulf Conflict*, 88.

31. Bush and Scowcroft, *World Transformed*, 334.

32. Memorandum for William F. Sittman from Richard N. Haass, "Minutes of NSC Meeting on Iraqi Invasion of Kuwait, 5 August 1990," 18 August 1990, OA/ID CF00873, Richard N. Haass Files, Working Files-Iraq, National Security Council, George Bush Presidential Library.

33. Schwarzkopf and Petre, *It Doesn't Take a Hero*, 346.

34. Thomas A. Keaney and Eliot A. Cohen, *Revolution in Warfare? Air Power in the Persian Gulf* (Annapolis, MD: Naval Institute Press, 1995), 4. This book is an unclassified summary of the multi-volume Gulf War Air Power Study led by Cohen and commissioned by Secretary of the Air Force Donald Rice in 1991.

35. For an analysis of CIA's unique bureaucratic position, situated between the executive and legislative branches of government, see Robert M. Gates, "The CIA and Foreign Policy," *Foreign Affairs* 66 (Winter 1987/88): 215–230

36. U.S. News & World Report, *Triumph Without Victory*, 150.

37. Letter, William H. Webster to Les Aspin, 10 January 1991, OA/ID CF 01361, Virginia Lampley Files, National Security Council, George Bush Presidential Library.

38. Gordon and Trainer, *Generals' War*, 139.

39. Freedman and Karsh, *Gulf Conflict*, 288.

40. Keaney and Cohen, *Revolution in Warfare?* 108.

41. Ibid., 108.

42. Rick Atkinson, *Crusade: The Untold Story of the Persian Gulf War* (Boston: Houghton Mifflin,1993), 86.

43. Powell, *My American Journey*, 468.

44. Atkinson, *Crusade*, 88.

45. Gordon and Trainor, *Generals' War*, 230.

46. Ibid., 230.

47. Freedman and Karsh, *Gulf Conflict*, 220.

48. Keaney and Cohen, *Revolution in Warfare?* 71.

49. Gordon and Trainor, *Generals' War*, 183.

50. Freedman and Karsh, *Gulf Conflict*, 321.

51. Keaney and Cohen, *Revolution in Warfare?* 67.

52. Atkinson, *Crusade*, 144–145.

53. Keaney and Cohen, *Revolution in Warfare?* 73.

54. Ibid., 78.

55. Schwarzkopf and Petre, *It Doesn't Take a Hero*, 319.

56. Keaney and Cohen, *Revolution in Warfare?* 40–41.

57. Atkinson, *Crusade*, 345.

58. Ibid., 266.

59. Ibid., 346.

60. Ibid., 347.

61. U.S. House of Representatives, Committee on Armed Services, Subcommittee on Oversight and Investigations, "Intelligence Successes and Failures in Operations Desert Shield/Storm," August 1993, 4 and 31. Hereafter cited as House Report. CIA published an unclassified study "Operation Desert Storm: A Snapshot of the Battlefield" in September 1993, which graphically depicts the highlights of battle in the Kuwait theater of operations.

62. Powell, *My American Journey*, 474.

63. House Report, 4.

64. House Report, 7.

65. Andrew, *For the President's Eyes Only*, 533.

66. House Report, 30.

67. The author is indebted to Robert Gates for reminding him of this important distinction. For a discussion of the role of secrets and mysteries in intelligence estimates, see Joseph S. Nye, Jr., "Peering Into the Future," *Foreign Affairs* 73 (July/August 1994): 82–93.

68. Robert M. Gates, *From the Shades: The Ultimate Insider's Story of Five Presidents and How They Won the Cold War* (New York: Simon and Schuster, 1997), 560. ✦

Reprinted with permission from Richard L. Russell, "CIA's Strategic Intelligence in Iraq," *Political Science Quarterly* 117 (Summer 2002): 191–207.

Part III

Intelligence Analysis

Hamlet: "There are more things in heaven and
earth Horatio,
Than are dreamt in your philosophy!"

—*Shakespeare*, Hamlet, *1.5.167–169*

The hardest and most unforgiving task in the intelligence cycle is analysis. It is difficult because the fundamental problem facing intelligence analysts is that all information is inherently ambiguous. Most raw data about the world around us reaches us without any indication about its importance, its inherent meaning, or what it portends for the future. It is up to analysts to place this information in its historical context, in the context of current events, or in an appropriate analytical framework to uncover its meaning and significance so that policymakers or senior military officers can respond appropriately. Yet analysts sometimes lack the appropriate theoretical or historical framework to identify signals, lack accurate information about what is about to happen, and must deal with noise—misleading or superfluous information about coming events (Wohlstetter 1962). In fact, the dominant view among observers is that failures of intelligence are inevitable and that when they occur, important signals are always found in the intelligence pipeline that embarrass analysts and lead to much acrimony about the latest intelligence failure.

To avoid surprise, intelligence analysts often have to use old information to predict the future. Information about ship movements or what happened at some clandestine meeting, for example, might reach them hours or even weeks after actual events, but analysts have to use this rather dated information to gain insight into an even more distant future. In a sense, they are in a race to use old information to predict what is about to unfold, before events catch them by surprise. The target of intelligence analysts always has a head start in the race, and sometimes analysts fail to close the information gap before it is too late. The history of surprise is in fact replete with warnings that were *almost* issued in time: A message warning of the possibility of hostile Japanese action, for instance, reached the U.S. Navy commander at Pearl Harbor just as the attackers headed for home. Intelligence analysts thus face a deadline, but they can never be quite sure how much time they have left before their effort to develop an accurate estimate of the future is literally overtaken by events.

On the rare occasions when they obtain clear indications of what is about to happen, analysts also have to be wary. Opponents often use denial (efforts to hide their true intentions or operations) and deception (inaccurate information about current operations and intentions) to mislead analysts. Denial and deception can take many forms. Sometimes it is best to hide information from the prying eyes of reconnaissance satellites or agents on the ground so that accurate information fails to reach analysts. Sometimes intelligence targets will try to blend into their surroundings to try to make themselves appear innocuous. This is a good way to hide, because intelligence agencies lack the resources to monitor people, organizations, or states that appear to be engaged in routine and nonthreatening kinds of activities. Deception can also take the form of exaggerating one's capabilities in the effort to ward off attack or coerce opponents who might alter their policies because they mistakenly believe that they are in a weak military or diplomatic position. Denial and deception thus create a host of problems for analysts. When things sound too good to be true, analysts should suspect deception, because they face an opponent who would like to do nothing more than put their minds at ease while carrying out some nefarious scheme. When things become too quiet, analysts should suspect that collection systems might be failing to alert them to potential problems. For intelligence analysts, no news, or the fact that events seem to be going according to plan, is not necessarily good news.

Analysts also have to deal with the fact that the actions of some opponents might defy logic or be fundamentally irrational in that they fail to further the known objectives of the state or nonstate actor in question. Governments, militaries, bureaucracies, and terrorist syndicates have multiple decision centers, factions, and interests, and it is often difficult to harness all these individuals and organizations into unified and purposive behavior. Analysts might be correct in predicting what action an opponent should take, but they might turn out to be wrong when the opponent lacks the organizational or political wherewithal to carry out the predicted action. In other words, even if analysts discover what another state or nonstate actor intends to do, they cannot say categorically that it will occur, because the other party might not be able to implement its plan.

States or nonstate actors who seek to surprise their opponents often do so out of desperation. They generally lack the military, diplomatic, or economic resources to achieve their objectives without the force multiplier offered by surprise. They want to present their opponents with a *fait accompli*, then hope they will reach a negotiated settlement before their opponents rally to reverse the gains obtained from using surprise. The fact that state and nonstate actors can launch what amounts to a reckless gamble creates real problems for intelligence analysts. States and nonstate actors wishing to achieve surprise are engaged in an extraordinarily risky enterprise, which often, with good reason, looks implausible to intelligence analysts. Prior to the Cuban Missile Crisis, for example, analysts at the CIA predicted that the Soviet Union would not place offensive missiles in Cuba, because such an action would prompt a strong reaction from the United States and prove to be counterproductive. In effect, analysts recognized the possibility that the Soviets might place offensive missiles in Cuba, but they dismissed this course of action as implausible because it entailed too much risk from the Soviet perspective (Wirtz 1998).

The risk inherent in the effort to gain the element of surprise, according to Michael Handel, creates a paradox that works against intelligence analysts:

"The greater the risk, the less likely it seems, and the less risky it becomes. In fact, the greater the risk, the smaller it becomes" (Handel 1977, 468). So even when intelligence analysts detect signals of what is about to happen, they often dismiss these signals as too fantastic to be credible. Or even worse, they find it impossible to convince senior officials that the opponent is about to launch what appears to be a hare-brained operation. It might be impossible to improve on the Bard, but this might be a good way to think about the challenge of intelligence analysis: There are, in fact, more things in life than we can dream of; the opponent is likely to pick one of them and to try to hide it from us, and analysts will have extraordinary difficulty convincing senior officials that something bad is about happen.

Impediments to Accurate Analysis

Only the most creative and diligent minds can succeed as analysts. Good analysts have to be able to step outside the conventional military, diplomatic, and bureaucratic wisdom of their day to see vulnerabilities and opportunities that others might be tempted to exploit. They also face real-time constraints when it comes to generating their analysis. Estimates have to be accurate and delivered to officials or military officers in time to be used effectively.

Over the years, scholars and intelligence professionals have worked hard to understand general challenges in the process of intelligence analysis and the specific kinds of problems that can trip up analysts. Often, these studies come in the aftermath of spectacular events, and they tend to focus on the problems that seem to have contributed to the latest failure of intelligence. After Pearl Harbor, for instance, it appeared that a lack of "all-source" intelligence might have contributed to intelligence failure, so the Central Intelligence Agency was created to guarantee that at least one organization would have access to all of the data collected by the U.S. intelligence community. Although it is still too early to know what reforms will follow in the aftermath of the September 11, 2001 tragedy, it is likely that information gathered by local and federal law enforcement agencies will eventually be integrated into the all-source intelligence picture available to analysts and government officials. Despite the episodic attention that intelligence analysis receives, scholars and practitioners seem most concerned about problems that are idiosyncratic to intelligence analysis and about the constraints created by the limits of human cognition and organizational pathologies.

Idiosyncratic Challenges

Although intelligence analysis shares many similarities with journalism or academic research, several aspects of turning raw data into finished intelligence are unique and create special problems for analysts. A host of these idiosyncratic challenges exist. Probably the best-known challenge is the "cry wolf" syndrome. Analysts have to be careful about repeatedly issuing warnings that fail to materialize, because policymakers are likely to stop heeding alerts if they turn out to be false alarms. Responding to warning also is not without costs. Forcing an opponent to respond repeatedly to false alarms is a good way to create operational, financial, and political strains that soften it up for the real initiative. The "ultra" syndrome, named after the intelligence obtained from decrypted Nazi radio communications in World War II, occurs when analysts become overly dependent on highly valuable intelligence gained from a credible and reliable source. At a critical moment, however, the source might fail to produce important information for any number of reasons, and analysts might be caught without other sources or methods to track important developments. Alternatively, analysts might take the absence of information from a credible source as evidence that nothing important is going on, a judgment that can lull them into a false sense of security even when other indicators suggest that trouble is brewing (Kam 1988).

Because developing estimates of what is going to happen in the future is so difficult and unforgiving, analysts and the intelligence production process can fall into routines that are reassuring but that in the end prove to be highly counterproductive. Intelligence reports that are supposed to provide insight into future events can sometimes become reports on what has happened in the recent past or compilations of reports about past activities. Instead of offering a glimpse into the future, finished intelligence can take on a historical quality by summarizing events over the last few days or weeks. This "historical intelligence" often carries greater weight than more speculative intelligence about the future, because it is grounded in real evidence about past events. Information about what *has* happened is far more credible to the reader than information about what *might* happen.

A similar type of problem emerges when intelligence estimates become a matter of routine, involving the repeated assertion of key analytical judgments without recognition of either the passage of time or changing circumstances. Intelligence estimates having to do with the development of weapons systems often fall into this trap. For instance, in the years immediately following World War II, it was widely assumed that the Soviet Union would need about five years to acquire an atomic bomb. This estimate was repeated in 1946, 1947, 1948, and 1949—the year that the Soviets actually detonated their first nuclear device. Apparently, analysts lost track of the fact that the five-year window at the heart of their analysis was not a moving target but was instead pegged to 1945. The "five-year window" actually is rather common in intelligence estimates—especially in predictions of how long it might take for a state or nonstate actor to develop chemical, biological, or nuclear weapons and associated delivery systems—because it allows analysts to draw attention to a problem without setting in motion difficult political, economic, or military actions to deal with it. By predicting something that might happen in the relatively distant future, one can still claim that a warning was given, without forcing policymakers to act immediately to solve the problem.

The Limits of Human Cognition

Humans everywhere share one thing that transcends culture, history, and politics: human cognition and psychology. Whether they are leaders or led, highly educated or poorly educated, world travelers or stay-at-home country bumpkins, they all share the same cognitive biases and patterns of perception. Analysts, however, must struggle to overcome their own psychological presets if they are going to avoid cognitive pitfalls that often bedevil the analytic process.

First, people generally do not realize that their initial perception of the world occurs without much conscious awareness. Although cognitive psychologists might cringe at this explanation, our minds use what amounts to a pattern recognition program to help order the world around us and to bring a reality we recognize to our conscious mind (Heuer 1999). Without this precognition, we would be condemned to forever revisit first principles, to spend all our time just interpreting our sensory perceptions. If this situation were to occur, it would be extraordinarily difficult for us to learn or to generalize across various experiences and events. But because this precognition is extremely powerful, it can be dangerous from the analyst's perspective. If his or her mind places incoming data into the wrong pattern, the analyst will find it difficult to reinterpret the data in a more useful way or in a way that better corresponds to reality.

Second, how we interpret events or others' actions is often shaped by a series of cognitive biases. When others do something that has a negative effect on us, we tend to see them as evil people who intended to harm us, but when we do something that has a negative impact on others, we tend to see ourselves as having no choice in the matter, as being boxed in by circumstances. This thinking pattern is known as the *fundamental attribution error*. Similarly, people tend to take too much credit for the good things that happen and take too little blame when bad things happen. These biases complicate analytical work, because they prevent analysts from recognizing weaknesses that can be exploited by opponents or ways their own country is contributing to a deteriorating international situation. People also tend to interpret information in terms of what is on their mind when they receive the information or what comes to mind when they hear the information. Individuals interpret the world around them not based on the collected wisdom of humankind but in terms of living memory and experience, especially the vivid events that happen in their lives. This phenomenon is known as the *availability principle*. Thus, the life experiences and educational background of analysts is critical to the process of producing finished intelligence, because analysts have to compare incoming information with the historical and theoretical knowledge they possess to generate a useful estimate.

The key point to remember about the impact of human cognition on intelligence analysis is that the human mind tends to fill in the missing pieces of information, sometimes in ways that are difficult for analysts to recognize. For instance, *mirror imaging* often is a problem for analysts. That is, it generally is difficult for them to see the world from another person's perspective, especially when their differences with the person are created by a lack of shared cultural or historical perspective. But in the absence of clear information about what motivates others, analysts will "mirror image" by projecting their own values and motivations onto others in an effort to interpret these others' behavior. Analysis based on mirror imaging rarely is productive, because it tends to place data in a wrong analytical framework, which easily produces misleading estimates.

Organizational Pathologies

Because most intelligence analysis takes place in an institutional setting, bureaucracy itself can have a negative impact on the process of creating finished intelligence. Analysts can become preoccupied with defending institutional turf by keeping analysts from other organizations from undertaking work that replicates or contradicts their estimates. Organizations have a keen interest in preventing others from encroaching on their mission and issue domain, because they are interested in preserving their slice of the budgetary pie. Defending an organization's past positions on a given issue can also get in the way of honest estimates of a developing situation; it is difficult to admit that past estimates might have been inaccurate, because such an admission would call into question the usefulness of current intelligence products.

Organizations also have to create the proper working atmosphere to encourage analysts to take risks and to think "outside the box," to use a popular phrase. Although a full discussion of the issue of intelligence politicization must wait for Part IV, we should mention here that organizations must send a message to their rank and file that those who make bold predictions will not suffer negative consequences if their estimates fail to materialize. Intelligence organizations must cultivate independent thinkers, even if they sometimes ignore bureaucratic decorum to make their opinions known. Indeed, if signals can always be found somewhere in the intelligence production process in the aftermath of an analytic failure, more often than not an "intelligence dissenter" can be found in the organization, someone who bucked the conventional wisdom and predicted accurately what was about to happen. An organization that can empower these dissenters so that their views obtain a fair hearing can greatly improve its performance. Of course, too much free thinking can produce disorder, acrimony, and a failure to reach a conclusion or consensus that policymakers might put to good use (Odom 2003). Striking a balance between consensus and healthy debate is a never-ending struggle for those who manage the production of finished intelligence.

Intelligence organizations are also prone to specific bureaucratic problems related to the process of intelligence production. Secrecy and compartmentalization lie at the heart of intelligence analysis; after all, this is what distinguishes secret organizations from other organizations (newspapers, television networks, Internet sites) that disseminate information to government officials, military officers, and the general public. Secrecy can impede analysis, because as information becomes increasingly sensitive, the number of analysts who have the necessary clearances to view the information diminishes. Moreover, finished intelligence based on highly sensitive sources often is distributed only to a limited number of individuals; these restrictions can have negative consequences if the people who can put the information to good use are not given access to finished intelligence.

Compartmentalization also is an effort to restrict the dissemination of information within intelligence organizations. If a hostile agent penetrates an organization by becoming a trusted agent or operative, compartmentalization prevents that person from gaining access to all the secrets kept by an agency. But compartmentalization impedes the efforts of analysts to develop a comprehensive intelligence estimate. If various analysts are allowed to look at only a small piece of the intelligence puzzle, will they know who else holds the other critical pieces, or will they ever be able to figure out the whole picture from just a few pieces of information?

The Readings

The articles that follow provide a sense of the difficult challenges faced by intelligence analysts. Few articles shape an entire intellectual endeavor, but "Analysis, War, and Decision," by Richard Betts of Columbia University, made that type of contribution to the field of intelligence analysis. The careful reader will detect that many of the themes raised in this opening essay are expressed forcefully and clearly in Betts' analysis. In describing the cognitive, idiosyncratic, and bureaucratic challenges faced by analysts, Betts states that it is not possible to use organizational reforms to overcome all of these problems simultaneously, because making progress in resolving one type of problem only makes other problems worse. Eliminating false alarms, for example, only makes it more likely that analysts will fail to respond to signals of real danger. Betts' article is probably best known for his bold judgment, made at the outset of the piece, that intelligence failures are inevitable and that despite the resources invested and the reforms undertaken, it is realistic to expect only marginal improvements in the performance of intelligence organizations. But his article also offers an outstanding overview of the problems that can creep up as analysts try to place raw intelligence in some useful context and convince policymakers that they should act on their estimates.

Although the information revolution has transformed how we live and work, use of the enormous volume of information now available on the World Wide Web or from commercial sources has been hotly debated within the intelligence community. Many intelligence professionals minimize the role and use of open-source intelligence ("osint") because it seems to threaten their *raison d'être:* the collection, analysis, and dissemination of classified information. It also causes them embarrassment when they are scooped by the news media: CNN is an ever-present companion in intelligence and policy shops throughout the U.S. government. In "Open Source Intelligence," Robert D. Steele, perhaps the world's leading advocate of osint, describes how this particular "int" can contribute not only to the making of foreign and defense policy and to the production of finished intelligence but also to the general betterment of humankind. Steele describes the

various kinds of insights that can be gained from information contained on the Web and how this information can be applied in a variety of governmental and nongovernmental applications. Although osint plays an ever-increasing role in the process of producing finished intelligence, whether analysts will find an effective way to cull important information from the Web is a question that remains up in the air.

In a candid description of not only what life is like for a senior policymaker but also how intelligence can contribute to policymaking itself, Ambassador Robert D. Blackwill explains how analysts from the Office of European Analysis (EURA) supported him as he represented U.S. interests in various forums. Blackwill's description of 18-hour workdays and an inability to pay attention to anything not related to the immediate problem in his in-box should change the minds of those who think the life of a senior official is glamorous. "A Policymaker's Perspective on Intelligence Analysis" also describes how Blackwill found finished intelligence directed toward a general audience of no particular value and how he cultivated personal and professional relationships to obtain outstanding staff and analytical support from EURA. Blackwill tells a rare story in the literature on the nexus between intelligence and policy, a story of an outstanding intelligence success. Even though it appears mundane, it really is no small accomplishment. Blackwill describes the bureaucratic obstacles that had to be overcome and the personal sacrifices that had to be made by analysts to create a useful exchange between intelligence professionals and policymakers.

Shlomo Gazit offers a systematic overview of the relationship between intelligence professionals and policymakers in "Intelligence Estimates and the Decision-Maker." Gazit agrees with Blackwill that intelligence requires a reciprocal or two-way relationship between those in charge of making policy and those in charge of intelligence, and he highlights his observations about theory and organization with examples drawn from the Israeli experience. He also offers a fine discussion of the different types of estimates that intelligence analysts prepare and of the limits of each type of analysis. Gazit demonstrates that analysts and policymakers have different perspectives and needs and that to be useful, intelligence professionals must find ways to bridge the gap between them. It is not sufficient for analysts to develop accurate estimates. An effective relationship has to be in place between policymakers and analysts before the moment of crisis when clear and accurate communication becomes a matter of life and death.

The final essay explores the performance of intelligence organizations in moments of crisis. Ephraim Kahana's "Early Warning Versus Concept: The Case of the Yom Kippur War 1973" describes the failure of Israeli intelligence to warn of an impending Arab attack. Kahana describes how human cognition influences judgment and perception by examining in detail how the analytical framework shared by Israeli intelligence professionals and policymakers—"the concept," to borrow Kahana's term—shaped the way information was interpreted on the eve of the Yom Kippur War. Echoes of the failure of Israeli intelligence to anticipate the attack continue to reverberate within the Israeli defense and intelligence communities today, and the study of the failure has greatly enhanced our common understanding of warning and surprise. ✦

9

Analysis, War, and Decision: Why Intelligence Failures Are Inevitable

Richard K. Betts

The history of diplomatic and military affairs is riddled with instances when intelligence analysts failed to provide timely warning of what was about to unfold. Betts presents a strong explanation of why intelligence failures are inevitable, as well as insights into the myriad challenges that analysts must overcome to offer useful estimates of future events. In arguing that the nature of intelligence analysis prevents all but modest improvements in the performance of intelligence organizations, Betts offers a compelling argument that continues to serve as the conventional wisdom on the limits of intelligence reform and analysis.

Military disasters befall some states, no matter how informed their leaders are, because their capabilities are deficient. Weakness, not choice, is their primary problem. Powerful nations are not immune to calamity either, because their leaders may misperceive threats or miscalculate responses. Information, understanding, and judgment are a larger part of the strategic challenge for countries such as the United States. Optimal decisions in defense policy therefore depend on the use of strategic intelligence: the acquisition, analysis, and appreciation of relevant data. In the best-known cases of intelligence failure, the most crucial mistakes have seldom been made by collectors of raw information, occasionally by professionals who produce finished analyses, but most often by the decision makers who consume the products of intelligence services. Policy premises constrict perception, and administrative workloads constrain reflection. Intelligence failure is political and psychological more often than organizational.

Observers who see notorious intelligence failures as egregious often infer that disasters can be avoided by perfecting norms and procedures for analysis and argumentation. This belief is illusory. Intelligence can be improved marginally, but not radically, by altering the analytic system. The illusion is also dangerous if it abets overconfidence that systemic reforms will increase the predictability of threats. The use of intelligence depends less on the bureaucracy than on the intellects and inclinations of the authorities above it. To clarify the tangled relationship of analysis and policy, this essay explores conceptual approaches to intelligence failure, differentiation of intelligence problems, insurmountable obstacles to accurate assessment, and limitations of solutions proposed by critics.

I. Approaches to Theory

Case studies of intelligence failures abound, yet scholars lament the lack of a theory of intelligence.[1] It is more accurate to say that we lack a positive or normative theory of intelligence. Negative or descriptive theory—the empirical understanding of how intelligence systems make mistakes—is well developed. The distinction is significant because there is little evidence that either scholars or practitioners have succeeded in translating such knowledge into reforms that measurably reduce failure. Development of a normative theory of intelligence has been inhibited because the lessons of hindsight do not guarantee improvement in foresight, and hypothetical solutions to failure only occasionally produce improvement in practice. The problem of intelligence failure can be conceptualized in three overlapping ways. The first is the most reassuring; the second is the most common; and the third is the most important.

1. Failure in Perspective

There is an axiom that a pessimist sees a glass of water as half empty and an optimist sees it as half full. In this sense, the estimative system is a glass half full. Mistakes can happen in any activity. Particular failures are accorded disproportionate significance if they are considered in isolation rather than in terms of the general ratio of failures to successes; the record of success is less striking because observers tend not to notice disasters that do not happen. Any academician who used a model that predicted outcomes correctly in four out of five cases would be happy; intelligence analysts must use models of their own and should not be blamed for missing occasionally. One problem with this benign view is that there are no clear indicators of what the ratio of failure to success in intelligence is, or whether many successes on minor issues should be reassuring in the face of a smaller number of failures on more critical problems.[2] In the thermonuclear age, just *one* mistake could have apocalyptic consequences.

2. Pathologies of Communication

The most frequently noted sources of breakdowns in intelligence lie in the process of amassing timely data, communicating them to decision makers, and impressing the latter with the validity or relevance of the information. This view of the problem leaves room for optimism because it implies that procedural curatives can eliminate the dynamics of error. For this reason, official post mortems of intelligence blunders inevitably produce recommendations for reorganization and changes in operating norms.

3. Paradoxes of Perception

Most pessimistic is the view that the roots of failure lie in unresolvable trade-offs and dilemmas. Curing some pathologies with organizational reforms often creates new pathologies or resurrects old ones;[3] perfecting intelligence production does not necessarily lead to perfecting intelligence consumption; making warning systems more sensitive reduces the risk of surprise, but increases the number of false alarms, which in turn reduces sensitivity; the principles of optimal analytic procedure are in many respects incompatible with the imperatives of the decision process; avoiding intelligence failure requires the elimination of strategic preconceptions, but leaders cannot operate purposefully without some preconceptions. In devising measures to improve the intelligence process, policy makers are damned if they do and damned if they don't.

It is useful to disaggregate the problem of strategic intelligence failures in order to elicit clues about which paradoxes and pathologies are pervasive and therefore most in need of attention. The crucial problems of linkage between analysis and strategic decision can be subsumed under the following categories:

1. Attack Warning

The problem in this area is timely prediction of an enemy's immediate intentions, and the "selling" of such predictions to responsible authorities. Major insights into intelligence failure have emerged from catastrophic surprises: Pearl Harbor, the Nazi invasion of the U.S.S.R., the North Korean attack and Chinese intervention of 1950, and the 1973 war in the Middle East. Two salient phenomena characterize these cases. First, evidence of impending attack was available, but did not flow efficiently up the chain of command. Second, the fragmentary indicators of alarm that did reach decision makers were dismissed because they contradicted strategic estimates or assumptions. In several cases hesi-

tancy in communication and disbelief on the part of leaders were reinforced by deceptive enemy maneuvers that cast doubt on the data.[4]

2. Operational Evaluation

In wartime, the essential problem lies in judging the results (and their significance) of interacting capabilities. Once hostilities are under way, informed decision making requires assessments of tactical effectiveness—"how we are doing"—in order to adapt strategy and options. In this dimension, the most interesting insights have come from Vietnam-era memoirs of low-level officials and from journalistic muckraking. Again there are two fundamental points. First, within the context of a glut of ambiguous data, intelligence officials linked to operational agencies (primarily military) tend to indulge a propensity for justifying service performance by issuing optimistic assessments, while analysts in autonomous non-operational units (primarily in the Central Intelligence Agency and the late Office of National Estimates) tend to produce more pessimistic evaluations. Second, in contrast to cases of attack warning, fragmentary tactical indicators of *success* tend to override more general and cautious strategic estimates. Confronted by differing analyses, a leader mortgaged to his policy tends to resent or dismiss the critical ones, even when they represent the majority view of the intelligence community, and to cling to the data that support continued commitment.[5] Lyndon Johnson railed at his Director of Central Intelligence (DCI) at a White House dinner:

> Policy making is like milking a fat cow. You see the milk coming out, you press more and the milk bubbles and flows, and just as the bucket is full, the cow with its tail whips the bucket and all is spilled. That's what CIA does to policy making.[6]

From the consensus-seeking politician, this was criticism; to a pure analyst, it would have been flattery. But it is the perspective of the former, not the latter, that is central in decision making.

3. Defense Planning

The basic task in using intelligence to develop doctrines and forces for deterrence and defense is to estimate threats posed by adversaries, in terms of both capabilities and intentions, over a period of several years. Here the separability of intelligence and policy, analysis and advocacy, is least clear. In dealing with the issue of "how much is enough" for security, debates over data merge murkily into debates over options and programs. As in operational evaluation, the problem lies more in data mongering than in data collecting. To the extent that stark generalizations are possible, the basic points in this category are the reverse of those in the previous one.

First, the justification of a mission (in this case, preparedness for future contingencies as opposed to demonstration of current success on the battlefield) prompts pessimistic estimates by operational military analysts; autonomous analysts without budgetary axes to grind, but with biases similar to those prevalent in the intellectual community, tend toward less alarmed predictions.[7] Military intelligence inclines toward "worst-case" analysis in planning, and toward "best-case" analysis in operational evaluation. (Military intelligence officials such as Lieutenant General Daniel Graham were castigated by liberals for *under*estimating the Vietcong's strength in the 1960's but for *over*estimating Soviet strength in the 1970's.) Air Force intelligence overestimated Soviet air deployments in the "bomber gap" controversy of the 1950's, and CIA-dominated National Intelligence Estimates (NIE's) underestimated Soviet ICBM deployments throughout the 1960's (overreacting, critics say, to the mistaken prediction of a "missile gap" in 1960).[8]

Second, in the context of peacetime, with competing domestic claims on resources, political leaders have a natural interest in at least partially rejecting military estimates and embracing those of other analysts who justify limiting allocations to defense programs. If the President had accepted pessimistic CIA operational evaluations in the mid-1960's, he might have withdrawn from Vietnam; if he had accepted pessimistic military analyses of the Soviet threat in the mid-1970's, he might have added massive increases to the defense budget.

Some chronic sources of error are unique to each of these three general categories of intelligence problems, and thus do not clearly suggest reforms that would be advisable across the board. To compensate for the danger in conventional attack warning, reliance on worst-case analysis might seem the safest rule, but in making estimates for defense planning, worst-case analysis would mandate severe and often unnecessary economic sacrifices. Removing checks on the influence of CIA analysts and "community" staffs[9] might seem justified by the record of operational evaluation in Vietnam, but would not be warranted by the record of estimates on Soviet ICBM deployments. It would be risky to alter the balance of power systematically among competing analytic components, giving the "better" analysts more status. Rather, decision makers should be encouraged to be more and less skeptical of certain agencies' estimates, *depending on the category of analysis involved.*

Some problems, however, cut across all three categories and offer a more general basis for considering changes in the system. But these general problems are not very susceptible to cure by formal changes in process, because it is usually impossible to disentangle intelligence failures from policy failures. Separation of intelligence and policy making has long been a normative concern of officials and theorists, who have seen both costs and benefits in minimizing the intimacy between intelligence professionals and operational authorities. But, although the personnel can be segregated, the functions cannot, unless intelligence is defined narrowly as the collection of data, and analytic responsibility is reserved to decision makers. Analysis and decision are interactive rather than sequential processes. By the narrower definition of intelligence, there have actually been few major failures. In most cases of mistakes in predicting attacks or in assessing operations, the inadequacy of critical data or their submergence in a viscous bureaucracy were at best the proximate causes of failure. The ultimate causes of error in most cases have been wishful thinking, cavalier disregard of professional analysts, and, above all, the premises and preconceptions of policy makers. Fewer fiascoes have occurred in the stages of acquisition and presentation of facts than in the stages of interpretation and response. Producers of intelligence have been culprits less often than consumers. Policy perspectives tend to constrain objectivity, and authorities often fail to use intelligence properly. As former State Department intelligence director Ray Cline testified, defending his analysts' performance in October 1973 and criticizing Secretary Kissinger for ignoring them:

> Unless something is totally conclusive, you must make an inconclusive report . . . by the time you are sure it is always very close to the event. So I don't think the analysts did such a lousy job. What I think was the lousy job was in bosses not insisting on a new preparation at the end of that week [before war broke out] . . . the reason the system wasn't working very well is that people were not asking it to work and not listening when it did work.[10]

II. Basic Barriers to Analytic Accuracy

Many constraints on the optimal processing of information lie in the structure of authority and the allocation of time and resources. Harold Wilensky argues persuasively that the intelligence function is hindered most by the structural characteristics of hierarchy, centralization, and specialization.[11] Yet it is precisely these characteristics that are the essence of any government. A related problem is the dominance of operational authorities over intelligence specialists, and the trade-off between objectivity and influence. Operators have more influence in decision making but are less capable of unbiased interpretation of evidence because they have a vested interest in the success of their operations; autonomous analysts are more disinterested and usually more objective, but lack influence. Senior generalists at the policy level often distrust or discount the judgments of analytic professionals and place more weight on reports from operational sources.[12] In response to this phenomenon, the suggestion has been made to *legislate* the requirement that decision makers consider analyses by the CIA's Intelligence Directorate (now the National Foreign Assessment Center) before establishing policy.[13] Such a requirement would offer no more than wishful formalism. Statutory fiat cannot force human beings to value one source above another. "No power has yet been found," DCI Richard Helms has testified, "to force Presidents of the United States to pay attention on a continuing basis to people and papers when confidence has been lost in the originator."[14] Moreover, principals tend to believe that they have a wider point of view than middle-level analysts and are better able to draw conclusions from raw data. That point of view underlies their fascination with current intelligence and their impatience with the reflective interpretations in "finished" intelligence.[15]

The dynamics of decision are also not conducive to analytic refinement. In a crisis, both data and policy outpace analysis, the ideal process of staffing and consultation falls behind the press of events, and careful estimates cannot be digested in time. As Winston Churchill recalled of the hectic days of spring 1940,

> The Defence Committee of the War Cabinet sat almost every day to discuss the reports of the Military Coordination Committee and those of the Chiefs of Staff; and their conclusions or divergences were again referred to frequent Cabinets. All had to be explained or reexplained; and by the time this process was completed, the whole scene had often changed.[16]

Where there is ample time for decision, on the other hand, the previously mentioned bureaucratic impediments gain momentum.[17] Just as information processing is frustrated by constraints on the time that harried principals can spend scrutinizing analytic papers, it is constrained by the funds that a government can spend. To which priorities should scarce resources be allocated? The Schlesinger Report of 1971, which led to President Nixon's reorganization of U.S. intelligence, noted that criticisms of analytic products were often translated into demands for more extensive collection of data, but

"Seldom does anyone ask if a further reduction in uncertainty, however small, is worth its cost."[18] Authorities do not always know, however, which issues require the greatest attention and which uncertainties harbor the fewest potential threats. Beyond the barriers that authority, organization, and scarcity pose to intelligence lie more fundamental and less remediable intellectual sources of error.

1. Ambiguity of Evidence

Intelligence veterans have noted that "estimating is what you do when you do not know,"[19] but "it is inherent in a great many situations that after reading the estimate, you will still not know."[20] These observations highlight an obvious but most important obstacle to accuracy in analysis. It is the role of intelligence to extract certainty from uncertainty and to facilitate coherent decision in an incoherent environment. (In a certain and coherent environment there is less need for intelligence.) To the degree they reduce uncertainty by extrapolating from evidence riddled with ambiguities, analysts risk oversimplifying reality and desensitizing the consumers of intelligence to the dangers that lurk within the ambiguities; to the degree they do not resolve ambiguities, analysts risk being dismissed by annoyed consumers who see them as not having done their job. Uncertainty reflects inadequacy of data, which is usually assumed to mean *lack* of information. But ambiguity can also be aggravated by an *excess* of data. In attack warning, there is the problem of "noise" and deception; in operational evaluation (particularly in a war such as Vietnam), there is the problem of overload from the high volume of finished analyses, battlefield statistics, reports, bulletins, reconnaissance, and communications intercepts flowing upward through multiple channels at a rate exceeding the capacity of officials to absorb or scrutinize them judiciously. (From the CIA alone, the White House received current intelligence dailies, Weekly Reports, daily Intelligence Information Cables, occasional Special Reports and specific memoranda, and analyses from the CIA Vietnam Working Group.) Similarly, in estimates for defense planning, there is the problem of innumerable and endlessly refined indices of the strategic balance, and the dependence of assessments of capabilities on complex and variable assumptions about the doctrine, scenarios, and intentions that would govern their use.

Because it is the job of decision makers to decide, they cannot react to ambiguity by deferring judgment.[21] When the problem is an environment that lacks clarity, an overload of conflicting data, and lack of time for rigorous assessment of sources and validity, ambiguity abets instinct and allows intuition to drive analysis. Intelligence can fail because the data are too permissive for policy judgment rather than too constraining. When a welter of fragmentary evidence offers support to various interpretations, ambiguity is exploited by wishfulness. The greater the ambiguity, the greater the impact of preconceptions.[22] (This point should be distinguished from the theory of cognitive dissonance, which became popular with political scientists at the time it was being rejected by psychologists.)[23] There is some inverse relation between the importance of an assessment (when uncertainty is high) and the likelihood that it will be accurate. Lyndon Johnson could reject pessimistic NIE's on Vietnam by inferring more optimistic conclusions from the reports that came through command channels on pacification, interdiction, enemy casualties, and defections. Observers who assume Soviet malevolence focus on analyses of strategic forces that emphasize missile throw weight and gross megatonnage (Soviet advantages); those who assume more benign Soviet intentions focus on analyses that emphasize missile accuracy and numbers of warheads (U.S. advantages). In assessing the naval balance, Secretary of Defense Rumsfeld focused on numbers of ships (Soviet lead), and Congressman Les Aspin, a critic of the Pentagon, focused on total tonnage (U.S. lead).

2. Ambivalence of Judgment

Where there are ambiguous and conflicting indicators (the context of most failures of intelligence), the imperatives of honesty and accuracy leave a careful analyst no alternative but ambivalence. There is usually *some* evidence to support any prediction. For instance, the CIA reported in June 1964 that a Chinese instructor (deemed not "particularly qualified to make this remark") had told troops in a course in guerrilla warfare, "We will have the atom bomb in a matter of months."[24] Several months later the Chinese did perform their first nuclear test. If the report had been the only evidence, should analysts have predicted the event? If they are not to make a leap of faith and ignore the data that do not mesh, analysts will issue estimates that waffle. In trying to elicit nuances of probability from the various possibilities not foreclosed by the data, cautious estimates may reduce ambivalence, but they may become Delphic or generalized to the point that they are not useful guides to decision. (A complaint I have heard in conversations with several U.S. officials is that many past estimates of Soviet objectives could substitute the name of any other great power in history—Imperial Rome, 16th-century Spain, Napoleonic France—and sound equally valid.) Hedging is the legitimate intellectual response to ambiguity, but it can be politically coun-

terproductive, if the value of intelligence is to shock consumers out of wishfulness and cognitive insensitivity. A wishful decision maker can fasten onto that half of an ambivalent analysis that supports his predisposition.[25] A more objective official may escape this temptation, but may consider the estimate useless because it does not provide "the answer."

3. Atrophy of Reforms

Disasters always stimulate organizational changes designed to avert the same failures in the future. In some cases these changes work. In many instances, however, the changes persist formally but erode substantively. Standard procedures are constant. Dramatic failures occur only intermittently. If the reforms in procedure they have provoked do not fulfill day-to-day organizational needs—or if, as often happens, they complicate operations and strain the organization's resources—they fall into disuse or become token practices. After the postmortem of North Korea's downing of a U.S. EC-121 monitoring aircraft in 1969, there was, for several months, a great emphasis on risk assessments for intelligence collection missions. Generals and admirals personally oversaw the implementation of new procedures for making the assessments. Six months later, majors and captains were doing the checking. "Within a year the paperwork was spot-checked by a major and the entire community slid back to its old way of making a 'quick and dirty' rundown of the JCS criteria when sending in reconnaissance mission proposals."[26] The downing of the U-2 over the Soviet Union in 1960 and the capture of the intelligence ship *Pueblo* in 1968 had been due in part to the fact that the process of risk assessment for specific collection missions, primarily the responsibility of overworked middle-level officers, had become ponderous, sloppy, or ritualized.[27] At a higher level, a National Security Council Intelligence Committee was established in 1971 to improve responsiveness of intelligence staff to the needs of policy makers. But since the subcabinet-level consumers who made up the committee were pressed by other responsibilities, it lapsed in importance and was eventually abolished.[28] A comparable NSC committee that *did* serve tangible day-to-day needs of consumers to integrate intelligence and policy—the Verification Panel, which dealt with SALT—was more effective, but it was issue-oriented rather than designed to oversee the intelligence process itself. Organizational innovations will not improve the role of intelligence in policy unless they flow from the decision makers' views of their own needs and unless they provide frequent practical benefits.

None of these three barriers are accidents of structure or process. They are inherent in the nature of intelligence and the dynamics of work. As such, they constitute severe constraints on the efficacy of structural reform.

III. The Elusiveness of Solutions

If they do not atrophy, most solutions proposed to obviate intelligence dysfunctions have two edges: in reducing one vulnerability, they increase another. After the seizure of the *Pueblo*, the Defense Intelligence Agency (DIA) was reprimanded for misplacing a message that could have prevented the incident. The colonel responsible developed a careful microfilming operation in the message center to ensure a record of transmittal of cables to authorities in the Pentagon. Implementing this check, however, created a three-to-four hour delay—another potential source of failure—in getting cables to desk analysts whose job was to keep reporting current.[29] Thus, procedural solutions often constitute two steps forward and one step back; organizational fixes cannot transcend the basic barriers. The lessons of Pearl Harbor led to the establishment of a Watch Committee and National Indications Center in Washington. Although this solution eliminated a barrier in the communication system, it did not prevent the failure of timely alert to the Chinese intervention in Korea or the 1973 October War, because it did not eliminate the ambiguity barrier. (Since then, the Watch Committee has been replaced by the DCI's Strategic Warning Staff.) DIA was reorganized four times within its first ten years; yet it continued to leave most observers dissatisfied. The Agranat Commission's review of Israel's 1973 intelligence failure produced proposals for institutional reform that are striking because they amount to copying the American system of the same time—which had failed in exactly the same way as the Israeli system.[30] Reform is not hopeless, but hopes placed in solutions most often proposed—such as the following—should be circumscribed.

1. Assume the Worst

A common reaction to traumatic surprise is the recommendation to cope with ambiguity and ambivalence by acting on the most threatening possible interpretations. If there is *any* evidence of threat, assume it is valid, even if the *apparent* weight of contrary indicators is greater. In retrospect, when the point of reference is an actual disaster attributable to a mistaken calculation of probabilities, this response is always justifiable, but it is impractical as a guide to standard procedure. Operationalizing worst-case analysis requires extraordinary expense, it risks being counterproductive if it is effective (by provoking enemy countermeasures or pre-emption), and it is likely to be ineffective because routinization will discredit it. Many Israeli observers deduced from the 1973 surprise that defense planning could only rest on the assumption that no attack warning will be available, and that precautionary mobilization should always be undertaken even when there is only dubious evidence of impending Arab action.[31] Similarly, American hawks argue that if the Soviets' intentions are uncertain, the only prudent course is to assume they are seeking the capability to win nuclear war.

In either case, the norm of assuming the worst poses high financial costs. Frequent mobilizations strain the already taut Israeli economy. Moreover, countermobilization can defeat itself. Between 1971 and 1973, the Egyptians three times undertook exercises similar to those that led to the October attack; Israel mobilized in response, and nothing happened. It was the paradox of self-negating prophecy.[32] The Israeli Chief of Staff was sharply criticized for the unnecessary cost.[33] The danger of hypersensitivity appeared in 1977, when General Gur believed Sadat's offer to come to Jerusalem to be a camouflage for an Egyptian attack; he began Israeli maneuvers in the Sinai, which led Egypt to begin maneuvers of its own, heightening the risk of accidental war.[34] To estimate the requirements for deterrence and defense, worst case assumptions present an open-ended criterion. The procurement of all the hedges possible for nuclear war-fighting—large increments in offensive forces, alert status, hardening of command-control-and-communications, active and passive defenses—would add billions to the U.S. defense budget. Moreover, prudent hedging in policy should be distinguished from net judgment of probabilities in estimates.[35]

Alternatively, precautionary escalation or procurement may act as self-fulfilling prophecies, either through a catalytic spiral of mobilization (à la World War I) or an arms race that heightens tension, or doctrinal hedges that make the prospect of nuclear war more "thinkable." Since evidence for the "action-reaction" hypothesis of U.S. and Soviet nuclear policies is meager, and arms races can sometimes be stabilizing rather than dangerous, the last point is debatable. Still, a large unilateral increase in strategic forces by either the United States or the Soviet Union would, at the least, destroy the possibility of gains desired from SALT. A surprise attack or defeat make the costs of *under*estimates obvious and dramatic; the unnecessary defense costs due to *over*estimates can only be surmised, since the minimum needed for deterrence is uncertain. Worst-case analysis as a standard norm would also exacerbate the "cry wolf" syndrome. *Unambiguous* threat is not an intelligence problem; rather, the challenge lies in the response to fragmentary, contradictory, and dubious indicators. Most such indicators turn out to be false alarms. Analysts who reflexively warn of disaster are soon derided as hysterical. General William Westmoreland recalled that the warnings that had been issued before the 1968 Tet Offensive were ignored. U.S. headquarters in Saigon had each year predicted a winter-spring offensive, "and every year it had come off without any dire results. . . . Was not the new offensive to be more of the same?"[36]

Given the experience of intelligence professionals that most peace-time indicators of suspicious enemy activity lead to nothing, what Colonel who has the watch some night will risk "lighting up the board" in the White House simply on the basis of weak apprehension? How many staffers will risk waking a tired President, especially if they have done so before and found the action to be needless? How many distracting false alarms will an overworked President tolerate before he makes it clear that aides should exercise discretion in bothering him? Even if worst-case analysis is promulgated in principle, it will be compromised in practice. Routinization corrodes sensitivity. Every day that an expected threat does not materialize dulls receptivity to the reality of danger. As Roberta Wohlstetter wrote of pre-Pearl Harbor vigilance, "We are constantly confronted by the paradox of pessimistic realism of phrase coupled with loose optimism in practice."[37] Seeking to cover all contingencies, worst-case analysis loses focus and salience; by providing a theoretical guide for everything, it provides a practical guide for very little.

2. Multiple Advocacy

Blunders are often attributed to decisionmakers' inattention to unpopular viewpoints or to a lack of access to higher levels of authority by dissident analysts. To reduce the chances of such mistakes, Alexander George proposes institutionalizing a balanced, open, and managed process of debate, so that no relevant assessments will be submerged by unchallenged premises or the bureaucratic strength of opposing officials.[38] The goal is unobjectionable, and formalized multiple advocacy certainly would help, not hinder. But confidence that it will help systematically and substantially should be tentative. In a loose sense, there has usually been multiple advocacy in the U.S. policy process, but it has not prevented mistakes in deliberation or decision. Lyndon Johnson did not decide for limited bombing and gradual troop commitment in Vietnam in 1965 because he was not presented with extensive and vigorous counterarguments. He considered seriously (indeed solicited) Under Secretary of State George Ball's analysis, which drew on NIE's and lower-level officials' pessimistic assessments

that any escalation would be a mistake. Johnson was also well aware of the arguments by DCI John McCone and the Air Force from the other extreme—that massive escalation in the air war was necessary because gradualism would be ineffective.[39] The President simply chose to accept the views of the middle-of-the-road opponents of *both* Ball and McCone.

To the extent that multiple advocacy works, and succeeds in maximizing the number of views promulgated and in supporting the argumentive resources of all contending analysts, it may simply highlight ambiguity rather than resolve it. In George's ideal situation, the process would winnow out unsubstantiated premises and assumptions about ends-means linkages. But in the context of data overload, uncertainty, and time constraints, multiple advocacy may in effect give all of the various viewpoints an aura of empirical respectability and allow a leader to choose whichever accords with his predisposition.[40]

The efficacy of multiple advocacy (which is greatest under conditions of manageable data and low ambiguity) may vary inversely with the potential for intelligence failure (which is greatest under conditions of confusing data and high uncertainty). The process could, of course, bring to the surface ambiguities where false certainty had prevailed; in these cases, it would be as valuable as George believes. But if multiple advocacy increases ambivalence and leaders do *not* indulge their instincts, it risks promoting conservatism or paralysis. Dean Acheson saw danger in presidential indecisiveness aggravated by debate: " 'I know your theory,' he grumbled to Neustadt. 'You think Presidents should be warned. You're wrong. Presidents should be given confidence.' "[41]

Even Clausewitz argued that deference to intelligence can frustrate bold initiative and squander crucial opportunities. Critics charged Henry Kissinger with crippling U.S. intelligence by refusing to keep analysts informed of his intimate conversations with foreign leaders.[42] To do so, however, would have created the possibility of leaks and might thereby have crippled his diplomatic maneuvers. It is doubtful that Nixon's initiative to China could have survived prior debate, dissent, and analysis by the bureaucracy.

It is unclear that managed multiple advocacy would yield markedly greater benefits than the redundancy and competitiveness that have long existed. (At best it would perfect the "market" of ideas in the manner that John Stuart Mill believed made liberalism conducive to the emergence of truth.) The first major reorganization of the American intelligence community in 1946–1947 emphasized centralization in order to avert future Pearl Harbors caused by fragmentation of authority; the latest reorganization (Carter's 1977 extension of authority of the Director of Central Intelligence over military intelligence programs) emphasized centralization to improve efficiency and coherence. Yet decentralization has always persisted in the overlapping division of labor between several separate agencies. Recent theorists of bureaucracy see such duplication as beneficial because competition exposes disagreement and presents policy makers with a wider range of views. Redundancy inhibits consensus, impedes the herd instinct in the decision process, and thus reduces the likelihood of failure due to unchallenged premises or cognitive errors. To ensure that redundancy works in this way, critics oppose a process that yields coordinated estimates—negotiated to the least common denominator, and cleared by all agencies before they are passed to the principals. George's "custodian" of multiple advocacy could ensure that this does not happen. There are, of course, trade-off costs for redundancy. Maximization of competition limits specialization. In explaining the failure of intelligence to predict the 1974 coup in Portugal, William Hyland pointed out, "if each of the major analytical components stretch their resources over the same range, there is the risk that areas of less priority will be superficially covered."[43]

The problem with arguing that the principals themselves should scrutinize numerous contrasting estimates in their integrity is that they are constantly overwhelmed by administrative responsibilities and "action items"; they lack the time to read, ponder, and digest that large an amount of material. Most intelligence products, even NIE's, are never read by policy makers; at best, they are used by second-level staffers as background material for briefing their seniors.[44] Consumers want previously coordinated analyses in order to save time and effort. In this respect, the practical imperatives of day-to-day decision contradict the theoretical logic of ideal intelligence.

3. Consolidation

According to the logic of estimative redundancy, more analysis is better than less. Along this line of reasoning. Senate investigators noted critically that, as of fiscal year 1975, the U.S. intelligence community still allocated 72 percent of its budget for collection of information, 19 percent for processing technical data, and less than 9 percent for production of finished analyses. On the other hand, according to the logic of those who focus on the time constraints of leaders and the confusion that results from innumerable publications, quantity counteracts quality. The size of the CIA's intelligence directorate and the complexity of the production process "precluded close association between policy makers and analysts, between the intelligence product and policy informed by intelligence analysis."[45] For the sake of clarity and acuity, the intelligence bureaucracy should be streamlined.

This view is consistent with the development of the Office of National Estimates (ONE), which was established in 1950 and designed to coordinate the contributions of the various organs in the intelligence community for the Director of Central Intelligence. DCI Walter Bedell Smith envisioned an operation of about a thousand people. But William L. Langer, the scholar Smith imported to organize ONE, wanted a tight group of excellent analysts and a personnel ceiling of fifty. Langer prevailed, and though the number of staff members in ONE crept upwards, it probably never exceeded a hundred in its two decades of existence.[46] Yet ONE could not eliminate the complexity of the intelligence process; it could only coordinate and integrate it for the production of National Intelligence Estimates. Other sources found conduits to decision makers (to Cabinet members through their own agencies, or to the President through the National Security Council). And some policy makers, though they might dislike the cacophony of multiple intelligence agencies, were suspicious of the consolidated NIE's, knowing that there was pressure to compromise views in order to gain agreement. Over time, the dynamics of bureaucracy also blunted the original objectives of ONE'S founder. From a cosmopolitan elite corps, it evolved into an insular unit of senior careerists from the CIA. The National Intelligence Officer system that replaced ONE reduced the number of personnel responsible for coordinating NIE's, but has been criticized on other grounds such as greater vulnerability to departmental pressures. Bureaucratic realities have frustrated other attempts to consolidate the intelligence structure. The Defense Intelligence Agency was created in 1961 to unify Pentagon intelligence and reduce duplicative activities of the three service intelligence agencies, but these agencies regenerated themselves; in less than a decade they were larger than they had been before DIA's inception.[47]

The numerous attempts to simplify the organization of the analytic process thus have not solved the major problems. Either the streamlining exercises were short-lived, and bureaucratization crept back, or the changes had to be moderated to avoid the new dangers they entailed. Contraction is inconsistent with the desire to minimize failure by "plugging holes" in intelligence, since compensating for an inadequacy usually requires *adding* personnel and mechanisms; pruning the structure that contributes to procedural sluggishness or complexity may create lacunae in substantive coverage.

4. Devil's Advocacy

Multiple advocacy ensures that all views held by individuals within the analytic system will be granted serious attention. Some views that should receive attention, however, may not be held by anyone within the system. Virtually no analysts in Israel or the United States believed the Arabs would be "foolish" enough to attack in 1973. Many observers have recommended institutionalizing dissent by assigning to someone the job of articulating apparently ridiculous interpretations to ensure that they are forced into consideration. Establishing an official devil's advocate would probably do no harm (although some argue that it may perversely facilitate consensus-building by domesticating true dissenters or providing the illusory comfort that all views have been carefully examined;[48] worse, it might delude decision makers into believing that *uncertainties* have been resolved). But in any case, the role is likely to atrophy into a superfluous or artificial ritual. By the definition of the job, the devil's advocate is likely to be dismissed by decision makers as a sophist who only makes an argument because he is supposed to, not because of its real merits. Institutionalizing devil's advocacy is likely to be perceived in practice as institutionalizing the "cry wolf" problem; "There are limits to the utility of a 'devil's advocate' who is not a true devil."[49] He becomes someone to be indulged and disregarded. Given its rather sterile definition, the role is not likely to be filled by a prestigious official (who will prefer more "genuine" responsibility); it will therefore be easier for policy makers to dismiss the arguments. In order to avert intelligence failures, an analyst is needed who tells decision makers what they don't want to hear, dampening the penchant for wishful thinking. But since it is the job of the devil's advocate to do this habitually, and since he is most often wrong (as would be inevitable, since otherwise the conventional wisdom would eventually change), he digs his own grave. If the role is routinized and thus ritualized, it loses impact; but if it is not routinized, there can be no assurance that it will be operating when it is needed.

Despite the last point, which is more important in attack warning than in operational evaluation or defense planning, there is a compromise that offers more realistic benefits: *ad hoc* utilization of "real devils." This selective or biased form of multiple advocacy may be achieved by periodically giving a platform within the intelligence process to minority views that can be argued more persuasively by prestigious analysts outside the bureaucracy. This is what the President's Foreign Intelligence Advisory Board and DCI George Bush did in 1976 by commissioning the "Team B" critique of NFE's on Soviet strategic objective sand capabilities. Dissenters within the intelligence community who were skeptical of Soviet intentions were reinforced by a panel of sympathetic scholars, with a mandate to produce an analysis of their own.[50] This controversial exercise, even if it erred in many of its own ways (as dovish critics contend), had a major impact in promoting the reexamination of premises and methodology in U.S. strategic estimates. The problem with this option is that it depends on the political biases of the authorities who commission it. If it were balanced by a comparable "Team C" of analysts at the opposite extreme (more optimistic about Soviet intentions than the intelligence community consensus), the exercise would approach regular multiple advocacy, with the attendant limitations of that solution. Another variant would be intermittent designation of devil's advocates in periods of crisis, when the possibility of disaster is greater than usual. Since the role would then be fresh each time, rather than ritualized, the advocate might receive a more serious hearing. The problem here is that receptivity of decision makers to information that contradicts preconceptions varies inversely with their personal commitments, and commitments grow as crisis progresses.[51]

5. Sanctions and Incentives

Some critics attribute intelligence failures to dishonest reporting or the intellectual mediocrity of analysts. Suggested remedies include threats of punishment for the former, and inducements to attract talent to replace the latter. Other critics emphasize that, will or ability aside, analytic integrity is often submerged by the policy makers' demands for intelligence that suits them; "the NIE sought to be responsive to the evidence, not the policy maker."[52] Holders of this point of view would institutionalize the analysts' autonomy. Unobjectionable in principle (though if analysts are totally unresponsive to the consumer, he will ignore them), these implications cannot easily be operationalized without creating as many problems as they solve.

Self-serving operational evaluations from military sources, such as optimistic reports on progress in the field in Vietnam or pessimistic strategic estimates, might indeed be obviated if analysts in DIA, the service intelligence agencies, and command staffs were credibly threatened with sanctions (firing, nonpromotion, reprimand, or disgrace). Such threats theoretically could be a countervailing pressure to the career incentives analysts have to promote the interests of their services. But, except in the most egregious cases, it is difficult to apply such standards without arbitrariness and bias, given the problem of ambiguity; it simply encourages an alternative bias or greater ambivalence. Moreover, military professionals would be in an untenable position, pulled in opposite directions by two sets of authorities. To apply the sanctions, civil authorities would have to violate the most hallowed military canon by having civilian intelligence officials interfere in the chain of command. In view of these dilemmas, it is easier to rely on the limited effectiveness of redundancy or multiple advocacy to counteract biased estimates.

Critics concerned with attracting better talent into the analytic bureaucracy propose to raise salaries and to provide more high-ranking positions (supergrades) to which analysts can aspire. Yet American government salaries are already very high by academic standards. Those who attribute DIA's mediocrity (compared to CIA), to an insufficient allocation of supergrades and a consequent inability to retain equivalent personnel are also mistaken; as of 1975 the difference in the grade structures of DIA and CIA had been negligible.[53] And the fact that CIA analysts cannot rise to a supergrade position (GS-16 to 18) without becoming administrators is not convincing evidence that good analysts are underpaid; GS-15 salaries are higher than the maximum for most tenured professors.

Non-military analysts, or high-ranking soldiers with no promotions to look forward to, have fewer professional crosspressures to contend with than military intelligence officers. But an analyst's autonomy varies inversely with his influence, and hortatory injunctions to be steadfast and intellectually honest cannot ensure that he will be; they cannot transcend political realities or the idiosyncrasies of leaders. Richard Helms notes that "there is no way to insulate the DCI from unpopularity at the hands of Presidents or policy makers if he is making assessments which run counter to administrative policy. That is a built in hazard of the job. Sensible Presidents understand this. On the other hand they are human too." Integrity untinged by political sensitivity courts professional suicide. If the analyst insists on perpetually bearing bad news, he is likely to be beheaded. Helms himself succumbed to policy makers' pressures in compromising estimates of the MIRV capabilities of the Soviet SS-9 missile in 1969, and the prospects for Cambodia in 1970.[54] The same practical psychological constraints are reflected in an incident in which Chief of Naval Operations Elmo Zumwalt, who had already infuriated Nixon and Kissinger several times with his strategic estimates) was determined to present yet another unwelcome analysis; Secretary of Defense Schlesinger dissuaded him with the warning, "To give a briefing like that in the White House these days would be just like shooting yourself in the foot."[55]

6. Cognitive Rehabilitation and Methodological Consciousness

The intertwining of analysis and decision and the record of intelligence failures due to mistaken preconceptions and unexamined assumptions suggest the need to reform the intelligence consumers' attitudes, awareness, and modes of perception. If leaders were made self-conscious and self-critical about their own psychologies, they might be less vulnerable to cognitive pathologies. This approach to preventing intelligence failure is the most basic and metaphysical. If policy makers focused on the methodologies of competing intelligence producers, they would be more sensitive to the biases and leaps of faith in the analyses passed to them.

> In official fact-finding . . . the problem is not merely to open up a wide range of policy alternatives but to create incentives for persistent criticism of evidentiary value.[56]

Improvement would flow from mechanisms that force decision makers to make explicit rather than unconscious choices, to exercise judgment rather than engage in automatic perception, and to enhance their awareness of their own preconceptions.[57]

Unlike organizational structure, however, cognition cannot be altered by legislation. Intelligence consumers are political men who have risen by being more decisive than reflective, more aggressive than introspective, and confident as much as cautious. Few busy activists who have achieved success by thinking the way that they do will change their way of thinking because some theorist tells them to. Even if they could be forced to confront scholarly evidence of the dynamics of misperception it is uncertain that they could consistently internalize it. Preconception cannot be abolished; it is in one sense just another word for "model" or "paradigm"—a construct used to simplify reality, which any thinker needs in order to cope with complexity. There is a grain of truth in the otherwise pernicious maxim that an open mind is an empty mind. Moreover, the line between *perception* and *judgment* is very thin, and consumers cannot carefully scrutinize, compare, and evaluate the methodologies of competing analyses, for the same prosaic reason (the problem of expertise aside) that impedes many proposed reforms: they do not have the *time* to do so. Solutions that require principals to invest more attention than they already do are conceptually valid but operationally weak. Ideally, perhaps, each principal should have a Special Assistant for Rigor Enforcement.

Although most notable intelligence failures occur more often at the consuming than the producing end, it is impractical to place the burden for correcting those faults on the consumers. The most realistic strategy for improvement would be to have intelligence professionals anticipate the cognitive barriers to decision makers' utilization of their products. Ideally, the Director of Central Intelligence should have a theoretical temperament and personal skills in forcing unusual analyses to the attention of principals; he might act as George's "custodian" of the argumentation process. To fulfill this function, the DCI should be not only a professional analyst and an intellectual (of the twelve DCI's since 1946, only James Schlesinger met those criteria, and he served for only three months), but also a skilled bureaucratic politician. These qualifications seldom coincide. The DCI's coordinating staff and National Intelligence Officers should be adept at detecting, making explicit, and exposing to consumers the idiosyncrasies in the assessments of various agencies—the *reasons* that the focus and conclusions of the State Department's Bureau of Intelligence and Research differ from those of DIA, or of naval intelligence, or of the CIA. For such a procedure to work, the consumers would have to favor it (as opposed to negotiated consensual estimates that would save them more time). There is always a latent tension between what facilitates timely decision and what promotes thoroughness and accuracy in assessment. The fact that there is no guaranteed prophylaxis against intelligence failures, however, does not negate the value of incremental improvements. The key is to see the problem of reform as one of modest refinements rather than as a systematic breakthrough.

IV. Living With Fatalism

Organizational solutions to intelligence failure are hampered by three basic problems: most procedural reforms that address specific pathologies introduce or accent other pathologies; changes in analytic processes can never fully transcend the constraints of ambiguity and ambivalence; and more rationalized information systems cannot fully compensate for the predispositions, perceptual idiosyncrasies, and time constraints of political consumers. Solutions that address the psychology and analytic style of decision makers are limited by the difficulty of changing human thought processes and day-to-day habits of judgment by normative injunction. Most theorists have thus resigned themselves to the hope of marginal progress, "to improve the 'batting average'—say from .275 to .301—rather than to do away altogether with surprise."[58]

There is some convergence in the implications of all three ways of conceptualizing intelligence failures. Mistakes should be expected because the *para-*doxes are not resolvable; minor improvements are possible by reorganizing to correct *pathologies,* and despair is unwarranted because, seen *in perspective,* the record could be worse. Marginal improvements have, in fact, been steadily instituted since World War II. Although many have indeed raised new problems, most have yielded a net increase in the rationalization of the system. The diversification of sources of estimates of adversaries' military power has grown consistently, obviating the necessity to rely exclusively on military staffs. The resources and influence of civilian analysts of military data (principally in the CIA's Office of Strategic Research but also in its Directorate of Science and Technology) are unparalleled in any other nation's intelligence system. At the same time, the DCI's mechanism for coordinating the activities of all agencies—the Intelligence Community Staff—has grown and become more diverse and representative, and less an extension of the CIA, as more staffers have been added from the outside. In 1972, a separate Product Review Division was established within the staff to appraise the "objectivity, balance, and responsiveness" of intelligence studies on a regular basis. It has conducted postmortems of intelligence failures since then (the Yom Kippur War, the Cyprus crisis of 1974, the Indian nuclear test, and the seizure of the *Mayaguez*).[59] (Previously, postmortems had been conducted by the analysts who had failed, a procedure that hardly guaranteed objectivity.)

Within the Pentagon, capabilities for estimates relevant to planning were enhanced with the establishment of an office for Net Assessment, which analyzes the significance of foreign capabilities in comparison with U.S. forces. (CIA, DIA, and NIE's only estimate foreign capabilities.) Civilian direction of military intelligence was reinforced by an Assistant Secretary of Defense for Intelligence after the 1970 recommendation of the Fitzhugh Commission, and an Under Secretary for Policy in 1978. Experiments in improving communication between producers and consumers have been undertaken (such as, for example, the testing of a Defense Intelligence Board in late 1976). The dominance of operators within the intelligence community has also waned—especially since the phasing out of paramilitary operations in Southeast Asia and the severe reductions in size and status of CIA's covert action branch that began in 1973. Dysfunctions in the military communications system, which contributed to crises involving intelligence collection missions in the 1960's (the Israeli attack on the U.S.S. *Liberty* and North Korea's seizure of the *Pueblo*) were alleviated (though not cured) by new routing procedures and by instituting an "optimal scanning system" in the Pentagon.[60] Statistical analyses of strategic power have become progressively more rigorous and comprehensive; as staffs outside the executive branch—such as the Congressional Budget Office—have become involved in the process, they have also become more competitive.[61]

Few of the changes in structure and process have generated more costs than benefits. (Some critics believe, however, that the abolition of the Office and Board of National Estimates and their replacement with National Intelligence Officers was a net loss.) But it is difficult to prove that they have significantly reduced the incidence of intelligence failure. In the area of warning, for instance, new sophisticated coordination mechanisms have recently been introduced, and since the institution at the time of the 1974 Cyprus crisis of DCI "alert memoranda"—"brief notices in a form which cannot be overlooked"[62]—no major warning failure has occurred. But the period of testing is as yet too brief to demonstrate that these adaptations are more effective than previous procedures. In the area of operational evaluation, it is clear that there was greater consciousness of the limitations and cost-ineffectiveness of aerial bombardment during the Vietnam War than there had been in Korea, due largely to the assessments made by the offices of Systems Analysis and International Security Affairs in the Pentagon and Secretary of Defense McNamara's utilization of CIA estimates and contract studies by external analytic organizations.[63] Yet this greater consciousness did not prevail until late in the war because it was not consensus; Air Force and naval assessments of bombing effectiveness contradicted those of the critical civilian analysts. Nor has the elaboration and diversification of analytical resources for strategic estimates clearly reduced the potential for erroneous planning decisions. Determination of the salience and proper weight of conflicting indicators of strategic power and objectives or of the comparative significance of quantitative and qualitative factors is inextricable from the political debate over foreign policy: uncertainties always remain, leaving the individual's visceral fears or hopes as the elements that tilt the balance of judgment.

Although marginal reforms may reduce the probability of error, the unresolvable paradoxes and barriers to analytic and decisional accuracy will make some incidence of failure inevitable. Concern with intelligence failure then coincides with concern about how policy can hedge against the consequences of analytic inadequacy. Covering every hypothetical vulnerability would lead to bankruptcy, and hedging against one threat may aggravate a different one. The problem is thus one of priorities, and hedging against uncertainty is hardly easier than resolving it. Any measures that clarify the cost-

benefit trade-offs in policy hedges are measures that mitigate the danger of intelligence failure.

One reasonable rule in principle would be to survey the hypothetical outcomes excluded by strategic premises as improbable but not impossible, identify those that would be disastrous if they *were* to occur, and then pay the price to hedge against them. This is no more practicable, however, than the pure form of worst-case analysis, because it requires willingness to bear and inflict severe costs for dubious reasons. Escalation in Vietnam, after all, was a hedge against allowing China to be tempted to "devour" the rest of Southeast Asia. The interaction of analytic uncertainty and decisional prudence is a vicious circle that makes the segregation of empirical intelligence and normative policy an unattainable Platonic ideal.

In the simplest situation, the intelligence system can avert policy failure by presenting relevant and undisputed facts to non-expert principals who might otherwise make decisions in ignorance. But these simple situations are not those in which major intelligence failures occur. Failures occur when ambiguity aggravates ambivalence. In these more important situations—Acheson and Clausewitz to the contrary—the intelligence officer may perform most usefully by *not* offering the *answers* sought by authorities, but by offering *questions*, acting as a Socratic agnostic, nagging decision makers into awareness of the full range of uncertainty, and making the authorities' calculations harder rather than easier. Sensitive leaders will reluctantly accept and appreciate this function. Most leaders will not; they will make mistakes, and will continue to bear the prime responsibility for "intelligence" failures. Two general values (which sound wistful in the context of the preceding fatalism) remain to guide the choice of marginal reforms: anything that facilitates dissent and access to authorities by intelligence producers, and anything that facilitates skepticism and scrutiny by consumers. The values are synergistically linked; one will not improve the use of intelligence without the other. (A third value, but one nearly impossible to achieve, would be anything that increases the time available to principals for reading and reflection.)

Intelligence failures are not only inevitable, they are natural. Some are even benign (if a success would not have changed policy). Scholars cannot legitimately view intelligence mistakes as bizarre, because they are no more common and no less excusable than academic errors. They are less forgivable only because they are more consequential. Error in scholarship is resolved dialectically, as deceptive data are exposed and regnant theories are challenged, refined, and replaced by new research. If decision makers had but world enough and time, they could rely on this process to solve their intelligence problems. But the press of events precludes the luxury of letting theories sort themselves out over a period of years, as in academia. My survey of the intractability of the inadequacy of intelligence, and its inseparability from mistakes in decision, suggests one final conclusion that is perhaps most outrageously fatalistic of all: tolerance for disaster.

Questions for Further Discussion

1. Why is it so difficult to strike the correct balance in undertaking intelligence reforms?

2. Why is it impossible to overcome many of the problems faced by intelligence analysts?

3. Who in the intelligence community should play the role of "devil's advocate"?

4. How might net assessment contribute to better intelligence analysis?

Endnotes

1. For example, Klaus Knorr, "Failures in National Intelligence Estimates: The Case of the Cuban Missiles," *World Politics*, XVI (April 1964), 455, 465–66; Harry Howe Ransom, "Strategic Intelligence and Foreign Policy," *World Politics*, XXVII (October 1974), 145.

2. "As that ancient retiree from the Research Department of the British Foreign Office reputedly said, after serving from 1903–50: 'Year after year the worriers and fretters would come to me with awful predictions of the outbreak of war. I denied it each time. I was only wrong twice.' " Thomas L. Hughes, *The Fate of Facts in a World of Men—Foreign Policy and Intelligence-Making* (New York: Foreign Policy Association, Headline Series No. 133, December 1976), 48. Paradoxically, "successes may be indistinguishable from failures." If analysts predict war and the attacker cancels his plans because surprise has been lost, "success of the intelligence services would have been expressed in the falsification of its predictions," which would discredit the analysis. Avi Shlaim, "Failures in National Intelligence Estimates: The Case of the Yom Kippur War," *World Politics*, XXVIII (April 1976), 378.

3. Compare the prescriptions in Peter Szanton and Graham Allison, "Intelligence: Seizing the Opportunity," with George Carver's critique, both in *Foreign Policy*, No. 22 (Spring 1976).

4. Roberta Wohlstetter, *Pearl Harbor: Warning and Decision* (Stanford: Stanford University Press 1962); Barton Whaley, *Codeword Barbarossa* (Cambridge: The M.I.T. Press 1973); Harvey De Weerd, "Strategic Surprise in the Korean War," *Orbis*, VI (Fall 1961); Alan Whiting, *China Crosses the Yalu* (New York: C1 Macmillan 1960); James F. Schnabel, *Policy and Direction: The First Year* (Washington, D.C.: Department of the Army 1972), 61–65, 83–85, 274–78; Michael I. Handel, *Perception, Deception, and Surprise: The Case of the Yom Kippur War* (Jerusalem: Leonard Davis Institute of International Relations, Jerusalem Paper No. 19, 1976); Shlaim (fn. 2); Abraham Ben-Zvi, "Hindsight and Foresight: A Conceptual Framework for the Analysis of Surprise Attacks," *World Politics*, XXVIII (April 1976); Amos Perlmutter, "Israel's Fourth War, October 1973: Political and Military Misperceptions," *Orbis*, XIX (Summer 1975); U.S. Congress, House, Select Committee on Intelligence [hereafter cited as HSCI], *Hearings, U.S. Intelligence Agencies and Activities: The Performance of the Intelligence Community*, 94th Cong., 1st sess., 1975; Draft Report of the House Select Committee on Intelligence, published in *The Village Voice*, February 16, 1976, pp. 76–81.

5. David Halberstam, *The Best and the Brightest* (New York: Random House 1972); Morris Blachman, "The Stupidity of Intelligence," in Charles Peters and Timothy J. Adams, eds., *Inside the System* (New York: Praeger 1970); Patrick J. McGarvey, "DIA: Intelligence to Please," in Morton Halperin and Arnold Kanter, eds., *Readings in American Foreign Policy: A Bureaucratic Perspective* (Boston: Little, Brown 1973); Chester Cooper, "The CIA and Decision-Making," *Foreign Affairs*, Vol. 50 (January 1972); Sam Adams, "Vietnam Cover-Up: Playing War With Numbers," *Harper's*, Vol. 251 (June 1975); Don Oberdorfer, *Tet!* (Garden City, N.Y.: Doubleday 1971). For a more detailed review, see Richard K. Betts, *Soldiers, Statesmen, and Cold War Crises* (Cambridge: Harvard University Press 1977), chap. 10.

6. Quoted in Henry Brandon, *The Retreat of American Power* (Garden City, N.Y.: Doubleday 1973), 103.

7. Betts (fn. 5), 160–61, 192–95. On bias within CIA, see James Schlesinger's comments in U.S., Congress, Senate, Select Committee to Study Governmental Operations with Respect to Intelligence Activities [hereafter cited as SSCI], *Final Report, Foreign and Military Intelligence*, Book I, 94th Cong., 2d sess., 1976, 76–77.

8. *Ibid.*, Book IV, 56–59; William T. Lee, *Understanding the Soviet Military Threat: How CIA Estimates Went Astray* (New York; National Strategy Information Center, Agenda Paper No. 6. 1977), 24–37; Albert Wohlstetter: "Is There a Strategic Arms Race?" *Foreign Policy*, No. 15 (Summer 1974); Wohlstetter, "Rivals, But No Race", *Foreign Policy*, No. 16 (Fall 1974); Wohlstetter, "Optimal Ways to Confuse Ourselves," *Foreign Policy*, No. 20 (Fall 1975). There are exceptions to this pattern of military and civilian bias: see *ibid.*, 185–188; Lieutenant General Daniel Graham, USA (Ret.), "The Intelligence Mythology of Washington," *Strategic Review*, IV (Summer 1976), 61–62, 64; Victor Marchetti and John Marks, *The CIA and the Cult of Intelligence* (New York: Knopf 1974), 309.

9. The U.S. intelligence *community* includes the CIA, Defense Intelligence Agency (DIA), National Security Agency, the intelligence branches of each military service, the State Department Bureau of Intelligence and Research, the intelligence units of the Treasury and Energy Departments, and the FBI. Before 1973, coordination for national estimates was done through the Office of National Estimates, and since then, through the National Intelligence Officers. The Intelligence Community Staff assists the Director of Central Intelligence in managing allocation of resources and reviewing the agencies' performance.

10. HSCI, Hearings (fn. 4), 656–57.

11. Wilensky, *Organizational Intelligence* (New York: Basic Books 1967), 42–62, 126.

12. *Ibid.*, *passim* The counterpoint of Cooper (fn. 5) and McGarvey (fn. 5) presents a perfect illustration.

13. Graham Allison and Peter Szanton, *Remaking Foreign Policy: The Organizational Connection* (New York: Basic Books 1976), 204.

14. Quoted in SSCI, *Final Report* (fn. 7), I, 82.

15. *Ibid.*, 267, 376; SSCI, *Staff Report, Covert Action in Chile 1963–1973*, 94th Cong., 1st sess., 1975, 48–49. The Senate Committee deplored the tendency of decision makers to focus on the latest raw data rather than on refined analyses, a practice that contributed to the intelligence failure in the 1974 Cyprus crisis. SSCI, *Final Report* (fn. 7), I, 443. But the failure in the October War was largely due to the *reverse* phenomenon: disregarding warning indicators because they contradicted finished intelligence that minimized the possibility of war. HSCI Draft Report (fn. 4), 78; Ben-Zvi (fn. 4), 386, 394; Perlmutter (fn. 4), 453.

16. Churchill, *The Gathering Storm* (Boston: Houghton Mifflin 1948), 587–88.

17. "Where the end is knowledge, as in the scientific community, time serves intelligence; where the end is something else—as in practically every organization but those devoted entirely to scholarship—time subverts intelligence, since in the long run, the central institutionalized structures and aims (the maintenance of authority, the accommodation of departmental rivalries, the service or established doctrine) will prevail." Wilensky (fn. 11), 77.

18. Quoted in SSCI, *Final Report* (fn. 7), I, 274.

19. Sherman Kent, "Estimates and Influence," *Foreign Service Journal*, XLVI (April 1969), 17.

20. Hughes (fn. 2), 43.

21. "The textbooks agree, of course, that we should only believe reliable intelligence, and should never cease to he suspicious, but what is the use of such feeble maxims? They belong to that wisdom which for wane of anything better scribblers of systems and compendia resort to when they run out of ideas." Carl von Clausewitz, *On War*, ed. and trans. by Michael Howard and Peter Paret (Princeton: Princeton University Press 1976), 117.

22. Robert Jervis, *The Logic of Images in International Relations* (Princeton: Princeton University Press 1970), 132; Jervis, *Perception and Misperception in International Politics* (Princeton: Princeton University Press 1976), chap, 4; Floyd Allport, *Theories of Perception and the Concept of Structure* cited in Shlaim (fn. 2), 358. Cognitive theory suggests that uncertainty provokes decision makers to separate rather than integrate their values, to deny that inconsistencies between values exist, and even to see contradictory values as mutually supportive. John Steinbruner, *The Cybernetic Theory of Decision* (Princeton: Princeton University Press 1974), 105–8.

23. See William J. McGuire, "Selective Exposure: A Summing Up," in R. P. Abelson and others, eds., *Theories of Cognitive Consistency* (Chicago: Rand McNally 1968), and Irving L. Janis and Leon Mann, *Decision Making: A. Psychological Analysis of Conflict, Choice, and Commitment* (New York: Free Press 1977), 213–14.

24. CIA Intelligence Information Cable, "Remarks of the Chief of the Ranking Military Academy and Other Chinese Leaders on the Situation in South Vietnam," June 25, 1964, in Lyndon B. Johnson Library National Security Files, Vietnam Country File [hereafter cited as LBJL/NSF-VNCF], Vol. XII, item 55.

25. See for example, U.S. Department of Defense, *The Senator Gravel Edition: The Pentagon Papers* (Boston: Beacon Press 1971) [hereafter cited as Pentagon Papers],Vol. II, 99; Frances Fitzgerald, *Fire in the Lake* (Boston: Atlantic-Little, Brown 1972), 364; Special National Intelligence Estimate 53–64, "Chances for a Stable Government in South Vietnam," September 18, 1964, and McGeorge Bundy's covering letter to the President, in LBJL/NSF-VNCF, Vol. XIII, item 48.

26. Patrick J. McGarvey, *CIA: The Myth and the Madness* (Baltimore: Penguin 1974), l6.

27. David Wise and Thomas B. Ross, *The U-2 Affair* (New York: Random House 1962), 56, 176, 180; Trevor Armbrister, *A Matter of Accountability* (New York: Coward-McCann 1970), 116–18, 141–45, 159, 187–95; U.S. Congress, House, Committee on Armed Services, *Report, Inquiry Into the U.S.S. Pueblo and EC-121 Plane Incidents* [hereafter cited as *Pueblo and EC-121 Report*], 91st Cong., 1st sess., 1969, 1622–24, 1650–51; U.S. Congress, House, Committee on Armed Services, *Hearings, Inquiry Into the U.S.S. Pueblo and EC-121 Plane Incidents* [hereafter cited as *Pueblo and EC-121 Hearings*], 91st Cong., 1st sess., 1969, 693–94, 699–700, 703–7, 714, 722, 734, 760, 773–78, 815–l6.

28. SSCI, *Final Report* (fn. 7), I, 61–62; HSCI Draft Report (fn. 4), 82.

29. McGarvey (fn. 26), 16.

30. Shlaim (fn. 2), 375–77. The proposals follow, with their U.S. analogues noted in parentheses: appoint a special intelligence adviser to the Prime Minister (Director of Central Intelligence) to supplement the military chief of intelligence; reinforce the Foreign Ministry's research department (Bureau of Intelligence and Research); more autonomy for non-military intelligence (CIA); amend rules for transmitting raw intelligence to research agencies, the Defense Minister, and the Prime Minister (routing of signals intelligence from the National Security Agency); restructure military intelligence (creation of DIA in 1961); establish a central evaluation unit (Office of National Estimates). On the U.S. intelligence failure in 1973, see the HSCI Draft Report (fn. 4) 78–79.

31. Shlaim (fn. 2), 379; Handel (fn. 4), 62–63.

32. *Ibid.*, 55.

33. Shlaim (fn. 2), 358–59. The Israeli command estimated a higher probability of attack in May 1973 than it did in October. Having been proved wrong in May, Chief of Staff Elazar lost credibility in challenging intelligence officers, complained that he could no longer argue effectively against them, and consequently was unable to influence his colleagues when he was right. Personal communication from Michael Handel, November 15, 1977.

34. *Washington Post*, November 27, 1977, p. A17.

35. Raymond Garthoff, "On Estimating and Imputing Intentions," *International Security*, II (Winter 1978), 22.

36. Westmoreland, *A Soldier Reports* (Garden City, N.Y.: Doubleday 1976), 316. See the postmortem by the President's Foreign Intelligence Advisory Board, quoted in Herbert Y. Schandler, *The Unmaking of a President* (Princeton: Princeton University Press 1977), 70, 76, 79–80.

37. Wohlstetter (fn. 4), 69.

38. George, "The Case for Multiple Advocacy in Making Foreign Policy," *American Political Science Review*, Vol. 66 (September 1972). My usage of the term multiple advocacy is looser than George's.

39. Henry F. Graff, *The Tuesday Cabinet* (Englewood Cliffs, N.J.: Prentice-Hall 1970), 68–71; Leslie H. Gelb with Richard K. Betts, *The Irony of Vietnam: The System Worked* (Washington, D.C.: Brookings, forthcoming), chap. 4; Ball memorandum of October 5, 1964, reprinted as "Top Secret; The Prophecy the President Rejected," *Atlantic Monthly*, Vol. 230 (July 1972);

McCone, memorandum of April 2, 1965, in LBJL/NSF-VNCF, Troop Decision folder, item 14b.

40. Betts (fn. 5), 199–202; Schandler (fn. 36), 177. George (fn. 38), 759, stipulates that multiple advocacy requires "no major maldistribution" of power, influence, competence, information, analytic resources, and bargaining skills. But, except for resources and the right to representation, the foregoing are subjective factors that can rarely be equalized by design. If they are equalized, in the context of imperfect data and time pressure, erroneous arguments as well as accurate ones will be reinforced. Non-expert principals have difficulty arbitrating intellectually between experts disagree.

41. Quoted in Steinbruner (fn. 22), 332.

42. Clausewitz (fn. 21), 117–18; HSCI, *Hearings* (fn. 4), 634–36; William J. Barnds, "Intelligence and Policymaking in an Institutional Context," in U.S. Commission on the Organization of the Government for the Conduct of Foreign Policy [hereafter cited as Murphy Commission], *Appendices* (Washington, D.C.: G.P.O., June 1975), Vol. VII, 32.

43. HSCI, *Hearings* (fn. 4), 778.

44. SSCI, *Final Report* (fn. 7), IV, 57; Roger Hilsman, *Strategic Intelligence and National Decisions* (Glencoe, Ill.: Free Press 1956), 40. During brief service as just a low-level staff member of the National Security Council, even I never had time to read all the intelligence analyses relevant to my work.

45. SSCI, *Final Report* (fn. 7), I, 344, and IV, 95 (emphasis deleted).

46. Ray S. Cline, *Secrets, Spies, and Scholars* (Washington, D.C.: Acropolis 1976), 20.

47. Gilbert W. Fitzhugh and others, *Report to the President and the Secretary of Defense on the Department of Defense, By the Blue Ribbon Defense Panel* (Washington D.C.; G.P.O., July 1970), 45–46.

48. Alexander George, "The Devil's Advocate: Uses and Limitations," Murphy Commission, *Appendices* (fn. 42), II, 84–85; Jervis, *Perception and Misperception* (fn. II), 417.

49. *Ibid.*, 416.

50. U.S. Congress, Senate, Select Committee on Intelligence, Report, *The National Intelligence Estimates A-B Team Episode Concerning Soviet Capability and Objectives*, 95th Cong., 2d sess., 1978; *New York Times*, December 36, 1976, pp. 1, 14; *Washington Post*, January 2, 1977, pp. A1, A4.

51. George H. Poteal, "The Intelligence Gap: Hypotheses on the Process of Surprise," *International Studies Notes*, III (Fall 1976), 15.

52. Cline (fn.46), 140.

53. SSCI, *Final Report* (fn. 7), I, 352. A valid criticism is that military personnel systems and promotion standards penalized intelligence officers, thus encouraging competent officers to avoid intelligence assignments. This situation was rectified in the service intelligence agencies by the early 1970's, but not within DIA. *Ibid.* Betts (fn. 5), 196–97.

54. SSCI, *Final Report* (fn. 7), I, 77–81. See also U.S., Congress, Senate, Committee on Foreign Relations, *Hearings, National Security Act Amendment*, 92d Cong., 2d sess. 1972, 14–24.

55. Zumwalt, *On Watch* (New York: Quadrangle 1976), 459.

56. Wilensky (fn. 11), 164.

57. Jervis, *Perception and Misperception* (fn. 22), 181–87.

58. Knorr (fn. I), 460.

59. SSCI, *Final Report* (fn. 7), I, 276, and IV, 85; U.S., Congress, House, Committee on Appropriations, *Hearings, Supplemental Appropriations for Fiscal Year 1977*, 95th Cong., 2d sess., 1977, 515–621; *Washington Post*, February 15, 1977, p. A6; Paul W. Blackstock, "The Intelligence Community Under the Nixon Administration," *Armed Forces and Society*, I (February 1975), 238.

60. Joseph C. Goulden, *Truth Is the First Casualty* (Chicago: Rand McNally 1969), 101–4; Phil G. Goulding, *Confirm or Deny* (New York: Harper & Row 1970), 130–33, 269; *Pueblo and EC-121 Hearings* (fn. 27), 646–47, 665–73, 743–44, 780–82, 802–3, 865–67, 875, 880, 897–99; *Pueblo and EC-121 Report* (fn. 27), 1654–1656, 1662–67; Armbrister (fn. 27), 196ff, 395; U.S. Congress, House, Committee on Armed Services, Report, *Review of Department of Defense Worldwide Communications: Phase I*, 92d Cong., 1st sess., 1971, and *Phase II*, 2d sess., 1972.

61. See, for example, James Blaker and Andrew Hamilton, *Assessing the NATO/Warsaw Pact Military Balance* (Washington, D.C.: Congressional Budget Office, December 1977).

62. SSCI, *Final Report* (fn. 7), I, 61; Thomas G. Belden, "Indications, Warning, and Crisis Operations," *International Studies Quarterly*, XXI (March 1977), 192–93.

63. *Pentagon Papers*, IV, 111–12, 115–24, 217–32. CIA critiques of bombing results begin even before the Tonkin Gulf crisis. CIA/OCI, Current Intelligence Memorandum, "Effectiveness of T-28 Strikes in Laos," June 26, 1964; CIA/DDI, Intelligence Memorandum, "Communist Reaction to Barrel Roll Missions," December 29, 1964. But ambivalence remained even within the CIA, which occasionally issued more sanguine evaluations—e.g., CIA Memorandum for National Security Council, "The Situation in Vietnam," June 28, 1965 (which McGeorge Bundy called directly to the President's attention), and CIA/OCI, Intelligence Memorandum, "Interdiction of Communist Infiltration Routes in Vietnam," June 24, 1965. (All memoranda are in LBJL/NSF-VNCF, Vol. I, item 5, Vol. III, items 28, 28a, 28b, Vol. VI A, items 4, 5, 8.) See also *Pentagon Papers*, IV, 71–74. See also the opposing assessments of the CIA, the civilian analysis in the Pentagon, and the Joint Chiefs in NSSM-I (the Nixon Administration's initial review of Vietnam policy), reprinted in the *Congressional Record*, Vol. 118, part 13, 92d Cong., 2d sess., May 10, 1972, pp. 16749–836. ✦

10
Open Source Intelligence

Robert D. Steele

Although open source intelligence (OSINT) always has existed, the information revolution now provides citizens, intelligence analysts, and government officials with easy access to an enormous volume of information, data that were gathered and manipulated at great expense only by government agencies just a few short decades ago. Steele describes various types of information available on the World Wide Web and explains how these sources can be exploited by intelligence organizations to supplement the classified information they traditionally rely on as a basis for their estimates.

Executive Summary

Open Source Intelligence (OSINT) is the only discipline that is both a necessary foundation for effective classified intelligence collection and analysis, and a full multi-media discipline in its own right, combining overt human intelligence from open sources, commercial imagery, foreign broadcast monitoring, and numerous other direct and localized information sources and methods not now properly exploited by the secret intelligence community. OSINT is uniquely important to the development of strategic intelligence, not only for the government, but for the military, law enforcement, business, academia, non-governmental organizations, the media, and civil societies including citizen advocacy groups, labor unions, and religions for the simple reason that its reliance on strictly legal and open sources and methods allows OSINT to be shared with anyone anywhere, and helps create broader communities of interest through structured information sharing.

It can be said that at the strategic level in particular, but at all four levels of analysis (strategic, operational, tactical, and technical) generally, the secret intelligence communities of the world are inside-out and upside-down. They are inside-out because they persist in trying to answer important questions with unilaterally collected secrets, rather than beginning with what they can learn from the outside-in: from the seven tribes[1] and the 90+ nations that form the Coalition. They are upside down, at least in the case of the United States of America (USA) and selected other major powers, because they rely too much on expensive overhead satellite systems, instead of bottom-up ground truth networks of humans with deep historical, cultural, and localized knowledge.

In the long-run, I anticipate that OSINT will displace 80% of the current manpower and dollars devoted to secret sources & methods, and that this will offer the taxpayers of the respective nations a Return on Investment (RoI) at least one thousand times better than what is obtained now through secret sources and methods. A proper focus on OSINT will alter the definition of "national" intelligence to embrace all that can be known from the seven tribes across both the home nation and the coalition nations, and will dramatically reform intelligence, electoral processes, governance, and the application of the national, state, and local budgets in support of the public interest.

Strategically, OSINT will restore informed engaged democracy and moral capitalism, a new form of communal capitalism, in America and around the world. OSINT is, at root, the foundation for the emergence of the World Brain, and the empowerment of the public.

The bulk of this chapter will focus on OSINT and intelligence reform at the strategic level, but it is essential that the reader appreciate the implications of OSINT for electoral, governance, and budgetary reform so as to better realize the enormous implications of the revolution in intelligence affairs[2] for which OSINT is the catalyst.

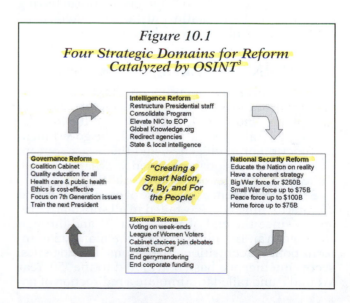

Figure 10.1
Four Strategic Domains for Reform Catalyzed by OSINT[3]

Intelligence Reform
Restructure Presidential staff
Consolidate Program
Elevate NIC to EOP
Global Knowledge.org
Redirect agencies
State & local intelligence

Governance Reform
Coalition Cabinet
Quality education for all
Health care & public health
Ethics is cost-effective
Focus on 7th Generation issues
Train the next President

"Creating a Smart Nation, Of, By, and For the People"

National Security Reform
Educate the Nation on reality
Have a coherent strategy
Big War force for $250B
Small War force up to $75B
Peace force up to $100B
Home force up to $75B

Electoral Reform
Voting on week-ends
League of Women Voters
Cabinet choices join debates
Instant Run-Off
End gerrymandering
End corporate funding

The impetus for reform across all four strategic domains could emerge from within any one of the four. If the economy collapses and the war on Iraq combined with an attack on Iran cause a clear and present danger to emerge in the form of global Islamic counter-attacks that are asymmetric and indiscriminate as well as widespread, we can anticipate not just the ejection of the extremist Republicans, but also of the complacent and equally corrupt and ignorant Democrats.[4]

There is a growing awareness within the public, described by some as "smart mobs," or "wisdom of the crowds," or—our preferred term—Collective Intelligence, that it is now possible for individuals to have better intelligence based on open sources and methods, that is being made available to—or acknowledged by—the President.[5] We will see, within the next four years, a dramatic increase in both historical accountability,[6] and current accountability for actions impacting on future generations and other communities.

Electoral reform will be inspired by citizens realizing that both the Republican and Democratic parties have become corrupt as well as inept at representing the public interest.

Governance reform will be inspired by citizens realizing that in today's world, we need a networked model of governance that elevates intelligence to the forefront—decisions must be made in the public interest and be sustainable by consensus and conformance to reality, not purchased by bribery from special interests who seek to loot the commonwealth and/or abuse their public power to pursue the ideological fantasies of an extremist minority.

Budgetary reform will be inspired by citizens who understand that we still need to be able to defend ourselves, but that waging peace worldwide is a much more cost effective means of both deterring attacks and of stimulating sustainable indigenous wealth that is inherently stabilizing.

OSINT and Intelligence Reform

Open Source Intelligence (OSINT) should be, but is not, the foundation for all of the secret collection disciplines, and it could be, but is not, the foundation for a total reformation of both the governmental function of intelligence, and the larger concept of national and global intelligence, what some call Collective Intelligence or the World Brain.[7]

Secret intelligence, inclusive of covert action and counterintelligence, has failed in all substantive respects since the end of World War II and through the Cold War. In failing to meet the mandate to inform policy, acquisition, operations, and logistics, secret intelligence has contributed to the "50 Year Wound"[8] and failed to stimulate a redirection of national investments from military capabilities to what General Al Gray, then Commandant of the Marine Corps, called "peaceful preventive measures."[9]

Secret intelligence became synonymous with clandestine and secret technical collection, with very little funding applied to either sense-making information technologies, or to deep and distributed human expertise. The end result at the strategic level can be described by the following two observations, the first a quote and the second a recollected paraphrase:

Daniel Ellsberg speaking to Henry Kissinger:

"The danger is, you'll become like a moron. You'll become incapable of learning from most people in the world, no matter how much experience they have in their particular areas that may be much greater than yours" [because of your blind faith in the value of your narrow and often incorrect secret information].[10]

Tony Zinni speaking to a senior national security manager:

"80% of what I needed to know as CINCENT I got from open sources rather than classified reporting. And within the remaining 20%, if I knew what to look for, I found another 16%. At the end of it all, classified intelligence provided me, at best, with 4% of my command knowledge."[11]

Secret intelligence may legitimately claim some extraordinary successes, and we do not disagree with Richard Helms when he says that some of those successes more than justified the entire secret intelligence budget, for example, in relation to Soviet military capabilities and our counter-measures.[12] However, in the larger scheme of things, secret intelligence failed to render a strategic value to the nation, in part because it failed to establish a domestic constituency, and could be so easily ignored by Democratic presidents and both ignored and manipulated by Republican presidents.[13]

In this first section, we will briefly review both the failings of each aspect of the secret intelligence world, and summarize how OSINT can improve that specific aspect.

History

The history of secret intelligence may be concisely summarized in relation to three periods:

- **Secret War.** For centuries intelligence, like war, was seen to be the prerogative of kings and states, and it was used as a form of "war by other means," with spies and counter-spies, covert actions and plausible deniability.[14]

- **Strategic Analysis.** During and following World War II, Sherman Kent led a movement to emphasize strategic analysis. Despite his appreciation for open sources of information, and academic as well as other experts, the clandestine and covert action elements of the Office of Strategic Services (OSS) and the follow-on Central Intelligence Group (CIG) and then Central Intelligence Agency (CIA), grew out of control, well beyond what President Harry Truman had envisioned when he sponsored the National Security Act of 1947.[15]

- **Smart Nation.** Since 1988 there has been an emergent movement, not yet successful, but increasingly taking on a life of its own in the private sector outside of government. Originally conceptualized as an adjunct to secret intelligence, a corrective focus on open sources long neglected, it was soon joined by the Collective Intelligence movement that has also been referred to as "smart mobs" or "wisdom of the crowds," or "world brain." H. G. Wells conceptualized a world brain in the 1930's. Quincy Wright conceptualized a world intelligence center in the 1950's. Others have written about smart nations, collective intelligence, global brain, and the seven tribes of intelligence.[16]

Although the U.S. Intelligence Community has individuals that respect the value of open sources of information, and every major commission since the 1940's has in some form or another called for improved access to foreign language information that is openly available, the reality is that today, in 2006, the United States of America (USA) continues to spend between $50 billion and $70 billion a year on secret collection, almost nothing on all-source sense-making or world-class analysis, and just over $250 million a year on OSINT. This is nothing less than institutionalized lunacy.

The future history of secret intelligence is likely to feature its demise, but only after a citizen's intelligence network is able to apply OSINT to achieve electoral, governance, and budgetary reform, with the result that secret intelligence waste and defense acquisition waste will be converted into "waging peace" with peaceful preventive measures and a massive focus on eliminating poverty, disease, and corruption, while enabling clean water, alternative energy, and collaborative behavior across all cultural boundaries.[17]

Requirements

Requirements, or Requirements Definition, is the single most important aspect of the all-source intelligence cycle, and the most neglected. Today, and going back into history, policymakers and commanders tend to ignore intelligence, ask the wrong questions, or ask questions in such a way as to prejudice the answers. There are three major problems that must be addressed if we are to improve all-source decision support to all relevant clients for intelligence.

1. **Scope.** We must acknowledge that all levels of all organizations need intelligence. We cannot limit ourselves to "secrets for the President." If we fail to acknowledge the needs of lower-level policy makers, including all Cabinet members and their Assistant Secretaries; all acquisition managers, all operational commanders down to civil affairs and military police units; all logisticians; and all allied coalition elements including non-governmental organizations, then we are not being professional about applying the proven process of intelligence to the decision-support needs of key individuals responsible for national security and national prosperity.

2. **Competition.** We must acknowledge that open sources of information are vastly more influential in the domestic politics of all nations, and that it is not possible to be effective at defining

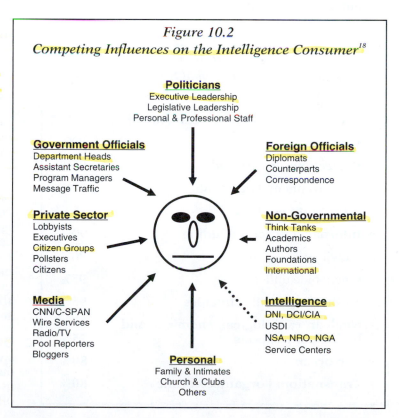

Figure 10.2
Competing Influences on the Intelligence Consumer[18]

Politicians
Executive Leadership
Legislative Leadership
Personal & Professional Staff

Government Officials
Department Heads
Assistant Secretaries
Program Managers
Message Traffic

Foreign Officials
Diplomats
Counterparts
Correspondence

Private Sector
Lobbyists
Executives
Citizen Groups
Pollsters
Citizens

Non-Governmental
Think Tanks
Academics
Authors
Foundations
International

Media
CNN/C-SPAN
Wire Services
Radio/TV
Pool Reporters
Bloggers

Intelligence
DNI, DCI/CIA
USDI
NSA, NRO, NGA
Service Centers

Personal
Family & Intimates
Church & Clubs
Others

requirements for secret intelligence decision-support in the absence of a complete grasp of what is impacting on the policy makers, managers, and commanders from the open sources world. Consider Figure 10.2 (p. 139).

3. **Focus.** Third, and finally, we must acknowledge that at the strategic level, our focus must of necessity be on long-term threats and opportunities that are global, complex, inter-related, and desperately in need of public education, public recognition, and public policy that is sustainable, which is to say, non-partisan or bi-partisan. Consider, for example, the following findings from the Report of the High-level Panel on Threats, Challenges and Change, *A more secure world: Our shared responsibility.*[19]

The average utility and relevance of OSINT to these global threats is—on the basis of my informed estimate—82.5%, which comes very close to the generic "80–20" rule. We must conclude that any nation that persists in spending 99.9 percent of its intelligence funds on collecting secrets,[20] and less than one half of one percent of its intelligence funds on OSINT, is quite literally, clinically insane (or insanely corrupt) at the highest levels.

In all three of the above cases, only OSINT can deliver a solution that is affordable, practical, and infinitely shareable with all stake-holders both in and out of government.

Figure 10.3
OSINT Relevance to Global Security Threats

- **Economic and social threats including**   **95%**
  - poverty,   99%
  - infectious disease and   95%
  - environmental degradation   90%
- **Inter-State conflict**   **75%**
- **Internal conflict, including**   **90%**
  - civil war,   80%
  - genocide and   95%
  - other large-scale atrocities   95%
- **Nuclear, radiological, chemical, and biological weapons**   **75%**
- **Terrorism**   **80%**
- **Transnational organized crime**   **80%**

Collection

Secret collection has made three fundamental mistakes across several generations of management:[21]

1. **Denigrated OSINT.** It chose to ignore open sources of information, assuming that the consumers of intelligence were responsible for their own OSINT, and that OSINT would not impact on secret collection. In fact, OSINT can dramatically reduce the cost and the risk, and increase the return on investment in secret sources and methods, simply by helping with targeting, spotting, assessment, validation, and the over-all strategic context of what needs to be collected "by other means." It merits very strong emphasis that this failure to respect open sources of information falls into three distinct forms:

- Complete disrespect for history in all languages. There is no place within the U.S. Government where one can "see" all Chinese statements on the Spratley Islands, or all Iranian statements on the competing Caliphate concept, or all Brazilian statements on alternative energy sources. We simply do not compute history, and consequently what little we know about current events and threats is known is isolated ignorance of history.

- Complete abdication of any responsibility for monitoring, understanding, and engaging sub-state or transnational entities as major factors in both international affairs, and as threats or potential allies in domestic security and prosperity.

- Finally, almost complete abdication for more nuanced topics other than standard political-military calculations, with very important sustained failures to collect information on socio-economic, ideo-cultural, techno-demographic, or natural-geographic matters. This has been compounded by an extraordinary laziness or ignorance is relying almost exclusively on what can be stolen or obtained readily in English—the USA simply does not "do" the key 31 languages,[22] much less the totality of 185 languages necessary to understand the sub-state threat and the global network of cause and effect.

2. **Official Cover.** We have relied almost exclusively, at least in the USA, on "official cover" for our spies, and known trajectories for our satellites. Non-Official Cover (NOC), which does not offer any form of diplomatic or other official

immunity from incarceration or eviction, has been treated as too expensive, too complicated, and not worthy of full development. The result has been the almost total compromise of all U.S. secret agents and case officers overseas, as well as their varied not-so-secret thefts of the codebooks of other nations. We not only don't know what we don't know, we are in denial about the basic fact that what we do know has been compromised.

3. **Failure to Process.** Finally, and this applies to both clandestine human collection and secret technical collection, we have failed, with deliberate ignorance at the management level, to devote any resources of significance to processing—to sense-making. Today, eighteen years after the needed functionalities for an all-source analytic desktop toolkit were published, we still do not have a desktop analytic toolkit. Today, despite major advances in the private sector with respect to machine-speed translation, and machine-speed statistical, pattern, and predictive analysis, the large majority of our classified intelligence analysis is still done the old-fashioned way: reading at human speed, cutting and pasting, attempting to make sense of vast volumes of secret information while lacking equivalent access to vast volumes of open source information (and especially open source information in any language other than English), limited by the physics of the 24-hour day.

OSINT combines the proven process of intelligence with the ability to collect, process, and analyze all information in all languages all the time. We collect, at best, 20% of what we need to collect, at 99% of the cost, and we spill most of that for lack of processing capabilities. It can be said, as an informed judgment, that Washington is operating on 2% of the relevant strategic information necessary to devise, implement, and adjust national strategy.[23] We should not be sending spies where schoolboys can go, nor should we be ignoring scholarship in all languages.

There will still be a need for selected clandestine human operations, especially against organized crime and translation terrorist groups, but they will need to shift toward non-official cover, and multinational task forces. Secret technical collection will need to emphasize commercial collection first, dramatically refocus secret collection, and shift the bulk of the future resources toward processing—making sense of what we do collect—and toward close-in technical collection inclusive of beacons for tracking bad guys and bad things.

Collection Management will require draconian reform. Instead of defaulting to the tasking of secret collection capabilities, an enlightened collection manager will first determine if they can FIND the information for free in their existing stores of knowledge; then determine if they can GET the information for free from an allied government or any of the seven tribes; and then determine if they can BUY the information from a commercial provider, ideally a localized provider with direct indigenous access, in the time and with the operational security (e.g. cover support plans) appropriate to the need. Only if the first three options are unsuited to the need should the collection manager be tasking secret sources and methods, and even that will have to change to accommodate new possibilities from multinational secret task forces able to leverage the collection capabilities of varied countries, many of them vastly superior to the USA when it comes to both deep cover clandestine human penetrations, and the related ability to place close-in secret technical collection devises.[24]

OSINT is, without question, the catalyst for a revolution in how we collect intelligence.

Processing

Apart from our failure to actually invest in processing (known within the US Intelligence Community as Tasking, Processing, Exploitation, and Dissemination, or **TPED**), we have made three consistent mistakes over time that have made it virtually impossible, and now unaffordable, to actually do automated all-source analysis:

1. **No Standards.** We failed to establish data standards that could be used at the point of entry for both secret and open sources of information. This applies to both information sources, and information software. Not only was the intelligence community much too slow to adopt commons standards such as eXtended Markup Language (XML) Resource Description Framework (RDF), Web Ontology Language (OWL), Simple Object Access Protocol (SOAP), today it is either ignorant of or reluctant to move ahead aggressively with Open Hypertextdocument System (OHS)[25] and eXtended Markup Language Geospatial (XML Geo). The obsession with security, and the pathology of limiting contracts to the established firms in the military-industrial complex who profit from proprietary softwares and human "butts in seats" rather than real-world low-cost answers, can be blamed for the chasm between the secret intelligence world and the real world of open sources and standards.

2. **No Geospatial Attributes.** In the fall of 1988 it was made known to the U.S. Intelligence Community and clearly articulated by the author to a meeting of the General Defense Intelligence Program (GDIP), that in the absence of geospatial attributes for every datum entering the all-source processing system (actually an archipelago of private databases), that machine-speed all-source analysis and fusion would be an impossibility. Despite this, the individual secret collection disciplines of clandestine human intelligence (HUMINT), signals intelligence (SIGINT), and imagery intelligence (IMINT) refuse to do anything other than persist with their human analytic reporting that provides date-time-group (DTG), and geographic place names where known, but no standard geospatial attributes for relating information to a map. Today Google Earth is being used in extraordinary ways to visualize relationship databases of real estate, shipping, and other important topics, and the individual citizen is light years ahead of the average "cut and paste" analyst at the federal, state, and local levels.

3. **No Integration.** There is no one single place where all known information comes together. Despite critical concerns raised by every Congressional and Presidential commission since the 1940's, the U.S. Intelligence Community has continued to be "flawed by design,"[26] and persisted in the turf wars between the Central Intelligence Agency (CIA) and the Federal Bureau of Investigation (FBI), between the FBI and the Drug Enforcement Administration (DEA), between FBI and the Department of Justice (DoJ), and between the Departments of State and Defense. Within the Department of Defense (DoD), the services have not only competed with one another, but actively conspired to fabricate and manipulate intelligence to exaggerate the threats relevant to their budget share. A corollary of this abysmal situation is that processing within the stovepipes has been focused on the delivery of documents rather than on making sense of all of the information in the aggregate. With the exception of selected efforts at the National Security Agency, the Army's Intelligence and Security Command, and the U.S. Special Operations Command, virtually all civilian and military analysts are still in cut and paste mode, and do not have the tools for pattern or trend analysis or anomaly detection, much less predictive analysis.

In processing, it is machine speed translation and statistical analysis, based on standards and global distributed information integration, that permits early warning, anomaly detection, and structured analysis that can be completed in a timely—that is to say, relevant—manner. OSINT is where the real innovation is occurring, and I anticipate that within ten years, the secret world will be sharply restricted to no more than 20% of its present cost and size, while the balance of the funding is re-directed to a mix of OSINT that can be shared with anyone, and peaceful preventive measures in lieu of a heavy metal military.

Among the corrective measures required in secret processing, which OSINT will facilitate, are a shift toward the Internet as the common operating environment; the adoption of open source software to provide a generic access and collaborative sharing environment for all seven tribes;[27] the development of 24/7 "plots" at every level of governance in which all information can be seen in time and geospatial context;[28] and the creation of a national skunkworks with an anti-trust waiver for the public testing and certification of all open sources, softwares, and services. Rapid promulgation of free wireless within urban areas and in the Third World will help accelerate both sharing in the North and West, and uploading of useful information from the East and South.

Analysis

In evaluating the failure of analysis, it is important to understand that most U.S. analysts are too young, too inexperienced in the real world, and too isolated from foreign or even U.S. private sector experts, to realize that the secret information they are receiving is out of context, often wrong, and largely irrelevant to strategic analysis. Their managers are too busy trying to be promoted or to win bonuses or please the White House (or the representative of the White House, the Director of Central Intelligence (DCI)). As a result, the strategic analysis vision of Sherman Kent has been dishonored and largely set aside. There have been three major failures in analysis over time.

1. **Hire Young.** The intelligence management philosophy in both the national civilian hires and at the military theater and service center levels has combined "hire to payroll" with obsessive lazy security parameters that have resulted in an analytic population that is largely young, white, and mostly bereft of overseas experience and especially long-term residency in foreign countries. On the one hand, budgets have been used to hire low and promote over time, treating analysis as an entry-level hiring challenge rather than a mid-career sabbatical challenge; this has been deeply and pathologi-

cally influenced by a low-rent security philosophy that has combined paranoia over foreign contacts (and relatives), with an unwillingness to spend the time and thoughtfulness necessary to clear complicated individuals who have led complicated lives. This personnel management failure stems from the larger philosophical management failure, which confuses secrets with intelligence, and thus demeans expertise from the open source world while assuming that young analysts will succeed because they have access to secrets, rather than because of any application of analytic tradecraft such as might take twenty years to refine.

2. **Hard Target Focus.** In keeping with the military-industrial complex and its desire to profit from the Cold War, the national and military intelligence communities devoted virtually their entire budgets and most of their manpower to the "hard targets" (generally, Russia, China, Iran, India, Pakistan, Libya, and—hard to believe but true—Cuba). They ignored all of the "lower tier" issues and Third World countries,[29] and also focused only on very big threats, not on very big opportunities for peaceful preventive measures where a few dollars invested in the 1970's might have eradicated Anti-Immune Deficiency Systems (AIDS) or dependency on Middle Eastern oil. This was of course in keeping with policy preferences, and even when the CIA did excellent work (for example, accurately forecasting the global AIDS epidemic), it could safely be ignored because its work was not available to the public or even to most Members of Congress. A very important consequence of this narrow focus was the complete failure to ensure that all of the sources of national power—diplomatic, informational, military, economic (DIME)—were funded, acquired, fielded, and applied in a coherent and timely manner. The entire military-industrial-intelligence complex has been skewed toward a heavy metal military—a few big platforms or big organizations—that are only relevant 10% of the time. We are completely unprepared for, we are not trained, equipped, or organized, for small wars, waging peace, or homeland defense. This is still true—truer than ever—in the aftermath of 9-11 and the invasions and occupations of Afghanistan and Iraq.

3. **Local Now.** Finally, U.S. Intelligence (and many foreign intelligence communities) focused on the local now instead of the global future. "Current Intelligence" dominated the President's Daily Briefing (PDB), and over time longer-term research fell by the wayside. This problem was aggravated by a draconian editing process in both the national civilian and theater or service level military, where a twelve month research project could be subject to eighteen month editing cycles, such that the work was out of date or thoroughly corrupted by the time it was finally released to a relatively limited number of policymakers. With most of the intelligence products being released in hard-copy, or messages that were printed out and not saved electronically, the overall impact of U.S. intelligence production, and especially Codeword production, must be judged as marginal.[30]

OSINT is "the rival store."[31] Whereas I spent the first eighteen years of my campaign to foster an appreciation on OSINT and focusing on the urgency of integrating OSINT into secret sources toward improved all-source analysis, I plan to spend the next eighteen years burying 80% of the classified world. They are too expensive, too irrelevant, and pathologically anti-thetical to the new and correct Swedish concept of Multinational, Multiagency, Multidisciplinary, Multidomain Information Sharing (M4IS).[32] OSINT analysis will in the future be the benchmark by which classified sources and methods are judged to be relevant and cost-effective, or not. The Director of National Intelligence (DNI) has chosen to remain focused on secrets for the President. So be it. OSINT, from a private sector and non-governmental foundation, will capture all the other consumers of intelligence. The day will come when "clearances" are severely devalued and open source access—international open source access in all languages all the time—is ascendant. The DCI must serve all levels of the government, all seven tribes, and must balance between open and closed sources so as to inform decision-makers—and their publics—in order to preserve and enhance the long-term national security and prosperity of the USA. Secret sources and methods—and the existing military—have demonstrably failed in both regards.

Analytic tradecraft notes are available online and should be consulted.[33] All-source analysts should not be hired until they have first proven themselves as masters of all open sources in all languages relevant to their domain and not be considered for mid-career hire unless they are one of the top 25 cited authorities in the field. They must know how to leverage their historian, their librarian, and the Internet. They must know how to identify and interact with the top 100 people in the world on their topic, regardless of citizenship or clearances. Finally, they must understand that they are—and must be—trained to be—managers of customer relations and requirements definition; of open sources; of external experts; and of classified collection management. Analysts must know and practice the "new rules" for the new craft of intelligence, with specific reference to being able to actually do forecasting, establish strategic generalizations, and drill down to the neighborhood and tribal levels, not simply hover at the nation-state level.[34]

Covert Action

Covert action consists of agents of influence, media placement, and paramilitary operations. Covert action assumes two things that may once have been true but are no longer true: that an operation can be carried out without its being traced back to the USA as the sponsor; and that the fruits of the operation will be beneficial to the USA. In each of these three areas, the USA has acted with great disdain for the normal conventions of legitimacy, accountability, morality, and practicality, and today the USA is suffering from what is known as "blow-back"—it is reaping the dividends from decades of unethical behavior justified in the name of national security, but unfounded upon any substantive grasp of long-term reality.

1. **Agents of influence** are individuals bribed covertly who are charged with getting their governments or organizations to pursue a course of action that the USA deems to be necessary, but that may not be in the best interests of the indigenous public or its government. Regardless of what one may think of the local country and its government and public, what this really means is that agents of influence are responsible for disconnecting local policies from local realities, and imposing instead a reality or choice selected by the US Government. This is inherently pathological. There are certainly some success stories—support to Solidarity in Poland, for example, but this was a capitalization on the fall of communism, not the cause.

2. **Media placement** uses individuals, generally foreign journalists, who are bribed covertly to create and publish stories that communicate an alternative view of reality, one sanctioned by the US Government but generally at odds with the actual facts of the matter. There is a constructive side to media placement, for example the promulgation of information about atrocities committed by dictators or Soviet forces, but generally the US Government supports most of the dictators it deals with, and reserves this tool for deposing individuals that dare to oppose predatory immoral capitalism or virtual colonialism. Consequently, most media placement activities consist of propaganda seeking to manipulate rather than deliver the truth. Media placement by spies should not be confused with Public Diplomacy by diplomats or Strategic Communication by the military—the latter two are overt truth-telling missions, although misguided practitioners may occasionally stray into propaganda and the manipulation of the truth.[35]

3. **Paramilitary operations** are not only direct assaults on the sovereignty of other nations, but they tend to bring with them black markets, drug running, money laundering, corruption, and the proliferation of a culture of violence and the small arms with which to do indiscriminate violence. The Phoenix program of assassinations in Viet-Nam, the support to the contras and the mining of the Nicaraguan harbors (an act condemned by the World Court), the arming of the Islamic fundamentalists for jihad in Afghanistan, join the planned overthrows of the governments of Chile, Guatemala, Iran, as causes of long-term and costly "blow-back." Of all of these, Iran is the most interesting. Had we allowed the nationalization of the oil in Iran and the fall of the Shah, we might today have both a non-fundamentalist Iran as a bulwark against the radicals from Saudi Arabia, but we might also be less dependent on oil, and less subject to the whims of the extraordinarily corrupt Saudi regime and its US energy company allies.

OSINT is the anti-thesis of all three forms of covert action. As David Ignatius noted so wisely in the 1980's, overt action rather than covert action delivers the best value in both the short and the long run. Promulgating the tools for truth—cell phones, wireless access, access to the Internet—is a means of fostering informed democracy and responsible opposition. It is also a means of creating stabilizing indigenous wealth. OSINT provides a historical and cultural foundation for achieving multi-cultural consensus that is sustainable precisely because it is consensual. As Jonathan Schell documents so well in *The Unconquerable World: Power, Nonviolence, and the Will of the People,* there are not enough guns in the world for force our way or protect our borders.[36] Only by fostering legitimacy, morality, charity, and full participation of all, can we stabilize the world to the mutual benefit of the USA and the rest of the world.

OSINT, in addition to being vastly superior to covert action as a means for establishing reasonable goals that are sustainable over time, is also very well suited to documenting the extraordinary costs of historical covert actions. Only now is the public beginning to understand the lasting damage caused by the US sponsorship of assassination attempts against Fidel Castro, capabilities that were ultimately turned against the unwitting President, John F. Kennedy, and his brother Robert. We have sacrificed our national values, and our international credibility at the alter of covert action, and we are long overdue for a deep "truth and reconciliation" commission that evaluates the true costs of covert action, and that then defines much more narrowly the conditions and protocols for engaging in covert action in the future.

Counterintelligence

Strategic counterintelligence is completely distinct from tactical counterintelligence.[37] In strategic counterintelligence, one is looking for emerging threats at the strategic level, not individual penetrations of specific organizations. This is an area where OSINT should, but does not, shine. The US Intelligence Community—and consequently the US policy community—have completely missed the end of cheap oil, the end of free water, the rise of Bin Laden and the rise of pandemic disease, even global warming, precisely because national counterintelligence was focused obsessively on penetrating foreign security services, and not on the strategic environment where natural and other threats of omission and commission were to be found. There are three areas where strategic counterintelligence can benefit considerably from comprehensive OSINT, inclusive of the digitization and statistical analysis of all available historical information.

1. **National education.** Thomas Jefferson said that "A Nation's best defense is an informed citizenry." This is absolutely correct, and even more so today, when central bureaucracies are no match for agile networked transnational groups. The USA has failed to understand the strategic implications of its lack of border control, its mediocre educational system designed to create docile factory workers, and the trends toward obesity, insularity, and indifference that characterize the bulk of the population today. We have gone hollow for lack of focus.

2. **Environment.** The Singapore military was stunned by the emergence of Severe Acute Respiratory Syndrome (SARS), but unlike the U.S. military—they got it. They realized they were responsible for defending Singapore against all threats, not just man-made or man-guided threats, and added national health and border security against airborne, waterborne, and human or animal borne diseases, to their charter. Similarly, the Singapore police have an extraordinarily nuanced and enlightened understanding of their global and regional information needs and responsibilities in relation to deterring and resolving all forms of crime impacting on Singapore. In the USA, and globally with dire consequences for the USA, there are threats associated with the environment and how it changes (including water, energy, and raw material resources) that are simply not understood, not acknowledged, and not being acted upon responsibly by any US Administration, be it Democratic or Republican.[38]

3. **Ideology.** There are two ideological threats to US security today, one external, the other internal. The two together are very troubling. Externally, the radical and violent fundamentalist stream of Islam has been armed and energized by jihad in Afghanistan, in Chechnya, and in Iraq. Other small jihads in Indonesia, the Philippines, and southern Thailand, as well as selected locations in Muslim Africa, add to this threat. Internally, US Christian fundamentalists—these are the people that graduated from rote reading of the Bible to the Left Behind fiction series—have assumed a terribly excessive importance in extremist Republican circles, in part because the Texas corporate energy interests chose to make common cause with them. The Middle East, oil, and the almost cult-like extreme religious right, have hijacked American democracy. The American left, nominally but not intelligently led by the Democratic party (which is as corrupt as the Republican party, but more inept), meanwhile, abandoned faith and God and the sensible calming effect of religion as a foundation for community and ethics.[39] The American ideology of capitalism has also been corrupted. Immoral predatory capitalism, and pathologically inept formulas for "developmental economics" as imposed on failed states by the International Monetary Fund (IMF) and the World Bank, have given rise to populism and other forms of indigenous resistance now witting of the collusion between their corrupt elite and immoral foreign capitalism that are in combination looting the commonwealth of many peoples.[40]

In all three of these cases, OSINT has an extraordinary role to play. Under the leadership of Congressman Rob Simmons (R-CT-02), a moderate Republican with an extraordinarily deep background in both intelligence and on the Hill, the campaign continues for a national Open Source Agency funded at $3 billion per year, under the auspices of the Department of State (as a sister agency to the Board of Governors that controls the Voice of America and other public diplomacy outlets). However, fully half the budget is intended to fund fifty Community Intelligence Centers and networks across the country (each receiving $30 million at Full Operating Capability or FOC). These centers are needed for two reasons: first, to provide 119 and 114 numbers for citizen mobilization (119 alerts all cell phones within a 5 kilometer radius) and citizen neighborhood watch inputs (114 receives cell phone photos, text messages, any form of information, all with geospatial and time tags); and second, to serve as dissemination nodes for transmitting to all schools, chambers of commerce, churches and synagogues and mosques, labor unions, civil advocacy groups, and so on, the wealth of "real world" information to be collected, processed, and shared, free via the Internet, by the Open Source Agency. This will impact very favorably on the environment, as these centers will help citizens at the county, state, and regional levels understand, with precision, where each of them stands with respect to access to clean water, alternative energies and related lifestyle choices, and global threats to their children and grandchildren based on easy access to the actual U.S. federal budget in relation to real world threats and needs. Militarism will be reduced, poverty and disease will be eliminated, and the USA can rejoin the community of nations as force for good. Finally, all competing ideologies can be subject to scrutiny and understanding, and the majority of Americans who are not part of the nutty right can come together consensually to limit the damage these people can do to the Republic, while also holding their political and corporate allies accountable for serving America as a whole rather than a lunatic fringe element.

Dramatically redirecting national intelligence toward OSINT will substantially reduce the cost of secrecy, estimated by the Moynihan Commission as being on the order of $6 billion a year (probably closer to $15 billion a year today),[41] and will also eliminate perhaps 70% of the costs associated with establishing the trustworthiness of individuals being considered for clearances. The security and clearance system of the U.S. Government is broken beyond repair. Not only does it take over two years from most investigations to be completed, but they are generally sub-standard investigations that go through the motions and generally do not detect basic aberrations, such as a fascination with child pornography and online molestation of children, as was the case recently with a senior manager in the Department of Homeland Security. The fact is that most sheriffs and other state and local officials are not "clearable" for a variety of reasons, and we may as well recognize that not only is OSINT better suited for most national intelligence information sharing, but we really do not need most of the grotesquely expensive and dysfunctional Top Secret "compartments" (over 400 of them, half in the civilian world and half in the military world) and all the attendant costs, including the costs of ignorance stemming from compartmented information not being shared. At least at the strategic level, we need a national intelligence system where we are less concerned about betrayal from within, and more focused on emerging strategic threats to our long-term security and prosperity, threats that must not be limited to man-made capabilities, but include animal borne diseases and other environmental conditions that tend to be shut out from national security decision processes.

Accountability, Civil Liberties, and Oversight

As all of the preceding sections should have made clear, OSINT is the essential contributing factor to dramatically improving the accountability and oversight of the U.S. Intelligence Community and the policymakers, acquisition managers, and operational commanders that respond to White House Direction. OSINT is also a means of dramatically enhancing not just civil liberties, but civic engagement in the practice of democracy. By providing citizens at every level with structured OSINT on any issue for any zip code or other geographic grouping, and by making it possible for citizens to immediately connect with other like-minded citizens and with accountable officials, OSINT in practice is an enabler of a new form of constant engaged informed democracy. Civil liberty infractions will be broadcast or podcast, rapidly aggregated, and civil pressure brought to bear. By harnessing citizens are part of the "home guard" and empowering them with immediate and understandable access to indications and warning information, we will dramatically improve the reporting of relevant information, and—through the Community Intelligence Centers—be able to process, make sense of, and act on—or discount—the "bottom up" dots that I am convinced will comprise at least 50% of the relevant dots needed to prevent the next 9-11.

It is also important to emphasize that at the strategic level, we need to be concerned not just with accountability and oversight of secret intelligence, but with the much larger issue of whether Congress and the Executive are being responsible in representing the public interest. For this reason we include very brief but vital sections at the end of this chapter on OSINT and electoral reform, governance reform, and budgetary reform. OSINT is the ultimate resources for citizens to hold their government accountable, and to protect their civil liberties over time.

Strategic Warning

Although CIA has done some fine work on global threats, and I particular like the work done under John Gannon as Assistant Director of Central Intelligence for Analysis & Production (*Global Trends 2015*, which led to *Global Trends 2020*),[42] on balance the U.S. Intelligence Community has failed abysmally at strategic warning because of some fundamental operational and philosophical failures.[43]

Operationally, despite fifty years of extraordinarily generous funding for multi-billion dollar satellite systems, the U.S. Intelligence Community still cannot do wide area surveillance, real-time change detection, or "the last mile" inclusive of seeing into urban area, under jungle canopy, and into the deep ravines of mountainous terrain.

Philosophically U.S. Intelligence has been a disaster in strategic terms. The cult of secrecy limited "intelligence" to "secrets for the President" and left everyone else, from Cabinet-level leaders to military acquisition manager and operational commanders, to Governors and Mayors, completely without "decision-support." Perhaps worse, the U.S. Intelligence Community has refused to recognize the seven tribes of intelligence, shutting out, for the most part, state and local officials with overseas knowledge, business travelers, academics, non-governmental observers, journalists, labor union leaders, religious travelers, and so on. The obsession with government secrecy over public sharing has cost this Nation fifty years of time—the one strategic factor that can not be bought nor replaced[44]—and at least 3 billion souls of good will. U.S. Intelligence is a small part of the overall federal government, and it merits comment that most of our problems today cannot be blamed on U.S. Intelligence as much as on a corrupt Congressional and Executive all too eager to ignore, for example, the Peak Oil warnings of 1974-1979 in order to keep the bribes going and the public docile. This is not, however, to excuse the U.S. Intelligence Community, in as much a focus on OSINT from 1988 onwards would have done much to illuminate and correct the policy errors that benefited from secrecy, obscurity, and public inattentiveness.

Strategic Sharing

The U.S. Intelligence Community is incapable today, five years after 9-11, of creating a single consolidated watch list of suspected terrorists. The U.S. Government as a whole is incapable of sharing everything that it knows for lack of collaborative mindsets, willing management, interoperable systems, and coherent data sets. There are three primary impediments to the U.S. Intelligence Community ever being able to share readily:

1. **High Side Security.** The obsession with security is occasioned in part by the fact that the secret intelligence world, even though it has "compartments," has never learned to disaggregate secret from non-secret information. Everything is stored at the "high side," at the highest possible level of security, meaning that nothing can be shared with anyone who is not cleared for the highest level of security, however unclassified the information might be.

2. **Third Party Rule.** The secret world has for decades operated under a "third party rule" that prohibits the sharing of any information received from one party, with another party. This rule is extremely detrimental to multi-lateral sharing, and imposes enormous time, manpower, and dollar costs when something needs to be shared and the sharing must be coordinated. The default condition of the secret world is "do not share."

3. **Legacy Systems.** As John Perry Barlow noted in an article in *Forbes,*[45] if you want to see the last remnants of the Soviet Empire, go visit the CIA and look at their computer systems. The U.S. Intelligence Community as a whole is still mired in 1970's technology managed by 1950's mind-sets, totally out of touch with 21st Century information networks, both machine and human.

OSINT is going to be the catalyst for M4IS and strategic sharing. OSINT is the only discipline that can easily distribute the collection, processing, and analysis burden across all coalition nations (e.g. the ninety nations comprising the U.S. Central Command coalition), and also the only discipline whose products can easily be shared with non-governmental organizations as well as state and local authorities all over the world who will never qualify for "clearances." It will be our challenge in the next eighteen years to develop an alternative global intelligence community that relies almost exclusively on "good enough" open sources, and that consequently forces the secret world into proving its "added value" in relation to cost, risk, and time, on every topic, every day.

Emerging Prospects

Apart from increased public access to the Internet, inclusive of electronic mail, the deep web, and the dramatically increased availability of free multi-media communications and information sharing capabilities, several factors are supportive of a displacement of secret sources and methods by open sources and methods:

1. **Digitization.** It is a mistake to believe that all relevant information is being digitized today. Tribal histories (e.g. those from Iraq) and vast quantities of important information are still being produced in Industrial Era mediums, and Friday sermons by Islamic imans as well as the sermons by all the other faiths, are not part of the digital revolution. In strategic terms, however, digitization is extremely important for three reasons:

   • Most current information from mainstream and niche media as well as individual publishers and bloggers, in all languages, is now available digitally.

   • Historical information, including policy and financial statements of great importance to specific nations, industries, organizations, and tribes, can now be affordably and effectively digitized.

   • Hand-held devices are rapidly becoming a primary means of collecting and sharing information, with imminent prospects of being able to harness, selectively, all that any group of individuals can see and hear and think, and is willing to upload as needed.

2. **Visualization.** Digital information, including historical information, can now be visualized, not only in relation to content analysis and links between paragraphs and among individuals, but in relation to a geospatial foundation such as Google Earth provides in rudimentary but quite compelling terms. This is moving OSINT well beyond secret sources and methods because it can draw on a much greater body of information and expertise in real time, and apply all modern machine analytic tools with fewer security, legal, and policy constraints. The centralized unilateral secret bureaucracies are losing ground—rapidly—to distributed open multinational networks.

3. **Peer-to-Peer (P2P).** "Ground truth" is taking on a whole new meaning as individuals exercise the power to share complex information directly with one another, eliminating the intermediary journals, web sites, and government or media offices that in the past have played the role of editor, judge, and broker of meaning and value.

The power of OSINT at the strategic level can simply not be exaggerated nor underestimated for the simply reason that it harnesses the distributed intelligence of the Whole Earth, in real time as well as in historical memory time, across all languages and cultures. There isn't a bureaucracy in the world that can match its networked power. To drive that point home, consider the game of baseball. In today's secret environment, government bureaucrats accustomed to unlimited budgets and secret methods continue to try to win the game by bribing a player (Clandestine Intelligence), putting a "bug" in the dug-out (Signals Intelligence), trying to "sniff" the direction and speed of the ball (Measurements & Signatures Intelligence), or taking a satellite picture of the field every three days (Imagery Intelligence). The new craft of intelligence requires integrates the audience. It uses the collective wisdom of all the participants. It encourages the crowd to participate. Open source intelligence harnesses what *everyone* sees and knows. It changes the rules of the game. Any catch in the stands is an out. *That* is how we win against asymmetric opponents who know our Achilles' heels all too well.

OSINT and Electoral Reform

The USA is a Republic. An extraordinary characteristic of Republics is that voters have the power to dissolve the government should it become so ineffective or destructive as to warrant its termination. The Constitution, and the voters, are the foundation of the American democracy, not the three branches of government. If the Executive is mendacious, the Congress is corrupt, and the Judiciary is so unrepresentative of the values of the people as to be a mockery of Justice, then the public has the power to change the rules of the game for elections. It is OSINT that can be used by citizens to break away from the Republican and Democratic parties, and develop new networked means of demanding minimalist changes such as suggested by Ralph Nader and enhanced by the author: voting on week-ends so the poor don't lose work; restoring the League of Women Voters as the arbiters of multi-party debates; demanding that Presidential candidates announce their Cabinets in advance of the election, and including at least the Secretaries of Defense and State, and the Attorney General, in Cabinet-level debates; applying the instant run-off concept to ensure a true majority election; and of course ending gerrymandering and corporate funding for any elected official.

OSINT and Governance Reform

Government at the Federal level has become incompetent, and is wasteful of the taxpayer dollar for two reasons: special interest corruption both in Congress (bribery) and in the Executive (revolving-door favoritism); and an industrial era structure that is largely disconnected from reality to the point that ideological fantasy can supplant a reasoned policy process. At a minimum, the Republic needs a Coalition Cabinet and some means of assuring the citizenry that Presidents will not be able to simply appoint cronies from their own party; the Executive needs to be restructured to provide for integrated policy development, not just national security policy development; strategic planning focused out seven generations (over 200 years) must be demanded and be publicly transparent and accountable; and the fundamentals of national power must be mandated: quality education for all, health care for all, and an end to poverty at home. Presidents and their teams must be elected for their ability to govern rather than campaign. OSINT will make all of this possible, sooner than later if a national Open Source Agency is created as a new fourth branch of government, independent of Congress and the Executive, with a lifetime appointment for its Director, and a Board of Directors comprised of former Presidents, Leaders of the Senate and House, and retired Supreme Court Justices.

OSINT and Strategic Budgetary Reform

Finally, we come to budgetary reform. OSINT has already made it clear that we have a Department of Defense costing $500 billion a year (not counting the cost of the war in Iraq) that is relevant to only 10% of the threat (state on state warfare), that is largely incompetent at small wars and homeland defense, and that we are, as a Republic, not investing properly in peaceful preventive measures inclusive of the spread of participatory democracy and moral capitalism. The RoI on our "Big War" military is not only not there, the existence of that Big War force leads ignorant Presidents and their mendacious Vice Presidents to seek out wars as an option for capturing "cheap" oil (never mind the cost in blood, spirit, and treasure). The American Republic specifically, and all other countries, are long over-due for what I call "reality-based budgeting." OSINT will restore sanity and sensibility to the public treasury and how it is applied.

There is, in the immortal words of Arnie Donahue[46] in 1992, "plenty of money for OSINT." There is also plenty of money for participatory democracy and moral capitalism. Our problem has been that we have allowed the mandarins of secrecy to pretend to be informing the President, rather narrowly and very expensively, while failing to demand that the Republic develop a public intelligence capability suitable for directing public policy and public spending in an intelligent sustainable manner.

9-11, the Iraq War, and the varied accomplishments—or crimes—of the Bush Administration may stand in history as a bright turning point in the history of the Republic. One doubts that anything less might have awakened the somnolent public.

Questions for Further Discussion

1. Which of the Seven Tribes named by Steele will benefit most from Osint?

2. Why does secret information carry such a cachet within the intelligence community?

3. How can Osint help eliminate poverty?

4. What risks do policymakers run if they increase their reliance on Osint?

Endnotes

1. The "seven tribes" are a concept developed by the author and include government, military, law enforcement, business, academia, the ground truth tribe (non-governmental organizations and the media), and the civil sector tribe (citizen advocacy groups and societies, labor unions, and religions).
2. This term, "Revolution in Intelligence Affairs," is abused by loosely-educated individuals who know nothing of revolution and little of all-source intelligence. For a critique of the abuse of the term, and a discussion of the three options for intelligence reform, see the author's "Intelligence Affairs: Evolution, Revolution, or Reactionary Collapse," *International Journal of Intelligence and Counterintelligence* 19/1 (Spring 2006). In a forthcoming issue the author comments on "Intelligence in Denial."
3. NIC: National Intelligence Council. EOP: Executive Office of the President. It is important to observe that the Global Knowledge organization, now called an Open Source Agency, is intended to be completely independent of both Presidential and Congressional manipulation. This chart is discussed in more detail in the final section on Governance Reform. This illustration is drawn from "Citizen in Search of a Leader" as prepared 8 January 2003 and posted to <www.oss.net>. Additional detail on each reform domain can be found in that document.
4. This is a practical professional discourse on OSINT, not a political diatribe, but it is essential for those who have the most to gain from OSINT, citizens, to understand that the extremist Republicans have driven out the moderate Republicans (including the author) while the inept Democrats have alienated both the conservative Democrats and the New Progressives. For an excellent and erudite discussion of why the prevailing mood of the country may well be "a pox on both parties," see Peter Peterson, *RUNNING ON EMPTY: How The Democratic and Republican Parties Are Bankrupting Our Future and What Americans Can Do About It* (New York: Farrar, Straus and Giroux , 2004). Peterson was a Cabinet Secretary under Nixon and Chairman of the Council on Foreign Relations. He joins numerous other moderate Republicans who have published books dismissive of the Republican Party as it has been hijacked by the religious extremists, the neoconservatives, and corporate war-profiteers. The Democratic leadership is equally corrupt, but so inept

as to be incapable of either governing or holding the Republicans accountable.

5. Howard Rheingold, *SMART MOBS: The Next Social Revolution* (New York: Basic Books, 2003); James Surowieki, *The Wisdom of the Crowds* (New York: Anchor Books, 2005); and Pierre Levy, *Collective Intelligence: Mankind's Emerging World in Cyberspace* (New York: Perseus Books, 2000). Three other essential references are H. G. Wells, *World Brain* (London: Ayer, 1938), Howard Bloom, *GLOBAL BRAIN: The Evolution of Mass Mind From the Big Bang to the 21st Century* (New York: Wiley Books, 2001), and Tom Atlee, *The Tao of Democracy: Using Co-Intelligence to Create a World That Works for All* (San Francisco: Writer's Collective, 2003). Robert Steele addresses the concepts and doctrine for actually "doing" collective public intelligence in *THE NEW CRAFT OF INTELLIGENCE: Personal, Public, and Political* (Oakton, Virginia: OSS, 2002).

6. It is now clearly documented that both the White House and the Senate knew that Peak Oil was upon us during varied hearings conducted from 1974-1979, and deliberately concealed this fact from the public, and failed to alter energy policy, in order to avoid alarming citizens or angering them over prices, while continuing to reap the rich dividends of bribery from the oil companies. This is a single specific example of where retrospective impeachments would be appropriate as a means of putting all elected officials that they will be held accountable not just today, but into the future as their treasonous betrayal of the public trust becomes known.

7. There are 20,000 pages on OSINT at <www.oss.net>, and a one-page list of key familiarization links covering history, context, practice, policy, and reference are at <www.oss.net/BASIC>. To this day, the secret intelligence world refers with disdain to OSINT as "Open Sores."

8. The single best book on the cost of the Cold War is Derek Leebaert's *The Fifty-Year Wound: How America's Cold War Victory Has Shaped Our World* (Boston: Back Bay Books, 2003). Chalmers Johnson has written two books in this genre, the first and most recent more methodical than the second: *The Sorrows of Empire: Militarism, Secrecy, and the End of the Republic* (New York: Metropolitan Books, 2004), and *Blowback: The Costs and Consequences of American Empire* (New York: Owl Books, 2004 re-issue). See my partial list of books on blowback at <http://tinyurl.com/qrcdu>. An entire literature on "why people hate America" has been developing, along with US-based critiques of immoral capitalism and virtual colonialism.

9. General Alfred M. Gray, Commandant of the Marine Corps, "Global Intelligence Challenges in the 1990's," in *American Intelligence Journal* (Winter 1988–1989). Despite four years of effort by the Marine Corps, the National Foreign Intelligence Board (NFIB) and the Military Intelligence Board (MIB) refused to address General Gray's recommendations that we change our priorities from worst-case least probably to most probable emerging threats, and that we invest in open sources. Had we done so from 1988–2000, in those twelve years we would probably have collected enough open sources in Arabic and other languages to understand the threat represented by Bin Laden in terms compelling enough—because they were *public*—to mandate sustained effective action by all relevant national capabilities.

10. Daniel Ellsberg, *SECRETS: A Memoir of Vietnam and the Pentagon Papers* (London: Viking Books, 2002). This is his recollection of his words to Henry Kissinger, then National Security Advisor to President Richard Nixon. The three pages on the pathological effects of falling prey to the cult of secrecy, on pages 237–239, should be forced rote memorization for all who receive clearances.

11. General Tony Zinni, USMC (Ret.), former Commander-in-Chief, U.S. Central Command (CINCCENT), as recounted to the author on 4 April 2006 by a very prominent individual close to varied National Security Council and defense personalities, who desires to remain anonymous.

12. As recounted in Richard Helms, *A Look over My Shoulder: A Life in the Central Intelligence Agency* (New York: Random House, 2003)

13. Cf. Robert Steele, *ON INTELLIGENCE: Spies and Secrecy in an Open World* (AFCEA, 2000, Oakton, Virginia: OSS, 2003) with a Foreword by Senator David Boren (D-KS), whose efforts to reform national intelligence in 1992 were undone by a combination of Senator John Warner (R-VA) and Secretary of Defense Dick Cheney. The book remains the single most comprehensive public critique of the shortfalls of the secret world. For a list of other books critical of the past and offering a vision for the future, see my varied lists at Amazon.com.

14. Cf. Walter Laqueur, *A World of Secrets: The Uses and Limits of Intelligence* (New York: Basic Books, 1985). Many other books give accounts of secret warfare going back into time, but culminating in the behind the lines operations in World War II, and then the "dirty tricks" of the 20th Century.

15. Sherman Kent, *Strategic Intelligence for American World Policy* (Princeton: Princeton, 1951). This is a classic. In reality, Kent did not achieve his vision for two reasons: because the clandestine service took over the Central Intelligence Agency and subordinated the analysts, and because in so doing, they cut the analysts off from the world of open sources that were the mainstay of Kent's vision in the first place.

16. Robert Steele is the primary author on the concept of "smart nation." Among the early works were "Creating a Smart Nation: Information Strategy, Virtual Intelligence, and Information Warfare," in Alan D. Campen, Douglas H. Dearth, and R. Thomas Goodden (contributing editors), *CYBERWAR: Security, Strategy, and Conflict in the Information Age* (Fairfax, Virginia: AFCEA, 1996); "Creating a Smart Nation: Strategy, Policy, Intelligence, and Information," *Government Information Quarterly* (Summer 1996); "Reinventing Intelligence: The Vision and the Strategy," *International Defense & Technologies* (December 1995), bilingual in French and English; and "Private Enterprise Intelligence: Its Potential Contribution to National Security," paper presented to the Canadian Intelligence Community Conference on "Intelligence Analysis and Assessment," 29 October 1994, reprinted in *Intelligence and National Security* (Special Issue, October 1995), and also in a book by the same name, 1996.

17. The sections that follow deliberately relate OSINT to reform of the secret elements of the intelligence cycle. Complete multi-media lectures, a total of eight, are easily accessed via <www.oss.net/BASIC>.

18. A variation of this chart appears on page 53 of the author's *ON INTELLIGENCE, supra note 13.* It is based on differing renditions as used by Greg Treverton in teaching the Intelligence Policy Course at Harvard

University in the 1980's, and Jack Davis teaching at CIA on challenges to intelligence analysis effectiveness.

19. (New York: United Nations, 2004), The endeavor benefited from the participation of The Honorable LtGen Dr. Brent Scowcroft, USAF (Ret), former national security advisor to President George Bush. Terrorism is ninth out of the ten high-level threats. The report, 264 pages, can be seen at <http://www.un.org/secure world/report2.pdf>.

20. It merits comment that according to the *Report* of the Commission on the National Imagery and Mapping Agency, as published in December 1999, most of the intelligence money is spent on esoteric collection systems, and almost none at all is spent on actually making sense out of the collected information.

21. The author has served in the clandestine service (six tours, three overseas), supported strategic signals intelligence acquisition operations, and been a member of the Advanced Program and Evaluation Staff (APEG) with responsibilities for national level validation of current and future secret imagery collection programs.

22. The languages that the OSS and its partners use to follow terrorism and other topics properly are as follows: Arabic, Aramaic, Berber, Catelan, Chinese, Danish, Dari, Dutch, English, Farsi, Finnish, French, German, Indonesian, Irish, Italian, Japanese, Korean, Kurdish, Kurmanji, Norwegian, Pashto, Polish, Portuguese, Russian, Serbian, Spanish, Swedish, Tamil, Turkish, and Urdu. Arabic variations include Andalusi Arabic (extinct, but important role in literary history); Egyptian Arabic (Egypt) Considered the most widely understood and used "second dialect"; Gulf Arabic (Gulf coast from Kuwait to Oman, and minorities on the other side); Hassaniiya (in Mauritania); Hijazi Arabic; Iraqi Arabic; Levantine Arabic (Syrian, Lebanese, Palestinian, and western Jordanian); Maghreb Arabic (Tunisian, Algerian, Moroccan, and western Libyan); Maltese; Najdi Arabic; Sudanese Arabic (with a dialect continuum into Chad); and Yemeni Arabic.

23. This is a very serious indictment of both the policy community and the intelligence community. It is based on direct observation in three Embassies overseas (three tours), on a second graduate thesis on strategic and tactical information management for national security, and on eighteen years of advocacy during which over 40 governments have been helped to enhance their access to and exploitation of open sources of information.

24. The author spent a tour in the Collection Requirements and Evaluations Staff (CRES) at the CIA, and also consulting in the 2000–2001 timeframe to ICMAP, the attempt by the Deputy Director of Central Intelligence for Administration (DDCI/A) to reduce duplicative tasking of the varied classified collection disciplines. Neither CIA nor the new Open Source Center have a full grasp of how to access all information in all languages all the time, and ICMAP continues to focus on triage among the classified systems, without regard for what can be found, gotten, or bought.

25. This is the only standard that may not be readily apparent when this chapter is published. Invented by Doug Englebart, also the inventor of the mouse and hypertext, this standard enables linkage of related content to take place at the paragraph level, which also allows copyright compliance to be executed at the paragraph level, for pennies instead of dollars. The Information Economy Meta Language (IEML), invented by Professor Pierre Levy of Canada, is the emerging standard for language-independent meta-tagging.

26. Amy Zegart, *Flawed by Design: The Evolution of the CIA, JCS, and NSC* (Stanford: Stanford, 2000).

27. It is a fact that 90% of the information that we need to gain access to is controlled or obtainable by non-governmental, academic, civil, and generally foreign organizations that cannot afford the gold-plated and generally pathologically dysfunctional information technology systems that the beltway bandits have been selling to the secret world for decades. In order to create a global information sharing environment where we can get much more than we give in the way of content (what we can provide is processing power), it is essential that we establish generic open source software suites of tools, such as the Defense Advanced Research Projects Agency (DARPA) has done with STRONG ANGEL, so that all relevant contributors can join the Open Source Information System (OSIS) via inexpensive collaborative toolkits and access ports.

28. Information technology has not been an obstacle to the creation of 24/7 "plots" but rather mind-sets and bureaucratic inertia. For a stimulating and truly enlightening account of both the early mistakes and later successes of the British in World War II in using "plots" to track and anticipate the movements of submarines (a skill applicable to today's terrorists), see Patrick Beesley, *Very Special Intelligence: The Story of the Admiralty's Operational Intelligence Centre, 1939–1945* (London: Greenhill, 2000). As with all books cited, a summative review by Robert Steele, with key points itemized, can be read at Amazon.

29. Despite General Gray's concern in 1988, and years of effort by the author that culminated in testimony to the Aspin-Brown Commission resulting in a finding that our access to open sources was "severely deficient" and should be a "top priority" for funding; and despite a report commissioned by DCI George Tenet and delivered by Boyd Sutton in July 1997 on "The Challenge of Global Coverage"—a report recommending that $1.5 billion a year be spent on open sources as an insurance policy, consisting of $10 million a year on each of 150 topics of lower tier countries spawning terrorism, crime, disease, and other ills, Tenet, his predecessors, and his successors have consistently refused to focus on anything other than secrets for the President. The Global Coverage report is easily accessible via <www.oss.net/BASIC>.

30. There are a handful of books that really emphasis the importance of history and the continuing strategy relevance of historical factors including morality and birth control (or not). Among them: Will and Ariel Durant, *The Lessons of History* (New York: Simon & Schuster, 1968), Richard Neustradt and Ernest May, *Thinking In Time : The Uses Of History For Decision Makers* (New York: Free Press, 1988), and Stewart Brand, *The Clock of the Long Now: Time and Responsibility: The Ideas Behind the World's Slowest Computer* (New York: Basic Books, 2000), John Lewis Gaddis, *The Landscape of History : How Historians Map the Past* (Oxford: Oxford, 2004). Included here are two books on the strategic implications of losing history, and failing to notice fact: Robert Perry, *Lost History: Contras, Cocaine, the Press & 'Project Truth'* (San Francisco: Media Consortium, 1999), and Larry Beinhart, *Fog Facts: Searching for Truth in the Land of Spin* (New York: Nation Books, 2005).

31. This term was first used by Alvin Toffler to describe the author, his company, and OSINT. See the chapter on "The Future of the Spy" in which 5 of the 12 pages are focused on OSINT, in *War and Anti-War: Making Sense of Today's Global Chaos* (New York: Warner Books, 1995). All of the books by the Tofflers, who now write as a team, are relevant to the information era, but *Powershift: Knowledge, Wealth, and Power at the Edge of the 21st Century* (New York: Bantam Books, 1991) is rather special.

32. This term (M4IS) was first introduced by the Swedes at the Third Peacekeeping Intelligence Conference held in Stockholm in December 2004. The Swedes have replaced the Canadians as the neutral third party of choice.

33. Goggling for "analytic tradecraft" is always useful. The actual notes from Jack Davis can be accessed via <www.oss.net/BASIC>.

34. As with all observations in this chapter, the specifics are easily accessible via <www.oss.net/BASIC>, in this case as "New Rules for the New Craft of Intelligence," under Practice, where other guides to analytic tradecraft may also be found.

35. Cf. Robert Steele, *INFORMATION OPERATIONS: All Information, All Languages, All the Time* (Oakton, Virginia: OSS, 2006) and-more focused on the military as well as free, *INFORMATION OPERATIONS: Putting the I Back Into DIME* (Strategic Studies Institute, February 2006). The latter is easily found by Googling for the title.

36. Jonathan Schell, *The Unconquerable World: Power, Nonviolence, and the Will of the People* (New York: Owl Books, 2004).

37. The author spent a tour at the national level responsible for offensive counterintelligence against a denied area county, and was also responsible for global oversight of recruitment efforts against all representatives of the same government.

38. In general the reader is referred to the 770+ books reviewed by the author at Amazon over the past five years. Dr. Col Max Manwaring, USA (Ret) has edited *Environmental Security and Global Stability: Problems and Responses* (Lanham, Maryland: Lexington Books, 2002) and there is an entire literature on ecological economics as well as on the health of nations, relating disease, poverty, and the environment.

39. On this vital topic, see on the internal threat, two books: Kevin Philips, *American Theocracy: The Peril and Politics of Radical Religion, Oil, and Borrowed Money in the 21st Century* (New York: Viking Books, 2006), and Michael Lerner, *The Left Hand of God: Taking Back Our Country From the Religious Right* (New York: Harpers, 2006). On the external threat, while there are numerous books on radical Islam, the best overall discussion of ideology as a means of changing the pecking order among social groups, and

grabbing real estate and resources, is offered by Howard Bloom, *The Lucifer Principle: A Scientific Expedition Into the Forces of History* (Boston: Atlantic Monthly, 1997). The book includes a prescient discussion of Sunni versus Shiite, as well as of religion as an ideology used to capture resources.

40. Among the most obvious and hard-hitting current references on immoral capitalism are Clyde Prestowitz, *Rogue Nation: American Unilateralism and the Failure of Good Intentions* (New York: Basic Books, 2004), John Perkins, *Confessions of an Economic Hit Man* (New York: Plume Books, 2005), William Greider, *The Soul of Capitalism: Opening Paths to a Moral Economy* (New York: Simon & Schuster, 2004), and, most recently, Jeffrey Sachs, *The End of Poverty: Economic Possibilities for Our Time* (New York: Penguin Books USA, 2006). There is a separate literature on "virtual colonialism" and the inner anger that a U.S. military presence inspires, particularly in Muslim countries.

41. *Report of the Commission on Protecting and Reducing Government Secrecy* (Washington, D.C.: GAO, 1997), available at <http://www.fas.org/sgp/library/moynihan/>.

42. Both are available online.

43. No disrespect is intended in neglecting to address the standard works on strategic warning. The author's concept of strategic warning is much broader than now exists within both the secret intelligence world, and the academic world that writes *Modern Strategy* (Oxford: Oxford, 1999). An eight point summary is at Amazon. A superb monograph on strategy (83 pages) by Dr. Col (Ret) Harry (Rich) Yarger, "Strategic Theory for the 21st Century," is easily found online by Googling the author and title.

45. John Perry Barlow, "Why Spy?" in *Forbes*, 10/07 2002, at <http://www.forbes.com/asap/2002/1007/042.html>.

46. At the time, Donahue was the ranking director with the Office of Management and Budget (OMB) for all Command and Control, Communications, Computing, and Intelligence (C4I), and one of a handful of individuals with all of the codeword clearances. His boss, Don Gessaman, the ranking civil servant at OMB for National Security inclusive of Programs 50 (International Relations) and 150 (Defense), guided the establishment of Code M320 for defense expenditures on OSINT in 2000. OSINT is seen by the IC as a threat that should not be out-sourced, and by OMB as a function that can be accomplished in the private sector and therefore should be out-sourced to the fullest extent possible. ✦

Reprinted with permission from Robert D. Steele, "Open Source Intelligence," in Loch K. Johnson, ed., *Strategic Intelligence, Vol. 2: The Intelligence Cycle: From Spies to Policymakers* (New York: Praeger, 2007), 95–122.

11

A Policymaker's Perspective on Intelligence Analysis

Robert D. Blackwill and Jack Davis

As Robert D. Blackwill reveals in this interview with CIA analyst Jack Davis, the life of a senior policy official in the U.S. government—in this case, an ambassador—can be overwhelming. Policymakers must focus on the pressing issues of the day, leaving little time to study broad-gauged intelligence reports. What officials need, and what Blackwill sought out, was a team of analysts who were willing to respond directly to his requests for information. Blackwill offers the reader a glimpse into the lives of policymakers and analysts as they interact.

Sherman Kent, in *Strategic Intelligence for American World Policy,* his path-breaking effort to join intelligence doctrine and practice for post-World War II America, concluded that:

> There is no phase of the intelligence business which is more important than the proper relationship between intelligence itself and the people who use its products. Oddly enough, this relationship, which one would expect to establish itself automatically, does not do this. It is established as a result of a great deal of conscious effort . . .[1]

Despite guidance from Kent and numerous subsequent authors, the terms of engagement between intelligence analyst and policymaker are still ill-defined doctrinally and thus practiced as much to suit the immediate preferences of the players on both sides of the relationship as to meet the fundamental demands of sound policymaking. The quest to join sage principle—*what should work*—to solid practice —what does—is more important than ever in post-Cold War America, as resources for intelligence support of policymaking are cut back more rapidly than responsibilities.

The original pillar of Ambassador Blackwill's doctrinal views on intelligence and policy was self-interest—his effort to make the relationship work for him personally under trying conditions. He served as Special Assistant to the President and Senior Director for European and Soviet Affairs, National Security Council Staff, during 1989–90, a tumultuous period that witnessed the collapse of the Soviet Union and the reshaping of Europe. The more lasting pillar is his concern for the national interest—a belief that the United States can ill afford prevailing patterns of ineffective ties between experts on events overseas and policymakers in Washington.

Some Key Points

The Ambassador's framework for defining the requirements for sound intelligence-policy relations consists of four key points:

- Roughly 90 percent of what passes for national security analysis in the US Government, including structured study of events overseas, is done by intelligence analysts.

- The national interest requires that this effort be effectively joined to the policymaking process.

- The officials who carry most of the day-to-day burden of policymaking on key issues are so besieged by time-consuming responsibilities that decisions on how much to stay informed on events overseas and in what way are narrowly based on self-interest in managing the pressures and getting the job done.

- Intelligence professionals have to carry nearly all the burden to convince each key policy official that they are committed to servicing his or her analytic needs via customized expert support.

Thus, to meet their responsibilities in promoting the national interest, intelligence professionals have to become expert not only on substantive issues but also on serving the self-interest of policy professionals by providing specialized analytic support.

A Shaky Start

I first met the Ambassador in November 1987, when he was teaching in the CIA-funded Kennedy School Seminar on Intelligence and Policy. He seized the attention of the class of some 30 Directorate of Intelligence (DI) division chiefs and managers from elsewhere in the Intelligence Community by asserting that as a policy official he never read DI analytic papers. Why? "Because they were nonadhesive." As Blackwill explained, they were written by people who did not know what he was trying to do and, so, could not help him get it done:

> When I was working at State on European affairs, for example, on certain issues I was the Secretary of State. DI analysts did not know that—that I was one of a handful of key decision-makers on some very important matters. Why bother to read what they write for a general audience of people who have no real responsibility on the issue.

More charitably, he now characterizes his early periods of service at the NSC Staff and in State Department bureaus as ones of "mutual ignorance":

> DI analysts did not have the foggiest notion of what I did; and I did not have a clue as to what they could or should do.

An unpromising start. Yet during his 1989–90 NSC Staff tour. Ambassador Blackwill—by the lights of DI analysts working with him on European affairs—raised analyst-policy relations to an exemplary level. Time after time, the DI's Office of European Analysis (EURA) provided much-needed intelligence support under stringent time constraints. In a tribute with resonance in the hometown of the Washington Redskins, Blackwill called the EURA crew his "analytic hogs," opening up holes in the line for him to run through. At least one EURA analyst considers this period "the most exciting and meaningful" of his career.

The balance of this article consists of the Ambassador's replies to my questions.

From Mutual Ignorance to Mutual Benefit

Q: What caused your apparent change of mind about the utility of DI analysis?

A: I had started to rethink my position even before our 1987 classroom encounter. As chief negotiator for the MBFR talks,[2] I worked closely for the first time with Agency analysts—those assigned to the US delegation. They regularly came up with information and interpretations that helped me sharpen my approach to the individual negotiating issues. When I gave them a special task, they delivered to suit my schedule, even if it meant considerable inconvenience to them.

One more matter important to negotiators, and to heavily engaged policymakers generally. Unlike other intelligence people I had worked with in the past, including those from State, my informal talks about possible US tactical initiatives with CIA analysts from the Arms Control Intelligence Staff did not end up in the *Washington Post*.

My understanding of the role of intelligence was also broadened by my work at Kennedy School. In addition to the CIA seminar, I collaborated with Professors Ernest May and Richard Neustadt on a course called "Assessing Other Governments." Here, the importance of country expertise, of language skills, of perspective and a sense of history were underscored by well-documented case studies. Then there was the survival factor. I knew soon after [President] Bush's election in November 1988 that I was to be selected for the NSC Staff job on both Europe and the USSR. This meant longer hours and more pressures for me than ever before. Frankly, I was concerned about forgetting what my 10-year-old daughter looked like. So I sat down in Cambridge and planned how I was going to interact with Executive Branch colleagues, with Congress, with the press—and with intelligence. I decided that in my own self-interest I had to arrange to get as much support as practical from Agency analysts.

Q: Why Agency analysts?

A: You mean besides the fact there are many more of them in my areas of responsibility than in the other intelligence outfits? My experience at State convinced me that INR [Bureau of Intelligence and Research] works for the Secretary. I suppose it is the same at Defense. I judged that Agency analysts would be much more likely to provide close and continuous support to an NSC Staff director.

Back to State. From my White House perspective, the State Department almost never met a deadline it could not miss. Then there is also the confidentiality factor. As I said earlier, your musings about possible policy initiatives are not leaked to the press by the DCI to shoot down your policy.

The most important consideration is that Agency analysts are better informed about individual countries than anyone else in the [US] Government. And I judged they had the wit—the historical perspective I spoke of—to interpret this information for my benefit and the President's benefit. I just had to determine whether they had the professional interest and enterprise to be responsive to my overtures.

Let me expand on one point. Intelligence analysts—essentially DI analysts—do 90 percent of the analysis by the USG on foreign affairs. Policy officials, even those with academic backgrounds, are too busy with more pressing matters.

In some administrations, the most heavily engaged and influential policy officials on any given issue spend 90 percent of their time assessing their policy competitors in Washington. I am talking here about getting ready to leverage competing Administration officials, not just Congress. Busy decision-makers concentrate what little time they have for foreign policy analysis on narrowly focused aspects of key agenda issues—often how to deal effectively with their foreign counterparts. Let me tell you any policy official who can do his own research on all aspects of an issue, cannot be very important—because he is not fully engaged in the coalition-building and power-leverage games essential for getting serious policy work done in Washington.

And there is no second team. If Agency analysts do not do the work of keeping up with developments overseas that the decisionmakers need to know about, it does not get done. It was in my self-interest to see if I could get those analysts working for me, to help me keep up with a broad range of developments I could not possibly follow on my own.

What Works, and What Does Not

Q: You have mentioned self-interest a couple of times.

A: Let me explain. The policymakers who count the most—those five to 10 on any issue who have the most power for getting anything done, decided, implemented—work much harder than intelligence analysts. During 1989–90, I was often at my desk from 7 in the morning till 10 at night. Others at the NSC Staff, Brent Scowcroft and Bob Gates for instance, started even earlier.[3] Unlike analysts we had no evening tennis games. No weekends.

Even with these hours, as I indicated, I needed help to stay informed. But it had to be the right kind of help. I could not afford to read intelligence papers because this or that intelligence agency was entitled to produce them. It did not matter to me how much work the Agency had put into its products, or how polished they were in scholarly terms. In fact, I could not afford the time to read intelligence papers written by personal friends and colleagues. I could only read intelligence products tailored to help me get through my substantive schedule. There was no other rational choice.

Q: The old issue of "adhesive analysis."

A: You asked, so let me unload here. During my [1989–90] NSC tour, the Agency was still putting out gobs of analytic products that I never read. During the two years I did not read a single [National Intelligence] estimate. Not one. And except for Gates, I do not know of anyone at the NSC who did. The reason, at least for me, is simple. There was no penalty to be paid for not reading an NIE. It did not cost you anything in terms of getting done the most important policy things you had to get done.

The same goes for your other general audience papers. I got them, but I did not read them. I am sure somebody did or you would not bother to put them out. Let me grant without hesitation that there is a lot you put out for good reason that has nothing to do with policymakers at my level. I think however that you ought to consider the cost-benefit ratios of producing papers that are read mostly by specialists at the desk level at State and Defense, or

by policy officials with general interest but no direct say on an issue.

Q: What about the NID [*National Intelligence Daily*]? I've heard a number of NSC Staff members praise its utility over the years.

A: Of course, I was interested in the PDB [*President's Daily Brief*] because President Bush read it. As for the NID, I would spend, literally, 60 seconds a day on it. This was a defensive move. I wanted to know in advance what would likely be leaked to the press by readers in Congress. Other than that, there was, again, no cost to me, no penalty, from not having read the NID.

Q: What did you read, aside from what you commissioned directly from DI analysts?

A: Despite what you hear about policymakers not having time to read, I read a lot. Much of it was press. You have to know how issues are coming across politically to get your job done. Also, cables from overseas for preparing agendas for meetings and sending and receiving messages from my counterparts in foreign governments. Countless versions of policy drafts from those competing for the President's blessing. And dozens of phone calls. Many are a waste of time but have to be answered, again, for policy and political reasons.

Q: Let's turn to what you commissioned from DI analysts.

A: One more minute, please, on what I did not find useful. This is important. My job description called for me to help prepare the President for making policy decisions, including at meetings with foreign counterparts and other officials. One thing the Agency regularly did was send me memos on the strategic and tactical agendas of foreign officials; in effect, what they wanted from the United States. Do you think that after I have spent long weeks shaping the agenda, I have to be told a day or two before the German foreign minister visits Washington why he is coming?

O.K. What did I want from analysts? I want their reading of what is going on in the domestic affairs of country "X" or "Y"—countries the President is planning to visit to advance foreign policy or countries from which we are going to receive important visitors to discuss problems and bilateral strategy, or countries on which, for one reason or another, we feel a need to get US policy into better shape.

What is going on domestically in these countries that could have an impact on how the President's counterparts and my counterparts will behave? What pressures are they under at home? Although I knew the national security issues cold, I could not become expert on all important issues affecting Germany or France or Italy at the national level, much less at the provincial or state levels. DI analysts knew this, and they helped me bone up on what

I needed to understand to nuance and sharpen the US approach.

You also have to consider that President Bush, as a political animal, was naturally interested in the domestic politics of other leaders, even when there was no pressing bilateral business on the table.

Q: We variously call this "opportunity analysis," or "value-added analysis." Sometimes we call it "targeted tactical analysis."

A: I never put a label on it. Your terms are all good ones. Incidentally, the MacEachin metaphor you told me, about scouts and coaches, is also useful.[4] Yes, intelligence analysts should help key policymakers make the best game plan by telling them what they do not know or appreciate sufficiently. Regarding my own needs, this was mostly, as I said, on the domestic politics of the countries I was dealing with.

Whatever label you put on it, the service I got on Europe from EURA was superb and invaluable. As you know, when I traveled to Europe, EURA analysts prepared a daily cable for me on key developments. They got it to me first thing in the morning European time, which means they worked late into the night in Washington to get it done. I appreciated that immensely. Once a senior State Department colleague joined me for breakfast in Brussels as I was reading my very own newsletter. He studied it with great interest and asked me where it came from. I chose not to give him a clear answer.

EURA people met without exception whatever deadlines I set for informal memos while I was in Washington. They also were responsive and quick with some major projects I laid on with little advance notice. My only problem with their written work is sometimes the text had gone through too many levels of review and began to read like a NID article. If I wanted a NID article, I could read one. What I wanted was the analyst's unvarnished response to my questions. After I made this point, the incidence of overpolished papers diminished.

Q: What about briefings?

A: Yes, because you get a chance to ask questions, briefings can be more helpful than memos. Here, too, I got first-rate customized service. Whenever I asked for briefings in my office, the analysts who came were both informed and responsive. Really terrific people.

Again, I was mostly interested in domestic affairs in this and that country. From time to time, though, I would ask the analysts in my office what the response of a European government would be to the policy initiatives the President was considering or that I was thinking of recommending to the President. Their unrehearsed responses here were also useful. I always hesitated to put such requests into writing for fear of leaks to the press. I learned you can trust DI analysts. They were well informed. Ready to help. And they kept their traps shut.

Q: That sounds like a good advertisement for DI analysts.

A: You bet. They were expert on their subjects. They were responsive to my needs. And they did not leak my confidences to the press.

Politicization Not an Issue

Q: Did your NSC Staff colleagues resent your close ties to DI analysts?

A: Not that I was aware of. The people who worked for me, rather than being resentful, made use of EURA support on their own.

Q: What about this kind of closeness pushing analysts across the line into policymaking?

A: Again, I saw no problem with EURA analysts. When I asked, they provided advice on tactics to support an established policy. They were good at that too. But the EURA people did not get into policy prescription. And where it did happen on occasion with others, when intelligence people started recommending policy, I pushed them back.

Q: What about telling you what you wanted to hear, or avoiding bad news?

A: Not a problem. I wanted their help in avoiding setbacks as well as for advancing policy goals. If there were negative developments I had to know about, they let me know. We had trust going both ways.

I would like to continue with this for a minute. I know during the Gates confirmation hearings [for DCI during 1991] the media were full of charges of analysts writing to please policymakers. My experience was different. I would argue that at least in my experience close professional relationships encouraged frankness—not politicization. But I know it does not always turn out that way.

Just as top policy aides have got to deliver bad news to the President when called for, intelligence people have got to have the intellectual courage to tell key policy officials that something is not working, or is not going to work. It is tough, really tough, to stop a policy failure based on ignorance of the ground truth. Intelligence analysts have got to rise to this challenge. I am not talking about shouting it from the rooftops. NSC directors are especially resentful when Congress is told bad news before they have a chance to think about it. But limited distribution memos should work. Private briefings might be even better, since that gives the policy official a chance to ask questions.

Often it is important to decisionmakers to know how to get to the least bad outcome, to limit the damage. I think options papers work very well here, especially if they are delivered after bad news forces key policymakers to focus on an issue. Somalia is a good example. The analysts could table a paper or lay on a briefing outlining three possible outcomes six months down the road, and what opportunities, leverage, and so forth the United States has to influence the outcome.

Intelligence and Policy Tribes

Q: Why do not more overworked policy officials lean on Agency analysis the way you did?

A: I guess some do, though I do not personally know of any case quite like mine with EURA. The absence of a pattern of effective relations probably reflects a combination of professional differences and mutual ignorance about what really makes the relationship work.

I am not the only policy official who decided that too many intelligence products still are nonadhesive. They are, or were when I last served, too long and complex. Analysts love words and complexities; it is one of their strengths. Good policymakers are driven by the need to take action. They need problems broken down, simplified. You and I have been through this before, and you can probably make a better list of tribal differences than I can. The key still is getting close enough to the individual policymaker to find out what he needs.

Policymakers do not as a rule know what intelligence analysts can do for them. They read Estimates, think pieces, the NID, and say, in effect, "What does this have to do with *my* problems"? They do not see it as their job to teach analysts how to be helpful. Besides, they would not have the time.

Q: How did your counterpart NSC Staff senior directors stay informed, and, for that matter, others in the Bush administration who were the kinds of key hands-on policy officials you think the Agency should cultivate?

A: The only honest answer is, I do not really know. I was too busy with my own affairs. But I seriously doubt that any of them [during 1989–90] received the kind of customized support from the Agency that I am talking about.

Q: This seems to bother you.

A: Yes. As a citizen and taxpayer it sure does. I am talking here about the national interest. Let's go back to my statement that the Intelligence Community does 90 percent of foreign affairs analysis in the USG.

Policy choices are made and policy actions are taken whether or not the expertise of analysts is brought to bear. But how can anyone argue that we should pay for this expertise and not make use of it?

I do not mean to say it is all the analysts' fault, but I am fully prepared to argue that if an analyst's work does not have an impact on policymaking as a process, including in the long run, he or she is taking pay under false pretenses. A lot that you do is useful to someone. You have to make it more useful to those who count.

Let me say this: the Agency's understanding of the world is probably needed more today than ever. The world and the challenges the United States faces are changing so rapidly. Also, the new [Clinton] administration does not seem to have yet defined its policy approach. The costs of tribal tensions between analysts and policymakers—mutual ignorance, really—may be rising.

At a Lower Level

Q: Much of what you have had to say relates to officials at your level, the NSC senior director and departmental assistant secretaries and above. What about one level down—deputy assistant secretaries, office directors?

A: I would say, much the same. Find out who counts—the five or 10 midlevel officials who have the most influence on more senior decisionmakers—and cultivate close relations with them. Trade customized support for access to the real agenda, and so forth.

A Program for the DI

Q: How would you combine your various recommendations for Agency analysts into a program? If you were advising the DCI or DDI, what measures would you propose to enhance the effectiveness of relations between analysts and policy decisionmakers?[5]

A: Thank you for letting me know in advance this question was coming. It is a good question, and I have given it considerable thought. Let's see if the seven measures I have sketched out add up to a program.

1. Identify the 30 or so senior policy officials who count—those who really carry weight with administration Cabinet officers on key foreign policy issues. These officials, usually assistant secretaries in policy departments or special assistants to the President on the NSC Staff, regularly set the thinking of NSC principals on major policy decisions. As a rule, these are the assessors of foreign governments, or the analysts of last resort. To contribute to sounder policymaking, intelligence analysts have to reach this group. Remember, the list of policy

notables has to be carefully worked out and kept up to date, because office titles do not always reflect real policy weight.

2. Approach the policy officials who count as if they were motivated solely by self-interest. Their self-interest has to be worked on because they are just too busy to allow either institutional considerations or personal friendships to determine their attitude toward intelligence analysts.

3. Learn as much as you can about each senior official. Study them as carefully as you do foreign leaders. For example, read everything they have written on the subjects in their policy portfolios. Check them out through mutual contacts.

4. Take the initiative to establish ties. This is an essential obligation of intelligence managers, because policy officials will rarely seek them out.

   - For new appointees, send a letter asking for an appointment and spelling out your areas of expertise and the services you are ready to extend.

   - For serving officials, anticipate a major pending visit or event and offer to send over your analysts for a briefing on any one of several related aspects. For example, if the prime minister from Denmark is to visit the President, the DI manager should signal that he will bring over his Denmark analyst to fill the policymaker in on any gaps in understanding in time for the latter to prepare briefing memos for his or her principal, be it the Secretary of State or the President.

   - Whenever DI managers know of travel plans by a key policy official, offer to send over country analysts who can fill in the official's knowledge on areas of his choice.

   - Have the DCI set up luncheon meetings in town (CIA Headquarters is just too inconvenient), at which analysts and their managers can establish their credentials as entrepreneurial experts.

5. Customize intelligence papers and briefings to solidify the relationship. Many policy officials, overwhelmed by the volume both of their activities and of seemingly important information, will welcome specialized newsletters. They will welcome even one-page summaries of key events overseas that provide the kind of information and analysis they want at the time of day or week they prefer to set aside for keeping up with developments. For the same reason—

fear of being overwhelmed—many will welcome customized briefings and memos relating to their policymaking responsibilities on matters on which the DI country analyst is much better informed than they can be or than anyone else in the government. Give them something they will really miss if they do not get it.

6. Place the best and most promising analysts on tours in the policy world. The Agency could offer, free of charge, 50 first-rate people to policy officials around town. Intelligence officers can learn something about how to use intelligence resources effectively by reading about policymaking. You can learn some more by periodic visits to a policymaker's office. But the best way to learn about a different bureaucracy is just the same as the best way to learn about any alien tribe—go live with them for a couple of years.

7. Reward those managers and analysts who are successful in gaining and maintaining access. As a rule, once a win-win relationship takes hold, momentum will keep it going. Once the policy official knows the intelligence unit can and will deliver support when it is needed, he will provide in exchange access to the real policy agenda. But policy officials come and go, and the Agency has to take care of those with talent at starting over again with newcomers who, as almost always will be the case, will not seek you out.

Final Thoughts

Q: How do you stay informed on events overseas these days, while working again at Kennedy School?

A: My main current interest is Russian politics and military affairs. I have been spending one week per month in Russia, dealing directly with the General Staff. While at Harvard, I spend a couple of hours each morning on the Internet. It is amazing how much good information and worthwhile commentary is out there for those with the interest and the time. While at the NSC, I had the interest but not the time.

Internet, CNN, increasing visits by all sorts of Americans. The competition for the DI analyst is becoming much stronger. This means you are going to have to work much harder to find a comparative advantage. How do you get more expertise—living there, of course, language, and history?

I worry a bit about this. Just as you cannot rely on quality alone to get your job of informing policy done, you cannot rely only on access. In fact, marketing without a quality product to deliver is worse than passivity.

Q: Final question. At the end of a long day, which is it, working for more expertise, or for more access?

A: The answer, I suppose, is more efficiency. I imagine a textbook breakdown would have the analysts spending 40 percent of their time on collection and other activities for building expertise, 30 percent on analysis and writing—putting things together, and 30 percent on assuring impact on the policymaking process. I never managed an analytic unit, and this is just a guess. I do not think you are anywhere near the last 30 percent.

One final thought occurs to me. Managers in particular should spend enough time establishing and keeping up effective links to the policymaking world that they begin to feel guilty about not having enough time for their other duties. It is that important.

Questions for Further Discussion

1. Why are policymakers often dissatisfied with the analysis they receive from the intelligence community?

2. Why is it difficult for policymakers to obtain useful analysis and information from intelligence analysts?

3. Should policymakers view the intelligence community as an extension of their own staff?

4. Will the "information revolution" help analysts build constructive relationships with policymakers?

Endnotes

1. Princeton University Press (1949), p. 180.
2. Mutual and Balanced Force Reduction negotiations between NATO and the Warsaw Pact.
3. Scowcroft was Special Assistant to the President for National Security Affairs. Robert M Gates, subsequently Director of Central Intelligence, was then Deputy Special Assistant.
4. Douglas A. MacEachin, currently CIA's Deputy Director for Intelligence, uses the scout-coach metaphor for analyst-policymaker relations to underscore that it is the scout's responsibility to help the coach prepare to win the game and not to predict the outcome of the game before it is played.
5. This question was communicated in a letter sent in October 1991 and answered in an interview in November 1991. The DI has been moving in the recommended direction for several years. When the interviewer showed an outline of Blackwill's program to DDI Douglas MacEachin (October 1993) he said, "I guess Bob [Blackwill] and I agree." ✦

Reprinted with permission from Jack Davis, "A Policymaker's Perspective on Intelligence Analysis," *Studies in Intelligence* 38 (1995): 7–15.

12

Intelligence Estimates and the Decision-Maker

Shlomo Gazit

All too often, intelligence professionals never interact with policymakers until some crisis thrusts them together in an unsteady and uncertain discourse. Shlomo Gazit highlights the importance of establishing what he describes as a "reciprocal relationship" between analysts and policymakers and ways to bridge the gap between them. He also notes that accurate estimates will have little effect if analysts fail to break through the clutter of everyday pressures that can distract policymakers from the emerging threats they face.

Time and again, for one reason or another, the problems of Intelligence hit the headlines. An event or statement focuses attention once again on the public debate: What constitutes an intelligence estimate? What is its value? How reliable is it? Time after time numerous opinions are aired—for the most part by people unacquainted with intelligence and its inner workings. These opinions merely confuse the issue and breed fanciful expectations which are bound to be shattered. To complicate matters further, the fields of activity and responsibility of intelligence—in both information-gathering (collection) and research (analysis)—are many and extensive, and almost all are completely hidden from public view.

Nothing to Do With Fortune-Telling

In antiquity (and to this day, in some countries) kings and generals used to act on the advice of diviners or fortune-tellers. Not so the statesmen and army commanders of today. Nevertheless, they find it hard to accept a situation in which nobody can foretell the future for them. Many of them hope, or

delude themselves, that the intelligence system serving them can fulfill this purpose.

Intelligence is a valuable instrument, and it can make an immense contribution to the success or failure of any political or military move. For that very reason, it is imperative for decision-makers to be highly knowledgeable on the subject of intelligence, being of necessity its principal consumers. Here we will discuss that narrow field which is in dispute—the intelligence estimate.

I will open by stating unequivocally what we, who have grown up within the framework of intelligence, have repeatedly insisted: An intelligence estimate has nothing to do with fortune-telling. The very term 'intelligence estimate' signifies an estimate based on intelligence, which means that intelligence must limit itself to two areas:

- Specifically stating what may be expected, based on hard information about the other side's resolutions.

- Presenting the possibilities, based on knowledge of the other side's general intentions and the optimal technical feasibilities at its disposal.

Here is an example from the military field. An operation order is accompanied by an intelligence estimate (or an intelligence annex). This estimate, in its entirety, is a presentation of possibilities:

- The forces available to the other side that may interfere and disrupt the military operation.

- The available weapon-systems and their operational characteristics.

- The possible timetable of intervention.

This is clearly not an attempt to predict the course of events. On the contrary, it can be stated with near certainty that these 'possible courses of action' available to the enemy will never materialize, the most drastic, severe and perilous possibilities having been deliberately chosen for presentation. Furthermore, what really happens depends, of course, on the decisions made by the other side, their timing, their rate of implementation, the combat readiness of their forces and their speed of action. The true test of intelligence does not lie in whether these possibilities actually occur, but in whether forces of whose existence intelligence was unaware come into play, or if their speed of intervention exceeds the intelligence forecast.

For instance, before the 'Entebbe Operation' (July 1976), intelligence pointed out the existence of Ugandan MIG fighters at the Entebbe airport and the possibility (even though of low probability) that they could be used to shoot down the fleet of Israeli

Hercules transports during the flight north after the rescue. Israel's government, basing its decision on these data and the estimate, ordered the destruction of the MIGs on the ground to ensure the safe return flight of the task force and the hostages.

Decisions made by political or military leaders should rely on intelligence to a great degree, but in no circumstances should intelligence be the sole factor in making a decision. This is something the intelligence analyst should recognize and understand. To put it bluntly, the decision-maker has a perfect right to disregard the advice of intelligence. There are always additional considerations, and it is his responsibility to evaluate them all and introduce his personal priorities.

What are these additional considerations? First in order of priority are varying national strategies and policies. Under the same conditions, two different party leaderships or two different characters may come up with two different solutions for a problem, despite identical intelligence data. In June 1982, following a Palestinian terrorist attempt to assassinate the Israeli ambassador in London, the combination of Mr Begin as Prime Minister, Mr Sharon as Minister of Defense and General Eitan as Chief of the General Staff precipitated war against Lebanon. Two years later, when Israel's political leadership counted Mr Peres as Prime Minister, Mr Rabin as Minister of Defense and General Levy as Chief of Staff, a different decision would most probably have been made, not only because of the different personalities involved, but principally because they represent different policies and strategies. Either decision, however, would have been legitimate.

Next in order come internal considerations, which have little to do with enemy intelligence. These may even include military considerations, such as the rating of one's own military forces. How does one evaluate their capability? Their training and their state of readiness? Their morale?

Finally, internal politics play a part. It is quite legitimate for a politician to ask how a certain decision would affect his personal position of leadership, or if it would compromise his standing as Prime Minister. Would it endanger his position within his own party? Would it break up the government coalition or, on the contrary, strengthen it? These are all perfectly legitimate considerations. Economic considerations also carry weight. What is the price of a certain decision to the economy's stability and is it affordable? Israel recently went through a very painful decision-making process with regard to ending the 'Lavie' project, Israel Aircraft Industries' attempt to develop and produce a new, modern and sophisticated combat-aircraft for the Israeli Air Force. Despite the purely military character of the project (with an important impact on the future balance of forces and air superiority), the consideration which carried most weight was a purely economic one.

A Reciprocal Relationship: Intelligence–Decision-Makers

This description, and the concrete example given, serve to illustrate one aspect of the reciprocal relationship between intelligence, especially the intelligence estimate, and the decision-maker (military commander or civilian statesman). The simplistic approach holds that a good intelligence collection system and a good intelligence evaluation system are enough to produce good military and political decisions. Actually, things are not that simple. Furthermore, it is surprising how little awareness there is of the real and difficult problems involved. It is surprising how many intelligence people and statesmen remain ignorant of the problem and do not understand the complications that may arise, and as a result, of course, fail to reap the maximum benefit from the relationship.

True, decisions cannot be based on non-existent intelligence information. If it has not been collected and has not found its way into the intelligence estimate (written or verbal), it cannot be used as the basis for a decision.

True, decision-makers (civilian or military) may disregard intelligence estimates for one or more of those additional considerations which have nothing to do with the 'enemy' column in the total situation appraisal—considerations of which intelligence is neither required nor expected to take any account. Indeed, for decision-makers consciously to decide against an intelligence estimate is entirely legitimate, with the emphasis on 'consciously.' This means that the decision-maker knows and understands the intelligence estimate but has found reason to decide against it. This is not the case when a decision contrary to the intelligence estimate is made unknowingly—whether because an estimate was never asked for or delivered, or arrived too late, or whether the decision-maker never got around to reading it or misunderstood it when he did.

This is what the reciprocal relationship between decision-makers and intelligence primarily means: how to ensure that intelligence will properly serve the decision-maker and supply his needs.

The intelligence analyst has two 'twin brothers' who do very similar work in a very similar way. One of these is the journalist, the other is the academic scholar. From personal experience, I can say that all three produce very similar papers. Reading the documents on any given subject, one can hardly tell which was written by whom. Yet there is a substantial difference derived from their respective clients and different designated readers. The intelligence analyst prepares his papers for a single customer—the decision-maker he serves. His papers have no further distribution; the general public will never see them (except, of course, in official archives after 25 years or more). But this 'single client' character marks a very important difference: if the academic scholar proves to be wrong, no harm is done. He publishes a new paper explaining the reasons for his mistake, and other scholars, in quoting the previous paper, add footnotes mentioning that the analysis proved to be wrong. For the journalist, things are even easier. He can entirely ignore his own mistakes, which will be forgotten by the time tomorrow's headlines appear. It is not the same for the intelligence analyst. If he proves to be wrong on a cardinal issue, he will doubtless hang for it, quite literally in some regimes. In Israel, thank God, he will only be fired.

The intelligence man, much like the academic researcher and the journalist, has a 'marketing' problem—how to ensure the acceptance of the intelligence estimate. 'Acceptance' means both that it be delivered to its destination and that it be cognitively accepted, analysed and understood.

The first sense of acceptance is physical, technical. It means being delivered in time to the proper consumer, the one who must hear or read it (and not being detained or blocked at some lower administrative level). And arriving in an acceptable way, which means that the form, the 'packaging,' is of considerable importance, quite similar to the marketing of any other product.

The second sense of 'acceptance,' the cognitive sense, means being assimilated and understood. All aspects and ramifications of the intelligence estimate must be understood. For this purpose there must be routine recourse between the two factors, routine discussion and deliberation. This is why the 'chemistry' between the decision-maker and his intelligence man is so important. Without it there can be no mutual trust, and no chance of the intelligence estimate being accepted.

How can this be achieved? The answer is far from simple, and perhaps in large degree due to the fact that the investment of money or resources cannot help in this field.

Awareness of the Problem

The answer and the key to the problem lie in awareness of the need of developing such a reciprocal relationship.

The military decision-maker rises through the ranks and learns, beginning at the lowest level of command, how to work in co-operation and direct liaison with intelligence. The subject of intelligence has an important place in every military school or course. These not only deal with and impart an understanding of intelligence and its possibilities, but do not neglect the importance of staff work. What constitutes good, proper staff work? What is routine battle procedure? What are the Planning and Orders' groups? And, of course, what function does intelligence serve within this procedure? It is obvious that within the military the intelligence officer generally takes his place as the commander's constant and steadfast right-hand man.

The civilian decision-maker, the statesman, on the other hand, generally rises to the top through a party apparatus—an entirely civilian framework in which the main subject, and the necessary condition for success, is skillful navigation through the party machinery and power blocs. Men who rise through this separate chain of command lack the experience, understanding and training for their jobs as coordinators, initiators and directors of government staff work. It is only to be regretted that there is no Command and Staff College serving the civilian system and supplying its needs. Furthermore, ministers (and quite often prime ministers) who have graduated to their posts directly from the party apparatus are immediately embroiled in a heavy workload; even if there were such a college, they could not take the time off from their activities to attend such courses. Here and there exceptions are to be found, typical to a great extent of the Israeli political system. These exceptions involve bringing in people from networks outside the limited party system directly to assume high posts within the political system. Occasionally some of these men have had suitable experience in previous positions.

How then can awareness be created in these conditions? It can, especially if there is a willingness to invest in long term planning and training of upper echelon government workers. There is no difficulty in identifying the offices and paths of promotion through which the next generation of high-level government administrators will rise. These people can be specially trained for their future positions and for handling government and state staff work. Such special schools do not exist in Israel; not only has the Civil Service Commission not considered establishing such a central government facility but Israeli universities have no teaching program aimed at this goal.

Lacking such teaching institutions, the problem can be tackled immediately to some extent through a program of short courses, each devoted to a specific topic. But in this case it is important that these courses be attended by key figures within the upper levels of government service (under-secretaries, director-generals, personal aides, etc.).

Regardless of supplementary courses, it is of the utmost importance that the decision-maker be invited and brought on an introductory tour of the intelligence system. The visit should be unrelated to and uninfluenced by current affairs and problems; its purpose is to stimulate awareness. Such a visit can contribute the decision-maker's understanding of the intelligence system at his disposal. It can provide opportunities for framing the desired relationship with the network and for a frank discussion which may include analysis of established procedure, criticism and suggested improvements.

Getting the decision-maker to make such a visit is no easy task. Devoting time to this purpose, indulging in frank conversation (with no recriminations)—these are things to which he may not be accustomed. If it cannot be done properly, at the very least it should be done with the men closest to the decision-maker—his chief of staff, personal assistant, or military aide. A comprehensive visit by these people may serve as a useful substitute if on their return to duty they remain aware of, and capable of pointing out to their chief, what they have learned during their visit. Possibly, given time, they may be able to persuade the decision-maker himself to undertake such a tour.

Another suggestion, which may be of great help if it can only be accomplished, is for the intelligence system to try to 'plant' its own man at the decision-maker's side. These decision-makers, arriving at their posts inexperienced and unacquainted with the network at their disposal, search for professional assistants (people outside the party) to help them, usually from within the military. Experience shows that intelligence men often make the best assistants.

Not all intelligence service heads recognize the importance of having such an 'agent.' Often enough they are sorry to lose one of their best and brightest officers. Yet a good man in the right place is a priceless asset. Such a man can solve many problems by his very presence alongside the decision-maker.

During my term of office as director of military intelligence, I used such 'agents' for several tasks. The most common and routine of these was to communicate through them in order to emphasize certain points in the daily report, points which I thought the decision-maker (Minister of Defense or Prime Minister) should be made aware of. And in return, these 'agents' communicated to us the comments and reactions of the 'boss' to our reports with regard to the substance of our analysis or questions of form and style. Such feedback greatly enhances the intelligence report's chances of acceptance.

Once in a while I would ask them to convene a special meeting, 'initiated' by the Minister of Defense or the Prime Minister, to discuss certain developments across the border which I considered intriguing and important. And last, though this happened not more than two or three times during my five years in office, I sometimes asked for a special and confidential meeting with the Prime Minister, bypassing the Chief of Staff and the Minister of Defense, in order to brief him personally and ensure that he was aware of the full picture before giving his approval to certain proposals brought forward by the defense establishment. In all such cases, my intervention persuaded the Prime Minister to overrule the proposition. I did not enjoy doing it, but at the time I believed, and still do today, that I had no alternative in the circumstances and that this was the true sense of my responsibility as national intelligence adviser to the government and the Prime Minister.

A Two-Way Relationship

As stated previously, the relationship between intelligence and the decision-maker should ensure, as far as possible, correct decision-making. It is not enough to have a good intelligence collection system or a good intelligence evaluation system, even if the latter should deliver its estimate in time. Optimal utilization of intelligence capabilities is only possible as the result of a close, two-way relationship. The decision-maker has to understand that he is responsible for guiding the activities of the intelligence system subordinate to him. Intelligence cannot function within a vacuum; it must be told what to search for, what interests and is required by the decision-maker. In professional jargon this is known as EEI (Essential Elements of Information), and it should come from above and always be up-to-date. Again and again, developments take place that interest and influence the decision-maker. In many cases intelligence remains unaware of these developments unless informed of them by the decision-maker.

Often enough decision-makers have a tendency to neglect to inform their subordinate networks, thus denying themselves better service. Two examples will serve to demonstrate this problem.

As will be remembered, in the summer and autumn of 1956 Israel began to collaborate with the governments of France and Britain, culminating in the Sinai Campaign of October 1956. All contacts were conducted covertly, and the entire Israeli Foreign Ministry (with the exception of the Foreign Minister herself, Golda Meir) was kept in the dark. Thus, the principal factor responsible for evaluating the response of the superpowers (i.e., the Israeli ambassadors to Washington and Moscow) was unable to make its contribution and deliver appraisals on this important matter. Even Israel's ambassadors to Paris and London were kept in the dark and were unable to express their opinion about the allies in whom Israel was about to put its trust.

In the summer of 1977 the Likud came to power. The new Foreign Minister, Moshe Dayan, viewed one subject as the focal point of his job: negotiating with Arab leaders to achieve Arab–Israeli peace agreements. Within this framework, Dayan met with Dr Hassan Touhami, Egyptian President Anwar Sadat's envoy, in Morocco. Both the Foreign Ministry and military intelligence were kept out of the picture. Needless to say, no account from above was given on this matter, and no attempt was made to verify the positions presented by Touhami against other sources. The intelligence estimate dealing with Egypt's expected courses of action analysed Cairo's quandary but failed to point out one possibility: peace negotiations.

True, when covert contacts are being conducted, secrecy must be kept to prevent leaks that may imperil those contacts. There is no doubt that the intelligence network must be guided prudently and that parties to secrets must be kept to a necessary minimum, but the opposite extreme should be shunned as well.

The EEI originating with the decision-maker should achieve its aim. The decision-maker should not be laconic. He must explain what is bothering him and detail the background to his request, all as clearly as possible. Furthermore, circumstances permitting, putting the question in writing should not be allowed to suffice; a process of response, interrogation and correction is to be desired. A misunderstood question cannot produce the required answer.

The decision-maker who has become acquainted with the intelligence network at his service will not hesitate to make demands upon it, posing questions that require special efforts. There need be no fear of burdening the system. On the contrary, the character of intelligence people is such that they derive great satisfaction from being able to complain about their heavy workloads.

This point can only be emphasized. I assume it is no secret that analysts serving the intelligence community receive modest salaries (this being definitely true of Israel), nor do these good public servants enjoy the advantages of public exposure. They just love their work. And their greatest satisfaction comes from knowing that their work is appreciated, and that they have provided some direct input for their country's major decisions. If you ask your analyst to prepare a special report for one of the decision-makers, he will always grumble and complain how busy and overworked he is, but he will go home and proudly tell his family and friends 'how sorry he is to cancel all plans for the weekend, but he has to work on something very special for the coming weekly meeting of the Israeli Cabinet on Sunday.' Yes, that makes him the happiest person in the world.

The key to a successful two-way relationship lies in the rapport between the parties. Decision-makers can function effectively regardless of the 'chemistry,' or lack of it, between them and most of their subordinates. But this does not hold true for their heads of intelligence. If no give-and-take develops, the desired result cannot be achieved.

This 'chemistry' should encourage the development of regular working procedures that are the key to success. The most important point is to base the relationship on direct contact, not on mediators or strictly written communication. Intelligence reports should not be anonymous. The decision-maker should know who is responsible so that he can turn to him with questions for clarification, and the intelligence man should always be entitled to maintain direct contact with the decision-maker whenever necessary. Incidentally, when an intelligence man is permanently stationed alongside the decision-maker, he can serve as an important element in encouraging such direct contacts. It is within his power to relay impressions both ways which will invite contact for needed clarification.

The decision-maker should conduct a 24-hour-a-day, open-door policy, allowing the intelligence head to call or contact him if he feels he has an important communication. Furthermore, the intelligence man can 'barge in' knowing full well that he will not be given a dressing-down for bothering the decision-maker unnecessarily. The right 'chemistry' is the required precondition. Not everyone is willing to be awakened in the middle of the night or bothered at unsociable hours. Both sides must be clearly aware of what such a relationship entails and refrain from abusing it.

The patience to listen is another element in the 'chemistry.' Not infrequently we will find an intelligence man presenting his appraisal to a decision-maker who has stopped listening, whose patience has expired. The fault may not always lie with the decision-maker. Rhetorical style, monotonous intonation, manner of presentation—these may all be factors in the success or failure of the interchange.

And of course, the highest expression of the reciprocal relationship is the right to state unpopular opinions. Few decision-makers are willing to listen to criticism and appraisals contrary to their actions and decisions. But the intelligence man who is forbidden to speak his mind cannot perform his job properly. A decision-maker who declines such opinions slams the door in the face of views that may save him from grave mistakes. The intelligence man, in doing his duty, must maintain the position of devil's advocate.

Integration in the Decision-Making Process

It is important that the intelligence man participate in decision-making consultations on national security issues. Just as it would be unthinkable for military staff work to be conducted without the participation of an intelligence officer, so it is unthinkable that government-level consultations on such issues should take place without the participation of an intelligence representative. His importance in such forums is threefold.

In the first place, such national security deliberations, like military staff work, should begin with a presentation of the intelligence picture. This can consist of the enemy's situation, intentions, deployment and possible courses of action. Where a military move is not under consideration, the intelligence picture will present the political map and its ramifications with regard to the subject being discussed and decided. The intelligence man's second function in such deliberations is to be present and ready to answer any questions that may arise. It can never be foretold what subjects, problems and questions may arise in such discussions, and it is vitally important that an authorized representative be there who is capable of providing immediate answers. In addition, though it demands a great deal of prudence and tact, an intelligence man present, even if only as an observer, can respond to and remark upon mistaken premises and unfounded proposals that may be brought up. Finally, his third role comes in the second stage—after a decision has been made—to provide feedback and to try to sustain the process with estimates of the possible responses of the various factors. Needless to say, this too must be accomplished with great tact.

In this last stage of the decision-making process intelligence risks being branded with a 'defeatist' label. This is unavoidable, for its function is always to point out the most severe and dangerous possibilities. The test of the intelligence network with regard to possible responses is not, and should not be, whether its direst forecasts have come to pass or not. Indeed the intelligence man, like any other, would be happy to see these forecasts come to naught. The test is whether responses are made that intelligence did not foresee or give warning about.

We all certainly remember the Maronite massacre in the Palestinian refugee camps of Sabra and Shatila in Lebanon. Intelligence's failure was in not providing warning—after the decision had been made to allow the Christian Phalangists into the camps for mopping-up operations—that a massacre might result. There is no doubt, as the Kahan Commission of Inquiry report specifically points out, that this failure was not the result of an incorrect appraisal, but rather of improper staff work, whereby intelligence was excluded from deliberations and its estimate not consulted.

Intelligence men bear a heavy burden of responsibility. They perpetually walk a tight rope. One danger is that intelligence will present its estimates so that they may be covered from all directions, that is in such a way as to make everything seem both possible and plausible. An intelligence estimate that is nothing but an inventory of existing possibilities will contribute little to the formulation of a reasoned decision. Another danger, no less severe, lies at the other extreme. There is always some risk that intelligence men will lose their objectivity. Indeed, their participation in political deliberations and close contact with decision-makers may lead to an identification with policy to such an extent that they may ignore facts and dangers that contradict that policy. That wretched term, 'conception,' which proved the undoing of intelligence just before the outbreak of the Yom Kippur War in 1973, certainly expressed such a relationship to no small degree.

There is no perfect cure, I am afraid, for this problem. One must understand that the analyst is part and parcel of his general environment and the society in which he lives. In his deliberations he not only relies on intelligence data but is exposed to the same media communications, to the same general moods and feelings, and, of course, has an instinctive loyalty to his superiors. The best we can do is to be aware of the danger and the pitfalls involved. There is one partial remedy, easy to recommend but very difficult to implement—that is, to invite 'outside' analysts to give their advice. The best of these are to be found in the academic world, such as are not privy to any confidential data. The difficulty in implementation is twofold. First, the existing bureaucracy, warning against having 'outsiders' involved in any secret intelligence consultation. Second, of course, comes the fear of hurting the feelings of one's own dedicated and hard-working analysts. In Israel, however, things have been simplified; almost all the needed scholars are part of our intelligence reserve forces.

Sure enough there are two opposed conceptions of the role of intelligence within the decision-making process. One exclusively limits it to a presentation of the picture with regard to the enemy, the other sees intelligence as a full and active partner in proposing courses of action for 'our forces' to the decision-maker.

There are arguments in favor of both views. In Israel, especially within the military, the intelligence officer has traditionally been a full partner in the formulation of proposals and decisions. At the political level no uniform picture presents itself. It can be said that each prime minister has his or her own style. At any rate, it is clear that the risk of total identification with policy on the part of the intelligence officer is minimized to the extent that intelligence's role is exclusively limited to a presentation of the picture with regard to the enemy.

True, there is an internal contradiction between the importance of two-way contact, the close and direct relationship between the decision-maker and his intelligence head, and the wish to retain measured, objective appraisal. Unfortunately, there are no simple solutions, and we must learn to live within this world of contradictions.

Working Techniques

The routine of reciprocal relationship consists of awareness, 'chemistry,' and the small techniques of working procedure. This may not seem the place to discuss such trifles, but sometimes there are no arguments and no problems in principle as regards the working relationship yet things go wrong because of these minor aspects.

Just as routine working procedure should not be entirely based on written communication, so it should not be solely based on oral communication either. The decision-maker who finds the time every day to take in intelligence reports will never be found. It is also important for the intelligence system to sum up its thoughts and appraisals in an organized manner. But the danger lies primarily in the first direction: statesmen are busy people, so used to perusing or skimming over a great quantity of written material that they easily become accustomed to a routine of written reports only.

When Golda Meir was Prime Minister of Israel (1969–74), Mrs Lou Kedar was her personal secretary, in charge of Mrs Meir's mail and documents. Every day Mrs Kedar would go through all the incoming reports and mail, do the necessary screening and decide what the Prime Minister was to see personally. Mrs Kedar used to separate all papers and place them in identical files—one, very thin, would go to the Prime Minister, the other, three or four times heavier, was handled by Mrs Kedar herself. One day when Mrs Meir was leaving her office in a hurry, she passed by Lou Kedar's desk and accidentally picked up the wrong file. The next morning Mrs Meir returned the file and told her secretary:

You know, Lou, there was something most unusual about yesterday's file. It took me some four hours to work through the papers; but on the other hand it was so much more interesting than the stuff you give me every day. . . .

The dangers in this case are numerous but we will only mention the principal ones. First of all, one can never know if, and what, the decision-maker has really read. Many heads of state ask one of their assistants to serve as a 'reader'; he classifies the material and decides which of it, and what part thereof, ends up on the decision-maker's desk. No system can function without such assistants, but they should never be allowed to take over the process.

Secondly, a routine of face-to-face meetings is needed to extract the EEI from the decision-maker. The chances that the decision-maker himself will find the time and invest the effort in formulating comprehensive queries on matters of interest to him are slim indeed. But this is not true of open conversation, in which the intelligence man can directly comprehend the decision-maker's problems and questions and certainly focus issues unambiguously.

Thirdly, without a working relationship that includes unmediated contact there can be no open-door policy on the part of the decision-maker, and we have already remarked upon the importance of this element.

Finally, written communication leaves no room for deliberation, clarification and laying emphasis upon things beyond what is written in the report. In many cases such clarifying discussions play an important role in the decision-making process.

Another important technique is for intelligence to suggest and implement a routine of meetings with the decision-maker unconcerned with ongoing policy-making. Such meetings can be devoted to the discussion of a subject chosen by the decision-maker or at his discretion, and attended by intelligence professionals who can shed light on the subject from various viewpoints. On the decision-maker's side, his partners in policy-making can take part in the meetings. This routine can contribute a great deal in three ways: first of all, of course, in teaching, recognizing and understanding the fundamental problems behind daily political decisions. Second, only through such meetings can decision-makers learn and evaluate the information intelligence has. Such meetings will awaken and encourage interest in the field of daily contact, not only enriching the store of information at the decision-maker's disposal but strengthening the reciprocal relationship as well. Third, such meetings are important for maintaining morale in the intelligence network's personnel.

Yet another technique: in many cases there is a tendency to limit contact with the decision-maker to the head of intelligence only. Sometimes it is the decision-maker who is responsible; many decision-makers disapprove of large meetings with lower-level representatives and are only willing to admit ministers or heads of service. But sometimes this is the attitude of the head of intelligence himself, perhaps as the result of a lack of self-confidence. For in company with the real expert his relative ignorance and superficial knowledge are sure to be exposed on every single subject. Of course, before such a meeting with the decision-maker, he conducts a preliminary discussion with his own people in order to analyse the subject, formulate a position and be prepared as best he can. But no preliminary discussion can take the place of the expert, who can immediately add, propose and criticize.

A final technical subject, but one of the utmost importance, is the demand decision-makers (almost without exception) that intelligence reports and reviews be delivered in 'telegraphic' style, within a limited number of pages. This demand may be justified as far as the busy decision-maker is concerned but it rankles with intelligence people who find it hard to confine themselves to this constraint. On the other hand, it is clearly difficult to condense all the information and its ramifications into the space of one or two pages. The solutions—and these depend on the character and style of each individual decision-maker—involve various techniques. It seems there is no escape from preparing two or three versions of every intelligence report; the first containing an outline within the required limits, the second slightly more detailed, and the third containing an in-depth analysis of selected topics.

Other methods may be integrated instead of having recourse to physical separation; each subject can be reviewed using an 'amplified title' immediately followed by the full text. Different colored paper can be used systematically, each color always representing one version of review. The intelligence report can include recommendations where the in-depth review is to be preferred.

As previously stated, the subject may be technical and minor to a degree, but insofar as the key to intelligence work lies in the relationship between the decision-maker and his intelligence man, the form of the written account is a major element in this relationship. In ensuring the cognitive acceptance of intelligence estimates, these minor techniques can play a very significant role.

The Limitations of Intelligence

One of the central problems in the relationship between decision-makers and intelligence is awareness and understanding of the limitations of intelligence. The political leaders of the modern world have of course stopped seeking out the advice of diviners, but in looking for another agency to serve this purpose and finding it in intelligence they are making a grave mistake. The intelligence man cannot predict the future. His training and experience enable him to present in an intelligent manner the information the system has acquired about the adversary's reasoning and intentions, and to evaluate possible enemy actions.

It is incumbent upon both the intelligence network and the decision-maker to understand what an intelligence estimate is, and furthermore to distinguish between various types of estimate. No instance is exactly like another, and each has its own characteristics, its own limitations and possibilities.

Intelligence estimates can be schematically divided into four categories. Though the term 'intelligence estimate' suits all four, there are basic differences in the quality of the data involved, and therefore the decision-maker's expectations must vary according to the type of estimate.

1. Estimate of Decisions Already Made

There is only one case in which intelligence may be expected and required to provide a definite prognostication, and this is when an appraisal is requested with regard to actions or failures on the other side stemming from decisions that have already been made. It may be hoped, even expected, that good intelligence work will find out as soon as possible or recognize moves that are a result of the decision by telltale indications. This is not an easy matter. Many of these decisions, especially where strategic military moves are concerned, are made secretly with the specific intention of concealment, deception and surprise. Experience has shown that many such tricks succeed, to the vexation of intelligence people and decision-makers alike.

The combined attack of the Egyptian and Syrian armies on 6 October 1973 is no doubt one of the more prominent examples (and has already entered the classical literature of attempts at surprise and deception). The decision to attack was made at the highest political level—by the presidents of the countries involved—months before Yom Kippur. Israeli intelligence was unaware of this decision and provided no warning. This failure was threefold. In the first place, the information-collection system failed to obtain, and provide in time, clear and unambiguous information about the decision. Second, the evaluating system failed in its faulty interpretation of the ominous signals of impending attack, explaining them as part of the seasonal strategic maneuvers in Egypt. Third, the presentation of the case to the decision-makers was mistakenly over-confident and reassuring, making it hard for them to decide upon suitable preventive measures, despite the uncertainty about a possible attack.

We are principally interested in the third failure. If intelligence men had explained the problems involved in differentiating between preparations for war and preparations for strategic exercise, if the style of presentation had been less confident, if decision-makers had been less reliant on the infallibility of intelligence, the necessary precautionary steps might yet have been taken to meet the danger.

One of the tragedies of those days is that there were people who wanted to, and did, give warning, but their voices were drowned out and did not reach those who should have heard them. These warnings proved to be in vain.

2. Estimate of Possible Reactions

In the second situation, the estimate of possible responses, intelligence cannot be expected to provide an explicit account of future events. The reason for this is simply that no intelligence information in the realm of decision or action can indicate decisively what is liable to happen.

We are dealing with the other side's response to an expected development. This may be a response to action we intend to initiate in the near future, or to a development over which we have absolutely no control. Of course the main difficulty lies in the fact that intelligence cannot base its estimate on reliable information supplied by the collection system. We are required to appraise in advance, to guess or forecast a decision which our adversary will make in the future. Even if we do have information, from the most highly authorized sources and acquired in whatever fashion, as to how the other side plans to act in a given hypothetical situation, we must treat it with a number of reservations; nothing can guarantee that in the future, when the decision is required, identical circumstances will prevail.

We will survey two examples of such situations. Both have to do with our part of the world and both were not foreseen by intelligence in time.

The first example is the Six-Day War. The Israeli Intelligence appraisal did not anticipate an all-out war in the summer of 1967. The intelligence analysis, which was based on the most reliable information, held that the Arab armies were not yet ready to initiate a wide-ranging military move that might embroil them in a full-scale war. Therefore—as long as their preparations remained to be completed—they would prefer to postpone their attack for a year or two at least. This appraisal remained in force despite the process of escalation that characterized Arab–Israeli relations in the year and a half preceding the war. Two factors added fuel to the fire. The first was the decision of the Arab Summit Conference about the diversion of the Jordan headwaters (the Banias and the Hazbani) and steps taken by the Syrian government to implement that decision. The second factor was the appearance of the El Fat'h organization, whose first terrorist operation was carried out in January, 1965. The organization's operations against various Israeli targets began the era of organized Palestinian terrorism.

Could anyone have foreseen and anticipated that these two factors would drag the entire Middle East into war? Information from intelligence-gathering sources certainly did not indicate any such thing. There was no Arab element that wished to become involved in war at that stage. The attempted intelligence estimate had to analyse the balance of military power and come to the conclusion that a hostile Arab initiative made no sense. (Furthermore, retrospective analysis of the results of the Six-Day War verify this appraisal.) The only element that might have wanted a war, from a theoretical viewpoint at least, was Israel. Needless to say, Israel was as surprised by the sudden, radical escalation and the train of events beginning in May 1967 as all the other elements involved.

At the same time Israel played an important role in the process of escalation. Israeli military acts against the Syrians responsible for the diversion of the Jordan River headwaters, as well as retaliations against the bases from which Palestinian terrorists penetrated into Israel across the ceasefire lines, statements by Israeli leaders warning the rulers of Damascus—all these forced the Arab side to embark upon a counter-deployment and provided the basis for mistaken intelligence estimates in Arab capitals, and Moscow as well.

In April–May 1967, it seemed that war with Syria was imminent, and a collusion of Russian and Egyptian interests formed to prevent it. In these conditions the concentration of Egyptian forces in the Sinai Peninsula could have been anticipated as a deliberate response to the situation on the Syrian border to halt the escalation there. The Middle East had experienced a similar situation in 1961 when the Egyptians had concentrated forces in the Sinai in response to an Israeli attack on the Syrian position of Tawafik in the Golan Heights, and had thus successfully halted escalation.

But in 1967 events took an entirely different turn. The key figures involved had changed, their responses were different, and quick and unrestrained escalation resulted on the Israeli–Egyptian front. At first forces were concentrated on both sides of the border, then came the Egyptian ultimatum and the removal of the UN emergency force. This last step prompted the Egyptian decision to occupy Sharm el-Sheikh, in this way blockading the shipping route to Eilat which had been open for about ten years. This last development made war inevitable.

Could these developments have been foreseen? Could anyone have anticipated this chain of unpremeditated responses? Even if intelligence had correctly appraised the situation and pointed out in April–May that it might deteriorate into a state of war, there was no way of proving it.

Now for the second example. We have already mentioned the intelligence failure before the Yom Kippur War. But the intelligence appraisal also failed in another way. The combined attack of Egypt and Syria on 6 October 1973 stimulated chain reactions throughout almost the entire Arab world. Among these responses was one step that shook the whole world: the Arab oil embargo. On the face of it, this step could have been foreseen. In 1967, in the wake of the Six-Day War, a first Arab oil embargo had already been attempted. At the time it had been a fiasco that left almost no impression. Perhaps for the very reason that the previous attempt was so dimly remembered, there was justification for assuming that the Arabs would not risk making an empty threat again. The 1973 oil embargo succeeded beyond expectations. It revealed an awesome Arab weapon that was to influence events in the region for years, indeed to this day. The intelligence appraisal totally ignored this possibility and danger.

Again, can intelligence be blamed? The embargo was a retaliatory step that had already failed once. Even had it been remembered and pointed out, it is quite likely that the intelligence estimate would have made little of the danger it posed.

3. Estimate of Results of Processes

In appraising the results of a process—even less than in appraising the response to an act—there is no significance to earlier decisions made by either side. Here we are placed after the decisions of those concerned have already been made (although in all probability additional decisions will be made, of course, in attempts to influence the process). What is demanded of the intelligence man in this case is like sitting down at the roulette table after the wheel has already been spun and attempting to determine whether the ball will settle on red or black.

In attempting to appraise such results the intelligence collection system can contribute little information in advance. From such information we can, of course, learn about the basic balance of forces, and determine, according to the laws of probability, that there is a two-to-one chance in favor of red. But the result itself will be determined by the 'players' themselves, by the forces they actually commit to the engagement, and perhaps, in no lesser degree, by their relative determination. By the way, often

there is no doubt as to the long-term process but questions arise about imminent developments.

Let us take Lebanon as an example. For years and years all students of the country repeatedly insisted that Lebanon's internal situation was simply impossible. The compact that had at one time been accepted for regulating the relations between the country's religions and ethnic groups could not possibly keep emotions in check. Furthermore, the compact's very rigidity had become a major obstacle, for the demographic and political reality stood in stark contrast to the findings of the census made in the 1930s.

It did not take much acumen to predict that Lebanon would suffer a severe internal crisis; the difficulty lay in determining when. Such was the position for approximately 40 years, although when civil war broke out in 1975 many were surprised. But Lebanon is also an excellent example of our central problem—attempting to appraise the result of a process. Here we are witness to a process that began with inter-religious conflicts in 1975. Since that time we have seen astounding reversals. Who still remembers that Palestinian units first entered Lebanon in order to restore order and contain the Muslim leftists, or that Syrian forces came to protect the Christians and actually fought against and defeated the leftist and Palestinian opposition?

In the first few years after 1975, Israeli's policy was unequivocal: no direct involvement in the internal Lebanese conflict (weapons and training supplied to the Phalangists were supposed to enable them to solve their problems on their own). After two years of bitter civil war there was a relative lull. Other than limited local clashes, all sides were waiting for the next round, and quite certain that it would arrive. In June 1982, IDF forces entered Lebanon. In a total reversal of previous policy, Israel and the IDF became factors directly influencing developments in Lebanon.

It is doubtful whether Israeli Intelligence estimates foresaw this development, and not only because it was the result of one factor out of the many acting on and influencing the Lebanese process. This factor took the initiative and as a result in the special circumstances created, dramatically influenced the turn of events. The other reason that prevented this development from being included in the intelligence estimate is that intelligence does not study the factor that played the major role in this case—its own government's policies.

Even today Lebanon's affairs are far from settled. And, today, no less than in 1983, it is still hard to foresee and appraise the results of the internal process within that country. They will be determined by the individuals involved, by the governments involved, and by contending political and military forces and many other factors whose identity, power and possible behavior we cannot always predict.

Let us take two more examples of processes that have played themselves out in the not too distant past.

The Vietnam War ended over ten years ago. The United States and its armed forces suffered heavy losses, the American expeditionary force was evacuated and the Saigon regime collapsed. Could this result have been foreseen with any certainty? The balance of military power was certainly in favor of the Americans. The failure was not a result of the military engagement.

The first factor, and perhaps the most critical, was the American gamble on the wrong 'horse.' The South Vietnamese regime was rotten and corrupt; the country's leaders did not attempt, and were perhaps unable, to win broad popular support for themselves personally and for their policies. American attempts to build up a local civilian infrastructure proved fruitless.

The second factor was the failure of American leadership to explain the importance of the Far Eastern conflict adequately to the American public, to the West and to the free world. In this way a democratic country was forced to wage a war with no support at home. Draft-dodging, desertion and a constantly growing protest movement eventually produced a search for a way out at any price, even if it involved sacrificing an ally in the field.

The American intelligence community did not warn the leaders in Washington that the war would end in such utter failure. Furthermore, even if this had been the appraisal of some, it must have been highly disconcerting to them, for—even within American democracy—it is no simple matter to promulgate an intelligence estimate contrary to declared government policy.

Existing organizational frameworks of a military-political nature, whether in the USA or elsewhere, are not up to the problems. None of these countries has an agency responsible for objective, frank and trenchant appraisal of the complex which constitutes respective power (meaning not merely the quantitative balance of military forces). It is no coincidence that no such framework exists, for by its very establishment it would take responsibility for appraisal of respective power out of the hands of the certified political leadership, and may occasion conflict between this leadership and the body responsible for objective appraisal. Of course, there are various academic research institutions, but these do not have the formal status of responsibility for such an appraisal, or the necessary binding authority. In fact, they are nothing but another

source—even if more thorough and better grounded—of journalistic analysis.

Our second example is the sequence of events that led to the fall of the Shah's regime in Iran and the rise of the Ayatollah Homeini to power. There was no difficulty in pointing out the dangers threatening the Shah's rule (just as the dangers threatening the regimes in many other countries in the Middle and Far East, in Africa or in Latin America, may be pointed out today without our being able to tell if or when they will come to pass).

The Israeli embassy in Teheran was more sensible of what was happening than the American embassy. So Israeli intelligence was able to warn the Americans, as early as April–May 1978, of the danger threatening the regime in Teheran. The Americans, trusting in their in-place representatives, took no heed of this warning. In retrospect the Israeli appraisal was proved right. But were these developments inevitable? It is quite possible that had the Shah taken a few steps, at the right time, he might have succeeded in stemming the tide and staying in power, at least until the next crisis.

Furthermore, in the Iranian crisis the principal factor was, of course, the Shah himself. As long as this experienced ruler who had overcome numerous crises did not seem worried, was there any reason for a pessimistic intelligence estimate?

These two examples return us to our central topic, the reciprocal relationship between decision-makers and intelligence. American intelligence in Vietnam and Iranian intelligence were limited in their appraisals, exactly like Israeli intelligence in the Lebanese context—they did not study or appraise and were not allowed to refer to their own governments' decisions. Indeed, when intelligence does refer to its own leaders, in many cases it does so as an active partner committed to mutual policy. It is almost inconceivable that Iranian intelligence would have put forward a critical estimate of the Shah.

In all the many consultations that dealt with the situation in Iran and the regime's disintegration, it is doubtful whether a real expert on Iran, the Shah or the Ayatollah Homeini was ever summoned to take part in meetings with the President or the National Security Council. The 'system' blocked any such experts, and limited itself to heads of services only.

4. Estimate of Long-Term Developments

Long-term intelligence estimates (five or ten years) have a relative advantage over appraisals of current affairs: it is easier to point out trends and processes than to give exact answers. And of course, it is doubtful whether anyone will remember the estimate in the years to come (including the person responsible for it).

Clearly, long-term estimates cannot be based on specific information collected or concrete decisions made. An attempt to analyse what might happen in the future can be made on the basis of familiarity with essential data and the various factors and trends that influence, or may influence, the course of development. Intelligence information about these essentials, factors and trends is of paramount importance. It provides the analyst with the various elements which decision-makers will also have to take into account. But this equation has two unknowns. The first, of course, is those elements that will accrue or change their relative weight, in the course of time, which may upset an estimate based on current information. The second stems from the fact that policy is not an exact science. No two statesmen will make the same decision in a given situation. Each statesman has his own inclinations, standards and preferences. And in this fourth situation, like the previous one, the result is also influenced by the acts and decisions of other relevant factors.

In 1976 Israeli intelligence had already begun examining and considering whether a real change had taken place in the attitudes of Arab leadership in general and Egypt in particular toward a peaceful settlement with Israel. The question Israeli intelligence asked itself was whether Israel had once again confined itself to a conception. Was the basic premise—that the Arab world was intent on Israel's annihilation—still valid? Was there any basis for the supposition that all Arab talk of peace and negotiations was nothing but masquerade? Even though intelligence did not have reliable, proven tools for investigating these developments, the intelligence estimate determined that there had been changes in the style of expression, semantic changes, but no real, profound alteration was detected. Nevertheless the estimate asserted that even if the change was semantic and tactical, if such talk persisted it could eventually have a cumulative effect on Arab public opinion.

At approximately the same time the intelligence estimate dealt with the expected Egyptian position nearing October 1978, when three years were to have expired from the signing of the interim Israeli–Egyptian agreement in Sinai, which Egypt considered to be of three years' duration. The estimate determined that in the absence of a new and different agreement (then we still spoke in terms of a 'cessation of hostilities or state of war' rather than peace) there was almost no chance of a new interim agreement in Sinai acceptable to both sides, and that therefore Egypt would have no choice but to resort to arms again.

History, as we well know, took a different turn. In November 1977, we witnessed Anwar Sadat's dramatic visit to Jerusalem and the Egyptian–Israeli peace process began. The storm of opposition in Egypt and the Arab world on the eve of Sadat's visit showed they were no less surprised there than in Israel. The resignation of the Egyptian Foreign Minister, Fahmi, in protest against Sadat's decision, indicates to what extent this step seemed unnatural and unexpected even in the highest echelons of the Egyptian government.

Later intelligence analysis left no doubt that Sadat's policy was the result of a personal decision, a decision that had not been discussed, examined or accepted by any forum within the ruling circles of Cairo. It did not rest on any broad, Arab consensus. On the contrary, Sadat, who knew his people well, believed he could bend them to his will and force his decision on them. Has Sadat's policy found any broad backing? Has it been accepted by popular opinion? The years that have gone by are too short a time to give any unequivocal answer. Sadat's assassination was certainly not a reassuring sign.

Several years ago reliable security sources in Israel expressed the opinion that Syria was planning to launch an attack against Israel in the summer of 1982. Not being privy to such information, I admit this estimate seemed to me unwarranted. The military evidence and considerations did not seem to indicate such a Syrian initiative. We do not know, and no details regarding this matter have been published, whether this appraisal belonged to the first category of estimates and was based on reliable information (meaning that a Syrian decision had already been made and uncovered by Israeli intelligence), or whether this was an estimate of trends falling into the fourth category. If the latter, then there was certainly room for argument and dissension about the appraisal.

Today, in the wake of the Lebanese War, it is doubtful if we will ever know whether a real danger existed. At any rate, in examining the functioning of Israeli Intelligence at the time we must ask at least two questions. First, was intelligence, or at least those responsible for the estimate, privy to the secret of Israel's intent to interfere directly in the Lebanese conflict? Obviously without this information it would have been hard to come to the proper conclusion. Second, if intelligence had indeed been in the secret, to what extent was it conceptually tainted with the same faith that drove Israeli leadership to this intervention, and subject to a distorted view that precluded presentation of an objective analysis? These two questions are once again directly related to the whole web of relations between leaders and intelligence.

An understanding of the problems pertaining to the four different situations is an essential, though sadly often deficient, element in the reciprocal relationship between decision-makers and intelligence men in everything concerned with intelligence estimates. It is imperative that both sides work out this matter, on both the conceptual-theoretic level and the pragmatic level, when discussing and examining any concrete estimate.

Two conditions are equally dangerous in decision-maker–intelligence relations. One is blind trust in the intelligence estimate on the part of the decision-maker. The other is total mistrust, based on the failings of an estimate that never had a chance of being properly and reliably presented in the first place. Differences between decision-makers and intelligence men should not center on the use of such terms as 'high' or 'low' probability, but on the nature and value of the estimate, on the problem with which intelligence is trying to deal and the chances of finding definitive answers to it.

The subject does not generally receive much mention. Most professional literature deals with the problems of intelligence itself, disregarding the special role the reciprocal relationship has in the decision-making process. This relationship can be instrumental in achieving maximum utilization of the system's potential, but it can also be an obstacle depriving decision-makers of information and appraisals even though they be in the hands of intelligence.

Appendix:
Operation Peace for Galilee

The civil war in Lebanon started some 13 years ago. It was an eruption of hostilities which gave vent to the very old feud between Christian factions on the one hand and a coalition of leftist Muslim forces, Palestinian organization and Druze militias on the other. The war has been characterized by the most horrible atrocities and massive murders committed by both parties.

In July 1981, following severe clashes between Palestinian militias and Israeli forces along the Lebanese border, a cease-fire was concluded through American mediation. According to this agreement the Palestinian organizations undertook a complete cessation of terrorist acts against Israel. However, under the umbrella of the agreement, Palestinians began to establish a gigantic military build-up in southern Lebanon. There was no doubt that, sooner or later, this build-up would enable terrorist acts against Israeli targets to be renewed, with the Palestinians well prepared and protected behind the border. An Israeli preventive military move against this new build-up was inevitable.

The war started on 6 June 1982 following a Palestinian terrorist attack on the Israeli ambassador to London. In retaliation, Israel aircraft hit Palestinian targets in south Lebanon. This generated a massive Palestinian missile and artillery attack against Israeli civilian targets south of the Lebanese border.

The Israeli government's response was Operation Peace for Galilee. This aimed to destroy the Palestinian build-up in south Lebanon. At a later stage Israeli forces joined Christian forces near Beirut, but following strict orders, the IDF were careful not to enter west Beirut, which served as the main stronghold for the Palestinian and Muslim militias. Tough bargaining brought an agreement according to which all military forces (Syrian, Muslim and some 15,000 Palestinians) evacuated west Beirut by land and by sea.

On 14 September there was a dramatic and unexpected development. Basheer Jemayel, the newly elected president of Lebanon, was killed when an explosion demolished the Phalangist headquarters in east Beirut. Fearing quick deterioration in Beirut, Israel ordered the IDF into the western Muslim part of the city. Two days later, Phalangist units were permitted to move into two refugee camps (Sabra and Shatilla), to uncover and apprehend all Palestinian militias hiding in the camps. The ensuing atrocities, committed by the Phalangists in the camps, attracted world-wide attention at the time, as well as stormy reactions within Israel. After some hesitation, the Israeli cabinet initiated an official judiciary enquiry into the atrocities and into Israel's involvement and responsibility.

Israeli decision-making at the time, as described in the official report of the commission of enquiry, may serve as a fine example for the complexity of relations between the decision-maker and the military in general and intelligence in particular. In the three major decisions—to initiate a major offensive into Lebanon, to occupy west Beirut and to allow Phalangist mop-up in the camps—we may analyse and examine the principles, the rules and the preferred procedures for the correct inter-relationship between the decision-maker and his intelligence adviser.

The Initiation of the War in Lebanon

Operation Peace for Galilee (OPG) was aimed at destroying the Palestinian military build-up in south Lebanon. It rapidly developed into a war aiming to link up with the Christians in the north to impose a new order in Lebanon, and to

a. establish indisputable Christian rule over the country;

b. remove all Syrian and Palestinian forces from Lebanon (preferably together with most of the Palestinian refugees);

c. establish normal peace relations between Israel and Lebanon.

This decision was adopted *in spite of the intelligence evaluation*. It is, of course, the decision-maker's privilege not to accept an intelligence analysis or evaluation, provided that this is done consciously and after thorough consideration. Unfortunately, this was not true of the above decision:

1. Israeli intelligence did not accept the political thesis based on overestimating the capability or reliability of the Christian-Maronite militias, neither as a future political ally of Israel nor as to their operational-military performance, and least of all, as to their future participation in the fighting. This intelligence evaluation was never allowed to be presented to the cabinet and was never confronted with the opposite position.

2. The basic assumption behind OPG was that Israel could destroy the Palestinian military build-up and that the mass of Palestinians in Lebanon would move out of the country in general and out of south Lebanon in particular. Intelligence did not entertain this assumption. Past experience has taught us that Palestinian militias were always avoiding military confrontation and that OPG would end with minimal Palestinian casualties. On the other hand, political limitations would not permit the evacuation of the Palestinians out of Lebanon. This evaluation was never brought for discussion or to a conscious cabinet decision.

3. The two main decision-makers, Minister of Defense Sharon and Prime Minister Begin, did their best to exclude General Saguy, the Director of Military Intelligence (DMI) from the relevant cabinet meetings and did not give him a chance to present his evaluation. In some cases, Mr Zippori, the Minister for postal services, a retired Brigadier General and former deputy Minister of Defense, insisted on inviting intelligence to open the cabinet discussions, preceding a political decision (as is routine and normal with all military planning-groups). On a personal level, General Saguy had good and long-standing relations with both Mr Begin and General Sharon, but this was not enough to allow the sort of 'chemistry' giving intelligence the right to present *unpopular* positions.

4. Israeli intelligence was not informed of relevant political discussions, did not partake and did not receive complete and detailed reports which could influence its evaluations:

   a) Political talks between senior Israeli politicians and Lebanese leaders of the Maronite organisations were organized by Mossad representatives, in charge of the clandestine liaison in Lebanon. The Mossad, in this role, served neither as an intelligence collection agency nor as an evaluation one. Not having diplomatic relations with Lebanon, these delegates fulfilled a 'diplomatic' role, and were affected by the classic diplomatic ailment of being biased and presenting a non-realistic picture of their Lebanese counterparts. Israeli decision-makers became confused and could not differentiate between the Mossad as a major intelligence agency, and the Mossad in its diplomatic role. The absurdity of this confusion was best expressed by General Hoffi, the head of the Mossad, who did not accept the evaluation of his own people, and did not rely on their reports.

   b) General Sharon visited the US and had several meetings just before OPG; the most important one with Secretary of State Al Haig. His report of these meetings was incomplete, and gave a false impression as if the US supported a major Israeli military operation in Lebanon. Israeli intelligence was again excluded, and did not receive the complete and detailed report of the meetings.

5. During the war itself, the cabinet did not have a chance to receive a full intelligence report and analysis (in most cases, intelligence was not even present at the meetings). This omission is even more striking when we know that the DMI presented a most detailed evaluation of the possible military move in Lebanon some three weeks earlier (13 May), in front of the IDF military leadership, with the Chief of Staff and the Minister of Defense both present.

The Occupation of West Beirut

In the afternoon of 14 September 1982 the Phalangist headquarters in Beirut were blown up by opponents of the newly elected president, Basheer Jemayel. It was some six hours before it was made known that Basheer was among the dead. Once this was confirmed, Israel ordered the IDF to occupy west Beirut (the Muslim–Palestinian stronghold).

One can understand the urgency for such a decision, which did not allow convening a regular cabinet meeting first. It was imperative that the forces move in before daylight and before Christian fanatics had time to initiate indiscriminate atrocities against Muslims and Palestinians. Indeed, between 10 p.m., when Basheer's death was recognized, to 3 a.m. when the IDF were already entering west Beirut, it was practically impossible to spend the 3–4 hours necessary for convening a meeting and reaching a decision. However:

1. The decision was taken following many telephone conversations between the Prime Minister, the Minister of Defense and the Chief of Staff. There was no effort to bring together the main actors (including the above three)—the Foreign Minister, the DMI and the head of the Mossad. It should have been quite easy to have the above six in one place, for the duration of the crisis.

2. The Israeli general staff is well organized to set up a special Command Post (CP) with all the decision-makers present. As a routine, such a CP serves the MOD and the military authorities. The military secretary to the PM is also present, and it is his duty to keep the PM updated. One has to understand that while all ministries in Israel are in Jerusalem, the MOD, together with IDF headquarters, are in Tel Aviv. Had such a CP been established, then all procedural problems would have been resolved. It would have been good to have present, as routine, the personal representation of the Foreign Minister too. This would allow complete co-ordination between the main concerned parties of the cabinet.

3. There is no record of the many telephone conversations which took place that night. Nobody took notes at the time and nobody bothered to have a record made on the following morning. One may argue that the importance of such records is mainly for the future historian or to satisfy a formal enquiry, but such records have at least two additional purposes:

   a) A formal record of a conversation has to define in clear and precise terms what was discussed and what decision was reached. We all know how many conversations end up with each party having a different version of the decision.

   b) Such a record does serve as reference to whoever needs to know the decision, and one day ask for the written record without bothering the decision-makers. This is a most important co-ordination tool.

4. In the circumstances, it is no wonder that the official enquiry found many discrepancies between the various testimonies, leaving three unanswered questions:

   a) What were the IDF goals in entering west Beirut?

   b) How were the IDF to treat the Palestinian refugee camps?

   c) Had the Christian militias any role during the phase of entering west Beirut and the immediate mop-up?

5. During these discussions, three central figures were not consulted:

   a) The Foreign Minister was not updated, he was not consulted, and nobody thought that such a decision ought to be discussed with Washington, or even that Washington should be notified about Israel's decision to enter west Beirut (such a notification would have been far beyond courtesy, following the leading role Washington played in reaching the July agreement on Beirut).

   b) The DMI, who carries the formal responsibility for the Israeli national intelligence evaluation, did not participate in the discussions and his opinions neither asked nor heard as to the possible consequences of such an entry from a strategic, as well as from a political, point of view.

   c) The head of the Mossad was not consulted. As the agency in charge of the liaison with the political and military leadership in Lebanon, one should have asked Mossad to report on Christian reactions following the assassination, as well as to their possible intentions and plans for revenge.

Phalangist Mop-Up in the Refugee Camps

The original order to occupy west Beirut did not specify what should be done with the refugee camps. Operation order No. 6, issued 36 hours later (on Thursday, 16 September), did clearly specify that the IDF should not enter the camps. The mop-up of the camps was the responsibility of Lebanese forces (either army or militias).

The MOD and the Chief of Staff, at least one day earlier, have reached the decision to allow the Phalangists to do the job. This decision was distributed in writing only within the military; it was sent out on the 16th and reached the DMI on the 17th. The Foreign Minister and the Head of the Mossad were not among the recipients. Now, in contrast to the earlier decision to enter west Beirut, there was no urgency attached to this decision. It could have been brought up for discussion at all echelons. It should have been discussed, at least, on the military level with the DMI and the Mossad, and on the political level with the PM and the Foreign Minister. It seems that there was no intention to circumvent anyone. It was simply the result of a faulty procedure to reach such a decision while visiting the divisional CP, overlooking one of the camps from the rooftop of the building. It is a deep-rooted tradition with the IDF for the most senior commanders to be as frequently as possible with the troops, to have first-hand impressions and to make decisions on the spot. The advantages of this procedure are of course:

1. Up-to-date and reliable information, independent of the system's slow, clumsy distorting process of reporting.

2. Consulting with the field commanders, without wasting their time and interfering with their duties.

3. A very important boost to the morale of the troops to see the VIPs among them.

On the other hand, one should not underestimate the dangers and the disadvantages of such a tradition.

1. While field commanders may all be there, one can never expect all staff officers and all political leaders to be present and to have their opinion.

2. Many such decisions suffer from the 'seeing red' syndrome. A decision taken at the scene of the fighting is very often biased because of the immediate and emotional impact of the sounds and sights of the battle-scene, not allowing a careful and comprehensive consideration of all factors before the decision.

Had this decision been brought for a formal discussion, it is fairly obvious that both the DMI and the Mossad would have raised their strong reservations, warning against the unavoidable atrocities which would be committed by the Christian militias. The Israeli decision would probably have been a different one.

We have been reviewing three major Israeli decisions, all related to Operation Peace for Galilee, all three suffering severely from the defects that characterize faulty relations between decision-makers and their intelligence systems. There was nothing wrong with the Israeli collection-activity regarding Lebanon; there was nothing wrong with the intelligence analysis and evaluation on Lebanon. The necessary data were all there, the recommendations proved to be sober and realistic. Israel's real problem during that crisis was just that for a variety of reasons, affecting the existing relations between the top decision-makers and the heads of their intelligence services, circumstances in 1982 made it impossible for the Israeli cabinet to have a balanced discussion and consideration before its decisions. We all know today the unfortunate consequences.

Epilogue

The report of the commission was brought before the cabinet for adoption. It carried personal recommendations as well as organizational ones. Unfortunately the personal recommendations, dealing with the MOD, with the chief of staff, with the DMI and some others, overshadowed the cabinet's discussion. And the outcome was that the organizational recommendations were never really discussed, and obviously no changes were introduced.

Questions for Further Discussion

1. Why do politicians need to be introduced to the intelligence community?

2. Why is it difficult for intelligence analysts to estimate foreign responses to national policies and initiatives?

3. Why is it important for intelligence analysts to supplement written reports with personal briefings to policy makers?

4. When are intelligence analysts likely to be viewed as defeatists by policymakers? ✦

Reprinted with permission from Shlomo Gazit, "Intelligence Estimates and the Decision-Maker," *Intelligence and National Security* 3 (July 1988): 261–267.

13

Early Warning Versus Concept: The Case of the Yom Kippur War 1973

Ephraim Kahana

In the aftermath of surprise, intelligence professionals and policymakers are often haunted by the fact that disaster might have been avoided if they had just interpreted available and, in hindsight, highly credible evidence differently. In this study of Israeli intelligence performance prior to the 1973 Yom Kippur War, Kahana describes how the analytic framework ("The Concept") that dominated Israeli perceptions of events in the fall of 1973 led both analysts and officials to misinterpret information about the threats they faced.

Early warning in strategic intelligence studies can be defined as 'Informing decisions makers about the enemy's future actions, in a time span ensuring the possibility of taking of steps previously evaluated as adequate to neutralize advantages that the enemy may obtain from surprise, and thereby frustrating the surprise move.'[1] Surprise may be defined as 'the occurrence of an unexpected event, or alternatively, the non-occurrence of an expected event.'[2]

Following the Yom Kippur War, the Agranat Commission (the commission of inquiry into the circumstances of that war) concluded that Aman (acronym of the Hebrew *Agaf Modi'in*, namely Intelligence Branch) had failed to provide an early warning, as required by decision-makers, that the war was going to start.[3]

A document entitled 'Annual Intelligence Evaluation,' submitted by the head of Aman, Major General Aharon Yariv, to the Chief of Operations, Major General Yisrael Tal, in June 1972, stated among other things that Aman could be expected to provide the General Staff with warning of an Egyptian

attack 36 hours in advance if Egypt were to make preparations, and that a similar warning could be given of a Syrian attack, but with lower likelihood.

Such warnings would be provided on the basis of methods of collecting information about war preparations. The basic assumption of the Aman document was that the organization of the Egyptian Army for a large-scale operation would involve military preparations spanning at least six days. These indications, General Yariv believed, would make it possible to provide an early warning. General Yariv added a caveat, namely that if the military preparations were conducted against the background of prolonged tension or a large-scale military exercise, then the military trends and moves would not be clear-cut.[4]

A similar note was sounded in the evaluation made by Major General Eli Zeira in the spring of 1973. Zeira, who succeeded Yariv as head of Aman, replied to a question from Prime Minister Golda Meir regarding what warning provisions he could provide of Egyptian military action. Eli Zeira distinguished three possible modes of action by the Egyptians, one of which was the crossing of the Suez Canal. In this regard he claimed: 'I am certain that we will know about it in advance, and will be able to give warning several days ahead.'[5] When questioned by the Prime Minister, as to the means used to derive such a warning, he said: 'By the preparations: the preparations cannot be hidden.'[6]

Yet on other occasions Zeira was also heard to voice reservations. At a conference of Israel Defense Forces (IDF) corps commanders in spring of 1973 he stressed that despite his confidence in the ability to give a warning, planning should not rule out a situation of no warning, and appropriate planning measures should be undertaken.[7] In fact, until the last moment Zeira was not entirely convinced that a war was about to erupt, and all the decision-makers were similarly unconvinced.[8]

The question is, therefore, whether in formal terms any reasonable intelligence officer would have been able to forecast the outbreak of war within the time frame suggested in the 'Annual Intelligence Evaluation' of June 1972.[9] The following discussion attempts to answer this question and to examine the obstacles that made the provision of early warning an almost impossible task.[10] However, I will focus primarily upon 'the Concept' as the highest in the ranking order of pitfalls that await intelligence analysis. The term 'the Concept' (*ha-konceptzia* in Hebrew) was coined by the Agranat Commission for investigation of the Yom Kippur War debacle.[11]

Ha-konceptzia (the Concept) and Its Growth Process

Ha-konceptzia (the Concept) as the main paradigm guiding Aman's analysis, was composed of two components. These two components were rooted in what were widely agreed to be rational assumptions:

1. Egypt would not embark on war against Israel unless it could first assure itself the capability of attacking Israel's chief military airfields, by long-range Sukhoi bombers and Scud missiles, in order to paralyze the Israeli Air Force. The Egyptian component of the Concept was not an assessment by Israeli Intelligence analysts of the Egyptian capabilities nor was it an assessment of how the Egyptians considered their capabilities. The Egyptian component of the Concept was Humint information provided to the Mossad secret service by an Egyptian top source (hereafter, the Top Source).[12]

It was exactly what every intelligence officer wishes to get but very rarely does get. The Top Source voluntarily offered his services to Mossad after the Six Day War (June 1967) and provided information on what the Egyptian government and military command believed regarding their ability to win an all-out war against Israel.

The information was supported by authentic protocols of Egyptian government meetings. According to the information provided by the Top Source the Egyptian leadership and army did not believe that they could win an all-out war against Israel as long as they had not obtained the military capability they considered vital for success, namely, Scud missiles and long-range bombers.[13]

2. Syria would not embark on a full-scale attack against Israel except simultaneously with Egypt.[14] The Syrian component of the Concept was based on the assessment of Aman's analysts. It is worth stressing that this factor pertained before the Yom Kippur War, and it still pertains today; it has never been disproved. Syria has never waged war on Israel alone.

According to Aman's analysts, the key component was therefore the Egyptian, namely, that as long as Egypt did not believe in its ability to win an all-out war against Israel, it would not start one, and that Syria would not wage war alone. The Syrian component was therefore contingent upon the Egyptian component.

Aman's assessment in 1973 was based on the assumption that should Egypt acquire the needed bombers and Scud missiles at any time, for instance, in the following year, it would then take two years for these weapons to be absorbed and become operational. Therefore, Aman recommended to the Israeli leadership to be prepared for war in 1975. The probability of war in 1973 was deemed low.[15]

With the hindsight of almost 30 years, it may be stated with certainty that the Concept in respect to Egypt was accurate only until about October 1972. At that time, by a process and not a *volte face*, Sadat changed his mind and decided not to await delivery of the Soviet weapons. He had become increasingly convinced that the Egyptian Army was able to win an all-out war against Israel and could proceed to occupy the territory of the Sinai desert under the cover of massive protection by surface-to-air (SA) missiles.[16]

To advance the process towards war, Sadat replaced his Minister of War, General Mohammed Sadik, who opposed a military move in the absence of the protection of Scud missiles and bombers, with General Ahmed Ismail.[17] Sadat's change of strategy was unknown to the Israeli intelligence community at that time; it became known only after the war.[18]

Even after Sadat had changed his strategy, however, Aman continued to receive information from the Top Source, although the delivery of the information became less frequent and the content more sparse and shallow. It was of lower quality in that it was less authentic and not supported by documents as before. In any event, the Top Source's information until the Yom Kippur War continued to maintain that the Egyptian leadership did not believe in its ability to win an all-out war against Israel without Scud missiles and long-range bombers. The Concept remained static until the outbreak of the Yom Kippur War even though the reality had radically changed during this critical period.[19]

Concepts, when they become a dominant paradigm of human thinking, acquire an inherent strength. A concept or perception, as Jervis and Lebow stated, can be changed either when one gets new unequivocal information that runs counter to one's perception or when a changed reality hits one in the face.[20]

This was not the case with any of the information collected by Aman's Signals Intelligence (Sigint) department or by the Mossad. No item of information unequivocally contradicted the existing position. Moreover, three events of the 'cry-wolf scenario' served as tests of the Concept, and in the end supported and reinforced it.[21]

1. The first test was in November–December 1971. At that time, Aman received information from what were considered reliable sources that Egypt had resolved to go to war at the end of 1971. In addition, President Sadat publicly

declared 1971 as the 'Year of Decision.' The information was checked by Aman's Analysis section which concluded that Sadat did not plan to go to war at that time. Indeed, war did not erupt in 1971, reaffirming the tenets of the Concept.[22]

2. The second test providing support for the Concept was in December 1972. As in 1971, Humint maintained that Egypt was going to launch a war in December 1972. The Analysis section studied the warnings and the facts, checked them against the Concept, and concluded that Sadat would not start a war at that time. Again, sure enough, there was no war in 1972. The actual events that year were indeed in harmony with the Concept and with information received from a diplomat who had access to the Egyptian leadership. This diplomat reported that he had been present at a diplomatic function where he heard that Sadat, despite his repeated declaration that 1972 was the 'Year of Decision,' was farther than ever before from being ready to realize this threat of war. It seemed to the diplomat that Sadat had in fact come to terms with the situation of 'no war and no peace.'[23]

3. Finally, in March 1973, the Israeli intelligence community received information that Egypt was making preparations for a war which it intended to launch against Israel by April. Then came news that the attack had been postponed until May. At that time signs indicated that Egypt was conducting a major military mobilization and exercises. Beirut's *Al-Nahar* newspaper reported that many Egyptian troops were being transferred from Cairo to the Canal Zone and that Sadat, finally convinced that war was the only solution, was holding secret meetings with his high command.[24]

Following an evaluation of the situation by Aman's Analysis section, Zeira, head of Aman, concluded that Egypt wished to create the impression that its back was against the wall and that it had no alternative but to go to war.[25] He claimed that Egypt's purpose in creating such an atmosphere of pre-war tension was to exert pressures on the superpowers before their expected summit meeting. They undoubtedly wished to avoid war, and in that case they should be encouraged to insist on a diplomatic process and to impose an arrangement on Israel. Zeira added that Egypt's military command assessed that its forces were inferior to those of Israel and Egypt would not be able to derive positive results from a war. Therefore, according to Zeira, the probability of a war low, although it did exist.

The IDF Chief of Staff, Lieutenant General David Elazar accepted Amans assessment that the probability of a war was low, but added 'Instinctively, I feel that this time it is more serious than previous warning . . .' He observed that 'likelihood' was a dynamic concept and was contingent upon specific developments. Several factors were pushing towards war, among them the political stalemate and Egypt's disappointment with the United States and its decision to supply Israel with arms. Therefore, Sadat's purpose was to threaten Israel in advance of the forthcoming summit meeting. He might suffice with the warning but he might also estimate that the situation would allow him to launch a short war that would not cause him damage, but it would thrust the Middle East into the headlines. Above all, Egypt's determination to go to war could be so powerful that it might outweigh rational considerations.[26]

Therefore, the Chief of Staff decided to take the necessary steps based on the assumption that there was the possibility of war, albeit slight, and that the likelihood was dynamic.[27]

The Minister of Defense, Moshe Dayan, assessed that Egypt's intention was to make moves towards a diplomatic process.[28] The question remaining was whether the Egyptian believed that threats would suffice or whether they would open fire to move the process forward. Dayan added that the measures taken by Egypt so far indicated its plan to go to war. He based this argument mainly on the fact that Sadat had dispatched Hafez Ismail, head of the Egyptian National Security Council, to Washington to meet Henry Kissinger, the US National Security Council Adviser, to request that he exert pressure on Israel for a diplomatic solution to the conflict; However, Ismail's mission bad failed.[29] Therefore, Dayan believed, Egypt saw matters as being an impasse; a diplomatic settlement was deemed unlikely, which left the military option as the only way out.[30]

This was the first time that the Concept began to weaken. Consequently, decision-makers did not automatically adopt Aman's assessment. The Chief of Staff decided that his move should be based on the dynamics of likelihood, and he declared a 'blue-white alert,' namely, partial mobilization of the reserves and a military alert along the Suez Canal.[31] In the end, no Egyptian attack materialized and the cost of the partial mobilization was estimated between $13 and $18 million.[32]

The Concept received a boost from the general atmosphere in Israel, especially after the victory of the Six Day War, with the Arabs stereotyped as incapable of overcoming Israeli forces. This was a widespread belief in Israeli society in general and in the IDE in particular. This stereotype was frequently given public expression by Prime Minister Golda

Meir through the maxim 'Our situation has never been better.'[33] The Minister of Defense made the same point repeatedly in military forums and public speeches, In August 1973 he stated: 'There is a large gap between us and the Arabs. It is a qualitative gap. Because of the quality of our manpower, the gap will not be closed for many years.'[34]

In the IDE this attitude was supported by the following findings:

1. At a meeting between a group of Aman intelligence officers and a senior Israel Air Force combat pilot, the latter stressed that the Israel Air Force had found the solution to the problem of the Egyptian SA missiles.[35]

2. Shortly before the Yom Kippur War Aman conducted a study on the Egyptian POWs of the Six Day War. Aman concluded that the Arab officers and soldiers were inferior to and less intelligent than their Israeli counterparts.[36] On a visit by Aman officers to the Canal Zone the Israeli commanders there showed self-assurance and appeared quite confident that Egyptian troops and tanks would be incapable of crossing the Bar-Lev line, especially under Israeli fire.[37]

On 18 July 1972 Sadat ordered the withdrawal of Soviet military personnel from Egypt. By 6 August, 15,000–20,000 Soviet military advisers, pilots, and missile crews had left Egypt. Only approximately 3,000 Soviet missile technicians and other instructors remained in the country. This measure was interpreted by Aman as weakening the Egyptian capability to go to war.[38] In addition, plenty of information published in the Western press and the Arab press reinforced Aman's view of the Egyptians and their military inferiority to the Israeli Army.

All of these circumstances bore on conclusions reached by the officers of Aman's Analysis section. By the eve of the Yom Kippur War, the Concept had grown strong; but it was wrong.

The Concept and Its Erosion Process

At the end of August 1973 Israeli intelligence received information that a delegation of Soviet experts had visited Syria and reported to the Syrian leadership that the Syrian Army would be able to occupy the Golan Heights in a couple of hours, according to the balance of forces at that time. Israeli intelligence already knew that the Syrians were carrying out a large-scale military exercise for occupying the Golan Heights. On 30 August Aman obtained information that Syria and Egypt had received their expected weapons: surface-to-sur-face Frog missiles for Syria and surface-to-surface Scud missiles for Egypt.[39]

On 4 September the Syrians started to intensify their activity along the border of the Golan Heights with more artillery and infantry battalions. In addition to these signs, the first concrete strategic warnings of Egyptian and Syrian preparations to start war in a very short time began reaching the Israeli intelligence community from mid-September 1973. Bar-Joseph enumerates more than 11 strategic warnings.[40]

However, several of these were contradictory. According to the first warning in mid-September, Egypt's intention was to start the fighting at the end of 1973. Later it was added that President Assad of Syria had agreed to embark upon war toward the end of 1973, as proposed by Sadat. However the Top Source continued to report that Sadat wished for three more years of quiet.[41]

The identities of the various Humint sources are still top secret, and for good reason, but, some public sources have revealed the identity of several of them. Admiral Fulvio Martini, a previous head of the Italian intelligence services, was very close to Mossad. When traveling to Arab countries he would carry a concealed camera to photograph Arab military installations for the Israelis.[42]

One of the Mossad operators was a professor of languages who flew into Israel on 4 October, bringing photocopies of the Egyptian-Syrian war plans bearing the codename of the war, 'Operation Badr.'[43] Ibraim Sahin, an Egyptian, provided concrete confirmatory-type warnings about Egyptian army movements in the Canal Zone; he was arrested by the Egyptian authorities after the war and sentenced to death.[44] The identification of these first two sources should be treated very circumspectly.

The most senior source, although not an Israel agent, was King Hussein of Jordan. His identity is no longer secret, as General Zeira referred to the King in his book and mentioned his name explicitly in a seminar on the Yom Kippur War.[45] Hussein met Prime Minister Golda Meir at a Mossad guest house in north Tel Aviv on 25 September 1973 and warned her that 'the Syrian army is in [sic] occupying [an] attack position,' adding that he suspected these moves were being coordinated with Egypt. The King recommended that Israel accept a diplomatic solution to the conflict in order to avoid a military conflagration.[46] The next day, 26 September, the King conveyed the same warning through the CIA, and it reached the Mossad on 30 September.[47]

For all that, the Concept was by then so solid and powerful that it seemed that even if President Sadat himself met Mrs Meir and informed her that he was about to hurl his army against Israel, Meir would probably ask him if he had long-range bombers and Scud missiles to strike Israel's military airfields. Hearing President Sadat reply in the negative Mrs Meir would no doubt say, 'Okay, when you get these weapons come and see me again and we'll talk.'

Hussein's warning was strategic, though it gave no exact timing. But it was taken sufficiently seriously for Prime Minister Meir to telephone Dayan that same evening for an assessment of its gravity. Zeira, at Dayan's request, checked the warning against the Concept and found it exaggerated. Moreover, since the warning was not unequivocal, Aman's reassessment gave Meir a sense of calm. The Prime Minister left Israel the following day, 26 September, to attend the Socialist International at Strasbourg.

Recently Zeev Schiff, a leading Israeli journalist for the daily *Ha'aretz*, reported that Lieutenant Colonel Zusia Knizer, head of the Jordanian section in Aman, who was present at the meeting between Meir and Hussein behind a glass wall, regarded the King's message as a serious warning. That evening he reported it to his colleague, Lieutenant Colonel Avi Yaari, head of the Syrian section, in contravention of a clear order to classify the meeting. The latter alerted the Israeli Northern Command.[48] The following day, both officers were rebuked by the deputy head of Aman in charge of analysis. Brigadier General Aryeh Shalev: Knizer for disobeying an order and Yaari for alerting the Northern Command without cause.[49]

Moreover, there is evidence that Dayan considered Hussein's warning serious enough.[50] On the morning of 26 September, Dayan asked the Chief of Staff to find solutions for the possibility that Syrian forces might be able to overrun an Israeli settlement or military post without an early warning. The emphasis was on a limited operation, given Aman's assessment that Syria would not attempt to occupy the Golan Heights without Egypt.

In fact, what was taking place on the Syrian side of the border had attracted the attention of the Israeli defense leadership even before Hussein's warning. As previously noted, signs indicating some change in the status quo had begun to appear in the region since the middle of August 1973, when Syria had started to intensify it deployment of SA missiles on the Golan Heights. From the beginning of September, Syria had been enlarging its ground forces deployed on the Golan Heights.[51] On 13 September, Israeli aircraft were on a photographic reconnaissance mission over Latakia when they encountered Syrian fighters. In the ensuing airbattle over the Mediterranean, 13 Syrian MiGs were shot down.[52] This was the biggest Israeli-Syrian air battle since the Six Day War in 1967. From that point onward, Syrian retaliation was expected by the Israeli side.[53]

A further sign of Israeli concern was evident on 24 September at an IDF general staff meeting. The chief of Northern Command, Major General Yizhak Hofi, noted that he was disturbed by events on the Syrian side of the border, even though the issue was not on the meeting's agenda.[54] Hofi maintained that the Syrians could launch a surprise strike without any possibility that the Northern Command would be properly prepared. He added that with no early warning system in place and with no ground obstacles, there was a danger that Syrian jets could reach Israel's heartland quickly. Hofi said, that 'recently Syria had thickened and thinned the line' without his knowledge in real time. If Syria's SA missiles were moved up to the front line, this might cause increased problems of response by the Israel Air Force.[55] Hofi therefore recommended the immediate enlargement of Israeli ground forces on the Golan Heights.

The matter before the Israeli military leadership, then, was not the content of Hussein's warning but its interpretation, especially in regard to the indications on the Golan Heights. At the 26 September general staff meeting, Zeira assessed the probability of a Syrian operation as low due to fear of IDF retaliation. The only explanation offered by Zeira for the Syrian actions was that they were taken in response to the shooting down of their 13 fighters, or as a preventive measure in case of any further IDF operation.[56] The Chief of Staff excluded any possibility of a Syrian attempt to occupy the Golan Heights without Egyptian involvement in the war—which was one of the components of the Concept. While he admitted that gaining warning of a limited operation would be very difficult to achieve, he claimed that having early warning of an all-out war was all but guaranteed.

From that point, all decisions were based on the assumption of a limited operation and not a war. The measures decided on by the Chief of Staff were to place the Air Force on attack alert and reinforce the Golan Heights with two tank companies and one artillery battery.[57] The Minister of Defense added that steps should not be taken due to assessment of the probability of a limited operation, but due to warnings of a possible Syrian attempt to occupy an Israeli post or settlement on the Golan Heights. The position of the Chief of Staff, which was adopted by Dayan, was based on Zeira's assessment.[58] In sum, the Israeli defense authorities were confident that an early warning would be available in case of a full-scale Syrian attempt to occupy the Golan Heights. The steps taken were merely against a limited action whose likelihood was considered low.

On the same day, 26 September, the first news reached Aman of Egyptian troop movements towards the Canal Zone, probably for large-scale maneuvers or an exercise. Now, the likelihood of an all-out Syrian attack on the Golan Heights was dismissed because of Syrian dependency of Egypt, and the indications of warlike intentions by Egypt were likewise dismissed in view of the assumption regarding the Egyptian components of the Concept. No observations were made in the opposite direction, namely that the Syrian measures might have indicated that something was going on in Egypt. This information, however, was soon to come.

Following Hussein's second warning through CIA channels, the General Staff convened again on 30 September. The King's message relayed that battle procedures had reached the level of battalion commanders and that the main points of the plan of attack had been delivered.[59] At the same time, concrete information reached Aman about the Egyptian Army's plan to hold large-scale maneuvers from 1 to 7 October; troops and equipment were being moved to the Canal Zone.[60]

Despite this information, Aman's assessment remained the same: Egypt had no real motive at that time to launch a war, and the Egyptians' preparations were in fact just for a military exercise. However, firmly believing in Syrian dependence on Egypt's initiation of war, Aman could not explain the Syrian emergency array or the advance of attack aircraft, except to say that Syria might be planning to occupy an Israeli military post or civilian settlement in reprisal for the loss of its aircraft. The Aman approach still focused only on a limited operation, with the chances even of that deemed hardly likely.

However, the Deputy Chief of Staff, Major General Yisrael Tal challenged Aman's assessment, suggesting that the real threat presented by the Syrians was not revenge for downing of their 13 MiGs but occupation of the Golan Heights. Tal was the first to raise the issue of a large-scale Syrian military operation rather than a limited operation. His reasoning was based on information that President Hafez Assad had postponed the war from May to September, *inter alia,* due to shortage of matériel. Therefore he requested an examination of whether Syria had completed its SA missile deployment on the Golan Heights, and if so, an explanation of its meaning. Taken together, the events of recent days had led him to conclude that Syria had long been planning to occupy the Golan Heights. He urged that steps be taken in the face of the potential risks rather than on the basis of what was considered a low probability.[61]

Tal therefore recommended the mobilization of reserves and reinforcement of the Golan Heights defenses with a regular armored brigade. The Chief of Staff did not concur with his deputy's assessment, but he did decide on reinforcement of the Golan Heights. This was by an artillery battalion and an entire armored battalion of the 7th Tank Brigade rather than two companies from that brigade which had already been sent to the Golan Heights by an earlier decision.

Following the clear warning on the night between 30 September–1 October, the General Staff convened again on the morning of 1 October.[62] According to the information that had reached General Zeira, the intention of Egypt and Syria was to launch a war against Israel on 1 October under Egyptian command.[63] While the information had not been submitted to the Chief of Staff and the Minister of Defense during the night, it had been checked by Aman's analysts who in the end preferred the Concept and concluded that there was no immediate threat of war.[64] In retrospect Aman's assessment that night proved correct and war did not break out on 1 October. Additional information that the Egyptian exercise was in fact a disguise for war intentions reached Aman.[65] However, its analysts continues to reject the possibility, adhering firmly to the Concept.

The Chief of Staff likewise based his decision on the assumption that in the event of a limited operation, the IDF would destroy the Syrian Army in 48 hours, and that recognition of this would probably deter Syria from initiating any such operation.[66]

Following the Chief of Staff's decision, the Minister of Defense added that there were no substantive signs for a war about to be started by Syria. However, Dayan suggested that attention be paid to the heavy Syrian deployment and the fact that the Israeli settlements were located on the Golan Heights. He asked the Chief of Staff to find a solution to the possibility that a Syrian force might try to penetrate the thin IDF defense line in order to occupy a settlement. Accordingly, the Chief of Staff ordered reinforcement of the Golan Heights by yet another armored battalion and an artillery battalion, as well as the laying of landmines along the frontier. Plans were also make for retaking any part of the Golan Heights that might be occupied.[67]

Following a meeting between the Minister of Defense and the Chief of Staff on 2 October, the latter checked with Aman for the significance of the Syrian-Egyptian activity. Aman's assessment of the Egyptian activity was that it was an exercise only. Regarding the Syrian deployment, Aman admitted that it had no explanation, but maintained that Syria had no intention of attacking.[68]

However, the Chief of Staff asked Aman about the reliability of the information that Syria would not start war without Egypt. Aman's reply was as follows:

(1) We do not know for sure of Syria's intentions. (2) There was general information from a source [the reference is to King Hussein] and more detailed information from the Americans based on it. (3) A verbal message from another source in Egypt [apparently the Top Source] warned of the intention of opening an Egyptian-Syrian attack on 1 October. (4) Aman had no adequate additional indications that may attest that the Syrian army indeed had aggressive intentions in the short term. (5) According to Aman's evaluation the state of emergency was chiefly put in place on account of growing fears of Israel. (6) In Aman's opinion Syria did not estimate that it could risk a general war with Israel, or to go to war without Egypt [the Concept was still in force]. (7) An additional possibility of low likelihood was that the state of emergency had been declared because of the Syrian intention to conduct some kind of reprisal for the downing of its aircraft, and the emergency array would provide Syria with maximal defense against our response.[69]

On 2 October the Israeli inner Cabinet was convened at the Prime Minister's office at the request of the Minister of Defense to discuss Aman's reply. Aman was represented by the deputy head of Aman for analysis, Brigadier General Aryeh Shalev, as the head of Aman was ill. Shalev presented Aman's assessment, based on the Concept.[70] But the Prime Minister asked if Egypt, contrary to the existing assessment, would start a war and if Syria would join in; or might matters be the reverse, namely Syria would be the first to attack Israel and Egypt would tie Israeli forces down in the south.[71] Shalev replied that Syria wanted to occupy the Golan Heights, but Assad was thought to be pragmatic and calculating, and he was aware that the balance of forces was not in his favor. It was ascertained that the IDF could exploit a Syrian move to advance as far as Damascus.[72]

In this regard the Minister of Defense raised several issues for consideration, *inter alia* the Syrian SA missile deployment. If the Syrians were afraid that Israel would strike back at their hinterland, then why had they deployed the missiles on the Golan Heights rather than around Damascus? The answer, which Dayan himself suggested, was that the Syrians probably needed the SA missile batteries as cover for an attack.[73]

Dayan's second subject for consideration was that in contrast to Egypt, which would have to move SA missile batteries up to the Canal Zone, the Syrians could occupy the Golan Heights without needing to advance their SA missiles to the front line. By taking such action, the Syrians, according to Dayan, might regain their lost honor—a very tempting notion for them. His third question was whether, in case of a Syrian attack, the IDF would be able to deploy about 150 tanks within 24 hours and to attack sensitive targets in the Syrian rear.[74]

Aman's assessment was indicative that the Concept was still in force: although Syria wished to occupy the Golan Heights, Assad was too pragmatic and calculating to risk a general war with Israel, being aware that the balance of forces was not in his favor. However, three events in the domain of information collection were able to undermine the Concept, albeit not completely.

First, on 4 October, at about 3.00 p.m., the Aman's Sigint section intercepted a phone call involving the Iraqi Ambassador in Moscow who had close relations with the Soviet leadership. In his conversation he reported the Soviet intention to evacuate the families of the Soviet advisers in Syria and Egypt following information received by the USSR leadership of an imminent Egyptian-Syrian attack against Israel.[75]

Second, this possibility of a full-scale Egyptian-Syrian attack was also conveyed to the head of Mossad, Zvi Zamir, by the Top Source, through his handling officer in Europe. According to one version, this information reached the head of the Mossad at 2.00 a.m. on 5 October; the Top Source insisted on providing further details only at a face-to-face meeting with the head of the Mossad.[76]

According to another version the information reached Zamir late in the afternoon of 4 October.[77] If the latter version is correct, it means that the two above pieces of information reached the Israeli intelligence community simultaneously, and this should indeed have set the alarm bell ringing. In any event at about 5:00 a.m. on 5 October, Zamir flew out on a small airliner to London to meet the Top Source.

The third event to undermine the Concept was information collected by aerial photography on 4 October. Its interpretation on 5 October revealed that the Egyptian deployment along the Canal was more significant than had been previously thought. Reconnaissance along the Syrian front also showed additional deployment of five to six artillery battalions, bringing the total to 130 artillery batteries and 760 tanks. Referring to the enlarged deployment, the Minister of Defense observed that

from the numbers alone you could have a heart attack. . . . There are 1100 [artillery] guns, as against 802 guns on September 25, an *addition of 308 guns*.[78] (emphasis added).

Following these three events in the era of information, Aman altered its assessment from no war to 'low probability.'[79] However, it should be emphasized that in the Cabinet meeting of the morning of 5 October, Zeira stated explicitly that 'technically the Egyptians and the Syrians are ready, prepared, and able to start a war at any time.'[80]

With respect to the intentions of the Egyptians and the Syrians to start a war, the main piece of information that aroused doubts was the hurried evacuation of the families of the Soviet advisers, from both Syria and Egypt.[81] As the head of Aman put it, 'but for the evacuation, I would be convinced that they were not going to attack but are in a state of fear.'[82] Zeira said that Aman had three alternative explanations for the evacuation: (1) the Soviets knew that Egypt and Syria were going to attack and ordered the evacuation so as not to risk harm befalling Soviet citizens, as well as to signal Syria and Egypt that the Soviets did not support this attack; (2) Syria and Egypt feared that Israel was going to attack them, but if this were so, Zeira added, they could seek verification from the United States and try to influence Israel not to go ahead; (3) a rift might have opened between the Soviets and the Syrians, but Zeira felt that this was not a reasonable possibility because the Soviets were leaving Egypt as well.[83] In the event, the last two explanations proved wrong and only the first turned out to be right.

In any case, Zeira concluded that it was more likely than not that war would be avoided.[84] Zeira's position was adopted by the Chief of Staff, who claimed that if Egypt and Syria were going to attack Israel the Israeli intelligence community would probably get indication of it, *inter alia* from the Top Source. He knew that the head of the Mossad was going to meet him.[85] Nevertheless, the Chief of Staff decided to prepare for war without any further early warning.[86] The preparations proposed by the Chief of Staff were that regular troops would halt an attack on the front line together with the Air Force, and mobilization of the reserves was to be made ready.[87]

On these grounds, the Chief of Staff decided to declare a Stage 3 alert, for the first time in several years, and to dispatch the 7th Tank Brigade up to the Golan Heights and an artillery brigade to Sinai. The decision on mobilizing the reserves would be taken in the light of additional indications that the head of the Mossad would presumably bring from London.[88]

The Minister of Defense approved the Chief of Staff's decision and recommended reporting to the United States on the imminent Soviet evacuation and requesting the American administration to sound out its significance from the Soviets themselves. It was also recommended that the United States be told of the Israeli assessments of greater probability of war and be asked to warn Egypt that Israel was aware of its intentions and was ready from them. The Prime Minister approved these rec-

ommendations and authorized the Minister of Defense to mobilize the reserves if the need arose during the Yom Kippur fast without convening the government.[89]

To summarize, 5 October, the day before the war broke out, was a day of uncertainty, where the total exclusion of the possibility of war was replaced by its assessment as being of low probability. The basis for the decision reached was on the one hand uncertainty, and on the other hand the certainty that if Egypt and Syria decided to start a war an early warning would be obtained in due time. The steps were taken as interim measures until more information reached the Israeli intelligence community, on the assumption of sufficient time being available to upgrade the alert for the regular troops and the Air Force.

The final piece of information regarding the outbreak of war was conveyed to the head of the Mossad late on Yom Kippur Eve (5 October) and reached the Israeli decision makers only at 4.30 a.m. on 6 October, namely early in the morning of the day the war was to begin. However, even this information was not definite.[90] It stated that Egypt and Syria were technically ready to attack; but there was still a slight doubt. According to the information, Sadat was still wavering and the final order to go to war had not yet been given.[91] There was a chance, albeit slight, of war being prevented.

Only at 7.00 a.m. on 6 October, with a further message from the Top Source that the war was to begin, was it understood that the war would start before sunset. In fact it erupted at 1.55 p.m. It is still not known if the message was misunderstood by any link in the chain of the Israeli intelligence community, and interpreted as 'sundown,' namely the precise hour of 6.00 p.m. on that October day. 'Sunset' is a looser term; in October it is about 5.20 p.m. Two other possibilities are that the Top Source simply did not know the exact time of the onslaught, or that he was a double agent.[92]

Even after receipt of this information from the Top Source, the assessment of the head of Aman was that Sadat was not in an international or internal position to launch an attack, knowing that he would lose any war that might break out. Sadat, according to Zeira, might be deterred, perhaps by Israel's mobilizing the reserves or by conveying him a message that his intentions were known.[93]

The Chief of Staff, however, decided that measures should be taken under the assumption that war was going to break out. The emphasis here is on the Chief of Staff's assumption of this, not his knowledge.[94] He asked the Minister of Defense to authorize the call-up of the entire reserve combat force and to order the Air Force to deliver a preemptive strike.[95] But the Minister of Defense remained hesitant in view of the Top Source's message that Egypt might still be deterred without military action. Therefore, he recommended that the IDF take only defensive measures and avoid any that might be interpreted as moving towards war.[96] His argument was that the international community; especially the United States, might blame Israel for causing an escalation towards war.[97]

Because of the difference of opinion between the Chief of Staff and the Minister of Defense early on the morning of 6 October, they decided to ask the Prime Minister to resolve the issue.[98] The Prime Minister, after hearing both views, namely that an outbreak of a war was likely, though not certain, sought the optimal position for Israel. Such a position should embody the best operational possibilities in the case that war did break out, but it should avoid any measures that might be interpreted as an Israeli move towards war. She believed that a preemptive strike would be considered such a move, while calling up the reserves would not.

In the meanwhile, the United States government had to be persuaded that Egypt and Syria were about to launch a war; then Israel would not be charged with escalation and a preemptive strike might be possible. At the same time, a message should be conveyed to the United States asking that Egypt and Syria be informed of Israel's knowledge regarding their intentions; this might deter them.[99] Time, however, was running out faster than realized. The war started at 1.55 p.m.

It should be noted that throughout the morning of 6 October until that hour, Aman still doubted that war was going to break out; the Chief of Staff Elazar chose to act as if war was certain; the Minister of Defense was unsure and wary of undertaking any measures that might present Israel as pushing towards war. Prime Minister Meir's decision was based on the political considerations of the Minister of Defense and the military considerations of the Chief of Staff.

In sum, the measures that were taken went forward on the *assumption* that war was going to start but not under any *certainty* of it. The Concept, while eroded, remained all-powerful, so much so that even when the war began at 1.55 p.m. on 6 October the feeling was that it was going to be just one or two days of battle at most, not an all-out conflagration.[100]

Conclusions

A close examination of the case of the Yom Kippur War reveals how difficult it is to abandon a firm concept, even though it is wrong. The result in this case was that the decision-makers were not provided with early warning in due time and a surprise

occurred, despite an abundance of good and relevant information that is unusual in the history of before-war case studies. This, in turn, raises two main questions: (1) Why did the decision-makers rely so heavily on Aman's analysts for early warning? (2) Is it possible to learn lessons from the Yom Kippur intelligence failure so as to prevent future surprises?

The answer to the first question concerns the development of strategic intelligence after World War II. Strategic intelligence was developed during the nuclear age together with the doctrine of deterrence. Both deterrence and strategic intelligence were deemed to serve a country's status quo policy.

The logic of the connection between deterrence and strategic intelligence is based on the assumption that while the enemy has no need to initiate a war in the absence of a reason, such as territorial expansion, the enemy may initiate the war for that or different reasons. Therefore, deterrence should be employed to convince the enemy that initiating a war carries an intolerable price. However, as is well known from well-developed theories of deterrence, it is impossible to know the enemy's exact cost-benefit matrix. Hence, the logic is that once deterrence fails, strategic intelligence will hopefully provide a warning in due time that the enemy is about to strike.

This was the logic of the Cold War. Even as status quo preserver, one should be prepared for war as if the enemy were about to attack. Israel as a status quo state, adopted the doctrine of deterrence and made intensive use of strategic intelligence in order to avoid war. However, Israel's setup was based mainly on conventional deterrence, which is more problematic than nuclear deterrence: no one is ready yet to pay the price of nuclear war. The price of conventional war, as history illustrates, is widely regarded as more bearable.

By favoring the doctrine of deterrence and early warning, Israel left itself vulnerable in the Yom Kippur War.[101] The doctrine of early warning, as noted above, was one of the basic components in Israel's response to its national security predicament. Originally, early warning by the Israeli intelligence community informed the decision-makers and the military command of any gathering threat. Early warning had nothing to do with intentions, and any physical threat required a suitable response.

In the 'Annual Intelligence Evaluation' document submitted by Aman to the Chief of Staff in June 1972, the possibility of providing early warning referred only to a gathering threat. However, from then until the outbreak of the Yom Kippur War the sense of early warning apparently altered, to refer to the enemy's intentions.[102]

Prior to the start of the Yom Kippur War the comprehensive early warning referred to the gathering threat. At the Cabinet meeting of 5 October, Major General Zeira explicitly warned that 'technically the Egyptian and the Syrians are ready, prepared, and able to start a war at anytime.' This was undoubtedly a major intelligence success regarding the gathering threats.[103] But he also referred to the Egyptians' intentions, assessing that the likelihood of their starting a war was low. Therefore, the decision-makers elected to put off a decision to mobilize the reserves until further information concerning the Egyptian intention was received.

As to the second question, there are two views. One maintains that following a surprise like that of the Yom Kippur, the Israeli intelligence services studied and will keep on studying the lessons of the failure, and there will be no more surprises. However, in light of the answer to the first question it seems that immunity to surprises is impossible to achieve. The Yom Kippur War represents a single case study of a failure of providing early warning concerning the enemy's intention.

As history shows, there have been numerous instances of surprises and failures to provide early warning, before and after the Yom Kippur War. Early warning apparently may be compared to deterrence. One can demonstrate the failure of deterrence, and also the failure of early warning, but it is impossible to point out the success of deterrence or the success of early warning. One can never be sure that a surprise has been prevented as a result of the early warning. An early warning might always be a false warning, and if the situation indeed deteriorates, it might be due to unnecessary mobilization on the part of the side that got early warning, which thereby escalates the war unintentionally.

It may be impossible to be immune to surprises, and excessive reliance on early warning, especially early warning with respect to intentions, might be considered little more than gambling.[104] Phrasing it in formal terms, one can assert that no reasonable intelligence officer was able to forecast the war under the conditions of the eve of the Yom Kippur War.

Questions for Further Discussion

1. Do you think the Israeli experience prior to the Yom Kippur War was unique, or does a "concept" often drive intelligence estimates?

2. Are the preconceived images and theories that influence intelligence estimates easily overcome by contradictory information?

3. Was it rational for Egypt to attack Israel? Does this perception of rationality influence analysts' estimates?

4. Could a devil's advocate overcome the influence of a "concept" on intelligence analysts?

Endnotes

1. Based on the definition of T. G. Belden, 'Indications: Warning and Crisis Operations,' *International Studies Quarterly* 21/1 (March 1977) pp.181–98.
2. Based on the definition of Robert Jervis, 'Roundtable: Communicating Warning to Foreign Policy-makers in the Post-Cold War Era: Impediments and Perspectives,' 37th Annual Convention on 'Where to Next in International Studies,' San Diego: CA, 16–20 April 1996. Previous studies about the Yom Kippur War surprise dealt with perception and misperception of surprise. See: Abraham Ben-Zvi, 'Between Warning and Response: The Case of the Yom Kippur War,' *International Journal of Intelligence and Counterintelligence* 4/2 (Summer 1990) pp.227–42. Also: Abraham Ben-Zvi, 'Perception, Misperception and Surprise in the Yom Kippur War: A Look at the New Evidence,' *Journal of Conflict Studies* 15/2 (Fall 1995) pp.5–29. And Abraham Ben-Zvi, 'The Dynamics of Surprise: The Defender's Perspective,' *Intelligence and National Security* 12/4 (Oct. 1997) pp.113–44. Avi Shlaim discussed in general the intelligence estimates failure on the eve of the Yom Kippur War without dwelling on the concept: Avi Shlaim, 'Failures in National Estimates: The Case of the Yom Kippur War,' *World Politics* 28/3 (April 1976) pp.348–80.
3. *Report of the Commission of Inquiry into the Events of the Yom Kippur War, Additional Partial Reports and Complementary Matter to the Partial Report, Arguments and Complementary Matter to the Partial Report of April 1974*, p.60 (Hebrew) (hereafter The Agranat Commission).
4. Zvi Lanir, *Fundamental Surprise: The National Intelligence Crisis* (Tel Aviv: Hakibbutz Hame'uhad 1983) p.28 (Hebrew).
5. The Agranat Commission (note 3) p.149.
6. Ibid. p.150.
7. Lanir, *Fundamental Surprise* (note 4).
8. The Agranat Commission (note 3) pp.135–6.
9. On the legal theory of the reasonable man, see H.L. Hart, *The Concept Law* (Oxford: OUP 1988) p.39. Also on the reasonable man in Anglo-Saxon law, see G. Fletcher, 'The Right and the Reasonable,' *Harvard Law Review* 98 (III) 1984–85, p.949.
10. There are various pitfalls in intelligence analysis, e.g., *mirror image*— assuming that the subject of analysis will act in the same way that the analyst would; *stereotyping*—generalizing too much from specific known facts to a general situation; *problems of information*—including overload of information and noise. See Philip Knightley, *The Second Oldest Profession: Spies and Spying in the Twentieth Century* (NY: Penguin 1988) pp.387–9. 'Noise' means irrelevant and misleading information. The term was borrowed for intelligence by Wohlstetter from electricity, where it means that in a lead with a given diameter only a certain amount of signals can pass through, and more signals that pass, the more noise that passes through too. See C. E. Shannon and W. Weaver, *The Mathematical Theory of Communication* (Urbana: Univ. of Illinois Press

1949). There are also problems of *timelines*, meaning that the intelligence analysis does not reach those who can use it in due time. See Gordon Prange, *At Dawn We Slept* (NY: Penguin 1981). *Politicization* is also found, namely the tailoring of intelligence analysis to fit the assumptions and prejudices of decision-makers. See Angelo Codevilla, *Informing Statecraft: Intelligence for a New Century* (NY: The Free Press 1992) p.335. *Problems of relations* between analysis and decision-makers and between collectors and analysts are regarded as another pitfall for analysis. See James Woolsey, 'Intelligence Quotient: The Mission of the CIA in a New World,' *Harvard Intelligence Review* (Fall 1994) p.37, and Codevilla, *Informing Statecraft, supra*, p.391.

11. The Agranat Commission (note 3) pp.60–1.
12. The identification of the Top Source is still classifieds but some details of his identity do exist. The Top Source was a young Egyptian, in 1969 in his late twenties or early thirties. He was the right-hand man of President Nasser and after Nasser's death he continued as such with President Sadat. Interview with Maj. Gen. (Res.) Eli Zeira, Zahala, 27 Jan. 1999.
13. In origin, the Concept was that of the president of Egypt, Anwar Sadat, and was presented to Israeli intelligence by the Top Source, accompanied by authentic protocols of meetings of the Egyptian government. The Concept as transmitted by the Top Source consisted of the following tenets: (a) Egypt and Syria would start a war against Israel if the political conditions of a return to the 1967 borders as laid down in UN Security Council Resolution 242 were not met; (b) the military condition that Egypt set for launching a war at its own initiative was a change in the balance of air power, in which Israel enjoyed decisive superiority. To change this balance, Egypt needed advanced fighters capable of striking Israeli airfields flying low, as well as Scud ground-to-ground air missiles that would constitute a threat to additional targets in the Israeli rear and would deter Israel from attacking civilian targets deep in Arab countries. Confirmation of this Egyptian concept was obtained by Aman also through Sigint, which acquired the content of a secret dispatch from Sadat to Brezhnev. In it Sadat wrote, 'In our frequent talks I have pointed out that there is need for us to possess deterrent weapons, which will cause the enemy to hesitate about attacking us in depth. . . . Without deterrent weapons we will not be capable of operating militarily.' These positions were confirmed by Sadat in his book *In Search of Identity: An Autobiography* (Glasgow: Fontana/Collins 1978) p.419, and cited by Eli Zeira in his book *The October 73 War: Myth Against Reality* (Tel Aviv: Yedioth Aharonoth 1993) p.87. The Agranat Commission adopted the term 'the Concept,' referring to the Israeli conception consisting of two elements. The first was the Egyptian one, based on information passed on to the Israeli intelligence community by the Top Source. Note that information obtained from the Top Source was transferred to the Analysts section of Aman. All intelligence went there first so that the decision-makers would get the final, processed product without being deluged by mounds of raw material. However, because of the great interest shown by the Israeli decision-maker in the information from the Top Source it was forwarded as raw material, only translated from Arabic, directly to the Chief of Staff, the Minister of Defense, the Prime Minister, and the Minister Ylsrael Galili. Amnon

Dankner, 'Grandma Cooked Porridge' *Maariv*, 19 Sept 1998, p.23 (Hebrew).
14. The Agranat Commission (note 3) p.60.
15. On the basis of this assumption Aman recommended that Israel be prepared for war in 1975.
16. Mohamed Heikel, *The Road to Ramadan* (London: Collins 1975) pp.157, 181.
17. Ibid.
18. Ibid. pp.180–1; Zeira, *The October 73 War* (note 13) p.91.
19. The Concept, as applied by the Agranat Commission, was no doubt intended as a paradigm for the grounds on which a scientist constructs theories. As Kuhn has pointed out, supplanting paradigms is extremely difficult; it is like changing existing concepts or beliefs. See Thomas S. Kuhn, *The Structure of Scientific Revolutions* (Univ. of Chicago Press 1962).
20. Robert Jervis, *Perceptions and Misperceptions in International Politics* (Princeton UP 1976) pp.117–86. Especially, see the chapter entitled 'Failure to Recognize the Influence of Pre-Existing Beliefs,' pp.181–6. Richard Ned Lebow, *Between Peace and War: The Nature of International Crisis* (Baltimore: John Hopkins UP 1981) pp.148–228.
21. The Agranat Commission (note 3) p.66.
22. One of the common explanations at the time as to why war did not break out then was that Sadat's limited attack planned against Shann El-Sheikh had to be canceled due to the outbreak of the India-Pakistan War. Sadat felt that this would divert world attention from the Egyptian attack. Chaim Hertzog, *The War of Atonement* (Tel Aviv: Yedioth Aharonoth 1974) p.65. However, as far as we know today, no positive evidence was found that Sadat indeed intended to start a war in 1971, despite his declaration that 1971 would be the Year of Decision.
23. Ms Esther Herlitz, Israel's ambassador to Copenhagen during the late 1960s, developed good relations with the international diplomatic community in Denmark. One of the diplomats with whom Herlitz had excellent relations was a Catholic ambassador (his name and identity are still classified). Herlitz kept up contact and correspondence with this ambassador after she returned to Israel and became a Member of Knesset. The diplomat in question later became his country's ambassador to Cairo. Using Rome as a mail route, in the absence of relations between Israel and Egypt, he wrote regularly to Herlitz about the mood and atmosphere in Egypt. Shiomo Nakdimon, *Low Probability: A Narrative of the Dramatic Story Preceding the Yom Kippur War and the Fateful Events that Followed* (Tel Aviv: *Revivim* 1982) p.28 (Hebrew).
24. *Al-Nahar.* 29 May 1973.
25. The Agranat Commission (note 3) p.70.
26. Arie Braun, *Moshe Dayan and the Yom Kippur War* (Tel Aviv: Yedioth Aharonoth 1992) p.20.
27. Ibid. p.24.
28. Ibid. pp.22–3.
29. Ibid. p.25; Nakdimon, *Low Probability* (note 23) pp.24–5.
30. Nakdimon (note 23) p.31.
31. Lanir, *Fundamental Surprise* (note 4) p.19; Braun, *Moshe Dayan* (note 26) p.25.
32. Hanoch Bartov, *Dado: 48 Years and 20 Days More* (Tel Aviv: Sifriat Maariv 1978) Vol. 1.
33. Dankner (note 13) p.23.
34. Ibid.
35. Ephraim Kam, 'Intelligence in Advance of War,' Lecture delivered at a Study Day on 'Earthquakes or Hu-

man Activity: The Yom Kippur War 25 Years After,' Herzl Institute, Univ. of Haifa, 4–5 Nov. 1998 (Hebrew).

36. Ibid.
37. Ibid.
38. Neil Catch, *The Israeli Intelligence Failure in the Yom Kippur War* (Los Angeles: Univ. of Southern California 1983) p.7.
39. Israel Tal, *National Security: The Few Against the Many* (Tel Aviv: Dvir 1996) pp.169–72.
40. Uri Bar-Joseph, 'The Yom-Kippur Surprise and Its Origins,' *Ma'arakhot*, Vol. 361, Nov 1998, p.14 (Hebrew).
41. Braun (note 26) p.35 (Hebrew).
42. In 1973 Fulvio served as head of the analysis department in Italian military intelligence Oded Granot, 'Former Head of Italian Intelligence Services, Admiral Fulvio Martini, Reveals for the First Time, to *Maariv*, the Cooperation between Him and the Israeli Mossad: "I Spread a Security Network for Mossad People All over the World".' Granot quotes Martini from his book Fulvio Martini, *Nome in Codice: Ulisse*, in *Maariv*, 19 Sept. 1999 (Hebrew). The story of the cooperation between the head of Italian intelligence and Israeli intelligence is told, without mention of his name, by: Victor Ostrovsky, *By Way of Deception* (NY: St Martin 1990) p.208.
43. Badr is the name of the battle in which Muhammed and his companions first captured Mecca. Richard Deacon, *The Israeli Secret Service* (London: Sphere Books 1979) p.291.
44. Gad Shimron, *The Mossad and its Myth* (Tel Aviv: Keter Publishing House 1996) p.128 (Hebrew).
45. Zeira, *The October 73 War* (note 10) p.98 (Hebrew). Also: Eli Zeira, lecture delivered at a panel on 'The Concept and the Surprise' at a symposium on the Yom Kippur War in a year perspective, The Leonard Davies Institute for International Relations, The Hebrew Univ., Jerusalem, 27 Oct. 1998 (Hebrew).
46. See, e.g. Shlomo Nakdimon, 'Hussein Told Golda: The Syrian Army Was Moving into Attack Positions,' *Yedioth Aharonoth*, 29 Sept. 1993, p.l4. See also Zeev Schiff, 'A Forein Ruler Warned: The Intelligence and Golda Meir Ignored,' *Ha'aretz*, 15 Sept. 1993, p.5b (Hebrew).
47. The Agranat Commission (note 3) p.12.
48. Zeev Schiff, 'Was There a Warning?' *Ha'aretz*, 12 June 1998, p.16 (Hebrew).
49. Ibid.
50. Braun (note 26) p.36.
51. Ibid. p.34.
52. Ibid. p.35.
53. Ibid.
54. Ibid. p.38.
55. Ibid. pp.38–41.
56. Ibid. pp.40–1.
57. Ibid. p.40.
58. Ibid.
59. Ibid. p.44.
60. Ibid. p.46.
61. Ibid. p.44.
62. Ibid. pp.45–6.
63. Ibid. p.45.
64. Ibid. pp.45–6.
65. Ibid. pp.47–9.
66. Ibid. p.46.
67. The Agranat Commission (note 3) p.13.
68. Ibid.
69. Interview with Maj. Gen. (Res.) Eli Zeira, Zahala, 27 Jan 1999.
70. Braun (note 26) p.51.
71. Ibid. p.53.
72. Ibid. p.52.
73. Ibid. p.53–4.
74. Ibid. pp.54–5.
75. Interview with Brig. Gen. (Res.) Yoel Ben-Porat, head of Aman's Sigint section verbal communication, Ramat Hasharon, 14 Dec. 1998. See also The Agranat Commission (note 3) p.21.
76. Shlomo Nakdimon,'12 Days before Yom Kippur Golda Meir received Personal Information: Egypt and Syria Are Coordinating War,' *Yedioth Aharonoth*, 8 Oct. 1989, pp.6–7. Also *Yedioth Aharonoth*, 24 Oct 1989 and *Hadashot*, 24 Sept. 1993 (all Hebrew).
77. Interview with Ben-Porat (note 75). See also Yossi Mellnan and Dan Raviv, *The Imperfect Spies: The History of Israeli Intelligence* (London: Sidgwick & Jackson 1981) p.218.
78. The Agranat Commission (note 3) pp.21, 136, 310.
79. Braun (note 26) p.60; The Agranat Commission (note 3) p.22.
80. Tal, National Security (note 39) p.210.
81. The Agranat Commission (note 3) p.22.
82. Ibid.
83. Braun (note 26) p.66; Hertzog, *The War of Atonement* (note 22) p 70.
84. The Agranat Commission (note 3) p.22.
85. Nakdimon, *Low Probability* (note 23) p.88.
86. Hertzog (note 22) p.70.
87. Ibid. Also: The Agranat Commission (note 3) pp.40–1, 273.
88. Braun (note 26) p.67; Nakdimon (note 23) p.88.
89. The Agranat Commission (note 3) pp 39–43.
90. Brau (note 26) p.68.
91. Ian Black and Benny Morns, *Israel's Secrets War: A History of Israel's Intelligence Services* (London: Futura 1991) pp.287–8. See also Dankner (note 33) p.62; Zeira (note 10) pp.123–4.
92. There is evidence that the Top Source left Egypt for Europe one day prior to the decision on the precise hour of starting the war by presidents Sadat and Assad. On the other hand, Zeira has hardly any doubts that the Top Source was a double agent. According to the identity of the Top Source, which is known to Zeira, the Top Source should have known the exact hour of the beginning of the war. Interview with Zeira (note 69). Furthermore it was a primary Soviet doctrine to operate double agents, and the Egyptians adopted it. According to this view, after a fairly long period of silence the Top Source contacted his Mossad handlers to mislead the Israeli intelligence community Interview with Zeira (note 69). Zeria (note 10) p.62; Dankner (note 33) p.62.
93. Hertzog (note 22) p.70.
94. Bartov, *Dado* (note 32) Vol.2.
95. From the transcript of conversation at 6.15 of the morning of Yom Kippur l973 between Minister of Defense Dayan and the Chief of Staff (CoS) David (Dado). Elazar emerges that the talk proceeded smoothly, with jokes being cracked and without any sense of eve-of-war urgency. The CoS asked the Minister of Defense for approval to mobilize all the reserve troops and to deliver a preemptive air strike again the Syrian Air Force. Dayan replied that he was entirely opposed to a preemptive strike, and asked the CoS why he needed general mobilization of the reserves for a war that was supposed to begin 12 hours later [then it was believed

that opening salvos of the war would be fired at 6 o'clock in the evening]. Elazar replied with a joke. He was, he said, reminded of the Jew who emerged from a brothel at a very early morning hour. When asked what he was doing there so early he said that he was due to have a very busy day and he wanted to get that out of the way. About the mobilization of the reserves, the CoS said that they would be required for stage of counter-attack, so he wanted to begin already in the morning with the mobilization to get that out of the way. It is worth nothing that the sense of superiority and self confidence caused the CoS and the Minister of Defense to believe that for the blocking stage the standing army might be enough. Dayan retorted, 'You don't mobilize the entire reserve array [just] on the basis of what Zvika Zamir [that is, the Top Source] knows.' Dado persisted: 'I want to call up the entire array of divisions so that we can push them back and move into a counter-attacks as early as possible. Incidentally, a mobilization of this sort might make the Arabs abandon their planned attack.' Dayan replied, 'You can do that with 30,000 men you don't need 500,000. I'm in favor of calling up only the forces essential for defense.' 'A Jew Out of a Whorehouse: What Moshe Dayand and David Elazar Chatted about on Yom Kippur Morning 1973,' *Ha'aretz*, 1 Jan 1999. See also The Agranat Commission (note 3) p.43.

96. Bartov (note 32) Vol. 2, p.14.
97. Ibid. Vol. 2, p.15.
98. Braun (note 26) p.70.
99. Bartov (note 32) pp.20–5.
100. Braun (note 26) pp.87–8.
101. This is reminiscent of Sir Arthur Conan Doyle's account of Baskerville's attempt to protect his home by locking all doors and windows. One day, he decided to strengthen these defenses even more by stationing a watchdog in a kennel in the yard: He expected that if a burglar tried to break in, the dog would bark, thereby providing a warning. After a while, when Baskerville had got used to the dog and burglars had not shown up, he assumed that he could rely on the dog's barking and stopped locking his doors and windows. One night, however, burglars did approach the house, and for some reason, the dog did not even bark. Luckily for them, they found the doors and windows unlocked and no other deterrents to their accomplishing their mission.
102. In Feb. 1960 the doctrine of early warning was tested by Israel for the first time and failed. On 18 Feb., Egyptian forces started to move to the Sinai desert and Is-

raeli intelligence was unaware of this fact. The information reached Israeli intelligence four days later, after the Egyptian forces were deployed in the Sinai desert. The Chief of Staff did not ponder likely Egyptian intentions, and he and the government decided to upgrade the level of alert, to partially mobilizing the reserves and to deploying the standing army along Israel's southern border with Egypt. Although early warning was not provided in due time the military command and the decision-makers decided to take measures according to the gathering threat rather than on the basis of assessment of Egyptian intentions. Prior to the Six Day War Israeli intelligence began to engage in providing early warning in respect of the enemy's intentions, and failed. The assessment of me Egyptians' intentions was that as long as Egypt was engaged in Yemen, Egypt would not deploy forces in Sinai so there was no real threat in the Sinai desert on 14 May 1967. Egypt deployed its forces in the Sinai desert deliberately and overtly, so early warning was not tested. But the assessment in respect of the Egyptian's intentions proved wrong. The Israeli response was based on the new situation of gathering threat, namely moving forces towards the southern border with Egypt, regardless of the Egyptian intention. The result was a spiraling escalation. Egypt closed the Tiran Straits to Israeli shipping and deployed more forces in the Sinai desert; finally without assessing Egyptian intentions, Israel undertook the measure of a preemptive strike.
103. The threat had been gathering for some time, certainly since the end of the Six Day War, but it gained an intensity in the period under review.
104. If, nevertheless, one wants to take into account intentions, the right people to do so are probably the decision makers themselves, who might assess the political strategic moves of their counterparts across the border better than the military intelligence experts. On the eve of the Yom Kippur War Israeli intelligence tried to assess the Egyptian decision on whether to go to war or not on the basis of the military components, namely to forecast strategic decisions on the basis of two items of weaponry: long-range bombers and surface-to-surface missiles. ✦

Reprinted with permission from Ephraim Kahana, "Early Warning Versus Concept: The Case of the Yom Kippur War 1973," *Intelligence and National Security* 17 (Summer 2002): 81–104.

Part IV

The Danger of Intelligence Politicization

Hamlet: "Do you see yonder cloud that's almost
in shape of a camel?"
Polonius: "By th' mass and 'tis, like a camel in-
deed."
Hamlet: "Methinks it is like a weasel."
Polonius: "It is backed like a weasel."
Hamlet: "Or, like a whale?"
Polonius: "Very like a whale."

—*Shakespeare*, Hamlet, 3.2.378–384

Intelligence politicization is a complex phenomenon. The literature on intelligence suggests that
politicization occurs when intelligence analysis is
either deliberately or inadvertently skewed to give
policymakers the results they want, not the unvarnished truth about the situation at hand. For intelligence analysts and managers, politicization is considered a mortal sin, a fundamental violation of
their commitment to provide policymakers with
honest answers and estimates. The U.S. intelligence
community is supposed to be isolated from the political fray so that analysts and managers can tell
policymakers the truth without fear of recrimination, no matter how unpleasant or politically damaging the truth might be to policymakers. The grand
bargain within the intelligence community is that
analysts will not meddle in politics and policy, and
policymakers will not ask or force analysts to "cook
the books" to guarantee that analysis supports their
policy or political preferences.

Sherman Kent is the intelligence professional
best known for championing this separation of intelligence analysis from policy. In his writings, published in the immediate postwar period, Kent, a historian who was in charge of the CIA's Office of

National Estimates, warned that it would be a mistake for analysts to get too close to policymakers,
because their analysis would inevitably be influenced by policymakers' political agendas. Above all,
Kent (1949) argued that analysts have to maintain
their objectivity if their estimates are to have any
value. Intelligence professionals often champion
Kent's view of the importance of analytical objectivity, because it empowers them to pursue their intellectual and analytical interests to their logical—and
sometimes even illogical—conclusions. Much in
the same way that academic freedom empowers intellectuals to champion unpopular causes or to offer unpleasant observations about contemporary
society, isolating analysts from policymakers allows
intelligence professionals to set their own research
agendas. From the viewpoint of intelligence professionals, Kent's emphasis on objectivity and analytical detachment makes perfect sense. After all, who
is better able to set research agendas than analysts
themselves?

Too much analytical detachment or too little interaction between analysts and policymakers, however, virtually guarantees that finished intelligence
will fail to address the issues that fill policymakers'
in-boxes. Forced to focus on issues of immediate
importance, policymakers simply ignore "academic" analyses—i.e., anything that fails to address
the problems that preoccupy them. Repeated complaints that intelligence lacks relevance has led to
calls for the production of "actionable" intelligence,
estimates that policymakers will find useful in developing and executing current policy. This view is
most closely associated with Robert Gates, a former
Director of Central Intelligence. Gates and his supporters believe that relevance, not just objectivity,
should govern intelligence production and that

intelligence managers should shape finished intelligence so that it meets the needs of policymakers. According to those who embrace this perspective, intelligence managers, by interacting closely with policymakers and with a view of all intelligence assets, can create relevant finished intelligence from a variety of sources. The intelligence manager, not the analyst, would create the questions addressed in finished intelligence and sometimes even shape the answers. In a speech to analysts at the CIA in 1992, Gates explained what amounted to a revolutionary vision of the future of intelligence production:

> Unwarranted concerns about politicization can arise when analysts themselves fail to understand their role in the process. We do produce a corporate product. If the policymaker wants the opinion of a single individual, he can (and frequently does) consult any of a dozen outside experts on any given issue. Your work, on the other hand, counts because it represents the well-considered view of an entire directorate and, in the case of National Estimates, the entire intelligence community. Analysts . . . must discard the academic mindset that says their work is their own. (quoted in Betts 2002, 64)

It appeared to many analysts that Gates' vision of actionable intelligence guaranteed that intelligence would be politicized. If intelligence mangers tailored intelligence analysis to meet policymakers' agendas, mangers could be expected to generate a series of leading questions that would produce answers that would support existing political or policy preferences.

What is the correct balance between objective and actionable intelligence? How detached or engaged should analysts be in the policymaking process? These questions are generating much debate among academics, elected officials, and intelligence professionals. Although the most effective balance between these two positions depends on the issues at stake, the personalities involved, and the bureaucratic and political climate, it does appear that the debate itself becomes most acute at times of policy failure or when the intelligence community is out of step with changing political realities.

Sources of Politicization

Although politicization can take a variety of forms, scholars focus on three ways in which the production of finished intelligence can be corrupted by undue policy or political influence. First, analysts can be directly pressured to emphasize findings that support the policies and preferences of officials or to ignore issues that could cause political or personal embarrassment. Sometimes this pressure comes in direct requests to support existing policy. Because they are viewed by most observers as inherently credible and not influenced by the wishes of officials, intelligence findings can be used to terminate political debate or to gain political support. Thus, this type of politicization is best viewed as corruption of the intelligence process, because intelligence analysts are considered politically detached observers and are supposed to stand above the political fray and provide honest estimates. By contrast, other sources of politicization are produced by human frailty or organizational pathologies, not the direct manipulation of the intelligence process for political gain.

Charges that the intelligence production has been subjected to direct manipulation for political reasons emerged in the immediate aftermath of Gulf War II, when conclusive evidence supporting administration claims that Saddam Hussein had an active program to produce weapons of mass destruction (WMD) and a large stockpile of these weapons failed to materialize. Critics of the Bush Administration claimed that "worst case thinking," if not outright manipulation, dominated the interpretation of every scrap of evidence collected about Iraqi weapons programs and that most of this spin was concocted by administration officials looking to justify military actions against the kleptocracy that ruled in Iraq. Although some members of the intelligence community have suggested that the intelligence picture was far less conclusive than many administration officials suggested, most seem to stand by their general assessments of Iraq's overall desire to acquire and possess chemical, biological, and nuclear weapons. It is up to future historians to tell us whether the cup was really "half full," "half empty," or "completely drained" in terms of Iraq's chemical, biological, or nuclear capability and exactly who was responsible for "overselling" the Iraqi WMD threat.

Second, senior officials and officers sometimes give subtle and not-so-subtle cues to intelligence managers and analysts about the kinds of analyses they welcome or abhor. If intelligence consumers fawn over or reward analysts who provide them with encouraging reports but dismiss, berate, or punish analysts who bring them disconcerting news, they will send a powerful signal to analysts everywhere. Analysts will line up to provide consumers with positive estimates but shrink from the prospect of reporting bad news. Given the nature of senior leadership—only the most intractable problems and disputes are resolved at the top of the bureaucratic hierarchy—it takes an exceptional official to welcome the receipt of another negative report and to thank the bearer of bad news. Exceptional leaders cultivate a reputation for demanding the unvarnished truth from their staffs, and they make sure that not just the bearers of good news are recognized for outstanding efforts.

An interesting example of this second type of politicization occurred during the Vietnam war. General William C. Westmoreland, commander of U.S. Military Assistance Command, Vietnam (MACV), had asked his command historian to produce a study of sieges throughout history to generate some insights into the North Vietnamese effort to overwhelm the U.S. Marine firebase at Khe Sanh, which was located just below the demilitarized zone that separated North from South Vietnam. The command historian was asked to study the matter and to deliver a briefing to the MACV staff. After describing various battles that had occurred throughout history, the historian concluded that the news was not good for the Marines: Most besieged fortresses fell because the attacker retained mobility. Needless to say, the news shocked the officers present at the briefing. When it concluded, Westmoreland thanked the historian for his report and turned to the staff, saying that now that they had heard the worst-case assessment, he would no longer tolerate anyone thinking, planning, or acting as if the siege of Khe Sanh would end in defeat. Whatever his motives, Westmoreland virtually guaranteed that whoever was in that room that day would think twice before bringing the boss bad news in the future.

Third, analysts can skew their estimates to advance their professional interests, attack their personal or professional rivals, or simply advance their careers. They can ignore negative trends or mistakes, especially if they are about to transfer into another organization or receive a promotion. It is better to leave one's position on a high note than to draw negative attention to problems that can jeopardize an otherwise positive record, especially at critical times. No news is always good news to those in charge of running a large organization; deciding not to rock the bureaucratic boat rarely damages one's career prospects. Politicization in this sense is really a form of careerism: Analysts or intelligence managers place a greater emphasis on enhancing their job prospects than on fulfilling their responsibilities. Sometimes conflict between professional responsibilities and personal interests occurs when analysts' findings call into question the performance or policies of their home organization or institution. Making senior officials aware of analyses that undermine the preferences or priorities of one's home institution is fraught with professional danger, and few people will persevere in the face of opposition from virtually everyone they encounter in the workplace.

John McCone's performance as director of the Central Intelligence Agency in the months leading up to the Cuban Missile Crisis provides an outstanding example of someone who did not allow concerns about his interests and reputation to get in the way of his responsibilities. During the summer of 1962, a consensus emerged among CIA analysts that it was unlikely that the Soviets would place offensive missiles in Cuba, and this finding was reported officially to policymakers in Special National Intelligence Estimate (SNIE) 85-3-62, "The Military Buildup in Cuba." McCone, however, became increasingly concerned about the possibility that the United States might suffer some sort of intelligence failure related to Cuba, as the Soviets attempted to shroud their activities on the island in secrecy. Despite the CIA's official estimate, an estimate that was reported to the most senior officials in the Kennedy administration, McCone pushed agency analysts to repeatedly reassess their judgments about Soviet activities in Cuba. McCone was less concerned about his reputation or his agency's track record for being correct and more interested in preventing the president from being caught by surprise by some nefarious scheme (Usowski 1988).

Intelligence Is Politics?

Politicization is a charge often leveled when intelligence estimates actually support one political position over another. In other words, when analysts "hit their mark" and produce timely finished intelligence that addresses matters of national importance and debate, charges are sometimes raised that someone has unduly influenced the intelligence process or that analysts are following their own policy or political agenda at the expense of objectivity. According to Richard Betts:

> For issues of high import and controversy, any relevant analysis is perforce politically charged, because it points to a policy conclusion. Various disputes—about which elements of information are correct, ambiguous, or false; which of them are important, incidental, or irrelevant; in which context they should be understood; and against which varieties of information pointing in a different direction they should assess—are in effect, if not in intent, disputes about which policy conclusion stands or falls. (Betts 2002, 60)

Because intelligence estimates are inherently credible, individuals who oppose findings that are adverse to their political position have to attack the objectivity of the intelligence process, not the inherent validity of the analysis. After all, few people have access to the classified materials used to develop intelligence estimates, so it is difficult for most observers to validate the intelligence community's findings through independent analysis. Ironically, when intelligence estimates have a political impact and help shape policy—the very goal of the intelligence community—some people interpret that effect as evidence that the process must have been corrupted to serve political ends.

A variation of this phenomenon occurs when analysts themselves cry foul when their estimates are ignored by policymakers. This situation usually occurs when analysts warn policymakers of impending policy failure or indicate that past estimates were inaccurate and in need of significant revision. There are a variety of reasons, however, that policymakers might choose not to act on specific estimates. They might have information from other sources that provides different perspectives on current issues, or they might believe the effort to utilize the intelligence by changing policy might create more problems than are solved. In this sense, analysts break the grand bargain inherent in the relationship between the intelligence community and policymakers by going public in an effort to use estimates to shape policy.

The Readings

In the selections that follow, the authors explore politicization in its various forms. In the first selection, Harry Howe Ransom turns the whole issue of politicization on its head by describing how information is power and is thus an inherently political issue. Intelligence, according to Ransom, is the "subject, object, and instrument of power politics." For Ransom, the degree to which politicization can be avoided is directly related to the degree to which consensus exists within policymaking circles about the ends and means of foreign policy. When little consensus exists, everything about intelligence appears to be politicized, because policy and political partisans judge every issue involving the intelligence community in terms of whether it favors or hurts their political position. Ransom also offers the hypothesis that when threats to national security are high and are likely to be exacerbated by poor intelligence, the threat of politicization will decline, because policymakers and politicians will realize that they depend on accurate intelligence estimates. We might also add that when threats are high, intelligence politicization is a recipe for disaster.

In his analysis of a dispute that occurred between analysts at the CIA and military intelligence officers in Vietnam over estimates of enemy troop strength, James Wirtz addresses a dispute over intelligence politicization that lasted for decades and that moved from classified meetings in Saigon to American television and finally to a Manhattan courtroom. In "Intelligence to Please?" he describes the allegations made by CIA analyst Sam Adams that the Johnson Administration deliberately tried to suppress estimates suggesting that they had underestimated the numerical strength faced on the battlefields of Vietnam, thereby contributing to the shock of the Tet Offensive. Wirtz describes the arcane art of estimating an opponent's "order of battle," the course and issues at stake in the dispute, and which position in the dispute seems to be best supported by the evidence drawn from prisoners of war and captured enemy documents.

In the final selection, Glenn Hastedt explores the controversial terrain of unauthorized disclosure of classified information. Using the second Iraqi war as a case study, he describes the variety of ways secret information becomes a matter of public discourse through leaks and examines the motives of policymakers for using leaks to advance policy positions. Hastedt also identifies the circumstances—increased media coverage, institutional rivalry, and foreign policy debate—that lead policymakers to use intelligence leaks as a powerful tool to influence political discourse in Washington, D.C. ✦

14

The Politicization of Intelligence

Harry Howe Ransom

In this overview of how politicization occurs within the intelligence community, Ransom suggests that politicization is inherent in the production of intelligence because information is crucial to gaining and preserving political power. Ransom argues that intelligence politicization is not an anomaly, but a "natural" relationship that emerges between policymakers and analysts. What has to be identified and explained, in Ransom's view, are the conditions necessary for intelligence organizations to provide policymakers with estimates that are not designed simply to support them in their partisan battles.

I. Introduction

Knowledge can convey political power. Plausibly, then, an agency of government charged with collecting secret information overseas and supplying knowledge to decision makers will be drawn into politics. For politics is about power. Politics and intelligence seem fated for an inter-relationship. Note that several past leaders of the Soviet KGB, an information apparatus, have been executed. Closer to home, the presidential election campaigns of 1976, 1980 and 1984 saw intelligence policy and operations as issues for debate. And the investigations of intelligence by Senate and House select committees and by a presidential (Rockefeller) commission in 1975–1976 took place in a highly-charged political atmosphere. By 1975 it was obvious that intelligence was politicized.[1] Political leadership in foreign affairs inevitably involves the use of privileged, or secret, information. The institution that plays a major role in providing that information may be assumed to be highly vulnerable to politicization.

The United States Central Intelligence Agency, however, was designed, in keeping with American management doctrines, to be policy neutral. The CIA was to be made up of experts providing information relevant to policy, but not advice. The agency's goal is to report reality about foreign affairs with policy-neutral objectivity. The CIA was created with the intention that its intelligence assessments would be produced by persons with no stake in a president's campaign promises, in particular weapons systems, or foreign policies.

"Perhaps the strongest cultural trait common to all CIA analysts," the chairman of the National Intelligence Council and CIA Deputy Director for Intelligence has written, "is a very deep sensitivity to the dangers of politicization."[2]

My guiding hypothesis in this essay, based as much upon intuitive judgment as upon concrete evidence (a difficult problem for anyone studying secret intelligence) is that intelligence is subject, object, and instrument of power politics.

Assertions that the strategic intelligence function of government has become politicized have been frequently heard, particularly since the 1980 presidential election. Widespread discussion of the CIA's alleged "politicalization" could be regarded as *prima facie* evidence of politicization. The purpose in this essay is to suggest ways to think about the intelligence role in an American system of government that is by design highly politicized.

The term politicization has multiple meanings.[3] The primary meaning is that when an agency or an issue has become politicized it has become a point of contention between organized political groupings, normally political parties. This can be categorized as partisan politicization. Competing ideologies—or preferred values—enter into role definitions or policy choices in the process of politicization. Another feature of politicization is popularization, or publicity, which generates public debate over ends and means. In this case we often have bipartisan politicization. A matter is politicized when it becomes involved in public policy choices and the ordering of power. As used here, politicization normally refers to conditions external to the bureaucracy and therefore excludes bureaucratic or "turf" politics, although these sometimes become involved in external politicization. Another form of politicization occurs when intelligence estimates are influenced by imbedded policy positions. When preferred policies dominate decision making, overt or subtle pressures are applied on intelligence systems, resulting in self-fulfilling intelligence prophecies, or in "intelligence to please" that distorts reality. Illustrative examples are given in the cases analyzed below.

II. The Political Life of the CIA

The main point about the early years of the CIA is that the agency was born in a nonpartisan atmosphere. A dominant founding concept was that the agency would be detached from partisan politics. While considerable controversy developed about the organizational arrangements for central intelligence, such controversy did not divide itself into partisan political groupings. Furthermore, little publicity, or public attention, was given to the sometimes bitter bureaucratic infighting over where central intelligence should be located. Another feature of the early years is the fact that the first directors of the CIA and its predecessor, the Central Intelligence Group, were military professionals, normally assumed to be detached from partisan politics. So it seems accurate to say that the CIA was born of nonpartisanship.

This was because by 1947, a Cold War consensus had been generated. Consensus wars provide the "best of times" for intelligence agencies. If war or threat of war is the health of the state, so it is a good time for intelligence systems, which flourish when the wartime spirit prevails.   *9/11 reflection*

Censorship, albeit voluntary, prevails, and secrecy is the norm. But when a consensus about the ends and means of foreign policy fades, perhaps inevitably in the American separation of powers system, the last bastion of political neutrality—the intelligence system—will be threatened by politicization. This becomes more likely when there is a lack of conceptual clarity about the functions of intelligence, which lack will be reflected in ambiguous organizational arrangements for secret intelligence.

At the end of World War II a central intelligence organization was proposed, to be created independent of the armed services and State Department. Bitter bureaucratic controversy greeted this proposal, but political partisanship was not a part of the controversy. Two years elapsed before the internecine bureaucratic conflict was settled in a compromise truce, and President Truman sent Congress a proposal largely drafted by military professionals that became the National Security Act of 1947. The more publicized issue at the time was armed forces "unification" and how much authority a Secretary of Defense should have. The proposed establishment of a Central Intelligence Agency as part of this reorganization of the national security structure created no political conflict between the two major political parties; there was little publicity about intelligence; and most of the controversy involved bureaucratic turf protection behind closed doors.

Concern was expressed by a few members of Congress, both Republican and Democrat, about the possibility that the proposed Central Intelligence Agency might become a domestic political police force (*Gestapo* was the term some used). This concern was voiced prominently by the *Chicago Tribune*, which may have been expressing a neo-isola-

tionist view, abetted by possible leaks from sources within the FBI, which was concerned about its future intelligence role. These concerns were met by the managers of the bill in the House and Senate who gave explicit assurance that the CIA would operate overseas only, and would have no security functions within the United States. Thus the strict constructionists and civil libertarians were from the start apparently motivated more by principle than party allegiance; others were motivated by the desire to protect existing organizational jurisdictions.

The first two Directors of Central Intelligence were military professionals—Rear Admiral Roscoe Hillenkoetter and General Walter Bedell Smith. The temporary Central Intelligence Group, 1945–1947, was also headed by military professionals. And so from 1947 to 1953, the formative years in the evolution of the new central intelligence system, nonpartisanship prevailed because military professionals held these positions of intelligence leadership, detached from political partisanship. Their appointments were in keeping with the doctrine that intelligence leadership and policy were above, or outside of, partisan politics. Intelligence was generally seen as too important, sensitive and technical a matter to be left to the politicians. More significant, however, was that a strong foreign policy consensus existed in the nation.

Allen W. Dulles became the first civilian to head the Central Intelligence Agency, early in Eisenhower's first term as president. A Republican, Dulles had been Deputy Director of the CIA since August 1951. His appointment as Director by the Eisenhower Administration did not suggest a party patronage handout. In testimony to Congress on the proposed Central Intelligence Agency, Dulles declared that "whoever takes the post of Director of Central Intelligence should make that his life's work." Accordingly a director should be detached from partisan politics and be expected, in his words, to " 'take the cloth' of the intelligence service." It is likely that he was influenced by the British model, where early heads of the British Secret Intelligence Service were professionals, generally holding long tenure.

During his long tenure as Director of Central Intelligence, Dulles was confronted with a Congress much of the time under Democratic Party control. Dulles was required to practice a nonpartisan approach to intelligence policy operations, but Congress was not an aggressive watchdog. Assuming the presidency in 1961, John F. Kennedy in the spirit of nonpoliticization asked Dulles to stay on as director. The Bay of Pigs fiasco in April of 1961 destroyed Kennedy's confidence in Dulles' leadership. Even so, some months passed before Dulles was replaced in order to separate the intelligence leadership from policy failures.

President Kennedy chose John McCone. an active Republican shipbuilder and former chairman of the Atomic Energy Commission as the new director of Central Intelligence. Kennedy was more interested in finding a tough-minded administrator than in making a symbolic statement of nonpartisanship, but the McCone appointment served as a bipartisan gesture. The point is that political partisanship was clearly not a criterion for selection to the important position of director of Central Intelligence, although public relations may have been a concern. Yet the McCone nomination became politicized.

A small group of liberal Democrats led by Senator Eugene McCarthy opposed McCone's confirmation on the Senate floor. McCone allegedly was not an adequately objective observer of world politics. Senator McCarthy and his allies saw McCone as blindly anti-Communist, intolerant of views dissenting from his own, and not the person best qualified to be the president's eyes and ears regarding world affairs. But bipartisanship prevailed on the McCone nomination, and endorsed by the Democratic-controlled Senate Committee on Armed Services, McCone was confirmed by a 71 to 12 vote. Ten of the negative votes were by Democrats. McCone served until April 1965.

In choosing a director, President Johnson followed the Kennedy formula of seeking a person of demonstrated administrative skill rather than sophisticated person knowledgeable in world politics. Johnson had shown little interest in the intelligence system up to this point. He nominated Vice Admiral William F. Raborn, Jr., who had managed successfully the development of the *Polaris* sea-launched ballistic missile. His nomination was uncontested; it had no particular foreign policy implications. Raborn was quickly confirmed without contest by the Senate. Raborn served without distinction for little more than a year. President Johnson nominated as his replacement a man whose qualifications were distinctly different from Raborn's. Richard Helms was the first professional intelligence person to be named CIA Director. Allen Dulles was to some degree experienced in intelligence, but primarily he was a lawyer. Helms was a career CIA officer. His appointment to the top position was in keeping with the doctrine of non-politicization. When Nixon became president he wanted to replace Helms. Nixon associated Helms with Georgetown liberals and was said to feel ill at ease with him, states Henry Kissinger, who reports he opposed Helms' removal because of the danger of turning the directorship into a patronage plum which would change with each incoming president. Helms

was the originator of the "honorable men" label which he advocated for intelligence professionals. His concept was that you choose as leaders persons you can trust; insulate them from the partisan struggles of the Executive Branch and Congress; and call upon them for objectives estimates of the world situation. As "honorable men" they would maintain a high degree of secrecy; serve constituted authority; keep clear-eyed watch on foreign adversaries; and participate when necessary in a "plausible denial" system which protected politically accountable decision makers and required, on occasion, false or dissembling testimony, even to Congressional committees. Helms could hold to this doctrine and adhere to its rules so long as the bipartisan spirit prevailed, but as director he often had to walk a political tight rope, particularly when the Nixon administration made attempts to use the CIA for partisan ends. But when bipartisanship began to evaporate, he ultimately found himself in trouble, not in the partisan political arena but in the courts.[4] The rules and assumptions began to change in the late 1960s. The foundations of bipartisanship were becoming shaky; foreign policy consensus began to fade.

Richard Helms' nonpartisan stance eventually complicated his relationship with Richard Nixon. The president replaced him in February 1973 with James Schlesinger, whose ideological posture may have led Nixon to believe that this conservative former economics professor might be more pliable, or at least more ideologically sympathetic. Schlesinger was skilled in the ways of Washington bureaucracy, having headed the Atomic Energy Commission. He also had conducted a special study for the president of administrative problems of the intelligence system. Schlesinger proved to be the most puritanical of CIA Directors, ordering that a confidential internal study be made of potential wrongdoing, past and present, including violations of the law of the CIA's legislative charter. From this came a document, to be known as "The Family Jewels," a detailed report of questionable activities in which the CIA had been engaged over the years. But Schlesinger served barely six months as director before being named Secretary of Defense. Nixon turned next to William E. Colby, another intelligence careerist who, like Helms, had spent most of his adult life as a CIA officer, including service in Vietnam where he headed the "Phoenix" program designed to destroy the Viet Cong substructure in South Vietnam. Colby's role in this ruthless effort caused 13 senators to vote against his confirmation on August 1, 1973. But 83 voted to confirm. Colby bore the brunt of the controversies that followed the leaking of major contents of the "Family Jewels" report to the *New York Times* in December 1974. President

Nixon had appointed Colby with no prior personal conversation with him before he became director.[5] This may be categorized as the ultimate in nonpartisanship; alternatively some saw it as Nixon's symbolic personal disparagements of the CIA. When Nixon earlier had tried to misuse the agency in his efforts to cover up the Watergate scandal, he was rebuffed. He may have, unconsciously, dismissed the agency as not useful for the exercise of presidential power.

The CIA was born in the year that President Truman declared the existence of a Cold War. From 1947 until 1967 the agency was essentially insulated from partisan political conflict. It remained immune from politicization for multiple reasons: a foreign policy consensus prevailed, secrecy normally expected by an intelligence agency was maintained, and, congressional knowledge and monitoring of intelligence operations was very limited. The CIA had survived what is routinely described as a "fiasco" at the Bay of Pigs because the Cold War foreign policy consensus remained strong, and presidents were permitted a free hand in clandestine operations, even in the face of monumental policy failure. The Vietnam War in its later stages, followed by Watergate, was a manifestation both of the breakdown in foreign policy consensus and the removal of the doctrinal insulation that had protected the CIA from partisan political controversy.

As America's intervention in Indochina evolved in the 1960s, so began a gradual deterioration of the wall of separation between the CIA and partisan politics. As earlier noted there was a flurry of partisan politics when President Kennedy replaced Allen Dulles with John McCone as CIA Director in late 1961, at which time a small band of liberal Democrats in the Senate opposed McCone's Senate confirmation. When Nixon became president, his natural urge was to replace Richard Helms, who earlier had become the first intelligence professional to be named CIA head. But Nixon's advisers warned him that such a change would politicize the agency, and Helms remained. The Watergate scandal, which exposed President Nixon's internal efforts to use the CIA to protect the president's personal political power, was the event opening the floodgates of CIA politicization. With Watergate it became clear that an agency like the CIA constituted a dangerous presidential instrument of secret power.

No review will be made here of all of the Watergate related events as they pertain to the CIA. The main point is that the Watergate disclosures exposed the vulnerability of CIA to politicization by an administration choosing to disregard the traditional intelligence ethic. Watergate led to the internal investigation of CIA's practices, primarily those in the 1960s. When the results of this investigation became publicly known, a political Pandora's box was opened for the CIA. The agency then found itself subject to intensive investigation by a presidential commission (Rockefeller) and separate, congressional select committees. With these developments, the CIA was in the midst of heated political controversy and became truly, in the cliche, a political football. In the process of detailed studies, hearings, and reports on the record of U.S. intelligence agencies (with most attention centering on the CIA), intelligence policy decisions came to be influenced by ideology, partisan politics, political ambition, and media "news" values. In the process, the tradition of bipartisanship or political neutrality with regard to secret intelligence was abandoned. Intelligence policy, organization, and systems for accountability became a matter of widespread political debate; public opinion polls indicated widespread popular concern with the past management of the intelligence system and with the need for reforms.

Accordingly, in the 1976 campaign for the presidency, the CIA and its organization, management and accountability were made major campaign issues. The Democratic Party platform for 1976 stipulated that covert action was to be permitted "only in the most compelling cases." "[A]ssassination must be prohibited," "thorough Congressional oversight instituted," and "intelligence abuses corrected."[6] The Republican platform, in a brief paragraph on intelligence, defensively promised to "withstand partisan efforts to turn any part of our intelligence system into a political football." But the Republicans implicitly defended covert action and suggested vaguely the need to tighten intelligence security. Even more important from the viewpoint of politicization was that Carter, when elected president, moved to appoint his own CIA director, Theodore Sorensen, a politician rather than an intelligence professional. (He was, of course, replacing a politician, George Bush, whom President Ford had named to the post.) In an unusual move, the Senate refused to go along with President Carter's nominee and the President was, in fact, forced to return to the traditional appointment of a politically neutral naval professional, Admiral Stansfield Turner.

Without question, the policy and leadership of the CIA had become a partisan issue, strongly correlated, it would seem, with the degree of foreign policy consensus existing in the nation. This became dramatically clear in 1979 when the Republican National Committee issued a broadside condemning Democrats in Congress for weakening the intelligence system. As chairman of the GOP National Committee, Bill Brock issued a statement declaring that under the Carter administration there had been "harmful miscalculations, massive intelligence failures, and setbacks in our foreign policy."[7] President Carter's proposals for reorganizing the intelligence community—most of which had failed of enactment—were condemned by the Republicans as likely to result in "politicizing" the intelligence system. Here for the first time, a national party committee had blamed the other major party for intelligence failures and mismanagement. True, President Carter had made intelligence abuses an issue in his 1976 campaign. But the distinctive point is that he had not blamed Republicans for what he saw as past intelligence abuses. A further point to note, therefore, is that intelligence policy can be politicized in a non-partisan way; so it can be politicized in a partisan manner, illustrating two categories of politicization.

The Republican advisory subcommittee that drafted the study that was to become the basis for GOP criticism of the Democrats, cited above, ironically had advocated the necessity for structuring the intelligence system so as to insulate it from "political influence" and revision of staffing concepts so that directors are appointed for fixed terms to guarantee their "political independence."[8] The ultimate irony, of course, was that when the Republican candidate became president in 1980 his nominee for the CIA directorship was his national campaign director, William J. Casey, the most partisan appointment, symbolically at least, in CIA's history. By this act, by giving the CIA director Cabinet status, and by Mr. Casey's conduct in the office, the CIA had become politicized in multiple ways.

As CIA Director, William J. Casey has been an activist intelligence chief. His definition of the role of intelligence, however, has occurred in the context of foreign policy dissensus. The CIA role in Central America, particularly, has been the subject of almost daily newspaper headlines since 1981 and a matter for frequent congressional debate. Proposed congressional legislation and debates on the CIA's role in carrying out foreign policy have further politicized the agency, to an unprecedented degree, in recent years. Not only has "covert" action been the subject of partisan political controversy, but CIA's information, for example, on the degree of Nicaraguan, or Cuban, or Soviet Russian intervention in the Central American political scene, has been politicized. And votes in Congress have often been divided along partisan lines, even with the usual undisciplined party deviations. The high degree of politicization that has occurred in recent years cannot be attributed entirely to the Reagan administration's, or Director Casey's interpretations of the CIA's role. But Mr. Casey has been heard to say that he is "not a purist" on the question of being involved in policy matters; he has not hesitated to give "poli-

cy" speeches and numerous published interviews and has noted that he holds Cabinet status.

In sum, the political life of the CIA has been a checkered one since 1947. While the intelligence profession has never seemed to waver from its conception of role—political neutrality—the presidency and congress have demonstrated a lack of conceptual clarity about the functions of intelligence. Certainly the creation of permanent committees in the House and Senate to participate, in effect, in all aspects of intelligence policy, budgets, and operations may be said to have institutionally, and inevitably, politicized central intelligence. This means we cannot take at face value an abstract role model picturing the intelligence agency as parapolitical. The ill-advised marriage of intelligence collection—analysis—estimates with covert action has further complicated role theory. An astute observer of the intelligence scene, Thomas Powers has written:

> Intelligence is the most political of professions. In the United States, as in every other country, it is subjected to endless attempts at meddling by every sort of special interest across the spectrum of domestic politics. . . . The history of the CIA can be written as a history of the attempts to politicize the Agency, some of them of appalling crudity, and more than a few successful.[9]

Powers exaggerates the politicization in other countries, where agencies normally operate in well-guarded secrecy. In the United States, politicization of the CIA is primarily a feature of the post-Vietnam, post-Watergate period. The record suggests that between 1947 and 1968, a foreign policy consensus both protected the CIA from aggressive congressional or media scrutiny and provided, as well, a high wall of separation between intelligence and domestic politics.

III. Examples of the Problem

Next will be offered examples illustrating the proposition that since knowledge is power and the political process involves power, intelligence estimates and operations sometimes become deeply involved in policy and process. This can happen in different ways, as examples of estimates of the Communist enemy in Vietnam, estimates of Soviet strategic power and intentions, and the intelligence failure in Iran will demonstrate. No attempt is made here to present definitive case studies of each of the three events analyzed. They will be sketched briefly as illustrative examples of the many facets of politicization. Each of the cases continues to be under intense study by scholars and participants.

A. The Nature and Size of the Enemy in Vietnam

In 1966–67 a controversy developed within U.S. government intelligence circles about the nature and size of the enemy in Vietnam. Details of this dispute first were exposed in 1975 when Sam Adams, a former CIA analyst, published an article in *Harper's* magazine (1975) asserting that the military command in Vietnam had deliberately misrepresented the size of Communist forces in South Vietnam. In essence, the CIA's estimates of enemy strength were nearly twice those officially estimated by the U.S. Military Assistance Command, Vietnam, commanded (1964–68) by General William Westmoreland. Westmoreland and other officials rejected civilian intelligence estimates, arguing that the CIA estimates included insurgent groups having no substantial military capacity which were not classifiable as "fighters."

This dispute went to the heart of American strategy in Vietnam, based as it was upon the goal of attrition and of gradually reducing the enemy's capability and will to pursue its revolution. The Vietnam War remains today a battleground among historians and foreign policy analysts. Was the administration's and Westmoreland's strategy based upon inaccurate calculations; was this a colossal intelligence blunder? Was the president deliberately misled by military officials wanting to send home encouraging news? If the CIA's pessimism rather than the military's more optimistic stance had prevailed, would the United States have withdrawn from the war sooner? And, the question that was given widespread publicity by a CBS television documentary and a subsequent lawsuit: Was there, in the words of CBS,

> a conspiracy at the highest levels of American military intelligence to suppress and alter critical intelligence on the enemy in the year leading up to the Tet offensive?

To put this complex intelligence issue as a simple question: Were the military intelligence figures manipulated to anticipate the presumed taste of political leaders at home, in which case we see intelligence politicized to a major degree; or was this simply a case of varying judgments about the capabilities and intentions of an enemy? During the lengthy trial, from October 1984 to February 1985, in which General Westmoreland sued CBS for libel as a result of its television documentary arguing that the General had engaged in a conspiracy to falsify enemy strength for political purposes, a revealing amount of testimony in the Westmoreland/CBS trial tended to support the argument that the military had in effect imposed a ceiling, determined by concern with politics at home, on estimates of enemy strength. But no conclusive evidence was presented in the trial that the military estimates were deliberately tailored for political purposes. There is no doubt from the record that the administration and military officials in the field feared that a demonstration of lack of military progress by U.S. forces in South Vietnam would aid the growing number of opponents of the war. Throughout the summer and fall of 1967, elaborate efforts were made to produce compromise estimates that would bring together CIA and military differences.

The central point in this whole story, however, is that throughout the debate over enemy strength the president and his advisers were attempting to rally public and congressional support for the war by demonstrating progress and encouraging hope for a successful ending in the near future. The simple fact was that estimates showing an increased enemy military strength, however calculated, stood in the way of demonstrating "light at the end of the tunnel." General Westmoreland knew that the political leadership hoped for, and public opinion demanded, good news. The CIA's estimates of greater enemy strength were bad news.

On January 30, 1968, the North Vietnamese communists launched what is now known as the Tet offensive, coordinated attacks against every major city in South Vietnam. Communist soldiers were pictured on American home television screens inside the American Embassy compound in Saigon. Even though the ultimate outcome of the Tet offensive, surprising in its ferocity and scope, was militarily catastrophic for North Vietnam, the Viet Cong earned the decisive victory of the war by winning a spectacular psychological victory over American public opinion. The public had been fed a heavy diet of optimism, encouragement and progress reports by its military and civilian leadership. And suddenly the enemy appeared to be strong enough to attack on all fronts.

The Viet Cong shattered the image of American progress and hopes for an early conclusion to the war. The Tet offensive reopened the "order of battle" dispute among civilian and military intelligence analysts. By March of 1968, CIA estimates of total Communist military and guerilla forces in South Vietnam ranged as high as 600,000, a figure which many military men found incredible. CIA officials for their part suspected that the military estimates continued to be tailored for political purposes. No real agreement was ever reached by the contending sides, despite great efforts to achieve compromise. Indeed, no agreement on the issue exists today, as evidenced by earnest testimony by both sides in Westmoreland's unsuccessful libel suit against

CBS. But if Westmoreland did not win, neither did CBS, which, in effect, settled out of court without final and convincing validation of its conspiracy hyperbole. The question of how to count the enemy was a perplexing intelligence problem in the Vietnam war. Whatever the truth in the matter, the case demonstrates the interrelatedness of intelligence and policy, and the inevitable interaction, in a free society not fighting a consensus war, of intelligence and politics.

B. Estimating Soviet Military Power

Another example demonstrating the confluence of ideology, politics and intelligence is estimates of Soviet military power. We saw in the Westmoreland/CBS case an illustration of the alleged military conspiracy to underestimate enemy strength for domestic political purposes. The so-called "Team B" episode illustrates efforts of the military and their allies to engage in "worst case" estimates of Soviet military strength in order to influence policy.

The CIA was created to institutionalize the intelligence ethic of policy neutrality. The State Department or the Pentagon, with all of their experts on foreign and military matters—and with their separate intelligence staffs—were expected to be policy advocates. In pursuit of pure objectivity, the Board of National Estimates was created within the CIA with its Office of National Estimates as a totally independent staff arm; independent, that is, of departmental vested interests. The individual analyst drafting estimates in theory worked behind the protective walls of policy independence, detached from partisan or vested interest pressures. Ultimately the Board of Estimates and its staff were abolished, in 1973, for many reasons. Perhaps most important was that independent national estimates limited the policy options of activist decision makers. In other words, the facts sometimes got in the way of what the leadership wanted to do. Henry Kissinger in *White House Years* put it this way: "In my experience the CIA developed rationales for inaction much more frequently than for daring thrusts."[10]

More to the point were criticisms that the CIA record in predicting accurately the development of Soviet strategic military forces was poor. Senator Malcolm Wallop reviewed his perception of the record in 1978 as follows:

> While the Soviets were beginning the biggest military buildup in history, the NIEs judged that they would not try to build up as many missiles as we had. When the Soviets approached our number, the NIEs said they were unlikely to exceed it substantially; when they exceeded it substantially, the NIEs said they would not try for decisive superiority—the capability to fight and win a nuclear war. Only very recently have the

NIEs admitted the possibility as an 'elusive question.' Now the NIEs say the Soviets may be trying for such a capability but they cannot be sure it will work.[11]

In place of the Board of National Estimates, the position of National Intelligence Officer was created in 1973. The NIO was to be responsible for producing a particular estimate. It was hoped that estimates would be sharper and less compromised to meet all views; that those in charge of estimates would be more specialized; accountability more focused; and, some would say, estimates more relevant to—if not supportive of—policy concerns. The number of NIOs has varied from 8 to 17 in recent years. There are NIOs for areas, e.g., the Soviet Union; for functional matters, e.g., counter-terrorism; and for at-large officers. Initially, NIOs were not given an independent staff but called upon the resources of the intelligence community. In recent years the National Intelligence Council has been created, giving NIOs an institutional existence, now with a staff—the NIC Analytical Group. Also in recent years, the NIOs have come under the jurisdiction of the CIA director, which in some ways would seem to decrease their independence from politics.[12]

Even with these reorganizations, the estimating system came under sharp criticism from those who were convinced that the CIA was underestimating the development of Soviet strategic military capabilities. In the latter part (1975) of the Ford Administration, the President's Foreign Intelligence Advisory Board, took issue with the CIA's general posture suggesting that the Soviet Union was not militarily superior to the United States, nor was it seen as planning to wage and win a nuclear war. The PFIAB, weighted heavily with foreign policy hardliners, persuaded the new CIA director, George H. W. Bush, a former chairman of the Republican National Committee and ambitious for the presidency, to appoint a group of outsiders to evaluate the CIA estimates on Soviet military strength and come up with independent findings. After reviewing the CIA's estimates, this group—known as Team B—concluded that the CIA (Team A) had systematically underestimated the strategic military capability of the Soviet Union. This came to be known as the "Team A–Team B" controversy. Controversy over Soviet estimates had been commonplace within the government for a quarter of a century. But appointment of an outside group, dominated by hard-line ideologists, was a novel and much criticized move, since the outside group was in no way ideologically balanced. Indeed, it was a phalanx composed primarily of men soon to become leaders of the influential Committee on the Present Danger.[13]

The Team B group ended up challenging CIA's findings on Soviet strength, not so much on capabilities as on intentions. The group assumed that the Soviet Union was bent on world domination, was preparing to fight and win a nuclear war, had undertaken a formidable civil defense effort, was aiming for nuclear superiority over the United States, and that a "window of vulnerability" confronted U.S. strategic forces. It saw CIA analysts as caught up in "mirror-imaging" U.S. strategic posture and doctrine when estimating future capabilities and intentions of the Soviet Union.

The Team B episode demonstrates a novel way in which intelligence can be politicized. A minority view on Soviet power and intentions was foisted upon the intelligence system. What was missing, of course, a Team C, made up of arms control enthusiasts with different assumptions about Soviet goals and capabilities. Former CIA Director Stansfield Turner has provided a good summary of this episode, capped by some knowledgeable advice:

A new technique of competitive analysis was attempted in 1976. This was the so-called A-Team, B-Team competition. Two analytic groups were organized to study U.S. and Soviet military capabilities. Team A was the CIA's normal analytic group on this subject. Team B was composed of outsiders with a right-wing ideological bent. The intention was to promote competition by polarizing the teams. It failed. The CIA team, knowing that the outsiders on B would take extreme views, tended to do the same in self defense. When B felt frustrated over its inability to prevail, one of its members leaked much of the proceedings to the press. My reluctance to use this team approach was criticized, but I believe that pitting extremists against one another can only lead to poor results. Instead, extremist views should be permitted to emerge from the analytic effort to be included as a minority view in the report.[14]

The Team B episode illustrates one way in which intelligence can be politicized. This is not to suggest that politicization is inherently destructive of accurate intelligence. But if benefits exist in such a method of competitive intelligence, clearly there are also costs.

C. Intelligence Failure in Iran: Example of Politicization?

In 1978 the CIA informed the President that the Shah of Iran, obviously buffeted by internal unrest, was secure in his position for the foreseeable future. The Shah was deposed in an internal revolution shortly thereafter. Was this failure in forecasting the result of politicization? Was this an example of an intelligence agency offering the leadership "intelligence to please?"

In 1978 President Carter had sincerely toasted the Shah as the head of "an island of stability in one of the most troubled areas of the world." In the words of the president's national security adviser, "the fall of the Shah was clearly a political calamity for President Carter."[15] The question before us is whether the intelligence system, realizing that this would be the case, was consciously or unconsciously influenced to forecast that such a calamity would not happen.

Few contest the judgment that American comprehension of the political situation was a significant failure of intelligence. Zbigniew Brezezinski recalls in his memoirs, "the intelligence system gave the president little preparation for the shock that the sudden disintegration of Iran was for him, as well as for the rest of us."[16] The case of the unexpected collapse of the Shah is an example of one special type of intelligence politicization.

Understanding the true nature of this failure with only limited access to the record is difficult. Various participants have supplied a variety of presumably self-serving memoirs. Fortunately, the staff of the U.S. House of Representatives Select Committee on Intelligence undertook a study in late 1978 and issued a report in January 1979. The report is based upon interviews with CIA managers and analysts, officials in the Department of State, the Defense Intelligence Agency and National Security Agency, and an analysis of current intelligence archives. What emerges are some significant insights, including the following:

First, collection and analysis of information from Iran was inadequate. Reports of anti-Shah demonstrations were greeted with complacency in Washington. The power of the religious opposition, which later came to be the ruling group, was seriously underestimated. Also misinterpreted was the depth of popular, middle-class opposition to the Shah. Put simply, the data flow from Iran was incomplete and misleading; its interpretation at intelligence headquarters was unsophisticated and complacent.

Second, U.S. foreign policy in the Persian Gulf region was anchored to the Shah's survival. A deliberate policy of no contact with opposition elements was in effect because of fears of antagonizing the Shah, who himself feared clandestine activities by the CIA within his realm. Policy makers were not asking the intelligence system to assess the strength of the Shah; they simply assumed that the Shah would prevail over opposition elements indefinitely. In sum, policy makers were unconsciously politicizing intelligence. Because U.S. policy was firmly fixed on assumptions that the Shah was secure, the decision-making system was incapable of absorbing information that would challenge such assumptions.

One can retrospectively sift through the vast amount of intelligence "paper" available to decision makers and find warning signals. State Department *Morning Summaries*, for example, noted the seriousness of disturbances in Iran. These were received daily at the White House for the President's eyes. White House reaction to such signals was not to ask for more detailed analysis of the Shah's stability. The question of removing restrictions that had been placed on CIA clandestine collection in Iran was not considered, out of fear of displeasing the Shah. Put more simply, political leaders seemed to demand only good news from Iran. And intelligence agencies were prone albeit unconsciously to report what they think—or know—leaders want to hear. Yet the intelligence system felt the sting of presidential displeasure after the event. President Carter in November 1978 penned a handwritten note to his national security advisers, including the CIA Director. With pointed reference to his surprise at events in Iran, he told them: "I am not satisfied with the quality of political intelligence." In his memoirs Zhigniew Brezezinski takes credit for this presidential note. Quoting from his diary he notes he was

> really appalled by how inept and vague Stan Turner's comments on the crisis in Iran were. This reinforces my strong view that we need much better political intelligence.[17]

Is Iran simply another case of intelligence failure, carrying with it—like Pearl Harbor in 1941 and Korea in 1950—world-shaking consequences? A simple positive answer would be misleading because it would ignore the role of policy and political leadership in the failure, and it would also ignore the subtle ways intelligence becomes politicized by unquestioning policy assumptions. The conclusion of the House Select Committee on Intelligence seems valid. It found that

> in the case of Iran, long-standing U.S. attitudes toward the Shah inhibited intelligence collection, dampened policy makers' appetite for analysis of the Shah's position, and deafened policymakers to the warning implicit in available current intelligence.[18]

Furthermore, the left hand of the CIA—the dominant covert action branch—had put the Shah in power and he was the CIA's man; the CIA was a principal booster of the Shah. Meanwhile the right hand of the CIA—the analytic branch—failed to provide policy-free information about the Shah's position. Such a system provided few incentives to challenge the conventional wisdom, or to substitute facts for preferences.

The man in charge of central intelligence during the Iranian crisis was Stansfield Turner as Director of Central Intelligence. In his memoirs, he analyzes the intelligence failure.

He admits there were two fundamental factors that the Carter administration, as well as earlier administrations, had failed to identify. One was the growing dissatisfaction with the Shah, and the other was the rising appeal of Islamic fundamentalism. There was a failure to see that a variety of dissident groups would coalesce under Khomeini. While dissidence was recognized, the primary failure was to assume that the Shah, who controlled a powerful Army, police force and ruthless secret intelligence service, would not be able to use these instruments of state power to maintain control.

Turner's most telling comment is:

> U.S. policy in the area of the world was so dependent on the Shah that it was all too easy for us to assume that he would do what was necessary to play the role we had in mind for him.[19]

Admiral Turner gives insight into other aspects of the intelligence failure regarding Iran. One factor is that intelligence analysis live in a rarified atmosphere where there is "excessive emphasis of the use of secret data as opposed to open information."[20] As a long-range trend, Turner notes, there was relatively little secret information that was relevant, and intelligence analysts tend to be disdainful of outside scholars as "second opinions" from experts. Furthermore, the CIA was short on specialized analytic skills pertinent to Iran, particularly the skills of sociologists and anthropologists. Another factor was the "inherent conservatism of a large bureaucracy."[21] Turner suggests that more "probability" estimating would have been useful, but he found the bureaucracy resistant to innovative analytic methods.

Most significantly, Turner's experience led him to observe: "The White House was repeatedly insensitive . . . to the importance of protecting the apolitical credibility of intelligence."[22] It would seem clear that however subtle, unconscious or indirect, the White House had politicized intelligence and induced failure.

IV. Conclusions

Questions were posed at the outset as to whether intelligence agencies are inevitably drawn into politics; whether assignment of policy implementation (covert action) automatically politicizes; or whether policy neutrality is either a necessity or a reasonable expectation for intelligence agencies.

Our task has been to compare, in the interest of behavioral generalization, the abstract intelligence model of policy neutralism with the observed reality of how things really work. Unquestionably, intelligence doctrine calls for policy neutrality in that crucial stage of the intelligence process of reporting the facts, and making judgments about the unknown. The axiom that intelligence should be strictly separate from policy, in the words of a veteran intelligence official "is as hallowed in the theology of intelligence as the doctrine of separation of church and state is in the U.S. Constitution."[23] That is an interesting analogy, but it will be quickly observed that the question of precisely where to draw the line separating church and state in the American polity is a matter of constant contention. So it is with intelligence and politics.

Lyndon Johnson reportedly once observed:

Policy making is like milking a fat cow. You see the milk coming out, you press more and the milk bubbles and flows, and just as the bucket is full, the cow with its tail whips the bucket and all is spilled. That's what the CIA does to policy making.[24]

In Lyndon Johnson's metaphor, the CIA is performing its idealized function, reporting the facts even if it informs leaders that policy is wrong or not working; even if it causes domestic political problems; or endangers the political security of the leadership in power. But the CIA's intelligence record in Vietnam, to which President Johnson had been referring, was not stellar. True, the CIA was often in conflict with the military regarding order of battle figures (strength of the enemy). But at crucial points, the CIA seems to have compromised with the military on the strength of the enemy for political rather than intelligence moves. The result was that at crucial periods of the Vietnam War, the strength of the enemy was underestimated by half.[25]

Recall that my guiding hypothesis in this essay, based as much upon intuitive judgment as upon concrete evidence, has been that intelligence is subject, object and instrument of power politics.

It is the subject of politics in the sense that those seeking access to political power must gain access to information in the process. Information is a key to power; information gives advantage; information provides the means for gaining power.

Once power is attained, intelligence becomes the object for maintaining power. Intelligence must remain exclusive, both in the domestic and international sense. Access to intelligence is strictly limited to those holding power. Maintenance of secrecy thus becomes an imperative, not just to persons exercising responsible political leadership (access to intelligence secrets is a primary bade of that power) but also to the nation state, which tries vigorously to maintain intelligence secrecy as a requirement of national security.

And finally, intelligence is also an instrument of political power in the sense that agents of secret intelligence (spies) function in the dual role as agents of political influence. This became a major function of an intelligence agency, particularly when military power reached the stage of being too destructive to have political utility. This may explain why the clandestine arm of the CIA came to dominate the agency in the Cold War years, and even today seems to preoccupy CIA leadership.[26] Once an intelligence agency is called upon to implement foreign policy—such as overthrowing an unfriendly government, conducting paramilitary operations, buying an election, or waging psychological warfare—the agency automatically becomes politicized; neutrality impossible. And so it may be concluded that intelligence is extricably intertwined with politics, no more so than when the intelligence agency is used to carry out policy. Allison and Szanton remind us that it is a "law of bureaucratic behavior" as well as a universal tendency that "agencies with operational responsibilities produce analyses that support their operating programs."[27]

And yet the doctrine of policy neutrality remains the guiding ethic of central intelligence. And so the analytical challenge is to suggest when such doctrine will prevail, and when it will be overcome by the political variables pressing upon it.

What, then, are the identifiable factors determining the degree of politicization that will characterize the intelligence system at any given time? A number of factors, or variables, may be identified that interact to affect the degree of isolation from politics permitted for intelligence systems.

First is the international environment. As suggested at the outset, a national consensus about the ends and means of foreign policy will produce a setting in which an intelligence agency can adhere to its ideal of policy neutrality and of insulation from politics. The behavior of other nations perceived as adversaries is certainly one feature of the international environment that will be an important conditioning factor. When a consensus in perceiving the nature of the foreign threat breaks down/or is weak, the intelligence system may be expected to lose its immunity from politicization.

A second factor is American political culture, which will interact with the consensus perceptions of the external factors. Americans are ambivalent about secret agencies of government. Common assumptions about the threat of an external enemy move the shared value of the citizen's right to know in the direction of acceptance of secrecy and censorship. The greater the demand for openness and accountability in government, which demand rises in times of perceived peace, the greater the probability of politicization of intelligence. When the Cold War consensus that lasted from 1947–1967 began to evaporate, so did the media and Congressional reluctance to debate publicly intelligence policy, organization, operations, and product. Put simply, in times when no national security emergency is perceived, it is the natural tendency of American political culture to politicize intelligence.[28]

A third factor is the governmental structure for intelligence. Internal bureaucratic conflict over "turf" as well as disagreements over estimates have characterized the intelligence system from the start. By the definitions suggested this does not constitute politicization. But internal bureaucratic struggles, in which the "leak" to the news media is sometimes a weapon, can quickly politicize intelligence, for it commonly leads to public debate over intelligence-related issues, and often divides political parties or factions within parties. Executive-legislative separation of powers is an institutional invitation to intelligence politicization. Perhaps it is the single most important factor nurturing politicization. The institutionalization of intelligence oversight in the House and Senate may have permanently politicized intelligence, but the degree to which this is so will be influenced by the other factors listed here.

The idiosyncratic or personality factor will be another important variable determining politicization. This is so particularly with regard to the personality of the director of Central Intelligence. Who that person is, how the director is chosen, the Director's personal definition of role, and the director's ideological persuasions—all will affect the degree of politicization.

In sum, a behavioral generalization is that in times of consensus war, cold or hot, when national unity exists and political bipartisanship prevails, an intelligence agency will come closest to applying its doctrinal orthodoxy of policy neutrality. But when the varied interests of America's plural society are at odds over the ends and means of foreign policy—particularly the means—the intelligence system tends to become politicized. In such a situation, the intelligence system is less likely to function at maximum efficiency.

Finally, the purpose of intelligence—accurate information promptly communicated—will most likely be fulfilled when:

- Executive-legislative cooperation is genuine.

- There are no weak links in the intelligence process "chain."

- The presidency is acutely sensitive to the dangers of a politicized intelligence system.

- American political culture incorporates some understanding that the greatest threat to national security is a misinformed or ill-informed political leadership.

Questions for Further Discussion

1. Was the failure to anticipate the fall of the Shah based more on a reluctance to acknowledge a harsh reality or on politicization?

2. Do you think it is reasonable to believe that the position of the Director of the Central Intelligence Agency, or today, the Director of National Intelligence, can be separated from partisan politics?

3. Does the "Team B" concept increase or decease the politicization of intelligence?

4. How might intelligence professionals themselves be a source of politicization?

Endnotes

1. J. Leiper Freeman, "Investigating the Executive Intelligence: The Fate of the Pike Committee," *Capitol Studies*, Fall, 1977, pp. 103–117. See also Loch K. Johnson, *A Season of Inquiry: The Senate Intelligence Investigation* (Lexington, KY: The University Press of Kentucky, 1985).
2. Robert M. Gates, "Is the CIA's Analysis Any Good?" *Washington Post National Weekly Edition*, Dec. 31, 1984, p. 29.
3. These distinctions suggested by Frances Hudson Oneal of Vanderbilt University.
4. Thomas Powers, *The Man Who Kept the Secrets*, (New York: Knopf, 1971). For Henry Kissinger's comments see *White House Years* (Boston: Little, Brown, 1979) p. 36.
5. William E. Colby, *Honorable Men* (New York: Simon and Schuster, 1978) pp. 342–344.
6. *Congressional Quarterly Almanac 1976*, Washington, D.C.: Congressional Quarterly News Service, 1977, p. 869.
7. Republican National Committee, Press Release, Aug. 6, 1979. Policy Paper, Intelligence Subcommittee, Advisory Council on National Security and International Affairs, p. 1.
8. *Ibid.*, pp. 5–6.
9. Powers, *op. cit.*, pp. 57–58.
10. Kissinger, *op. cit.*, p. 37.
11. U.S. Congress, 95th Cong. 2d Sess., Senate Select Committee on Intelligence Report, Subcommittee on Collection, Production and Quality, "The National Intelligence, A-B Team Episode" (Washington, D.C.: GPO, 1978) p. 13.
12. Jeffrey T. Richelson, *The U.S. Intelligence Community* (Cambridge, Mass.: Ballinger, 1985) pp. 330–331.
13. Charles Tyroler, II, ed., *Alerting America: The Papers of the Committee on the Present Danger* (Washington, D.C.: Pergamon-Grassey's, 1984).

14. Stansfield Turner, *Secrecy and Democracy: The CIA in Transition* (Boston: Houghton Mifflin, 1985) p. 251.

15. Zbigniew Brzezinski, *Power and Principle* (New York: Farrar, Straus and Giroux, 1983) p. 398.

16. *Ibid.*, p. 396.

17. *Ibid.*, p. 367.

18. U.S. Congress, 96 Cong. 1st Sess., House Select Committee on Intelligence, "Iran: Evaluation of the U.S. Intelligence Performance Prior to November 1978," Staff Report (Washington, D.C.: GPO, 1979) pp. 6–7.

19. Turner, *op. cit* p. 115.

20. *Ibid.*, p. 116.

21. *Ibid.*, p. 124.

22. *Ibid.*, p. 120.

23. Hans Heymann, "The Intelligence-Policy Relationship," in Alfred C. Mauer, et al., editors, *Intelligence Policy and Process* (Boulder, CO: Westview Press, 1985) p. 57.

24. Quoted by Henry Brandon, *The Retreat of American Power* (Garden City, NY: Doubleday, 1973) p. 103.

25. Powers, *op. cit.*, pp. 183–196.

26. Anne Karalekas, "History of the Central Intelligence Agency," in William M. Leary, *The Central Intelligence Agency: History and Documents* (University, AL: University of Alabama Press, 1984) pp. 13–119.

27. Graham Allison and Peter Szanton, *Remaking Foreign Policy: The Organizational Connection* (New York: Basic Books, 1976) pp. 194–195.

28. Harry Howe Ransom, "Strategic Intelligence and Intermestic Politics," pp. 299–319 in Charles W. Kegley, Jr. and Eugene R. Wittkopf, editors, *Perspectives on American Foreign Policy* (New York: St. Martin's, 1983) pp. 299–319. *See also* Ransom, "Intelligence and Partisan Politics," in Alfred C. Mauer, Marion D. Tunstall, and James M. Keagle, editors, *Intelligence Policy and Process* (Boulder, CO: Westview Press, 1985). A number of other essays in this collection are relevant to this study, particularly the contributions of Morton Halperin, Roger Hilsman, Mark M. Lowenthal, Robert Jervis, Stafford T. Thomas, Glenn Hastedt, Loch K. Johnson, James D. Austin, and Michael Handel. ✦

Reprinted with permission from Harry Howe Ransom, "The Politicization of Intelligence," in Stephen J. Cimbala, ed., *Intelligence and Intelligence Policy in a Democratic Society* (Dobbs Ferry, New York: Transnational, 1987): 25–46.

15

Intelligence to Please? The Order of Battle Controversy During the Vietnam War

James J. Wirtz

Ironically, debates about classified intelligence estimates often become a matter of public knowledge as participants make disagreements public to garner support for their positions. In this account of a dispute that occurred within the U.S. intelligence community on the eve of the 1968 Tet offensive, Wirtz explores charges made by Samuel Adams, a CIA analyst, that a conspiracy existed to prevent accurate information about enemy troop strength from reaching senior members of the Johnson Administration.

Although dozens of interservice and bureaucratic disputes occurred during the Vietnam war, one relatively minor debate has emerged to take a major place in the mythology of the conflict. A controversy over the contents of the Enemy Order of Battle—an intelligence report that identified enemy units and estimated North Vietnamese and Viet Cong (VC) troop strength—continued decades after the original confrontation between analysts at the Central Intelligence Agency (CIA) and officers working at the headquarters of the Military Assistance Command, Vietnam (MACV). At the heart of the debate stood the allegation made by a CIA analyst, Sam Adams, that a "conspiracy at the highest levels of American military intelligence" prevented an increase in the estimates of enemy strength contained in the Order of Battle, thereby contributing to the surprise and setbacks suffered by U.S. forces during the 1968 Tet offensive.[1] The charges, fully articulated by Adams in an article published in *Harper's* in May 1975, were repeated during hearings held by the Pike Committee in December of the same year.[2]

His claims captured widespread attention, however, when they served as the basis of a CBS News documentary.[3] The assertions made in the program led General William C. Westmoreland, the commander of MACV at the time of the controversy, to take legal action which ultimately resulted in the *Westmoreland vs. CBS* litigation.[4] Even today, these allegations continue to exert a pull on the imaginations of interested Americans.

Given the notoriety attained by the Order of Battle controversy and the place it has achieved in the literature on the Vietnam war, the purpose of this article is to offer some judgments not only about the charges leveled by Adams but also about the conditions that existed within the American intelligence community on the eve of the Tet offensive.[5] In part one of the analysis, both the MACV and CIA positions on the Order of Battle question will be identified. The events that marked the course of the debate also will be described, including the compromise over estimates that was eventually produced.

In part two, an evaluation of each side's position, based upon evidence uncovered during the Tet offensive, will be undertaken. Additionally, this section will evaluate the evidence supporting Adams's charges of conspiracy and the presence of a similar problem, the "intelligence to please" syndrome. This syndrome can occur when intelligence analysts are directly pressured by policy makers to produce estimates that support an ongoing program or a preferred initiative, a situation similar to the conspiracy alleged by Adams. Conversely, the syndrome also can be linked to less diabolical causes: intelligence analysts sometimes supply estimates that support a given course of action because they simply desire to please policy makers.[6] Three questions will be addressed by this section of the analysis: Whose Order of Battle estimates appear to be more accurate in hindsight? Did a conspiracy exist to prevent the higher estimates championed by CIA analysts from reaching senior policy makers? Did a desire to please policy makers lead analysts to produce estimates that demonstrated that ongoing efforts were succeeding?

Part three explains the imperatives that drove MACV and the CIA to contest this issue bitterly. Drawn from the bureaucratic politics literature, the explanation asserts that the Order of Battle debate, which was driven by organizational definitions of who constituted an enemy combatant, was used as an instrument by CIA analysts to challenge the prevailing assumptions that governed the debate over America's policy in Southeast Asia. Finally, the conclusion will offer some judgments not only about the controversy created by the Order of Battle debate, but also about some of the problems that plagued American intelligence on the eve of the Tet offensive.

Who Was the Enemy?

Order of Battle estimates are an important part of the intelligence product available to commanders. Not only do they keep track of specific enemy units, but they also provide an approximation of the number of forces that could be faced in battle. By monitoring the combat histories and positions of particular units, analysts can estimate the quality of the forces arrayed on a given area of the battlefield. This type of information would help in planning an offensive: attacks could be directed against places held by "green" units or forces that have recently suffered heavy casualties. Conversely, the movement of well rested or battle-hardened units to a given sector could be an indication that an opponent is preparing an offensive. In any event, history suggests that disaster is the likely outcome when commanders conduct operations without an accurate estimate of the forces facing them.[7]

As important as these estimates always have been to commanders, Order of Battle intelligence was even more important to U.S. officers during the Vietnam war. In part, this importance was generated by the drive to monitor the conflict through quantitative measures: Secretary of Defense Robert McNamara's well-known predilection toward systems analysis was accommodated in the effort to measure progress in the war.[8] Although they were resisted initially by the military, quantitative measures—the best known is the infamous and unreliable body count—were used to evaluate a variety of programs. Progress in the pacification effort, for example, was measured with the Hamlet Evaluation System (HES), a questionnaire completed periodically by commanders as a basis for judging progress in winning the "hearts and minds" of the South Vietnamese peasants.[9] Because of this emphasis on quantitative analysis, Order of Battle estimates, which traditionally incorporated a numerical component, held a place of prominence in the overall intelligence picture developed by analysts working at MACV.

Order of Battle estimates also were important because they measured progress in achieving one of the fundamental objectives set for American forces during the February 1966 Honolulu conference. To "attrit, by year's end, VC/NVA [North Vietnamese Army] forces at a rate as high as their capability to put men into the field," was the goal adopted by senior military and political officials who attended this meeting.[10] Westmoreland, in his general order issued for 1967, also emphasized the attrition ob-

jective embodied in U.S. military strategy.[11] Even though the adoption of this goal appears to be a recipe for stalemate, the objective was pursued vigorously by the American military. Order of Battle estimates—which summarized the results of the body count, estimates of North Vietnamese infiltration, VC recruitment, and the status of specific enemy units—were used to measure progress in achieving the attrition objective.

In developing Order of Battle estimates, analysts at MACV monitored four different types of enemy units: NVA forces, VC main force units, VC local force units, and VC irregular forces (which included guerrilla, self-defense, and secret self-defense forces).[12] These forces were placed into categories according to which element of the communist command hierarchy controlled them and also according to their function: combat units (sometimes called maneuver units); combat support units; administrative service units; irregular units; and units that served as the VC political infrastructure.[13] Even though hundreds of pages of intelligence were produced every month to monitor changes in dozens of specific enemy units, the overall results of this analysis were presented in a few lines contained in the Monthly Order of Battle Summary (see Table 15.1).

Although the exact numbers presented in the Monthly Order of Battle Summaries give an impression of accuracy and seem innocuous enough, to analysts and officers working at MACV, these calculations contained both hidden problems and far-reaching implications. Analysts would have identified two limitations that called into question the accuracy of these apparently exact results. First, the conservative methodology adopted to monitor infiltration and to identify newly formed VC units—at least two captured documents and/or two prisoner interrogation reports had to confirm the existence of the unit before it was added to the Order of Battle—tended to skew estimates. Delays of two to three months or even longer might occur between the time an NVA unit entered the country and the time its presence was reflected in the official estimate of enemy strength. Enemy casualties, however, were quickly deducted from the Order of Battle. Second, many members of the intelligence community, including analysts at MACV, would have admitted that secrecy and the continuous metamorphosis taking place within VC irregular units and the VC infrastructure reduced the accuracy of their assessments of these forces. In contrast, analysts believed that their estimates of the strength of combat, combat support, and administrative support units were reasonably accurate. Since they were organized along conventional mili-

Table 15.1
Monthly Order of Battle Summaries
(Missing Extracts Unavailable)

Extract from Monthly Order of Battle Summary as of 31 July 1967

Maneuver	Combat Support	Administrative Service	Irregulars	Political	Grand Total
108,757	12,235	24,863	112,760	39,175	297,790
(46,125)*	(8,660)	(400)			(55,185)

Extract from Monthly Order of Battle Summary as of 31 August 1967

Maneuver	Combat Support	Administrative Service	Irregulars	Political	Grand Total
105,822	12,705	25,653	112,760	39,175	296,115
(43,920)	(8,140)	(400)			(52,460)

Extract from Monthly Order of Battle Summary as of 31 October 1967

Maneuver	Combat Support	Administrative Service	Irregulars	Political**	Grand Total
102,397	14,155	38,000	81,300		235,852
(44,040)	(9,660)	(400)			(54,100)

Extract from Monthly Order of Battle Summary as of 31 December 1967

Maneuver	Combat Support	Administrative Service	Irregulars	Political**	Grand Total
100,651	14,505	37,725	71,700		224,581
(44,539)	(10,010)	(125)			(55,674)

Extract from Monthly Order of Battle Summary as of 31 January 1968

Maneuver	Combat Support	Administrative Service	Irregulars	Political**	Grand Total
100,836	14,180	37,725	72,605		225,346
(45,684)	(9,935)	(125)			(55,744)***

* NVA strength shown in parentheses.

** Political category dropped from Order of Battle.

*** In addition to those NVA in NVA units there are approximately ten to twelve thousand NVA in VC units.

Source: "Extract from MACV Order of Battle Summary August 1–31,1967," Joint Exhibit #195P; "Extract from MACV Order of Battle Summary October 1–31, 1967," Joint Exhibit #198S; "Extract from MACV Order of Battle Summary December 1–31, 1967," Joint Exhibit 198S; "Extract from MACV Order of Battle Summary January 1–31. 1968," Joint Exhibit #198TT; all contained in *Vietnam: A Documentary Collection—Westmoreland v. CBS* (New York: Clearwater Publishing Co., 1985).

tary lines, it was easier to monitor changes in these units.[14]

In terms of the far reaching implications raised by the Order of Battle, estimates produced after June 1967 carried a message that is not apparent to contemporary readers: they could be interpreted as evidence that the United States was winning the war. Colonel Daniel Graham, an analyst assigned to MACV J-2 (intelligence) demonstrated in his controversial Crossover Memo that the "crossover point" had been reached during June 1967. Numerous claims had been made previously about attaining the crossover point, but following Graham's work, analysts and officers at MACV generally accepted the notion that enemy losses exceeded replacements gained from recruitment and infiltration. Graham's Crossover Memo formed the basis of the June Measurement of Progress Report (MOP) which stated officially that the crossover point had been reached in South Vietnam.[15]

How did this claim about reaching the crossover point indicate that the United States was winning the war? A comparison of subsequent Order of Battle reports (see Table 15.1) to the July 1967 estimate shows how Graham's analysis was reflected in estimates of enemy strength. Even though there is a slight increase in overall enemy strength between December 1967 and January 1968 (765 or about .035 percent), the total estimate of the number of troops in communist ranks declines significantly between July 1967 and January 1968. In July, enemy strength was placed at 297,790, but by the eve of the Tet offensive, the estimate of communist strength was only 225,346. By definition, the military had attained one of its primary goals in Vietnam: the attrition objective set at the Honolulu conference had been achieved. During the summer of 1967, senior officers and analysts at MACV began to use Order of Battle estimates to demonstrate that American forces were winning the war. In the words of Colonel Charles Morris, one of Graham's colleagues at

MACV: "we honestly believed . . . that we had reached the crossover point . . . Danny Graham and all of us thought the enemy was out of men."[16]

Sam Adams and the Skeptics at the CIA

By the summer of 1967, CIA analysts, in contrast to officers at MACV. had established a record of skepticism about achieving American goals in Southeast Asia.[17] Several factors probably contributed to the differences in the assessments offered by individuals working for these organizations. MACV analysts focused on battlefield events, while CIA analysts tended to integrate political, economic, and social developments into their judgments about the conflict. Analysts working at CIA headquarters also enjoyed a degree of detachment that was not available in Saigon. CIA analysts had the luxury of focusing on the big picture, while analysts working at MACV concentrated on supporting the day-to-day conduct of military operations. In addition, it was less onerous for CIA analysts to identify weaknesses in the American war effort: the U.S. military and not the intelligence community was largely responsible for the implementation of U.S. policy in Vietnam. CIA analysts could identify problems without calling into question the efficacy of the programs implemented by their organization.[18]

Disagreement over Order of Battle estimates, however, was not primarily responsible for this divergent perspective about progress in the war. In fact, CIA analysts relied on MACV estimates of enemy strength. Order of Battle analysis not only was a military bailiwick, it also was a massive enterprise. Senior agency officials decided not to use their comparatively limited resources in what would have amounted to a very small attempt to duplicate the work of dozens of MACV analysts who were able to draw upon the resources of the Defense Intelligence Agency (DIA) and the National Security Agency (NSA). CIA analysts settled for attaching their qualifications to the estimates produced by the military.[19]

Sam Adams, an enterprising young Harvard graduate who made his reputation as an analyst during the 1960 crisis in the Congo, was largely responsible for the Order of Battle estimates that were produced by the CIA. Toward the end of 1966, Adams concluded his own examination of VC strength. He used documents captured from the VC to develop a detailed estimate of VC strength in Binh Dinh province, the largest and most populated province in South Vietnam. Adams determined that at least one VC organization was not reflected in the MACV Order of Battle: the VC were busy recruiting teenagers to serve with a part-time organization called the assault youth, but this type of unit was not counted in the MACV estimate.[20]

When Adams used these captured documents to conduct his own estimate of VC strength, especially the strength of irregular units and the VC infrastructure, the results were shocking. Adams developed a detailed assessment of the number of individuals in these VC units in Binh Dinh province, and then he multiplied his results by the number of provinces in South Vietnam. Adams's analysis, which focused on the irregular and clandestine units maintained by the VC, yielded the number 600,000 as a conservative estimate for the total enemy strength in South Vietnam. Adams analysis was over twice the size of the official estimate carried in the MACV Order of Battle (277,150 as of 3 January 1967).[21]

Adams's analysis did not generate much controversy during the first half of 1967, even though CIA officials used his work as the basis of the agency's view of the MACV Order of Battle. In fact, George Carver, Adams's boss at the CIA, informed Richard Helms, the director of Central Intelligence (DCI), and Walt Rostow, the president's national security adviser, that "the MACV Order of Battle . . . is far too low and should be raised, perhaps doubled." Rostow then suggested to General Earle Wheeler, chairman of the Joint Chiefs of Staff, that the interested parties should meet to discuss the issue.[22] As a result, a conference was held during February 1967 on Order of Battle issues. During the meeting, it appears that MACV analysts actually sympathized with the position taken by Adams. Colonel Gains B. Hawkins, in charge of conducting estimates of enemy strength for MACV, placed enemy strength at 500,000. A CIA-MACV compromise over the issue actually appeared possible for a time.[23]

The debate began to heat up, however, by about mid-year. An official estimate issued by the CIA in May 1967 stated that in contrast to the MACV Order of Battle, which listed irregular force strength at 113,000, an accurate estimate for this category was "more likely in the neighborhood of 190–200,000. . . ."[24] Moreover, Adams's hand can be detected in another observation offered by this estimate:

> it appears that [the] strength of the insurgent apparatus in South Vietnam, instead of totaling 292,000 as listed in the 15 May 1967 OB [Order of Battle], may actually be in the half-million range.[25]

The critique contained in this widely disseminated document did not go unnoticed by analysts at MACV. Its existence undermines Adams's charge that a conspiracy prevented the presentation of information that indicated that estimates were in need of upward revision.

The Battle Over Estimates

The controversy over the Order of Battle began to emerge in June 1967; efforts to prepare a draft of the Special National Intelligence Estimate (SNIE) 14.3–67 entitled, "Capabilities of the Vietnamese Communists for Fighting in South Vietnam," catalyzed the debate. SNIE 14.3–67 was a formal assessment produced by the entire intelligence community and was intended to "estimate the capabilities of the Vietnamese Communists to conduct military operations in South Vietnam over the next year or so."[26] Obviously, an assessment of enemy strength would play a part in SNIE 14.3–67, and CIA analysts wanted the document to reflect their estimate of the strength of VC forces. MACV analysts, however, were no longer willing to bargain with the skeptics at the CIA over a compromise concerning the strength of the VC irregulars. Instead, MACV analysts adopted a vastly different approach to the discrepancy between estimates.

MACV proposed eliminating several types of units that were counted in the irregular category contained in the Order of Battle. In other words, MACV suggested that the VC self-defense and secret self-defense forces, the units Adams claimed were underestimated in MACV estimates, should be dropped altogether from assessments of enemy strength, including the estimate prepared for SNIE 14.3–67. In response to this suggestion, Agency analysts cabled Saigon:

Headquarters analysts would find solution to OB problem, as proposed, totally unworkable. Self Defense and Secret Self Defense Militia simply cannot be dropped or ignored in the official OB or in public releases on enemy strength. . . . In our view, it is time to be realistic in public as in private with nature of enemy force we are facing.[27]

The positions adopted by both sides in this controversy are easy to discern from the blizzard of cable traffic generated by the debate. The MACV position, which was supported by analysts at the DIA, rested on several arguments. First, MACV officers questioned the feasibility of developing an accurate assessment of these clandestine VC units; they claimed that a lack of hard data would turn any attempt to calculate the strength of these forces into an exercise in speculation. As Daniel Graham noted years after the war, even the effort to make a distinction between guerrilla units was not realistic:

You didn't know how many . . . guerrillas there were, let alone have some guy out there in the boonies tell you, "I just saw a guerrilla, and we believe that he was a member of the self-defense militia, or the assault youth, or the village self-protection." . . . as far as the guys who were giving

us direct reports from the field, no way . . . they could tell one guerrilla from another.[28]

Second, MACV officers argued that even if an accurate assessment was possible, it was not appropriate to include many VC units—including the self-defense, secret self-defense, and assault youth—into an Order of Battle that accounted for combat units. According to General Creighton Abrams, deputy commander of MACV:

From the intelligence viewpoint, the inclusion of SD [self-defense] and SSD (secret self-defense] strength figures in an estimate of military capabilities is highly questionable. These forces contain a sizable number of women and old people. They operate entirely in their own hamlets. They are rarely armed, have no real discipline, and almost no military capability. They are no more effective in the military sense than the dozens of other nonmilitary organizations which serve the VC cause in various roles.[29]

MACV was claiming that it was inappropriate to include thousands of South Vietnamese civilians—open and covert supporters of the VC cause—in the Order of Battle, thereby designating them as a legitimate military target. To be fair, civilians who supported the South Vietnamese cause would then have to be included in the allied Order of Battle, but this idea was rejected as preposterous by officers assigned to MACV. The American military simply preferred not to designate the civilians living in VC controlled areas as enemy combatants.[30]

Third, no matter how they looked at it, MACV officers believed that the acceptance of the CIA position would produce a public relations disaster. On the one hand, senior officers at MACV were concerned that a major increase in the Order of Battle would generate public and media criticism, especially in light of MACV reports of progress in the war. Not only would a massive increase in the estimates contained in the Order of Battle add to the credibility gap with the American public, but they also believed that it would undermine the Johnson administration's confidence in their conduct of the war. Westmoreland's initial reaction to the proposal to increase estimates of enemy strength—"What am I going to tell the press? What am I going to tell the Congress? What am I going to tell the President?"—reflects the idea that an increase in the estimate would be interpreted as evidence of military incompetence or as an attempt to end a long-standing effort to mislead Americans.[31] Westmoreland informed General Wheeler that "no possible explanation could prevent the erroneous conclusions that would result" from a significant increase in the estimates contained in the Order of Battle.[32]

On the other hand, MACV officers were worried that the disclosure of the increased estimate would leave them open to another charge: they were pushing for an increase in the Order to Battle to bolster their requests for additional forces. Westmoreland was sensitive to this charge, because he had earlier been accused by a senior official in the Johnson administration of following this type of strategy to secure additional forces for his command.[33] Other senior officers also were worried about this type of problem. For example, when improvements in the method of counting enemy-initiated incidents were applied retroactively by MACV analysts and produced a sharp increase, as opposed to a previously reported decrease in enemy-initiated incidents over the past year, they received a sharp warning from the chairman of the Joint Chiefs of Staff (JCS):

> I note . . . that some feeling exists within your [Westmoreland's] headquarters that there is a relationship between statistical bookkeeping . . . and decisions concerning future strength levels. I feel certain this does not reflect your own views, but for the record, you can assure those who hold such dangerous views that any requirements for additional forces which are well and clearly justified will receive a fair hearing at this and higher levels regardless of the way statistics on enemy activity are running, and that any attempts to "weight the dice" can only result in trouble for us all.[34]

One way or another, an increase in the Order of Battle estimate would rebound to the detriment of the war effort by reducing confidence in the military's conduct of the war.

In contrast, CIA analysts noted that MACV concerns about the impact of higher estimates on official Washington and the American public were not really justified:

> We think it possible that Saigon authorities are overemphasizing difficulty of explaining jump in figures adequately to "high levels" in Washington. Several CIA studies and some by other intelligence components have broached probability that estimates are upcoming which will be much higher. Questions we get from high levels involve when community is going to come up with these new assessments.[35]

They also argued that the failure to include the approximately 120,000 members of the VC self-defense and secret self-defense forces in American estimates of enemy strength would undermine the allied war effort. Analysts claimed that these forces formed a manpower pool that MACV analysts failed to consider as they worked on their crossover calculations. MACV, according to CIA analysts, probably subtracted many dead self-defense force members

from estimates of the number of individuals in the more conventional NVA and VC units, thereby skewing the calculations that measured progress towards the attrition objective. Analysts stated that the inclusion of self-defense and secret self-defense forces in the Order of Battle would depict a more realistic and accurate picture of the strength and nature of the communist forces fighting in South Vietnam.[36]

Efforts to arrange a compromise between MACV and the CIA broke down on 18 August when the CIA's Office of National Estimates (ONE) included in a draft of the SNIE the estimate of 120,000 for the strength of the self-defense forces and secret self-defense forces. This information prompted a flurry of protest from Robert Komer, General Davidson (MACV J-2), General Abrams, and Westmoreland. In response to this protest the JCS asked Helms, in his capacity as chairman of the United States Intelligence Board, to send a team of personal representatives to Saigon to settle the dispute. The CIA team, composed of George Carver, William Hyland, Dean Moor, and Sam Adams, arrived in Saigon on 8 September. The effort to reach a compromise was about to collapse when Helms, who was anxious to avoid a split SNIE (whereby separate MACV/DIA and CIA figures would be presented), stepped in and apparently encouraged Carver, who was the head of the CIA delegation, to drop the CIA's insistence on quantifying the self-defense and secret self-defense forces. Westmoreland agreed to the compromise on 14 September 1967.[37]

The compromise between MACV and the CIA was tenuous at best, although it was reflected in the estimates produced by MACV starting in October 1967 (see Table 15.1). Since CIA representatives only succeeded in obtaining MACV's agreement to provide them with a copy of the June 1967 Crossover Memo, they apparently felt shortchanged. Moreover, CIA analysts took a dim view of a draft of a proposed MACV press briefing, which they received on 10 October 1967. They believed that the briefing violated the tenets of the September compromise, because it implied that there was greater certainty about Order of Battle estimates than was justified, further played down the role of self-defense and secret self-defense forces, and stated that the intelligence community had generally overestimated the size of enemy forces arrayed against the allies, whereas SNIE 14.3–67 stated that the analysts had historically underestimated communist strength. CIA representatives suggested that the agency should attempt to distance itself from what they considered to be the unsupportable statements offered by MACV analysts. The compromise remained effective, however, until the issue re-emerged with a vengeance in the aftermath of the Tet offensive.[38]

The Controversy in Perspective

Although the intelligence community avoided a split SNIE, the temporary resolution of the Order of Battle debate left an important question unresolved. Did the MACV or the CIA estimate of enemy strength provide the best approximation of the forces faced by Americans in South Vietnam? In hindsight, neither estimate proved to be exact, but the MACV assessment was much closer to reality than the analysis developed by Adams. Evidence for the MACV position emerged in the aftermath of the Tet offensive.

The Tet offensive, launched amid the celebration of Vietnam's sacred holiday, was an extremely ambitious enterprise: it engulfed 39 of South Vietnam's 44 provincial capitals, five of its six autonomous cities, and 71 of its 245 district capitals in serious fighting.[39] In launching this go-for-broke offensive, the communists employed virtually all of the military forces under their control, including walking wounded and teenagers equipped with weapons still covered in packing grease. The maximum estimate of the number of communist troops that participated in the attacks, however, is only 85,000.[40] Renata Adler, who followed the *Westmorland v. CBS* proceedings in detail, has already asked the obvious question raised by Adams's analysis: "What were the remaining five hundred and fifteen thousand [communist troops] doing during Tet?"[41]

Even though it can never be determined exactly, it would appear that MACV analysts might have overestimated communist combat strength by as much as 20 percent. The actual size of the force available to the communists (based upon a two-to-one ratio between support personnel and estimates of participants in the battle) probably ranged from a low of about 180,000 to a high of about 250,000. The number contained in the 31 January 1968 Order of Battle—225,346—appears reasonable, however, given this simple rule of thumb estimate. (See Table 15.1.) In contrast, Adams's estimate of 600,000 is a gross overestimation of communist strength (combat forces combined with partially armed civilian supporters) in South Vietnam.

Where did Adams go wrong in his analysis? Apparently, his central assumption proved to be inaccurate: the captured documents that formed the basis of his study did not provide an accurate description of the status of VC irregulars. In fact, these documents might have been fabricated, not to mislead the Americans but to demonstrate to superiors that cadre in the field had met recruitment and organizational quotas set by senior commanders.

In the aftermath of the Tet attacks, for example, none of the POWs and defectors that fell into allied hands claimed to be members of the assault youth, self-defense, and secret self-defense forces, despite the fact that the CIA even warned interrogators to allow former VC to answer questions about their organizational affiliation without prompting.[42] In a 22 April 1968 cable to Admiral U.S. Grant Sharp, commander in chief, Pacific, Westmoreland explained:

> . . . we questioned a representative cross section of prisoners we picked up during the Tet offensive. Not one has admitted to being a member of any of the organizations which CIA would quantify as 'the insurgency base.'[43]

Moreover, one senior NVA officer stated that he decided to surrender after he discovered that the several units of assault youth that he was supposed to lead in combat were nowhere to be found.[44] The fact that the South Vietnamese population failed to support the VC in their attacks also stands in evidence against Adams's assertion that the communists had a force of 600,000 soldiers and supporters in the country. Ninety percent of the POWs captured during the attacks claimed that they received no aid from South Vietnamese civilians. Admittedly, it was in the interest of the POW to answer the question in this way to avoid implicating compatriots, but only 2 percent claimed that they received unsolicited help during an attack that was designed to elicit support from the South Vietnamese.[45]

Apparently, Adams's analysis reflected the total number of combatants in the broadest sense of the term available to the communists, combined with the potential pool of strength available to the VC (the total number of individuals who might have supported the communist cause). In hindsight, Adams might be forgiven for making this mistake. The North Vietnamese and VC leadership, in hoping that the South Vietnamese population would revolt in support of the Tet offensive, made a similar error. VC cadre working in the south, according to Douglas Pike, created

> in the minds of the people in the North a very strong view that anti-Americanism was on the rise, which it was . . . [but] it wasn't as bad as was being reported.[46]

In other words, both Adams and the North Vietnamese might have been misled by the same types of reporting turned in by southern cadre.[47]

A Conspiracy?

In terms of the main question raised by Adams in the aftermath of the controversy, conclusive evidence can be provided to demonstrate that a conspiracy to prevent an increase in Order of Battle estimates did not exist at the highest levels of American intelligence. In fact, the inaccuracy of Adams's accusation can be illustrated in two ways. First, as the description of the debate over estimates of enemy strength demonstrates, Adams's charges received a fair hearing from senior members of the intelligence community and senior members of MACV. DCI Helms and General Westmoreland, the commander of MACV, were not only aware but personally involved in the debate over the Order of Battle. Adams's analysis was not summarily rejected by officials, but was instead the focus of a bruising bureaucratic debate. Moreover, if a conspiracy existed to suppress Adams's analysis, it was not an efficient one: at one point CIA analysts admitted that the entire intelligence community knew that a debate over the Order of Battle was taking place. In fact, MACV officers were concerned that the story about the existence of a dispute in the intelligence community might find its way into the media, reducing public trust in the individuals conducting the war. The *New York Daily News* correspondent in Saigon already had learned that the Order of Battle might be increased.[48] In other words, the dispute over the Order of Battle propagated the ideas Adams championed.

Second, even in the strictest sense, Adams's analysis was disseminated in at least one formal CIA report—the May 1967 estimate, which stated that enemy strength in South Vietnam might total as much as 500,000. He also succeeded in preventing MACV from ignoring the need to account in SNIE 14.3–67 for the possible existence of several kinds of clandestine VC units. Officers at MACV, after all, would have preferred to sweep this problem under the rug. These are not small accomplishments for a relatively junior player who also happened to be wrong.

Did this conspiracy at the highest levels of American intelligence, which included officers at MACV, prevent accurate information from reaching senior members of the Johnson administration? Indeed, if members of the intelligence community deliberately misled the president or his advisers about the status of communist forces, then Adams's charges of conspiracy might be accurate. The documentary record, however, demonstrates that this simply is not the case.

MACV and CIA analysts were not alone in attempting to estimate enemy strength in South Vietnam. Apparently, NSA analysts not only monitored the movement of North Vietnamese soldiers down the Ho Chi Minh trail, but also monitored VC communications in an effort to calculate the number of VC units that were active and to monitor the movements of these forces. Information obtained from the NSA, however, was supplied directly by this agency to the White House. Members of the MACV staff, or the CIA for that matter, could not prevent these estimates from reaching the president and his senior advisers.[49]

The president was honestly and accurately informed not only about the debate over the Order of Battle, but also about the overall uncertainty involved in developing estimates of enemy strength. In a cover memo that summarized the findings of SNIE 14.3–67, Helms informed Johnson about the Order of Battle debate:

> The new estimate has been produced through an exhaustive process of analysis including detailed consultations in Saigon between the Embassy and MACV and a team from the Washington Community headed by my personal representative. . . . The new estimate is sensitive and potentially controversial primarily because the new strength figures are at variance with our former holdings. Much of the past data on overall Communist capabilities in Vietnam has turned out to be unreliable and many of the figures have turned out to be too low . . . we have not been able to find a reliable basis for reconstructing Communist strength figures retrospectively to provide a true standard of comparison between present and Communist strength as it actually was a year ago. . . . I have considered not issuing this Estimate and after considerable consultation, believe this would be a mistake . . . too many people are aware that the exercise to get agreed figures has been going on. In short, the charge of bad faith or unwillingness to face the facts would be more generally damaging than the issuance of this document which can stand on its own feet.[50]

Adams lost in his attempt to gain complete acceptance of his inaccurate estimates but the president was made aware generally of his efforts and the issues at stake.

Despite the fact that senior members of the Johnson administration were aware of the Order of Battle controversy, several junior officers who served as intelligence analysts testified during the *Westmoreland vs. CBS* litigation that estimates that reflected an increase in enemy strength had been arbitrarily blocked or altered by their immediate superiors.[51] Other individuals who were not involved in the litigation also have described similar events, which seem to substantiate the overall veracity of Adams's position, including its conspiratorial overtones. For example, Robert Simmons, a junior officer who worked on Order of Battle estimates at the Headquarters of II Field Force Vietnam (II FFV), has stated:

> Intelligence officers were under a great deal of pressure in the fall of 1967 to produce statistics that proved the war was going well. . . . Order of

Battle officers . . . were told in late October that their holdings did not reflect progress results expected in General Westmoreland's Combined Campaign Plan and that these figures were to be "reassessed." When their reassessments still did not satisfy the requirement for progress, the ranking intelligence officer in II FFV, personally changed the figures before forwarding them to Saigon.[52]

Even though a connection seems to exist between the charges raised by Adams and these incidents, the relationship is largely coincidental. The experiences cited by these officers have little to do with the accusations leveled by Adams that conspiracy existed at "the highest levels of American intelligence."[53] None of the available evidence indicates that the individuals who suppressed these estimates based their actions on orders issued by officers at MACV. Instead, several other incentives probably motivated the alteration of estimates at the grass roots level.

First, the six month tour of duty for officers placed a premium on demonstrating results in an extremely short period of time. Officers were loathe to report fluctuations of enemy strength in their area of responsibility. They might have reasoned that negative reporting could act as a black mark on their record, preventing the necessary ticket punch needed for promotion.[54] Second, the emphasis given to quantitative measures of progress was generally viewed with disdain by officers who were busy with the actual conduct of military operations. Since they believed that these numbers could not provide an accurate reflection of the situation they faced, they might have reasoned that it was foolhardy to risk their careers over quantitative analyses that they regarded as worthless.[55] Third, army officers confronted tremendous institutional pressure to demonstrate that the policies adopted by their service were succeeding. In other words, institutional loyalty corrupted the analytical-policy distinction that should have been maintained in the military's evaluation of its own performance. In effect estimates produced by junior officers were manipulated, but the officers who changed these estimates were probably responding to personal or institutional imperatives and not the dictates of a deeply rooted conspiracy to mislead senior officials.[56]

The stories told by these junior analysts, however, embody both manifestations of the intelligence-to-please syndrome. Estimates were deliberately altered, but the officers who suppressed reports that conflicted with the expectations of higher authorities were not acting under orders. Instead, officers who were eager to please their superiors changed reports to accommodate the expectations of senior commanders. Even though these incidents probably did little to affect the overall intelligence picture, they do reflect a breakdown in the delicate balance between intimacy and detachment that should exist between commanders and intelligence advisers. Military intelligence is highly prone to this type of problem, because officers seem to lose their sense of objectivity when they are required to evaluate the performance of their own service and commanders.

Explaining the Controversy

Although they had no way of knowing at the time, agency analysts would have been pleased with one of the comments about SNIE 14.3–67 offered to the president by Walt Rostow: "this is a conservative estimate."[57] Interpreted in this manner, SNIE 14.3–67 would have represented a victory for CIA analysts. They might have lost the battle over estimates of enemy strength, but they had taken the first step in limiting MACV claims of progress in the war. The issue driving the Order of Battle controversy was not the disagreement over the size of the forces arrayed against the allies in South Vietnam. Instead, it was an argument about which organization would be allowed to set the ground rules governing discourse about the war.

A simpler explanation for the controversy can, of course, be suggested. MACV's resistance to CIA meddling with its estimates of enemy strength might be explained by bureaucratic imperatives. Organizations can be expected to resist the efforts of other bureaucracies to encroach on their domain. MACV analysts also considered the CIA critique of their estimates to be amateurish: Adams, after all, was suggesting that old men, women, and children should be counted on the same list that tallied battle-hardened and highly capable NVA soldiers.

Indeed, organizational definitions of who constituted a combatant loomed large in the debate. MACV tended to take a narrow view of the issue, arguing that only males who were armed, fought full-time, and were under the control of higher authority should be counted as combatants. In comparison, CIA analysts took a broader view of the issue that reflected political realities more than traditional military criteria. MACV officers, however, did not initially maintain that Order of Battle analysis was none of the CIA's concern. In fact, their first response was favorable. CIA efforts to study the "VC Political Order of Battle" would allow MACV analysts to concentrate on what they considered to be important, the assessment of the NVA and VC forces organized along conventional lines.[58]

Because the military did not object to the CIA's initial foray into the Order of Battle business, the controversy over estimates of enemy strength, although influenced by differences in the CIA's and MACV's definition of the term combatant, was not prompted by a desire to protect organizational prerogatives. Instead, the bureaucratic struggle that took place between MACV and the CIA resembles the type of event captured by the political process theories advanced by Roger Hilsman, Samuel Huntington, Richard Neustadt, and Warner Schilling.With one important caveat, these theories—reflected in Graham Allison's notion that "players . . . make government decisions not by a single, rational choice but by the pulling and hauling that is politics"—can explain the forces driving the debate over estimates.[59] Allison's explanation takes the rules of the bureaucratic game as a given, but in fact the rules of the game were being contested by MACV and the CIA.[60]

The Order of Battle controversy was a struggle to determine which organization would be able to set the agenda concerning debate about the war: MACV wanted a positive agenda, based upon the ideas of progress and impending success; while the CIA desired a pessimistic agenda that highlighted the relative lack of progress in South Vietnam compared to the resources that had been devoted to the conflict. The organization that lost this struggle would be put on the defensive. It would then have to shoulder the additional burden of proof by first demonstrating how its claims indicated that the prevailing wisdom was wrong.

What kind of evidence would support the contention that the Order of Battle debate was just an instrument in the struggle to determine which assumption would govern debate about the war? Was the United States winning or losing in Vietnam? First, both sides in the debate agreed that there was tremendous uncertainty surrounding an estimate of the VC units that were the focus of Adams's analysis. The majority of CIA analysts and senior agency officials, for example, did not give their unqualified support to Adams's findings. They recognized that Adams's estimates, extrapolated from a detailed study of only one province, were weak. Because so little was known about the clandestine VC units, they also recognized that by changing the assumptions employed by Adams, other analysts could produce different but equally plausible results.[61] Moreover, MACV analysts would have agreed with the idea that the effort to estimate the strength of these VC units was difficult and that it was impossible to develop an exact assessment. MACV and CIA analysts could agree to disagree, creating a situation that was ripe for a compromise that could satisfy everyone except Adams. In fact, SNIE 14.3–67 was produced through compromise: it incorporated the numbers championed by MACV accompanied by the qualifications suggested by the CIA.

Second, just weeks before the Order of Battle controversy reached its peak, MACV analysts made a claim that the crossover point had been reached. The attrition objective had been achieved and by definition the United States was winning the war in Vietnam. MACV analysts always have pointed out, however, that Adams's analysis would have had no effect on their crossover calculations. In a sense they are absolutely correct; the attainment of the crossover point just indicated that enemy losses now exceeded replacements. This number could have been reached if the enemy had 600,000 or 225,000 troops. Yet, this claim does contain a disingenuous element: by projecting a continuous net reduction of two to three thousand soldiers per month from the Order of Battle (for example, the October estimate listed 224,581 for total enemy strength) Westmoreland was able to make the assertion in November 1967 that in two years the American commitment in South Vietnam could be scaled down.[62] If current trends continued. communist forces would have declined to a total strength of about 150,000 (224,581 – 72,000 [3000 per month loss x 24 months] = 152,581). In contrast the light at the end of the tunnel was not so bright if one accepted Adams's analysis: it would take more than twelve years before American forces could begin to withdraw from South Vietnam (600,000 – 432,000 (3000 per month loss x 144 months] = 168,000). If Adams's analysis was accepted, MACV's claim of progress and impending success, based upon achieving the crossover point, would have appeared ludicrous. In effect, CIA officials and analysts used the Order of Battle issue to attempt to undermine claims of progress made by MACV based on crossover calculations.

Although the facts mustered by the CIA in questioning the military's claims of progress in the war were wrong, the general thrust of its critique of American policy has been vindicated by events. Over the years, the American public has been strongly attracted to this aspect of the controversy, especially as the arcane arguments that fueled the debate become increasingly shrouded by the mists of time. Americans are enamored with the image of a lone individual, Sam Adams, struggling against bureaucratic inertia to change the agenda governing discourse on Vietnam. When viewed from this perspective, his charges of conspiracy and malfeasance seem to explain the general failure of American policies in Southeast Asia. In a sense, Adams's accusations serve as a response to the stab-in-the-back thesis that has been suggested by some to explain the Vietnam debacle. The military, according to this argument, did not lose on the battlefields of Vietnam, but in the living rooms of America.[63] Adams's charges suggest that American policies in Vietnam failed not because they were badly conceived, poorly implemented, or lacked sufficient public support. Instead, members of the American military sowed the seeds of the Vietnam fiasco when they deliberately altered and suppressed information that indicated that their policies were failing.

Conclusion

If Adams's estimates were so wrong and his accusations of conspiracy unfounded, then why does his story continue to exert such a strong attraction? One could accuse General Westmoreland, DCI Helms, General Abrams, or senior members of their staffs of bad judgment and even stupidity. But to charge them with deliberately attempting to prevent accurate information from reaching members of the Johnson administration is absurd. Adams's refusal to recognize that honest differences of opinion could exist in the realm of intelligence analysis led him to an error rare among individuals with experience in large governmental organizations. He claimed that the workings of a conspiracy offered a better explanation of the shortcomings of intelligence analysis than human frailty or organizational pathologies.

History will probably depict Adams as a tragic figure who tilted at windmills, a man, according to his colleague George Carver, "who was often in error but seldom in doubt."[64] Adams's estimates were wrong, but he served as the point man for a CIA position that appears to be supported by subsequent events. In a sense, many Americans, including several observers of the Vietnam war, believe that Adams fought for a noble cause. Given this assumption, it is easy for them to ignore the fact that the substance of the claims made by Adams and the CIA were incorrect. Yet, as long as Americans focus on the assertions made by Adams, they will fail to recognize the real tragedies embodied in the debate over enemy strength.

First, most CIA and MACV analysts never looked beyond the bureaucratic ramifications of the controversy: analysis was replaced by continuous recrimination when institutional priorities were threatened. No effort was made to exploit Order of Battle analyses in a way that would assist the actual prosecution of the war. Ironically, Americans only questioned each other about the discrepancy between the estimates contained in captured documents used by Adams and the analyses produced by the best efforts of the entire intelligence community. Instead, MACV and the CIA should have at-

tempted to exploit this discrepancy for intelligence purposes and not as a weapon in bureaucratic battle. In other words, they might have tried to determine what might happen if the communists actually believed the figures that were contained in their secret communications. The Americans might have attempted to identify the opportunities that could become available if the communists possessed an exaggerated sense of their own capabilities. For instance, analysts at both the CIA and MACV dismissed as unrealistic VC calls for civilian help in upcoming attacks (which turned out to be the Tet offensive), because they correctly estimated that the communists lacked widespread support. If they had realized that communist documents indicated that this support was available, they might have recognized one of the warnings they possessed about the impending attacks. In an atmosphere charged by bureaucratic battle, however, this type of analysis was simply not undertaken within the intelligence community.

Second, junior analysts began to champion vigorously their estimates in the policy debates conducted by senior officials. Instead of simply informing their superiors of the conclusions that they had drawn from the analysis of raw data, according to Tom Cubbage, they wanted senior officials ". . . to accept and to act on their intelligence product, no matter what the consequences."[65] A policy-to-please syndrome, to coin a phrase, emerged when analysts pressured intelligence consumers to modify policies in response to estimates. In a strange turn of events, analysts who only focused on small aspects of the war somehow managed to convince themselves and others that they were qualified to address the most important questions of strategy confronting the allies. As a result, the tasks faced by senior officers and officials were complicated by the repeated need to respond to the policy and bureaucratic implications of every turn in the debate over the Order of Battle. Under these circumstances, the Order of Battle controversy became a self-sustaining phenomenon that exerted a disproportionate and ultimately counterproductive influence over commanders and analysts. Mundane efforts to use information to better prosecute the war simply fell by the wayside.

Third, the intelligence-to-please syndrome influenced estimates of enemy strength, especially those produced by officers working as analysts. Personal and institutional considerations apparently influenced the decisions made by middle-level officers to shape the reports produced by junior analysts in a way that supported the policies adopted by the American military. In fact, the Order of Battle controversy demonstrates that military institutions engaged in intelligence work are likely to experience the breakdown in the distinction between intelligence analysis and policy formulation that is at the heart of the intelligence-to-please syndrome. It is extremely difficult for individuals to resist the pressures that emerge when they are asked to evaluate information directly bearing on the performance of their own organizations. Yet, Americans were not prepared in Fall 1967 to deal with the problems generated by civil-intelligence-military relations.[66]

In sum, the negative consequences supposedly produced by Adams's alleged conspiracy pale in comparison to the existing state of affairs within the American intelligence community on the eve of the Tet offensive. Indeed, a breakdown in the distinction between the roles played by intelligence analysts and policy makers produced a situation far more detrimental to American aims in Southeast Asia than the workings of any conspiracy. Ultimately, the Order of Battle controversy created a situation in which the paper war fought in the bureaucracies of Washington and Saigon sometimes took precedence over the shooting war occurring on the battlefields of Vietnam.

Questions for Further Discussion

1. What is "intelligence to please"? Is it different than politicization?

2. What is "policy to please"?

3. What causes intelligence analysts to become preoccupied with the fine points of their analyses, leading them to lose focus on the "big picture"?

4. What special burdens do analysts face in writing estimates when influences resulting from their own institutions or from national policy affect the situation they are reporting on?

Endnotes

1. This is how Mike Wallace characterized the gist of Adam's charges. See "The Uncounted Deception," transcript of 23 January 1982 broadcast on CBS Television Network, 1, listed as Joint Exhibit #1 in *Vietnam: A Documentary Collection—Westmoreland v. CBS* (New York: Clearwater Publishing, 1985; hereafter refered to as *Westmoreland*).

2. Sam Adams, "Vietnam Coverup: Playing War With Numbers," *Harper's*, May 1975, 41–73; and Proceedings of the House Select Committee on Intelligence, 94 Cong. 1st sess., *U.S. Intelligence Agencies and Activities: The Performance of the Intelligence Community* (Washington, DC: U.S. Government Printing Office [hereafter GPO], 1975), 683–692. Although Adams's charges of conspiracy gained the most notoriety and were greeted with the most skepticism by senior government officials, many working-level officials at the CIA, State Department, Defense Intelligence Agency

and even MACV initially found his estimates of enemy strength to be credible. I am indebted to George Allen for emphasizing the importance of this observation.

3. "The Uncounted Enemy; A Vietnam Deception," transcript of 23 January 1982 broadcast on CBS Television Network,1, Joint Exhibit #1 in *Westmoreland*.

4. For a description of the litigation and the issues raised about the role of the media in the controversy, see Renata Adler, *Reckless Disregard: Westmoreland vs. CBS et al; Sharon vs. Time* (New York: Knopf, 1986); Bob Brewin and Sydney Shaw, *Vietnam on Trial: Westmoreland vs. CBS* (New York: Atheneum, 1987); T. L. Cubbage. *"Westmoreland vs. CBS: Was Intelligence Corrupted by Policy Demands?"* in Michael Handel, ed., *Leaders and Intelligence* (London: Frank Cass, 1989), esp. 138–164; and Michael A. Hennessey, "The Uncounted Enemy: A Vietnam Deception Revisited" in David A. Charters and Maurice A. J. Tugwell, eds., *Deception Operations: Studies in the East-West Context* (London: Brassey's 1990), 373–392.

5. Because of the gravity of the accusations leveled by Adams, even scholars who doubted the veracity of his claims address his charges. See Leslie H. Gelb with Richard K. Belts. *The Irony of Vietnam: The System Worked* (Washington, DC: The Brookings Institution, 1978), 131. Neil Sheehan's almost gratuitous reference to Adams's efforts to change the MACV Order of Battle is an example of how the incident has entered the mythology of the war. See Neil Sheehan, *A Bright Shining Lie: John Paul Vann and America in Vietnam* (New York: Random House, 1988), 696.

6. For a discussion of the intelligence-to-please syndrome, see Ariel Levite, *Intelligence and Strategic Surprises* (New York: Columbia University Press, 1987), 16–17; Ephraim Kam, *Surprise Attack: The Victim's Perspective* (Cambridge, MA: Harvard University Press, 1988), 208–209; Handel, ed., *Leaders and Intelligence*, 5.

7. During the fall of 1944, for example, the British 1st Airborne Division conducted a parachute assault against the Rhine River crossing near the city of Arnhem. The division was virtually wiped out, however, when the 9th SS Panzer Division, which was resting in the vicinity of Arnhem, engaged the lightly equipped British paratroopers. Senior British commanders "underestimated" the German presence near Arnhem. For the complete story, see Cornelius Ryan, *A Bridge Too Far* (New York: Simon & Schuster, 1974).

8. The epitome of this fascination with numbers and the use of systems analysis not only to monitor but to prosecute the war more effectively (that is, generate high body counts) can be found in Julian J. Ewell and Ira A. Hunt, *Sharpening the Combat Edge: The Use of Analysis to Reinforce Military Judgment* (Washington, DC: Department of the Army, 1974). For a fine critique of this emphasis on quantitative measures, see Martin Van Creveld, *Command in War* (Cambridge, MA: Harvard University Press, 1985), 252–254.

9. For a discussion of the HES, see Douglas S. Blaufarb, *The Counterinsurgency Era: U.S. Doctrine and Performance* (New York: Free Press, 1977), 248–249; and Timothy J. Lomperis, *The War Everyone Lost—And Won* (Baton Rouge: Louisiana State University Press, 1984), 70–71.

10. For the attrition objective set at the 1966 Honolulu Conference, see "1966 Program to Increase the Effectiveness of Military Operations and Anticipated Results Thereof," (drafted by Bill Bundy and John McNaughton) Joint Exhibit #215D in *Westmoreland*.

For a description of the importance of this memo in terms of the American ground strategy for the war, see "Letter from Westmoreland to E.H. Simmons, 27 May 1978," Joint Exhibit #215B, 3, in *Westmoreland;* William C. Westmoreland, *A Soldier Reports* (Garden City, NY: Doubleday, 1976), 160–161; and "BDM Study Vol VI," Joint Exhibit #318A, 3–26, 3–27 in *Westmoreland.*

11. MSG, COMUSMACV, 2412272 Jan 67, Subj: Command Guidance, in Headquarters United States Military Assistance Command, Vietnam, Command History 1967 vol. I (San Francisco: Headquarters USMACV, 1968), 326.

12. The American intelligence community accepted the following definitions for these units: VC main force (MF) units were directly subordinate to Central Office for South Vietnam (COSVN) or VC HQ, a VC military region HQ, or subregion HQ; VC local force units were directly subordinate to a provincial or district party committee and normally operated only within a specified VC province or district; NVA units were formed, trained, and designated by North Vietnam as an NVA unit and were composed completely or primarily of North Vietnamese; irregulars were organized units composed of guerrilla, self-defense. and secret self-defense forces subordinate to village and hamlet level VC organizations that performed a wide variety of missions in support of VC activities. Their regulars also served as a manpower base for both NVA and VC combat units. Guerrillas were full-time forces organized into squads or platoons that did not always stay in their village or hamlet. They usually engaged in tax collection, propaganda, terrorism, sabotage, or the protection of village party committees. Self-defense forces were paramilitary units that defended hamlets and villages controlled by the VC. These forces did not leave their home areas, and they performed their duties (propaganda, construction, and home area defense) on a part-time basis. Secret self-defense forces were a clandestine VC organization that conducted the same type of operations in villages under the control of the government of Vietnam (GVN) that were conducted by self-defense forces in VC controlled areas. See USMACV Ac of S J-2, PERINTREP (Periodic Intelligence Report), February 1967, vi–vii (hereafter referred to as PERINTREP and date).

13. The American intelligence community accepted the following definitions for these categories. "Maneuver units: infantry, armor, security, sapper and reconnaissance elements from platoon level upward, regardless of subordination. Combat support units: fire support, anti-aircraft, and technical service units organized at battalion level and above and not classified under administrative services. Separate fire support companies are classed as combat support. Administrative service units: military personnel in identified COSVN, military region, military subregion, province, and district staffs, and rear service technical units of all types directly subordinate to these headquarters," PERINTREP, February, 1967, vi.

14. These are the major weaknesses of Order of Battle estimates that were identified by members of the Defense Intelligence Agency, the National Security Agency, the Central Intelligence Agency, MACV, the Office of the Secretary of Defense, and officers attached to the HQ of the Commander in Chief Pacific. See "Report of the Honolulu Conference to Standardize Methods for Developing and Presenting Statistics on Order of Battle, Infiltration Trends and Estimates, 6–11 February 1967," Joint Exhibit #227, 8, contained in *Westmore-*

land. For an insightful discussion of the problem, see Bruce Palmer, *The 25-Year War* (Lexington: University Press of Kentucky, 1984), 79.

15. For Graham's description of how he conducted his "crossover analysis," see Daniel O. Graham, Oral History I, 24 May 1982, interviewed by Ted Gittinger, 7, 9, Lyndon Baines Johnson Library, Austin, TX. For a discussion of Graham's June 1967 Crossover Memo, which served as the basis of the claim made in the June 1967 MOP that the crossover point had been reached, see "Adams' William Westmoreland Chronology," Joint Exhibit #64. 11–12; "Adams' James Meacham Chronology," Joint Exhibit #58, 39, both in *Westmoreland* and Daniel O. Graham's testimony contained in *U.S. Intelligence Agencies and Activities: Risks and Control of Foreign Intelligence,* 1682. For a discussion of the contents of the June 1967 MOP, see Douglas Kinnard, *The War Managers* (Hanover NH: University Press of New England, 1977), 69–70. The MACV Measurement of Progress Report was issued on a monthly basis by MACV J-3 and was based on selected data on VC personnel and weapons losses, VC initiated incidents, the number of Hoi Chanhs (defectors), and Order of Battle data on combat, support, irregular, and political personnel. The MOP was distributed to National Agencies higher and lateral commands, subordinate MACV commands, and "other" addressees. See "Report of the Honolulu Conference to Standardize Methods for Developing and Presenting Statistics on Order of Battle, Infiltration Trends and Estimates," Joint Exhibit #227; "Annex C-Index of Current Periodic Reporting on Enemy Strength, Dispositions, Gains, Losses, and Base Areas," C-4, both in *Westmoreland.* In a 28 April 1967 meeting with the president, for example, Westmoreland had made a more limited claim about reaching the crossover point in all but the two northern most provinces of South Vietnam. See *The Pentagon Papers as Published by the New York Times* (New York: Bantam Books), 568; "William Westmoreland Interview Transcript" with Mike Wallace, 17 May 1981, Joint Exhibit #349, 23–24, in *Westmoreland.*

16. "Criles Notes on Charles Morris Telephone Interview" (no date), Joint Exhibit #37A, 2–3, in *Westmoreland.* It should be noted, however, that Morris also stated that enemy losses no longer exceeded replacements by the late fall of 1967 because of an increase in NVA infiltration.

17. For an example of this skepticism, which includes the assertion that the crossover point had not been reached, see "5/23/67, Central Intelligence Agency, 'The Vietnam Situation: An Analysis and Estimate,'" Joint Exhibit #347, in *Westmoreland.*

18. Daniel Graham confirms this division of responsibilities between MACV and the CIA. See Graham, *Oral History I,* 32.

19. For example, in the May 1967 CIA assessment, analysts cited MACV numbers but noted that the estimates presented in the MACV Order of Battle were extremely conservative. See Daniel O. Graham, *Oral History II,* 8 November 1982, interviewed by Ted Gittinger, Lyndon Baines Johnson Library, 2. On the reasons why the CIA never devoted the resources needed to duplicate MACV Order of Battle estimates, see "Monograph by Allen 'Indochina War—1950–1975,'" Joint Exhibit #313, 312, in *Westmoreland.* On the role of the NSA see Graham, Oral History I, 15.

20. John Ranelagh, *The Agency: The Rise and Decline of the CIA* (New York: Simon & Schuster, 1987) 455, 459;

"Monograph by Allen 'Indochina War—1950–1975,'" Joint Exhibit #313, 312; and "Memo 12/2/66 from Adams to Chief, Indochina Division," Joint Exhibit #222, 3, both in *Westmoreland*. Adams began his examination of VC strength following the conclusion of a study he conducted of VC desertion rates. Adams estimated that between 50,000 and 100,000 VC deserted their units every year. When this figure was combined with the approximately 150,000 casualties the allies inflicted on the enemy every year, Adams's analysis indicated that the war should have been coming to a close because of VC losses (270,000 – 250,000 = 20,000). Adams, after being told by George Allen that the official estimate of enemy strength was "suspect" started his work on the VC Order of Battle. See Cubbage, "*Westmoreland vs. CBS*." 125–126; and Adams, "Vietnam Coverup," 41–42.

21. Adams stated that in comparison to the number carried by the MACV Order of Battle, "the 248 number of Viet Cong is closer to 600,000, and perhaps more." See "Memo 12/19/66, from Adams to Director OCI [Office of Current Intelligence]," Joint Exhibit #2244, 2, in *Westmoreland*. For a more formal statement of Adams's position and the report of the number contained in the MACV Order of Battle on 3 January 1967, see "Memo 1/11/67 from Carver to Deputy Director for Intelligence," Joint Exhibit #226, in *Westmoreland*.

22. Cubbage, "*Westmoreland vs. CBS*," 128. Needless to say, the fact that these senior officials were aware of the possibility that the Order of Battle was in need of revision, even before the issue became heated, provides strong evidence against Adams's conspiracy thesis.

23. Thomas Powers, *The Man Who Kept the Secrets: Richard Helms and the CIA* (New York: Knopf, 1979), 187–189. Powers states that this conference was held in mid-January 1967, but the official report issued at the end of the conference states that it was held between 6–11 February 1967.

24. "5/23/67, Central Intelligence Agency, 'The Vietnam Situation; An Analysis and Estimate,'" II-1.

25. Ibid., II-2.

26. "SNIE 14.3–67 Capabilities of the Vietnamese Communists For Fighting in South Vietnam, 13 November 1967,"Joint Exhibit #273, I, in *Westmoreland*. For a discussion of SNIEs and National Intelligence Estimates (NIEs), see Walter Laqueur, *A World of Secrets* (New York: Basic Books, 1985), 32–37; and Richard K. Betts, "Strategic Intelligence Estimates; Let's Make Them Useful," *Parameters* 10 (December 1980): 20–26.

27. "Cable 6/2/67 from Adams to Sandine," Joint Exhibit #239B, 1–2, in *Westmoreland*.

28. Graham, *Oral History II*, 15.

29. "Cable 8/20/67 from Abrams to Wheeler, Sharp, Westmoreland," Joint Exhibit #252B, 1–2, in *Westmoreland*.

30. "George Allen 5/25/81 Interview Transcript," Joint Exhibit #7, 9; "Adams' Notes on William Westmoreland," Joint Exhibit #191, 57; and "William Westmoreland Interview Transcript," with Mike Wallace 17 May 1981, Joint Exhibit #349, 30, in *Westmoreland*. George Allen maintains that this position on VC irregulars was not held by all officers at MACV; some believed that the self-defense and the secret self-defense forces did pose a serious military threat. See "Monograph by Allen 'Indochina War—1950–1975,'" Joint Exhibit #313.

31. "Gains Hawkins 3/8/81 Interview Transcript," Joint Exhibit #9, 67; and "William Westmoreland Interview Transcript" with Mike Wallace 17 May 1981, Joint Exhibit #49, 29–30, both in *Westmoreland*.

32. "Cable 8/30/67 from Westmoreland to Wheeler, Sharp," Joint Exhibit #253A, in *Westmoreland*.

33. Paul Nitze made this accusation. See Westmoreland, *A Soldier Reports*, 193, 416.

34. "Cable 3/11/67 from Wheeler to Westmoreland," Joint Exhibit #233, 4, in *Westmorland*.

35. "Cable 6/2/67 from Adams to Sandine," Joint Exhibit #239B, 2–3, in *Westmoreland*.

36. For a characteristic example of the position taken by CIA analysts on the Order of Battle issue, see "Cable 9/12/67 from Carver to Helms," Joint Exhibit #258AA, in *Westmoreland*.

37. For the protests against ONE'S move, see "Cable 8/19/67 from Komer to Carver," Joint Exhibit #250; "Cable 8/19/67 from Davidson to Godding," Joint Exhibit #251A; "Cable 8/20/67 from Abrams to Wheeler, Sharp, Westmoreland," Joint Exhibit #252B; "Cable 8/20/67 from Westmoreland to Wheeler, Sharp," Joint Exhibit #253A; and "Cable 8/25/67 from Westmoreland to Sharp," Joint Exhibit #255. For the JCS request to have the DCI (Helms) settle the dispute and for the personnel he sent to Vietnam on his behalf, see "Cable 8/29/67 from Carver to Saigon," Joint Exhibit #220BB. For a discussion of the meetings between the CIA delegation and MACV representatives, see "Cable 9/11/67 from Carver to Helms," Joint Exhibit #256B; "Cable 9/12/67 from Carver to Helms," Joint Exhibit #258E; "Cable 9/12/67 from Carver to Helms," Joint Exhibit #258AA; "Cable 9/13/67 from Carver to Helms," Joint Exhibit #259B; and "Cable 9/14/67 from Carver to Helms,"Joint Exhibit #260B. For the claim that Helms compromised with MACV over the Order of Battle estimate in order to avoid a "split" NIE, see "Monograph by Allen 'Indochina Wars—1950–1975,'" Joint Exhibit #313; 315, all in *Westmoreland*.

38. For Carver's requests to MACV for a copy of the "Crossover Memo," see "Cable 9/12/67 from Carver to Helms," Joint Exhibit #258E, 3. CIA analysts eventually received a copy of the June 1967 MACV "Crossover Memo" sometime in early November 1967. See "11/14/67 Ron Smith re: The Crossover Memo," Joint Exhibit #710. For a copy of the proposed MACV press briefing, see "Memo 10/10/67 from Henkin to Carver," Joint Exhibit #263. For the reaction of analysis at CIA Headquarters to the proposed MACV press briefing, see "Memo 10/11 /67 from Walsh to Carver," Joint Exhibit #265A; and "Memo 10/13/67 from Carver to Goulding," Joint Exhibit #266, all in *Westmoreland*.

39. Herbert Y. Schandler, *The Unmaking of a President* (Princeton, NJ: Princeton University Press, 1977), 74.

40. Although estimates of the number of communist soldiers participating in the Tet offensive vary, Daniel Graham states that 85,000 was the largest estimate that was ever brought to his attention. See Graham, *Oral History I*, 11. The low estimate of the number of communist soldiers participating in Tet—58,000—was turned in by the CIA. See "2/68 CIA Memo on Communist Units Participating in Tet Offensive," Joint Exhibit #713, 1, in *Westmoreland*. In an interview with the author, George Allen noted that the CIA estimate of 58,000 for the number of soldiers participating in the offensive was made soon after the eruption of the Tet attacks and was based upon limited information.

41. Adler, *Reckless Disregard*, 202.

42. For the warning to field interrogators, see "Cable 2/18/68 from Carver to Saigon," Joint Exhibit #296A, in *Westmoreland*.
43. "4/22/68 Westmoreland Cable to Sharp and Wheeler," Joint Exhibit #403, in *Westmoreland*.
44. Graham, *Oral History II*, 16.
45. Douglas Pike, "The Tet Offensive: A Setback for Giap, But Just How Big?" *Army* 18 (April 1968): 61.
46. Douglas Pike. *Oral History I*, 4 June 1981, interviewed by Ted Gittinger, 36, Lyndon Baines Johnson Library, Austin, TX.
47. Pike and Graham both make this point. See Pike, "The Tet Offensive," 61; and Graham, *Oral History I*, 11.
48. "Cable 8/20/67 from Abrams to Wheeler, Sharp, Westmoreland," in *Westmoreland*, 2.
49. Ranelagh, *The Agency*, 459; and "Russell Cooley 4/9/81 Interview," Joint Exhibit #11, 6, in *Westmoreland*.
50. "11/15/67 Memo From Rostow to LBJ," [including Memo from Helms] Joint Exhibit #963, 3, in *Westmoreland*.
51. Brewin and Shaw, *Vietnam on Trial*, 29–30.
52. Robert Ruhl Simmons "Tet 1968: The Political Ingredients of Military Defeat," (Unpublished Paper, Harvard University, 1978), 17–18; Deborah Fitts, "Robert Simmons Recalls Enemy Strength Tinkering," *The Westerly Sun*, 18 February 1985. Tim Lomperis also has described a similar experience that occurred while he was a junior analyst attached to MACV Headquarters in 1973. See Lomperis, *The War Everyone Lost—and Won*, 71–72. II Field Force was a major Headquarters that commanded American forces in the provinces that surrounded Saigon.
53. On this point, see Adler, *Reckless Disregard*, 239–240.
54. On this point, see Edward N. Luttwak, *The Pentagon and the Art of War* (New York: Simon and Schuster, 1984), 196; and Patrick J. McGarvey, "DIA: Intelligence to Please" in Morton Halperin and Arnold Kanter, eds., *Readings in American Foreign Policy* (Boston: Little, Brown, 1973), 318–328.
55. For a similar point, see Van Creveld, *Command in War*, 254–255.
56. On the pressures faced by officers who serve as intelligence analysts and evaluate the performance of their particular service, see Michael Handel, "The Politics of Intelligence," *Intelligence and National Security* 12 (October 1987): 18; and Gelb with Betts, *The Irony of Vietnam*, 309.
57. "11/15/67 Memo from Rostow to LBJ," (including Memo from Helms) Joint Exhibit #963, 2, in *Westmoreland*.
58. Adler makes this observation about the attitude of officers engaged in Order of Battle work for MACV. See Adler, *Reckless Disregard*, 113.
59. Graham T. Allison, *Essence of Decision* (Boston: Little, Brown, 1971), 144; Roger Hilsman, "The Foreign-Policy Consensus: An Interim Report," *Journal of Conflict Resolution*, 3 (December 1959): 361–382; Roger Hilsman, *To Move a Nation* (Garden City, NY: Doubleday, 1967), esp. parts 1, 2, and 10; Samuel P. Huntington, *The Common Defense: Strategic Programs in National Politics* (New York: Columbia University Press, 1961); Richard Neustadt, *Presidential Power: The Politics of Leadership* (New York: John Wiley, 1960); and Warner Schilling, "The Politics of National Defense: Fiscal 1950" in Warner R. Schilling, Paul T. Hammond, and Glenn H. Snyder, eds., *Strategy, Politics and Defense Budgets* (New York: Columbia University Press, 1962).
60. Allison, *Essence of Decision*, 170.
61. Ranelagh, *The Agency*, 459–460. In fact, during his testimony at the *U.S. v. Russo and Ellsberg* litigation in early 1973, Adams even admitted the difficulties inherent in estimating VC strength: "Now, even in the guerrillas . . . you are not absolutely sure how many to count. The same problem arises with the Self-Defense, Secret Self-Defense and particularly the Political Cadre. . . . It is very difficult to decide who to count." See Adler, *Reckless Disregard*, 196; and Cubbage, "*Westmoreland vs. CBS*," 136–137.
62. Westmoreland made the prediction during an address to the National Press Club in Washington, DC. See "21 November 1967 Westmoreland Speech to the National Press Club," Joint Exhibit #360, 9, in *Westmoreland*.
63. Jeffrey P. Kimball, "The Stab-in-the-Back Legend and the Vietnam War," *Armed Forces and Society* 14 (Spring 1988); 433–458.
64. Carver quoted in Adler, *Reckless Disregard*, 199.
65. Cubbage, "*Westmoreland vs. CBS*," 167.
66. Michael Handel has already noted that the topic of civil-military-intelligence relations largely remains unexamined. He has called for the development of a theoretical framework, patterned after Samuel Huntington's *The Soldier and the State*, to study this relationship. See Handel, ed., *Leaders and Intelligence*, 4. ✦

Reprinted with permission from James J. Wirtz, "Intelligence to Please? The Order of Battle Controversy During the Vietnam War," *Political Science Quarterly* 106 (Summer 1991): 239–263.

16
Public Intelligence

Glenn Hastedt

In this discussion of the controversial issue of intelligence "leaks," Glenn Hastedt explores why policymakers go public with classified information. Moving beyond the often-voiced complaint that leaks have a fleeting effect but can seriously compromise intelligence "sources and methods," Hastedt provides an analysis of circumstances that turn policymakers toward "public intelligence." He finds that there is no single motive or objective behind the effort to use classified information to bolster policy positions. By identifying a new realm of interaction among the intelligence community and policymakers, Hastedt suggests that leaks of classified information are an increasingly common form of intelligence politicization.

'We were almost all wrong.' This was the conclusion reached by David Kay about the assertion that Iraq possessed weapons of mass destruction.[1] Kay was the United States' top weapons inspector in the period leading up to the Iraq War and his admission pointed to the presence of a serious intelligence failure on the part of the US intelligence community. Intelligence analysis by governments is conducted in secret. This is true regardless of whether the sources used are open or restricted and whether the analysis is competitive or consensual. Our thinking about intelligence takes this context of secrecy as its foundational reference point. Yet intelligence does not always remain secret. On occasion it becomes public. A review of instances where intelligence has become public shows that it does so in a variety of ways. The two key dimensions are whether it is contested or not and whether it is sustained over time or an isolated occurrence. Four patterns emerge: promotional, orchestrated, warring, and entrepreneurial. This stands in sharp contrast to the almost universal tendency to combine all such instances under the single heading of 'leaks'. Doing so obscures the underlying dynamics of public intelligence, the forces that give rise to it, and the potential consequences that public intelligence has for secret intelligence. The need for systematic attention to public intelligence is seen both in past examples of its occurrence and most recently by the manner in which intelligence was used during the buildup to the Iraq war.

Public Intelligence

Conventional accounts of intelligence failures focus on the dynamics of the intelligence process and the inherent difficulty of anticipating events in world politics.[2] These explanations are inadequate because the world of 'secret' intelligence coexists with the world of 'public' intelligence. Its internal dynamics contributes both to the occurrence of specific intelligence failures and, if unchecked, to cumulative degradation of the overall quality of intelligence.

Public intelligence is not a new phenomenon but it is one that has risen in prominence due to several reinforcing changes in the complexion of American politics. By public intelligence we refer to secret intelligence that has become part of the societal debate over the conduct of American foreign policy. One is the change in the nature of legislative-executive relations in foreign policy. The period of bipartisanship, to the extent that it existed, has long since ended. So too has the notion of two presidencies in which the president was de facto granted far greater powers to deal with foreign policy issues than he was to deal with domestic policy problems. In their place we find presidents and legislators suspicious of each other's agenda and in competition to control the direction of American foreign policy. These conflicts are most pronounced in periods of divided government but are present even when one party is in control of both branches. Contributing to this institutional competition is the lack of a foreign policy consensus among the public at large or elites. The broad areas of agreement on the content and conduct of American foreign policy that existed prior to the Vietnam War has yet to be reconstructed. If anything the passage of time and repeated controversies over the use of force have deepened the dividing lines on foreign policy and made them more evident. Finally, there is the changed nature of media coverage of foreign policy events. The advent of 24 hour per day/seven days per week news programming with its heavy emphasis on breaking news, visual images, and instant (and conflicting) expert opinion places great obstacles in the way of an administration's efforts to demonstrate that it is on top of a situation, present its foreign policy in a positive light, speak with one voice, and avoid the appearance of engaging in ad hoc policy making.

These three features, institutional rivalry, lack of foreign policy consensus, and increased media coverage, combine to create a foreign policy making environment that accentuates the normal advantage held by immediate policy questions and current intelligence over long-range issues. It also favors the politics of confrontation and competition over that of problem solving. Placed in this setting secret intelligence becomes a tantalizing resource not simply for its ability to shed light on a situation but for its ability to alter the political logic by which decisions are made in the broader political arena. But in order to do so, it must stop being secret and become public.

Secret intelligence becomes public intelligence through unauthorized leaking of secret intelligence, the sanitized release of secret material, or public references to sources and analyses. It does not become public in a uniform manner. We can distinguish between four different patterns depending upon whether the leaked intelligence emerges in a sustained or episodic fashion and whether or not it is contested. The four patterns are presented in Table 16.1.

Table 16.1
Patterns of Public Intelligence

		Time Frame	
		Episodic	Sustained
Contested	*Uncontested*	**Promotional**	**Orchestrated**
	Contested	**Entrepreneurial**	**Warring**

When secret intelligence is leaked in an episodic manner and is uncontested then public intelligence is promotional intelligence. Here we have secret intelligence being made public largely on a 'one-shot' basis and under circumstances where it is not countered by the leaking of contrary secret intelligence. The essential purpose of public intelligence under these circumstances is either to draw attention to oneself or to a policy problem, or to defend or distance oneself from a policy failure. President Dwight Eisenhower made intelligence public in this fashion in the aftermath of the failed Paris Summit meeting with Nikita Khrushchev. In a nationally televised address from the Oval Office he showed a U-2 photograph of the North Island Naval Air Station in San Diego. Trying to build support for his open skies program he noted: 'I show you this photograph as an example of what could be accomplished through United Nations aerial surveillance.' In releasing this photo he rejected calls from his advisors that he make public actual U-2 photographs

of the Soviet Union. Nevertheless, releasing even these photos made public a secret intelligence capability.[3]

On 14 April 1969 a North Korean MIG fighter shot down a US navy aircraft in international airspace. Intelligence concluded that the attack was a command and control accident. The Nixon administration adopted a different position. It held the North Korean attack to be calculated and premeditated. In a news conference a few days after the attack Nixon asserted the North Koreans knew what they were doing 'because we know what their radar showed. We, incidentally, know what the Russian radar showed'. This was the first public revelation of American capabilities to read North Korean and Russia radar systems.[4]

Another example of promotional public intelligence comes from late in the Ford administration. The B Team report on Soviet strategic capabilities was completed on 2 December 1976. This report was highly critical of the intelligence community's established view of the Soviet threat. Within a few weeks its conclusions were leaked to the press.[5] The incoming Carter administration engineered its own promotional leak of intelligence. On 18 April 1977 Carter delivered a nationwide address in which he stressed the seriousness of the energy crisis facing the United States. To support his cause he released a declassified 18-page CIA report, 'The International Energy Situation: Outlook to 1985'. The Senate Select Committee on Intelligence publicly challenged the conclusions of the report but it did say the episode had 'understandably given rise to questions about his [Carter's] use of intelligence'.[6]

President Reagan engaged in promotional public intelligence in trying to garner support for his 'Star Wars' initiative. In a nationally televised March 1983 speech he denounced the Soviet Union as an 'evil empire'. Two weeks later he went on television and put forward his strategic defense initiative. In the course of his presentation he made public a wide range of imagery intelligence that included photos of a large Soviet Sigint station in Cuba, Soviet arms shipments to Cuba and Nicaragua, and the construction of an airfield on Grenada.[7]

More recently promotional public intelligence surfaced in 1998. The United States and North Korea were engaged in a complex diplomatic enterprise as the Agreed Framework began to come undone. The *New York Times* ran a prominent story asserting that 'U.S. intelligence agencies had detected a huge secret underground complex in North Korea that they believed to be the centerpiece of an effort to revive the country's frozen nuclear weapons program, according to officials who have been briefed on the intelligence information'.[8] The origins of the story have been linked to the head of the Defense Intelligence Agency who regularly gave information to Republican congressmen. Two days after it appeared the Pentagon said the site was a large hole in the ground and said it had no evidence that North Korea was not abiding by the Agreed Framework.

When secret intelligence is contested and episodic in public then it becomes entrepreneurial intelligence. As with promotional public intelligence, entrepreneurial intelligence involves a burst of leaked intelligence focused on a specific issue. This time, however, more is involved here than drawing attention to a situation. Public intelligence is entrepreneurial in the sense that it is being used in a competitive environment. The opponent, so to speak, is not inertia or a policy stream that appears to be set in motion without opposition. Here, public intelligence is used in a competitive environment in which both sides to a dispute are using intelligence to advance or block a policy. The objective is to convince consumers (policy makers) that their position is superior politically or strategically to that being offered by a competitor. A prime example comes from the Carter administration and the 'discovery' of a Russian combat brigade in Cuba by the National Security Agency.

The Central Intelligence Agency (CIA) gave an ominous interpretation to this revelation. When briefed on the situation Senator Frank Church, who was in a difficult and ultimately unsuccessful re-election campaign, went public with the story. Church was a highly visible and outspoken opponent of US foreign policy in Vietnam and the Third World. In 1975 he was named chair of the Senate Select Committee to Study Governmental Operations with Respect to Intelligence Activities. It investigated allegations of CIA abuses of power and assassination plots. Now Church was on the political defensive. He was accused of being soft on communism for meeting with Fidel Castro. Church went public with this intelligence as a means of re-establishing his foreign policy credentials. He then demanded that Strategic Arms Limitation Talks (SALT II) be cancelled unless the brigade left immediately. President Carter responded by going on television and stating 'we have concluded, as the consequences of intensified intelligence efforts, that a Soviet combat brigade is currently stationed in Cuba . . . it is not an assault force. . . its purpose is not clear . . . this status quo is not acceptable'. Not surprisingly his statement did not effectively counter Church's charges. In fact, the reality was that Kennedy had agreed in 1963 that a Soviet brigade could remain in Cuba. Carter refused to admit that

his administration and the intelligence community had forgotten this. Instead twice more Carter would go on television referencing intelligence in an attempt to establish that his administration was on top of matters and that the situation did not present a security threat. One time he declared: 'American intelligence has obtained persuasive evidence that . . . it presents no threat to us.' The other time he spoke of increasing American intelligence capabilities.[9]

A third situation emerges when leaked intelligence is carried out on a sustained basis and is uncontested. In this instance public intelligence is orchestrated intelligence. Secret intelligence is being leaked on a systematic basis in order to advance a policy position. More often than not orchestrated public intelligence will emanate from the executive branch. It has greater access to the products of the intelligence community and it is responsible for the selection and execution of foreign policy. In situations where public intelligence is orchestrated no significant amount of countering public intelligence or assertions relating to intelligence capabilities or analysis are aired to challenge the position being advanced although the position itself may be challenged by Congress or other political actors.

One example of orchestrated public intelligence occurred during the missile gap controversy in the late 1950s over the relative strengths of the US and Soviet nuclear forces. Beginning in the mid 1950s the Air Force began providing a 'steady stream of sensitive information' to sympathetic members of Congress. Foremost among them were Senators Henry 'Scoop' Jackson and Stuart Symington who frequently aired alarmist interpretations of the situation.[10] Symington often referred to information in National Intelligence Estimates (NIEs) that contradicted the Eisenhower administration's less alarmist position on the issue. One such instance was in 1958 when in rejecting the administration's estimates of Soviet missile strength he publicly asserted that he had 'other' intelligence on the matter.

Intelligence also made its way to the press. Joseph and Stuart Alsop repeatedly referred to intelligence reports and capabilities in their articles and columns. In 1956 they wrote that 'it could positively be stated that no Soviet Inter-Continental Ballistic Missile (ICBM) test had not yet occurred' but that American intelligence routinely underestimated Soviet nuclear developments by two years and that current American intelligence estimates predicted a test in 1958. In 1957 Stuart Alsop followed with a column in which he stated that the United States possessed 'convincing evidence' that the Soviet Union had tested an experimental version of a very long range ballistic missile. The story was confirmed a few days later by the *New York Times*. In

1958 one of their columns leaked the projected range of the Soviet ICBMs contained in intelligence estimates. In 1957 *Newsweek* ran a story on DCI Allen Dulles and an NIE prediction that the Soviet Union would have an operational ICBM capability by the end of 1959.

The Kennedy administration engaged in the practice of orchestrated public intelligence during the Cuban missile crisis. The first public showing of intelligence came in Great Britain on 23 October 1962. Prime Minister Harold Macmillan had requested that the BBC be permitted to show photos of missile sites in order to build support for the American position in the British public. American intelligence officials had convinced Secretary of Defense Robert McNamara not to release these pictures for fear of giving the Soviet Union information they might lack on the state of American photo reconnaissance capabilities. Yet the Kennedy administration soon used photo intelligence to build its case at the United Nations with great effect. On 25 October Adlai Stevenson, the American ambassador to the United Nations, displayed a series of U-2 photographs documenting the construction of Soviet missile sites at San Cristobal and Guanajay.[11]

Another example of orchestrated intelligence comes from the Reagan administration. It involved the North Korean attack on a South Korean jet liner, KAL 007, on 1 September 1983. The plane had veered off course into Soviet airspace when it was shot down. The Reagan administration was first to go public with the announcement. Secretary of State George Shultz stated there was no doubt that the pilot of the North Korean MIG knew he was attacking a civilian airliner because Russian radar had tracked KAL 007 for two hours and the pilot had reported the shoot-down to authorities on the ground. Soon after Shultz's statement it became increasingly clear to American intelligence officials that the attack actually may have been an accident. The administration, however, pressed ahead with its case. On 4 September President Reagan played Sigint recordings of conversations between the pilot and authorities detailing his actions leading up to firing his missile and his reaction to destroying KAL 007. Reagan made these excerpts public the next day. Jeanne Kirkpatrick then used a longer excerpt from the Sigint intercepts in making the American case at the United Nations.

Finally, secret intelligence may become public intelligence when it is leaked on a sustained and contested basis. The result is warring intelligence. The competition need not be equal but the overall effect of having contending accounts of a situation emerge from secret intelligence over a protracted period of time is to preclude the emergence of a clear end point to the policy debate. Rather than pursuing a 'sale' and moving on to other policy issues, here the opposing sides are involved in a siege in which the objective is to wear challengers down to the point where their opposition is no longer politically significant. Warring intelligence is not inevitable even where a policy debate exists. Secrecy may hold in parts of the national security establishment and its oversight system even when intelligence is becoming public from other parts.

One long running episode of warring intelligence centered on the state of the US-Soviet strategic balance in the late 1960s. By the late 1960s the focus of this policy debate had shifted from the performance capabilities of the Soviet Anti-Ballistic Missile (ABM) system to the need for an American ABM system and the capabilities of the Soviet SS-9. The technical issue here was whether or not the SS-9 had multiple warheads or multiple independently targeted warheads. The political issue was whether or not to fund the Safeguard ABM system requested by the Nixon administration. Much testimony was presented to Congress including assertions by Secretary of Defense Melvin Laird as to the need for the Safeguard system. After listening to the conflicting testimony Senator Albert Gore publicly asserted that the 'National Intelligence Estimate does not concur with the statements made by Dr. Foster [Director of Defense, Research and Engineering at the Pentagon] and by Mr. Laird'. Laird was publicly on record as having asserted that the Soviet Union was undertaking an arms buildup that would give it a first strike capability against the United States. Shortly after Gore's statement information on the contents of a new estimate were leaked to the press revealing CIA disagreements with the Pentagon over the extent of the SS-9's capabilities.

In a June 1969 press conference Nixon sought to build public support for the Safeguard system by publicly referencing secret intelligence. He asserted:

> in recommending Safeguard, I did so based on intelligence information at that time. Since that time new intelligence information with regard to the Soviet success in testing multiple entry vehicles . . . has convinced me that Safeguard is even more important . . . there isn't any question that it [SS-9] has a multiple weapon and that its footprints indicate that it just happens to fall in somewhat the precise area in which our Minuteman silos are located.[12]

Laird went on the offensive in March 1970 when he charged that 'for some time, the Soviet forces which became operational in a given year have often exceeded the previous intelligence projections for that year'. To support his case Laird released the national estimate projections for 1966–70.[13] Later that year, Laird showed reporters film of Soviet multiple warhead tests to bolster his case.[14]

Warring intelligence also surfaced during the Reagan administration. It came into office determined to change the direction of American foreign policy toward Central America from one emphasizing human rights to one centered on halting the spread of communism through the region. El Salvador was the first target for this reversal in policy. In 1981 the State Department released a White Paper citing documents considered to be authoritative as indicating that in late 1980 the Soviet Union and Cuba agreed to deliver weapons to the Marxist guerrillas operating in that country. Secretary of State Alexander Haig stated that this was an example of unprecedented risk taking on the part of the Soviet Union and a challenge to the future of American-Soviet relations. Instead of galvanizing American support for a policy change the White Paper provoked great debate. Soon after its release *New York Times* columnist Flora Lewis wrote of the existence of a 29-page dissenting paper within the intelligence community. Among the arguments it made was that intelligence not supporting the administration's desired change in policy was suppressed. Later news stories questioned the translation of various materials cited and Haig's allegations that the intelligence available pointed to unprecedented Soviet risk taking. In March 1982, as the El Salvadoran elections neared, the Reagan administration released some previously classified intelligence reports to bolster its position. In congressional testimony Haig described the intelligence as providing 'overwhelming and unrefutable' evidence that the Salvadoran guerrillas were under foreign control. To further its case the State Department publicly presented an alleged Nicaraguan rebel leader operating in El Salvador. Much to the embarrassment of the State Department he recanted his story. Next the administration released intelligence photos showing a military buildup in Nicaragua. The photos were from an SR 71A spy plane rather than a satellite to try and protect its true capabilities. The potential benefits of this revelation were quickly negated by a *Washington Post* story that the administration had secretly authorized the spending of $19 million to train a 500-person paramilitary force to attack Nicaraguan power plants and bridges as well as disrupt the flow of weapons to El Salvador. There was further damaging news for the administration in November when *Newsweek* ran a story revealing the existence of a covert war to overthrow the Nicaraguan government and the US involvement in training and organizing the Contra rebel forces in Honduras. The culmination of this political conflict in which warring intelligence played a central part was the passage of the Boland Amendment that barred the use of US funds to overthrow the Nicaraguan government.

Characteristics and Consequences of Public Intelligence

Regardless of which of these four forms public intelligence takes, it has a set of common characteristics. First, public intelligence is incomplete intelligence. It is intelligence out of context. The purpose of public intelligence is not to tell the whole story but to highlight a certain aspect of a policy problem. Second, public intelligence is action prompting. Good intelligence needs to be policy relevant but it does not dictate policy. Public intelligence takes on an oracle quality in which it appears to be revealing some divine truth that theretofore has been hidden from view. It gives the impression that great dangers await unless some now self-evident action is taken. Third, public intelligence is accusatory. The guilty party changes. It may be a policy maker who has failed to take appropriate action, another country that has not lived up to its word, or an intelligence agency that has not performed up to standard. Fourth, public intelligence lacks nuance. Under the best of circumstances it is difficult to express the level of certainty that exists in intelligence analysis and to highlight those aspects of a situation that are known and those that are unknown. Public intelligence is presented with an aura of certainty and conviction. All of the uncertainty that surrounds the analytic process is absorbed leaving an absolutist quality. Finally, there is little, if any, penalty for being wrong. Public intelligence achieves its desired impact not through the qualities of good 'secret' intelligence presented earlier but through the ability to move the public debate and the range of acceptable policy options. In this respect the reach and staying power of bad news far exceeds that of good news. It becomes the intelligence of choice regardless of its insightfulness.

Beyond distorting the analytic process and the intelligence product that emerges from it, these characteristics of public intelligence contribute to intelligence failures in other ways. Public intelligence makes achieving consensus more difficult because it raises the stakes for organizations and individuals by calling into question their competence and integrity. This is most notably the case where leaks are systematic and lead to blame laying and scapegoating. The challenge to consensus building exists at multiple levels. Not only does it affect the ability of highly visible policy makers to work out policy agreements, it also complicates the efforts of those working anonymously within the intelligence community to forge a consensus on how to interpret the information they have. Beyond making the achievement of consensus more difficult, public intelligence has the potential for reducing viable policy options. It does so both by presenting a problem in stark black and white terms and in ways that lend themselves to first case thinking. This creates the potential for masking a policy failure under the guise of an intelligence failure. Finally, another consequence is the loss of credibility for intelligence products. The cumulative effect of making intelligence public over time and across policy arenas is to call into question the value of future intelligence and produce calls for the reform and restructuring of the intelligence community. The danger is that the organizational reforms will not address (and cannot address) all the factors that contributed to the intelligence failure. As a consequence not only will there be the inevitable future intelligence failure but there may also occur a spiraling public distrust of intelligence.

Public Intelligence and the Iraq War: A Case Study

The George W. Bush administration engaged in a campaign of orchestrated public intelligence in the lead-up to the Iraq War that was part of the administration's broader campaign to build support for the war. It was not an entirely one-sided campaign as doubts were expressed about the quality of the intelligence being cited by the administration. The challenges did not, however, take the form of leaked secret intelligence or the release of sanitized secret intelligence. They either were public rebuttals based on conclusions reached by others who examined the same data or secret doubts raised by intelligence agencies. In the case study that follows both the intelligence made public by the administration and commentary about its accuracy are presented.

The campaign to build support for the war began in August 2002 with two comments made by Vice President Cheney. The first came on 7 August. Responding to a question at the Commonwealth Club in San Francisco, Cheney said 'it is the judgment of many of us that in the not too-distant future he [Saddam Hussein] will acquire nuclear weapons'. In a speech to the National Convention of the Veterans of Foreign Wars on 26 August which referenced intelligence in highlighting the threat posed by Saddam Hussein, Cheney stated 'there is no doubt that Saddam Hussein has weapons of mass destruction'. He continued, 'we now know that Saddam has resumed his efforts to acquire nuclear

weapons. Among other sources we've gotten this from firsthand testimony from defectors, including Saddam's own son-in law, who was subsequently murdered at Saddam's direction'. Hussein Kamel, Saddam's son-in-law, managed Iraq's special weapons program until he defected to Jordan in 1995. He was killed in February 1996. The actual information he gave contradicted Cheney's public interpretation of it. Kamel stated Iraq's uranium enrichment program had not been restarted after the 1991 Persian Gulf War.[15]

Also in August 2002 under the direction of Chief of Staff Andrew Card the Bush administration set up a White House Iraq Group (WHIG) to ensure that the various parts of the White House were working in harmony on Iraq.[16] The group met weekly. Its members were Karl Rove, the president's senior political advisor; Karen Hughes, Mary Matlin, and James Wilkinson, communications strategists; Nicholas Calio, legislative liaison; Condoleezza Rice, national security advisor and her deputy Stephen Hadley; and I. Lewis Libby, Cheney's chief of staff. In a 6 September interview with the *New York Times* Card hinted that the purpose of the unit was to sell the war. He observed, 'from a marketing point of view, you don't introduce new products in August'.[17]

WHIG formed a strategic communications task force to work on speeches and white papers dealing with Iraq. The first White Paper produced, 'A Grave and Gathering Danger: Saddam Hussein's Quest for Nuclear Weapons', went through at least five drafts but was never published. Working with administration officials beyond those in WHIG the document brought together intelligence reports and press clippings. It contained the claim that Iraq 'sought uranium oxide, an essential ingredient in the enrichment process from Africa'. It claimed that a satellite photograph shows 'many signs of the reconstruction and acceleration of the Iraqi nuclear program'. And it stated that 'since the beginning of the nineties, Saddam Hussein has launched a crash program to divert nuclear fuel for . . . nuclear weapons'. None of these assertions was accurate but all would appear in later administration statements. The claim that Iraq sought uranium from Africa was false. The second claim left out a statement by United Nations Chief Weapons Inspector Hans Blix that 'you don't know what's under them [the buildings in the photos]'. The third claim was presented as if referring to the current situation rather than the early 1990s as was actually the case.

President Bush and British Prime Minister Tony Blair met at Camp David on 7 September and each made public pronouncements regarding the seriousness of the threat. Blair cited a report from the International Atomic Energy Agency (IAEA) showing 'what's been going on at the former weapons sites' and Bush said an IAEA report placed Iraq 'six months away from developing a [nuclear] weapon. I don't know what more evidence we need'. Neither reference was to a contemporary IAEA report. In Blair's case he was referencing news reports. President Bush was citing an IAEA report written in 1996 and updated in 1998 and 1999. It stated that

> based on all credible information to date, the IAEA has found no indication of Iraq having achieved its program goal of producing nuclear weapons or of Iraq having retained a physical capacity for the production of weapon usable nuclear material or having clandestinely obtained such material.

The report did say that before the Gulf War Iraq was six months to a year away from having a nuclear capacity.

The following day the *New York Times* quoted anonymous administration officials on Iraq's possession of aluminum tubes whose specifications made them ideally suited as component parts of a centrifuge. That morning Rice, Cheney, Rumsfeld, and Secretary of State Colin Powell made appearances on TV talk shows. Rice stated on CNNs 'Late Edition' that 'we do know that there have been shipments going . . . into Iraq, for instance of aluminum tubes that really are only suited to . . . nuclear weapons programs, centrifuge programs'. She noted that 'there will always be some uncertainty about how quickly he can acquire nuclear weapons . . . but we don't want the smoking gun to be a mushroom cloud'. Cheney on NBC's 'Meet the Press' in speaking of the Iraqi nuclear program said 'increasingly we believe the United States will become the target'. Rumsfeld on CBS's 'Face the Nation' asked viewers to imagine an 11 September with weapons of mass destruction.[18]

Next to speak for the administration was President Bush. At the United Nations on 12 September he repeated the charge that Iraq 'has made several attempts to buy high strength aluminum tubes used to enrich uranium for a nuclear weapon. Should Iraq acquire missile material, it would be able to build a nuclear weapon within a year'. Seized shipments were cited as proof. To buttress its case, the same day that Bush addressed the UN the administration released a background paper, 'A Decade of Deception and Defiance: Saddam Hussein's Defiance of the United Nations'. Included in the section on 'the Development of Weapons of Mass Destruction' were already public references to a 2001 Iraqi defector who said he visited 20 chemical, biological, and nuclear weapons facilities there and a public re-

port by the International Institute for Strategic Studies purporting to show that Saddam Hussein could build a bomb in months if he were able to obtain the necessary missile material.

One week after Bush spoke to the UN, Rumsfeld told the Senate Armed Services Committee that 'at this moment' Iraq was trying to obtain the material needed to complete a nuclear weapon. On 26 September President Bush continued this theme of certainty stating 'the Iraq regime possesses biological and chemical weapons. The Iraq regime is building the facilities necessary to make more biological and chemical weapons'. The president's comments came around the same time a classified Defense Intelligence Agency document concluded that 'no reliable information on whether Iraq is producing or stockpiling chemical weapons or whether Iraq has or will establish its chemical agent facilities'.[19]

The charge that Iraq sought aluminum tubes in order to produce nuclear material originated within the US government with a CIA engineer-turned-analyst.[20] It was presented to UN nuclear inspectors in January 2002. His interpretation was not uniformly accepted by the intelligence community. Centrifuge scientists working for the Department of Energy were among those who rejected it. Controversy within the intelligence community over how to interpret the purpose of the aluminum tubes continued until September 2002 when it became necessary to take a position in the NIE that was about to be released. When put to a vote the Energy Department and State Department's Bureau of Intelligence and Research said no. The four other intelligence agencies participating in the deliberations, the Defense Intelligence Agency, the National Image and Mapping Agency, the National Security Agency, and the CIA, said 'yes'. The NIE was released affirming the interpretation stating that 'most analysts' believed the aluminum tubes were intended for a centrifuge.

The validity of these allegations was quickly challenged. The Institute for Science and International Security (ISIS) in a report cited by the *Washington Post* asserted that 'by themselves, these attempted procurements are not evidence that Iraq is in possession of, or even close to possessing nuclear weapons. . . . They do not provide evidence that Iraq has an operating centrifuge plant'.[21] The IAEA report also charged, and the administration acknowledged, that not all in the intelligence community agreed with the administration's public assessment of the situation.

In early March 2003, prior to the beginning of the war, Mohamed El Baradei, director general of the IAEA, rejected the Bush administration's assertion that Iraq had sought to purchase aluminum tubes in order to produce nuclear-grade material. The IAEA undertook an intensive investigation into the aluminum tubes allegation after it returned to Iraq in November. Its preliminary conclusion, reached in January 2003, was that the aluminum tubes were 'not directly suitable' for centrifuges. More likely they were to be used in the production of conventional artillery rockets. In its March report the IAEA noted that Iraq had tried unsuccessfully for 14 years to make these 81 mm tubes that would resist corrosion and perform well. In the course of these failures they had progressively raised the technical standards of the tubes they sought. Additionally, the ISIS concluded that the presence of 'anodized' features in the tubes that Powell would report to the UN in February 2003 actually increased the likelihood that they were for rockets and not centrifuges. The Institute reported that Powell's staff was briefed on this point prior to the address.[22]

The assertion that Iraq was trying to obtain 'significant quantities of uranium from Africa' emerged in a 50-page intelligence report released by British Prime Minister Tony Blair on 24 September.[23] The report also indicated that Iraq could deploy nerve gas and anthrax weapons within 45 minutes of being ordered to do so by Saddam Hussein. On the question of Iraq's ability to build a nuclear weapon the report put forward a one to two year time frame should UN sanctions be lifted. President Bush said Iraq could do so within one year. The report became the center of controversy after David Kelly, a senior British weapons expert, committed suicide on 18 July 2003 following his testimony to a parliamentary committee investigating a BBC report that Blair's government had 'sexed up' the report by exaggerating the claim that Iraq could deploy chemical or biological weapons in 45 minutes. Kelly was the suspected source of this allegation. Evidence revealed that Kelly had made a more subtle argument, similar to one that American intelligence officials would make regarding the accuracy of the Bush administration's caricature of Iraq's weapons of mass destruction capability. He told another BBC reporter that 'it was a statement that was made and it just got all out of proportion. . . . In the end it was just a flurry of activity and it was very difficult to get comments in because people at the top of the ladder didn't want to hear some of the things'. Memos revealed that the phrase 'may be able to deploy' became 'are able to deploy'.[24] Kelly concluded that he did not think Blair's staff was being 'willfully dishonest' but that they had changed the wording for 'public consumption', 'to put things into words that the public will understand'.[25]

On 2 October, between President Bush's address to the United Nations and his speech in Cincinnati on 7 October in which he stated 'the evidence indicates Iraq is reconstituting its nuclear weapons program' and that 'satellite photographs reveal that Iraq is rebuilding facilities at sites that have been part of its nuclear program in the past', the administration released a White Paper based on the classified NIE it had just produced. Entitled, 'Iraq's Weapons of Mass Destruction Program', its lead 'key judgment' was that 'if left unchecked it [Iraq] probably will have a nuclear weapon during this decade'. In the body of the text it stated:

> Baghdad could produce a nuclear weapon within a year if it were able to procure weapons-grade missile material abroad. Baghdad may have acquired uranium enrichment capabilities that could shorten substantially the amount of time necessary to make a nuclear weapon.[26]

The White Paper repeated the conclusion expressed by Bush on 26 September that Baghdad 'has chemical and biological weapons' and that it 'has begun renewed production of chemical warfare agents'. The White Paper also contained maps and aerial photographs and made the case that new construction facilities were related to Iraq's nuclear program. One month before the war began personnel on the ground were able to verify that this interpretation was inaccurate.

In Bush's 7 October speech the president stated: 'we have discovered through intelligence that Iraq has a growing fleet' of unmanned aircraft and worried they might be targeted on the United States. He also asserted that in 1998 'information from a high-ranking Iraqi nuclear engineer who had defected revealed that despite his public promises, Saddam Hussein had ordered his nuclear program to continue'. This could, Bush continued, provide weapons of mass destruction to terrorist groups or allow Iraq to attack the United States. Left unsaid in these intelligence revelations was the fact that the defector, Khidhir Hamza, while he defected in 1998, had not worked in Iraq's nuclear program since 1991 and the conclusion that Iraq could attack the United States was counter to secret congressional testimony provided by the CIA. This testimony was declassified after Bush's speech. In it the CIA rated as 'low' the possibility that Iraq would initiate a chemical or biological attack on the United States but might take the 'extreme step' of assisting terrorist groups if provoked.[27]

The next major salvo involving the orchestrated use of public intelligence came in President Bush's 28 January 2003 State of the Union Address. In it he stated: 'the British government has learned that Saddam Hussein recently sought significant quantities of uranium from Africa'. Shortly after the 11 September 2001 terrorist attacks the CIA received information from Italy's Military Intelligence and Security Service that in February 1999 Iraq's ambassador to the Vatican had openly traveled to Niger and a few other African states. No particular importance was attached to the trip at the time. Now Italy's intelligence service raised the possibility that the purpose of the mission was to purchase uranium ore, Niger's major export.

The report was not met with widespread credence within the intelligence community for a number of reasons, including the absence of corroborating documentation. The report was, however, stovepiped to high ranking administration officials including Vice President Cheney who would engage in a 'year long tug of war' with the agency over the truthfulness of the Italian theory. By early 2002 public references to Iraq's attempted purchase of uranium were appearing. The CIA stated 'Baghdad may be attempting to acquire materials that could aid in reconstituting its nuclear weapons program' in a declassified report given to Congress shortly after the president's State of the Union address. Powell told the House International Affairs Committee that 'with respect to the nuclear program, there is no doubt that the Iraqis are pursuing it'.

In an effort to resolve questions over the report's authenticity the CIA arranged for retired Ambassador John Wilson to fly to Niger to investigate the matter in February 2002. The trip lasted eight days and Wilson concluded the allegations were without merit. He could find no evidence that a document arranging for such a sale was signed and concluded that there was not any uranium available for export since all of it had been pre-sold. The first press accounts of Wilson's trip surfaced 15 months after his trip and the affair quickly became entangled in revelations from the White House that Wilson's wife was a CIA employee. The allegations were first publicly refuted just prior to the beginning of the Iraq War when IAEA Director Mohamed El Baradei declared key documents that had been given to the IAEA in February 2003 by the CIA to be forgeries. The CIA had come into possession of these documents in October 2002 when an Italian journalist turned them over to the American embassy in Rome. It considered the documents to be of 'dubious authenticity' and little value since they contained no new information.[28]

After the war had ended, in July 2003, it was revealed that on two occasions in October 2002 the CIA raised strong doubts about the Niger-Iraq uranium connection. The CIA warned in memos that the allegation that Iraq had tried to acquire 500 tons of uranium from Niger rested on weak evidence and was not particularly significant. It also came to light that DCI George Tenet called Steven Hadley, Condoleezza Rice's assistant, the day before President Bush's 7 October Cincinnati speech and got him to agree to remove this reference ('The regime

has been caught attempting to purchase substantial amounts of uranium oxide from sources in Africa') from that speech.[29]

Still, this same reference appeared in Bush's State of the Union address in slightly altered form. A few days before the speech Robert Joseph, a presidential assistant for nonproliferation, asked the CIA if the reference to Iraq's attempted purchase of 500 tons of uranium from Niger could be included in the State of the Union address. Alan Foley, the CIA official contacted, objected to mentioning Niger and the specific amount. Joseph agreed but countered by suggesting that more general language could be used, noting the British intelligence report's less precise language. Foley responded that the CIA had objected to this formulation too but the British went ahead with it using their own sources.[30]

Public intelligence was at the heart of Secretary of State Powell's 5 February 2003 address to the UN Security Council. A few days before the speech, he cautioned observers that he would not present a 'smoking gun'. In making his case, however, he affirmed that 'every statement I make today is backed up by sources, solid sources. . . . These are not assertions. What we are giving you are facts and conclusions based on solid intelligence'. Powell was accompanied by DCI George Tenet in a move intended to symbolize the certainty of the information that he presented in his 90-minute multimedia presentation that included photographs, intercepted phone conversations, and charts linking Iraq to al-Qaeda.

Powell stated: 'we know from sources that a missile brigade outside Baghdad was dispersing rocket launchers and warheads containing biological agents to various locations'. UN weapons inspector David Kay would later report that he found no evidence that 'any chemical weapons were present on the battlefield, even in small numbers'. Powell also asserted that the United States has 'satellite photos that indicate banned materials have recently been moved from a number of Iraqi weapons of mass destruction facilities'. The material Powell identified was used for hazardous material transfers. Missiles identified in the photos were later destroyed by UN weapons inspectors. Powell also affirmed that 'we have first hand descriptions of biological weapons factories on wheels and rails'. President Bush would later cite the capture of two of these facilities as proof that Iraq had weapons of mass destruction.[31] UN weapons inspectors concluded that they were not suitable for this purpose and the CIA also had its doubts. He claimed that 'we know Iraq has embedded key portions of its illicit chemical weapons infrastructure within its legitimate civilian industry'. Kay reported that evidence indicates Iraq did not have a large centrally controlled chemical weapons program after 1991 and that all remaining stocks were destroyed after 1995. Finally, Powell stated: 'we have detected one of Iraq's newest UAVs [unmanned aerial vehicles] in a test flight that went 500 kilometers . . . Iraq could use these small UAVs . . . to deliver biological agents to its neighbors or if transported to other countries, including the United States'. Iraq did have a large UAV program. It was used for surveillance. Kay stated that it did not have a deployment capability and had not successfully been mounted with a chemical sprayer.

President Bush would publicly reference intelligence at least twice more before the war began. In his 8 February 2003 radio address to the nation he stated: 'we have sources that tell us that Saddam Hussein recently authorized Iraqi field commanders to use chemical weapons'. Then, in delivering his final ultimatum to Iraq on 17 March, the president told the nation that 'intelligence gathered by this and other governments leaves no doubt that the Iraq regime continues to possess and conceal some of the most lethal weapons ever devised'.[32]

Iraq War Public Intelligence Post Mortem

The characteristics and consequences of public intelligence identified earlier were on display in the buildup to the Iraq War and the postwar debate. The incompleteness of the public intelligence was evident in the outdated nature of much of the information on Iraq's weapons of mass destruction program and the controversial nature of the interpretations given to it. After the war Paul Wolfowitz acknowledged there had been a tendency to emphasize weapons of mass destruction because of differences in the administration over the strength of other charges such as its ties to al-Qaeda.[33] The public intelligence was action-prompting. It was used to paint a picture of grave and imminent threat. Additional on-site weapons inspections would take too much time. Congressional authorization of military actions could not wait until after the November elections but had to be given before then.

The public intelligence was accusatory. Saddam Hussein was the villain. It was his actions that public intelligence documented. He had created the foreign policy problem facing the United States. Moreover, since he had demonstrated a ruthless willingness to use military force, repeatedly broken his word and engaged in deception there could only be one interpretation of his actions. On 2 December 2003 White House press secretary Ari Fleischer observed that 'Saddam Hussein would be misleading the world' by denying that he had weapons of mass destruction. 'You've heard the president say repeatedly that he has chemical and biological weapons'.[34] Public intelligence was presented in absolute terms.

Intelligence analysts noted that they were not responsible for the manner in which it was presented to the public. One senior official stated that 'the president's speechwriters took "literacy license" with intelligence'.[35] Another said 'we were careful about language, and it's not fair to accuse the analysts for what others say about our material'.[36] After the war the administration took two different positions on the strength of the intelligence it used. Wolfowitz expressed both views. On one occasion he asserted 'there was no oversell'.[37] On another he commented 'If there's a problem with intelligence . . . it doesn't mean anybody misled anybody. It means that intelligence is an art and not a science'.[38] Finally, public intelligence such as that concerning the aluminum tubes or the attempted purchase of uranium from Niger continued to be aired even as support for these interpretations from the intelligence community disappeared. They continued to be good stories even though they were based on bad intelligence.

Turning to the broader consequences of public intelligence, evidence of scapegoating was easy to find. For three weeks in July 2002 a battle raged over who was responsible for the '16 words' in Bush's 2003 State of the Union address that referenced Iraq's attempt to buy uranium from Africa. Initially President Bush and national security advisor Condoleezza Rice blamed the CIA. DCI Tenet accepted responsibility for the statement. The laying of blame on the CIA did not end the controversy. By the end of the month Bush accepted 'personal responsibility' for the matter. In February 2004 Tenet made a public speech at Georgetown University in which he defended the CIA's analysis of information before the war and rejected charges that political considerations had affected the intelligence product. Never, he said, did the intelligence community say 'there was an imminent threat' and that 'no intelligence agency thought that Iraq's efforts had progressed to the point of building an enrichment facility or making missile material. We said such activities were a few years away'.[39]

Public intelligence also limited options. In February 2004, Colin Powell commented that he did not know if he would have recommended an invasion of Iraq had he known that it did not possess a stockpile of banned weapons.[40] Powell is speaking to the accuracy of the intelligence but, in part, this misses the point. Public intelligence directs our attention not to its accuracy but the manner in which intelligence is used. What made changing direction difficult is the way in which public intelligence raises the stakes of a decision and casts problems in simple terms. Here, public intelligence was being used—and being used by the president—to justify war. And, as Walter Pincus noted in his *Washington*

Post article on the allegation that Iraq tried to buy uranium in Africa, Bush kept repeating the charge because by the time he gave his 2002 State of the Union address 'almost all other evidence had either been undercut or disproved by UN inspectors in Iraq'.[41] It was all he had left. If intelligence was preventing a shift in policy it was not secret intelligence that was doing so but public intelligence.

Loss of confidence in the intelligence community was not long in coming. Congressional investigations were launched into the quality of the intelligence available to the Bush administration in the period leading up to the war and how intelligence was used by the White House.[42] Overseas, the Polish government expressed concern that it had been misled by prewar intelligence claims. Perhaps most telling, the accuracy of the intelligence community's prewar assessments became part of a larger questioning of its abilities in the 9-11 Commission's public hearings into that day's tragedies.

Conclusion

The surprise Japanese attack of 7 December 1941 on Pearl Harbor cemented in the minds of policy makers the importance of information for the conduct of American foreign policy. Yet for many years little scholarly attention was given to intelligence. It was a largely unexamined area of American national security policy. In one sense we are far removed from this state of neglect. Memoir accounts by intelligence professionals and policy makers have provided us with great insight into the role played by intelligence and intelligence organizations in the making of American foreign policy. Congressional hearings and investigations have provided still another entry point into the practice of intelligence. Case studies of surprise have generated concepts and frameworks that permit comparisons across time and space. As a consequence we are now able to move beyond identifying and debating the elements of intelligence and begin to explore creating theories of intelligence.[43] At the same time there are still gaps in our understanding of intelligence. One of these is the political reality that not all intelligence remains secret. Sometimes it becomes public intelligence. The framework presented here demonstrates that there is no single pattern to the process by which secret intelligence becomes public intelligence. It is not enough to simply refer to it as leaked intelligence. Further development of theories of intelligence must incorporate this public dimension of intelligence into its analysis if our understanding of the interplay of intelligence and policy is to move forward. The case study of orchestrated intelligence in the lead-up to the Iraq War presented here highlights one pattern of public intelligence. It reveals the underlying characteristics of public intelligence and demonstrates the negative consequences it has for the intelligence function and the ability of intelligence agencies to provide credible and timely advice to policy makers.

Questions for Further Discussion

1. What is promotional intelligence?

2. Under what circumstances should policymakers release classified information to the public?

3. Did policymakers deliberately mislead the public about alleged Iraqi activities in Niger, or did their statements accurately reflect intelligence estimates?

4. Is there a single process whereby secret intelligence becomes public?

Endnotes

1. 'Kay: "We were almost all wrong" ', *Washingtonpost.com*, 28 January 2004, 12:50 pm.
2. See Mark Lowenthal, *Intelligence: From Secrets to Policy*, 2nd edn. (Washington, DC: Congressional Quarterly Press, 2003), pp.108–10; Shlomo Gazit, 'Intelligence Estimates and the Decision Maker', *Intelligence and National Security*, 3 (1988), pp.261–7; and Alfred Maurer et al. (eds.), *Intelligence: Policy and Process* (Boulder: Westview Press, 1985).
3. Christopher Andrew, *For the President's Eyes Only: Secret Intelligence and the American Presidency from Washington to [H.W.] Bush* (New York: Harper Collins 1995), p.249.
4. Ibid., p.357.
5. Ibid., p.424.
6. Ibid., p.432.
7. Ibid., p.471.
8. Chalmers Johnson, *Blowback: The Costs and Consequences of American Empire* (New York: Owl Books 2000), p.134.
9. Andrew, *For the President's Eyes Only* (note 3), p.445.
10. John Prados, *The Soviet Estimate* (Princeton, NJ: Princeton University Press 1986), p.59.
11. Andrew, *For the President's Eyes Only* (note 3), pp.295–8.
12. Ibid., pp.357–8.
13. Prados, *The Soviet Estimate* (note 10), p.193.
14. Ibid., p.195.
15. Sounding the Drums of War, *The Washington Post*, 10 August 2003, p.A9.
16. Barton Gellman and Walter Pincus, 'Depiction of Threat Outgrew Supporting Evidence', *The Washington Post*, 10 August 2003, p.A1.
17. Ibid.
18. Sounding the Drums of War, *The Washington Post*, 10 August 2003, p.A9.
19. Dana Priest and Walter Pincus, 'Bush Certainty on Iraq Arms Went Beyond analysts' Views', *The Washington Post*, 7 June 2003, p.A1.

20. Gellman and Pincus, 'Depiction of Threat Outgrew Supporting Evidence' (note 16).
21. Joby Warrick, 'Evidence on Iraq Challenged', *The Washington Post*, 19 September 2003.
22. Joby Warrick, 'Some Evidence on Iraq Called Fake', *The Washington Post*, 3 March 2003.
23. Glenn Frankel, 'Blair: Iraq Can Deploy Quickly', *The Washington Post*, 25 September 2002.
24. Glenn Frankel, 'Blair Aides Shaped Iraq Dossier', *The Washington Post*, 23 August 2003, p.A14.
25. 'British Court Hears Arms Expert on Tape', *The Washington Post*, 14 August 2003, p.A12.
26. Iraq's Weapons of Mass Destruction Programs, October 2002. <www.cia.gov/cia/reports/iraq>.
27. Dana Milbank, 'For Bush, Facts Are Malleable', *The Washington Post*, 22 October 2002.
28. Walter Pincus and Dana Priest, 'U.S. Had Uranium Papers Earlier', *The Washington Post*, 18 July 2003, p.A1.
29. Walter Pincus and Mike Allen, 'CIA Got Uranium Mention Cut in Oct', *The Washington Post*, 13 July 2003, p.A1; Dana Milbank and Walter Pincus, 'Bush Aides Disclose Warning From CIA', *The Washington Post*, 23 July 2003, p.A1; and Walter Pincus, 'Bush Team Kept Airing Iraq Allegation', *The Washington Post*, 8 August 2003, p.A10.
30. Pincus and Priest, 'U.S. Had Uranium Papers Earlier' (note 28).
31. Mike Allen, 'Bush: "We Found Banned Weapons",' *The Washington Post*, 31 May 2003.
32. Dana Milbank, 'Bush Remarks Confirm Shift in Justification for War', *The Washington Post*, p.A1. 1 June 2003, p.A18.
33. Karen DeYoung and Walter Pincus, 'U.S. Hedges on Finding Iraqi Weapons', *The Washington Post*, 29 May 2003, p.A1.
34. Milbank, 'Bush Remarks Confirm Shift in Justification for War' (note 32).
35. Gellman and Pincus, 'Depiction of Threat Outgrew Supporting Evidence' (note 16).
36. 'Transcript: CIA Director Defends Iraq Intelligence', *Washingtonpost.com*, 5 February 2004.
37. DeYoung and Pincus, 'U.S. Hedges on Finding Iraqi Weapons' (note 33).
38. Walter Pincus and Dana Priest, 'Lawmakers Begin Iraq Intelligence Hearings', *The Washington Post*, 19 June 2003, p.A16.
39. A transcript of his comments is available at <washington post.com>: 'Tenet: Analysts Never Claimed Imminent Threat Before War'.
40. Glenn Kessler, 'Powell Says New Data May Have Affected War Decision', *The Washington Post*, 3 February 2004, p.A1.
41. Walter Pincus, 'Bush Faced Dwindling Data on Iraq Nuclear Bid', *The Washington Post*, 16 July 2003, p.A1.
42. Dana Priest, 'House Probers Conclude Iraq War Data Was Weak', *The Washington Post*, 28 September 2003, p.A1; and Walter Pincus, 'Intelligence Weaknesses Are Cited', *The Washington Post*, 29 November 3002, p.A18.
43. See, for example, Loch Johnson, 'Preface to a Theory of Strategic Intelligence', *International Journal of Intelligence and Counterintelligence*, 16 (2003), pp.638–63; and David Kahn, 'An Historical Theory of Intelligence', *Intelligence and National Security*, 16 (2001), pp.79–92. ✦

Reprinted with permission from Glenn Hastedt, "Public Intelligence: Leaks as Policy Instruments—The Case of the Iraq War," *Intelligence and National Security* 20 (September 2005): 419–439.

Part V

Intelligence and the Policymaker

Barnado: "Sit down awhile
And let us once again assail your ears,
That are so fortified against our story."

—*Shakespeare*, Hamlet, *1.1.31–33*

Policymakers—elected officials, career civil servants, and senior military officers—have an extraordinarily important part to play in the intelligence cycle. They are the individuals who must develop or change policy in response to the estimates and reporting produced by the intelligence community. Without effective communication among policymakers and intelligence analysts and managers, there is simply no way to put intelligence to good use in making and conducting foreign or defense policy.

Lines of Communication

Although the September 11 tragedy is reshaping the lines of communication between the intelligence community and policymakers, intelligence managers and analysts direct most of their efforts toward five clients within the U.S. government. First and foremost is the president and his immediate staff. The relationship with this client is crucial and is often handled personally by the Director of National Intelligence (DNI). Occasionally, when the issues are important or the topics under consideration are complex or highly technical, the DNI (or, prior to 2005, the DCI) will bring analysts to the White House or the old Executive Office Building to brief the president or members of his staff. In the past, some DCIs were not particularly welcome at the White House, but most have served as the Chief Intelligence Officer to the president.

Second, the intelligence community maintains close links with the National Security Council (NSC), which supports the president in his conduct of U.S. foreign and defense policy. The NSC is staffed by military officers, political appointees, career civil servants, and intelligence professionals who are experts on various issues and regions. The intelligence community supports the NSC as it works to coordinate foreign and defense policy across a variety of government agencies and the military services and as it monitors policy implementation.

Third, intelligence managers and analysts have traditionally forged relationships with political appointees and senior career civil servants throughout the Defense and State departments. In the Defense Department, the intelligence community focuses on providing information to the civilians within the Office of the Secretary of Defense and the military officers who fill the ranks of the Joint Staff. These contacts within cabinet departments and with the Joint Staff are important, because these individuals make recommendations that are used by top staffers directly supporting the president in the formulation of national policy. These officials also make sure their own organizations work faithfully to implement policy generated by senior members of the administration. In the aftermath of September 11, interaction is also increasing with the Departments of Justice, Commerce, Treasury, Agriculture, and Homeland Security, under the guidance of the DNI.

Fourth, the intelligence community interacts with individual members of Congress, Congressional committees, and their staffs. In this role, intelligence managers provide not only finished intelligence to elected officials but also information related to Congressional oversight of the activities of the intelligence community (Lowenthal 2006).

The intelligence community also is a great contributor to the *interagency process,* a system of consultations between mid-level officials over the formulation and conduct of foreign and defense policy. All organizations with a vested interest in the policy at hand are asked to arrive at a consensus that they can support. The interagency process can be cumbersome because it must accommodate multiple players with a variety of interests and because it gives tremendous power to holdouts—organizations that demand specific concessions to move forward with policy. The interagency process thus affects the intelligence community in two ways: (1) by the policies that flow from the interagency process, and (2) by contributing intelligence materials that influence the nature of the interagency debate. Because they share the same long-term perspective on policy, career civil servants and intelligence professionals often have more common positions with each other in interagency debates than they do with the political appointees who face severe time constraints in terms of achieving their objectives.

The Role of Policymakers

Policymakers obviously need to use intelligence to advance national objectives, but they also play an important part in other functions of the intelligence cycle. Policymakers often have a great deal to say when it comes to setting intelligence requirements—that is, identifying topics that should be of interest to the intelligence community when it comes to collecting data and producing finished intelligence. Policymakers generally leave the technical and often arcane process of collecting information to intelligence professionals, although they sometimes intervene if intelligence operations pose grave political or military risks. The U-2 reconnaissance program attracted the attention of senior officials because of the risks of using aircraft to overfly Soviet or Cuban territory in the late 1950s and early 1960s. Policymakers can also turn to the intelligence community with specific requests for information that help them devise policy or political positions, a process that can lead to frustration if policymakers hold unrealistic expectations about intelligence capabilities. Policymakers tend to think that experts and information on just about everything reside somewhere within the intelligence community, an expectation that ignores budgetary and bureaucratic reality (Lowenthal 2006). The risk of intelligence politicization also looms large if policymakers begin to see intelligence as simply another weapon in partisan politics.

The intelligence community would not exist if it were not for policymakers' need to make foreign and defense policy. But intelligence managers sometimes are wary of policymakers and worry about sharing too much sensitive intelligence. There is always a risk that officials will leak classified information to the media. Officials "leak" for a variety of reasons (see Glenn Hastedt's chapter on "public intelligence" in this volume). Sometimes they leak classified information to score political points by bolstering their position or damaging the position of their opponents. Sometimes they leak information to focus government or public attention on a problem they believe is being overlooked. Sometimes they leak information because they like to feel important; journalists might even be expected to return a favor by putting a positive news spin on one's pet policy or by writing a favorable story about one's performance in office. Most of the time, the information that is leaked is of transient importance. However, some leaked information can cause grave damage to national security or destroy the effectiveness of intelligence programs created at enormous expense. A September 1971 *Washington Post* article written by Jack Anderson is a case in point. Anderson wrote that U.S. intelligence organizations, in Operation GUPPY, were intercepting telephone calls made by Politburo members from their limousines as they drove around Moscow (Anderson 1973). Soon after the report, the transmissions ceased. What is maddening from the perspective of the intelligence community is the fact is that these "leakers" are rarely if ever identified, reprimanded, or prosecuted for releasing classified information. Most intelligence officials probably would wish that Anderson had not written the story, but they are most critical of the government official (who of course might have been a member of the intelligence community) who gave Anderson the piece of information in the first place.

Occasionally, the president and his closest advisers decide to reveal classified information as part of a deliberate effort to build public and international support for national policy. Today, the public has almost come to expect that U.S. administrations will present their case using classified information—radio intercepts, pictures taken from reconnaissance satellites, or even agent reports. Although the president is within his rights to authorize the use of classified material in a public forum to support national policy, members of the intelligence community consider this type of action to be a mixed blessing. They recognize the enormous impact that classified information can have on public opinion, but they worry that using current intelligence in this way can compromise sources and methods. In other words, revealing classified information provides clear indications to opponents about how the intelligence community collects and analyzes data. Even though it might seem unlikely that publicly revealing a reconnaissance photo can do lasting damage, revelations of classified data can have a cumulative effect. Over time, those targeted by the intelligence community can build a good picture of how information is gathered and analyzed, allowing them to identify and rectify vulnerabilities that were being exploited for the purposes of intelligence collection. Intelligence managers and analysts focus on these long-term consequences when classified data are made public. They tend to worry that their future ability to collect and analyze information is being mortgaged to meet today's political demands.

Intelligence for the Policymaker

The relationship between the intelligence community and policymakers also varies in terms of the nature of the information supplied to senior officials. *Warning intelligence* informs policymakers about direct and immediate threats to national security or the impending failure of foreign policy. To produce warning intelligence, however, someone has to designate exactly what needs to be monitored. Intelligence analysts would prefer for policymakers to give them a list of people, places, or things that should be watched closely, while policymakers would rather deliver blanket orders to the intelligence community to take all necessary steps to avoid being surprised. If a warning needs to be delivered, analysts then face the problem of getting busy policymakers to pay attention to what at first glance might appear to be some minor disturbance (after all, warnings of potential disasters always appear less threatening than actual disastrous events). Sometimes, analysts face the opposite problem: They have to communicate to policymakers that signs of impending danger are overblown. Analysts have to place alarming news or diplomatic reporting in an analytical or historical context, and sometimes they have to convince policymakers not to overreact to events that appear threatening. Warning intelligence also works best when standard procedures are in place to communicate quickly and credibly to senior officials. Given the difficulty of getting people to pay attention to disturbing information, it also helps to have some sort of feedback mechanism in place so that analysts can be assured that their warnings have been received and understood.

Policymakers also rely on the intelligence community for *current intelligence*. Compared with other finished intelligence products, current intelligence—the *National Intelligence Daily* (NID) and *President's Daily Brief* (PDB)—resembles newspaper reporting. Working on the NID is a lot like working as a journalist at a major newspaper or television network. The NID and PDB are best thought of as classified newspapers, with feature articles and shorter "news stories" about important current and upcoming events. Analysts involved in the production of this current intelligence face many challenges, especially those created by competing news organizations. Given the advent of global news networks, Internet communications, and satellite television phones, current intelligence can be easily "scooped" by global media outlets, much to the chagrin of intelligence analysts. Instead of trying to beat the news cycle (an impossible task given the fact that cable news networks are monitored in offices throughout the government), intelligence analysts comment on the veracity of media stories or provide additional insights based on classified information. Current intelligence is unlikely to tell policy experts new information about their specific fields of expertise, but it does provide them with a body of knowledge about events that are affecting other parts of the government.

Analysts also conduct *basic research*—major research products that can take months to complete. They undertake these "term papers" to gain expertise or to respond to specific questions raised by policymakers. Basic research helps analysts place current events in their correct historical or political context and provides them with the background needed to identify and trace the impact of obscure issues that can undermine well-crafted policies. Unless policymakers ask for these basic research reports directly, however, they are unlikely to read them and often respond negatively to in-boxes that seem to be filled with an endless stream of detailed intelligence reports. When it comes to intelligence, policymakers value brevity and relevance. The challenge for intelligence managers is to make sure that basic research is delivered to policymakers who would be interested in the report—i.e., individuals who already are experts in the field addressed by the research.

Intelligence estimates—the National Intelligence Estimates (NIEs), for example—are formal intelligence reports produced by the entire intelligence community to support key policy decisions. These estimates require close coordination with policy agendas because they attempt to single out and explore the key issues on which some policy hinges. To be useful, these estimates have to be closely coordinated with policy agendas, a situation that requires policymakers to provide the intelligence community with the lead time necessary to perform the analysis. Accusations about politicization of the intelligence process are most likely to emerge with intelligence estimates, because they are directly linked to issues of political or policy importance.

Finally, policymakers, to the consternation of intelligence professionals, sometimes request raw intelligence—agent reports, reconnaissance photographs, or intercepted communications—so that they can evaluate these materials themselves. Dissemination of this kind of information is risky from the perspective of intelligence managers, because it can easily compromise the sources or methods used to collect and analyze raw intelligence. But it is the timing of these requests that is especially disconcerting to intelligence professionals; the requests usually occur in moments of crisis, when information flows increase and critical decisions have to be made on short notice. When it matters most, policymakers or senior military commanders want to serve as their own chief intelligence analyst; they want to view raw data to make up their own minds about its meaning. But policymakers rarely have the expertise or knowledge to place raw intelligence in its proper context or to judge the authenticity or accuracy of the information, and a crisis is a poor time to attempt to develop that skill set. The best policymakers and senior officers resist the urge to serve as their own chief intelligence analyst and instead bombard analysts and managers with a series of questions to assess the degree to which they are confident in their assessments (Hulnick 1986).

Getting Over the Rough Spots

One important perspective that separates career intelligence officers from policymakers who are political appointees is a different perception of the time available to accomplish the tasks before them. Political appointees are under pressure to show results quickly, or at least to demonstrate some progress on vexing issues before the next election. Intelligence professionals tend to see policy cycles in a longer perspective. In the rush to gain results, policymakers want support from the rest of the "career bureaucracy" to gain their policy objectives quickly. By contrast, intelligence analysts are less interested in the success of a specific policy per se and more interested in preserving the long-term effectiveness of the relationship between the intelligence and policy communities; they are likely to cry foul if they are pressured to supply intelligence to be used as ammunition in the political fray.

This difference in perspectives about time constraints and objectives creates several rough spots in the relations between elected officials and intelligence professionals. Policymakers want clear recommendations from the intelligence community and complain when finished intelligence tends to survey the range of possible future contingencies and policy outcomes. When intelligence analysts hedge their bets, policymakers suspect some sort of bias, especially when the reservations voiced by analysts conflict with policymakers' preferences. Policymakers, especially those with minimal government experience, often know little about how intelligence estimates are developed. Without knowing the individuals responsible for the analysis, they are sometimes not sure of how seriously to take various finished intelligence reports. As a result, they are reluctant to accept intelligence judgments that conflict with their preferences, which are of course the very findings that should enter into the policy formulation process. The intelligence community sometimes exacerbates this problem by carefully choosing the language used in estimates to suggest subtle differences in the confidence it has in key findings. These subtle variations are often lost on policymakers who know little of the distinctions that are being made. Additionally, policymakers are unlikely to wade through stacks of current intelligence reports and research papers in search of relevant material and often become frustrated by the need to cull through mountains of paperwork to get to a few useful nuggets of information (Hulnick 1986).

When dealing with policymakers, analysts also encounter their own problems. It is difficult to monitor the twists and turns in the debate over policy to guarantee that intelligence reports and estimates are relevant. Standardized intelligence products do little to address the concerns or needs of individual policymakers and are often ignored. Policymakers will also ignore information if it fails to address the issue that is filling their in-box at a given moment. If left to their own devices, policymakers tend to ask for opinions about policy options, advice which is beyond the purview of intelligence managers and analysts (Hulnick 1986).

The Readings

In the selections that follow, our contributors shed light on the relationship between policymakers and the intelligence community. Michael Herman addresses the fundamental question posed by the interaction between intelligence and policy: Does intelligence actually influence policy? Herman peers into the decision-making "black box" to describe the factors that influence the impact of intelligence on policy. He also identifies the various ways intelligence can be expected to shape diplomacy in peacetime and land, air, and naval operations in wartime. He suggests that outstanding intelligence alone rarely produces diplomatic coups or military victory but that intelligence has a cumulative impact on a country's fortunes in peace and war.

In "Tribal Tongues: Intelligence Consumers, Intelligence Producers," Mark Lowenthal, a former senior official in the U.S. intelligence community, suggests that even though policymakers and intelligence professionals are on the same team, they do not always follow the same playbook. Lowenthal describes how different organizational pressures and bureaucratic cultures shape the way policymakers and intelligence professionals view their roles and relationships, creating a gap that is often diffi-

cult to bridge in practice. Lowenthal also makes the key observation that policymakers have a great deal to do with influencing the quality and timeliness of the intelligence they receive, even though they are often unaware of the way they shape intelligence inputs into the policymaking process.

The final selection consists of an extract from the final report of the Aspin-Brown Commission (1996). It underscores the necessity for policymakers to provide guidance to intelligence officers with respect to the informational needs of those holding high office. "Intelligence agencies cannot operate in a vacuum," the report underscores. ✦

17

Intelligence and National Action

Michael Herman

Herman suggests that many things can influence what goes on inside the "black box" of policymaking in peacetime and in war. It is difficult, in his view, to estimate the exact role intelligence plays in shaping many foreign policy decisions. Intelligence serves to educate policymakers and military officers about the complexities of the political issues they face; and, in wartime, the fate of entire campaigns can turn on the possession of superior intelligence.

Rational Action and the Intelligence Dimension

Intelligence is produced to influence government action, however remotely. Before the modern system developed Clausewitz was inclined to discount it in warfare; important things could never be known with sufficient reliability at sufficient speed. 'Many intelligence report are contradictory; even more are false, and most are uncertain. . . . In short, most intelligence is false.'[1] The commander's intuition and willpower were better foundations for generalship.

This was before the growth of organized, permanent collection and analysis, and by the second half of the century there were more positive views about intelligence. A British book in 1895 agreed with Clausewitz that 'it is beyond the nature of things to avoid getting meagre, inexact or false information,' but contradicted him by adding ' . . . for all that he [the commander] must strive to acquire as much positive intelligence as he can, as it is on this alone that he can base his most important resolutions.'[2]

From this came the modern belief in intelligence as an indispensable component of decision-taking. In his book Kent portrayed it as the essence of rational government.

Our policy leaders find themselves in need of a great deal of knowledge of foreign countries.

They need knowledge which is complete, which is accurate, which is delivered on time, and which is capable of serving as a basis for action.[3]

This needed applied scholarship:

Research is the only process which we of the liberal tradition are willing to admit is capable of giving us the truth, or a closer approximation to the truth, than we now enjoy.[4]

Intelligence-based action was the antithesis of leadership by ideology.

I do not wish to be the one who rejects all hunches and intuitions as uniformly perilous, for there are hunches based on knowledge and understanding which are the stuff of highest truth. What I do wish to reject is intuition based upon nothing and which takes off from the wish.

Intelligence represented rationality, and the statesman who rejected it

should recognize that he is turning his back on the two instruments by which western man has, since Aristotle, steadily enlarged his horizon of knowledge—the instruments of reason and scientific method.[5]

Intelligence also received similar though more muted approval in military orthodoxy; at about the same time as Kent wrote his book, the British Chiefs of Staff listed 'Maintaining our Intelligence Organisations at a high standard of efficiency' among the 'Fundamentals' of post-Second World War defence.[6] Writers on military matters have propounded intelligence as the force multiplier and optimizer. According to Michael Handel,

Good intelligence will act as a force multiplier by facilitating a more focused and economical use of force. On the other hand, when all other things are equal, poor intelligence acts as a force divider by wasting and eroding strength. In the long run, therefore, the side with better intelligence will not only use its power more profitably but will also more effectively conserve it.[7]

R. V. Jones has written similarly that

The ultimate object of intelligence is to enable action to be optimized. The individual or body which has to decide on action needs information about its opponent as an ingredient likely to be vital in determining its decision; and this information may suggest that action should be taken on a larger or smaller scale than that which otherwise would be taken, or even that a different course of action would be better.[8]

The intelligence dimension has still not been integrated into writing on the nature of war; reading the enemy's mind is still neglected in the literature on generalship. Official texts still tend to place intelligence in the second rather than first rank of military attributes.[9] Nevertheless there is no dissent from the general idea that it is one of the keys to successful military action.

Gathering and using intelligence is also part of what is now expected of modern government's adherence to rational procedures in other matters. Intelligence failure is a regular subject for media investigation, as are governments' failures to act on what they get, as in the British Matrix-Churchill case. A participant in the Washington intelligence-policy process wrote in 1976 that

> In recent years the institutionalization of intelligence in Washington has become so irreversible, the processes themselves so pervasive, the products so indispensable, the penalties for spurning them so disagreeable and most of the intelligence officers so durable that the policy-maker must suffer intelligence gladly.[10]

The official statement of the United States Security Strategy in 1990 saw intelligence as 'the "alarm bell" to give us early warning of new developments and new dangers even as requirements grow in number and complexity.'[11]

Other governments also publicize the links between intelligence and national security. The British government made vivid pronouncements about the importance of Sigint to defend the 1984 ban on national trade unions at GCHQ. GCHQ was 'one of the security and intelligence agencies on which our national security, and to a degree that of our allies, depends.'[12] It played 'a unique and vital role in the security of the United Kingdom.'[13] The ban was imposed only because of 'the critical importance and special nature of the work.'[14] Despite the political controversy about the ban, the agency's importance was not contested by the government's opponents.[15]

This might suggest that there is little more to be said. Every government has an intelligence system to make it better informed than it would be without it. Wise governments note intelligence's indications of risks, rather as private organizations pay for and use the risk assessments available on a commercial basis. What intelligence produces may well be incomplete, inaccurate or positively misleading in particular cases; but decision-takers that use it regularly are likely to have a better track-record than those that manage without it, just as government statistics for all their faults give leaders something better than guessing. Intelligence's role is to collect the information and build up the special knowledge needed to understand 'them' and not 'us.' The mere fact of incorporating intelligence's inputs into a regular decision-making process entails some government commitment to rationality and concern for reality. Except by those who believe like Marxists that

events are shaped by great historical forces and not the quality of individual decisions, it may seem that intelligence's effect can almost be taken as read.

But not quite. Even if intelligence is useful, those setting its budgets have to decide *how* useful it is; how much does it really matter? This entails some understanding of the intelligence-decision couplings, and whether they give special support to particular actions. This chapter considers these two aspects of intelligence's value.

Decisions as Black Boxes

Set-piece decision-taking might be expected to have an easily observable intelligence-decision linkage; thus military doctrine emphasizes methodical decision-taking, with specified intelligence inputs (as EEIs or Essential Elements of Information) and clear decision outputs.[16] Yet in practice it is not clear what causes what. The intelligence input may well be 'soft' rather than 'hard' data, embodying uncertainty, alternatives and speculation. Intelligence forecasts may themselves alter the situations on which they forecast. As well as clear-cut government decisions there are also all kinds of less structured ones and reflex reactions, as well as decisions not to do anything. There are also the constraints on action. Even if intelligence points to what should be done it may be impossible to do it; the best warnings of attack may lead to no action if there is nothing that can be done.

Even when there are identifiable intelligence inputs and decision outputs, the decision thought-process tends to be a mystery, like a black box with no external indication of its internal circuitry. Decision-takers cope with complex information and analysis through short-cuts, 'satisficing' and 'bounded rationality.'[17] Decisions are 'framed' by extraneous factors besides formal information inputs.[18] 'Information is only one of the many resources which policy-makers use to reach a decision.'[19] Besides information and forecasts, decisions involve judgment, political sense, leadership and determination in pursuing objectives.

> In a sense, rational or analytical decision-taking stands as an ideal to which decision systems aspire. The conditions in which foreign policy operates, however, make this goal impossible.[20]

Thus foreign policy is not a simple translation of objectives into decisions in the light of information. It

involves complex processes in which values, attitudes, and images mediate perceptions of reality provided by various sources of information. . . . The components of any definition of a situation will vary with conditions in the system, internal political structure, degree of urgency in a situation, and political roles of policy makers.[21]

In short there are no clear wiring diagrams for the connections between intelligence items and specific action. Intelligence may be ignored, as when the British command ignored the intelligence on German deployments just before the Arnhem assault.[22] Governments can cut intelligence communities out of sensitive decisions altogether, as seems to have happened over the Israeli invasion of the Lebanon in 1982.[23] The British JIC process was similarly insulated from the planning for the 1956 Suez operation.[24] If intelligence is used, users consciously and unconsciously *select* from what is presented to them. Some users like Kissinger value secret single-source material but are uninterested in all-source assessment, preferring to be their own assessors.[25] Even diligent users who pay attention to everything interpret intelligence's careful expressions of uncertainty and alternatives in the light of their own prejudices. 'Interested policy-makers quickly learn that intelligence can be used the way a drunk uses a lamp post—for support rather than illumination.'[26] Intelligence's ideal is to transfer its own analyses, forecasts and estimates of probabilities to the user's consciousness *in toto*. But it is doing well if it ever gets near it. The decision-taking black box works through selectivity.

The effect of intelligence therefore depends on its institutional reputation and the personal chemistry between practitioners and users. Studies of Allied military leaders in the Second World War suggest that their initial experience of it determined their subsequent attitudes.[27] In one historian's view, the collective record of Allied leaders in the Second World War left a lot to be desired, for a variety of reasons: lack of knowledge and training; wariness after unfortunate earlier experiences; the determination of authoritarian personalities to impose their own will.[28]

Thus intelligence is at the mercy of users' unpredictable attitudes towards it; but it tries to make its own luck with them through persuasion, personal relations and marketing. One purpose of some routine intelligence output is to get users accustomed to it and build up credibility for the future. But it can never regard users' minds as blank sheets on which it can write whatever it chooses. Its presentation of its product always has to have an eye to its users' preconceptions. Even so, users' absorption is selective.

Education and Conditioning

The coupling between specific intelligence and identifiable decisions is however only one way in which intelligence affects action. Intelligence-driven decisions tend to come from the cumulative effect of successions of reports, not from individual items.[29] Studies of information bring out the time-lags in information's effects; it is not consumed once and for all like a material product, but has recurrent and unpredictable 'waves of usefulness,'[30] or it may never be used at all. Information is inherently wasteful: 'virtually every flow of knowledge may have its admixture of waste, some of the effort of producing it proving either abortive or superfluous.'[31] No one knows in advance what will turn out to be useful or how it will be used. There is the observation that government information as a whole works not instrumentally but indirectly, affecting action by seepage and 'enlightenment,' providing an intellectual setting for actions rather than their precise raw material.[32]

In all these respects intelligence is the same as other information. [There is a] spectrum between intelligence reports intended as users' background, like weekly summaries, and the assessments geared to specific use. Most intelligence is produced as background current-repotorial reports and short-term forecasts meeting intuitive criteria of 'relevance' and 'significance.' Those in CIA who produce the *President's Daily Briefing* and the *National Intelligence Daily* do not expect them to lead regularly to immediate action, any more than newspapers expect to change the world with every issue. Of all the contents of daily and weekly high-level intelligence summaries only a minute proportion feed directly into decisions. The same applies to the even more voluminous single-source services direct to users. There are also the intelligence efforts devoted to surveillance for warning against unlikely events; the voluminous near real-time flows of reports against Soviet military activities during the Cold War were almost completely useless (in the sense that they led to no action), but fully justified as warning trip-wires.

Consequently the role of most intelligence is not driving decisions in any short term, specific way, but contributing to decision-takers' general enlightenment; intelligence producers are in the business of educating their masters. Education provides knowledge that may influence unforeseeable future decisions; a background item today turns out to be useful tomorrow or next year. Intelligence has the same unpredictable effects as information in newspapers. Enlightenment works at the level of 'the policies which precede policy . . . [which] lie in the area of predispositions and felt associations which exist in men and hover in institutions.'[33] Negatively, it reduces the proportion of users' action based on misconceptions; knowledge drives out error.

Arranging this mental furniture merges into influencing decision-takers' style and psychology. One of the effects of Western Allies' high-grade intelligence in the second half of the Second World War was simply to reduce uncertainty in decision-taking and support methodical strategies of systematically seeking overwhelming local superiority and planned risk-reduction, without constant worries about being surprised and the need to insure against it.

These factors complicate the intelligence-decision coupling. Intelligence producers cannot peer too far into all the varieties and unpredictability of use. In large part they have the techniques of educators. Their best normal test of value is simply whether users say that what they have been given has interested them; hard evidence from them of actual use is a bonus. This 'soft' criterion complicates critical attempts to evaluate intelligence investments as value for money.

. . . [S]ome generalizations can be attempted now on the kinds of decisions intelligence supports in war and peace.

War

Optimization and Transformation

Wartime intelligence is now well documented, but historians still have the problems of reconstructing actual effects. Some leaders acknowledge intelligence debts more than others; Montgomery never acknowledged his to Ultra.[34] Yet war provides the best laboratory for intelligence. Victory is a clear objective; intelligence has an unambiguous role of understanding the enemy; it has a higher priority than in peace and attracts more talent. Language for evaluating it is available in the arithmetic of war, casualties, material losses, territory and time. Thus the British official historian of the Second World War has quantified the effect in terms of time, and has argued that British and US cipher-breaking shortened the war in Europe by three or four years.[35]

Generalizations about wartime effects are still not easy. Obviously intelligence alone does not make for victory without force to use it. Better Allied intelligence in the early years of the Second World War would not have avoided defeats by more effective German forces, though it might have reduced the scale of disaster. Whether intelligence is good or bad has to be judged by two standards. One is its accuracy in an absolute way compared with reality, and the other is its quality compared with the opponent's; it is possible for both sides to have good or bad intelligence about the other.[36] The effects may not be the same at the strategic, operational

and tactical levels of command; and at a tactical level the combat information . . . (like the effects of radars in air warfare) gets mixed up with intelligence proper. Intelligence effects also operate via the commanders' personalities and psychology; Signet in the Pacific War 'led aggressive risk-takers to become even more audacious but it led cautious ones to become not more prudent but rather more calculated.'[37] In any case intelligence is only part of overall 'command performance.'[38] The Germans in capturing Crete in 1941 showed superior 'command fluency,' but their intelligence within it was inferior.[39]

But with all these qualifications two complementary intelligence dimensions can be suggested. The main one has already been indicated: the optimization of resources, in ways that lend themselves to quantification, or at least to analogies in quantified terms. Commanders' descriptions of the added value produced by good intelligence tend to be as the equivalent of so many extra troops, aircraft or warships. They are partly rhetorical but nevertheless provide some indication of scale. War is partly a matter of 'the concentration of superior forces at the decisive time and place,' coupled with the corollary of 'economy of effort,' or not wasting resources.[40] On the effect on command:

> With accurate information, uncertainty about the surrounding environment can be reduced and decisions affecting the readiness, movement, and application of military force can be taken with clearer understanding of the likely costs and benefits. If processed and delivered promptly, information can also provide more time for these decisions to be taken and, moreover, implemented with successful results. Overall it permits a clearer assessment of a situation, generates policy choices to achieve a specific outcome, and allows those choices to be weighed for their relative payoff.[41]

Or, briefly, 'information can help military organizations to handle their resources efficiently.'[42]

Thus the basic arithmetic of Second World War strategy in Europe was manpower and numbers of divisions. Germany underestimated total Soviet resources, overestimated those of Britain and the USA (through Allied deception) and got its military planning wrong. It believed that the Western Allies had twice as many divisions as they actually had, and allocated between one-and two-thirds of its scarce resources in France and Southern Europe to guard against non-existent dangers.[43] The Allies got the calculations right. The measured style of their offensives and the German failures against them illustrate intelligence as the arithmetical optimizer. If 'the effective distribution of superior resources was in large part the key to the Allies' success in the

Second World War,'[44] then good intelligence was an important contributory factor.

Obviously there are various degrees of this optimization. Yet occasionally it seems to move to another dimension, in which intelligence moves from optimization towards *transformation* effects. Intelligence not only optimizes but also determines the nature of operations and campaigns as well as the outcomes; the war is in some real sense an intelligence war. This transformation has not been explored and there is no ready-made typology for it, but three examples can be suggested.

One is where the style of combat in land warfare with a low force-to-space ratio emphasizes movement and surprise, transcending material power. Luttwak describes a dialectic between two styles of strategy: attrition based on the direct deployment of strength, and 'relational manoeuvre' for 'the application of some selective superiority against presumed weaknesses, physical or psychological, technical or organizational.'[45] The blitzkrieg effect of the second is 'above all *the unbalancing of command decisions* [italics in original].'[46] Its deep penetration battle is 'an information race.'[47] The military aim in war of movement is often expressed as 'getting inside the enemy's decision-cycle' so that he is always overtaken.

Hence battle incorporating this information race can turn particularly on intelligence, for both the attacker and defender. The success of the German blitzkrieg in France in 1940 was based on mobile forces and a superior C³I system, which included accurate intelligence assessments of French vulnerability in the Ardennes and better battlefield intelligence as the campaign progressed.[48] By contrast Britain was not geared to exploit sufficiently quickly the Sigint that was then becoming available. Sufficient intelligence—in speed of delivery as well as quality—may be a necessary condition for effective fluid warfare of this kind.

Another example of transforming effects may be maritime warfare, if intelligence is able to provide advance warning of enemy movement, rather than just current positions. As far back as the Armada intelligence has guided the strategic mobilization and deployment of British fleets. In the early months of the First World War the Grand Fleet was forced by the German submarine threat to withdraw to its Scottish bases, and the successful German bombardment of East Coast ports in late 1914 could have led to a consistent German strategy of bombardment, attacks on British coastal trade and interference with cross-Channel support for the forces in France. To be able to counter such operations the Grand Fleet had to be able to weigh anchor at its northern bases at the same time as the German fleet left its North Sea ports. After the end of 1914

British codebreaking was able to provide its fleet with the warning needed. The resulting Battle of the Dogger Bank in early 1915 dissuaded the Germans from further operations of this kind.[49] Intelligence was the basis of a successful reactive use of British sea power.

Intelligence can also determine the ways in which sea power can be used offensively. In the Second World War the British use of maritime power to interdict Axis seaborne supplies to North Africa turned on deciphered messages giving advance information of convoy movements.[50] In a rather different way decipherment by both sides influenced the Battle of the Atlantic's style as a battle with long-distance shore-based control on both sides, turning on concentrating U-boat wolf-pack attacks on the one hand and re-routing convoys on the other. In these maritime examples, in one way and another, intelligence not merely increased effectiveness but influenced the character of operations.

A third kind of operations transformed or at least heavily influenced by intelligence is long-range bombardment, including strategic air attack. Bombardment needs targets and some assessment of vulnerabilities and effects. Its modern ranges are such as to need intelligence for them, not just the visual observation and other combat information that sufficed as 'artillery intelligence' in the First World War. Hence intelligence is a major determinant of bombardment's form. The strategic air offensive against Germany in the Second World War depended on targeting and bomb damage assessments from airborne photographic reconnaissance. Sigint on the German forces' oil shortages eventually produced the successful concentration on oil targets in the war's final year.[51] US satellite and conventional imagery had similar effects on the air offensive in the Gulf War. The strategy of any long distance bombardment is driven at least partly by the state of target intelligence.

Attacks and Defence

Whether intelligence is optimizing or transforming, there is still the question whether it favours attack or defence. Attackers use surprise, and David Kahn has argued that intelligence is the classical counter to it.[52] Intelligence is 'essential to victory only in defense . . . [It] is a defining characteristic of defense; it is only an accompanying characteristic of offense.'[53] After its initial disasters, the USA's exploitation of the Japanese naval cipher helped it in effective strategic defence in the Pacific in 1942, including the Battle of Midway.[54] Precise intelligence on German plans of attack helped the British to save Egypt at Alam Haifa in 1942, 'Montgomery won his first battle by believing the intelligence with which he was furnished.'[55] Intelligence superiority by the intended victim leaves the surpriser open to ambush. It enabled the British to inflict heavy losses on Rommel's last spoiling attack in the North African campaign, at Medenine, 'surprise had been indispensable for the success of the [German] plan, and Rommel had indeed attacked in the belief that the Eighth Army was unready.'[56] It facilitated defence and counter-stroke on a bigger scale in the Battle of Kursk and its aftermath.[57] High quality intelligence made a major contribution to the British defence of Malaysia in the operations against Indonesian 'confrontation' in 1963–6, 'a satisfactory and successful campaign, skillfully and economically conducted.'[58] At the end of his study of German intelligence in the Second World War, Kahn has suggested that over the centuries Britain has tended to have effective intelligence in conflicts with continental European states because

> this balance-of-power policy, which is a reactive, or defensive, technique, requires intelligence to succeed . . . each nation's attitude toward intelligence may be seen as an expression of its geography and its internal dynamics. Britain was a sea power, essentially defensive . . . she needed intelligence. Germany was a continental power. . . . Her armies, attacking, did not require intelligence. And so she failed to develop it.[59]

This is a thought-provoking theory. Yet in practice intelligence superiority can also favour the offence. The Germans' reading of British naval ciphers during the invasion of Norway in 1940 favoured the aggressor. The Japanese triumph in planning Pearl Harbor depended partly on good local target intelligence on the US anchorage and its defences. In early 1944 Sigint on Japanese deployments led Admiral Nimitz to aim the US attack on the Marshall Islands at Kwajalein, in the centre of the group, instead of the perimeter islands as had been expected.[60] More generally, Sigint in the Pacific 'allowed the United States to defeat Japan far more speedily and at lower cost' in its recapture of island bases.[61] Similarly intelligence superiority was the foundation of the Allies' successful strategic deception over the Normandy invasion in 1944. Even apart from the effects of deception, intelligence on the enemy's defensive positions can do something to counteract the defender's inherent advantages, as in the way the Normandy success owed much to the detailed intelligence put together on beaches and defensive positions. In general terms, good intelligence's ability to help the aggressor to achieve local superiority should be as important as its potential for warning the defender against surprise. Further study of the theory may indeed show that intelligence's warning value to the defender can be equalled by its ability to tell the attacker whether he is about to achieve surprise or not, thereby giving him the option of avoiding what would otherwise be a 'surprise failure.'

Strength and Weakness

Rather the same ambiguity emerges from the relationship between intelligence and material strength. In facilitating the effective use force intelligence might seem to be of relatively greater value to the weak than the strong. Ferns argues persuasively that the German 'fire brigade' strategy after autumn 1942 of deploying elite forces to defeat Allied attacks or force expensive battles of attrition depended on advance warning:

> There is a direct correlation between the success of German intelligence and operations throughout the last three years of the war. Whenever Germany did correctly assess the intentions of its foes, whether around Monte Cassino in the spring of 1944 or directly to the east of Berlin in February 1945, its forces had their maximum effect, indeed they demonstrated the feasibility of German defensive strategy. . . . Indeed had the German Army possessed the Allies' intelligence, it might well have forced a stalemate in Europe.[62]

But the evidence about intelligence's special importance to the weak seems as unproven as its affinity with defence. Examples of successful campaigns by weaker sides guided by effective intelligence are quite hard to come by. From the Second World War the predominant impression is that the Allies' intelligence superiority coincided with their superior material resources from 1942 onwards.

This suggests some other possible conclusions. One is that, besides optimizing the use of military power, wartime intelligence can itself be partly a reflection of it. Allied Second World War intelligence superiority was itself nourished in some ways by the military superiority which it supported. Thus its imagery depended on air superiority. It was the battlefield victors, not the vanquished, who benefited most from POW interrogation and captured documents. Those with effective command of the sea were consistently more successful at capturing the crucial cryptographic material for parts of naval cipher-breaking.

Another is that the development of effective wartime intelligence takes time, but gets a particular impetus from defeat in the early years of war;[63] military men need a sharp shock to overcome their lack of intelligence interest and competence. The Allies' disasters in the early stages of the Second World War were more potent intelligence teachers than success was to the Axis. On the German side even the considerable naval crypt-analytic successes in the first half of the war were never absorbed into a properly integrated intelligence system.[64] For Britain on the other hand Alam Haifa in 1942

> saw operations welcome intelligence into full partnership for the first time.... Hitherto "... information about the enemy was frequently treated as interesting rather than valuable. We had had good intelligence before; henceforth we were going to use it."[65]

In the same way the vast Japanese successes of 1941–42 perhaps blinded them to their intelligence inefficiency.

Peace

Knowledge is part of peacetime state power or influence, it is

> a resource which some societies may be able to exploit more successfully than others.... Those who know more, and can manipulate what others know, have more power.... Knowledge and ideology structures, it can be argued, are vital frameworks of foreign policy, not merely peripheral additions to it.[66]

Intelligence is part of this decision-takers' contact with reality. But in peacetime the effects are more diffuse than in war; and success and failure are themselves often debatable. A writer inclined to be critical of the effects of intelligence on high policy concluded with the careful judgment that

> Intelligence may not be able to find the truth; even less may it be able to persuade others that it has found it. But keeping the players honest, not permitting disreputable arguments to thrive, pointing out where positions are internally contradictory or rest on tortured readings of the evidence would not be a minor feat. While it would not save the country from all folly, it would provide more assistance than we get from most instruments of policy.[67]

Perhaps one principal effect is simply to encourage decision-takers towards a style based on evidence and analysis, rather than intuition and conviction. This is part—not an unimportant part—of rational leadership.

However it is even harder than in war to generalize on where it most matters. Intelligence's peacetime successes tend to remain secret, but some peacetime conclusions can be offered. First, parts of nominal peace are simply less violent versions of war, and intelligence there has extensions of its wartime power for the application of force. Thus it is central to counter-terrorism and negates terrorism's characteristics of invisibility and surprise. Defeating terrorism usually depends on intelligence success and not the force available; sometimes, as

in the Northern Ireland campaign, military force has intelligence-gathering as a principal aim. The most sustained and effective use of tactical intelligence in peacetime since the Second World War has probably been in Israeli campaigns against Arab terrorism, the ability to take counter-action has helped to set the terms of its relationships with the Arab world. On the analogy with war intelligence on terrorism is a transforming element.

Second, apart from intelligence's influence on particular decisions, there is the cumulative influence on national standing of having well-informed policies. This has been particularly relevant to Britain as a nation of declining economic power wishing nevertheless to maintain world status. The Foreign Secretary claimed in 1992 that 'In recent years Britain has punched above her weight in the world. We intend to keep it that way.'[68] Intelligence has been one element in this position. Good intelligence has helped Britain to play bad hands with some finesse.

Third, effects on the actual conduct of diplomacy have some parallels with wartime use. Tactical intelligence support adds to certainty and confidence in foreign policy execution; as already quoted from Hibbert, it gives immediacy, practicality and focus to existing general conclusions.[69] It has been claimed that after Britain ceased to intercept and decipher foreign diplomatic dispatches in 1844

> British diplomacy necessarily suffered, and the loss of foreign interceptions in 1844 helps to explain the contrast between previous success and subsequent failures, illustrated for example by Palmerston's career.'[70]

Christopher Andrew had argued that French diplomacy was less effective in the years immediately before 1914 than hitherto, since German diplomatic ciphers had been made unreadable after a French indiscretion.[71] Decrypted telegrams which provided most of the Turkish delegation's correspondence contributed to British negotiating tactics at the Lausanne conference in 1922–23.[72] The literature about intelligence focuses on how if affects policy. But in practice the main effects are more tactical, at least for diplomatic intelligence sent to Foreign Offices and their posts. As Ferris has put it, 'practice, intelligence rarely affects the determination of policy—although it does happen. Frequently however it does affect its execution of policy.'[73]

Fourth, there is intelligence's role as defence against peacetime surprise. The diplomatic equivalent of military surprise is not part of most foreign affairs. 'Unlike military men, diplomats and run-of-the-mill political leaders do not like to surprise each other.'[74] But there is some deliberate surprise in peacetime, pre-empting normal reactions; examples include Hitler's re-militarization of the Rheinland in 1936, the 1939 Nazi-Soviet Pact, the US-Chinese rapprochement of 1971, Sadat's expulsion of Soviet advisers in 1972, and his peace initiative with Israel in 1977. Intelligence may fail in this warning role, as in the British failure to detect the making of the Nazi-Soviet Pact.[75] But it is some counterweight to surprise tactics.

These points suggest that intelligence's general peacetime effect is to optimize national positions, not transform them. Yet there is a serendipity factor. The greatest single coup produced by an item of diplomatic intelligence was the British use of the deciphered Zimmerman telegram as a lever in securing the United States' entry to the First World War. This emerged unpredictably from what had previously been an unspectacular line of German diplomatic traffic. Arguably the firm intelligence on Libyan support for terrorism in April 1986, leading to the US air attack aimed at the Libyan leadership, was a similar case of a relatively small (but authentic) piece of intelligence having a big result. Most use of intelligence consists of undramatically optimizing national influence; but sometimes—often unpredictably—it is crucial, transforming peacetime action in the way it sometimes transforms war. Perhaps in some ways it is like medicine; doctors in general practice are said to spend most of their time on things that affect patients' quality of life, but occasionally their role is life-saving. Intelligence has something of the same variation.

Summary

Intelligence's justification is that it influences action in useful ways. But these uses are very varied: some reports are used immediately, while others are useful in the distant future; many more reports influence decisions through their cumulative effects; others still have long-term educational or psychological value. Warning surveillance is a precaution against what may never happen.[76] Much intelligence is never used at all. In all these ways it is like other information.

Nevertheless the effect is to optimize national strength and international influence, on varying scales. In war it assists the effective use of force. Sometimes in war (and counter-terrorism) it goes further and transforms the ways in which action takes place. In peace its effects are often in diplomatic execution rather than the making of foreign policy. In both war and peace intelligence's consistent impacts are its cumulative relatively unsurprising contributions to effectiveness and influence. Overlaying any regular patterns there is serendipity or luck.

These are central points for assessing intelligence's importance. However there are the other effects listed at the beginning of this chapter. These can be considered in what follows.

Questions for Further Discussion

1. Why is it difficult to predict the role played by intelligence in policymaking?

2. If intelligence does not drive short-term decisions, how does it influence policy (if at all)?

3. What role does intelligence play in managing national resources?

4. What are some differences between wartime and peacetime intelligence?

Endnotes

1. Carl von Clausewitz, *On War* (Princeton: Princeton University Press, 1976) (ed. and trans. by M. Howard and P. Paret), p. 117. For discussion of Clausewitz's view see D. Kahn, 'Clausewitz and Intelligence' in M. Handel (ed.) *Clausewitz and Modern Strategy* (London: Cass, 1986), pp.117–26.
2. Col. G. A. Furse, *Information in War* (London: Clowes, 1895), p. 12.
3. S. Kent, *Strategic Intelligence for American World Policy* (Hamden, Conn.: Archon Books, 1965 edition), p. 5.
4. Kent, *Strategic Intelligence for American World Policy*, pp. 155–6.
5. Kent, *Strategic Intelligence for American World Policy*, pp. 203, 206.
6. Chiefs of Staff Report on Future Defence Policy, 22 May 1947, reproduced in M. Dockrill, *British Defence Since 1945* (Oxford: Blackwell, 1989), p. 135.
7. M. Handel, 'Intelligence and Military Operations,' *Intelligence and National Security* (Special Issue: 'Intelligence and Military Operations') vol. 5 no. 2 (April 1990), p. 69.
8. R. V. Jones, 'Intelligence and Command' in M. I. Handel (ed.), *Leaders and Intelligence* (London: Cass, 1989), p. 288.
9. Thus there is no reference to intelligence in the current British army's 'Principles of War' in *Design for Military Operations—The British Military Doctrine* (Army code 71451, 1989), Annex A. Its 'Information Requirements' (p. 46) emphasize the dangers of having too much information rather than too little.
10. T. L. Hughes, *The Fate of Facts in the World of Men—Foreign Policy and Intelligence-Making* (New York: The Foreign Policy Association Headline Series no. 233, December 1976), p. 22.
11. *National Security Strategy of the United States* (The White House: March 1990), p. 22.
12. Sir Geoffrey Howe (Secretary of State for Foreign Affairs) in the GCHQ debate, 27 February 1984, *Hansard*, col. 25.
13. Lord Trefgarne in the Lords' debate on the same subject, 8 February 1984, *Hansard*, col. 1254.
14. Lord Trefgarne, from the same speech, *Hansard*, col. 1259.
15. For the present author's views on the issue see M. E. Herman, 'GCHQ De-Unionisation 1984,' *Public Policy*

and Administration vol. 8 no. 2 (summer 1993), commenting on H. Lanning and R. Norton-Taylor, *A Conflict of Loyalties: GCHQ 1984–1991* (Cheltenham, Glos.: New Clarion Press, 1991). Lanning and Norton-Taylor are strongly opposed to the union ban at GCHQ but do not dispute the importance of the work.

16. EEIs (Essential Elements of Information) are deemed as 'critical information requirements at a theatre's various levels of command.' They are 'identified in operational doctrine in peacetime and regularly refined.' (Design for Military Operations—The British Military Doctrine, p. 46.)
17. See for example H. A. Simon, *Administrative Behaviour* (New York: Macmillan, 1959). In this and subsequent work Simon 'showed that the assumptions that economic rationality made about human capacities, knowledge and information-processing procedures were quite unreasonable. The consequence was his model of "bounded rationality" . . . [that] argued (what was later proved) that individuals limit the alternatives considered, value their information-processing costs more highly than assumed, and settle for a process of "satisficing," that is, they assure themselves that the consequences of their decisions will be "good enough" for their purposes and proceed accordingly.' R. E. Lane, *The Market Experience* (Cambridge: Cambridge University Press, 1991), p. 47.
18. For references and discussion see Lane, *The Market Experience*, chapters 3 and 6, especially pp. 52 and 100.
19. R. Davidson and P. White (eds.), 'Introduction' in *Information and Government* (Edinburgh: Edinburgh University Press, 1988), p. 5.
20. M. Clarke, 'The Foreign Policy System: a Framework for Analysis' in M. Clarke and B. White, *Understanding Foreign Policy: The Foreign Policy Systems Approach* (Aldershot, Hants: Elgar, 1989), p. 53.
21. K. J. Holsti, *International Politics: A Framework for Analysis* (Englewood Cliffs, N.J.: Prentice-Hall, 1983 edition), p. 355.
22. B. Urquhart, *A Life in Peace and War* (London: Weidenfeld and Nicolson, 1987), pp. 72–6.
23. S. Gazit, 'Intelligence Estimates and the Policy-Maker' in M. Handel (ed.). *Leaders and Intelligence* (London: Cass, 1989), pp. 282–7.
24. *The Naval Review* vol. 79 no. 4 (October 1991), pp. 356–61 (private accounts).
25. For criticism of this propensity of Kissinger's, see R. S. Cline, 'Policy Without Intelligence,' *Foreign Policy* no. 17 (winter 1974–5).
26. Hughes, *The Fate of Facts in a World of Men*, p. 24.
27. Handel, *Leaders and Intelligence*.
28. H. C. Deutsch, 'Commanding Generals and the Use of Intelligence' in Handel, *Leaders and Intelligence*, pp. 194–260.
29. See for example the account of the accumulation of evidence on German missile development in R. V. Jones, *Most Secret War: British Scientific Intelligence 1939–1945* (London: Hamish Hamilton, 1978), chapters 38 and 44.
30. F. Machlup, *Knowledge and Knowledge Production* (Princeton: Princeton University Press, 1980), p. 174 note.
31. Machlup, *Knowledge and Knowledge Production*, p. 177.
32. Davidson and White (eds.), 'Introduction,' *Information and Government*, p. 2.
33. Hughes, *The Fate of Facts in a World of Men*, p. 13.

34. Deutsch, 'Commanding General and the Use of Intelligence,' pp. 211–15.
35. K. H. Hinsley, 'British Intelligence in the Second World War' in C. Andrew and J. Noakes (eds.), *Intelligence and International Relations 1900–45* (Exeter: University of Exeter Press, 1987), p. 218.
36. For this point, and illuminating discussion of intelligence and command, see J. Ferris and M. I. Handel, 'Clausewitz, Intelligence, Uncertainty and the Art of Command,' *Intelligence and National Security* vol 10 no.1 (January 1995), pp. 40–1. But note also the 'intelligence-security contest' and 'counterintelligence contest' to be discussed in chapter 10. In it offensive intelligence superiority tends to produce better information security for its own side than the enemy's, and intelligence inferiority the reverse. Good intelligence has defensive applications which degrade the enemy's collection.
37. Ferris and Handel, 'Clausewitz, Intelligence, Uncertainty and the Art of Command,' p. 40.
38. B. G. Blair, *Strategic Command and Control: Redefining the Nuclear Threat* (Washington D.C.: Brooking Institution, 1985), pp. 1–13, and P. B. Stares, *Command Performance: the Neglected Dimension of European Security* (Washington D.C.: Brookings Institution, 1991), chapters 1–3 'Command performance' is Stares' term (as is 'command influence' in what follows).
39. A. Beevor, *Crete* (London: Murray, 1991), part two. The Sigint evidence of the German plan of attack was passed to the Allied commander, but apparently with orders prohibiting him from acting on it; these are discussed in detail in R. Bennett, *Behind the Battle: Intelligence in the War with Germany* (London: Sinclair-Stevenson, 1994), pp. 281–4. Nevertheless it was command failure that lost the battle. It was said after the war that 'a hundred extra wireless sets would have saved Crete.' (Quoted by Stares, *Command Performance*, p. 57.)
40. *Design for Military Operations—The British Military Doctrine* Annex A (Principles of War), p. 68.
41. Stares, *Command Performance*, p. 19.
42. J. Ferns, 'Ralph Bennett and the Study of Ultra,' *Intelligence and National Security* vol. 6 no. 2 (April 1991), p. 480.
43. For German calculations of Soviet manpower see B. Wegner, 'The Tottering Giant: German Perceptions of Soviet Military and Economic Strength for "Operation Blau" (1942)' in C. Andrew and J. Noakes (eds.). *Intelligence and International Relations 1900–45*, pp. 293–311. For conclusions on the campaign in the West see Ferns, 'Ralph Bennett and the Study of Ultra,' p. 477.
44. J. Gooch (ed.), *Decisive Campaigns of the Second World War* (London: Cass, 1990), p. 3.
45. E. N. Lunwak, *Strategy: the Logic of War and Peace* (Cambridge, Mass.: Belknap, Harvard, 1987), p. 94. For related ideas of momentum in war and its psychological leverage, see R. Simkin, *Race to the Swift* (London: Brassey, 1985).
46. Lunwak, *Strategy*, p. 108.
47. Luttwak, *Strategy*, p. 106.
48. Stares, *Command Performance*, pp. 25–6. But note that in this and other examples of the 'information race' intelligence and combat information (see previous chapter) are both involved.
49. P. Becsly, *Room 40: British Naval Intelligence 1914–18* (London: Hamish Hamilton, 1982), pp. 308–9.

50. F. H. Hinsley with E. E. Thomas, C. F. G. Ransom and R. C. Knight, *British Intelligence in the Second World War* vol. II (London: HMSO, 1981), pp. 319–24.

51. F. H. Hinsley with E. E. Thomas, C. A. G. Simians and C. F. G. Ransom, *British Intelligence in the Second World War* vol. III part 2 (London: HMSO, 1988), chapter 54. The Bletchley view was that this 'may have been the outstanding service rendered by Special Intelligence to the strategic air war in Europe' (p. 497).

52. As argued in G. J. A. O'Toole, 'Kahn's Law: A Universal Principle of Intelligence, *Journal of Intelligence and Counterintelligence* vol. 4 no. 1 (spring 1990).

53. D. Kahn, *Hitler's Spies* (London: Arrow paperback edition, 1980), p. 510, quoted in O'Toole, 'Kahn's Law: A Universal Principle of Intelligence,' p. 39.

54. R. Lewin, *The American Magic: Codes, Ciphers and the Defeat of Japan* (London: Penguin, 1983), chapters 4–7.

55. Sir Edgar Williams (Montgomery's Chief Intelligence Officer), quoted in R. Bennett, *Behind the Battle: Intelligence in the War with Germany 1939–45* (London: Sinclair-Stevenson, 1994), p. 100.

56. Hinsley, *British Intelligence in the Second World War* vol. II, p. 596.

57. See D. M. Glantz, 'Soviet Operational Intelligence in the Kursk Operation,' *Intelligence and National Security* vol. 5 no. 1 (January 1990).

58. For references to this cross-border intelligence see Lord Carver, *Seven Ages of the British Army* (London: Grafton, 1984), pp. 310–13.

59. Kahn, *Hitler's Spies*, p. 513.

60. Lewin, *The American Magic*, p. 195.

61. Ferns and Handel, 'Clausewitz, Intelligence, Uncertainty and the Art of Command,' p. 35.

62. Ferris, 'Ralph Bennett and the Study of Ultra,' p. 481.

63. I owe this suggestion to John Prestwich, ex-Bletchley.

64. M Bennett, *Behind the Battle*, p. 174.

65. Bennett, *Behind the Battle*, p. 100, quoting Sir Edgar Williams.

66. C. Farrands, 'The Context of Foreign Policy Systems: Environment and Structure' in Clark and White, *Understanding Foreign Policy*, pp. 95–6.

67. R. Jervis, 'Strategic Intelligence and Effective Policy' in A. S. Parson, D. Stafford and W. K. Wark (eds.). *Security and Intelligence in a Changing World: New Perspectives for the 1990s* (London: Cass, 1991), pp. 179–80.

68. Douglas Hurd, 'Making the World a Safer Place; Our Priorities' (*Daily Telegraph*, 1 January 1992), quoted by W. Wallace, 'British Foreign Policy after the Cold War,' *International Affairs* vol. 68 no. 3 (July 1992), p. 438.

69. Chapter 5, note 35.

70. K. Ellis, *The Post Office in the Eighteenth Century* (Oxford: Oxford University Press, 1958), p. 141.

71. C. Andrew, 'Codebreakers and Foreign Offices' in C. Andrew and D. Dilks, *The Missing Dimension* (London: HarperCollins, 1995), pp. 37–8.

72. K. Jeffrey and A. Sharp, 'Lord Cuzon and Secret Intelligence' in Andrew and Noakes, *Intelligence and International Relations 1900–1945*.

73. J. Ferris, 'The Historiography of American Intelligence,' *Diplomatic History* vol. 19 no. 1 (winter 1995), p. 97.

74. M. Handel, *The Diplomacy of Surprise: Hitler, Nixon, Sadat* (Cambridge, Mass.: Harvard University Center for International Affairs, 1981), p. ix.

75. For a summary of British intelligence on the Soviet-German negotiations see D. C. Watt, *How War Came: The Immediate Origins of the Second World War 1938–1939* (London: Heinemann, 1989), pp. 372–4. For a fuller treatment of this British intelligence failure see the same author's article, 'An Intelligence Surprise: the Failure of the Foreign Office to Anticipate the Nazi-Soviet Pact,' *Intelligence and National Security* vol. 4 no. 3 (July 1989), pp. 512–34. For Soviet use of information from an agent in the Foreign Office's communications section, see Watt's 'Francis Herbert King: A Soviet Source in the Foreign Office,' *Intelligence and National Security* vol. 3 no. 4 (October 1988).

76. Warning surveillance is sometimes spoken of as insurance. Lawrence Freedman has pointed out in a different context that insurance policies do not stop accidents happening or equip one to cope with them; instead they give compensation. Warning is a precaution against surprise rather than post facto compensation. [L. Freedman, 'The Use and Abuse of Threats,' *Brassey's Defence Yearbook* (London: Brassey's, 1995), pp. 4–5]. ✦

Michael Herman, "Intelligence and National Action," in his *Intelligence Power in Peace and War* (Cambridge: Cambridge University Press, 2001): 137–155. Reprinted with the permission of Cambridge University Press.

18

Tribal Tongues: Intelligence Consumers, Intelligence Producers

Mark M. Lowenthal

Lowenthal suggests that the bureaucratic cultures of the policymaking and intelligence communities often form a significant barrier when it comes to the relationship between the consumers and producers of intelligence. Both policymakers and intelligence professionals are preoccupied with the demands of their own positions and tend to believe that their motivations and objectives are shared by everyone. "Tribal Tongues" offers many insights into the way policymakers and intelligence professionals view the *real world* around them.

In the Aftermath of the Cold War and the Gulf War there has been much soul-searching in the executive and Congress concerning the organization and role of the intelligence community: How should it be organized? Which issues should it be covering? What are the emerging issues that should be addressed now? These are of course important questions. But they tend to by-pass more fundamental issues within the intelligence community that are of a more permanent—and thus, perhaps—more important nature because they deal with how the community functions and fulfills its role on a daily basis. One of these is the relationship between the intelligence consumers and the intelligence producers.

Most analyses of the U.S. intelligence process pay lip service to the consumer-producer relationship. Although occasional serious forays on the subject exist, such as Thomas Hughes's *The Fate of Facts in the World of Men*,[1] most either ignore or downplay the importance of this relationship as a significant shaper of intelligence *throughout* the so-called intelligence process, starting with collection and ending with its final consumption.

A major problem is that the consumer-producer relationship resembles that of two closely related tribes that believe, mistakenly, that they speak the same language and work in the same manner for agreed outcomes. Reality, when viewed from either perspective, suggests something wholly different. Indeed, one is often reminded of George Bernard Shaw's quip about Britons and Americans being divided by a common tongue.

We All Want the Same Thing

Most policymakers (i.e., consumers) work on the assumption of basic support throughout the government for their various policy initiatives, including support by the intelligence community. The first problem lies in the very word *support*. For policymakers, this means a shared and active interest and, if necessary, advocacy. This runs counter, however, to the intelligence community's long-standing position not to advocate any policy. Rather, the intelligence community tends to see itself, correctly or not, as a value-free service agency, although at its upper levels the line begins to blur.

Second, the intelligence community, like all other parts of the permanent government bureaucracy, has a "we/they" view of its political masters. The intelligence community is part of the *permanent* government; those making policy are politically driven *transients*, even when nominated from within the professional ranks of agencies. Indeed, with the exception of the uniformed military, nowhere else in the entire foreign policy and defense apparatus can there be found as many career officials at such senior levels as in the intelligence community. They can sometimes be found at the level equivalent to deputy secretary and clearly predominate at and below the level equivalent to assistant secretary.

Compounding this professional versus political, "we/they" conflict is the fact that consumers can and do advocate policy initiatives that run athwart intelligence community preferences. For example, the political demands for visibly intrusive arms-control monitoring methods, regardless of their minimal contribution to verification, pose real dangers for counterintelligence. The need to go public with information in order to justify policy initiatives or to brief foreign officials in order to build international support for policies often poses dangers to intelligence sources and methods. Such confrontations must often be resolved at the cabinet level and, although there will be some cutting and pasting to accommodate intelligence concerns, the overall policy will generally prevail. This is as it should be within the U.S. system of government. At the same time, it deepens the "we/they" syndrome.

Finally, the two groups have very different interests at stake. A successful policy is what the consumers were hired to create and execute. The intelligence community's reputation however, rests less on the success of any policy than on its ability to assist in the formation of that policy and to predict potential outcomes—both good and bad. The producers are only vulnerable if the policy is perceived as failing because the intelligence support was in some way lacking. Ironically, the intelligence community is rarely given credit if the policy succeeds. In part, this is a self-fulfilling outcome given the distance the producers cultivate from the process; in part, it is the natural bureaucratic phenomenon of scrambling for honors.

The Value of a Free Commodity: Priceless or Worthless?

Intelligence products arrive in the consumers' limousines, pouches, and in boxes every morning and evening. They are part of the established routine. These products are, for their readers, basically cost-free subscriptions that were never ordered and never have to be paid for, perks of the job. High-level policy consumers have no real sense of either budgetary or mission/manpower cost to their departments or agencies for the very existence of these products, even if some of the products come from entities that they control. Thus, the secretary of defense will rarely be faced with a significant trade-off between required intelligence programs for the Defense Intelligence Agency and the National Security Agency versus next year's weapons procurement, nor will the secretary of state have to juggle the Bureau of Intelligence and Research's budget against prospective embassy closings.

Intelligence production, for the consumers, exists somewhere beyond their ken, as if unseen gnomes labor to produce the papers that magically arrive. If the analyses are good, all the better; if they are not, consumers are unlikely to advocate redirecting some of their resources to improving them.

Moreover, the very regularity with which these products appear has a lulling effect. The standard items—the *National Intelligence Daily*, the *Secretary's Morning Summary*—are essentially newspapers. Anyone who has read yesterday's edition or watched last night's 11:00 p.m. news can predict what is likely to be covered in this morning's edition. Indeed, while these publications are all lumped together as part of the "current intelligence" emphasis of the intelligence community, in reality they represent items that can safely be given to customers the next day. They are not urgent warnings or long-awaited breakthroughs, items that scream "read me now." Rather, they are part of the daily routine.

To break through this lulling effect, intelligence has to be able to prove to its consumers that it brings "value added" to the steady drone of information, analysis, and opinion that comes from both within and beyond the intelligence community. But one bureau or agency's memo looks much like another's, unless you bother to read them and assess them. How do you assure that, if only one will be read, it's yours? In reality, the unstated value added that intelligence producers bring is their sources. But, for very good reasons, raw intelligence is rarely presented to consumers. The intelligence is given context and comment, analysis that again makes it look like everyone else's.

How does the producer break out of this trap? One way is simply packaging, designing products that *do* scream for attention when there is a truly important piece of intelligence or a fastbreaking event about which the producers know first. The second is establishing a track record, although this still depends on whether the consumer reads intelligence analyses and remembers who was right and who was wrong.

In the end, consumers incur no real and regular penalty for ignoring this daily flow of information. In managing their day, high-level consumers establish methods to cut down on reading extraneous material. At the very highest levels, a large portion of daily intelligence products probably falls into this category. These consumers assume that their subordinates will read what they must within their areas of responsibility and that truly urgent items will come to their attention.

Consumer Behaviors That Matter

In reality, the intelligence consumer does more than just consume. He or she is not some eager, expectant eye and mind waiting at the end of the intelligence process. The consumer helps set the agenda, from intelligence priorities, to collection, to format.

Agenda

Consumers have their own sets of priorities and preferences, issues in which they are deeply interested, those in which they must take an interest by their nature, and those they would just as soon ignore. If they bother to communicate these preferences to the intelligence producers (a rare enough occurrence), and the producers respond accordingly, then the entire intelligence process has already been influenced. Although producers will not cease to try to cover all the issues that *they* believe are important, only those intelligence officers with a taste for abuse and a desire to be ignored will try to force these on an unwilling consumer. This can put producers in an awkward position, especially if the subject in question is one they feel quite strongly deserves attention. It can also run athwart the intelligence community's "warning function," namely, the requirement that it look ahead for issues—especially sleepers—that have the potential to become grave concerns.

Collection

The most senior consumer, the president, can also determine what gets collected and what does not for reasons of policy beyond the preferences of the intelligence producers. The U.S. policy in the shah's Iran of having no contact with the mullahs,[2] or President Jimmy Carter's termination of U-2 flights over Cuba, both come to mind.

'What Don't I Know?'

To the producer, the ideal consumer is one who knows what he doesn't know. Unfortunately, this quality can be hard to come by. It is understandable that senior officials dislike admitting areas of ignorance within their fields of responsibility. Those who do, however, have a clear advantage, especially if they are willing to take steps, among them requested analyses and briefings, to remedy the situation. Similarly, it is important for the consumers to distinguish between what they must know, what they'd like to know, and what is simply enjoyable but unnecessary. Failure to do this well, and continually, can lead to one of two traps—either consuming too much time on some subjects or too little on others. Given the primacy of time management, this should be a crucial skill for the harried consumer. Once this skill is acquired, and its results communicated to the producers, it again establishes priorities and agendas.

Dealing With Uncertainty

Neither producers nor consumers like intelligence gaps. At best they are annoying; at worst they can be both crucial and frightening. They do exist, however, and are often responsible for uncertainties in estimates and analyses. As strange as it may seem, such uncertainties appear to be very difficult to convey, at least in English. "If/then" constructions can become long laundry lists covering all the possibilities, without regard to likelihood; "on the one hand/on the other hand" often creates octopuses of sentences—too many hands spoil the analyses. The absence of an easily used subjunctive really hurts.

Unfortunately, consumers often interpret these very real problems of limited sources and uncertain outcomes as pusillanimity on the part of producers. "They have a best guess," consumers suppose, "they're just hedging so they won't be wrong." The inability on the part of producers to convey adequately the cause and nature of uncertainty and ambiguity tends to alienate a largely dubious audience.

'Shooting the Messenger'

This consumer behavior is as old as recorded history—if the messenger brings bad news, kill him. Unfortunately, it still happens. The messenger is not killed; he is first berated and then, on subsequent occasions, ignored. In part this consumer behavior stems from the darker side of the "we all want the same thing" syndrome. Once consumers have figured out that they and their intelligence people do *not* all necessarily want the same thing, they become suspicious of the producers. Do they have their own agenda for their own dark reasons? If they are not actively supporting me are they working against me? Unfortunately, the delivery of "bad news," usually some piece of intelligence or an analysis that questions preferred or ongoing policies, fits this more paranoid view all too well.[3]

What, however, is the producer's alternative? Suppress the intelligence and risk having the consumer blindsided or even badly embarrassed, a sure blow to credibility? Better to err on the side of caution and risk opprobrium, knowing full well that this, too, can harm credibility. Either way, the outcome largely rests on the intelligence's reception by the consumers, on their maturity, experience, and willingness to be challenged by people who are not a threat to their policies.

The Consumer as Analyst

Consumers are, by and large, a self-confident group. They have achieved fairly exalted and responsible positions through either the trial by fire of long professional careers or through the hurly-burly of private enterprise or partisan politics. No matter the route, they assume that it is not just connections and luck that have brought them to their current positions. This self assurance is all to the good, although it can lead to some aberrant behavior.

The first such behavior has to do with issues of long standing regarding which the consumer believes that he or she knows as much, if not more, than the intelligence analysts. Certainly, assistant secretaries of state for Europe, the Near East, and so on, are likely to have spent a large portion of their professional careers on these issues, and they probably know some of the key players in the region on a personal basis. Interestingly, the same perception eventually takes hold of senior officials dealing with Soviet issues, regardless of their previous experience. At least two factors are at work here. First, the long-standing nature of the U.S. rivalry with the Soviets lends an air of familiarity, whether deserved or not. Second, after about two years in office, the average secretary of state has met with his Soviet counterpart more than half a dozen times and probably feels he has greater insight into Soviet thinking than do "ivory tower" analysts who have only seen the Soviet Union from 150 miles up.[4] The recent upheaval in the Soviet Union and Eastern Europe may have tempered the first attitude, now that the familiar signposts of relations have gone. This probably results, however, in increased emphasis on the second attitude, the value of high-level, face-to-face contacts over analysis by those more remote from events.

For this type of reaction the "value-added" question becomes paramount. What can the producer bring to the issue that is new, insightful, and useful? Here, the natural inclination, if not necessity, to hedge analyses works against the producer and only serves to reinforce the prejudice of the consumer.

The second "consumer-as-analyst" behavior manifests itself during those periods of intense activity usually misnamed crises. Suddenly, the premium for current intelligence rises dramatically; consumers will often cry out for the "raw intelligence." There is the sudden assumption that at moments like these, trained intelligence analysts will somehow get in the way, that they will, perhaps inadvertently, distort the incoming information. Ideally, the intelligence officers should resist, offering to come back in several minutes with some sort of analysis or context along with the raw intelligence. Quite simply, consumers are probably less well suited at these moments to serve as their own analysts. Their ability to assess objectively and dispassionately what is happening is usually inverse to the importance of the issue, its intensity, and the amount of time they have been dealing with it. This is not to say that consumers have nothing of analytical value to bring to the process, including during crises. They should not, however, act to cut off the contributions of professional expertise. At worst, they will get an alternative point of view that they are always free to reject.[5]

The Assumption of Omniscience

For the United States as a global power, it is difficult to find many issues or regions that are not of at least some minimal interest. For the consumer this translates into the erroneous assumption that somewhere in the labyrinths of the intelligence community there is at least one analyst capable of covering each issue that comes along.

The source of this assumption is most likely a conceit derived from the expectation that U.S. interests must be matched by U.S. capabilities, that intelligence managers must know that *all* bases should be covered. Interestingly, this runs counter to the often heard criticism (and accepted folk wisdom) that the intelligence community has traditionally spent too much time and effort on the Soviet target, to the disadvantage of less sexy albeit no less important issues.

Unfortunately, there is no safe way for the producers to correct the assumption of omniscience. The intelligence community is loath to admit that it is not true and is fearful of the criticism that will ensue if this is discovered. Yet, in a world of unlimited issues and limited intelligence resources gaps are unavoidable. How resources are allotted either to close or to allow gaps remains a murky process based on past experience and known or—more likely—perceived consumer interest. Too often this process degenerates into a debate over the size of the intelligence budget, raising the suspicion among consumers (and congressional overseers) that cries of insufficient coverage are in reality pleas for more resources that will be redirected to areas that the intelligence community sees fit. Were the producers, however, to address the issue forthrightly and ask consumers, say down to the assistant secretary level, for a list of issues that had to be covered and those that could be given shorter shrift, it is unlikely that they would get consensus. Here again the "free commodity" issue is at work, only now consumers would be asked to give up something that they had always received, even if they had never had any great use for it.

Inevitably, one of the issues that has long been considered below the threshold will suddenly require attention. With a little luck there may be an analyst somewhere who has at least passing familiarity with it. This is the moment when the producers hope to shine, to prove the "value added" they bring to the process. If they succeed, however, they also reinforce the omniscience assumption, which sooner or later will be found, painfully, to be false.

The Absence of Feedback

Intelligence consumers have neither the time nor the inclination to offer much feedback on what they are getting or not getting. This stems from several sources. First, the throwing of bouquets is not a habit in government nor should it be expected.[6] Second, there is rarely enough time. As soon as one problem is solved or crisis ended, it is time to move on to the next. But the absence of feedback enforces the producers' image of top consumers as "black holes," into which intelligence is drawn without any sense of the reception or effect. The result is to deny the producers any guidance as to how they are doing.

At the same time, it must be admitted that, despite calls on their part for feedback, many in the intelligence community are quite content with the status quo. They do not favor "report cards"; they fear that they will only hear the negative and not receive any praise; they are concerned lest feedback becomes a means by which consumers would try to affect the content of intelligence to elicit greater support for policies. None of this needs to happen if the feedback process is honest and regularized.

There also would be genuine benefits. The intelligence community is made up of analysts who largely enjoy their work and who believe, as individuals, that the issues they cover are worthy of attention. At the working level, however, they exist in relative isolation, without any reference point as to how well their work fulfills its purported purposes among the consumers. Analysts will continue to work on what they believe to be relevant and important unless or until consumers offer guidance as to preferences, needs, and style. In short, producers need to be told how best to shape their products and focus for the consumers, but the initiative for doing so remains with the consumers.[7]

Feedback is also an area where Congress, in its oversight role, can be helpful. Congress has, in the past, reviewed important policy issues for which intelligence was a major factor and has offered objective assessments of the quality of intelligence and the uses to which it was put by consumers. The Senate Select Committee on Intelligence, for example, offered a critique of the famous Team A-Team B competitive Soviet analysis and called the exercise worthwhile but flawed in its execution. This same committee also found that President Jimmy Carter's release of Central Intelligence Agency analysis of Soviet oil prospects was largely driven by his own political needs.[8] Similarly, the House Permanent Select Committee on Intelligence offered a scathing review of intelligence on Iran prior to the fall of the shah. The same committee's review of intelligence prior to the Mariel exodus from Cuba concluded that U.S. surprise on that occasion was not due to lack of intelligence warnings.[9]

Such a service is quite useful and can be done by Congress objectively and without partisan rancor. However, the two Select Committees on Intelligence also have limits on their time and cannot provide this sort of review regularly. Congress is an intelligence consumer as well, although it is not privy to the full extent of the analyses that flow to policymakers in the executive. Thus, Congress can supplement feedback from consumers but cannot fully substitute for it.

Producer Behaviors That Matter

Just as the consumer does more than consume, the producers do more than simply collect, analyze, and produce. Their behavior also affects the product and the perceptions held by the consumers.

Current Versus Long-Term Intelligence

All intelligence agencies, managers, and analysts are constantly tugged between the need for current intelligence and the desire to write long-term intelligence. Thomas Hughes portrayed the struggle as one of "intelligence butchers" (current intelligence, done in short, sharp chops of material) versus "intelligence bakers" (long-term intelligence, done in prolonged melding and blending). As cute as Hughes's model is, it gives the mistaken impression that the choice of which type of intelligence to emphasize lies with the producers. This tends not to be so. Rather, it is the very nature of how foreign and defense policy is handled by consumers that drives the choice. Intelligence producers claim not to be bothered by this consumer preference for current intelligence, but this too is not entirely correct.

Current intelligence (i.e., tonight, tomorrow, this week) will always dominate. That is the very nature of the U.S. policy process. It is very "now" oriented, creating a series of difficult choices among issues all crying for attention. Indeed, there is very little sense of completion, because each issue laid to rest has too many successors waiting for attention as well. The drive of current events even tends to distort the notion of "long-term" analysis, which becomes the next ministerial meeting, the next arms-control round, the next summit, next year's budget process at best.

Much lip service is given by both producers and consumers to the need for long-term intelligence. Yet nothing in their daily lives indicates what use they would make of such intelligence if it existed. For consumers it would represent luxury items, things to be read when or if the press of current business allowed. For producers it would mean just a chance to be more wrong at a greater distance from the events—a constant concern.

Some will argue that the intelligence community already produces long-term analyses in the form of the National Intelligence Estimates (NIEs). But what is the function of the NIEs? In theory they represent the best judgment of the entire intelligence community on major issues, as conveyed by the director of central intelligence to the president. Some NIEs are done at the request of consumers, most often a fast-track or Special NIE (SNIE, pronounced "snee"). Other NIEs are done at the suggestion of an intelligence organization or are initiated by national intelligence officers, who perceive a need among consumers.

But beyond their impressive name and theoretical status, do NIEs really influence long-term policies? Or are they, in the scathing words of the House Permanent Select Committee on Intelligence, "not worth fighting for"?[10] It is difficult to find many NIEs that have substantially influenced ongoing policy debates. Various intelligence agencies participate earnestly in the NIE game largely to keep track of their brethren and to preserve their own points of view. NIEs are important simply because they exist and not because of any great value that they regularly add to the process. More often they serve either as data bases for budget justifications (in the case of the annual NIE on Soviet programs) or as the source of self-serving and often misleading quotations for use by consumers during policy debates.

Although both producers and consumers constantly cry out for more long-term and less current intelligence, it remains unclear that the outcry has any substance beyond a general and unsubstantiated belief that, if it were produced, long-term intelligence would give greater coherence to policy.

Portraying Uncertainty

One of the most difficult problems that producers face on a daily basis is the need to portray uncertainty. Every issue that is analyzed has gaps, unknown areas, competing plausible outcomes. As much as producers would like to be able to predict with finality, they both know that it is rarely possible and tend to write so as to cover, at least minimally, less likely outcomes so as not to be entirely wrong.

Portraying this in writing can be difficult. In the absence of a widely used subjunctive tense, producers use other techniques: "perhaps, although, however, on the one hand/on the other hand, maybe." There is nothing intrinsically wrong with any of these, although their net effect can be harmful for several reasons.

First, their use becomes habitual, creating written safety nets that allow the producers to keep all their bets covered. Second, and perhaps more important, they strike the consumer, especially with repetition, as "weasel words," efforts by the producers to avoid coming down on one side or another of any issue.

Producers do not spend enough time or effort explaining why these uncertainties remain. Consumers, being thus uninformed, tend to revert to their omniscience syndrome and see pusillanimity instead.

The Perceived Penalty for Changing Estimates

Producers do not like to be wrong, but they realize they are fallible. They also, however, do not like having to make changes in estimates, fearful of the cost to their credibility with the consumers. Wide swings are especially anathema; better to adjust one's estimates gradually, to bring the consumers along slowly to the new view. Thus, if for years the estimate has said "*T* is most likely," and producers now believe that "*Z* is most likely," few will want to jump directly from *T* to *Z*. Instead, they would rather move slowly through *U*, *V*, *W*, *X* and *Y*, preparing the consumer for the idea that *Z* is now correct.

In this case, the perception may be worse than the reality. Most consumers, if properly prepared as to why there is a change (new data, new sources, new models, and so on), are likely to accept it unless changes become so regular a phenomenon as to raise serious questions.[11] Again, it is largely an issue of communications, of adequately explaining the uncertainties inherent in any estimate and the factors that have led to the change. Unfortunately, the outcome is so dreaded that the process rarely takes place.

Miracles Versus Saints

One of the necessary premiums put on all intelligence writing (with the exception of some NIEs) is brevity. Less is more when dealing with overly busy readers. Unfortunately, this runs counter to the desire burning within nearly every analyst to tell as much of the story as possible, to give the reader background, context and, in part, to show off. (For example: "You can't really understand the FMLN insurgency in El Salvador unless you go back to the Spanish land grants of the sixteenth century." A plausible point, but not an analysis that any busy reader is likely to read.)

Analysts tend not to err on the side of brevity. It becomes, therefore, the task of the intelligence production managers to edit material down to a suitable length. Analysts must be admonished to "just tell the miracles, and not the lives of all the saints involved in making them happen."

The miracles versus saints problem, however, also poses a difficult managerial decision. Analysts cannot write about the miracles with any facility until they have mastered the lives of the saints. Managers therefore have to be flexible enough to allow their analysts the time to study, and even to write about the saints, if only for use in background papers sent to other analysts. But this time must not be allowed to conflict with ongoing demands for written products, including those about the very miracles in question. It's a tough call, but one that has a payoff later on.

Jaded Versus Naive

Given a choice between appearing jaded or naive on a given subject, the average intelligence professional will choose to appear jaded at least nine times out of ten. No one wants to appear to be the new kid on the block. Instead, analysts act as though they have seen it all and done it all before. This is especially troublesome in group meetings with peers, where appearances matter.

What this means, in terms of analysis, is that few situations are treated as being truly new, regardless of their nature. But some situations *are* new or different and do require analysis that has not been done before. A nuclear power plant blows up catastrophically; the Chinese sell intermediate-range ballistic missiles; or the Soviet Union allows its East European satellites to remove their Communist governments. By taking the jaded approach analysts force themselves, first of all, to play catch-up to situations that are ongoing, having initially wasted time playing them down. Moreover, they allow themselves to appear less than perspicacious before their consumers and now must spend time explaining away their previous stance, for which there may be little justification beyond mind-set.

The fix here is apparently simple—approach issues with a more open mind. But how can this be implemented? It cannot be institutionalized or even easily taught. It largely depends on production managers who continually ask skeptical questions, forcing their analysts to rethink. It is not easy, but it is achievable.

'Covering the World'

This is the producers' version of the agenda issue. At most times there will be more issues crying out for attention than resources available to cover them all adequately. Producers, however, do not want to let any one of these issues slip, in part out of concern that they will choose the wrong ones and not be ready if they become more important or if consumer interest is suddenly piqued. Interestingly, this behavior on the part of producers only reinforces the consumers' belief in the intelligence community's omniscience. Feedback from consumers is an essential ingredient in making choices. If this is absent, however, then the intelligence producers must decide, knowing they cannot cover everything. They must also be able to distinguish, which they sometimes do not, between issues genuinely requiring serious attention and those that do not. They may also find as noted earlier, that there are important issues that consumers do not want to ad-

dress. Here, the producers are torn, their professional responsibilities and best judgment at odds with the political realities. Overall, producers tend to side with covering more than less.

Reporting 'No Change'

Although the intelligence community cannot cover everything, it does keep track of more issues than most of its consumers can or want to deal with. Because of the limits on space in written products and the consumers' time, much goes unreported. But a second filtering process also takes place. On issues that are not "front burner" but are still of some interest, analysts will choose not to report developments or, more significantly, the lack of developments. The absence of activity is taken to mean the absence of any need to report.

There is value, however, to reporting periodically (admittedly at long intervals) on these issues and nondevelopments. If the analysts or managers know that the Rumanian nuclear program is of interest but that nothing new has happened in the last six months, there is nothing wrong with reporting that to consumers. What is the effect of such a report? First, it shows the consumer that the producers are alert, that they are tracking areas of interest beyond the self-evident. Second, it allows consumers to check off that issue on their mental lists. They can assume, probably correctly, that the producers will alert them to any change. For the moment, they need not worry about it. There is, however, a cost to such reporting, in that it tends to reinforce the consumers' omniscience assumption. Still, the net effect remains a positive one, albeit infrequent.

The Absence of Self-Analysis

This is the flip side of the absence of consumer feedback. Like everyone else in the government, intelligence analysts and officials are busy people. As soon as one crisis ends they move on to the next with very little reflection on what worked and what did not. Nor do they spend much time trying to sort out why certain analyses in certain situations work well and others do not, why warnings and indicators flag proper attention in some cases but not others, why the synergism of collection resources works for this topic or region and not for that.

Admittedly, genuine critical self-examination is difficult. The payoff for having it done more regularly, not by "outside" reviewers in the intelligence community but by the analysts and their supervisors themselves, is a much clearer insight into their institutional behaviors and processes that can greatly improve their work and their ability to serve the consumers.

Conclusion

The production and use or disuse of intelligence as part of the policy process is the net result of several types of mind-sets and behavior within and between two groups that are more disparate than most observers realize. Moreover, the disparity is more likely to be appreciated by one group, the intelligence producers, than it is by the intelligence consumers. As argued here, the consumers play a much greater role *throughout* the intelligence process and at all stages in that process than is customarily realized. Certain aspects of the gap between these two groups will never be bridged. Other aspects, like the issue of supporting policy, *should* never be bridged. Nonetheless, there remains much that can be done—even within current structures and processes—to improve communications between the two groups. The views expressed in this article are the author's and not attributable to any government agency.

Questions for Further Discussion

1. What accounts for the differences in perspectives between the permanent government and the political government?

2. What is the "value-added" problem faced by intelligence analysts and managers?

3. Why is it so difficult to correct a mistaken estimate?

4. How should the intelligence community report on "nondevelopments"?

Endnotes

1. Thomas Hughes, *The Fate of Facts in the World of Men* (New York: Foreign Policy Association, 1976).
2. See Gary Sick, *All Fall Down* (New York: Penguin Books, 1985), pp. 36, 64, 91, 104–105.
3. Needless to say, not all paranoia is unjustified. There have undoubtedly been instances in which intelligence analysts have tried to work against policies with which they disagreed. Most analysts, however, and certainly their senior supervisors know the severe penalty for being caught in such a compromising position and would most often prefer to avoid it, even at the risk that the policy will go forward. Most often, the cost to future credibility far outweighs the value of stopping one specific policy initiative.
4. During the first U.S.-Soviet ministerial meeting of the Bush administration, the deputy national security adviser, Robert Gates, who has spent a considerable part of his intelligence career as a Soviet analyst, was in Moscow for the first time. President Mikhail Gorbachev reportedly kidded Gates, asking him if the Soviet Union looked different from the ground than it did from satellites.

5. There is evidence that President George Bush, perhaps reflecting his past tenure as director of central intelligence, has a predilection for "raw traffic" and that he likes to sort out differences among reporting on his own without a sifting by lower-level analysts. See Andrew Rosenthal, "White House Aims to Sharpen Role in Panama Plots," *New York Times*, October 13, 1989, p. A-8; and Maureen Dowd, "2-Summit Plan Reflects Bush Style: Intense (Relaxed) Personal Diplomacy," *New York Times*, November 6, 1989, p. A-14.
6. Feedback is so rare that, when it occurs, the effect can often be comical. When one senior official noted his pleasure over a piece of intelligence analysis, the initial reaction among those responsible was, first, elation, quickly followed by doubts. Was this memo so good, they wondered, or was it that all of the others that received no such notice were so bad?
7. The President's Foreign Intelligence Advisory Board (PFIAB), a group of outside experts that reviews both intelligence analysis and operations, provides such guidance. It was PFIAB, for example, that suggested the Team A-Team B competitive analysis. However, PFIAB meets infrequently, reportedly once a month, and remains somewhat removed from the daily needs of producers. It cannot substitute entirely for direct producer feedback.
8. See Senate Select Committee on Intelligence, *The National Intelligence Estimates AB Team Episode Concerning Soviet Strategic Capability and Objectives and The Soviet Oil Situation: An Evaluation of CIA Analyses of Soviet Oil Production*, 95th Cong., 2d sess. 1978.
9. See House Permanent Select Committee on Intelligence, *Iran: Evaluation of U.S. Intelligence Performance Prior to November 1978*, 96th Cong., 1st sess., 1979, and *Cuban Emigres: Was There a U.S. Intelligence Failure?* 96th Cong., 2d sess., 1980.
10. See House Permanent Select Committee on Intelligence, *Iran*.
11. There have been cases, however, in which wide swings did hurt credibility. In the mid-1970s U.S. intelligence estimates of the portion of Soviet gross national product devoted to defense went from 6 to 7 percent in the mid-1970s to 10 to 15 percent, leading some consumers to question the validity of the new estimates as well. Critics in Congress suspected that the change was created to support the Ford administration's larger defense budget. See John W. Finney, "Soviet Arms Outlay May Be Bigger Slice of Pie Than Once Thought," *New York Times*, February 23, 1976, p. 13, and "U.S. Challenged on Arms Estimate," *New York Times*, March 8, 1976, p. 11. When the intelligence community repeated its estimate a year later, this threatened to discomfit the plans of the new Carter administration, which was in the midst of its review of Presidential Review Memorandum #10 on U.S. strategy. In drawing up PRM-10, Carter administration officials purposely excluded some of the premises that they saw driving the new estimates. See Hedrick Smith, "Carter Study Takes More Hopeful View of Strategy of U.S.," *New York Times*, July 8, 1977, p. A-1. ✦

Reprinted with permission from Mark M. Lowenthal, "Tribal Tongues: Intelligence Consumers, Intelligence Producers," *Washington Quarterly* 15 (Winter 1992): 157–168.

19

The Need for Policy Guidance

Aspin-Brown Commission

It is said that policymakers get the intelligence they deserve. Without specific requests from senior policy officials, the intelligence community is left to its own devices when it comes to selecting intelligence requirements and targets. As the Aspin-Brown Commission noted, the intelligence community is sometimes left without any guidance. This is especially the case when the National Security Council reconstitutes itself with the change of administrations; during this period, senior officials are diverted from their normal duties of conducting routine oversight and helping to establish desired intelligence requirements and targets. The Commission recommended dedicated committees, lodged in the NSC, to set long-term intelligence needs and to evaluate intelligence priorities periodically in the face of a changing strategic landscape.

Intelligence agencies cannot operate in a vacuum. Like any other service organization, intelligence agencies must have guidance from the people they serve. They exist as a tool of government to gather and assess information, and if they do not receive direction, chances are greater that resources will be misdirected and wasted. Intelligence agencies need to know what information to collect and when it is needed. They need to know if their products are useful and how they might be improved to better serve policymakers. Guidance must come from the top. Policymaker direction should be both the foundation and the catalyst for the work of the Intelligence Community.

The drafters of the National Security Act of 1947 understood the importance of such guidance in creating the National Security Council (NSC).[1] The NSC was created to coordinate the policies and functions of the departments and agencies of the Government relating to all aspects of national security, including the intelligence function.

Since then, each Administration has created its own structure and procedures to meet the policy objectives and management styles of the President and his senior advisers responsible for national security. Historically, intelligence information has made significant contributions to the substantive work of the NSC, whatever its structure; but where top-level guidance for intelligence requirements and policies is concerned, the role of the NSC and its staff has varied.

In some Administrations, formal NSC committees composed of cabinet-level officials have been established to provide guidance on intelligence matters. Such committees have been supported by a small professional staff within the NSC. In other Administrations, the national security advisor has delegated most intelligence issues to a senior member of the NSC staff. In some Administrations, the NSC principals and/or staff have taken an active and consequential role in providing guidance on intelligence matters; in others, they have served principally to coordinate the intelligence response during times of crises.

Intelligence as an NSC Function From the Nixon Administration to the Present

President Richard M. Nixon took office in 1969 and created an NSC structure shortly thereafter. Not until 1971, however, did his Administration create an "Intelligence Committee," one of the four top committees within the NSC responsible for providing policy guidance on national security issues. In addition, the NSC structure during the Nixon Administration contained a separate committee to approve and coordinate covert actions (the 40 Committee).

In 1975, the blue-ribbon "Commission on the Organization of the Government For the Conduct of Foreign Policy" (the Murphy Commission) reviewed this structure and found it largely ineffective. The Murphy Commission recommended that the NSC Intelligence Committee "should be actively used as the principal forum for the resolution, short of the President, of the differing perspectives of intelligence consumers and producers, and should meet frequently for that purpose."

In 1976, almost two years into his presidency, President Gerald R. Ford issued a new Executive Order on intelligence, abolishing the existing NSC structure on intelligence and creating in its place a "Committee on Foreign Intelligence" (CFI). This new Committee was composed of the Director of Central Intelligence, the Deputy Secretary of Defense for Intelligence, and the Deputy Assistant to the President for National Security Affairs. The Administration directed this committee to "control budget preparation and resource allocation" for national intelligence, as well as to establish priorities for collection and production. The Executive Order spelled out several specific tasks the CFI should accomplish, among them giving direction on the relationship between tactical and national intelligence and providing "continuing guidance to the Intelligence Community in order to ensure compliance with policy direction of the NSC."

This structure proved short-lived. President Ford remained in office less than a year thereafter, and his successor, President Jimmy Carter, immediately replaced the existing NSC apparatus with a two-committee structure consisting of a Policy Review Committee (PRC) and a Special Coordinating Committee (SCC). Depending upon the subject matter under consideration, the PRC would be chaired by, and composed of, different Administration officials, including the DCI when it addressed intelligence issues. The SCC was chaired by the National Security Advisor, and addressed the review and policy considerations of special activities, including covert action.

In 1978, President Carter provided more specific guidance on intelligence matters and issued a separate Executive Order on intelligence. It stipulated that the PRC, when dealing with intelligence matters, would be responsible for the establishment of requirements and priorities for national foreign intelligence, review of the intelligence budget, and the periodic review and evaluation of intelligence products. It was also charged with submitting an annual report on its activities to the NSC.

Three years later when he assumed office, President Ronald Reagan abolished the Carter NSC structure without creating a separate standing committee on intelligence, relying instead on a separate element on the NSC staff. He also signed Executive Order 12333, a broad statement of intelligence responsibilities and policies, which provided that the NSC "shall act as the highest Executive Branch entity that provides review of, guidance for, and direction to the conduct of all national foreign intelligence, counterintelligence, and special activities, and attendant policies and programs."

Later, as part of a reorganization of the NSC staff, a series of "Senior Interagency Groups" (SIGs) were created, one of which dealt with intelligence. Chaired by the DCI, the "SIG-I" was chartered to establish requirements and priorities for national foreign intelligence, review the program and budget for national intelligence as well as proposals for sensitive operations.

In 1989, President George Bush eliminated the Reagan NSC structure, and returned to a two-Committee structure, consisting of a "Principals Committee" and a "Deputies Committee." The Principals Committee was chaired by the National Security Advisor; the Deputies Committee, by his Deputy. A separate staff office coordinated intelligence programs.

Two years into the Administration, the NSC conducted the first in-depth review of intelligence requirements. The document that instituted the review, known as "National Security Review-29," noted that "senior policy makers traditionally have neglected their critical role in setting intelligence priorities and requirements." It produced a lengthy list of government-wide intelligence requirements, but it failed to assign priorities in a way that usefully guided collection efforts or the allocation of resources.

In 1993, President Bill Clinton took office. He retained the "Principals Committee/ Deputies Committee" structure to coordinate major foreign policy issues and created a system of "Interagency Working Groups" to handle more routine issues. A separate staff office coordinated intelligence activities. In April, 1995, a new presidential directive was issued which, for the first time, stated in priority order what a President considered to be his intelligence requirements and established a working group of mid-level policy officials to review more regularly intelligence policies and requirements.

Shortcomings of the Past

The Commission sees several shortcomings in the historical process described above. The institutional role played by the NSC in providing guidance and direction for intelligence activities has varied widely. Often substantial lapses occur at the change of Administrations when there is no guidance at all. As a result, a consistent level of guidance concerning appropriate roles for intelligence, as well as the guidance establishing requirements and priorities for collection and analysis, has, all too often, been missing.

In practice, the NSC's structures created to perform such functions often have foundered. Senior officials, such as cabinet secretaries or their deputies, who represent their respective departments and agencies at NSC-level meetings, usually have little or no background in intelligence and are inundated by the press of other duties. Intelligence is too often viewed as a support function that is "someone else's responsibility." Subordinates are increasingly sent to meetings in place of principals, and meetings become progressively less frequent. As a result, a true "consumer driven" intelligence process has never fully evolved within the NSC, regardless of the Administration in office.

The Commission believes the NSC as an institution should provide clearer guidance for intelligence, through regular tasking and a better organizational framework for handling intelligence issues. Several close allies visited by the Commission during its inquiry have effective mechanisms at the senior levels of governments to ensure that their intelligence agencies receive timely, ongoing guidance from the political level. In Great Britain, for example, a Cabinet-level office known as the Joint Intelligence Committee (JIC) brings together senior British policymakers and intelligence officials on a weekly basis. The JIC, functioning since 1936, is responsible for setting intelligence priorities on an ongoing basis, and for producing a weekly intelligence summary. Members include the principal producers and consumers of intelligence. While clearly the work and value of structures such as the JIC are facilitated where the government is considerably smaller than the U.S. Government and principally staffed by career civil servants, the Commission believes the concept embodied in the JIC can also be made to work in the United States.

What Needs to Be Done

The Commission recognizes that every President must be free to use and structure the National Security Council as he or she sees fit, including the performance of its statutory role to provide direction to the Intelligence Community. From the Commission's standpoint, however, the particular structure decided upon by a president is less important than a clear and consistent understanding and implementation of the roles it should perform. Even when Administrations change, the functions of the NSC should not. Top-level direction to intelligence agencies would be greatly strengthened by a more institutionalized role for the NSC, one that is not rewritten every two or four years. The more the role of the NSC varies, the more difficult it is to develop and sustain working relationships that provide clear, frequent direction for intelligence and guidance for its collection and analytic efforts.

In the view of the Commission, the institutional role played by the NSC structure should include setting the policy guidelines for intelligence activities, stating what the intelligence agencies are expected to do and what they should not do. The NSC structure should clarify, for example, whether intelligence agencies should collect economic intelligence or analyze intelligence on the environment, whether they perform analysis of publicly-available information, and what rules should govern intelligence-gathering where allied and friendly governments are concerned.

The institutional role of the NSC also should include providing guidance for ongoing intelligence collection and analysis, to say what is needed and when, clarifying what is helpful and not helpful. What are the issues on the "front burner" for the President and other policymakers? What information would fill a void? On what subjects is intelligence adding little of value? Where does intelligence have access to information that would be of considerable value, but is not being collected?

It should also be the institutional role of the NSC (but not the NSC staff by itself) to assess, from time to time, the performance of the Intelligence Community in satisfying their substantive needs as policymakers, reporting its conclusions, as appropriate, to the President.

In the section that follows, the Commission proposes a two-tier NSC structure for carrying out these roles. It is intended as a model for this and future Administrations.

Whatever NSC structure may be adopted for intelligence, however, it must not interfere with the direct reporting relationship between the President and the Director of Central Intelligence, which must be preserved. The importance to the intelligence function of having a strong relationship between the President and the DCI cannot be overemphasized. The Commission was consistently told by former DCIs that where their relationship was strong, it had repercussions across the entire Government, including the Congress, giving vitality and purpose to the whole enterprise. Conversely, where the relationship was weak, it took a heavy toll on the esprit and influence of the Intelligence Community.

3-1. The Commission recommends the establishment within the National Security Council of a "Committee on Foreign Intelligence" (CFI), chaired by the Assistant to the President for National Security Affairs and including the Director of Central Intelligence, the Deputy Secretary of State and the Deputy Secretary of Defense. The Chair should invite other senior officials to attend as may be appropriate given the meeting agenda.

The CFI should meet at least semi-annually and provide guidance to the DCI for the conduct of intelligence activities, to include establishing overall requirements and priorities for collection and analysis. Appropriate NSC staff should formulate the agendas and supporting materials for these meetings, with NSC members and their staffs providing such assistance as may be required. The CFI should report annually to the President on its activities.

3-2. The Commission recommends that a "Consumers Committee" be established as a subordinate element of the CFI. This Committee should be chaired by the Deputy Assistant to the President for National Security Affairs and should include senior representatives at the Undersecretary level of the parent CFI members as well as senior representatives of other princi-

pal intelligence producers and consumers within the Government, e.g. the Secretaries of Commerce and Treasury, the U.S. Trade Representative. The Consumers Committee should meet at least monthly and provide continuous, ongoing guidance with respect to the priorities for intelligence collection and analysis to meet the needs of the Government. The Consumers Committee should monitor and periodically report to the CFI with respect to how well the Intelligence Community is meeting the needs of consumers, identifying gaps and shortcomings where appropriate. The NSC staff should be responsible for formulating the agendas and supporting materials for each meeting, with NSC members and their staffs providing such assistance as may be required.

The Commission opted for this bifurcated approach for several reasons. The Commission believes that the major overarching issues in the intelligence area are best left to a small group, consisting of the principal cabinet officers who are responsible for, and the users of, intelligence. The Commission believes such a group should be chaired by the National Security Advisor because he can approach the issues from the viewpoint of the President and has responsibility for coordinating national security matters on his behalf.

However, it is unrealistic to expect such a senior group to play an active role in setting ongoing requirements and priorities for intelligence-gathering and analysis. This function necessarily requires more frequent meetings and must be carried out at a lower level of representation. Membership should be at a high enough level so that the participant can represent the policies of his or her agency or department, but also at a level where the participant can be a regular attendee at the monthly meetings. Whoever may be designated, however, should have or be able to obtain a grasp of the overall intelligence requirements and priorities of the department or agency they represent.

The Commission believes that a forum outside the Intelligence Community (but including a representative of the Intelligence Community) should evaluate the substantive contributions made by the intelligence agencies. Hence, this role is suggested for the Consumers Committee. This is a function that the NSC has not performed in the past but is needed for the effective operation of the Intelligence Community.

Finally, the Commission does not contemplate that either the CFI or its subordinate Consumers Committee would perform oversight or management functions. The DCI would continue to report to the President and not to either of these commit-

tees. The function of both bodies would be to provide guidance to the Director of Central Intelligence and, through him, to the Intelligence Community as a whole. If disagreements arose which could not be resolved inside the NSC structure, each cabinet-level official would retain the right to appeal to the President.

The President's Foreign Intelligence Advisory Board

While not a part of the NSC structure, the President has another body at his disposal to provide advice on intelligence matters-the President's Foreign Intelligence Advisory Board (PFIAB). First created by Executive Order in 1961, the PFIAB is charged with advising the President with respect to the quality, quantity, and adequacy of intelligence collection, analysis, counterintelligence, and other activities.[2] The PFIAB is also authorized to assess the adequacy of management, personnel and organizational arrangements in the intelligence agencies. Composed of private citizens, usually with some government experience, the number of PFIAB members has varied from one Administration to another.[3]

Historically, the PFIAB often has produced insightful and critical reports. Early boards were instrumental in analyzing and promoting the technical developments of the 1960s which revolutionized intelligence gathering. In the last several years, the PFIAB has looked at issues such as personnel practices within intelligence agencies and intelligence-sharing with multinational organizations.

The Commission supports the continuation of the PFIAB but believes that its role would be enhanced and its contributions more significant if it sought to perform functions that are not being performed elsewhere, either by the NSC or within the Intelligence Community itself. The Commission has noted in the course of its inquiry that very little thought is given by the Intelligence Community to the future, to finding creative technical or managerial solutions to the problems of intelligence or focusing on long-term issues and trends. By virtue of its membership, the PFIAB appears uniquely positioned to serve this function by bringing to bear the experience and expertise of the private sector and respected former government officials. Presidents must ensure that persons appointed to the Board have the qualifications necessary to perform this role and an adequate staff capability to support them.

Questions for Further Discussion

1. What are the problems that have troubled the National Security Council's effort to guide the intelligence community?

2. Do you think that the National Security Council should be the government organization charged with evaluating the intelligence community's support to policymakers? If not, who should?

3. What might account for the conclusion that intelligence managers rarely focus on the long-term trends and issues facing the intelligence community?

4. Do you think the risks of politicization will increase if the policymakers spend more time evaluating the usefulness of intelligence?

Endnotes

1. The statutory members of the NSC are the President, the Vice President, the Secretary of State, and the Secretary of Defense. Secretaries and Deputy Secretaries of other Executive departments may also serve on the NSC at the pleasure of the President. The present NSC includes the Secretary of the Treasury, the U.S. Ambassador to the United Nations, the U.S. Trade Representative, the Assistant to the President for National Security Affairs, the Assistant to the President for Economic Policy, and the Chief of Staff to the President.

   The Chairman of the Joint Chiefs is principal military adviser to the NSC and may attend and participate in NSC meetings. The Director of Central Intelligence also may attend and participate.

   The NSC is served by a staff headed by the Assistant to the President for National Security Affairs (who is often referred to as the National Security Advisor). The composition and organization of the NSC staff are left to the discretion of the President.

2. The PFIAB replaced an earlier "President's Board of Consultants on Foreign Intelligence Activities" that had been created by President Eisenhower in 1956. The PFIAB was disbanded in 1977 by President Carter but reconstituted by President Reagan in 1981.

3. The current Executive Order governing the PFIAB, E.O. 12863 (Sept. 13, 1993), limits membership to 16 individuals. ✦

Reprinted from the Commission on the Roles and Capabilities of the United States Intelligence Community (the Aspin-Brown Commission), *Preparing for the 21st Century: An Appraisal of U.S. Intelligence* (Washington, D.C.: U.S. Government Printing Office, March 1, 1996): 29–35.

Part VI

Covert Action

Hamlet: ". . . And there put on him
What forgeries you please . . ."
    —*Shakespeare*, Hamlet, *2.1.19–20*

*C*overt action (CA) may be defined as those activities carried out by national governments or other organizations, such as terrorist groups, to secretly influence and manipulate events abroad. The emphasis is on indirect, nonattribution, clandestine operations; the role of the government or other entity engaged in covert action is neither apparent nor publicly acknowledged (Godson 1996; Prados 1986; Treverton 1987). This approach to advancing one's interests is also sometimes referred to as the "Third Option"—between sending in the Marines on the one hand and relying on the diplomatic corps to achieve one's goals on the other hand. The use of military force is "noisy" and likely to draw a quick reaction from adversaries, as well as stir up criticism at home, while diplomacy can be notoriously slow and often ineffectual. Thus, covert action has a special appeal to some policy officials; with this tool, they can move rapidly and in relative quiet, avoiding lengthy debate over tactics and broader objectives (hence, another euphemism for CA: the "quiet option"). Covert action has the added advantage of usually costing less than a major military buildup.

The Evolution of Covert Action in the United States

The use of covert action is older in the United States than the nation itself, having been used extensively by the colonial insurgents during the Revolutionary War (Knott 1996). The revolutionaries secretly urged France to aid the war effort by providing the colonial rebels with covert arms, and General George Washington initiated a campaign of propaganda against his British military adversaries. Soon after the founding of the new nation, President Thomas Jefferson secretly supplied arms to insurgents in Tripoli as a means for fermenting a coup against the unfriendly throne of the Bashaw, and President James Madison authorized paramilitary operations against the Spanish in Florida. During the Civil War, the North and the South both used covert actions for spreading propaganda and supplying arms to sympathizers.

Not until World War II, though, did the United States begin to carry out covert actions in a more concerted manner. President Franklin D. Roosevelt established an Office of Strategic Services (OSS) to engage not only in espionage but also in the sabotage of bridges and railroad tracks in Germany, the dissemination of propaganda, and the support of resistance groups. Although the OSS was disbanded after the war, President Harry S. Truman understood the importance of intelligence—Pearl Harbor had taught him—and he created the Central Intelligence Agency (CIA, or "the Agency") in 1947. The statutory language of the National Security Act of that year left open the possibility that the new Agency might be called on to engage in operations beyond the collection of intelligence. Without mentioning covert action explicitly, the law stated that the CIA had authority to "perform such other functions and duties related to intelligence affecting the national security as the National Security Council may from time-to-time direct."

The immediate challenge of the Soviet Union and its avowed intent to spread communism far and wide turned the Truman Administration toward this ambiguous phrase in the National Security Act. The administration interpreted the language broadly as an invitation to unleash the CIA to fight against Soviet expansion and the activities of other communist countries and movements. In the late 1940s and early 1950s, secret funding went to pro-Western labor unions, political parties, and publishers in Europe; anticommunist dictators in Latin America; and pro-Western factions in Asia, Africa, and the Middle East. By the end of the 1960s, the Agency had hundreds of operations under way around the world. During the major overt wars in Korea (1950–53) and Vietnam (1964–75), the budgets grew for CIA paramilitary or secret warlike operations in those nations.

When the United States withdrew from the unpopular war in Vietnam, funding for covert action began a downward slide, accelerated by the attempted misuse of the CIA by the Nixon Administration during the Watergate affair in 1973–74 and by investigative disclosures in 1975 that the Agency had spied on American citizens and tried to subvert the democratically elected president of Chile (Salvador Allende). When President Jimmy Carter entered office in 1977, the CIA's covert action budget had fallen to less than 5 percent of the Agency's funding (in contrast to over 50 percent during the Vietnam war). President Carter kept the budget at that level initially, but following the Soviet invasion of Afghanistan in 1979, he increased the funding for covert action sixfold.

When the Reagan Administration came into power, this secret instrument of foreign policy entered its heyday. The Reagan Doctrine, a term coined by the media, entailed an all-out covert struggle led by the CIA against communist partisans around the world—especially in Nicaragua and Afghanistan but also in El Salvador, Angola, Cambodia, and Eastern Europe, and against the Soviet Union itself.

The Iran-*contra* scandal (1987), in which the Reagan Administration resorted to covert actions in Iran and Nicaragua without proper reporting to Congress and in defiance of a law (the Boland Amendment) strictly prohibiting such operations in Nicaragua, discredited the CIA generally and covert action in particular. The budget for CA dropped to its lowest levels since the opening months of the Cold War: less than 1 percent of the Agency's annual budget (Johnson 1996). The funding remained at this level throughout the first Bush Administration and rose modestly when the Clinton Administration turned to the CIA for help with its foreign policy woes in Haiti, Africa, and the Balkans.

It would take the terrorist attacks against the United States on September 11, 2001, to really stimulate the covert action budget, which began a rapid rise in the name of combating world terrorism. The use of CIA paramilitary operations against the Taliban regime in Afghanistan, in tandem with overt military operations by the indigenous Northern Alliance and U.S. bombing missions, opened a new chapter in America's reliance on covert action. Events in Afghanistan in 2001–02 pointed to a successful triple-threat formula for the accomplishment of U.S. foreign policy objectives: a combination of pinpoint bombing, local allied insurgents, and paramilitary operations conducted by the CIA and Pentagon Special Forces. This formula was applied in Iraq in 2003, although in the context of a much larger overt U.S. invasion force in this second Persian Gulf War.

The Methods of Covert Action

Covert action takes four forms, often used in conjunction with one another: propaganda (psychological warfare operations, or "psy ops"), political operations, economic operations, and paramilitary (PM) operations—with the last including assassination as a subset. These activities are estimated to have accounted for 40, 30, 10, and 20 percent, respectively, of the total number of covert actions during the Cold War (Johnson 1989). Paramilitary operations were, however—and continue to be—by far the most expensive and controversial form of CA.

Propaganda

During the Cold War, the open instrument of U.S. propaganda was the United States Information Agency (USIA), which released, through American embassies abroad, a vast amount of information about the United States and its objectives. As a supplement to this overt flow of information, the CIA (following presidential directives) inserted comparable, often identical, themes into secret media channels around the world. As with the USIA releases, the CIA's propaganda was in almost all cases (98 percent) accurate, if partial to the policies of the United States; about 2 percent of the propaganda was false ("black").

Indigenous agents ("media assets") secretly working for the CIA in foreign countries—journalists, radio and television commentators, op-ed and magazine writers, book authors—expressed "their" views through local media channels, although the material was often written verbatim for them in their native tongues by propaganda specialists in the Operations Directorate at CIA Headquarters in Langley, Virginia. Local audiences understandably looked on these seemingly homegrown sources of information—their own newspapers—as far more credible than USIA press releases. In return for these services, the media assets would receive cash payments and travel stipends from their local CIA "case officer," who normally operated out of the American embassy in the nation's capital. During the height of the Cold War, the CIA made 70 to 80 insertions into various media outlets each day—a great tidal wave of information flowing secretly from Agency headquarters into hundreds of hidden channels around the globe.

In tightly controlled totalitarian regimes where it was difficult (if not impossible) to recruit local media assets, the CIA relied on infiltrating propaganda. Such efforts could be quite primitive, including the lofting of air balloons to carry speeches, magazines, books, and transistor radios into forbidden territories where—thanks to these airborne deliveries—a deprived citizenry might have the opportunity to read about the outside world. Most of the balloons aimed at the U.S.S.R. crashlanded in that empire's vast expanse, with unknown but probably negligible effects. The CIA also dispatched airplanes to drop leaflets over isolated regimes or transmitted radio broadcasts (sometimes from makeshift stations in remote jungles). Most successful were the radio transmissions directed toward the Soviet Union and other adversaries, especially those conducted by Radio Free Europe (RFE) and Radio Liberty (RL), operating in Munich initially under the auspices of the CIA, until their secret ties with intelligence were leaked to the press in the early 1970s, at which point the U.S. government provided overt funding for the radio stations. Supporters credit these stations with having helped to sustain hope behind the Iron Curtain among dissident groups and slowly, but steadily, abetting the erosion of support for the Communist party in Moscow and Eastern Europe. Critics are less sure that they contributed much to the fall of the Soviet Union.

Although the CIA's secret propaganda operations against the Soviet Union and China during the Cold War have been praised by some in the United States and Europe, its operations in the developing world have been subjected to widespread criticism. The best known and most controversial example is Chile during the 1960s (Treverton 1987). In the Chilean presidential election of 1964, the CIA spent $3 million to mar the reputation of Salvador Allende, the Socialist candidate with suspected ties to Moscow. On a per capita basis, this amount was equivalent to the expenditure of $60 million in a U.S. presidential election at the time, a staggering level of funding likely to decide the outcome of a presidential election whether in Chile or the United States. The CIA managed to thwart Allende's election in 1964, but he

persevered and in 1970 won the presidency in a free and open election.

The CIA then turned to a range of propaganda and other covert actions designed to destroy Allende's regime. The Agency poured $3 million into the country to support anti-Allende secret propaganda between 1970 and 1973, in the form of press releases, radio commentary, films, pamphlets, posters, leaflets, direct mailings, paper streamers, and vivid wall paintings conjuring images of Communist tanks and firing squads that would supposedly soon become a part of life in Chile. Printing hundreds of thousands of copies, the CIA blanketed the country, which is predominantly Catholic, with an anti-Communist pastoral letter written many years earlier by Pope Pious XI. The effect was to substantially weaken the Allende government.

Another successful CIA propaganda operation took place in Central America in 1954. The Agency set up a radio station in the mountains of Guatemala. Local media assets began to broadcast the fiction that a revolution had erupted and that the people of Guatemala were joining the movement in large numbers; meanwhile, other CIA recruits began a march against the pro-Communist dictator Jacobo Arbenz. With a speed that surprised even the CIA instigators, the reports became something of a self-fulfilling prophecy, and the hapless Arbenz, panicked by the mythical prospect of the masses storming his palace, resigned before a shot was fired. This bloodless coup was a heady experience for covert action advocates, coming only seven years after the establishment of the CIA and on the heels of a similar victory in Iran (though one that relied on clandestine political maneuvering as well as propaganda). It began to seem as though the world could be transformed toward a pro-Western orientation by Madison Avenue public relations techniques, secretly applied.

Despite these early successes, the CIA's use of propaganda has had its share of critics. Early in the Cold War, the CIA funded the National Student Association inside the United States as part of its propaganda operations. The purpose was to encourage young Americans to travel abroad and counter Soviet efforts at manipulating international student conferences. Critics were enraged, though, by this trespassing of the CIA into the activities of groups within the United States, an activity strictly prohibited by the Agency's founding statute. The specter of influencing American audiences, not just foreign countries, arose again when it became public that the CIA was sponsoring the publication of anti-Communist books written by Soviet defectors as well as U.S. authors. The idea of American students and writers on the payroll of a secret intelligence agency struck civil libertarians as beyond the pale.

So did the revelation that the CIA had journalists on its payroll. The estimates ranged from three dozen, conceded by the Agency, to over 400 alleged by investigative reporters. Furthermore, it came to light that the CIA had secretly encouraged its U.S. media assets to write negative reviews of books published by American authors critical of the Agency. Some of George Orwell's worst fears appeared to have come true in the United States.

Troublesome, too, was the notion of "blowback" or "replay": the insertion of propaganda abroad only to have it waft back to U.S. audiences by way of American correspondents innocently reading CIA media plants in foreign newspapers and reporting this information to American readers. Critics raised doubts as well about the propriety of placing secret propaganda into the media outlets of fellow democracies. The U.S.S.R. and Communist China, yes, because their citizens had no access to accurate information about the world, their masters had no compunction about manipulating their own media, and the regimes were hostile toward the United States. But Denmark, France, and Germany seemed a different story—at least for critics, if not for the CIA's Operations Directorate.

Sometimes the Agency's propaganda operations looked as though they had been crafted by an imaginative descendent of Franz Kafka. As a means for discrediting Fidel Castro of Cuba, one CIA plan (according to the public testimony of an intelligence officer before a U.S. Senate investigating committee in 1975) consisted of

> spreading the word that the Second Coming of Christ was imminent and that Christ was against Castro [who] was anti-Christ. And you would spread this word around Cuba, and then on whatever date it was, that there would be a manifestation of the thing. And at that time—this is absolutely true—and at that time just over the horizon there would be an American submarine which would surface off of Cuba and send up some starshells. And this would be the manifestation of the Second Coming and Castro would be overthrown. (Church Committee 1975b)

The CIA called this operation "Elimination by Illumination." Fortunately, someone in the higher reaches of the Agency had the good sense to cancel this absurd exercise before it was attempted.

Political Covert Action

Governments also carry out covert actions—or "special activities," as the United States likes to clothe the concept in its official and (rare) public references to the subject—of a political nature. Secret payments to friendly foreign politicians and bureaucrats are one example. Critics scorn this method as nothing less than bribery to advance America's national interests around the world. Advocates, however, prefer a more sanguine interpretation: not bribery, but rather stipends for the advancement of global democracy—what British intelligence officers in Her Majesty's Secret Service refer to affectionately as "King George's cavalry."

According to the public record, during the Cold War the CIA's political sponsorships included political parties, individual politicians, or dictators in (from a longer, mostly classified list) Italy, Jordan, Iran, Ecuador, El Salvador, Angola, Chile, West Germany, Greece, Egypt, Sudan, Suriname, Mauritius, and the Philippines. The secret funds were used to win the favor of influential government officials, to help win elections for pro-Western factions (Italy was a heated electoral battleground in the early days of the Cold War), to recruit and build parties and regimes opposed to communism, and to strengthen labor unions in opposition to Communist party takeovers (again, Italy and the rest of Europe was pivotal).

Propaganda and political covert action are meant to work hand-in-glove, and sometimes both are subsumed under the "political" label. Some offices in the CIA's Operations Directorate take on the attributes of a political campaign headquarters, with intelligence officers engaged in the mass production of brochures, speeches, placards, campaign buttons, and bumper stickers (never mind that campaign buttons look a little out of place on tribal warlords or that some of the developing countries where the bumper stickers are sent may have only a few automobiles). Their common purpose during the Cold War was to persuade important foreign officials to turn a favorable eye toward the United States and away from the Soviet Union—or, more recently, away from adversaries such as Saddam Hussein in Iraq or the global network of Al Qaeda terrorist organizations. In this sense, the Cold War and the era since may be thought of as a subterranean political struggle between the United States and its enemies abroad, in which intelligence organizations have waged a clandestine war to win the hearts and minds of people around the world and to place into government positions men and women of an ideological persuasion compatible with America's interests.

Economic Covert Action

A further weapon in a nation's arsenal of clandestine operations is the use of subversion against an adversary's means of economic production. During its campaign to ruin Allende, the CIA provided financial support to factions within Chile for the purposes of encouraging strikes—especially against the trucking industry—that would roil the regime in commercial chaos. Earlier, during the Kennedy Administration, the CIA planned to undermine Soviet-Cuban relations by lacing 14,125 bags of sugar bound from Havana to Moscow with an unpalatable (though harmless) chemical substance. At the eleventh hour, a White House aide learned of the proposal and, deeming it excessive, put a stop to it (Wicker 1966).

In the conduct of economic covert action, foreign currencies may be counterfeited, the world price of trading commodities depressed (especially harmful to one-crop economies, as in the case of Cuba's reliance on sugarcane), harbors mined to discourage commercial shipping (carried out by the Johnson and Nixon Administrations against North Vietnam and by the Reagan Administration against the Marxist regime in Nicaragua), electrical power lines and oil-storage tankers dynamited (again, North Vietnam and Nicaragua), oil supplies contaminated (North Vietnam), and even clouds seeded in an effort to disrupt weather patterns over the enemy's territory (in North Vietnam, to no effect).

Today, a prime target of economic dislocation is an adversary's computer systems. With skillful hacking ("cyberwarfare"), a nation's or group's financial transactions can be left in disarray, its bank assets stolen, its communications hopelessly tangled, and its military command-and-control capabilities frozen—an electronic assault that could be at least as dislocating as a military attack.

Paramilitary Covert Action

While some of the covert actions we've mentioned earlier can be quite devastating (such as the mining of harbors), paramilitary or warlike operations are usually the most extreme and controversial forms of a nation's secret foreign policy. They can involve large-scale "secret" warfare—something of an oxymoron, since the extensive use of military force against an adversary does not stay secret for long, as the "quiet option" soon becomes noisy (an overt-covert action). The CIA's Special Operations Group (SOG), a subsidiary of its Operations Directorate, sponsored many guerrilla wars during the Cold War. From 1963 to 1973, the Agency backed the Hmong (Meo) tribes of North Laos in a war against the Communist Pathet Lao, who served as puppets of North Vietnam. The two sides fought to a draw, before the United States finally withdrew from the struggle. From the public record alone, it is clear that the CIA has also supported pro-Western insurgents in Ukraine, Poland, Albania, Hungary, Indonesia, China, Oman, Malaysia, Iraq, the Dominican Republic, Venezuela, North Korea, Bolivia, Thailand, Haiti, Guatemala, Cuba, Greece, Turkey, Vietnam, Afghanistan, Angola, and Nicaragua.

In these operations, the CIA's main role was to provide advice and weaponry. Anti-Communist dissidents during the early stages of the Cold War became the beneficiaries of a wide range of arms shipments from the United States, compliments of the CIA, including high-powered rifles, suitcase bombs, fragmentation grenades, rapid-fire machine guns, 64-mm antitank rockets, .38-caliber pistols, .30-caliber M-1 carbines, .45-caliber submachine guns, tear-gas grenades, and supplies of ammunition. When the Reagan Administration came into office, it funneled through the CIA a reported $3 billion worth of weaponry to anti-Soviet fighters in Afghanistan (the *mujahideen,* or "soldiers of god"). Among the weapons were sophisticated shoulder-held Stinger and Blowpipe missiles capable of bringing down Soviet bombers. This "secret" supply of armaments to the *mujahideen* is said to have been an important consideration in Moscow's decision to withdraw from its losing "Vietnam" war in Afghanistan.

Since the end of the Cold War, the CIA has provided substantial amounts of arms and financial support to a new list of pro-U.S. factions, especially in the Middle East, the Balkans, and South Asia. Recipients have included the Iraqi National Congress, an umbrella group of insurgents opposed to Saddam Hussein's regime; opponents of Serbian expansion in Bosnia and Kosovo; and the Northern Alliance, along with other anti-Taliban factions, following the 2001 terrorist attacks against the United States that were widely thought to have been masterminded by Al Qaeda cells based in Afghanistan. In the 2002–03 war to root out Al Qaeda and Taliban forces from Afghanistan, the CIA introduced the use of unmanned aerial vehicles (UAVs) such as the Predator, equipped with cameras and Hellfire missiles to spot and quickly eliminate enemy forces—the newest, and highly lethal, approach to paramilitary operations.

As part of its paramilitary operations, the CIA is extensively involved in the training of foreign soldiers to fight on behalf of U.S. interests. These programs have entailed the training of foreign soldiers for guerrilla warfare, as well as counterterrorism. The CIA's military advisers for such purposes are often borrowed from the Department of Defense (DoD) and given nonofficial battlefield gear, a conversion known by insiders as "sheepdipping." The CIA's paramilitary program includes support to the Department of Defense in the development of the Pentagon's own unconventional warfare capability, known as Special Operations (or "Special Ops" for short) and carried out by elite Special Forces. For example, the CIA has provided armaments to the

DoD for covert sales abroad. Some of the weapons sold to Iran by the Defense Department in the notorious arms-sale scandal of 1986–87 (the Iran-*contra* affair) had their origin in the CIA's paramilitary arsenal.

Moreover, the CIA provides training for military and police units in the developing world, particularly security personnel responsible for the protection of their nation's leaders. Among the skills taught at Camp Perry, the Agency's training facility in Virginia, are lessons in how to protect communications channels and the techniques of "executive driving" (designed to impart spin-away steering skills for maneuvering an automobile through terrorist roadblocks).

During those rare moments when the United States is not involved in the support of paramilitary wars in one place or another (as in the early years of the Carter Administration), the CIA's Special Operations Group bides its time by carrying out training operations for its own personnel and by maintaining its military hardware (including a small navy and air force). Above all, SOG is kept busy in its added responsibility to provide support for intelligence collection operations, especially in remote regions like the mountains of Afghanistan, where U.S. paramilitary officers have recently developed geographic expertise and contacts with local warlords.

Assassination Plots

A special category within the realm of paramilitary operations is the assassination of individual foreigners—needless to say a subject fraught with controversy. This option has gone by a number of euphemisms, used in hushed tones within the government of the United States: "executive action," "terminate with extreme prejudice," or "neutralize." At one time during the Cold War, proposals for assassination were screened by a special unit within the CIA called the "Health Alteration Committee." (Its counterpart in the Soviet Union was the KGB's "Department of Wet Affairs.")

Fidel Castro was America's prime target for death during the Kennedy Administration, although none of the plots against him succeeded. Another target for "health alteration" during the Kennedy years was Patrice Lumumba, the Congolese leader. Members of a rival Congolese faction beat the CIA to the punch, however, and murdered Lumumba for their own political reasons related to an internal power struggle. In 2003, the CIA launched a Hellfire missile from a Predator platform hovering at 10,000 feet above the deserts of Yemen, destroying an automobile filled with suspected Al Qaeda members. The occupants, including one who turned out to be an American citizen, died a fiery death. The Preda-

tor had become a potent instrument of CIA paramilitary covert actions.

A Balance Sheet

Since the outbreak of the Cold War and the establishment of the CIA in 1947, covert action has exercised a fascination on most presidential administrations. But what have been the results? This question may be answered according to practical outcomes and ethical considerations. With respect to practicalities, a further distinction must be made between the short-term and long-term consequences of covert action.

The practical results have been mixed. Sometimes covert action has led to stunning successes for the United States, at least over the short term. In Europe in the immediate aftermath of World War II (particularly in Greece and Italy), in Iran (1953), in Guatemala (1954), and less spectacularly throughout Latin America in the 1950s, covert action played a major role in thwarting Communist and Marxist political leaders and movements—often sponsored openly or covertly by the U.S.S.R. Over the short run, the CIA also chalked up notable successes in Laos (1963–73), Afghanistan (1982–88), Panama (1989, toppling the corrupt dictator General Manuel Antonio Noriega), and Afghanistan and Iraq (2001–03).

Yet, the lasting value of some of these "victories"—the long-term consequence—has been questionable. Iran is hardly a close friend of the United States today; Guatemala and Panama are as poor and repressive as ever; the first Afghanistan intervention brought the Taliban regime to power, which in turn supported the Al Qaeda terrorist organization; and the second Afghanistan and Iraq interventions are unlikely to have brought global terrorism to a halt (although in Afghanistan it took a useful step in that direction). Earlier there were the Bay of Pigs fiasco, the madcap plots to dispatch Fidel Castro (exploding cigars, secret powders designed to make his charismatic beard fall out), the pouring of millions of dollars into the sinkhole of the Angolan civil war, and the Iran-*contra* scandal and its dismissal of the Constitution. Along the way came the CIA's abandonment of temporary allies in a string of anti-Communist paramilitary operations, including the freedom fighters in Hungary and at the Bay of Pigs, the South Vietnamese who aided the CIA and ended up buried in cemeteries throughout Saigon as the United States fled Indochina, the Meo tribesman in Laos, the Khambas in Tibet, the Nationalist Chinese in Burma, and the ever-suffering Kurds.

On practical grounds, perhaps the best conclusion one can draw based on the empirical record is that covert action (like overt economic sanctions or aerial bombing) sometimes succeeds and sometimes fails. Its chances seem best when the objectives are limited, when strong opposition groups already exist within a target nation or group, and, in the case of paramilitary operations, when it is aided and abetted by overt precision bombing and elite DoD Special Forces on the ground.

The Readings

In the first article of this section, Kevin A. O'Brien provides insights into the clandestine political operations of both the CIA and the Soviet KGB during the Cold War. He finds that the CIA was better at some covert actions than the KGB, but less good at others. The CIA was able to carry out political covert actions over a wider portion of the globe than the KGB, but the KGB proved more effective in the conduct of paramilitary operations. Both intelligence organizations directed successful propaganda operations.

Former Senator Frank Church (D, Idaho), who in 1975 led a searing investigation into legal violations of the intelligence agencies, argues in the next selection that the covert action instruments of the CIA during the Cold War were "put to the service of reactionary and repressive regimes that can never, for long, escape or withstand the volcanic forces of change." A strong critic of most covert actions during the Cold War, Senator Church nonetheless saw a potential role for this approach, say, if a timely clandestine intervention were able to avert a nuclear holocaust or if covert action might aid the people of another nation in their struggle against an unpopular Marxist regime.

James A. Barry, a former CIA officer, likewise addresses the pros and cons of covert action. Applying just-war theory to the study of covert action, Barry establishes a checklist of safeguards to ensure that clandestine interventions abroad comport with some degree of ethical standards. High on his list: The covert action has to be "approved by the president, after due deliberation within the Executive Branch, and with the full knowledge and concurrence of appropriate members of the Congress." No more Iran-*contra* affairs. ✦

20

Interfering With Civil Society: CIA and KGB Covert Political Action During the Cold War

Kevin A. O'Brien

The Cold War was in large part a subterranean battle between the intelligence services of the two superpowers, the United States and the Soviet Union, as carried out by their premier intelligence services: the CIA and the KGB. O'Brien examines the political dimension of covert actions undertaken by these two intelligence behemoths, and he draws conclusions about the successes and failures of both nations in their conduct of secret foreign policy.

> We are at the beginning of an age in which it will be insisted that the same standards of conduct and responsibility for wrong done shall be observed among nations and their governments that are observed among the individual citizens of civilized states.
>
> —*Woodrow Wilson, 1917*

> The status of world-power is inseparable from its responsibilities.
>
> —*Winston Churchill, 1958*

The Cold War has been defined as a war carried on by means short of sustained, overt, military confrontation. This implicitly conveys the understanding that the confrontation between the Western world, dominated by the United States, and the Communist bloc, dominated by the Soviet Union, was covert in nature, resorting more often than not to non-military means in an attempt to undermine the authority of the opposing Power while maintaining control and influence over its own sphere. Within the period 1945 to 1991, both Powers developed their security and intelligence services as a mechanism by which this confrontation could be carried out. In the United States, the Central Intelligence Agency (CIA) was founded in 1947 for the purpose of intelligence collection and dissemination. In the USSR, following Stalin's death in 1953, the Komitet Gosudarstvennoi Bezopasnosti (KGB) was reorganized out of the previous intelligence and security services.

Both services soon rapidly developed covert action arms that far outweighed their intelligence collection missions. In the case of the KGB, such activity had been the mainstay of the previous incarnations of Soviet security (*Cheka*, GPU, OGPU, NKVD, MGB, MVD). The U.S. had only recently developed such an ability with the Office of Strategic Services. Covert Action (CA) or, as the Soviets call it, 'active measures,' during the Cold War symbolized the ideological conquest for the soul of the world that was the basis of the rivalry between the Western and Soviet (including the East bloc Communist) intelligence services. Loch Johnson defines CA as the 'third option' between diplomacy and open warfare.[1] The scope of CA is very broad; in general, it comprises 'actions carried out abroad in support of national foreign policy objectives so that the role of the [government] is not apparent or acknowledged publicly.'[2] This definition will suffice for the purposes of both the CIA and the KGB.

There are four types of CA: propaganda, political CA, economic CA, and paramilitary CA.[3] Richard Bissell further broke these down to (1) political advice, (2) subsidies to an individual, (3) financial support and 'technical assistance' to political parties, (4) support of private organizations, (5) covert propaganda, (3) 'private' training, (7) economic operations, and (8) paramilitary operations.[4] The focus here is on covert political action (CPA). Gregory F. Treverton has defined CPA as 'attempts to change the balance of political forces in a particular country, most often by secretly providing money to particular groups.'[5] Paul Blackstock has further broken down CPA into three stages: infiltration-penetration, forced disintegration, and subversion-defection. Infiltration ('the deliberate/planned penetration of political and social groups within a state by agents of an intervening power for manipulative purposes') as well as subversion ('the undermining of detachment of the loyalties of significant political and social groups within the victimized state, and their transference, under ideal conditions, to

267

the symbols and institutions of the aggressor') are the most relevant here.[6] Additional elements of CA fall under other categories, including covert economic or military action, as well as propaganda disinformation. Paramilitary CA (such as assassination and the overthrow of governments) occasionally cross the line into CPA.

Many types of organizations have been utilized by both the CIA and KGB under the auspices of CPA.* Both have attempted to influence political parties throughout the world in an effort to directly or indirectly undermine the influence of the other, as well as to further consolidate U.S. or Soviet interests in the region. Social organizations, such as student groups, international front organizations and legitimate bodies, and proxy armies have been founded, penetrated and funded by both services. Media outlets, individuals and services have been utilized either knowingly or unwittingly by the CIA and, perhaps to a lesser extent, the KGB. And finally, various corporate organizations and associations were used as fronts for CIA or KGB activities throughout the globe. Individuals also played a role in this confrontation through such aspects as 'false-flag recruitment,' agents of influence, defectors and disinformation agents.

Origins and Goals

The origins of the policies related to the use of civil society in the Cold War lay with the governments of both the United States and the Soviet Union. The main concern of the United States during the early days of the Cold War was 'the global challenge of Communism'; it was 'to be confronted wherever and whenever it seemed to threaten [U.S.] interests.'[7] To this end, the Clandestine Action Service (CAS) was established within the CIA as a complementary branch to the Office of Policy Coordination (OPC) in 1947–1948, and was given the task of 'rolling back' Communism in Europe.[8] The OPC, founded on the encouragement of George Kennan, was originally intended to 'undercut debilitating strikes by Communist trade unions and election advances by Communist parties.'[9] These operational roles were laid out in the National Security Act of 1947, as well as in directives like NSC 10/2 and NSC 5412/2.[10] This policy can be clearly summarized in three points: (1) create and exploit problems for international Communism; (2) discredit international Communism and reduce the strength of its parties and organizations; and (3) reduce international Communist control over any area of the world.[11] Victor Marchetti stated that, more specifically, 'in most countries . . . the United States policy [was] usually to maintain the status quo, so most [CIA] subsidies [were] designed to strengthen the political base of those in power.'[12] However, Gabriel Kolko feels that

> The credibility of American military power and the emergence of geopolitical analogies and linkages in the form of the domino theory soon subjected U.S. behavior and policies in many areas to new influences that paralleled and sometimes outweighed the more traditional narrower assessments of the economic and political stakes involved in success or failure, action or inaction, in some nation or region.

This in turn led to

> A growing number of de facto and formal alliances with Third World surrogates . . . raising for the first time the United States' increasing dependence on inherently unstable men and regimes.[13]

In the former Soviet Union and Russia, the KGB and its related intelligence services have been carrying out such actions since the time of the Revolution. Clandestine political action is considered to be 'the central thrust of the Kremlin's [foreign policy] . . . the leaders' prime executor of such policies is . . . the KGB.'[14] Since 1945, the United States has been referred to as the KGB's 'Main Adversary,' a designation indicating the primary focus of all its activities, and as such policies were designed to take this into consideration.[15] KGB goals were not laid out as clearly in the sources as those of the CIA, but from what is available, its aims did not seem to differ much from those of the CIA. Generally, an effort was made to influence the world toward a policy of friendliness for their parent states. The KGB became the Kremlin's main arm in dealing with world Communism, justifying the control it exerted over all aspects of international Communism (client regimes, front organizations, proxy armies, etc.) by stating that 'to ignore the activities of international progressive public movements . . . may isolate and weaken national revolutionary forces . . . fraught with the danger of defeat.'[16]

Contemporary politics had a great deal to do with the origins of the intelligence policies. During the late 1940s and into the 1950s, Europe was the CIA's prime concern. Reconstruction was being carried out in Western Europe, but Communist influence was strong. Politically, in Italy and France, the Communists threatened to destabilize the post-war political and economic balance that the United States was attempting to establish throughout the Western world. Communist unions and organizations posed serious threats to the economic and social welfare of a rebuilding Europe. Thus, the policies of the CIA were to stabilize Western politics as much in favor of the U.S. while simultaneously destabilizing and removing any elements that could threaten economic reconstruction. During this time the Clandestine Action Service (CAS) was developed: By 1954, with the consolidation of American power in Europe and the full development of the CIA's paramilitary capacity, the Agency turned its focus onto the Third World, never again undertaking paramilitary CA against the USSR.[17] This shift of focus from Eastern European to the underdeveloped countries during the 1960s was due to (a) the reinforcement of the 'Iron Curtain' and construction of the Berlin Wall, lessening the availability and opportunities to use classic forms of intelligence collection, leading to heavier reliance on electronic intelligence, and (b) the general development of increased concern with policies in the Third World, and the attendant shift on events and competition made on the Third World.[18] Furthermore, following African decolonization, CIA activity on the continent increased 56 percent between 1959 and 1963 due to fears of Soviet encroachment on these newly-independent states.[19] Finally, by the mid-late 1970s, after the exposure of many CIA activities conducted during the late 1960s and 1970s, the CIA had supposedly curtailed its activities, bringing them more in line with current U.S. government policies.

On the Soviet side, much the same policies were followed for much the same reasons. The USSR wished to establish its influence throughout as much of the globe as possible; in the 1940s and early 1950s, it centered on Europe. But, as with the CIA, the KGB shifted its focus to the Third World during the 1950s and 1960s, attempting to establish influence in this uncultivated area. One of the most significant Soviet defectors to the CIA, Anatoli Golitsyn, stated that in 1959 the KGB's primary mission had changed from conventional espionage to 'covert statecraft': the use of agents and other mechanisms to achieve the USSR's geopolitical goals.[20] In addition, a major aspect of the relationship between the KGB and its proxies was that the KGB was itself the 'sword' of another organization, the Communist Party of the Soviet Union (CPSU). All actions undertaken by the KGB internationally throughout the period were coordinated with the International Department of the Central Committee of the CPSU; the KGB was the conduit for implementing the internationalist policies of the CPSU. The KGB branch that carried out these activities was Department D (later Service A) of the First Chief Directorate; it coordinated action directly with the International Department.[21] This relationship emerged out of the pre-World War II policies of the Comintern: (a) developing international organizations with the 'basic aims of promoting the national Communist parties; (b) propagating the Soviet line; and (c) developing political forces subservient to Moscow.'[22]

Implementation

Having examined how the policies of the CIA and KGB developed in relation to each other, and the factors that affected those policies, each category can be examined individually, to analyze the implementation of these policies as they related to specific issues.

I. Political Parties

A prime mechanism for implementing these CIA and KGB policies was the use of political parties and forces during the Cold War. Gregory Treverton states that certain political parties (most often right-wing or centrist) were supported by the CIA during elections, when their existence was threatened, or when there was an opportunity to alter the power balance in a country where the U.S. had interests.[23]

A. Continental Europe

Even though this policy was implemented globally, there were significant differences between its application in Europe and in the Third World by both services. As to Europe, Gabriel Kolko asserts that

> U.S. collaboration with Europe's colonial powers was not merely based on Washington's desires to see European economic reconstruction and cooperation with its plans for an integrated international economy. It was also strategic and political, involving the desire to rebuild Europe's military power against the USSR as well as to keep Communists and the more militant Socialists out of power in the NATO states themselves.[24]

Elections, as Loch Johnson states, were often nothing more than hidden struggles between the CIA and KGB to secure the government for their respective countries. Following the development of CA, interest was primarily focused on influencing elections. CPA in this context consisted mainly of financial aid to friendly politicians and bureaucrats abroad.[25] Within the European context, there were no political parties created by the CIA. But, a great deal of influencing was carried out under the auspices of the first policy: i.e., the establishment where possible of Western electoral systems throughout Europe, and the opening up of Europe to ensure the development and continuation of economic reconstruction along lines friendly to the U.S. The primary example of this was the funding of the Christian Democrats in Italy during the 1948 elections; Treverton states that this set a precedent of 'election projects' which became central to all nonmilitary CA.[26] CPA was developed even further under Allen Dulles in the 1950s: his personal interests in securing democracy against the Soviets in Eastern and Western Europe led to a CPA dominance of CIA during the 1950s, through direct influence on parties and politicians in Western Europe.[27] This continued throughout the years: the CIA reportedly gave more than $1 million to the Secretary-General of Christian Democrats, Amintore Fanfani, in the 1970 elections. Over $800,000 was given to General Vito Miceli, the leader of the neo-fascist MSI and former head of Italian military intelligence. All in all, between 1948 and 1975, over $75 million was spent by the CIA on Italian elections, $10 million in the 1972 elections alone. Even following the Church Committee Report of the U.S. Senate (1976), President Gerald R. Ford approved an additional $6 million for the next election.[28]

Another example is the Federal Republic of Germany (FRG). The aim of CPA operations within the FRG has always been to establish or revive anti-Communist, pro-American institutions, while discrediting and destroying left-opposition movements. To this end, the CIA has supported extensively the Christian Democratic Union (CDU) and, reportedly, the Social Democratic Party (SPD) over the years.[29] Overall, funding and political intervention was carried out by the CIA because its budget was 'black,' or hidden; therefore, the Agency was agreeable to undertaking activities which might be considered 'wasteful' if carried out by other groups. Through the concept of plausible denial built into CA, the U.S. government was able to become involved without many of the groups or individuals involved even knowing where funding was coming from.[30] Another example of this type was U.S. support of the Christian Democrats in Portugal after April 1974.[31]

The KGB has been less active in this field than the CIA; nevertheless, KGB activities related to political parties in Europe have been significant. In general, foreign Communist Parties were used as 'auxiliaries' by the KGB, as well as recruiting grounds.[32] (There is no evidence to indicate that the CIA penetrated these Communist Parties, although logically this would have often been the case.) For example, a great number of the activities of the French Communist Party were directed from Moscow, and used as a means of penetrating the French government.[33] Document No. 907/PR (8Dec77) of the Moscow KGB Centre's instructions to its stations ('The Copenhagen Residency's PR line Work Plan for 1978') states the main thrust of active measures was to be political influence and penetration in Denmark.[34] Overall, despite an indication of attempts made to influence the socialist parties of Western Europe, in general (with the possible exception of the British Labor Party) the KGB has had little success in influencing any non-Communist party in Western Europe.[35] With the demise of the Soviet Union and the reorganization of the KGB by Russian President Boris Yeltsin, the question must be raised as to what direction these parties, particularly in France and Italy, are now taking.

B. The Third World Arena

In the Third World, the use of political parties was significantly different. Whereas in Europe, influence over party organizations was carried out purely along ideological lines, in the Third World a different pattern emerged. The CIA apparently operated under the belief that if a party was not aligned with Washington, and was not 'helped along' toward that end, then it would automatically fall into Moscow's camp. Nothing could be further from the truth. The KGB, in contrast, generally helped Communist and Socialist movements in the Third World, but, almost without exception, only when they were linked to paramilitary formations involved in wars of 'national liberation.'

John Prados has called the CIA-supported parties 'third force' political movements; they were generally non-communist and non-fascist, and preferably anti-communist and politically moderate (usually designated as Christian Democrats). In Latin America, they were usually associated with established oligarchies, and in Africa and Asia with tribes. In instances where no 'third force' existed, one was created. Examples of these were the Committee for the Defense of National Interests (Laos), and the Committee for a free Albania. Holden Roberto and later Jonas Savaimbi in Angola, and Joseph Mobutu in the Congo, also received aid for their movements. Such minorities often did little to satisfy general, popular aspirations, and often led to further upheaval and, as in Laos, additional obligations for U.S. support. They were generally perceived as 'agents of American power.'[36]

The most obvious case of CIA involvement with Third World political parties is that of Chile. Political control and penetration throughout the Organization of American States (OAS) was attempted, to legitimatize U.S. 'anti-Communist' actions throughout the western hemisphere, but the effort was largely unsuccessful. In Chile, the CIA intervened in every election between 1963 and 1973. During Popular Unity coalition government, the Christian Democrats and the National Party were funded with more than $4 million from the CIA; at the same time, money was used to try to lure away factions from the coalition. In 1964, $2.6 million was given to the candidate Eduardo Frei (who later won) to prevent Salvador Allende and the socialists from gaining power.[37]

Several more examples can be cited. Between 1961 and 1969, Holden Roberto, the leader of the largest anti-Communist party in Angola, the FNLA, was heavily funded by the CIA and received non-military materiél. Simultaneously, a rival group, UNITA, under Jonas Savimbi, was supported by the CIA. BOSS, the South African intelligence service,[38] received CIA assistance. Egypt's Gamal Abdel Nasser was contacted and offered aid by the CIA in 1959 after his falling-out with the Soviets.[39] Joseph Mobutu was funded to take power in the Congo in 1965 following the CIA-supported assassination of Patrice Lumumba in January 1961. And in the Philippines, the CIA created NAMFREL in 1951 to build support for its candidate Ramon Magsaysay in the upcoming elections, spending more than $1 million on his campaign to counter the Huks and the leftist candidate Elpidio Quirino.[40]

But these were not the only types of political organizations supported by the CIA. Victor Marchetti has stated that the 'CIA will support and direct neofascist forces if necessary in order to counter Socialist power.' This is exactly what happened in Chile with General Pinochet.[41]

On the Soviet side, there seem to be fewer examples of political support throughout the Third World by the KGB. One clear example is supported by the KGB until 1973 of the MPLA in Angola.[42] The head of the dominant faction in the Afghanistan Communist Party, Babrak Karmal, was a KGB agent. Moscow Center was reported to have a number of agents directly in Nasser's entourage, including Egypt's head of intelligence.[43] Finally, Nelson Mandela's African National Congress (ANC) was clearly penetrated by the KGB through the ANC's close links with the South African Communist Party.[44]

In general, neither the KGB nor the CIA were very successful in their usage of political parties in the Third World. The United States and, to a lesser extent, the Soviet Union failed to understand the nature of Third World socialist movements and their links to international ideologies. The end result more often than not was the creation of further problems for the individual service, whether on a massive scale such as Indochina and Afghanistan, or on a smaller scale such as Central America or Angola. As Prados states, one problem with working through proxies is that of suffering political liabilities as a result of their acts, another is the obvious lack of full or even sufficient control over these 'allies.' Examples of such problems include the drug smuggling carried out by the Indonesian military regime, Li Mi's Chinese in Burma, and Vang Pao's Meo.[45]

II. Front Organizations

Unlike the use of political parties, use of front organizations (FOs) by both the CIA and KGB was widespread throughout the whole of the Cold War. These organizations took on different guises, depending on the requirements of the period, the intended action, and the hoped-for outcome. Here, once again, the KGB acted quite often as a filter for other Soviet organizations (primarily the International Department of the CPSU), and thus, even in instances where an FO was not a direct part of the KGB, it was linked thereby to other organizations. In the case of the CIA, however, the vast majority of these FOs were direct appendages of the Agency. Only FO and related individuals active in operations against or in a foreign state will be dealt with; those used for other purposes (for example, domestic recruiting) will not be considered here. Six categories of FO (or related) will be examined. But first, specific policies must be reviewed regarding how the CIA and KGB saw the usefulness of front organizations.

The CIA's policy was to base its support on a wide range of groups and institutions (besides political parties) in various countries in order to 'shift the balance of [a] country's politics by countering groups perceived as threatening to American interests and aiding those friendly to the United States.'[46] The Soviets had originated FO with the GRU (Soviet military intelligence) in the 1920s in order to obtain money and economic considerations without evidence that these were going to the USSR.[47] Their policy was articulated in the March 1926 statement from the Comintern, advocating

> creating a whole solar system of organizations and smaller committees around the Communist Party . . . actually working under the influence of the Party, but not under its mechanical control.

The overall task of these FOs was to 'advance the cause of Soviet Communism, to defend the policies of the Soviet Union . . . and to attack the policies of those it opposes.' They were also used to recruit agents, provide covers for 'illegals,' and to 'mold and manipulate public opinion.'[48] Most of the FOs that the Soviets used during the Cold War were legitimate at their founding, but were 'captured' by the Soviets during the period 1945–1949.

A. Proprietary Corporations

In general, the CIA's corporate front organizations or 'Delaware Corporations'** were known as *proprietaries*.[49] Document 1984-000081 discusses air proprietaries, as well as other FOs. These took on many different guises and forms through the Cold War, depending on geography, mission and time. The best-known type of proprietary was the air corporation. Several of these were established during the wars in Indochina, and in relation to the conflict between Formosa (Taiwan) and Communist China. The first proprietary Civil Air Transport (CAT)[50], was used in South-East Asia in operations involving Li Mi's Nationalist Chinese forces, as well as in support of the French in Indochina (e.g., Operation SQUAW II). This shortly led to a plan for the formation of an International Volunteer Air Group (IVAG) in South-East Asia, later to become Air America.[51] The CIA incorporated a holding company, Pacific Corporation, to serve as a management firm for CAT; it employed 20,000 people. Once Air America was founded, it too was placed under Pacific Corp. There were many spin-off air proprietaries from CAT and Air America. Two of them, Air Asia, developed in Taiwan, and Southern Air Transport, were placed after 1963 under a newly-formed CIA office with Air America called the Executive Committee for Air Proprietary Operations (EXCOMAIR).[52] Air America was very successful in Laos and Thailand during CIA and Special Forces operations there, moving 2500 tons a month by 1968 in support of the Meo. It also rescued as many downed airmen as the USAF.[53]

Another region where FOs were extensively used was in Central America. During the war with Nicaragua, the CIA used fictitious fronts for purchasing equipment, such as Investair Leasing, Armairco, and Shenandoah Airleasing, as well as corporations for purchasing arms, e.g., RM Equipment Co. Summit Aviation was linked to the CIA during the 1980s with operations in El Salvador and Honduras.[54] Double-Chek Corporations [sic], listed as a brokerage firm in the Florida government records, was in reality a recruiting front for pilots flying against Cuba after 1959. Many of the pilots flying B-26s out of Central America against Cuba were recruited by another company, Caribbean Marine Aero Corp (Caramar), a CIA proprietary.[55] The sale of arms to Iran has been called a mess of 'corporate networks with shells on top of shells.' For example, Udall Corporation owned Santa Elena, a corporation that maintained aircraft at Hopango; Lake Resources collected all monies and ran the Iranian side of the operations. Corporate Air Services provided the aircrews for the transport, and the flight operations were arranged by Stanford Technology Trading Group International. All of these were CIA proprietaries.[56] St. Lucia Airways, although denying it, has been conclusively tied to the Iran operations, as well as to operations in Angola and the Congo (Zaire). In Africa, Intermountain Aviation carried out CIA air operations in Portuguese Africa. And, although not direct proprietaries, Pan African Airlines (Nigeria) and Africair (Africa/Caribbean) were CIA assets.[57] Most of these air proprietaries were, at one time or another, controlled through a company called Aero Associates, under George Doole, Jr., until his 1971 retirement.[58]

As far as other types of corporate fronts, Washington's Robert Mullen and Co. was used to provide covers for CIA personnel in Stockholm, Mexico City and Singapore; in 1971, Mullen set up a subsidiary operation with the Agency called Interprogress, Ltd.[59] In Taiwan, CIA operations were carried out under the name of Western Enterprises, Inc., which soon became well known to everyone. It was then changed to 'Department of the Navy.'[60] Southern Capital and Management Corporation in Washington was a CIA proprietary managing a $30 million investment portfolio—this became widely known as 'The Insurance Complex.' United Business Associates in Washington was a FO of the CIA used to fund corporate development in the Third World in order to 'offset the Communists from moving in.'[61] In 1952, the CIA was supported by the United Fruit Company in developing plans to carry out a coup against Jacobo Arbenz in Guatemala, but it never carried them through.[62] Finally, one of the CIA's best known FOs was Zenith Technical Enterprises, the Miami corporation used to organize, direct, fund and carry out Operation MONGOOSE, the CIA's war against Castro.[63] The only other type of corporate organization known to have been used was banks. The Hialeah-Miami Springs Bank, Bankers Trust Co. of New York, and Royal Bank of Canada were all used by the CIA as financial fronts for various operations.[64]

In contrast, no evidence has been found to indicate that the Soviets, pioneers of the corporate FO with Arcos (All-Russian Co-operative Society) in London in 1921,[65] continued with corporate fronts following 1945. The few exceptions were in KGB use of 'covers,' to be discussed later.

B. Communications Media

The second category of FO is that of media usage by the intelligence services. Many different methods of media manipulation were used by the CIA and the KGB. The policies behind media usage were clear: general propaganda and support of one's own policies were the goal. To achieve this, the CIA used

> networks of several hundred foreign individuals . . . who provide[d] intelligence for the CIA and at times attempt to influence foreign opinion through the use of covert propaganda. These individuals provide[d] the CIA with direct access to a large number of foreign newspapers and periodicals, press services and news agencies, radio and television stations, commercial book publishers, and other foreign media outlets.[66]

For the KGB, a distinction was made between propaganda and disinformation: propaganda has been described as 'directly attributed to the Soviets, the satellites, the client states, or the obviously predisposed.' Disinformation, on the other hand, is

> seldom attributable to these sources and depends on its false attribution to an ally, to 'discovered' classified documents that purport to reveal plans to attack the USSR and to other rumors, forgeries and orchestrated deceptions with enough verifiable content to raise serious doubts among allies.[67]

Reed Irvine has pointed out that 'the extension of Communist control over vast areas and populations since the end of the Second World War has owed more to the propaganda and disinformation offensive of the Communist countries than to the power of their arms.'[68]

Agency documents CIA 1984-000089/87/85/83, and CIA 1980-90C all provide verification of this usage of media assets by the CIA.[69] There is ample evidence of the same type of activity by the KGB. The primary direct usage of the media was that of radio. The best-known CIA use of radio as a propaganda tool concerned Radio Free Europe (RFE) and Radio Liberty (RL). RFE was established by the CIA in 1949 out of the National Committee for a Free Europe; RL was established out of the American Committee for Freedom for the Peoples of the USSR in 1951;[70] they were funded and run by the CIA until the early 1970s.[71] In 1953, the stations began 'saturation broadcasting' to overcome Soviet jamming. The policy behind RFE/RL was the assumption that they would 'be more effective if the role of the [USG] was not apparent'.[72] The CIA also founded 'Voice of Liberation' radio as part of its successful coup in Guatemala in 1954;[73] Radio Nejat (Liberation) out of the Front from the Liberation of Iran to which it reportedly paid $100,000 per month in 1982;[74] and Radio Swan, established under the Gibraltar Steamship Corporation in Miami, against Cuba from 1960 until 1969.[75] These later became Radio Americas and Vanguard Service Corp. respectively after the 1962 Bay of Pigs invasion.

The KGB never used radio to the extent the CIA did. It preferred to carry out its 'active measures' in disinformation and propaganda through surrogates in the Communist world, and through influencing the print press. The aim behind such usage was the propagating of the Soviet line, the encouragement of negative reactions to their opponents, and the recruitment and development of agents. This was done through a number of methods. The prime method was the planting of *dezinformatsia* in neutral papers either knowingly or unknowingly. An example of this was the late-1960s reporting in the Bombay *Free Press Journal* of alleged U.S. use of bacteriological weapons in Indochina. This story was picked up by the *Times* of London in 1968, as well as other Western print media.[76] London's *New Statesman* was unwittingly used in November 1982 to discredit U.S. Ambassador to the United Nations Jeane Kirkpatrick by linking her with BOSS, South African military intelligence.[77] The Soviets also influenced the media to better their leaders' images: stories picked up by *Time* and *Newsweek* during Yuri Andropov's tenure as Chairman of the KGB stated that he was 'a closet liberal' who 'speaks English well,' 'collects big band records and relaxes with American novels,' and 'sought friendly discussions with dissident protesters.'[78]

The KGB also used press agencies or personnel that were actually KGB fronts or agents. For example, the *Novosti* Press Agency acted as 'one of the vehicles for Soviet "active measures" and provide[d] cover posts for many KGB officers abroad,' employing approximately thirty to forty officers.[79] Communist press bureaus and outlets across Europe were used to support measures in the Soviet Union (such as the purported 'Doctors' Plot' against Josef Stalin in 1953). The KGB used the Danish journalist Arne Petersen between 1973 and 1981 to direct attacks against the British Conservative Party, Prime Minister Margaret Thatcher, and other anti-Soviet elements in British politics through pamphlets and articles either written by himself or by KGB Service A under his name.[80] John Barron states that out of the approximately five-hundred Soviet journalists abroad, the majority were intelligence officers, and the minority, who weren't free to travel outside of the USSR without KGB authorization, could not refuse a request by the KGB to carry out an 'assignment.'[81]

The CIA used similar methods, but not to the same extent as the KGB. Following his appointment as Director of Central Intelligence (DCI) in 1953, Allen W. Dulles expressed the desire to use the press for both intelligence collection and propaganda.[82] The CIA relied on U.S. journalists to carry out 'their desire to help their country.'[83] Loch Johnson maintains that the CIA uses a vast network of reporters, magazines, electronic media, and other media personnel to supplement official information from the U.S. government to promote Washington's current policies through quiet channels. The media can help or harm foreign political figures or organizations, as happened to Chile's Salvador Allende.[84] The CIA has stated that it has 'assets who are employed by, or have access to media outlets'; these can be either foreign employees of U.S. publications, Americans in the U.S. news media, or foreign nationals employed by foreign media outlets.[85] These journalists have a 'clandestine relationship of one sort or another' with the CIA, either by official (known by Langley) or unofficial contacts with journalists abroad that are not listed with the

Agency offices.[86] The journalist Carl Bernstein claimed that more than 400 U.S. journalists secretly carried out CIA activities from 1952 to 1976. The Church Committee disclosed 50 for the same time period, and CIA official sources put the number at 36.[87]

As well as using journalists directly, the CIA funded and otherwise supported huge numbers of newspapers, journals and other print media over the course of the Cold War. Some, including its funding of *Der Monat* (FRG), *Encounter* (UK), and the *Daily American* (Rome),[88] was within the context of direct rivalry with the Soviets. Others, like *El Mercurio* (Chile), and *Elimo* and *Salongo* (Angola),[89] were to promote CIA interests in a specific region of the globe in support of other operations. During the Vietnam War, the CIA allegedly wrote whole articles on the war for *The Economist*.[90] Additional examples of this type are funding the FNLA in Angola with $300,000 in 1975 to develop a radio station and newspaper,[91] and the establishment of the news organization *Forum World Features* (FWF) under Brian Crozier in the United Kingdom. FWF was originally set up under the Congress for Cultural Freedom and placed under a CIA proprietary, Kern House Enterprises. By keeping its ownership secret, 'journalists' from FWF could go anywhere under full accreditation and supply CIA propaganda openly. In 1970, a splinter group was founded in London, the *Institute for the Study of Conflict,* under joint CIA-Secret Intelligence Service (SIS) control. The Institute was not used for propaganda purposes, but to give academic respectability to old anti-Communist clichés through its journal *Conflict Studies*.[92] Finally, publishing was funded by the CIA, some overtly and some covertly. As Marchetti states,

> Financing books is a standard technique used by all intelligence services. Many writers are glad to write on subjects which will further their own careers, and with a slant that will contribute to the propaganda objectives of a friendly agency.[93]

Many books, such as *The Deception Game, The Dynamics of Soviet Society*, and *The Foreign Aid Programs of the Soviet Bloc and Communist China* were commissioned by the CIA. Other books, supposedly written by Soviet personnel, such as *The Penkovskiy Papers,* were in reality written by the CIA and placed under someone else's name.[94] There is great suspicion that *Khrushchev Remembers: The Glasnost Tapes* is, in reality, of this type.[95]

C. Social Groups

Both the CIA and the KGB equally used social organizations as FOs. The basic trend in this category was one of directly balancing off each other: when the KGB used a social organization oriented around students, the CIA would attempt to establish a counter organization.

In 1967, *Ramparts* published an expose of CIA activities relating to student, religious and media groups.[96] The magazine revealed that the CIA had been funding 80 percent of the budget of the National Students Association between 1952 and 1967 in an attempt to counter Soviet efforts to mobilize world youth. More than 250 U.S. students were 'sponsored by the CIA to attend youth festivals in Moscow, Vienna and Helsinki, and were used for missions such as reporting on Soviet and third world personalities or observing Soviet security practices.'[97] Academics were also used; the CIA admitted to 'using several hundred American academics, who in addition to providing leads and . . . making introductions for intelligence purposes, occasionally write books and other material to be used for propaganda purposes abroad. Beyond these, an additional few score are used in an unwitting manner for minor activities.'[98] One individual funded directly by the CIA was Giovanni Cardinal Montini (later Pope Paul VI) who promoted orphanages in Italy. The thinking was that

> if such institutions were adequately supported, many young people would be able to live well there and so would not one day fall into Communist hands.[99]

Other types of sponsorship included spending $20–30 million annually to finance anti-Communist groups (cultural, youth, labor unions, etc.) in Italy,[100] and sending £380,000 between 1947 and 1953 to the European Market Movement through the CIA-controlled American Committee on a United Europe, the same organization that spent £1.34 million on the European Youth Campaign in 1951, a response to the Communist Youth Rally.[101]

One of the largest CIA social FOs was the Congress for Cultural Freedom (CCF). Founded in 1950, it was used in the UK to support politicians seeking to move the Labour Party away from policies of pacifism and nationalization.[102] In 1967, a CIA employee admitted that the agency had been providing the CCF with more than $1 million annually since 1950. The CCF was also active in fomenting the democratic opposition to Spanish dictator Francisco Franco.[103] Anti-Communist trade unions were heavily funded by the CIA in Europe and the Third World.[104] Other social FOs that received funding from the CIA were the American Society for a Free Asia, used as a pressure group to push the U.S. government to action against unfriendly Communist regimes;[105] the National Front for the Salvation of Libya, funded by both the CIA and Saudi Arabia, which attempted to overthrow Muammar Quadaffi in 1984;[106] the *Patria y Libertad*, the Society for Manufacturing Development (SOFOFA), the Confederation of Private Organizations (CAP), and the National Front of Private Activity (FRENAP), all in Chile, funded to influence the 1973 elections.[107]

The KGB was just as actively involved as CIA in this arena. In 1921, Lenin introduced the idea of propagating Communism through trade unions, youth organizations, and other social groups.[108] Many Soviet front organizations have existed throughout the twentieth century; they emerged out of Willi Münzenberg's 'Innocents' Clubs' of the 1920s, where individuals were recruited to the Communist cause.[109] Since 1945, the KGB has been more concerned with rallying specific social groups throughout the globe. In 1965, 11 social FOs were officially linked to the USSR. Included were the World Federation of Trade Unions and the International Union of Students in Prague, the International Organization of Journalists (Prague), the World Federation of Scientific Workers (London), the World Federation of Teachers' Unions (Prague), and the Women's International Democratic Federation (East Berlin).[110] More regionally, such organizations as the Nigerian Trade Union Congress and the Afro-Asian People's Solidarity Organization were funded and utilized by the KGB.[111]

The single largest social FO used by the KGB was the World Council of Peace/International Institute for Peace (WCP/IIP). Originally, it was penetrated but not controlled by the KGB; not until the mid-1960s did the KGB begin to actively control it. The WCP was expelled from Paris in 1951 for 'fifth column activities.' From Prague it went to Vienna, where it was banned in 1957 for 'activities directed against the interest of the Austrian state.' Its headquarters were finally established in Helsinki in 1968.[112] Headed at one time by the Indian Communist Romesk Chandra, the WCP sponsored various peace conferences. Claiming to be funded by international peace movements, in reality it received over $50 million annually through the KGB, and even achieved recognition from the UN and UNESCO.[113]

Another key social FO used by the KGB was the International Association of Democratic Lawyers, used in mid-1988 to circulate a story stating the 'U.S. agents are butchering Latin American children and using their bodies for organ transplants.'[114] This disinformation was picked up by the press in over 50 countries. One of the most often misrepresented KGB social FOs were the peace movements in Western Europe. Although the KGB often claimed responsibility for 'encouraging' these movements (such as the Campaign for Nuclear Disarmament responsible for the protest at Greenham Common), its aid could not have motivated them

any further for, according to Christopher Andrew, they were already in the 1980s very intensely anti-United States.[115]

III. Proxies and Covers

Proxy armies and covers were often used by both the CIA and KGB. The use of proxy armies and paramilitary formations was equal on both sides. There are many examples of such groups. The CIA supported paramilitary formations in Indochina, Angola, Nicaragua, El Salvador, Ethiopia, Afghanistan, and many other regions. The KGB, almost without exception, supported proxy armies in the same areas opposed to those the CIA supported. This is the clearest use of this type of FO.

But other methods were used by both sides. The CIA directly trained the members of the South Vietnamese government's police force in a $25 million project at Michigan State University;[116] this program was one of many developed under the cover of the U.S. Agency for International Development (USAID). Begun in 1952, USAID sent 'public safety missions' to over thirty-eight nations between 1955 and 1962. By 1973, over 73,000 foreign police personnel had been trained. That year, however, Congress banned USAID from continuing such operations, and the project was taken over covertly by the Agency.[117] SAVAK, Iran's security service, was created and trained by the CIA as a means of gathering information on the USSR in exchange for helping repress dissident activity against the Shah's regime.[118] Reinhard Gehlen's intelligence network in post-war West Germany (called 'The Org') was used by the CIA to train Baltic emigres and refugees to carry out paramilitary covert action against the Soviets. These agents acted in concert with the Ukrainian partisan groups NTS and OUN in operations against the Soviets in Poland, the Baltics and the USSR itself. Eisenhower's Task Force-C programs in the 1950s had included the development of a Volunteer Freedom Corps, employing cadres of European emigre fighters, as an aspect of 'roll-back.' But they failed miserably during the late-1940s and early 1950s.[119] Finally, Vang Pao's *Armée Clandestine*, made up of Meo units backed by Operation WHITE STAR Green Beret forces, was used to combat Pathet Lao forces in Laos. Police Aerial Resupply Units (PARU) were active, not to be confused with the Provincial Reconnaissance Unit (PRU) used in the PHOENIX Project in Indochina. This aid continued successfully until the 1970 revelations regarding the secret war in Laos.[120]

Although Soviet use of proxy armies in the Third World was very similar to that of the CIA there were some notable differences. The KGB usually influenced, and often controlled, the armies of client-states such as Cuba, Angola, Afghanistan, Ethiopia through replicated Soviet Political Administrations which placed informers throughout the armies' ranks.[121] The main difference arose in the KGB's use of 'friendly' intelligence services. The KGB directly controlled the intelligence and security services of all the Soviet bloc countries, and used the intelligence services of client-states, such as Libya. This was done to 'give distance and deniability in potentially embarrassing operations,' as well as to carry out 'false-flag' recruitment.[122] Examples of this are the KGB's direction to the StB (Czech intelligence) to 'cause conflict and exploit tension between individual countries, even countries that recently gained their independence.'[123] As well, the East German (GDR) *Staatsicherheitsdienst* (SSD) was used between 1959 and 1960 as *agents provocateurs* to try and destabilize West Germany (FRG) by infiltrating agents into Jewish areas to desecrate graves, spray swastikas on property, and other similar acts. In 1968, the KGB took direct control of Cuba's DGI in a secret agreement with Fidel Castro.[124] The KGB also used paramilitary front organizations through international terrorism. Although never directly controlled by the KGB, terrorist organizations such as the Red Brigades in Italy and the Baader-Meinhof Gang in the FRG, were indirectly-sponsored by Moscow Center. This was most often accomplished through surrogate intelligence services, such as the GDR's MFS and Romania's DIE. Links existed as well between these organizations and the Palestine Liberation Organization (PLO), as well as the Provisional Irish Republican Army (IRA) for a number of years.[125] No evidence can be found to indicate a similar relationship between the CIA and its allies, although the argument has been made that the agency supported terrorist groups in Central America.

The final category is that of cover. Close similarities exist between the CIA and KGB use of covers in their operations. Both services made extensive use of press covers for their operations and officers, but the Soviets appear to have done so more frequently. CIA1984-000091 states that

> the number of Communist intelligence agents . . . under official cover abroad . . . is considerably in excess of the number of American intelligence operators under similar cover.[126]

CIA1984-000083 states that 'American journalistic cover is now in use by the [CIA].'[127] This often leads to a serious problem. As Loch Johnson explains, 'cover' is a problem because many different types of societal groups (journalists, missionaries,[128] diplomats) do not want CIA agents masquerading under their profession as this compromises and possibly endangers themselves.[129] Certain corporations have been used for cover as well, including the Psycho-

logical Assessment Associates, Inc., in Washington that provided covers for CIA agents overseas.[130]

The KGB employed cover in much the same way, using corporations such as Aeroflot and the news agency TASS,[131] as well as the traditional use of the diplomatic service as cover. Peter Deriabin points out that organizations such as 'Friendship Societies/Leagues' and 'Bureaus of Technical Assistance' attached to Soviet embassies and trade missions were covers for KGB operations and officers.[132] The journal *New Times* was a clear example of use of the press: of the twelve correspondents allowed in the West, ten were KGB officers.[133] Finally, even previously believed legitimate organizations have become suspect: John Barren maintains that the Institute for the Study of the USA and Canada, attached to the USSR Academy of Sciences, was a front for the KGB acting through the CPSU's International Department.[134]

The KGB differed in its use of covers from the CIA in the area of disinformation and defectors. Although there were a number of legitimate defectors from the KGB over the course of the Cold War, there was an even larger number of 'dangles,' as Edward Jay Epstein calls them. These KGB officials apparently 'defected' to the CIA, only to later be revealed as 'triples,' returning to the Soviets after planting a great deal of misleading information on CIA debriefing officers. Prime examples of this have allegedly included Yuri Nosenko in the 1960s, Vitaly Yurchenko in the 1980s, and the two CIA assets in the Soviet mission to the UN, code-named 'Fedora' and 'Top-Hat.'[135] These elaborate deception schemes were the hallmark of the KGB; there was no evidence found to indicate anything similar carried out by the CIA or any of its Western allies. More recently, Nosenko, 'Fedora,' and 'Top-Hat' have been accorded legitimacy, further complicating assessment of their defections and collaboration with the CIA and FBI.[136]

Assessing Success

There are several levels at which intelligence success or failure can be assessed. Treverton raises the question as to whether CPA successes were more 'apparent than real,' and if real, then at what cost?[137] At the general level, the CIA was successful in carrying out many of its operations through the use of front and political organizations. As John Prados points out, almost without exception, the CPA carried out by the CIA forced the Soviets and the Chinese (the specific opponents named in NSC 5412) to respond in kind without escalation to open military confrontation.[138] This seems to contradict the general assumption that CIA covert actions were more often than not failures in the long or short term.

More specifically, limited operations were never allowed to stay limited due to the problem of ever-escalating commitments, the quagmire of covert action. Thus, even though limited covert actions in Angola in 1975 and Nicaragua in 1980 were initially limited to preventing the consolidation of a Marxist government in one case, and of harassing the Sandinista regime to prevent its continued support of guerrillas in El Salvador, they eventually escalated to such a level that failure was inevitable unless the next step, military intervention, was taken.[139] At this level, the CIA had some debacles (Indochina, Cuba) but as well a number of limited successes (Chile, Western Europe).

Propaganda operations had certain successes: Guatemala is one of the most obvious. But even here, the CIA admitted in a post-mortem assessment that Communism was never a real threat in Guatemala; there was no evidence of contacts with the Soviets.[140] But these 'successes' later led to failures or 'problems that rebounded in the face of the [U.S. government].'[141] As far as media successes, opponents of propaganda or psychological warfare argue that if overt means had failed, it was unlikely that the target would be persuaded by covert use of media organs. The problem of 'blow-back' is also of concern; information planted abroad finds its way back into domestic press sources, deceiving one's own citizens.[142] The question is raised as well as to why the U.S. Information Agency does not carry out a propaganda role since its mission is overt and aimed at spreading U.S. views anyway.[143]

In assessing individual operations, the CIA comes up lacking. Mistakes were often made in the planning stages, pre-determining failure. In Libya, for instance, the CIA bypassed the best potential replacement for Quadaffi, and in Iran no attempts were made to penetrate religious groups prior to the Khomeini Revolution.[144] In funding support to resistance groups in Tibet, Afghanistan, and Indochina, large portions of CIA assistance were soaked up while still in transit due to corruption. And in certain operations, follow-up support could not be granted for various reasons. This was most evident in the link between Radio Free Europe (RFE) and the Hungarian uprising of 1956. RFE broadcast vague hints about possible Western assistance to students and workers in Budapest prior to the revolt; however, once the uprising began, RFE was forced to sit by helplessly and listen to broadcasts from Budapest charting the slaughter. An estimated 30,000 Hungarians died in the Soviet suppression.[145]

Soviet successes were more apparent than those of CIA. In the years following World War II, KGB use of paramilitary fronts linked to deception operations in Eastern Europe forced the CIA to establish a Counterintelligence Staff under James Angleton in 1954.[146] Generally, the KGB's social FOs were by-and-large successful in that they always forced the CIA to react, one step *behind* the KGB. The World Peace Council (WPC) was very successful in coordinating world opinion through its leadership of many other social FOs, particularly against the U.S. during the Vietnam War. Obviously, it was not solely responsible for the results. But the WPC's influence ultimately failed in 1989 when it admitted that 90 percent of its funding came from the Soviets.[147] Other perceived successes were in reality distinct from KGB operations. For example, during the 1984 elections, the KGB launched an anti-Reagan propaganda campaign using the slogan *Reagan: eto voina!* ('Reagan Means War!'). Anti-U.S. reaction to Ronald Reagan's re-election was claimed by the KGB as a sweeping success; however, the fact that the KGB slogan went unused everywhere points to another area where the KGB had little to do with world opinion.[148] But the KGB was successful in gaining recognition for most of its social FOs by the UN, UNESCO, United Council of Churches, and other international bodies. This was largely accomplished through the use of Third World surrogates to influence colleagues and decisions. Outside of the known social FOs, many splinter committees, action groups, subsidiary organizations and the like emerged to carry out much the same work as their parent bodies, but without apparent Soviet involvement.[149]

A Shade of Difference

Clearly, both the CIA and KGB interfered with civil society during the Cold War. Yet, an obvious global imbalance existed between CIA and KGB operations. The CIA by the 1980s had effected a much greater outreach than the KGB. Where the CIA generally dealt with any non-Communist political organizations that would further its cause, the KGB dealt almost exclusively with Communist parties in an attempt to further world Communism. But both powers were simply looking out for their own interests and using whatever vehicles necessary to fulfill and secure those interests. John Prados has concluded that,

> in all these CIA operations, there is a lesson . . . the United States acts in its own interests, which are those of a Great Power. There is little true identity of interest between the restive local minority and the Great Power.[150]

This could easily be said for the KGB and the Soviet Union as well. As far as front organizations are concerned, the Soviets proved themselves much more adept than the CIA at developing and wielding social FOs internationally. The use of the media for propaganda, cover and influence was equally successful on both sides. But where the CIA generally failed in its use of proxy armies, the KGB can be said to have been successful in its use of surrogate intelligence services and armies to spread the Soviet point of view.

All in all, during their Cold War confrontation, both the CIA and the KGB intervened extensively in civil society in order to further the aims of the individual service and Power. But, more often than not, the interests of the Power impeded the interests of the world. As Victor Marchetti, a former CIA officer and writer put it, 'We wanted to export democracy. We exported fascism instead. Democracy is like religion: it cannot be imposed. It can be spread only if those who preach it practice it.' [151]

Questions for Further Discussion

1. What methods of covert action did the Soviet Union use during the Cold War?

2. How successful was the Soviet Union in the conduct of covert action?

3. How would you compare and contrast the approaches of the two superpowers to covert action?

4. Do you think that Russia continues to engage in global covert actions, now that the Cold War is over? If so, what would be its targets and purposes?

   * The term CPA will henceforth denote all types of covert action related to the subject-area, including propaganda/disinformation, direct political influencing, paramilitary support and use of social organizations where related to the Cold War confrontation, and any other categorical topic covered in this study.

   ** Most CIA corporate FOs were incorporated in Delaware due to its more lenient regulations regarding corporations (Marchetti, 1989; p. 118).

Endnotes

1. Loch Johnson, *America's Secret Power: The CIA in a Democratic Society* (Oxford, 1989), p. 17.
2. Ibid. p. 18.
3. Ibid. p. 1.
4. Victor Marchetti and John D. Marks, *The CIA and the Cult of Intelligence* (New York, 1980), p. 38.
5. Gregory F. Treverton, *Covert Action: The Limits of Intervention in the Postwar World* (New York, 1987), p. 13.
6. Paul W. Blackstock, *The Strategy of Subversion: Manipulating the Politics of Other Nations* (Chicago, 1964), pp. 43–44, 56.
7. Johnson, n1, p.19.

8. Gabriel Kolko, *Confronting the Third World: United States Foreign Policy 1945–1980* (New York, 1988), p. 51; Ray S. Cline, *Secrets, Spies and Scholars: Blueprint of the Essential CIA* (Washington, 1976), p. 103; Richard Bissell states that the merging of the OPC with the CAS led to a blurring of the lines between the two functions of the CIA and eventual domination of CA over the collection mission (Marchetti and Marks, p. 329).
9. United States Senate, *Final Report of the Select Committee to Study Governmental Operations With Respect to Intelligence Activities*, Book I: *Foreign and Military Intelligence*, p. 145; Book IV: *Supplementary Detailed Staff Reports on Foreign and Military Intelligence*, p. 29.
10. John Prados, *Presidents' Secret Wars: CIA and Pentagon Coven Actions from World War II Through Iranscam* (New York, 1988), pp. 29, 112–113.
11. Philip Agee, 'Where Do We Go From Here?' in Philip Agee and Louis Wolf (eds.) *Dirty Work: The CIA in Western Europe* (Secaucus, 1978), p. 260.
12. Marchetti, n4, p. 40.
13. Kolko, n8, p. 5.
14. Peter Deriabin and T. H. Bagley, *KGB: Masters of the Soviet Union* (New York, 1990), p. 383.
15. Christopher Andrew and Oleg Gordievsky, *KGB: The Inside Story* (Toronto, 1990).
16. Deriabin, n14, p. 387.
17. Prados, n10, p. 468.
18. Marchetti, n4, pp. 330–331.
19. United States Senate, Book IV, n9, p. 68.
20. Edward Jay Epstein, *Deception: The Invisible War Between the KGB and the CIA* (Toronto, 1989), p. 78.
21. Andrew, n15, pp. 57–58, 420, 384–385.
22. William R. Corson and Robert T. Crowley, *The New KGB: Engine of Soviet Power* (New York, 1985), p. 278.
23. Treverton, n5, p. l9.
24. Kolko, n8, p. 18.
25. Johnson, n1, pp. 26, 101.
26. Ibid. pp. 25–26; Treverton, n5, p. 20.
27. Johnson, n1, p. 102.
28. Victor Marchetti in *Panorama*, 'The CIA in Italy: An Interview with Victor Marchetti', *Dirty Work*, p. 170; Agee, 'Where Do We Go From Here?' p. 267.
29. Philip Agee and *Information Dienst*, 'West Germany: An Interview With Philip Agee,' *Dirty Work*, pp. 185–186
30. Treverton, n5, pp. 211–212.
31. Philip Agee, 'The CIA in Portugal,' *Dirty Work*, pp. 67–68.
32. Edward Van der Rhoer, *The Shadow Network* (New York, 1983) pp. 6–8.
33. Andrew, n15, p. 334.
34. Christopher Andrew and Oleg Gordievsky (eds.), *More 'Instruction from the Centre': Top Secret Files on KGB Global Operations 1975–1985* (London, 1992), pp. 29–31.
35. Chapman Pincher, *The Secret Offensive—Active Measures: A Saga of Deception, Disinformation, Subversion, Terrorism, Sabotage and Assassination* (London, 1985), pp. 2–3, 7–12.
36. Prados, n10, pp. 469–470.
37. Treverton, n5, p. 20; Kolko, n8, p. 217.
38. Kolko, n8, pp. 196, 242.
39. Andrew, n15, p. 412.
40. Kolko, n8, pp. 64, 105, 195.
41. Marchetti, n28, 'The CIA in Italy,' p. 172.
42. Kolko, n8, p. 242.
43. Andrew, n15, pp. 413, 480.
44. Ibid. pp. 466–468.

45. Prados, n10, pp. 469–470.
46. Treverton, n5, p. 21.
47. Epstein, n20, p. 26; Corson, n22, p. 278.
48. Iain Phelps-Fetherston, *Soviet International Front Organizations* (New York, 1965), pp. 1, 2.
49. For a full discussion of the CIA's use of proprietaries, see United States Senate, Book I, n9, pp. 124–126.
50. For a complete discussion of CAT, see Marchetti, n4, pp. 121–124.
51. Prados, n10, pp. 114–115, 116; Lyman B. Kirkpatrick, Jr., *The U.S. Intelligence Community: Foreign Policy and Domestic Activities* (New York, 1973), p. 119n; for a complete discussion of Air America, as well as subsidiaries like Air Asia, see Marchetti, n4, pp. 126–129.
52. Prados, n10, p. 231.
53. Ibid. pp. 176–278.
54. Ibid. pp. 375, 408, 431–432.
55. Marchetti, n4, p. 120.
56. Prados, n10, p. 450.
57. Ibid. pp.237, 375; John Marks, 'The CIA's Corporate Shell Game,' *Dirty Work*, p. 130, for a complete discussion of Intermountain, see Marchetti, n4, pp. 126–129.
58. Marchetti, n4, pp. 121, 133.
59. John Marks, 'How To Spot a Spook,' *Dirty Work*, p. 37.
60. David Wise and Thomas B. Ross, *The Invisible Government* (New York, 1964), p. 109.
61. John Marks, 'The CIA's Corporate Shell Game,' *Dirty Work*, pp. 127, 130.
62. Treverton, n5, pp. 102–105.
63. Marks, 'The CIA's Corporate Shell Game,' n61, p. 137; Prados, n10, pp. 195, 211.
64. Wise, n60, pp. 83, 90, 283, 285.
65. Arcos was funded through Amtorg (New York) and Wostwag (Hamburg), two fronts for the Comintern, and supported by the Cheka. It was later expelled from the UK for aversion, sabotage, political intrigue, etc. (Corson, n22, p. 283; Andrew, n15, p. 82).
66. United States Senate, Book I, n9, p. 192; Johnson, n1, p. 186.
67. Corson, n22, p. 379.
68. Pincher, n35, p. 1.
69. For a discussion of the CIA's use of the media, see United States Government , Book I, n9, pp. 191–201.
70. Prados, n10, pp. 34–35; Marchetti, n4, pp. 119, 146–149.
71. Prados, n10, p.123; Johnson, n1, p.23.
72. Cline, n8, p. 128.
73. Treverton, n5, p. 15.
74. Prados, n10, p. 377.
75. Marchetti, n4, p. 119; Wise, n60, p. 335.
76. Andrew, n15, p. 419.
77. Ibid. p. 491.
78. Ibid. p. 406.
79. Ibid. pp. 419, 527.
80. Ibid. pp. 346, 495; John Barron, *KGB Today: The Hidden Hand* (New York, 1983), p. 277.
81. Barron, n80, p. 261.
82. Johnson, n1, p. 184.
83. CIA1984-000091.
84. Johnson, n1, p. 22.
85. CIA1984-000089/87/85.
86. CIA1984-000083, CIA 1980-9C.
87. Johnson, n1, p. 185; United States Congress, Book I, n9, p. 192.
88. Johnson, n1, p. 186.
89. Treverton, n5, pp. 14–15, 19.
90. Johnson, n1, p. 197.
91. Treverton, n5, p. 17.
92. Steve Weissman, 'The CIA Makes the News,' *Dirty Work*, pp. 206–208.
93. Johnson, n1, pp. 158–159: this was highly contested by the House Judiciary Committee on Civil and Constitutional Rights who considered this to be operating in the U.S., specifically forbidden activity under the CIA's legislative mandate; Marchetti, n4, p. 153.
94. Marchetti, n4, pp. 144, 152–153.
95. Ibid. pp. 154–156, 156–157.
96. CIA 1978-225F
97. Kirkpatrick, n51, p. 153; United States Government, Book I, n9, p. 184; Marchetti, n4, p. 41; Richard Fletcher, 'How CIA Money Took the Teeth Out of British Socialism,' *Dirty Work*, p. 198.
98. United States Senate, Book I, n9, p. 189; further discussion of this is Johnson, n1, pp. 162–163.
99. Marchetti, 'The CIA in Italy,' n28, p. 169.
100. Ibid., pp. 168–169.
101. Weissman et al., 'The CIA Backs the Common Market,' *Dirty Work*, pp. 202, 203.
102. Fletcher, n97, p. 188.
103. Fletcher, pp. 195, 199; Cambio 16, 'The CIA in Post-Franco Spain,' *Dirty Work*, p. 142.
104. Johnson, n1, p. 26; Treverton, n5, p. 19.
105. Prados, n10, p. 154.
106. Ibid. p. 383.
107. Treverton, n5, pp. 140–141.
108. Phelps-Fetherston, n48, p. 1.
109. Andrew, n15, pp. 57–58.
110. Phelps-Fetherston, n48, pp. 3–4.
111. Richard Deacon, *A History of the Russian Secret Service* (London, 1972), p. 513; Barron, n80, pp. 264–265.
112. Andrew, n15, pp. 359, 419.
113. Ibid. pp. 419–420.
114. Ibid. p. 530.
115. Ibid. pp. 490, 492, 506.
116. Johnson, n1, p. 157; this was exposed in a 1966 issue of *Ramparts;* Kirkpatrick, n51, p. 151.
117. Kolko, n8, pp. 50–51, 131, 210.
118. Ibid. p. 269.
119. Prados, n10, pp. 40–41, 55–58, 120–121.
120. Ibid. pp. 269–294, 271, 291.
121. Deriabin, n14, p. 388.
122. Epstein, n20, pp. 282, 283–290.
123. Deriabin, n14, p. 363.
124. Andrew, n15, p. 384; Van der Rhoer, n32, pp. 11–12.
125. Deriabin, n14, pp. 358–359.
126. CIA 1984-000091.
127. CIA 1984-000083.
128. For a discussion of the CIA's use of religious groups, see United State Senate, Book I, n9, pp. 201–204.
129. Johnson, n1, pp. 70, 186 (journalists).
130. Marks, 'How To Spot a Spook,' n59, p. 38.
131. Deacon, n111, p. 490: in 1967 the manager of Aeroflot in Holland was arrested for espionage; in 1969, TASS personnel were expelled from Belgium for the same reason.
132. Deriabin, n14, p. 357.
133. Ibid. p. 391.
134. Barron, n80, p. 265.
135. Epstein, n20, p. 4.
136. See David Wise, *Nightmover: How Aldrich Ames Sold the CIA to the KGB for $4.6 Million* (New York, 1995), p. 67.
137. Treverton, n5, p. 22.
138. Prados, n10, p. 466.
139. Treverton, n5, p. 22.
140. Kolko, n8, p.105.

141. Prados, n10, pp. 465–466.
142. Johnson, n1, p. 69.
143. Ibid. p.196.
144. Ibid. p. 84; Prados, n10, p. 383.
145. Prados, n10, pp. 469–470, 125.
146. Epstein, n20, p. 41.
147. Andrew, n15, pp. 420, 528.
148. Ibid. p. 494.
149. Deriabin, n14, p. 364.

150. Prados, n10, p. 467.
151. Marchetti, 'The CIA In Italy,' n28, p. 173. ✦

Reprinted with permission from Kevin A. O'Brien, 'Interfering With Civil Society: CIA and KGB Covert Political Action During the Cold War,' *International Journal of Intelligence and Counterintelligence* 8 (Winter 1995): 431–456.

21

Covert Action: Swampland of American Foreign Policy

Senator Frank Church

The chairman of the Senate Intelligence Committee that investigated intelligence abuses in 1975–76 finds in the excesses of the CIA abroad the symptoms of an illusion of American omnipotence that entrapped and enthralled the nation's presidents throughout the Cold War. Writing in the middle of the Cold War, the Senator saw no place for bribery, blackmail, abduction, or assassination in America's relations with the rest of the world.

Two hundred years ago, at the founding of this nation, Thomas Paine observed that "Not a place upon earth might be so happy as America. Her situation is remote from all the wrangling world." I still believe America remains the best place on Earth, but it has long since ceased to be "remote from all the wrangling world."

On the contrary, even our internal economy now depends on events far beyond our shores. The energy crisis, which exposed our vulnerable dependence upon foreign oil, made the point vividly.

It is also tragic but true that our own people can no longer be made safe from savage destruction hurled down upon them from the most hidden and remote regions on Earth. Soviet submarines silently traverse the ocean floors carrying transcontinental missiles with the capacity to strike at our heartland. The nuclear arms race threatens to continue its deadly spiral toward Armageddon.

In this dangerous setting, it is imperative for the United States to maintain a strong and effective intelligence service. On this proposition we can ill-afford to be of two minds. We have no choice other than to gather, analyze, and assess—to the best of our abilities—vital information on the intent and prowess of foreign adversaries, present or potential. Without an adequate intelligence-gathering apparatus, we would be unable to gauge with confidence our defense requirements; unable to conduct an informed foreign policy; unable to control, through satellite surveillance, a runaway nuclear arms race. "The winds and waves are always on the side of the ablest navigators," wrote Gibbon. Those nations without a skillful intelligence service must navigate beneath a clouded sky.

With this truth in mind, the United States established, by the National Security Act of 1947, a Central Intelligence Agency to collect and evaluate intelligence, and provide for its proper dissemination within the government. The CIA was to be a clearing house for other U.S. intelligence agencies, including those of the State Department and the various military services. It was to be an independent, civilian intelligence agency whose duty it was, in the words of Allen Dulles, CIA Director from 1953–1961:

> To weigh facts, and to draw conclusions from those facts, without having either the facts or the conclusions warped by the inevitable and even proper prejudices of the men whose duty it is to determine policy and who, having once determined a policy, are too likely to be blind to any facts which might lend to prove the policy to be faulty.

"The Central Intelligence Agency," concluded Dulles, "should have nothing to do with policy." In this way, neither the President nor the Congress would be left with any of the frequently self-interested intelligence assessments afforded by the Pentagon and the State Department to rely upon.

In its efforts to get at the hard facts, the CIA has performed unevenly. It has had its successes and its failures. The CIA has detected the important new Soviet weapons systems early on; but it has often over-estimated the growth of the Russian ICBM forces. The CIA has successfully monitored Soviet adherence to arms control agreements, and given us the confidence to take steps toward further limitations; but it has been unable to predict the imminence of several international conflicts, such as the 1973 Arab-Israeli War. In a word, though it deserves passing marks for its intelligence work, the CIA has certainly not been infallible.

While one may debate the quality of the agency's performance, there has never been any question about the propriety and necessity of its involvement in the process of gathering and evaluating foreign intelligence. Nor have serious questions been raised about the means used to acquire such information, whether from overt sources, technical devices, or by clandestine methods.

What has become controversial is quite unrelated to intelligence, but has to do instead with the so-called covert operations of the CIA, those secret efforts to manipulate events within foreign countries in ways presumed to serve the interests of the United States. Nowhere are such activities vouchsafed in the statutory language which created the Agency in 1947. "No indication was given in the statute that the CIA would become a vehicle for foreign political action or clandestine political warfare," notes Harry Howe Ransom, a scholar who has written widely and thought deeply about the problems of intelligence in modern society. Ransom concludes that "probably no other organization of the federal government has taken such liberties in interpreting its legally assigned functions as has the CIA."

The legal basis for this political action arm of the CIA is very much open to question. Certainly the legislative history of the 1947 Act fails to indicate that Congress anticipated the CIA would ever engage in covert political warfare abroad.

The CIA points to a catch-all phrase contained in the 1947 Act as a rationalization for its operational prerogatives. A clause in the statute permits the Agency "to perform such other functions and duties related to intelligence affecting the national security as the National Security Council may, from time to time, direct." These vague and seemingly innocuous words have been seized upon as the green light for CIA intervention around the world.

Malignant Plots

Moreover, these interventions into the political affairs of foreign countries soon came to overshadow the Agency's original purpose of gathering and evaluating information. Just consider how far afield we strayed.

For example:

- We deposed the government of Guatemala when its leftist leanings displeased us.

- We attempted to ignite a civil war against Sukarno in Indonesia.

- We intervened to restore the Shah to his throne in Iran, after Mossadegh broke the monopoly grip of British Petroleum over Iranian oil.

- We attempted to launch a counter-revolution in Cuba through the abortive landing of an army of exiles at the Bay of Pigs.

- We even conducted a secret war in Laos, paying Meo tribesmen and Thai mercenaries to do our fighting there.

All these engagements were initiated without the knowledge or consent of Congress. No country was too small, no foreign leader too trifling, to escape our attention.

- We sent a deadly toxin to the Congo with the purpose of injecting Lumumba with a fatal disease.

- We armed local dissidents in the Dominican Republic, knowing their purpose to be the assassination of Trujillo.

- We participated in a military coup overturning the very government we were pledged to defend in South Vietnam; and when Premier Diem resisted, he and his brother were murdered by the very generals to whom we gave money and support.

- We attempted for years to assassinate Fidel Castro and other Cuban leaders. The various plots spanned three Administrations, and involved an extended collaboration between the CIA and the Mafia.

Whatever led the United States to such extremes? Assassination is nothing less than an act of war, and our targets were leaders of small, weak countries that could not possibly threaten the United States. Only once did Castro become an accessory to a threat, by permitting the Soviets to install missiles on Cuban soil within range of the United States. And this was the one time when the CIA called off all attempts against his life.

The roots of these malignant plots grew out of the obsessions of the Cold War. When the CIA succeeded the Office of Strategic Services of World War II, Stalin replaced Hitler as the Devil Incarnate. Wartime methods were routinely adopted for peacetime use.

In those myopic years, the world was seen as up for grabs between the United States and the Soviet Union. Castro's Cuba raised the specter of a Soviet outpost at America's doorstep. Events in the Dominican Republic appeared to offer an additional opportunity for the Soviets and their allies. The Congo, freed from Belgian rule, occupied the strategic center of the African continent, and the prospect of Soviet penetration there was viewed as a threat to U.S. interests in emerging Africa. There was a great concern that a communist takeover in Indochina would have a "domino effect" throughout Asia. Even the lawful election in 1970 of a Marxist president in Chile was still seen by some as the equivalent of Castro's conquest of Cuba.

In the words of a former Secretary of State, "A desperate struggle [was] going on in the back alleys of world politics." Every upheaval, wherever it occurred, was likened to a pawn on a global chessboard, to be moved this way or that, by the two principal players. This led the CIA to plunge into a full range of covert activities designed to counteract the competitive efforts of the Soviet KGB. Thus, the United States came to adopt the methods and accept the value system of the "enemy." In the secret world of covert action, we threw off all restraints. Not content merely to discreetly subsidize foreign political parties, labor unions, and newspapers, the Central Intelligence Agency soon began to directly manipulate the internal politics of other countries. Spending many millions of dollars annually, the CIA filled its bag with dirty tricks, ranging from bribery and false propaganda to schemes to "alter the health" of unfriendly foreign leaders and undermine their regimes.

Nowhere is this imitation of KGB tactics better demonstrated than in the directives sent to CIA agents in the Congo in 1960. Instructions to kill the African leader Lumumba were sent via diplomatic pouch, along with rubber gloves, a mask, syringe, and a lethal biological material. The poison was to be injected into some substance that Lumumha would ingest, whether food or toothpaste. Before this plan was implemented, Lumumha was killed by Congolese rivals. Nevertheless, our actions had fulfilled the prophesy of George Williams, an eminent theologian at the Harvard Divinity School, who once warned, "Be cautious when you choose your enemy, for you will grow more like him."

Allende 'Unacceptable'

The imperial view from the White House reached its arrogant summits during the Administration of Richard Nixon. On September 15, 1970, following the election of Allende to be President of Chile, Richard Nixon summoned Henry Kissinger, Richard Helms, and John Mitchell to the White House. The topic was Chile. Allende, Nixon stated, was unacceptable to the President of the United States.

In his handwritten notes for this meeting, Nixon indicated that he was "not concerned" with the risks involved. As CIA Director Helms recalled in testimony before the Senate Committee, "The President came down very hard that he wanted something done, and he didn't care how." To Helms, the order had been all-inclusive. "If I ever carried a marshal's baton in my knapsack out of the Oval Office," he recalled, "it was that day." Thus, the President of the

United States had given orders to the CIA to prevent the popularly elected President of Chile from entering office.

To bar Allende from the Presidency, a military coup was organized, with the CIA playing a direct role in the planning. One of the major obstacles to the success of the mission was the strong opposition to a coup by the Commander-in-Chief of the Chilean Army, General Rene Schneider, who insisted that Chile's constitution be upheld. As a result of his stand, the removal of General Schneider became a necessary ingredient in the coup plans. Unable to get General Schneider to resign, conspirators in Chile decided to kidnap him. Machine guns and ammunition were passed by the CIA to a group of kidnappers on October 22, 1970. That same day General Schneider was mortally wounded on his way to work in an attempted kidnap, apparently by a group affiliated with the one provided weapons by the CIA.

The plot to kidnap General Schneider was but one of many efforts to subvert the Allende regime. The United States sought also to bring the Chilean economy under Allende to its knees. In a situation report to Dr. Kissinger, our Ambassador wrote that:

> Not a nut or bolt will be allowed to reach Chile under Allende. Once Allende comes to power we shall do all within our power to condemn Chile and the Chileans to utmost deprivation and poverty, a policy designed for a long time to come to accelerate the hard features of a Communist society in Chile.

The ultimate outcome, as you know, of these and other efforts to destroy the Allende government was a bloodbath which included the death of Allende and the installation, in his place, of a repressive military dictatorship.

Why Chile? What can possibly explain or justify such an intrusion upon the right of the Chilean people to self-determination? The country itself was no threat to us. It has been aptly characterized as a "dagger pointed straight at the heart of Antarctica."

Was it to protect American owned big business? We now know that I.T.T. offered the CIA a million dollars to prevent the ratification of Allende's election by the Chilean Congress. Quite properly, this offer was rejected. But the CIA then spent much more on its own, in an effort to accomplish the same general objective.

Yet, if our purpose was to save the properties of large U.S. corporations, that cause had already been lost. The nationalization of the mines was decided well before Allende's election; and the question of compensation was tempered by insurance against confiscatory losses issued to the companies by the U.S. government itself.

No, the only plausible explanation for our intervention in Chile is the persistence of the myth that communism is a single, hydraheaded serpent, and that it remains our duty to cut off each ugly head, wherever and however it may appear.

Ever since the end of World War II, we have justified our mindless meddling in the affairs of others on the ground that since the Soviets do it, we must do it, too. The time is at hand to re-examine that thesis.

Before Chile, we insisted that communism had never been freely chosen by any people, but forced upon them against their will. The communists countered that they resorted to revolution because the United States would never permit the establishment of a communist regime by peaceful means.

In Chile, President Nixon confirmed the communist thesis. Like Caesar peering into the colonies from distant Rome, Nixon said the choice of government by the Chileans was unacceptable to the President of the United States.

The attitude in the White House seemed to be: If—in the wake of Vietnam—I can no longer send the Marines, then I will send in the CIA.

What Have We Gained?

But what have we gained by our policy of consummate intervention, compared to what we have lost?

- A "friendly" Iran and Indonesia, members of the OPEC cartel, which imposes extortionate prices on the Western World for indispensable oil?

- A hostile Laos that preferred the indigenous forces of communism to control imposed by Westerners, which smacked of the hated colonialism against which they had fought so long to overthrow?

- A fascist Chile, with thousands of political prisoners languishing in their jails, mocking the professed ideals of the United States throughout the hemisphere?

If we have gained little, what then have we lost? I suggest we have lost—or grievously impaired—the good name and reputation of the United States from which we once drew a unique capacity to exercise matchless moral leadership. Where once we were admired, now we are resented. Where once we were welcome, now we are tolerated, at best. In the eyes of millions of once friendly foreign people, the United States is today regarded with grave suspicion and distrust.

What else can account for the startling decline in American prestige? Certainly not the collapse of our military strength, for our firepower has grown immensely since the end of World War II.

I must lay the blame, in large measure, to the fantasy that it lay within our power to control other countries through the covert manipulation of their affairs. It formed part of a greater illusion that entrapped and enthralled our Presidents: the illusion of American omnipotence.

Nevertheless, I do not draw the conclusion of those who now argue that all U.S. covert operations must be banned in the future. I can conceive of a dire emergency when timely clandestine action on our part might avert a nuclear holocaust and save an entire civilization.

I can also conceive of circumstances, such as those existing in Portugal today, where our discreet help to democratic political parties might avert a forcible take-over by a communist minority, heavily subsidized by the Soviets. In Portugal, such a bitterly-unwanted, Marxist regime is being resisted courageously by a people who earlier voted 84 percent against it.

But these are covert operations consistent either with the imperative of national survival or with our traditional belief in free government. If our hand were exposed helping a foreign people in their struggle to be free, we could scorn the cynical doctrine of "plausible denial," and say openly, "Yes, we were there—and proud of it."

We were there in Western Europe, helping to restore democratic governments in the aftermath of World War II. It was only after our faith gave way to fear that we began to act as a self-appointed-sentinel of the status quo.

Then it was that all the dark arts of secret intervention—bribery, blackmail, abduction, assassination—were put to the service of reactionary and repressive regimes that can never, for long, escape or withstand the volcanic forces of change.

And the United States, as a result, became ever more identified with the claims of the old order, instead of the aspirations of the new.

The remedy is clear. American foreign policy, whether openly or secretly pursued, must be made to conform once more to our historic ideals, the same fundamental belief in freedom and popular government that once made us a beacon of hope for the downtrodden and oppressed throughout the world.

Questions for Further Discussion

1. Why is Senator Frank Church so critical of U.S. covert actions?

2. Does he see any need for covert action at all in the conduct of American foreign policy?

3. Against what nations was covert action directed by the United States, according to Senator Church?

4. What kinds of covert action, if any, do you think are morally acceptable for the United States, and under what conditions? ✦

Reprinted with permission from Frank Church, "Covert Action: Swampland of American Foreign Policy," *Bulletin of the Atomic Scientists* 32 (February 1976): 7–11.

22

Covert Action Can Be Just

James A. Barry

Exploring the use of covert action from the point of view of just-war theory, Barry establishes benchmarks for judging the morality of this controversial form of secret foreign policy. He eschews the use of highly invasive clandestine operations but advances an ethical justification for certain forms of covert action.

In 1954, President Dwight Eisenhower appointed a panel to make recommendations regarding covert political action as an instrument of foreign policy. The panel, headed by General Jimmy Doolittle, included the following statement in its report:

> It is now clear that we are facing an implacable enemy whose avowed objective is world domination by whatever means and at whatever cost. There are no rules in such a game. Hitherto acceptable norms of human conduct do not apply. If the United States is to survive, long standing American concepts of "fair play" must be reconsidered. We must develop effective espionage and counterespionage services and must learn to subvert, sabotage and destroy our enemies by more clever, more sophisticated means than those used against us. It may become necessary that the American people be made acquainted with, understand and support this fundamentally repugnant philosophy.[1]

Today, this conclusion of the Doolittle report appears exaggerated—even its authors were uncomfortable with the "repugnant philosophy" they deemed necessary—and fortunately America did not abandon its moral traditions much less "acceptable norms of human conduct." Nevertheless, covert political action did become an important tool of U.S. policy, and the threat of international communism was so compelling a rationale that most covert action operations needed no more specific justification. This objective was used to justify covert coups, assassination attempts, and other activities that in hindsight appear reprehensible. These actions—pursued under a crusading variant of *Real-politik*—seem to many today to be questionable in their objectives and disproportionate to the threat.

The cold war justification for covert action began to draw fire, in part because of the late 1960s opposition to the Vietnam War and in part because of the revelation of abuses by the Central Intelligence Agency (CIA) such as assassination plots against foreign leaders. As a result of those revelations, greater attention was paid to managing covert actions. But, until recently, the adequacy of the Soviet threat to justify covert action was not seriously doubted in Washington.

Covert Action and the New World Order

Since the dismantling of the Berlin Wall, the abortive coup in the Soviet Union, and the dissolution of the Soviet empire, this once compelling anticommunist rationale for covert action has lost all validity. But this is not to say that the United States should eschew the method of covert action. The Gulf War shows that aggression by hostile states remains a threat. And other challenges—such as terrorism, narcotics trafficking, and the proliferation of weapons of mass destruction—are likely to require the United States to consider covert responses.

What, then, would replace the cold war justification that has shaped covert action policy since the founding of the Central Intelligence Agency?

One approach to assessing the justification for intervention overseas, an approach that has received renewed attention in recent years, derives from the natural law tradition and those rules regarding the use of force by states that fall under the rubric of "just-war theory." Just-war theory was used extensively by the Bush administration to explain its decision to go to war, under United Nations auspices, against Iraq.[2] More recently, a symposium of jurists, philosophers, theologians, government officials, and military officers affirmed that just-war theory is useful in evaluating low-intensity conflict.[3]

Just-War Theory: Traditional and Modern Formulations

Just-war doctrine can be traced to Saint Augustine in the fourth century A.D., and especially to Saint Thomas Aquinas, who codified it in the thirteenth century. Just-war theory is a set of moral guidelines for going to war (the so-called *jus ad bellum*), and a set of moral guidelines for the conduct of hostilities (*jus in bello*).[4] Though associated with Catholic scholars, just-war theory is not a religious teaching but rather part of a moral tradition,

286

dating from Aristotle, a tradition that emphasizes ethical consideration in decision making.

According to Thomas, the act of going to war must have the following three characteristics if it is to be a moral act: the action must be ordered by proper authority; the cause must be just; and there must be an intention of promoting good or avoiding evil.[5] Later authorities added three further criteria: the action must be a last resort and peaceful alternatives (negotiations, sanctions, and so forth) must be exhausted or judged ineffective; there must be a reasonable probability of success anticipated; and the damage which the war entails must be expected to be proportionate to the injury or the injustice which occasions it.[6]

Once these conditions are met, according to this formulation of just-war theory, the belligerent is subject to two further constraints in his conduct of the war: his actions must be discriminate, that is, directed against the opponent not against innocent people; and the means of combat must be proportionate to the just ends envisioned and under the control of a competent authority.[7]

The first of these constraints has been further refined, under the so-called "principle of double effect," to encompass situations in which injury to innocent parties is unavoidable. Under this principle, a belligerent may permit incident evil effects. However, the action taken must not be evil in itself; the good effect and not the evil effect, must be intended; and the good effect must not arise out of the evil effect, but both must arise simultaneously from the action taken.[8]

Modern political theorists in the just-war tradition have focused primarily on the criterion of just cause. The majority favors the view that the only justifiable cause for war is to repel aggression. Traditionally, however, there were two others: to retake something wrongfully taken and to punish wrongdoing.[9] Another area of debate has been whether forcible intervention could be justified in order to reform a state's political system, for example, in the case of flagrant human rights abuses.[10]

Just-War Theory and Covert Action

One former intelligence practitioner, William Colby, has argued that "a standard for selection of covert actions that are just can be developed by analogy with the long-standing effort to differentiate just from unjust wars."[11] And former Director of Central Intelligence (DCI) William Webster has noted that in its deliberations the CIA's Covert Action Review Group explores three key questions regarding a proposed covert action: "Is it entirely consistent with our laws? Is it consistent with American values as we understand them? And will it make sense to the American people?"[12]

With respect to the latter two considerations, a reformulation of the just-war criteria in common sense terms would probably appeal to the American people. It seems fair to conclude that the people would support a covert action if:

The action is approved by the president, after due deliberation within the Executive Branch, and with the full knowledge and concurrence of appropriate members of the Congress;

The intentions and objectives are clearly spelled out, reasonable, and just;

Other means of achieving the objectives would not be effective;

There is a reasonable probability of success; and

The methods envisioned are commensurate with the objectives.

Further, it is reasonable to presume that the American people would approve of methods that minimize injury (physical, economic, or psychological) to innocent people, are proportionate to the threat, and under firm U.S. control.[13]

Those who advocate or approve such covert actions, however, bear the additional burden of demonstrating why they must be conducted secretly. As ethicist Sissela Bok has pointed out, every state requires a measure of secrecy to defend itself, but when secrecy is invoked citizens lose the ordinary democratic checks on those matters that can affect them most strongly.[14] In addition, as Charles Beitz has argued, a special problem of operational control can arise when intermediaries (especially foreign agents) are employed—because their aims may differ from ours, and because the chain of command may be ambiguous or unreliable.[15] Finally, most covert actions will necessarily lack the public legitimacy and legal status under international law of a declared, justifiable war. This makes it incumbent on those advocating such actions to take into account the consequences of possible public misunderstanding and international opprobrium.

Just War and the Chile Case of 1964

Reverend John P. Langan, S.J., of the Kennedy Center for Ethics and Public Policy, Georgetown University, notes that just-war theory has both material and formal aspects, and that the formal aspects, such as just intention and proportionality are applicable to a broad range of situations where one has to do harm to another, including punishment, surgery, and—by extension—political or economic intervention.[16] It would appear that the framework of just-war theory could be useful for making choices regarding covert actions, since they can cause suffering or moral damage, as war causes physical destruction. To explore this, consider how the guidelines would have applied to covert U.S. interventions in Chile in 1964 and 1970.[17]

Background

As part of its worldwide buildup of covert action capabilities in the early 1950s, the CIA established a capacity to conduct covert propaganda and political influence operations in Chile. In 1961, President John Kennedy established the Alliance for Progress to promote growth of democratic institutions. He also became convinced that the Chilean Christian Democratic Party shared his belief in democratic social reform and had the organizational competence to achieve this goal, but lacked the resources to compete with parties of the Left and Right.

U.S. Intentions

During 1961, the CIA established relationships with key political parties in Chile, as well as propaganda and organizational mechanisms. In 1962, the Special Group (the interagency body charged with reviewing covert actions) approved two CIA proposals to provide support to the Christian Democrats. The program was intended to strengthen democratic forces against the Socialist challenge from Salvador Allende Gossens, who was supported by the Soviet Union and Cuba. When President Lyndon Johnson succeeded Kennedy, he continued the covert subsidies, with the objective of making Chile a model of democracy, and preventing nationalization of Chilean branches of American corporations.

The Chilean presidential election of 1964 was a battle between Allende and Eduardo Frei Montalva, a liberal Christian Democrat. The election was viewed with great alarm in Washington. The *New York Times* compared it to the Italian election of 1948, when the communists had threatened covertly to support democratic parties. Similarly, in 1964, the Johnson administration intervened in Chile, according to the Church Committee Report, to prevent or minimize the influence of Marxists in the government that would emerge from the election. Cord Meyer, a former CIA covert action manager, argued that the intervention was intended to preserve Chile's constitutional order.

Policy Approval

In considering the 1964 election operation, the Johnson administration used the established mechanism, the interagency Special Group. By 1963, according to Treverton, the Special Group had developed criteria for evaluating covert action proposals. All expenditures of covert funds for the 1964 opera-

tion (some $3 million in all) were approved by the Group. (There is no indication that the Congress approved these expenditures or was even informed in detail of the operation.) In addition, an interagency committee was set up in Washington to manage the operation and was paralleled by a group in the U.S. embassy in Santiago. Meyer contends that covert intervention on behalf of Christian Democratic candidates had very wide support in the administration, and the Church Committee confirms that the covert action was decided upon at the highest levels of government.

Other U.S. Activities

Covert action by the CIA was an important element, but not the only aspect of U.S. policy. Chile was chosen to become a showcase of economic development programs under the Alliance for Progress. Between 1964 and 1969, Chile received well over a billion dollars in direct, overt U.S. aid—more per capita than any other country in the hemisphere. Moreover, funding to support the Frei candidacy was funnelled overtly through the Agency for International Development, as well as secretly through the CIA. Frei also received covert aid from a group of American corporations known as the Business Group for Latin America.

Probability of Success

That the 1964 covert action had a reasonable probability of success is evident from the outcome—Frei won a clear majority of the vote, 56 percent. According to Church Committee records, a CIA post-mortem concluded that the covert campaign had a decisive impact. It is not clear from available records whether a calculation of the likelihood of success was part of the decision-making process. According to Treverton, the CIA was required under Special Group procedures to make such an estimate, and it is likely that their view would have been optimistic, since they had penetrated all significant elements of the Chilean political system.

Methods Employed

In the 1964 election operation the CIA employed virtually its entire arsenal of non-lethal methods:

> Funds were passed through intermediaries to the Christian Democrats.

> The CIA provided a consultant to assist the Christian Democrats in running an American-style campaign, which included polling, voter registration, and get-out-the-vote drives.

> Political action operations, including polls and grass roots organizing, were conducted among important voting blocs, including slum dwellers,

peasants, organized labor, and dissident Socialists.

CIA-controlled assets placed propaganda in major Chilean newspapers, and on radio and television; erected wall posters; passed out political leaflets; and organized demonstrations. Some of this propaganda employed "scare tactics" to link Allende to Soviet and Cuban atrocities.

Other assets manufactured "black propaganda"—that is, material falsely attributed to Allende's supporters and intended to discredit them.[18]

Constraints Imposed

Significant constraints were imposed, however. Paramilitary and other lethal methods were not employed. The CIA rejected a proposal from the Chilean Defense Council to carry out a coup if Allende won. The Department of State turned down a similar proposal from a Chilean Air Force officer. Moreover, the Special Group turned down an offer from American Businessmen to provide funds for covert disbursement. According to the Church Committee, the Group considered this "neither secure nor an honorable way of doing business."

Covert Action and the 1970 Election

Under Chilean law, Frei could not serve two consecutive terms as president. As the 1970 elections approached, therefore, the United States faced a dilemma. The Christian Democrats had drifted to the left, and were out of step with the view of President Richard Nixon's administration. The conservative candidate, Jorge Alessandri, was not attractive, but there was even greater concern about an Allende victory.

The CIA began to warn policy makers early in 1969 that an Allende victory was likely. In March 1970, the 303 Committee (successor to the Special Group) decided that the United States would not support any particular candidate, but would conduct a "spoiling operation" aimed at discrediting Allende through propaganda. The effort failed when Allende won a slim plurality in the September 4 election. Since no candidate won a clear majority, the election was referred to a joint session of Congress, which in the past had always endorsed the candidate who had received the highest popular vote. The joint session was set for October 24, 1970.

U.S. Intentions

Senior U.S. officials maintained that their preoccupation with Allende was defensive and aimed at allaying fears of a communist victory both abroad and at home. Henry Kissinger, then assistant to the president for national security affairs, later noted

that what worried the United States was Allende's proclaimed hostility and his perceived intention to create "another Cuba." Nixon stated in a *New York Times* interview:

> There was a great deal of concern expressed in 1964 and again in 1970 by neighboring South America countries that if Mr. Allende were elected president, Chile would quickly become haven for Communist operatives who would infiltrate and undermine independent governments throughout South America.[19]

The intelligence community, however, offered a more subtle analysis of the threat. According to an assessment by the CIA's Directorate of Intelligence:

> Regarding threats to U.S. interests, we conclude that:
>
> 1. The U.S. has no vital national interests in Chile. There would, however, be tangible economic losses.
>
> 2. The world balance of power would not be significantly altered by an Allende government.
>
> 3. An Allende victory would, however, create considerable political and psychological costs:
>
>   a. Hemispheric cohesion would be threatened by the challenge that an Allende government would pose to the OAS, and by the reactions that it would create in other countries. We do not see, however, any likely threat to the peace of the region.
>
>   b. An Allende victory would represent a definite psychological setback to the U.S. and a definite psychological advance for the Marxist idea.[20]

When Allende won a plurality of the popular vote, the thrust of U.S. covert action shifted to preventing his accession to the presidency by manipulating the congressional vote, by another political gambit, or by support for a military coup.

Policy Approval

Until the middle of September, management of the covert action against Allende was entrusted to the 40 Committee (a new name for the 303 Committee), which Kissinger headed. After the popular vote, the committee asked Edward Korry, the U.S. ambassador in Santiago, for a "cold-blooded assessment" of the likelihood of mounting a coup and organizing an effective opposition to Allende. With negative evaluations from both Korry and the CIA, the committee explored a so-called "Rube Goldberg" gambit in which Alessandri would be elected by the Congress, then resign allowing Frei to run in a second election. The ploy was turned down.

By this time, Nixon had taken a personal role. On September 15, Donald Kendall, chief executive officer of Pepsi Cola, and Augustine Edwards, an influential Chilean publisher who had supported Frei during the 1964 election, communicated their alarm at the prospect of an Allende victory to the Nixon administration. According to Kissinger, Nixon was alarmed by their views and decided that more direct action was necessary. He called in DCI Richard Helms and ordered the CIA to play a direct role in organizing a military coup. Further, Helms was told not to coordinate CIA activities with the Departments of State and Defense and not to inform Ambassador Korry. The 40 Committee was not informed, nor was the Congress. This activity was called "Track II," to distinguish it from the 40 Committee program, "Track I."[21]

Other U.S. Activities in Chile

Track II was a carefully guarded secret, but U.S. displeasure with the prospect of an Allende victory was not. According to Kissinger, all agencies were working to prevent the election. The Chilean government was threatened with economic reprisals, and steps were taken to inform the Chilean armed forces that military aid would be cut off. Separately from the CIA's efforts, several large American companies had financed Alessandri's campaign. One company, ITT, offered the CIA $1 million, but Helms turned it down.

Probability of Success

When Helms left the Oval Office on September 15, he had a page of handwritten notes. The first entry read "less than one in ten chance of success." His pessimistic assessment was echoed by Ambassador Korry. According to his correspondence with the Church Committee, Korry consistently warned the Nixon administration that the Chilean military was no policy alternative. From Santiago, according to Church Committee documents, the CIA reported: "Military action is impossible; the military is incapable and unwilling to seize power. We have no capability to motivate or instigate a coup." (This view apparently was based on an evaluation of the military's political will; in 1973 the armed forces showed their capability by removing Allende from power.)

The CIA's view was shared by the managers of Track II. According to David Phillips, chief of the CIA's Chile Task Force, both he and his supervisor were convinced that Track II was unworkable. The Deputy Director for Plans, Thomas Karamessines, was adamant that the Agency could not refuse the assignment, but briefed Nixon several times on the progress of the operation, always pessimistically.[22]

Methods Employed

Although both Track I and Track II were intended to prevent Allende's taking power, they employed different methods. Track I included funding to bribe Chilean congressmen, propaganda and economic activities, and contacts with Frei and elements of the military to foster opposition to Allende. Track II was more direct, stressing active CIA involvement in, and support for, a coup—without Frei's knowledge. The CIA specifically offered encouragement to dissident Chilean military officers who opposed Allende but who recognized that General Rene Schneider, the Chilean Chief of Staff would not support a coup. These dissidents developed a plan to kidnap Schneider and take over the government, and this became known to CIA officials. Two unsuccessful kidnap attempts were made; on the third attempt, on October 22 1970, General Schneider was shot and subsequently died. Both the Church Committee and the Chilean inquiry concluded that the weapons used were not supplied by the United States, and that American officials did not desire or encourage Schneider's death. Neither, however, did they prevent it.

Constraints Imposed

Unlike the 1964 effort, the 1970 covert operation did not involve extensive public opinion polling, grass roots organizing, or direct funding of any candidate. Moreover, Helms made clear that the assassination of Allende was neither feasible nor politically acceptable, and when a right-wing Chilean fanatic, General Arturo Marshall, offered to help prevent Allende's confirmation, the CIA declined because of his earlier involvement in bombings in Santiago.

Evaluating the 1964 and 1970 Chile Operations

A just-war theorist reviewing the two covert operations would likely reach two conclusions. First, the 1964 operation was more justifiable than the 1970 activity. And, second, both operations would have benefited from a more rigorous application of the *jus ad bellum* and *jus in bello* criteria.

U.S. authorities probably would have considered that their covert intervention in the 1964 election was generally consistent with the *jus ad bellum*. It had clear objectives, which the administration would have likely considered akin to repelling aggression (preservation of an important democratic force in Chile and defense against the establishment of another communist stronghold in the Western hemisphere). These were set by President Kennedy based on his assessment of the commonality of U.S.

and Chilean interests. While not a last resort, it was conducted in the context of an overall overt policy (the Alliance for Progress). It was likely to be successful; was limited in scope and used political methods generally proportionate to the perceived threat in that they were essentially the same as those used by the USSR. It was approved in accordance with the established procedures. In retrospect, the process would have been morally strengthened if Congress had been consulted, even though there might have been an increased risk of causing the operation to fail owing to leaks.

Some doubts can be raised regarding consistency with the *jus in bello*. The need for "scare tactics" and "black propaganda" is not obvious. (If indeed Allende's affinities to the USSR and Cuba were on the public record, promulgation of this truthful information should have been adequate.) As Bok notes, lying and deception carry a "negative weight" and require explanation and justification.[23] If not clearly necessary to respond to Cuban or Soviet activities, such deceptive actions would not meet the test of proportionality.

The 1970 "Track II" operation, in contrast, violated virtually all of the just-war guidelines. Its objective was clear (prevent Allende's confirmation), but little thought apparently was given to the consequences for the Chilean people or political system. The normal process was bypassed, and Nixon made the fateful Track II decision in a state of high emotion.[24] No expert believed that success was likely. The methods chosen were initially inadequate (the "spoiling operation") and, subsequently, when support for coup-plotting took center stage, the intermediaries could not be controlled. Although injury to innocent parties was a foreseeable outcome of the coup, no advance provision was made to prevent or minimize it. In light of the intelligence assessment that the United States lacked vital interests in Chile, it is hard to rationalize support for a potentially violent military coup as a proportionate response.

In sum, the Chile case shows that just-war theory can provide a useful framework for evaluating political action by asking penetrating questions: Is the operation directed at a just cause, property authorized, necessary, and proportionate? Is it likely to succeed, and how will it be controlled? Is it a last resort, a convenience, or merely an action taken in frustration? In the case of the 1964 operation, the answers to most of these questions were satisfactory; in 1970, they were not.

Reforms Since the 1970s

In the more than two decades since Track II, significant improvements have been made in control-ling covert action. The doctrine of "plausible deniability," which allowed senior officials to disclaim responsibility for their actions, has been replaced by one intended to secure direct presidential accountability. Since the Hughes-Ryan Amendment of 1974, a series of laws has been enacted requiring the president personally to "find" that proposed covert actions are important to the national security, and to report such operations to Congress in a timely manner. (Debate has continued over what constitutes timely notification.) In the wake of the Iran/*contra* scandal more stringent procedures were implemented by the Executive Branch and then by Congress.

Under the current system, established by the Reagan administration in 1987 and refined by legislation in 1991, a written Finding must be signed before a covert action operation commences, except that in extreme circumstances an oral Finding may be made and then immediately documented in writing. A Memorandum of Notification (MON), also approved by the president, is required for a significant change in the means of implementation, level of resources, assets, operational conditions, cooperating foreign countries, or risks associated with a covert action. Each Finding or MON includes a statement of policy objectives; a description of the actions authorized, resources required, and participating organizations; a statement that indicates whether private individuals or organizations or foreign governments will be involved; and an assessment of risk. A Finding or MON is reviewed by a senior committee of the National Security Council (NSC), and by the NSC Legal Advisor and Counsel to the President. Copies of Findings and MONs are provided to the Congress at the time of notification, except in rare cases of extreme sensitivity.[25]

An Approach for the 1990s

These reforms are positive, because they provide for broader consultation, a legal review, presidential accountability, and Congressional involvement in covert action decisions. However, the content of Findings and MONs, as described above, leaves much to be desired from the perspective of just-war theory. The Chile case suggests that explicit attention to the key questions raised by just-war guidelines can strengthen the ethical content of covert actions. In short, the current system addresses the legality, feasibility, and political sensitivity of proposed covert actions. It does not ensure that they are right according to an ethical standard.

The United States would be well-served by establishing a policy process modeled after the just-war criteria. To do this, the current procedures should be revised so that, at each stage in the covert action approval process, difficult questions are asked about the objectives, methods, and management of a proposed operation. It is equally important that they be answered in detail, with rigor, and in writing—even (perhaps especially) when time is of the essence. Covert operators are reluctant to commit sensitive details to paper, but this is essential if the United States is to meet high standards of accountability when the easy rationalization of fighting communism is no longer available.

A decision-making process structured explicitly around just-war criteria lines is, in many ways, simply a restatement of Webster's criteria of consistency with law, American values, and public mores. In that sense, just-war criteria merely reiterate the obvious and make explicit the goals that the United States has striven towards in its reforms of the covert action process since the mid-1970s. But there is value to building a more systematic framework for substantive debate, even if many of these questions are already considered in the CIA's Covert Action Review Group, the senior NSC groups or the oversight committees. The questions of concern include:

Just Cause: Exactly what are the objectives of the operation? Is it defensive—to repel an identifiable threat—or is it intended to redress a wrong, to punish wrongdoing, or to reform a foreign country?

Just Intention: What specific changes in the behavior or policy of the target country, group, or individual does Washington seek? What will be the likely result in the target countries and in other countries? How will the United States or the international community be better off?

Proper Authority: Who has reviewed the proposal? Are there dissents? What is the view of intelligence analysts on the problem being considered? Have senior government officials discussed the proposal in detail? Has the Congress been advised of all significant aspects of the covert activity? If notification has been restricted, what is the justification?

Last Resort: What overt options are being considered? What are their strengths and weaknesses? Why must the proposed activity be secret?

Probability of Success: What is the likelihood that the action will succeed? What evidence is available? Are there differing views of the probability of success?

Proportionality: Why are these methods necessary? Are they the same as those being used by the adversary, or are they potentially more damaging or disruptive? If so, what is the justification?

Discrimination and Control: What steps will be taken to safeguard the innocent against death, injury, economic hardship, or psychological damage? What will be done to protect political institutions and processes against disproportionate damage? If some damage is inevitable, what steps are being taken to minimize it? What controls does Washington exercise over the agents to be employed? What steps will be taken if they disregard our directions? What steps will be taken to protect the agents, and what are our obligations to them? How will the operation be terminated if its objectives are achieved? How will it be terminated if it fails?

Each of these questions should be investigated in the initial approval process, and in periodic reviews by the NSC and the oversight committees.

The Casuistry of Covert Action

Critics of just-war theory note that, in the hands of advocates the criteria can deteriorate into mere rationalizations of intended actions. Scholars acknowledge that moral reasoning is especially complex and difficult in cases involving politics and international affairs.[26] Just-war theory, then, can be exceedingly useful as an organizing principle, but—in itself—does not necessarily provide clear answers.[27] How can this inherent uncertainty be minimized?

William Colby has suggested giving special attention to the criteria of just cause and proportionality.[28] With respect to just cause, a recent report by a panel of distinguished scholars has recommended that covert action should be undertaken only in support of a publicly articulated policy.[29] Open, public debate would go a long way toward determining whether a proposed course of action could be construed as a just cause. The need for such debate is so fundamental that, if secrecy or political fear prevents it, this in itself would seem to be grounds for rejection of any suggested operation.

Assessments of proportionality cannot have recourse to the same open scrutiny, because they involve secret methods. Nevertheless, proposed activities must pass strict tests of consistency with American values. Loch Johnson has attempted to rank-order various types of covert operations into a "ladder of escalation" and he introduces a useful concept of "thresholds" that involve different degrees of risk and interference in foreign countries.[30] Following Johnson, proposed covert activities could be arrayed for debate under thresholds of increasing ethical concern:

Limited Concern would arise if the means would cause minimal damage to people or the political system: Examples might be the benign provision of truthful information; support to existing political forces; or intervention to keep elections honest.

Significant Concern would arise from the use of methods that could cause psychological damage or disrupt the political system: Examples might be a manipulative use of information; the rigging of elections or other distortion of political processes; or the creation of new political forces or strengthening of existing ones out of proportion to their indigenous support.

Serious Concern would result from lying or other techniques that could cause personal suffering or economic hardship: Examples might be the deceptive use of information; non-lethal sabotage; or economic disruption.

Grave Concern would attend any operation involving loss of life or major change in a political system: Examples might be the use of lethal force; or forcible changes in government.

The greater the level of concern, the greater the obligation on the advocate of covert action to show why the proposed method is necessary.

Policy Implications

The end of the cold war means that U.S. policy on covert action can no longer be based on sweeping generalities. Covert interventions abroad should be less frequent; each proposed action must be justified on a case-by-case basis, and on its own merits. Adopting a covert action management system that makes explicit use of the guidelines and thresholds above would move the process substantially in this direction.

Under these guidelines, the types of covert actions that involve the gravest moral risks—lethal force and forcible changes of government—would be reserved for the clearest threats to U.S. security or for redressing the most serious abuses of human rights. The bias would be towards the lower levels of intervention—primarily propaganda and political action programs that carry less risk of destruction and moral damage. This would mean that the United States would have less need for a standing capability for large-scale covert infrastructure of covert action programs to provide a base for mobilization if necessary.

Though the principle is not derived, strictly speaking, from just-war guidelines, it is equally important that the United States keep faith with its foreign agents. Indeed, a morally rigorous approach would strongly discourage any covert action in which the United States raises the hopes of its supporters overseas, only to abandon them when the political will to continue the operation is lost.

U.S. officials would be required to level with their agents about the risks of an operation, the probability of success, and the steps that would be taken to safeguard their interests.

The just-war guidelines set a higher ethical standard than a policy based solely on *Realpolitik*. Although the recommended process would likely result in far fewer covert actions, there is no reason to believe that the United States would be prevented from responding to serious threats. Kissinger's high-handed disproportionate manipulation of the Chilean political system would have been prohibited. But other types of covert action, carefully crafted and keyed to the interests they are intended to support, would still be possible. Moreover, they would likely receive greater political support, and thus have a greater likelihood of success, than some of the poorly thought out, unfocused programs that have occurred in the past. In sum, there is no necessary contradiction between a systematic, thoughtful process for managing covert action and a realistic appraisal of national interest.

Conclusion

Such an application of the just-war framework would not end controversy regarding covert action, nor prevent inappropriate or unethical actions. The claim for a conscious application of just-war guidelines is modest: it will help to make more rigorous Webster's common-sense criteria, and to improve the quality of decisions regarding one of the most controversial aspects of U.S. national security policy. Reforming the process along the lines suggested would signal that the United States is concerned—even in secret activities—with issues of right and wrong and not merely with power. It would promote openness and accountability, and underscore that we firmly reject the "repugnant philosophy" of the Doolittle Report.

Questions for Further Discussion

1. How does Barry relate "just-war theory" to the subject of CIA covert actions?

2. To what extent does Barry find covert actions morally acceptable for the United States?

3. What methods of covert action did the United States use against the Allende regime in Chile, and how effective were they?

4. What would be the consequences of prohibiting all forms of U.S. covert action? How about just certain kinds of covert action? Which would you prohibit and which would you keep?

What criteria would you use to make these judgments?

Endnotes

1. "Report of the Special Study Group [Doolittle Committee] on the Covert Activities of the Central Intelligence Agency. September 30, 1954 [excerpts]" in William M. Leary, ed., *The Central Intelligence Agency, History and Documents* (University, Alabama: The University of Alabama Press, 1984), p. 144.

2. See James Turner Johnson and George Weigel, *Just War and the Gulf War* (Washington, D.C.: Ethics and Public Policy Center, 1991).

3. *Symposium on Moral and Legal Constraints on Low-Intensity Conflict,* Sponsored by the Office of the Assistant Secretary of Defense for Special Operations and Low Intensity Conflict, US. Naval War College, Newport, Rhode Island, April 9–10, 1992.

4. National Conference of Catholic Bishops, *The Challenge of Peace* (Washington, D.C.: U.S. Catholic Conference, 1983), pp. 25–29. (Hereafter, National Conference of Catholic Bishops, *The Challenge of Peace.*)

5. Thomas Aquinas, *Summa Theologica,* trans. Joseph Rickaby, S. J. (London: Burns and Gates, 1892), Question XL, Article I. (Hereafter, Aquinas, *Summa Theologica.*)

6. National Conference of Catholic Bishops, *The Challenge of Peace,* pp. 29–32.

7. Aquinas, *Summa Theologica,* Q. XLI, Art. I.

8. Paul Ramsey, *War and the Christian Conscience* (Durham, N.C.: Duke University Press, 1969), pp. 47–48.

9. The classic modern work on just-war theory is Michael Walzer, *Just and Unjust Wars* (New York: Basic Books, 1977).

10. Charles R. Beitz, "Recent International Thought," *International Journal,* Spring 1988, p. 190.

11. William E. Colby, "Public Policy, Secret Action," *Ethics and International Affairs,* 1989, p. 63. (Hereafter, Colby, "Public Policy, Secret Action.")

12. William Webster, address to the Eighth Circuit Judicial Conference, July 12, 1991. Mimeographed transcript of remarks made available by the Public Affairs Office of the Central Intelligence Agency.

13. See Donald Secrest, Gregory G. Brunk, and Howard Tamashiro, "Moral Justification for Resort to War With Nicaragua: The Attitudes of Three American Elite Groups," *Western Political Quarterly,* September 1991, pp. 541–59.

14. Sissela Bok, *Secrets: On the Ethics of Concealment and Revelation* (New York: Pantheon Books, 1982), p. 191.

15. Charles R. Beitz, "Covert Intervention as a Moral Problem," *Ethics and International Affairs,* 1989, pp. 49–50.

16. John P. Langan, letter to the author dated May 28, 1992.

17. The following discussion is drawn primarily from documents of the Church Committee, which investigated CIA covert actions in the mid-1970s, as well as from memoirs of some of the participants and other government officials and commentators. (These include William Colby, Henry Kissinger, Cord Meyer, David Atlee Phillips, and Arthur Schlesinger.) A summary of the Church Committee's findings, and recommendations for reform, can be found in Gregory Treverton, *Covert Action: The Limits of Intervention in the Postwar World* (New York: Basic Books, 1987). A case study based on Treverton's research has been published by the Carnegie Council on Ethics and International Affairs: *Covert Intervention in Chile, 1970–73,* Carnegie Council on Ethics and International Affairs, 1990.

18. United State Senate, *Staff Report of the Select Committee to Study Government Operations with Respect to Intelligence Activities: Covert Action in Chile, 1963–73* (Washington D.C.: U.S. Government Printing Office, 1975), pp. 15–17.

19. *New York Times,* March 12, 1976.

20. Assessment dated September 7, 1970, declassified and quoted in the Church Committee report.

21. The U.S. decision process is described in detail in the Church Committee Report, *Alleged Assassination Attempts Involving Foreign Leaders,* as well as in Kissinger's memoirs and John Ranelagh, *The Agency: The Rise and Decline of the CIA* (New York: Simon and Schuster, 1986), pp. 514–20.

22. David Atlee Phillips, *The Night Watch* (New York: Ballentine Books, 1977), pp. 283–87.

23. Sissela Bok, *Lying: Moral Choice in Public and Private Life* (New York: Random House, 1978), p. 30.

24. See Alberto R. Coll, "Normative Prudence as a Tradition of Statecraft," *Ethics and International Affairs,*1991, pp. 36–37.

25. *National Security Decision Directive(NSDD) 286,* partially declassified on December 15, 1987, *Intelligence Authorization Act, Fiscal Year 1991,* Title VI.

26. Joseph Boyle, "Natural Law and International Ethics," in Terry Nardin and David Mapel, eds., *Traditions of International Ethics* (Cambridge: Cambridge University Press, 1992), p. 115.

27. The author is indebted to Joel Rosenthal of the Carnegie Council on Ethics and International Affairs for this point. (Letter to the author dated May 12, 1992.)

28. Colby, "Public Policy, Secret Action," p. 63.

29. *Report of the Twentieth Century Fund Task Force on Covert Action and American Democracy* (New York: Twentieth Century Press, 1992), p. 8.

30. Loch K. Johnson, "On Drawing a Bright Line for Covert Operations," *American Journal of International Law,* April 1992, p. 286. ✦

Reprinted with permission from James A. Barry, "Covert Action Can Be Just," *Orbis* 37 (Summer 1993): 375–390.

Part VII

Counterintelligence

Polonius: "Your bait of falsehood takes this carp
   of truth . . ."
   —*Shakespeare*, Hamlet, *2.1.60*

Although it was never directly mentioned in the National Security Act of 1947, America's secret agencies quickly adopted a second intelligence mission in support of their primary mission of intelligence collection and analysis: namely, the protection of America's secrets from espionage by hostile, and sometimes even friendly, foreign powers. This mission is known as *counterintelligence* (Church Committee 1976; Godson 1996; Johnson 1987; Zuehlke 1980). The purpose of counterintelligence (CI) is to uncover and thwart foreign intelligence operations directed against the United States, especially infiltration by foreign agents.

Defined more formally, counterintelligence is the

knowledge needed for the protection and preservation of the military, economic, and productive strength of the United States, including the security of the Government in domestic and foreign affairs against or from espionage, sabotage, and all other similar clandestine activities designed to weaken or destroy the United States. (Commission on Government Security 1957, 48–49)

Counterintelligence specialists wage nothing less than a secret war against antagonistic intelligence services and terrorist organizations—the latter task a subsidiary of CI known as *counterterrorism* (CT). As a CI expert noted in testimony before the Church Committee (1975a, 163): "In the absence of an effective U.S. counterintelligence program, [adversaries of democracy] function in what is largely a benign environment."

The Concerns of Counterintelligence

Over the years, the United States has faced numerous adversaries, from British Redcoats and Barbary Pirates in the early days to the Soviet Red Army and Al Qaeda terrorists in the modern era. In the midst of the Cold War, over 1,000 Soviet officials were on permanent assignment in the United States, according to FBI figures (Church Committee 1975a, 163). Among them, the FBI identified over 40 percent as members of the KGB or GRU, the Soviet civilian and military intelligence units. Estimates on the number of unidentified intelligence officers lurking in the United States raised this figure to over 60 percent of the Soviet "diplomatic" representation, and some defector sources have estimated that 70–80 percent of Soviet Embassy officials in Washington, D.C., and Soviets assigned to the United Nations in New York City had intelligence connections of one kind or another.

The opening of American deepwater ports to Russian ships in 1972 gave the Soviet intelligence services "virtually complete geographic access to the United States," a counterintelligence specialist testified before the Church Committee. In 1974, for example, over 200 Soviet ships with a total crew complement of 13,000 officers and men called at 40 deepwater ports in the United States. Various exchange groups provided additional opportunities for Soviet intelligence gathering within the United States. Some 4,000 Soviets entered the United States as commercial or exchange visitors on an annual basis during the latter decades of the Cold War, and the FBI identified over 100 intelligence officers among the approximately 400 Soviet students who attended American universities during this period as part of an East-West student exchange program. In addition, in the 1970s, the United States experienced a sharp increase in the number of Soviet immigrants to the United States, along with a rise in East-West commercial exchange visitors. Recently, the co-chair of a joint investigative committee on intelligence expressed shock at the FBI estimates on the number of suspected Al Qaeda terrorists and sympathizers who continued to move about inside the United States after the September 11, 2001, attacks (Pelosi 2002).

Foreign intelligence agents have attempted to recruit U.S. executive branch personnel and Congressional staff members. They have also tried to steal secrets in America regarding weapons systems as well as commercial activities and strategies (Johnson 1989). The most elusive counterintelligence threat has been from "illegal" agents, who have no easily detectable contacts with their intelligence service. The problem of "illegals" is summarized by the FBI as follows:

> The illegal is a highly trained specialist in espionage tradecraft. He may be a [foreign] national and/or a professional intelligence officer dispatched to the United States under a false identity. Some illegals [may be] trained in the scientific and technical field to permit easy access to sensitive areas of employment.
>
> The detection of . . . illegals presents a most serious problem to the FBI. Once they enter the United States with either fraudulent or true documentation, their presence is obscured among the thousands of legitimate emigrés entering the United States annually. Relatively undetected, they are able to maintain contact with [their foreign masters] by means of secret writing, microdots, and open signals in conventional communications that are not susceptible to discovery through conventional investigative measures. (Church Committee 1976, 164)

The espionage activities of nations and terrorist cells against the territory of the United States, as well as its citizens, troops, diplomats, and interests abroad, are extensive and relentless, especially by the Soviet Union during the Cold War and today by an assortment of "rogue nations" and terrorist organizations—not to mention Russia, China, and even traditional America allies such as France. To combat these threats, America's counterintelligence officers have developed sophisticated investigative techniques to obtain information about adversaries (at home and abroad) and to guard the U.S. intelligence agencies. The task is difficult technically; moreover, the targeting of counterintelligence operations can raise sensitive legal and ethical questions at home. "U.S. counterintelligence programs, to be both effective and in line with traditional American freedoms," a CIA official told the Church Committee (1975a, 164),

must [on the one hand] steer a middle course between blanket, illegal, frivolous and unsubstantiated inquiries into the private lives of U.S. citizens, and [on the other hand] excessive restrictions which will render the Government's counterintelligence arms impotent to protect the nation from foreign penetration and covert manipulation.

Counterintelligence as a Product: Information About 'The Enemy'

Counterintelligence is both a product and an activity. The product is reliable information about all hostile foreign intelligence services and other threats, such as Al Qaeda cells within the United States. It is necessary to understand the organizational structure of the enemy, its key personnel, its methods of recruitment and training, and the details of specific operations. The efforts of intelligence services through the world to conceal such information from one another, through various security devices and elaborate deceptions, creates what former CIA Chief of Counterintelligence James Angleton (borrowing a line from the poet T. S. Eliot) referred to as a "wilderness of mirrors."

Counterintelligence as an Activity: Counterespionage and Security

As an activity, CI consists of two matching halves: counterespionage and security. *Counterespionage* (CE) is the offensive, or aggressive, side of counterintelligence. It involves identifying specific adversaries and developing detailed knowledge about the operations they are planning or conducting. Counterespionage personnel must then attempt to block these operations by infiltrating the hostile service, an operation known as a "penetration," and by using sundry forms of manipulation. Ideally, as in jujitsu, the thrust of the hostile operation is turned back against the enemy.

Security is the passive, or defensive, side of counterintelligence. It entails putting in place static defenses against all hostile and concealed operations aimed at the United States, regardless of who might be attempting to carry them out. Security defenses include screening and clearance of personnel and establishment of programs to safeguard sensitive intelligence information—in a phrase, the administration of security controls. The objectives are to defend the personnel, installations, and operations against enemy intelligence services and terrorists.

Among the specific defensive devices used for information control by counterintelligence officers are security clearances (consisting of thorough inquiries into the backgrounds of job candidates), polygraphs, locking containers, security education, document accountability, censorship, camouflage, and codes. Grim-faced uniformed guards with German shepherds patrol the electrified fences at the CIA's headquarters, and, inside, polygraph experts administer tests of loyalty to all new recruits and, periodically for seasoned intelligence officers, cross-examine them on whether they have had any associations with foreigners. The polygraph has produced uneven results. Several traitors have been able to fool the machines, among them Aldrich H. Ames, a Russian recruit at the heart of the CIA (discovered in 1994 and now in prison for life). On occasion, though, polygraph sessions have uncovered treasonous behavior, and not long ago they even elicited a confession from a nervous would-be employee that he had murdered his wife and buried her body in his back yard.

Beyond armed guards and watchdogs, devices for physical security include fences, lighting, general systems, alarms, badges, and passes. The control of a specific area relies on curfews, checkpoints, and restricted zones. As a CIA counterintelligence officer has observed (Church Committee 1975a, 166), the security side of counterintelligence "is all that concerns perimeter defense, badges, knowing everything you have to know about your own people," while the counterespionage side "involves knowing all about foreign intelligence services—their people, their installations, their methods, and their operations—so that you have a completely different level of interest."

Counterintelligence as Organization

At the CIA, the Office of Security is responsible for protecting that agency's personnel and installations, while counterespionage operations are largely the preserve of the Operations Directorate and its CI staff (which has personnel overseas using official or nonofficial cover). To combat terrorism more effectively, DCI William J. Casey established a Counterterrorism Center (CTC) in 1986. Despite its preponderance of CIA personnel, the center has 24 officers from a dozen other agencies, including the FBI and the Department of State (the two most important links); the Department of Defense; the Secret Service; the Department of Energy; the Bureau of Alcohol, Tobacco and Firearms; the Naval Investigative Service; the Federal Aviation Agency (another vital participant in this mission); the National Security Agency; the Immigration and Naturalization Service; and, most recently, the new Department of Homeland Security.

A senior officer in the center has remarked:

The whole concept behind the CTC was to bring elements from all four [CIA] Directorates together and put them under one single chain-of-command, so that we'd have all the necessary resources together to tackle the problem. In addition, we brought in these detailees from outside [the CIA], so that we'd have a very close relationship with the intelligence community. These people can pick up a secure [telephone] line and cut through the bureaucratic thickets that we normally face. (Johnson 2000, 177)

The 1993 bombing of the World Trade Center in New York City and the 1995 bombing of a federal building in Oklahoma City, as well as bombings at the U.S. embassies in Kenya and Tanzania in 1998, led Congress to fund expansively those agencies combating terrorism, including the CTC (even though it did not deal with U.S. domestic terrorism—exclusively the FBI's preserve, until the 9/11 attacks). After September 11, 2001, the steady funding for counterterrorism became a flood. Despite funding and sophisticated organizations, some forms of terrorism are nearly impossible to stop, such as a suicide attack carried out by an individual or a group prepared to die in the cause (as happened against Egyptian President Anwar Sadat in 1979, the U.S. Marine base in Lebanon in 1983, and the Israeli Embassy in Buenos Aires in 1992, and with the events of September 11, 2001).

In combating terrorism, the CTC has worked closely with the Nonproliferation Center (both located at the CIA), since each has a mandate to curb the use of dangerous weapons against mass populations. Both centers have concluded that a terrorist organization is more likely to use biological or chemical weapons against the United States, or a radioactive "dirty" bomb, rather than a fission or fusion nuclear device. The NPC concentrates on the supply side of the weapons problem, trying to stem the flow of weapons at the origins of production and distribution; the CTC focuses on the demand side, frustrating terrorist groups from acquiring weapons or weapons material (uranium, plutonium, or chemical-biological substances) in the first place.

The most important defense against terrorism is information about its likely occurrence, so that law enforcement officials can intercede before an attack takes place. To this end, the perfection of humint and other collection methods stands at the top of the CTC's priorities—especially the infiltration of terrorist organizations or the wooing of a defector from the enemy's camp. These are difficult tasks, as modern terrorist organizations are sophisticated, tightly controlled, and acutely aware of the CTC's aspirations.

In growing frustration over the failure of the CTC and the FBI to adequately share counterterrorism information with each other both before and after the 9/11 attacks on the United States, President George W. Bush established a new Terrorist Threat Integration Center (TTIC) in 2003. As the president said in his State of the Union Address that year, the purpose of the TTIC was "to merge and analyze all threat information in a single location." Continued the president: "In order to better protect our homeland, our intelligence agencies must coexist like they never had before." The TTIC incorporates the CIA and FBI counterterrorism units along with representatives involved in counterterrorism from throughout the government. The precise structure and mission of the TTIC remains foggy, however, and riven with bureaucratic bickering—much like the new Department of Homeland Security (with its obvious interest in counterintelligence matters). Among the confusions was how the TTIC would relate to the CIA's Counterterrorism Center, which has a comparable mission.

The Penetration and the Double Agent

Several kinds of operations exist within the rubric of counterespionage (the more aggressive side of counterintelligence). One, however, transcends all the others in importance: the *penetration,* or, in the common vernacular, the "mole." Since the primary goal of counterintelligence is to contain the intelligence services and saboteurs of the enemy, it is desirable to know his plans in advance and in as much detail as possible. This logical, but challenging, objective may be achieved through a high-level infiltration of an adversary's intelligence service or government, or of a terrorist cell. As DCI John McCone observed in 1963 during the Cold War, "Experience has shown penetration to be the most effective response to Soviet and Bloc [intelligence] services" (Church Committee 1975a, 167).

Furthermore, a well-placed infiltrator in a hostile intelligence or terrorist camp may be better able than anyone else to determine whether one's own service has been penetrated by an outsider. A former director of the Defense Intelligence Agency (DIA) has emphasized that the three principal programs used by the United States to meet, neutralize, and defeat hostile penetrations are penetrations of America's own, the security screening and clearance of personnel, and efforts to physically safeguard sensitive intelligence information (Carroll Report of 1964, cited by the Church Committee 1976, 167).

Methods of infiltrating the opposition service take several forms. Usually the most effective and desirable penetration is recruitment of an agent-in-place. He or she is already in the employment of an enemy intelligence service or a terrorist group.

Ideally, the agent-in-place will be both highly placed and susceptible to recruitment by the United States. The prospective recruit—say, a Pakistani diplomat at the U.N. with suspected ties to remnants of the Taliban regime in Afghanistan (and, therefore, possible ties to Al Qaeda)—is approached and asked to work for "the government" of the United States (in fact, the CIA or the FBI). Various inducements may be used to entice the recruit. Money is the most popular bait since the Cold War, while during the Cold War foreigners—notably disaffected individuals inside the intelligence services of the Soviet Bloc—would sometimes spy for the United States purely out of a sense of anti-Communist ideology or disenchantment over the misdirection of communism by Joseph Stalin and other Soviet dictators. The importance of money as a trigger for treason in the post-Cold War era was recently illustrated in the United States. In 2003, Brian P. Regan, an intelligence analyst with access to spy satellite technology and a $100,000 credit card debt, was convicted of plotting to sell to Iraqi officials the coordinates of U.S. satellite targeting in the Persian Gulf region.

If recruitment is successful, an agent-in-place operation can be highly fruitful, since the agent is presumably already trusted within his or her organization and will have unquestioned access to key secret documents. Jack E. Dunlap, who worked at and spied on the National Security Agency in the 1960s, is a well-known example of a Soviet agent-in-place within the U.S. intelligence service during the Cold War. His handler was a Soviet Air Force attaché at the Soviet Embassy in Washington. A single penetration can be an intelligence goldmine, as were Kim Philby (inside MI6, British foreign intelligence), Aldrich H. Ames (CIA), Robert P. Hanssen (FBI) for the Soviet Union, and Col. Oleg Penkovsky (KGB) for the United States.

Another method of infiltration is the double agent. Double agents, however, are costly and time-consuming, and they are risky, because the loyalty of the agent remains a question mark, with double-crosses being commonplace. The running of double agents involves much pure drudgery with few dramatic results, as new information must be constantly and painstakingly checked against existing files. Moreover, passing credible documents back to the enemy to ensure the credibility of the double agent can be a major undertaking. The operations must appear plausible to the adversary, so—to make fake papers seem realistic—the genuine article must be provided now and again. In this process, classified documents must be cleared—typically a slow and contentious activity, since intelligence agencies are reluctant to release any classified information to an outsider. "This means letting a lot of good stuff go to the enemy, without much in return," complained a CIA counterintelligence officer to a Senate Committee (Church Committee 1976, 168).

To accomplish each of these tasks, hard work, careful planning, and considerable staff resources are necessary. The extraordinary staffing requirements of double-agent operations restricted the capacity of the British to run many of them during World War II—only approximately 150 for the entire period of the war and no more than about 25 at any one time—even though the task was eased significantly by the ability of the British to read German secret ciphers throughout most of the war (Masterman 1972).

The Defector

Almost as good as the agent-in-place, and less troublesome to manage than the double agent, is the "defector with knowledge." In this case the challenge consists of a skillful interrogation and validation of the defector's bona fides (as usual), but without the worrisome, ongoing requirement to provide the agent with a credible mix of false and genuine documents along with other logistical support. Although an agent-in-place is preferable because of the ongoing useful information he or she can provide, often an agent-in-place does not want to accept the risk of staying in place—especially in nations where the security is sophisticated and the execution of traitors swift and often painful. The agent's usual preference is to defect to safety in the United States. As a result, agents-in-place are harder to come by in tightly controlled totalitarian regimes with robust counterintelligence services of their own; defection is more likely. In contrast, agents-in-place are more easily recruited in the developing nations, where sophisticated security that might discover them is often lacking.

Defectors recruited overseas by the CIA are occasionally brought to the United States and resettled if they are considered highly important (that is, someone likely to provide valuable ongoing information or someone who has already provided vital information and now seeks exfiltration to avoid capture and execution in his or her own country). The FBI is notified and, after the CIA completes its interrogation, FBI counterintelligence officers may interrogate. Terrorists captured in the United States are normally interrogated first by the FBI, then by the CIA; the process is vice versa for terrorists captured abroad. Sometimes the bona fides of a defector remain in dispute for many years, as in the case of Yuri Nosenko, who defected from the U.S.S.R. soon after the assassination of President John F. Kennedy in 1963. The FBI viewed Nosenko as a legitimate defector; the CIA's chief of counterintelligence worried, however, that Nosenko was really a false defector, sent to the United States to sow disinformation.

The Deception Operation

The penetration (mole) or double agent is closely related to another important counterespionage method: the *deception operation*. Simply stated, the deception is an attempt to give the enemy a false impression about something, causing him to take action contrary to his own interests. Fooling the Germans into a believing that D-Day landings would occur in the Pas de Calais rather than in Normandy is a classic example of a successful deception operation during World War II.

Deception is related to penetration, because U.S. agents-in-place operating within foreign intelligence agencies or terrorist groups can serve as an excellent channel through which misleading information can flow to the enemy. So moles and double agents can serve as both collectors of intelligence and instruments of deception. In another illustration of an approach to deception, the CIA might allow a hostile foreign penetration into its own intelligence service and then carefully feed false information through him or her back to the enemy.

Other Counterintelligence Techniques

Counterespionage operations also include surreptitious surveillance of various kinds (for instance, audio, mail, physical, and "optical"—that is, photography), as well as interrogation (sometimes keeping the subject incommunicado until his or her bona fides are verified). Part and parcel of the CE trade are decoding of secret messages sent by an adversary to a mole, trailing suspected agents, observing "dead drops" (the exchange of material, such as secret documents or instructions, between a spy and his handler), and photographing individuals entering opposition embassies or at other government locations. At the Arlington Cemetery funeral of CIA officer Richard Welch in 1975, Eastern European diplomats were discovered among the media corps snapping photographs of CIA officers (and their automobile license plates) who were attending the burial service. Since the focus of offensive counterintelligence is disruption of the enemy service, provocation can be an important element of counterespionage, too. This approach involves harassment of an adversary, such as publishing the names of his agents or sending a troublemaking false defector into his midst who is in reality an agent provocateur.

Counterintelligence and Research

Good research is critical to effective counterintelligence. It involves amassing encyclopedic knowledge on suspected foreign spies, including American citizens associated (wittingly or unwittingly) with hostile intelligence services or terrorist organizations. Such research can step over the line of protected civil liberties in the United States unless care is taken by the intelligence agencies to honor the law and the rights of citizens.

Counterintelligence officials also have a responsibility for preparing guidelines regarding interrogation of defectors. The matter of counterintelligence interrogation methods has been controversial, raising the question of what techniques should be permissible in a democracy. In 2003, the CIA captured in Pakistan Kahlid Sheikh Mohammed, the suspected mastermind of the Pentagon and World Trade Center attacks two years earlier. Immediately, media accounts around the world (including in the United States) speculated that he might be mistreated—even tortured—by his CIA handlers. Officials within the CIA responded that no brutal force would be used, not the least because psychological pressure was considered more effective. Former CIA officers speculated that the Al Qaeda strategist would be subjected to sleep deprivation; if he cooperated, he would be given rewards, such as good food, rest, and a television. They conceded, though, that while there would be no stretching on the rack, the captured terrorist might be forced to sit or stand in awkward or painful positions for hours at time—"torture lite."

The line between acceptable and unacceptable interrogation techniques is not well defined and in the light of the savage 9/11 attacks is apt to be smudged by interrogators who may be angry about past attacks as well as concerned about the possibility of another sudden strike against the United States unless warning information is extracted quickly from the subject. "There was a before 9/11 and there was an after 9/11," Cofer Black, the head of the CIA's Counterterrorism Center, has said. "After 9/11, the gloves came off" (Harden 2003, A1). Abu Zubaydah, another top Al Qaeda leader captured in Pakistan after the September 11, 2001 attacks, was on painkillers because of a pistol shot to the groin; until he began to cooperate, interrogators held back his full medication. Reports suggest that other Al Qaeda suspects have been chained, naked and hooded, to the ceiling; routinely kicked to keep them awake; and shackled so tightly that blood flow is halted. Most alarming are charges that two Al Qaeda prisoners were killed during interrogation at a U.S. military base in Afghanistan, beaten to death with blunt instruments (Campbell 2003, 1). If the

assertion is proved true, the interrogators would be subject to U.S. civil and military prosecutions. Those being interrogated can also be threatened with the prospect that they will be turned over to a government allied with the United States that is known to have a decidedly malevolent approach to interrogation and few, if any, laws on the subject (Egypt, for example).

Counterintelligence officials also study such subjects as use of proprietary companies by foreign intelligence services or terrorist cells, and the organization and methods of those who practice terrorism. Further, they analyze defector briefs and, if they suspect that internal classified documents have been compromised, they help ascertain who had access and what secrets might have been lost (the latter a process called "damage assessment").

Counterintelligence and Liaison

Liaison among U.S. counterintelligence services, at home and abroad, is vital as well, as no single CI organization can do its job alone. The relationship among CI units is especially important for the United States, because counterintelligence—with all its intricacies and deceptions—requires close coordination among agencies and sharing of records; yet, traditionally, the American intelligence "community" has been organizationally fragmented. Thus, a liaison system to overcome these centrifugal forces is crucial. This need for coordination is especially important between CIA and FBI counterintelligence units, since the CIA has foreign jurisdiction and the FBI domestic, but they must jointly monitor the movements of foreign spies who travel in and out of these two jurisdictions. Sometimes this coordination has suffered spectacular failures. In 1970, for example, FBI Director J. Edgar Hoover terminated formal liaison with the CIA and all other CI units in the government because of a disagreement over how to handle a particular East European defector. Far more tragically, the FBI and the CIA proved unable to share information effectively about the whereabouts of Al Qaeda terrorists just prior to the attacks against the World Trade Center and the Pentagon in 2001, losing track of two known to be inside the United States weeks before the attacks.

Liaison with foreign intelligence services overseas can undergo strain, too. Each nation fears that the intelligence services of its allies have been infiltrated by hostile agents and, therefore, that the ally should not be given sensitive information. Nonetheless, cooperation does take place, since all intelligence services seek information and—with precautions—will take it where they can get it, if the information is useful.

Counterintelligence and Accountability

The counterintelligence mission is among the most secretive of all intelligence activities—the heart of the onion. Its tight compartmentalization makes proper supervision a challenge for lawmakers and executive overseers. The most disquieting chapter in U.S. counterintelligence occurred during the 1960s when America's secret agencies began to spy at home, against the very people they had sworn to protect (Johnson 1985). In the midst of the Cold War, the CIA generated a data bank on 1.5 million U.S. citizens, almost all of whom were simply exercising their First Amendment rights to dissent against the war in Vietnam. Many had their mail intercepted and read, their telephones tapped, their day-to-day activities monitored. The NSA intercepted every cable sent overseas or received by Americans. The FBI carried out 500,000 investigations of so-called subversives (again, mainly Vietnam war dissenters, plus civil rights activists and even Klan members added to the "enemies list"), without a single case ending in a court conviction.

During this period, FBI agents wrote anonymous letters meant to incite violence among African Americans. The Bureau's counterintelligence program, labeled "Cointelpro," involved not only spying on but harassing civil rights activists and Vietnam war dissidents, in an attempt to fray or break family and friendship ties. A campaign to wreck America's civil rights movement stood at the center of Cointelpro.

The overzealous pursuit of counterintelligence threatened the very foundations of American democracy, undermining basic U.S. laws and the constitutional right to free expression. Only when the CIA's transgressions leaked to the press in 1974, triggering a Congressional inquiry, did these illegal operations by the CIA, the FBI, the NSA, and military intelligence units come to a halt. Counterintelligence—so vital to the nation's security—had strayed, and Americans were again reminded of Madison's warning (etched on the walls of the Library of Congress) that "power, lodged as it must be in the hands of human beings, is ever liable to abuse." A democracy cannot remain free without having strong accountability over its counterintelligence corps. The proper balance between security and civil liberties was tested again after the 9/11 attacks, when the second Bush Administration initiated warrantless wiretaps against American citizens inside the United States and critics cried foul, perceiving this privacy intrusion as a violation of the Foreign Intelligence Surveillance Act of 1978.

The Readings

In this section, Stan A. Taylor and Daniel Snow review the motivations of 139 American traitors during the Cold War, as well as how they were unmasked. The authors found money to be the most prevalent motive for treason, although during the 1950s some Americans spied for the Soviet Union out of attraction to communist ideology. With respect to the post-Cold War era, Taylor and Snow note that treason continues and that materialism remains the primary motivation. As for improvements in capturing spies, the authors give considerable credit to the establishment of better electronic surveillance procedures in the United States as a result of the passage of the Foreign Intelligence Surveillance Act in 1978.

The second selection is drawn from a Senate Select Committee on Intelligence report on the discovery in 1995 of a Soviet/Russian mole in the CIA: Aldrich Hazen Ames, the most devastating counterintelligence failure in the history of the Agency. The damage caused by Ames' treachery, and how counterintelligence officials finally tracked him down, are the subjects of this fascinating, if disheartening, report.

In the final selection in this part of the book, former CIA officer and counterintelligence specialist Frederick L. Wettering analyzes the weaknesses of contemporary counterintelligence in the United States. "The overall record of United States counterintelligence at catching spies is not good," he writes. He calls for a "sea change" in American political attitudes in order to overcome the "bureaucratic rivalries, American ethics and mores, and operational realities" that currently retard an aggressive approach to protecting America and its legitimate secrets. ✦

23

Cold War Spies: Why They Spied and How They Got Caught

Stan A. Taylor and
Daniel Snow

Why do some people commit treason against their own country? Taylor and Snow examine this question and find that the answer is simple enough: for money. They note, too, that the United States has become somewhat more effective in catching American traitors, as a result of improvements in electronic surveillance procedures.

The purpose of this study is to ask why certain Americans decided to betray their country and how it is that they were caught. While the general intelligence literature has grown rapidly, not much has been written about traitors as a class or group.[1] Several books have been written about Soviet citizens who have betrayed their government, particularly about those who have defected to the West.[2] And a fair amount has been written about specific Americans who have betrayed their government, particularly the famous cases.[3] But beyond the well-known cases, often little exists except one or two short newspaper articles on specific traitors. And as a *category*, very little has been written about Americans who have betrayed their government and revealed classified information to other states.[4]

For this research, we created a database consisting of 139 Americans who have been *officially* charged with spying against their government. We have attempted to include all who either began their treason or were caught during or immediately after the Cold War.[5] To the best of our knowledge, this is a fairly complete list. Obviously, undetected traitors are not included and we have also left out moles or penetration agents—foreign agents who have entered America legally or illegally and have attempted to penetrate national security organizations—unless they acquired US citizenship and were caught. We have relied solely on public information and realize that this may not present the entire picture. But more information is publicly available than is generally realized. We collected information about 40 variables associated with each case. These variables included: date of birth, date of arrest, personal habits (gambling, drinking, and drug habits), sexual preferences, how they were recruited, and a range of other variables. . . .[6]

Why They Spied

Models of Espionage

Some scholars have developed highly sophisticated models which, they believe, explain espionage.[7] These models consider various psychological attributes, situational factors, and behavioral chains, coupled with insight from several academic disciplines. Others adopt rather simple models.[8] Nearly all such attempts to explain espionage, however, focus on two areas: factors associated with the individual and factors associated with the situation. No single explanation adequately explains treason nor any other human action. Even the most treasonous of individuals must have access to classified information before it can be pilfered. And only a small percentage of those who do have access to classified information (fewer than .001 percent) ever commit treason.[9]

Our research suggests that nearly all motivations can be grouped into four categories—money, ideology, ingratiation, and disgruntlement. Of these four, money and disgruntlement appear to be growing in importance and ideology and ingratiation appear to be waning (see Figure 23.1).[10] We also consider a few additional, and probably idiosyncratic, variables which we believe cannot be overlooked, especially when combined with other motives.

Money

Money appears to be the most prevalent motive for betrayal in recent American history. William Webster, when he was Director of Central Intelligence (DCI), told a reporter that he had not known of a traitor since 1986 who had been motivated by anything beyond money.[11] 'It was a truism of the 1980s that ideology was out; materialism was in.'[12]

Our data reveal that financial gain has been the primary motivation in 55.4 percent of all cases of Cold War espionage, by far the single most prevalent motive. This counts those whose intent was to get money even though they may have been arrested before any money changed hands. When linked with secondary factors (disgruntlement, ideology,

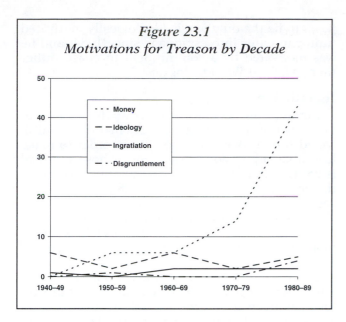

Figure 23.1
Motivations for Treason by Decade

etc.) money was the motive in 62.6 percent of the 139 cases. Seventy-one percent of enlisted personnel were motivated *solely* by money. Until military pay raises in the early 1980s, pay for low ranking military personnel was traditionally meager and many of our cases turned to espionage merely to pay outstanding debts or to allow them to live more stylishly.[13] Rather than turn to family, friends, or banks for loans, they turned to the KGB or related services.

It is difficult to know precisely how much money was involved in each case. Unless the foreign intelligence services revealed how much they paid, or unless the captured spy kept careful records of his or her payments, many dollar amounts are estimates. From what is known, it appears that 17 were paid between $10,000 and $100,000, seven were paid between $100,000 and $1,000,000, and four were paid over $1,000,000.[14] The recent American traitor Aldrich Ames typifies this financial motive. Ames related that he 'felt a great deal of financial pressure' and that it was stress from this pressure that led him to conceive 'a scam to get money from the KGB.'[15] The scam got out of hand and Ames continued to betray his country. His reports to the KGB cost at least ten human lives, compromised scores of intelligence operations, and earned him at least $1,397,300.[16] Ames' vulnerability to monetary temptation is revealed in the crass 'Publisher's Clearinghouse'-like document given him by his Russian handlers. This piece of paper tallied the money and prizes available to him for his continuing service. . . .

The prevalence of avarice in these cases is remarkable. Thomas Patrick Cavanagh was sentenced to life imprisonment on 23 May 1985 for his involvement in espionage. Cavanagh was an engineer for Northrop Corporation who was working on what was called 'quiet' radar techniques. Facing serious financial crises, he contacted what he thought was a KGB agent and offered him information for $25,000. As was often the case in our research, the 'KGB agent' was an FBI undercover agent and Cavanagh was arrested. His explanation is typical of many of those who were trying to get into the espionage business for monetary gain. Cavanagh matter-of-factly suggested that since he did not know how to rob a bank, he instead offered classified documents to a foreign country. 'There was this piece of paper. I thought it might be worth $25,000. I took the avenue of least resistance. I didn't have the foggiest idea of how to rob a bank.'[17]

William Bell was arrested in 1981 for providing classified information about sensitive technologies being developed at Hughes Aircraft to Polish intelligence. After being arrested, Bell was asked if he supported or had sympathies for the Polish government. 'No,' he replied, 'Mr Zacharski [his Polish handler] had found a fool who needed money. I had a weak spot. He took advantage of me.'[18]

The prevalence of financial motivation may reflect increasing materialism and greed, but it also says something about recruitment techniques. All intelligence officers are taught to involve money as quickly as possible when dealing with potential or actual assets. When money is exchanged and a receipt is signed, the semblance of a contract is created. A reporting relationship based on ideology, revenge, or other motives is not entirely under the control of the case officer and is less stable.

Ideology

Conventional wisdom suggests that while most Soviet citizens betrayed their country for ideological reasons, Americans have done so solely for money. As with most conventional wisdom, this generalization is not entirely true. In fact, all traitors, regardless of national origin, have reacted to somewhat similar changing social circumstances. Many early traitors in the West appeared to be motivated by ideological considerations—at least to the degree that anyone acts on single motivation. In Britain, all of the members of the Cambridge ring (Philby, Burgess, Maclean, Blunt, and Cairncross) were attracted to communism early in life. In the United States, the Rosenbergs, Klaus Fuchs, Alger Hiss, and Lauchlin Curry, as well as the much later Larry Wu-Tai Chin, had all been at one time members of the Communist Party.[19]

But after the famous atomic spies cases in the early 1950s, the number of Americans who spied for ideological reasons dropped dramatically. And those that do appear are not the typical cases of communist sympathizers. Several international events seem to be responsible for this trend—revelations about the horrors of Stalin were verified in the 1950s and Soviet violence in Hungary and other Eastern European countries did much to disabuse ideological communists in the West of the purity of the Soviet version of Marxism.

Ultimately, it appears, capitalist materialism prevailed over Marxist materialism—when historical and dialectical materialism failed, avarice was always ready to step in. On both sides of the Iron Curtain, money came to replace beliefs as a motive for betrayal. While Oleg Penkovsky risked his life in the late 1950s and early 1960s to betray what he believed was an evil political system, Victor Belenko, who flew his MiG-25 from the Soviet Union to Hokkaido in 1976, was more anxious to escape his dreary family life and line his pockets with large sums of money.[20]

In about 23.7 per cent of 139 cases, we find ideology to be a primary motive. Even in these cases, other motives were apparent. For example, the Chinese-American, Larry Wu-Tai Chin, who joined the Communist Party in China in 1942 seems to illustrate the allure of money more than the allure of ideology. Chin may have begun as an agent-in-place for the Chinese communists, but the longer he lived in the West, the more he continued his espionage in order to maintain his rather opulent life style.

Jonathan Jay Pollard and Anne Henderson-Pollard also illustrate this shading of motives. The Pollards originally contacted Israeli military personnel and agreed to pass information Jonathan would obtain from the US Navy. Pollard's Zionist sympathies seem to have prompted his original betrayal, but, as with Chin, before long Pollard was attracted to the $30,000 per year he was promised by his Israeli contacts.

But over the last 15 years, ideology has almost disappeared as a motive. Only six individuals appear to have entered into espionage for ideological reasons since 1980, five of whom appear to have been motivated *solely* by ideological considerations. Thomas Dolce (who actually began spying in late 1979) wanted to support the white-dominated South African government; Glenn Souther developed Marxist leanings while in college; Jeffrey Carney spied for East Germany, essentially because of his anti-American feelings; Michael Moore wanted to defect to the USSR while serving as an American seaman in the Philippines; Frederick Hamilton's desire to end the perennial border dispute between Peru and Ecuador led him to give US electronic intercepts to Ecuadorian officials; and Robert Kim, a naturalized US citizen born in South Korea, appears to have been a mole. In fact, Hamilton appears to be the only *purely* ideologically motivated traitor to enter into espionage since 1984, and he was motivated by a commitment to peace rather than to a Cold War ideology.

Ingratiation

Ingratiation becomes a motive when information is betrayed to foreign sources in order to fulfill friendship or love obligations or in order to make favorable impressions on someone whose approval is desired. In our database, ingratiation figured as the primary motive in eight, or 5.8 percent, of the cases. This is not enough cases to allow broad conclusions, but it does appear that ingratiation is declining as a motive. Ingratiation, especially sexually motivated ingratiation, may be a relic of the Cold War.

The use of same- or opposite-sex 'honey traps' to attract and, if necessary, blackmail potential traitors has been a favorite theme of novelists and scriptwriters, but has been little understood and vastly overrated by them. In our database, there are only four cases of betrayal brought on by blackmail and they are spread over many years—1951, 1960, 1970, and 1984. Ingratiation's effectiveness may be judged by the handful of spies who were motivated by it. Though there is no publicly-available evidence to support it, we believe that if we had a record of every KGB, or related service, attempt to attract a potential traitor through some variety of friendship, the list would be much longer than it is in our database which counts only those who succumbed and were caught.

The case of the only FBI agent ever arrested for treason illustrates this motive. Richard Miller was recruited by the FBI in 1963 and served in New York, Puerto Rico, Florida, and California. In 1981 he was given a counterintelligence position in the Los Angeles FBI office. His past performance had been far from stellar and he had been suspended twice for weighing more than FBI guidelines allowed. Moreover, his marriage was disintegrating. After a series of extra-marital affairs, in May 1984 Miller met Svedana Ogorodnikov, who described herself to Miller as a KGB major. Miller became emotionally and sexually involved with her. Miller was arrested on 2 October 1984 and, after three separate trials, was convicted of espionage. Miller argued throughout the trials that he was trying to ingratiate himself with Ogorodnikov for counterintelligence purposes, but two different judges and even a member of Miller's family believed that the KGB had capitalized on Miller's emotional needs and compromised his career through seduction.[21]

Ingratiation's decline probably results from several developments. One is the end of the Cold War. Clearly, if Soviet and East European secret service defectors are to be believed, various forms of seduction were part of the KGB espionage arsenal.[22] One prominent Soviet defector suggested that compromise and coercion based on various levels and types of friendship were techniques in which KGB officers were well-trained.[23] Moreover, seductions and sexual affairs now can have graver medical consequences than they did for much of the Cold War. Also, the instability of the international system and the fast pace of technological developments make long-term spy operations less useful. Effective and efficient intelligence operations today require short-time success and do not allow long-term development of relationships. Finally, the role of sex in espionage has always attracted more attention than it merited. American secret services have found that happy and well-adjusted family men and women make better agents than those who are sexually promiscuous, emotionally impaired, and susceptible to blackmail.[24]

Disgruntlement

Like money, disgruntlement is a motive of growing importance. By disgruntlement we refer to the sense of personal dissatisfaction that stems from feelings of being overlooked, overworked, and under-appreciated. No cases of disgruntlement occurred in the 1940s, and virtually none occurred in the 1950s. However, as the military and defense industry grew, the likelihood of disgruntled employees taking revenge against their employers by betraying secrets also grew. Disgruntlement has grown in importance in the last five years.[25] Disgruntlement was the primary motive in 2.9 percent of our 139 cases. People entrusted by their government with classified information are given a unique ability to exact revenge on that government if it offends them.

If we consider those who, though not completely disgruntled, were not entirely 'gruntled' (to borrow from Oscar Wilde), then disgruntlement becomes a more prevalent motive. Disgruntlement comes from a variety of sources. Often, disgruntled because of low pay, individuals have attempted to supplement their income through selling information. We classified these cases as motivated by disgruntlement rather than by greed. In other cases, dissatisfaction with their treatment would lead individuals to treason. The case of Daniel Walter Richardson illustrates the latter point. Richardson was described in reports as a mediocre soldier, and in August 1987 was demoted from tank instructor to tool room manager for his chronic tardiness. Shortly after, he called the Soviet embassy in Washington and offered to sell them defense information. The FBI intercepted this call and, posing as the KGB, was able to stage a meeting with Richardson. At this meeting, Richardson turned over a training manual and circuitry from an M-1 tank. Richardson illustrates disgruntlement leading to a desire for revenge and followed by an attempt to sell secrets for money.

Other cases illustrate this pattern. Allen John Davies left the Air Force in 1984 as a result of poor job performance. Two years later he tried to get revenge by attempting to sell classified information to Soviet agents. A disgruntled ex-CIA employee, Edwin G. Moore, followed a similar path. Unhappy about his failure to be promoted in the CIA, Moore collected ten boxes of classified documents and attempted to sell them to Soviet diplomats in Washington.

There is an interesting parallel between disgruntlement as a motive for espionage and disgruntlement as a motive for leaking classified or confidential information. Leaking is virtually a national pastime in Washington. Hardly a week passes without some public revelation of information that was meant to be confidential or private. Every president since Eisenhower has complained about the debilitating and discouraging effects of leaking. One in-depth study of several cases of unauthorized leaks revealed that disgruntlement and revenge are the primary motives of such leaking.[26]

Other Factors

Other factors account for the remaining 12.2 percent of our cases. As with more common motives, when combined with other motives these miscellaneous factors figure in a larger percentage of espionage cases. But as a sole or primary motivation, they are rare. Some, however, deserve comment.

One under-appreciated motive is fantasy. We were surprised by the number of spies who appear to have developed an addiction to the mystique of espionage. We call this the 'James Mitty' syndrome because it combines the allure of a James Bond lifestyle with a Walter Mitty sense of fantasy.

Two cases illustrate this motivation. William Kampiles was a young man who was so attracted to the life of espionage that he sought a position with the CIA's Directorate of Administration in March 1977 and was assigned to cable. When he did not get selected as a case officer in the Directorate of Operations, he concocted a plan through which he thought he could prove to his bosses that he had all of the skills necessary to be a case officer. Seeing a classified document left lying on a filing cabinet one night, he stole it, fled to Greece, and eventually sold it to the Soviet Embassy.[27] His logic was that as soon as he was hired by the KGB, he could confess to the CIA and become a double agent.

Jeffery Loring Pickering was convicted of espionage in 1983 and was described as a person who fantasized about espionage. Even in the many cases where money, disgruntlement, or ideology was the primary motive, we were surprised to notice the large number of cases where an obsession with excitement and intrigue, or a fascination with spying, blended and shaded with other motives.

Though closely related to disgruntlement, a desire to bolster one's ego or self-importance also played a role in some cases. For example, Samuel Loring Morison was hired as an analyst for the Navy Intelligence Support Center (NISC) in 1974. Described by his peers as an 'oddball genius' and an 'eccentric patrician,' Morison considered himself to be above many of the rules that governed the handling of sensitive information. In 1978, two years after he was hired by the NISC, Morison became involved with Jane's Defense Weekly as a part-time editor. Morison regularly pushed the security limits until, in 1984, he provided Jane's with three secret US satellite-photos of a Soviet submarine under construction. Jane's published the pictures, revealing some of the resolution capabilities of the ultra-secret KH-11 spy satellite. Morison's principle motivation for doing this was to impress his higher-ups at Jane's.

Kinship was a factor in several cases. In the famous Walker case, John Walker involved both his brother and his son. Kinship even played a factor in the demise of the Walker ring—it was his former wife who reported John's spying to the FBI. The Pollard case involved kinship ties, Edward Howard's escape required his wife's complicity, and Aldrich Ames' wife was also convicted of spying.

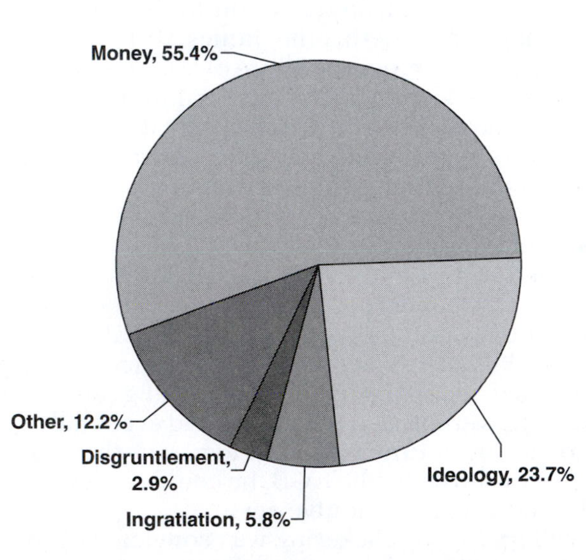

In summary, people enter into treason for a variety of reasons and any attempt to classify risks oversimplification since every human being is unique and no human act is ever motivated by a single factor. However, the cases in our database suggest that avarice, disgruntlement (including job dissatisfaction, desires to harm to one's employer and alienation), ideology, and ingratiation explain the overwhelming number of cases of treason. The next question, however, is how they are caught.

How They Got Caught

Many counter-intelligence methods are closely guarded. But one can imagine that they are somewhat similar to crime detection methods. Known foreign intelligence service officers in the United States are kept under close surveillance and embassies and other buildings, particularly those of hostile states, are monitored. It is widely suspected that telephone calls and correspondence with certain embassies and individuals might also be monitored. But until 1978, one of the most frequently-used law enforcement techniques for detecting criminal behavior was not available to the intelligence community. That technique was electronic surveillance.

Foreign Intelligence Surveillance Act

In order to address that problem, Congress passed the Foreign Intelligence Surveillance Act (FISA) in 1978. This act established warrant-like procedures to authorize electronic surveillance of foreign powers and their agents.[28] The effect of FISA on the detection and conviction of American traitors has been overlooked by intelligence scholars. The authors of the most thorough study yet published, for example, conclude that they 'cannot determine' why the government was more successful in the 1980s that it had been earlier in catching espionage attempts.[29] Our data suggest that FISA played a major role in this development.

From the end of World War II up to 1978, many changes were made to the procedures governing electronic surveillance for domestic criminal purposes. But the procedures for authorizing the collection of electronic surveillance for national security purposes remained the same—presidential authorization. Although presidents believed they had extremely broad powers to authorize warrantless electronic surveillance for national security purposes, that practice suffered from two significant problems. First, there were many abuses. Presidents and other senior government officials could order electronic surveillance and place entities of

Figure 23.2
Motivations for Treason

Money, 55.4%

Other, 12.2%

Disgruntlement, 2.9%

Ingratiation, 5.8%

Ideology, 23.7%

foreign governments located in the United States or their agents, as well as US persons suspected of spying for these entities, under the most intrusive of electronic surveillance techniques without court issued warrants. These techniques, especially when conducted against US persons, exceeded the 'unreasonable search and seizure' and 'probable cause' requirements of the Fourth Amendment. But, as long as national security was invoked, senior government officials were willing to overlook constitutional niceties and condone this questionable behavior.

Second—and from a counter-intelligence point of view, perhaps more serious—the evidence obtained through arguably illegal monitoring techniques was often rejected by American courts.[30] Thus, many who engaged in treason against the United States found evidence against them either rejected by courts or found decisions against them overturned by higher courts. Aware of this latter fate, the Federal Bureau of Investigation (FBI) became reluctant to use evidence obtained in this manner in courts.

A series of lower court decisions between 1971 and 1977 accepted the Executive's argument that warrantless national security-related electronic surveillance could lawfully be authorized by the President or . . . the Attorney General. . . . In several cases, however, surveillances were found to be unlawful when courts retrospectively disagreed with the judgments of Executive officials as to whether national security, rather than law enforcement, objectives were being served by warrantless electronic surveillance.[31]

Moreover, the government became reluctant to seek normal surveillance warrants through open court procedures for three reasons. First, to do so might result in unwanted 'publicity about the secret information and [establish] the fact of its loss.'[32] To convince a regular court to issue a warrant required publicly proving the significance of that information, a task which often could not be done without revealing other classified information relating to it. Second, purchased secret information is often viewed suspiciously by the government that buys it. That government does not know whether it is false information made up just to make a sale, misinformation given purposely to mislead it, or valuable secret information which might enhance its national security. Corroboratory information revealed in an open warrant procedure tends to confirm the veracity and importance of the purloined information. And, third, and perhaps most importantly, to reveal enough information to obtain a warrant in an open court might compromise the sources and methods through which the information was obtained.

FISA changed all of this. It created a special court procedure that is 'consistent with the "reasonable search" requirement of the Fourth Amendment.'[33] Under FISA, the Department of Justice was not bound by the traditional 'probable cause' standard required to obtain warrants in normal criminal cases. Yet, at the same time, it was bound by specified procedures which protected civil liberties by banning electronic surveillance of Americans merely on the order of a government official under a loosely defined national security standard.

[FISA] established comprehensive legal standards and procedures for the use of electronic surveillance to collect foreign intelligence and counter-intelligence within the United States. The Act provided the first legislative authorization for wiretapping and other forms of electronic surveillance for intelligence purposes against foreign powers and foreign agents in this country. It created the Foreign Intelligence Surveillance Court comprised of seven federal district judges, to review and approve surveillances capable of monitoring United States persons who are in the United States.[34]

In general, FISA has been supported both by law enforcement agencies as well as by most civil libertarians. Evidence obtained under FISA has been accepted in courts as long as it satisfied the foreign intelligence and counterintelligence requirements of the act and as long as the procedural requirements of the act were met. Perhaps the most thorough constitutional justification of FISA can be found in *United States v. Duggan* (743 F.2d 59[2d Cir. 1984]) where both Fourth and Fifth Amendment challenges to this kind of electronic surveillance were addressed by the court.[35]

FISA allows the government to obtain a court order authorizing electronic surveillance, but to do so in a non-public setting which protects national security information and intelligence methods from foreign scrutiny. The problems of the earlier warrant procedure were overcome while at the same time American citizens were assured that their government could not 'spy' on them capriciously.

Record of FISA

The record of FISA is good and may say more about the increase in successful espionage prosecution in recent years than other explanations. For example, 'between 1965 and 1974, an average of 177 warrantless national security surveillances were approved annually by the Attorney General.'[36] The FISA Court, by contrast, approved an annual average of 530 surveillances between 1980 and 1994 (see Table 23.1).

Given the length of time necessary to put together a solid court case for treason, the surge of

Table 23.1
Foreign Intelligence Surveillance Act Court-Surveillance Orders Issued

Year	FISA Orders Issued
1979 (partial year)	207
1980 (first full year)	319
1981	431
1982	475
1983	583
1984	635
1985	587
1986	573
1987	512
1988	534
1989	546
1990	598
1991	593
1992	484
1993	511
1994	575

Source: United States Senate Select Committee on Intelligence and Administrative Office of the US Court System.

espionage cases in 1984 and 1985 may be attributable to the impact of the FISA court. It is also obvious why 1984 is often referred to as 'The Year of the Spy' and the 1980s as 'The Decade of the Spy.' In the Ames case, for example, the FBI was searching for a penetration agent in the CIA as early as 1987. After dropping the investigation in 1989, they began again in 1991 and identified Ames as the traitor in March 1993, but did not arrest him until February 1994. Even after learning that Ames was the long sought KGB agent-in-place, it took nearly a year to complete the evidence necessary for a trial.[37]

Until all of the classified information relating to the detection and arrest of each case is made public, it is difficult to document the precise contribution of the FISA legislation. But the raw numbers do suggest that FISA made a significant difference in the government's ability to detect and prosecute traitors. Clearly, the Carter administration's decision to prosecute espionage more vigorously also contributed to the higher arrests in the mid-1980s, but that new vigor would not have been possible without FISA.

Excluding those who defected and were not caught, from 1945 to 1977, 23 percent of the detected spies were caught during their first attempt at espionage, suggesting that many continued their espionage for longer periods of time. From 1978 to date, however, 38 percent have been caught in their first foray into espionage. This probably reflects not only increasing skills on the part of counterintelligence agents, but also the role of FISA in making electronic surveillance more available and usable in court.

Physical Searches

To make matters even worse for traitors, Congress recently adopted legislation creating FISA-like procedures covering physical searches, a category that was explicitly left out of the 1978 FISA Act. In 1980, then Attorney-General Benjamin Civiletti asked that requests for national security-related physical search authorizations also be considered under FISA. A few physical search authorizations were actually approved by the FISA court even though the original legislation was specifically limited to electronic surveillance. Several earlier attempts to include physical searches under the FISA procedures failed.

In 1981, however, the Reagan administration convinced the USA court that it had no authority to approve applications for physical searches. It is somewhat ironic that 'the only government request that the FISA Court has ever rejected was done at the insistence of the Executive Branch itself.'[38]

Following Aldrich Ames's arrest in 1994, however, both public opinion and the mood of Congress changed regarding physical searches. Physical searches are now under the FISA procedures and the government can obtain court orders authorizing access to phone records, banking information, and other personal data by following the procedural requirements of FISA.[39] Prior to this change, it was easier to tap a telephone than to obtain telephone records.

Faulty Tradecraft

In any discussion of why spies are caught, one often overlooked motive deserves mention. After reading as much data as was available about our 129 cases, we are amazed at the poor level of tradecraft, even abject stupidity, displayed in many cases. This is especially apparent among one-time-sellers, but even among those with some understanding of tradecraft, foolish blunders played a significant role in their eventual detection. One worries, in fact, that an especially acute spy with good tradecraft might be very difficult to catch. But even spies with some tradecraft skills (Walker, Howard, and Ames, for example) made foolish mistakes, perhaps stemming from feelings of overconfidence, which often betrayed them. Since 1976, at least 16 of the spies in our database telephoned or walked into the Soviet Embassy and asked if they would like to buy some secrets. In every case the FBI, who had intercepted the calls, met these would-be spies, bought what they had to offer, and then arrested them. In one case, the budding traitor threw a package of classified material with a note in it asking for money over the wall of the Soviet Embassy. The Soviets thought it was a bomb and called the Washington fire department who came and collected the material. Aldrich Ames, one of the most recent traitors, paid $540,000 cash for a home while earning a $62,000-a-year salary. Robert Haguewood walked into a bar and started talking to a stranger on an adjacent stool about his desire to sell classified information to the Soviets. The man was an off-duty policeman. Time and time again, these spies would engage in activities that any thinking person would avoid.

Intelligence After the Cold War

Some have wondered whether clandestine intelligence gathering and counterintelligence activities are needed in the post-Cold War world. Senator Daniel Patrick Moynihan, former member of the Senate Intelligence Committee, has introduced legislation that would assign most of the CIA's current functions to State, Defense, and other government departments and change the focus of most intelligence gathering operations to open sources.[40] Less draconian is the proposal of former CIA director Stansfield Turner, who has proposed significant shifts in priorities in the US intelligence community. Admiral Turner believes that economic intelligence ought to be the primary goal of the intelligence community, and that it should reorganize its efforts to reflect that new priority.[41]

Others, however, might remind us of Lord Palmerston's adage, first expressed in the House of Commons in 1848, that there are no eternal enemies and there are no eternal friends, there are only eternal interests. If that is the case, then all states will continue to gather information about other states, and all states will try to protect against that collection. Even without the Soviet challenge, intelligence gathering will continue and counterintelligence efforts will still be necessary. In fact, the collection of both open- and denied-source information may be more important now than it was during the Cold War.

Stanley Hoffmann once said that as the 'physics of power declines, the psychology of power rises.'[42] That is, as the material elements of power become less capable of shaping and determining events, then perceptions and images become more important. And as perceptions and images become more important, then what Joseph Nye call 'soft power' becomes more important.[43] With the end of the Cold War, the eggs of power—particularly nuclear weapons—have become relatively less important. But that merely forces attention to the hens that make that power possible—the economies and social and political developments of other states.

This logic suggests that all nations will continue to collect clandestine intelligence information and that all nations will need to protect against that activity through counterintelligence efforts. What has changed is the nature of the intelligence desired. Strategic intelligence—information about abilities and intentions of hostile or potentially hostile states—is still important. But information about general social, economic, and political conditions of states has become perhaps even more significant. What used to be called non-strategic intelligence may be the new strategic intelligence.[44] In the information age, information, indeed, may be the principle commodity of international relations.

The recent case of Aldrich Ames, who may be the most damaging traitor in all American history, suggests two conclusions. First, treason is still possible, even after the Cold War. Ames began his treason in 1991, and continued to sell classified information to non-Communist Russia even after the Soviet Union collapsed in 1989. He was identified as a Russian asset in March 1993, but not arrested until February 1994.[45] His activities were celebrated in Moscow, but will be condemned in the United States for years to come.[46] Within the last 15 years, we know of attempts by France, Israel, Japan, Germany, and South Korea to gather denied information about the United States.

Second, while some isolated cases of ideologically motivated treason may still be found, most recent treason has been motivated by cupidity and avarice. Knowing how difficult it is to change institutional directions, one can only speculate whether the profile of traitors that existed during the years that James Angleton headed the CIA's counterintelligence efforts made it more or less difficult to identify non-ideological traitors. Angleton headed counterintelligence efforts over the very two decades during which our data suggest ideology was declining and other motives becoming more important. Clearly, current counterintelligence profiles must pay more attention to the kinds of motivations we have discussed.[47] As a thoughtful reviewer of an earlier version of this article suggested, it may have been difficult for the CIA to find people like Ames when it was searching for people like Philby.

Postscript: Since this article was submitted, Harold J. Nicholson (CIA), Earl E. Pitts (FBI) and Robert C. Kim (office of Naval Intelligence) have been accused, but not convicted, of espionage. In all three cases, money appears to be the primary motivation.

Questions for Further Discussion

1. What are the primary motivations that lead people to spy against their own nation? How would you describe what these individuals have in common, if anything?

2. How have these motivations changed over time, and why?

3. How has the United States caught those engaged in treason?

4. How can one balance the needs of counterintelligence and security, on the one hand, and civil liberties, on the other hand? Has the Foreign Intelligence Surveillance Act achieved this balance when it comes to wiretaps?

Endnotes

1. The prolific writer Rebecca West published one of the early and interesting books on treason. In her *The Meaning of Treason* (NY: Viking 1946) and *The New Meaning of Treason* (ibid. 1964), West discusses some specific British traitors during World War II. Her Epilogue in both volumes is a good introduction to the concept of ideological treason. See also Chapman Pincher, *Traitors* (London: Penguin 1988) for a more lengthy discussion of treason.

2. See e.g. Gordon Brook-Shepherd, *The Storm Petrels: The First Soviet Defectors, 1928–1938* (London: Weidenfeld 1977) and the same author's *The Storm Birds: Soviet Postwar Defectors* (NY: Harcourt Brace Jovanovich 1989). The best bibliography for both first- and second-hand accounts of Soviet defectors and Western agents-in-place is Raymond G. Rocca and John J. Dziak, *Bibliography on Soviet Intelligence and Security Services* (Boulder, CO: Westview 1985).

3. See e.g. John Barron, *Breaking the Ring: The Bizarre Case of the Walker Family Spy Ring* (Boston: Houghton Mifflin 1987), Wolf Blitzer, *Territory of Lies: The Exclusive Story of Jonathan Jay Pollard* (NY: Harper & Row 1989), and Robert Lindsey, *The Falcon and the Snowman* (NY: Simon & Schuster 1979).

4. Of the recent books, Theodore R. Sarbin *et al.* (eds.) *Citizen Espionage: Studies in Trust and Betrayal* (Westport, CT: Praeger 1994) is, by far, the best generally available trade book. The Defense Personnel Security Research Center, created by the Dept. of Defense in the wake of several security breaches in 1984 and 1985 and located at Monterey, California, has published several reports, primarily for use within the defense community. See, for example, Susan Wood and Martin F. Wiskoff, *Americans Who Spied Against Their Country Since World War II* (Monterey, CA: Def. Pers. Security Res. Center). See also, Thomas B. Allen and Norman Polmar, *Merchants of Treason* (NY: Delacourt 1988), Ronald Kessler, *Spy vs. Spy: Stalking Soviet Spies in America* (NY: Scribner's 1988), Pincher, *Traitors* (note 1), and Robert J. Lamphere and Tom Shachtman, *The FBI-KGB War: A Special Agent's Story* (NY: Random House 1986). Most of these works are somewhat anecdotal and earlier works consider only a few cases.

5. Several deified databases obviously exist; however, we have had access to none of them. By far the best and most thorough analysis of espionage cases is Wood and Wiskoff, *Americans Who Spied* (note 4). Their database was created from unclassified information; however, their study was conducted under government contract and they had cooperative personnel at all of the intelligence agencies with whom they dealt. Their database included cases through 1990, while ours includes cases through 1996. As a contracted study, their report was not as widely distributed as it should have been. But any student of treason should obtain it. No research on American traitors would be possible were it not for the valuable contributions made by the Defense Personnel Security Research Center and the Dept. of Defense Security Institute. The latter's *Recent Espionage Cases* is the only data available on some spies. Our rather narrow definition of traitor as an American citizen who was charged with treason caused us to omit several early ideological spies whose prosecution was considered too sensitive by the government. For example, we have not included William Weisband, an NSA spy, because he was charged only with failing to report to a grand jury even though he was a known spy. We have not included cases of economic espionage in our database unless the traitor was charged by the government under espionage acts. We did not include the case of two Connecticut company executives who sold carbon-carbon technologies and equipment to Indian defense-related organizations. They were convicted of violating export laws, but were not charged with espionage. Similar cases are discussed in Peter Schweizer, *Friendly Spies: How America's Allies Are Using Industrial Espionage to Steal Our Secrets* (NY: Atlantic Monthly Press 1993).

6. On 11 July 1995 the National Security Agency released communications relating to the Rosenberg case which could not have been made public at the time without compromising sensitive collection techniques. See David Kahn, 'VENONA Messages and Atomic Bomb Espionage,' in *World Intelligence Review* (formerly *Foreign Intelligence Literary Scene*) 14/2 (1995) p.1 and Lamphere and Shachtman, *FBI-KGB War* (note 4).

7. See e.g. the excellent article by Carson Eoyand, 'Models of Espionage,' in Sarbin, *Citizen Espionage* (note 4) Ch.4.

8. See e.g. the MICE model (motivation, ideology, compromise or coercion and ego) first described by KGB defector Stanislav Levchenko, *On The Wrong Side: My Life in the KGB* (Washington, DC: Pergamon-Brassey's 1988).

9. Herbig accepts the figure of 3 million Americans holding security clearances in the 1980s. See Katherine L. Herbig, 'A History of Recent American Espionage,' in Sarbin, *Citizen Espionage* (note 4) p.45. Approximately 30 were charged with espionage during the same time period.

10. Joseph P. Parker and Martin F. Wiskoff, *Temperament Constructs Related to Betrayal of Trust* (Monterey, CA: Def. Pers. Security Res. Center 1991) p.50.

11. 'US Finds it Difficult to Catch Spies Who Sell Out For Cash, Not Ideology,' *Wall Street Journal*, 30 June 1986, p.26, quoted in Sarbin, *Citizen Espionage* (note 4) p.51.

12. Herbig, 'A History of Recent American Espionage' (note 9) p.51.

13. See ibid. p.53.

14. Wood and Wiskoff, *Americans Who Spied* (note 4) p.55.

15. The quotation is from an FBI transcript interview with Ames and is reported in US Congress, Senate, Select Committee on Intelligence, *An Assessment of the Aldrich H. Ames Espionage Case and Its Implications*

for *U.S. Intelligence*, S. Rpt. 103-90, 103d Cong., 2d sess. (Washington, DC: 1994) p.11.

16. See US Senate, *An Assessment of the Aldrich H. Ames Case* (note 15) p.39. *U.S. News & World Report*, 6 March, 1995, p.50, claims Ames' revelations could have resulted in 30 deaths.

17. *The San Francisco Examiner*, 21 June 1987, p.1. Also cited in Herbig (note 9) p.54.

18. United States, Senate, Select Committee on Intelligence, *Meeting the Espionage Challenge: A Review of United States Counterintelligence and Security Programs*, Report 99-522, 98th Cong., 2d sess. (Washington, DC, 1986), p.118.

19. For many of the insights in this section, I am indebted to Herbig (note 9).

20. John Barron, *MIG Pilot: Lt. Victor Belenko's Final Escape* (NY: Reader's Digest Press l980) is the most complete account of Belenko's delivery of the Soviet Foxbat jet fighter into Western hands.

21. Most of the information on Richard Miller is taken from articles in the *Los Angeles Times* by William Overend published on 24 Oct. 1985, 7 Nov. 1985 and 15 July 1986. Mr. James McQuivey also interviewed Miller's son Paul in 1991 and used that interview in a class case study of Miller that is in the authors' possession.

22. 'The use of sex to lure and entrap potential agents is known to be a technique of Soviet and bloc intelligence services,' according to George C. Constantinides, *Intelligence and Espionage: An Analytical Bibliography* (Boulder, CO: Westview 1983) p.292. But Constantinides rightly discredits David Lewis' *Sexpionage: The Exploitation of Sex by Soviet Intelligence* (NY: Harcourt Brace 1976) for being based on 'a potpourri of fact, rumor, and speculation,' p.292.

23. Levchenko, *On the Wrong Side* (note 8).

24. Joseph P. Parker and Martin F. Wiskoff, *Temperament Constructs Related to Betrayal of Trust* (Monterey, CA: 1991), pp.32–35.

25. Herbig (note 9) p.50.

26. See Martin Linsky, *How the Press Affects Federal Policymaking: Six Case Studies* (NY: Norton 1986).

27. Kampiles sold for $3,000 a technical manual for the KH-11, an overhead reconnaissance satellite, a highly classified US secret. This satellite, the capabilities of which were unknown to the Soviets, provided real-time photographs in high resolution. Had Kampiles known the significance of his information, he could have sold the manual at a considerably higher price.

28. Public Law 95-511. This legislation passed Congress as S. 1566. Electronic surveillance refers to wire taps, television monitoring, hidden microphones, electronic tracing devices, and other electronic means to gather evidence. S. 1566 did not address the question of physical searches.

29. Wood and Wiskoff, *Americans Who Spied* (note 4) pp.A12 and A13.

30. Americo R. Cinquegrana, 'FISA: A Reformist Success Story,' in *Foreign Intelligence Literary Scene* 8/6 (1989) p.2.

31. Ibid. p.2.

32. Herbig (note 9) p.64. The case of William Weisband, mentioned in note 5 above, illustrates this principle. Had Weisband been caught after passage of FISA, prosecution would have been possible.

33. US Senate, *Foreign Intelligence Surveillance Act of 1978*, Report No. 95-701, 95th Cong., 2d sess. (Washington, DC: 1978) p.9.

34. US Senate, *The Foreign Intelligence Surveillance Act of 1978: The First Five Years*, Report 98-660, 98th Cong., 2d sess. (Washington DC 1984) p.1.

35. FISA has survived unscathed over 20 challenges in various court cases. See, for example, *United States v. Falvey*, 540 F. Supp. 1306,1314 (E.D.N.Y. 1982), *United States v. Megahey*, No. 83-1313, 2d cir. 8 Aug. 1984, and *United States v. Belfield*, 692 F. 2d 141 (D.C. Cir. 1982). These and other cases are discussed in United States Senate, Foreign Intelligence Surveillance Act (note 34).

36. Cinquegrana, 'FISA' (note 30).

37. US Senate, *Assessment of the Aldrich H. Ames Case* (note 15).

38. Cinquegrana (note 30) p.12.

39. This is contained in Section 303 of S. 2056. See, United States, Senate, Select Committee on Intelligence, *The Counterintelligence and Security Enhancements Act of 1994*, Report 103-296, 103d Cong. 2d sess. (Washington, DC 1994) p.8.

40. Moynihan explained the rationale for his legislation on Public Television's *MacNeil/Leher News Hour* on 13 Feb. 1995. The text of this discussion is available on Lexis/Nexis, 15 Feb. 1995.

41. Stansfield Turner, 'Intelligence for a New World Order,' *Foreign Affairs* 70 (Fall 1991), pp.151–152.

42. Stanley Hoffmann, 'Perceptions, Reality, and the Franco-American Conflict,' in John C. Farrell and Asa P. Smith (eds.), *Image and Reality in World Politics* (NY: Columbia UP 1967) p.58.

43. Joseph S. Nye, Jr., 'Soft Power,' *Foreign Policy* No.80 (Fall 1990), pp.153–171.

44. In 1976 and 1977, the Senate Intelligence Committee, on the urging of then member Senator Adlai Stephenson, III, undertook a lengthy study of so-called non-strategic intelligence—general information about the social, economic, and political conditions within the Soviet Union. In the wake of criticism of the intelligence community for its failure to see more clearly the pending collapse of the Soviet Union in 1989, the strategic importance of general social, economic, and political information now seems more apparent.

45. Literally hundreds of newspaper and magazine articles have been written about the Ames case. Undoubtedly, scores of books will follow, not to mention TV miniseries and movies. But the best brief official record is found in United States Senate, *An Assessment of the Aldrich H. Ames Espionage Case* (note 15).

46. It appears his KGB managers even sent him photographs of the 'beautiful land' on which his country house (dacha) would be located when he had to end his treason. See 'The Cold War's Last Spy,' *U.S. News and World Report*, 6 March 1995, p.59.

47. Angleton continues to have supporters and detractors. Perhaps the most objective review of the literature about Angleton can be found in 'Of Moles and Molehunters: A Review of Counterintelligence Literature, 1977–92' written by Cleveland C. Cram and published as an intelligence monograph by the CIA's Center for the Study of Intelligence in 1993. ✦

Reprinted with permission from Stan A. Taylor and Daniel Snow, "Cold War Spies: Why They Spied and How They Got Caught," *Intelligence and National Security* 12 (April 1997): 101–125.

24

Treachery Inside the CIA

Senate Select Committee on Intelligence

In 1994, the U.S. Senate Select Committee on Intelligence (SSCI) conducted an investigation into America's most damaging counterintelligence failure: the treachery of Aldrich H. Ames inside the Central Intelligence Agency. This chapter provides a look at the Committee's findings.

In the end, regardless of what the Committee may recommend or what Congress may enact, fundamental change will come only if the Director of Central Intelligence, supervisors at all levels, and the employees of the CIA bring it about. The Committee intends to monitor the Agency's progress in this regard, but the leadership must come from within.

The Committee undertook its inquiry not for the purpose of assessing individual blame—which is the exclusive responsibility of the Executive branch—but rather to learn what had gone wrong and to evaluate the institutional lessons to be learned from the Ames case. Nevertheless, the Committee believes that the recent actions taken by the Director of Central Intelligence, R. James Woolsey, against past and current CIA officials implicated in the Ames case warrant comment.

On March 10 of this year, Director Woolsey appeared before the Committee in closed session to outline his interim responses to the Ames case. One area for reform which was cited by the Director was "management accountability." According to the Director: "[T]o my mind, this is very much at the heart of the entire matter." The Committee strongly shares this view.

Despite the CIA Inspector General's recommendation that 23 current and former CIA officials be held accountable for the Agency's failure to prevent and detect Ames' espionage activities, Director Woolsey chose only to issue letters of reprimand to 11 individuals—7 retired and 4 current Agency employees. None of the individuals cited by the Inspec-

tor General was fired, demoted, suspended or even reassigned as a result of this case. In response to what was arguably the greatest managerial breakdown in the CIA's history, the disciplinary actions taken by the Director do not, in the collective experience and judgment of the Committee, constitute adequate "management accountability."

All Committee Members believe that the Director's disciplinary actions in this case are seriously inadequate and disproportionate to the magnitude of the problems identified in the Inspector General's report. It is clear, given the immense national security interests at stake, that there was "gross negligence"—both individually and institutionally—in creating and perpetuating the environment in which Ames was able to carry out his espionage activities for nine years without detection.

The Committee is concerned about the message that Director Woolsey's mild disciplinary actions will send to the overwhelming majority of CIA employees who are dedicated, conscientious, patriotic, and hard-working professionals, many of whom are exposed daily to risk and hardship. For the current employees who were faulted by the Inspector General for their role in the Ames case to remain in their grades and positions falls far short of the level of accountability expected by the Committee. Indeed, in the wake of the Director's decision, many professionals within the Intelligence Community have contacted the Committee to register the same sentiment.

As this report documents, the failures evident in the Ames case were numerous and egregious. While it might be argued that the majority of individuals cited by the Inspector General were guilty of acts of omission rather than commission, the seriousness of these omissions cannot be overstated. The failures of the individuals cited by the Inspector General led to the loss of virtually all of CIA's intelligence assets targeted against the Soviet Union at the height of the Cold War. Ten of these agents were executed. The inability of the CIA to get to the bottom of these losses in a timely way was itself a significant management failure.

If there is not a higher standard of accountability established by DCIs, then a repeat of the Ames tragedy becomes all the more likely. Management accountability within the Intelligence Community should be no less than the highest levels found elsewhere in the Executive branch. Director Woolsey's actions do not meet this standard.

Having noted in strong terms the magnitude of CIA's failures, the Committee would be remiss not to point out what went right. A traitor, responsible for heinous acts of espionage, was identified and convicted. He has been imprisoned for life. In the end, this was accomplished by the work of a small group of CIA and FBI personnel who took part in what became a long and arduous inquiry—for some, lasting almost nine years. At least one member of this group appears to have pushed from the very beginning to get to the bottom of the 1985 compromises. It was his impetus that eventually put the investigation back on track in 1991. Over time, the scope and pace of the investigation had taken many twists and turns, some caused by the KGB and some by internal factors beyond the control of the investigators themselves. The commentary which follows is not intended to diminish in any way what was ultimately accomplished by this dedicated group of investigators and analysts.

Finally, the Committee notes that its recommendations are based upon the situation that pertained through early 1994. Director Woolsey has promulgated some new policies since then and has announced his intention to institute still others. While the Committee believes in general that stronger measures are needed, it is too early to pass judgment on the Director's recent actions.

The Failure to 'Fix' Past Counterintelligence Problems

The counterintelligence function at the CIA is weak and inherently flawed. Despite repeated internal and external reports which have recognized a longstanding cultural problem with the counterintelligence function, CIA managers have, judging from the Ames case, failed to fix it.

In particular, the Committee was struck by the number of internal and external studies undertaken after 1985—which became known as the "Year of the Spy" following the exposure of spies John Walker, Ronald Pelton, Edward Lee Howard, and Jonathan Pollard—which pointed out the systemic and deeply-rooted problems in the CIA's conduct of counterintelligence.

As summarized by the recent report of the CIA Inspector General, these internal and external reports over the years focused on common themes:

> That a counterintelligence career was held in low esteem at the CIA and did not attract high caliber officers. This was, in part, because officers gained promotions by agent recruitments, not by analyzing problems in recruitment operations;
> That there was an ambiguous division of responsibility for counterintelligence among CIA offices;
> That counterintelligence information was not being shared properly among CIA components; and
> That CIA was reluctant to share counterintelligence information fully and in a timely manner with the FBI. (IG Report, pp. 16–22)

The poor state of counterintelligence at the CIA in the mid-1980s can be explained in part by the reaction to the so-called "Angleton era." James Angleton had been the head of the Counterintelligence Staff of the CIA from 1954 until 1974 (when he was involuntarily retired by DCI William Colby). He became convinced that the KGB had penetrated the CIA. Accordingly, Angleton was suspicious of virtually every Soviet agent who was recruited by the CIA and suspicious of every CIA officer responsible for such recruitment. On occasion, his suspicions led to CIA officers being fired without adequate justification.

While several of the officers who had been unjustly fired were later compensated, the counterintelligence function was effectively undermined by the negative reaction to Angleton's relentless pursuit of spies, particularly within the Soviet-East European (SE) Division of the Directorate of Operations, which had the principal responsibility for recruiting Soviet agents for the CIA.

In addition, there appears to have been an excessive focus within the Directorate on the recruitment of intelligence sources to the exclusion of counterintelligence concerns. Few officers wanted to go into counterintelligence because promotions and recognition came from successful recruitments, not from questioning, or identifying problems with, ongoing operations. Further, there was an image of a "corporate elite" constructed among these officers which led them to dismiss too readily the possibility of a spy among them.

By all accounts, these attitudes were prevalent within the Directorate of Operations at the time Ames sabotaged the Agency's Soviet operations in the summer of 1985, and they greatly contributed to management's failure to focus upon the CIA employees who had had access to the compromised cases (as explained in detail below).

The CIA made some efforts to address these shortcomings after "the Year of the Spy." In 1988, the head of the counterintelligence staff was made an "Associate Deputy Director" in the Directorate of Operations, and was double-hatted as the head of a new Counterintelligence Center (CIC). The CIA and FBI also signed a new Memorandum of Understanding (MOU) in 1988, which provided, at least on paper, for improved sharing of information in counterintelligence cases.

But these new bureaucratic "trappings" for the counterintelligence function did not overcome the fundamental problems which continued to be cited in reports issued in the 1990s. Despite the formation of a "lead office" for counterintelligence and the 1988 MOU with the FBI, the sharing of counterintelligence information between CIA components and with the FBI continued to be a serious problem, as was clearly evident in the Ames case.

In conclusion, the Committee finds that, despite repeated internal and external reports which recognized a longstanding cultural problem in the counterintelligence function, the CIA failed to implement adequate solutions. Indeed, the Committee believes the fundamental problems persist.

Recommendation No. 1: The Director of Central Intelligence should revise the CIA's strategy for carrying out the counterintelligence function. The Director should institute measures to improve the effectiveness of counterintelligence to include (a) establishing as a requirement for promotion among officers of the Directorate of Operations, service in a counterintelligence or counterintelligence-related position during their careers; (2) establishing incentives for service in a counterintelligence position; (3) instituting effective and comprehensive counterintelligence training for all officers of the Directorate of Operations and for appropriate officers assigned elsewhere in the CIA; and (4) ensuring adequate access to ongoing foreign intelligence operations by those charged with the counterintelligence function. The Committee will make this a "special interest area" for purposes of oversight until it is satisfied the weaknesses noted above have been adequately addressed.

The Failure to Deal With Suitability Problems

As the Ames case all too clearly demonstrates, the CIA Directorate of Operations is too willing to dismiss, deny, or ignore suitability problems demonstrated by its officers.

From the outset of his career at the CIA, Ames demonstrated serious suitability problems which, over the years, should have led his supervisors to reassess his continued employment. These problems included drunkenness, disregard for security regulations, and sloppiness towards administrative requirements. In the years immediately before he began to commit espionage and during the rest of his career, his supervisors were aware of his personal and professional deficiencies, but did not make his problems part of his official record, nor act effectively to correct them. Despite his recognized unsuitability, there is little evidence that his assignments, activities, or access to sensitive information were in any way limited as a result.

Prior to Ames's assignment to the counterintelligence staff of the SE Division in 1983, his supervisor in Mexico City sent a message to CIA headquarters recommending that Ames be counseled for alcohol abuse when he returned. While Ames's supervisor

recognized a chronic problem, the message to headquarters apparently stemmed from an incident which occurred at an official reception at the U.S. Embassy where Ames was drunk and became involved in a loud argument with a Cuban official. On another occasion, Ames was involved in a traffic accident in Mexico City and was so drunk he could not answer police questions nor recognize the U.S. Embassy officer sent to help him. In fact, based upon recent interviews with his colleagues, Ames was notorious for long, alcoholic lunches, often slurring his speech when he returned to the office. None of this behavior prompted any serious effort to correct the problem while Ames was overseas, or when he later returned to CIA headquarters.

In April 1983, when CIA headquarters asked Ames's supervisors in Mexico City whether Ames qualified for a staff position in another Latin American country, they recommended against it, citing his alcohol problem, his failure to do financial accountings, and his generally poor performance. Nevertheless, six months later, when a former supervisor of Ames requested him to fill a position in the SE Division at headquarters—the most sensitive element of the Directorate of Operations—there is no indication that Ames' alcohol problem or poor performance were ever noted. Indeed, Ames was placed in a position which provided him access to the identities of virtually all of the Soviet intelligence officers by the CIA without his new supervisors being aware of the problems he had had in Mexico City.

The alcohol abuse counseling that Ames ultimately did receive upon his return to headquarters amounted to one conversation with a counselor, who, according to Ames, told him that his case was not a serious one when compared to many others in the Directorate of Operations.

In 1983, during the assignment in Mexico City, Ames also began an extra-marital relationship with a Colombian national, Rosario Casas Dupuy (hereinafter "Rosario"), herself a recruited asset of the CIA. Over time, the seriousness of their relationship became apparent to several of Ames's colleagues, but this never led to any action by Ames's supervisors, despite the fact that CIA regulations prohibit sexual relationships with recruited assets and require that reports of "close and continuing" relationships with foreign nationals be submitted by employees. Despite the security implications of this relationship, the violation of Agency regulations was ignored.

In fact, Ames did not file an official report concerning his relationship with Rosario until April 1984, four months after she came to the United States to live with him. Indeed, it appears that until their marriage in August 1985, Ames (still married to his first wife) and Rosario continued to live together, without any perceptible concern being registered by the CIA. While the counterintelligence staff recommended in February 1985, that in view of the anticipated marriage, Ames be moved to a less sensitive position, nothing changed. Ames continued in the same position.

While his alcohol problem abated during this assignment to the SE Division—at least as a matter of attracting official attention—it resurfaced during his assignment in Rome. He was known among colleagues for his long, alcoholic lunches, for sleeping at his desk, for often slurred speech, and generally as a marginal performer. On one occasion, after an Embassy reception, he was so drunk that he passed out on a street and awakened in a hospital. While his supervisor was unhappy, this incident did not become part of Ames' record, nor does it appear that this episode led to counseling or any serious reevaluation of Ames' fitness for continued service. Indeed, the same supervisor extended Ames' tour in Rome for a third year.

Over his career, Ames repeatedly demonstrated carelessness and disdain for security requirements. In 1975, while on his way to meet a CIA source in New York, Ames left a briefcase of classified materials identifying the source on a subway train. Although the briefcase was ultimately recovered, it might well have compromised the source's relationship with the CIA. In the fall of 1984, he brought Rosario to CIA housing where CIA undercover officers were staying, in violation of security regulations. In August 1985, he took her to the safe house where the Soviet defector Yurchenko was being debriefed, again in violation of security procedures. In Rome, he was known to prepare classified reports at home. During his assignments at CIA headquarters between 1989 and 1994, he was occasionally found in other CIA offices where he had no reason to be, and with materials he had no reason to have.

He was equally negligent throughout his career in complying with the administrative requirements imposed on officers of the Directorate of Operations, such as submitting financial accountings for the cases he was handling.

Despite these and other incidents, Ames never received a single official reprimand during his 31-year career at the CIA. Indeed, most of the incidents and shortcomings which have come to light since Ames was arrested were never made a matter of official record. Once on board, his fitness to serve in the Directorate of Operations was never reevaluated.

The Committee appreciates that intelligence officers of the Directorate of Operations are often placed in jobs and situations with stresses and strains that far exceed those of the average government employee. But these positions also demand self-control and personal discipline. Particularly in overseas assignments, it may be impossible to separate an intelligence officer's private life from his or her public, official one. A single misstep can prove his undoing or that of other officers.

It is the Committee's perception, which the Ames case confirms, that the Directorate of Operations has been far too willing to dismiss or ignore flagrant examples of personal misconduct among its officers. Excessive drinking and extra-marital relationships with sources have all too often been seen as part of the job, rather than as indicators of problems. Security concerns are too often dismissed as the bureaucratic whining of small-minded administrators. All too often an officer who has been through training, gone through the polygraph examination, and had an overseas assignment, is accepted as a "member of the club," whose fitness for assignments, promotions, and continued service becomes immune from challenge.

Director Woolsey, in a recent speech, said that the "culture" of the directorate must be changed. The Committee shares that view. Such change will not come solely by changing regulations or personnel. It will come only when supervisors at every level of the directorate take seriously their responsibilities as managers. Personal misconduct should be documented. Officers who do not meet acceptable standards of personal behavior should not be assigned to sensitive positions nor qualify for supervisory positions. Personal shortcomings should be factored into consideration of promotions and bonus awards. While officers with personal problems should be given an opportunity, as well as appropriate assistance, to rehabilitate themselves, failing that, their employment with the directorate, if not with the Agency itself, should be terminated.

Recommendation No. 2: The Director of Central Intelligence should ensure that where evidence of suitability problems comes to the attention of supervisors, it is made a matter of official record and factored into the consideration of assignments, promotions, and bonus awards; that efforts are made to counsel and provide assistance to the employee where indicated, and, if the problem persists over time, the employment of the individual is terminated. The Committee will make this a "special interest area" for purposes of oversight until it is satisfied these policies have been instituted and are being observed within the Directorate of Operations.

Recommendation No. 3: The Director of Central Intelligence should, in particular, take prompt and effective action to deal with what appears to be a widespread problem of alcohol abuse by ensuring that CIA employees experiencing such problems are identified and are put into effective counseling and/or treatment. During this period, these employees should be suspended from their duties until they have demonstrated to a qualified professional their fitness to return to service. Should their problems continue, their employment should be terminated.

Recommendation No. 4: The Director of Central Intelligence should institute, consistent with existing legal authority, an "up or out" policy for employees of the CIA, similar to that of the Foreign Service, without waiting for the report required by section 305 of the Intelligence Authorization Act for Fiscal Year 1995, pertaining to the Intelligence Community as a whole. Chronically poor performance should be grounds for dismissal from the Agency. If the Director decides not to institute such a policy and does not provide a persuasive rationale to the Committee for his decision, the Congress should enact legislation requiring such a policy during the next Congress.

Recommendation No. 5: The Director of Central Intelligence should review and revise the performance appraisal reporting system of the CIA, to include a review of the factors upon which employees are rated and the grading system which now exists, to institute a system which reflects more accurately job performance. Where supervisors are concerned, their rating should include an assessment of how well they have supervised the performance and development of their subordinates.

The Failure to Coordinate Employees' Operational Activities

The Ames case provides a striking example of CIA supervisors failing to critically evaluate the contacts of an operations officer—with known personal shortcomings and in an extremely sensitive position—with Soviet officials in 1984 and 1985. Further, the fact that Ames virtually ceased submitting reports of such contacts, in violation of standard Agency procedures, never became known to his SE Division supervisors or made part of his official record.

In 1984, while occupying a position within the SE Division which gave him access to the identities of Soviet agents working with the CIA and FBI, Ames, with the approval of his immediate supervisor, began making contacts with Soviet Embassy officials in Washington, D.C. According to testimony received by the Committee, it was not infrequent that Directorate of Operations Officers at CIA headquarters were asked to "help out" other CIA elements that had responsibility for establishing relationships and maintaining contacts with foreign individuals located in the Washington area.

The Committee has been advised that Ames's senior supervisors in the SE Division were unaware that he was having these meetings and would have disallowed them had they known.

In any event, to permit a person in Ames's position, and someone with the personal and professional shortcomings already noted, to meet alone with Soviet Embassy officials substantially increased the risk of the disaster that eventually occurred. It provided Ames with an opportunity that he otherwise may not have had, or may have had difficulty in contriving on his own.

After June 1985, after his espionage activities had begun, Ames repeatedly failed to submit reports of his contacts with Soviet officials. While his failure prompted complaints from the FBI, the CIA element that Ames was supporting failed to bring this to the attention of his supervisors in the SE Division, nor was it reflected in his official record. Again, had Ames' SE Division supervisors been aware of his failure to file these reports, it may have alerted them to a possible problem. Since the advancement of Directorate of Operations officers depends upon their official reporting, the failure to file such reports should have suggested something was amiss.

A similar failure occurred during his assignment in Rome. While his supervisor was aware that he was meeting alone with Soviet officials in Rome (one of whom was Ames' KGB contact), Ames explained his failure to file reports of such meetings on the basis that he had obtained little worthwhile information. This apparently was enough to satisfy the supervisor.

Recommendation No. 6: The Director of Central Intelligence should revise the policies and procedures governing the operational activities of CIA officers to ensure that these activities are better supervised, controlled, coordinated, and documented.

The Failure to Apply a Structured Methodology to the Investigation of Intelligence Compromises

The most puzzling deficiency in the Ames case was the failure, in the wake of the 1985–86 compromises, to aggressively investigate the possibility that CIA had been penetrated by a KGB spy.

Certainly by the fall of 1986, the CIA was aware that it had suffered a disaster of unprecedented proportions which was not explained by the defection of Edward Lee Howard. Within a matter of months, virtually its entire stable of Soviet agents had been imprisoned or executed. In the days of the Cold War, Soviet operations represented the Agency's principal *raison d'etre*. There were no operations which had greater importance to its mission. The CIA was left virtually to start from scratch, uncertain whether new operations would meet the same fate as its old ones.

To be sure, these compromises involved extremely sensitive agents. There was a need for discretion in terms of how the matter was handled. But this does not explain or excuse the Agency's tentative, tepid response. Initially, some CIA officers could not believe that the KGB would "roll up" all of CIA's sources at once if the KGB had a source in the CIA who was still in place. Taking some comfort that new operations appeared to be surviving, some believed the problem had gone away. But this in no way explains the seeming lack of urgency to get to the bottom of what had gone so drastically wrong.

The obvious place to begin would have been with the CIA employees who had had access to the information which had been compromised. At least one official in the SE Division made a strong plea to his supervisors at the time that they needed to "investigate it, not study it." But this did not happen. The CIA task force created in October 1986, undertook what was largely an analytical review of the compromised cases. The task force did oversee an Office of Security review of personnel who had served in Moscow, but no broader examination was made of all CIA officers who had had access to the compromised cases. No systematic effort was made to identify and investigate problem employees and their activities, as was eventually done in 1991–92.

Later, the CIA came to suspect that the KGB was running ploys against them, purposely suggesting reasons for the compromises other than a penetration of the CIA itself. Even then, however, any sense of urgency was lacking. CIA analysts waited for things to happen, for more information to surface. They continued to analyze and conjecture. There was no clear sense of purpose, no clear methodology, and no clear sense of what was required to get to the bottom of the compromises.

In a related counterintelligence investigation of a report suggesting that the KGB may have recruited a source in a particular office in the CIA, a CIA investigator conducted a systematic investigation of over 90 employees who were assigned to that office. The inquiry took more than year. But investigators did not conduct the same type of inquiry of the CIA employees who had had access to the information that was actually compromised in 1985 until 1991–1992.

The FBI was officially brought into the case in October 1986, when the CIA learned that two sources recruited by the FBI had been compromised. But the two agencies worked their investigations separately, despite the likelihood that the compromises were caused by the same source (whether it be human or technical).

While the FBI and CIA task forces regularly exchanged information on the compromises and on the progress of their respective analyses, they never performed a systematic assessment, together, of the CIA employees who had had access to the compromised information, until mid-1991.

Why CIA management during the 1986–1991 period did not attach more importance or urgency to getting to the bottom of the 1985 compromises is incomprehensible to the Committee. While CIA Director William Casey and Deputy Director for Operations (DDO) Clair George, who were in office at the time the compromises occurred, reportedly regarded them as "a huge problem," the Agency's response was to create a 4-person team to analyze the problem. No one believed there was a basis for bringing in investigators from the FBI at this juncture, apparently because CIA was unable to pin responsibility on a particular CIA employee.

While Casey and George became deeply enmeshed in the Iran-contra scandal in the fall of 1986 and spring of 1987, this circumstance does not explain, in the view of the Committee, why a problem so close to the heart of the CIA's mission was not given more attention by senior management. Indeed, once Casey and George departed the scene, it does not appear that their successors—either as DCI or as DDO—gave the inquiry any particular emphasis or priority. DCI William Webster, his deputy Robert M. Gates, and the new DDO Richard Stolz were briefed on the compromises in 1988, but did not delve deeply into either the nature of the problem (which was now several years old) or what the Agency was doing to resolve it.

Due to the extraordinary sensitivity of this inquiry, there was only one junior investigator from the Office of Security assigned to the case from 1985 until 1991. He was responsible for investigating all counterintelligence leads and reports coming in which involved CIA employees. After he began to develop information regarding Ames' unexplained affluence in the fall of 1989, he was diverted from this investigation for a nine-month period, first for training and then to handle other leads. There was no one else assigned to pick up the Ames leads. Nor was consideration given to having the FBI pick up the leads, despite the fact that the information now focused upon a particular CIA employee within the United States.

While the Committee believes that the investigator in question made a good faith effort to work the leads he was given, he was essentially self-trained and, because of the compartmented nature of the investigation, was given very little help and guidance. Overworked and overloaded, he did not use all of the investigative techniques he might have utilized to get at Ames' financial situation. Indeed, the statutory authority invoked by the CIA in 1992 to obtain access to Ames' bank records was available to the Agency in 1989. Had this authority been utilized at the time information was received concerning Ames's unexplained affluence, it might well have led to his detection at a much earlier stage. The investigator also apparently made no effort to develop information regarding Ames's unexplained affluence during his assignment in Rome. Efforts to verify the financial condition of Ames's in-laws in Bogota were shoddy and ineffective, producing inaccurate information which supported rather than exposed Ames's contrived explanation.

The Committee does not think it fair to hold the investigator assigned to the case solely responsible for these failures. CIA managers simply failed to assign enough investigators to such an important task and failed to provide them with sufficient legal and administrative support to ensure that all appropriate avenues would be explored and all appropriate investigative authorities utilized. Since the professional investigative expertise of the FBI was effectively spurned during this period, insufficient resources and expertise were brought to bear on the case.

The Committee believes that those in charge of the CIA during the 1986–1991 period—Director William Casey, Acting Director and later Deputy Director Robert Gates, Director William Webster, and Deputy Director and later Acting Director Richard Kerr—must ultimately bear the responsibility for the lack of an adequate investigative response to the 1985 compromises. Whatever they may have personally understood the situation to be, they were in charge. It was their responsibility to find out what was being done to resolve the 1985 compromises. Based upon the information available to the Committee, they failed to do so.

Their failure is especially disheartening when one realizes that the information developed in August 1992, which finally focused the investigation on Ames—correlating his bank deposits in 1985 and 1986 with his meetings with Soviet officials—was available to investigators since 1986. Unfortunately, no one asked for it, even when alerted to Ames's unexplained affluence in October 1989.

Although the 1985–86 compromises represented a unique situation for the CIA, the Ames case demonstrates the lack of a clear *modus operandi* for dealing with situations where intelligence sources are known to have been compromised.

Recommendation No. 7: The Director of Central Intelligence should establish procedures for dealing with intelligence compromises. At a minimum, these procedures should entail a systematic analysis of all employees with access to the relevant information and, if suspects are identified, provide an investigative methodology to determine whether there is evidence of unexplained affluence, unreported travel, unreported contacts, or other indicators of possible espionage. This type of systematic analysis should begin when a known compromise occurs, not after CIA has eliminated the possibility of a technical penetration, or after CIA has narrowed the range of possible suspects to one or two employees. Analysis and investigation should be undertaken on the basis of access and opportunity, and should not be delayed waiting for evidence on culpability.

Recommendation No. 8: Pursuant to section 811 of the Intelligence Authorization Act for Fiscal Year 1995, the FBI should be notified immediately of any case where it is learned that an intelligence source has been compromised to a foreign government, regardless of whether the CIA believes at the time that there is a basis for an FBI counterintelligence or criminal investigation of a particular employee or employees. The CIA should also coordinate with the FBI subsequent investigative actions involving employees potentially involved in the case in order not to prejudice later criminal or counterintelligence activities of the FBI and in order to benefit from the investigative assistance and expertise of the FBI.

Recommendation No. 9: The Director of Central Intelligence should require that all employees assigned as counterintelligence investigators have appropriate training, experience, and supervision which ensures, at a minimum, such investigators will be familiar with, and know how to utilize, the investigative authorities available to the CIA and the FBI.

Recommendation No. 10: CIA management must ensure that adequate analytical and investigative resources are assigned to counterintelligence cases, and that other kinds of staff assistance (e.g., legal support, administrative support) are made available. In turn, those involved in these cases must ensure that their needs are communicated to their supervisors. The Inspector General of the CIA should periodically assess the counterintelligence cases of the CIA to ensure that adequate resources are being afforded to particular cases.

Recommendation No. 11: The status of significant counterintelligence investigations must be regularly briefed to senior Agency officials, including the Director of Central Intelligence. Such briefings should include an explanation of the resources and expertise being brought to bear upon a particular case.

The Failure to Expedite the Inquiry After 1991

The period after the CIA and FBI decided to join forces in June 1991—compared with the period between 1985 and 1991—was relatively intense and focused. For the first time, investigators conducted a systematic review of the CIA employees who had had access to the compromised information, and there was an intensive, productive effort to link Ames and other priority suspects to the compromises.

Yet even during this phase, the investigation took an inordinate amount of time and was plagued by past inefficiencies. The joint investigative unit still had only four people (two from each agency); and there was still a lone CIA investigator working with them. While members of the joint investigative unit did obtain support from the CIA Office of Security and the FBI Washington Metropolitan Field Office, they were still but a few people carrying an extraordinarily demanding workload.

In August 1991, the joint investigative unit developed a list of 29 CIA employees for priority scrutiny. Ames was at the top of the list.

Yet the first letters to go out to financial institutions requesting access to Ames's financial records did not go out until June 1992, almost 10 months later.

In August 1992, when investigators correlated the records of Ames's bank deposits with what was known about Ames's 1985 meetings at the Soviet Embassy, the joint investigative unit suspected they had their man. When they learned in October of Ames's Swiss bank accounts, their suspicions were confirmed.

But according to the Inspector General's report, this crucial information was not presented to FBI headquarters until January 1993. It was explained to the Committee that the joint investigative unit was looking at possible suspects in addition to Ames. But this still does not explain why significant information pertaining to Ames was not passed contemporaneously to the FBI, particularly given the presence of two FBI agents on the joint investigative unit.

On the basis of the work of the joint investigative unit—which culminated in the March 1993 Skylight/playactor report—the FBI assembled an investigative team and tasked the team members to acquaint themselves with the facts. The FBI began an intensive investigation of Ames shortly thereafter. The Committee was advised in the course of its investigation that FBI headquarters had determined that the earlier information developed on Ames by the joint investigative unit did not meet the standards for an intensive FBI investigation. The Committee believes, however, that there was ample evidence by October 1992, to reasonably suggest that Ames was acting in 1985 (and thereafter) as an agent of the Soviet Union. The FBI's hesitation resulted in a six-month delay before the FBI began to apply the full array of its investigative capabilities against Ames. Once applied, they produced impressive results. Indeed, the FBI investigative team from the Washington Metropolitan Field Office, together with the CIA, did a superb job in bringing the investigation to a successful conclusion.

Recommendation No. 12: The Director of the FBI should ensure that adequate resources are applied to counterintelligence cases involving the CIA and other federal agencies, and that FBI headquarters is apprised immediately of significant case developments which could form the basis for the FBI's opening an intensive counterintelligence investigation.

Recommendation No. 13: The Attorney General and the Director of the FBI should review the FBI's guidelines for the conduct of counterintelligence investigations to determine whether clearer guidance is needed in determining whether a subject of a counterintelligence inquiry is acting as an agent of a foreign power.

Failure to Restrict the Assignments and Access to Suspects in Counterintelligence Cases

The Ames case reveals glaring weaknesses in the CIA's procedures for dealing with the career assignments of employees who are under suspicion for compromising intelligence operations. The CIA failed to restrict Ames's assignments and access even after information surfaced in 1989 which indicated Ames was a possible counterintelligence problem.

In September 1989, after a poor tour in Rome, which was known to the managers in the SE Division, his SE superiors allowed Ames to return to the SE Division and assigned him to the office supporting to all Soviet and East European operations in Europe, a position affording him broad access to sensitive information. He remained assigned to the SE Division until August 1990. During this period, investigators learned about Ames's unexplained affluence and developed information regarding several large bank deposits and a particularly large currency exchange. Yet none of this appears to have had any bearing on Ames's continued assignment or access during this period.

In fact, at the end of this assignment, notwithstanding his own poor performance record (he was then ranked 3rd from the bottom among 200 officers in his rating group), Ames was appointed to serve on a promotion board for mid-level CIA operations officers. This assignment gave him access to the personnel records of an entire class of mid-level CIA operations officers.

In October 1990, SE Division managers reassigned Ames to the Counterintelligence Center (CIC) because he had performed poorly and they wanted him out of the Division. Apparently, supervisors in the CIC knew Ames was a poor performer and were aware that questions had been raised about his unexplained affluence. Yet they believed they could manage the problem. After his arrest, these officials recognized that Ames' position had given him access to data which identified virtually every double agent operation controlled by the United States. It is unclear how or why this access was permitted. It is clear that despite the security concerns raised about Ames, his CIC supervisors did not ascertain or evaluate the extent of his access at the time.

In April 1991, while Ames was assigned to the CIC, the Office of Security carried out an updated background investigation of Ames. The results of this investigation were evaluated and shared with the investigator assigned to the special task force. Reflecting interviews with his co-workers in Rome and his Arlington, Virginia neighbors, the investigation produced information that Ames had frequent contacts in Rome with Soviet and East European officials not fully explained by his work requirements, frequently violated security regulations by leaving his safe open and doing classified work at home, and lived far beyond his CIA salary in both Rome and Arlington. (One of those interviewed went so far as to say that he would not be surprised if Ames were a spy.)

Inexplicably, the CIA security officer who reviewed the investigative report evaluated it as "raising no CI concerns" and the task force investigator assigned to the case did not regard the report as providing any new information. Ames retained his security clearance and his job in the Counterintelligence Center, and no further action was taken to follow-up on the information developed in this report. Indeed, the special task force members viewed the investigative report, together with the favorable results of the April 1991 polygraph, as giving Ames "a clean bill of health."

In September 1991, despite having been "booted out" of the SE Division a year earlier, and despite the special task force inquiry then underway, Ames was allowed to return to the SE Division to conduct a special study of the KGB. While the study itself did not call for particularly sensitive access, Ames once again was given access to the personnel and records of the SE Division.

In December 1991, he was assigned to the Counternarcotics Center (CNC) where he remained until his arrest in 1994. This apparently was the first assignment made on the basis of the security concerns about Ames. But due to the sensitivity of the investigation into the 1985–86 compromises, CNC senior managers were not told of the investigation or the suspicions about Ames until the beginning of the FBI's intensive investigation in 1993. Even then, there was little or no effort made to evaluate and control the extent of Ames' access to classified information. Indeed, investigators later learned that Ames had computer access to a vast range of classified information that did not pertain to counternarcotics. Moreover, when a computer upgrade was installed in November 1993, it provided Ames with the capability to "download" vast quantities of information onto computer discs which he could take out of the building. Fortunately, Ames was arrested before he was able to pass these discs to his KGB handlers. But the fact that he was provided this capability at all at a time when his arrest was imminent is indicative of the CIA's lack of attention to this security problem.

Recommendation No. 14: The Director of Central Intelligence should establish procedures to inform current and prospective supervisors about employees under suspicion in counterintelligence cases. While the need to protect the secrecy of the investigation is essential, as well as the need to protect the employees themselves from unfair personnel actions, the assignment of employees under suspicion without frank consultations at the supervisory level increases the likelihood of serious compromises and leads to conflict between CIA elements.

Recommendation No. 15: The Director of Central Intelligence should issue procedures to require, in any case in which an employee is under suspicion for espionage or related activities, that a systematic evaluation be made of the employee's access to classified information, and that appropriate and timely actions be taken to limit such access. While care must obviously be taken to ensure that such actions do not tip off the employee that he or she is under suspicion, the failure to evaluate the access of an employee in these circumstances may eventually result in damage that might have been prevented.

Recommendation No. 16: The Director of Central Intelligence should establish more stringent criteria for CIA employees serving on promotion and assignment boards, which, among other things, prevent the appointment to such panels of employees with poor performance records or records of suitability problems.

Deficiencies in Security Procedures

The Ames case demonstrated numerous deficiencies in the CIA's use of the polygraph, its control over classified documents and materials, and its coordination of security and counterintelligence functions.

The Polygraph

Ames was able to pass polygraph examinations in 1986 and 1991 with relative ease. Although deeply involved in espionage activities, he was able to answer questions such as whether he worked for a foreign intelligence service, or had contacts with foreign nationals which he failed to report, without showing signs of deception.

The CIA Inspector General's report faults the 1986 examination, finding that the examiner was "too chummy" with Ames. When Ames showed a slight reaction to a question asking whether he had ever been "pitched," i.e., asked to work for a foreign intelligence service, the examiner appeared to readily accept his explanation that he was concerned about being "pitched" in his upcoming assignment in Rome.

The 1991 polygraph examination, according to the Inspector General's report, was deficient in that the examiners (there were two separate sessions) were not sufficiently familiar with the existing information on Ames' unexplained affluence, or with the information developed in the April 1991 background investigation of Ames. The examination was also deficient in that the investigator assigned to the special task force had not participated directly in the examination process, and there had been no prior planning in terms of how the CIA would handle the situation if Ames suddenly made damaging admissions.

According to Ames's debriefings, he did not take drugs or use any particular technique to pass the polygraph examinations. Acting on the advice of the KGB, he tried only to be cooperative and stay as calm as he could. Since he was acquainted with how polygraph examinations were conducted, he also was able to manipulate the process to prevent a "problem" from arising.

If Ames's account is true, it seems to indicate problems beyond those cited by the Inspector General's report, i.e. that examiners should be better informed and prepared. Indeed, it suggests that the CIA's reliance on the results of polygraph examinations needs to be far more circumspect than in the past.

Recommendation No. 17: The Director of Central Intelligence should tighten polygraph procedures to make the polygraph more useful. Such procedures should include random examinations instead of exams at regular intervals, with little or no prior notice, and variations in the polygraph technique. These procedures should also ensure that polygraph examinations involving employees under suspicion are carefully planned and constructed, and that appropriate prior notification is made to the Federal Bureau of Investigation if such cases have potential criminal implications. In addition, the Director should review the policies applicable to the training, supervision, and performance appraisal of polygraph examiners to ensure that polygraph examinations are conducted in a professional manner and produce optimum results.

Recommendation No. 18: The Director of Central Intelligence should institute a fundamental reevaluation of the polygraph as a part of CIA's security program. As the Ames case demonstrates, the polygraph cannot be relied upon with certainty to detect deception. This necessarily puts far more reliance on other aspects of the security process, e.g., background investigations, supervisory reporting, psychological testing, financial reporting, etc. The DCI's review should also include a reevaluation of the use of inconclusive polygraph test results. Even where the polygraph does indicate deception, such information is often useless unless damaging admissions are also obtained from the subject. The Committee believes that if an employee with access to particularly sensitive information does not make such admissions but continues to show deception to relevant questions after adequate testing, there should be additional investigation of the issues in question to attempt to resolve them. Should such investigation fail to do so, the CIA should have the latitude, without prejudice to the employee, to reassign him or her to less sensitive duties.

Control of Classified Documents and Materials

The Ames case also demonstrated gaps in the control of sensitive classified information. Ames was able—without detection—to walk out of CIA headquarters and the U.S. Embassy in Rome with bags and envelopes stuffed with classified documents and materials. Many of the classified documents he passed to his KGB handlers were copies of documents that were not under any system of accountability. Ames did not even have to make copies of them. In his last job in the Counternarcotics Center at the CIA, Ames was able to "download" a variety of classified documents onto computer discs and then simply remove them to his home. When he attended a conference in Turkey in 1993, he brought a lap-top computer to do work in his hotel room.

This apparently raised no security concern among those familiar with the incident. He was also able to visit offices he had no reason to be in, and gain access to information he had no business seeing.

In the late 1970s, the CIA instituted a policy calling for random and unannounced spot-checks of personnel leaving Agency compounds. But the policy was discontinued soon thereafter due to the inconvenience caused to those subject to such searches.

Ames recounted later that his KGB handlers were amazed at his ability to gain access to sensitive operations and take large bundles of classified information out of CIA offices without arousing suspicion, a sad commentary on the laxness of security at the CIA.

Recommendation No. 19: The Director of Central Intelligence should reinstate the policy making persons leaving CIA facilities subject to random searches of their person and possessions, and require that such searches be conducted unannounced and periodically at selected locations. Such searches should be conducted frequently enough to serve as a deterrent without unduly hampering the operation of the facilities involved.

Recommendation No. 20: The Director of Central Intelligence should institute computer security measures to prevent employees from being able to "download" classified information onto computer diskettes and removing them from CIA facilities. In addition, existing policies for the introduction, accountability, dissemination, removal, and destruction of all forms of electronic media should be reevaluated. The ability of the CIA's security managers to "audit" specific computer-related functions in order to detect and monitor the actions of suspected offenders should be upgraded.

Recommendation No. 21: The Director of Central Intelligence should institute a policy requiring employees to report to their supervisor any instance in which a CIA employee attempts to obtain classified information which the CIA employee has no apparent reason to know. In turn, supervisors should be required to report to the CIA Counterintelligence Center any such case where a plausible explanation for such a request cannot be ascertained by the supervisor.

Recommendation No. 22: The Director of Central Intelligence should institute new policies to improve the control of classified documents and materials within the CIA. In particular, the Directorate of Operations should undertake an immediate and comprehensive review of its practices and procedures for compartmenting information relating to clandestine operations to ensure that only those officers who absolutely need access can obtain such information. Further, the Directorate should estab-lish and maintain a detailed, automated record of the access granted to each of its employees.

Coordination of Security and Counterintelligence

The Ames case demonstrated a serious division between security and counterintelligence activities in the CIA. Even though an investigator from the Office of Security (OS) participated in the investigation of the 1985–86 compromises under the auspices of the Counterintelligence Center (CIC), he failed to coordinate properly with OS with respect to Ames' 1991 polygraph examination. OS had initiated a background investigation of Ames in March 1991, but went ahead with the polygraph in April without the benefit of the background investigation. As it turned out, the background investigation provided significant information about Ames that was largely ignored by the investigator assigned to the CIC in light of Ames's passing the polygraph examination.

Citing senior security officials, the Inspector General's report noted there had always been a "fault line" in communications between the CIC and its predecessors, and the OS. The CIC had not always shared information regarding its counterintelligence investigations and had failed to make use of OS's investigative expertise. Indeed, the search to find the cause of the 1985 compromises might have moved more quickly from analysis to investigation if there had been better coordination between security and counterintelligence.

The Inspector General's report also found "a gradual degradation" of the resources and authority given the security function since 1985, concluding that "this degradation has adversely affected the Agency's ability to prevent and deter activities such as those engaged in by Ames. . . ." The Committee shares the view that this decline has been too great, too precipitous. The Committee had recommended an increase in personnel security funding for the CIA and other agencies for Fiscal Year 1995, but was unable to sustain its initiative due to the lack of interest shown by the agencies involved.

Responding to the continuing problem of CIA offices failing to share pertinent information on CIA personnel with one another, Director Woolsey recently created a new Office of Personnel Security that combines elements of the old Office of Personnel, the Office of Medical Services, and the Office of Security. While this consolidation may facilitate the sharing of information regarding suitability problems, it may also hamper the exchange of counterintelligence information from the CIC and may further dilute the security function, particularly the expertise of security investigators.

The Committee believes that the personnel security function should be preserved with a separate office. Routine monitoring of Agency employees from a security perspective remains an important function and one that must be accomplished without carrying a presumption that persons are under suspicion. An effective personnel security program would deter potential traitors, limit the burden on counterintelligence investigators and result in faster, more effective counterintelligence investigations.

Recommendation No. 23: The Director of Central Intelligence should reexamine the decision to combine the Office of Security with the other elements of the CIA's new personnel center, and should ensure sufficient funding is provided to the personnel security function in Fiscal Year 1995 and in future years. The Director should also clarify the relationship between security and counterintelligence, specifying their respective functions and providing for effective coordination and cooperation between them.

Failure to Advise the Oversight Committees

The CIA failed to notify the congressional oversight committees in any meaningful way of the compromises of 1985–1986, as required by applicable law.

Indeed, in the hearings held annually on counterintelligence matters and in numerous staff briefings on the subject from 1985 until 1994, the massive compromises of 1985–86 were never once mentioned by representatives of the CIA or the FBI.

Based upon the recollections of individuals, there were two occasions when the 1985–86 compromises were alluded to in discussions with Members or staff of the Senate Select Committee on Intelligence (SSCI). The first mention came during a staff visit to Moscow in December 1988. The second occurred in 1992 during a visit to Moscow by two Members of the Committee. But on each occasion, the information provided was fragmentary and anecdotal and did not specifically address what was being done by the CIA about the problem. Informal staff efforts to follow-up on each of these conversations were put off by the CIA.

The Committee strongly believes that both the CIA and the FBI had an obligation to advise the oversight committees at the time of the 1985–86 compromises. Section 502 of the National Security Act of 1947 specifically requires intelligence agencies to report to the oversight committees "any significant intelligence failure." The compromises of 1985–86 resulted in a virtual collapse of CIA's Soviet operations at the height of the Cold War. According to the SE Division officer's memorandum of November, 1986, the evidence was at that point "overwhelming" and clearly indicated a problem of disastrous proportions. The oversight committees were responsible for funding the activities of the Directorate of Operations. They should have been formally notified pursuant to section 502 of the National Security Act of 1947.

The Need for Continued Follow-up

Many of the problems identified by the Committee are deep-seated and pervasive, and will not be solved easily or quickly. Yet these problems are too important and too integral to the functioning of an agency with important national security responsibilities not to merit continuing and intensive scrutiny by both CIA managers and the congressional oversight committees.

While the Committee intends to make the CIA's response to this report an area of "special oversight interest" in the years ahead, the Committee also directs the Inspector General of the CIA to provide the Committee, through the Director of Central Intelligence, with a report no later than September 1, 1995, and annually thereafter, on the CIA's progress in responding to the recommendations contained in this report and to the continuing counterintelligence and security challenges that the CIA faces.

Questions for Further Discussion

1. What was Aldrich Ames' motivation for spying against the United States from inside the CIA?

2. How was he apprehended? Why did it take so long?

3. Do you think other instances of treason could happen inside the government today? What are the best approaches to prevent this from happening again?

4. Why has counterintelligence often been the neglected stepchild among intelligence activities? ✦

Reprinted from "An Assessment of the Aldrich H. Ames Espionage Case and Its Implications for U.S. Intelligence," Staff Report, Select Committee on Intelligence, U.S. Senate, 103d Cong., 2d. Sess. (November 1, 1994), pp. 53–72.

25

Counterintelligence: The Broken Triad

Frederick L. Wettering

An expert on counterintelligence formerly with the CIA, Wettering sees U.S. counterintelligence as a discipline in disarray. Radical reforms are in order, he argues, beginning with changes in American political attitudes toward counterintelligence, along with greater cooperation among counterintelligence specialists throughout the intelligence community.

> There is one evil I dread and that is their spies . . . I think it a matter of some importance to prevent them from obtaining intelligence about our situation.
>
> —George Washington, 24 March 1776

United States counterintelligence is alive, but not well. Its triad of three essential functions is: protecting secrets, frustrating attempts by foreign intelligence services to acquire those secrets, and catching Americans who spy for those foreign intelligence services. The first of these functions is in effect broken, that is, not being performed. The second and third operate haphazardly at best, so that counterintelligence is not being effectively conducted by U.S. counterintelligence agencies today. In fact, it has never been effectively conducted.

The reasons for this conclusion go to the nature of American society, which, from its inception, has been suspicious of a too-powerful federal government. In addition, the anti-government reaction of the American public (and the U.S. Congress) in the 1960s and 1970s to the Vietnam War, Watergate, COINTELPRO abuses of the FBI, and revelations about apparent CIA abuses of American norms and laws revealed in the Pike and Church Committee Reports had catastrophic effects on counterintelligence. Other causes include the generally uncooperative nature of bureaucracies, and their special dislike of security and counterintelligence, the liti-gious nature of contemporary Americans, and the national cultural bias against informing and informers.

Counterintelligence officers, especially at the Central Intelligence Agency (CIA), tend to dismiss the protection of secrets as "merely" security. Indeed, in the counterintelligence profession "security" officers are looked down on as poor cousins who have to deal with safe closings and employee thefts rather than the exciting business of catching spies. This hubris has resulted in a split throughout both the federal government and the private sector which has resulted in two bureaucracies: "security" and "counterintelligence." Yet, physical and personnel security are actually major components of counterintelligence.

CIA officers tend to put other activities under the rubric of counterintelligence. One is protection of intelligence collection operations by tightening up tradecraft and vetting sources carefully. This is, in reality sui generis, so much a part of the intelligence collection operations that it is excluded here. In this journal a few years back, a former colleague, George Kalaris, also mentioned recruitment of foreign intelligence officers as a major function of offensive counterintelligence.[1] CIA operations officers like to split counterintelligence into "offensive" measures, primarily recruitment and double agent operations, which they see as fun to do and really important; and "defensive" measures, such as surveillance, personnel and physical security, investigations, and police work, which they see as drudge work done by the FBI and security personnel. But this definition is too dismissive of much of what counterintelligence is all about. Kalaris also mentioned counterterrorism and denial and deception efforts as part of counterintelligence. These latter two functions have developed into separate intelligence disciplines, and thus, they too will not be discussed here.

The Functions of Counterintelligence

I. Protecting Secrets

The obvious first responsibility of counterintelligence is to protect information, usually classified and hereafter referred to as secrets considered important to national security. Two aspects to this function are: physical security, which involves keeping secrets away from all except those who need to be aware of them, and personnel security, which involves making sure that the people who are made aware of secrets protect those secrets responsibly. Other security measures include ethnic recruiting, technical security issues, and encryption.

Physical security. Much of physical security is obvious, and involves mechanical measures—safes, passwords, identification badges, security guards, alarms, and related measures. But the very latest in all physical security measures is now available for sale to foreign buyers, thus giving them the opportunity to study these systems and devise countermeasures. Indeed, the United States government has given modern security technology away to such intelligence adversaries as Russia, under the rubric of facilitating the safeguarding of Russian nuclear materials.[2]

The most obvious physical security measures are the keeping of potential foreign spies away from secret information by denying them access or proximity, and preventing American and other spies from walking off with them. There is a long, rich history of foreign spies collecting information while working as foreign employees of the U.S. Government or contractor firms, using building construction as a point of attack, and using visitors to facilities that house secrets. Exit control, that is, preventing spies from walking off with secret papers, film, and diskettes, is yet another problem area in security.

Foreign employees. In 1938, J. Edgar Hoover, the Director of the Federal Bureau of Investigation (FBI), sent a Special Agent Beck to the U.S. Embassy in Moscow to examine security there. He reported that secrets, including code books and sensitive correspondence, were left unguarded. Local Russian employees, all in the pay of the NKVD (the Soviet security service, predecessor of the KGB) had access everywhere and to everything, including the code room.[3] Tyler Kent, a young American code clerk at the time, had an NKVD-supplied bimbo (the KVD/KGB calls them "swallows") in his bed in the embassy, as did many other American officials.[4] He subsequently was recruited by the NKVD. Five decades later, in 1987, FBI counterintelligence expert David Majors visited the U.S. Embassy in Moscow and found the physical situation little improved.[5] Despite several embarrassments and subsequent tightening of security, in March 1997, a naked Russian soldier was found in the shower of the U.S. charge d'affaires' residence within the guarded compound. He was apparently an army deserter who had no trouble scaling the wall and entering the residence.[6] Even now, while a handful of supersecure "Inman" embassies (named for former National Security Agency [NSA] Director Admiral Bobby Inman) have been constructed, the vast majority of U.S. diplomatic missions remain sadly vulnerable in terms of physical security.

Construction or renovation of offices abroad has its own physical security perils, best exemplified by the U.S. embassy in Moscow. In 1953, the embassy was moved to an apartment building, which was re-constructed using local workers. It was also unguarded at night. In 1964, forty secret microphones were discovered built into its walls, as well as a secret tunnel leading out of the basement.[7] In constructing the new U.S. embassy chancery building in Moscow in 1979, State Department bureaucrats incredibly allowed all materials to be provided locally, from Russian suppliers. Unsurprisingly, the building was riddled with hundreds of listening devices. This embarrassment to the State Department is still standing in Moscow inside the U.S. compound.[8] Building construction remains a problem for U.S. government and contractor offices overseas.

For decades, U.S. counterintelligence officials from the FBI, CIA, and State Department pleaded with State Department diplomats to eliminate or curtail the access of hundreds of local employees at the U.S. embassies and consulates inside the former Warsaw Pact nations of Eastern and Central Europe. Everyone involved was fully aware that all these local employees were reporting to the KGB (or its equivalent services). Yet, the "professionals" at the State Department refused to fire them or restrict their access.[9] The problem was not confined to the Warsaw Pact. For example, in 1979 a foreign employee of the American embassy in Paris was caught stealing classified documents and fired.[10]

The hiring of foreign nationals in the United States poses its own security problems. French intelligence, for example, regularly sought to place employees within targeted U.S. firms with high-tech secrets.[11] Chinese intelligence regularly uses its scientists in U.S. firms as intelligence sources and collectors.[12]

In fact, foreign employees can expect to be targeted by their home intelligence services if they occupy positions with access to secrets either abroad or in the United States. The U.S. counterintelligence community needs to be better prepared to deal with this fact.

Visitors. When the Cold War was declared over in 1993, shortly after the demise of the Soviet Union, physical security safeguards at installations housing secrets, such as they were, were greatly relaxed. Even before that, in 1985, the Director of Central Intelligence raised concerns about the U.S. Department of Energy's (DOE) foreign visitors program, as did the General Accounting Office in its reports in 1988 and 1997.[13] The 1999 President's Foreign Intelligence Advisory Board's (PFIAB) Special Report cited numerous instances of sloppy or nonexistent safeguarding of classified material at the Department of Energy (DOE) nuclear weapons laboratories.[14] Paul Redmond, a former head of CIA counterintelligence, noted on television on 12 December 1999, that after 1993 the State Department issued non-escort badges to several foreign officials, including those from Russia. Redmond also noted that the director of the Defense Intelligence Agency did the same thing with foreign military attaches, including Russians, giving them free run of the Pentagon.[15] Surprisingly, they, in fact, had similar access in the 1970s, and used it to steal anything they could lay hands on, according to a KGB officer.[16] Redmond also reminded viewers of a 1998 incident when an entire day's worth of top secret intelligence reports was taken from Secretary of State Madeleine Albright's office by an unidentified man and has never been recovered, nor has the man been identified.[17]

According to information in the 1999 Defense Authorization Bill, 6,398 foreigners visited the three DOE "weapons labs" (Los Alamos, Sandia, and Lawrence Livermore, where nuclear and other weapons research and development is conducted and weapons information is archived) in 1998. Of these, 1,824 were from countries involved in arms proliferation or espionage, such as China, Russia, and India.[18] Once the matter became a national sensation in early 1999, DOE Secretary Bill Richardson, under pressure from Congress, mandated a temporary ban on all foreign visitors to these labs. The 1999 Report of the House Select Committee (Cox Committee) which investigated Communist Chinese espionage, stated authoritatively that

> The PRC (Peoples' Republic of China) also relies heavily on the use of professional scientific visits, delegations, and exchanges to gather sensitive technology.[19]

But less than six months later Secretary Richardson (incredibly) announced that visits—including long-term visits—of foreign nationals to DOE labs would resume.[20]

Dr. Bruce Alberts, president of the National Academy of Sciences and a leading critic of the DOE ban, stated that it was "unfair to foreign scientists," would cause other countries to impose bans on American scientists, would affect U.S. ability to implement and verify nuclear arms agreements, and would affect the ability of the labs to attract first-rate scientific talent.[21] Dr. Rodney Nichols, president of the New York Academy of Sciences, while giving lip service to zero tolerance for lax security and espionage, seemed to miss the connection with foreign visitors when he stated that "an overzealous security bureaucracy, shutting down thousands of productive exchanges every year, must not be tolerated."[22] This mindset that science is more important than secrets or counterintelligence is pervasive at the DOE.

Exit control. Other government agencies are equally negligent regarding physical security. Fawn Hall (the former secretary to Oliver North at the National Security Council during the Ronald Reagan Administration) admitted to Congress that she removed secret papers from the Old Executive Office White House complex by concealing them in her clothing. Aldrich (Rick) Ames, a CIA officer, downloaded secrets onto a floppy diskette on his Agency computer and left the premises with them in his pocket. Jonathan Pollard regularly walked out of the U.S. Naval Intelligence Support Center with his briefcase full of secret papers destined for the Israelis.[23] Other western democracies suffer from the same problems. Recently, a senior officer of Canadian intelligence reportedly left a computer diskette containing the names of confidential informants and contacts in a phone booth, while a Royal Canadian Mountie had a list of informants (and his revolver) stolen from the trunk of his car.[24]

As the 1999 special investigative report of the President's Foreign Intelligence Advisory Broad (Rudman Report) noted,

> Every administration set up a panel to review the national labs. The problem is that nothing is done. . . . Security and counterintelligence responsibilities have been 'punted' from one office to the next.[25]

This, unfortunately, is indicative of government in general. Even the most elementary of precautions—keeping potential intelligence agents away from facilities and personnel with secrets—appears beyond the capabilities of the U.S. counterintelligence and security communities, as does stopping employees from exiting offices with secrets.

Personnel security. The essence of personnel security is to determine that those who have access to secrets as a result of their jobs are people of sufficient probity and responsibility who will safeguard that data. Here, the counterintelligence community has traditionally failed badly, and continues to do so. Key elements of personnel security counterintelligence are background investigations and reinvestigations, polygraph examinations, and the "need to know" principle. Numerous other programs involve the detection of employees with problems such as alcohol and substance abuse, financial problems, and marital problems that might affect their performance as custodians of classified information, and mechanisms to assist separated employees find new jobs. These important elements also address some major causes of why an American might spy, but being widespread and generally noncontroversial matters, they will not be discussed further here.[26]

Background investigations. A basic step in the personnel security process is the background investigation, required when someone is proposed for a security clearance which gives access to secrets. Historically, this counterintelligence tool has been very poorly used, thereby allowing several hundred members of the U.S. Communist Party and supporters of the Soviet Union, who had been recruited by Soviet intelligence in the 1930s and 1940s, into sensitive and senior positions in such agencies as the State, Treasury, Agriculture, and Justice Departments, and the Office of Secret Services (OSS), to spy for the USSR. These inroads were documented in detail by John Earl Haynes, Harvey Klehr, and Fridrikh Firsov in the groundbreaking book *The Secret World of American Communism* (Yale University Press, New Haven, CT, 1995). Their information was confirmed by the release of the NSA's "Venona" communications intercepts.

In 1995, 50,000 firms were working as United States government contractors, conducting classified research or production, and 3.2 million secret or above security clearances had been issued.[27] The Defense Department recently admitted that it currently has a huge backlog of new clearance investigations and reinvestigations. The Pentagon also disclosed that over 2.4 million military, civilian, and contractor employees hold defense security clearances (the government-wide figure is over 3 million). Of that total, about 524,000 hold "top secret" clearances and 1.8 million hold "secret" clearances.[28] Many of these employees have been given "temporary" access, pending the completion of the background investigation.

People who do background investigations are not usually well-paid, and the job has no career prospects. Civil liberties concerns have blocked investigators from access to employees' bank accounts and investments, as well as lifestyles. The sheer number of employees with sensitive access precludes any double check of employee-volunteered information unless the subject comes under suspicion from other investigative leads. As a result, background investigations tend to be cursory, usually involving an interview of the references the applicant listed, as well as verification of employment, academic records, and checking the person's name with various law enforcement agencies for criminal records.

Classic examples of poor background investigations include the case of Sergeant Jack Dunlap, who worked at the NSA and spied for the KGB for at least three years (1960–1963). Paid a modest military salary of $100 per week, Dunlap had a pleasure boat, a Jaguar, and two Cadillacs in his driveway. Counterintelligence officers became fully aware of Dunlap's espionage only after his suicide in 1963, when secret materials were found in his garage.[29] Larry Wu-Tai Chin had over $700,000 in real estate holdings, dropped $96,000 while gambling in Las Vegas, and was repeatedly audited by the Internal Revenue Service (IRS), all of which went unnoticed by the CIA.[30] NSA defectors William Martin and Bernon Mitchell, homosexuals who had serious lifestyle problems, went undetected by NSA.[31] Thirty years later, Rick Ames drove a Jaguar, lived in a $500,000 home fully paid for, and had an extravagant lifestyle, yet he passed a CIA reinvestigation, which included a new background check.[32]

Recent reforms as a result of the Ames case give U.S. law enforcement investigators greater access to financial and investment data, and provide for greater FBI control over personnel security at the CIA, but this is useful only in the investigation of people who have already come under Counterintelligence scrutiny. The sheer volume of information cannot be routinely checked, and is thus of little value to basic Counterintelligence. Private contractors are not exempt from poor personnel security practices: the cases of Christopher Boyce, James Harper, William Bell, and Thomas Cavanagh, all contractor spies, stand testament to this.[33] The number of people to be screened is beyond the capabilities of the U.S. Counterintelligence establishment (including contractors), and there is little prospect of change.

Reinvestigations. To the best of my knowledge, only the CIA, FBI, and NSA routinely reinvestigate employees after a certain number of years. Other agencies do it on a random basis. And some never reinvestigate. When an employee acquires a top secret or special access clearance to highly compartmented information, a reinvestigation is supposed to take place every five years (for example: the Department of Energy "Q" clearance giving its holder access to nuclear secrets). The Pentagon recently admitted to being more than 905,000 reinvestigations behind.[34] A DOE study showed that from 1947 to 1972 over one million Q clearances were applied for, with only 0.2 percent turned down.[35] Many investigators have indicated that this reinvestigation is often a mere review of an individual's file, without any new field investigation. Again, the numbers defeat the counterintelligence investigators. Even special clearances are widely handed out. Because of a lack of personnel and budget, as well as civil liberties concerns, reinvestigations are not a serious counterintelligence check.

Polygraph examinations. Polygraph examinations serve three separate counterintelligence purposes. First, they intimidate would-be disclosers of secrets from doing so for fear of being caught. Second, when used on a routine basis they can reveal deceptions which can lead to confessions, or at least more intensive scrutiny. Third, they can be used as a follow-up investigative tool should a person come under suspicion from other means. Examples of all three are available: Chinese spy Larry Wu-Tai Chin retired from the CIA rather than face a periodic re-investigation and polygraph examination. Sergeant Jeffrey Carney, a spy for East Germany's Stasi, changed jobs to avoid having to undergo a polygraph test. The CIA maintains that Harold Nicholson, a spy for the KGB and SVR (the latest incarnation of the KGB's foreign intelligence component), came to the attention of counterintelligence officers when he failed a routine re-polygraph exam.[36] CIA secretary Sharon Scranage, when confronted with a failed re-polygraph, confessed to giving information to her Ghanaian lover.[37] NSA's Jack Dunlap, mentioned earlier, committed suicide following an unsatisfactory polygraph which had aroused counterintelligence suspicions of him.[38] Los Alamos scientist Wen Ho Lee reportedly failed a polygraph on what are known as counterintelligence (CI) questions (for example, unreported contact with foreign officials and passage of information) which (belatedly) played a part in his investigation.[39]

The polygraph is a vital tool of counterintelligence, yet it is opposed by most Americans, including legislators and the courts. Only a handful of government agencies use it. During my years on the National Security Council staff (1981–1984), I and others argued vociferously for polygraph examinations for all who read the most sensitive intelligence, primarily to find out who was leaking very sensitive information to the press. This suggestion actually made it into a draft Presidential order, but Secretary of State George Shultz threatened to resign if it were to be applied to the State Department. Certain senior White House aides also expressed opposition, for easily imaginable reasons. The idea was quietly dropped.

In the wake of a massive leak of U.S. nuclear weapons secrets, Energy Secretary Richardson announced in June 1999 that 12,000 DOE weapons laboratory scientists would henceforth be polygraphed.[40] An ensuing loud outcry from scientists and legislators resulted in that order being gutted.[41] In December 1999, Richardson reversed himself, stating that only a few hundred scientists would eventually (over a five-year period) face a polygraph exam.[42] New Mexico Senators Pete V. Domenici and Jeff Bingaman supported the protesting scientists, and publicly questioned the polygraph's reliability.[43] U.S. Supreme Court Justice Clarence Thomas, speaking on an 8 to 1 Court ruling disallowing polygraph results as evidence in military courts martial (*U.S. v. Scheffer*), stated "There is simply no consensus that polygraph information is reliable." Justice John Paul Stevens, in dissent, noted studies indicating that Defense Department studies show that polygraphs have an accuracy rating of about 90%, which is comparable to

fingerprint identification.[44] But American attitudes concerning civil liberties, distrust of government, and disrespect for secrets of any kind make mandatory routine polygraph examinations only a pipedream of counterintelligence officers, not a reality.

Need to know principle. "Need to know" is an axiom of counterintelligence, requiring that employees be given access only to those secrets that they need to know and no others. A variation is known as "compartmentation," that is, restricting access to secret information to only those with a need to know. It has never worked in practice, despite periodic reforms demanding that it be rigorously enforced. The 1986 U.S. Senate Select Committee Report, "Meeting the Espionage Challenge: A Review of Counterintelligence and Security Programs," was one such futile effort insisting on a new effort to implement the need to know principle.

From time to time, certain categories of information are restricted, but inevitably the readership list grows and grows. A classic example is the CIA's *National Intelligence Daily*, a daily summary of overnight intelligence items designed for the members of the National Security Council. Readership eventually grew to the thousands. In 1998 its publication was suspended because a number of entries regularly found their way into the daily newspapers, especially Bill Gertz's column in the *Washington Times*. Doubtless, within a short time, a similar publication will develop a wide readership.

The proliferation of special access clearances is another example of the laxity of compartmentation. The 1999 PFIAB Special Report noted that one weapons lab in 1990 and 1991 had granted "Q" clearances to more than 2,000 employees who did not need access to the information.[45] The CIA, burned by Rick Ames's access to vast areas of intelligence outside his "need to know," has made a major effort to tighten up computer access, but at the same time is promoting functional "centers" covering areas such as counterintelligence, counterterrorism, and nonproliferation, thereby merging operations and intelligence personnel in one functional office and widely expanding the circle of knowledge of sensitive intelligence and operations. Counterintelligence reforms at CIA after the Ames scandal resulted in, among other things, a wider dissemination of CIA secrets to the FBI and to the National Counterintelligence Center (NACIC), a multi-agency organization.

Defense against ethnic recruiting. Counterintelligence defense against the targeting of ethnic Americans needs a separate assessment. Most of the more than 50 foreign intelligence services which operate in the United States (and numerous others which operate against Americans when they are abroad), practice ethnic recruiting, that is, seek to recruit persons of the same ethnic background as the foreign intelligence officer. A classic example is the Robert Kim case. Kim, a Korean-American working as a Navy intelligence analyst, was persuaded by the South Korean military attaché to give him Pentagon secrets.[46] Russia, China, India, and Israel are avid practitioners of this tactic, with the Chinese taking it to the extreme of recruiting only ethnic Chinese.[47]

Yet attempts to warn hyphenated Americans of this danger have been met with outcries of discrimination. Despite the fact that in 1998 Peter Lee, a Los Alamos laser scientist, confessed to passing secrets to China, the investigation of Wen Ho Lee produced an immediate outcry of discrimination from various Chinese-American organizations (as well as the PRC).[48] The same thing happened to television reporter Connie Chung when, in 1995, she broadcast a report that many PRC visitors were performing intelligence missions. After vociferous protests from Sino-American groups, she was forced to apologize on air, and subsequently lost her anchor job on the CBS Evening News.[49]

Even stating the fact that foreign intelligence organizations practice ethnic recruiting has come under attack. In 1993, a Hughes Company security briefer was forced to publicly apologize when his warning about the PRC's targeting of Chinese Americans resulted in protests from Chinese-American groups.[50] When a Defense Department security officer wrote in a 1995 study that the Israeli services targeted American Jews, Jewish organizations, led by B'nai B'rith, demanded that heads roll.[51] The analysis was quite correct, and was repeated in a General Accounting Office (GAO) study of economic espionage in 1996.[52] Fearing political incorrectness if not persecution, the GAO identified Israel only as "Country A" in the study. The targeting of ethnic Americans by foreign intelligence services is a reality, but the discomfort of Americans in discussing, thinking about, or dealing with it will continue to inhibit Counterintelligence measures.

Infosec. Computer security is often termed "infosec" in governmentese. Any number of senior counterintelligence officials, including FBI Director Louis Freeh, have warned that the computers which house U.S. secrets are very vulnerable. The Cox Committee Report noted that at DOE "classified information had been placed on unclassified networks, with no system for either detection or reliable protection."[53] The 1999 PFIAB Special Report added a long list of computer security shortcomings.[54] Simple yet effective measures, such as removing the disk drives so as to prevent copying of data to disks, done by the CIA after Ames's espionage became confirmed, is not widespread in government. Russian intelligence hackers penetrated

Defense Department establishments and DOE laboratories. An early penetration effort at DOE, done by hackers in the pay of the KGB, was chronicled by Cliff Stoll in his book *The Cuckoo's Egg.*[55] In 1998, a hacker group calling themselves "Masters of Downloading" bragged publicly that they had stolen the means to cripple U.S. military communications, a claim denied by the Pentagon.[56]

More serious threats recently came from Russia and China. An FBI investigation, called "MOONLIGHT MAZE," noted in 1999 that Russian hackers had penetrated Defense Department and other government agency computers, as well as those of contractors.[57] After the United States inadvertently bombed the PRC embassy in Belgrade, Yugoslavia, in early 1999, Chinese hackers reportedly attacked U.S. Defense computer sites, allegedly revealing an astonishing 3,000–4,000 "back doors" into U.S. computer systems that had apparently been created by Chinese agents.[58] The FBI subsequently admitted that its new infosec unit, the National Infrastructure Protection Center (NIPC), is badly under strength.[59] The NIPC was created as a result of President Bill Clinton's 1998 Presidential Decision Directive (PDD-63) to protect the national infrastructure.

In addition to professional intelligence hackers, an increasing number of dangerous semiprofessional hacker groups are targeting research sites. One such group, Milw0rm, boasted in 1997 of penetrating the Indian government's classified nuclear research site, a feat repeated by three teenage hackers in 1998, while Global Hell members attacked the White House and FBI websites. Many hacker groups, such as LOpht, Phrack, Masters of Downloading, Cult of the Dead Cow, Global Hell, the Chaos Computer Club, Milw0rm, and others maintain websites where they openly share hacking tips, while others provide free of charge the latest state-of-the-art software hacking tools, such as "SATAN" and "Back Orifice." Hacker magazines, both on-line and over the counter, such as *2600* and *Phrack,* also offer hacking tips.

In sum, the offense, represented by both intelligence service hackers and semi-professional private groups, is well ahead of counterintelligence defense in terms of protecting computer information security, and is likely to stay ahead in the foreseeable future.

TSCM. Technical security countermeasures (TSCM) are a collection of technical efforts to detect the technical penetrations of facilities by foreign intelligence services to collect intelligence. The best-known are the electronic audio listening devices, or bugs. TSCM is a standby collection technique for all major intelligence and security services. The United States has proven particularly vulnerable to this technical espionage. Widely known is the story of the reproduction of the great seal of the United States hanging in U.S. Ambassador George Kennan's office in the Moscow embassy which, in 1952, was discovered to have a listening device concealed therein.[60]

TSCM measures usually involve trained technicians who, using both sophisticated electronic and x-ray devices, as well as painstaking physical examination, "sweep" an area to discover any such devices. In 1944, the very first TSCM sweep uncovered 120 microphones in the Moscow embassy. In 1962, another 40-odd were uncovered in another sweep. Before the new U.S. chancery was occupied in the late 1970s, sweepers found a very large number of listening devices built into walls, girders, and other parts of the building.[61] In a late 1960s case called "Gunman," CIA technicians discovered that IBM electric typewriters in the Moscow embassy had been bugged by the Soviets so that the electronic radiations could and were being detected by Soviet receivers which could convert the signals into keystrokes.[62]

A solid defense measure was introduced in the 1970s, both at home and abroad, with special acoustically-shielded rooms, often called "bubbles," being installed. These counter-audio and other techniques and hardware are excellent counterintelligence measures. But they are expensive, still too few in number, and unwieldy to use on a daily basis, and thus fall victim to the American character trait of not doing anything that makes demands on resources which might be "better" used elsewhere, and which calls for sacrificing certain "freedoms." The problem is compounded by the huge number of U.S. facilities under attack, not just by the Russians but by most world services.

TSCM simply has far too few resources dedicated to it compared to the breadth of the attacks. Sweeps, even of highly-threatened facilities, are made too infrequently. The problem continues: as recently as December 1999, Department of State security officials discovered a Russian listening device planted in a seventh floor (executive level) conference room at the State Department.[63] The number of facilities to be swept is far too huge for the very limited number of "sweepers," who burn out quickly, and other measures such as bubbles. As a result, this form of counterintelligence is a recurring failure.

Encryption. Encryption of communications is a wonderful counterintelligence tool, but like sweep teams and bubbles is not used nearly enough to secure U.S. secrets. Despite the fact that the National Security Agency supplies effective and widespread encrypted communications instruments and methods, U.S. communications are under massive intercept attack by Russian (and other) signals intelligence (sigint) units. KGB defector Vasily Mitrokhin devotes several pages of his book, *The Sword and The Shield*, to the great intelligence gains of these (sigint) efforts against U.S. communications.[64] He notes that the Russians maintained signals intelligence sites located in Soviet diplomatic installations to listen in on telephone calls, telexes, faxes, cellular phone calls, radio communications (via radio, microwave, and satellite signal intercept capabilities). Other Soviet (sigint) listening sites were located in Mexico City and Lourdes, Cuba, where both the SVR (successor to the KGB's foreign intelligence arm) and GRU have maintained a massive collection of antennas and personnel even subsequent to the fall of the USSR. To expect that Russia has closed any of these installations since Mitrokhin's defection is unrealistic. Other defectors have confirmed Mitrokhin's disclosure that Americans are very open in discussing secrets on unprotected communications channels, despite the wide availability of encrypted, secure communications.[65] In the 1999 Kosovo fighting, Serbian forces were able to evade much NATO bombing damage because they were reportedly listening in on U.S. pilots' radio chat which gave away targets in advance.[66]

Part of the problem is the sheer volume of communications involved in, for example, a military deployment. But another part of the problem is the American cultural trait of avoiding any counterintelligence procedure that is too intrusive or value-conflicting. The end result is continuing failure to protect American secrets, despite yeoman efforts by counterintelligence agencies and the NSA.

Other measures. Many corporations now routinely monitor employee e-mail. But several government agencies and contractors refuse to do so, even though many of their personnel openly correspond electronically with colleagues overseas, including Russia and China. Similarly, regular scrutiny of telephone and fax records is rare. The security, rather than counterintelligence, officers generally charged with conducting these measures are often both untrained and legitimately concerned about possible violations of employees' rights and their own personal liability. Photocopy machines in areas where classified information is developed and stored are uncontrolled throughout the federal government. Routine "trash trawling," the examination of employees' trash, is considered anathema unless done by a law enforcement agency. Firewalls on computers are weak or nonexistent. (Some government offices inexplicably use a firewall made in Israel.)

Attempts to rectify these situations are usually met by passive resistance and noncompliance.

Overworked and undertrained security officers cannot enforce such other measures. Foreign nationals on most staffs are generally untouchable. And in private industry and at American universities, they often come either free or inexpensively from foreign firms and governments.

II. Frustrating Foreign Intelligence Operatives

The second major function of counterintelligence is to frustrate the efforts of foreign intelligence operatives to steal U.S. secrets. This can be accomplished in numerous ways: expelling them or denying them entry; controlling their movements and access; surveilling them by physical and/or electronic observation; and using "double agents" to preoccupy and mislead them. A key precondition to these efforts is knowing who the operatives are.

Knowing who they are. Essential parts of any counter-intelligence effort are good record-keeping and the sharing of information among agencies. This aspect of counterintelligence has been improved as a result of reforms in the aftermath of the Ames case. A widespread knowledge exists in the overall counterintelligence community about the known and suspected foreign intelligence officers, and the modus operandi of the foreign intelligence services. But information concerning visitors who may be known or suspect intelligence collectors is not well-circulated. Until 1998 foreign visitors to U.S. weapons laboratories went largely unreported to DOE counterintelligence, especially after 1993 and the perceived ending of the Cold War.

Record-keeping is the heart of any counterintelligence program. The U.S. counterintelligence community has had excellent records, built up mostly from painstaking debriefings of intelligence defectors and assets, as well as examination of the results of double-agent cases and the surveillance of intelligence officers. During the Cold War there was also widespread sharing among NATO allies of information on Warsaw Pact intelligence personnel. Identification and record-keeping are made difficult by the use of non-official cover by foreign spies, and by the use of nonprofessionals to collect intelligence— a major modus operandi of the Chinese services.

Recently, cooperation among Western services has cooled somewhat, as allies now also consider themselves competitors engaging in economic espionage against each other. The expulsions of alleged CIA officers from France in 1995 and Germany in 1997 are indicative of this new wariness.[67]

Expelling or denying entry to intelligence officers. The single most effective counterintelligence technique the United States or any other state used to suppress foreign spying is the expulsion or denial

of entry to others' intelligence officers, but the positive results are generally short-term. Most intelligence personnel operate with the protection of diplomatic status, or "official cover," as it is known in the business. But even as "diplomats," their visa requests always receive extra scrutiny by counterintelligence services. During the Cold War, NATO counterintelligence officials cooperated in exchanging information on hostile intelligence officers, and in denying visas to known or heavily-suspect intelligence operatives. This seriously handicapped the Warsaw Pact services.

Mass expulsion of intelligence officers is also effective in seriously damaging espionage operations, at least for a time. For example, KGB operations were crippled in Britain in 1971 when Prime Minister Edward Heath authorized the expulsion, with publicity, of 105 KGB and GRU personnel. In 1986, President Ronald Reagan authorized the FBI to mount a similar effort in which 80 KGB and GRU officers under diplomatic cover were expelled from the United States. In his book on the KGB, written in collaboration with British scholar Christopher Andrew, KGB defector Oleg Gordievsky, a former head of the KGB office in Britain, states that in 1971 "the golden age of KGB operations came to an end. The London residency never recovered from the 1971 expulsions."[68] Yet, according to former CIA counterintelligence chief Paul Redmond, despite heavy expulsions, the Russian intelligence presence in the United States today is as large or larger than at the height of the Cold War.[69]

If expulsions with publicity and visa denials are so successful, why are they not done more often? The answer is twofold: first, the foreign governments always retaliate, although not always proportionately. More important, such expulsions seriously damage relations with the state whose suspect diplomats have just been expelled. Important bilateral and multilateral agreements, and trade relations—the basic elements of diplomacy and state-to-state relations—are put at risk. Mutual hostilities increase, and diplomatic "hawks" are encouraged. As a result, presidents, prime ministers, and especially foreign ministries and the State Department, almost always oppose such expulsions. The CIA also opposed the 1986 expulsions, fearing retaliation. The customary method is to ask, without fanfare, that detected intelligence officers quietly leave the country. Occasionally, an intelligence officer involved in an operation deemed particularly damaging may be expelled with publicity. For example, Stanislav Borisovich Gusev, a Russian diplomat caught remotely operating a listening device in the State Department, was expelled for espionage on 8 December 1999.[70] But earlier that year, three Russian diplomats had been quietly expelled without publicity. The bottom line is that mass ex-pulsions with fanfare can cripple a foreign state's espionage effort for a time, but the diplomatic cost is almost always too high for leaders to accept such recommendations.

Using physical surveillance. Physical surveil-lance, the most common technique of counterintel-ligence agencies worldwide, is very labor intensive and boring, and positive results are few and far be-tween. It can be divided into three parts: static sur-veillance, mobile surveillance, and electronic and other surveillance.

a. Static surveillance. Static or fixed-point sur-veillance is observation of a place, perhaps a sus-pect's residence, or a "choke-point," where suspects regularly have to pass, or, more commonly, the chancery building of a foreign embassy whose per-sonnel include intelligence officers. These surveillances have three purposes: to alert a mobile surveillance team when a subject exits or passes by so that the team might pick the suspect up; to chronicle a suspect's movements and/or visitors; and to attempt to identify would-be spies walking into a foreign embassy to volunteer their services. The results admirably serve the first two purposes of counterintelligence; that is why surveillance ex-ists on most major embassies (including American embassies) around the world.

The third purpose, catching prospective spies, is, frankly, not well-served. For example, in the United States, the most important volunteer spies have walked through the front door of the Russian chan-cery on 16th Street in Washington, D.C., to offer their services without being identified by the FBI. Martin and Mitchell, Dunlap, Ronald Pelton, Ed-ward Lee Howard, and Robert Lipka are perfect ex-amples. The FBI has, however, caught some "bot-tom-feeder," or low-level (and dumb), would-be spies who made the mistake of calling or writing to the Soviet embassy to volunteer their services, or somehow drew attention to themselves while visit-ing that embassy. Charles Anzalone, Kurt Lessen-thien, Randy Jeffries, and Thomas Cavanagh made the mistake of phoning and writing to the Soviet embassy, not realizing that the FBI has means of de-tecting call-ins and write-ins.[71] Edwin Moore tossed a package of secrets over the wall of the embassy compound with a note offering his services. Thinking it might be a bomb, KGB security officers turned the package over to the police unopened.[72]

In the main, static surveillance has a very narrow window of usefulness to counterintelligence, and is better suited to watching suspects and catching low-level would-be spies than to catching hereto-fore undiscovered real spies coming in off the street.

b. Mobile surveillance. Mobile surveillance can be done in many ways: on foot, cycle, vehicle, and air-craft. The classic Hollywood-style "tail" is on foot, exemplified in the old spy movie *Walk East on Bea-con.* This type of surveillance, very common world-wide, is designed for two purposes: to intimidate and discourage a suspect from undertaking an ille-gal act relating to espionage, and catching the sus-pect in the act of undertaking some aspect of espio-nage.

Mobile surveillance is extremely labor intensive, and therefore prevalent in Third World countries where manpower is not a problem. It is often com-bined with fixed-point surveillance and/or elec-tronic surveillance. Following a well-trained intelli-gence operative without revealing the surveillance is extremely difficult. This is not a problem if the purpose is to intimidate. Both the KGB and FBI have long practiced close and obvious surveillance of foreign diplomats suspected of being intelligence officers. But officers of major intelligence services are given extensive training in surveillance detec-tion and evasion techniques, and are rarely intimi-dated. The autobiographies of a Polish and a Soviet intelligence officer assigned to spy in the United States reveal that, while each had great respect for FBI surveillance, both were confident they could beat it when necessary.[73] The FBI's surveillance re-cord is mixed. A large number of Soviet and Russian intelligence officers have been caught by the Bu-reau while committing an intelligence act (most of-ten involving putting things in or taking some out of a "dead drop"—a place to conceal money, docu-ments, film, etc.) Similarly, some real spies have been caught this way. But rarely will a spy be caught without having first come under suspicion by some other means.

FBI surveillance, unfortunately, has missed some big ones. In 1947, Hoover's most wanted man, Gerhard Eisler (an East German Comintern agent working with the U.S. Communist Party), eluded FBI surveillance while on trial and fled by ship.[74] In 1985, Ed Howard (CIA-trained in surveillance de-tection and evasion) evaded FBI surveillance and fled to Mexico.[75] Even the FBI's elite surveillance team, called the "Super-Gs," was beaten by Rick Ames (also CIA-trained and FBI-trained as well) who managed to elude surveillance, load a dead drop with a devastating package of stolen secrets, and then signal (often with a chalk mark) his KGB handler that the drop was loaded.[76]

The Hollywood idea that both the spy and han-dler will be caught *in flagrante delicto* by counter-intelligence surveillants is, frankly, no longer a reality when it concerns important spies and major intelli-gence services. In 1959, it was still possible; FBI sur-veillance of the USSR's Washington embassy GRU officers caught them in a meeting with U.S. Army Lt. Colonel William Whalen, who was later convicted as a Soviet spy.[77] But today, foreign intelligence services respect current FBI surveillance capabilities and avoid face-to-face meetings with their spies within the United States. Important spies are no longer met in-country but rather abroad, in a safer environment, usually by a highly-trained officer of an elite, highly-compartmented part of the foreign intelligence service. Only when intelligence officers get sloppy (as does happen, surprisingly, but usually with spies of lesser importance) do counterintelligence forces have a real chance to catch them in the act with their spy. In summary, mobile surveillance has serious limitations in terms of catching important spies or frustrating foreign intelligence officers. It does have some deterrent effect which results in foreign intelligence services moving the spy business quickly offshore.

c. Electronic and other surveillances. Electronic surveillance by means of telephone taps (teltaps) or electronic listening devices (bugs), and other forms of surveillance, such as "mail covers" (intercepts), serve to frustrate foreign intelligence officers by identifying their contacts, and either subsequently blocking their communications or enabling them to be converted to "double agents." Electronic devices also assist mobile surveillance with such tools as "beacons" which broadcast the location of a vehicle or item. Cell phone taps can also pinpoint a location. The famous 0. J. Simpson low-speed motor vehicle chase is an example. The California police initially located him through his cell-phone, which constantly broadcast its location when turned on.

These special surveillance tools are very useful to counterintelligence. Teltaps and bugs can serve other purposes besides discovering contacts or tracing the movements of suspects. They are a primary means of collecting evidence of espionage when a suspect is identified as a spy or a foreign diplomat as an intelligence officer. They can also tell much about the character of an intelligence officer, perhaps enabling counterintelligence personnel to target him/her for recruitment.

In terms of frustrating espionage efforts, the utility of electronic and other devices is limited, and presupposes that foreign intelligence officers will meet a real or would-be spy in the United States. Intelligent would-be spies (the most dangerous) know the dangers of meeting a foreign intelligence officer in the United States (a testimony to the FBI's overall effectiveness and intimidatory effect). Instead, as Harold Nicholson and others did, they will meet in another country, where surveillance may be less likely or effective.

III. Catching American Spies

The overall record of United States counterintelligence at catching spies is not good. Approximately 100 Americans have been caught and convicted of espionage since World War II. A number of others were caught but not convicted, or even not prosecuted, given the very rigorous American legal requirements to prove espionage. The FBI noted in 1997 that it had over 200 active espionage cases under investigation and 800 economic espionage cases.[78] Anecdotal reports suggest that the large quantity of information given U.S. counterintelligence from just two sources, KGB defector Vitaly Mitrokhin and the CIA-captured East German "Stasi" (State Security Agency) files, puts the number of still not uncovered American spies at several hundred.

Author Ronald Kessler, citing unidentified FBI sources, earlier claimed the number is "more than 1,000."[79] The Stasi files alone held data on 13,000 spies, including some nine Americans, according to *Der Spiegel* magazine.[80] The then-CIA Director James Woolsey stated on the NBC television program *The Today Show* in 1994 (probably reflecting on Mitrokhin's information, which had been smuggled to Britain in 1992) that there were large numbers of leads to people who undertook espionage in the Cold War, in the United States and elsewhere, and in several parts of the U.S. government.[81] Woolsey attributed these leads to information obtained after the collapse of Communist governments in Eastern Europe, particularly East Germany (a clear reference to the Stasi files), and probably information from Hungary and Czechoslovakia which led to the wrap-up of the five sergeants of the Clyde Lee Conrad spy ring in the 1980s. The famous "Venona" decryptions of Soviet intelligence messages during World War II leave yet unidentified 178 Russian code names of American spies.[82]

The most effective sources of identification of U.S. spies are defecting foreign intelligence officers and the spies themselves. The second most effective is the decryption of coded messages, primarily electronic. The third most effective are CIA and other intelligence efforts to acquire this information, including attempts to recruit foreign agents who have such knowledge. A fourth is through double agents. Last are the methods described earlier.

Gifts of information. The United States and Russia have both benefited from unwarranted bonanzas when extraordinarily well-informed intelligence officers, spies, and informants have volunteered their services and/or information. Aldrich Ames just about wiped out the stable of U.S. spies in Russia (estimated at around 20) when he gave their names to a Russian contact and asked for $50,000 in return.[83] CIA acquisition of the East German State Security (Stasi) files has resulted in the arrest and trial of four Americans who had worked for Stasi during the Cold War, as well as hundreds of Germans.[84] Most of the information on the Conrad spy ring of five army sergeants was probably from CIA acquisition of foreign intelligence files. In fact, a majority of the great "successes" of counterintelligence have been gifts from volunteers. KGB defector Reino Hayhanen gave up Soviet illegal "Colonel Rudolf Abel" (true name Willie Fischer).[85] Polish defector Michal Goleniewski gave up MI6 spy George Blake, Harry Houghton, and West German BND spies Hans Feife and Hans Clemens.[86] Vitaly Yurchenko gave the FBI and CIA Edward Howard and Ronald Pelton.[87] Chinese defector Yu Shensan gave up Larry Wu-Tai Chin to the CIA.[88] A Polish CIA spy revealed the spying of contractors William Bell and James Harper.[89] FBI spy Earl Pitts was identified by a defector, Russian diplomat Rollan Dzheikiya.[90] NSA spy Sergeant David Boone was almost certainly identified by Mitrokhin. NSA spy Ronald Lipka was uncovered when his former KGB case officer, Oleg Kalugin, identified him too closely in his memoirs.[91] KGB senior officer Oleg Gordievsky gave up Norwegian diplomat Arne Treholt and the entire British stable of KGB agents when he defected. The "red diaper" spies (so named because of their affiliation with Communism at a young age), Marie Squillicote, Kurt Stand, and James Dark, were uncovered by the Stasi files.[92]

In fact, the history of U.S. counterintelligence is replete with deus ex machina gifts. In 1938, a naturalized American, William Sebold, born in Germany, reported his recruitment by German Abwehr, and through his efforts the FBI identified over 60 German agents in the United States. The eight German spies who were landed on Long Island from a submarine during World War II were not caught by the FBI's clever efforts, as Director Hoover announced at the time, but because one of the eight phoned the FBI and gave himself up and betrayed his comrades.[93] In 1938, Whittaker Chambers gave State Department Assistant Secretary Adolph Berle a list of GRU spies in the State Department, including Alger Hiss, Lawrence Duggan, and Noel Field. Berle wrote a memo for his diary, incredibly warned Duggan, and then dropped the matter.[94] Hoover refused to even speak to Chambers, who was not believed credible until interviewed by Congress in 1948 (and when his information became confirmed by the Venona intercepts). Similarly, Elizabeth Bentley gave the FBI the names of over 70 NKVD (KGB) agents, but she was not fully believed until the Venona information began verifying her statements in 1948. In 1943, a disgruntled KGB officer sent the FBI an anonymous letter completely identifying every Soviet intelligence officer in Washington D.C.[95] In 1945, the defecting GRU code clerk Igor Gouzenko gave U.S. and Canadian authorities the names of several important GRU spies, including its entire Canadian stable of agents. Vasily Mitrokhin, a KGB archivist, may have presented the greatest gift of all when he defected in 1992—thousands of pages of KGB archives, with clues to hundreds of Soviet spies.[96]

The careers of many spies could have been far shorter and much less damaging had the American counterintelligence community only listened to disgruntled spouses and ex-spouses. The most damaging spy to the United States has been, beyond a shadow of a doubt, John Walker—a judgment shared by former KBG officers Gordievsky and Mitrokhin. Walker spied for the USSR from 1967 to 1985. Yet the damage he did could have been lessened had the FBI paid better attention to two telephone calls: from his ex-wife Barbara and daughter Laura reporting his espionage.[97] In 1982, Patrizia di Palma, the Italian ex-wife of Glenn Souther, a major KGB spy with access to U.S. Navy strategic secrets, reported his espionage to the Naval Investigative Service. Her claim went uninvestigated and Souther spied for three more years before fleeing to the Soviet Union.[98] The wife of Douglas Groat, a CIA official charged in 1998 with passing secrets to a foreign power, stated that she notified the FBI in 1985 that he had passed secrets to two foreign operatives. She claimed she was interviewed by two FBI agents, but her allegations were dismissed because Groat had left her a few months before.[99] These incidents reflect a serious lack of counterintelligence training, and perhaps some male sexist behavior in discounting allegations from a credible source.

The U.S. counterintelligence record on reception of defectors and other volunteers is not strong. Defectors have come to the United States and not been debriefed on a timely basis, if at all, starting with Georgi Agabekov in 1930, an OGPU (an early version of the KGB) *rezident* who was murdered by the OGPU in 1939. A top GRU officer, "Walter Krivitsky" (true name Samuel Ginsberg), fled to the United States in 1937 to avoid Stalin's death purges. He had no serious reception from the FBI or any other government agency, and had to tell some of his story through a book, *Stalin's Agent,* and articles sold to the now defunct *Saturday Evening Post* magazine. His death in 1941 was almost certainly an NKVD or GRU "hit" to silence him.[100] At the same time, a top NKVD intelligence general, "Alexander Orlov" (true name Leiba Felbin), fled to the United States, also to avoid Stalin's death purges. Orlov was not interviewed by the FBI until 1953, when he sold a denunciation of Stalin to *Life* magazine. An outraged Hoover belatedly ordered an interview, but Orlov successfully concealed his extensive knowledge of Soviet spies from both FBI and CIA interrogations.[101]

More recently, key volunteers have been turned away. Oleg Penkovsky, "the spy who saved the world," was turned away from America's Moscow embassy in 1960.[102] Worse still, spies seeking asylum have been returned to certain execution. Igor Gouzenko was almost given back to the Russians by the Canadians in 1945. To America's national shame, KGB defector Yuri Nosenko was badly and illegally mistreated for three years in the United States, and defector Yuri Loginov, a KGB illegal, was returned from South Africa in 1969 to the Soviets (and was immediately executed) because James Angleton and the CIA were mesmerized by the paranoid ravings of a previous defector, Anatoly Golitsyn.[103] Lastly, in 1991, the CIA's Soviet Operations Chief, Milton Bearden, ordered his field personnel not to accept KGB volunteers, which probably explains why Mitrokhin finally went to the British for asylum.[104]

A strong case can be made that the large majority of the most important spy cases went undetected until someone told the United States about them. This reflects little credit to the entire American counterintelligence community.

Decoding breakthroughs. The biggest bonanza of all came in 1948 when the Army Security Agency, later to become the National Security Agency (NSA), began to solve Soviet wartime intelligence messages that had been intercepted but not previously decoded. These Venona messages ultimately identified by code name some 350 spies. Nearly half of them were identified, including the famous nuclear spies Klaus Fuchs and Ted Hall. The British spy ring known as the "Cambridge Five": Kim Philby, Guy Burgess, Donald Maclean, Anthony Blunt, and John Cairncross were also identified from Venona.

Earlier, in 1940, the British had decoded German military intelligence (Abwehr) messages encoded on the "Enigma" machine, and were able to identify and neutralize or turn every German spy in Britain. Such decoded messages rarely give the name of the spy, but provide clues to his identity, thereby making the counterintelligence community's job much easier. While these breakthroughs are few and far between, when they occur, the counterintelligence forces are given a tremendous leg up in neutralizing the espionage efforts of the target country.

CIA and other agency collection efforts. In 1991, the CIA reportedly purchased the East German Stasi's files, which provided clues to the identification of 13,000 East German spies, from a Russian transport officer in charge of shipping them out of East Germany.[105] Various CIA and FBI recruitments of foreign intelligence officers have identified other officers and their spies. These operations are major sources of counterintelligence leads, but further discussion of this properly belongs in a discussion of intelligence collection, not counterintelligence.

Double agents. Double agents are spies who fall into either of two categories: (a) foreign spies who have been discovered and subsequently agree to work for their counterintelligence captors to avoid penalties; (b) or "dangles," controlled sources who are dangled in front of a foreign intelligence officer, often by directly volunteering to spy, in hopes that the officer will bite and attempt to recruit the dangle. From such agents a counterintelligence officer hopes to learn the identity, method of operation, and spy equipment provided by the intelligence service to "their" spy. The effort also offers an opportunity to preoccupy the other side's officers, keeping them occupied and without time to chase valid targets. Lastly, it offers opportunities for disinformation. The British used their best double agent, codenamed GARBO, to effectively confound the German leadership about the Normandy landings in 1944.[106]

Disinformation has become a separate, "hot" new discipline in the U.S. intelligence community. But information obtained from such double agents is often minimal. Intelligence officers have learned not to expose their best techniques to new, volunteer sources, and to be suspicious of their information. Dangles and double agents must produce good intelligence information or they will be dropped. And making real secrets available to give away in such fashion is often difficult. Only double agents from current or previously denied areas, such as Cuba, East Germany, or the former Soviet Union, have proven really effective because so little is or was known about their countries and governments, and almost any information has been welcomed by intelligence analysts.

Double agents are time-consuming, and the payoff generally so slight, that as a rule the CIA avoids them, leaving them to the military intelligence and the FBI.

IV. Why U.S. Counterintelligence Does Not Work

There are three reasons why United States counterintelligence methods do not work. The first is a problem with U.S. law. The second deals with two American cultural traits which have assumed the importance of fixed and binding customs, or "mores." The third has to do with traditional bureaucratic behavior.

a. U.S. law problems. Since the 1950s Supreme Court under Chief Justice Earl Warren and even earlier, United States espionage law has posed major burdens on the counterintelligence community. Prevailing law is based primarily on the 1917 Espionage Act (now 18 US Code 794) which requires that four elements be proven before an espionage conviction can occur: The accused person must (1) knowingly communicate or deliver to (2) a foreign entity (3) material related to national security (third requirement) with (4) intent to injure the United States, for the advantage of the foreign entity, or for personal gain. For a counterintelligence service to develop and prove all four parts, absent a confession or catching the suspect "in the act," is extraordinarily difficult. For example, a State Department official, Felix Bloch, was observed secretly meeting a known Soviet intelligence officer and passing him papers.[107] But, the U.S. government was unable to prove that the papers contained national security information, and thus Bloch was not even tried. Months and even years of observing a suspect are often required in order to build up a case which would stand up in court. Yet, during this period the spies continue to spy, and, as Ames did, cause even further damage.

Of the many leads to spies provided to U.S. counterintelligence by the Stasi files and Mitrokhin papers, only a handful have yet been brought to trial, largely because meeting the four conditions of proof is difficult when counterintelligence receives information of espionage in years gone by. That explains, for example, why Ted Hall was not prosecuted for his nuclear spying for the KGB in the 1940s.[108] It also explains why FBI agents had to pose as foreign intelligence officers to nail Earl Pitts, Daniel King, Robert Lipka, Robert Boone, and the "red diaper babies."[109]

Even when all four elements appear to have been developed, the government faces the additional problem of the right of "discovery." This first arose at the Judith Coplon trial in 1948. Coplon had been caught passing notes containing classified information to her KGB lover. Her lawyers successfully demanded, under the right of discovery, all FBI files remotely related to the case. J. Edgar Hoover reluctantly agreed, but was so outraged by the negative public reaction to material in the FBI files revealed by the defense that he ordained that the FBI no longer would risk arresting a suspect unless all vital information was protected, and would result in a "slam-dunk" prosecution. One reason why Coplon's conviction was later overturned was that the U.S. government refused to make public the Venona material which identified her as a spy.[110]

This threat of exposure of secret information obtained by the defense under discovery motions is called "greymail." In 1980, Congress, at the urging of the counterintelligence community, provided some relief from greymail by passing the Classified Information Procedures Act (CIPA), which allows the government to present the material ex parte and in camera to the judge, that is, secretly, without the defense present. But this does not relieve the government from giving the defense classified information that is directly relevant, and fear of exposure of this information still constrains counterintelligence agencies and government prosecutors. This fear reportedly inhibited the government from trying both Oliver North and CIA Costa Rica station chief Joseph Fernandez during the Iran-Contra investigations, and to a downgrading of the charges against Douglas Groat.[111]

b. American mores. Alexis de Tocqueville in his treatise on the American people, *Democracy In America*, noted in 1830 that democracies are not good at secrecy or perseverance in foreign affairs. Tocqueville had it right: the sad truth is that Americans do not like or respect secrets. Newspapers are full of leaks of classified information, even from the highest levels of government.

Revelations of secrets are often inadvertent: Ronald Reagan, when denouncing the 1986 terrorist bombing of the "La Belle" discotheque in Berlin, blamed Libya and inadvertently revealed that the NSA had intercepted Libyan communications, a secret of the highest magnitude. Scientist George Keyworth admitted that he had perhaps talked too much about the neutron bomb to Chinese scientists during a visit to China in 1980 but felt no remorse, claiming the information was "just physics."[112] Congressman Robert G. Torricelli (D., New Jersey) made public classified information about Central America, and was shortly thereafter elected to the U.S. Senate. Senator Daniel Patrick Moynihan (D., New York) has attacked government secrecy as undermining the accountability of government to the people, a serious point which has great validity.

Taken together, these are indications of a profound cultural trait which has become one of America's mores, which Webster's Dictionary defines as "the fixed customs or folkways of a particular group that are morally binding upon all members and necessary to its welfare and preservation."

A second U.S. cultural trait is the dislike of informers. Most children are taught that it is bad to "tattle" on others. During the controversy over President Bill Clinton's affairs ABC anchorman Jack Ford, a former practicing attorney, explained on a television show why everyone loathed Linda Tripp, stating that in his experience no jury member likes an informer, and that jurors tend to disregard informer-supplied information.[113] This trait, also a "mor," has serious counterintelligence implications. Defectors are often not well received, and their information is not considered strong evidence in an espionage trial. People are also disinclined to report on others. Sergeant Jeffrey Carney noted that a colleague walked in on him photographing secret documents, but never reported it.[114]

A third "mor" is American distrust of government. This goes back to the beginning of U.S. history as a nation. The federal government was hopelessly weak under the Articles of Confederation because Americans feared a strong central government. Only after the tacking on of a Bill of Rights was the Constitution ratified by the crucial states of New York and Virginia. The writings and statements of Thomas Jefferson and James Madison warn consistently against a strong central government. In modern history, civil libertarians have allied themselves with civil rights advocates and political conservatives in attempting to limit the powers of federal government, as is very well documented by Gary Wills in *A Necessary Evil: A History of American Distrust of Government* (New York: Simon & Schuster, 1999).

The misbehavior and malfeasance of recent Presidents certainly has fed this distrust, as have the exposed transgressions of the FBI and the CIA. The very fact that the United States had neither an intelligence nor a counterintelligence agency for most of its history stands testament to this view. Since the 1960s Hollywood has fed the American fear of government, and especially the FBI, CIA, and NSA, in a plethora of feature films.

c. Bureaucratic behavior. Students of organizational behavior affirm that bureaucracies never give up "turf" or authority. The common bureaucratic response to a shortcoming is to ask for more money and create new bureaucratic entities. That behavior has occurred in the counterintelligence community, most recently in 1994 after the Ames case surfaced. President Clinton, in Presidential Decision Document 24, reshuffled and renamed several counterintelligence coordinating committees. Congress voted lots more money for the FBI and CIA counterintelligence bureaucracies. An FBI officer was put in charge of a new bureaucracy, the National Counterintelligence Center (separate from the CIA's counterintelligence center and the new FBI counterintelligence center), and other FBI officers were inserted at the top level in the CIA's counterintelligence and security offices. This has somewhat improved bureaucratic and organizational communications, albeit largely one way, from CIA to the FBI. The FBI is legendary for not sharing its information with any other agency.

In addition, the FBI has been moving aggressively in the last decade in bureaucratically usurping the authority of its rivals. The FBI attempted a takeover, partly successful, of the Drug Enforcement Administration. In the counterintelligence field, the FBI has upset the intent of the 1947 National Security Act, as well as several Presidential executive orders which mandated that the Bureau would be in charge of counterintelligence at home, with CIA in charge abroad. The FBI has obtained a congressional mandate to investigate terrorist crimes against Americans abroad, and has leveraged this and other congressional grants of authority to challenge the CIA in foreign countries.

In the last two years the FBI has opened many new overseas offices, seriously contesting traditional CIA turf in dealing with foreign intelligence and security organizations.[115] This has created further bureaucratic muddle and moved the FBI into operations where it has little expertise nor a necessary freedom of action. Sam Papich, a senior FBI officer, stated in response to Senate legislation (the Boren-Cohen Bill) which would have given all counterintelligence authority to the FBI, that the FBI was incapable of doing CIA duties abroad, which necessarily involve breaking the laws of foreign countries.[116] The author and journalist Mark Riebling noted that three "solutions" have been proposed for U.S. counterintelligence problems: give all counterintelligence to the FBI (supported by then Senators Dennis DeConcini, [D., Arizona], William Cohen [R., Maine], and David Boren [D., Oklahoma]); give all counterintelligence to the CIA (supported by Congressman Larry Combest [R., Texas]); or create a third, "super" organization which would command both the FBI and CIA in counterintelligence (variations attributed to Kenneth de Graffenried, former CIA counterintelligence officer Newton "Scotty" Miler, and former National Security Adviser Anthony Lake).[117] My thesis is that none of these will work bureaucratically or politically. The best that can be reasonably expected is some improvement in coordination between the CIA's overseas collection and counterintelligence roles and the FBI's domestic counterintelligence role. And the swing toward throwing more authority at the FBI to a large degree adds to the bureaucratic muddle and will not improve counterintelligence, merely competition.[118]

Notably, after each major spy scandal, counterintelligence coordination improves between agencies. Some of the reforms have also improved interagency communication. But basic bureaucratic behavior consistently precludes developing an efficient counterintelligence system. This was best evidenced when, in 1981, de Graffenried became the Intelligence Director on the National Security Council Staff. He was committed to creating a single effective counterintelligence czar or oversight staff to mandate coordination between the FBI and

CIA, and otherwise improve coordination and training in those agencies. But in his seven years on the White House Staff, de Graffenried, even with his incredible talent, and despite his best efforts and the authority of his office was able to achieve only minor, piecemeal reforms.[119] Bureaucratic inertia and self-defense was too strong.

V. Sea Change Needed

> When you're catching spies, you have a bad counterintelligence service. When you're not catching spies, you have a bad counterintelligence service. You can't have it both ways!
>
> —*Judge William Webster, former Director of Central Intelligence*

An examination of its component parts shows United States counterintelligence to be indeed broken. Bureaucratic rivalries, American ethics and mores, and operational realities show that a truly effective U.S. counterintelligence program cannot be effected without a sea change in American political attitudes.

Questions for Further Discussion

1. According to Wettering, what are the primary goals of counterintelligence?

2. How can one share intelligence more effectively—a core recommendation of committees investigating the 9/11 intelligence failure—while at the same time maintaining the principles of "need to know" and compartmentation?

3. What forms of counterintelligence tradecraft does Wettering find most effective?

4. Why is Wettering skeptical about the successful practice of counterintelligence by the United States?

Endnotes

1. George Kalaris and Leonard McCoy, "Counterintelligence for the 1990s." *International Journal of Intelligence and Counterintelligence*, Vol. 2, No. 2, Summer 1987, pp. 179–187.
2. Energy Secretary Bill Richardson's Address to the National Press Club, 3 March 1999.
3. Letter from J. Edgar Hoover to Major General Edwin M. Watson, Secretary to the President, dated 13 December 1940, which forwarded the attached Beck memorandum to President Roosevelt. See also Ambassador Charles "Chip" Bohlen's recollections of lax security in his memoirs, *Witness To History* (New York: W. W. Norton, 1973), especially p. 15.
4. Ray Bearse and Anthony Read, *Conspirator: The Untold Story of Tyler Kent* (New York: Doubleday, 1991), p. 36. See also the Beck Report (footnote 1) for discussion of Embassy employees Donald Nichols, John Morgan, Sylvester Huntkowski, and James Lewis and their Soviet paramours.
5. Mark Riebling, *Wedge: The Secret War Between the FBI and CIA* (New York: Alfred A. Knopf, 1994), p. 351.
6. Reuters, cited in *Toronto Globe and Mail*, 21 March 1997.
7. Ronald Kessler, *Moscow Station: How the KGB Penetrated the American Embassy* (New York: Pocket Books, 1989), pp. 29–30.
8. Ibid., pp. 107–109.
9. Ibid., pp. 12–16.
10. Frank Greve, "In the World of Espionage, France Emerges as U.S. Adversary," *Philadelphia Inquirer*, 24 October 1992. Also, same author and paper, 18 April 1993.
11. Peter Schweitzer, *Friendly Spies: How America's Allies Are Using Economic Espionage to Steal Our Secrets* (New York: Atlantic Monthly Press, 1993), pp. 96–126.
12. Nicholas Eftimiades, *Chinese Intelligence Operations* (Annapolis, MD: Naval Institute Press, 1994), pp. 28–29. See also Vernon Loeb, "Chinese Spy Methods Limit Bid to Find Truth, Officials Say," *Washington Post*, 21 March 1999, and Bill Gertz, "Big Rise in Chinese Visitors Poses an Intelligence Threat," *Washington Times*, 18 January 1992.
13. See General Accounting Office, GAO/RCED-87-72, *DOE Reinvestigation of Employees Has Not Been Timely*, 1987, and GAO/RCED 89–31, *Major Weaknesses in Foreign Visitor Controls At Weapons Laboratories*, 1989.
14. President's Foreign Intelligence Advisory Board Report (Rudman Commission), *Science at Its Best, Security at Its Worst: A Report on Security Problems at the U.S. Department of Energy*, June 1999 (henceforth PFIAB Report). My copy was obtained from the Federation of American Scientists (FAS) website, <www.fas.org>, making page citation problematical. See p. 11 of the chapter "Recurring Vulnerabilities" in the FAS download.
15. Paul Redmond interview, *NBC Meet the Press*, 12 December 1999. See also Bill Gertz, "Pentagon Lets in Russians," *Washington Times*, 22 June 1993.
16. Yuri Shvets, *Washington Station: My Life as a KGB Spy in America* (New York: Simon & Schuster, 1994), p. 35.
17. Redmond interview, NBC's "Meet the Press." See also, "State Department Tightens Security After Loss of Secret Documents," *Washington Post*, 20 March 1998.
18. William Broad and Judith Miller, "Scientists Criticize Limits on Foreign Visitors to Laboratories," *New York Times*, 3 December 1999.
19. *U.S. National Security and Military/Commercial Concerns With the Peoples' Republic of China.* Select Committee, United States House of Representatives, (Washington, D.C.: U.S. Government Printing Office, 1999) Vol. 1, p. 39 (hereafter, Cox Report).
20. Broad and Miller, op cit.
21. Ibid.
22. Ibid.
23. Ruth Sinai, "It's Not So Hard to Walk Out with Secret Documents," Associated Press, 5 August 1993.
24. John Grey, "Gaffes Damage Intelligence Agency's Image," *South China Morning Post*, 6 December 1999.
25. PFIAB Report. The citation is found at the section entitled "Root Causes," p. 5.

26. Lynn Fischer, "Espionage: Why Does It Happen?," *Security Awareness Bulletin*, Department of Defense Security Institute (DoDSI), Number 1-94, pp. 1–8.

27. Christopher Andrew and Oleg Gordievsky, *KGB: The Inside Story of Its Foreign Operations from Lenin to Gorbachev* (London: Hodder and Stoughton, 1990), p. 381.

28. Walter Pincus, "Huge Backlog for Security Checks Tied to Pentagon Computer Woes," *Washington Post*, 30 November 1999. See also, Walter Pincus "900,000 People Awaiting Pentagon Security Clearances," *Washington Post*, 20 April 2000.

29. Norman Polmar and Thomas B. Allen, *Spy Book: The Encyclopedia of Espionage* (New York: Random House, 1997), p. 179.

30. The Maldon Institute, "America's Espionage Epidemic," Washington D.C., 1996, pp. 22–23.

31. On Martin and Mitchell, see Polmar and Allen, op. cit., pp. 356, 372.

32. On Ames, see Ibid, p. 22.

33. See Ibid., pp. 56 (Bell), 83 (Boyce), 104 (Cavanagh), 254 (Harper).

34. Pincus, "Huge backlog...."

35. U.S. Department of Energy, *Counterintelligence Newsletter*, 1997, p. 4.

36. David Wise, "The Spy Who Sold the Farm," *GQ Magazine*, March 1998, p. 294.

37. Maldon Institute, op. cit. pp. 30–33.

38. Andrew and Gordievsky, op. cit., p. 381.

39. Bob Drogin, "Secrets, Science Are Volatile Mixture at Los Alamos," *Los Angeles Times*, 1 April 1999.

40. Vernon Loeb, "Polygraphs Start for 5,000 at Energy," *Washington Post*, 21 June 1999.

41. Walter Pincus and Vernon Loeb, "Lie Tests Anger Lab Scientists," *Washington Post*, 23 September 1999.

42. Walter Pincus and Vernon Loeb, "Energy Chief to Allow Foreign Scientists to Visit Labs," *Washington Post*, 3 December 1999.

43. Vernon Loeb, "Senators Challenge Energy Polygraph Plan," *Washington Post*, 26 September 1999.

44. David G. Savage, "High Court Bars Use of Polygraph Test as Defense," *Los Angeles Times*, 1 April 1998. See also Aaron Epstein, "Ruling Rejects Lie Detector Evidence," *Philadelphia Inquirer*, 1 April 1998.

45. PFIAB Report, p. 8 of the section, "Recurring Vulnerabilities."

46. Brooke Masters, "Va. Man Sentenced to 9 Years in Spy Case," *Washington Post*, 12 July 1997.

47. Former FBI China analyst Paul Moore, quoted in Vernon Loeb, "Inside Information," *Washington Post*, 18 October 1999. Also see Paul Moore, "Spies of a Different Stripe," *Washington Post*, 31 May 1999.

48. Erik Eckholm, "China Detects Racism in U.S. Report on Spying," *New York Times*, 1 June 1999. Also, Fox Butterfield and Joseph Kahn, "Chinese in U.S. Say Spying Casts Doubt on Their Loyalties," *New York Times*, 16 May 1999, and David Stout, "Lee's Defenders Say Scientist Is Victim of Witch Hunt Against China," *New York Times*, 11 December 1999.

49. *New York Times*, 23 October 1994, p. 36.

50. Ralph Vartabedian, "Asian-American Workers View Hughes Memo as Ethnic Insult," *Los Angeles Times*, 27 July 1993.

51. Kevin Galvin, "Jewish Group Protests ... ," Associated Press, 29 January 1996.

52. General Accounting Office, GAO/T-NSIAD-96-114, *Economic Espionage: Information on Threat from U.S. Allies*, 28 February 1996.

53. Cox Report, Vol. 1, p. 94.

54. PFIAB Report, p. 9 of section "Recurring Vulnerabilities."

55. Cliff Stoll, *The Cuckoo's Egg* (New York: Simon & Schuster, 1989).

56. Chris Albritton, Associated Press, 28 April 1998.

57. Roberto Suro, "FBI Cyber Squad Termed Too Small," *Washington Post*, 1 October 1999.

58. Lisa Hoffman, *Washington Times*, 24 October 1999.

59. Roberto Suro, op. cit.

60. Kessler, *Moscow Station*, p. 25.

61. Christopher Andrew and Vasily Mitrokhin, *The Sword and The Shield: The Mitrokhin Archive and the Secret History of the KGB* (New York: Basic Books, 1999), pp. 338, 342.

62. Mark Reibling, *Wedge*, p. 361.

63. David A. Vise and Steve Mufson, "State Dept. Bug Seen as Major Security Breach," *Washington Post*, 9 December 1999.

64. Andrew and Mitrokhin, op. cit, pp. 337–354.

65. Juan Tamayo, "Soviets Spied on Gulf War Plans from Cuba, Defector Says," *Miami Herald*, 3 April 1998.

66. Dana Priest, "Serbs Listening in on NATO," *Washington Post*, 1 May 1999.

67. Terry Atlas, "French Spy Charges Highlight Trade Wars," *Chicago Tribune*, 23 February 1995, and Alan Cowell, "Bonn Said to Expel U.S. Envoy Accused of Economic Spying," *New York Times*, 10 March 1997.

68. Andrew and Gordievsky, pp. 523–524.

69. Redmond, *Meet the Press*.

70. David A. Vise and Vernon Loeb, "State Department Bugged: Russian Accused of Spying," *Washington Post*, 9 December 1999.

71. "Rendezvous at the Cockatoo: The Cavanagh Case," *Security Awareness Bulletin*, No. 1-86, December 1985, Department of Defense Security Institute (DoDSI), Richmond, Va., p. 2.

72. *Recent Espionage Cases: Summaries and Sources*, July, 1997, DoDSI Richmond.

73. Shvets, *Washington Station*, pp. 40–41, 53–56; Pawel Monat and John Dille, *Spy in the U.S.* (New York: Berkeley, 1961), pp. 22–28, 46–53; Ronald Kessler, *Spy vs. Spy* (New York: Scribner's, 1988), pp. 36–37, 124–125.

74. Robert Lamphere and Tom Schachtman, *The FBI-KGB War: A Special Agent's Story* (New York: Random House, 1986), p. 64. Also, Max Lowenthal, *The Federal Bureau of Investigation* (New York: William Sloane, 1950), p. 433.

75. David Wise, *The Spy Who Got Away* (New York: Random House, 1988), pp. 198–205.

76. Excerpt from *The Enemy Within*, by Tim Weiner, David Johnson, and Neil Lewis, published in *Rolling Stone*, 29 June 1995, p. 34. See also *Betrayal: The Story of Aldrich Ames, American Spy*, same authors (New York: Random House, 1995) pp. 228–229.

77. William Corson and Robert Crowley, *The New KGB: Engine of Soviet Power*, (New York: William Morrow, 1985), p. 461.

78. Michael Sniffen, "FBI Is Conducting 200 Spy Investigations," Associated Press, 2 February 1997. See also Frank Swoboda, "Economic Espionage Rising, FBI Director Tells Congress," *Washington Post*, 29 February 1996.

79. James Rowley, "FBI Seeking Scores of Once-KGB Spies, Book Says," Associated Press, 3 August 1993. The author is quoting from Ronald Kessler's book, *The FBI*.

80. *Washington Post*, 22 November 1998.

81. Bill Gertz, "Woolsey Expects Exposure of More Spies," *Washington Times,* 20 April 1994.

82. John Earl Haynes and Harvey Klehr, *VENONA: Decoding Soviet Espionage in America* (New Haven, CT: Yale University Press, 1999), p. 339.

83. Weiner, Johnson and Lewis, *Betrayal,* p. 37.

84. The four Americans who worked for Stasi and have been tried are the three "Red Diaper" spies, Kurt Stand, Marie Squillicote, and James Michael Clark, and an American nuclear researcher in Germany (tried by the Germans), Jeffrey Schevitz. Stand, Squillicote, and Clark confessed; while Schevitz admitted spying, he also unsuccessfully claimed that he was a double agent for the CIA. See the public indictment of Squillicote et. al. See also Tim Weiner, "Spies Just Wouldn't Come in from The Cold," *New York Times,* 15 October 1997; Jamie Dettmer "Stasi Lured Americans to Spy for E. Germany," *Washington Times,* 14 November 1994; and Terence Petty, "American Arrested as Suspect Spy for Former East Germany," Associated Press, 5 May 1994.

85. Lamphere and Schachtman, p. 273.

86. Jeffrey Richelson, *A Century of Spies: Intelligence in the Twentieth Century* (New York: Oxford University Press, 1995), pp. 272–274. Also, Andrew and Mitrokhin, p. 438.

87. Richelson, pp. 390–391.

88. Ibid., pp. 395–396.

89. Ibid., p. 375.

90. Walter Pincus, "Paper Cites ex-Soviet Envoy in Spy Hunt," *Washington Post,* 27 December 1996.

91. Andrey Streletsky, "Another Russian Spy Arrested," *Moscow Nezavisimaya Gazeta,* 27 February 1996. See also Oleg Kalugin and Fen Montaigne, *The First Directorate: My 32 Years in Intelligence and Espionage Against the West* (New York: St. Martin's Press), pp. 82–83.

92. Walter Pincus, "FBI Finds Leads in Files of Former East German Spy Service," *Washington Post,* 11 October 1997.

93. The German cases have been well-documented in a Columbia House television history series titled "Spies" that has run on several channels. The History Channel has also done documentaries on the ill-fated German spies.

94. Sam Tanenhaus, *Whittaker Chambers: A Biography* (New York: Random House, 1997), pp. 162–163.

95. Jim Wolf, "Anonymous 1943 Letter to FBI Unmasked Soviet Spies," Reuters, 3 October 1996.

96. See Andrew and Mitrokhin, op. cit.

97. John Barren, *Breaking the Ring* (Boston: Houghton Mifflin, 1987), pp. 42–44.

98. Ronald Kessler, *The Spy in the Russian Club* (New York: Scribner's, 1990), pp. 49–51.

99. James Risen, "Warning on Spy Ignored, Ex-Wife Says," *Los Angeles Times,* 8 April 1998.

100. For a discussion of Krivitsky's death, see Eugene Lyons, *The Red Decade* (Arlington House, 1941), pp. 378–379.

101. John Costello and Oleg Tsarev, *Deadly Illusions* (New York: Crown, 1993), pp. 340–341. The book discusses Orlov's career and how he evaded revealing any NKVD secrets.

102. Jerrold L. Schecter and Peter Deriabin, *The Spy Who Saved the World* (New York: Scribners, 1992), pp. 5–6.

103. Chris Steyn, "Ex-KGB General Meets Former State Security Chief," *Johannesburg Star,* 23 September 1995. See also Corson and Crowley, *The New KGB,* pp. 350–351.

104. James Risen, "An Extraordinary Link for Archenemies in Spying," *Los Angeles Times,* 31 December 1997.

105. Jamie Dettmer, "Stasi Lured Americans to Spy in E. Germany," *Washington Times,* 14 November 1994.

106. J. C. Masterman, *The Double-Cross System in the War of 1939–1945* (New Haven, CT: Yale University Press, 1972), pp. 156–157.

107. David Wise, "Was Oswald a Spy, and Other Cold War Mysteries," *New York Times Magazine,* 6 December 1992, p. 36.

108. See Joseph Albright and Marcia Kunstel, *Bombshell: The Secret Story of America's Unknown Atomic Spy Conspiracy* (New York: Random House, 1997), for a semi-confession from Hall to his spying.

109. On Pitts, see Charles W. Hall and Ann O'Hanlon, "Espionage Suspect Depicted as Eager to Sell His Loyalty," *Washington Post,* 19 December 1996; "Navy Petty Officer Charged with Giving Secrets to Russia," Reuters/*Orlando Sentinel,* 30 November 1999 (King); William Carlen, "How the FBI Broke Spy Case That Baffled Agency for 30 Years," *Wall Street Journal,* 21 November 1996 (Lipka); James Risen, "Spy Agency's ex-Analyst Arrested," *New York Times,* 14 October 1998 (Boone); Brooke Masters, "DC Couples' Spymaster Testifies," *Washington Post,* 9 October 1998.

110. Lamphere and Schachtman, *The FBI-KGB War,* pp. 100–104; 107–123.

111. In Raymond Bonner, "Prosecution Will Mean Tug of War Over Secrets," *New York Times,* 11 December 1999.

112. James Risen, "In China, Physicist Learns, He Tripped Between Useful Exchange and Security Breach," *New York Times,* 1 August 1999.

113. Jack Ford on MSNBC's "Imus in the Morning," 17 December 1999.

114. Jeff Stein, "The Mole's Manual," *New York Times,* 5 July 1994. See also "Turning a Blind Eye to Spies," *Harper's Magazine,* September 1994, p. 16.

115. R. Jeffrey Smith and Thomas Lippman, "FBI Plans to Expand Overseas," *Washington Post,* 20 September 1996.

116. Riebling, *Wedge,* p. 458.

117. Ibid., p. 459.

118. Jim McGee, "The Rise of the FBI," *Washington Post Magazine,* 20 July 1997, pp. 10–15, 25–26.

119. See Kenneth de Graffenried, "Building for a New Counterintelligence Capability: Recruitment and Training," in Roy Godson, *Intelligence Requirements for the 1980s: Counterintelligence* (Washington, D.C.: National Strategy Information Center, 1980), pp. 261–272. Also, see Mark Riebling, *Wedge,* pp. 349, 364, 393, 395, 399, 455–456, 459. ✦

Reprinted with permission from Frederick L. Wettering, "Counterintelligence: The Broken Triad," *International Journal of Intelligence and Counterintelligence* 13 (Fall 2000): 265–299.

Part VIII

Accountability and Civil Liberties

Hamlet: "Come, come, and sit you
down, you shall not budge,
You go not till I set you up a glass
Where you may see the inmost part of you."

—*Shakespeare*, Hamlet, 3.4.17–20

Virtually every nation in the world has a secret intelligence apparatus, whether just a few agents in key foreign capitals (if the nation is poor) or a vast network of humans and machines for spying around the world (if the nation is affluent). By collecting information from abroad and by engaging in the companion activities of counterintelligence and covert action, an intelligence establishment can help provide a shield against external threats—what the first President George Bush, a former Director of Central Intelligence (DCI), liked to call the nation's "first line of defense."

The Special Case of Intelligence

In most nations, intelligence agencies are treated as exceptions from the rest of government. They are cloaked in secrecy, allowed exceptional access to policymakers, and given leeway to get the job done—even if that means breaking laws overseas (almost always the case) and engaging in unsavory activities that would be deemed inappropriate for other government agencies. From the beginning, the United States embraced this laissez-faire philosophy for intelligence activities, even as its leaders sought to "bind down" the rest of the government "with the chains of the Constitution" (as Thomas Jefferson expressed the theory of checks and balances in his draft of the Kentucky Resolu-

tions in 1798). The Founders well understood the dangers from abroad to the new Republic and were willing to grant broad discretionary powers to America's intelligence officers as they endeavored to protect the nation from foreign threats.

As the United States matured and its intelligence service expanded in the aftermath of World War II, this hands-off philosophy continued. The Cold War against the communist world required a strong and flexible intelligence shield; in the nuclear age, a nation might not survive another surprise attack like the one that shook the nation at Pearl Harbor. A top secret study group reported to the Eisenhower Administration in 1954 that

> we are facing an implacable enemy whose avowed objective is world domination by whatever means and at whatever cost. There are no rules in such a game. Acceptable norms of human conduct do not apply. We must develop effective espionage and counterespionage services. We must learn to subvert, sabotage and we must destroy our enemies by more clear, more sophisticated and more effective methods than those used against us. (Church Committee 1976, 9)

In light of these hostile conditions, the CIA and its fellow agencies would have to be set loose to fight the communists. If the United States were to win this ideological battle, often fought "in the back alleys of the world" (as Secretary of State Dean Rusk often described this hidden side of the Cold War), America's intelligence agencies would have to be as tough and as effective as anything the Soviet Union could field.

This is not to say the CIA was without supervision, even in this warlike climate (however "cold"). Most of its activities were approved by the White

House and were reported, in broad outline at least, to small oversight subcommittees in the House and Senate. The approvals were highly discretionary, however, allowing DCIs broad scope to fill in the details in this struggle against communism; and reporting to Congress was usually sketchy, perfunctory, and frequently rebuffed. "No, no, my boy, don't tell me," a leading Senator overseer, John Stennis (D, Mississippi), told DCI James R. Schlesinger in 1973 when he tried to provide a full accounting of the CIA's operations abroad. "Just go ahead and do it, but I don't want to know!" (Johnson 2000, 202).

Model democracy or not, the United States would follow the practice of other nations—democracies and dictatorships alike—in placing the secret agencies outside the normal framework of governmental supervision. If Americans were to be secure, a hostile world demanded no less.

An Abrupt Change of Philosophy

In 1975, this philosophy of intelligence exceptionalism changed dramatically, a rare occurrence in this or any other government. The shift resulted not from any sudden sea change in world affairs; that would not happen until the dissolution of the Soviet Empire in 1991. Rather, the stimulus arose from revelations at home regarding alleged abuses of power by the CIA (Johnson 1980, 1985, 1989; Smist 1994). Looking into charges of malfeasance published by the *New York Times*, government investigators uncovered a startling number of transgressions during this season of inquiry known as the "Year of Intelligence" (or what many intelligence officers recall more ruefully as the "Intelligence Wars").

The horrors that emerged from the investigations included assassination plots against foreign leaders; illegal mail openings, wiretaps, and interception of international cable traffic; intelligence files on over a million American citizens; improper drug experiments and unlawful sequestering of dangerous chemicals and biological materials; a master spy plan to conduct surveillance against Vietnam war dissenters in the United States; intelligence infiltration into a wide range of groups in American society, from universities to religious and media organizations; incitement of violence against African American groups; and covert actions abroad aimed not just at autocracies but at democratically elected regimes as well.

The effects of this breathtaking catalog of secret government excesses were profound. From then on, America's support for a muscular, unbound intelligence capability would have to compete with another value long central to the rest of America's government: liberty—safeguarding the American

people against the power of their own government, not only foreign governments. Beginning in 1975, the nation's leaders undertook an unprecedented experiment to balance security and liberty with respect to its secret agencies. In contrast, most other democracies continued to shelter their intelligence services under a special status outside the purview of parliamentary overseers.

The Experiment in Accountability Unfolds

In the United States, reformers shed the traditional exceptionalism bestowed on intelligence in favor of a new kind of experiment in an intelligence partnership between the legislative and executive branches. America's intelligence agencies could be subjected to the norms of rigorous accountability, a hallmark of constitutional government (Currie 1998; Snider 1997). This era of enhanced supervision, following 30 years of benign neglect by Congress, began with the establishment of three new oversight panels: a Senate Select Committee on Intelligence (SSCI, in 1976), a White House Intelligence Oversight Board (IOB, 1976), and a House Permanent Select Committee on Intelligence (HPSCI, 1977).

The Congressional committees have authority to hold hearings on intelligence matters, whether routine or in response to charges of impropriety; to scrutinize annual budgets line by line; to inspect intelligence facilities at home and abroad; to draft intelligence legislation; and, in the Senate, to conduct confirmation hearings on nominations for the office of DCI and other top intelligence managers. On behalf of the president, the IOB carries out special inquiries into allegations of abuse.

The thoroughness with which these groups pursue their duties depends on how much media attention is focused on claims of wrongdoing, as well as on the philosophy of members toward the concept of intelligence accountability (for some, an oxymoron). Among the members of these three panels, a few have expressed the view that intelligence should return to its status as a special case, with only the lightest supervision from Capitol Hill. They join the chorus of antireformers inside and outside the government who look on the new oversight as an exercise in "micromanagement"—too many legislative fingers clumsily probing into delicate intelligence operations that require quickness, skill, and secrecy for success.

Barry Goldwater (R, Arizona) provides an example of the antireformist view. Ironically having risen to the chairmanship of the Senate Intelligence Committee, whose creation he opposed, the Senator opined in 1982: "When it comes to covert operations, it would be best if they [the CIA's leaders] did-

Part VIII ◆ Introduction 343

n't have to tell us anything." The antireformers complain, too, that legislators cannot be trusted with the nation's secrets; loquacious by nature, politicians will invariably babble—perhaps inadvertently, or even on purpose if they oppose a secret operation (a "leak item veto"). Senator Goldwater viewed his own legislative chamber as a place with "more leaks than the men's room at Anhauser-Busch" (Johnson 1996, 52).

In rebuttal, pro-reformers are quick to recite the litany of abuses uncovered in 1975 that led to new oversight in the first place. They echo James Madison's warnings about the corrupting nature of power and the need to have "ambition counteract ambition" (*Federalist Paper* No. 51), pitting one branch of government against another. They dismiss the micromanagement criticism, noting that—despite the tightened supervision—secret operations have moved swiftly forward when necessary. They argue, too, that leaks from Capitol Hill (as opposed to the executive branch) have been few and insignificant.

The very existence of this debate over intelligence reform raises eyebrows in most countries. Leaders overseas, even in fellow democracies, find it difficult to understand why the United States would intentionally seek to handicap its intelligence agencies—just as they failed to understand why Americans insisted on pursuing the Watergate investigation in 1974, at the expense of discrediting their own government and driving an incumbent president from office in shame.

Even at home, the experiment has hardly been a smooth evolution toward some golden mean of accountability agreed on by everyone. On the contrary, it has been characterized by fits and starts. Among the enduring features have been an executive order prohibiting assassination plots against foreign leaders (1976); a Foreign Intelligence Surveillance Act (1978), which establishes judicial safeguards against overzealous wiretaps for purposes of national security; strict reporting requirements, which force the secret agencies to keep Congressional overseers informed of intelligence operations and the discovery of abuse inside their high walls; persistent questioning by lawmakers and staff that requires intelligence managers to explain and defend their budgets and programs; and expectations on Capitol Hill that intelligence reports will be shared with the Congressional intelligence committees on the same footing as executive officials.

More contentious has been the question of when the intelligence agencies should inform Congress about their operations, especially controversial covert actions designed to manipulate foreign governments. Should the reports come before or after these operations are launched? After demanding "prior notification" in a 1980 statute, lawmakers retreated somewhat (under pressure from President George H. W. Bush in 1991) to the current prescription of prior reporting in most cases but with an escape hatch for the president of a couple of days delay in times of emergency. Any delay, though, must be fully explained to the two oversight committees at the time the report is sent to Congress. This strikes most people as a sensible compromise and is a good illustration of the constructive debate on intelligence between the legislative and executive branches of government that has gone on since 1975.

Balancing Liberty and Security: An Unfinished Story

The current equilibrium between liberty and security in the intelligence domain has failed to satisfy everyone. On the reform side, some have called for the abolition of the CIA, particularly in light of its failure to predict the U.S.S.R.'s disintegration in 1991 (although it did better in tracking the Soviet decline, especially the economic dimension, than is usually acknowledged). On the antireform side, the criticism of legislative micromanagement continues, with commentators advocating a repeal of the assassination prohibition; the unprecedented use of the Peace Corps as a cover for CIA officers abroad; the adoption of media, academic, and clerical credentials by intelligence officers; and more aggressive participation in coups d'état against regimes deemed unfriendly to the United States—all activities deemed inappropriate by reformers in 1975 (Johnson 2002). A central goal of the antireformers remains dismantlement of the three oversight panels, removing what they see as undue constraints on the intelligence agencies.

Even those not on the extremes of this debate have raised troubling questions about the success of the experiment. At times the secret agencies have simply ignored Congress and the IOB, as if the new oversight rules were so much flotsam in the wake of the ship of state as it plows through the turbulent seas of international affairs. During the Iran-*contra* affair of the Reagan Administration (a full decade into the new oversight), the staff of the National Security Council (NSC) bypassed Congress to raise secret funds for its covert actions in Nicaragua from foreign potentates and private citizens within the United States, making a mockery of Congress' power of the purse and, therefore, of constitutional government. Officers of the CIA and the NSC staff also lied to legislative investigators about their involvement in the affair. When the less-than-forthright nature of his testimony became clear, one high-ranking CIA officer proffered this gloss: he had been "technically correct, if specifically evasive." This is not exactly the sort of comity the new spirit of intelligence partnership and accountability was meant to engender.

More recently, the CIA failed to inform legislative overseers of its ties to Col. Julio Roberto Alpirez in Guatemala, an unsavory agent charged with murder. Further, the National Reconnaissance Office (NRO) misled legislators about major cost overruns in its new headquarters buildings, as well as the NRO's improper accumulation of unspent appropriated funds. Although less serious than the blow struck against democratic procedures by the Iran-*contra* affair, neither of these cases did anything to nurture the bonds of trust and cooperation between the branches that are so vital for accountability to succeed.

While the intelligence agencies have occasionally transgressed against both the spirit and the letter of the law behind the new oversight, Congress, too, has been far from perfect in meeting its responsibilities. Some members and staff have been dedicated overseers, trying to make the balance between liberty and security succeed. They have pored over intelligence budgets and asked probing questions of intelligence officials during open and closed hearings. Others, though, have been distracted, perhaps less interested in the subject, facing a tough reelection bid, or simply true believers in the pre-1975 philosophy of laissez-faire for the secret agencies. Keeping the balance has required the devotion of at least a few individuals willing to dedicate the necessary time to maintain the eternal vigilance that is the price of liberty, and usually there have been a few lawmakers so disposed—but not many. Particularly important have been the attitudes of the chairs of the House and Senate intelligence committees, and that has been a mixed record: Some have been dynamic overseers while others have been rather passive.

A Qualified Success

With the major exception of Iran-*contra*—an appalling lapse in accountability from which, presumably, the nation has learned some lessons—the watchdogs on the oversight panels have been sufficient in number and commitment to make the experiment a qualified success, unless one believes that secret agencies ought to be abolished or, at the opposite extreme, that they should be given the broad leeway they once enjoyed. Although the current state of intelligence accountability is still imperfect and subject to ongoing debate and adjustment (like democracy itself), most government officials and observers agree that it represents a workable balance between the two important values of security and liberty.

Certainly most people who have closely examined the subject value the contribution made by secret agencies to America's security. During the Cold War, the eyes and ears of these agencies helped keep a third world war at bay by providing a reasonably clear understanding of Soviet military capabilities and activities. Indeed, the modern espionage capabilities of both superpowers greatly reduced anxieties and the likelihood of hair-trigger responses on either side of the Iron Curtain. Moreover, no one wants to see a return to the abuses of power by the secret agencies that were revealed to the American people by the Church Committee during the Year of Intelligence.

Close followers of intelligence issues also understand that the key to a stronger U.S. intelligence capability lies not in upsetting the current oversight arrangements that were so carefully hammered out on the anvil of experience by bipartisan majorities over the years since 1975. Rather, improved performance will require organizational and attitudinal changes within the executive branch. The needed reforms include, above all, further strengthening of the DCI's authority over community-wide budgets and appointments. Otherwise, the intelligence "community" will remain a collection of tribal fiefdoms with little interest in working together and sharing information.

Even more important to the success of American intelligence will be a willingness on behalf of policymakers to clarify their precise intelligence needs to the secret agencies in a timely fashion, then listen with an open mind to the findings of these agencies. This seemingly simple and obvious requirement has, nonetheless, become the Achilles heel of American intelligence—especially the problem of listening. All too often policymakers have shunted aside accurate intelligence that failed to conform with their preconceptions or ideological preferences or, worse still, have exaggerated the intelligence they have received in order to bolster their policy arguments. This charge has been made by critics of the administrations of President George W. Bush and U.K. Prime Minister Tony Blair with respect to the possible existence of weapons of mass destruction in Iraq in 2003. Both are said to have hyped the threat to gain public support for a military invasion.

An Immutable Principle for Democracies

A free government must maintain security from foreign and internal threats or it will not survive, but it must have liberty at home as well. A true democracy depends on both. In his memoir, former DCI Robert M. Gates (1996) writes,

> . . . some awfully crazy schemes might well have been approved had everyone present [in the White House] not known and expected hard questions, debate, and criticism from the Hill. And when, on a few occasions, Congress was kept in the dark, and such schemes did proceed, it was nearly always to the lasting regret of the presidents involved. (p. 559)

Here is another reminder of the necessity for checks on the use of executive power—especially secret executive power. Accountability is a tenet of free government that remains as valid today as it did when it animated the thinking of the Founders and the writing of the American Constitution over 200 years ago.

The Readings

In the first selection, Gregory F. Treverton spells out the importance of bringing the intelligence agencies into the normal framework of American government, facing the rigors of accountability just like the more open agencies have always experienced. He refers to the new intelligence oversight as an "uncompleted experiment" and notes that the new procedures, though certainly an improvement on the overlook approach of an earlier era, are still "no guarantee against stupid presidential decisions" (such as the Iran-contra affair).

Frederick P. Hitz, an attorney and former CIA Inspector General, offers a rather different view, as the title of his article suggests: "Unleashing the Rogue Elephant: September 11 and Letting the CIA Be the CIA." In 1975, Senator Frank Church, who had just learned about the CIA's involvement in assassination plots against foreign leaders, accused the Agency on a national television news show of behaving like a rogue elephant on a rampage. Hitz seeks fewer restraints on the intelligence agencies so they can combat terrorism more energetically, though he is quick to add that "it is equally important that these changes not throw the CIA back into the pre-1974 era of limited Congressional oversight and little executive branch accountability that led to earlier excesses." The debate over where to draw the line between security and liberty is ongoing, with Hitz seeking to place it a little more toward the security side.

Just as intelligence reform has become a lively topic since the mid-1970s, so has attention to the ethics of intelligence operations. Are there moral standards spies should obey, or is to speak of ethics in the same breath as intelligence an absurdity? E.

Drexel Godfrey, Jr. takes on this question and emphasizes that "at the heart intelligence is rooted in the severest of ethical principles: truth telling." He takes the reader through a series of ethical dilemmas related to espionage, counterintelligence, and covert action, then ends where he began: underscoring the paramount need for the CIA's leadership "to establish beyond question the capacity of its experts and its facilities to seek and find the truth, or the nearest approximation of the truth possible." The importance of a factual orientation for intelligence agencies is why, in 2003, the allegations in the United States and the United Kingdom that perhaps the intelligence services of both nations had not been entirely forthright about the danger—or lack of danger—posed by the Saddam Hussein regime in Iraq struck a raw nerve with intelligence scholars and, indeed, with the general public. If the intelligence process were distorted through exaggerations either by intelligence officers or the policy officials they served, who could play the vital role of the truth seeker in a democratic government? The controversy casts a shadow in both nations over the legitimacy of the intelligence agencies and the trustworthiness of decision makers who may have misused intelligence reports.

In the next piece, a legal counsel in the CIA, Frederic F. Manget, examines the role of the third branch of government in intelligence matters: the judiciary. "In effect," he observes, "the judicial review of issues touching on intelligence matters has developed into a system of oversight." Manget reports that the federal courts have not been shy to assert their authority over the intelligence agencies when individual rights may have been jeopardized by intelligence operations. In such cases, judges routinely require intelligence officials to visit the courthouse and explain their activities. "Nothing concentrates the mind and dampens excess so wonderfully," he writes, "as the imminent prospect of explaining one's actions to a federal judge"—another safeguard for liberty envisioned by the Founders when they created the judicial branch of government.

In the following selection, Loch K. Johnson offers a history of the Church Committee investigation in 1975, which opened a Pandora's box of intelligence threats to civil liberties in the United States. The safeguards against future intelligence abuse established by the committee "have endured," Johnson argues, "and, on most occasions, they have brought greater sobriety to the conduct of intelligence operations at home and abroad. Someone beyond the walls of the secret agencies is now steadily watching their activities; would-be violators of the public trust know they might be caught—a vital check on abuse." Johnson's study of intelligence abuses uncovered in the mid-1970s is a reminder of how the darkest stain on the U.S. intelligence ledger came about as a result of the fear of communism that gripped the nation during the Cold War.

Fear has frequently been the reason the government has tilted, from time to time, too far toward security at the expense of liberty: the fear of the Japanese that led President Franklin D. Roosevelt to authorize the internment of Japanese American citizens during World War II; the fear of communists that produced the witch hunts of the House Un-American Activities Committee and, later, of Senator Joseph McCarthy; the fear of student dissent that led to CIA spying at home during the Vietnam war; the fear of civil rights activists that inspired the FBI's Cointelpro; and the fear of terrorism that could now lead to the trampling of civil liberties for Arab Americans and other minorities in the search for Al Qaeda supporters inside the United States. Of course, Japanese sabotage was a legitimate concern during the World War II, just as communism was

during the Cold War. Moreover, some students broke the law during the Vietnam war era, even robbing banks and murdering bank guards to support their radical activities. But there are lawful ways to deal with criminal acts without resorting to mass internments, Congressional hearings guided less by evidence than innuendo, illegal surveillance, secret harassment of citizens, and jailing of terrorist suspects without legal counsel or formal charges. The goal is to maintain security while preserving democracy, not by turning a democracy into a totalitarian state.

Finally, this part ends with a series of viewpoints on the use of the National Security Agency for warrantless wiretapping in the United States—a controversial issue during the confirmation hearings for CIA Director Gen. Michael V. Hayden, who served as NSA Director at the time the wiretaps were initiated by the George W. Bush Administration. These perspectives were written originally for a Yale University School of Law "debate" on the matter. ✦

26
Intelligence: Welcome to the American Government

Gregory F. Treverton

For most of America's history, intelligence agencies were treated differently from the rest of the government. Their operations were considered too sensitive for normal procedures. Yet when the intelligence agencies were accused in 1974 of abusing their powers by engaging in spying at home, reformers argued that the time had come to bring the dark side of government more into the sunlight of stricter accountability. Treverton examines the merits of viewing intelligence organizations as a regular part of America's government, as subject to constitutional safeguards as any other department or agency.

Congress was deeply engaged in intelligence at the beginning of the Republic: in 1775 the Second Continental Congress set in motion covert operations to secure French supplies for Washington's army. The next year Thomas Paine, the first congressional "leaker," was dismissed for disclosing information from the Committee of Secret Correspondence. For the next century and a half, however, the congressional role lapsed. A disengaged America had little need for foreign intelligence, and for the first thirty years after World War II the preeminence of the president and the imminence of the cold war induced Congress to leave intelligence to the executive, for better or worse.

Events of the 1970s changed that. Since then, the role of Congress in intelligence matters has increased dramatically, and the intelligence community has become like the rest of the government. In the intelligence agencies' relations with Congress, especially, they are coming to resemble the Agriculture or Commerce departments. The House and Senate Intelligence committees have become, like other committees on Capitol Hill, the patrons as well as the overseers of "their" government agencies.

Intelligence officials are finding, as have other members of the executive branch before them, that congressional patrons who control purse strings are also tempted to tell them how to run their business. For their part, members of Congress find secret oversight politically awkward. In the words of Republican Senator William Cohen, then vice-chairman of the Senate Intelligence Committee: "It's not exactly a Faustian bargain, . . . But if we wish to have access, we are bound."[1]

The paradox of secret oversight by the branch of government meant to be characterized by open debate is sharpest in the realm of covert action. There, intelligence officials are tempted to see their congressional overseers as potential leakers, while the overseers fear being misled or deceived or becoming responsible, in secret, for covert actions they cannot easily stop even if they oppose them.

Yet the oversight process has not worked badly even for covert action; ironically, the recent Iran-contra debacle is testimony to that judgment even as it also testifies to the limits whereby process can impose wisdom on the making of American public policy. This grappling over secret *operations* gets the headlines; as a vexing constitutional question, it merits them.

However, covert action is only a small part of oversight, and despite the publicity accorded it, the balance between executive and Congress in the making of foreign policy is probably more affected by a related change: Congress now receives virtually the same intelligence *analysis* as the executive. One senior Central Intelligence Agency (CIA) official described the agency as "involuntarily poised equidistant between the executive and legislative branches."[2] Asking whether intelligence agencies can serve both masters is shorthand for a wider question about the implications of intelligence joining an American government in which the fault lines sometimes divide along the executive-legislative gap but often cut across it.

'Plausible Denial' and the 'Buddy System'

Since its first serious investigations of intelligence in the mid-1970s, Congress has become steadily more involved in secret operations. Its most recent investigations into the Iran-contra affair, however, testify to the continuing puzzles, constitutional and procedural. These questions run through all of foreign affairs but are sharper in the realm of intelligence.

The investigations in the mid-1970s began very much in the shadow of Watergate; the press was full of intimations that intelligence agencies had acted outside the law, beyond the ken of Congress and the control even of presidents. Democratic Senator Frank Church, the chairman of the Senate investigating committee, likened the CIA to a "rogue elephant on the rampage."[3] In the event, the committees did not find much evidence of rogue elephants in the CIA or other agencies involved in foreign intelligence, like the National Security Agency or the Defense Intelligence Agency.[4]

Yet the committees did find a troubling looseness in the control of covert action. Part of the problem was CIA abuse of so-called plausible denial, a practice intended to protect the American government, a practice also abused by Oliver North and John Poindexter during the arms sales to Iran in the 1980s. A second part of the problem was a kind of "buddy system" in which oversight consisted of informal conversations between the director of central intelligence (DCI) and a few senior members of Congress. Neither plausible denial nor the buddy system emerged because the CIA had broken free of its political masters. Rather, they emerged because that was how successive administrations and Congress had wanted it.

In 1975, testifying before the Senate committee—often called the "Church committee" after its chairman—about charges that the CIA had tried to kill Fidel Castro, former DCI Richard Helms was vivid in describing plausible denial and almost plaintive in drawing its implications:

> It was made abundantly clear . . . to everybody involved in the operation that the desire was to get rid of the Castro regime and to get rid of Castro . . . the point was that no limitations were put on this injunction . . . one . . . grows up in [the] tradition of the time and I think that any of us would have found it very difficult to discuss assassinations with a President of the U.S. I just think we all had the feeling that we're hired out to keep those things out of the Oval Office.[5]

If he had ever thought he would later have to testify before Congress about what he had done, Helms reflected, he would have made sure that his orders were clear and in writing.

By their own testimony, not a single member of the National Security Council (NSC) outside the CIA knew of, much less authorized, those plots.[6] Even inside the CIA, officials spoke with each other about these operations only in riddles. And if they spoke of them at all with those outside the CIA charged with approving covert operations, they did so indirectly or in circumlocutions. Thus, in 1975 the Church committee spent hours trying to unravel

whether terse references in documents to "disappear" or "direct positive action" or "neutralize" referred to assassination. It could not be sure. And that was precisely the point of plausible denial. Those CIA officials who spoke in circumlocutions could feel they had done their duty as they understood it. Their political superiors could understand what they would, ask for more information if they desired, but also forebear from asking. If things went awry, they could, if they chose, disclaim knowledge and do so more or less honestly.

These effects of plausible denial are extreme in the instance of the Cuban assassination plots, but similar effects ran through covert actions of the 1950s and 1960s. Dean Rusk, who served Presidents Kennedy and Johnson as secretary of state, observed that he routinely knew little of CIA operations: "I never saw a budget of the CIA, for example."[7] Of thousands of covert action projects between 1949 and 1968, only some 600 received consideration outside the CIA by the National Security Council body then charged with reviewing covert operations.

For its part, the American Congress was more interested in making sure the CIA had what it needed in the fight against communism than in overseeing its operations. The fate of several congressional initiatives for improving oversight that came to naught in these early years is eloquent testimony to the mood of the time and the temper of Congress. In early 1955 Democratic Senator Mike Mansfield, later chairman of the Foreign Relations Committee, introduced a resolution calling for a joint oversight committee. The resolution had thirty-five cosponsors. It also had the strong opposition not only of the executive but also of the "club" of senior senators. In hearings on the resolution, Mansfield elicited the following comment from Senator Leverett Saltonstall, the ranking Republican on the Armed Services Committee:

> It is not a question of reluctance on the part of the CIA officials to speak to us. Instead, it is a question of our reluctance, if you will, to seek information and knowledge on subjects which I personally, as a Member of Congress and as a citizen, would rather not have, unless I believed it to be my responsibility to have it because it might involve the lives of American citizens.[8]

In April 1956 the resolution was voted down, 59–27, with a half dozen cosponsors voting against it.

The debate did, however, result in the creation of formal CIA subcommittees in both Armed Services committees. Yet the buddy system remained largely unchanged. Allen Dulles, the near legend, was DCI until the Bay of Pigs fiasco in 1961; relaxed and candid with senior members, he had their absolute trust. In the Senate Armed Services Committee, Senator Richard Russell appointed to the formal subcommittee those senators with whom he had been meeting informally on CIA matters— Saltonstall and Harry Byrd. Later he added Lyndon Johnson and Styles Bridges. When, in 1957, the Appropriations Committee formed a subcommittee for the CIA, its members were Russell, Byrd, and Bridges. They both authorized and appropriated, often at the same meeting. Most CIA business continued to be conducted as before—by Dulles and Russell, meeting informally.

The Climate Changes

The Bay of Pigs marked the end of an era for the CIA. It was a stunning defeat for an agency known only for success. Dulles and his deputy, Richard Bissell, were eased out of their jobs. Yet neither executive procedures for, nor congressional oversight of, intelligence changed all that much.

A decade later, with the big expansion in covert action in Asia as the war in Vietnam heated up, the executive branch undertook somewhat more formal procedures. For instance, the NSC body charged with reviewing covert action (after 1970 called the 40 committee) considered operations in Chile on 23 separate occasions between March 1970 and October 1973, the period surrounding the presidency of Salvador Allende. Still, in numbers, most covert action projects continued not to be approved by anyone outside the CIA. By the early 1970s only about a fourth of all covert actions came before the NSC review body.[9]

During the 1960s more committees of Congress were receiving more information from the CIA than in the early days; however, about clandestine operations the CIA did not often volunteer information and Congress did not often ask. The role of Congress had not moved from receiving information to overseeing operations. In 1961 after the Bay of Pigs, and again in 1966, Democratic Senator Eugene McCarthy attempted unsuccessfully to revive the idea of a CIA oversight committee.

Watergate and Chile, coming on the heels of the war in Vietnam, changed all that. So did the passing of a congressional generation and the enacting of internal reforms that dispersed authority away from committee chairmen. The buddy system, smooth and private, had depended on a handful of congressional barons. Thus, as a former CIA director of congressional liaison put it, "When Chairmen Russell, [Carl] Hayden, [Mendel] Rivers, and [Carl] Vinson retired between 1965 and 1971, CIA's congressional constituency retired with them."[10] Or as William Colby, the DCI at the time of the first congressional investigations, later recalled:

There had been a time when the joint hearing held by the Senate's intelligence subcommittees would have been deemed sufficient [to end the matter]. Senators with the seniority and clout of [John] McClellan and [John] Stennis then could easily have squelched any demands for farther action on the part of their junior colleagues. But this was no longer the case.[11]

Congress's disinclination to ask about secret operations was the first change. Neither reticence nor deference were hallmarks of the congressional class of 1974, elected as Watergate played out on the nation's television screens. Congress passed the Hughes-Ryan act of 1974, the operative paragraph of which reads:

No funds appropriated under the authority of this or another Act may be expended by or on behalf of the [CIA] for operations in foreign countries, other than activities intended solely for obtaining necessary intelligence, unless and until the President finds that each such operation is important to the national security of the United States and reports, in a timely fashion, a description and scope of such operation to the appropriate committees of the Congress.[12]

From the verb "finds" came the noun "finding"—a written document bearing the president's signature. As was often the case, Congress sought to change the pattern of executive action not by making specific decisions but rather by changing the process by which decisions were made. The Hughes-Ryan act was intended to end the abuse of plausible denial displayed in the Cuban assassination plots, which seemed to have confused procedures within the executive—and deluded Congress—more than it protected anyone.

Hughes-Ryan required the president to put his name and his reputation on the line. It was meant to ensure that there would be no future wrangles such as those over assassinations. Covert actions, wise or stupid, would reflect presidential decision; there would be no doubt that someone was in charge. It also meant that members of Congress would find it harder to assert that they had been kept in the dark. Less often could they speechify in professed ignorance of covert action. The "appropriate committees" now became six: the Intelligence subcommittees of Armed Services and Appropriations in both houses plus the Foreign Affairs and Foreign Relations committees.

Tending the 'Government's' Secrets

A year later Congress established the Church committee and a parallel investigating committee in the House, chaired by New York Democrat Otis Pike. Those committees, the Church committee in particular, represented an innovation in constitutional relations between the executive and Congress.[13] At the heart of the wrangling between the committees and the Ford administration over access to classified documents lay a constitutional issue: were those secret documents, written and classified by the CIA or State, the property of the executive only? Or were they the "government's" documents, to which Congress should have access on terms decided by it and which could be declassified by its decision as well as that of the executive? Popular usage mirrors ambiguity about what constitutes "the government," particularly in foreign affairs. Constitutionally, Congress is a coequal branch of the government, yet people often speak of "the government" more narrowly to refer to a particular administration in power.

The committees did not resolve the question of who controlled documents. In the nature of the system, they could not. But Congress and the executive did move a long way toward the view that even in matters of clandestine operations, Congress has its own right to the "government's" secret documents and that it bears the responsibility that goes with that right.

The Ford administration was a grudging partner in adjusting the constitutional bargain. A few in the administration, Colby foremost among them, believed the changes were fundamentally correct; others felt that, given the public mood, the administration simply had no choice. The administration had something of a dual approach to the Church committee. At one level, that of executive prerogatives in foreign affairs, it was opposed to the investigation and its results. It held, thus, that publication of an interim report on assassinations was not only wrong but also a mistake that would harm the reputation of the United States. At another level, however, it was prepared to work with the committee, particularly to protect intelligence sources and methods. In that regard the administration and the committee shared an interest; the committee had no reason to want to endanger intelligence methods or agents' lives. In the case of the assassination report, the issue boiled down to whether the committee would publish the names of some thirty-three CIA officers. The administration argued that publishing the names would tarnish reputations and might, in one or two instances, endanger the individuals in question. Colby even took the issue to district court.

In the end, the committee and the administration reached a sensible compromise. The committee agreed to delete the names of twenty of the officers, required for neither the substance nor the credibility of the report. The remaining names were left in. Most were those of senior officers and were already in the public domain. The committee felt, moreover, that senior officials should be held publicly accountable for their actions. Like most compromises, it pleased neither side fully but was one with which both could live.[14]

In seeking to establish its position, the Church committee was assiduous about leaks. Not a single secret worth mention got out.[15] The same could not be said of the Pike committee, whose entire final report leaked into the press in 1976 after the fall House had voted not to release it until the president certified that it did not contain information that would harm U.S. intelligence activities.[16]

When the House, like the Senate, later decided to establish a permanent intelligence committee, the Pike committee experience, which had created acrimony not only between the committee and the administration but within the House as well, was much on the House's collective mind. As one sophisticated former suffer observed: "The message from the House was clear: no more fiascos. The new . . . committee would have to stay in line; the honor of the House was at stake."[17]

The House did not agree to a permanent committee until 1977, a year after the Senate. The vote was closer—227–171 in the House, compared with 75–22 in the Senate; and the House committee was granted less autonomy and control over classified information. For instance, the Senate committee was authorized to disclose classified information over the president's objection, while in the House that right rested with the full body. The House committee was also smaller and more partisan—13 members, nine of them Democrats, in a House of 435, compared with 15, eight Democrats, in a Senate of 100. The House Democrats were chosen by the Speaker, not the majority caucus, evidence of a desire to retain control. By contrast, the Senate committee, following the relatively bipartisan approach of the Church committee, made the ranking minority member the vice-chairman, a unique arrangement in Congress.

Initially, the two congressional investigations resulted only in two new permanent oversight committees, increasing the number of congressional overseers of intelligence from six committees to eight, albeit ones with more access to information. Yet the institutional legacy of permanent select committees in each house of Congress has turned out to be an important one. The committees established the principle of rotating memberships, limiting tenures to six years in the House and eight in the Senate, to broaden their representation within Congress, thus guarding against a recurrence of the buddy system in image or in fact.

Reflecting their different lineages, the Senate committee was initially more self-confident in its approach to oversight. A cadre of members and staff from the Church committee moved to the new permanent committee, while the House started afresh, staffed mostly by ex-intelligence officials. Over time, however, the House staff, though smaller and divided along partisan lines, acquired the reputation of being more professional, especially in those aspects of oversight that seldom find their way into headlines—budgets, collection systems, and intelligence products.

Over time, too, the committees were stamped by the styles and personalities of their chairmen as well as by the character of their parent bodies. The House committee was chaired in the 1980s by Edward Boland and Lee Hamilton, members of experience and stature in the legislature by comparison with their counterparts on the Senate side, Republican David Durenberger and Democrat Patrick Leahy. The Republican ascendance to control of the Senate in 1980 not only brought new young senators to control of the committee, but also shifted the focal point for congressional scrutiny of secret operations to the House. And it frayed cooperation between the two committees.

By the latter half of the 1980s, with the Democrats again in control of the Senate, the Senate committee reflected its parent body in being less partisan than the House. Its Democrats were mostly moderates, senators like David Boren, Sam Nunn, and Ernest Hollings, who had few counterparts on the House committee. Some of those moderate Democrats, especially southerners, were attracted to the Intelligence Committee as a way to become active in foreign affairs without acquiring the liberal taint of the Foreign Relations Committee.

The Carter administration, disinclined from the start to resort to covert action, found its intelligence relations with Congress easy. It first pressed the House to establish a permanent intelligence committee, then cooperated with Congress in passing the Intelligence Oversight Act of 1980, the most important law in the realm of covert action. The act cut back the executive's reporting requirements for covert action to the two Intelligence committees; eight committees were too unwieldy for both executive and Congress, and virtually invited executive charges of being "too leaky." At the same time, however, the act charged the two committees with informing other relevant committees, especially Foreign Affairs, Foreign Relations, and the two Appropriations committees. It also made clear that Congress wanted to be notified of all covert actions, not just those carried out by the CIA; secret executive recourse to other agencies, in particular the military, was denied.

Congress also tiptoed toward prior notification of covert action; the "timely fashion" of the Hughes-Ryan act, which allowed notification after the fact (within twenty-four hours came to be the understanding), became "fully and currently informed," including "any significant anticipated intelligence activity" in the 1980 act. Yet notifying Congress still was not a "condition precedent to the initiation" of covert action. And the act gave the president another escape hatch, for in emergencies he was permitted to limit notice to eight members—the chairmen and ranking minority members of the Intelligence committees, the Speaker and minority leader of the House, and the majority and minority leaders of the Senate—the "gang of eight" or the "eight wise men," depending on the describer's inclinations.

The 'Covert' War in Central America

The tussle between executive and Congress, which had been restrained when operators and overseers shared the view that the covert instrument should be used sparingly, grew more passionate with the surge of covert actions in the 1980s. The Reagan administration came into office determined to make covert assistance to "freedom fighters" around the world a key element of its global pressure on the Soviet Union. Strikingly, in light of what came later, Reagan's executive order 12333 gave the CIA full responsibility for covert actions except in time of war or by specific presidential instruction.[18]

With the new administration, however, attitudes changed more than directives or procedures. One congressional staffer referred to men like NSC staffer Lieutenant Colonel Oliver North as "field grades," people eager for action, long on energy, but short on political savvy. William Miller, the staff director of both the Church committee and the first permanent Senate Intelligence Committee, observed that the CIA and its sister agencies were led in the late 1970s by people who had been through the experience of investigation and reform. They were "so immersed in the constitutional questions that they could recite chapter and verse. Questions of law and balance occurred naturally to them." By contrast, the Reagan leadership was dominated by "advocates, people who were always trying to get around the roadblocks, who were looking for a way to get it done."[19]

In Central America, the long reign of the Somoza family in Nicaragua had come to an end in 1979, bringing to power the regime's armed opponents, the Sandinista National Liberation Front, in uneasy partnership with a range of civilian opposition groups. Early in its tenure, the Reagan administration charged that the Sandinistas were becoming a base for Cuban and Soviet subversion in the region and, specifically, that they were shipping arms to guerrilla opponents of the U.S.-supported government of El Salvador. At first, the Sandinistas were confronted primarily by remnants of Somoza's hated National Guard who had found sanctuary in Honduras, but over time several of the Sandinistas' original allies fell out with the government. One of them opened a new anti-Sandinista front operating out of Costa Rica.

Congressional opposition to the administration's course in Nicaragua grew in direct proportion to the breakdown in congressional-executive relations. The administration sought to unite the Sandinistas' armed opponents—dubbed the contras—and to support them. Yet the purpose of that covert support seemed a moving target, which suggested to Congress either confusion or deception. In November 1981 President Reagan signed National Security Council Decision Directive 17 proposing to build a force of contras to interdict arms shipments from Nicaragua to the rebels in El Salvador. However, the directive, when turned into a finding, contained language—"engage in paramilitary . . . operations in Nicaragua, and elsewhere"— that seemed to permit almost anything.[20] The congressional Intelligence committees first made clear in their classified reports on the CIA budget that they opposed covert efforts to overthrow the Sandinista government or Nicaragua. Then, at the end of 1982, they put that language, as the Boland amendment, publicly into the appropriations bill. Named for Edward P. Boland, then chairman of the House Intelligence Committee it stipulated that no money could be used "for the purpose of overthrowing the Government of Nicaragua or provoking a military exchange between Nicaragua and Honduras."[21]

The aims of America's covert intervention remained in dispute while the war intensified, especially as the CIA opened a second front in Costa Rica. In response, Boland and the House shifted their focus from appropriations to authorization, proposing not to limit covert action in Nicaragua but to end it. The House voted to do so in July 1983. However, the Senate Intelligence committee, with the Republicans in the majority, was prepared to approve more money if the administration would be precise about its objectives. The administration "thoroughly scrubbed" a new finding, which was signed in September 1983.[22]

In October the House again voted to end the contra program but at year's end the House-Senate conference compromised, accepting the revised presidential finding, which expanded the American aim from halting arms flows from Nicaragua to pressuring the Sandinistas to negotiate with their neighbors. However Congress capped funding at $24 million, enough for one year's operations, thus requiring the administration to return to Congress before the end of the fiscal year if it wanted the program to continue.[23]

Any limited American objective seemed less plausible after revelations early the next year that the CIA itself had mined Nicaraguan harbors. The mining, a new phase in the covert war, was itself an act of war and one that threatened the shipping of both American allies and the Soviet Union. The operation was approved by the president in the winter, probably in December 1983.[24] The Sandinistas protested on January 3, 1984, that the contras were laying mines in Nicaraguan harbors, and the rebel leaders, who plainly had no capacity to lay mines on their own, finally learned their lines and announced on January 8 that they would do so.

On January 31, 1984, DCI William Casey met with the House Intelligence committee and mentioned the mining, though the meeting was primarily about releasing further funds for the overall contra project. The House committee apparently did not share its information with its Senate colleagues, although the CIA may have briefed several members of the Senate committee and its staff. The Senate, however, was pushing toward its February recess, and the administration twice asked for a delay so that Secretary of State George Shultz could also attend. As a result, a full briefing of the Senate committee was delayed, and many, perhaps most, members remained unaware of the operation, especially of the direct CIA role in it.

Casey first met with the full Senate Intelligence committee on March 8, for over an hour, but this meeting too dealt primarily with authorizing the release of funds, over which the Intelligence committee was fighting a jurisdictional battle with Appropriations. Only one sentence dealt with the mining, and it, like the rest of the briefing, was delivered in Casey's inimitable mumble.[25] Many on the committee did not learn of the mining until a month later, and then almost by accident.

Casey nodded toward the letter of the law with his brief reference, but the episode angered even Senator Barry Goldwater, the Republican committee chairman and a man not known for his opposition to covert action. He had not understood the reference. When he learned about the mining operation, once the committee staff received a full briefing on April 2, he was furious. His letter to Casey, which leaked into the press, was notable for its unsenatorial prose as well as for its displeasure: "It gets down to one, little, simple phrase: I am pissed off!"[26] In the wake of this episode, the Senate committee moved toward the House's position, and Congress cut off further covert assistance with a second Boland amendment enacted into law in October 1984, thus rejecting the president's request for $21 million more.

By the end of 1984 the House of Representatives had voted three times against paramilitary aid, only to have the operation rescued by House-Senate conferences. Yet despite these losses, the Reagan administration was succeeding in framing the debate on its own ground. Americans' deep ambivalence—their fears of U.S. involvement competed with their distaste for the Sandinistas—left covert support standing as a "middle option," cheap in money and American blood, and hard for members of Congress, even Democrats, to vote against lest they be branded "soft on communism" by a popular president.

In early 1985 President Reagan again asked for aid to the contras, this time for $14 million. The House again voted down the aid after a sharp debate. However, when Sandinista leader Daniel Ortega unwisely journeyed to Moscow just after the vote, those Democrats who had voted against covert aid looked soft and foolish. They responded by enacting economic sanctions, largely symbolic, against Nicaragua. In August 1985 Congress compromised on $27 million in "nonmilitary" aid to the contras; this was not to be administered by the CIA, and the agency was barred from direct contact with the contras or assistance in their training. Congress did not restore CIA funding for this purpose until October 1986.

This off-again, on-again funding, deeply frustrating to those in the Reagan administration most committed to the contras, bred circumventions of the congressional restrictions—efforts suspected in press accounts as early as the spring of 1985. The second Boland amendment applied to the CIA, the Defense Department, and "any other agency or entity involved in intelligence."[27] Some in the administration felt it did not prevent the NSC staff or other officials from seeking aid from other sources. By early 1984, as the $24 million ran out, the president directed the NSC staff, in the words of national security adviser Robert McFarlane, "to keep the contras together 'body and soul.'" Casey and other officials began to approach governments ranging from Israel to Brunei to Saudi Arabia and quietly canvassed private sources in the United States, South Korea, Taiwan, and Latin America. That private support totaled some $34 million during the period of the aid cutoff.[28]

By May 1984, when the congressional appropriation ran out, Oliver North, the NSC staff's deputy director for political-military affairs, had become coordinator of the private support, dubbed "the

Enterprise" by those involved. In October when Congress barred any CIA involvement, the agency issued a "cease and desist" order to its stations. Nevertheless, about a dozen CIA officers remained involved in North's operation, apparently construing his role to signify White House authorization. By the fall of 1985, North was overseeing the shipping of privately purchased arms to the contras and the construction of a secret airfield in Costa Rica. North, who also called his operation "Project Democracy," relied on a network of conservative organizations and ex-military men, one of whom, retired general Richard V. Secord, was also a key conduit for arms sales to Iran.

In the fall of 1986 a Beirut newspaper published a bizarre account of a secret mission to Iran the previous May by former national security adviser McFarlane. The account, which first seemed another piece of partisan Middle East nonsense, turned out to be true. McFarlane's delivery of U.S. weapons to Iran was part of a sequence running back to August 1985. The first two shipments had been made by Israel, through middlemen, with U.S. approval and assurance that depleted Israeli stocks would be replenished. The operation, also managed day to day by North, was so closely held that even the CIA was at first cut out, though Casey himself was central. Critical meetings were held with no analytic papers prepared beforehand and no record of decisions kept afterward.

North sought and received CIA help in November 1985 when, in a comedy of errors, Secord could not get one shipment through Portugal to Israel. When he heard of the CIA involvement, John McMahon, the agency's deputy director, angrily barred any further CIA involvement without a presidential finding. The next month the president signed one finding to provide retroactive approval for the shipments; the new national security adviser, Admiral John Poindexter, destroyed that finding a year later because, he later testified, it would have been embarrassing to the president.[29]

The president approved another finding on January 17, 1986, "to establish contact with moderate elements within and outside the Government of Iran by providing these elements with arms, equipment and related materiel." However, the accompanying background paper, prepared by North, was explicit about the link to getting U.S. hostages out of Lebanon:

> This approach . . . may well be our *only* way to achieve the release of the Americans held in Beirut. . . . If all of the hostages are not released after the first shipment of 1,000 weapons, further transfers would cease.[30]

In February, American arms were first shipped directly from the United States by the CIA to Israel for transfer to Iran. Three other shipments were made, the last in late October. In all, some 2,000 TOW antitank weapons, as well as other weapons and spare parts were sold to Iran. Three U.S. hostages were released, but three more were taken during the course of the operation.

The strange tale became more bizarre when it was revealed that the profits of the Iranian arms sales had been diverted to support the Nicaraguan contras. The arms had been sold to Iran for nearly $16 million more than the CIA had paid the Pentagon for them. In a scheme masterminded by North, the profits were then laundered through Swiss bank accounts, to be drawn on by the contras. When the scheme was revealed, North was fired, and his boss, Poindexter resigned.

The story unfolded first through an executive investigating panel, named by the president in December 1986 and chaired by former Senator John Tower. Then Congress began a joint Senate-House investigation in January 1987, which treated the nation to the spectacle of public testimony by the central figures, most notably Oliver North, through the hot summer of 1987. The focus of both investigations was narrowly the diversion of profits from the Iran arms sales to the contras: had the president authorized or known of it? This charge remained unproven. The investigations, however, did what Congress had been unable, in part unwilling, to do before—unravel the trail of private support for the contras.

The narrow initial focus broadened further through the criminal trials of McFarlane, North, and Poindexter. McFarlane, distraught to the point of breakdown by what had been done, pleaded guilty to lying to Congress. North, the loyal soldier to the end, asserted his innocence; he was found guilty of destroying documents and other charges but not of deceiving Congress. North's light sentence reflected the discrediting of what had been the administration's primary defense, one accepted by the Tower panel: that the wrongdoing was the result of a small cabal centered on North. North plainly was central, but just as plainly the circle of those involved was wider than the administration wanted to acknowledge.

Sources of Tension:
External and Internal

The sources of tension in the intelligence role of Congress are displayed in this history. They are both external and internal to Congress. The houses of Congress not only share a distrust of the executive, no matter which party is in power, but they are also jealous of each other. The two Intelligence committees do not automatically share information, as is apparent in the case of the mining of Nicaragua's harbors. Working together is all the harder if, as in this case, there is both disagreement on the merits and partisan division: Democrats controlled the House, Republicans the Senate from 1980 until 1986. In December 1985, during the time CIA assistance was cut off, the Intelligence committees did approve some money for "communications" and "advice" to the contras, subject to conditions negotiated with the committees. There then ensued an exchange of letters suggesting that the two chairmen were uncertain—or disagreed—over what was permitted and what was proscribed.[31]

Moreover, despite their authority, the Intelligence committees do not monopolize oversight of covert operations. Because covert actions are foreign policy, the Foreign Affairs and Foreign Relations committees have an interest in their authorization; because they cost money, the Appropriations committees have their stakes. The tracks of both sets of jurisdictional battles are visible in the Nicaraguan episode.

However, the sharper tensions arise between Congress and the executive. Even with good will in both branches, congressional overseers have to get deeply into the details of ongoing operations, which is hard for them and uncomfortable for covert operators in the executive branch. Critical details can fall between the cracks: it may be that Senate committee members, like Goldwater, simply were not paying attention when Casey mumbled about the mining. Even their staffs are hard-pressed to keep up with the details of forty-odd covert actions. As one staffer close to the process put it: "How can you know which detail will jump up and bite you? Things move fast. How long did the mining take from beginning to end? A few weeks."[32]

For members, oversight remains something of an unnatural act. They are not hard to interest in intelligence; the lure of secrecy and the mystique of covert operations are a powerful tug on their attentions. At the beginning of the One-hundredth Congress in 1987, 60 members of the House signed up for four openings on the Intelligence Committee. Given rotating memberships, chairs can come quickly; Republican Senator Dave Durenberger became chairman of the Senate committee after only six years. Still, the assignment is one among many, whatever its fascination. Members have little political reason to become involved, still less to take responsibility for particular operations. Politicians' temptation to use their special access to information on morning talk shows competes uneasily with the disciplines of committee membership. Sometimes the special access is, in political terms, more a burden than an asset; as Senator Daniel K. Inouye, the first chairman of the permanent Senate Intelligence Committee, observed, in words not much different from Saltonstall's thirty years before: "How would you like to know a very, very high official of a certain government was on our payroll?"[33]

On balance, members have resolved the contest between responsibility and self-promotion or credit taking in favor of the former. The temptations of the latter are always there, and the dividing line is fine, but the penalties for being seen to traverse it are high: recent incidents demonstrate both these points. In early 1987 Senator Patrick Leahy, the chairman of the Senate Intelligence Committee, was forced to resign his chairmanship after leaking an unclassified but not yet released version of the committee's Iran-contra report. His action was unwise, but by the standard applied to Leahy, the executive branch would be depopulated. In 1988 House Speaker Jim Wright told a reporter that he had "received clear testimony from CIA people that they have deliberately done things to provoke an overreaction on the part of the Government in Nicaragua."[34] He was not the first to characterize American policy in that way, he later denied he had leaked secret testimony, and the incident was later overshadowed by his other ethical problems. But at the time, invoking the CIA as the source was enough to earn him a storm of criticism.

Iran-contra provides most graphic testimony to the tensions in the congressional role when the committees confront a determined president, especially if they themselves are of divided mind. Administrations, especially one as committed to covert operations as the Reagan administration, are bound to want the flexibility of broad, general findings that give the CIA room to adapt to changing circumstances. Congress is almost equally bound to be wary of signing a blank check, particularly when the administration is committed. McGeorge Bundy, who ran the NSC review committee for the Kennedy and Johnson administrations, emphasized by understatement in 1975 the difficulty reviewers outside the CIA confront:

> I think it has happened that an operation is presented in one way to a committee . . . and executed in a way that is different from what the committee thought it had authorized.[35]

Norman Mineta, a charter member of the House Intelligence Committee, put his frustration more colorfully in speaking of the executive: "They treat us like mushrooms. Keep us in the dark and feed us a lot of manure."[36]

At more than one point in the Iran-contra affair, administration officials deceived Congress. The January 1986 arms sales finding was explicit: do not tell Congress. The congressional overseers did not find out about the operation until the following autumn—not "fully and currently informed" by anyone's definition. Earlier, the Intelligence committees responded to press accounts that the ban on aid to the contras was being circumvented. In August 1985, for instance, the House asked the administration about North's activities. The response drafted by McFarlane and North and signed by the former, said that at no time did I or any member of the National Security Council staff violate the letter or spirit of the restrictions.[37]

That is outright deception, even granting some ambiguity in the wording of the ban. Did the wording mean no administration official could seek other sources of aid? If so, how could Congress enforce the ban? Its means were limited, as they are in more normal cases. Even if the committees are united in their opposition to an operation, they cannot easily stop it, for if the administration is determined to proceed it can fund the operation for a year from the CIA Contingency Reserve.[38] Congress has in two cases resorted to public legislation banning covert action—the Boland amendments and the 1976 Clark-Tunney amendment on Angola. These were signs that it did not trust the administration, or its designated overseers of covert action, or both.

In the instance of aid to the contras, however, Congress's will was also limited. In part, it was reluctant to take on a popular president even on a controversial issue. The reluctance is customary in relations between the executive and Congress, even if the president is less popular than Reagan; unless the president is plainly out of step with the American people, members of Congress do not like to confront the presidency. The House Intelligence Committee, like its parent body, was sharply divided over aid to the contras; in later votes, whichever side captured a group of thirty-odd swing votes, mostly Democratic and mostly conservative southerners, carried the day. The Senate although wavering, probably had a consistent majority favoring aid in principle.

In those circumstances, it is perhaps less surprising that the committees were halfhearted in inquiring into violations of the ban that their later, retrospective investigations framed the issues narrowly or that Congress breathed an audible sigh of relief that Reagan had left the presidency by the time new revelations during the trials of his former aides might have raised questions of impeachment.

Limits to the System

Aid to the contras was as divisive within the Intelligence committees as it was in the nation, but almost every other covert action has elicited a near consensus, even within the House committee. The congressional overseers have been informed of the covert action and recorded their views; presidents cannot lightly ignore those views, especially if they are held by senior committee members in both parties. Lest the president miss the point, the committees can take a formal vote to underscore their view. More than once, apparently, such votes have induced a president to rescind approval of an operation.[39]

In other cases the committees have said, in the words of one staff member, "Hey, do you know how risky that is?"[40] Hearing an affirmative response, they have let the program go ahead despite their doubts. They did so in the case of Angola, letting the administration resume covert aid to Jonas Savimbi's UNITA (Union for the Total Independence of Angola, in its Portuguese acronym) in 1986 to the tune of some $15 million a year; they did so in that case despite the fact that Lee Hamilton, the House Intelligence committee chairman, took his personal opposition to the House floor.

The Reagan administration wanted to make use of covert action much more frequently than did its predecessor, and the oversight committees, reflecting the mood of Congress and probably of the American people as well, assented to that expansion of covert action. The centerpiece of the Reagan program was aid to the resistance in Afghanistan, begun under the Carter administration, which came to total more than a half billion dollars a year by 1986. Indeed, Congress was if anything ahead of the executive, appropriating unrequested additional money for the resistance in 1983 and pressing the administration to deliver more sophisticated weaponry.

In a sense the system "worked" even in the instance of arms sales to Iran. In deciding to sell, the president pursued a policy that was opposed by his secretaries of state and defense and about which he was afraid to inform the congressional oversight committees. Those should have been warning signals aplenty that the policy was unwise.

If presidents are determined to do something stupid, they will find someone, somewhere, to do it.

In seeking to circumvent the requirements of process, the president, it appears, also set himself up for deception. It was he who was not told when the Iran and contra operations crossed. Keeping Congress in the dark also encouraged looseness within the executive, just as it did a quarter century earlier in the CIA's attempted assassinations of Fidel Castro. North and Poindexter mistakenly construed plausible denial after their own fashion, much the same as Helms and his colleagues had, keeping their president ignorant in order to protect him. Although convinced the president would approve the use of proceeds from the Iranian arms sales for the contras as an "implementation" of his policy, Poindexter "made a very deliberate decision not to ask the President" so that he could "insulate [him] from the decision and provide some future deniability."[41]

When the president's closest advisers become the operators, the president loses them as a source of detached judgment on the operations. They become advocates; not protectors of the president (even if he does not quite realize his need for protection). So it was with McFarlane and Poindexter; once committed, they had reason to overlook the warning signals thrown up by the process. Excluding Congress also excluded one more "political scrub," one more source of advice about what most Americans would find acceptable.

In circumventing the ban on aid to the contras, the Reagan administration's approach to Congress was more one of contempt than of exclusion. An isolated act or two of aiding the contras would have been a close call, given the ambiguity of the ban. But close congressional votes do not excuse establishing "the Enterprise." Poindexter and North were explicit in their later testimony before Congress: "I simply did not want any outside interference," and "I didn't want to tell Congress anything," they said, respectively.[42]

"The Enterprise" is the most troubling piece of the entire story, one the congressional investigations paused over far too briefly. It was an attempt to escape congressional oversight entirely, to construct a CIA outside the American government. As North put it: "Director Casey had in mind . . . an overseas entity that was . . . self-financing, independent of appropriated monies."[43] The idea was dangerous, but the price the administration eventually paid for it was high. If covert actions are to be undertaken, they should be done by the agency of government constructed to do them—the Central Intelligence Agency. It has both the expertise and the accountability.

Information and the Balance of Power

Disputes over secret operations between Congress and the executive have grabbed the headlines, yet the day-to-day balance of power between the two branches has been more affected by the sharply increased availability of intelligence analysis to Congress. This latter change has coincided with the tug-of-war over operations and so has been obscured by it. However, Congress now receives nearly every intelligence item the executive does. In this way, too, the intelligence agencies are coming to have a more customary relationship with Congress, but one that is more awkward for them than for the Agriculture or Commerce departments.

Intelligence agencies, the CIA in particular, were conceived as servants of their executive masters. It bears remembering that *the* intelligence issue in the early postwar period was not operations; rather it was avoiding another Pearl Harbor. That problem was what to do about fragmented intelligence that could neither sort out signals of warning from surrounding "noise" nor make the warning persuasive to senior officials of government. This problem, along with the balkanized way the separate armed services had fought World War II, begat the National Security Council. It also begat the sequence of efforts to coordinate American intelligence, beginning with the Central Intelligence Group in 1946.

Congress was a promoter of these changes but essentially a bystander to them. As in other areas of government, it used laws to shape processes in the executive branch. Long after it had tried to centralize and formalize the intelligence process in the executive, it left its own oversight of intelligence and its role in receiving intelligence information informal and fragmented. Changing congressional attitudes toward operations both coincided with and produced an altered view of intelligence products. If Congress was to know about and judge covert operations, it was logical to assess them in light of the intelligence premises on which they were based.

Some numbers suggest the extent of the change over the past decade. Virtually everything the CIA produces goes to the two Intelligence committees, and most also goes to the Foreign Affairs, Foreign Relations, Armed Services, and Appropriations committees. All eight committees receive the CIA "newspaper," the National Intelligence Daily (NID). The CIA alone sends some 5,000 reports to Congress each year and conducts over a thousand oral briefings.[44] By contrast, CIA records show only twenty-two briefings to Congress (on topics other than covert action) about Chile in the decade 1964–74.[45] Overall, the CIA gave perhaps a hundred briefings a year to Congress in the mid-1970s.[46]

What is true of CIA analyses is also the case in varying degrees for the products of other intelligence agencies. Just as the Intelligence committees get a biweekly list of new CIA publications, they receive indexes from the Defense Intelligence Agency (DIA), along with the DIA daily summary.[47] The National Security Agency provides weekly summaries of signals intelligence. Committee staffers can get access to "raw" intelligence, like defense attache or CIA agent reports, by special request, although in the most sensitive cases these must be made by the committee chairman to the DCI. People move in both directions from committee staffs to intelligence community analyst jobs, and occasionally committee staffers get friendly calls from intelligence community analysts suggesting that they ask for a particular item.

The change is marked enough without overstating it. Because intelligence is available on Capitol Hill does not mean it is read. Congress is an oral culture, while written products are the intelligence analyst's predilection. If they read, members of Congress, like their counterparts in the executive, will turn to the *New York Times* and *Washington Post* before they pick up the NID. The committees, especially the Intelligence committees, are tightly compartmented in their handling of classified material, which means that getting access to some intelligence is at least a bother. And since knowledge is power and access prestige, Hill staffers who receive intelligence may hold it, not share it.

The people within the intelligence community who conduct the briefings or write the reports are analysts, not operators. They are more professorial than conspiratorial in temperament. They work for the CIA's Directorate of Intelligence, not its Directorate of Operations, and they tell their neighbors openly that they work for the CIA or for the State Department's Bureau of Intelligence and Research or the Pentagon's DIA.

They get much of their information about foreign governments the same way academics do, through reading periodicals or transcripts of media monitored openly by the Foreign Broadcast Information Service. In addition they have access to two sets of secret sources—diplomatic cables sent by State Department officers abroad and raw intelligence, such as agent reports produced by the CIA's Directorate of Operations or foreign communications monitored secretly by the National Security Agency.

The change is dramatic for these analysts, many of whom had never dealt with Congress before a decade ago and all of whom have been steeped in a professional culture that separates intelligence from policy lest the former be biased or politicized through contact with the latter. When the subject is technical and, preferably, out of the limelight, briefing Congress is a welcome chance to educate another set of consumers. Yet the analysts recognize that members of Congress, like executive officials, seldom are disinterested consumers of information.

They seek it as leverage, often to be used against the executive that is the analysts' ostensible master. If the subject is politically hot, like Central America in the 1980s, the experience is painful, the sense of being manipulated keen.

Congress as Lever or Ally?

Sometimes, Congress listens to intelligence analysis when the executive will not. In such cases, benefits and risks are two sides of the same coin. In June 1987, Representative Duncan Hunter smashed a Toshiba radio-cassette player on the steps of the Capitol. The purpose of his stunt was attention: Toshiba and a Norwegian firm had deliberately sold the Soviet Union milling equipment that would make Soviet submarines quieter, hence harder to track. Hunter charged that the $17 million sale might "cost the West $30 billion to regain the superiority we lost."[48] The Toshiba bashing was the culmination of a series of events in which the CIA's Technology Transfer Assessment Center (TTAC) had, in effect, hawked its analyses around Washington.

The story began not with TTAC but with a disaffected Japanese employee who took the story of the Toshiba sale to COCOM, the Paris-based export control organization comprising the NATO allies and Japan. Staffers at COCOM, however, accepted Toshiba's word that it had sold only permitted technology. The employee then took his story to the U.S. embassy in Tokyo, which put him in touch with TTAC. The first stop for TTAC was the State Department, which made a diplomatic "demarche" to Japan. Like most such demarches, it was, however, brushed off for want of hard information. Moreover, the State Department looked askance at TTAC: TTAC's desire to control the issue left its colleagues at State's Bureau of Intelligence and Research feeling cut out, and policy officials at State were nervous about the repercussions of the issue on relations with two allies. Yet the tradition of CIA independence, plus TTAC's control of the issue, made it difficult for State to influence what TTAC said.

The next stop was the Defense Department, where Undersecretary Fred Iklé, a willing listener, agreed to take the issue up in his forthcoming trip to Japan. For Iklé the issue was one among several, not primary, and his trip produced little more than the demarche. But Iklé's office, briefed by TTAC and now with a better case in hand, in turn briefed Senator Jake Gam, a kindred hard-liner on technology transfer. At about the same time, December 1986, mention of this "major technology transfer" appeared in classified written briefings to the two Intelligence committees. Word was spreading.

Within two months the issue was public. First it went again to COCOM, where this time TTAC briefed representatives of the fifteen member nations. As Japan and Norway responded, Washington buzzed with rumors of a big new case. In late February the House Armed Services seapower subcommittee was briefed on the issue, and the next month, at hearings on the omnibus trade bill, Iklé's deputy, Richard Perle, referred obliquely to an export control violation he "could go into in a classified hearing." A week later the conservative *Washington Times* broke the story, quoting unnamed officials "outside the government."

From then on, TTAC did not lack audiences; it had more than it wanted. Members of Congress outbid each other in proposals for retaliating against the wrongdoers, especially Toshiba, for Norway had acted to defuse the issue by admitting guilt and working with the United States. In the end, the weight of other interests at play in U.S.-Japanese relations began to be felt, and congressional leaders cooperated with the executive in enacting sanctions against Toshiba that, while sounding tough, were relatively mild.

The kind of interaction with Congress reflected in the Toshiba affair was uncharted water. On one hand, Guy DuBois, the principal TTAC analyst, sought to hold to the traditional line between intelligence and policy: "Once you state a position, how that position affects policy . . . is not your business."[49] On the other hand, DCI Casey had given TTAC a mandate that was more than providing information; it was to be a player in a quasi-prosecutorial process. In that sense, its information was to be nearly self-implementing: if it could prove guilt then that would frame the response. Congress was not the principal prosecutor, but telling it was a way to make sure someone paid attention.

The Toshiba case coincided with William Webster's arrival as DCI, replacing the late William Casey; plainly, Webster's main mission was repairing relations with Congress after Iran-contra. "To Webster," the TTAC analyst recalled, "Congress has an insatiable appetite and to the extent we can, we satisfy it." Moreover, "if a Congressman finds out that you decided not to be completely forthcoming," the credibility of the CIA could be damaged. The CIA's role, however, was not simply responding to congressional requests: "If they ask a stupid question, tell them it's stupid, then tell them what the smart question is and answer it."

It is still rare for Congress to be the lead consumer of intelligence. Most of the time Congress's effect is indirect. Since Congress will also know what the executive knows, executive officials are prudent to pay attention to intelligence lest they be skewered by Congress for the failure. Consider the contrast between the fall of the shah of Iran in 1978 and the departure from the Philippines of President Ferdinand Marcos in 1986.[50] The experience with the shah had taught policy officials in both the executive and Congress not to dismiss unwelcome news about Marcos, nor to assume, as they had about the shah, that Marcos knew his politics better than Washington did. That the Philippine opposition—moderate, Catholic, and U.S.-educated—was both much more accessible to intelligence collection and much more acceptable than Iran's mullahs made the lesson easier to learn.

The Philippine crisis moved more slowly than the Iranian, beginning in earnest with the assassination of opposition leader Benigno Aquino on the airport tarmac in Manila as he returned from the United States in August 1983. The intelligence community concluded that if Marcos had not ordered the assassination, it almost certainly had been done on his behalf. From then on the Philippines was on the congressional agenda almost as much as it was on that of the executive. The contrast with Iran could hardly be sharper; a 1979 House Intelligence committee postmortem on the Iran case contains not a single reference to Congress.[51]

The State Department worried about Congress in the instance of Toshiba, but in the instance of the Philippines the East Asia "mafia" in the executive—including State, Defense, and the NSC—welcomed congressional pressure as a way to persuade *their bosses*, not least the president, that Marcos might have to go. An August 1985 Senate Intelligence Committee report concluded that "the Marcos government is unlikely to pursue the changes necessary to stop the economic hemorrhaging, to slow or halt the insurgency or to heal the major lesions that are infecting the political process."[52] Later in the year, the links between Congress and the executive were tightened when one Senate Foreign Relations Committee staffer moved to the intelligence community to be national intelligence officer for East Asia and the Pacific.

Another Senate Foreign Relations Committee staff member described the interaction:

> The people in the State Department were using us, the Foreign Relations Committee, to get their point across in the White House. They were delighted when (Chairman Richard] Lugar decided to write a letter, not to Marcos but to the President of the United States. In other words, we laid it right on the President; We shifted our focus from the President of the Philippines to the President of the United States.

In November 1985, Marcos called a snap election for February 1986. The opposition managed to unite to name Aquino's widow, Corazon, as its presi-

dential candidate. In December 1985 the intelligence community was still predicting a narrow Marcos victory, but by January 1986 it labeled the election too close to call, and on the eve of the vote it actually predicted an Aquino victory while also betting that Marcos would fix the results if need be. On January 30 President Reagan announced a bipartisan mission of U.S. election observers, cochaired by Lugar.

The effect of Congress's access to intelligence was most evident in the crunch. Most of the U.S. observers witnessed fraud by the ruling party, but as late as February 11, as votes trickled in, Reagan commented that the United States was concerned about both violence and "the possibility of fraud, although it could have been that all of that was occurring on both sides," a quote that so pleased Marcos that he had it shown over and over on Philippine television.[53]

At this point, the intelligence community was told, in effect, to put up or shut up. It responded with convincing proof of massive fraud by Marcos's party. Thus the administration had to act in the knowledge that Congress would soon have the same proof. Its options—to ride out the storm with Marcos, for instance—were correspondingly constrained. By February 15 the White House had dropped the "fraud on both sides" line, and on the 17th Lugar called for Marcos to resign.

Judgments about whether the sharing of intelligence with Congress creates more consensus or less, let alone whether it produces wiser policy or more foolish, are hard to make and inevitably subjective. In retrospect, if the departure of Marcos is regarded as a success, the fact that Congress knew what the executive did seems to have contributed to that success. Unwise options were foreclosed, and senior officials, especially the president, had to see the election as it was, not as they might wish it to be: Congress was watching. At the end, sharing intelligence about what Marcos had done in stealing votes made a compelling case and was enough to produce consensus.

In the case of Nicaragua, however, if shared intelligence produced a more enlightened debate, it surely did not produce consensus. This issue, like so many others, turned not on what the Sandinistas did but on what their actions meant, implied, or portended. On those latter questions, even good intelligence assessments are seldom convincing. Officials in the executive and Congress disagreed, unsurprisingly, despite looking at the same data and reading the same analyses of it.

So far, there is little evidence of analysts cutting their cloth to suit congressional consumers. However, it may simply be that the congressional role is new. A cynic would say that analysts always hedged their bets, and critics would argue that analysts feel the most formidable pressures to change assessments from their bosses in the executive branch. Analysts did not soften the news in the Philippines even though it was unwelcome to some in the administration; nor did TTAC hold back in the Toshiba case because the State Department did not much like its assessment (and Congress liked it too much). In the heat of the debate over Nicaragua, the House Intelligence Committee, while generally praising intelligence community performance, certainly did not feel it had been pandered to—quite the contrary.[54]

The Special Case of Verification

The more direct role of intelligence agencies in the political process is especially apparent in battles over arms control verification. Since the Senate must ratify treaties, verification is plainly an issue for Congress. Treaty supporters and opponents, as well as those who seek a way out by voting against the treaty without being labeled against arms control, all use verification as an argument. In the process they seek, understandably, to push decisions about what is finally a political issue—whether existing monitoring arrangements provide for adequate verification—onto the technical intelligence agencies, which in turn want, again understandably, to confine their role to describing those monitoring arrangements.

Verification was not an issue during the debate over SALT I in 1972, but charges of Soviet violations of that treaty, as well as the much more ambitious aims of SALT II, raised the issue five years later. Accordingly, in 1977 the Senate Foreign Relations Committee asked the Intelligence Committee for a thorough review of monitoring capabilities. The report was relatively sanguine. It appeared verification would not, after all, be a stumbling block in the ratification debate.[55]

Then, in March 1979 the United States lost access to monitoring facilities in Iran. Verification returned to the agenda, especially for the fence sitters, prominent among whom was Senator John Glenn, who said he could not support the treaty until the lost capabilities were replaced. The Intelligence Committee's final report, released on the eve of the floor debate, distinguished between the treaty's numerical limits and many of its qualitative constraints that could be monitored with high confidence, and several qualitative limits for which confidence was relatively low.[56]

Opponents zeroed in on the low-confidence provisions, while supporters pointed to the committee judgment that the treaty itself would enhance America's ability to monitor the treaty limits. The ratification vote boded to be a close-run thing, due largely to verification issues, but the whole debate was rendered moot by the Soviet invasion of Afghanistan. President Carter withdrew the treaty from Senate consideration.

In 1988 the Senate Intelligence Committee's unanimous judgment was decisive in removing verification as an issue in the discussion over the Intermediate Nuclear Forces (INF) treaty.[57] The treaty itself both embodied the most elaborate verification arrangements ever negotiated and simplified verification by eliminating weapons systems entirely, not merely reducing them in number. In its report approving the INF treaty, the committee explicitly opened the debate on a future strategic arms treaty by observing that strategic reductions would be far more demanding to monitor than those in the INF treaty.

The committee report also sought to protect the intelligence community by noting that verification is not simple, nor does it alone settle whether a treaty is desirable; a bad treaty that can be verified is still a bad treaty. It also distinguished carefully between monitoring and verification—the former an intelligence community responsibility, the latter a judgment by the executive of whether Soviet behavior as reported by the community is compatible with the treaty.[58]

Clients and Patrons

Yet another sign that the intelligence community has joined the American government is that the institutional relations that have grown up between intelligence agencies and their congressional overseers have come to resemble those between domestic agencies and their congressional committees. Although the committees can be sharply critical of their agencies—witness covert actions or particular "intelligence failures"—in general the interests of the overseers and those overseen run parallel. The creation of the two intelligence oversight committees was thus the best thing that ever happened to the intelligence community, even if the heat of specific disputes sometimes has obscured that fact for intelligence officials.

The committees and their staffs have created a pool of people knowledgeable about intelligence and able to serve as advocates throughout the two chambers. By the time both new committees had been formed, in 1977, only 3 percent of House and 20 percent of Senate incumbents had served on the then-existing oversight subcommittees of Appropriations and Armed Services. Ten years later the percentages were 8 and 43. Over the period between 1980, when the Intelligence committees became the budget authorizers for intelligence, and 1986, the

CIA budget more than doubled, growing faster than the defense budget. The total budget for the intelligence community nearly tripled, reaching close to $20 billion.[59]

Indeed, the committees have been accused of becoming as much protectors of the intelligence community as overseers—a risk that runs through all relations between Congress and executive agencies. It is true that the base of knowledge among members and staff does build understanding. The difference between the congressional investigations of intelligence in the mid-1970s and the Iran-contra panel was, for better or worse, striking: the latter was narrow, disciplined, and, Oliver North excepted, boring, with no visible sentiment for ending covert operations, much less for dismantling the CIA.

The bulk of the increase in the intelligence budget has gone for expensive satellites and other technical collection systems, where the role of Congress and the link to arms control have been central. The fall of the shah underscored the need for better human intelligence and analysis, and the closing of the Iranian monitoring sites showed just how fragile U.S. technical collection could be. As members of the Intelligence committees came to know what U.S. intelligence can do, they naturally became sympathetic to what more it could do with more money. That was particularly the case in monitoring arms control, for if judgments about verification are subjective, those about monitoring are less so: if existing systems provide 50 percent confidence in monitoring some aspect of Soviet weaponry, the argument that an additional system would increase the confidence to 80 percent can be relatively straightforward.

For example, in its report on the INF treaty, the Senate Intelligence Committee prefaced its positive judgment about verification with this statement on behalf of new technical collection systems needed to verify a future strategic arms treaty: "The Committee feels that this potential gap between intelligence capabilities and intelligence requirements must be appreciated by Members of the Senate."[60] As is typical of the multifaceted relations between committees and agencies, the committee apparently had in mind not only systems the intelligence community eagerly sought, but also ones about which it had doubts.

Other cases of congressional involvement, departures in the realm of intelligence, also look more familiar in the domestic sweep of executive-congressional relations. A good example is counterintelligence. Early in the Reagan administration the breaking wave of spy scandals elicited a number of dramatic proposals from political officials in and around the White House. Most of these ideas were judged excessive or unwise by career counterintelli-

gence professionals; the Senate Intelligence Committee came to share that judgment, and careerists and Congress cooperated in beating back the proposals.

Later in the administration, concern remained high, fed by evidence that the new U.S. embassy in Moscow was riddled with eavesdropping devices. By then, cooler heads had come to the fore in the White House, and the Senate committee now sided with them about counterintelligence even as Congress and the White House were at loggerheads over aid to the contras.[61] The committee became a player in the administration debate, siding with those who proposed to take strong measures (the FBI and part of the CIA) against those who worried that Soviet retaliation could hinder America's ability to run foreign policy (State and the CIA's espionage managers). Liberals on the committee were persuaded to the FBI view both because they came to believe the administration was not doing enough and because they wanted to demonstrate that their attitude toward the intelligence agencies was not purely negative, that they could say "yes" as well as "no."

Joining the government means pluses and minuses for the intelligence community that are familiar from the experience of domestic agencies. For instance, for most of its history the CIA was better at understanding foreign governments than its own. One congressional staffer described Clair George, the CIA director of congressional affairs during the contra affair and a career clandestine service officer, as a man convinced that "Washington was a foreign country and he was the station chief in hostile terrain, mounting operations against the Congress."[62] Joining the American government provides both sympathetic guides to and experience in reconnoitering that terrain.

The negative side is also familiar: the more "your" congressional committees know, the more able they are to help you, but also the more they are tempted to tell you how to do your business. The Intelligence committees have been voracious requirers of reports even if, like other committees, they receive more than they can digest. Like other committees, they have also been tempted to "micromanage"; the line between oversight and management can blur, especially perhaps if the subject to be managed is exciting.

To be sure, micromanagement is relative, and the intelligence budget is not subject to anything like the intrusions of, say, the Armed Services committees into the defense budget. The CIA, for instance, has all training lumped under a single budget line item. Still, the CIA is coming to look like other agencies of government, for good and ill. Simple aging has made it more bureaucratic in any case, but congressional oversight has abetted that tendency.

Projects conceived one year do not get approved until the next. Even minor operations require major paperwork. And despite renewed fondness for covert action on the part of American administrations, CIA officers retain an anxious eye on their political masters outside the executive; no one wants to be a subject of the next congressional investigation. The CIA is becoming more cautious; its officers want authorization in writing. On balance, the caution is a benefit, but it has come at some cost to the entrepreneurial spirit of the CIA.

Open Questions

The process of intelligence becoming a more ordinary part of the government is an uncompleted experiment. It is not, however, reversible. It was inevitable that the intelligence community would come to resemble the rest of the government as the conditions that spawned it as an exception changed: the waning of the deepest fears of the cold war, the loss after the Bay of Pigs of the CIA's image of mastery, the tarnishing of the presidency by Watergate, and the rise of investigative journalism. Perhaps the most important changes are internal to Congress, for intelligence oversight had been the quintessential working of the congressional club. When age removed those few committee chairmen from Congress, and reform meant that they would not be replaced, intelligence's relation to Congress was bound to change.

In 1954 when news of the covert operation to overthrow Guatemala's President Jacobo Arbenz leaked out, it was the leak that was discredited, not the operation. In *Time's* overheated prose, the revelations were "masterminded in Moscow and designed to divert the attention . . . from Guatemala as the Western Hemisphere's Red problem child."[63] Not so three decades later, not even if the initial leak was in Beirut in Arabic.

The government that intelligence has joined is a divided one, its divisions institutionalized. The executive-legislative division is the most obvious but not always the most important. In areas like agriculture or commerce, for instance, it is taken for granted that, whether particular observers like it or not, executive agencies and congressional committees serve essentially the same domestic constituencies. Those agencies and committees then contend within their respective arenas against representatives of other constituencies.

Intelligence analysis, by contrast, represents no conventional domestic interest groups. It is a source of advice about foreign countries. Offering advice within a single branch is political enough. Whether the intelligence community can sustain its credibility in offering advice across two branches, often in sharp contention remains to be seen. Congress may come to feel it wants its own intelligence analysts, as it came into another area of advice, the budget, to feel it required its own budgeteers, the Congressional Budget Office. A Congressional Intelligence Office does not seem imminent, however. It would ensue, if it did only from a bitter conflict between the executive and Congress. Nor is there is a stream of congressional action whose shape and deadlines would argue for an in-house intelligence service comparable to the one that exists for the budget.

Yet it is instructive, and perhaps a little fearsome, to contemplate, now that Congress and intelligence analysts are acquainted, just how perfect they are for each other. The lives of foreign policy officials in the executive are dominated by their in-boxes; for them, analysis is a nuisance unless they can be sure it will support their predilections. Moreover, when assistant secretaries average not much more than a year in tenure, neither they nor intelligence analysts have much incentive, or much opportunity, to take the measure of each other.

By contrast, members of Congress, and still more their staffs are not so driven by their in-boxes. Their quest to signify means a hunt for information and for issues, just what intelligence analysts have to offer. And career paths in Congress and intelligence fit together neatly, most members are, in effect, elected for life if they choose and the tenures of their senior staffers are much longer than those of assistant secretaries,

Arrangements linking Congress to intelligence analysis are portentous but will change only gradually, for the most part out of the spotlight and out of the headlines. The focal point of conflict between the two branches will remain covert operations. There, in the nature of both constitutional and political reality, the conflict cannot be resolved, for it runs to the heart of foreign policy: balancing the responsibility of Congress with the primacy of the president.

The 1988 debate over when Congress would be notified of covert actions is illustrative of that fact. On its face the debate seemed almost trivial: both sides agreed that normally the president should inform the committees of a covert action in advance if possible, within a day or so of its start; and so the debate was over whether the forty-eight-hour requirement would be binding or not. Both sides cited examples to suit their preferences: proponents of a mandatory requirement cited arms sales to Iran, opponents, an offer by Canada during the Carter administration to help in smuggling U.S. hostages out of Iran but only if the U.S. Congress were not notified.[64]

Like most debates about intelligence, the argument was about not only the powers of the president but also about where to strike the balance between expediency and accountability. Over the past two decades the balance has moved toward accountability, and in one sense the Iran-contra affair can be seen as confirmation that the evolution has worked tolerably well. Yet there can be no full resolution to the dilemma, for secret operations inescapably raise the trade-off between democratic, thus open, process and effective, hence secret, foreign policy.

Observers fearful that increased congressional involvement poses a risk to secrecy have proposed combining the separate House and Senate committees into one joint intelligence committee. The idea of a joint committee, however, is misdirected. While a single committee might give the president less justification for excluding Congress as "too leaky," Congress has not been leaky, certainly not by comparison with the executive.

The disadvantage of having two committees is the risk of miscommunication: witness the mining of the Nicaraguan harbors. Yet given the institutional jealousies of the two houses, the advantages of two committees—their different personalities, different priorities, and a greater claim to credibility in their respective houses—outweigh that risk. Moreover, the greatest risk to oversight is that the overseers will become co-opted. So it was by all accounts with an earlier joint committee, the Joint Atomic Energy Committee. Having two points of oversight, and even a certain amount of competition between them, reduces the chance that the overseers will become only the patrons of those they oversee.

Congress neither desires nor is able to approve every covert action in advance. Apart from constitutional questions, the process is simply too slow: Congress's instruments are blunt. One way to increase congressional control over controversial operations would be to require the Intelligence committees to approve any withdrawal from the CIA Contingency Reserve. That would be uncomfortable for the committees in that it would put them more directly on the line in the eyes of their congressional colleagues, but it would at least spare them the discomfort of having to choose between silent opposition to an operation and public exposure of it.

When administrations feel secrecy is at a premium, they can resort to informing only the "gang of eight," a procedure that had been used only once by mid-1988.[65] Had relations between Casey and the committees been better, the Reagan administration might have done so in the instance of Iranian arms sales. That would not necessarily have resulted in wiser policy, for it is conceivable that the gang of eight would have been seduced down the path from geostrategic interests to releasing hostages just as the president was. But the subsequent debate would then have been about the wisdom of the policy, not about whether Congress was deceived.

In the future, major covert actions will be overt, as was aid to the contras or to the resistance in Afghanistan. The controversy over them will spill into public, even if they are not propelled there by the executive. If some options are thereby foreclosed, at least the choices will be openly debated. Administrations will have to make evident how those covert programs support coherent public policies. And because major covert actions will not remain secret, presidents will be well advised, before the fact, to ask themselves whether the covert action could bear the test of disclosure: would it still seem sensible once it were public?

The views of congressional overseers will give the president a good indication of what the public would think if it knew of the operation. If the administration is out of step with what the public will accept, as in the case of arms sales to Iran, it may learn that in advance, rather than being punished by Congress after the fact. If the public is divided or confused, as with aid to the contras, the administration probably can have its way. This process is about the best we can do. It is, as Iran-contra testifies, no guarantee against stupid presidential decisions or the resulting public scandals.

Questions for Further Discussion

1. What does Treverton mean when he writes: "Welcome to the American Government"?

2. What have been the main sources of tension between Congress and the executive branch over intelligence activities?

3. How optimistic is Treverton—and are you—about the chances for successful Congressional accountability for intelligence operations?

4. Have lawmakers become too meddlesome when it comes to sensitive intelligence activities, or have they provided a valuable safeguard against the abuse of secret power?

Endnotes

1. Quoted in Susan F. Rasky, "Walking a Tightrope on Intelligence Issues," *New York Times*, October 11, 1988, p. A26.
2. Quoted in "Taking Toshiba Public," Case C15-88-858.0, Harvard University, Kennedy School of Government, 1988, p. 5.

3. At a press conference at the Capitol, July 19, 1975, quoted in Gregory F. Treverton, *Covert Action: The Limits of Intervention in the Postwar World* (Basic Books, 1987), p. 5.

4. The committees did find some rogue elephants in domestic intelligence activities, especially those of the Federal Bureau of Investigation.

5. *Alleged Assassination Plots Involving Foreign Leaders*, An Interim Report of the Senate Select Committee to Study Governmental Operations with Respect to Intelligence Activities, S. Rept. 94-465, 94 Cong. 1 sess. (Government Printing Office, 1975), p. 149. (Hereafter cited as *Assassination Report*.)

6. See *Assassination Report*, p. 108ff.

7. Richard B. Russell Library, Oral History No. 86, taped by Hughes Cates, February 22, 1977, University of Georgia, Athens, Georgia, cited in Loch K. Johnson, *America's Secret Power: The CIA in a Democratic Society* (Oxford University Press, 1989), p. 108.

8. Quoted in "History of the Central Intelligence Agency," in *Supplementary Detailed Staff Reports on Foreign and Military Intelligence*, bk. 4, *Final Report*, S. Rept. 94-755, Senate Select Committee to Study Governmental Operations with Respect to Intelligence Activities, 94 Cong. 2 sess. (GPO, 1976), p. 54.

9. *Covert Action in Chile, 1963–1973*, Committee Print, Senate Select Committee to Study Governmental Operations with Respect to Intelligence Activities, 94 Cong. 1 sess. (GPO, 1975), pp. 41–42.

10. David Gries, "The CIA and Congress: Uneasy Partners," *Studies in Intelligence* (September 1987), p. 77. This is an unclassified article in a CIA journal. In the original, "Vinson" is rendered "Vincent," a typographical error that is, perhaps, inadvertent testimony to just how foreign the Congress was to the CIA.

11. William Colby and Peter Forbath, *Honorable Men: My Life in the CIA* (Simon and Schuster, 1978), pp. 402–03.

12. Officially, Foreign Assistance Act of 1974, sec. 32 (88 Stat. 1804).

13. For an intriguing account of the Senate Select Committee, see Loch K. Johnson, *A Season of Inquiry: The Senate Intelligence Investigation* (University Press of Kentucky, 1985).

14. For instance, Colby regards the outcome as "not unreasonable." See Colby and Forbath, *Honorable Men*, p. 429.

15. The Church committee was more often the victim of leaks than the perpetrator. See Johnson, *Season of Inquiry*, pp. 206–07.

16. It was published by the *Village Voice* as "The CIA Report the President Doesn't Want You to Read," February 16 and 23, 1976.

17. Loch Johnson, "The U.S. Congress and the CIA: Monitoring the Dark Side of Government," *Legislative Studies Quarterly*, vol. 5 (November 1980), pp. 491–92.

18. The order was printed in *New York Times*, December 5, 1981, pp. 18–19.

19. Interview, January 16, 1986.

20. This account is drawn primarily from the subsequent congressional investigation, *Report of the Congressional Committees Investigating the Iran-Contra Affair with Supplemental, Minority, and Additional Views*, H. Rept. 100-400, S. Rept. 100-216, 100 Cong. 1 sess. (GPO, 1987) (hereafter cited as *Iran-Contra Affair*); and from the earlier *Report of the President's Special Review Board* (known as the Tower commission after its chairman, former Senator John Tower) (GPO, 1987). (Hereafter cited as *Tower Commission*.) The NSC documents are quoted in *Washington Post*, March 10, 1982.

21. *Report of the Select Committee on Intelligence, U.S. Senate, Jan 1, 1983 to Dec. 31, 1984*, S. Rept. 98-665, 98 Cong. 2 sess. (GPO, 1984), pp. 4–5. (Hereafter *Intelligence Report*.)

22. The phrase is Oliver North's, quoted in *Iran-Contra Affair*, p 3.

23 The House-Senate conference report spoke of Nicaragua "providing military support (including arms, training, and logistical, command and control, and communications facilities) to groups seeking to overthrow the Government of El Salvador." See *Intelligence Report*, pp. 6–7.

24. See Stephen Kinzer, "Nicaraguan Says No Mines Are Left in Nation's Ports," *New York Times*, April 13, 1084, p. Al; Philip Taubman, "How Congress Was Informed of Mining of Nicaragua Ports," *New York Times*, April 16, 1984, p. A1; and Bernard Gwenzman, "C.I.A. Now Asserts It Put Off Session with Senate Unit," *New York Times*, April 17, 1984, p. A1. See also the account in *Intelligence Report*, p. 4ff.

25. Interviews with Intelligence Committee staff members, January 1987.

26. The letter was dated April 9; see Joanne Omang and Don Oberdorfer, "Senate Votes, 84–12, to Condemn Mining of Nicaraguan Ports," *Washington Post*, April 11, 1984, p. A16.

27. *Iran-Contra Affair*, p. 41.

28. The quote and the estimate are both from *Iran-Contra Affair*, pp. 37 and 4, respectively.

29. *Iran-Contra Affair*, p. 7.

30. The finding is printed in *Tower Commission*, pp. B60, B66 (emphasis in the original).

31. *Tower Commission*, p. III-22.

32. Interview, January 9, 1986.

33. As quoted in "Overseeing of C.I.A. by Congress Has Produced Decade of Support," *New York Times*, July 7, 1986, p. A10.

34. Quoted in Susan F. Rasky, "Walking a Tightrope," *New York Times*, October 11, 1988, p. A26.

35. Quoted in Johnson, *America's Secret Power*, p. 125.

36. Quoted in Martin Tolchin, "Of C.I.A. Games and Disputed Rules," *New York Times*, May 14, 1984, p. A12.

37. *Iran-Contra Affair*, p. 123.

38. Interview with CIA officials, August 1986 and January 1987.

39. One reported instance was an operation in Suriname in early 1983. See Philip Taubman, "Are U.S. Covert Activities Best Policy on Nicaragua?" *New York Times*, June 15, 1983, p. A1.

40. Interview, January 9, 1987.

41. Testimony before the Iran-Congress investigation, quoted in *Iran-Contra Affair*, p. 271.

42. *Iran-Contra Affair*, p. 19.

43. *Iran-Contra Affair*, p. 333.

44. Robert M. Gates, "The CIA and American Foreign Policy," *Foreign Affairs*, vol. 66 (Winter 1987–88), p. 224; and Gries, "The CIA and Congress," p. 78.

45. *Covert Action in Chile*, p. 49.

46. "Taking Toshiba Public," p. 5.

47. The information in this paragraph derives from interviews with congressional staffers conducted principally in September 1988.

48. "Taking Toshiba Public," p. 1.

49. This and subsequent quotes from DuBois are from "Taking Toshiba Public."

50. The source for this account is W. E. Kline, "The Fall of Marcos," Case C16-88-868.0, Harvard University, Kennedy School of Government, 1988.

51. See *Iran: Evaluation of U.S. Intelligence Performance Prior to November 1978*, Committee Print, Subcommittee on Evaluation of the House Permanent Select Committee on Intelligence, 96 Cong. 1 sess. (GPO, 1979).

52. This and the following quote are from "The Fall of Marcos," pp. 18–19.

53. "The Fall of Marcos," p. 20.

54. See *U.S. Intelligence Performance on Central America: Achievements and Selected Instances of Concern*, Committee Print, Subcommittee on Oversight and Evaluation of the House Permanent Select Committee on Intelligence, 97 Cong. 2 sess. (GPO, 1982).

55. See Stephen J. Flanagan, "The Domestic Politics of SALT II: Implications for the Foreign Policy Process," in John Spinier and Joseph Nogee, eds., *Congress, the Presidency and American Foreign Policy* (Pergamon Press, 1981), pp. 63–64.

56. *Principal Findings on the Capabilities of the U.S. to Monitor the SALT II Treaty*, Committee Print, Senate Select Committee on Intelligence, 96 Cong. 1 sess. (GPO, 1979).

57. *The INF Treaty Monitoring and Verification Capabilities*, S. Rept. 100-318, Senate Select Committee on Intelligence, 100 Cong. 2 sess. (GPO, 1988).

58. *INF Treaty*, S. Rept. 100-318, p. 5.

59. Numbers of members and the CIA budget are from Gries, "The CIA and Congress," p. 78. The total intelligence community budget is an estimate, compiled from interviews and published sources.

60. *INF Treaty*, S. Rept. 100-318, p. 3.

61. See, for instance, *Meeting the Espionage Challenge: A Review of United States Counterintelligence and Security Program*, S. Rept. 99-522, Senate Select Committee on Intelligence, 99 Cong. 2 sess. (GPO, 1986).

62. Interview, January 18, 1987.

63. *Time*, February 8, 1954, p. 36.

64. *Intelligence Oversight Act of 1988*, H. Rept. 100-705, 100 Cong. 2 sess. (GPO, 1988), pt. 1, pp. 56–57. See also Dick Cheney, "Covert Operations: Who's in Charge," *Wall Street Journal*, May 3, 1988. However, a subsequent investigation by the Senate Intelligence Committee left doubt that the Canadian example actually happened.

65. *Intelligence Oversight Act of 1988*, H. Rept. 100-705, p. 11. ✦

Reprinted with permission from Gregory F. Treverton, "Intelligence: Welcome to the American Government," in Thomas E. Mann, ed., *A Question of Balance: The President, the Congress, and Foreign Policy* (Washington, DC: The Brookings Institute, 1990): 70–108.

27

Unleashing the Rogue Elephant: September 11 and Letting the CIA Be the CIA

Frederick P. Hitz

The year 1975 was a watershed in the history of U.S. intelligence. That year the secret agencies were subjected to three serious inquiries into their activities, in response to newspaper allegations that they had engaged in illegal activities—most notably, spying at home. Called a "rogue elephant" by one of the leading investigators, the CIA found itself facing new restrictions and reporting requirements, as lawmakers attempted to leash the Agency. Over the next 25 years, intelligence reformers and antireformers debated the proper level of supervision, in hopes of maintaining accountability without stifling the effectiveness of intelligence officers. Hitz argues that the leash on the CIA is too tight and suggests ways to improve effectiveness without eroding civil liberties.

Media outlets have argued that the United States has had an "intelligence failure," decrying the intelligence community for failing to warn the American people of the September 11 attacks on the World Trade Center in New York and on the Pentagon in Virginia. In addition, there is constant clamor that the Central Intelligence Agency (CIA) has been unwisely stifled since the Church Committee hearings of 1975–76[1] and the resultant executive orders of Presidents Ford, Carter, and Reagan that sought to govern the conduct of intelligence activities.[2] There is a cry to unleash the CIA from its perceived legal and policy restrictions and permit it to fight the terrorist threat facing the United States on terms that will succeed against this pernicious force. Some of this impetus comes from a rash of recent studies such as the report of the bipartisan National Commission on Terrorism (NCT), which urged the Director of Central Intelligence (DCI) to modify the current guidelines restricting the recruitment of agents with spotty human rights records, when applied to terrorist informants, with the assertion that "one cannot prowl the back streets of states where terrorist incidents occur and recruit only nice people."[3]

Have the CIA and other intelligence community entities been unwisely constrained in their abilities to pursue the terrorist target by outmoded policies dating from the Cold War? This article will examine four potential modifications to such policies. One possible change is to loosen restraints on the CIA in the recruitment of so-called "dirty assets." A second is to grant domestic law enforcement powers to the CIA to better pursue the terrorist target. Third, the government could repeal the prohibition in Executive Order 12,333 of assassination in peacetime. Finally, impediments could be removed that currently prevent the use of agents in special categories such as journalists, clerics, and academics, if the need is great and cooperation is voluntary. Each possibility will be addressed in turn.

The theme underlying this analysis will be one of balancing. Our need to gather better intelligence about threats posed to the United States and the international community by transnational terrorist groups must be weighed against the constraints imposed by current United States law and practice, the U.S. Constitution, and our status as a constitutional democracy.

I. Recruitment of 'Dirty Assets'

To some degree, the argument over the use of unsavory assets is misleading. By definition, spies are liars, law-breakers, and traitors. They may not be violating U.S. law in supplying CIA spymasters with intelligence information about their own country's defenses or political decision-making, but they are surely violating the laws of the country that they are betraying. John Le Carre wrote with much accuracy when he crafted Alee Leamas' reply to his girlfriend's complaint about using a villain as an agent of East German intelligence:

> What do you think spies are: priests, saints and martyrs? They're a squalid procession of vain fools, traitors too, yes; pansies, sadists and drunkards, people who play cowboys and Indians to brighten their rotten lives. Do you think they sit like monks in London, balancing the rights and wrongs?[4]

Guidelines were established in 1995 that directed CIA case officers in the field to balance human rights and other criminal violations committed by their agents against the positive intelligence supplied or likely to be supplied by these agents. The unintended intersection of several different global and domestic developments after the 1991 collapse of the Soviet Union has prompted confusion over these guidelines and their implementation.

At the end of the Cold War, the then-Deputy Director of Operations (DDO) at the CIA, Richard Stolz, observed that the Directorate probably had more reporting agents on its payroll than it needed to deal with the new post-Soviet world. Always sensitive to the accusation from the ranks that the quantity of spy recruitments counted more than the quality, Mr. Stolz sought to reverse this perception by instituting an asset validation system. Under this asset validation system, pursuant to agreed principles relating to the value and number of intelligence reports produced by a given spy, the Directorate of Operations (DO) could trim its roster of non-reporting or marginally-reporting agents. Mr. Stolz retired before he could evaluate the results of his validation system, so the Inspector General (IG) of the CIA made it the subject of one of his periodic inspections of the Directorate of Operations in 1994. The Office of Inspector General (OIG) concluded in its 1994 inspection report that the Directorate had made a substantial start at validating its agent base and eliminating marginal producers in some offices, but there had not been complete buy-in by other offices. Thus, it was recommended that the DCI lend his support to the effort.[5]

At about the same time, the *New York Times* reported that an agent on the CIA's payroll in Guatemala had been involved in the murder of an American citizen inn-keeper and the husband of an American citizen.[6] Even though subsequent investigations by the CIA, OIG and the President's Intelligence Oversight Board both concluded that neither CIA employees nor Guatemalan Colonel Julio Alpirez had been involved in the murders of the two Americans, the reports found that CIA headquarters and the U.S. Congress had been inadequately informed about human rights violations by agents in Guatemala. The CIA had on its payroll several agents whose human rights records were notoriously poor, and they were not producing much positive intelligence information on drug trafficking or other post-Cold War targets to justify their salary or retention.[7] Out of these reports, and the disciplinary measures taken by DCI John Deutch pursuant to them, came the infamous 1995 guidelines concerning the recruitment of foreign intelligence assets with egregious human rights records. The CIA Office of General Counsel drafted a regulation requiring headquarters' involvement in the recruitment or retention of spies with unsatisfactory human rights records or a record of substantial criminal violations.[8] Although originally intended as a "sanity check" for field agents to enable them to advocate the retention of a spy with dirty hands who nonetheless had ample potential to aid U.S. intelligence collection, the regulation became an invitation to do nothing in an allegedly risk-averse CIA culture. Because spy runners had more on their plates overseas than they could possibly accomplish, it has apparently become easier not to seek a waiver (which in some instances had to go to the DCI for approval) and let the relationship with the malefactor expire.

In any event, that is history. Congress urged the CIA to alter the "dirty hands" guidelines to encourage risk-taking in the recruitment of assets knowledgeable about terrorism after September 11.[9] The DCI has responded by eliminating the requirement of a DCI waiver in the recruitment or retention of dirty assets, leaving that to a dialogue between the field agent and the DDO. Importantly, however, the Agency has retained the requirement of an audit trail in these cases in recognition of a need for some explanation to headquarters why a dirty asset ought to be on the payroll. Left untouched is § 1.7(a) of E.O. 12,333 requiring senior officials of the intelligence community to

> [r]eport to the Attorney General possible violations of federal criminal laws by employees and of specified criminal laws by any other person as provided in procedures agreed upon by the Attorney General and the head of the department or agency concerned, in a manner consistent with the protection of intelligence sources and methods, as specified in those procedures.[10]

Presumably this would still cover knowledge by an American spy runner of an agent's involvement in the death of an American citizen or a U.S. person (an alien legally residing in the United States).

II. Granting Domestic Law Enforcement Powers to the CIA

When the CIA was created in 1947 out of the elements of the wartime Office of Strategic Services (OSS), it was statutorily prohibited from having "police, subpoena, law-enforcement powers, or internal security functions."[11] This was due to President Truman's aversion to creating an American gestapo and some fancy footwork by Federal Bureau of Investigation head J. Edgar Hoover, who was determined to keep the fledgling CIA on a short leash if he could not accrue overseas intelligence powers for his own organization.[12]

For the first two decades of the CIA's existence, the prohibition on the exercise of domestic law enforcement powers was not controversial. The CIA's mission was clearly overseas, countering the spread of Stalinist Communism first in Europe, then in the Far East, and soon all over the globe. It concentrated on clandestine reporting and analysis of political and economic events overseas for the President and his senior policymakers. Congress had little oversight or interest in means used to achieve what was universally considered laudable ends. Lawmakers encouraged the CIA in covert action projects designed to roll back the sweep of Communism, and otherwise remained largely supportive, from a distance, of the Agency's overseas mission.

The Vietnam War and the presidential terms of Lyndon Johnson and Richard Nixon saw a breakdown in the consensus of support for the CIA in Congress and the American public. Part of this breakdown was caused by revelations in *Ramparts* magazine, Seymour Hersh's articles for the *New York Times,* and Congressional hearings conducted by Senator Frank Church (D-Idaho) and Congressman Otis Pike (D-N.Y.) beginning in 1974. These three sources of information indicated the CIA had become substantially involved in domestic activity during its short history.[13] Revealed for the first time to the American public was the CIA's involvement with the National Student Association, the establishment of proprietary domestic foundations to support anti-Communist activity abroad, and an operation aptly named CHAOS designed to infiltrate American student organizations opposed to the Vietnam War to determine if there were foreign links. It was out of this pungent stew that the current system of congressional oversight for the intelligence agencies was ladled. Congressional initiatives reinforced the presidential executive orders mentioned earlier. The new congressional oversight committees, the House Permanent Select Committee on Intelligence (HPSCI) and the Senate Select Committee on Intelligence (SSCI), made it clear in the Intelligence Authorization Act for Fiscal Year 1981 that they wanted to be kept "fully and currently informed of all intelligence activities" by the intelligence agencies.[14] Congress's purposes also included conformity by the CIA with the statutory ban on domestic law enforcement activities.

The principal force pulling the CIA into the domestic arena prior to the end of the Cold War was its shared jurisdiction with the FBI in counterintelligence matters involving U.S. citizens and U.S. persons. The FBI clearly has primacy in counterintelligence investigations conducted within the borders of the United States, but the responsibility is shared for suspected CIA spies like Aldrich Ames. Furthermore, many domestic cases have overseas connections that are often the province of the CIA to investigate. Advances in technological surveillance in recent years have complicated matters further,

blurring the lines between that which is clearly domestic and foreign, when information from both domains can easily be intercepted by both organizations.

The U.S. Constitution's Fourth Amendment prohibition against "unreasonable searches and seizures"[15] extends to counterintelligence cases involving U.S. citizens and U.S. persons. When, however, the U.S. government proposes to conduct surveillance of an individual suspected of being the "agent of a foreign power," it can do so without presenting itself to an Article III court or magistrate, under the terms of the Foreign Intelligence Surveillance Act (FISA) of 1978.[16] Instead, the government can go to the special FISA court and obtain a warrant as long as "the primary purpose" for the surveillance is "to obtain foreign intelligence information."[17] If the government believes that there is enough evidence to support a possible criminal prosecution, as it did in the Ames investigation, then the government must go to an Article III court or magistrate to obtain criminal warrants before proceeding with the surveillance.[18] (The government never obtained Article III judicial warrants in the Ames case. Although Mr. Ames's attorney intended to challenge this in court, the case never went to trial.)

Since the end of the Cold War, however, the CIA's mission has changed radically. The principal targets of intelligence concern are no longer just political and economic developments abroad that impinge on American national interests, but terrorism, the proliferation of weapons of mass destruction, and drug-trafficking, all of which have domestic law enforcement ramifications. Well before September 11, the CIA sat alongside colleagues from domestic law enforcement agencies (such as the FBI, the Drug Enforcement Administration (DEA), Customs, and the Bureau of Alcohol, Tobacco and Firearms (ATF) of the Treasury Department in DCI Centers dealing with counterterrorism, counternarcotics, and counterintelligence issues. Today, the movement of people, money, and illegal goods can proceed seamlessly from country to country, including the United States—a negative byproduct of globalization. Any distinction between the requirements of domestic law enforcement and foreign intelligence gathering are becoming hopelessly blurred in these new world disorders of terrorism and proliferation.

Arguably, the United States has just taken a major step in resolving the ancient question of "should spies be cops?" in the affirmative with passage of the USA PATRIOT Act.[19] Along with the creation of an Office of Homeland Security, this Act represents a decision on the part of the President and the Congress that the nation expects its defenders to be proactive in the struggle against terrorism of all kinds. Instead of merely responding to threats and criminal acts after they happen, the USA PATRIOT Act seeks to create the basis for prevention. Unquestionably, the gathering and analysis of foreign intelligence is intended to play a prominent role in this mix, and a greater involvement of the intelligence community and CIA in domestic law enforcement proceedings is inevitable.

Let us quickly examine several of the legal changes in the USA PATRIOT Act and their consequences for the intelligence community. Section 203 of the Act amends Rule 6(e)(3)(c) of the Federal Rules of Criminal Procedure to permit disclosure of grand jury information when the matters involve "foreign intelligence and counterintelligence."[20] Such disclosures can be made

> to any Federal law enforcement, intelligence, protective, immigration, national defense, or national security official in order to assist the official receiving that information in the performance of his official duties.[21]

Although these disclosures may be used by the recipient "only as necessary in the conduct of that person's official duties,"[22] this represents a major departure from the traditional legal principle of grand jury secrecy. Although this provision is bound to be tested in the courts, grand jury secrecy has never been absolute; if the executive branch establishes some safeguards in the use of grand jury material, section 203 may pass constitutional muster given the enormity of the threat posed to American citizens by international terrorist attacks.

Less clear is what happens to the line separating the CIA from domestic law enforcement when it is sitting at the elbow of the FBI and the Immigration and Naturalization Service, trying to help make a criminal case against a U.S. person based upon a seamless chain of evidence provided by foreign sources and domestic informants.

Section 504 of the Act amends the FISA to permit consultation between intelligence officials conducting FISA-approved surveillance efforts and law enforcement officials.[23] The matters to be consulted upon must pertain to terrorist threats, but there is opportunity for definitional creep as the pressure for preventive action in this area of concern intensifies.

Finally, section 218 of the Act further amends the FISA to change the standard with which the FISA court will grant authority to conduct foreign intelligence surveillance.[24] Instead of the "primary purpose" test, section 218 amends the certification by the government to require only that foreign intelligence be "a significant purpose" for the FISA surveillance or physical search.[25] This change allows the scope of permitted national security surveillance to creep close to the boundaries of Fourth Amendment limitations. The fact that the domestic legal authority prohibition continues to haunt these determinations also means that the executive branch will have to exercise great care to specify guidelines for the application of these significant statutory changes.

My view is that the CIA should squarely address the inconsistencies that its new foreign intelligence mission is creating and seek legislative clarification and amendment of the prohibition against domestic law enforcement powers. It is better to seek an alteration of its 1947 charter to account for the new realities of its role in combating terrorism, proliferation of weapons of mass destruction, and drug-trafficking. This route of caution and clarification is preferable to being forced to change as a consequence of judicial action, which will understandably focus more on the rights of Americans than the difficulty of the anti-terrorist mission.

III. Repealing the Prohibition of Assassination

No issue has generated more heat and produced less light than the feckless debate as to whether the provisions in Executive Order 12,333 prohibiting direct and indirect participation in assassination by the U.S. Government and its employees should be rescinded.[26]

Previously, presidents contemplating a military response to an attack on Americans have successfully argued that their powers under the U.S. Constitution as Commander in Chief and executor of the nation's laws[27] gave them ample authority to strike back at the attackers, even if the strike was likely to kill the head of state or commander who may have authorized the attack. President Ronald Reagan's bombing of Muammar Qaddafi's compound in Libya in 1986—after the United States recovered signal intercepts implicating Libyan intelligence officers in the bombing of a Berlin discotheque in which several U.S. soldiers were killed—might have been justified as death incident to a military action had Qaddafi died in the strike. Likewise, President Bill Clinton's response to terrorist attacks on the U.S embassies in Dar-es-Salaam and Nairobi in 1998, in which a pharmaceutical factory in Sudan and a terrorist training camp in Afghanistan were destroyed by U.S. cruise missiles (the latter strike having been directed at the supposed perpetrator, Osama bin Laden), could also have been justified as death incident to military action.

There is little doubt in the wake of the September 11 attacks and the Joint Resolution of Congress of September 14 authorizing the use of force[28] that the efforts of the United States to capture or destroy Osama bin Laden and the Al Qaeda network will be governed by the Joint Resolution, the constitutional authorities of the President, and the laws of war, rather than Executive Order 12,333's provisions prohibiting assassination.

What activity then *is* affected by these executive order provisions? The answer would appear to be political assassinations occurring in peacetime. For that reason, it is worth reviewing the final report of the Church Committee in 1975, which first gave rise to the prohibitions of peacetime political assassinations.[29] Church concluded that the "cold-blooded, targeted, intentional killing of an individual foreign leader has no place in the foreign policy of the U.S."[30] The Church Report documented involvement by the U.S. Government in assassination plots against five foreign leaders during the 50s, 60s, and early 70s, four of whom died violently at the hands of others.[31] In fact, no foreign leader was assassinated by U.S. operatives, but it was not for want of trying. Indeed, the failures came about largely as a consequence of a lack of developed competence in this line of work by the CIA. The first conclusion one draws from this record is that the CIA did not relish the task of assassination planning. It was not what intelligence officers signed up to do, and they were not very good at it.[32]

Second, what happens if the plot is successful? Who would succeed Saddam Hussein if we assassinated him? Might any new leader be worse than the assassinated one? Although it was not the result of assassination, when President Arbenz decamped from Guatemala in 1954 as a consequence of U.S-sponsored covert action, the United States became the de facto guarantor of his incompetent successor, Castillo Armas. Guatemala, in effect, became a ward of the United States for the next forty-five years because the United States had chosen to intervene to replace an elected leader. So much for plausible deniability.

Third, if the United States starts down the road of political assassination for its own foreign policy goals, what will stop other nations from targeting our leaders for assassination? What does it say about our respect for the law of nations and our own adherence to the rule of law?[33] I agree with the Church Committee's conclusion that "[i]t may be ourselves that we injure most if we adopt tactics 'more ruthless than the enemy.'"[34] Short of war, the Committee noted, "assassination is incompatible with American principles, international order, and morality."[35]

Fourth, there is little evidence that retaliating against terrorists by assassinating their leaders is an effective deterrent to future terrorist acts. Assassination appears to beget assassination, if we are guided by the example of the Israelis. Assassination has been no more successful in the struggles between the IRA and the Protestant majority in Northern Ireland, or those of the Basque separatists in Northern Spain.

Finally, if the U.S. chooses to embark upon a course of political assassination in peacetime to nip a potential future Hitler in the bud, who makes the judgment that any given leader is another Hitler? Who exercises control, and what audit trail will exist to establish accountability for the decision?

I would like to see the answers to these questions before the executive order banning assassinations is lifted, especially since there appears to be ample authority in the hands of the President to pursue the September 11 attackers under both the Joint Resolution of Congress of September 14 and the U.S. Constitution.

IV. Prohibition on Recruitment of Journalists, Clerics, and Academics

As controversial and unproductive as lifting the ban on peacetime assassinations would be, the removal of the barriers against the intelligence community's use of journalists, clerics, and academics would be equally controversial but, unlike assassinations, could be productive.

Use of so-called "angel" assets, including Peace Corps and USAID workers, by the CIA fell into disfavor at the same time that the Church and Pike committees were holding hearings on the CIA's behavior and Seymour Hersh was writing exposes on the CIA's "family jewels" in the *New York Times*. The *Times* editorialized in 1996 that from the Agency's creation in 1947 until the Church and Pike Committee investigations in 1975, about fifty journalists were paid by CIA for their services at various times.[36] In addition, foreign correspondents and CIA station chiefs often swapped information informally, and many other journalists were used as "unwitting sources" of intelligence information.[37] At the time of the investigations, there were eleven CIA officers working under journalistic cover provided by fifteen news organizations.[38]

As a result of the controversy engendered by the revelations of Agency use of journalistic cover, then-DCI George H. W. Bush issued regulations in 1976 limiting the CIA's use of the clergy and the media.[39] The regulations provided that the CIA would not enter into any paid or contractual relationships with full or part-time U.S.-accredited journalists or any similar clandestine relationships with clergymen or missionaries.[40] The regulations did not prohibit, however, the gathering of information "volunteered" by journalists or clergy, or the use of journalistic or clerical cover.[41]

One year later, in recognition of the "special status afforded the press under the Constitution," then-DCI Stansfield Turner promulgated stricter regulations prohibiting "any relationship" with full or part-time U.S.-accredited journalists, as well as non-journalist staff employees of the print media, without the express approval of their senior management.[42] The 1977 regulations also prohibited the use of any U.S. media organization as cover for Agency employees or activities.[43] Like the 1976 regulations, the Turner policy permitted voluntarily-supplied information from journalists. Unlike the Bush regulations, however, the new policy established a small loophole allowing the DCI to make exceptions to the stated prohibitions in the event of an emergency.[44]

This two-sentence loophole remained buried for nearly twenty years until the Council on Foreign Relations presented its report on intelligence reform at the end of the Cold War. It included a suggestion that the CIA rethink its policy on non-official cover and reconsider the use of journalistic cover.[45] In response, then-DCI John Deutch made the disclosure, startling to many, that the CIA had in fact used the loophole on several occasions since the regulations were enacted.[46]

The firestorm that ensued in Congress led to the insertion in the Intelligence Authorization Act of FY 1997 of section 309, which declares it to be the "policy" of the United States that the intelligence community may not use a U.S.-accredited correspondent of a U.S. news media organization for intelligence purposes unless the President or the DCI signs a waiver that such use is "necessary to address the overriding national security interest of the United States."[47] Voluntary cooperation by a journalist is still permitted as long as it is in writing.[48] Unstated is any congressional position on journalistic cover.

In the aftermath of September 11, the President and Congress are obliged to raise again the issue of the use of "angel" assets and the cover they might provide. As observers call for greater flexibility and creativity from the intelligence community, especially in the recruitment and deployment of non-official cover human sources of intelligence, it seems arbitrary and absurd to rule out any potential method of getting close to Al Qaeda and other anti-American terrorist networks. To be sure, consideration of the privileged position certain professions

occupy under the U.S. Constitution should continue to carry weight, but the waiver provision set forth in section 309 provides a sensible solution to a tough problem. Under section 309, the waiver and finding procedure is sufficiently cumbersome and weighty that it is unlikely to be invoked on a casual basis, and the requirement that a proposed waiver must go to the HPSCI and the SSCI insures a measure of accountability. Furthermore, it contemplates that the individuals involved in the intelligence gathering activity will only do so on a voluntary basis. I would broaden the section 309 test to all of the "angel" asset categories: clerics, academics, and Peace Corps and USAID workers.

From this, it is clear that some changes in the laws and rules governing intelligence activities are necessary for the intelligence community to be successful in its struggle to prevent international terrorist acts, especially those directed at Americans. By the same token, it is equally important that these changes not throw the CIA back into the pre-1974 era of limited congressional oversight and little executive branch accountability that led to earlier excesses. The terrorist threat need not become an excuse for abusing the rights of Americans. If the failure to warn of the September 11 attacks indeed constitutes a massive "intelligence failure"[49] these changes will not alone save the day for the CIA and the intelligence community. A greater understanding of the cultures and circumstances in the Near East and South Asia that produced Osama bin Laden and Al Qaeda will be of far greater importance in sharpening human source intelligence operations against terrorism and fundamentalist Islam than changing the rules under which the intelligence community operates. To accomplish this mission successfully, U.S. intelligence will have to do it the old fashioned way. It will have to learn the languages, spend time on the ground, get its hands dirty, and listen to chatter in the bazaar.[50]

Questions for Further Discussion

1. What does Hitz mean when he uses the phrase "rogue elephant"? Is the CIA a rogue elephant? Has it been? Could it be?

2. Evaluate Hitz's argument about repealing the executive order that currently prohibits assassination plots by the CIA against foreign heads of state.

3. Should journalists, clerics, and scholars be used by the CIA for intelligence purposes? If so, under what conditions and guidelines?

4. How would you contrast Senator Church's views with those of Mr. Hitz?

Endnotes

1. The hearings were conducted by Senator Frank Church (D-Idaho) after revelations by the CIA and in the media of CIA violations of rights of American citizens, etc. *See* SELECT COMM. TO STUDY GOVERN-MENTAL OPERATIONS WITH RESPECT TO INTEL-LIGENCE ACTIVITIES, ALLEGED ASSASSINATION PLOTS INVOLVING FOREIGN LEADERS, S. REP. NO. 94-465 (1975).

2. President Ford promulgated Executive Order (E.O.) 11,905, which was followed by E.O. 12,306 under President Reagan. *See* Exec. Order No. 11,905, 41 Fed. Reg. 7703 (Feb. 18,1976); Exec. Order No. 12,306, 46 Fed. Reg. 29,693 (June 1, 1981). These orders were superseded by E.O. 12,333, which was promulgated by President Reagan and is still in effect *See* Exec. Order 12,333, 46 Fed. Reg. 59,941 (Dec. 4,1981).

3. Vernon Loeb, *Panel Advocates Easing CIA Rules on Informants: Agency Disputes Commission Finding*, WASH. POST, June 6,2 000, at A25.

4. John Le Carre, THE SPY WHO CAME IN FROM THE COLD 246 (1963).

5. The IG report on the asset validation system remains classified.

6. *See* Tim Weiner, *Guatemalan Agent of C.I.A. Tied to Killing of American*, NY TIMES, March 22, 1995, at Al; *see also* Tim Weiner, *Shadowy Alliance—A Special Report; in Guatemala's Dark Heart, CIA Lent Succor to Death*, NY TIMES, April 2, 1995, at A1.

7. *See* INVESTIGATIONS STAFF, OFFICE OF INSPECTOR GENERAL, CENTRAL INTELLIGENCE AGENCY, REPORT NO. 95-0024-IG, REPORT OF INVESTIGATION: GUATEMALA 2 (1995); INTELLIGENCE OVERSIGHT BOARD, REPORT ON THE GUATEMALAN REVIEW 4 (1996).

8. *See* Walter Pincus, *CIA Steps Up 'Scrub Down' of Agents: Agency May Weigh Rights Violations Against Value of Information*, WASH. POST, July 28, 1995, at A25.

9. *See* Intelligence Authorization Act for Fiscal Year 2002, Pub. L. No. 107-108, 115 Stat. 1394 (2001).

10. Exec. Order No. 12,333, *supra* note 1, at 59,945.

11. National Security Act of 1947 § 102a, 50 U.S.C. § 403 (1994).

12. *See* Christopher Andrew, FOR THE PRESIDENT'S EYES ONLY 156 (1995).

13. *See id.* at 405.

14. § 501(a), Pub. L. No. 66-450, 94 Stat. 1975,1981 (1980) (codified as amended at 50U.S.C. 413 (1994)).

15. U.S.CONST. amend. IV.

16. 50 U.S.C. § 1805 (1994).

17. 50 U.S.C. §§ 1804(a)(7)(B), 1823(a)(7)(B); United States v. Duggan, 743 F.2d59, 77 (2d Cir. 1984); *see also* United States v. Nicholson. 955 F. Supp. 588, 591 (E.D. Va. 1997) (holding that a FISA physical search was "constitutionally indistinguishable from the FISA-authorized electronic surveillance unanimously upheld by federal courts"); United States v. Bin Laden, 126 F. Supp 2d 264, 285 (S.D.N.Y. 2000).

18. *See* United States v. Truong Dinh Hung, 629 F.2d 908, 915-16 (4th Cir. 1980), *cert. denied*, 454 U.S. 1144 (1982).

19. Uniting and Strengthening America by Providing Appropriate Tools Required to Intercept and Obstruct Terrorism Act (USA PATRIOT Act) of 2001, Pub. L. No. 107-56, 115 Stat. 272 (2001).

20. USA PATRIOT Act § 203(a)(1)(i), 115 Stat. at 279; *see generally* Sara Sun Beale & James E. Felman, *The Consequences of Enlisting Federal Grand Juries in the War on Terrorism: Assessing the USA PATRIOT Act's Changes to Grand Jury Secrecy*, 25 HARV. J.L. & PUB. POL'Y 699 (2002).

21. *Id.*

22. § 203(a)(1)(ii), 115 Stat. at 279.

23. § 504, 115 Stat. at 364-65.

24. § 218,115 Stat. at 291.

25. *Id.*

26. *See* Exec. Order 12,333, *supra* note 2, at 59,592.

27. *See* U.S. CONST. art. II, §§ 2-3.

28. Joint Resolution to Authorize the Use of United States Armed Forces Against Those Responsible for the Recent Attacks Launched Against the United States, Pub. L. No. 107-40, 115 Stat, 224 (2001).

29. *See* SELECT COMM. TO STUDY GOVERNMENTAL OPERATIONS WITH RESPECT TO INTELLIGENCE ACTIVITIES, *supra* note 1.

30. *Id.* at 6.

31. *See id.* at 4.

32. *See* John Ranelagh, THE AGENCY: THE RISE AND DECLINE OP THE CIA 336 (1986).

33. *See* SELECT COMM. TO STUDY GOVERNMENTAL OPERATIONS WITH RESPECT TO INTELLIGENCE ACTIVITIES, *supra* note 1, at 258, 282.

34. *Id.* at 259.

35. *Id.* at 1.

36. *See*, Editorial, *No Press Cards for Spies*, N.Y. TIMES, Mar. 18, 1996, at A14.

37. *See id.*

38. "Assets" are generally defined as sources that provide information to intelligence agencies as part of a salaried relationship that is based on gifts, reimbursement of expenses, or regular financial payments. There may or may not be an element of control. "Cover" is the use of employment, name, or facilities of any non-official U.S. organization to provide an identity for CIA employees or activities.

39. *See The CIA and the Media: Hearings Before the Subcomm. on Oversight of the House Permanent Select Comm. on Intelligence*, 95m Cong; 331-32 (1978). For a list of the ways in which intelligence agencies cooperate with journalists, *see* Lt. Col. Geoffrey B. Demarest, *Espionage in International Law*, 24 DENV. J. INT'L. L. & POL'Y 321, 345 (1996).

40. *See The CIA and the Media: Hearings Before the Subcomm. on Oversight of the House Permanent Select Comm. on Intelligence*, *supra* note 39.

41. *See id.*

42. *See id.* at 333.

43. *See id.*

44. *See id.* at 334.

45. *See* COUNCIL ON FOREIGN RELATIONS, MAKING INTELLIGENCE SMARTER: THE FUTURE OF U.S. INTELLIGENCE (1996).

46. Former DCI Turner admitted to approving the use of journalists three times but asserted that on at least one occasion the permission was not used. *See* Walter Pincus, *Turner: CIA Nearly Used a Journalist in Teheran*. WASH. POST., Mar. 1, 1996, at A15. Deutch stated that he had not used the loophole at all during his ten-

ure. *See* 142 CONG. REC. 12,153 (1996) (letter from DCI John Deutch).

47. Intelligence Authorization Act for Fiscal Year 1997 § 309, Pub. L. No 104-293, 110 Stat. 3461, 3467 (codified at 50 U.S.C. 403-7 (Supp. 1997)).

48. *See id.*

49. I continue to believe that it is rather a "failure of intellect" as Harlan Ullman argued skillfully last October. Harlan Ullman, *Intellect Over Intelligence*, FIN. TIMES, Oct. 19, 2001, at 17.

50. The author has written an op-ed piece on this subject. *See* Frederick P. Hitz, Editorial, *Not Just a Lack of Intelligence, a Lack of Skills*, WASH. POST, Oct. 21, 2001, at B3. ✦

Reprinted with permission from Frederick P. Hitz, "Unleashing the Rogue Elephant: September 11 and Letting the CIA Be the CIA," *Harvard Journal of Law & Public Policy* 25 (2002): 756–781.

28
Ethics and Intelligence

E. Drexel Godfrey, Jr.

Is a discussion of intelligence and ethics in the same breath an oxymoron? Some would say yes, but others, including Godfrey, maintain that even in this dark domain one must have certain limits of restraint—at least in nations like the United States that have long displayed a concern for morality in the making of foreign policy decisions. For Godfrey, the litmus test for a moral intelligence agency is whether it tells the truth in its service to policy officials.

I

The three-year public agony of the Central Intelligence Agency may be coming to an end. Richard Helms has been convicted, the President has issued a new set of regulations restricting certain surveillance activities, and the torrent of public exposes by "insiders" seems to be abating. What remains to be seen is whether the traumas suffered since the sweeping congressional investigations began in 1975 have made any significant impact on the heart and guts of the Agency.

There are some suggestions, of course, that nothing much has changed. When Mr. Helms returned from receiving a suspended sentence, he was given a hero's welcome by an indulgent group of ex-colleagues. Simultaneously the announced intention of Admiral Stansfield Turner, the present Director, to reduce Agency operational personnel by several hundred was met by smear campaigns so powerful that the President soon felt obliged to publicly declare his continuing support for the Admiral. These responses from traditional intelligence officers may not be all that significant, however. Angry reactions to reductions in force are not, after all, new in Washington. Any pruning of career public servants can result in mid-level bureaucrats making high-level mischief.

The Helms case was quite another matter. Far from resolving any of the deeper issues of recent Agency conduct, it did not even address them. The case did, however, expose the persistent failure of several administrations to establish appropriate congressional arrangements for the exercise of intelligence operations. All postwar Presidents have permitted Directors of Central Intelligence to appear before congressional committees in the full knowledge that they would be closely questioned about secret operations approved and placed under tight security restrictions by the National Security Council. A long tradition had been built up over the years with the leaders of the Congress itself, that the facts concerning political operations (or clandestine intelligence operations) should be revealed only to selected members of Congress, and denied to formal committees at least in open session.

From time to time efforts were made by individual Presidents, or their staffs, to reach an accommodation with Congress that would reduce the vulnerability of CIA officials, caught between the professional obligation for secrecy and the legislative thirst for candor. No true resolution of this dilemma was achieved until President Ford declared for candor and so instructed Mr. Helms' successor. By then, of course, Mr. Helms had presented the testimony on operations in Chile, to a Senate committee, which a federal judge subsequently found to be not only misleading but false.

Not unnaturally many intelligence officials felt their ex-Director had been victimized. In a narrow sense he had. Lacking a presidential mandate to reveal the full nature of the U.S. involvement in the Chilean elections, Mr. Helms opted to give testimony that was less than truthful.

The irony of the case, however, is not that Mr. Helms was forced to choose between two ethical imperatives, one honoring his oath of secrecy, the other telling the truth. Far more significant is the fact that because it focused on such a narrow issue—and one where responsibility for the sorry turn of events could be laid as much at the doors of a succession of Presidents and leaders of Congress as to the Agency Director—the trial and judgment ignored a whole range of ethical problems concerning intelligence practices in a free society.

II

To some the mere juxtaposition of ethics and intelligence may appear to be a contradiction in terms. But at heart intelligence is rooted in the severest of ethical principles: truth telling. After all, the end purpose of the elaborate apparatus that the intelligence community has become is to provide the policymaker with as close to a truthful depiction of a given situation as is humanly possible. Anything less is not intelligence. It may be useful opinion—in some cases it may even be more accurate than prevailing intelligence—but if it is, the opinion maker is lucky, or in the particular instance possessed of more facts and sharper judgmental skills than the professional intelligence officer. Even the CIA has long recognized the centrality of truth telling. As a contributor to *Foreign Affairs* observed several years ago, the motto of the CIA chosen by the doughty old Presbyterian, Allen Dulles, is "And the Truth Shall Make You Free."[1]

Even as the motto was being chosen in the mid-1950s, however, the point was being lost and the purpose of the Agency corrupted. Perhaps because of the personality of Mr. Dulles and his operational successes in Switzerland during World War II, emphasis on activities having little or nothing to do with the pursuit of truth grew to preoccupy the CIA. The Church Committee's excellent report on intelligence activities makes it abundantly clear that foreign operations won top priority under Mr. Dulles' leadership; worse, foreign operations expanded from a tiny "psych warfare" section of the clandestine collection division to absorb a major share of the Agency's budget, its personnel, and skills. Operations both foreign and domestic, with a host of concomitant and now familiar malpractices, became the bread and butter of the Agency during the 1950s and 1960s.[2]

To accept the approximation of truth as the purpose of intelligence is one thing. To accept the methods by which truth can be obtained poses ethical dilemmas. The truth, after all, is often a set of facts, or concrete physical entities, or intentions, which the party with whom they are entrusted will guard jealously as a precious, not to say sacred, element of the national preserve. Ferreting out the truth under these circumstances often requires means and techniques not ordinarily employed in human intercourse.

At this point the ethical absolutist is compelled to say: "Exactly, an ethical society should renounce foreign intelligence altogether; given the new Administration's emphasis on human rights, domestic intelligence might best be scuttled, too." In this formulation the argument that other nations will not cease intelligence gathering activities simply because the United States renounces them, carries little weight. Ethical conduct is a force of its own; powerful nations lead by example; renunciation of intelligence gathering would be an act of moral courage with untold beneficial international consequences, etc.

But we are not all ethical absolutists. Value trade-offs are probably the best that most people in an uncertain world will accept. And it is because intelligence offers security that bizarre methods to obtain it are acceptable to most. Foreign policy making without an intelligence input of some kind would be capricious; in the uncharted waters of world crisis situations it would be scandalously foolhardy. It follows that the more ambiguous the international situation, the greater the value of intelligence in the decision-making process. Put another way, of course, this means that where intelligence does not add to international security, but rather, say to the obsessive comfort of knowing more about Ruritania than even the Ruritanians, or where it merely facilitates the feeding of salacious tidbits about foreign leaders to inquisitive Presidents, questionable methods to collect it are not acceptable.

The security returns of intelligence are probably inestimable, and they are welcomed by both world superpowers and tacitly condoned by almost all active participating nations on the world stage. Satellites monitor the missile developments of the superpowers; microwave telephone messages between foreign embassies and capitals are intercepted for critical information. Without technology of this kind in the hands of both the United States and the Soviet Union, there would of course have been no SALT talks; there would not now be any form of SALT agreement. Nikita Khrushchev implied just this when he half seriously suggested to President Eisenhower in 1958 that the two countries exchange intelligence chiefs. Both leaders recognized that inspections in each other's countries would probably be out of the question for many years to come; each knew that in order to make any progress on arms limitation he would have to rely on the safety of his own intelligence monitoring system and avert his eyes to monitoring by the other.

In a world where the two great powers can no longer guarantee international stability and where weaponry is no longer the exclusive currency of power, intelligence monitoring must sweep targets other than the principal antagonist—e.g., China or the Middle East. It must also be as concerned with economic and energy considerations as missiles. But the principle governing the choice of targets remains the same. Intelligence must promote international security, or the ethical compromises necessary to accommodate the requisite collection methods cannot and should not be stomached.

Intelligence monitoring substitutes for full faith and credit between nations, and technology provides a pitiful but workable substitute for the joyful conditions of a distant One World. The tensions of the nation-state system are, in other words, held in bounds not only by diplomacy and by mutual common sense but by carefully calibrated monitoring systems.

Assuming, then, that intelligence can help toward security in a dangerous international order, how can the intelligence function be carried out at the least risk to other values in our society? To put this most succinctly, how can a professional intelligence service operate so that officials within it perform their roles in an ethical manner? Most public officials would prefer that this be the case; certainly most private citizens expect nothing less.

The traditional easy answer, of course, is that in international affairs a double standard operates. What is unacceptable human behavior at home or in one's own society can be forgiven in dealings with foreign societies or with the representatives abroad of those societies. War is the ultimate expression of this double standard. But the assassination of foreign leaders in peacetime stretches the standard furthest, beyond, as is now wholly agreed, its breaking point. Under the shelter of the double standard, self-justification usually takes the form of: "Someone's got to do the dirty work"; or "Distasteful as the task was, it served the national purpose." On examination both statements contain implicit assertions by the makers of ethical standards. This, then, is the nub of the matter.

Foreign intelligence is not, by and large, conducted by people lacking the capacity to recognize ethical standards, but standards are lowered to accommodate the perceived national purpose. Once lowered, they can be more easily lowered a second time, or they can be lowered further and further as routine reduces ethical resistance to repugnant activities. This is the area of human dynamics where yesterday's managers of the intelligence community have been the most irresolute. Management rarely blew the whistle on subordinates. When subordinates succeeded in operations of questionable morality, they were as often rewarded with promotions as reprimanded for using dubious methods.

A high management official of one intelligence agency—in this case the FBI—blurted out to the Church Committee an incredibly candid confession of amorality. In response to questions as to whether any supervisory official of the Bureau had voiced reservations about the legitimacy of the infamous Operation Cointelpro (active disruption of citizen groups) he answered:

> We never gave any thought to this line of reasoning, because we were just naturally pragmatists. The one thing we were concerned about was this: Will this course of action work; will we reach the objective that we desire to reach? As far as legality is concerned, morals or ethics, it was never raised by myself or anyone else. I think this suggests really that in government we are amoral.[3]

To disagree with this official's conclusion is easy; to refute the implicit charge that government itself contributes to, if not insists on amorality, is more

difficult. Presumably, the official, like most Americans, entered government service with some sense of ethics and acceptable norms of moral behavior. He came to believe, apparently, that the responsible intelligence officer should not concern himself with such matters. They are, he said, irrelevant to the conduct of his government business.

III

Most professions, such as the law and medicine, have for centuries provided themselves with failsafe systems to ensure that ethical norms are not compromised out of existence, or rusted from misuse. Some of these systems work better than others, some are susceptible to corruption themselves and a few are mere shams, but the fact that they exist and generally are taken seriously by the members of the profession is critically significant. At the very least, it means that there are limits to a professional's freedom and that those limits are defined by ethical codes sanctioned by colleagues.

A profession whose end purpose it is to root out the truth cannot afford to resist asking where its limits should be set. However, the intelligence professional has in the past operated under the simple guideline, "don't get caught." Recently there have been signs that suggest that the intelligence community is busily, if somewhat ponderously, groping towards a limit-setting policy for its professionals.

The business of limit setting will not be easy, particularly for the centerpiece of the community, the CIA, and specifically for its large clandestine services element. It will not be easy because of the grim ethos of clandestine collection and operations, developed long before orbiting photographic satellites or sophisticated interception systems were ever conceived. That ethos is rooted in a concept as old as human society: the weak or the vulnerable can be manipulated by the strong or the shrewd. Human intelligence collection is a major preoccupation of the clandestine service. Simply put, this is the process of extracting from others information or national assets they would not willingly part with under normal circumstances.

In some cases the creation of appropriate circumstances is relatively easy. This is where the source is a willing volunteer acting out of his own sense of patriotism. Anti-Soviet emigre Hungarians providing detailed information on Russian military units occupying their country fall into this category. The clandestine officer must provide the means whereby the emigre can return to his country. By and large the clandestine officer can content himself with the knowledge that the Hungarian is as anxious to reenter his homeland illegally as he is anxious to have him make the effort.

But the highest art in tradecraft is to develop a source that you "own lock, stock and barrel." According to the clandestine ethos, a "controlled" source provides the most reliable intelligence. "Controlled" means, of course, bought or otherwise obligated. Traditionally it has been the aim of the professional in the clandestine service to weave a psychological web around any potentially fruitful contact and to tighten that web whenever possible. Opportunities are limited, but for those in the clandestine service who successfully develop controlled sources, rewards in status and peer respect are high. The modus operandi required, however, is the very antithesis of ethical interpersonal relationships.

Sometimes the information obtained by these methods can be important. It is, however, rarely of critical importance. At best it may provide a measure of confirmation of some already suspected development or fill in a missing piece of a complex mosaic of facts. There have been occasions when controlled sources have been successful in snatching internal documents off high-level desks in their own governments, but even in these instances the "take" has not been earthshaking. Perhaps the faintly disappointing record of achievement by clandestine operatives is explainable in bureaucratic terms. Well-placed officials with immediate access to critical policymaking circles—and for the most part this means they are part of the policymaking process—are generally well rewarded by and well satisfied with their own governments. If they were not, they would not hold powerful positions. The main targets for clandestine collectors are usually second and third-level officials who may not be fully privy to policy developments.

Finally, there is the human consideration. Most controlled sources are ambivalent about the roles they are obliged to play. On the one hand, there may be gratification that their retainer fees enable them to reduce some crushing personal debts, or to meet other expenses incurred as a result of weaknesses or personal misjudgments. On the other hand, they will almost certainly feel a sense of guilt in betraying trusts they are expected not to betray; they may also feel more than a little self-loathing that they have been too weak to resist being used by those who pay them or blackmail them. How these feelings subconsciously affect what they report and how they report is anybody's guess. It is at least possible that the clandestine officer who "owns" a controlled source may not have the extraordinary asset that his "tradecraft" teaches him he should have.

Quality of information obtained aside, a fundamental ethical issue concerning clandestine human collection remains. That issue is the impact on the clandestine officer of his relationship with his source. The former's bread and butter is the subversion of the latter's integrity. The officer is painstakingly trained in techniques that will convert an acquaintance into a submissive tool, to shred away his resistance and deflate his sense of self-worth. Of course, the source may be thoroughly cynical, even a venal merchant of his country's privacy, and in that case the task of the clandestine officer is less burdensome—although he may come to find the relationship just as repellent as if the source had slowly and resistingly been bent to compliance. Whatever the chemistry between the two individuals, collector and source, or perhaps more pointedly, dominant and dominated, the biggest loser is the one whose ethical scruples are most damaged in the process. Depending on the techniques he may have to use to bring the source under control and maintain that relationship, the biggest loser may be the clandestine officer.

Another prime concern of the clandestine services is the development of methodologies and devices to thwart the defensive measures of other intelligence agencies and other national political systems. While much of this activity is purely technical electronic engineering, a significant investment has also been made in such exotica as "truth drugs," complex psychological warfare strategies, bizarre bugging devices and the like. Some of these devices and techniques have been used with profit and success by clandestine officers operating overseas; others have proved impractical in the field or have stalled on the drawing board as development costs got out of hand. But the search for new ways to penetrate other societies goes on. Today's drug experimenters (if there are indeed any left) may become tomorrow's experts in long-range behavior modification processes.

Whatever the state of these arcane arts, they have two things in common. First, their purpose is almost always to facilitate the manipulation of man by man. In this sense they are not dissimilar in effect and impact to the process of controlled source development. Secondly, the practitioners of these arts and the "psych warfare" experts are obliged by the very nature of their trade to presume that they are operating in hostile environments. The end point of their efforts, after all, is to bypass normal authority, or at the least, to use semi-legal means to overcome obstacles placed in their path by the authorities of other nations. The professional premise of the officers engaged in these practices, then, is the constructive use of illegality. While revolutionaries around the world have lived long and comfortably with this paradox, it is quite another matter for sober and presumably accountable U.S. public servants to be exposed to its temptations.

In this connection it is important to note that over the years officers whose careers have primarily been spent in clandestine activities have occupied the preeminent roles in the management of the CIA. At least until recently, when heavy reductions in clandestine staff were ordered by the current Director, Admiral Stansfield Turner, roughly two-thirds of the highest executive positions at any given time were filled by officers whose careers blossomed in the clandestine services. Years of hardening in the ugly business of source control and penetration of foreign capitals have surely taken their toll. Little wonder that the CIA's top leadership did not traditionally spend much time setting "limits" on the Agency's activities. Little wonder that management developed a process of compartmentalizing what it recognized to be questionable activities. The most bizarre operations, such as Chaos (to be discussed below) and human drug experimentation, have been traditionally walled off even from other Agency colleagues whose questions might have been embarrassing. Mr. Helms himself testified before the Church Committee that in many instances the CIA's General Counsel was simply excluded from knowing of the existence of particularly exotic activities and operations.[4] The inference is inescapable that he was shut off out of fear that he would, as he had occasionally done in the past, advise that the operations overstepped legal limits. Similarly, the Church Committee report makes clear that even the recommendations of the Agency's elaborate Inspector General system could be, and sometimes were, rejected by the Agency Director.[5]

Thus, a picture emerges of a highly compartmentalized bureaucracy whose direction has been largely controlled by officials with long experience in the seduction of other human beings and societies. Not immoral or even without ethics standards themselves, they had lost the habit of questioning where they should set limits on their official conduct. And other officers who might have been expected to remind them of these limits were kept in ignorance. This state of affairs is particularly distressing when it involves an organization where high premiums are paid for inventiveness, for "outsmarting the opposition."

In an organizational context where the edge of possibility is bounded only by the stretch of the imagination, special arrangements for limit setting are necessary. Each management level of the clandestine services, from the most immediate and parochial to the highest, should have an officer who plays the role of "nay-sayer." His task would be to review operational plans for their ethical consequences and occasionally to remind the imaginative subordinate that daring and innovativeness must sometimes bow to prudence. Every organization has informal "nay-sayers" seeded through its ranks. In traditional bureaucracies they are almost always negative influences, cruel stiflers of initiative and zeal. In intelligence organizations, institutional "nay-sayers" could have just the opposite effect: they could be critical to a rediscovery of ethically acceptable limits of activity.

IV

That element of the CIA whose job it is "to tell the truth," as opposed to collecting the truth overseas, is the overt Intelligence Directorate. It would appear at first glance to have the easier job. But this is not necessarily so. For one thing, truth is rarely simple fact; it is almost always a combination of fact and judgment and as such almost always subject to second guessing. The intelligence analyst has no monopoly on wisdom and prescience, but he does have one advantage. He is not subject to the policy considerations of the operating departments, such as State and Defense. He is, in this respect, free to call the shots as he sees them, whether or not they substantiate or confirm some fundamental premise of U.S. policy. Ignoring the policy assumptions of the Administration in a search for the most defensible judgment can be an unhappy affair, as those analysts who toiled through the Vietnam years can testify. While support from Agency superiors for the views of the analysts was strong during the Johnson and Nixon Administrations, the analytic product—that is, the truth as the analysts saw it—was not always palatable to higher consumers. The "truth" more often than not implicitly cast doubt on the outcome of the U.S. efforts in Indochina. Reaction to such judgments at White House and National Security Council levels was at worst unfriendly, and at best indifferent.

Nevertheless, the obligation remains for the analytic component of the CIA to produce what it believes to be the least assailable version of a given situation and its consequences for the future course of events. In this lonely and sometimes scorned pursuit, there are ethical pitfalls no less severe than those encountered by the overseas clandestine collectors.

A case in point is the unusual episode surrounding the studies of radical youth produced by the Agency at the demand of both Presidents Johnson and Nixon in the late 1960s and early 1970s. The original order for such a study coincided with one of the peak points in protest against the Vietnam War, protests conducted in Europe and the Far East as well as in the United States. When the order was first relayed to the Agency by Walt Rostow, then National Security Special Assistant to the President, it was accompanied by the hypothesis that the protest actions were so vociferous and so universal that they must be orchestrated by communists. Dubious at best, this became the principal theme of the first study and the several successive versions that were subsequently ordered. The Agency undertook, in other words, to determine whether communist instigation lay behind the worldwide protests.

The first edition of the study concluded that there had been no discernible communist involvement in the student protests, with a purely theoretical aside that, at least as far as U.S. student protests were concerned, there were a variety of justifications for protest that made communist intervention unnecessary. The study was ill received by the White House. In effect, it was rejected out of hand with the pointed question: "Are you sure of your conclusions? Have you turned over every rock?" These injunctions were to be repeated twice more as the Agency, confident of its original judgments, tried to produce the evidence, or demonstrate the absence of evidence, that would similarly persuade two reluctant Presidents and a host of presidential advisors.

The costs to the CIA of "turning over every rock" were shatteringly high. The dearest cost was the decision to expand greatly the patently illegal "Operation Chaos," which had begun modestly with the intention of collecting evidence for the analysts preparing the first version of the student paper. To this end U.S. agents under control of the Clandestine Services, counterintelligence component were infiltrated into student groups within the United States and abroad. Once again the operation was carefully compartmentalized so that few even of the most senior Agency officials were aware of its existence—including those responsible for the production of the study. When the first study was rejected, Chaos was built up into a sizable operation, with access to computer technology and a network of overseas and domestic employees keeping book on many thousands of U.S. and foreign students. Not only was the Agency's legislative charter, which mandates only overseas espionage, violated, but so too were privacy rights of thousands of young Americans.

The second cost was a natural concomitant of the first. As more and more "rocks got turned over," the pursuit of evidence became an end in itself. A tendency developed among the collectors to believe that if they hunted long enough and assiduously enough, some communist involvement might be found, and if it were, the President would be satisfied. In short, the collection effort lost perspective. Had it found communist affiliations—say, in the leadership of a particular student organization—it would not have been of much significance given the overwhelming negative findings elsewhere in the

great majority of student movements. The notion that an assertion can be converted to a truth if there is one scrap of positive evidence to support it is dangerous nonsense—in this case nonsense entertained by desperate Presidents and abetted by officials who might better have said: "We have turned over enough rocks, Mr. President." Thus, at the end of the unhappy affair called Chaos, one side of the Agency was unwittingly engaged in what was a corruption of the search for truth, to say nothing of extensively illegal activities, while the other side of the Agency was frenetically trying, under heavy fire, to stick to its best judgment.

In retrospect, it can be rationalized that all the actors in this unhappy drama were victims of the curious political climate of Washington as the Vietnam conflict ground to a conclusion. The psychological ingredients were all there: bureaucratic weariness with a clearly failing U.S. policy to which the Agency had already committed much of its manpower energies for a decade was one. Presidential frustration as various ways out of the dilemma were closed off was another. When all is said and done, however, there can only be one satisfactory explanation for the Agency's plunge into massive illegal activities. Top management had the means, the manpower and the mind-set to do the President's bidding and to do it without arousing suspicion or inviting investigation. Only in the waning days of Chaos (and the War) did complaints from lower echelons of the Agency begin to be registered around Washington. What top management lacked was the habit of limit setting, the reflex that warns of dangerous consequences—not of being found out, but of transgressing minimal ethical standards. Presidents can perhaps be forgiven for obsessiveness, but for the servants of Presidents, particularly those whose business is truth, the first duty is to guard against those personal and institutional frailties that make a mockery of the search for truth.

V

Is it possible, then, to introduce, or better to revive, a sense of ethics in the intelligence community? Certainly much can be accomplished simply by strong leadership that sets an appropriate tone. Presumably some efforts are being made in this direction now. But rhetoric alone cannot do the job that is required. Some specific prescriptions are offered in the following paragraphs.

The time would appear ripe, from the perspective both of history and the complexities of a world where energy resources, food supply and technological sophistication carry as much, if not more weight than weapons superiority, for the intelligence community to get out of political operations.

The massive investment in these activities in recent years has paid off only rarely in terms of advancing U.S. interests. At times, as in the Congo, they have done more to confuse and unsettle an already fluid situation than to stabilize it. Some operations have probably cost the United States goodwill for years to come. Cost-benefit factors apart, political operations are often, although not always, illegal activities in which the greatest skill is to thwart the established authorities of foreign countries. To live clandestinely, to manipulate others, to distress the political ecology of another society—these are all activities that induce an amoral view of life. While they may or may not produce critical effects in the countries where they are undertaken, they almost certainly will affect those who engage in them. They are, finally, activities that have little or nothing to do with intelligence.

It can be argued that there are occasions, or there may be occasions, when political action of a clandestine nature may be the only feasible way to produce a desirable circumstance beneficial not only to the instigating country, but to a larger portion of the world's peoples. One can imagine, for example, such operations, mounted in South Africa, that might have positive consequences throughout the southern part of the continent. U.S. policy interests could be served at the same time as the interests of South Africa's neighbors. Indeed, there have been occasions when massive infusions of U.S. funds and skills have turned the tide in tightly balanced and critical political contests. Support for the noncommunist parties in Italy and France in 1948 comes to mind as does the far less obtrusive (and, one gathers, predominantly European) support in 1975 for democratic elements threatened by hard-line (and Soviet-supported) Communists in Portugal.

The opportunity for U.S. intervention in political events of high international significance would not be lost by the abolition of a political operations capability. Private citizens recruited for the occasion have carried out such tasks for Presidents before and could again. On the other hand, there could be two salutary consequences for the United States in abandoning political operations as an ongoing activity of the CIA. First, Presidents would have to shoulder the burden themselves and create ad hoc arrangements for each instance. This would almost certainly sharpen their discrimination and force them to concentrate on interventions with the highest chance of success and the least chance of exposure. Second, the elaborate network of clandestine operators currently in place could be drastically reduced. No longer would it be necessary to nurture and maintain agents around the world on a contingency basis. The temptation to indulge in operational mischief of low or ambiguous priority for the sake of keeping agents alert would be foreclosed.

Many of the arguments used to question the efficacy and suitability of political operations can be applied to the process of human clandestine intelligence collection. The product is not all that impressive; the moral damage to the collectors is high; intelligence tends to be collected as an end in itself; and there is always the risk of exposure. Nevertheless, intelligence must be collected in selected areas and against specific subject targets. Technology is now the workhorse of the collection business and it should remain so. The present Director has in effect recognized this evolution in collection methods; he has justified his reduction of covert officers on this ground. Photographic and audio satellites and other interception devices are immensely expensive, but they have the advantage of doing only minimal damage to the ethical standards of the operators and processors. As noted above, technological intelligence collection is in at least one highly significant area—that of arms limitation control—tacitly accepted as essential to security by both superpowers.[6]

Of course, even with the phasing down of clandestine human collection, the need will remain for residual capability in certain esoteric collection techniques. Atmospheric conditions in some geographic locations may be so unfavorable that short-range collection devices will be needed to supplement "stand-off" equipment, such as satellites. There will always be the need for personnel skilled in the techniques of situating these devices. Similarly, there must be those who can exploit the defector or the "walk-in" source.

Counterintelligence is another field of clandestine intelligence activity which probably cannot be dispensed with for some years to come. But if counterintelligence is to survive, it should be organized on a purely defensive basis as a protection against foreign penetration of the U.S. intelligence services and their technical capabilities. It should be a small, lean component with a sophisticated understanding not only of the technological capabilities of major foreign intelligence services, but also of those countries' political dynamics. Far from being walled off from other Agency components as in the past, it should be a vital part of Agency life, as much to gain from exposure to varying points of view as to influence those points of view.

A vigorous reexamination of the entire collection function, both in terms of techniques and targets, would be salutary at this point in the intelligence community. Collection that goes beyond what the satellite and the intercept station provide cannot be forsaken altogether. Indeed, it should be improved with renewed emphasis on (a) analytic collection and (b) the old-world expertise of the open dialogue replacing the controlled source. Collectors with the training to mine and exploit technical materials in archives and specialized libraries or statistical centers could be the intelligence pick-and-shovel men of the future.

For those tightly closed societies where access to such material is almost completely denied to the United States, a different methodology will be necessary. Third-country officials with some access privileges in the host country must be assiduously cultivated, but (breaking with past practice) in an open and reciprocal manner. Collectors with substantive knowledge of their data targets should be authorized to disseminate "trading materials" to their foreign counterparts in exchange for hard-to-get data and technical material. This will be a delicate business. Maladroit handling of such negotiations could result in even tighter controls over information by the host country. Needless to say, negotiations could not be conducted in the target country without risking the expulsion of third-country nationals. New expertise in content evaluation both of the materials desired by the United States and the data to be used as trading currency will have to be developed.

At the higher levels of intelligence collection—that is, gaining insight into the sensitive complex of issues concerning political, economic and military developments in a target country—emphasis should be on the old-fashioned method of diplomatic dialogue. Reports that contribute to an understanding of social or economic trends or that sort out shifting national priorities are almost always more significant and useful than the one-shot item that reveals a specific decision or records some finite act. "Think pieces" have traditionally been the preserve of the ambassador or senior Foreign Service official. Their quality has, however, been uneven; they suffer from irregularity. Part of the problem is that few Foreign Service officers stay long enough on a single posting to become in-depth analytical experts. Only a few of the largest embassies have enjoyed the luxury of having one such person on their staffs for a number of years. What is being proposed here is that CIA officers fill the roles of permanent in-country experts. These would be senior officials, chosen for their substantive familiarity with the political and economic cultures of the countries to which they are posted. They would be expected to cultivate openly the widest circle of acquaintances and to report selectively both to headquarters and the ambassador. Clandestinity would give way to substantive expertise.

The finely trained and highly skilled clandestine collection officer with years of service in the field is likely to scoff at these suggestions. It has always been the contention of the clandestine collector that overt techniques could indeed uncover immense amounts of data about the capabilities of a foreign nation target, but that the intentions and plans of the same country could only be unlocked by controlled penetrations. There is, of course, some truth to this proposition. Final and critical decisions—e.g., to go to war with a neighbor, to begin the development of nuclear weaponry—are so tightly held and originate from such complex motivations that they do not suddenly spring off printed pages being turned by a lonely researcher. On the other hand, neither have such decisions been revealed with any great degree of success by penetration agents in the past.

Once the CIA has begun to turn itself around by the actions suggested above, it will have taken the most painful steps. But backsliding into old habits and behavior patterns will surely occur unless other, less dramatic moves are made. The influence of the clandestine service in the Agency remains strong and, given the sheer weight of numbers, it will have a significant voice in internal Agency affairs for years to come. Something of the flavor of how that voice might express itself can be inferred from the hero's welcome given to Richard Helms when he appeared at a reception of recently retired covert officers fresh from his conviction in federal court. The old methods of compartmentalization and tightly controlled operations have become a way of life not easily shaken in the insular bureaucracy of an intelligence service. Radical rearrangements of traditional procedures must be considered.

At the least the Inspector General's function should be strengthened, as the Church Committee has recommended. Specifically, this officer's role should be expanded beyond its traditional one of internal control and response to employee complaints. One ex-Agency official who is a careful student of its recent history has suggested the creation of an ombudsman accessible to employees who felt they were being used in improper activities.[7] This would be a helpful addition to the Inspector General's staff, freeing him for the vital task of constructively intervening in questionable plans and programs throughout the Agency.

Similarly, the Legal Counsel must be given more steel to put under his velvet glove, particularly when his rulings are ignored or overturned by the Director. Traditionally matters of legal propriety have been referred to the Legal Counsel by other senior officers when and if they chose to do so; in effect his role has been passive. It should be a relatively simple internal matter to reverse this pattern. President Ford followed up one Church Committee recommendation by giving the Legal Counsel access to the

Executive Oversight Board in the event that one of his rulings was ignored by the Director. This is a significant step in strengthening the legal review function in the Agency.

VI

A more sweeping structural change for the Agency has been suggested from time to time. This would entail a complete divorce of overt and covert intelligence activities. Overt functions (analysis, reporting, estimates, etc.) would be aggregated under one organizational roof and covert functions (collection, operations, counterintelligence, technical development of human control devices, etc.) under another. The objective behind such proposals has usually been to remove from the intelligence end product the taint of the methods used to obtain the raw data, in other words to strengthen the dignity and credibility of the Agency's truth-telling function.

There are merits to these suggestions, but perhaps the optimum time for divorce has passed. Indeed, if political operations were now eliminated and clandestine collection minimized, the temptation to breach ethical standards by the clandestine services would be reduced significantly. Moreover, cutting the clandestine services adrift would result in the concentration in one organization of most of those officers—now at high positions—who have been exposed to the highest ethical risks. Backsliding would be a great temptation, managerial control an administrator's nightmare.

But the measures discussed above will amount to little more than tinkering if not buttressed by a radical new personnel policy that places a premium on ethical values. Beyond native intelligence, recruitment criteria have in the past emphasized such psychological factors as stability, intellectual curiosity and phlegm. Once selected on the basis of favorable readings on these counts, the candidate had, of course, to survive the polygraph test—a final screening against the possibility of penetration by a foreign agent or a duplicitous adventurer. To this battery a test of ethical values should be added.

Law enforcement agencies in a few communities have provided something of a model in an area almost as contentious. A handful of larger police departments have been including in their selection procedures a "violence test" for rookie candidates.[8] The tests are basically psychological, designed to determine which applicants, in the normal course of their duties, would resort too readily to heavy-handed or bullying tactics. The results are not yet wholly clear—in part, one suspects, because there is little or no reinforcement of the desired value level as the new patrolmen become acculturated by their older colleagues, who possessed badges years before consideration of behavior patterns became a professional concern.

An ethics test could be constructed from an array of situational choice problems inserted into the Agency's selection instruments. Such problems would present difficult ethical decision choices for the test-taker in a variety of interpersonal and organizational settings. To prevent the job applicant from tilting his answers toward problem solutions he presumes the testers are seeking the questions would have to be scattered throughout the various portions of the questionnaires used—psychological, intelligence, etc. All ethics questions could then be selected out of the various test parts and reviewed separately. One hopes that a rough profile of the applicant's personal ethical standards could be obtained by this device, but at best it would probably do no more than single out applicants with unacceptably low or hopelessly confused ethical standards. Follow-up tests for those who enter the Agency and have served for several years would be considerably more difficult to design, but they are not beyond the skills of Agency psychologists.

Surely this is slippery ground. One man's ethical floor may be another's ethical ceiling. Who is to define what the acceptable level of ethical beliefs should be? How would Agency management keep its ethical sights straight in a period of rapidly changing moral values? The issues raised are immensely difficult, but dismissing the concept will not solve the problem of the current low estate of the Agency in the public mind. Tackling the problem head on would, if nothing else, constitute a clear signal of top Agency management's concern to current employees, prospective recruits and the general public.

VII

Finally, the real purpose of intelligence—truth telling—must be placed at the center of Agency concerns. This is a harsh prescription; it is certainly the most difficult objective of the lot. But it must be the principal purpose of Agency leadership to establish beyond question the capacity of its experts and its facilities to seek out and find the truth, or the nearest approximation of the truth possible. Public cynicism will have to be dispelled before this is possible; it will take time. There are no easy paths to this objective. Indeed, the present mood of the public toward the Agency militates against its succeeding. The best graduate students do not gravitate to the Agency; its name is suspect in much of academia; business and professional groups are fearful of association.

Where such circumstances exist they must be met with new and probably at first none too credible approaches. Insistence on being primarily in the business of truth telling will not automatically convince the skeptic that it is so. But CIA leadership that condones no other competing role and that demands that ethical questions be asked before internal Agency policies are decided upon will have made a beginning in the long journey back to public accountability. None of these steps, of course, would avert the damage that an unscrupulous President, intent on misusing intelligence talents, could produce. Only loud, angry public resignations by intelligence leaders could in such a case underscore a professional's ethical commitment to truth.

Questions for Further Discussion

1. Is the phrase "intelligence ethics" oxymoronic?

2. Is there a moral "bright line" across which you would not allow the CIA or other U.S. intelligence agencies to pass in its conduct of secret operations abroad?

3. What rules would you set, if any, for the detention, extraordinary rendition, and interrogation of individuals who might know something about Al Qaeda activities?

4. What do you think Godfrey would have to say about Hitz's views on assassination?

Endnotes

1. Chester L Cooper, "The CIA and Decision-Making," *Foreign Affairs*, January 1972, p. 223.
2. *Final Report of the Select Committee to Study Governmental Operations with Respect to Intelligence Activities*, U S Senate. 94th Cong , 2nd sess., April 14, 1976, seven volumes.
3. Testimony of William Sullivan. *Final Report, op cit.*, Book II, p. 141.
4. *Final Report, op. cit.*, Book I, p. 282.
5. *Ibid*, p. 286.
6. Harry Rositzke in "America's Secret Operations: A Perspective," *Foreign Affairs*, January 1975, pp 334–51, has presented a sophisticated view of the remaining need for clandestine human intelligence and counterintelligence collection. And Herbert Scoville, Jr., writing from a consumer's viewpoint (as I do) has laid I think the right strew on the predominant need for technological methods today, "Is Espionage Necessary for our Security?," *Foreign Affairs*, April 1976, pp. 482–95.
7. See Harry Rositzke, *CIA's Secret Operations*, New York. Reader's Digest Press, 1977, Chapter 13.
8. The "Machover DAP" test is one frequently used to detect overly aggressive personalities. Sophisticated screening instruments are described in the publication *Police Selection and Career Assement*, issued by the Law Enforcement Assistance Administration, National Institute of Law Enforcement and Criminal Justice, U.S. Dept of Justice, 1976. ✦

Reprinted with permission from E. Drexel Godfrey, Jr., "Ethics and Intelligence," *Foreign Affairs* 56 (April 1978): 624–642.

29

Another System of Oversight: Intelligence and the Rise of Judicial Intervention

Frederic F. Manget

The judicial branch of government is a latecomer to the world of intelligence; but, as Manget notes, it is now very much a part of that world. The courts provide yet another check on intelligence abuse. Judges frequently interact with lawyers from the intelligence community, probing the activities of the secret agencies with questions about what they are doing and why.

"Perhaps the best way to give you a conception of our power and emplacement here is to note the state and national laws that we are ready to bend, break, violate, and/or ignore. False information is given out routinely on Florida papers of incorporation; tax returns fudge the real sources of investment in our proprietaries; false flight plans are filed daily with the FAA; and we truck weapons and explosives over Florida highways, thereby violating the Munitions Act and the Firearms Act, not to speak of what we do to our old friends Customs, Immigration, Treasury, and the Neutrality Act. . . . As I write, I can feel your outrage. It is not that they are doing all that—perhaps it is necessary, you will say—but why . . . are you all this excited about it?"

—*Norman Mailer,* Harlot's Ghost

It is actually not such an exercise in glorious outlawry as all that. But the belief is widely held be-yond the Beltway, in the heartland of the country and even in New York, that the intelligence agencies of the US Government are not subject to laws and the authority of judges. No television cop show, adventure movie, or conspiracy book in two decades has left out characters who are sinister intelligence officials beyond the law's reach.

The reality, however, is that the Federal judiciary now examines a wide range of intelligence activities under a number of laws, including the Constitution. To decide particular issues under the law, Federal judges and their cleared clerks and other staff are shown material classified at the highest levels. There is no requirement that Federal judges be granted security clearances—their access to classified information is an automatic aspect of their status. Their supporting staffs have to be vetted, but court employees are usually granted all clearances that they need to assist effectively the judiciary in resolving legal issues before the courts.

Judges currently interpret the laws that affect national security to reach compromises necessary to reconcile the open world of American jurisprudence and the closed world of intelligence operations. They have now been doing it long enough to enable practitioners in the field to reach a number of conclusions. In effect, the judicial review of issues touching on intelligence matters has developed into a system of oversight.

FI, CI, and CA

Intelligence has several components. The authoritative statutory definition of intelligence is in Section 3 of the National Security Act of 1947, as amended, and includes both foreign intelligence and counterintelligence. Foreign intelligence means information relating to the capabilities, intentions, or activities of foreign governments or elements thereof, foreign organizations, or foreign persons. Counterintelligence means information gathered and activities conducted to protect against espionage, other intelligence activities, sabotage, or assassinations conducted by or on behalf of foreign governments or elements thereof, foreign organizations, or foreign persons, or international terrorist activities.

Covert action is also often lumped with intelligence because historically such activity has been carried out by parts of the Intelligence Community agencies, most notably by CIA. Covert action is now defined as activity of the US Government to influence political, economic, or military conditions abroad, where it is intended that the role of the US Government will not be apparent or acknowledged publicly, but not including traditional foreign intelligence, counterintelligence, diplomatic, law enforcement, or military activities.

Official Accountability

The term "oversight" describes a system of accountability in which those vested with the executive authority in an organization have their actions reviewed, sometimes in advance, by an independent group that has the power to check those actions. In corporations, the board of directors exercises oversight. In democratic governments, the classic model of oversight is that of the legislative branches, conducted through the use of committee subpoena powers and the authority to appropriate funds for the executive branches. Legislative oversight is unlimited, by contrast with the model of judicial oversight described here, which is limited.

Legislative oversight is policy related, as opposed to judicial oversight and its concern with legal questions. And legislative oversight tends toward micromanagement of executive decisions, where judicial oversight is more deferential. But a rule of thumb for a simple country lawyer is that when you have to go and explain to someone important what you have been doing and why, that is oversight, regardless of its source. Today, Intelligence Community lawyers often do just that. But it has not always been that way.

Past Practices

Until the mid-1970s, judges had little to say about intelligence. Because intelligence activities are almost always related to foreign affairs, skittish judges avoided jurisdiction over most intelligence controversies under the political question doctrine, which allocates the resolution of national security disputes to the two political branches of the government. This doctrine was buttressed by the need to have a concrete case or controversy before judges, rather than an abstract foreign policy debate, because of the limited jurisdiction of Federal courts. The doctrine was further developed in the Federal Court of Appeals for the DC Circuit by then Judge Scalia, who wrote that courts should exercise considerable restraint in granting any petitions for equitable relief in foreign affairs controversies.

In addition, American intelligence organizations have historically had limited internal security functions, if any. Before CIA's creation, most intelligence activity was conducted by the military departments. In 1947, the National Security Act expressly declined to give CIA any law enforcement authority: "... except that the Agency shall have no police, subpoena, or law enforcement powers or internal security functions"—a prohibition that exists in the

same form today. Without the immediate and direct impact that police activity has on citizens, there were few instances where intelligence activities became issues in Federal cases.

There is even a historical hint of an argument that, to the extent that intelligence activities are concerned with the security of the state, they are inherent to any sovereign's authority under a higher law of self-preservation and not subject to normal judicial review. Justice Sutherland found powers inherent in sovereignty to be extra-constitutional in his dicta in the *Curtiss-Wright* case.

Even that good democrat Thomas Jefferson wrote to a friend,

> A strict observance of the written laws is doubtless *one* of the high duties of a good citizen, but it is not *the highest* (emphasis in original). The laws of necessity, of self-preservation, of saving our country, by a scrupulous adherence to written law, would be to lose the law itself, with life, liberty, property and all those who are enjoying them with us: thus absurdly sacrificing the end to the means. . . .

This sense that somehow secret intelligence activities were governed by a higher law of self-preservation no doubt added to the Federal judiciary's reluctance to exert its limited jurisdiction in such areas.

Increasing Scrutiny

In the 1970s this reluctance began to dwindle, driven by a number of causes. After the Watergate affair, the activities of the executive branch came under a growing and skeptical scrutiny by the press, the public, and Congress. This scrutiny blossomed into the Church and Pike Committee investigations of CIA, as well as the Rockefeller Commission report on CIA activities.

The Federal judiciary was following right behind, in part due to a natural extension of the judicial activism that began in the 1960s. The expansion of due process rights of criminal defendants meant that judges would examine in ever-increasing detail the actions of the government in prosecutions. The American tendency to treat international problems as subject to cure by legal process became even more pronounced, and the Intelligence Community found itself increasingly involved in counterterrorism, counternarcotics, and nonproliferation activities of the law enforcement agencies of the US Government.

The other cause was simply the increasing number of statutes that Congress passed dealing with CIA and the Intelligence Community. The more statutes there are on a particular subject, the more judicial review of the subject there will be. For example, in the late 1970s, Congress began to pass annual authorization bills for the Intelligence Community which generally contained permanent statutory provisions, a practice that continues today.

Congress Weighs In

Congressional inroads on all types of executive branch foreign affairs powers also increased in the 1970s. The constitutional foreign affairs powers shared by the executive and legislative branches wax and wane, but it seems clear that Congress began to reassert its role in international relations at that time.

The War Powers Resolution and the series of Boland Amendments restricting aid to the Nicaraguan Contras in the 1980s were statutory attempts by Congress to force policy positions on a reluctant executive branch. The Hughes-Ryan Amendment required notification of oversight committees about covert actions. When Congress passes laws to prevail in disagreements in foreign affairs, more judicial review will occur. De Tocqueville was right—all disputes in the United States inevitably end up in court.

The result is the current system of judicial oversight of intelligence. By 1980, then Attorney General Benjamin Caviled could write that,

> Although there may continue to be some confusion about how the law applies to a particular matter, there is no longer any doubt that intelligence activities are subject to definable legal standards.

It is not nearly so comprehensive as legislative oversight, because Federal courts still have jurisdiction limited by statute and constitution. But it does exist in effective and powerful ways that go far beyond the conventional wisdom that national security is a cloak hiding intelligence activities from the Federal judiciary.

Criminal Law

Federal judges are required to examine the conduct of the government when it becomes a litigated issue in a criminal prosecution, and almost every case involves at least one such issue. Intelligence activities are no exception. What makes those activities so different is that they almost always require secrecy to be effective and to maintain their value to US policymakers.

The need for secrecy clashes directly with conventional US trial procedures in which most of the efforts on both sides of a case go into developing the pretrial phase called discovery. As a result, Federal judges review and decide a number of issues that

regularly arise in areas where democratic societies would instinctively say that governmental secrecy is bad. The pattern has developed that judges review intelligence information when protection of its secrecy could affect traditional notions of a fair trial.

For example, it would be manifestly unfair if the government could, without sanctions, withhold secret intelligence information from defendants that would otherwise be disclosed under rules of criminal procedure. In fact, under both Federal Rule of Criminal Procedure 16 relating to discovery and the *Brady* and *Giglio* cases, Federal prosecutors are required to turn over certain materials to the defense, regardless of their secrecy.

For a number of years, judges fashioned their own procedures to balance competing interests. In the *Kampiles* case, the defendant was charged with selling to the Russians a manual about the operation of the KH-11 spy satellite. The trial court did not allow classified information to be introduced at trial. The court issued a protective order after closed proceedings in which the Government presented evidence of the sensitive document that was passed to the Soviet Union, and of the FBI's counterintelligence investigation into the document's disappearance. The court of appeals upheld the espionage conviction based upon the defendant's confession that he had met with and sold a classified document to a Soviet intelligence officer and upon sufficient other evidence to corroborate the reliability of the defendant's confession.

CIPA

The Classified Information Procedures Act (CIPA) was passed in 1980 to avoid ad hoc treatment of the issues and to establish detailed procedures for handling such classified information in criminal trials. It was a response to the problem of grey-mail, in which defendants threatened to reveal classified information unless prosecutions were dropped or curtailed. Before passage of CIPA, the government had to guess the extent of possible damage from such disclosures because there were no methods by which classified information could be evaluated in advance of public discovery and evidentiary rulings by the courts.

Under CIPA, classified information can be reviewed under the regular criminal procedures for discovery and admissibility of evidence before the information is publicly disclosed. Judges are allowed to determine issues presented to them both *in camera* (nonpublicly, in chambers) and *ex parte* (presented by only one side, without the presence of the other party).

Under CIPA, the defendant is allowed to discover classified information and to offer it in evidence to the extent it is necessary to a fair trial and allowed by normal criminal procedures. The government is allowed to minimize the classified information at risk of public disclosure by offering unclassified summaries or substitutions for the sensitive materials. Judges are called upon to balance the need of the government to protect intelligence information and the rights of a defendant to a fair trial. This is an area in which democratic societies would want judicial scrutiny of governmental assertions of national security equities, in order to preserve constitutional due process guarantees.

Looking at Surveillance

Judges also scrutinize intelligence activities in areas involving surveillance. Because of the Fourth Amendment guarantee against unreasonable searches and seizures, intelligence collection also is reviewed under standards applied to search warrants. The Federal judiciary has been reviewing surveillance in the context of suppression of evidence hearings for many years. For example, the issue of electronic surveillance was considered in 1928 in the Supreme Court case of *Olmstead*, which held that the government could conduct such surveillance without a criminal search warrant. In 1967 the Supreme Court overturned *Olmstead*, and the government began to follow specially tailored search warrant procedures for electronic surveillance.

FISA

In 1978 the Foreign Intelligence Surveillance Act (FISA) was passed to establish a secure forum in which the government could obtain what is essentially a search warrant to conduct electronic surveillance within the United States of persons who are agents of foreign powers. FISA requires that applications for such orders approving electronic surveillance include detailed information about the targets, what facts justify the belief that the targets are agents of foreign powers, and the means of conducting the surveillance.

Applications are heard and either denied or granted by a special court composed of seven Federal district court judges designated by the Chief Justice of the United States. There is a three-member court of review to hear appeals of denials of applications.

Thus, judges conduct extensive review of foreign-intelligence-related electronic surveillance operations before their inception. Intrusive collection techniques make this area especially sensitive, and their review by Federal judges is important to reconciling them with Fourth Amendment protections against unreasonable searches. In the Intelligence Authorization Act for Fiscal Year 1995, the FISA procedures were expanded to apply to physical searches.

Pleading Government Authorization

In another area, judges review secret intelligence activities in the context of whether defendants were authorized by an intelligence agency to do the very actions on which the criminal charges are based. Under rules of criminal procedure, defendants are required to notify the government if they intend to raise a defense of government authorization. The government is required to respond to such assertions, either admitting or denying them.

Should there be any merit to the defense, the defendant is allowed to put on evidence and to have the judge decide issues that arise in litigating the defense. This satisfies the notion that it would be unfair to defendants, who could have been authorized to carry out some clandestine activity, if they could not bring such secret information before the court.

For example, in the case of *United States v. Rewald*, the defendant was convicted of numerous counts of bilking investors in a Ponzi scheme. Rewald maintained that CIA had told him to spend extravagantly the money of investors in order to cultivate relationships with foreign potentates and wealthy businessmen who would be useful intelligence sources. The opinion of the Ninth Circuit Court of Appeals panel that reviewed the convictions characterized Rewald's argument as his principal defense in the case, and in fact Rewald did have some minor contact with local CIA personnel, volunteering information from his international business travels and providing light backstopping cover for a few CIA employees.

Rewald sought the production of hundreds of classified CIA documents and propounded more than 1,700 interrogatories, but after reviewing responsive records and answers, the trial court excluded most of the classified information as simply not relevant under evidentiary standards. The Ninth Circuit panel noted that, "This court has examined each and every classified document filed by Rewald in this appeal." It subsequently upheld the District Court's exclusion of the classified information at issue.

In two more recent criminal cases—the prosecutions of Christopher Drougoul in the BNL affair and in the Teledyne case related to Chilean arms dealer Carlos Cardoen—press accounts have noted that the judges in both cases heard arguments from the defendants that sensitive intelligence and foreign policy information should be disclosed in those prosecutions as part of the defense cases. The press accounts further state that in both cases the judges disagreed, and, after reviewing the information at issue, ruled against the defendants.

The significance is not that the defendants lost their arguments, but that they had the opportunity to litigate them before a Federal judge. The Department of Justice does not prosecute defendants while the Intelligence Community denies them the information they need to have a fair trial. Who decides what a fair trial requires? An independent Federal judge, appointed for life, who reviews the secrets.

Civil Law

Criminal law has the most direct and dramatic impact on individual citizens, but civil law also requires judicial intervention in numerous cases where intelligence activities, and the secrecy surrounding them, become issues. Private civil litigants may demand that the government produce intelligence information under the laws requiring disclosure of agency records unless they are specifically exempted. Individual civil plaintiffs may bring tort actions against the government under the Federal Tort Claims Act based on allegations that secret intelligence activities caused compensable damages. Private litigants may sue each other for any of the myriad civil causes of action that exist in litigious America, and demand from the government information relating to intelligence activities in order to support their cases.

In all such instances, Federal judges act as the arbiters of government assertions of special equities relating to intelligence that affect the litigation. Private civil litigants may not win their arguments that such equities should be discounted in their favor, but they can make their arguments to a Federal judge.

For example, under the Freedom of Information Act (FOIA) and the Privacy Act, there are exceptions to the mandatory disclosure provisions that allow classified information and intelligence sources and methods to be kept secret. Courts defer extensively to the executive branch on what information falls within those exceptions, but there is still a rigorous review of such material. CIA prepares public indexes (called *Vaughn* indexes, after the case endorsing them) describing records withheld under the sensitive information exceptions that are reviewed by the courts.

If those public indexes are not sufficient for a judge to decide whether an exception applies, classified *Vaughn* indexes are shown to the judge *ex parte* and *in camera*. If a classified index is still not sufficient, then the withheld materials themselves can be shown to the judge.

Other FOIA Requests

The *Knight* case illustrates this extensive process. The plaintiff filed an FOIA request for all information in CIA's possession relating to the 1980s sinking of the Greenpeace ship *Rainbow Warrior* in the harbor in Auckland, New Zealand, by the French external intelligence service. CIA declined to produce any such records, and the plaintiff filed a suit to force disclosure. Both public and classified indexes were prepared by CIA, and, when they were deemed by the court to be insufficient for a decision in the case, all responsive documents were shown in unredacted form to the trial judge in her chambers. Her decision was in favor of the government, and it was affirmed on appeal. Historian Alan Fitzgibbon litigated another FOIA request to CIA and the FBI for materials on the disappearance of Jesus de Galindez, a Basque exile and a critic of the Trujillo regime in the Dominican Republic who was last seen outside a New York City subway station in 1956. The case was litigated from 1979 to 1990, and, during the process, the district court conducted extensive *in camera* reviews of the material at issue. That pattern has been repeated in numerous other cases.

Thus, in areas where Federal laws mandate disclosure of US government information, Federal judges review claims of exemptions based on sensitive intelligence equities.

State Secrets Privilege

Federal courts also have jurisdiction over civil cases ranging from negligence claims against the government to disputes between persons domiciled in different states. In such cases, litigants often subpoena or otherwise demand discovery of sensitive intelligence-related information. The government resists such demands by asserting the state secrets privilege under the authority of *U.S. v. Reynolds,* a Supreme Court case that allowed the government to deny disclosure of national security secrets. Other statutory privileges also protect intelligence sources and methods. Judicial review of US Government affidavits that assert the state secrets privilege is regularly used to resolve disputed issues of privilege.

In *Halkin v. Helms,* former Vietnam war protesters sued officials of various Federal intelligence agencies alleging violation of plaintiffs' constitutional and statutory rights. Specifically, they alleged that the National Security Agency (NSA) conducted warrantless interceptions of their international wire, cable, and telephone communications at the request of other Federal defendants. The government asserted the state secrets privilege to prevent disclosure of whether the international communications of the plaintiffs were in fact acquired by NSA and disseminated to other Federal agencies.

The trial court considered three *in camera* affidavits and the *in camera* testimony of the Deputy Director of NSA, and the case was ultimately dismissed at the appellate level based on the assertion of the privilege. The plaintiffs had their day in court. They lost the case, but they had the full attention of both trial and appellate Federal court judges on the assertion of governmental secrecy.

Allegations of Abuse

Federal courts also adjudicate the substance of legal claims brought by private citizens alleging abusive governmental actions. For example, in *Birnbaum v. United States,* a suit was brought under the Federal Tort Claims Act by individuals whose letters to and from the Soviet Union were opened and photocopied by CIA in a mail-opening program that operated between 1953 and 1973. Plaintiffs were awarded $1,000 each in damages, and the award was upheld on appeal.

In *Doe v. Gates,* a CIA employee litigated the issue of alleged discrimination against him based on his homosexuality. Doe raised two constitutional claims—whether his firing violated the Fifth Amendment equal protection or deprivation of property without compensation clauses. He was heard at every Federal court level, including the U.S. Supreme Court. The judicial review even included limited evidentiary review pursuant to cross-motions for summary judgment. (The case has been litigated for years and is not yet final, but the government is expected to prevail.)

In two more recent cases, the chance of losing litigation over alleged gender-based, discrimination led the parties to settle claims with one female officer in the CIA's Directorate of Operations (the "Jane Doe Thompson Case") and with a class of female operations officers in CIA. The settlements made moot a full judicial review of all government actions, but both sides clearly believed that judicial review would occur.

The First Amendment

Federal judges also look at First Amendment protections of freedom of speech and the press as they relate to intelligence. One context is the contract for nondisclosure of classified information that employees, contractors, and others sign when they are granted access to sensitive information by agencies of the Intelligence Community. The contract requires prepublication review of non-official writings by the government in order to protect sen-

sitive information. That is a prior restraint on publication which was challenged in two separate lawsuits by former CIA employees Victor Marchetti and Frank Snepp. After extensive appellate review, the contract restrictions on freedom of speech were held reasonable and constitutional. It is clear that Federal courts will entertain claims of First Amendment violations from Intelligence Community employees, and will examine the claims closely.

For example, in 1981 a former CIA officer named McGehee submitted an article to CIA for prepublication review pursuant to a secrecy agreement he had signed in 1952, when he joined the Agency. The article asserted that the CIA had mounted a campaign of deceit to persuade the world that the "revolt of the poor natives against a ruthless U.S.-backed oligarchy" in El Salvador was really "a Soviet/Cuban/Bulgarian/Vietnamese/PLO/Ethiopian/Nicaraguan/International Terrorism challenge to the United States." McGehee offered a few examples of CIA operations to support his assertion; some were deemed classified by the Agency, and permission to publish those portions of the article was denied.

McGehee sued, seeking a declaratory judgment that the CIA prepublication and classification procedures violated the First Amendment. He lost, but the DC Circuit Court of Appeals stated: "We must accordingly establish a standard for judicial review of the CIA classification decision that affords proper respect to the individual rights at stake while recognizing the CIA's technical expertise and practical familiarity with the ramifications of sensitive information. We conclude that reviewing courts should conduct a *de novo* review of the classification decision, while giving deference to reasoned and detailed CIA explanations of that classification decision." When individual rights are affected, Federal courts have not been reluctant to assert oversight and require Intelligence Community agencies to visit the courthouse and explain what they are doing.

The second context involving the First Amendment is government attempts to restrain publication of intelligence information by the press. When *The Pentagon Papers* were leaked to the news media in 1971, the attempt to enjoin publication resulted in the Supreme Court case of *New York Times v. U.S.* Because of the number of individual opinions in the case, the holding is somewhat confusing. Nonetheless, it seems clear that an injunction against press publication of intelligence information will not only be difficult to obtain but also will subject any petition for such relief to strict scrutiny by the Federal courts.

Conclusions

The exposure of Federal judges to intelligence activities leads to a number of conclusions. One is that judicial oversight operates to an extent overlooked in the debate over who is watching the Intelligence Community. Judicial oversight is limited compared to unlimited Congressional oversight. Judicial oversight deals with legal issues, as opposed to policy issues. Judges are deferential to the executive branch in intelligence matters, something not often true of Congress. But judges do act as arbiters of governmental secrecy in a powerful way.

The basic conundrum for intelligence is that it requires secrecy to be effective, but government secrecy in a Western liberal democracy is generally undesirable. Government secrecy can destroy the legitimacy of government institutions. It can cripple accountability of public servants and politicians. It can hide abuses of fundamental rights of citizens. In fact, secret government tends to excess.

In the United States, Federal judges counterbalance the swing toward such excess. In those areas most important to particular rights of citizens, they act as arbiters of governmental secrecy. The Federal judiciary ameliorates the problems of government secrecy by providing a secure forum for review of intelligence activities under a number of laws, as surrogates for the public.

The developing history of judicial review of intelligence activities shows that it occurs in those areas where government secrecy and the need for swift executive action conflict with well-established legal principles of individual rights: an accused's right to a fair criminal trial; freedom from unreasonable searches and seizures; rights of privacy; freedom of speech and the press.

Judges thus get involved where an informed citizenry would instinctively want judicial review of secret intelligence activities. The involvement of the Federal judiciary is limited but salutary in its effect on executive branch actions. Nothing concentrates the mind and dampens excess so wonderfully as the imminent prospect of explaining one's actions to a Federal judge. The Constitution's great genius in this area is a system of government that reconciles the nation's needs for order and defense from foreign aggression with fundamental individual rights that are directly affected by intelligence activities. Those nations currently devising statutory charters and legislative oversight of their foreign intelligence services might do well to include an independent judiciary in their blueprints. Federal judges are the essential third part of the oversight system in the United States, matching requirements of the laws to intelligence activities and watching the watchers.

Questions for Further Discussion

1. Do you think there is a proper role for the judicial branch in the supervision of intelligence activities?

2. Which organization do you think provides the best safeguards against the misuse of secret power by the CIA and other intelligence agencies: the National Security Council, the Office of the DNI, the Congress, the courts, or the media?

3. What kinds of intelligence activities are covered by the FISA Court?

4. What are some reasons that the court system may not provide a strong check on the executive branch when it comes to intelligence operations? ✦

Reprinted with permission from Frederic F. Manget, "Another System of Oversight: Intelligence and the Rise of Judicial Intervention," *Studies in Intelligence* 39 (1966): 43–50.

30

Congressional Supervision of America's Secret Agencies: The Experience and Legacy of the Church Committee

Loch K. Johnson

Aformer assistant to Senator Frank Church, who led the Senate inquiry into alleged CIA abuses of power in 1975, Johnson reviews the experiences of that investigation and gauges the contribution made by the Church Committee to the search for a proper balance between security against America's enemies and the civil liberties of its own citizens.

Keeping an Eye on the Hidden Side of Government

For purposes of gathering and interpreting information from around the world, the United States created thirteen major agencies during the Cold War, known collectively as the "intelligence community" and led by a Director of Central Intelligence (DCI). Seven of the agencies have a predominantly military mission and are within the jurisdiction of the Defense Department (among them, the National Security Agency or NSA, which gathers signals intelligence); five are associated with civilian departments, such as the Federal Bureau of Investigation (FBI) within the Justice Department; and one, the Central Intelligence Agency (CIA), stands alone as an independent entity answerable directly to the president (Lowenthal 1992;

Richelson 1999). Together, these agencies comprise the largest cluster of information-gathering organizations in American history, and rivalled in world history only by the intelligence apparatus of the Soviet Union during the Cold War and Russia today.

Concealed from public scrutiny, America's intelligence agencies pose a major challenge to the idea of government accountability in a democratic society (Ransom 1970, 1975; Johnson 1986). This essay examines the failure of legislative supervisors to hold the intelligence community in check during the Cold War, leading to a significant erosion of civil liberties in the United States. It explores as well the prerequisites necessary to lessen the probability of the further abuse of power by the secret agencies.

A Conceptual Framework

An extensive literature exists on the subject of congressional control over administrative agencies, commonly referred to as legislative oversight (e.g., Aberbach 1990; Ogul 1976; Scher 1963). As Spence notes (1997), positive theorists and quantitative empiricists have pointed to the capacity of lawmakers to shape the environment of agency decision-making in such a way as to align bureaucrats toward the goals of oversight committees on Capitol Hill. For instance, Calvert, McCubbins, and Weingast (1989), as well as McCubbins *et al.* (1989), maintain that executive agencies are essentially "hard-wired" at their statutory inception to honor legislative intentions (*ex ante* control). Moreover, they posit, lawmakers have potent sanctions that may be used to punish rogue bureaucratic behavior, notably the power of the purse to reduce funding for recalcitrant agencies (*ex post* control).

Theorists emphasize as well that organized interest groups provide an added safeguard to assist lawmakers in thwarting errant bureaucrats who fail to uphold original legislative mandates. Lobbyists set off "fire alarms" to alert members of Congress when agencies have violated expected norms (McCubbins and Schwartz 1984). Media reporting on agency activities can serve a similar function. Moreover, lawmakers and their staff can engage in "police patrolling," that is, a more active and direct monitoring of agency activities through persistent hearings and less formal dialogues with agency personnel.

Yet, in contrast to these roseate theories on the efficacy of legislative oversight, a more extensive body of research that stretches over four decades of scholarly reporting offers quite a different impression. From this point of view, lawmakers have engaged in oversight only sporadically and half-heartedly (Bibby 1968; Ransom, 1970, 1977; Dodd and Schott 1979, 170–184; Johnson 1994). This failure of accountability has stemmed chiefly from a lack of motivation among members of Congress to immerse themselves in oversight activities, such as hearings and detailed budget reviews. For lawmakers, greater political advantage lies in the passage of legislation, where credit-claiming—vital to re-election—is more visible to constituents (Mayhew 1986).

Further, representatives have often been reluctant to become involved in (and, thus, responsible for) controversial agency decisions; better to keep a distance from potential trouble (Walden 1970). Information asymmetries have contributed as well to the failure of oversight, giving agencies room to maneuver as lawmakers remain unaware of informal rules, internal memoranda, and private deals struck inside the vast domains of the executive departments (Spence 1997, 200).

The Special Case of Intelligence

With respect to the intelligence agencies, the limited relevance of the safeguards heralded by the positivists and quantitative empiricists is manifest. In the first place, the statutory rules established for the secret agencies by the National Security Act of 1947 (50 U.S.C. 401) are broadly worded and often ambiguous. In one clause, for instance, this statute grants the CIA with authority to "perform such other functions and duties related to intelligence affecting the national security as the President or the National Security Council may direct . . . "—not exactly a tight legislative leash.

As for the appointment power, it is true that lawmakers have closely examined the credentials of some DCI nominees, rejecting a hand full over the years in hotly debated hearings (as with the donnybrook over the failed nomination of Anthony Lake during the Clinton Administration). Yet, the Office of DCI is notoriously weak. The DCI is head of the CIA, but exercises only marginal control over the dozen other agencies in the community. Their separate chiefs have extensive discretionary authority and are seldom subjected to the kind of legislative scrutiny directed toward on DCI nominations (Johnson 2000).

Fire alarms set off by lobbyists or by media reporters are unreliable, too. Few interest groups exist in this policy domain, and those that do (the Boeing corporation, for instance, which manufactures surveillance satellites) are rarely able to discuss whatever grievances they may have in public, given the classified nature of their work. And as Dana Priest, the *Washington Post*'s correspondent with an intelligence beat, has remarked (2003), the "high walls" of the intelligence agencies make it very difficult to report on intelligence activities. These walls are important to protect the nation's secrets from foreign spies; however, they have the effect, too, of isolating the intelligence agencies from the normal processes of legislative accountability envisioned in the Constitution (Article I), the *Federalist Papers* (e.g., No. 51), and various Supreme Court opinions (among the most famous, Justice Brandeis's comments in *Myers v. U.S.*, 272 U.S. 52 [1926]).

Police patrolling by Congress itself has been minimal, resulting from the lack of motivation by lawmakers in all policy domains, alluded to earlier. Specifically with respect to intelligence, members of Congress made it clear during the early stages of the Cold War that they were content to rely on the intelligence professionals to take care of business, with limited congressional supervision. The House and the Senate maintained small oversight subcommittees on the Armed Services and Appropriations Committees, but they met only infrequently and the questioning was typically brief if not perfunctory. One of the overseers, Leverett Saltonstall (D, Massachusetts), said on the floor of the Senate in 1956 that he was hesitant to "obtain information which I personally would rather not have, unless it was essential for me as a member of Congress to have it. . . ." (Holt 1995, 211).

Intelligence enjoyed a special dispensation since the days of the American Revolution (Knott 1996). The sense was that secret operations were too sensitive to be treated as normal government activities. The intelligence agencies would have to be kept apart; whether fighting Barbary pirates in the early days or communists during the Cold War, the nation would have to rely on the good intentions and sound judgment of its spymasters and professional intelligence officers.

The results of this "hands off" approach to intelligence supervision are probed here, using the methodologies of archival research, interviews with government officials, and participant observation as a scholar-in-residence on Capitol Hill. Lord Acton's venerable aphorism provides a working hypothesis: "Power corrupts and absolute power corrupts absolutely." To which he might have added, "especially secret power."

An Awakening

In 1974, a pivotal year in American politics, the nation had just withdrawn from the war in Vietnam and the ensuing Watergate scandal produced the first ever resignation of a president, Richard M. Nixon. It was a time of great turmoil and the confidence of Americans in their institutions of government began to plummet. Coming on top of these jarring experiences, the *New York Times* accused the CIA of spying at home.

In December, the newspaper's allegations produced a firestorm of public outrage (Colby 1978). Congressional offices received thousands of letters from citizens across the country. "Watergate might only be a prelude" to an even deeper assault on democracy, worried a constituent from Minnesota—a common theme in these mailings (Mondale 1975). A feeling of anger and dismay spread through the Congress. "To whom are the intelligence agencies responsible?" the fiery orator John Pastore (D, Rhode Island) demanded to know as he introduced a resolution calling for an investigation. On January 21, 1975, senators voted overwhelmingly in support of the resolution (Johnson 1986). The House launched its own inquiry as well, and, not to be left behind, so did the White House under the leadership of President Gerald R. Ford (Smist 1994). If the Orwellian charges were true, something had to be done.

The formal name of the investigative panel created by the Senate was the "Special Select Committee to Investigate Intelligence Activities," known less formally as the "Select Committee on Intelligence" or simply the Church Committee after its chairman, Frank Church (D, Idaho), with whom I served as a special assistant during the 16-month inquiry. A veteran of the Senate (elected at age 32, almost two decades earlier) and an expert on foreign affairs, Church was drawn chiefly to the accusation in the *Times* that dealt with CIA excesses overseas. Most of the others on the eleven-member panel were more concerned about the charges of domestic spying, particularly the next ranking Democrat Walter F. Mondale (Minnesota). Church asked him to lead a special subcommittee looking into this aspect of the Committee's investigation. The four additional Democrats on the Committee were Philip Hart of Michigan, Walter "Dee" Huddleston of Kentucky, Robert Morgan of North Carolina, and Gary Hart of Colorado. The Republican members included John Tower of Texas, Howard Baker of Tennessee, Barry Goldwater of Arizona, Charles Mathias of Maryland, and Richard Schweiker of Pennsylvania.

The charges of intelligence abuse came as a shock to lawmakers. This is not to say that they were unaware of problems that had cropped up in the intelligence community from time to time. Earlier reports had surfaced that the FBI kept extensive data banks on U.S. citizens, for example, and rumors were rife in the nation's Capitol about the personal files kept by Bureau Director J. Edgar Hoover on government officials, used to "encourage" their support of his programs and budgets (Ungar 1975). Yet, despite occasional revelations about intelligence improprieties (and dismay over the CIA's disastrous Bay of Pigs operation in 1961), no efforts toward reform had managed to gain the support of a majority in either chamber of Congress. Certainly none of the members of Congress serving in 1974 had ever suggested that America's secret agencies might be engaged in widespread spying against the very people they had sworn to protect (although in 1947 a few of their predecessors had expressed fears about this possibility when Congress passed the CIA's founding statute).

The paths of spies and lawmakers had seldom crossed. The FBI enjoyed the most frequent presence on Capitol Hill, having learned early the skills of legislative lobbying. Its officers came across as dedicated, hardworking public servants engaged in catching bank robbers, white-collar criminals, and Soviet spies. The drumbeat message from the Bureau was straightforward: its legitimate law enforcement and counterintelligence duties helped keep thugs, terrorists, and foreign agents at bay and deserved the approbation of the American people (Kessler 2003).

Moreover, lawmakers comforted themselves in the thought that both chambers had intelligence oversight subcommittees within the jurisdictions of the Armed Services and Appropriations Committees. These panels were supposed to monitor the nation's intelligence activities on behalf of the Congress, freeing the vast majority of lawmakers from concern—and culpability (Barrett 1998). Hence, when the allegations of abuse came to light in 1974, the public and their representatives in Washington were taken aback.

Mandate for Reform

The scope of the Church Committee investigation was staggering. The Senate Watergate Committee had taken over a year to examine just that single event; during the next eight months, Congress expected the Church Committee to probe a multitude of alleged intelligence abuses that had taken place over the past quarter century. Members of the Committee would eventually have to seek an additional eight-month extension to complete their work. As the Committee started up, it confronted one frustration after another, for the executive branch did its best to slow the pace of the inquiry. Compliance with the Committee's documents request would take time, the White House argued; the Committee would have to be patient. It seemed like the same old stonewalling that had plagued the Senate during its Watergate inquiry.

Slowly, however, the Church Committee managed to uncover revealing documents during the summer of 1975 and, at last, was prepared to hold public hearings in September. The initial focus was a master spy plan prepared for President Nixon by a young White House aide from Indiana by the name of Tom Charles Huston. Despites laws to the contrary (not to mention the first amendment to the Constitution), the so-called Huston Plan recommended using the nation's secret agencies to spy on Vietnam War dissenters. Huston and the intelligence chiefs who signed onto the Plan, including DCI Richard Helms and FBI Director Hoover, portrayed the United States as a nation under siege by student radicals. The document revealed, as Mondale observed during the hearings (U.S. Senate 1975), an "enormous, unrestricted paranoid fear about the American people."

The executive branch had concluded, wrongly, that the youthful dissenters were agents of Moscow. As a result, the United States would have to move outside the framework of the Constitution and the law; the legal system had become too confining in the struggle against the Soviet Union, itself unrestrained by a Bill of Rights. The enemy was sinister and lawless, so, the United States would have to become that way, too. Fire would have to be fought with fire. Yet, as Huston conceded in testimony before the Committee (U.S. Senate 1975), his spy plan raised the risk that the secret agencies would "move from the kid with a bomb to the kid with a picket sign, and from the kid with the picket sign to the kid with the bumper sticker of the opposing candidate. And you just keep going down the line."

The Committee's chief counsel, Frederick A.O. Schwarz, Jr. (grandson of the toy manufacturer) saw this chilling declension as the most important insight to emerge from the inquiry. "Government," he concluded (Schwarz 2000), "is going—inevitably and necessarily, I submit—to keep on going down that line, once it departs from suspected violation of the law as the only legitimate ground to investigate Americans."

The Huston Plan was just the first of many jolts to the Committee as it opened a Pandora's box of wrongdoing. One abuse after another came tumbling out as lawmakers and staff investigators shined a light into the hidden recesses of government (U.S. Senate 1976). Looking over the shoulder of the Church Committee, the American public discovered:

- The FBI had created files on over 1 million Americans and carried out over 500,000 investigations of "subversives" from 1960–74, without a single court conviction.

- NSA computers had monitored every cable sent overseas, or received from overseas, by Americans from 1947–75.

- The Internal Revenue Service had allowed tax information to be misused by intelligence agencies for political purposes.

- FBI agents had conducted a campaign to incite violence among African-Americans.

- An FBI counterintelligence program ("Cointelpro") had harassed civil rights activists and Vietnam war dissidents, in an attempt to fray and often break apart family and friendship ties.

Cointelpro

Senators on the Church Committee found Cointelpro deeply troubling. With its spying at home (Operation CHAOS), the CIA had also acted in a manner inconsistent with American laws and values; but Cointelpro stunned lawmakers, for it went beyond even domestic spying. Internal Bureau documents revealed that from 1956 to 1971 the FBI had carried out smear campaigns against individuals and groups across the country, simply because they had expressed opposition to the war in Vietnam, criticized the slow pace of the civil rights movement, or (quite the opposite) advocated racial segregation. The attacks were directed against people in all walks of life and of various political persuasions; the expansive hatred of the Bureau's leaders embraced black leaders and white supremacists alike, with critics of the war in Vietnam thrown in for good measure. As Mondale recalled, "no meeting was too small, no group too insignificant" to escape the FBI's attention (2000).

Among the thousands of Cointelpro victims was Dr. Anatol Rapoport, a gifted social scientist at the University of Michigan. He attracted the Bureau's attention because of his criticism of the war in Indochina and his "suspicious" origins (he had been born in Russia shortly before his parents immigrated to America early in the twentieth century). The FBI's agent in charge for the Ann Arbor area, responding to top secret directives from Bureau headquarters, set out to "neutralize" Professor Rapoport—a term used by the FBI to mean the harassment of an individual as a means for curbing his or her dissent. The Bureau mailed anonymous letters to senior administrators at the University, as well as to prominent citizens in Ann Arbor and throughout the state, claiming without a shred of evidence that Rapoport was, if not a communist, then at least an apologist for communism and a troublemaker. The letters were typically signed "a concerned citizen" or "a concerned taxpayers."

The Bureau also placed informants in Rapoport's classrooms to report on his "subversive" activities. He was to be embarrassed, discredited, and spied upon in whatever imaginative ways the FBI's special agent could devise. These pressures, whose underlying source Rapoport never comprehended (Rapoport 1975), eventually led him to resign from the University of Michigan and take up a faculty post at the University of Toronto. The FBI had won. Although he remained a critic of the war in Vietnam, Cointelpro had damaged Rapoport's career, drained him emotionally, strained his family and professional ties, and drove him from this country.

White supremacists also failed to fit into Hoover's Procrustean bed of conformity. The FBI sent another of its poisonous letters, this time written in Southern slang, to a wife of a Ku Klux Klan member, intimating that her husband was having an affair with another woman. The Klan, the women's liberation movement, socialists, the New Left, antiwar and civil right activists—all became enemies of the Republic whom the Bureau set out secretly to destroy (U.S. Senate 1976). In the Twin Cities, an FBI *agent provocateur* encouraged striking taxi drivers to construct a bomb for use in their battle against local teamsters; in California, a Bureau office boasted in a memorandum back to headquarters:

> Shootings, beatings, and a high degree of unrest continues to prevail in the ghetto area of southeast San Diego. Although no specific counterintelligence action can be credited with contributing to this overall situation, it is felt that a substantial amount of the unrest is directly attributable to this program.

One day in the middle of the Committee's inquiry, a staff aide came across Hoover's "Personal & Confidential" files at FBI Headquarters in Washington, D.C. (Gittenstein 2000). Most of the files had been destroyed by the Director's assistant, Johnny Moore, who starting burning the papers in reverse alphabetical order after Hoover died. Moore had gotten to "C" before being discovered and stopped by Bureau officials. In "B" was a file labeled "Black Bag Jobs." It contained documents that proved Hoover had wiretapped Dr. Martin Luther King, Jr., the famed civil rights leader, without the benefit of a court order. When the Church Committee investigator presented lawmakers with this and related papers, even the more sceptical among them began to realize: "My god, Hoover really did these things!"

Soft-spoken, bearded Philip Hart was one of the most influential members of the Committee (one of the Senate's three office buildings is now named after him). His struggle with cancer prevented him from attending most Committee meetings, but he found the strength to come to the opening hearing on the FBI. Hundreds of people filled the ornate Senate Caucus Room, site of famous investigations into the sinking of the Titanic, the Pearl Harbor attack, Joseph McCarthy's witch-hunt, and the recent Watergate scandal. With his frail body bent over the Committee bench, Hart listened intently to testimony from witnesses about Cointelpro. When it came time for him to speak, the cavernous hall fell silent as reporters and tourists strained to hear his weakened voice. He recalled that he had been sceptical when his own family of political activists had complained about how the FBI was trying to discredit opposition to the war in Vietnam. With his words cracking in emotion, Hart conceded that they had been right all along; he had been wrong to defend the Bureau. Not a soul stirred in the Caucus Room as he continued:

> As a result of my superior wisdom in high office, I assured them they are on pot—it just wasn't true. [The FBI] wouldn't do it. What you have described is a series of illegal actions intended to deny certain citizens their first amendment rights, just like my children said.

It was the most poignant moment in the Committee's inquiry.

Targeting Reverend King

Nor were lawmakers apt to forget other key FBI documents unearthed by the Committee. The most shocking to the Committee's members was an anonymous letter written by the Bureau, accompanied by a tape recording. As King travelled around the country, FBI agents had followed him and placed listening devices in his hotel room, recording compromising romantic liaisons. The Bureau then mailed the letter and tape to King in 1964, 34 days before he was to receive the Nobel Prize for Peace. In a ploy interpreted as an attempt by the FBI to push King into taking his own life, the letter read (U.S. Senate 1976):

> King, there is only one thing left for you to do. You know what it is. You have just 34 days in which to do it. (The exact number has been selected for a specific reason.) It has a definite practical significance. You are done. There is but one way out for you. You better take it before your filthy, abnormal fraudulent self is bared to the nation.

A month later, the Bureau sent a copy of the tape recordings to Mrs. King, who joined her husband in denouncing the blackmail attempt.

The goal of wrecking the civil rights movement stood at the heart of Cointelpro and the efforts to ruin Rev. King were relentless. All the elements of the Bureau's dark side came together as it directed its full surveillance powers against him. In tandem with the blackmail attempt, the Bureau initiated whispering campaigns to undermine the moral authority of the civil rights leader, and sent anonymous letters to newspapers that questioned his patriotism. The purpose, according to an FBI document, was to knock King "off his pedestal" (U.S. Senate 1976). Like Professor Rapoport, he would be "neutralized." Hoover pressured his subordinates to either rewrite their field reports on King, falsely labelling him the pawn of a Soviet agent—or else lose their jobs.

In 1964, the FBI bugged King's hotel suite at the Democratic National Convention, along with rooms occupied by delegates of the Mississippi Freedom Democratic Party, using this information to disrupt civil rights activists at the convention. Further, the Bureau blocked King from receiving honorary degrees, tried unsuccessfully to keep him from meeting with the Pope, planted an attractive female *agent provocateur* on his staff, and supplied friendly reporters with a stream of prurient stories about his private life (U.S. Senate 1976).

The Bureau continued to harass King until his final days. Committee investigators assigned to examine the case brooded darkly about the possibility of a Bureau set up to end the life of the civil rights leader. They wondered if, on a fateful trip to Memphis, King might have been "encouraged" by FBI media leaks to abandon plans to stay in a white-owned hotel and move instead to the less secure, black-owned Lorraine Hotel. The Committee never found any evidence to support this theory, but close associates of the slain civil rights continue to harbor suspicions about FBI and local law enforcement complicity in King's assassination (Pepper 2003). Andrew Young, for example, points to the quick removal of potential evidence from the murder scene, even the cutting down of bushes across the street from the Lorraine near the area where the fatal shots were fired (Young 2000). After King's death, when lawmakers began to consider whether his birthday should be made a national holiday, the FBI developed plans to brief selected members of Congress on how to stop the proposal.

During hearings into the King case, Senator Mondale asked the Committee's chief counsel, Schwarz: "Was there any evidence at any time that [the FBI] was suspicious that [Dr. King] was about to or had committed a crime?" The answer was "no." Mondale asked further: "Was he ever charged with fomenting violence? Did he ever participate in violence?" Again the answer was "no." Mondale

considered King the nation's greatest civil rights hero, an apostle of non-violence at a time in American history when there were tremendous pressures to use violence. King was a man of the cloth, acting from a deep sense of conviction—only to be treated by the FBI as a common criminal. "There is nothing in this case that distinguishes that particular action from what the KGB does with dissenters in that country [the U.S.S.R.]," he said in disgust during a Committee hearing (U.S. Senate 1976). He concluded: "I think it is a road map to the destruction of American democracy."

Schwarz remembers being "shocked" by the attacks on King:

> Here was a peaceful civil rights leader whom I admired as much as anybody in our history, and the FBI was trying to get him to commit suicide. The bureau called the Southern Christian Leadership Conference a black hate organization. The words were all upside down. (2000)

When the Attorney General in the Ford Administration, Edward H. Levi, former dean of the law school at the University of Chicago, came before the Church Committee, Mondale—who had evolved into the Committee's leading interrogator on matters of domestic intelligence—asked him what he intended to do about cleaning up the FBI mess. The AG's answers were far from what Committee members, most of whom had gone to law school and two of whom (Mondale and Morgan) had served as state attorneys general, expected to hear from the nation's chief law enforcement officer and a noted constitutional scholar. Levi sought unprecedented authority for the Bureau to act against a group or individual, before a crime was committed—the same slippery slope that had led to Cointelpro in the first place. He seemed to have forgotten that the job of the FBI was to focus on actual or suspected violations of the law, not just the expression of ideas. Levi had assumed the role of the Bureau's protector, while Mondale had taken on the role of the Committee's leading defender of civil liberties. A collision was inevitable.

Mondale suggested to the AG that his guidelines were "vaguely defined" and that, if they were not strengthened and codified into law, they "would be swept away as quickly as a sand castle is overrun by a hurricane" (U.S. Senate 1976). The temperature in the Senate Caucus Room rose as the two men confronted each other across the green-baize hearing table. When Levi resorted to an evasive answer, Mondale stared at him and said, "Well, I think that kind of arrogance is why we have trouble between the executive and the legislative branch." Levi replied, "I apologize to Senator Mondale if I appeared arrogant. I thought that someone else was appearing arrogant, but I apologize."

Mondale had put the AG on notice: the Committee was not going to be a push over; it would strenuously defend the liberties of American citizens. Despite this public confrontation, Mondale and Levi soon met privately and placed behind them any bad feelings, agreeing to work together in the crafting of FBI guidelines that would be acceptable both to the Committee and to the Justice Department. It was an important turning point in the investigation that led to constructive negotiations between the branches over proper guidelines for Bureau activities.

A Widening Gyre of Abuse

As the investigation unfolded, the Church Committee discovered just how far the violations of public trust had extended to the CIA and military intelligence units as well. For instance:

- The CIA had opened the mail to and from selected American citizens, which generated 1.5 million names stored in the Agency's computer bank (Operation CHAOS). No one was immune, not Leonard Bernstein, not John Steinbeck, not Arthur Burns; even Richard Nixon had made the CIA's "watch list."

- Army intelligence units had conducted investigations against 100,000 U.S. citizens during the Vietnam war era.

- The CIA had engaged in drug experiments against unsuspecting subjects, two of whom had died from side effects.

- The CIA had manipulated elections even in democratic regimes like Chile.

- The CIA had infiltrated religious, media, and academic organizations inside the United States.

- The CIA had plotted failed assassination attempts against Fidel Castro of Cuba and Patrice Lumumba, among other foreign leaders.

The CIA's assassination plots and drug experiments were as unacceptable to the Church Committee as the FBI's Cointelpro operations had been. The CIA had even resorted to the recruitment of mafia mobsters to assist in the plots against Castro.

In Joseph Conrad's *Heart of Darkness*, the protagonist Marlow discovers in the jungles of central Africa the savagery that had befallen upon his once civilized companion, Mr. Kurtz. Isolated in a primitive setting, Kurtz had succumbed to a steady moral deterioration. In the last hours of his life, he peered into his own soul and, confronting the decay, cried out in despair: "The horror! The horror!" The allegory suited the secret agencies. Removed from the rest of democratic society, they had descended into a primordial underworld, using methods deemed necessary to combat foreign enemies, then turning these dark arts against citizens at home whose only crime had been to express beliefs that the White House or the intelligence chiefs found objectionable. In this crusade, the secret agencies had adopted some of the tactics of the repressive regimes they opposed. To argue that the United States had to abandon liberty in the name of security was to say that the nation had to become more like its enemies in order to protect itself from them—a pernicious doctrine that the Committee rejected out of hand.

How could the intelligence community have strayed so far from its rightful duties and into this heart of darkness? The answer stemmed in part from the paranoia engendered by the Cold War, even though—as acknowledged by William Sullivan (1975), the top FBI agent in charge of Cointelpro—there were not enough communists in the United States to carry the smallest precinct in New Hampshire, let alone take over the country. Sullivan told the Committee that the secret agencies had been caught up in an anti-communist tide that swept aside safeguards against the misuse of power (just as, today, a war against global terrorism in the wake of the 9/11 attacks against the United States holds the danger of eroding civil liberties at home, especially for law-abiding Arab-Americans). As Sullivan recalled, during the FBI's operations against Rev. King,

> No holds were barred. We have used [similar] techniques against Soviet agents. [The same methods were] brought home against any organization against which we were targeted. We did not differentiate. This is a rough, tough business. (U.S. Senate 1976)

He added that never once had he heard a discussion about the legality or constitutionality of any aspect of the FBI's internal security program. His explanation: "We were just naturally pragmatic."

During the Committee's public hearings on the NSA and its interception of cables sent to and from U.S. citizens (Operation SHAMROCK), a revealing exchange took place between Senator Mondale and the NSA's deputy director, Benson Buffham (U.S. Senate 1975):

Mondale: Were you concerned about its legality?

Buffham: Legality?

Mondale: Whether it was legal.

Buffham: In what sense? Whether that would have been a legal thing to do?

Mondale: Yes.

Buffham: That particular aspect didn't enter into the discussion.

Mondale: I was asking you if you were concerned about whether that would be legal and proper.

Buffham: We didn't consider it at the time, no.

It was a response echoed by other agency representatives during the hearings. One of the Committee members asked Clark Clifford, who had helped to draft the charter for the CIA in 1947 and served as secretary of defense during the Johnson Administration, about constitutional protections against abuses. He replied, "Well, that was a different time when we could afford that."

Criticism of the intelligence agencies was widely considered unpatriotic. They had to be given broad discretionary powers if they were to be successful in subduing America's adversaries at home and abroad. As a consequence, the secret agencies took on the features of a political police, growing increasingly autonomous, insulated, and aggressive. As William W. Keller has written (1989, 154), the intelligence community became "a state within the state, which would not be bound by the constraints of the constitutional order."

Responsibility for the abuses did not fall on the intelligence community alone. Presidents of both parties used the secret agencies to spy on political adversaries. Lawmakers were derelict, as well, for permitting the growth of an inadequately supervised security state. Intelligence scholar Harry Howe Ransom has drawn the proper conclusion (1984, 21): the Congress had become "a sleeping watchdog." James R. Schlesinger, DCI in 1973, remembers his initial briefing to the small Senate oversight subcommittee of that day (1993). As he began his briefing, John Stennis (D, Mississippi) interrupted the DCI: "No, no my boy, don't tell me. Just go ahead and do it, but I don't want to know."

William Sullivan of the FBI testified about another influence that contributed to the lawlessness that gripped the intelligence agencies (U.S. Senate 1976). "During World War Two, we had grown up topsy-turvy," he said, "when legal matters were secondary to achieving victory against the Nazis. This mentality carried over easily into the new war against the communists." During the course of its inquiry, the Committee came across a telling top secret document that had been prepared for President Dwight D. Eisenhower (U.S. Senate 1976, 9). A key passage advised that in the war against communism:

. . . hitherto acceptable norms of human conduct do not apply. If the U.S. is to survive, long-standing American concepts of 'fair play' must be reconsidered . . . we must learn to subvert, sabotage, and destroy our enemies by more clear, more sophisticated and more effective methods than those used against us.

The underlying philosophy reminded Schwarz (2000), the Committee counsel, of Macbeth's words: inevitably, the invention returns home "to plague the inventor."

The FBI's skillful lobbying of lawmakers further warded off serious oversight. So did its clever promotion of a favorable public relations image, as with the television show *The FBI Story*, which starred the dashing actor Efrem Zimbalist, Jr. The FBI censored the program's scripts and CBS beamed the program into millions of living rooms each week during the 1960s. Self-promotion helped the Bureau gain remarkable popularity and independence, free from congressional probes and detailed laws to guide its activities (Ungar 1975).

Hannah Arendt's ever lingering "banality of evil" (1973) entered the picture, too. When asked by the Committee how he could have brought himself to participate in the Cointelpro operations, William Sullivan replied (U.S. Senate 1976):

I was so inured and accustomed to any damn thing I was told to do, I just carried it out and kept my resentment to myself. I was married and trying to buy a house with a big mortgage and raise a family.

The Church Committee came to the conclusion that the overwhelming majority of the men and women in the nation's intelligence agencies had consistently carried out their assignments with integrity and devotion to the law and constitutional principles. Some had given their lives in the defense of liberty. America owed its freedom in part to their dedication in the struggle against those who wish to harm the United States. Yet some intelligence officers had clearly overstepped the boundaries of law and propriety, and the Committee felt impelled to adopt measures that would help protect citizens against future abuses.

Steps Toward Reform

The initial congressional response to the CIA's domestic spying was to pass the Hughes-Ryan Act on December 31, 1974 (22 U.S.C. 2422). This statute, which marks the beginning of the new era of intelligence accountability, required the president to review and authorize (in a "finding") every important CIA covert action, then report to Congress on those he had approved. Prior to the Hughes-Ryan law, pinning down responsibility for covert action was, observed Mondale during the Church Committee inquiry, "like nailing jello to a wall." With this statute in place, there would be no more plausible denial; no more vanishing paper trails. It was the first attempt since the creation of the CIA to place meaningful limits on its activities.

The Congress then began its formal investigations, with probes by the Church Committee in the Senate and the Pike Committee in the House (led by Otis Pike, D, New York, and concentrating on the quality of intelligence reporting, as opposed to the Church Committee focus on charges of abuse). Along with the inquiry conducted by the White House (the Rockefeller Commission, led by Vice President Nelson Rockefeller), the congressional committees did much to educate the American people on the importance of more meaningful intelligence supervision.

In May 1976, the Church Committee presented 96 proposals for reform of domestic intelligence alone, many of which were adopted by the Congress. The most significant, affecting both domestic and foreign intelligence, was the creation of a permanent Senate Select Committee on Intelligence (SSCI). As Mondale noted at the time (1976), "If there is one lesson that our Committee felt above all must be learned from our study of the abuses which have been reported, it has been the crucial necessity of establishing a system of congressional oversight." The Senate had put into place a potentially effective standing committee, equipped with a large and experienced professional staff, devoted to monitoring the secret agencies day-by-day and reviewing their programs and budgets with a fine-tooth comb.

The creation of an intelligence oversight committee in the Senate was not an easy task, opposed as it was by the White House, the intelligence agencies, and even a few members of the Church Committee on the Republican side (Tower, Goldwater, and Baker). In floor debate on the proposal, Church and Mondale stressed the necessity of providing the new committee with annual budget authorization, realizing that without the power of the purse as leverage over the intelligence community no form of accountability would succeed. Opponents introduced a number of weakening amendments; but, one-by-one, they were defeated and on May 19, 1976, by a vote of 72-to-18, the Senate created the new intelligence oversight committee. It was a remarkable achievement. Institutional inertia normally carries the day in the Congress, yet the Church Committee had been able to bring about a major power shift. Responsibility for supervision of the intelligence agencies would be largely removed from the jurisdiction of the Armed Services Committee and given the closer attention it warranted.

Not to be left behind, President Ford set up an Intelligence Oversight Board (IOB) in the White House in 1976, and (also by executive order in the same year) he prohibited further assassination plots against foreign leaders. In 1977, the House established an intelligence oversight committee of its own, patterned after the Senate model and designated the House Permanent Select Committee on Intelligence (HPSCI).

Many of the reforms advanced by the Church Committee and eventually adopted were of a technical nature, dealing with FBI investigative methods and how they should be employed without violating the civil liberties of American citizens. Others were broader, including the recommendation that the CIA clarify and sharply limit its ties to U.S. journalists. The Committee proposed a single eight-year term limit on the directorship of the FBI; no more imperial czars like Hoover, who served an incredible forty-eight years in that capacity. The Congress eventually settled on a ten-year term. The Committee recommended as well that the Office of Professional Responsibility (OPR), established in reaction to the Watergate scandal, be given legal status, thereby providing it firmer footing to probe allegations of abuse inside the intelligence agencies. During the Carter Administration, the President bestowed upon Vice President Walter Mondale extensive responsibilities over intelligence issues, especially with respect to the FBI and domestic intelligence matters. In turn, Mondale and the new AG, Griffin Bell of Georgia, relied upon OPR to oversee intelligence activities (Mondale 2000; Bell 1982). The attorneys in OPR were expected to investigate fully any allegations of intelligence misconduct, reporting their findings and conclusions to the Vice President and the AG.

Since the Carter years OPR has been less actively involved in intelligence oversight, as its responsibilities broadened to investigate charges of misconduct across the policy board. Its attorneys are expected as well as to represent the government in litigation and to provide legal advice to the AG, which places OPR in a "precarious position in the Justice Department because it threatens the prerogatives of the prosecuting divisions. . . ." (Elliff 1979). Contributing to OPR's demise as a vigorous intelligence overseer has been the fact that no president and or vice president since the Carter years have been as focused on questions of intelligence accountability as were Jimmy Carter and Walter Mondale. The creation of an inspector general at the Department of Justice has further diminished the influence of OPR. Nevertheless, the Office has played a useful mediating role at times between the

FBI and the prosecuting divisions in the Justice Department (Elliff 1979, 169); and it has conducted some important investigations into charges of wrongdoing in the Department, including an inquiry into alleged financial improprieties by FBI Director William Sessions during the Reagan Administration (Kessler 2002, 277–283).

The Church Committee also proposed that all non-consensual electronic surveillance, mail-opening, and unauthorized entities be conducted only with the authority of a judicial warrant, instead of allowing the White House and the intelligence agencies to use such invasive tools at their own discretion. Further, the Committee stressed that the threshold for FBI investigations should be sufficiently high to ensure that only groups with a record of violence would be targeted for intelligence gathering; and the Committee took a strong stand, in addition, against the conduct of intelligence operations inside the United States by the CIA or any other foreign-oriented component of the intelligence community. In 1978, as urged by the Church Committee, Congress passed the Foreign Intelligence Surveillance Act (FISA; 50 U.S.C. 1801–1811), which provided for a special FISA court to review wiretap requests. The third branch of government, too, was now firmly in the business of intelligence oversight.

The Legacy of the Church Committee

Soon after the investigation, historian Henry Steele Commager observed (1976, 32) that the indifference of the intelligence agencies to constitutional restraint was "perhaps the most threatening of all the evidence that [emerged] from the findings of the Church Committee." The inquiry was able to focus citizen awareness on this threat, creating a foundation of public support indispensable for the reform measures subsequently adopted by Congress and the executive branch. Legislators laid out the facts for the American people—a difficult and important duty in itself—about the extent of lawlessness that had overtaken the secret agencies. The Committee was unable to plumb to the depths of every intelligence abuse; it did not have time enough. Rather it laid out key findings that pointed to a pattern of wrongdoing, without trying to probe every specific allegation. This public airing proved thorough enough to bring about a sea change in attitudes throughout the intelligence community.

The Committee's central conclusion was clear and important: the law works. In every case where the secret agencies had violated the law, the Committee demonstrated how U.S. security objectives could have been achieved through legal means. As the Committee emphasized, security and liberty were compatible values in a democracy; it was possible to defend the nation without becoming a police state. Thoughtful intelligence officers began to understand how the unlawful activities of their agencies had actually interfered with the nation's legitimate intelligence and counterintelligence duties.

The Committee made it clear as well that the principle of accountability was valid even with respect to the hidden side of government—indeed, there most especially. The Senate and House intelligence oversight committees would now stand guard as watchmen to America's civil liberties, replacing the small and ineffectual subcommittees that the nation had relied upon before, only to see fail. Today as the nation's spymasters plan their secret operations, they must take into account the likely reactions of two full committees of elected representatives. This new relationship has strengthened the intelligence community by better defining its limits and responsibilities, and by tying the secret agencies closer to the values and beliefs of the American people and their surrogates in Congress. The resulting higher level of professionalism among the intelligence agencies has helped to restore public confidence and respect in their activities, a primary objective of the Church Committee.

The Committee conveyed to the American people that the Senate would stand up for their constitutional rights. " 'We can't slide back into the days of J. Edgar Hoover'—that was the message delivered by the Committee through its promulgation of guidelines and recommendations," recalls John Elliff, the Committee's top staff aide for the FBI side of the inquiry (2000). William E. Colby, DCI during the investigation, wrote afterward that the Church Committee had shed light on the boundaries "within which [the intelligence community] should, and should not, operate" (1976, 11). The current DCI, George Tenet, himself a former SSCI staff director, has similarly stated that the new oversight procedures represent ". . . our most vital and direct link to the American people—a source of strength that separates us from all other countries of the world" (1997).

Discussion and Conclusion

The importance of establishing intelligence oversight committee in the Senate and the House cannot be overemphasized. The protection of freedom requires daily attention; someone has to be continuously on guard. That "someone" in the world of intelligence now includes two permanent, well-staffed committees that concentrate exclusively on intelligence activities, not (as earlier) small, feckless subcommittees that occasionally reviewed the nation's secret operations as an adjunct to their principal duties. Robert M. Gates, a career intelligence officer and DCI under the first President Bush, has come to this conclusion about the new era of intelligence oversight (1997, 559):

> . . . some awfully crazy schemes might well have been approved had everyone present not known and expected hard questions, debate, and criticism from the Hill. And when, on a few occasions, Congress was kept in the dark, and such schemes did proceed, it was nearly always to the lasting regret of the presidents involved.

Here was the most vital result of the Church Committee's work: the establishment of safeguards to ensure that lawmakers are able to provide a check against abuses by the secret, not just the more open, agencies of government. This is not to say that the Church Committee created a fool-proof system of intelligence accountability. The Iran-*contra* affair of 1986–87 served as a reminder that even robust legislative safeguards are no guarantee against the misuse of power by determined conspirators in the executive branch (Cohen and Mitchell 1988). That scandal led to a further tightening of oversight procedures, however, including the creation of a CIA Office of Inspector General directly answerable to Congress (Kaiser 1994; Currie 1998).

The best assurance against future abuse lies, as the ancient philosophers realized, in the selection of individuals of the highest integrity for positions of power. Then, lawmakers and their staff on the oversight committees must maintain close watch over intelligence budgets and programs, posing detailed questions in hearings and probing fearlessly into any activities that seem untoward. Outside the executive branch, only Congress has the authority to insist on access to intelligence documents and testimony; if elected representatives lapse into complacency, the secret agencies will again drift toward autonomy and the arrogance that isolation breeds.

Even now there are signs that some have failed to learn this lesson of American democracy. A senior official in the Association of Retired Intelligence Officers opined in the wake of Iran-*contra* that those who had lied to legislators during that affair were right to have done so, since sensitive intelligence operations are none of Congress's business (cited in Turner 1991). In 1994, Senate overseers learned that the National Reconnaissance Office (NRO, a component of the intelligence community that builds and manages spy satellites) had run up $159 million in cost overruns for the construction of its new headquarters in Virginia, without properly informing lawmakers (*New York Times* 1994); and, in 1995, the CIA failed to report, as required by law, on its questionable ties to a suspected murderer in the Guatemalan military (*New York Times* 1996). Just in

the past two years, DCI Tenet resisted a probe by lawmakers on a special Senate-House Joint Committee of Intelligence into the failure of the intelligence community to warn the nation of the 9/11 attacks (see, e.g., Lewis 2002). The second Bush White House has stonewalled efforts by a commission to further investigate this subject and related weaknesses in U.S. security (Johnson 2003).

This backsliding emphasizes the need for renewed attention to the question of intelligence accountability. Still, these episodes notwithstanding, the safeguards set up by the Church Committee and the Ford Administration in 1976 have endured and, on most occasions, they have brought greater sobriety to the conduct of intelligence operations at home and abroad. Someone beyond the walls of the secret agencies is now steadily watching their activities; would be violators of the public trust know they might be caught—a vital check on abuse.

This nation must have strong and effective intelligence agencies; America's security depends on it. Yet that power has to remain within the framework of the Constitution, not relegated to some dark outside realm. This is all the more true in an age where the methods of spying are far more sophisticated than in the era of J. Edgar Hoover. Breaches of faith will occur again; such is the nature of the human condition. It is imperative, however, that responsible officials remain ever vigilant in their protection of lawful political activities, ensuring that citizens do not become the target of secret intimidation by the intelligence community. The constitutional right to free expression must remain the lynchpin of American democracy.

With the safeguards established in 1976, citizens of the United States are far less likely to suffer abuse at the hands of the secret agencies than during the earlier years of benign neglect. The effectiveness of the safeguards will continue to depend on the resolve of lawmakers to carry out their duties of accountability with fresh resolve, with a willingness to engage in day-to-day "police patrolling," and with a determination to preserve liberty at home even in the face of global terrorism.

Questions for Further Discussion

1. What triggered the Church Committee investigation in 1975?

2. What were the strengths and weaknesses of the Church Committee inquiry?

3. How has intelligence in the United States changed as a result of the Church Committee's probe?

4. What do you make of the argument that the Church Committee weakened American intelligence and made the nation vulnerable to the intelligence mistakes that were made in 2001 (9/11) and 2003 (Iraq)?

References

Aberbach, Joel D. 1990. *Keeping a Watchful Eye: The Politics of Congressional Oversight.* Washington, D.C.: The Brookings Institution.

Arendt, Hannah. 1973. *The Origins of Totalitarianism.* New York: Harcourt.

Barrett, David M. 1998. Glimpses of a Hidden History: Sen. Richard Russell, Congress and Early Oversight of the CIA. *International Journal of Intelligence and Counterintelligence* 11 (3): 271–99.

Bell, Griffin B., with Ronald J. Astrow. 1982. *Taking Care of the Law.* New York: Morrow.

Bibby, John F. 1968. Congress' Neglected Function. In *The Republican Papers,* edited by Melvin R. Laird, 477–488. New York: Anchor.

Calvert, Randall, Mathew D. McCubbins, and Barry R. Weingast. 1989. A Theory of Political Control and Agency Discretion. *American Journal of Political Science* 33 (3): 588–611.

Cohen, William S., and George J. Mitchell. 1988. *Men of Zeal: A Candid Inside Story of the Iran-Contra Hearings.* New York: Viking.

Colby, William E. 1976. After Investigating U.S. Intelligence. *New York Times,* February 26.

——, with Peter Forbath. 1978. *Honorable Men.* New York: Simon and Schuster.

Commager, Henry Steele. 1976. *Intelligence: The Constitution Betrayed.* New York Review of Books, September 30.

Currie, James. 1998. Iran-Contra and Congressional Oversight of the CIA. *International Journal of Intelligence and Counterintelligence* 11 (2): 185–210.

Dodd, Lawrence, and Richard Schott. 1979. *Congress and the Administrative State.* New York: Wiley.

Elliff, John T. 1979. *The Reform of FBI Intelligence Operations.* Princeton: Princeton University Press.

——. 2000. Author's telephone interview: April 14.

Gates, Robert M. 1997. *From the Shadows.* New York: Simon and Schuster.

Gittenstein, Mark. 2000. Author's telephone interview: April 14.

Holt, Pat M. 1995. *Secret Intelligence and Public Policy.* Washington, D.C.: CQ Press.

Johnson, Loch K. 1986. *A Season of Inquiry.* Lexington: University Press of Kentucky.

——. 1994. Playing Ball with the CIA: Congress Supervises Strategic Intelligence. In *Congress, the Executive, and the Making of American Foreign Policy,* edited by Paul E. Peterson, 49–73. Norman: University of Oklahoma Press.

——. 2000. *Bombs, Bugs, Drugs, and Thugs: Intelligence and America's Quest for Security.* New York: New York University Press.

——. 2003. Author's interviews with members and staff of the Kean Commission, Washington, D.C.: January–March.

Kaiser, Frederick M. 1994. Impact and Implications of the Iran-contra Affair on Congressional Oversight of Covert Action. *International Journal of Intelligence and Counterintelligence* 7 (2): 205–234.

Keller, William W. 1989. *Liberals and J. Edgar Hoover: Rise and Fall of a Domestic Intelligence State.* Princeton: Princeton University Press.

Kessler, Ronald. 2003. *The Bureau: The Secret History of the FBI.* New York: St. Martin's.

Knott, Stephen F. 1996. *Secret and Sanctioned: Covert Operations and the American Presidency.* New York: Oxford University Press.

Lewis, Neil. 2002. Senator Insists C.I.A. Is Harboring Iraq Reports. *New York Times,* October 4.

Lowenthal, Mark. 1992. *U.S. Intelligence: Evolution and Anatomy,* 2nd edition. Washington, D.C.: Center for Strategic and International Studies.

Mayhew, David. 1986. *The Electoral Connection.* New Haven: Yale University Press.

McCubbins, Mathew D., and Thomas Schwartz. 1984. Congressional Oversight Overlooked: Police Patrols and Fire Alarms. *American Journal of Political Science* 28 (1): 165–179.

——, Roger G. Noll, and Barry R. Weingast. 1989. Structure and Process, Politics and Policy: Administrative Arrangements and the Political Control of Agencies. *Virginia Law Review* 75 (3): 431–482.

Mondale, Walter F. 1975. Personal archives. (Church Committee), Minneapolis.

——. 1976. Personal archives (Church Committee), Minneapolis.

——. 2000. Author's interview, Minneapolis: February 17.

New York Times. 1994. Unsigned editorial, May 19.

——. 1996. Unsigned editorial, August 18.

Ogul, Morris S. 1976. *Congress Oversees the Bureaucracy: Studies in Legislative Supervision.* Pittsburgh: University of Pittsburgh Press.

Pepper, William F. 2003. *An Act of State.* Verso, London.

Priest, Dana. 2003. Remarks, Panel on Congress, Intelligence and Secrecy During War, Woodrow Wilson Center, May 9, Washington, D.C.

Ransom, Harry Howe. 1970. *The Intelligence Establishment.* Cambridge: Harvard University Press.

——. 1975. Secret Intelligence Agencies and Congress. *Society* 123(2): 33–38.

——. 1977. Congress and the Intelligence Agencies. In *Congress Against the President,* edited by Harvey C. Mansfield, 153–166. New York: Praeger.

——. 1984. CIA Accountability: Congress As Temperamental Watchdog. Paper, American Political Science Association Annual Convention, September 1, Washington, D.C.

Rapoport, Anatole. 1975. Author's interview, Toronto: September 21.

Richelson, Jeffrey T. 1999. *The U.S. Intelligence Community,* 4th edition. Boulder: Westview Press.

Scher, Seymour. 1963. Conditions for Legislative Control. *Journal of Politics* 25 (3): 526–551.

Schlesinger, James R. 1994. Author's interview, Washington, D.C.: June 16.

Schwarz, Frederick A. O., Jr. 2000. Author's interview, New York City: April 27.

Smist, Frank, Jr. 1994. *Congress Oversees the United States Intelligence Community,* 2nd ed. Knoxville: University of Tennessee Press.

Spence, David. 1997. Agency Policy Making and Political Control: Modeling Away the Delegation Problem. *Journal of Public Administration Research and Theory* 7 (2): 199–219.

Sullivan, William. 1975. Author's interview, Boston: September 21.

Tenet, George. 1997. Remarks, Panel on Does America Need the CIA? Gerald R. Ford Library, November 19, Ann Arbor, Michigan.

Turner, Stansfield. 1991. Purge the C.I.A. of K.G.B. Types. *New York Times*, October 2.

Ungar, Sanford. 1975. *FBI*. Boston: Atlantic Monthly Press.

U.S. Congress. 1987. Report on the Iran-*Contra* Affair. *Senate Select Committee on Secret Military Assistance to Iran and the Nicaragua Opposition and House Select Committee to Investigate Covert Arms Transactions with Iran*. S. Rept. 100-216 and H. Rept. 100-433, November.

U.S. Senate. 1975. Hearings. *Select Committee to Study Governmental Operations with Respect to Intelligence Activities* (Church Committee), 94th Cong., 2d. Sess., September–December.

——. 1976. Final Report. *Select Committee to Study Governmental Operations with Respect to Intelligence Activities* (Church Committee). S. Rept. 94–755, 95th Cong., 1st. Sess., May.

Walden, Jerrold L. 1970. The C.I.A.: A Study in the Arrogation of Administrative Power. *George Washington Law Review* 39 (3): 66–101.

Young, Andrew. 2000. Author's interview, Minneapolis: June 6. ✦

Reprinted with permission from Loch K. Johnson, "Congressional Supervision of America's Secret Agencies: The Experience and Legacy of the Church Committee," *Public Administration Review* 64 (January/February 2004): 3–14.

31
Warrantless Wiretaps

Yale University School of Law Symposium (Alan Dershowitz, Senator Conrad Burns, John J. Donohue, David B. Rivkin, Jr., Dakota Rudesill, Stephen A. Vaden, and Loch K. Johnson)

In 2005, the *New York Times* revealed the existence of a warrantless wiretapping program adopted by the second Bush Administration in the struggle against global terrorism. Opponents of the program argued that it violated the Foreign Intelligence Surveillance Act (FISA) of 1978, which set in place a formal legal requirement for all wiretaps and other surveillance used by the federal government for intelligence-gathering purposes. Supporters countered with the argument that in times of emergency, as currently faced by the United States, bypassing FISA had become necessary for the nation's security. Yale University's School of Law assembled some experts to discuss the pros and cons of these arguments, and their conclusions are presented in this selection.

A Stick With Two Ends
Alan Dershowitz

Civil libertarians shouldn't be afraid of technology. First, there is no way to stop it. Second, there is almost always a way of using technology to enhance civil liberties. Third, civil liberties always require the striking of an appropriate balance between freedom and security. Technology is, to paraphrase Dostoyevsky, a stick with two ends.

The recent disclosure of a massive data "mining" program being conducted by the NSA raises the most profound concerns about how to strike the appropriate balance. Surely it does not require that we ignore or discard a significant breakthrough in our ability to catch the bad guys before they blow us up. We should figure out a way of cabining this useful technology within the rule of law. This is a daunting task, because the technology does not fit neatly into our existing constitutional structure.

The Fourth Amendment reads as follows:

> The right of the people to be secure in their persons, houses, papers, and effects, against unreasonable searches and seizures, shall not be violated, and no Warrants shall issue, but upon probable cause, supported by Oath or affirmation, and particularly describing the place to be searched, and the persons or things to be seized.

Plainly, its language and history presuppose retail intrusions on individuals based on particularized probable cause or reasonableness. It was written for the technology of a time in which eavesdropping, mail openings and general searches were the feared intrusions. When electronic wiretapping was developed, the Supreme Court held that wiretaps must be conducted pursuant to search warrants and that the warrants must be based on probable cause. Moreover, the intrusion must be subjected to what is called a "minimization" requirement, under which only those portions of a conversation which are relevant to criminal conduct can appropriately be monitored. In 1978 Congress enacted the Foreign Intelligence Surveillance Act (FISA) to regulate the government's collection of "foreign intelligence" information in furtherance of U.S. counterintelligence. FISA has been broadened since 1978, but it still requires a showing—in advance if possible and after-the-fact if necessary—of particularized cause against individuals. It also requires careful recordkeeping that permits subsequent oversight and accountability. Although the FISA court has only rarely denied requests for national security wiretaps, the very existence of this court and the requirement of sworn justification serves as a check on the improper use of the powerful and intrusive technologies that are permitted in national security cases.

But what the National Security Agency is now doing is a far cry from retail intrusions based on individualized probable cause. According to the *New York Times*, the Bush Administration decided to bypass the FISA warrant process in order to "monitor the international telephone calls and international e-mail messages of hundreds, perhaps thousands, of people inside the United States without warrants over the past three years." The so-called "special collection program" is reported to have expanded in scope so quickly that, at any given time, around 500 Americans' phone and e-mail communications are being recorded. Surveillance of communications between "foreign powers" and "U.S. persons" used to be conducted by the FBI and based on individualized suspicion. The Administration now appears to be focused on the NSA-directed "data mining" of massive amounts of computer-recorded conversations and correspondences. This change is part of a general shift in priorities from after-the-crime deterrence to before-the-terrorism preemption.

The major problems with the NSA program are that we don't know what we don't know and that there is no accountability or external check on what is being done. We were made aware of the program by a *New York Times* report that acknowledged that it was withholding some information. There is almost certainly some additional information that the *Times* did not succeed in learning. Moreover, there may be other technologies and actions that are currently in use of which we're simply unaware.

Although we are assured by the administration that the NSA program is targeting only terrorists and those who talk to or work with them, we have no way of knowing that this is always the case. Remember that Richard Nixon tried to use the excuse of national security to spy on his political opponents. Nor was Nixon alone. Even the Kennedy administration authorized the bugging of Martin Luther King's hotel rooms. And the current administration has taken the position that classified national security information can be leaked in order to discredit a political opponent.

At the very least, the FISA law should be amended to require sworn justifications for the monitoring of any conversation or communication involving a citizen or permanent resident. It should also require precise recordkeeping, Congressional oversight and periodic public disclosure of the kind of general information that does not endanger national security but that does provide a basis for cost-benefit analysis. Finally, it should define the criteria for different levels of intrusion.

Some have wondered why I have been less of an absolutist about certain rights than other civil libertarians following the attacks of 9/11. There are several reasons. First, I eschew all absolutism, even with regard to civil liberties and human rights. As I have written elsewhere, I do not believe rights come from God, nature or any other external source. Rights are not "out there" waiting to be discovered. They are human inventions that grow out of human experiences. In a word, rights come from wrongs—from a recognition of past human mistakes or evils and a determination not to repeat them. Second, among the greatest threats to civil liberties is terrorism itself. Were the United States to become victim to another large scale, mass casualty terrorist attack—especially one involving biological, chemical or nuclear weapons—the first casualty would likely

be civil liberties. It is therefore in the interest of civil libertarians to encourage lawful, smart, proportional and moral technologies and actions that hold promise of reducing the likelihood of terrorist attacks, so long as these technologies and steps are consistent with essential liberties.

I agree with Benjamin Franklin's oft quoted, but largely misunderstood, dictum: "They that can give up essential liberty to obtain a little temporary safety deserve neither liberty nor safety." The key words, often deemphasized by those who invoke Franklin, are "essential liberty" and "a little temporary safety." Some liberties are more essential than others. Freedom of expression and dissent, for example, may be more essential to democracy than freedom to bear arms or to refuse to disclose one's identity when entering a public building. All liberty is a matter of degree, as is all safety. The essence of a democracy is to strike the appropriate balance, rather than to set up a clash of absolutes. This balance requires an assessment of the kind and degree of intrusions on liberty as well as assessment of the kind, degree, likelihood, and proximity of the danger sought to be prevented. It also requires a consideration of alternative means of reducing the feared danger. The feel of freedom should never be lost. Nor should the right to dissent ever be diminished.

Applying these criteria to the NSA program leads me to express the cautious conclusion that we should continue to employ and develop sophisticated technologies to secure information that could help us preempt terrorist attacks, but that we must take steps to construct a jurisprudence, grounded in the values of the Fourth Amendment, that strikes the appropriate balance between liberty and security. We have barely begun this daunting task.

Terrorism Surveillance Critical (With Oversight)
Senator Conrad Burns

All Americans should be outraged that the existence of the Terrorism Surveillance program was irresponsibly leaked to the *New York Times*. There's a reason our efforts in the Global War on Terror are classified—we cannot afford to advertise to terrorists our sources and methods. I believe the leak of this program is a direct threat to our national security and must be thoroughly investigated and prosecuted to the fullest extent.

First, this leak of national security information has made us vulnerable as a nation. Gathered intelligence indicates that Osama bin Laden stopped using satellite phones once he learned that we were listening to his communications. CIA Director Porter Goss, in a recent *Washington Post* editorial, called the leak "one of the most egregious examples of an unauthorized criminal disclosure of classified national defense information in recent years." As Goss said, "the bin Laden phone went silent" and now that the NSA Terrorist Surveillance program has been leaked, this tool is measurably less useful than before its exposure.

Second, I believe, from what I know right now, this program is absolutely critical to our national security, entirely reasonable, and must not be interrupted. In any war, collecting intelligence regarding your enemy's operations is necessary and, as such, is consistent with our efforts in both World Wars. I've been in many intelligence and defense briefings in my 18 years in the Senate, and the threat we face today is unlike any other in the history of the world. We must use all of the available technological advances that we possess in our arsenal.

Third, I agree with the President that if anyone inside America is communicating with an al Qaeda agent or suspected foreign terrorist, we have a responsibility to use that information to protect Americans. This program is not neighbors spying on neighbors. One party to the call must be outside the U.S. and one party must be a suspected terrorist. No exceptions.

I believe these are points all Americans and the Congress can agree on.

The Foreign Intelligence Surveillance Act (FISA) was not intended for the 21st century methods and tactics used by our terrorist enemies. Every president since Carter has utilized statutory authority and affirmative court decisions to operate outside FISA's jurisdiction. In a *Chicago Tribune* editorial, John Schmidt, a former Associate Attorney General under President Clinton, said "Bush's authorization (of) NSA electronic surveillance into phone calls and emails is consistent with court decisions and positions of the Justice Department under prior presidents."

In 2002, the FISA court ruled in the case of *U.S. v. Truong* that a federal "court, as did all other courts to have decided the issue, held that the President did have inherent authority to conduct warrantless searches to obtain foreign intelligence information." Indeed, the 4th Circuit Court of Appeals, in hearing the Truong case, decided "we agree that the Executive Branch need not always obtain a warrant for foreign intelligence surveillance." Going further, the 4th Circuit Court said, the "needs of the Executive are so compelling in foreign intelligence that a uniform warrant requirement would 'unduly frustrate' the President in carrying out his foreign affairs responsibility," and "the Executive (branch) possesses unparalleled expertise to make the decision to conduct foreign intelligence surveillance"

while "the Judiciary is largely inexperienced" in this area.

Beyond the legal questions, I believe the program does require oversight, and its current level of oversight is not adequate. As co-equal branches of government, the Constitution tasks Congress with oversight of the Executive branch as a check on executive power. Limited briefings to the so-called Gang of Eight are not what the Framers of the Constitution had in mind. That said, the members of the Gang of Eight, if they had serious reservations about the legal basis for the program, needed to have acted in the course of at least 12 briefings, rather than objecting now. As members of Congress, we have an obligation to represent our constituency, but more importantly to preserve, protect, and defend the country, and that includes the Constitution. We each have power here in Washington to effect change, and when we feel we need to do so, we must.

Ultimately, the legal basis for the program may rest with the courts. Senate Judiciary Committee Chairman Arlen Specter (R-PA) has suggested the entire program be taken to the FISA Court so its legal status may be decided once and for all.

I believe the President acted in the best interests of the country when he authorized the use of this program in the wake of 9/11. Five and a half years later the threat remains and the leak of this program comes at a time when we need to be at our strongest in protecting America.

Security, Democracy and Restraint
John J. Donohue

The revelation of the NSA's domestic spying program raises a host of legal and policy questions. On its face, the program would seem to run afoul of the 1978 Foreign Intelligence Surveillance Act (FISA), and the Bush Administration's puzzling and contradictory statements on this legal issue have not been reassuring. First, given the explicit prohibitions of the 1978 Act, the Administration's allusions to pre-FISA precedents for Presidential spying are inapposite. Second, the claims that Congress implicitly authorized such behavior as part of the grant of authority to pursue military action in Afghanistan and/or Iraq seem hollow in light of the Administration's assertion that the President had the constitutional authority to engage in this type of domestic surveillance even in the face of a direct legislative ban. Third, in the aftermath of 9/11, the Administration asked for—and received—various amendments to FISA, which raises the question of why a further FISA amendment to cover the NSA program was not sought. Finally, the President's explicit prepared statement in April 2004 that "When we're talking about chasing down terrorists, we're talking about getting a court order before we do so" raises legitimate questions about whether the Administration has been caught misleading the public and skirting the law.

Is there a benign explanation for the Administration's conduct? Two questions exist. First, does the spying program advance the legitimate interests of the nation by reducing the risk of terrorist attacks within the United States? While we now know that the Bush Administration did not adequately heed clear signs about Bin Laden's intentions to attack within the United States and the specific warnings about terrorist use of planes, we do have a record of almost four and one-half years without a subsequent terrorist attack. It is hard to know whether the NSA surveillance campaign played any role in resisting further attack, but there is at least some possibility that it has.

Second, even if the program is helpful, is there a justification for failing to seek Congressional authority or to at least consult with the appropriate Congressional committees? Perhaps extreme secrecy would be needed in this case, since any effort to overturn the law (or share information with Congress?) would tip off the enemy to the need to avoid electronic surveillance. But, Bin Laden knew years ago that his cell phone conversations were tapped by the United States, so one assumes that our enemies probably knew or expected that they were being tapped in communicating with individuals in the U.S. itself. Given that the argument for extreme secrecy is uncertain and the Administration's behavior in the wake of the revelations raises concerns about its consciousness of guilt, the dangers of the Administration's course of conduct become more troubling. The loyal opposition will necessarily worry that unlawful snooping—most ominously against political opponents—could result from such unchecked assertions of Presidential power. The Administration's conduct in numerous other instances—from the release of the name of an undercover CIA operative under circumstances suggesting an attempt to punish a political adversary to the array of errors and misstatements leading up to the war in Iraq—buttresses the concern that the Administration pursues its agendas without feeling the need to be candid with the American people.

One factor might count in the Administration's favor on the question of whether its actions and secrecy were justified—the decision of the *New York Times* not to reveal the program when it learned of it a year ago. Apparently, the Administration made its case to the *New York Times* that legitimate national security interests would be jeopardized if the program were revealed, and the *Times* accepted those representations. Unfortunately, the power of this arguably independent endorsement of the Administration's position has been somewhat undercut by the *Times'* admitted gullibility and/or culpability in erroneously pumping up the pre-war stories about Iraqi weapons of mass destruction at the behest of the White House. The *New York Times* may also have some explaining to do.

Now that the NSA program has been revealed, any cost to national security has presumably been paid, and the highest priority would seem to be to resolve how the nation's interests in security and democratic decision-making can both be appropriately protected. Given the allegations and evidence about prisoner abuse and torture, the need for the country to address openly the appropriate limits on the pursuit of national security is evident. It is worth remembering that many aggressive acts unilaterally taken by the U.S. in furtherance of short-term national security objectives have ended up imposing larger long-term costs. For example, Ronald Reagan's championing and arming of Bin Laden and the other Afghan "freedom fighters" as they battled the Soviet Union looks far more questionable today than it did back in the 1980s. The same can be said of the CIA's overthrow of the Mossadegh regime in Iran in 1953 that has had such unhappy long-term results. One suspects that a sober assessment of the full array of aggressive, unilateral U.S. foreign policy initiatives over the last half century might well reveal that actions that initially looked appealing to zealous executive-branch officials commonly produced scant benefits and large costs.

Much Ado About

David B. Rivkin, Jr.

The frenzy surrounding the NSA surveillance program is nothing short of remarkable. The legal and constitutional case supporting the President's actions is quite compelling, and even his harshest critics concede its policy value. Meanwhile, there is absolutely no evidence that the program has been abused or politicized in any way; if impropriety existed, the very same critics, who saw fit to leak information about the surveillance effort to the *New York Times*, would have promptly disclosed this evidence. Thus, the criticisms, even when stripped of partisanship and a hefty dose of anti-Bush sentiment, regrettably manifest a broad underlying problem that is plaguing our political and legal discourse—a veritable hostility towards all discretionary exercise of presidential power. This tendency is particularly dangerous at a time of a "long war" against a dangerous and determined Islamist adversary, when the need for such uniquely presidential policy attributes (e.g., speed and unity of design) is all the more palpable.

For a lawyer like myself, whose practice encompasses administrative law, the critics' efforts to portray the 1978 Foreign Intelligence Surveillance Act (FISA) as a regulatory straightjacket, that allegedly renders unlawful the NSA surveillance program, border on laughable. To begin with, FISA, far from being a comprehensive regulatory edifice, applies only to four specific surveillance scenarios. Indeed, since FISA applies to electronic surveillance, carried out for "foreign intelligence purposes," and the NSA surveillance program focuses exclusively on gathering military intelligence about parties who are waging war against us, it is not even clear that FISA is at all relevant—foreign intelligence is not the same as military intelligence.

Meanwhile, howls of outrage greet the Administration's assertion that the September 2001 congressional Authorization to Use Military Force ("AUMF") provided additional blessing for the Executive's collection of battlefield intelligence. But exactly the same argument—that the AUMF authorized the President to use all traditional aspects of war prosecution—was embraced by the Supreme Court in the Hamdi case. (In that case, the Administration foes argued that the AUMF, because it did not expressly refer to detention of enemy combatants, could not have overridden the so-called Non-Detention Act, which barred the incarceration of U.S. citizens without trial.) Collecting intelligence on one's enemy is certainly every bit as traditional an aspect of waging war as detaining captured enemy combatants. To emphasize, a perfectly plausible and defensible construction of the existing statutory authorities fully vindicates the President's surveillance program and does not require us to reach the constitutional issues.

But what about the Constitution? The politicians and journalists would have you believe that it is unprecedented for the Executive to invade the privacy of Americans without a warrant. Yet, even a cursory reading of the 4th Amendment suggests that searches and seizures can be undertaken without a judicial imprimatur, so long as they are reasonable. In a world where the government deploys random sobriety checkpoints to apprehend drunken motorists, where U.S. citizens returning to the United States are randomly searched by custom agents, and airline travelers are randomly selected for intrusive body searches—all of which clearly invade one's privacy and bodily autonomy and do so without a shred of probable cause—the notion that it is not reasonable to invade the privacy of some Americans' telephone conversations in order to prevent attacks in which thousands of Americans would be killed is self-evidently absurd.

To suggest that all of the intercept activities must be conducted pursuant to a warrant is not only impractical, given the need for urgent action, but also betrays a further fundamental misunderstanding of the Fourth Amendment. While the Executive can constitutionally carry out a "reasonable" search that infringes on personal privacy, a warrant cannot be granted by a court absent "probable cause." Applying the higher probable cause standard would mean the NSA could only surveil the conversations of full-fledged al Qaeda agents, leaving invaluable conversations among al Qaeda sympathizers unmonitored.

The broader problem with the critics is that discretionary presidential action lies at the heart of executive power. To suggest that the President can act only with judicial blessing would vitiate his key constitutional attributes. The Framers, who placed much importance on executive independence and went to great lengths to ensure that the Executive would not be dominated by the Legislature, would have been horrified by current efforts to make him the ward of the courts. This is not to suggest that we should not be concerned about abuses of executive power, which have certainly occurred in the past. However, the proper way to deal with such abuses is through political accountability, with both Congress and the American people vigilant over the President's actions. In a world of endemic leaks, this is not a particularly difficult undertaking. Presented with the evidence of wrongdoing, Congress can cut off funds for NSA surveillance and even impeach the President. The American people can punish him and his party at the polls. But accountability for abusing power is very different than preventing the legitimate use of power.

Domestic Surveillance and Distrust
Dakota Rudesill

The debate about warrantless surveillance of Americans by the NSA is not about whether Al Qaeda is a threat, nor whether we need to keep an ear to Osama's agents. Everyone agrees it is, and we should.

Nor is the debate about whether the NSA's precise (still classified) method of surveillance should be employed. If it is legal or can be made legal, it may well have merit.

The big question is not even whether this particular administration (which benefits from the service of countless able and honorable Americans) should be trusted to search our bytes without explicit authorization or robust oversight by Congress, and without the warrant requirements of the Fourth

Amendment and the Foreign Intelligence Surveillance Act.

Rather, the real issue is whether we should largely shelve a notion long at the core of American political thought: profound skepticism of government, especially when it acts in the name of national security.

FISA, and indeed our republic itself, are products of informed distrust. If we still agree with Hamilton that humanity is "ambitious [and] vindictive" and with Madison that government is "but the greatest of all reflections of human nature," then we ought not accept arguments that boil down to "just trust us." Weakening institutional checks leaves us little choice but to depend on the good intentions of the president's men rather than the rule of law.

The FISA law of 1978 struck a careful balance between the equally necessary but inherently conflicting imperatives of security and liberty: allowing surveillance while preventing a repeat of the wiretapping abuses of prior presidents via a warrant requirement and congressional oversight. Similarly, the Constitution created an Executive strong enough to protect the country, but sufficiently limited by co-equal Judicial and Legislative branches to prevent the kind of abuses of military power to which the British army subjected the Colonies.

The Constitution's separated, diffused, but in practical terms *shared* power regarding national security adds up to institutionalized skepticism. In contrast, the Administration seeks unitary, concentrated, exclusive power for the Executive—the kind of aggregation the Framers knew imperiled liberty.

The current Executive claims that it, without going to court, may decide whether its own electronic searches in the United States are legal under the Fourth Amendment. President Bush has cited "multiple safeguards to protect civil liberties" now in place within the Executive. Yet the Administration's own "unitary Executive" theory accords the president all Executive authority. How, then, do subordinates check a misguided president?

How would Congress? The Constitution explicitly grants the legislature not only sole appropriations power, but authority to make "all Laws which shall be necessary and proper" for "all . . . Powers vested" in the federal government, including "the Government and Regulation" of the Armed Forces. Remarkably, the Justice Department alleges that any law limiting presidential power to order warrantless military foreign intelligence surveillance in the United States of suspected terrorists would be *unconstitutional*—that is, not just challenged but *trumped* by the president's inherent wartime authority. This cannot be reconciled with the Constitution's purpose and plain text, which embody shared power.

Furthermore, when Congress's senior "Gang of Eight" was briefed about the NSA program in 2003, the Administration reportedly stipulated that they consult with no one else—not even the intelligence committee's legal and technical experts with top-level clearances who would draft any classified annex to an intelligence bill that would authorize, regulate, or de-fund the program. The Administration thus blocked Congress from acting regarding programs within its comprehensive legislative authority, executing a sort of pre-emptive veto.

Meanwhile, its public legal arguments add up to a post-enactment veto power. Consider: if the president's inherent constitutional authority, plus the generally worded post-9/11 Authorization for the Use of Military Force, gives him authority to wiretap in contravention of the plain text—indeed, the entire point—of a highly specific statute like FISA, where does his authority end? How many other laws passed by Congress and signed by prior presidents can Bush and his successors invalidate at will? What congressional powers remain intact regarding national security beyond appropriations, declaring war, ratifying treaties, and confirming nominations? Do even these?

If judicial and congressional institutional skepticism of state power in wartime is circumscribed so dramatically, we will get a system dominated by an Executive the people have fewer ways to check—and therefore little choice but to trust—between presidential plebiscites.

If ever there were a time for such unipolar government in America (and I doubt it), this is not it. We are witnessing tremendous expansion in the volume and searchability of personal electronic information. Major decisions about the balance between security and liberty are about to be made.

Executive dominance would mean that just one branch of government would be making most of the decisions. That would not reflect the Constitution's vision of shared national security power. Getting the liberty/security balance right in the electronic age will not be easy, but Congress must not abandon this challenge to the bona fides of any Executive—for Congress's own sake, and for ours.

Pre-9/11 Politicians in a Post-9/11 World
Stephen A. Vaden

How soon some of our elected leaders choose to forget! It was only 4½ years ago, following the attacks of 9/11, that the members of the U.S. Congress stood on the steps of the Capitol and sang *God Bless America*. Hands joined, they vowed to take any and all steps necessary to attack terrorist camps sheltering those responsible for the destruction of the

World Trade Center and the attack on the Pentagon while adapting America's intelligence capabilities to ensure such attacks never occurred again.

Fast forward to today and Democratic Party Chairman Howard Dean, heading into the midterm election, vowed as a campaign pledge that should his party take control of one or both houses of Congress, Democrats will grind the normal business of government to a halt to engage in endless hearings to investigate "the most corrupt administration since Warren Harding." Adding a bipartisan spirit, Judiciary Committee Chairman Arlen Specter summoned Attorney General Alberto Gonzales to answer a long series of accusatory questions.

This blast of Beltway huffing and puffing came about because President Bush had the audacity to determine that individuals located inside the U.S. calling persons overseas with suspected terrorist connections do not have a reasonable expectation of privacy.

Four years ago we were all in agreement—the "wall" separating domestic and foreign intelligence gathering had to be breached. The wall had produced fatal consequences. Fearful of running afoul of then-in-place FISA guidelines, FBI agents refused to request a search warrant that would allow them to investigate the contents of Al Qaeda terrorist Zacarias Moussaoui's computer hard drive. Thus, a computer belonging to a man now suspected of being the "Twentieth Hijacker" sat in a Minneapolis FBI office unexamined from August 16, 2001, until after the attacks. As the 9/11 Commission concluded, absent the "wall," FBI agents would have discovered files full of flight simulation programs and information on dispersing aerial pesticides.

We will never know whether the FBI could have followed the leads Moussaoui's computer would have provided to disrupt 9/11. A Washington which fetishized bureaucratic obstacles and believed that a fantastical wall separating the CIA from the FBI could also separate America from its enemies overseas never gave its top counterterrorist agents the chance. If the rhetoric of today's political discourse is to be believed, America looks set to make the same mistake all over again, rebuilding the obsolescent wall it just so recently razed.

Unfortunately, Congress only is engaged in doing what it does best: evading responsibility and passing the buck to the other two branches of government. Many of the proposed "solutions" to the "problem" of terrorist surveillance involve expanding the jurisdiction of the unelected and therefore unaccountable FISA court judges. Congress would like nothing more than to be able to continue its disturbing pattern of making ill-conceived public attacks on highly important and useful intelligence programs while washing its hands of its oversight responsibilities entirely. Congress must not be allowed to repeat the mistakes of the past and shirk its constitutional duties; the only thing worse than a preening politician in a suit is a pseudo-politician in a robe.

The Bush Administration's failure to force Congress to play its role in protecting America from terrorist attacks, not the Administration's institution of the NSA program, is the most troubling aspect of the current debate. Rather than bearing all the burden and blame itself, the Bush Administration should actively involve Congress in the management of our intelligence programs. President Bush has asserted without rejoinder that the Administration reviews the status of the NSA program every 45 days. Nothing stands in the way of the President's sending a subordinate to brief the House and Senate Intelligence Committees, or subcommittees thereof, on the status of the program at that same interval.

Such meetings would necessarily be subject to the strictest secrecy requirements. Members of the committees would be free at these meetings to raise objections and demand accommodations to any concerns about privacy or any other supposed rights violations occurring. However, the key difference would be that in this formalized consultative process, congressmen's words would actually stand a chance of having an effect, unlike the unthinking comments bandied about on *Meet the Press*. As classified minutes of these meetings would also be kept, advice that resulted in damaging limitations to our intelligence gathering capabilities (or, in the worst case scenario, allowing terrorists to exploit the resulting vulnerability to attack) could be traced back to its originator in an ensuing investigation. Then, the American public could render its verdict at the next election as to whether the intelligence capabilities sacrificed were indeed worth it.

What would keep members of Congress from using the classified briefings to continue their demagogic ways? One need only compare the measured reaction to the revelation of the NSA program of Group of Eight member and California Democratic Congresswoman Jane Harman to the vitriolic partisan response of House Minority Leader Nancy Pelosi to see the difference a little actual responsibility can make. Surveillance is not the problem. Political rhetoric stripped of common sense and accountability is.

NSA Spying Erodes Rule of Law
Loch K. Johnson

The Bush administration finds itself embroiled in controversy over whether its program of NSA spying, a highly classified operation leaked to the public in December 2004, is necessary and lawful in the struggle against terrorism. The cause of the furor is the President's authorization by secret executive order to allow the NSA to eavesdrop on Americans without first acquiring a warrant. Critics maintain that this right violates the intent of the Foreign Intelligence Surveillance Act.

The FISA statute stemmed from the findings of the Church Committee in 1975–76, a panel of inquiry into alleged domestic spying, led by Senator Frank Church (D, Idaho). The Committee discovered that the FBI had carried out 500,000 investigations into so-called subversives from 1960 to 1974 without a single court conviction; the CIA had engaged in extensive mail-openings inside the U.S. (Operation Chaos); and Army intelligence units had conducted clandestine inquiries against 100,000 U.S. citizens opposed to the war in Vietnam.

The NSA took part in this widespread assault against freedom and privacy at home. Its "Operation Shamrock" monitored every cable sent overseas or received by Americans from 1947 to 1975, and its "Operation Minaret" swept in the telephone conversations of an additional 1,680 citizens. The effects of such spying, as Senator Walter Mondale (D, Minnesota) noted in public hearings, was to "discourage political dissent in this country." None of these NSA wiretaps went through a judicial review. When Mondale asked the NSA deputy director whether he was concerned about the program's legality, the official replied with a look of embarrassment: "That particular aspect didn't enter into the discussions."

In light of these abuses, Congress worked with both Presidents Ford and Carter to craft reforms that would protect the civil liberties of Americans against improper uses of the intelligence agencies. The FISA law took aim directly at the problem of warrantless wiretaps by the NSA. No longer could presidents or their aides decide by themselves who in this nation would be subjected to electronic surveillance. Henceforth, an impartial court comprised of experienced judges would decide the merits of an administration's request for a national security wiretap.

The FISA Court has worked well over the years, although some critics have assailed it for too easily approving warrant requests—indeed, all but five of over 17,000 requests since its inception. But the Court is not just a rubber stamp. Administrations have been careful to seek warrants only when the case is strong and that is why the approval rate is high. If the requests of the current administration for wiretaps are as urgent as President George W. Bush has asserted, the Court would no doubt have granted approval.

The Administration has drawn upon three major arguments to defend its bypassing of FISA procedures. First, DOJ attorneys maintain that the President has an inherent constitutional authority to wiretap under the commander in chief clause. Yet many legal scholars have called into question that point of view. Justice Jackson's famous opinion in the Youngstown case concluded that a president's power is "at its lowest ebb" when in conflict with the "expressed or implied will of Congress." The FISA law was an express and specific effort by lawmakers to curtail warrantless wiretaps.

Second, the administration claims that in the wake of the 9/11 attacks Congress provided the president with "authorization for use of military force"—a blank check in the war against global terrorism. That authorization, though, said nothing about electronic surveillance of American citizens; rather it was intended to give the president authority to carry out military retaliation against Al Qaeda terrorists in Afghanistan and their host, the Taliban regime.

Finally, the administration argues that the warrant procedures in the 1978 law are slow and cumbersome, as well as out-of-date in the light of new technology; in the struggle against terrorists, the U.S. must be nimble and fast moving. The FISA law, however, is agile. Warrants can be obtained in hours or even minutes; moreover, in times of crisis, the executive branch is permitted leeway to conduct wiretaps immediately for as long as 72 hours, applying for a warrant at the end of that period. If the law needs updating, the proper remedy is to amend it, rather than undermining the rule of law by using a secret executive order to waive the FISA statute.

The Senate Judiciary Committee, which has held one hearing on the surveillance program, will need a strong backbone—and probably subpoenas—to find out about its full dimensions. It may turn out that, contrary to preliminary media reports, the NSA program has merit and should be continued; but Congress and the FISA Court have an obligation to review the program. Then, if necessary, lawmakers can seek an amendment to the FISA law to improve its effectiveness.

The U.S. must defeat Al Qaeda and its affiliated terrorist organizations, but at the same time we have to keep civil liberties intact. Excessive executive branch discretion is a slippery slope, as revealed by the Church Committee. It found that America's secret agencies began by focusing on legitimate national security threats, only to be drawn into political surveillance. Tom Charles Huston, the architect of Nixon's domestic spy plan to monitor anti-Vietnam War activists, conceded to Church Committee investigators: "The risk was that you would get people who would be susceptible to political considerations as opposed to national security considerations, or would construe political considerations to be national security considerations—to move from the kid with a bomb to the kid with a picket sign, and from the kid with the picket sign to the kid with the bumper sticker of the opposing candidate. And you just keep going down the line." This danger is why a judicial check on national security wiretapping is essential.

Questions for Further Discussion

1. Contrast the argument of President George W. Bush in favor of warrantless wiretapping in some circumstances with those of his critics who oppose this approach.

2. To what extent does this controversy over wiretapping by the National Security Agency (NSA) echo the concerns of reformers on the Church Committee in 1975?

3. Why does David Rivkin think that the controversy is "much ado about nothing"?

4. Is it possible to have effective oversight with respect to the NSA without revealing its modus operandi to America's enemies? ✦

Reprinted with permission from *Symposium, Opening Argument,* Yale University School of Law 1 (February 2006): pp. 1–8.

Part IX

Intelligence Activities in the Aftermath of the 9/11 and WMD Intelligence Failures

Polonius: "Hath there been such a time, I'd fain
   know that,
That I have positively said 'tis so,
When it proved otherwise?"
King: "Not that I know."

—Shakespeare, Hamlet, *2.2.153–155*

The September 11, 2001, terrorist attacks on the World Trade Center and the Pentagon and the failure of the U.S. intelligence agencies and key allied governments to assess accurately the status of Iraq's programs to develop weapons of mass destruction (WMD) on the eve of the Second Gulf War were transformational events for the U.S. intelligence community. Both events are widely considered to be intelligence failures, but more recent explanations of what went wrong are beginning to emerge. The history of these events highlights how the limits of intelligence collection and analysis, politics, and the interaction between intelligence professionals and policymakers led, in the 9/11 instance, to lethargy in the face of an acute threat posed by Islamic fundamentalists. In the WMD example, in contrast, the intelligence and policy communities displayed a strong interest and examined the available data at length. The 9/11 case suggests that the U.S. government fell victim to a fundamental intelligence mistake, failing to respond to valid threat indicators prior to the terrorist attacks. The government then made quite a different error in the WMD case, reaching the conclusion that Iraq was in the process of restarting its prohibited weapons program.

The September 11 Attacks

When the Islamic terrorist organization Al Qaeda used civilian airliners to attack the World Trade Center and the Pentagon, many observers believed that the U.S. intelligence community had obviously failed to generate the warnings needed to stop the terrorist group before it could strike. Because of the devastating effects of the attacks, many assumed that the intelligence mistakes leading up to 9/11 were complete and total. In fact, though, the intelligence community had been tracking Islamic fundamentalists for years and had generated a steady stream of estimates about the possibility of terrorist attacks directed against U.S. forces and interests overseas, as well as against the American homeland itself. The intelligence community recognized that Al Qaeda had emerged from the remnants of U.S.-supported *mujahideen* fighters, who had successfully battled Soviet forces occupying Afghanistan. The community also recognized that, in the aftermath of the Soviet defeat, some of these "holy warriors" had gravitated toward Osama bin Laden, a Saudi financier who had built a reputation as a construction expert in Afghanistan. Bin Laden's motivations and rhetoric have changed over time, but initially his anger seemed to have been directed toward what he believed was a corrupt Wahabi regime in Saudi Arabia. The American military presence in the Persian Gulf and Saudi Arabia, necessitated by the need to pressure Baghdad to end its

WMD programs following the first Gulf War, only fueled Bin Laden's hatred toward the Saudi Royal Family and the United States. Emboldened by its victory over the Soviets, Al Qaeda did not shy away from directly attacking the remaining superpower, the United States.

By the mid-1990s, the CIA had identified Bin Laden not only as an advocate of violence but also as someone who was willing to organize and direct attacks against U.S. interests. By 1998, he had become increasingly public about his intentions, issuing a *fatwa* and holding press conferences in which he called for attacks against Americans. In August 1998, Al Qaeda attacked U.S. embassies in Nairobi in Kenya and Dar es Salaam in Tanzania. In 2000, after a failed attempt to attack the USS *The Sulivans*, his followers launched a suicide attack against the USS *Cole*, moored in the Gulf of Aden off the coast of Yemen. This attack produced 50 American casualties and nearly sank the ship. Bin Laden talked openly about his ambitions, which were codified in an insightful article published by *Foreign Affairs* (Rashid 1999).

As the threats posed by Al Qaeda became realities, U.S. officials were confronted, too, with a series of warnings that the United States was not prepared or organized to meet the challenge of international terrorism. Findings from no less than 11 major commissions and studies addressed the topic of intelligence reform. Several of these studies offered recommendations to improve coordination between the FBI and the rest of the intelligence community. Reform was needed to eliminate the wall that separated U.S. law enforcement officers from intelligence officials, a division that made it difficult to respond to terrorist networks that crossed domestic and international boundaries. A report issued in 2000 by the National Commission on Terrorism, for example, proposed clarifying the FBI's authority to investigate terrorist groups; allowing the CIA access to Bureau informants linked to terrorist organizations; placing terrorism high on the agendas of officials at the CIA, FBI, and NSA; and establishing new procedures for the quick dissemination of terrorist information to national security officials (Zegart 2005). Few of these recommendations, however, were acted upon. When Al Qaeda operatives infiltrated the United States prior to September 11, 2001, they effectively exploited the seam running between the intelligence community and domestic law enforcement agencies.

U.S. officials and organizations were slow to respond to the emerging threat posed by Al Qaeda, as well as to warnings that the U.S. government was poorly organized to meet the threat posed by transnational terrorist networks. Long accustomed to dealing with the menace of a Warsaw Pact conventional assault across what was then the inter-German border, or the prospect of a strategic nuclear exchange with the Soviet Union, officials and organizations were late in understanding the rising menace of international terrorism and how it was beginning to exploit the communication and transportation networks made possible by the information revolution and globalization. Mass casualty terrorism was recognized as a possibility, but policymakers and scholars alike debated whether such extreme violence would actually be carried out by terrorist organizations, or even whether nonstate actors were capable of creating high-casualty events. Most observers concluded that the 1993 attack on the World Trade Center by Islamic fundamentalists and the 1996 Aum Shinrikyo sarin attack on the Tokyo subway were failures. Some analysts also argued that launching a mass-casualty incident could easily rebound to the detriment of a terrorist organization, mobilizing governments and publics alike to undertake increasingly harsh and effective measures to eradicate the masterminds of terrorism and their supporters.

By the time President Bill Clinton left office, intelligence analysts had developed an increasingly alarming picture of Al Qaeda's international reach and ambitions to wreak havoc on the United States. Rocked by scandal and afflicted by chronic hand wringing—Attorney General Janet Reno repeatedly warned that Al Qaeda might retaliate if attacked—the Clinton Administration failed to translate its growing recognition of the threat into effective action. When President George W. Bush arrived in Washington to begin his term of office, his staff (with its own foreign policy agenda) seemed slow to recognize the looming threat. Here Al Qaeda might have enjoyed a lucky break: Preparations for the 9/11 attacks roughly corresponded to the change of administrations in Washington, a time when the effectiveness of the U.S. government is reduced. Al Qaeda was able to capitalize on the fact that a new team was in the White House, busy moving in and holding its first meetings. The threat of transnational terrorism was rising to the top of the Bush Administration's agenda by the late summer of 2001, but by then it was too late.

The Iraq WMD Estimate

In the aftermath of the 9/11 attacks, debate about the possibility of mass-casualty terrorism was laid to rest and a new threat came into sharp focus: WMD terrorism. All eyes focused on Iraq and the possibility that Saddam Hussein's regime had restarted its program to develop nuclear weapons following the ejection of U.N. Special Commission (UNSCOM) inspectors in the late 1990s. Many feared that the interests of Saddam and Al Qaeda might coincide, leading to an alliance of convenience that could make Bin Laden's often-stated interest in WMD a reality. With this nightmarish, if somewhat far-fetched, scenario in the background, the Bush Administration apparently made the political decision that the risk of living with an Iraq armed with WMD outweighed the risk of taking direct action to bring about regime change in Iraq. Support for this decision was provided by the October 2002 Iraqi Weapons of Mass Destruction National Intelligence Estimate (NIE). Although the judgments of this NIE were heavily qualified (the estimate went into some detail about the limitations of its conclusions and the data used in reaching them), it was seen by most policymakers within the U.S. government as evidence that Saddam had again embarked on the path of obtaining nuclear weapons. Subsequent findings now suggest that the 2002 NIE was off the mark. No significant WMD programs were uncovered following the American and British invasion of Iraq in March 2003 that began the Second Gulf War and drove Saddam's Ba'athist regime from power. But by the time the weaknesses of the 2002 NIE were clear, the die had been cast.

The origins of the intelligence community's overestimate of Iraq's WMD capability probably can be found in its underestimation of Iraq's nuclear capabilities that became apparent following the First Gulf War (1990–91). Information obtained by U.S. forces in the immediate aftermath of that war, data gleaned from UNSCOM inspections, and the revelations of Hussein Kamil (Saddam's son-in-law, who for a time defected to the West) settled first-order questions about the suspected Iraqi WMD program: Saddam seemed to be interested in all types of WMD. With justification, the intelligence community concluded that information available to it before the First Gulf War really was just the tip of the iceberg and, at least until the mid-1990s, more data became available that painted an increasingly vivid picture of Iraq's previous WMD efforts. What emerged was a policy-intelligence consensus about Iraq's WMD: Saddam Hussein would do everything in his power to obtain mass-casualty weapons, and the full extent of Iraq's WMD program was being concealed by the regime. New data generally confirmed worst-case estimates of Iraq's WMD capability. This estimate and the baseline data used to assess Iraq's WMD programs did not significantly change beliefs inside the Bush Administration and most agencies in the intelligence community until the aftermath of the Second Gulf War, although U.N. weapons inspectors and a few elements inside the U.S. intelligence community raised doubts before the U.S.-led invasion in 2003.

A turning point for most analysts in the American intelligence community came with the ejection of UNSCOM inspectors in the late 1990s. Analysts concluded that the Iraqi regime, no longer hamstrung by the threat of detection by UNSCOM, would be able to restart its WMD programs and, given Saddam's objectives, probably *would* restart its WMD programs. What analysts failed to realize, however, was that the Iraqi regime had been subjected to nearly a decade of international sanctions, UNSCOM inspections, continuous overflights, and concerted preventive attacks (the First Gulf War and Operation Desert Fox) intended to destroy, disrupt, and dissuade further efforts to produce, store, train with, or equip a large-scale WMD arsenal. These actions had a profound effect on the ability and will of the Iraqi regime to continue its WMD programs. Nevertheless, Saddam Hussein and his henchmen continued to create suspicion that nefarious activities might be taking place beyond the view of the prying eyes of the U.S. and allied intelligence agencies. Without a true "net assessment" to evaluate the full effect of international policies against Iraq—and there is no agency in the U.S. government that evaluates the overall success of U.S. foreign and defense policy—developments in Iraq tended to be judged with an eye toward Iraq's past capabilities, which were based on data gathered in the early 1990s and reflected the status of Iraq's programs in the 1980s.

If Western analysts were going to accurately assess the changing nature of Iraq's WMD program and current capabilities, they needed to step outside this policy-intelligence consensus about Iraqi behavior (a problem similar to the one faced by Israeli analysts prior to the Yom Kippur War in 1973). This type of assessment is extraordinarily difficult, because analysts would have to abandon their own policy-analytical-historical context to evaluate available information in a detached way. The U.S. intelligence community failed to undertake this reassessment of Iraq's weapons policies and capabilities; no one in the government of the United States attempted to reassess the underlying assumptions behind the Iraq estimate of October 2002. No one realized that the policy-intelligence consensus was no longer falsifiable, because most of the positive—as well as the negative—evidence, quite possibly manipulated by Iraqi denial and deception operations, suggested the presence of a clandestine Iraqi nuclear program. If matters look cut-and-dried to intelligence analysts, suspicions should have been raised that results might have been a little *too* cut-and-dried. This did not occur, however, in terms of the Iraq NIE. Indeed, there were no "intelligence dissenters" to that document—individuals who objected to the consensus and tried to make their opinions known. No one inside the U.S. government stepped forward effectively to object to the data, analysis, or conclusions contained in the Iraq NIE—although behind the scenes some officials in the Department of State intelligence service (Intelligence and Research, or INR), in the Energy Department intelligence unit, and in Air Force Intelligence did raise objections, without success. By and large, the NIE was considered to be rather ho-hum.

The Readings

The readings in this section examine these two intelligence-policy failures. The first selection is excerpted from the 9/11 Commission Report. Chaired by Thomas H. Kean and Lee H. Hamilton, the commission produced a document that offers a riveting account of the events leading up to the September 11 tragedy. The report should be read in its entirety by everyone, but especially by students who were too young in 2001 to absorb the full shock of the events of that dark day. The sections of the Commission Report that we present here contain its recommendations for overcoming the organizational weaknesses of the U.S. government revealed on 9/11. They also highlight the global threat posed by the rise of transnational terrorist networks and outline a national strategy to meet that threat. The report also offers reforms needed to make effective defense, homeland security, and intelligence a reality.

The second reading is taken from the report of the Commission on the Intelligence Capabilities of the United States Regarding Weapons of Mass Destruction, a panel chaired by Laurence H. Silberman and Charles Robb. Our selection focuses on the intelligence community's weaknesses when it comes to analysis—inadequacies made clear by the 2002 Iraq NIE. The commissioners again offer a variety of managerial and organizational reforms to improve the work of intelligence analysts.

The third selection, written by Amy Zegart, addresses why government officials failed to put to good use the scores of suggestions for intelligence and security reform offered in the decade before the September 11 attacks by a series of official commissions and blue ribbon panels. In exploring the reasons for this "adaptation failure," Zegart raises an important issue for the future. Will the intelligence and policymaking communities embrace a continuous process of adaptation necessary to meet evolving security threats in the twenty-first century? Or do the seeds of tomorrow's intelligence failures lie in the haphazard applications of today's recommendations for intelligence reform?

In the final selection, Loch K. Johnson provides an analysis of the problems that bedeviled the intelligence community as it struggled with the threats posed by transnational terrorism and WMD proliferation, leading to analytic failures that contributed to the September 11 attacks and the Iraq NIE. Johnson organizes his analysis using the framework of the intelligence cycle, highlighting weak points in the intelligence production process that prevented the creation of timely and accurate estimates. His analysis also focuses on how the relationship between intelligence professionals and policymakers sometimes proved to be counterproductive. In response to the problems uncovered by his analysis, Johnson offers a series of recommendations for the intelligence and policymaking communities. ✦

32

9/11 Intelligence Failure

Kean Commission

The 9/11 Commission, chaired by former New Jersey Republican governor Thomas H. Kean and former Representative Lee H. Hamilton (D, Indiana), produced an influential account of the events surrounding the September 11, 2001, Al Qaeda attacks on the World Trade Center and the Pentagon. The report achieved best-selling status and remains a valuable research document on global terrorism. Our selection from the report identifies the nature of the terrorist threat facing the United States, the organizational reforms needed to meet this challenge, and national strategies that the commissioners believed should be adopted to keep terrorism at bay.

WHAT TO DO? A GLOBAL STRATEGY
Reflecting on a Generational Challenge

Three years after 9/11, Americans are still thinking and talking about how to protect our nation in this new era. The national debate continues.

Countering terrorism has become, beyond any doubt, the top national security priority for the United States. This shift has occurred with the full support of the Congress, both major political parties, the media, and the American people.

The nation has committed enormous resources to national security and to countering terrorism. Between fiscal year 2001, the last budget adopted before 9/11, and the present fiscal year 2004, total federal spending on defense (including expenditures on both Iraq and Afghanistan), homeland security, and international affairs rose more than 50 percent, from $354 billion to about $547 billion. The United States has not experienced such a rapid surge in national security spending since the Korean War.[1]

This pattern has occurred before in American history. The United States faces a sudden crisis and summons a tremendous exertion of national energy. Then, as that surge transforms the landscape,

comes a time for reflectio[n] programs and even agen[cies] are invented or redesig[ned] gaged citizens redefine th[eir] ernment, working thro[ugh] American republic.

Now is the time for th[is reflec]tion. The United State[s ...] *do*—the shape and obj[ect ...] cans should also consider *now to as [...]* their government in a different way.

Defining the Threat

In the post-9/11 world, threats are defined more by the fault lines within societies than by the territorial boundaries between them. From terrorism to global disease or environmental degradation, the challenges have become transnational rather than international. That is the defining quality of world politics in the twenty-first century.

National security used to be considered by studying foreign frontiers, weighing opposing groups of states, and measuring industrial might. To be dangerous, an enemy had to muster large armies. Threats emerged slowly, often visibly, as weapons were forged, armies conscripted, and units trained and moved into place. Because large states were more powerful, they also had more to lose. They could be deterred.

Now threats can emerge quickly. An organization like al Qaeda, headquartered in a country on the other side of the earth, in a region so poor that electricity or telephones were scarce, could nonetheless scheme to wield weapons of unprecedented destructive power in the largest cities of the United States.

In this sense, 9/11 has taught us that terrorism against American interests "over there" should be regarded just as we regard terrorism against America "over here." In this same sense, the American homeland is the planet.

But the enemy is not just "terrorism," some generic evil.[2] This vagueness blurs the strategy. The catastrophic threat at this moment in history is more specific. It is the threat posed by *Islamist* terrorism—especially the al Qaeda network, its affiliates, and its ideology.[3]

As we mentioned in chapter 2, Usama Bin Ladin and other Islamist terrorist leaders draw on a long tradition of extreme intolerance within one stream of Islam (a minority tradition), from at least Ibn Taimiyyah, through the founders of Wahhabism, through the Muslim Brotherhood, to Sayyid Qutb. That stream is motivated by religion and does not distinguish politics from religion, thus distorting both. It is further fed by grievances stressed by Bin

...dely felt throughout the Muslim ...st the U.S. military presence in the ...t, policies perceived as anti-Arab and an-...n, and support of Israel. Bin Ladin and ...st terrorists mean exactly what they say: to ...n America is the font of all evil, the "head of the ...ake," and it must be converted or destroyed.

It is not a position with which Americans can bargain or negotiate. With it there is no common ground—not even respect for life—on which to begin a dialogue. It can only be destroyed or utterly isolated.

Because the Muslim world has fallen behind the West politically, economically, and militarily for the past three centuries, and because few tolerant or secular Muslim democracies provide alternative models for the future, Bin Ladin's message finds receptive ears. It has attracted active support from thousands of disaffected young Muslims and resonates powerfully with a far larger number who do not actively support his methods. The resentment of America and the West is deep, even among leaders of relatively successful Muslim states.[4]

Tolerance, the rule of law, political and economic openness, the extension of greater opportunities to women—these cures must come from within Muslim societies themselves. The United States must support such developments.

But this process is likely to be measured in decades, not years. It is a process that will be violently opposed by Islamist terrorist organizations, both inside Muslim countries and in attacks on the United States and other Western nations. The United States finds itself caught up in a clash *within* a civilization. That clash arises from particular conditions in the Muslim world, conditions that spill over into expatriate Muslim communities in non-Muslim countries.

Our enemy is twofold: al Qaeda, a stateless network of terrorists that struck us on 9/11; and a radical ideological movement in the Islamic world, inspired in part by al Qaeda, which has spawned terrorist groups and violence across the globe. The first enemy is weakened, but continues to pose a grave threat. The second enemy is gathering, and will menace Americans and American interests long after Usama Bin Ladin and his cohorts are killed or captured. Thus our strategy must match our means to two ends: dismantling the al Qaeda network and prevailing in the longer term over the ideology that gives rise to Islamist terrorism.

Islam is not the enemy. It is not synonymous with terror. Nor does Islam teach terror. America and its friends oppose a perversion of Islam, not the great world faith itself. Lives guided by religious faith, including literal beliefs in holy scriptures, are common to every religion, and represent no threat to us.

Other religions have experienced violent internal struggles. With so many diverse adherents, every major religion will spawn violent zealots. Yet understanding and tolerance among people of different faiths can and must prevail.

The present transnational danger is Islamist terrorism. What is needed is a broad political-military strategy that rests on a firm tripod of policies to

- attack terrorists and their organizations;

- prevent the continued growth of Islamist terrorism; and

- protect against and prepare for terrorist attacks.

More Than a War on Terrorism

Terrorism is a tactic used by individuals and organizations to kill and destroy. Our efforts should be directed at those individuals and organizations.

Calling this struggle a war accurately describes the use of American and allied armed forces to find and destroy terrorist groups and their allies in the field, notably in Afghanistan. The language of war also evokes the mobilization for a national effort. Yet the strategy should be balanced.

The first phase of our post-9/11 efforts rightly included military action to topple the Taliban and pursue al Qaeda. This work continues. But long-term success demands the use of all elements of national power: diplomacy, intelligence, covert action, law enforcement, economic policy, foreign aid, public diplomacy, and homeland defense. If we favor one tool while neglecting others, we leave ourselves vulnerable and weaken our national effort.

Certainly the strategy should include offensive operations to counter terrorism. Terrorists should no longer find safe haven where their organizations can grow and flourish. America's strategy should be a coalition strategy, that includes Muslim nations as partners in its development and implementation.

Our effort should be accompanied by a preventive strategy that is as much, or more, political as it is military. The strategy must focus clearly on the Arab and Muslim world, in all its variety.

Our strategy should also include defenses. America can be attacked in many ways and has many vulnerabilities. No defenses are perfect. But risks must be calculated; hard choices must be made about allocating resources. Responsibilities for America's defense should be clearly defined. Planning does make a difference, identifying where a little money might have a large effect. Defenses also complicate the plans of attackers, increasing their risks of discovery and failure. Finally, the nation must prepare to deal with attacks that are not stopped.

Measuring Success

What should Americans expect from their government in the struggle against Islamist terrorism? The goals seem unlimited: Defeat terrorism anywhere in the world. But Americans have also been told to expect the worst: An attack is probably coming; it may be terrible.

With such benchmarks, the justifications for action and spending seem limitless. Goals are good. Yet effective public policies also need concrete objectives. Agencies need to be able to measure success.

These measurements do not need to be quantitative: government cannot measure success in the ways that private firms can. But the targets should be specific enough so that reasonable observers—in the White House, the Congress, the media, or the general public—can judge whether or not the objectives have been attained.

Vague goals match an amorphous picture of the enemy. Al Qaeda and its affiliates are popularly described as being all over the world, adaptable, resilient, needing little higher-level organization, and capable of anything. The American people are thus given the picture of an omnipotent, unslayable hydra of destruction. This image lowers expectations for government effectiveness.

It should not lower them too far. Our report shows a determined and capable group of plotters. Yet the group was fragile, dependent on a few key personalities, and occasionally left vulnerable by the marginal, unstable people often attracted to such causes. The enemy made mistakes—like Khalid al Mihdhar's unauthorized departure from the United States that required him to enter the country again in July 2001, or the selection of Zacarias Moussaoui as a participant and Ramzi Binalshibh's transfer of money to him. The U.S. government was not able to capitalize on those mistakes in time to prevent 9/11.

We do not believe it is possible to defeat all terrorist attacks against Americans, every time and everywhere. A president should tell the American people:

- No president can promise that a catastrophic attack like that of 9/11 will not happen again. History has shown that even the most vigilant and expert agencies cannot always prevent determined, suicidal attackers from reaching a target.

- But the American people are entitled to expect their government to do its very best. They should expect that officials will have realistic objectives, clear guidance, and effective organization. They are entitled to see some standards for performance so they can judge, with the help of their elected representatives, whether the objectives are being met.

Attack Terrorists and Their Organizations

The U.S. government, joined by other governments around the world, is working through intelligence, law enforcement, military, financial, and diplomatic channels to identify, disrupt, capture, or kill individual terrorists. This effort was going on before 9/11 and it continues on a vastly enlarged scale. But to catch terrorists, a U.S. or foreign agency needs to be able to find and reach them.

No Sanctuaries

The 9/11 attack was a complex international operation, the product of years of planning. Bombings like those in Bali in 2003 or Madrid in 2004, while able to take hundreds of lives, can be mounted locally. Their requirements are far more modest in size and complexity. They are more difficult to thwart. But the U.S. government must build the capacities to prevent a 9/11-scale plot from succeeding, and those capabilities will help greatly to cope with lesser but still devastating attacks.

A complex international terrorist operation aimed at launching a catastrophic attack cannot be mounted by just anyone in any place. Such operations appear to require

- time, space, and ability to perform competent planning and staff work;

- a command structure able to make necessary decisions and possessing the authority and contacts to assemble needed people, money, and materials;

- opportunity and space to recruit, train, and select operatives with the needed skills and dedication, providing the time and structure required to socialize them into the terrorist cause, judge their trustworthiness, and hone their skills;

- a logistics network able to securely manage the travel of operatives, move money, and transport resources (like explosives) where they need to go;

- access, in the case of certain weapons, to the special materials needed for a nuclear, chemical, radiological, or biological attack;

- reliable communications between coordinators and operatives; and

- opportunity to test the workability of the plan.

Many details . . . illustrate the direct and indirect value of the Afghan sanctuary to al Qaeda in preparing the 9/11 attack and other operations. The organization cemented personal ties among veteran jihadists working together there for years. It had the operational space to gather and sift recruits, indoctrinating them in isolated, desert camps. It built up logistical networks, running through Pakistan and the United Arab Emirates.

Al Qaeda also exploited relatively lax internal security environments in Western countries, especially Germany. It considered the environment in the United States so hospitable that the 9/11 operatives used America as their staging area for further training and exercises—traveling into, out of, and around the country and complacently using their real names with little fear of capture.

To find sanctuary, terrorist organizations have fled to some of the least governed, most lawless places in the world. The intelligence community has prepared a world map that highlights possible terrorist havens, using no secret intelligence—just indicating areas that combine rugged terrain, weak governance, room to hide or receive supplies, and low population density with a town or city near enough to allow necessary interaction with the outside world. Large areas scattered around the world meet these criteria.[5]

In talking with American and foreign government officials and military officers on the front lines fighting terrorists today, we asked them: If you were a terrorist leader today, where would you locate your base? Some of the same places come up again and again on their lists:

- western Pakistan and the Pakistan-Afghanistan border region

- southern or western Afghanistan

- the Arabian Peninsula, especially Saudi Arabia and Yemen, and the nearby Horn of Africa, including Somalia and extending southwest into Kenya

- Southeast Asia, from Thailand to the southern Philippines to Indonesia

- West Africa, including Nigeria and Mali

- European cities with expatriate Muslim communities, especially cities in central and eastern Europe where security forces and border controls are less effective

In the twentieth century, strategists focused on the world's great industrial heartlands. In the twenty-first, the focus is in the opposite direction, toward remote regions and failing states. The United States has had to find ways to extend its reach, straining the limits of its influence.

Every policy decision we make needs to be seen through this lens. If, for example, Iraq becomes a failed state, it will go to the top of the list of places that are breeding grounds for attacks against Americans at home. Similarly, if we are paying insufficient attention to Afghanistan, the rule of the Taliban or warlords and narcotraffickers may reemerge and its countryside could once again offer refuge to al Qaeda, or its successor.

Recommendation: The U.S. government must identify and prioritize actual or potential terrorist sanctuaries. For each, it should have a realistic strategy to keep possible terrorists insecure and on the run, using all elements of national power. We should reach out, listen to, and work with other countries that can help.

We offer three illustrations that are particularly applicable today, in 2004: Pakistan, Afghanistan, and Saudi Arabia.

Pakistan

Pakistan's endemic poverty, widespread corruption, and often ineffective government create opportunities for Islamist recruitment. Poor education is a particular concern. Millions of families, especially those with little money, send their children to religious schools, or madrassahs. Many of these schools are the only opportunity available for an education, but some have been used as incubators for violent extremism. According to Karachi's police commander, there are 859 madrassahs teaching more than 200,000 youngsters in his city alone.[6]

It is hard to overstate the importance of Pakistan in the struggle against Islamist terrorism. Within Pakistan's borders are 150 million Muslims, scores of al Qaeda terrorists, many Taliban fighters, and—perhaps—Usama Bin Ladin. Pakistan possesses nuclear weapons and has come frighteningly close to war with nuclear-armed India over the disputed territory of Kashmir. A political battle among anti-American Islamic fundamentalists, the Pakistani military, and more moderate mainstream political forces has already spilled over into violence, and there have been repeated recent attempts to kill Pakistan's president, Pervez Musharraf.

In recent years, the United States has had three basic problems in its relationship with Pakistan:

- On terrorism, Pakistan helped nurture the Taliban. The Pakistani army and intelligence services, especially below the top ranks, have long been ambivalent about confronting Islamist extremists. Many in the government have sympathized with or provided support to the extremists. Musharraf agreed that Bin Ladin was bad. But before 9/11, preserving good relations with the Taliban took precedence.

- On proliferation, Musharraf has repeatedly said that Pakistan does not barter with its nuclear technology. But proliferation concerns have been long-standing and very serious. Most recently, the Pakistani government has claimed not to have known that one of its nuclear weapons developers, a national figure, was leading the most dangerous nuclear smuggling ring ever disclosed.

- Finally, Pakistan has made little progress toward the return of democratic rule at the national level, although that turbulent process does continue to function at the provincial level and the Pakistani press remains relatively free.

Immediately after 9/11, confronted by the United States with a stark choice, Pakistan made a strategic decision. Its government stood aside and allowed the U.S.-led coalition to destroy the Taliban regime. In other ways, Pakistan actively assisted: its authorities arrested more than 500 al Qaeda operatives and Taliban members, and Pakistani forces played a leading part in tracking down KSM, Abu Zubaydah, and other key al Qaeda figures.[7]

In the following two years, the Pakistani government tried to walk the fence, helping against al Qaeda while seeking to avoid a larger confrontation with Taliban remnants and other Islamic extremists. When al Qaeda and its Pakistani allies repeatedly tried to assassinate Musharraf, almost succeeding, the battle came home.

The country's vast unpoliced regions make Pakistan attractive to extremists seeking refuge and recruits and also provide a base for operations against coalition forces in Afghanistan. Almost all the 9/11 attackers traveled the north-south nexus of Kandahar–Quetta–Karachi. The Baluchistan region of Pakistan (KSM's ethnic home) and the sprawling city of Karachi remain centers of Islamist extremism where the U.S. and Pakistani security and intelligence presence has been weak. The U.S. consulate in Karachi is a makeshift fortress, reflecting the gravity of the surrounding threat.[8]

During the winter of 2003–2004, Musharraf made another strategic decision. He ordered the Pakistani army into the frontier provinces of northwest Pakistan along the Afghan border, where Bin Ladin and Ayman al Zawahiri have reportedly taken refuge. The army is confronting groups of al Qaeda fighters and their local allies in very difficult terrain. On the other side of the frontier, U.S. forces in Afghanistan have found it challenging to organize effective joint operations, given Pakistan's limited capabilities and reluctance to permit U.S. military operations on its soil. Yet in 2004, it is clear that the Pakistani government is trying harder than ever before in the battle against Islamist terrorists.[9]

Acknowledging these problems and Musharraf's own part in the story, we believe that Musharraf's government represents the best hope for stability in Pakistan and Afghanistan.

- In an extraordinary public essay asking how Muslims can "drag ourselves out of the pit we find ourselves in, to raise ourselves up," Musharraf has called for a strategy of "enlightened moderation." The Muslim world, he said, should shun militancy and extremism; the West—and the United States in particular—should seek to resolve disputes with justice and help better the Muslim world.[10]

- Having come close to war in 2002 and 2003, Pakistan and India have recently made significant progress in peacefully discussing their longstanding differences. The United States has been and should remain a key supporter of that process.

- The constant refrain of Pakistanis is that the United States long treated them as allies of convenience. As the United States makes fresh commitments now, it should make promises it is prepared to keep, for years to come.

Recommendation: If Musharraf stands for enlightened moderation in a fight for his life and for the life of his country, the United States should be willing to make hard choices too, and make the difficult long-term commitment to the future of Pakistan. Sustaining the current scale of aid to Pakistan, the United States should support Pakistan's government in its struggle against extremists with a comprehensive effort that extends from military aid to support for better education, so long as Pakistan's leaders remain willing to make difficult choices of their own.

Afghanistan

Afghanistan was the incubator for al Qaeda and for the 9/11 attacks. In the fall of 2001, the U.S.-led international coalition and its Afghan allies toppled the Taliban and ended the regime's protection of al Qaeda. Notable progress has been made. International cooperation has been strong, with a clear UN mandate and a NATO-led peacekeeping force (the International Security Assistance Force, or ISAF). More than 10,000 American soldiers are deployed today in Afghanistan, joined by soldiers from NATO allies and Muslim states. A central government has been established in Kabul, with a democratic constitution, new currency, and a new army. Most Afghans enjoy greater freedom, women and girls are emerging from subjugation, and 3 million children have returned to school. For the first time in many years, Afghans have reason to hope.[11]

But grave challenges remain. Taliban and al Qaeda fighters have regrouped in the south and southeast. Warlords control much of the country beyond Kabul, and the land is awash in weapons. Economic development remains a distant hope. The narcotics trade—long a massive sector of the Afghan economy—is again booming. Even the most hardened aid workers refuse to operate in many regions, and some warn that Afghanistan is near the brink of chaos.[12]

Battered Afghanistan has a chance. Elections are being prepared. It is revealing that in June 2004, Taliban fighters resorted to slaughtering 16 Afghans on a bus, apparently for no reason other than their boldness in carrying an unprecedented Afghan weapon: a voter registration card.

Afghanistan's president, Hamid Karzai, is brave and committed. He is trying to build genuinely national institutions that can overcome the tradition of allocating powers among ethnic communities. Yet even if his efforts are successful and elections bring a democratic government to Afghanistan, the United States faces some difficult choices.

After paying relatively little attention to rebuilding Afghanistan during the military campaign, U.S. policies changed noticeably during 2003. Greater consideration of the political dimension and congressional support for a substantial package of assistance signaled a longer-term commitment to Afghanistan's future. One Afghan regional official plaintively told us the country finally has a good government. He begged the United States to keep its promise and not abandon Afghanistan again, as it had in the 1990s. Another Afghan leader noted that if the United States leaves, "we will lose all that we have gained."[13]

Most difficult is to define the security mission in Afghanistan. There is continuing political controversy about whether military operations in Iraq have had any effect on the scale of America's commitment to the future of Afghanistan. The United States has largely stayed out of the central government's struggles with dissident warlords and it has largely avoided confronting the related problem of narcotrafficking.[14]

Recommendation: The President and the Congress deserve praise for their efforts in Afghanistan so far. Now the United States and the international community should make a long-term commitment to a secure and stable Afghanistan, in order to give the government a reasonable opportunity to improve the life of the Afghan people. Afghanistan must not again become a sanctuary for international crime and terrorism. The United States and the international community should help the Afghan government extend its authority over the country, with a strategy and nation-by-nation commitments to achieve their objectives.

- This is an ambitious recommendation. It would mean a redoubled effort to secure the country, disarm militias, and curtail the age of warlord rule. But the United States and NATO have already committed themselves to the future of this region—wisely, as the 9/11 story shows—and failed half-measures could be worse than useless.

- NATO in particular has made Afghanistan a test of the Alliance's ability to adapt to current security challenges of the future. NATO must pass this test. Currently, the United States and the international community envision enough support so that the central government can build a truly national army and extend essential infrastructure and minimum public services to major towns and regions. The effort relies in part on foreign civil-military teams, arranged under various national flags. The institutional commitments of NATO and the United Nations to these enterprises are weak. NATO member states are not following through; some of the other states around the world that have pledged assistance to Afghanistan are not fulfilling their pledges.

- The U.S. presence in Afghanistan is overwhelmingly oriented toward military and security work. The State Department presence is woefully understaffed, and the military mission is narrowly focused on al Qaeda and Taliban remnants in the south and southeast. The U.S. government can do its part if the international community decides on a joint effort to restore the rule of law and contain rampant crime and narcotics trafficking in this crossroads of Central Asia.[15]

We heard again and again that the money for assistance is allocated so rigidly that, on the ground, one U.S. agency often cannot improvise or pitch in to help another agency, even in small ways when a few thousand dollars could make a great difference.

The U.S. government should allocate money so that lower-level officials have more flexibility to get the job done across agency lines, adjusting to the circumstances they find in the field. This should include discretionary funds for expenditures by military units that often encounter opportunities to help the local population.

Saudi Arabia

Saudi Arabia has been a problematic ally in combating Islamic extremism. At the level of high policy, Saudi Arabia's leaders cooperated with American diplomatic initiatives aimed at the Taliban or Pakistan before 9/11. At the same time, Saudi Arabia's society was a place where al Qaeda raised money directly from individuals and through charities. It was the society that produced 15 of the 19 hijackers.

The Kingdom is one of the world's most religiously conservative societies, and its identity is closely bound to its religious links, especially its position as the guardian of Islam's two holiest sites. Charitable giving, or *zakat*, is one of the five pillars of Islam. It is broader and more pervasive than Western ideas of charity—functioning also as a form of income tax, educational assistance, foreign aid, and a source of political influence. The Western notion of the separation of civic and religious duty does not exist in Islamic cultures. Funding charitable works is an integral function of the governments in the Islamic world. It is so ingrained in Islamic culture that in Saudi Arabia, for example, a department within the Saudi Ministry of Finance and National Economy collects zakat directly, much as the U.S. Internal Revenue Service collects payroll withholding tax. Closely tied to zakat is the dedication of the government to propagating the Islamic faith, particularly the Wahhabi sect that flourishes in Saudi Arabia.

Traditionally, throughout the Muslim world, there is no formal oversight mechanism for donations. As Saudi wealth increased, the amounts contributed by individuals and the state grew dramatically. Substantial sums went to finance Islamic charities of every kind.

While Saudi domestic charities are regulated by the Ministry of Labor and Social Welfare, charities and international relief agencies, such as the World Assembly of Muslim Youth (WAMY), are currently regulated by the Ministry of Islamic Affairs. This ministry uses zakat and government funds to spread Wahhabi beliefs throughout the world, including in mosques and schools. Often these schools provide the only education available; even in affluent countries, Saudi-funded Wahhabi schools are often the only Islamic schools. Some Wahhabi-funded organizations have been exploited by extremists to further their goal of violent jihad against non-Muslims. One such organization has been the al Haramain Islamic Foundation; the as-

sets of some branch offices have been frozen by the U.S. and Saudi governments.

Until 9/11, few Saudis would have considered government oversight of charitable donations necessary; many would have perceived it as interference in the exercise of their faith. At the same time, the government's ability to finance most state expenditures with energy revenues has delayed the need for a modern income tax system. As a result, there have been strong religious, cultural, and administrative barriers to monitoring charitable spending. That appears to be changing, however, now that the goal of violent jihad also extends to overthrowing Sunni governments (such as the House of Saud) that are not living up to the ideals of the Islamist extremists.[16]

The leaders of the United States and the rulers of Saudi Arabia have long had friendly relations, rooted in fundamentally common interests against the Soviet Union during the Cold War, in American hopes that Saudi oil supplies would stabilize the supply and price of oil in world markets, and in Saudi hopes that America could help protect the Kingdom against foreign threats.

In 1990, the Kingdom hosted U.S. armed forces before the first U.S.-led war against Iraq. American soldiers and airmen have given their lives to help protect Saudi Arabia. The Saudi government has difficulty acknowledging this. American military bases remained there until 2003, as part of an international commitment to contain Iraq.

For many years, leaders on both sides preferred to keep their ties quiet and behind the scenes. As a result, neither the U.S. nor the Saudi people appreciated all the dimensions of the bilateral relationship, including the Saudi role in U.S. strategies to promote the Middle East peace process. In each country, political figures find it difficult to publicly defend good relations with the other.

Today, mutual recriminations flow. Many Americans see Saudi Arabia as an enemy, not as an embattled ally. They perceive an autocratic government that oppresses women, dominated by a wealthy and indolent elite. Saudi contacts with American politicians are frequently invoked as accusations in partisan political arguments. Americans are often appalled by the intolerance, anti-Semitism, and anti-American arguments taught in schools and preached in mosques.

Saudis are angry too. Many educated Saudis who were sympathetic to America now perceive the United States as an unfriendly state. One Saudi reformer noted to us that the demonization of Saudi Arabia in the U.S. media gives ammunition to radicals, who accuse reformers of being U.S. lackeys. Tens of thousands of Saudis who once regularly traveled to (and often had homes in) the United States now go elsewhere.[17]

Among Saudis, the United States is seen as aligned with Israel in its conflict with the Palestinians, with whom Saudis ardently sympathize. Although Saudi Arabia's cooperation against terrorism improved to some extent after the September 11 attacks, significant problems remained. Many in the Kingdom initially reacted with disbelief and denial. In the following months, as the truth became clear, some leading Saudis quietly acknowledged the problem but still did not see their own regime as threatened, and thus often did not respond promptly to U.S. requests for help. Though Saddam Hussein was widely detested, many Saudis are sympathetic to the anti-U.S. insurgents in Iraq, although majorities also condemn jihadist attacks in the Kingdom.[18]

As in Pakistan, Yemen, and other countries, attitudes changed when the terrorism came home. Cooperation had already become significant, but after the bombings in Riyadh on May 12, 2003, it improved much more. The Kingdom openly discussed the problem of radicalism, criticized the terrorists as religiously deviant, reduced official support for religious activity overseas, closed suspect charitable foundations, and publicized arrests—very public moves for a government that has preferred to keep internal problems quiet.

The Kingdom of Saudi Arabia is now locked in mortal combat with al Qaeda. Saudi police are regularly being killed in shootouts with terrorists. In June 2004, the Saudi ambassador to the United States called publicly—in the Saudi press—for his government to wage a jihad of its own against the terrorists. "We must all, as a state and as a people, recognize the truth about these criminals," he declared, "[i]f we do not declare a general mobilization—we will lose this war on terrorism."[19]

Saudi Arabia is a troubled country. Although regarded as very wealthy, in fact per capita income has dropped from $28,000 at its height to the present level of about $8,000. Social and religious traditions complicate adjustment to modern economic activity and limit employment opportunities for young Saudis. Women find their education and employment sharply limited.

President Clinton offered us a perceptive analysis of Saudi Arabia, contending that fundamentally friendly rulers have been constrained by their desire to preserve the status quo. He, like others, made the case for pragmatic reform instead. He hopes the rulers will envision what they want their Kingdom to become in 10 or 20 years, and start a process in which their friends can help them change.[20]

There are signs that Saudi Arabia's royal family is trying to build a consensus for political reform, though uncertain about how fast and how far to go. Crown Prince Abdullah wants the Kingdom to join the World Trade Organization to accelerate economic liberalization. He has embraced the *Arab Human Development Report,* which was highly critical of the Arab world's political, economic, and social failings and called for greater economic and political reform.[21]

Cooperation with Saudi Arabia against Islamist terrorism is very much in the U.S. interest. Such cooperation can exist for a time largely in secret, as it does now, but it cannot grow and thrive there. Nor, on either side, can friendship be unconditional.

Recommendation: The problems in the U.S.-Saudi relationship must be confronted, openly. The United States and Saudi Arabia must determine if they can build a relationship that political leaders on both sides are prepared to publicly defend—a relationship about more than oil. It should include a shared commitment to political and economic reform, as Saudis make common cause with the outside world. It should include a shared interest in greater tolerance and cultural respect, translating into a commitment to fight the violent extremists who foment hatred.

Prevent the Continued Growth of Islamist Terrorism

In October 2003, reflecting on progress after two years of waging the global war on terrorism, Defense Secretary Donald Rumsfeld asked his advisers: "Are we capturing, killing or deterring and dissuading more terrorists every day than the madrassas and the radical clerics are recruiting, training and deploying against us? Does the US need to fashion a broad, integrated plan to stop the next generation of terrorists? The US is putting relatively little effort into a long-range plan, but we are putting a great deal of effort into trying to stop terrorists. The cost-benefit ratio is against us! Our cost is billions against the terrorists' costs of millions."[22]

These are the right questions. Our answer is that we need short-term action on a long-range strategy, one that invigorates our foreign policy with the attention that the President and Congress have given to the military and intelligence parts of the conflict against Islamist terrorism.

Engage the Struggle of Ideas

The United States is heavily engaged in the Muslim world and will be for many years to come. This American engagement is resented. Polls in 2002 found that among America's friends, like Egypt—the recipient of more U.S. aid for the past 20 years than any other Muslim country—only 15 percent of the population had a favorable opinion of the United States. In Saudi Arabia the number was 12 percent. And two-thirds of those surveyed in 2003 in countries from Indonesia to Turkey (a NATO ally) were very or somewhat fearful that the United States may attack them.[23]

Support for the United States has plummeted. Polls taken in Islamic countries after 9/11 suggested that many or most people thought the United States was doing the right thing in its fight against terrorism; few people saw popular support for al Qaeda; half of those surveyed said that ordinary people had a favorable view of the United States. By 2003, polls showed that "the bottom has fallen out of support for America in most of the Muslim world. Negative views of the U.S. among Muslims, which had been largely limited to countries in the Middle East, have spread. . . . Since last summer, favorable ratings for the U.S. have fallen from 61% to 15% in Indonesia and from 71% to 38% among Muslims in Nigeria."[24]

Many of these views are at best uninformed about the United States and, at worst, informed by cartoonish stereotypes, the coarse expression of a fashionable "Occidentalism" among intellectuals who caricature U.S. values and policies. Local newspapers and the few influential satellite broadcasters—like al Jazeera—often reinforce the jihadist theme that portrays the United States as anti-Muslim.[25]

The small percentage of Muslims who are fully committed to Usama Bin Ladin's version of Islam are impervious to persuasion. It is among the large majority of Arabs and Muslims that we must encourage reform, freedom, democracy, and opportunity, even though our own promotion of these messages is limited in its effectiveness simply because we are its carriers. Muslims themselves will have to reflect upon such basic issues as the concept of jihad, the position of women, and the place of non-Muslim minorities. The United States can promote moderation, but cannot ensure its ascendancy. Only Muslims can do this.

The setting is difficult. The combined gross domestic product of the 22 countries in the Arab League is less than the GDP of Spain. Forty percent of adult Arabs are illiterate, two-thirds of them women. One-third of the broader Middle East lives on less than two dollars a day. Less than 2 percent of the population has access to the Internet. The majority of older Arab youths have expressed a desire to emigrate to other countries, particularly those in Europe.[26]

In short, the United States has to help defeat an ideology, not just a group of people, and we must do so under difficult circumstances. How can the United States and its friends help moderate Muslims combat the extremist ideas?

Recommendation: The U.S. government must define what the message is, what it stands for. We should offer an example of moral leadership in the world, committed to treat people humanely, abide by the rule of law, and be generous and caring to our neighbors. America and Muslim friends can agree on respect for human dignity and opportunity. To Muslim parents, terrorists like Bin Ladin have nothing to offer their children but visions of violence and death. America and its friends have a crucial advantage—we can offer these parents a vision that might give their children a better future. If we heed the views of thoughtful leaders in the Arab and Muslim world, a moderate consensus can be found.

That vision of the future should stress life over death: individual educational and economic opportunity. This vision includes widespread political participation and contempt for indiscriminate violence. It includes respect for the rule of law, openness in discussing differences, and tolerance for opposing points of view.

Recommendation: Where Muslim governments, even those who are friends, do not respect these principles, the United States must stand for a better future. One of the lessons of the long Cold War was that short-term gains in cooperating with the most repressive and brutal governments were too often outweighed by long-term setbacks for America's stature and interests.

American foreign policy is part of the message. America's policy choices have consequences. Right or wrong, it is simply a fact that American policy regarding the Israeli-Palestinian conflict and American actions in Iraq are dominant staples of popular commentary across the Arab and Muslim world. That does not mean U.S. choices have been wrong. It means those choices must be integrated with America's message of opportunity to the Arab and Muslim world. Neither Israel nor the new Iraq will be safer if worldwide Islamist terrorism grows stronger.

The United States must do more to communicate its message. Reflecting on Bin Ladin's success in reaching Muslim audiences, Richard Holbrooke wondered, "How can a man in a cave outcommunicate the world's leading communications society?" Deputy Secretary of State Richard Armitage worried to us that Americans have been "exporting our fears and our anger," not our vision of opportunity and hope.[27]

Recommendation: Just as we did in the Cold War, we need to defend our ideals abroad

vigorously. America does stand up for its values. The United States defended, and still defends, Muslims against tyrants and criminals in Somalia, Bosnia, Kosovo, Afghanistan, and Iraq. If the United States does not act aggressively to define itself in the Islamic world, the extremists will gladly do the job for us.

- **Recognizing that Arab and Muslim audiences rely on satellite television and radio, the government has begun some promising initiatives in television and radio broadcasting to the Arab world, Iran, and Afghanistan. These efforts are beginning to reach large audiences. The Broadcasting Board of Governors has asked for much larger resources. It should get them.**

- **The United States should rebuild the scholarship, exchange, and library programs that reach out to young people and offer them knowledge and hope. Where such assistance is provided, it should be identified as coming from the citizens of the United States.**

An Agenda of Opportunity

The United States and its friends can stress educational and economic opportunity. The United Nations has rightly equated "literacy as freedom."

- The international community is moving toward setting a concrete goal—to cut the Middle East region's illiteracy rate in half by 2010, targeting women and girls and supporting programs for adult literacy.

- Unglamorous help is needed to support the basics, such as textbooks that translate more of the world's knowledge into local languages and libraries to house such materials. Education about the outside world, or other cultures, is weak.

- More vocational education is needed, too, in trades and business skills. The Middle East can also benefit from some of the programs to bridge the digital divide and increase Internet access that have already been developed for other regions of the world.

Education that teaches tolerance, the dignity and value of each individual, and respect for different beliefs is a key element in any global strategy to eliminate Islamist terrorism.

Recommendation: The U.S. government should offer to join with other nations in generously supporting a new International Youth Opportunity Fund. Funds will be spent directly for building and operating primary and secondary

schools in those Muslim states that commit to sensibly investing their own money in public education.

Economic openness is essential. Terrorism is not caused by poverty. Indeed, many terrorists come from relatively well-off families. Yet when people lose hope, when societies break down, when countries fragment, the breeding grounds for terrorism are created. Backward economic policies and repressive political regimes slip into societies that are without hope, where ambition and passions have no constructive outlet.

The policies that support economic development and reform also have political implications. Economic and political liberties tend to be linked. Commerce, especially international commerce, requires ongoing cooperation and compromise, the exchange of ideas across cultures, and the peaceful resolution of differences through negotiation or the rule of law. Economic growth expands the middle class, a constituency for further reform. Successful economies rely on vibrant private sectors, which have an interest in curbing indiscriminate government power. Those who develop the practice of controlling their own economic destiny soon desire a voice in their communities and political societies.

The U.S. government has announced the goal of working toward a Middle East Free Trade Area, or MEFTA, by 2013. The United States has been seeking comprehensive free trade agreements (FTAs) with the Middle Eastern nations most firmly on the path to reform. The U.S.-Israeli FTA was enacted in 1985, and Congress implemented an FTA with Jordan in 2001. Both agreements have expanded trade and investment, thereby supporting domestic economic reform. In 2004, new FTAs were signed with Morocco and Bahrain, and are awaiting congressional approval. These models are drawing the interest of their neighbors. Muslim countries can become full participants in the rules-based global trading system, as the United States considers lowering its trade barriers with the poorest Arab nations.

Recommendation: A comprehensive U.S. strategy to counter terrorism should include economic policies that encourage development, more open societies, and opportunities for people to improve the lives of their families and to enhance prospects for their children's future.

Turning a National Strategy Into a Coalition Strategy

Practically every aspect of U.S. counterterrorism strategy relies on international cooperation. Since 9/11, these contacts concerning military, law enforcement, intelligence, travel and customs, and financial matters have expanded so dramatically, and often in an ad hoc way, that it is difficult to track these efforts, much less integrate them.

Recommendation: The United States should engage other nations in developing a comprehensive coalition strategy against Islamist terrorism. There are several multilateral institutions in which such issues should be addressed. But the most important policies should be discussed and coordinated in a flexible contact group of leading coalition governments. This is a good place, for example, to develop joint strategies for targeting terrorist travel, or for hammering out a common strategy for the places where terrorists may be finding sanctuary.

Presently the Muslim and Arab states meet with each other, in organizations such as the Islamic Conference and the Arab League. The Western states meet with each other in organizations such as NATO and the Group of Eight summit of leading industrial nations. A recent G-8 summit initiative to begin a dialogue about reform may be a start toward finding a place where leading Muslim states can discuss—and be seen to discuss—critical policy issues with the leading Western powers committed to the future of the Arab and Muslim world.

These new international efforts can create durable habits of visible cooperation, as states willing to step up to their responsibilities join together in constructive efforts to direct assistance and coordinate action.

Coalition warfare also requires coalition policies on what to do with enemy captives. Allegations that the United States abused prisoners in its custody make it harder to build the diplomatic, political, and military alliances the government will need. The United States should work with friends to develop mutually agreed-on principles for the detention and humane treatment of captured international terrorists who are not being held under a particular country's criminal laws. Countries such as Britain, Australia, and Muslim friends, are committed to fighting terrorists. America should be able to reconcile its views on how to balance humanity and security with our nation's commitment to these same goals.

The United States and some of its allies do not accept the application of full Geneva Convention treatment of prisoners of war to captured terrorists. Those Conventions establish a minimum set of standards for prisoners in internal conflicts. Since the international struggle against Islamist terrorism is not internal, those provisions do not formally apply, but they are commonly accepted as basic standards for humane treatment.

Recommendation: The United States should engage its friends to develop a common coalition approach toward the detention and humane treatment of captured terrorists. New principles might draw upon Article 3 of the Geneva Conventions on the law of armed conflict. That article was specifically designed for those cases in which the usual laws of war did not apply. Its minimum standards are generally accepted throughout the world as customary international law.

Proliferation of Weapons of Mass Destruction

The greatest danger of another catastrophic attack in the United States will materialize if the world's most dangerous terrorists acquire the world's most dangerous weapons. . . . [A]l Qaeda has tried to acquire or make nuclear weapons for at least ten years. . . . [O]fficials worriedly discuss[ed], in 1998, reports that Bin Ladin's associates thought their leader was intent on carrying out a "Hiroshima."

These ambitions continue. In the public portion of his February 2004 worldwide threat assessment to Congress, DCI Tenet noted that Bin Ladin considered the acquisition of weapons of mass destruction to be a "religious obligation." He warned that al Qaeda "continues to pursue its strategic goal of obtaining a nuclear capability." Tenet added that "more than two dozen other terrorist groups are pursuing CBRN [chemical, biological, radiological, and nuclear] materials."[28]

A nuclear bomb can be built with a relatively small amount of nuclear material. A trained nuclear engineer with an amount of highly enriched uranium or plutonium about the size of a grapefruit or an orange, together with commercially available material, could fashion a nuclear device that would fit in a van like the one Ramzi Yousef parked in the garage of the World Trade Center in 1993. Such a bomb would level Lower Manhattan.[29]

The coalition strategies we have discussed to combat Islamist terrorism should therefore be combined with a parallel, vital effort to prevent and counter the proliferation of weapons of mass destruction (WMD). We recommend several initiatives in this area.

Strengthen Counterproliferation Efforts. While efforts to shut down Libya's illegal nuclear program have been generally successful, Pakistan's illicit trade and the nuclear smuggling networks of Pakistani scientist A. Q. Khan have revealed that the spread of nuclear weapons is a problem of global dimensions. Attempts to deal with Iran's nuclear program are still underway. Therefore, the United States should work with the international community to develop laws and an international legal regime with universal jurisdiction to enable the capture, interdiction, and prosecution of such smugglers by any state in the world where they do not disclose their activities.

Expand the Proliferation Security Initiative. In May 2003, the Bush administration announced the Proliferation Security Initiative (PSI): nations in a willing partnership combining their national capabilities to use military, economic, and diplomatic tools to interdict threatening shipments of WMD and missile-related technology.

The PSI can be more effective if it uses intelligence and planning resources of the NATO alliance. Moreover, PSI membership should be open to non-NATO countries. Russia and China should be encouraged to participate.

Support the Cooperative Threat Reduction Program. Outside experts are deeply worried about the U.S. government's commitment and approach to securing the weapons and highly dangerous materials still scattered in Russia and other countries of the Soviet Union. The government's main instrument in this area, the Cooperative Threat Reduction Program (usually referred to as "Nunn-Lugar," after the senators who sponsored the legislation in 1991), is now in need of expansion, improvement, and resources. The U.S. government has recently redoubled its international commitments to support this program, and we recommend that the United States do all it can, if Russia and other countries will do their part. The government should weigh the value of this investment against the catastrophic cost America would face should such weapons find their way to the terrorists who are so anxious to acquire them.

Recommendation: Our report shows that al Qaeda has tried to acquire or make weapons of mass destruction for at least ten years. There is no doubt the United States would be a prime target. Preventing the proliferation of these weapons warrants a maximum effort—by strengthening counterproliferation efforts, expanding the Proliferation Security Initiative, and supporting the Cooperative Threat Reduction program.

Targeting Terrorist Money

The general public sees attacks on terrorist finance as a way to "starve the terrorists of money." So, initially, did the U.S. government. After 9/11, the United States took aggressive actions to designate terrorist financiers and freeze their money, in the United States and through resolutions of the United Nations. These actions appeared to have little effect and, when confronted by legal challenges, the United States and the United Nations were often forced to unfreeze assets.

The difficulty, understood later, was that even if the intelligence community might "link" someone to a terrorist group through acquaintances or communications, the task of tracing the money from that individual to the terrorist group, or otherwise showing complicity, was far more difficult. It was harder still to do so without disclosing secrets.

These early missteps made other countries unwilling to freeze assets or otherwise act merely on the basis of a U.S. action. Multilateral freezing mechanisms now require waiting periods before being put into effect, eliminating the element of surprise and thus virtually ensuring that little money is actually frozen. Worldwide asset freezes have not been adequately enforced and have been easily circumvented, often within weeks, by simple methods.

But trying to starve the terrorists of money is like trying to catch one kind of fish by draining the ocean. A better strategy has evolved since those early months, as the government learned more about how al Qaeda raises, moves, and spends money.

Recommendation: Vigorous efforts to track terrorist financing must remain front and center in U.S. counterterrorism efforts. The government has recognized that information about terrorist money helps us to understand their networks, search them out, and disrupt their operations. Intelligence and law enforcement have targeted the relatively small number of financial facilitators—individuals al Qaeda relied on for their ability to raise and deliver money—at the core of al Qaeda's revenue stream. These efforts have worked. The death or capture of several important facilitators has decreased the amount of money available to al Qaeda and has increased its costs and difficulty in raising and moving that money. Captures have additionally provided a windfall of intelligence that can be used to continue the cycle of disruption.

The U.S. financial community and some international financial institutions have generally provided law enforcement and intelligence agencies with extraordinary cooperation, particularly in supplying information to support quickly developing investigations. Obvious vulnerabilities in the U.S. financial system have been corrected. The United States has been less successful in persuading other countries to adopt financial regulations that would permit the tracing of financial transactions.

Public designation of terrorist financiers and organizations is still part of the fight, but it is not the primary weapon. Designations are instead a form of diplomacy, as governments join together to identify named individuals and groups as terrorists. They also prevent open fundraising. Some charities that have been identified as likely avenues for terrorist financing have seen their donations diminish and their activities come under more scrutiny, and others have been put out of business, although controlling overseas branches of Gulf-area charities remains a challenge. The Saudi crackdown after the May 2003 terrorist attacks in Riyadh has apparently reduced the funds available to al Qaeda—perhaps drastically—but it is too soon to know if this reduction will last.

Though progress apparently has been made, terrorists have shown considerable creativity in their methods of moving money. If al Qaeda is replaced by smaller, decentralized terrorist groups, the premise behind the government's efforts—that terrorists need a financial support network—may become outdated. Moreover, some terrorist operations do not rely on outside sources of money and may now be self-funding, either through legitimate employment or low-level criminal activity.[30]

Protect Against and Prepare for Terrorist Attacks

In the nearly three years since 9/11, Americans have become better protected against terrorist attack. Some of the changes are due to government action, such as new precautions to protect aircraft. A portion can be attributed to the sheer scale of spending and effort. Publicity and the vigilance of ordinary Americans also make a difference.

But the President and other officials acknowledge that although Americans may be safer, they are not safe. Our report shows that the terrorists analyze defenses. They plan accordingly.

Defenses cannot achieve perfect safety. They make targets harder to attack successfully, and they deter attacks by making capture more likely. Just increasing the attacker's odds of failure may make the difference between a plan attempted, or a plan discarded. The enemy also may have to develop more elaborate plans, thereby increasing the danger of exposure or defeat.

Protective measures also prepare for the attacks that may get through, containing the damage and saving lives.

Terrorist Travel

More than 500 million people annually cross U.S. borders at legal entry points, about 330 million of them noncitizens. Another 500,000 or more enter illegally without inspection across America's thousands of miles of land borders or remain in the country past the expiration of their permitted stay. The challenge for national security in an age of terrorism is to prevent the very few people who may pose overwhelming risks from entering or remaining in the United States undetected.[31]

In the decade before September 11, 2001, border security—encompassing travel, entry, and immigration—was not seen as a national security matter. Public figures voiced concern about the "war on drugs," the right level and kind of immigration, problems along the southwest border, migration crises originating in the Caribbean and elsewhere, or the growing criminal traffic in humans. The immigration system as a whole was widely viewed as increasingly dysfunctional and badly in need of reform. In national security circles, however, only smuggling of weapons of mass destruction carried weight, not the entry of terrorists who might use such weapons or the presence of associated foreign-born terrorists.

For terrorists, travel documents are as important as weapons. Terrorists must travel clandestinely to meet, train, plan, case targets, and gain access to attack. To them, international travel presents great danger, because they must surface to pass through regulated channels, present themselves to border security officials, or attempt to circumvent inspection points.

In their travels, terrorists use evasive methods, such as altered and counterfeit passports and visas, specific travel methods and routes, liaisons with corrupt government officials, human smuggling networks, supportive travel agencies, and immigration and identity fraud. These can sometimes be detected.

Before 9/11, no agency of the U.S. government systematically analyzed terrorists' travel strategies. Had they done so, they could have discovered the ways in which the terrorist predecessors to al Qaeda had been systematically but detectably exploiting weaknesses in our border security since the early 1990s.

We found that as many as 15 of the 19 hijackers were potentially vulnerable to interception by border authorities. Analyzing their characteristic travel documents and travel patterns could have allowed authorities to intercept 4 to 15 hijackers and more effective use of information available in U.S. government databases could have identified up to 3 hijackers.[32]

Looking back, we can also see that the routine operations of our immigration laws—that is, aspects of those laws not specifically aimed at protecting against terrorism—inevitably shaped al Qaeda's planning and opportunities. Because they were deemed not to be bona fide tourists or students as they claimed, five conspirators that we know of tried to get visas and failed, and one was denied entry by an inspector. We also found that had the immigration system set a higher bar for determining whether individuals are who or what they claim to be—and ensuring routine consequences for violations—it could potentially have excluded, removed, or come into further contact with several hijackers who did not appear to meet the terms for admitting short-term visitors.[33]

Our investigation showed that two systemic weaknesses came together in our border system's inability to contribute to an effective defense against the 9/11 attacks: a lack of well-developed counterterrorism measures as a part of border security and an immigration system not able to deliver on its basic commitments, much less support counterterrorism. These weaknesses have been reduced but are far from being overcome.

Recommendation: Targeting travel is at least as powerful a weapon against terrorists as targeting their money. The United States should combine terrorist travel intelligence, operations, and law enforcement in a strategy to intercept terrorists, find terrorist travel facilitators, and constrain terrorist mobility.

Since 9/11, significant improvements have been made to create an integrated watchlist that makes terrorist name information available to border and law enforcement authorities. However, in the already difficult process of merging border agencies in the new Department of Homeland Security—"changing the engine while flying" as one official put it[34]—new insights into terrorist travel have not yet been integrated into the front lines of border security.

The small terrorist travel intelligence collection and analysis program currently in place has produced disproportionately useful results. It should be expanded. Since officials at the borders encounter travelers and their documents first and investigate travel facilitators, they must work closely with intelligence officials.

Internationally and in the United States, constraining terrorist travel should become a vital part of counterterrorism strategy. Better technology and training to detect terrorist travel documents are the most important immediate steps to reduce America's vulnerability to clandestine entry. Every stage of our border and immigration system should have as a part of its operations the detection of terrorist indicators on travel documents. Information systems able to authenticate travel documents and detect potential terrorist indicators should be used at consulates, at primary border inspection lines, in immigration services offices, and in intelligence and enforcement units. All frontline personnel should receive some training. Dedicated specialists and ongoing linkages with the intelligence community are also required. The Homeland Security Department's Directorate of Information Analysis and Infrastructure Protection should receive more resources to accomplish its mission as the bridge between the frontline border agencies and the rest of the government counterterrorism community.

A Biometric Screening System

When people travel internationally, they usually move through defined channels, or portals. They may seek to acquire a passport. They may apply for a visa. They stop at ticket counters, gates, and exit controls at airports and seaports. Upon arrival, they pass through inspection points. They may transit to another gate to get on an airplane. Once inside the country, they may seek another form of identification and try to enter a government or private facility. They may seek to change immigration status in order to remain.

Each of these checkpoints or portals is a screening—a chance to establish that people are who they say they are and are seeking access for their stated purpose, to intercept identifiable suspects, and to take effective action.

The job of protection is shared among these many defined checkpoints. By taking advantage of them all, we need not depend on any one point in the system to do the whole job. The challenge is to see the common problem across agencies and functions and develop a conceptual framework—an architecture—for an effective screening system.[35]

Throughout government, and indeed in private enterprise, agencies and firms at these portals confront recurring judgments that balance security, efficiency, and civil liberties. These problems should be addressed systemically, not in an ad hoc, fragmented way. For example:

What information is an individual required to present and in what form? A fundamental problem, now beginning to be addressed, is the lack of standardized information in "feeder" documents used in identifying individuals. Biometric identifiers that measure unique physical characteristics, such as facial features, fingerprints, or iris scans, and reduce them to digitized, numerical statements called algorithms, are just beginning to be used. Travel history, however, is still recorded in passports with entry-exit stamps called cachets, which al Qaeda has trained its operatives to forge and use to conceal their terrorist activities.

How will the individual and the information be checked? There are many databases just in the United States—for terrorist, criminal, and immigration history, as well as financial information, for instance. Each is set up for different purposes and stores different kinds of data, under varying rules of access. Nor is access always guaranteed. Acquiring information held by foreign governments may require painstaking negotiations, and records that are not yet digitized are difficult to search or analyze. The development of terrorist indicators has hardly begun, and behavioral cues remain important.

Who will screen individuals, and what will they be trained to do? A wide range of border, immigration, and law enforcement officials encounter visitors and immigrants and they are given little training in terrorist travel intelligence. Fraudulent travel documents, for instance, are usually returned to travelers who are denied entry without further examination for terrorist trademarks, investigation as to their source, or legal process.

What are the consequences of finding a suspicious indicator, and who will take action? One risk is that responses may be ineffective or produce no further information. Four of the 9/11 attackers were pulled into secondary border inspection, but then admitted. More than half of the 19 hijackers were flagged by the Federal Aviation Administration's profiling system when they arrived for their flights, but the consequence was that bags, not people, were checked. Competing risks include "false positives," or the danger that rules may be applied with insufficient training or judgment. Overreactions can impose high costs too—on individuals, our economy, and our beliefs about justice.

- A special note on the importance of trusting subjective judgment: One potential hijacker was turned back by an immigration inspector as he tried to enter the United States. The inspector relied on intuitive experience to ask questions more than he relied on any objective factor that could be detected by "scores" or a machine. Good people who have worked in such jobs for a long time understand this phenomenon well. Other evidence we obtained confirmed the importance of letting experienced gate agents or security screeners ask questions and use their judgment. This is not an invitation to arbitrary exclusions. But any effective system has to grant some scope, perhaps in a little extra inspection or one more check, to the instincts and discretion of well trained human beings.

Recommendation: The U.S. border security system should be integrated into a larger network of screening points that includes our transportation system and access to vital facilities, such as nuclear reactors. The President should direct the Department of Homeland Security to lead the effort to design a comprehensive screening system, addressing common problems and setting common standards with systemwide goals in mind. Extending those standards among other governments could dramatically strengthen America and the world's collective ability to intercept individuals who pose catastrophic threats.

We advocate a system for screening, not categorical profiling. A screening system looks for particular, identifiable suspects or indicators of risk. It does not involve guesswork about who might be dangerous. It requires frontline border officials who have the tools and resources to establish that people are who they say they are, intercept identifiable suspects, and disrupt terrorist operations.

The U.S. Border Screening System

The border and immigration system of the United States must remain a visible manifestation of our belief in freedom, democracy, global economic growth, and the rule of law, yet serve equally well as a vital element of counterterrorism. Integrating terrorist travel information in the ways we have described is the most immediate need. But the underlying system must also be sound.

Since September 11, the United States has built the first phase of a biometric screening program, called US VISIT (the United States Visitor and Immigrant Status Indicator Technology program). It takes two biometric identifiers—digital photographs and prints of two index fingers—from travelers. False identities are used by terrorists to avoid being detected on a watchlist. These biometric identifiers make such evasions far more difficult.

So far, however, only visitors who acquire visas to travel to the United States are covered. While visitors from "visa waiver" countries will be added to the program, beginning this year, covered travelers will still constitute only about 12 percent of all noncitizens crossing U.S. borders. Moreover, exit data are not uniformly collected and entry data are not fully automated. It is not clear the system can be installed before 2010, but even this timetable may be too slow, given the possible security dangers.[36]

- Americans should not be exempt from carrying biometric passports or otherwise enabling their identities to be securely verified when they enter the United States; nor should Canadians or Mexicans. Currently U.S. persons are exempt from carrying passports when returning from Canada, Mexico, and the Caribbean. The current system enables non-U.S. citizens to gain entry by showing minimal identification. The 9/11 experience shows that terrorists study and exploit America's vulnerabilities.

- To balance this measure, programs to speed known travelers should be a higher priority, permitting inspectors to focus on greater risks. The daily commuter should not be subject to the same measures as first-time travelers. An individual should be able to preenroll, with his or her identity verified in passage. Updates of database information and other checks can ensure ongoing reliability. The solution, requiring more research and development, is likely to combine radio frequency technology with biometric identifiers.[37]

- The current patchwork of border screening systems, including several frequent traveler programs, should be consolidated with the US VISIT system to enable the development of an integrated system, which in turn can become part of the wider screening plan we suggest.

- The program allowing individuals to travel from foreign countries through the United States to a third country, without having to obtain a U.S. visa, has been suspended. Because "transit without visa" can be exploited by terrorists to enter the United States, the program should not be reinstated unless and until transit passage areas can be fully secured to prevent passengers from illegally exiting the airport.

Inspectors adjudicating entries of the 9/11 hijackers lacked adequate information and knowledge of the rules. All points in the border system—from consular offices to immigration services offices—will need appropriate electronic access to an individual's file. Scattered units at Homeland Security and the State Department perform screening and data mining: instead, a government-wide team of border and transportation officials should be working together. A modern border and immigration system should combine a biometric entry-exit system with accessible files on visitors and immigrants, along with intelligence on indicators of terrorist travel.

Our border screening system should check people efficiently and welcome friends. Admitting large numbers of students, scholars, businesspeople, and tourists fuels our economy, cultural vitality, and political reach. There is evidence that the present system is disrupting travel to the United States. Overall, visa applications in 2003 were down over 32 percent since 2001. In the Middle East, they declined about 46 percent. Training and the design of security measures should be continuously adjusted.[38]

Recommendation: The Department of Homeland Security, properly supported by the Congress, should complete, as quickly as possible, a biometric entry-exit screening system, including a single system for speeding qualified travelers. It should be integrated with the system that provides benefits to foreigners seeking to stay in the United States. Linking biometric passports to good data systems and decisionmaking is a fundamental goal. No one can hide his or her debt by acquiring a credit card with a slightly different name. Yet today, a terrorist can defeat the link to electronic records by tossing away an old passport and slightly altering the name in the new one.

Completion of the entry-exit system is a major and expensive challenge. Biometrics have been introduced into an antiquated computer environment. Replacement of these systems and improved biometric systems will be required. Nonetheless, funding and completing a biometrics-based entry-exit system is an essential investment in our national security.

Exchanging terrorist information with other countries, consistent with privacy requirements, along with listings of lost and stolen passports, will have immediate security benefits. We should move toward real-time verification of passports with issuing authorities. The further away from our borders that screening occurs, the more security benefits we gain. At least some screening should occur before a passenger departs on a flight destined for the United States. We should also work with other countries to ensure effective inspection regimes at all airports.[39]

The international community arrives at international standards for the design of passports through the International Civil Aviation Organization (ICAO). The global standard for identification is a digital photograph; fingerprints are optional. We must work with others to improve passport standards and provide foreign assistance to countries that need help in making the transition.[40]

Recommendation: The U.S. government cannot meet its own obligations to the American people to prevent the entry of terrorists without a major effort to collaborate with other governments. We should do more to exchange terrorist information with trusted allies, and raise U.S. and global border security standards for travel and border crossing over the medium and long term through extensive international cooperation.

Immigration Law and Enforcement

Our borders and immigration system, including law enforcement, ought to send a message of welcome, tolerance, and justice to members of immigrant communities in the United States and in their countries of origin. We should reach out to immigrant communities. Good immigration services are one way of doing so that is valuable in every way—including intelligence.

It is elemental to border security to know who is coming into the country. Today more than 9 million people are in the United States outside the legal immigration system. We must also be able to monitor and respond to entrances between our ports of entry, working with Canada and Mexico as much as possible.

There is a growing role for state and local law enforcement agencies. They need more training and work with federal agencies so that they can cooperate more effectively with those federal authorities in identifying terrorist suspects.

All but one of the 9/11 hijackers acquired some form of U.S. identification document, some by fraud. Acquisition of these forms of identification would have assisted them in boarding commercial flights, renting cars, and other necessary activities.

Recommendation: Secure identification should begin in the United States. The federal government should set standards for the issuance of birth certificates and sources of identification, such as drivers licenses. Fraud in identification documents is no longer just a problem of theft. At many entry points to vulnerable facilities, including gates for boarding aircraft, sources of identification are the last opportunity to ensure that people are who they say they are and to check whether they are terrorists.[41]

Strategies for Aviation and Transportation Security

The U.S. transportation system is vast and, in an open society, impossible to secure completely against terrorist attacks. There are hundreds of commercial airports, thousands of planes, and tens of thousands of daily flights carrying more than half a billion passengers a year. Millions of containers are imported annually through more than 300 sea and river ports served by more than 3,700 cargo and passenger terminals. About 6,000 agencies provide transit services through buses, subways, ferries, and light-rail service to about 14 million Americans each weekday.[42]

In November 2001, Congress passed and the President signed the Aviation and Transportation Security Act. This act created the Transportation Security Administration (TSA), which is now part of the Homeland Security Department. In November 2002, both the Homeland Security Act and the Maritime Transportation Security Act followed. These laws required the development of strategic plans to describe how the new department and TSA would provide security for critical parts of the U.S. transportation sector.

Over 90 percent of the nation's $5.3 billion annual investment in the TSA goes to aviation—to fight the last war. The money has been spent mainly to meet congressional mandates to federalize the security checkpoint screeners and to deploy existing security methods and technologies at airports. The current efforts do not yet reflect a forward-looking strategic plan systematically analyzing assets, risks, costs, and benefits. Lacking such a plan, we are not convinced that our transportation security resources are being allocated to the greatest risks in a cost-effective way.

- Major vulnerabilities still exist in cargo and general aviation security. These, together with inadequate screening and access controls, continue to present aviation security challenges.

- While commercial aviation remains a possible target, terrorists may turn their attention to other modes. Opportunities to do harm are as great, or greater, in maritime or surface transportation. Initiatives to secure shipping containers have just begun. Surface transportation systems such as railroads and mass transit remain hard to protect because they are so accessible and extensive.

Despite congressional deadlines, the TSA has developed neither an integrated strategic plan for the transportation sector nor specific plans for the various modes—air, sea, and ground.

Recommendation: Hard choices must be made in allocating limited resources. The U.S. government should identify and evaluate the transportation assets that need to be protected, set risk-based priorities for defending them, select the most practical and cost-effective ways of doing so, and then develop a plan, budget, and funding to implement the effort. The plan should assign roles and missions to the relevant authorities (federal, state, regional, and local) and to private stakeholders. In measuring effectiveness, perfection is unattainable. But terrorists should perceive that potential targets are defended. They may be deterred by a significant chance of failure.

Congress should set a specific date for the completion of these plans and hold the Department of Homeland Security and TSA accountable for achieving them.

The most powerful investments may be for improvements in technologies with applications across the transportation modes, such as scanning technologies designed to screen containers that can be transported by plane, ship, truck, or rail. Though such technologies are becoming available now, widespread deployment is still years away.

In the meantime, the best protective measures may be to combine improved methods of identifying and tracking the high-risk containers, operators, and facilities that require added scrutiny with further efforts to integrate intelligence analysis, effective procedures for transmitting threat information to transportation authorities, and vigilance by transportation authorities and the public.

A Layered Security System

No single security measure is foolproof. Accordingly, the TSA must have multiple layers of security in place to defeat the more plausible and dangerous forms of attack against public transportation.

- The plan must take into consideration the full array of possible enemy tactics, such as use of insiders, suicide terrorism, or standoff attack. Each layer must be effective in its own right. Each must be supported by other layers that are redundant and coordinated.

- The TSA should be able to identify for Congress the array of potential terrorist attacks, the layers of security in place, and the reliability provided by each layer. TSA must develop a plan as described above to improve weak individual layers and the effectiveness of the layered systems it deploys.

On 9/11, the 19 hijackers were screened by a computer-assisted screening system called CAPPS. More than half were identified for further inspection, which applied only to their checked luggage.

Under current practices, air carriers enforce government orders to stop certain known and suspected terrorists from boarding commercial flights and to apply secondary screening procedures to others. The "no-fly" and "automatic selectee" lists include only those individuals who the U.S. government believes pose a direct threat of attacking aviation.

Because air carriers implement the program, concerns about sharing intelligence information with private firms and foreign countries keep the U.S. government from listing all terrorist and terrorist suspects who should be included. The TSA has planned to take over this function when it deploys a new screening system to take the place of CAPPS. The deployment of this system has been delayed because of claims it may violate civil liberties.

Recommendation: Improved use of "no-fly" and "automatic selectee" lists should not be delayed while the argument about a successor to CAPPS continues. This screening function should be performed by the TSA, and it should utilize the larger set of watchlists maintained by the federal government. Air carriers should be required to supply the information needed to test and implement this new system.

CAPPS is still part of the screening process, still profiling passengers, with the consequences of selection now including personal searches of the individual and carry-on bags. The TSA is dealing with the kind of screening issues that are being encountered by other agencies. As we mentioned earlier, these screening issues need to be elevated for high-level attention and addressed promptly by the government. Working through these problems can help clear the way for the TSA's screening improvements and would help many other agencies too.

The next layer is the screening checkpoint itself. As the screening system tries to stop dangerous people, the checkpoint needs to be able to find dangerous items. Two reforms are needed soon: (1) screening people for explosives, not just their carry-on bags, and (2) improving screener performance.

Recommendation: The TSA and the Congress must give priority attention to improving the ability of screening checkpoints to detect explosives on passengers. As a start, each individual selected for special screening should be screened for explosives. Further, the TSA should conduct a human factors study, a method often used in the private sector, to understand problems in screener performance and set attainable objectives for individual screeners and for the checkpoints where screening takes place.

Concerns also remain regarding the screening and transport of checked bags and cargo. More attention and resources should be directed to reducing or mitigating the threat posed by explosives in vessels' cargo holds. The TSA should expedite the installation of advanced (in-line) baggage-screening equipment. Because the aviation industry will derive substantial benefits from this deployment, it should pay a fair share of the costs. The TSA should require that every passenger aircraft carrying cargo must deploy at least one hardened container to carry any suspect cargo. TSA also needs to intensify its efforts to identify, track, and appropriately screen potentially dangerous cargo in both the aviation and maritime sectors.

The Protection of Civil Liberties

Many of our recommendations call for the government to increase its presence in our lives—for example, by creating standards for the issuance of forms of identification, by better securing our borders, by sharing information gathered by many different agencies. We also recommend the consolidation of authority over the now far-flung entities constituting the intelligence community. The Patriot Act vests substantial powers in our federal government. We have seen the government use the immigration laws as a tool in its counterterrorism effort. Even without the changes we recommend, the American public has vested enormous authority in the U.S. government.

At our first public hearing on March 31, 2003, we noted the need for balance as our government responds to the real and ongoing threat of terrorist attacks. The terrorists have used our open society against us. In wartime, government calls for greater powers, and then the need for those powers recedes after the war ends. This struggle will go on. Therefore, while protecting our homeland, Americans should be mindful of threats to vital personal and civil liberties. This balancing is no easy task, but we must constantly strive to keep it right.

This shift of power and authority to the government calls for an enhanced system of checks and balances to protect the precious liberties that are vital to our way of life. We therefore make three recommendations.

First, as we will discuss [starting on page 429], to open up the sharing of information across so many agencies and with the private sector, the President should take responsibility for determining what information can be shared by which agencies and under what conditions. Protection of privacy rights should be one key element of this determination.

Recommendation: As the President determines the guidelines for information sharing among government agencies and by those agencies with the private sector, he should safeguard the privacy of individuals about whom information is shared.

Second, Congress responded, in the immediate aftermath of 9/11, with the Patriot Act, which vested substantial new powers in the investigative agencies of the government. Some of the most controversial provisions of the Patriot Act are to "sunset" at the end of 2005. Many of the act's provisions are relatively noncontroversial, updating America's surveillance laws to reflect technological developments in a digital age. Some executive actions that have been criticized are unrelated to the Patriot Act. The provisions in the act that facilitate the sharing of information among intelligence agencies and between law enforcement and intelligence appear, on balance, to be beneficial. Because of concerns regarding the shifting balance of power to the government, we think that a full and informed debate on the Patriot Act would be healthy.

Recommendation: The burden of proof for retaining a particular governmental power should be on the executive, to explain (a) that the power actually materially enhances security and (b) that there is adequate supervision of the executive's use of the powers to ensure protection of civil liberties. If the power is granted, there must be adequate guidelines and oversight to properly confine its use.

Third, during the course of our inquiry, we were told that there is no office within the government whose job it is to look across the government at the actions we are taking to protect ourselves to ensure

that liberty concerns are appropriately considered. If, as we recommend, there is substantial change in the way we collect and share intelligence, there should be a voice within the executive branch for those concerns. Many agencies have privacy offices, albeit of limited scope. The Intelligence Oversight Board of the President's Foreign Intelligence Advisory Board has, in the past, had the job of overseeing certain activities of the intelligence community.

Recommendation: At this time of increased and consolidated government authority, there should be a board within the executive branch to oversee adherence to the guidelines we recommend and the commitment the government makes to defend our civil liberties.

We must find ways of reconciling security with liberty, since the success of one helps protect the other. The choice between security and liberty is a false choice, as nothing is more likely to endanger America's liberties than the success of a terrorist attack at home. Our history has shown us that insecurity threatens liberty. Yet, if our liberties are curtailed, we lose the values that we are struggling to defend.

Setting Priorities for National Preparedness

Before 9/11, no executive department had, as its first priority, the job of defending America from domestic attack. That changed with the 2002 creation of the Department of Homeland Security. This department now has the lead responsibility for problems that feature so prominently in the 9/11 story, such as protecting borders, securing transportation and other parts of our critical infrastructure, organizing emergency assistance, and working with the private sector to assess vulnerabilities.

Throughout the government, nothing has been harder for officials—executive or legislative—than to set priorities, making hard choices in allocating limited resources. These difficulties have certainly afflicted the Department of Homeland Security, hamstrung by its many congressional overseers. In delivering assistance to state and local governments, we heard—especially in New York—about imbalances in the allocation of money. The argument concentrates on two questions.

First, how much money should be set aside for criteria not directly related to risk? Currently a major portion of the billions of dollars appropriated for state and local assistance is allocated so that each state gets a certain amount, or an allocation based on its population—wherever they live.

Recommendation: Homeland security assistance should be based strictly on an assessment of risks and vulnerabilities. Now, in 2004, Washington, D.C., and New York City are certainly at the top of any such list. We understand the

contention that every state and city needs to have some minimum infrastructure for emergency response. But federal homeland security assistance should not remain a program for general revenue sharing. It should supplement state and local resources based on the risks or vulnerabilities that merit additional support. Congress should not use this money as a pork barrel.

The second question is, Can useful criteria to measure risk and vulnerability be developed that assess all the many variables? The allocation of funds should be based on an assessment of threats and vulnerabilities. That assessment should consider such factors as population, population density, vulnerability, and the presence of critical infrastructure within each state. In addition, the federal government should require each state receiving federal emergency preparedness funds to provide an analysis based on the same criteria to justify the distribution of funds in that state.

In a free-for-all over money, it is understandable that representatives will work to protect the interests of their home states or districts. But this issue is too important for politics as usual to prevail. Resources must be allocated according to vulnerabilities. We recommend that a panel of security experts be convened to develop written benchmarks for evaluating community needs. We further recommend that federal homeland security funds be allocated in accordance with those benchmarks, and that states be required to abide by those benchmarks in disbursing the federal funds. The benchmarks will be imperfect and subjective; they will continually evolve. But hard choices must be made. Those who would allocate money on a different basis should then defend their view of the national interest.

Command, Control, and Communications

The attacks on 9/11 demonstrated that even the most robust emergency response capabilities can be overwhelmed if an attack is large enough. Teamwork, collaboration, and cooperation at an incident site are critical to a successful response. Key decisionmakers who are represented at the incident command level help to ensure an effective response, the efficient use of resources, and responder safety. Regular joint training at all levels is, moreover, essential to ensuring close coordination during an actual incident.

Recommendation: Emergency response agencies nationwide should adopt the Incident Command System (ICS). When multiple agencies or multiple jurisdictions are involved, they should adopt a unified command. Both are

proven frameworks for emergency response. We strongly support the decision that federal homeland security funding will be contingent, as of October 1, 2004, upon the adoption and regular use of ICS and unified command procedures. In the future, the Department of Homeland Security should consider making funding contingent on aggressive and realistic training in accordance with ICS and unified command procedures.

The attacks of September 11, 2001 overwhelmed the response capacity of most of the local jurisdictions where the hijacked airliners crashed. While many jurisdictions have established mutual aid compacts, a serious obstacle to multi-jurisdictional response has been the lack of indemnification for mutual-aid responders in areas such as the National Capital Region.

Public safety organizations, chief administrative officers, state emergency management agencies, and the Department of Homeland Security should develop a regional focus within the emergency responder community and promote multi-jurisdictional mutual assistance compacts. Where such compacts already exist, training in accordance with their terms should be required. Congress should pass legislation to remedy the long-standing indemnification and liability impediments to the provision of public safety mutual aid in the National Capital Region and where applicable throughout the nation.

The inability to communicate was a critical element at the World Trade Center, Pentagon, and Somerset County, Pennsylvania, crash sites, where multiple agencies and multiple jurisdictions responded. The occurrence of this problem at three very different sites is strong evidence that compatible and adequate communications among public safety organizations at the local, state, and federal levels remains an important problem.

Recommendation: Congress should support pending legislation which provides for the expedited and increased assignment of radio spectrum for public safety purposes. Furthermore, high-risk urban areas such as New York City and Washington, D.C., should establish signal corps units to ensure communications connectivity between and among civilian authorities, local first responders, and the National Guard. Federal funding of such units should be given high priority by Congress.

Private-Sector Preparedness

The mandate of the Department of Homeland Security does not end with government; the department is also responsible for working with the private sector to ensure preparedness. This is entirely appropriate, for the private sector controls 85 percent of the critical infrastructure in the nation. Indeed, unless a terrorist's target is a military or other secure government facility, the "first" first responders will almost certainly be civilians. Homeland security and national preparedness therefore often begins with the private sector.

Preparedness in the private sector and public sector for rescue, restart, and recovery of operations should include (1) a plan for evacuation, (2) adequate communications capabilities, and (3) a plan for continuity of operations. As we examined the emergency response to 9/11, witness after witness told us that despite 9/11, the private sector remains largely unprepared for a terrorist attack. We were also advised that the lack of a widely embraced private-sector preparedness standard was a principal contributing factor to this lack of preparedness.

We responded by asking the American National Standards Institute (ANSI) to develop a consensus on a "National Standard for Preparedness" for the private sector. ANSI convened safety, security, and business continuity experts from a wide range of industries and associations, as well as from federal, state, and local government stakeholders, to consider the need for standards for private sector emergency preparedness and business continuity.

The result of these sessions was ANSI's recommendation that the Commission endorse a voluntary National Preparedness Standard. Based on the existing American National Standard on Disaster/Emergency Management and Business Continuity Programs (NFPA 1600), the proposed National Preparedness Standard establishes a common set of criteria and terminology for preparedness, disaster management, emergency management, and business continuity programs. The experience of the private sector in the World Trade Center emergency demonstrated the need for these standards.

Recommendation: We endorse the American National Standards Institute's recommended standard for private preparedness. We were encouraged by Secretary Tom Ridge's praise of the standard, and urge the Department of Homeland Security to promote its adoption. We also encourage the insurance and credit-rating industries to look closely at a company's compliance with the ANSI standard in assessing its insurability and creditworthiness. We believe that compliance with the standard should define the standard of care owed by a company to its employees and the public for legal purposes. Private-sector preparedness is not a luxury; it is a cost of doing business in the post-9/11 world. It is ignored at a tremendous potential cost in lives, money, and national security.

HOW TO DO IT? A DIFFERENT WAY OF ORGANIZING THE GOVERNMENT

As presently configured, the national security institutions of the U.S. government are still the institutions constructed to win the Cold War. The United States confronts a very different world today. Instead of facing a few very dangerous adversaries, the United States confronts a number of less visible challenges that surpass the boundaries of traditional nation-states and call for quick, imaginative, and agile responses.

The men and women of the World War II generation rose to the challenges of the 1940s and 1950s. They restructured the government so that it could protect the country. That is now the job of the generation that experienced 9/11. Those attacks showed, emphatically, that ways of doing business rooted in a different era are just not good enough. Americans should not settle for incremental, ad hoc adjustments to a system designed generations ago for a world that no longer exists.

We recommend significant changes in the organization of the government. We know that the quality of the people is more important than the quality of the wiring diagrams. Some of the saddest aspects of the 9/11 story are the outstanding efforts of so many individual officials straining, often without success, against the boundaries of the possible. Good people can overcome bad structures. They should not have to.

The United States has the resources and the people. The government should combine them more effectively, achieving unity of effort. We offer five major recommendations to do that:

- unifying strategic intelligence and operational planning against Islamist terrorists across the foreign-domestic divide with a National Counterterrorism Center;

- unifying the intelligence community with a new National Intelligence Director;

- unifying the many participants in the counterterrorism effort and their knowledge in a network-based information-sharing system that transcends traditional governmental boundaries;

- unifying and strengthening congressional oversight to improve quality and accountability; and

- strengthening the FBI and homeland defenders.

Unity of Effort Across the Foreign-Domestic Divide

Joint Action

Much of the public commentary about the 9/11 attacks has dealt with "lost opportunities.". . . These are often characterized as problems of "watchlisting," of "information sharing," or of "connecting the dots.". . . [T]hese labels are too narrow. They describe the symptoms, not the disease.

In each of our examples, no one was firmly in charge of managing the case and able to draw relevant intelligence from anywhere in the government, assign responsibilities across the agencies (foreign or domestic), track progress, and quickly bring obstacles up to the level where they could be resolved. Responsibility and accountability were diffuse.

The agencies cooperated, some of the time. But even such cooperation as there was is not the same thing as joint action. When agencies cooperate, one defines the problem and seeks help with it. When they act jointly, the problem and options for action are defined differently from the start. Individuals from different backgrounds come together in analyzing a case and planning how to manage it.

In our hearings we regularly asked witnesses: Who is the quarterback? The other players are in their positions, doing their jobs. But who is calling the play that assigns roles to help them execute as a team?

Since 9/11, those issues have not been resolved. In some ways joint work has gotten better, and in some ways worse. The effort of fighting terrorism has flooded over many of the usual agency boundaries because of its sheer quantity and energy. Attitudes have changed. Officials are keenly conscious of trying to avoid the mistakes of 9/11. They try to share information. They circulate—even to the President—practically every reported threat, however dubious.

Partly because of all this effort, the challenge of coordinating it has multiplied. Before 9/11, the CIA was plainly the lead agency confronting al Qaeda. The FBI played a very secondary role. The engagement of the departments of Defense and State was more episodic.

- Today the CIA is still central. But the FBI is much more active, along with other parts of the Justice Department.

- The Defense Department effort is now enormous. Three of its unified commands, each headed by a four-star general, have counterterrorism as a primary mission: Special Operations Command, Central Command (both head-

quartered in Florida), and Northern Command (headquartered in Colorado).

- A new Department of Homeland Security combines formidable resources in border and transportation security, along with analysis of domestic vulnerability and other tasks.

- The State Department has the lead on many of the foreign policy tasks. . . .

- At the White House, the National Security Council (NSC) now is joined by a parallel presidential advisory structure, the Homeland Security Council.

So far we have mentioned two reasons for joint action—the virtue of joint planning and the advantage of having someone in charge to ensure a unified effort. There is a third: the simple shortage of experts with sufficient skills. The limited pool of critical experts—for example, skilled counterterrorism analysts and linguists—is being depleted. Expanding these capabilities will require not just money, but time.

Primary responsibility for terrorism analysis has been assigned to the Terrorist Threat Integration Center (TTIC), created in 2003, based at the CIA headquarters but staffed with representatives of many agencies, reporting directly to the Director of Central Intelligence. Yet the CIA houses another intelligence "fusion" center: the Counterterrorist Center that played such a key role before 9/11. A third major analytic unit is at Defense, in the Defense Intelligence Agency. A fourth, concentrating more on homeland vulnerabilities, is at the Department of Homeland Security. The FBI is in the process of building the analytic capability it has long lacked, and it also has the Terrorist Screening Center.[43]

The U.S. government cannot afford so much duplication of effort. There are not enough experienced experts to go around. The duplication also places extra demands on already hard-pressed single-source national technical intelligence collectors like the National Security Agency.

Combining Joint Intelligence and Joint Action

A "smart" government would *integrate* all sources of information to see the enemy as a whole. Integrated all-source analysis should also inform and shape strategies to collect more intelligence. Yet the Terrorist Threat Integration Center, while it has primary responsibility for terrorism analysis, is formally proscribed from having any oversight or operational authority and is not part of any operational entity, other than reporting to the director of central intelligence.[44]

The government now tries to handle the problem of joint management, informed by analysis of intelligence from all sources, in two ways.

- First, agencies with lead responsibility for certain problems have constructed their own interagency entities and task forces in order to get cooperation. The Counterterrorist Center at CIA, for example, recruits liaison officers from throughout the intelligence community. The military's Central Command has its own interagency center, recruiting liaison officers from all the agencies from which it might need help. The FBI has Joint Terrorism Task Forces in 84 locations to coordinate the activities of other agencies when action may be required.

- Second, the problem of joint operational planning is often passed to the White House, where the NSC staff tries to play this role. The national security staff at the White House (both NSC and new Homeland Security Council staff) has already become 50 percent larger since 9/11. But our impression, after talking to serving officials, is that even this enlarged staff is consumed by meetings on day-to-day issues, sifting each day's threat information and trying to coordinate everyday operations.

Even as it crowds into every square inch of available office space, the NSC staff is still not sized or funded to be an executive agency. . . . [S]ome . . . problems . . . arose in the 1980s when a White House staff, constitutionally insulated from the usual mechanisms of oversight, became involved in direct operations. During the 1990s Richard Clarke occasionally tried to exercise such authority, sometimes successfully, but often causing friction.

Yet a subtler and more serious danger is that as the NSC staff is consumed by these day-to-day tasks, it has less capacity to find the time and detachment needed to advise a president on larger policy issues. That means less time to work on major new initiatives, help with legislative management to steer needed bills through Congress, and track the design and implementation of the strategic plans for regions, countries, and issues. . . .

Much of the job of operational coordination remains with the agencies, especially the CIA. There DCI Tenet and his chief aides ran interagency meetings nearly every day to coordinate much of the government's day-to-day work. The DCI insisted he did not make policy and only oversaw its implementation. In the struggle against terrorism these distinctions seem increasingly artificial. Also, as the DCI becomes a lead coordinator of the government's operations, it becomes harder to play all the position's other roles, including that of analyst in chief.

The problem is nearly intractable because of the way the government is currently structured. Lines of operational authority run to the expanding executive departments, and they are guarded for understandable reasons; the DCI commands the CIA's personnel overseas; the secretary of defense will not yield to others in conveying commands to military forces; the Justice Department will not give up the responsibility of deciding whether to seek arrest warrants. But the result is that each agency or department needs its own intelligence apparatus to support the performance of its duties. It is hard to "break down stovepipes" when there are so many stoves that are legally and politically entitled to have cast-iron pipes of their own.

Recalling the Goldwater-Nichols legislation of 1986, Secretary Rumsfeld reminded us that to achieve better joint capability, each of the armed services had to "give up some of their turf and authorities and prerogatives." Today, he said, the executive branch is "stove-piped much like the four services were nearly 20 years ago." He wondered if it might be appropriate to ask agencies to "give up some of their existing turf and authority in exchange for a stronger, faster, more efficient government wide joint effort."[45] Privately, other key officials have made the same point to us.

We therefore propose a new institution: a civilian-led unified joint command for counterterrorism. It should combine strategic intelligence and joint operational planning.

In the Pentagon's Joint Staff, which serves the chairman of the Joint Chiefs of Staff, intelligence is handled by the J-2 directorate, operational planning by J-3, and overall policy by J-5. Our concept combines the J-2 and J-3 functions (intelligence and operational planning) in one agency, keeping overall policy coordination where it belongs, in the National Security Council.

Recommendation: We recommend the establishment of a National Counterterrorism Center (NCTC), built on the foundation of the existing Terrorist Threat Integration Center (TTIC). Breaking the older mold of national government organization, this NCTC should be a center for joint operational planning and joint intelligence, staffed by personnel from the various agencies. The head of the NCTC should have authority to evaluate the performance of the people assigned to the Center.

- Such a joint center should be developed in the same spirit that guided the military's creation of unified joint commands, or the shaping of earlier national agencies like the National Reconnaissance Office, which was formed to organize the work of the CIA and several defense agencies in space.

NCTC—Intelligence. The NCTC should lead strategic analysis, pooling all-source intelligence, foreign and domestic, about transnational terrorist organizations with global reach. It should develop *net* assessments (comparing enemy capabilities and intentions against U.S. defenses and countermeasures). It should also provide warning. It should do this work by drawing on the efforts of the CIA, FBI, Homeland Security, and other departments and agencies. It should task collection requirements both inside and outside the United States.

- The intelligence function (J-2) should build on the existing TTIC structure and remain distinct, as a national intelligence center, within the NCTC. As the government's principal knowledge bank on Islamist terrorism, with the main responsibility for strategic analysis and net assessment, it should absorb a significant portion of the analytical talent now residing in the CIA's Counterterrorist Center and the DIA's Joint Intelligence Task Force—Combatting Terrorism (JITF-CT).

NCTC—Operations. The NCTC should perform joint planning. The plans would assign operational responsibilities to lead agencies, such as State, the CIA, the FBI, Defense and its combatant commands, Homeland Security, and other agencies. The NCTC should not direct the actual execution of these operations, leaving that job to the agencies. The NCTC would then track implementation; it would look across the foreign-domestic divide and across agency boundaries, updating plans to follow through on cases.[46]

- The joint operational planning function (J-3) will be new to the TTIC structure. The NCTC can draw on analogous work now being done in the CIA and every other involved department of the government, as well as reaching out to knowledgeable officials in state and local agencies throughout the United States.

- The NCTC should not be a policymaking body. Its operations and planning should follow the policy direction of the president and the National Security Council.

NCTC—Authorities. The head of the NCTC should be appointed by the president, and should be equivalent in rank to a deputy head of

---

Box 32.1

Consider this hypothetical case. The NSA discovers that a suspected terrorist is traveling to Bangkok and Kuala Lumpur. The NCTC should draw on joint intelligence resources, including its own NSA counterterrorism experts, to analyze the identities and possible destinations of these individuals. Informed by this analysis, the NCTC would then organize and plan the management of the case, drawing on the talents and differing kinds of experience among the several agency representatives assigned to it—assigning tasks to the CIA overseas, to Homeland Security watching entry points into the United States, and to the FBI. If military assistance might be needed, the Special Operations Command could be asked to develop an appropriate concept for such an operation. The NCTC would be accountable for tracking the progress of the case, ensuring that the plan evolved with it, and integrating the information into a warning. The NCTC would be responsible for being sure that intelligence gathered from the activities in the field became part of the government's institutional memory about Islamist terrorist personalities, organizations, and possible means of attack.

In each case the involved agency would make its own senior managers aware of what it was being asked to do. If those agency heads objected, and the issue could not easily be resolved, then the disagreement about roles and missions could be brought before the National Security Council and the president. ✦

---

a cabinet department. The head of the NCTC would report to the national intelligence director, an office whose creation we recommend below, placed in the Executive Office of the President. The head of the NCTC would thus also report indirectly to the president. This official's nomination should be confirmed by the Senate and he or she should testify to the Congress, as is the case now with other statutory presidential offices, like the U.S. trade representative.

- To avoid the fate of other entities with great nominal authority and little real power, the head of the NCTC must have the right to concur in the choices of personnel to lead the operating entities of the departments and agencies focused on counterterrorism, specifically including the head of the Counterterrorist Center, the head of the FBI's Counterterrorism Division, the commanders of the Defense Department's

Special Operations Command and Northern Command, and the State Department's coordinator for counterterrorism.[47] The head of the NCTC should also work with the director of the Office of Management and Budget in developing the president's counterterrorism budget.

- There are precedents for surrendering authority for joint planning while preserving an agency's operational control. In the international context, NATO commanders may get line authority over forces assigned by other nations. In U.S. unified commands, commanders plan operations that may involve units belonging to one of the services. In each case, procedures are worked out, formal and informal, to define the limits of the joint commander's authority.

The most serious disadvantage of the NCTC is the reverse of its greatest virtue. The struggle against Islamist terrorism is so important that any clear-cut centralization of authority to manage and be accountable for it may concentrate too much power in one place. The proposed NCTC would be given the authority of planning the activities of other agencies. Law or executive order must define the scope of such line authority.

The NCTC would not eliminate interagency policy disputes. These would still go to the National Security Council. To improve coordination at the White House, we believe the existing Homeland Security Council should soon be merged into a single National Security Council. The creation of the NCTC should help the NSC staff concentrate on its core duties of assisting the president and supporting interdepartmental policymaking.

We recognize that this is a new and difficult idea precisely because the authorities we recommend for the NCTC really would, as Secretary Rumsfeld foresaw, ask strong agencies to "give up some of their turf and authority in exchange for a stronger, faster, more efficient government wide joint effort." Countering transnational Islamist terrorism will test whether the U.S. government can fashion more flexible models of management needed to deal with the twenty-first-century world.

An argument against change is that the nation is at war, and cannot afford to reorganize in midstream. But some of the main innovations of the 1940s and 1950s, including the creation of the Joint Chiefs of Staff and even the construction of the Pentagon itself, were undertaken in the midst of war. Surely the country cannot wait until the struggle against Islamist terrorism is over.

"Surprise, when it happens to a government, is likely to be a complicated, diffuse, bureaucratic

---

Box 32.2
Members of the U.S. Intelligence Community

- Office of the Director of Central Intelligence, which includes the Office of the Deputy Director of Central Intelligence for Community Management, the Community Management Staff, the Terrorism Threat Integration Center, the National Intelligence Council, and other community offices
- The Central Intelligence Agency (CIA), which performs human source collection, all-source analysis, and advanced science and technology

National Intelligence Agencies

- National Security Agency (NSA), which performs signals collection and analysis
- National Geospatial-Intelligence Agency (NGA), which performs imagery collection and analysis
- National Reconnaissance Office (NRO), which develops, acquires, and launches space systems for intelligence collection
- Other national reconnaissance programs

Departmental Intelligence Agencies

- Defense Intelligence Agency (DIA) of the Department of Defense
- Intelligence entities of the Army, Navy, Air Force, and Marines
- Bureau of Intelligence and Research (INR) of the Department of State
- Office of Terrorism and Finance Intelligence of the Department of Treasury
- Office of Intelligence and the Counterterrorism and Counterintelligence Divisions of the Federal Bureau of Investigation of the Department of Justice
- Office of Intelligence of the Department of Energy
- Directorate of Information Analysis and Infrastructure Protection (IAIP) and Directorate of Coast Guard Intelligence of the Department of Homeland Security. ✦

---

thing. It includes neglect of responsibility, but also responsibility so poorly defined or so ambiguously delegated that action gets lost."[48] That comment was made more than 40 years ago, about Pearl Harbor. We hope another commission, writing in the future about another attack, does not again find this quotation to be so apt.

Unity of Effort in the Intelligence Community

In our first section, we concentrated on counterterrorism, discussing how to combine the analysis of information from all sources of intelligence with the joint planning of operations that draw on that analysis. In this section, we step back from looking just at the counterterrorism problem. We reflect on whether the government is organized adequately to direct resources and build the intelligence capabilities it will need not just for countering terrorism, but for the broader range of national security challenges in the decades ahead.

The Need for a Change

During the Cold War, intelligence agencies did not depend on seamless integration to track and count the thousands of military targets—such as tanks and missiles—fielded by the Soviet Union and other adversary states. Each agency concentrated on its specialized mission, acquiring its own information and then sharing it via formal, finished reports. The Department of Defense had given birth to and dominated the main agencies for technical collection of intelligence. Resources were shifted at an incremental pace, coping with challenges that arose over years, even decades.

[T]he resulting organization of the intelligence community . . . is outlined [in Box 32.2].

The need to restructure the intelligence community grows out of six problems that have become apparent before and after 9/11:

- *Structural barriers to performing joint intelligence work.* National intelligence is still organized around the collection disciplines of the home agencies, not the joint mission. The importance of integrated, all-source analysis cannot be overstated. Without it, it is not possible to "connect the dots." No one component holds all the relevant information.

  By contrast, in organizing national defense, the Goldwater-Nichols legislation of 1986 created joint commands for operations in the field, the Unified Command Plan. The services—the Army, Navy, Air Force, and Marine Corps—organize, train, and equip their people and units to perform their missions. Then they assign personnel and units to the joint combatant commander, like the commanding general of the

Central Command (CENTCOM). The Goldwater-Nichols Act required officers to serve tours outside their service in order to win promotion. The culture of the Defense Department was transformed, its collective mind-set moved from service-specific to "joint," and its operations became more integrated.[49]

- *Lack of common standards and practices across the foreign-domestic divide.* The leadership of the intelligence community should be able to pool information gathered overseas with information gathered in the United States, holding the work—wherever it is done—to a common standard of quality in how it is collected, processed (e.g., translated), reported, shared, and analyzed. A common set of personnel standards for intelligence can create a group of professionals better able to operate in joint activities, transcending their own service-specific mind-sets.

- *Divided management of national intelligence capabilities.* While the CIA was once "central" to our national intelligence capabilities, following the end of the Cold War it has been less able to influence the use of the nation's imagery and signals intelligence capabilities in three national agencies housed within the Department of Defense: the National Security Agency, the National Geospatial-Intelligence Agency, and the National Reconnaissance Office. One of the lessons learned from the 1991 Gulf War was the value of national intelligence systems (satellites in particular) in precision warfare. Since that war, the department has appropriately drawn these agencies into its transformation of the military. Helping to orchestrate this transformation is the under secretary of defense for intelligence, a position established by Congress after 9/11. An unintended consequence of these developments has been the far greater demand made by Defense on technical systems, leaving the DCI less able to influence how these technical resources are allocated and used.

- *Weak capacity to set priorities and move resources.* The agencies are mainly organized around what they collect or the way they collect it. But the priorities for collection are national. As the DCI makes hard choices about moving resources, he or she must have the power to reach across agencies and reallocate effort.

- *Too many jobs.* The DCI now has at least three jobs. He is expected to run a particular agency, the CIA. He is expected to manage the loose confederation of agencies that is the intelligence community. He is expected to be the analyst in chief for the government, sifting evidence and directly briefing the President as his principal intelligence adviser. No recent DCI has been able to do all three effectively. Usually what loses out is management of the intelligence community, a difficult task even in the best case because the DCI's current authorities are weak. With so much to do, the DCI often has not used even the authority he has.

• *Too complex and secret.* Over the decades, the agencies and the rules surrounding the intelligence community have accumulated to a depth that practically defies public comprehension. There are now 15 agencies or parts of agencies in the intelligence community. The community and the DCI's authorities have become arcane matters, understood only by initiates after long study. Even the most basic information about how much money is actually allocated to or within the intelligence community and most of its key components is shrouded from public view.

The current DCI is responsible for community performance but lacks the three authorities critical for any agency head or chief executive officer: (1) control over purse strings, (2) the ability to hire or fire senior managers, and (3) the ability to set standards for the information infrastructure and personnel.[50]

The only budget power of the DCI over agencies other than the CIA lies in coordinating the budget requests of the various intelligence agencies into a single program for submission to Congress. The overall funding request of the 15 intelligence entities in this program is then presented to the president and Congress in 15 separate volumes.

When Congress passes an appropriations bill to allocate money to intelligence agencies, most of their funding is hidden in the Defense Department in order to keep intelligence spending secret. Therefore, although the House and Senate Intelligence committees are the authorizing committees for funding of the intelligence community, the final budget review is handled in the Defense Subcommittee of the Appropriations committees. Those committees have no subcommittees just for intelligence, and only a few members and staff review the requests.

The appropriations for the CIA and the national intelligence agencies—NSA, NGA, and NRO—are then given to the secretary of defense. The secretary transfers the CIA's money to the DCI but disburses the national agencies' money directly. Money for the FBI's national security components falls within the appropriations for Commerce, Justice, and State and goes to the attorney general.[51]

In addition, the DCI lacks hire-and-fire authority over most of the intelligence community's senior managers. For the national intelligence agencies housed in the Defense Department, the secretary of defense must seek the DCI's concurrence regarding the nomination of these directors, who are presidentially appointed. But the secretary may submit recommendations to the president without receiving this concurrence. The DCI cannot fire these officials. The DCI has even less influence over the head of the FBI's national security component, who is appointed by the attorney general in consultation with the DCI.[52]

Combining Joint Work With Stronger Management

We have received recommendations on the topic of intelligence reform from many sources. Other commissions have been over this same ground. Thoughtful bills have been introduced, most recently a bill by the chairman of the House Intelligence Committee Porter Goss (R-Fla.), and another by the ranking minority member, Jane Harman (D-Calif.). In the Senate, Senators Bob Graham (D-Fla.) and Dianne Feinstein (D-Calif.) have introduced reform proposals as well. Past efforts have foundered, because the president did not support them; because the DCI, the secretary of defense, or both opposed them; and because some proposals lacked merit. We have tried to take stock of these experiences, and borrow from strong elements in many of the ideas that have already been developed by others.

Recommendation: The current position of Director of Central Intelligence should be replaced by a National Intelligence Director with two main areas of responsibility: (1) to oversee national intelligence centers on specific subjects of interest across the U.S. government and (2) to manage the national intelligence program and oversee the agencies that contribute to it.

First, the National Intelligence Director should oversee *national intelligence centers* to provide all-source analysis and plan intelligence operations for the whole government on major problems.

• One such problem is counterterrorism. In this case, we believe that the center should be the intelligence entity (formerly TTIC) inside the National Counterterrorism Center we have proposed. It would sit there alongside the operations management unit we described earlier, with both making up the NCTC, in the Executive Office of the President. Other national intelligence centers—for instance, on counterproliferation, crime and narcotics, and China—would be housed in whatever department or agency is best suited for them.

- The National Intelligence Director would retain the present DCI's role as the principal intelligence adviser to the president. We hope the president will come to look directly to the directors of the national intelligence centers to provide all-source analysis in their areas of responsibility, balancing the advice of these intelligence chiefs against the contrasting viewpoints that may be offered by department heads at State, Defense, Homeland Security, Justice, and other agencies.

Second, the National Intelligence Director should manage the national intelligence program and oversee the component agencies of the intelligence community. (See Figure 32.1.)[53]

- The National Intelligence Director would submit a unified budget for national intelligence that reflects priorities chosen by the National Security Council, an appropriate balance among the varieties of technical and human intelligence collection, and analysis. He or she would receive an appropriation for national intelligence and apportion the funds to the appropriate agencies, in line with that budget, and with authority to reprogram funds among the national intelligence agencies to meet any new priority (as counterterrorism was in the 1990s). The National Intelligence Director should approve and submit nominations to the president of the individuals who would lead the CIA, DIA, FBI Intelligence Office, NSA, NGA, NRO, Information Analysis and Infrastructure Protection Directorate of the Department of Homeland Security, and other national intelligence capabilities.[54]

- The National Intelligence Director would manage this national effort with the help of three deputies, each of whom would also hold a key position in one of the component agencies.[55]

  - Foreign intelligence (the head of the CIA).

  - Defense intelligence (the under secretary of defense for intelligence).[56]

  - Homeland intelligence (the FBI's executive assistant director for intelligence or the under secretary of homeland security for information analysis and infrastructure protection).

  Other agencies in the intelligence community would coordinate their work within each

of these three areas, largely staying housed in the same departments or agencies that support them now.

Returning to the analogy of the Defense Department's organization, these three deputies—like the leaders of the Army, Navy, Air Force, or Marines—would have the job of acquiring the systems, training the people, and executing the operations planned by the national intelligence centers.

And, just as the combatant commanders also report to the secretary of defense, the directors of the national intelligence centers—e.g., for counterproliferation, crime and narcotics, and the rest—also would report to the National Intelligence Director.

- The Defense Department's military intelligence programs—the joint military intelligence program (JMIP) and the tactical intelligence and related activities program (TIARA)—would remain part of that department's responsibility.

- The National Intelligence Director would set personnel policies to establish standards for education and training and facilitate assignments at the national intelligence centers and across agency lines. The National Intelligence Director also would set information sharing and information technology policies to maximize data sharing, as well as policies to protect the security of information.

- Too many agencies now have an opportunity to say no to change. The National Intelligence Director should participate in an NSC executive committee that can resolve differences in priorities among the agencies and bring the major disputes to the president for decision.

The National Intelligence Director should be located in the Executive Office of the President. This official, who would be confirmed by the Senate and would testify before Congress, would have a relatively small staff of several hundred people, taking the place of the existing community management offices housed at the CIA.

In managing the whole community, the National Intelligence Director is still providing a service function. With the partial exception of his or her responsibilities for overseeing the NCTC, the National Intelligence Director should support the consumers of national intelligence—the president and policymaking advisers such as the secretaries of state, defense, and homeland security and the attorney general.

We are wary of too easily equating government management problems with those of the private

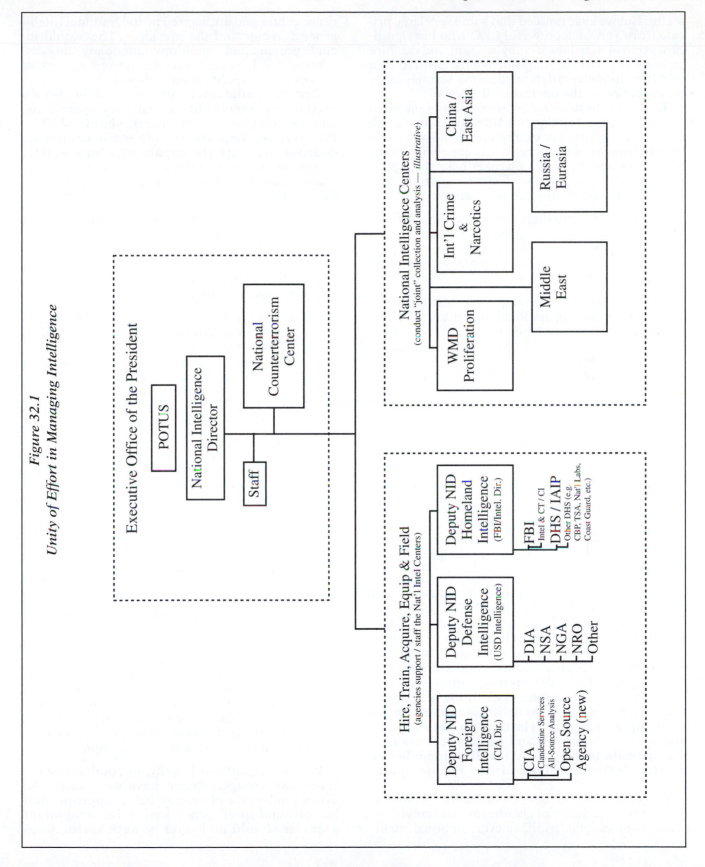

Figure 32.1
Unity of Effort in Managing Intelligence

sector. But we have noticed that some very large private firms rely on a powerful CEO who has significant control over how money is spent and can hire or fire leaders of the major divisions, assisted by a relatively modest staff, while leaving responsibility for execution in the operating divisions.

There are disadvantages to separating the position of National Intelligence Director from the job of heading the CIA. For example, the National Intelligence Director will not head a major agency of his or her own and may have a weaker base of support. But we believe that these disadvantages are outweighed by several other considerations:

- The National Intelligence Director must be able to directly oversee intelligence collection inside the United States. Yet law and custom has counseled against giving such a plain domestic role to the head of the CIA.

- The CIA will be one among several claimants for funds in setting national priorities. The National Intelligence Director should not be both one of the advocates and the judge of them all.

- Covert operations tend to be highly tactical, requiring close attention. The National Intelligence Director should rely on the relevant joint mission center to oversee these details, helping to coordinate closely with the White House. The CIA will be able to concentrate on building the capabilities to carry out such operations and on providing the personnel who will be directing and executing such operations in the field.

- Rebuilding the analytic and human intelligence collection capabilities of the CIA should be a full-time effort, and the director of the CIA should focus on extending its comparative advantages.

Recommendation: The CIA Director should emphasize (a) rebuilding the CIA's analytic capabilities; (b) transforming the clandestine service by building its human intelligence capabilities; (c) developing a stronger language program, with high standards and sufficient financial incentives; (d) renewing emphasis on recruiting diversity among operations officers so they can blend more easily in foreign cities; (e) ensuring a seamless relationship between human source collection and signals collection at the operational level; and (f) stressing a better balance between unilateral and liaison operations.

The CIA should retain responsibility for the direction and execution of clandestine and covert operations, as assigned by the relevant national intelligence center and authorized by the National Intelligence Director and the president. This would include propaganda, renditions, and nonmilitary disruption. We believe, however, that one important area of responsibility should change.

Recommendation: Lead responsibility for directing and executing paramilitary operations, whether clandestine or covert, should shift to the Defense Department. There it should be consolidated with the capabilities for training, direction, and execution of such operations already being developed in the Special Operations Command.

- Before 9/11, the CIA did not invest in developing a robust capability to conduct paramilitary operations with U.S. personnel. It relied on proxies instead, organized by CIA operatives without the requisite military training. The results were unsatisfactory.

- Whether the price is measured in either money or people, the United States cannot afford to build two separate capabilities for carrying out secret military operations, secretly operating standoff missiles, and secretly training foreign military or paramilitary forces. The United States should concentrate responsibility and necessary legal authorities in one entity.

- The post-9/11 Afghanistan precedent of using joint CIA-military teams for covert and clandestine operations was a good one. We believe this proposal to be consistent with it. Each agency would concentrate on its comparative advantages in building capabilities for joint missions. The operation itself would be planned in common.

- The CIA has a reputation for agility in operations. The military has a reputation for being methodical and cumbersome. We do not know if these stereotypes match current reality; they may also be one more symptom of the civil-military misunderstandings. . . . It is a problem to be resolved in policy guidance and agency management, not in the creation of redundant, overlapping capabilities and authorities in such sensitive work. The CIA's experts should be integrated into the military's training, exercises, and planning. To quote a CIA official now serving in the field: "One fight, one team."

Recommendation: Finally, to combat the secrecy and complexity we have described, the overall amounts of money being appropriated for national intelligence and to its component agencies should no longer be kept secret. Con-

gress should pass a separate appropriations act for intelligence, defending the broad allocation of how these tens of billions of dollars have been assigned among the varieties of intelligence work.

The specifics of the intelligence appropriation would remain classified, as they are today. Opponents of declassification argue that America's enemies could learn about intelligence capabilities by tracking the top-line appropriations figure. Yet the top-line figure by itself provides little insight into U.S. intelligence sources and methods. The U.S. government readily provides copious information about spending on its military forces, including military intelligence. The intelligence community should not be subject to that much disclosure. But when even aggregate categorical numbers remain hidden, it is hard to judge priorities and foster accountability.

Unity of Effort in Sharing Information

Information Sharing

We have already stressed the importance of intelligence analysis that can draw on all relevant sources of information. The biggest impediment to all-source analysis—to a greater likelihood of connecting the dots—is the human or systemic resistance to sharing information.

The U.S. government has access to a vast amount of information. When databases not usually thought of as "intelligence," such as customs or immigration information, are included, the storehouse is immense. But the U.S. government has a weak system for processing and using what it has. In interviews around the government, official after official urged us to call attention to frustrations with the unglamorous "back office" side of government operations.

In the 9/11 story, for example, we sometimes see examples of information that could be accessed—like the undistributed NSA information that would have helped identify Nawaf al Hazmi in January 2000. But someone had to ask for it. In that case, no one did. Or . . . the information is distributed, but in a compartmented channel. Or the information is available, and someone does ask, but it cannot be shared.

What all these stories have in common is a system that requires a demonstrated "need to know" before sharing. This approach assumes it is possible to know, in advance, who will need to use the information. Such a system implicitly assumes that the risk of inadvertent disclosure outweighs the benefits of wider sharing. Those Cold War assumptions are no longer appropriate. The culture of agencies feeling they own the information they gathered at taxpayer expense must be replaced by a culture in which the agencies instead feel they have a duty to the information—to repay the taxpayers' investment by making that information available.

Each intelligence agency has its own security practices, outgrowths of the Cold War. We certainly understand the reason for these practices. Counterintelligence concerns are still real, even if the old Soviet enemy has been replaced by other spies.

But the security concerns need to be weighed against the costs. Current security requirements nurture overclassification and excessive compartmentation of information among agencies. Each agency's incentive structure opposes sharing, with risks (criminal, civil, and internal administrative sanctions) but few rewards for sharing information. No one has to pay the long-term costs of overclassifying information, though these costs—even in literal financial terms—are substantial. There are no punishments for *not* sharing information. Agencies uphold a "need-to-know" culture of information protection rather than promoting a "need-to-share" culture of integration.[57]

Recommendation: Information procedures should provide incentives for sharing, to restore a better balance between security and shared knowledge.

Intelligence gathered about transnational terrorism should be processed, turned into reports, and distributed according to the same quality standards, whether it is collected in Pakistan or in Texas.

The logical objection is that sources and methods may vary greatly in different locations. We therefore propose that when a report is first created, its data be separated from the sources and methods by which they are obtained. The report should begin with the information in its most shareable, but still meaningful, form. Therefore the maximum number of recipients can access some form of that information. If knowledge of further details becomes important, any user can query further, with access granted or denied according to the rules set for the network—and with queries leaving an audit trail in order to determine who accessed the information. But the questions may not come at all unless experts at the "edge" of the network can readily discover the clues that prompt to them.[58]

We propose that information be shared horizontally, across new networks that transcend individual agencies.

• The current system is structured on an old mainframe, or hub-and-spoke, concept. In this older approach, each agency has its own database. Agency users send information to the database and then can retrieve it from the database.

- A decentralized network model, the concept behind much of the information revolution, shares data horizontally too. Agencies would still have their own databases, but those databases would be searchable across agency lines. In this system, secrets are protected through the design of the network and an "information rights management" approach that controls access to the data, not access to the whole network. An outstanding conceptual framework for this kind of "trusted information network" has been developed by a task force of leading professionals in national security, information technology, and law assembled by the Markle Foundation. Its report has been widely discussed throughout the U.S. government, but has not yet been converted into action.[59]

Recommendation: The president should lead the government-wide effort to bring the major national security institutions into the information revolution. He should coordinate the resolution of the legal, policy, and technical issues across agencies to create a "trusted information network."

- No one agency can do it alone. Well-meaning agency officials are under tremendous pressure to update their systems. Alone, they may only be able to modernize the stovepipes, not replace them.

- Only presidential leadership can develop government-wide concepts and standards. Currently, no one is doing this job. Backed by the Office of Management and Budget, a new National Intelligence Director empowered to set common standards for information use throughout the community, and a secretary of homeland security who helps extend the system to public agencies and relevant private-sector databases, a government-wide initiative can succeed.

- White House leadership is also needed because the policy and legal issues are harder than the technical ones. The necessary technology already exists. What does not are the rules for acquiring, accessing, sharing, and using the vast stores of public and private data that may be available. When information sharing works, it is a powerful tool. Therefore the sharing and uses of information must be guided by a set of practical policy guidelines that simultaneously empower and constrain officials, telling them clearly what is and is not permitted.

"This is government acting in new ways, to face new threats," the most recent Markle report explains. "And while such change is necessary, it must be accomplished while engendering the people's trust that privacy and other civil liberties are being protected, that businesses are not being unduly burdened with requests for extraneous or useless information, that taxpayer money is being well spent, and that, ultimately, the network will be effective in protecting our security." The authors add: "Leadership is emerging from all levels of government and from many places in the private sector. What is needed now is a plan to accelerate these efforts, and public debate and consensus on the goals."[60]

Unity of Effort in the Congress

Strengthen Congressional Oversight of Intelligence and Homeland Security

Of all our recommendations, strengthening congressional oversight may be among the most difficult and important. So long as oversight is governed by current congressional rules and resolutions, we believe the American people will not get the security they want and need. The United States needs a strong, stable, and capable congressional committee structure to give America's national intelligence agencies oversight, support, and leadership.

Few things are more difficult to change in Washington than congressional committee jurisdiction and prerogatives. To a member, these assignments are almost as important as the map of his or her congressional district. The American people may have to insist that these changes occur, or they may well not happen. Having interviewed numerous members of Congress from both parties, as well as congressional staff members, we found that dissatisfaction with congressional oversight remains widespread.

The future challenges of America's intelligence agencies are daunting. They include the need to develop leading-edge technologies that give our policymakers and warfighters a decisive edge in any conflict where the interests of the United States are vital. Not only does good intelligence win wars, but the best intelligence enables us to prevent them from happening altogether.

Under the terms of existing rules and resolutions the House and Senate intelligence committees lack the power, influence, and sustained capability to meet this challenge. While few members of Congress have the broad knowledge of intelligence activities or the know-how about the technologies employed, all members need to feel assured that good oversight is happening. When their unfamiliarity with the subject is combined with the need to preserve security, a mandate emerges for substantial change.

Tinkering with the existing structure is not sufficient. Either Congress should create a joint committee for intelligence, using the Joint Atomic Energy Committee as its model, or it should create House and Senate committees with combined authorizing and appropriations powers.

Whichever of these two forms are chosen, the goal should be a structure—codified by resolution with powers expressly granted and carefully limited—allowing a relatively small group of members of Congress, given time and reason to master the subject and the agencies, to conduct oversight of the intelligence establishment and be clearly accountable for their work. The staff of this committee should be nonpartisan and work for the entire committee and not for individual members.

The other reforms we have suggested—for a National Counterterrorism Center and a National Intelligence Director—will not work if congressional oversight does not change too. Unity of effort in executive management can be lost if it is fractured by divided congressional oversight.

Recommendation: Congressional oversight for intelligence—and counterterrorism—is now dysfunctional. Congress should address this problem. We have considered various alternatives: A joint committee on the old model of the Joint Committee on Atomic Energy is one. A single committee in each house of Congress, combining authorizing and appropriating authorities, is another.

- The new committee or committees should conduct continuing studies of the activities of the intelligence agencies and report problems relating to the development and use of intelligence to all members of the House and Senate.

- We have already recommended that the total level of funding for intelligence be made public, and that the national intelligence program be appropriated to the National Intelligence Director, not to the secretary of defense.[61]

- We also recommend that the intelligence committee should have a subcommittee specifically dedicated to oversight, freed from the consuming responsibility of working on the budget.

- The resolution creating the new intelligence committee structure should grant subpoena authority to the committee or committees. The majority party's representation on this committee should never exceed the minority's representation by more than one.

- Four of the members appointed to this committee or committees should be a member who also serves on each of the following additional committees: Armed Services, Judiciary, Foreign Affairs, and the Defense Appropriations subcommittee. In this way the other major congressional interests can be brought together in the new committee's work.

- Members should serve indefinitely on the intelligence committees, without set terms, thereby letting them accumulate expertise.

- The committees should be smaller—perhaps seven or nine members in each house—so that each member feels a greater sense of responsibility, and accountability, for the quality of the committee's work.

The leaders of the Department of Homeland Security now appear before 88 committees and subcommittees of Congress. One expert witness (not a member of the administration) told us that this is perhaps the single largest obstacle impeding the department's successful development. The one attempt to consolidate such committee authority, the House Select Committee on Homeland Security, may be eliminated. The Senate does not have even this.

Congress needs to establish for the Department of Homeland Security the kind of clear authority and responsibility that exist to enable the Justice Department to deal with crime and the Defense Department to deal with threats to national security. Through not more than one authorizing committee and one appropriating subcommittee in each house, Congress should be able to ask the secretary of homeland security whether he or she has the resources to provide reasonable security against major terrorist acts within the United States and to hold the secretary accountable for the department's performance.

Recommendation: Congress should create a single, principal point of oversight and review for homeland security. Congressional leaders are best able to judge what committee should have jurisdiction over this department and its duties. But we believe that Congress does have the obligation to choose one in the House and one in the Senate, and that this committee should be a permanent standing committee with a nonpartisan staff.

Improve the Transitions
Between Administrations

In . . . the transition of 2000–2001, . . . the new administration did not have its deputy cabinet officers in place until the spring of 2001, and the critical subcabinet officials were not confirmed until the summer—if then. In other words, the new administration—like others before it—did not have its team on the job until at least six months after it took office.

Recommendation: Since a catastrophic attack could occur with little or no notice, we should minimize as much as possible the disruption of national security policymaking during the change of administrations by accelerating the process for national security appointments. We think the process could be improved significantly so transitions can work more effectively and allow new officials to assume their new responsibilities as quickly as possible.

- Before the election, candidates should submit the names of selected members of their prospective transition teams to the FBI so that, if necessary, those team members can obtain security clearances immediately after the election is over.

- A president-elect should submit lists of possible candidates for national security positions to begin obtaining security clearances immediately after the election, so that their background investigations can be complete before January 20.

- A single federal agency should be responsible for providing and maintaining security clearances, ensuring uniform standards—including uniform security questionnaires and financial report requirements, and maintaining a single database. This agency can also be responsible for administering polygraph tests on behalf of organizations that require them.

- A president-elect should submit the nominations of the entire new national security team, through the level of under secretary of cabinet departments, not later than January 20. The Senate, in return, should adopt special rules requiring hearings and votes to confirm or reject national security nominees within 30 days of their submission. The Senate should not require confirmation of such executive appointees below Executive Level 3.

- The outgoing administration should provide the president-elect, as soon as possible after election day, with a classified, compartmented list that catalogues specific, operational threats to national security; major military or covert operations; and pending decisions on the possible use of force. Such a document could provide both notice and a checklist, inviting a president-elect to inquire and learn more.

Organizing America's Defenses in the United States

The Future Role of the FBI

We have considered proposals for a new agency dedicated to intelligence collection in the United States. Some call this a proposal for an "American MI-5," although the analogy is weak—the actual British Security Service is a relatively small worldwide agency that combines duties assigned in the U.S. government to the Terrorist Threat Integration Center, the CIA, the FBI, and the Department of Homeland Security.

The concern about the FBI is that it has long favored its criminal justice mission over its national security mission. Part of the reason for this is the demand around the country for FBI help on criminal matters. The FBI was criticized, rightly, for the overzealous domestic intelligence investigations disclosed during the 1970s. The pendulum swung away from those types of investigations during the 1980s and 1990s, though the FBI maintained an active counterintelligence function and was the lead agency for the investigation of foreign terrorist groups operating inside the United States.

We do not recommend the creation of a new domestic intelligence agency. It is not needed if our other recommendations are adopted—to establish a strong national intelligence center, part of the NCTC, that will oversee counterterrorism intelligence work, foreign and domestic, and to create a National Intelligence Director who can set and enforce standards for the collection, processing, and reporting of information.

Under the structures we recommend, the FBI's role is focused, but still vital. The FBI does need to be able to direct its thousands of agents and other employees to collect intelligence in America's cities and towns—interviewing informants, conducting surveillance and searches, tracking individuals, working collaboratively with local authorities, and doing so with meticulous attention to detail and compliance with the law. The FBI's job in the streets of the United States would thus be a domestic equivalent, operating under the U.S. Constitution and quite different laws and rules, to the job of the CIA's operations officers abroad.

Creating a new domestic intelligence agency has other drawbacks.

- The FBI is accustomed to carrying out sensitive intelligence collection operations in compliance with the law. If a new domestic intelligence agency were outside of the Department of Justice, the process of legal oversight—never easy—could become even more difficult. Abuses of civil liberties could create a backlash that would impair the collection of needed intelligence.

- Creating a new domestic intelligence agency would divert attention of the officials most responsible for current counterterrorism efforts while the threat remains high. Putting a new player into the mix of federal agencies with counterterrorism responsibilities would exacerbate existing information-sharing problems.

- A new domestic intelligence agency would need to acquire assets and personnel. The FBI already has 28,000 employees; 56 field offices, 400 satellite offices, and 47 legal attaché offices; a laboratory, operations center, and training facility; an existing network of informants, cooperating defendants, and other sources; and relationships with state and local law enforcement, the CIA, and foreign intelligence and law enforcement agencies.

- Counterterrorism investigations in the United States very quickly become matters that involve violations of criminal law and possible law enforcement action. Because the FBI can have agents working criminal matters and agents working intelligence investigations concerning the same international terrorism target, the full range of investigative tools against a suspected terrorist can be considered within one agency. The removal of "the wall" that existed before 9/11 between intelligence and law enforcement has opened up new opportunities for cooperative action within the FBI.

- Counterterrorism investigations often overlap or are cued by other criminal investigations, such as money laundering or the smuggling of contraband. In the field, the close connection to criminal work has many benefits.

Our recommendation to leave counterterrorism intelligence collection in the United States with the FBI still depends on an assessment that the FBI—if it makes an all-out effort to institutionalize change—can do the job. . . . [W]e have been impressed by the determination that agents display in tracking down details, patiently going the extra mile and working the extra month, to put facts in the place of speculation. In our report we have shown how agents in Phoenix, Minneapolis, and New York displayed initiative in pressing their investigations.

FBI agents and analysts in the field need to have sustained support and dedicated resources to become stronger intelligence officers. They need to be rewarded for acquiring informants and for gathering and disseminating information differently and more broadly than usual in a traditional criminal investigation. FBI employees need to report and analyze what they have learned in ways the Bureau has never done before.

Under Director Robert Mueller, the Bureau has made significant progress in improving its intelligence capabilities. It now has an Office of Intelligence, overseen by the top tier of FBI management. Field intelligence groups have been created in all field offices to put FBI priorities and the emphasis on intelligence into practice. Advances have been made in improving the Bureau's information technology systems and in increasing connectivity and information sharing with intelligence community agencies.

Director Mueller has also recognized that the FBI's reforms are far from complete. He has outlined a number of areas where added measures may be necessary. Specifically, he has recognized that the FBI needs to recruit from a broader pool of candidates, that agents and analysts working on national security matters require specialized training, and that agents should specialize within programs after obtaining a generalist foundation. The FBI is developing career tracks for agents to specialize in counterterrorism/counterintelligence, cyber crimes, criminal investigations, or intelligence. It is establishing a program for certifying agents as intelligence officers, a certification that will be a prerequisite for promotion to the senior ranks of the Bureau. New training programs have been instituted for intelligence-related subjects.

The Director of the FBI has proposed creating an Intelligence Directorate as a further refinement of the FBI intelligence program. This directorate would include units for intelligence planning and policy and for the direction of analysts and linguists.

We want to ensure that the Bureau's shift to a preventive counterterrorism posture is more fully institutionalized so that it survives beyond Director Mueller's tenure. We have found that in the past the Bureau has announced its willingness to reform and restructure itself to address transnational security threats, but has fallen short—failing to effect the necessary institutional and cultural changes organization-wide. We want to ensure that this does not happen again. Despite having found acceptance of the Director's clear message that counterterrorism is now the FBI's top priority, two years after 9/11 we also found gaps between some of the announced reforms and the reality in the field. We are concerned that management in the field offices still can allocate people and resources to local concerns that diverge from the national security mission. This system could revert to a focus on lower-priority criminal justice cases over national security requirements.

Recommendation: A specialized and integrated national security workforce should be established at the FBI consisting of agents, analysts, linguists, and surveillance specialists who are recruited, trained, rewarded, and retained to ensure the development of an institutional culture imbued with a deep expertise in intelligence and national security.

- The president, by executive order or directive, should direct the FBI to develop this intelligence cadre.

- Recognizing that cross-fertilization between the criminal justice and national security disciplines is vital to the success of both missions, all new agents should receive basic training in both areas. Furthermore, new agents should begin their careers with meaningful assignments in both areas.

- Agents and analysts should then specialize in one of these disciplines and have the option to work such matters for their entire career with the Bureau. Certain advanced training courses and assignments to other intelligence agencies should be required to advance within the national security discipline.

- In the interest of cross-fertilization, all senior FBI managers, including those working on law enforcement matters, should be certified intelligence officers.

- The FBI should fully implement a recruiting, hiring, and selection process for agents and analysts that enhances its ability to target and attract individuals with educational and professional backgrounds in intelligence, international relations, language, technology, and other relevant skills.

- The FBI should institute the integration of analysts, agents, linguists, and surveillance personnel in the field so that a dedicated team approach is brought to bear on national security intelligence operations.

- Each field office should have an official at the field office's deputy level for national security matters. This individual would have manage-

ment oversight and ensure that the national priorities are carried out in the field.

- The FBI should align its budget structure according to its four main programs—intelligence, counterterrorism and counterintelligence, criminal, and criminal justice services—to ensure better transparency on program costs, management of resources, and protection of the intelligence program.[62]

- The FBI should report regularly to Congress in its semiannual program reviews designed to identify whether each field office is appropriately addressing FBI and national program priorities.

- The FBI should report regularly to Congress in detail on the qualifications, status, and roles of analysts in the field and at headquarters. Congress should ensure that analysts are afforded training and career opportunities on a par with those offered analysts in other intelligence community agencies.

- The Congress should make sure funding is available to accelerate the expansion of secure facilities in FBI field offices so as to increase their ability to use secure email systems and classified intelligence product exchanges. The Congress should monitor whether the FBI's information-sharing principles are implemented in practice.

The FBI is just a small fraction of the national law enforcement community in the United States, a community comprised mainly of state and local agencies. The network designed for sharing information, and the work of the FBI through local Joint Terrorism Task Forces, should build a reciprocal relationship, in which state and local agents understand what information they are looking for and, in return, receive some of the information being developed about what is happening, or may happen, in their communities. In this relationship, the Department of Homeland Security also will play an important part.

The Homeland Security Act of 2002 gave the under secretary for information analysis and infrastructure protection broad responsibilities. In practice, this directorate has the job to map "terrorist threats to the homeland against our assessed vulnerabilities in order to drive our efforts to protect against terrorist threats."[63] These capabilities are still embryonic. The directorate has not yet developed the capacity to perform one of its assigned jobs, which is to assimilate and analyze information from Homeland Security's own component agencies, such as the Coast Guard, Secret Service, Transportation Security Administration, Immigration and Customs Enforcement, and Customs and Border Protection. The secretary of homeland security must ensure that these components work with the Information Analysis and Infrastructure Protection Directorate so that this office can perform its mission.[64]

Homeland Defense

At several points in our inquiry, we asked, "Who is responsible for defending us at home?" Our national defense at home is the responsibility, first, of the Department of Defense and, second, of the Department of Homeland Security. They must have clear delineations of responsibility and authority.

We found that NORAD, which had been given the responsibility for defending U.S. airspace, had construed that mission to focus on threats coming from outside America's borders. It did not adjust its focus even though the intelligence community had gathered intelligence on the possibility that terrorists might turn to hijacking and even use of planes as missiles. We have been assured that NORAD has now embraced the full mission. Northern Command has been established to assume responsibility for the defense of the domestic United States.

Recommendation: The Department of Defense and its oversight committees should regularly assess the adequacy of Northern Command's strategies and planning to defend the United States against military threats to the homeland.

The Department of Homeland Security was established to consolidate all of the domestic agencies responsible for securing America's borders and national infrastructure, most of which is in private hands. It should identify those elements of our transportation, energy, communications, financial, and other institutions that need to be protected, develop plans to protect that infrastructure, and exercise the mechanisms to enhance preparedness. This means going well beyond the preexisting jobs of the agencies that have been brought together inside the department.

Recommendation: The Department of Homeland Security and its oversight committees should regularly assess the types of threats the country faces to determine (a) the adequacy of the government's plans—and the progress against those plans—to protect America's critical infrastructure and (b) the readiness of the government to respond to the threats that the United States might face.

We look forward to a national debate on the merits of what we have recommended, and we will participate vigorously in that debate.

Questions for Further Discussion

1. How is the threat posed by Al Qaeda different from the threats posed by nation-states?

2. Do you think the recommendations proposed by the commissioners represent an effective response to the challenge posed by weapons of mass destruction in the hands of terrorists?

3. What do you think will be the main challenges faced by the National Counterintelligence Center in trying to coordinate an effective federal government response to transnational terrorist networks?

4. Why did the commissioners conclude that the U.S. intelligence community was badly organized to combat international and domestic terrorism?

Endnotes

1. For spending totals, see David Baumann, "Accounting for the Deficit," *National Journal*, June 12, 2004, p. 1852 (combining categories for defense discretionary, homeland security, and international affairs).

2. White House press release, "National Strategy for Combating Terrorism," Feb. 2003 (online at <www.whitehouse.gov/news/releases/2003/02/20030214-7.html>).

3. "Islamist terrorism is an immediate derivative of *Islamism*. This term distinguishes itself from *Islamic* by the fact that the latter refers to a religion and culture in existence over a millennium, whereas the first is a political/religious phenomenon linked to the great events of the 20th century. Furthermore Islamists define themselves as 'Islamiyyoun/Islamists' precisely to differentiate themselves from 'Muslimun/Muslims.'... Islamism is defined as an Islamic militant, anti-democratic movement, bearing a holistic vision of Islam whose final aim is the restoration of the caliphate.'" Mehdi Mozaffari, "Bin Laden and Islamist Terrorism," *Militaert Tidsskrift*, vol. 131 (Mar. 2002), p. 1 (online at <www.mirkflem.pup.blueyonder.co.uk/pdf/islamistterrorism.pdf>). The Islamist movement, born about 1940, is a product of the modern world, influenced by Marxist-Leninist concepts about revolutionary organization. "Islamists consider Islam to be as much a religion as an 'ideology,' a neologism which they introduced and which remains anathema to the ulamas (the clerical scholars)." Olivier Roy, *The Failure of Political Islam*, trans. Carol Volk (Harvard Univ. Press, 1994), p. 3. Facing political limits by the end of the 1990s, the extremist wing of the Islamist movement "rejected the democratic references invoked by the moderates; and as a result, raw terrorism in its most spectacular and destructive form became its main option for reviving armed struggle in the new millennium." Gilles Kepel, *Jihad: The Trail of Political Islam*, trans. Anthony Roberts (Harvard Univ. Press, 2002), p. 14.

4. Opening the Islamic Conference of Muslim leaders from around the world on October 16, 2003, then Malaysian prime minister Mahathir Mohamad said: "Today we, the whole Muslim ummah [community of be-

lievers] are treated with contempt and dishonour. Our religion is denigrated. Our holy places desecrated. Our countries are occupied. Our people are starved and killed. None of our countries are truly independent. We are under pressure to conform to our oppressors' wishes about how we should behave, how we should govern our lands, how we should think even." He added: "There is a feeling of hopelessness among the Muslim countries and their people. They feel that they can do nothing right. They believe that things can only get worse. The Muslims will forever be oppressed and dominated by the Europeans and Jews." The prime minister's argument was that the Muslims should gather their assets, not striking back blindly, but instead planning a thoughtful, long-term strategy to defeat their worldwide enemies, which he argued were controlled by the Jews. "But today the Jews rule the world by proxy. They get others to fight and die for them." Speech at the Opening of the Tenth Session of the Islamic Summit Conference, Oct. 16, 2003 (online at <www.oicsummit2003. org.my/speech_03.php>).

5. CIA map, "Possible Remote Havens for Terrorist and Other Illicit Activity," May 2003.

6. For the numbers, see Tariq interview (Oct. 20, 2003).

7. For Pakistan playing a key role in apprehending 500 terrorists, see Richard Armitage testimony, Mar. 23, 2004.

8. For Pakistan's unpoliced areas, see Tasneem Noorani interview (Oct. 27, 2003).

9. Pakistanis and Afghanis interviews (Oct. 2003); DOD Special Operations Command and Central Command briefings (Sept. 15–16, 2004); U.S. intelligence official interview (July 9, 2004).

10. Pervez Musharraf, "A Plea for Enlightened Moderation: Muslims Must Raise Themselves Up Through Individual Achievement and Socioeconomic Emancipation," *Washington Post*, June 1, 2004, p. A23.

11. For a review of ISAF's role, see NATO report, "NATO in Afghanistan," updated July 9, 2004 (online at <www.nato.int/issues/afghanistan>).

12. United States Institute of Peace report, "Establishing the Rule of Law in Afghanistan," Mar. 2004, pp. 1–3 (online at <www.usip.org/pubs/specialreports/srll7.html>).

13. For the change, see Lakhdar Brahimi interview (Oct. 24, 2003); U.S. officials in Afghanistan interview (Oct. 2003). For the request that the United States remain, see Kandahar province local leaders interview (Oct. 21, 2003). For the effect of the United States leaving, see Karim Khalili interview (Oct. 23, 2003).

14. Some have criticized the Bush administration for neglecting Afghanistan because of Iraq. Others, including General Franks, say that the size of the U.S. military commitment in Afghanistan has not been compromised by the commitments in Iraq. We have not investigated the issue and cannot offer a judgment on it.

15. Even if the U.S. forces, stretched thin, are reluctant to take on this role, "a limited, but extremely useful, change in the military mandate would involve intelligence sharing with civilian law enforcement and a willingness to take action against drug warehouses and heroin laboratories." United States Institute of Peace report, "Establishing the Rule of Law in Afghanistan," Mar. 2004, p. 17.

16. For barriers to Saudi monitoring of charities, see, e.g., Robert Jordan interview (Jan. 14, 2004); David Aufhauser interview (Feb. 12, 2004).

17. For the Saudi reformer's view, see Members of *majles al-shura* interview (Oct. 14, 2003).

18. Neil MacFarquhar, "Saudis Support a Jihad in Iraq, Not Back Home," *New York Times*, Apr. 23, 2004, p. A1.

19. Prince Bandar Bin Sultan, "A Diplomat's Call for War," *Washington Post*, June 6, 2004, p. B4 (translation of original in *Al-Watan*, June 2, 2004).

20. President Clinton meeting (Apr. 8, 2004).

21. For Jordan's initiatives, see testimony of William Burns before the Subcommittee on the Middle East and Central Asia of the House International Relations Committee, Mar. 19, 2003 (online at <www.house.gov /international_jrelations/108/burn0319.htm>). For the report, see United Nations Development Programme report, *Arab Human Development Report 2003: Building a Knowledge Society* (United Nations, 2003) (online at <www.miftah,org/Doc/Reports/Eng lishcomplete2003.pdf>).

22. DOD memo, Rumsfeld to Myers, Wolfowitz, Pace, and Feith, "Global War on Terrorism," Oct. 16, 2003 (online at <www.usatoday.com/news/washington/execu tive/rumsfeld-memo.htm>).

23. For the statistics, see James Zogby, *What Arabs Think: Values, Beliefs, and Concerns* (Zogby International, 2002). For fear of a U.S. attack, see Pew Global Attitudes Project report, *Views of a Changing World: June 2003* (Pew Research Center for the People and the Press, 2003), p. 2. In our interviews, current and former U.S. officials dealing with the Middle East corroborated these findings.

24. For polling soon after 9/11, see Pew Research Center for the People and the Press report, "America Admired, Yet Its New Vulnerability Seen as Good Thing, Say Opinion Leaders; Little Support for Expanding War on Terrorism" (online at <http://peoplepress. org/ reports/print.php3?ReportID=145>). For the quotation, see Pew Global Attitudes Project report, "War With Iraq Further Divides Global Publics But World Embraces Democratic Values and Free Markets," June 3, 2003 (online at <www.pewtrusts.com/ideas/ideas_ item.cfm?content_item_id=1645&content_type_ id=7>).

25. For the Occidentalist "creed of Islamist revolutionaries," see, e.g., Avishai Margalit and Ian Buruma, *Occidentalism: The West in the Eyes of Its Enemies* (Penguin Press, 2004).

26. We draw these statistics, significantly, from the U.S. government's working paper circulated in April 2004 to G-8 "sherpas" in preparation for the 2004 G-8 summit. The paper was leaked and published in *Al-Hayat*. "U.S. Working Paper for G-8 Sherpas," *Al-Hayat*, Feb. 13, 2004 (online at <http://english.daralhayat.com/ Spec/02-2004/Article-20040213-ac40bdaf-c0a8-01ed-004e-5e7ac897d678/story.html>).

27. Richard Holbrooke, "Get the Message Out," *Washington Post*, Oct. 28, 2001, p. B7; Richard Armitage interview Jan. 12, 2004).

28. Testimony of George Tenet, "The Worldwide Threat 2004; Challenges in a Changing Global Context," before the Senate Select Committee on Intelligence, Feb. 24, 2004.

29. U.S. Department of Energy Advisory Board report, "A Report Card on the Department of Energy's Non-proliferation Programs with Russia," Jan. 10, 2001, p. vi.

30. For terrorists being self-funding, see United Nations report, "Second Report of the [UN] Monitoring Group, Pursuant to Security Council Resolution 1390," Sept. 19, 2002, p. 13.

31. For legal entry, see White House report, Office of Homeland Security, "The National Strategy for Homeland Security," July 2002, p. 20 (online at <www.whitehouse.gov/homeland/book/index.html>). For illegal entry, see Chicago Council on Foreign Relations task force report, *Keeping the Promise: Immigration Proposals From the Heartland* (Chicago Council on Foreign Relations, 2004), p. 28.

32. The names of at least three of the hijackers (Nawaf al Hazmi, Salem al Hazmi, and Khalid al Mihdhar) were in information systems of the intelligence community and thus potentially could have been watchlisted. Had they been watchlisted, the connections to terrorism could have been exposed at the time they applied for a visa or at the port of entry. The names of at least three of the hijackers (Nawaf al Hazmi, Salem al Hazmi, and Khalid al Mihdhar), were in information systems of the intelligence community and thus potentially could have been watchlisted. Had they been watchlisted, their terrorist affiliations could have been exposed either at the time they applied for a visa or at the port of entry. Two of the hijackers (Satam al Suqami and Abdul Aziz al Omari) presented passports manipulated in a fraudulent manner that has subsequently been associated with al Qaeda. Based on our review of their visa and travel histories, we believe it possible that as many as eleven additional hijackers (Wail al Shehri, Waleed al Shehri, Mohand al Shehri, Hani Hanjour, Majed Moqed, Nawaf al Hazmi, Hamza al Ghamdi, Ahmed al Ghamdi, Saeed al Ghamdi, Ahmed al Nami, and Ahmad al Haznawi) held passports containing these same fraudulent features, but their passports have not been found so we cannot be sure. Khalid al Mihdhar and Salem al Hazmi presented passports with a suspicious indicator of Islamic extremism. There is reason to believe that the passports of three other hijackers (Nawaf al Hazmi, Ahmed al Nami, and Ahmad al Haznawi) issued in the same Saudi passport office may have contained this same indicator; however, their passports have not been found, so we cannot be sure.

33. Khallad Bin Attash, Ramzi Binalshibh, Zakariya Essabar, Ali Abdul Aziz Ali, and Saeed al Ghamdi (not the individual by the same name who became a hijacker) tried to get visas and failed. Kahtani was unable to prove his admissibility and withdrew his application for admission after an immigration inspector remained unpersuaded that he was a tourist. All the hijackers whose visa applications we reviewed arguably could have been denied visas because their applications were not filled out completely. Had State visa officials routinely had a practice of acquiring more information in such cases, they likely would have found more grounds for denial. For example, three hijackers made statements on their visa applications that could have been proved false by U.S. government records (Hani Hanjour, Saeed al Ghamdi, and Khalid al Mihdhar), and many lied about their employment or educational status. Two hijackers could have been denied admission at the port of entry based on violations of immigration rules governing terms of admission—Mohamed Atta overstayed his tourist visa and then failed to present a proper vocational school visa when he entered in January 2001; Ziad Jarrah attended school in June 2000 without properly adjusting his immigration status, an action that violated his immigration status and rendered him inadmissible on each of his six subsequent reentries into the United States between June 2000 and August 5, 2001. There were pos-

sible grounds to deny entry to a third hijacker (Marwan al Shehhi). One hijacker violated his immigration status by failing to enroll as a student after entry (Hani Hanjour); two hijackers overstayed their terms of admission by four and eight months respectively (Satam al Suqami and Nawaf al Hazmi). Atta and Shehhi attended a flight school (Huffman Aviation) that the Justice Department's Inspector General concluded should not have been certified to accept foreign students, see DOJ Inspector General's report, "The INS' Contacts with Two September 11 Terrorists: A Review of the INS's Admissions of Atta and Shehhi, its Processing of their Change of Status Applications, and its Efforts to Track Foreign Students in the United States," May 20, 2002.

34. John Gordon interview (May 13, 2004).

35. For a description of a layering approach, see Stephen Flynn, *America the Vulnerable: How the U.S. Has Failed to Secure the Homeland and Protect Its People From Terrorism* (HarperCollins, 2004), p. 69.

36. The logical and timely rollout of such a program is hampered by an astonishingly long list of congressional mandates. The system originated in the Illegal Immigration Reform and Immigrant Responsibility Act of 1996 and applied to all non-U.S. citizens who enter or exit the United States at any port of entry. Pub. L. No. 104-208, 110 Stat. 3009 (1996), § 110. The Data Management Improvement Act of 2000 altered this mandate by incorporating a requirement for a searchable centralized database, limiting the government's ability to require new data from certain travelers and setting a series of implementation deadlines. Pub. L. No. 106-215, 114 Stat. 337 (2000), § 2(a). The USA PATRIOT Act mandated that the Attorney General and Secretary of State "particularly focus" on having the entry-exit system include biometrics and tamper-resistant travel documents readable at all ports of entry. Pub. L. No. 107-56, 115 Stat. 272 (2001), § 1008(a). In the Enhanced Border Security and Visa Entry Reform Act, Congress directed that, not later than October 26, 2004, the attorney general and the secretary of state issue to all non-U.S. citizens only machine-readable, tamper-resistant visas and other travel and entry documents that use biometric identifiers and install equipment at all U.S. ports of entry to allow biometric authentication of such documents. Pub. L. No. 107-173, 116 Stat. 543 (2002), § 303(b).The Act also required that increased security still facilitate the free flow of commerce and travel. Ibid. § 102(a)(1)(C). The administration has requested a delay of two years for the requirement of tamper-proof passports. Testimony of Thomas Ridge before the House Judiciary Committee, Apr. 21, 2004 (online at <www.dhs.gov/dhspublic/display?theme=45&content=3498&print=true>). Program planners have set a goal of collecting information, confirming identity, providing information about foreign nationals throughout the entire immigration system, and ultimately enabling each point in the system to assess the lawfulness of travel and any security risks.

37. There are at least three registered traveler programs underway, at different points in the system, designed and run by two different agencies in the Department of Homeland Security (outside the U.S.VISIT system), which must ultimately be the basis for access to the United States.

38. For the statistics, see DOS report, "Workload Statistics by Post Regions for All Visa Classes," June 18, 2004. One post-9/11 screening process, known as Con-

dor, has conducted over 130,000 extra name-checks. DOS letter, Karl Hofmann to the Commission, Apr. 5, 2004. The checks have caused significant delays in some cases but have never resulted in visas being denied on terrorism grounds. For a discussion of visa delays, see General Accounting Office report, "Border Security: Improvements Needed to Reduce Time Taken to Adjudicate Visas for Science Students and Scholars," Feb. 2004. We do not know all the reasons why visa applications have dropped so significantly. Several factors beyond the visa process itself include the National Security Entry-Exit Registration System, which requires additional screening processes for certain groups from Arab and Muslim countries; the Iraq war; and perhaps cyclical economic factors. For the cost to the United States of visa backlogs, see National Foreign Trade Council report, "Visa Backlog Costs U.S. Exporters More Than $30 Billion Since 2002, New Study Finds," June 2, 2004 (online at <www.nftc .org/newsflash/newsflash.asp?Mode=View&article id=1686&Category=All>).

39. These issues are on the G-8 agenda. White House press release, "G-8 Secure and Facilitated Travel Initiative (SAFTI)," June 9, 2004 (online at <www.whitehouse .gov/news/releases/2004/06/ 20040609-51.html>). Lax passport issuance standards are among the vulnerabilities exploited by terrorists, possibly including two of the 9/11 hijackers. Three models exist for strengthened prescreening: (1) better screening by airlines, such as the use of improved document authentication technology; (2) posting of border agents or inspectors in foreign airports to work cooperatively with foreign counterparts; and (3) establishing a full preinspection regime, such as now exists for travel to the United States from Canada and Ireland. All three models should be pursued, in addition to electronic prescreening.

40. Among the more important problems to address is that of varying transliterations of the same name. For example, the current lack of a single convention for transliterating Arabic names enabled the 19 hijackers to vary the spelling of their names to defeat name-based watchlist systems and confuse any potential efforts to locate them. While the gradual introduction of biometric identifiers will help, that process will take years, and a name match will always be useful. The ICAO should discuss the adoption of a standard requiring a digital code for all names that need to be translated into the Roman alphabet, ensuring one common spelling for all countries.

41. On achieving more reliable identification, see Markle Foundation task force report, *Creating a Trusted Information Network for Homeland Security* (Markle Foundation, 2003), p. 72 (online at <www.markle.org>).

42. General Accounting Office report, *Mass Transit: Federal Action Could Help Transit Agencies Address Security Challenges*, GAO-03-263, Dec. 2002 (online at <www.gao.gov/new.items/d03263.pdf>).

43. The Bush administration clarified the respective missions of the different intelligence analysis centers in a letter sent by Secretary Ridge, DCI Tenet, FBI Director Mueller, and TTIC Director Brennan to Senators Susan Collins and Carl Levin on April 13, 2004. The letter did not mention any element of the Department of Defense. It stated that the DCI would define what analytical resources he would transfer from the CTC to TTIC no later than June 1, 2004. DCI Tenet subsequently told us that he decided that TTIC would have primary

responsibility for terrorism analysis but that the CIA and the Defense Intelligence Agency would grow their own analysts. TTIC will have tasking authority over terrorism analysts in other intelligence agencies, although there will need to be a board to supervise deconfliction. George Tenet interview (July 2, 2004). We have not received any details regarding this plan.

44. "TTIC has no operational authority. However, TTIC has the authority to task collection and analysis from Intelligence Community agencies, the FBI, and DHS through tasking mechanisms we will create. The analytic work conducted at TTIC creates products that inform each of TTIC's partner elements, as well as other Federal departments and agencies as appropriate." Letter from Ridge and others to Collins and Levin, Apr. 13, 2004.

45. Donald Rumsfeld prepared statement, Mar, 23, 2004, p. 20.

46. In this conception, the NCTC should plan actions, assigning responsibilities for operational direction and execution to other agencies. It would be built on TTIC and would be supported by the intelligence community as TTIC is now. Whichever route is chosen, the scarce analytical resources now dispersed among TTIC, the Defense Intelligence Agency's Joint Interagency Task Force—Combatting Terrorism (JITF-CT), and the DCI's Counterterrorist Center (CTC) should be concentrated more effectively than they are now.

The DCI's Counterterrorist Center would become a CIA unit, to handle the direction and execution of tasks assigned to the CIA. It could have detailees from other agencies, as it does now, to perform this operational mission. It would yield much of the broader, strategic analytic duties and personnel to the NCTC. The CTC would rely on the restructured CIA (discussed in the next section) to organize, train, and equip its personnel.

Similarly, the FBI's Counterterrorism Division would remain, as now, the operational arm of the Bureau to combat terrorism. As it does now, it would work with other agencies in carrying out these missions, retaining the JITF structure now in place. The Counterterrorism Division would rely on the FBI's Office of Intelligence to train and equip its personnel, helping to process and report the information gathered in the field.

The Defense Department's unified commands—SOCOM, NORTHCOM, and CENTCOM—would be the joint operational centers taking on DOD tasks. Much of the excellent analytical talent that has been assembled in the Defense Intelligence Agency's JITF-CT should merge into the planned NCTC.

The Department of Homeland Security's Directorate for Information Analysis and Infrastructure Protection should retain its core duties, but the NCTC should have the ultimate responsibility for producing net assessments that utilize Homeland Security's analysis of domestic vulnerabilities and integrate all-source analysis of foreign intelligence about the terrorist enemy.

The State Department's counterterrorism office would be a critical participant in the NCTC's work, taking the lead in directing the execution of the counterterrorism foreign policy mission.

The proposed National Counterterrorism Center should offer one-stop shopping to agencies with counterterrorism and homeland security responsibilities. That is, it should be an authoritative reference base on the transnational terrorist organizations: their people, goals, strategies, capabilities, networks of contacts and support, the context in which they operate, and their characteristic habits across the life cycle of operations—recruitment, reconnaissance, target selection, logistics, and travel. For example, this Center would offer an integrated depiction of groups like al Qaeda or Hezbollah worldwide, overseas, and in the United States.

The NCTC will not eliminate the need for the executive departments to have their own analytic units. But it would enable agency-based analytic units to become smaller and more efficient. In particular, it would make it possible for these agency-based analytic units to concentrate on analysis that is tailored to their agency's specific responsibilities.

A useful analogy is military intelligence. There, the Defense Intelligence Agency and the service production agencies (like the Army's National Ground Intelligence Center) are the institutional memory and reference source for enemy order of battle, enemy organization, and enemy equipment. Yet the Joint Staff and all the theater commands still have their own J-2s. They draw on the information they need, tailoring and applying it to their operational needs. As they learn more from their tactical operations, they pass intelligence of enduring value back up to the Defense Intelligence Agency and the services so it can be evaluated, form part of the institutional memory, and help guide future collection.

In our proposal, that reservoir of institutional memory about terrorist organizations would function for the government as a whole, and would be in the NCTC.

47. The head of the NCTC would thus help coordinate the operational side of these agencies, like the FBI's Counterterrorism Division. The intelligence side of these agencies, such as the FBI's Office of Intelligence, would be overseen by the National Intelligence Director we recommend later in this chapter.

48. The quotation goes on: "It includes gaps in intelligence, but also intelligence that, like a string of pearls too precious to wear, is too sensitive to give to those who need it. It includes the alarm that fails to work, but also the alarm that has gone off so often it has been disconnected. It includes the unalert watchman, but also the one who knows he'll be chewed out by his superior if he gets higher authority out of bed. It includes the contingencies that occur to no one, but also those that everyone assumes somebody else is taking care of. It includes straightforward procrastination, but also decisions protracted by internal disagreement. It includes, in addition, the inability of individual human beings to rise to the occasion until they are sure it is the occasion—which is usually too late. . . . Finally, as at Pearl Harbor, surprise may include some measure of genuine novelty introduced by the enemy, and some sheer bad luck." Thomas Schelling, foreword to Roberta Wohlstetter, *Pearl Harbor: Warning and Decision* (Stanford Univ. Press, 1962), p. viii.

49. For the Goldwater-Nichols Act, see Pub. L. No. 99-433,100 Stat. 992 (1986). For a general discussion of the act, see Gordon Lederman, *Reorganizing the Joint Chiefs of Staff: The Goldwater-Nichols Act of 1986* (Greenwood, 1999); James Locher, *Victory on the Potomac: The Goldwater-Nichols Act Unifies the Pentagon* (Texas A&M Univ. Press, 2003).

50. For a history of the DCI's authority over the intelligence community, see CIA report, Michael Warner ed., *Central Intelligence; Origin and Evolution* (CIA Center for the Study of Intelligence, 2001). For the Director's view of his community authorities, see DCI directive, "Director of Central Intelligence Directive 1/1: The Authorities and Responsibilities of the Director of Central Intelligence as Head of the U.S. Intelligence Community," Nov. 19, 1998.

51. As Norman Augustine, former chairman of Lockheed Martin Corporation, writes regarding power in the government, "As in business, cash is king. If you are not in charge of your budget, you are not king." Norman Augustine, *Managing to Survive in Washington: A Beginner's Guide to High-Level Management in Government* (Center for Strategic and International Studies, 2000), p. 20.

52. For the DCI and the secretary of defense, see 50 U.S.C. § 403-6(a). If the director does not concur with the secretary's choice, then the secretary is required to notify the president of the director's nonconcurrence. Ibid. For the DCI and the attorney general, see 50 U.S.C. § 403-6(b)(3).

53. The new program would replace the existing National Foreign Intelligence Program.

54. Some smaller parts of the current intelligence community, such as the State Department's intelligence bureau and the Energy Department's intelligence entity, should not be funded out of the national intelligence program and should be the responsibility of their home departments.

55. The head of the NCTC should have the rank of a deputy national intelligence director, e.g., Executive Level II, but would have a different title.

56. If the organization of defense intelligence remains as it is now, the appropriate official would be the under secretary of defense for intelligence. If defense intelligence is reorganized to elevate the responsibilities of the director of the DIA, then that person might be the appropriate official.

57. For the information technology architecture, see Ruth David interview (June 10, 2003). For the necessity of moving from need-to-know to need-to-share, see James Steinberg testimony, Oct. 14, 2003. The Director still has no strategy for removing information-sharing barriers and—more than two years since 9/11—has only appointed a working group on the subject. George Tenet prepared statement, Mar. 24, 2004, p. 37.

58. The intelligence community currently makes information shareable by creating "tearline" reports, with the nonshareable information at the top and then, below the "tearline," the portion that recipients are told they can share. This proposal reverses that concept. All reports are created as tearline data, with the shareable information at the top and with added details accessible on a system that requires permissions or authentication.

59. See Markle Foundation Task Force report, *Creating a Trusted Information Network for Homeland Security* (Markle Foundation, 2003); Markle Foundation Task Force report, *Protecting America's Freedom in the Information Age* (Markle Foundation, 2002) (both online at <www.markle.org>).

60. Markle Foundation Task Force report, *Creating a Trusted Information Network*, p. 12. The pressing need for such guidelines was also spotlighted by the Technology and Privacy Advisory Committee appointed by

Secretary Rumsfeld to advise the Department of Defense on the privacy implications of its Terrorism Information Awareness Program. Technology and Privacy Advisory Committee report, *Safeguarding Privacy in the Fight Against Terrorism* (2004) (online at <www.sainc.com/tapac/TAPAC_Report_Final_5-10-04.pdf>). We take no position on the particular recommendations offered in that report, but it raises issues that pertain to the government as a whole—not just to the Department of Defense.

61. This change should eliminate the need in the Senate for the current procedure of sequential referral of the annual authorization bill for the national foreign intelligence program. In that process, the Senate Armed Services Committee reviews the bill passed by the Senate Select Committee on Intelligence before the bill is brought before the full Senate for consideration.

62. This recommendation, and measures to assist the Bureau in developing its intelligence cadre, are included in the report accompanying the Commerce, Justice and State Appropriations Act for Fiscal Year 2005, passed by the House of Representatives on July 7, 2004. H.R. Rep. No. 108-576, 108th Cong., 2d sess. (2004), p. 22.

63. Letter from Ridge and others to Collins and Levin, Apr. 13, 2004.

64. For the directorate's current capability, see Patrick Hughes interview (Apr. 2, 2004). ✦

Reprinted from The 9/11 Commission (the Kean Commission), *Final Report of the National Commission on Terrorist Attacks Upon the United States* (New York: Norton, July 2004): 361–428.

33

WMD Intelligence Failure

Silberman-Robb Commission

History has demonstrated that the 2002 National Intelligence Estimate on Iraq's WMD programs was wrong. The analysts who wrote it failed to break through the existing analytic-policy consensus concerning the likely presence of nuclear, chemical, and biological weapons in Baghdad. A federal commission, chaired by Judge Laurence H. Silberman and U.S. Senator Charles Robb (D, Virginia), assessed the ability of the U.S. intelligence community to provide policymakers with accurate estimates of emerging WMD arsenals. Our selection from the commission report focuses on the suggestions offered by its members for managerial and organizational reforms to improve intelligence analysis.

Analysts are the voice of the Intelligence Community.

While intelligence failures can certainly result from inadequate collection, recent experience shows that they can also occur when analysts don't effectively assess all relevant information and present it in a manner useful to decisionmakers. Improving the business of analysis should therefore be a major priority of the new Director of National Intelligence (DNI).

. . . [O]ur recommendations—supported by vivid examples taken from our case studies—focus both on *integrating* analytical efforts across the Community and improving the overall *quality* of analysis.

The analytic effort in the Intelligence Community is hardly a monolithic enterprise; most of the Community's 15 organizations have at least one analytic component. Some of these agencies specialize in meeting the needs of particular users—notably the Defense Department's DIA and the State Department's INR. Some specialize in analyzing particular types of data—signals intelligence at NSA and geospatial intelligence at NGA. Some, such as the intelligence element of the Department of Energy, specialize in substantive intelligence topics, such as nuclear technology issues.

The separation of these analytic units serves a vital function; it fosters competitive analysis, encourages a diversity of viewpoints, and develops groups of analysts with different specialties. Any reform of the Community must preserve these advantages; our suggested move toward greater integration should not mean the homogenization of different viewpoints. Nevertheless, there is a great and growing need for Community analytic standards, interoperable and innovative technologies, access to shared information, and a common sense of mission. In many cases today, analysts in the 15 organizations are unaware of similar work being done in other agencies. Although analysts may develop working relationships with counterparts in other organizations, there is no formalized process or forum through which to do so. These dysfunctional characteristics of the current system must change; collaboration must replace fragmentation as the analytic community's primary characteristic.

Despite the fact that the analytic units are largely isolated and autonomous, we have been deeply impressed by pockets of excellence within them. The Community is blessed with a highly intelligent, dedicated analytic workforce that has achieved significant successes. We also note that, in response to Iraq-related failures, the Intelligence Community has recently undertaken several serious (although scattered) efforts to improve the overall quality and integrity of its analytical methods and products.

We conclude, however, that these strengths and reforms are too few and far between. Our investigation revealed serious shortcomings; specifically, we found inadequate Intelligence Community collaboration and cooperation, analysts who do not understand collection, too much focus on current intelligence, inadequate systematic use of outside experts and open source information, a shortage of analysts with scientific and technical expertise, and poor capabilities to exploit fully the available data. Perhaps most troubling, we found an Intelligence Community in which analysts have a difficult time stating their assumptions up front, explicitly explaining their logic, and, in the end, identifying unambiguously for policymakers what they *do not know*. In sum, we found that many of the most basic processes and functions for producing accurate and reliable intelligence are broken or underutilized.

This Commission is not the first to recognize these shortcomings—we trod a well-worn path. Again and again, many of the same obstacles to delivering the best possible analytic products have been identified. The Church Committee's 1976 report, the House Permanent Select Committee on Intelligence's 1996 study of the Intelligence Community in the 21st Century, the 1998 Rumsfeld Report side letter to the President, the 1999 Jeremiah Report, the Markle Foundation's 2003 Task Force, and the 9/11 Commission Report all pointed to the problems created by the poor coordination and resistance to information sharing among Intelligence Community agencies. Some studies, notably the 1996 report by the Council on Foreign Relations and the 1996 study by the Aspin-Brown Commission, noted the need to systematically engage in and use competitive analysis. As early as 1949, the Hoover Commission faulted the Intelligence Community for failing to improve relations with decision-makers, and these concerns were echoed by the Aspin-Brown Commission and, most recently, the Markle Foundation Task Force.[1] Finally, the House and Senate intelligence committees have both noted the problems the Intelligence Community faces in processing the collected information available to it, as well as the difficulty analysts have engaging in long-term analysis, given the press of daily demands.[2]

In other words, many of the problems we have identified have been apparent to observers of the Intelligence Community—and to the Community itself—for decades. Nevertheless, they have remained largely unresolved, due largely to institutional resistance to change, the classified nature of the work, and a lack of political will to enforce change.

We believe the creation of the Office of the DNI offers a unique opportunity to finally resolve many of these issues by infusing the analytic culture with new processes and Community standards. We believe that this new management structure can foster a new sense of community among analysts. Until the analytic community adopts a new approach, analysts at one agency will continue to be denied access to critical reporting from others; analysts will resist collaborating and coordinating across units; managers will persist in placing the need to answer the "daily mail" over the need to develop true expertise; and new commissions will be appointed in the wake of future intelligence failures. [W]e believe that the creation of Mission Managers will be an important factor in avoiding this grim outcome.

Our recommendations, therefore, focus on exploiting the opportunity presented by the new legislation and the creation of the Office of the DNI, as well as on instituting changes to the Community's culture that will improve analytic performance. In doing so, we offer specific suggestions for how the community of analysts can be better integrated without sacrificing all-important independent analysis, and how the Intelligence Community can ensure that analysts have the tools, training, and "tradecraft" practices to ensure that the analytic

---

Box 33.1

Achieving Community Integration Among Analysts

We believe that a principal goal of improving analysis should be to integrate the community of analysts while at the same time promoting independent—or competitive—analysis. In this sense, we believe a major challenge for the first Director of National Intelligence will be to foster more collaboration among analysts across the Community—that is, to bring the benefits of collaboration to daily support to the President, to strategic intelligence and warning, and to assistance to military, law enforcement, and homeland security efforts. In our view, there are five prerequisites to creating such a community:

- **Community standards** for analysis (analytic expertise, analytic performance, and analytic presentation to consumers) so that the work of any one analytic unit can be relied upon and understood by others;

- **A common analytic work environment** (a shared network, compatible tools, and a common filing system for products and work in progress) so that a DNI can know the state of intelligence on critical issues, and so knowledge and supporting data can be shared quickly and efficiently across the Community;

- **A group of "Mission Managers,"** acting on behalf of the DNI, to oversee the state of intelligence on designated priority issues (including the state of analytic skills and resources, the gaps in existing knowledge, strategies to fill those gaps, and the effectiveness of agreed upon collection strategies)—from a Community perspective;

- **A body of "joint" analysts** to work in concert with analysts across the Community—to help fill gaps in strategic research as distinct from current reporting, to prompt collaboration on tasks that merit a Community perspective, and to help spread sound analytic methods and standards; and

- **Daily intelligence support to the President,** without which the DNI would find it very hard to impose standards and priorities on organizations free to plead the exigencies of meeting immediate needs of important clients. ✦

---

community is prepared to meet today's and tomorrow's threats.

Managing the Community of Analysts

As we have discussed in our chapters on management and on collection, no single individual or office in today's Intelligence Community is responsible for getting the answers right on the most pressing intelligence issues of our day. We have recommended the creation of Mission Managers to fill this role, and they will perform a variety of essential tasks—including leading the development and management of collection strategies against high-priority intelligence targets. Because we believe that analysis must drive the collection process, it will be vital that Mission Managers also act as leaders in the analytic community. First and foremost, they must assess the strengths and weaknesses of analytic production in their areas of substantive responsibility.

These assessments will enable Mission Managers to develop strategic analysis plans to guide the Community's analytic efforts over the long term. Moreover, the assessments will guide Mission Managers in their role as chairs of Target Development Boards; their understanding of the gaps in analysts' knowledge will ensure that these gaps do in fact drive collection.

Armed with a clear understanding of where expertise resides in the Community, Mission Managers will also be able to foster competitive analysis. We expect that Mission Managers will ensure that finished intelligence routinely reflects the knowledge and competing views of analysts from all agencies in the Community. In particular, we expect that Mission Managers will encourage analysts to make differences in judgments, and the substantive bases for these differences, explicit in all finished products.

> **RECOMMENDATION 1** Mission Managers should be the DNI's designees for ensuring that the analytic community adequately addresses key intelligence needs on high priority topics.

To accomplish this, Mission Managers must have a comprehensive view of the skills and knowledge of the Community as a whole. The DNI should call on all agencies to provide—and regularly update—information about the knowledge and skills of their analysts, including their academic backgrounds, professional experiences, military experiences, and languages. The DNI's staff should make this information accessible through an easy-to-use directory and search tool. Mission Managers and agency heads would draw on this information to identify existing gaps, develop strategies to fill them, and create long-run strategic plans to avoid gaps on critical intelligence issues.

The model we envision is in stark contrast to the status quo, in which decisionmakers and analysts have little ability to find, track, and allocate analytic expertise. Although some efforts have been made to create such a database, ironically organizations have contributed information on the condition that other agencies not have access to their data. Our interactions with various agencies strongly suggest that the Intelligence Community still lacks a full understanding of the number, type, and skill-level of analysts in the various analytic organizations.[3] Therefore it is difficult to identify the gaps in expertise for purposes of hiring, training, supervising professional development, or managing day-to-day work. Today, line managers identify the gaps in expertise in their own analytic organizations, but little is done to understand gaps from the perspective of an entire agency, much less the entire Community. With so weak a grasp of the Community's analytic resources, it is no wonder that agencies have difficulty quickly aligning their resources to respond to crises.

Even in the area of counterterrorism, which has consistently received high level attention, agencies have struggled to establish a true Community analytic counterterrorism effort. The only way the Intelligence Community could bring together counterterrorism analytic expertise was to pull analysts away from their home agencies and house them together. From its inception, the Terrorist Threat Integration Center (now NCTC) faced fierce bureaucratic resistance in its efforts to do just this.

We believe a Mission Manager could respond to this or similar challenges more intelligently, quickly, and decisively. A Mission Manager would be able to (1) identify where analytic expertise resided and call on analysts from a variety of agencies to respond to critical questions; (2) identify and recommend to the DNI which analysts should be moved within or between agencies, if required in order to respond to a crisis; (3) "surge" on such a crisis, in the event that Community resources were insufficient, by tapping outside experts to contribute their expertise; (4) create a "virtual center" without physically co-locating analysts and without establishing a segregated and centrally-managed body to analyze a particular subject matter; and (5) clearly define organizational roles rather than letting bureaucratic dogfights, such as those surrounding TTIC, determine who has responsibility for which task. This, we believe, is how the analytical community should be managed.

Although Mission Managers would manage analysis by substantive area, they would not—in contrast to a center like the National Counterterrorism Center or the National Intelligence Council—actually *do* extensive intelligence analysis. Rather, a Mission Manager should coordinate and oversee decentralized analysis. By maintaining this separation of responsibilities, we believe that Mission Managers can prevent so-called "groupthink" among analysts. Indeed, we think fostering competitive analysis within the Community is a critical aspect of the Mission Manager's role.

We acknowledge that the Mission Managers will, if effective, interfere with the current autonomous management of analytic resources within individual organizations. But we see this as a strength, ensuring that members of the Community work together instead of at odds with one another. The risk, of course, is that a Mission Manager with a strong analytic viewpoint could reduce, rather than foster, competitive analysis. While this may sometimes happen—because Mission Managers must have substantive expertise to guide the Community's work—we expect Mission Managers to act more as facilitators of analytic products than as senior analysts. Consequently, their role most often should be to clearly present analytic viewpoints—including alternative views—to policymakers. If a Mission Manager fundamentally disagrees with the prevailing view in the Community, the Mission Manager could present his own view as an alternative, but he should not silence the perspective of other specialists in the Community.

Although not a precondition for success, our vision for Mission Managers ultimately requires a significant technological change—the creation of a "common work environment" for the community of analysts working on a topic. By "common work environment" we mean a shared information network with compatible computer tools and a common computer filing system for analytic products. Such technology is necessary to permit the Mission Manager to have full visibility into the emerging analytic work that is (or is not) being done on a topic, the basis for analytic assessments, and the degree of collaborative involvement between analysts and collectors. This common work environment will also enable greater collaboration between analysts in different agencies, as well as with the nucleus of analysts we recommend placing in the National Intelligence Council (see below).

A final note about managing the Intelligence Community's analysts: we recommend that one of the DNI's earliest undertakings be to have a senior advisor assess the Intelligence Community's medium- and long-term analytic needs, identify analytic gaps, and recommend ways to fill those gaps. And because the Intelligence Community's needs should be closely correlated with policymaker priorities, policymakers should be included in this assessment. Recommendations for correcting deficiencies might include such methods as targeted hiring, correcting national educational shortcomings, or contracting with outside experts.

Tapping Non-traditional Sources of Information

Analysts have large quantities of information from a wide variety of sources delivered to their desktops each day. Given the time constraints analysts face, it is understandable that their daily work focuses on using what's readily available—usually classified material. Clandestine sources, however, constitute only a tiny sliver of the information available on many topics of interest to the Intelligence Community. Other sources, such as traditional media, the Internet, and individuals in academia, nongovernmental organizations, and business, offer vast intelligence possibilities. Regrettably, all too frequently these "nonsecret" sources are undervalued and underused by the Intelligence Community. To be true all-source analysts, however, Community analysts must broaden their information horizons. We encourage analysts to expand their use of open source materials, outside experts, and new and emerging technologies.

To facilitate analysts' productive use of open source information, the Intelligence Community should create an organization responsible for the collection of open source information. . . . It merits emphasis here, however, that simply creating this organization is unlikely to be sufficient. Analysts who routinely receive clandestine reporting too often see unclassified reporting as less important, and they spend too little time reviewing and integrating data available through open sources. Analysts on lower priority accounts use open source materials because they have difficulty getting clandestine collectors to assist them, but even they receive little or no training on how to evaluate available open sources or find the best information most efficiently.

> **RECOMMENDATION 2** The DNI should create a small cadre of all-source analysts—perhaps 50—who would be experts in finding and using unclassified, open source information.

As the CIA increases its analytic workforce, a small number could be reserved and trained specifically in open source research. They could then be assigned to offices willing to experiment with greater use of open source material, where they would be expected to answer questions for and provide useful unclassified information to analysts. They would also produce their own pieces highlighting open source reporting but drawing on classified information as well.[4] We see these "evange-analysts" as essentially leading by example. They should show other analysts how to find and procure useful open source material, how to assess its reliability and biases, and how to use it to complement clandestine reporting.

We acknowledge that, given the demand for more analysts, there are real costs to designating even this small number as open source specialists. But we expect that the need for these specialized analysts will not be permanent. Over time, the knowledge this group has about open sources is likely to be absorbed by the general population of analysts—as a result both of their education outreach efforts and of the influx of younger, more technologically savvy analysts. As this happens, these open source specialists can be absorbed into the broader analytic corps.

In addition to this special cadre of analysts, the Community will need to find new ways to deal with the challenges presented by the growing availability of open source materials. Among these challenges is the critical problem of processing increasing numbers of foreign language documents.

> **RECOMMENDATION 3**   The DNI should establish a program office within the CIA's Open Source Directorate to acquire, or develop when necessary, information technologies to permit prioritization and exploitation of large volumes of textual data without the need for prior human translation or transcription.

Information technology has made remarkable advances in recent years. The private sector (without the same kinds of security concerns as the Intelligence Community) has led the adoption of technologies that are also critical to intelligence. Two areas show particular promise: first, machine translation of foreign languages; and second, tools designed to prioritize documents in their native language without the need for translation.

The Community will never be able to hire enough linguists to meet its needs. It is difficult for the Com-munity to predict which languages will be most in demand and to hire the necessary linguists in advance. And even an aggressive hiring and training effort would not produce an analytic workforce that can absorb the huge quantity of unclassified foreign language material available today.

Eventually, all analysts should have basic foreign-language processing tools easily available to them so that even those who are not language-qualified can pull pieces of interest and get a quick, rough translation. NSA has done pioneering work on machine translation and is pursuing a number of separate initiatives; the military services, CIA (including In-Q-Tel), and other agencies sponsor largely independent projects. There is an abundance of activity, but not a concerted, coherent effort, which has led to steady but slow development.

Advanced search and knowledge extraction technologies could prove to be even more valuable than machine translation (and of course, the two are very much related). We refer here to software that uses mathematical operations, statistical computations, and relational analyses to cluster documents and other data by subject, emphasis, and association in order to identify documents that are similar even when the documents do not use the same key words. Other types of software algorithms can discern concepts within a text; some can depict relationships between ideas or between factual statements based on an understanding of the word's meaning rather than merely searching for a word verbatim. As these tools mature, they will be invaluable to agencies that now find themselves collecting more information than they can analyze. They will also become essential to analysts caught in a similar avalanche of data.

The Intelligence Community has only begun to explore and exploit the power of these emerging technologies. The Intelligence Community's current efforts should be coordinated, consolidated where appropriate, directed, and augmented. Therefore, we suggest that the DNI establish a program office that can lead the Community effort to obtain advanced information technology for purposes of machine translation, advanced search, knowledge extraction, and similar automated support to analysis. This office would draw on the various initiatives in these areas dispersed throughout the Intelligence Community. It would work to avoid duplication of effort and would promote collaboration and cross-pollination. It would serve as a knowledge bank of state-of-the-art technology. It would also serve as a testbed, using open source information to experiment with software that has not yet been certified for classified environments. When appropriate, it would hand off successful technologies for use on classified networks. While we would place the program office in the new Open Source Directorate, where quick deployment seems most likely to occur, we recognize that NSA is a center of excellence for linguistics and technology, and it must surf a data avalanche every day. For that reason, we suggest that the program office be jointly staffed by NSA and CIA.

RECOMMENDATION 4 The Intelligence Community should expand its contacts with those outside the realm of intelligence by creating at least one not-for-profit "sponsored research institute."

We envision the establishment of at least one not-for-profit "sponsored research institute" to serve as a critical window into outside expertise for the Intelligence Community. This sponsored research institute would be funded by the Intelligence Community, but would be largely independent of Community management. The institute would both conduct its own research as well as reach out to specialists, including academics and technical experts, business and industry leaders, and representatives from the nonprofit sector and from Federally Funded Research and Development Centers.

Free from the demands created by the events of the day that burden those within the Intelligence Community, this sponsored research institute's primary purpose would be to focus on strategic issues. It would also serve as an avenue for a robust, external alternative analysis program. Whatever alternative analysis the Community undertakes internally—and we see this as essential—there must be outside thinking to challenge conventional wisdom, and this institute would provide both the distance from and the link to the Intelligence Community to provide a useful counterpoint to accepted views. In this vein, the DNI might consider establishing more than one such institute. By doing so, competitive analysis would be further promoted and healthy competition between the research institutes would help both from being co-opted by the Intelligence Community.

This sponsored research institute would eliminate some existing impediments to more extensive outreach. The institute would have a budget that would enable it to pay top experts unwilling to work for the lower rates typically offered by Intelligence Community components. Moreover, contractors linked to the institute would be available to all Intelligence Community components, avoiding any suggestion that contractors were tasked to provide as-

---

Box 33.2
Context Is Critical

Many of the intelligence challenges of today and tomorrow will, like terrorism or proliferation, be transnational and driven by non-state actors. Analysts who cover these issues will need to know far more than the inclinations of a handful of senior government officials; they will need a deep understanding of the trends and shifts in local political views, cultural norms, and economic demands. For example, analysts seeking to identify geographic areas likely to be receptive to messages of violence toward the United States will need to be able to distinguish such areas from those that, while espousing anti-U.S. rhetoric or advocating policies at odds with the interests of the United States, nevertheless eschew violent tactics.

Clandestine collectors, however, are poorly structured to fill the intelligence gaps these analysts face. Imagery is of little utility, and both signals and human intelligence are better positioned to provide insight into the plans and intentions of a few important individuals rather than broader political and societal trends.

As a result, analysts are supplementing clandestine collection not only with a greater reliance on open source material and outside experts, but also with their own expertise. To enable them to do so, the Intelligence Community must expand analysts' opportunities to travel and live overseas. And it must consider reforms to the security clearance process that often hampers recruitment of those with the most experience living and working among groups of interest to the Community. Failure to think creatively about how to develop an analytic cadre with a deep understanding of cultures very different from our own will seriously undermine the Community's ability to respond to the new and different intelligence challenges of the 21st century. ✦

---

sessments to support the views of a particular agency. Further, although the staff of the research institute would take recommendations from analysts for particular people to contact outside of the Community, we expect the staff itself to pull together possible contacts in critical fields, expanding the circle of those whose knowledge would be available to the Intelligence Community. The sponsored research institute could also become a center for funding nontraditional methods of assembling open source information. In our classified report we provide an example that cannot be discussed in an unclassified format.

Such a sponsored research institute is not the only way to capitalize on expertise from outside the Intelligence Community. Although the institute would expand the Community's ongoing outreach efforts, the Intelligence Community also needs to think more creatively and, above all, more *strategically* about how it taps into external sources of knowledge. This may include recognizing that the Community may simply not be the natural home for real expertise on certain topics. While economic analysts, for example, can and do play a valuable role in the Community, economists at the Federal Reserve, World Bank, or private sector companies investing millions in emerging markets are likely to have a better handle on current market conditions. Relying on these experts might free up Community resources to work more intensely on finding answers no one else has.

Each of these proposals assumes the Community will have access to existing experts, but that will not always be the case. As a result, the Community must also find ways to support the development of the external expertise it needs. One biosecurity expert remarked that what we really need is a major effort to foster publicly-minded experts to tackle the biothreats likely to face the United States in the future.[5] Title VI of the Higher Education Act, which supports language and area studies in universities, and the National Security Education Program (the Boren Program) might also help. We believe the Intelligence Community should think even more broadly about ways to meet national information needs.

Finally, analysts also need to take full advantage of currently available and underutilized non-traditional technical intelligence capabilities, like advanced geospatial intelligence techniques and measurement and signature intelligence (MASINT). Analysts would benefit from additional training and education to increase their awareness of new and developing collection techniques, so that they are able to effectively task these sources and use the information provided.

Managing the Influx of Information

As countless groups both inside and outside the Intelligence Community have commented, there is a dire need for greater information sharing—or, as we prefer to put it, information *access* in the Intelligence Community. . . .

But analysts not only need more information, they also need new ways to manage what is already available to them. Analysts today "are inundated and overloaded with information."[6] A study published in 1994 revealed that analysts on average had to scan 200 to 300 documents in two hours each day, just to discover reports worth writing about.[7] If we assume that relevant information has doubled for most analytic accounts over the past ten years (a gross understatement if open source information is considered)—and if we depend on analysts not just to pick reports to write about but instead to "connect the dots" among names, phone numbers, organizations, and events found in other documents—the typical analyst would need a full workday just to perform the basic function of monitoring new data.

The private sector is already using tools and techniques to handle the greatly increased flow of information in today's world; many of the best of these operate even before a user begins to look for relevant information. By the time an Internet user types search terms into Google, for example, the search engine has already done a huge portion of the work of indexing the information and sorting it by relevance. In fact, Google already has educated guesses about what information will be most useful regardless of the breadth of the user's search.

The Intelligence Community's widely used tools for processing raw intelligence traffic are far weaker. According to a senior official at CIA's In-Q-Tel, when analysts enter the Intelligence Community they discover that they have "left a world that was totally wired."[8] Today, an analyst looking for information on Intelligence Community computers is effectively performing a keyword search without any relevance ranking or additional context. The Community has been largely resistant to efforts to import tools from the private sector that offer new and different ways of using technology to exploit data.[9] While this resistance is often driven by legitimate concerns about security, these concerns can (and must) be overcome in the development of information technology for the Intelligence Community.

> **RECOMMENDATION 5** The Community must develop and integrate into regular use new tools that can assist analysts in filtering and correlating the vast quantities of information that threaten to overwhelm the analytic process. Moreover, data from all sources of information should be processed and correlated Community-wide *before* being conveyed to analysts.

The Intelligence Community is only in the beginning stages of developing effective selection, filtering, and correlation tools for its analysts, and more progress must be made. While in every case people are needed to see whether the proposed connections are real—and to be alert for intuitive but inchoate linkages—the Intelligence Community must more effectively employ technology to help draw attention to connections analysts might otherwise miss.

But better tools are not the whole answer. Time and again, tools introduced to the Intelligence Community have failed to take hold because the Community's analysts were accustomed to doing business a different way. We therefore believe there is a need to improve on the Community's long standing, but now outdated, basic approach to processing, exploiting, and disseminating information. In our view, the Intelligence Community needs processes that help analysts correlate and search large volumes of data after traditional dissemination by collectors but *before* the information overflows analysts' in-boxes.

Without such a change, we are afraid that analysts will be overwhelmed by piles of information through which they have little hope of sorting.

Fostering Long-Term Research and Strategic Thinking

Managers and analysts throughout the Intelligence Community have repeatedly expressed frustration with their inability to carve out time for long-term research and thinking. This problem is reinforced by the current system of incentives for analysts, in which analysts are often rewarded for the number of pieces they produce, rather than the substantive depth or quality of their production.

Analysts are consistently pressed to produce more pieces faster, particularly those for current intelligence publications such as the President's Daily Brief (PDB). One analyst told us that if an office doesn't produce for the PDB, its "cupboard is bare."[10] But constant pressure to write makes it hard for analysts to find time to do the research—and thinking—necessary to build the real expertise that underlies effective analysis. In one particularly alarming example, an Iraq analyst related that the demand for current intelligence became so acute that he not only gave up long-term research, but also stopped reading his daily in-box of intelligence reporting. That task was delegated to a junior analyst with no expertise on Iraq weapons of mass destruction issues who pulled traffic he thought might be of interest.[11] Although this is an unusually dramatic example, we provide additional classified statistics illustrating this problem in our classified report.

The drive to fill current publications can also crowd out work on strategic military and prolifera-

tion issues. As with long-term research, work on these issues may fall by the wayside as analysts respond to immediate, tactical policymaker interests. And strategic work may be discouraged simply because presenting it in a format usable by current intelligence publications is difficult or impossible. Technical assessments are generally seen as too cumbersome for daily intelligence and more difficult for the non-technical briefers to discuss should the President choose to have a dialogue on the issue. Although some of these products reach senior policymakers separately, the fact that they are typically excluded from the publication designed to inform the President about the most important issues of the day likely suggests to analysts that this work is not as highly valued as other topics.

Managers with whom we spoke are aware of the dearth of strategic, long-term thinking, and are seeking ways to remedy the problem. However, we think that part of the solution lies within the new office of the DNI.

> **RECOMMENDATION 6** A new long-term research and analysis unit, under the mantle of the National Intelligence Council, should wall off all-source analysts from the press of daily demands and serve as the lead organization for interagency projects involving in-depth analysis.

We recommend placing this new unit under the National Intelligence Council where analysts would be able to focus on long-term research and underserved strategic threats, away from the demands of current intelligence production. Although some analysts in this new organization would be permanently assigned, at least half—and perhaps a majority—would serve only temporarily and would come from all intelligence agencies, including those with more specialized analysts, such as NGA and NSA. Typically, analysts would have two-year assignments in the unit; in some cases, analysts may spend shorter periods in the organization, long enough to complete a single in-depth research project of pressing need. Because we expect the topics tackled by this group to be complex, collaboration with those outside the unit should be pervasive.

We envision the analysts located in this unit leading projects that bring in experts from across the Intelligence Community, as well as from outside the sphere of intelligence. This collaboration will enable the Intelligence Community to tackle broad strategic questions that sometimes get missed as many analysts focus on narrow slivers of larger issues. DIA analysts and managers, for example, told us that the current division of key analytical responsibilities among the various Department of Defense intelligence units at DIA, the service intelligence centers, and the unified commands makes it difficult for DIA to develop an integrated, strategic assessment of emerging security issues. We expect this new organization to fill such gaps.

Some might be concerned that this new analytic unit would create unhealthy barriers between those engaged in current intelligence and those conducting long-term research. But as proposed, this office avoids that division. Using the common technology infrastructure we propose, we expect that analysts in the new office would easily be able to draw on the insight of analysts still in their home offices who are working on current intelligence. Moreover, because analysts would rotate through this office and remain only for a short period of time, they would not run the risk of veering off into studying questions that might be intellectually interesting but are unlikely to be important to decisionmakers. These analysts would come to the office with an understanding of the pulse of current intelligence. Even more important, those same analysts would return to their line units, and the production of timely intelligence, with a greater depth of understanding of their accounts.

Rotations to this unit would also reinforce habits that should be second nature, but sometimes get lost in the daily press of business. Analysts would have time to think more carefully about their words, ensuring that terms used to express uncertainty or concerns about credibility were consistent over time and across accounts. We hope that this unit would also engage in alternative analysis—and that this would help to foster alternative analysis throughout the Intelligence Community. Moreover, rotations through this unit would foster a greater sense of community among analysts and spur collaboration on other projects as well.

Although this strategic analytic unit could be housed in a number of places, we believe that the NIC is best. First, the NIC remains today one of the few places within the Intelligence Community that focuses primarily on long-term, strategic thinking. Second, the NIC is already accustomed to working with analysts across the Community and is therefore likely to be seen as an honest broker—an organization that treats analysts from different agencies equally. Third, the NIC already regularly engages outside experts. Indeed, many National Intelligence Officers spend the bulk of their careers outside the intelligence field.

> **RECOMMENDATION 7** The DNI should encourage diverse and independent analysis throughout the Intelligence Community by encouraging alternative hypothesis generation as part of the analytic process and by forming offices dedicated to independent analysis.

Encouraging Diverse and Independent Analysis

Throughout our case studies we observed the importance of analysts clearly identifying and stating the basis for their assessments. But good analysis goes well beyond just saying what is known, what is unknown, and what an analyst thinks. It is critical that analysts find ways of routinely challenging their initial assumptions and questioning their conclusions—in short, of engaging in competitive (or, as we prefer to call it, independent) analysis.

We believe that diverse and independent analysis should come from many sources. In this vein we offer several recommendations that should foster diverse and independent analysis, most particularly our proposed long-term research and analysis unit in the National Intelligence Council, our proposed not-for-profit sponsored research institute, the preservation of dispersed analytic resources, and Community training that instills the importance of independent analysis.

To begin, we note ongoing efforts within the Intelligence Community that have provided valuable independent analysis. The CIA's Directorate of Intelligence, for example, currently has an organization that exclusively drafts "red cell" pieces—documents that are speculative in nature and sometimes take a position at odds with the conventional wisdom.[12] This office proved especially valuable in the context of Libya, for reasons we discuss in greater detail in our classified report but cannot discuss here.

We foresee our proposed long-term research and analysis unit augmenting such existing efforts. We envision the office conducting some of its own alternative analysis, working with analysts in their home offices to conduct independent analysis, and ensuring that analytic judgments are routinely challenged as new information becomes available. By both engaging in its own work and working in conjunction with other offices, we hope that the unit will help catalyze independent analysis throughout the Community and, in the long run, ensure that independent analysis becomes part of the standard way of thinking for all analysts.

Our envisioned not-for-profit sponsored research institute is another natural location for independent analysis to be conducted. In fact, a well-designed research institute should be ideal in that it would have close relationships with non-Intelligence Community experts, as well as easy access to large volumes of open source material. Similarly, the National Intelligence Council should further foster alternative analysis through a National Intelligence Estimate (NIE) process that promotes dissenting views. In our view, the NIE process today is designed to serve as a Community product and, as such, can sometimes become a consensus building process. We hope that the DNI will encourage the NIE drafters to highlight and explore dissenting opinions.

We must stress, however, the importance of fostering a culture of alternative analysis *throughout* the Intelligence Community, as opposed to centralizing the function in a single office (or even several offices). An office solely responsible for dissenting opinions is at risk of losing credibility over time, which would not make it an attractive place for analysts to work. Moreover, we are afraid that an office dedicated to independent analysis would—in the long run—end up having its own biases, and would not provide the diversity of views that we think is so important.

We thus recommend that the DNI give particular "red-team" or "devil's advocate" assignments to individuals or offices on a case-by-case basis, rather than trying to produce all alternative analysis through a separate office. By doing so, no individual or office would constantly bear the brunt of criticizing other analysts' work, nor would such alternative analysis be thought to be the sole responsibility of a single, stand-alone office. And while the DNI is statutorily required to assign an individual or entity responsibility for ensuring that the Community engages in alternative analysis,[13] this should not in our view artificially limit the locations in which such analysis occurs.

Perhaps most important, however, is the view that the Intelligence Community should not rely upon specialized "red team offices," or even individual "red team exercises" to ensure there is sufficient independent analysis. Rather, such independent analysis must become a habitual analytic practice for *all* analysts. The decentralization of the Intelligence Community's analytic bodies will naturally contribute to independent and divergent analysis, and we believe that the Mission Managers we propose will play a valuable role in identifying and encouraging independent analysis in their topic areas. But the Intelligence Community must also ensure that analysts across the Community are trained to question their assumptions and make their arguments explicit. Alternative analysis should be taught in the very first analyst training courses as a core element of good analytic tradecraft. It is to this topic—the training of analysts—that we next turn.

Improving Tradecraft Through Training

A common theme from our case studies is that the fundamental logical and analytic principles that should be utilized in building intelligence assessments are often inadequately applied. There are several reasons for this. Key among these is a leadership failure; managers of analysts have neglected to demand the highest standards of analytic craft. This management weakness has been compounded in recent years by the lack of experience among analysts, caused by the more than 33 percent decline in the number of analysts from the latter part of the 1980s through most of the 1990s. On top of the numerical reduction, many of the *best* analysts left during this period because they were the ones who could easily get jobs outside of government. The outflow of knowledge was even greater than the outflow of people.

The Intelligence Community started slowly to hire more analysts in the late 1990s, and recent congressional and executive branch actions are now resulting in further expansion of the analytic corps. As a result, the Intelligence Community is now populated with many junior analysts and few mentors. And the focus on current intelligence has meant that few analysts are given the time to develop expertise, while managers have little time to develop management and mentoring skills.

These difficulties have reduced the quality of finished intelligence. When we reviewed finished intelligence, we found egregious examples of poor tradecraft, such as using a piece of evidence to support an argument when the same piece also supported exactly the opposite argument—and failing to note this fact. In some cases, analysts also failed to update or correct previously published pieces, which led other analysts and policymakers to make judgments on faulty or incomplete premises.

But far and away the most damaging tradecraft weakness we observed was the failure of analysts to conclude—when appropriate—that there was not enough information available to make a defensible judgment.[14] As much as they hate to do it, analysts must be comfortable facing up to uncertainty and being explicit about it in their assessments. Thankfully, we have found several instances of recent efforts by individual analysts to clearly admit what they do and do not know. In particular, a recent National Intelligence Estimate used new processes to

> **RECOMMENDATION 8** The Intelligence Community must develop a Community program for training analysts, and both analysts and managers must prioritize this career-long training.

ensure that source information was carefully checked for accuracy before inclusion in the estimate. In addition, the Estimate clearly highlighted the intelligence collection gaps on the topic and analysts' level of confidence in their judgments. In our classified report we discuss the particulars of this Estimate in greater depth. Still, these efforts have not been institutionalized, nor are they widespread. We heard many times from users of intelligence that they would like analysts to tell them up front what they don't know—something that intelligence analysts apparently do too infrequently.

The Intelligence Community must reverse the erosion of analytic expertise that has occurred over the last 15 years. Analytic reasoning must be more rigorous and be explained in clearer terms in order to improve both the quality and credibility of intelligence. Specifically, analysts should take pains to write clearly, articulate assumptions, consistently use caveats, and apply standard approaches to sourcing. A renewed focus on traditional tradecraft methods needs to be augmented with innovative methodologies and tools that assist the analyst without inhibiting creativity, intuition, and curiosity.

This strengthening of the analytic workforce can only occur through a dedicated effort by the Intelligence Community to train analysts throughout their careers. A structured Community program must be developed to teach rigorous tradecraft and to inculcate common standards for analysis so that, for instance, it means the same thing when two agencies say they assess something "with a high degree of certainty." Equally important, managers and analysts must be held accountable for ensuring that analysts continue to develop expertise throughout their careers. The excuse, "I didn't have time for training," is simply unacceptable. This responsibility of both managers and analysts for continued tradecraft training should be made part of all performance evaluations.

Another critical element of training for analysts, and one that has been long lacking in the Intelligence Community, concerns their understanding of intelligence *collection*. Today, analysts receive too little training on collection capabilities and processes, and the training they do receive does not adequately use practical exercises to help analysts

---

Box 33.3
What Denial and Deception (D&D) Means for Analysis

State and non-state actors either with or seeking to develop WMD materials and technologies all practice robust denial and deception techniques against U.S. technical collection. We must significantly reduce our vulnerability to intelligence surprises, mistakes, and omissions caused by the effects of denial and deception (D&D) on collection and analysis. To do so, the Community must foster:

- **Greater awareness of D&D among analysts,** including a deeper understanding of what other countries know about our intelligence capabilities, as well as the D&D intentions, capabilities, and programs of those countries.

- **Greater specification by analysts of what they don't know and clearer statements of their degree of certainty.** Analysts should also work more closely with collectors to fully exploit untapped collection opportunities against D&D targets, and to identify and isolate any deceptive information.

- **Greater appreciation for the capabilities and limitations of U.S. collection systems.**

- **Greater use of analytical techniques that identify the impact of denial and the potential for deception.** Analysts must understand and evaluate the effects of false, misleading, or even true information that intelligence targets may have injected into the collection stream to deceive the United States. ✦

> **RECOMMENDATION 9** The Intelligence Community must develop a Community program for training managers, both when they first assume managerial positions and throughout their careers.

learn how to build effective collection strategies to solve intelligence problems. This fundamental ignorance of collection processes and principles can lead to serious misjudgments, and we recommend that the Intelligence Community strengthen analyst training in this area. In our classified report we point to areas in other intelligence agencies' training programs that we believe could be improved, but that cannot be discussed in an unclassified report.

Managerial training must also be vastly expanded throughout the Intelligence Community. Although scattered training is available, the Intelligence Community currently has no systematic, serious, or sustained management training program, and none that readily allows for cross-agency training—even though management problems can be similar across agencies. CIA managers, for example, receive a small portion of the training provided to their military counterparts.[15] And we are dismayed that some in the Intelligence Community resisted programs such as merit-based pay due to a mistrust of managers' ability to accurately and fairly measure performance.

Prospective managers should be given extensive management training before assuming their responsibilities, and current managers should be enrolled in refresher training courses on a regular basis. A well-trained management and leadership corps within the Intelligence Community is vital to the health of analysis (and collection), and the Community is currently suffering the consequences of its absence. To the degree that a few individuals at the CIA have already recognized this problem, and are designing programs to address it, we commend them.

Although we hesitate to prescribe any specific level of centralization for analytic and managerial training, we do suggest that some of the training be Community-wide, perhaps housed in our proposed National Intelligence University or done through an online education program.[16] We do so in full recognition that individual agencies may want to conduct their own training because their workforce requires specialized skills, and that some resist centralized training on the grounds that training should engender a strong affiliation among analysts for their particular agency.

Notwithstanding these objections . . . we believe that the creation of the DNI provides a unique opportunity to reconsider implementing some elements of Community training. The benefits will be enormous: it will teach common tradecraft standards, standardize teaching and evaluation, foster a sense of Community among analysts, and, we hope, provide analysts with a wider range of training opportunities throughout their careers. It may also create economies of scale in training costs. For these reasons, we strongly encourage joint training whenever feasible.

Making Analysis More Transparent

Training analysts and managers to use better "tradecraft" is only half the battle; rigorous analytic methods must be demanded in every intelligence product. One way of doing so—and at the same time ensuring that customers are confident in the intelligence they receive—is to make the analytic process more transparent. Although we recognize that real security issues make total transparency impossible, we fear that protecting sources and methods has resulted in the shrouding of analysis itself, not just the intelligence on which it is based. This tendency must, we believe, be actively resisted.

We recommend forcing analysts to make their assumptions and reasoning more transparent by requiring that analysis be well sourced, and that all finished intelligence products, either in paper or in digital format, provide citations to enable user verification of particular statements. This requirement is no more rigorous than that which is required in law, science, and the social sciences, and we see little reason why such standards should not be demanded of the Intelligence Community's analysts. Analysts are generally already expected to provide sources for internal review; including this information in finished analysis would simply increase the transparency of the process.

We further recommend that customers have access to the raw intelligence reporting that supports analytic pieces whenever possible, subject to legitimate security considerations. For many intelligence customers, especially senior policymakers and operators, a general description, such as State Department "diplomatic reporting" simply does not provide the confidence needed to take quick and decisive action.[17] Where a user accesses finished intelligence electronically, he should be able to link directly to at least some portion of the raw intelligence—or to underlying finished intelligence—to which a judgment is sourced.

Requiring that citations be routinely available and linked to source documents need not preclude analysts from making judgments or inferences; rather, the availability of such materials will simply enable users to distinguish quickly between those statements that are paraphrased summaries of intelligence reporting, and those that are analytic judgments that draw inferences from this reporting. Of course, some analysts might worry that such a system would essentially sideline the analyst,

> **RECOMMENDATION 10** Finished intelligence should include careful sourcing for all analytic assessments and conclusions, and these materials should—whenever possible in light of legitimate security concerns—be made easily available to intelligence customers.

making his or her work irrelevant because all of his or her hard calls could be "questioned" by returning to the original sources and performing the analysis independently. We do not, however, think this is inherently bad. Intelligence customers should be able to question judgments, and analysts should be able to defend their reasoning. In the end, such a reform should bolster the stature of good analysts, as policymakers and operators come to see their analytic judgments as increasingly accurate and actionable.

We recommend that the DNI create a system to electronically store sourced versions of analytic pieces and ensure that source information is easily accessible to intelligence users, consistent with adequate security permissions. Of course, to make such electronic storage and accessibility possible one needs first to have a truly integrated information sharing environment and shared information technology systems—a considerable challenge given the inadequacies of today's information technology environment. . . .

The DNI should also encourage the development of a system that enables Intelligence Community personnel to update intelligence information that has been judged to be unreliable, of increased or decreased certainty, or simply retracted. These updates must be electronically flagged in the intelligence reports themselves as well as any analytic products citing to the reports. Such tracking systems have existed in other fields for decades (*e.g.,* Lexis and Westlaw for the legal world).[18]

Above and beyond the technical constraints to implementing such a system, there are several barriers that have blocked these reforms in the past. For example, CIA's Directorate of Operations maintains a close hold on its highly sensitive reporting, often with good reason. Making this raw reporting accessible to policymakers and intelligence officers across the Community raises several security and counterintelligence-related concerns. Furthermore, it is questionable to what degree *all* policymakers will need access to raw reporting.

But none of these issues explains why the Intelligence Community's efforts in this vein are still in such a stage of infancy. While there will be information that cannot be provided to intelligence custom-

---

RECOMMENDATION 11 The analytic community should create and store sourced copies of all analytic pieces to allow readers to locate and review the intelligence upon which analysis is based, and to allow for easy identification of analysis that is based on intelligence reports that are later modified.

RECOMMENDATION 12 The DNI should develop and implement strategies for improving the Intelligence Community's science and technology and weapons analysis capabilities.

---

ers, many decisionmakers can and do read intelligence reporting at the same time as the analysts who receive it. Further, access to an analytic product is typically limited to those who are cleared to read the intelligence reports on which it is based. The easy availability of source information, related reporting, and other finished intelligence products, along with a system to clearly identify old intelligence that has been reconsidered in one way or another, will benefit both analysts and customers. Analysts will, we believe, do their work more meticulously and accurately, while customers will be able to better understand the products they receive and know whether the Community continues to stand behind the intelligence.

Improving Scientific, Technical, and Weapons Intelligence

A specific subset of analysts within the Intelligence Community is responsible for assessing emerging threats to U.S. interests resulting from advances in foreign science and technology (S&T) and weapons developments. Using specialized scientific and technical expertise, skills, and analytic methodologies, these analysts work on some of today's most important intelligence issues, including counterproliferation, homeland security, support to military operations, infrastructure protection, and arms control. We are therefore concerned that a recent Intelligence Science Board study concluded that the Intelligence Community's current S&T intelligence capability is "not what it could be and not what the nation needs."[19]

The Intelligence Science Board study and our own research found that the Intelligence Community's ability to conduct S&T and weapons analysis has not kept pace with the changing security environment.[20] The board's study noted the Intelligence Community was particularly vulnerable to surprise by "rapidly changing and readily available emerging technologies whose use by state and non-state actors, in yet unanticipated ways, may result in serious and unexpected threats."[21] The S&T areas of most concern include biological attacks, nuclear threats, cyber warfare, Chinese technology leapfrogging, and the impact of commercial technologies on foreign threats.[22] In addition, current analysis often fails to place foreign S&T and weapons developments in the context of an adversary's plans, strategy, policies, and overall capabilities that would provide customers with a better understanding of the implications for U.S. security and policy interests.[23] One senior Administration official interviewed by the Commission staff described the Intelligence Community's capability to conduct this kind of all-source S&T and weapons analysis as "pretty poor" and "mediocre at best."[24]

The state of the Intelligence Community's S&T and weapons analysis capabilities should be a key issue for the DNI, given the importance of these fields in providing warning and assessments of many of today's critical threats. In addition to hiring more analysts with technical and scientific skills and experience, the Intelligence Community would benefit from more contact with outside technical experts who could conduct peer reviews and provide alternative perspectives. In addition, resources should be set aside for conducting in-depth and multidisciplinary research and analysis of emerging technologies and weapon developments to help the Community keep pace with the ever-changing security environment. The use of analytical methodologies, such as red teaming, scenario analyses, and crisis simulations, to explore and understand the impact of new technologies and weapons on U.S. interests should also be encouraged to help analysts guard against technology surprise.

To ensure progress will be made in the future, we recommend that the DNI designate a Community leader for developing and implementing strategies for improving the Intelligence Community's S&T and weapons analysis capabilities. This person should report to the DNI on a periodic basis on the status of the Community's relevant capabilities and make recommendations on where further improvements are needed.

Serving Intelligence Customers

Analysts are the link between customers and the Intelligence Community. They provide a conduit for providing intelligence to customers and for conveying the needs and interests of customers to collectors. This role requires analysts to perform a number of functions. Analysts must assess the available information and place it in context. They must clearly and concisely communicate the information they have, the information they need, the conclusions they draw from the data, and their doubts about the credibility of the information or the validity of their conclusions. They must understand the questions policymakers ask, those they are likely to ask, and those they should ask; the information

needed to answer those questions; and the best mechanisms for finding that information. And as analysts are gaining unprecedented and critically important access to operations traffic, they must also become security gatekeepers, revealing enough about the sources for policymakers to evaluate their reporting and conclusions, but not enough to disclose tightly-held, source-identifying details.

Analysts fulfill these functions through interactions with a wide range of intelligence customers, who run the gamut in terms of rank, area of responsibility, and understanding of intelligence. "Typical" customers include not only the President and senior policymakers, but also members of Congress, military commanders, desk officers in executive agencies, law enforcement officers, customs and border patrol officials, and military units in the field. We do not attempt to examine each of these relationships, but we do note some challenges in this area. Specifically, we address how the Intelligence Community might modernize some customer relationships, some components of an "appropriate" relationship between analysts and customers, and how the President—and to a lesser degree other senior policymakers—should be supported.

Modernizing the Analyst-Customer Relationship

> **RECOMMENDATION 13**   The DNI should explore ways to make finished intelligence available to customers in a way that enables them—*to the extent they desire*—to more easily find pieces of interest, link to related materials, and communicate with analysts.

The Intelligence Community must distribute its products more efficiently and effectively. Today's policymaker receives intelligence in almost the same way as his 1985 predecessor; most intelligence products from the CIA's Directorate of Intelligence, for example, are still delivered in hardcopy. For some customers, this may remain the preferred method of receiving intelligence. For others with different needs or preferences—and we have heard from some of them—the Intelligence Community should consider ways to modernize intelligence distribution.

Some modernization has occurred; most notably, a limited number of Washington policymakers can access some intelligence products through the Defense Department's secure networks—JWICS and Intelink—at their desk. But the "populating" of these networks varies across agencies and by product type. For example, INR and DIA routinely place their publications on these secure networks, and a large percentage of finished intelligence products related to counterterrorism can be found online. By contrast, CIA sharply limits the use of its finished intelligence on these networks, citing the need to protect its human sources. And even when intelligence is available on electronic networks, the interfaces are clumsy and counterintuitive—far below the presentation of online publishers such as the *Washington Post*.

This state of affairs is markedly inferior to the state of the practice in private industry. Most customers of intelligence products cannot search electronic libraries of information or catalogues of existing products. They cannot query analysts in real time about needed information or upcoming products. They cannot link finished intelligence documents together electronically to create a reference trail. They cannot easily review research programs to provide suggestions or recommendations. They cannot explore thoughts and views with analysts in an informal online environment. They cannot read informal messages alerting them to new information which may include analysts' preliminary thoughts or judgments on an item. They cannot tailor information displays to their needs. They cannot reshape raw data into graphics and charts. They cannot access different intelligence media electronically.

This is not an area in which there is only one right answer; there are many ways to provide up-to-the-minute, in-depth information to policymakers in user-friendly formats. We also recognize that because of the dramatic effects an electronic system would have on the way the Intelligence Community does its work and because of substantial security concerns, any new program along these lines will require a great deal of additional thought and planning. Nevertheless, we believe that even in the relatively near future the benefits of an integrated electronic system will outweigh the risks, and it will become more necessary as a new generation of customers—with a preference for the flexibility of digital technology—reaches higher levels of government.

Components of the Analyst-Customer Relationship

Regardless of how customers receive intelligence, both analysts and customers have to recognize that certain exchanges between the two are appropriate and should be encouraged. Perhaps most importantly, we believe it is critical that customers engage analysts. It is the job of the analyst to express clearly what the analyst knows, what the analyst doesn't know, what the analyst thinks, and why—but if the analyst does not, the customer must insist that the analyst do so. If necessary, the customer should challenge the analyst's assumptions and reasoning. Because they are "keepers of the facts," analysts can play a decisive role in policy debates, a role that has temptations for analysts with strong policy views of their own. A searching examination of the underlying evidence for the analysts' factual assertions is the best way to reassure policymakers that the analysts' assertions are well-grounded. We reject any contention that such engagement is in itself inappropriate or that the risk of "politicizing" intelligence cannot be overcome by clear statements to analysts as to the purpose of the dialogue. When an analyst leaves a policymaker's office feeling thoroughly cross-examined and challenged to support his premises, that is not politicization; it is the system working at its best. Only through active engagement of this sort will intelligence become as useful as it can be.

Analysts also have a responsibility to tell customers about important disagreements within the Intelligence Community. We were told by some senior policymakers that it sometimes took weeks to get an answer to a question—not because the answer was difficult to obtain, but because analysts were hesitant to admit to Intelligence Community disagreement on an issue. This is not how intelligence should function. Analysts must readily bring disagreement within the Community to policymakers' attention, and must be ready to explain the basis for the disagreement. Such disagreement is often a sign of robust independent analysis and should be encouraged.

In addition to conveying disagreements, analysts must also find ways to explain to policymakers degrees of certainty in their work. Some publications we have reviewed use numerical estimates of certainty, while others rely on phrases such as "probably" or "almost certainly." We strongly urge that such assessments of certainty be used routinely and consistently throughout the Community. Whatever device is used to signal the degree of certainty—mathematical percentages, graphic representations, or key phrases—all analysts in the Community should have a common understanding of what the indicators mean and how to use them.

Finally, analysts and Intelligence Community leaders have a responsibility to take note, whenever possible, of what their customers are doing and saying, and to tell those customers when actions or statements are inconsistent with existing intelligence.

We do not mean to suggest that analysts should spend all of their waking hours monitoring policymakers, or that analysts should have a "veto" over policymaker statements. Rather, when aware of upcoming speeches or decisions, analysts should make clear that they are available to vet intelligence-related matters, and analysts should—when necessary—tell policymakers how their statements diverge from existing intelligence. Having fulfilled this duty, analysts must then let politically-accountable policymakers determine whether or not a statement is appropriate in light of intelligence judgments.

Serving the President and Senior Policymakers

The new legislation designates the DNI as the person primarily responsible for ensuring that the President's day-to-day intelligence needs are met.[25] This means that the Office of the DNI, not the Director of the Central Intelligence Agency, should have the final authority over the content and production of the President's Daily Brief (PDB)—or whatever other form intelligence support to the President may take.

We also believe that the DNI will have to work closely with the President and the National Security Council to reconsider how intelligence should best be presented to the President, because we are dubious that the PDB—in its current incarnation—is the right answer.

Our case studies, primarily Iraq, highlight several flaws indicating a need to rethink the PDB.[26] PDB pieces are typically limited by space constraints. While sophisticated, in-depth analysis can be presented in this abbreviated fashion, the task is considerably more difficult than drafting a more immediate, less research-intensive piece that updates the reader on current events and provides a more limited, near-term analytic focus. As a result, we worry that individual PDB articles fail to provide sufficient context for the reader. This view was reinforced by one senior intelligence officer's observation that policymakers are sometimes surprised to find that longer, in-depth intelligence reporting provides a different view from that conveyed by the PDB. The same individual noted that when a policymaker is given a piece of information about a certain subject, the policymaker will often ask questions about the information, leading to follow-up on that subject, thereby exacerbating the current intelligence bias.[27] Moreover, the PDB staff tends to focus on today's hot national security issues, or on issues that attracted the President's interest the last

---

> **RECOMMENDATION 14**   The President's Daily Brief should be restructured. The DNI should oversee the process and ensure a fair representation of divergent views. Reporting on terrorism intelligence should be combined and coordinated by the DNI to eliminate redundancies and material that does not merit Presidential action.

---

time they came up. This can lead to repeated reporting on a given topic or event; a drumbeat of incremental "hot news" articles affects a reader much differently than the same information presented in a longer, contextualized piece that explains the relationship between the various reports. Finally, the PDB sometimes includes excessively "snappy" headlines, which tend to misrepresent an article's more nuanced conclusions, and which are, in our view, unnecessary; a two or three-word indicator of the piece's subject (such as "North Korea-Nuclear") would tell policymakers which pieces were of most interest to them without obscuring the subtle contours of an issue raised in the text.

Having identified these potential problems, we are hesitant to suggest how the PDB process should be altered. Only the President can say for certain how often and in what format he prefers to receive national intelligence information. We do, however, recognize that the creation of the DNI will shift what has been a CIA-centric PDB process to more of a Community one—shepherded by the Office of the DNI.

Regardless of the structure of the PDB process, the DNI will need to respond to the demands of senior advisors and the President. We recommend that the DNI create an analytic staff too small to routinely undertake drafting itself, but large enough that its members would have expertise on a wide range of subjects. The staffers would task the appropriate experts and agencies to draft responses to decisionmaker requests. They could also perform last minute editing and would—in every case—ensure that the pieces reflect any differences of opinion in the Community.[28] In our view, it is simply not enough to present dissenting views from the Intelligence Community only in longer, more formal assessments like National Intelligence Estimates. Rather, because policymakers tend to be significantly influenced by daily intelligence products, we believe it is essential that those products offer as complete a perspective on an issue as is feasible. This is not to suggest that the production of each daily briefing for the President or others should recreate a mini-NIE process; in many cases, relatively few intelligence agencies need be involved. But when agencies have sharp differences, the DNI's analytic staff should be responsible for ensuring that the final memorandum clearly reflects these competing conclusions and the reasons for disagreement.

Equally important, we believe that the DNI should seek to combine—with the President's concurrence, of course—the three primary sources of intelligence that now reach the President. Currently, in addition to the PDB, the President receives the President's Terrorism Threat Report (PTTR), which is prepared by the National Counterterrorism Center and is appended to each day's PDB. The President may also be verbally briefed by the Director of the FBI who uses material from a "Director's Daily Report" prepared by his staff.

We have reviewed these materials and discussed the briefings with many regular participants. There are plainly redundancies that should be eliminated, but we are also concerned that the channels conveying terrorism intelligence are clogged with trivia. One reason for this unnecessary detail is that passing information "up the chain" provides bureaucratic cover against later accusations that the data was not taken seriously. As one official complained, this behavior is caused by bureaucracies that are "preparing for the next 9/11 Commission instead of preparing for the next 9/11." It may be difficult to stem this tide, but the new DNI is in the best position to bring order to the process. We recommend that the DNI be given clear responsibility for combining terrorism intelligence into a single, regular Presidential briefing (whether a daily briefing is required should depend on the pace of events). This briefing would resemble and would perhaps be combined into the PDB.

In the same vein, several senior officials told us that they read the PDB not so much for its content (for it often did not necessarily include especially critical information) as much as to stay apprised of matters on which the President is briefed. In this light, although the DNI and the PDB staff must be free to make a professional judgment about the intelligence to present on any given day, we recommend that the DNI encourage suggestions from policymaking agencies like State and Defense about topics that could usefully be presented in the President's briefing. By taking this step the PDB would likely become more attuned to a wider variety of pressing national security issues.

We fully recognize that the DNI's role calls for a delicate balance. It will be tempting for the DNI's analysts to become the primary drafters themselves, and analysts in individual agencies will continue to face demands from those in their chain of command to respond to requests directly. The former would turn the office of the DNI into one more analytic entity putting forward its own views. The latter problem recreates the situation we have today, which often results in a multiplicity of uncoordinated views appearing before senior decisionmakers. The DNI's analytic cadre, whose responsibility it is to understand and to put forward the views of the Community's experts, wherever located, must ensure that analytic differences in the Community are not suppressed and, equally important, are not presented to decisionmakers in a piecemeal fashion that forces senior officials to sort out the differences themselves.

Retaining the Best Analysts

The Intelligence Community is unlikely to have the funding necessary to rely exclusively—or even primarily—on economic incentives to recruit and retain the best and the brightest. The Community, however, has always offered analysts something more: the opportunity to play a role in shaping the decisions of the nation's top leaders and to help maintain the security of our nation. To the extent that the Community loses sight of this as a motivating factor for its employees, it loses its most valuable tool for recruitment and retention.

Recognize good performers. The Intelligence Community should look for ways to ensure that the best analysts are recognized both within the Community and by decisionmakers outside of the Community. The fact that the Community on the whole works in relative anonymity makes this recognition all the more necessary. Analysts who are viewed as experts get the opportunity to do exactly what analysts are hired to do—play a part in shaping U.S. policy. In turn, analysts who have the chance to sit face-to-face with top-level decisionmakers are motivated in a very personal way to do their best.

Provide travel, training, rotations, and sabbaticals. All analysts are not alike, and not all opportunities for professional development will appeal to all equally. But giving analysts time to do the things they most want to do, particularly when the activities also contribute to the development of their expertise, is beneficial to everyone. One DIA manager

> **RECOMMENDATION 15** The Intelligence Community should expand the use of non-monetary incentives that remind analysts of the importance of their work and the value of their contributions to national security.

told us that fully funding a robust travel budget would be far cheaper than paying salaries on a par with those paid by contractors, and would help a great deal in keeping analysts motivated and interested.[29] Other analysts are likely to find other activities more appealing, from full-time academic training, to policy rotations, to stints in the Office of the DNI or other agencies within the Community.

Permit careers to focus on the analysts' areas of interest. Analysts also differ in their preferred approaches to their careers. Some enjoy being generalists, moving among all types of accounts and bringing a fresh perspective; others have a strong interest in a certain type of analysis—such as conventional weapons—or an area of the world, and might choose to spend time on a variety of similar accounts. Still others seek to specialize on fairly focused subject matters. The Intelligence Community benefits from all of these career paths, and in the best of all worlds, analysts would be able to follow the one best suited to their interests. The nature of the intelligence business will never allow for such a perfect fit; some specialists will need to remain on an account after their interest in it has waned, and some analysts will be pulled from where they are happiest to respond to an emerging crisis. But the goal should be to get it right for as many analysts as possible. Doing so is an enormously powerful retention tool. Managers of technical analysts explained to us that they had a great deal of difficulty retaining analysts because they came in expecting to work on areas in which they had developed expertise, but were pulled by the demands of the job into other areas that they found less interesting.[30] We expect that the Mission Managers will be able to place more focused attention on long-range planning and generate an increased understanding of where knowledge and expertise reside—and thus better position the Community to respond to emerging crises in a thoughtful way and reduce the numbers of analysts forced into jobs they dislike.

Provide tools and support. Managers also complained that analysts often find that the tools and technology available in the Intelligence Community fall short of what they use in school, at home, or in the private sector.[31] Moreover, analysts across the board face declining administrative support. Among other things, analysts typically must do desktop publishing, maintain files of classified materials not available electronically, manage contracts, and perform logistical tasks associated with travel or training. In other words, analysts often view their counterparts in the private sector as having better tools and better support that enable them to spend their time and energy on core tasks. Giving analysts what they need to do their job and ensuring

that they spend their time as *analysts,* not clerks or administrative aides, would emphasize that their time and skills are valued.

Learning From Past Mistakes

The new intelligence reform legislation requires the DNI to assign an individual or entity the responsibility to ensure that finished intelligence products are timely, objective, independent of political considerations, based on all sources of available intelligence, and grounded in proper analytic tradecraft. In the course of conducting relevant reviews, this entity is further directed to produce a report of lessons learned.[32]

Iraq, Libya, and Afghanistan have offered opportunities for the Intelligence Community to compare its assessments with the ground truth and examine the sources of the disparities. We have already seen evidence that the lessons learned from Iraq are being incorporated by analysts covering other countries or intelligence topics. Analysts are increasingly careful to explain their analytical baseline in their products, and attribute the sources of intelligence underlying it. The Intelligence Community, analysts say, has adopted the "rule of elementary school math class," in that its analysts are dedicated to "showing our work" to prevent the "layering of analysis."[33]

This is an area in which the Intelligence Community should learn from the Department of Defense, which has an especially strong, institutionalized process for benefiting from lessons learned. In our classified report, we discuss a Defense Department "lessons-learned" study that we found particularly impressive, but that we cannot elaborate upon here. Intelligence Community lessons-learned efforts (such as CIA's Product Evaluation Staff) had less success, in part because they do not have sufficient resources or possess much prestige within intelligence agencies. Nor do we think that, in general, intelligence agencies should be responsible for "grading their own papers." The intelligence reform legislation recognizes the need for a separate body that conducts reviews of analysis, a welcome idea that should be fully embraced by the Community.

RECOMMENDATION 16 Examinations of finished intelligence should be routine and ongoing, and the lessons learned from the "post mortems" should be incorporated into the intelligence education and training program.

Conclusion

The changes that we recommend are significant departures from the current way in which the Community conducts the business of analysis. Some run counter to long-standing, embedded practices, and we are mindful that they may be resisted by analysts and managers alike. We believe, however, that these changes are essential to improving the Community's capability to accurately assess threats and to provide timely, relevant, thoughtful support to policymakers. Intelligence analysis faces unprecedented challenges; unprecedented measures to strengthen the analytical process are well warranted.

Questions for Further Discussion

1. What role do the commissioners see for "mission managers" in the intelligence community?

2. What role can outside experts play in the analytic process?

3. What can intelligence managers do to foster "long-range thinking" among analysts?

4. Do you think "denial and deception" is a significant problem for today's intelligence analysts? How can they counteract this problem?

Endnotes

1. U.S. Senate, *The Final Report of the Select Committee to Study Governmental Operations with Respect to Intelligence Activities* (April 26, 1976) (*i.e.,* Church Committee Report); Permanent Select Committee on Intelligence, U.S. House of Representatives, *IC21: Intelligence Community in the 21st Century* (1996); Commission to Assess the Ballistic Missile Threat to the United States (*i.e.,* Rumsfeld Commission), *Side Letter to the President* (March 18, 1999); CIA, *The Jeremiah Report: The Intelligence Community's Performance on the Indian Nuclear Tests* (June 1, 1998); Markle Foundation Task Force, *Creating a Trusted Information Network for Homeland Security* (Dec. 2003); National Commission on Terrorist Attacks Upon the United States, *Final Report of the National Commission on Terrorist Attacks Upon the United States* (*i.e.,* The 9/11 Commission Report) (2004); Council on Foreign Relations, *Making Intelligence Smarter: The Future of U.S. Intelligence: Report of an Independent Task Force* (1996); Commission on the Roles and Capabilities of the United States Intelligence Community (i.e., Aspin-Brown Commission), *Preparing for the 21st Century: An Appraisal of U.S. Intelligence* (1996); *Report of the Commission on Organization of the Executive Branch of the Government* (*i.e.,* Hoover Commission Report) (1949).

2. Staff review of House Permanent Select Committee on Intelligence and Senate Select Committee on Intelligence Markups of Intelligence Authorization Bills, 1991–2005.

3. Interview with senior intelligence official (Sept. 22, 2004).

4. The CIA has had similar programs in the past whereby the agency introduced analysts who were tools experts to work alongside other analysts. These analysts were just like their analytic colleagues, except that they were also specialists in how to use analytic technologies and could help counterparts learn to use these tools to structure research problems. CIA Office of Research and Development, *Office of East Asian Analysis Testbed Project Final Report* (Sept. 30, 1994).

5. Interview with biosecurity expert (Feb. 4, 2005).

6. Inter-agency Information Sharing Working Group, *Consolidated Report* (Dec. 14, 2004) at p. 5. We provided an additional footnote illustrating the magnitude of this challenge in our classified report.

7. CIA Office of Research and Development, *Office of East Asian Analysis Testbed Project Final Report* (Sept. 30, 1994).

8. Interview with senior In-Q-Tel official (Feb. 3, 2005). In addition, a senior manager of analysis told us he knew there is a need to make better use of open sources but that this could not be achieved without assistance in the form of preliminary correlation of the data. Interview with senior CIA DI official (Feb. 10, 2005).

9. Interview with senior In-Q-Tel official (Feb. 3, 2005).

10. Interview with CIA analysts (Jan. 24, 2005).

11. Interview with former CIA WINPAC analysts (Nov. 10, 2004).

12. These formal alternative analysis programs are also reinforced by the existence of multiple analytic units in the Community, which often reach different analytic conclusions.

13. The DNI is statutorily required to assign responsibility "for ensuring responsibility that, as appropriate, elements of the Intelligence Community conduct alternative analysis." Intelligence Reform and Terrorism Prevention Act of 2004 at § 1017, Pub. L. No. 108-458 (hereinafter "IRTPA").

14. Chapter Three (Afghanistan).

15. Interview with senior CIA official.

16. There currently exist several very successful joint training programs. The Joint Military Intelligence College, for example, currently operates a very successful program, a structured intermediate/advanced curriculum for Intelligence Community officers across the Community. At the same time, many similar efforts have failed for various reasons, including insufficient funding and lack of bureaucratic clout. The Defense Department Chancellor for Civilian Education's program is one such example of an unsuccessful cross-agency effort. Interview with former senior staff of the defunct Department of Defense Office of the Chancellor for Civilian Education and Development (Jan. 13, 2005).

17. Some, but not most, of the finished intelligence provided to the Commission included lists of reference numbers identifying particular sources, but we understand that such lists are not routinely provided to policymakers. In any case, these lists provide no indication of how one could determine which specific document supported facts included in the piece.

18. We recognize that the DO is currently working to establish Community procedures for such a system, and we commend this development. . . .

19. DCI Intelligence Science Board Task Force, *The State of Science and Technology Analysis in the Intelligence*

Community (April 2004) at p. xiii (hereinafter "ISB Report").

20. *Id.* at p. xiii; Interview with senior intelligence official (Oct. 7, 2004); Interview with senior DIA analyst (Sept. 23, 2004).
21. ISB Report at pp. 26–27.
22. *Id.* at p. 27.
23. *Id.* at pp. 26, 28; Interview with administration official (Sept. 30, 2004); Interview with administration official (Sept. 10, 2004).
24. Interview with senior administration official (Oct. 12, 2004).
25. IRTPA at § 1011.
26. In addition, several senior policymakers expressed concerns about the utility of the PDB in its current incarnation.
27. Interview with senior intelligence analyst (Nov. 8, 2004).
28. We understand that the CIA is already moving in this direction and we commend it for doing so.
29. Interview with DIA analysts and managers (Oct. 26, 2004).
30. *See, e.g.,* Interview with CIA WINPAC analysts (Oct. 14, 2004).
31. *Id.*
32. IRTPA at § 1019.
33. Interview with DIA analysts (Nov. 22, 2004). ✦

Reprinted from the Commission on the Intelligence Capabilities of the United States Regarding Weapons of Mass Destruction (the Silberman-Robb Commission), *Final Report* (Washington, D.C.: U.S. Government Printing Office, 2005), pp. 1–37.

34

Institutional Origins of the 9/11 Intelligence Failure

Amy B. Zegart

Diagnosing the problems that impede the production and dissemination of timely and accurate intelligence products is the beginning of any effort to reform the intelligence community. In this overview of the results of a series of blue ribbon panels and official commissions, Amy Zegart highlights the suggestions for reform that were available to government officials in the decade before the 9/11 tragedy—advice that might have improved the ability of the U.S. government to meet the threat posed by transnational terrorist networks. Zegart explains why so little progress was made in putting this advice to good use.

In January 2000, al-Qaida operatives gathered secretly in Malaysia for a planning meeting. The Central Intelligence Agency (CIA) was watching. Among the participants was Khalid al-Mihdhar, one of the hijackers who would later help to crash American Airlines flight 77 into the Pentagon. By the time the meeting disbanded, the CIA had taken a photograph of al-Mihdhar, learned his full name, obtained his passport number, and uncovered one other critical piece of information: al-Mihdhar held a multiple-entry visa to the United States.[1] It was twenty months before the September 11, 2001, terrorist attacks on the World Trade Center and the Pentagon. George Tenet, the director of central intelligence (DCI), later admitted that the CIA should have placed al-Mihdhar on the State Department's watch list denying him entry into the United States.[2] It did not until August 23, 2001, just nineteen days before the terrorist attacks and months after al-Mihdhar had entered the country, obtained a California motor vehicle photo identification card (using his real name), and started taking flying lessons.

The case of Khalid al-Mihdhar provides a chilling example of the subtle yet powerful effects of organization—that is, the routines, structures, and cultures that critically influence what government agencies do and how well they do it. Why did the CIA take so long to put this suspected al-Qaida operative on the State Department's watch list, especially given Director Tenet's earlier declaration that the United States was "at war" with al-Qaida, and when U.S. intelligence reporting throughout the spring and summer of 2001 revealed a dramatic spike in "chatter" about an upcoming terrorist attack?[3] The simplest answer is that keeping track of the whereabouts of foreign terrorists had never been standard practice or a high priority. For more than forty years, the Cold War had dominated both the thinking and operation of the CIA and the thirteen other agencies of the U.S. intelligence community.[4] When the Soviet Union fell in 1991 and the principal threat to U.S. national security changed, U.S. intelligence agencies were slow to change with it. Before September 11, none of these agencies had formal training programs or well-honed procedures to assist their intelligence officers in identifying dangerous terrorists and warning other U.S. government agencies about them before they reached the United States.[5] As one CIA employee told congressional investigators a year after the September 11 attacks, he believed it was "not incumbent" even on the CIA's Osama bin Laden unit to place individuals such as al-Mihdhar on the State Department's watch list.[6]

No organization is failure-proof, and no one will ever know whether the World Trade Center and Pentagon attacks could have been prevented. Evidence suggests, however, that the U.S. intelligence community showed a stunning inability to adapt to the rise of terrorism after the Cold War ended.

This article attributes the adaptation failure of U.S. intelligence agencies to three factors: the nature of bureaucratic organizations, which makes internal reform exceedingly difficult; the self-interest of presidents, legislators, and government bureaucrats, which works against executive branch reform; and the fragmented structure of the federal government, which erects high barriers to legislative reform.

The first section of the article considers whether the U.S. intelligence community adapted as well as could be expected during the 1990s, given the challenges and constraints that it faced. The second section examines the literature on organizational change and develops a framework for understanding why organizations fail to adapt. The third section, a case study of the CIA, describes how and why the agency adapted poorly to the growing terrorist threat between 1991 and 2001. The fourth section offers three conclusions from the preceding analysis. First, major reform of the U.S. intelligence community is difficult even after catastrophic failure.

Second, reform is likely to continue lagging behind external environmental demands. And third, dramatic improvements in U.S. intelligence capabilities require changing organizational routines and cultures as well as structures.

Determining Adaptation Failure: Change Versus Adaptation

The failure of U.S. intelligence agencies to meet the terrorist threat following the end of the Cold War was not immediately apparent. Some foreign policy leaders and intelligence officials argue that the dangers of the post-Cold War world were too opaque, too numerous, and too fluid for U.S. intelligence agencies to assess the terrorist threat more effectively than they did. According to this view, the danger posed by al-Qaida and other terrorist organizations may appear obvious in hindsight, but this was not the case before the September 11 attacks. As President Bill Clinton's national security adviser, Samuel Berger, put it, "History is written through a rearview mirror but it unfolds through a foggy windshield."[7]

Others point to evidence that U.S. intelligence agencies did, in fact, recognize the gravity of the terrorist threat, allocating resources and launching new programs to combat it years before September 11. According to former DCI Robert Gates, the U.S. intelligence community began to shift resources away from Soviet-related missions soon after the fall of the Soviet Union. Whereas in 1980, 58 percent of all intelligence resources was devoted to Soviet-related issues, by 1993, the figure had dropped to just 13 percent.[8] Although specific budgets are classified, resources appear to have been redirected to combat terrorism. Despite declining intelligence budgets during the 1990s,[9] direct spending on counterterrorism roughly quintupled.[10]

In addition, the CIA, the Federal Bureau of Investigation (FBI), and other intelligence agencies launched a number of new counterterrorism initiatives. These included the creation, in January 1996, of a special multiagency intelligence unit to track the activities of bin Laden and his network[11]; dramatic increases in the number of FBI offices overseas, with a focus on countries critical to fighting terrorism[12]; and a concerted effort to forge closer relationships with foreign intelligence services, which resulted in the disruption of terrorist cells in roughly twenty countries after 1997.[13] As Director Tenet concluded in February 2002, "This community has worked diligently over the last five years, and the American people need to understand that with the resources and authorities and priorities, the men and women of the FBI and the CIA per-

formed heroically." Tenet, in fact, strongly objected to the idea that the September 11 terrorist attacks signified an intelligence failure, adding, "When people use the word 'failure'—'failure' means no focus, no attention, no discipline—and those were not present in what either we or the FBI did here and around the world."[14] Tenet was not the only senior intelligence official to resist accusations that the September 11 attacks represented failure.[15] When asked how well the intelligence community had adapted to meet the terrorist threat, for example, another senior intelligence official answered, "I think before September 11th, I would have said exceptionally well . . . [now] I think we've done very, very well."[16] As these statements and examples indicate, U.S. intelligence agencies did make some internal changes in response to the end of the Cold War and the rise of the terrorist challenge.

Change, however, is not the same as adaptation. As sociologists have long pointed out, organizations are always changing.[17] The key issue is whether those changes matter, or more precisely, whether the rate of change within an organization keeps pace (or lags behind) the rate of change in its external environment.[18] Manifestation of this concept is more easily observed in the private sector, where responding to shifting market forces, consumer tastes, and competitive pressures can mean life or death for a firm. The concept may be less obvious, but no less important, for evaluating public sector organizations. The question is not: Are you doing anything differently today? But: Are you doing enough differently today to meet the challenges you face? Adaptation must be judged relative to external demands.

In the case of U.S. intelligence agencies, determining adaptation failure requires answering three questions: (1) did intelligence officials and policymakers recognize the gravity of the threat posed by al-Qaida before September 11, and if so, when? (2) did they understand the connection between the terrorist threat and the imperative for organizational change? and (3) to what extent did they achieve the organizational changes they believed were necessary? Timing is a crucial component. September 11 post mortems may highlight organizational deficiencies, but to make a strong case for adaptation failure, it is necessary to show that before September 11, intelligence officials and policymakers identified key organizational problems but did not succeed in fixing them.

The answers to the three questions above appear to be yes, yes, and only to a small degree. Many U.S. intelligence officials and policymakers recognized the threat, but were unable to achieve the intelligence reforms they believed were vital several years before the World Trade Center and Pentagon attacks.

Recognizing the Threat

In 1994 the DCI began delivering unclassified annual threat assessments to Congress. Analysis of these reports reveals that terrorism was identified as a significant threat to the United States every year from 1994 to 2001.[19] By 1998 terrorism ranked in the top tier of threats, alongside other transnational dangers such as the proliferation of weapons of mass destruction. The U.S. intelligence community became aware of bin Laden in the early 1990s, soon after he had founded al-Qaida, and was aggressively collecting intelligence on him by 1996.[20] A number of terrorist attacks and plots from 1991 to 2001 associated with Islamist groups also raised the profile of terrorism within the intelligence community and indicated that targets included the U.S. homeland.[21]

In 1998 concern for and warnings about a possible al-Qaida attack reached a heightened level inside the community. In February bin Laden issued a public *fatwa* encouraging attacks on Americans anywhere in the world.[22] In May he discussed "bringing the war home to America" in a public press conference.[23] And in August his terrorist network succeeded in carrying out two sophisticated, simultaneous, and devastating truck bomb attacks against the U.S. embassies in Nairobi, Kenya, and Dar es Salaam, Tanzania, killing 224 people and injuring 5,000 more.[24] Over the course of the year, U.S. intelligence agencies also received a number of reports indicating possible al-Qaida terrorist plots inside the United States. These events led CIA Director Tenet in December 1998 to issue a memo declaring war against Osama bin Laden. He wrote, "We must now enter a new phase in our effort against Bin Ladin. . . . We are at war . . . I want no resources or people spared in this effort, either inside CIA or the Community."[25] The House and Senate Intelligence Committees' Joint Inquiry into the September 11 attacks, a ten-month investigation that examined nearly 500,000 pages of documents and conducted 300 interviews, concluded that "Bin Ladin's declaration of war in February 1998 and intelligence reports indicating possible terrorist plots inside the United States did not go unnoticed by the Intelligence Community, which, in turn, advised senior officials in the U.S. Government of the serious nature of the threat."[26]

Tenet maintained his heightened level of concern in public addresses over the next three years. In 1999 he testified in open session before the Senate Armed Services Committee: "Looking out over the next year . . . there is not the slightest doubt that Usama Bin Ladin, his worldwide allies, and his sympathizers are planning further attacks against us. . . . I must tell you we are concerned that one or more of Bin Ladin's attacks could occur at any time."[27] In 2000 he told the Senate Select Intelligence Committee, again in open session, "Everything we have learned recently confirms our conviction that [bin Laden] wants to strike further blows against the United States. . . . We still believe he could strike without additional warning."[28] In his 2001 public threat assessment, the DCI bluntly warned, "The threat from terrorism is real, immediate, and evolving."[29] As one senior U.S. intelligence official lamented after September 11, "You know, we've been saying it forever, [bin Laden] wants to bring the fight here."[30]

Public statements and actions by policymakers during the 1990s suggest that they shared the intelligence community's assessment of the growing terrorist threat long before September 11. In 1993, after Islamic terrorists detonated a bomb in the World Trade Center parking garage, killing 6 and wounding more than 1,000, Attorney General Janet Reno declared that terrorism had become a major threat to U.S. national security interests.[31] Beginning in 1994, President Clinton mentioned terrorism in every one of his State of the Union addresses. In June 1997 the FBI's chief of International Terrorism Operations warned about the threat of an Islamic attack on U.S. soil in a public speech.[32] That same year, two different strategic assessments, the Pentagon's Quadrennial Defense Review and a report by the National Defense Panel, also included strong warnings about terrorist threats to the U.S. homeland.[33] In 1998 President Clinton delivered a major address at the opening session of the United Nations General Assembly in which he issued a forceful call to combat terrorism. Referring to terrorism as "a clear and present danger," the president said that the issue ranked "at the top of the American agenda and should be at the top of the world's agenda."[34] Less than a year later, U.S. Secretary of Defense William Cohen wrote an op-ed in the *Washington Post* in which he predicted a terrorist attack on U.S. soil.[35] In sum, the U.S. intelligence community's assessments of a growing terrorist threat did not go unnoticed. Senior policymakers across the national security establishment appear to have agreed with them.

Understanding the Imperative for Organizational Change

Evidence also suggests that U.S. policymakers understood the need for organizational changes to meet the terrorist threat. Between the fall of the Soviet Union and the September 11 attacks, six bipartisan blue-ribbon commissions,[36] three major unclassified governmental initiatives,[37] and three think tank task forces[38] examined the U.S. intelligence community, the FBI, and U.S. counterterrorism efforts. The commissions were chaired by well-respected leaders such as former Defense Secretary Harold Brown, Ambassador Paul Bremer, former Senators Gary Hart and Warren Rudman, and William Webster, former director of both the CIA and FBI. The three reports issued by governmental initiatives were President Clinton's 1993 and 1995 interagency National Performance Reviews; a 1996 House Intelligence Committee staff study that was the most comprehensive review of the intelligence community since the Church committee investigations into CIA abuses of the 1970s; and the FBI's 1998 Draft Strategic Plan. The think tank reports were produced by the Council on Foreign Relations, the Twentieth Century Fund, and the National Institute for Public Policy. All twelve were detailed, substantive examinations.

Although the reports addressed a variety of intelligence issues and problems, the common theme was the need for major change. The Council on Foreign Relations report noted in 1996 that "the intelligence community has been adjusting to the changed demands of the post-Cold War world for several years . . . [but] additional reform is necessary."[39] The report listed nearly forty recommendations that ranged from significant structural reforms to changes in personnel recruiting, training, and assignments. The 1996 House Intelligence Committee staff study found that the intelligence community suffered from a lack of "corporateness," or integration between individual agencies. The report noted, "Only intelligence, of all major government functions, is carried out by a very disparate number of agencies and organizations that are either independent of one another or housed in separate departments by officials whose main concerns are policy, not intelligence."[40] In particular, the report criticized what it saw as "the glaring gap" between the DCI's responsibilities and his authorities,[41] the "fundamental and urgent" need to improve the intelligence requirements process that sets agency priorities,[42] and the "internecine competition" between the various intelligence collection disciplines such as signals intelligence and human intelligence.[43] It issued eighty-two recommended reforms. Four years later, the Bremer commission warned that "international terrorism poses an increasingly dangerous and difficult threat to America." It urged the government to take immediate "steps to reinvigorate the collection of intelligence about terrorists' plans."[44] The commission's key recommendations included clarifying the FBI's authorities to investigate suspected terrorist groups; rescinding CIA guidelines that hindered the recruitment of terrorist informants; giving higher funding priority to counterterrorism efforts in the CIA, FBI, and National Security Agency; and establishing a new cadre of reports officers to distill and disseminate terrorism-related information quickly once it is collected. Indeed, the commission noted with concern that "U.S. intelligence and law enforcement communities lack the ability to prioritize, translate, and understand in a timely fashion all of the information to which they have access."[45] In total, the reports issued 340 recommendations to improve U.S. intelligence capabilities.[46] The imperative for organizational change was clear.

Failing to Change

To what extent were the studies' recommendations achieved? To be sure, gauging adaptation failure by examining the adoption of study recommendations has its limitations. Commissions may be created for the sole purpose of deflecting blame or delaying action rather than generating change, though this is far less often the case in national security affairs than most believe.[47] Even earnest efforts at reform often take a variety of forms, with some focusing on "the art of the possible" and others proposing more ideal and unlikely solutions. Examining the totality of study recommendations and their success, however, has the advantage of providing a rough, macro view of adaptation that does not rely on hindsight or impose ex post personal judgments of which reforms were better ideas than others. Asking what major consensus recommendations were made and whether these were implemented provides a useful, systematic first cut at the problem that goes beyond anecdotal evidence of failure.

The data indicate a widespread inability of U.S. intelligence agencies to adapt to the terrorist threat before the September 11 attacks. Of 340 recommendations for changes in the intelligence community, only 35 were successfully implemented, and 268—or 79 percent of the total—resulted in no action at all. Closer examination reveals surprising agreement on four major problems: the intelligence community's lack of coherence or "corporateness"; insufficient human intelligence; personnel systems that failed to align intelligence needs with personnel skills or encourage information sharing; and weaknesses in setting intelligence priorities. The twelve studies provided a menu of options to address these commonly identified problems. Yet policymakers left the intelligence community essentially intact. As the Hart-Rudman commission concluded in January 2001, "The dramatic changes in the world since the end of the Cold War . . . have not been accompanied by any major institutional changes in the Executive branch of the U.S. government."[48] The commission presciently predicted that these institutional deficiencies left the United States exceptionally vulnerable to a catastrophic terrorist attack.[49]

Explaining Failed Adaptation: Crossing the Theoretical Divide

Existing academic work does not offer a ready-made explanation for the failure of U.S. intelligence agencies to adapt to a changed external environment. On the one hand, organization theorists study organizational pathologies but focus almost exclusively on firms. On the other hand, political scientists examine national security affairs and bureaucracy but rarely treat intelligence agencies as dependent variables.[50] Taken together, however, these literatures provide the building blocks to construct a model of intelligence agency adaptation failure.

The Bottom Line of Organization Theory

Organization theory has long drawn a multidisciplinary crowd united by a common interest in understanding what organizations do, how they do it, and how well. Questions of organizational inertia,[51] evolution,[52] and learning[53] have generated rich and dynamic research programs over the past thirty years.

Although organization theory has much to offer, particularly about why organizations resist change even when it is clearly beneficial, the literature cannot be applied easily to the political realm. This is understandable. The field emerged with firms in mind and has remained focused on the private sector ever since. As Richard Cyert and James March noted in the introduction to their 1963 classic, *A Behavioral Theory of the Firm*, "We had an agenda. . . . We thought that research on economics and research on organizations should have something to say to each other."[54] The focus on business organizations continues. In his 1999 book, *Organizations Evolving*, Howard Aldrich criticizes the selection bias of organization theory. Notably, though, he is troubled by the inordinate attention paid to large publicly traded corporations instead of privately held businesses. Aldrich's idea of broadening organization theory is to include different kinds of businesses, not political organizations.[55] Because of the focus on firms, organization theory has developed without much attention to politics and power, forces that are crucial for understanding the development of government agencies.[56]

Consider, for example, the literature that appears most centrally related to the question of agency adaptation failure: population ecology. According to population ecologists, most organizations face strong pressures that make them resistant to change. Market forces, the competitive environment, technology, and consumer preferences all shift over time, but organizations are rarely good at shifting with them. Instead, population ecologists argue that innovations in organizational strategies and structures occur at the population level, through the birth of new organizations and the death of others. In other words, individual organizations do not adapt; populations do, with newer, fitter firms constantly replacing older, outdated ones through a process of natural selection.[57]

This approach is helpful in explaining the private sector, where firms routinely come and go. It is much less helpful, however, in understanding the public sector, where there is substantially less organizational churn. As many scholars have observed, government agencies are notoriously hard to eliminate because there are always interest groups and elected officials who have vested interests at stake.[58] In his pilot study comparing U.S. government agencies between 1923 and 1973, for example, Herbert Kaufman found that 85 percent of those in the 1923 sample were still in existence fifty years later.[59] By contrast, Aldrich found that in 1957, 398,000 businesses were created in the United States; about the same number were transferred to new owners; and almost as many failed.[60]

In addition, population ecology takes organizational inertia as a starting assumption rather than a dependent variable.[61] This is a serious weakness. If population ecologists are correct, and innovations are generated through the replacement of old organizations by new ones, then the imperative to understand what it is that keeps any single agency from adapting to environmental demands is all the greater in the public sector: the government is likely to be riddled with poorly performing agencies that persist because they are unchallenged by the threat of new entrants.

Finally, most research in population ecology consists of large-n studies of entire organizational populations, with little attention given to the role of individual choice, decisionmaking processes, or politics. The result is a strangely antiseptic theory of natural selection that seems to ignore the role of real people exercising real power. As Charles Perrow notes, "It is almost as if God does the negative and positive selecting."[62]

The Tally for Political Science

The political science literature suffers from a different problem. Rational choice approaches focus squarely on politics and power. Still largely unexamined, however, are the routines and cultures that develop within government bureaucracies and their resistance to change. Major work on U.S. government agencies in the 1980s and 1990s was produced by Congress scholars who were interested primarily in agencies as objects of congressional control, not as subjects of study in their own right. Using ideas from transaction cost economics, Mathew McCubbins, Barry Weingast, and other congressional dominance scholars argue that Congress controls the federal bureaucracy, and in surprisingly efficient ways.[63] Indeed, they contend that evidence usually thought to suggest poor oversight, such as sparsely attended congressional committee hearings, actually reveals oversight hard at work. Government bureaucrats know they must follow their congressional mandate or face the consequences. Congress therefore does not have to expend much effort monitoring them.

For the purposes of this analysis, the most serious limitation of the congressional dominance literature is its assumption that agencies can and do adapt. To say that Congress controls the bureaucracy is to say that agencies are, by and large, responsive to the preferences and demands of legislators. Much of the literature examines how legislators ensure that these preferences and demands are heeded—by building control mechanisms into the very design of government agencies, or by using (or threatening to use) existing controls such as withholding appropriations, or both.[64] The mechanisms may vary, but the logic is the same: government bureaucrats usually heed legislators' demands because they know, as McCubbins puts it, that "Congress holds the power of life or death in the most elemental terms."[65] The logic also suggests that when legislative preferences change significantly, bureaucracies should change, too. There is some evidence that they do.[66]

Notably, even critics of the congressional dominance literature agree that government agencies can adapt. Terry Moe, for example, argues that Congress is not alone in determining agency behavior; many factors, including presidents, interest groups, and courts, influence what agencies do.[67] Others argue that congressional dominance does not capture the degree of bureaucratic shirking, when agencies opt to pursue their own organizational interests instead of the interests of their congressional overseers. As David Epstein and Sharyn O'Halloran conclude, the literature on congressional-bureaucratic relations has reached something of an impasse in recent years: "The general consensus has been reached that legislators have more effective means of control than was previously realized, but bureaucrats still retain significant amounts of discretion in setting policy."[68]

All of this work suggests that agencies are out there, on the move, doing things. Usually agencies respond to congressional wishes; sometimes they pursue the interests of presidents and others in the political system; and sometimes they shirk to serve their own interests. Nowhere, however, is there a sense that government agencies may be unable to change. According to this literature, the challenge is to keep them from running amok. But the greater danger may be that agencies are stuck running in place.

A Model of Agency Adaptation Failure

Although neither organization theory nor rational choice theory offers a ready-made explanation of adaptation, each does provide the foundations for a general model of agency adaptation failure. Organization theory offers insights about intraorganizational impediments to reform, while rational choice theory helps to explain external impediments to reform.

Rather than viewing government agencies from without (i.e., as more limited public sector versions of firms or as objects of congressional control), I begin by assuming the bureaucracy's perspective. Heads of government agencies that are confronting a changing environment must answer two questions. First, how can they get the reforms they need in their agencies to keep pace with environmental demands? And second, what forces will hinder them from succeeding?[69]

There are three major sources of bureaucratic reform: (1) internal reforms made by the agency itself, whether in memos, speeches, revised guidelines, or sanctions of undesired behavior; (2) executive branch action, for example, executive orders, presidential directives, or efforts by executive branch officials outside the agency in question, such as the National Security Council; and (3) statutory reforms that require the involvement of both Congress and the executive branch.

Impediments to reform may emerge from both inside and outside the agency. Some reforms may fail because they challenge deeply held organizational values and threaten to alter established routines. Others may trigger opposition from competing government agencies that stand to gain or lose depending on the outcome. Proposed statutory changes that require the consent of multiple congressional majorities and the president bring institutional forces more centrally into play. Thus, developing a better understanding of agency adaptation failure requires combining the enduring realities operating within organizations with those operating outside them. More specifically, these are (1) the nature of organizations; (2) the rational self-interest of political officials; and (3) the fragmented structure of the U.S. federal government. Taken together, these three realities raise exceptionally high obstacles to agency change.

This approach, though not theoretically elegant, is analytically useful. The persistence of organizational habits, the unwillingness to veer from established routines, and the role of culture say little about why legislators have so rarely proposed statutory changes to the intelligence community, and why they have been opposed by colleagues in the House and Senate Armed Services Committees when they did. Conversely, examining only rational self-interest does not explain why, before the September 11 attacks, FBI agents preferred to keep case files in shoeboxes under their desks rather than entering them into computer databases; nor does it explain why, for a year and half, intelligence officials neglected to tell the State Department to include on its watch list a suspected al-Qaida operative with a multiple-entry U.S. visa in his passport.

The nature of organizations. The first route to agency reform is through the adoption of internal changes. Yet much of the work in organization theory argues that organizations do not change easily by themselves.[70] Examples abound. The U.S. Army kept a horse cavalry until World War II. Until the mid-1990s, U.S. Customs forms asked ships entering American ports to list the number of cannons on board, and federal law required the U.S. Agriculture Department to keep field offices within a day's horseback ride to everyplace in the United States. Even private sector firms, which have considerably more leeway over personnel decisions, more access to capital, and fewer management constraints than government agencies, do not fare well when changing circumstances require adjustment. Consider the most basic case: whether firms adapt enough to survive. Of the 5.5 million businesses tracked by the U.S. Census Bureau in 1990, only 3.8 million were still in existence four years later, a failure rate of 31 percent.[71] In New York City, more than 60 percent of all restaurants surveyed in the *Zagat* guide between 1979 and 1999 folded.[72] Between 2000 and 2003 more than 400 public companies, including Enron, Global Crossing, and Kmart, declared bankruptcy. As Aldrich points out, these and other findings about organizational adaptation failure are most likely understated because they tend to focus only on surviving firms and exclude all the organizations that never made it past the start-up phase.[73]

Government agencies are even less able than private sector businesses to make internal adjustments. First, they have more constraints, facing more conflicting missions with less managerial discretion and fewer resources than private sector firms do.[74] Any manager working for Coca Cola knows his mission is to sell soda—the more, the better. By contrast, for years U.S. Immigration and Naturalization Service officials were charged with helping some foreigners enter the United States while keeping others out. The most embattled chief executive officer answers only to a small group of influential investors, all of whom share the same goal: maximizing shareholder value of the firm. By contrast, even the new director of national intelligence (DNI), a position created in December 2004 to manage the U.S. intelligence community, serves a variety of intelligence consumers, from the president and his senior foreign policy advisers to the secretary of defense to 535 members of Congress.[75] Unlike a firm's shareholders, these policymakers have preferences and interests that often conflict. Caught between Democrats and Republicans, military hawks and civil libertarians, interventionists and isolationists, policy advocates and opponents, the new DNI, like DCIs before him, must navigate carefully, knowing that not everyone will be satisfied with his decisions.

Second, government agencies were not built to be adaptable. As James Q. Wilson and Joel Aberbach and Bert Rockman note, agencies are not designed to be especially nimble or innovative.[76] Instead, they are designed to be reliable and fair. Above all, reliability means ensuring that tasks are completed consistently and predictably, which is best guaranteed by having one organization repeatedly performing the same functions. The U.S. Postal Service has built the capacity to surge at Christmas time. Each state has a department of motor vehicles to issue driver's licenses. Assigning these tasks to a different agency every year would almost certainly result in more delays, lost mail, and perhaps even greater driver frustration. Government agencies are also designed to ensure fairness, by creating and adhering to rules and procedures about what benefits or services are provided to which citizens, regardless of their personal wealth, power, or political connections. The lines for government services may be long, but in principle everyone must stand in them.

Ironically, these attributes of bureaucracies create strong impediments to reform.[77] Standard operating procedures guarantee that the Social Security Administration mails benefit checks on time each month, and they help to ensure that every military pilot has the same rules of engagement in wartime. But they can also reduce the willingness and ability of agencies to deviate from established practices, even when such deviation may be more beneficial—a phenomenon that Barbara Levitt and James March refer to as a "competency trap."[78] The very characteristics that give an organization reliability and fairness reduce the probability of change.[79]

Finally, time is almost never on the side of government agencies that must adapt. All organizations become more resistant to change as routines, norms, and relationships become firmly established.[80] In addition, as Herbert Simon notes, the larger the number of organizations in a given system and the greater their level of interconnectedness, the harder it is for that entire system to adjust. Improvements must occur throughout the system at the same time to produce results.[81]

Government agencies that do not adapt on their own may be subjected to change from the outside, either through executive branch action or through legislation. In such cases, the rational self-interest of political actors and the fragmented structure of the federal government work to block success.

Rational self-interest of presidents, legislators, and national security bureaucrats. Government officials are constrained by the incentives and capabilities that come with their positions. Although individuals have their own ideas, skills, and policy preferences, institutional incentives and capabilities exert a powerful influence, making some courses of action easier and less costly than others. These incentives and capabilities explain why, before the September 11 attacks, no president championed intelligence reform, why legislators largely avoided or blocked it, and why national security agency bureaucrats opposed it.

Presidents have strong incentives to improve organizational effectiveness. To make their mark on history, they must make the bureaucracy work well for them. Perhaps even more important, presidents are also driven to enhance organizational effectiveness by the electorate, which expects far more of them than they can possibly deliver. Held responsible for everything from inflation to Iraqi democratization, presidents have good reason to ensure that government agencies adapt to changing demands as much and as fast as possible.[82]

Presidents, however, lack the capabilities to make the changes they desire. They have little time, limited political capital, few formal powers, and packed political agendas. Presidents therefore almost always prefer to focus their efforts on policy issues that directly concern (and benefit) voters, rather than on the arcane details of organizational design and operation. Tax cuts and Social Security lockboxes win votes, but no president ever won a landslide election by changing the CIA's personnel system. Moreover, presidents are especially reluctant to push for agency reforms in the absence of a crisis or in the presence of anticipated resistance. Presidents are thus loath to reform existing agencies through executive action or legislation. Although dozens of investigations, commissions, and experts identified shortcomings in the U.S. intelligence community between 1947 (when the CIA was created) and the September 11 terrorist attacks, no president attempted major intelligence reform.[83]

Self-interest leads most legislators to avoid tackling intelligence reform altogether or seek to block it. Legislators, like presidents, have little incentive to delve into the bureaucratic intricacies of intelligence agency design because doing so does not provide tangible benefits to voters back home.[84] Indeed, the weak electoral connection is one of the reasons congressional intelligence oversight committees until 2004 had term limits for their members, despite the fact that such limits hinder the development of expertise and despite repeated calls by commissions to abolish them. When crises do arise, intelligence committee members are rewarded more for holding hearings than taking corrective action. The Bay of Pigs, the congressional investigations into CIA abuses during the 1970s, the Iran-Contra scandal, and the Aldrich Ames spy case all triggered major investigations, but none produced fundamental change in the intelligence community. In addition, members of Congress care about maintaining the power of the institution. Generally, this means that legislators prefer executive arrangements that diffuse authority and capabilities; the more agencies in the executive branch, the more power bases can accrue in Congress to oversee them.

Finally, national security agency bureaucrats have their own interests at stake and powerful means to protect them. Whereas most domestic policy agencies operate in relatively autonomous spheres—the U.S. Forest Service, for example, has no reason to think about the design or operation of the Internal Revenue Service—U.S. national security agencies are more tightly connected. Policymaking inevitably crosses bureaucratic boundaries, involving diplomacy, the use of force, economic policy, and intelligence. In such a complex web, national security bureaucrats see reform as a zero-sum battle for agency autonomy and power. No national security agency wants to yield authority or discretion to another.[85]

The problems of decentralized democracy. Rational self-interest makes reform difficult; self-interest coupled with the decentralized structure of the U.S. federal government makes it more so. Some of the cherished features of American democracy impede effective agency design and raise obstacles to reform. Separation of powers, the congressional committee system, and majority rule have created a system that invites compromise and makes legislation hard to pass. This has two consequences for government agencies. First, political compromise allows opponents to sabotage the creation of any new agency from the start. As Terry Moe writes, "In the political system, public bureaucracies are designed . . . by participants who explicitly want them to fail."[86] Political compromise unavoidably leads to suboptimal initial agency design, even for national security agencies such as the CIA.[87] Indeed, critics who contend that the CIA is poorly suited to meeting the needs of the post-Cold War world are only partially right: the agency was not particularly well designed to meet the United States' Cold War needs. Opposed from the outset to the CIA's creation in 1947, existing intelligence agencies in the FBI, State Department, and military services succeeded in stripping the agency of any strong centralization powers. When the CIA was created in 1947, it was flawed by design.[88]

Second, the decentralized structure of American democracy means that the worst agency problems usually are the hardest to fix. Although agencies can make some changes on their own and can also be altered by unilateral presidential action, the most far-reaching reforms usually require new legislation. But legislative success is difficult even under the best of circumstances because it demands multiple majorities in both houses of Congress. As Philip Zelikow, executive director of the 9/11 commission, put it, "The most powerful interest group in Washington is the status quo."[89]

Summary. These three enduring realities—the nature of organizations, rational self-interest, and the fragmented federal government—provide a basic model for understanding why U.S. intelligence agencies failed to adapt to the pre-September 11 terrorist threat. U.S. government agencies are not built to change with the times. Because reform does not generally arise from within, it must be imposed from the outside. But even this rarely happens because all organizational changes create winners and losers, and because the political system allows losers many opportunities to fight back. Indeed, the greater the proposed change, the stronger the resistance will be. As a result, winners can never win completely. Organizational adaptation almost always meets with defeat, becomes watered down, or is postponed until the next crisis erupts.

The CIA Before September 11

Efforts to reform the Central Intelligence Agency in the post-Cold War period illustrate the three enduring realities. No sooner had the Soviet Union collapsed than calls were heard demanding an end to business as usual in the CIA. At first, these came from Senator Daniel Patrick Moynihan and other legislators who saw the CIA as a Cold War relic that should be abolished. But focus soon turned toward changing, not casting aside, the agency. Between 1992 and 1996, Congress twice attempted, but ultimately failed, to pass major reform of the intelligence community. During the same period, twelve public reports issued by blue-ribbon commissions, governmental reviews, and think tank task forces discussed shortcomings in the U.S. intelligence community, the FBI, and U.S. counterterrorism efforts more broadly.

Common Findings

Although the reports covered a variety of issues, they all identified four major problems within the U.S. intelligence community. The first was its lack of coherence or "corporateness." As the Council on Foreign Relations study noted, the organization and leadership of the intelligence community was a "structural oddity," with fourteen major agencies and no one in charge of them all.[90] Technically, the DCI was supposed to set broad strategies and coordinate efforts across these agencies (as well as run the CIA), but in reality the DCI held direct control over only 15 percent of the intelligence budget (the secretary of defense controlled the rest) and had weak management authority for allocating money, people, and programs to every agency outside the CIA. The reports' specific recommendations varied, but all offered ways to enhance intelligence community integration and coordination.

Second, ten out of twelve of these studies found that intelligence officials and policymakers did not devote enough attention to setting intelligence priorities.[91] To provide useful information, intelligence agencies require guidance from policymakers about which puzzles, people, and places rank higher on the priority list than others; about which surprises U.S. policymakers can live with; and about which ones they cannot. A robust mechanism for establishing and updating intelligence priorities, however, had never developed during the Cold War. And the Soviet Union's collapse, along with the emergence of new transnational threats, exacerbated these weaknesses. As a result, during the 1990s intelligence agencies had to cover more issues with fewer resources and little guidance about where to focus their efforts. In 1993 the president's National Performance Review found the system for establishing intelligence collection and analysis priorities to be a "jumble of loosely connected processes" that did not satisfy the needs of policymakers.[92] The 1996 House Intelligence Committee's staff study agreed, calling the prioritization process "one of the most vexing aspects of intelligence management" and the need for fixing it "fundamental and urgent."[93] Five years later the Hart-Rudman commission warned that the continued absence of an effective process for setting intelligence priorities was creating "dangerous tradeoffs between coverage of important countries, regions, and functional challenges."[94]

A third finding was the need to revitalize human intelligence capabilities. Nine of the twelve reports called for more aggressive human intelligence efforts to combat terrorism; two did not address the issue[95]; and only one, the Twentieth Century Fund report, advocated downgrading collection from human sources. Most frequently mentioned was the need to revise the CIA's 1995 guidelines that required prior approval from CIA headquarters before an individual suspected of human rights violations could be recruited as an asset—guidelines that had come to be known as the "scrub order" because they had led to the removal of hundreds of assets from the CIA's payroll.[96] Many of the reports also advocated improving the intelligence budgeting process so that resources could be more effectively matched against priorities-improvements that would have had the likely effect of redistributing some of the vast resources dedicated to technical intelligence systems to human intelligence activities.[97] In addition, the Aspin-Brown commission and the House Intelligence Committee staff reports recommended the revision of personnel incentives and restructuring of the intelligence community to ensure that human intelligence efforts could be more effectively and efficiently deployed against hard targets such as rogue states and transnational terrorist groups that are difficult to penetrate by other means.[98] Perhaps most radical, the National Institute for Public Policy report recommended stripping analysis functions from the CIA so that the agency could focus exclusively on human intelligence collection and even raised the possibility of disbanding the CIA's clandestine Directorate of Operations and replacing it with an entirely new clandestine service in order to address the directorate's long-standing cultural and management problems.[99]

Finally, the reports ranked personnel issues high on the list of concerns. As the House Intelligence Committee staff study bluntly concluded, "[The intelligence community] continues to face a major personnel crisis that it has, thus far, not addressed in any coherent way."[100] Although the specifics varied widely, two common themes emerged. First, the intelligence community lacked employees with the requisite skills to confront growing threats such as foreign terrorism.[101] Despite being technically exempt from a number of Civil Service regulations, intelligence agencies rarely fired poor performers. In addition, the Aspin-Brown commission noted that even when confronted with mandatory reductions in personnel in the early 1990s, intelligence agencies reached targets through attrition and voluntary retirement rather than through strategically focused cuts to keep the best talent and those with the most needed areas of expertise for a post-Cold War threat environment.[102] Second, intelligence officers too often stayed in their home agencies rather than building institutional bridges to other policymaking and intelligence agencies through temporary rotations. Three studies—the Aspin-Brown commission, the Council on Foreign Relations task force, and the House Intelligence Committee staff study—recommended that rotations to other agencies be required for intelligence officers to be promoted to senior ranks. Another three—the National Performance Review reports, the Twentieth Century Fund task force, and the FBI's 1998 Strategic Plan—urged the establishment of vigorous rotational assignments without requiring them for promotion. The need to realign the personnel skill mix and improve coordination through temporary tours of duty in other agencies received major attention in all but two of the reports.[103]

Common Failings

In all of these areas, the studies' recommendations went unheeded. In 2001 the intelligence community was 50 percent bigger than it was when the CIA was created in 1947, but the DCI had only slightly more power to oversee it. As the congressional Joint Inquiry into the September 11 attacks darkly concluded, "The inability to realign Intelligence Community resources to combat the threat posed by Usama Bin Ladin is a relatively direct consequence of the limited authority of the DCI over major portions of the Intelligence Community."[104] The 9/11 commission agreed, noting that the intelligence community "struggle[d] to collect on and analyze . . . transnational terrorism in the mid- to late 1990s" in large part because the community was a set of "loosely associated agencies and departmental offices that lacked the incentives to cooperate, collaborate, and share information."[105] Indeed, the intelligence community was so fragmented before September 11 that even Tenet's 1998 declaration of war against bin Laden and al-Qaida did not seem to have gotten much attention beyond the CIA's walls.[106]

The Joint Inquiry and 9/11 commission also found major deficiencies in the intelligence community's system for prioritizing collection and analysis. The Joint Inquiry noted that intelligence officials found the process "confusing" and "so broad as to be meaningless," with more than 1,500 formal priorities for the National Security Agency alone by

September 11.[107] The 9/11 commission concluded that the setting of clear intelligence collection priorities "did not occur" before the September 11 attacks.[108] Even some of those responsible for setting priorities agreed. Former National Counterterrorism Coordinator Richard Clarke noted that the White House "never really gave good systematic, timely guidance to the Intelligence Community about what priorities were at the national level."[109]

Despite calls to vastly upgrade human intelligence efforts, the CIA's clandestine Directorate of Operations continued to languish. In 1995 only twenty-five trainees became clandestine officers.[110] By the late 1990s, the Directorate of Operations had cut by nearly one-third the number of its personnel deployed overseas.[111] Today the CIA still does not have enough qualified case officers to staff many of its stations around the world.[112] In addition, the 1995 guidelines restricting recruitment of foreign assets remained in place until after September 11. Nor did funding priorities shift from technical intelligence systems to any significant degree. As one senior CIA official put it, "I'm cynical, but I think the reason people wanted to keep the [intelligence] budget secret was not to protect spies in Moscow, but because they didn't want people to know that 99 percent [of the budget] was stuck in some satellite."[113]

Personnel problems also continued. In 2001 only 20 percent of the graduating class of clandestine case officers were fluent in non-Romance languages.[114] Robert Baer, a veteran CIA clandestine case officer, noted that even after the 1998 U.S. embassy bombings, the CIA employed not one case officer who spoke Pashto, the dialect of the major ethnic group in Afghanistan, and still had none as of 2002.[115] The Joint Inquiry's findings are consistent with these assessments. The congressional panel concluded that before September 11, the intelligence community "was not prepared to handle the challenge it faced in translating the volumes of foreign language counterterrorism intelligence it collected. Agencies . . . experienced backlogs in material awaiting translation . . . and a readiness level of only 30% in the most critical terrorism-related languages used by terrorists."[116]

Nor have temporary rotations been commonly practiced. Although Director Tenet declared in the late 1990s that all intelligence officials were required to do a tour of duty in another intelligence agency before being promoted to the senior ranks, every agency, including the CIA, ignored him. Instead, intelligence agencies usually have filled these rotational positions with poor performers rather than rising stars. As one senior intelligence official lamented, "I often think of writing a vacancy notice [for temporary transferees to his agency] that says, 'only stupid people doing unimportant work need apply,' or 'send us your tired, your sluggish, your marginally brain dead.' "[117]

The Adaptation Failure Model Revisited

The adaptation failure model helps explain why recommendations to improve the four critical intelligence deficiencies described above were not implemented before September 11.

In 1992 and 1996, congressional intelligence committees attempted to enhance the intelligence community's corporateness by introducing legislation that would have dramatically strengthened the DCI's powers over the entire intelligence community. As expected, however, bureaucrats within the Department of Defense resisted these changes because they would have diminished the Pentagon's control over budgets, personnel, and the operation of key defense intelligence agencies. At the same time, both legislative proposals drew heavy fire from the House and Senate Armed Services Committees, whose own interests and power were threatened. And neither proposal had the strong support of President Clinton who, like his predecessors, was reluctant to press the issue against the vehement objections of the Defense Department and was more interested in pressing policy agendas on issues closer to home that promised more direct political benefits. Indeed, Clinton's focus on domestic issues was so strong that when a mentally unstable pilot crashed a Cessna airplane onto the White House lawn in 1994, aides joked that it was DCI James Woolsey trying to get the president's attention.[118]

The fragmented federal government ensured that reform opponents would succeed. In 1996 the pro-defense House National Security Committee stripped the Intelligence Committee's reform bill of virtually every measure designed to increase the DCI's power over military intelligence agencies. House Intelligence Committee Chairman Larry Combest chose not to send the bill to the floor in the face of such opposition. In the Senate, conflict between the Intelligence and Armed Services Committees proved even more acrimonious, with the same result. Unable to garner a majority in the Armed Services Committee for radical reform, the Intelligence Authorization Act of 1997 produced only minor changes across the intelligence community.[119]

Changes in the intelligence prioritization process required executive branch action. Here too reforms failed for reasons the model would expect. Although President Clinton issued a presidential decision directive in 1995 to establish intelligence priorities, the list was long and only grew longer with time. Despite provisions calling for an annual review, new priorities were added but old ones were never removed. The intelligence community was required to cover most issues and most places in the world. From the president's perspective, this made political sense. Held uniquely responsible for U.S. foreign policy, the president (and his top advisers) had strong incentives to gather information on every conceivable international problem because for them, no surprise was acceptable. Paradoxically, these incentives only made surprises more likely, by stretching the intelligence community too thin.

Finally, organizational factors help explain why the reports' recommendations for improvements in human intelligence and personnel systems were not made through internal reforms. Natural resistance to change, the persistence of old routines, and cultural obstacles to implementing new ideas ran deep. Although many intelligence officials, policymakers, and experts saw the need for ramping up human intelligence efforts in the 1990s, the CIA seemed unable to escape from the 1970s, when congressional investigations into CIA covert operations pushed the agency to reign in its clandestine efforts. Baer and other veteran CIA clandestine operators have described a culture of excessive risk aversion that, together with the Cold War's end, led to a crippling of human intelligence capabilities during the 1990s.[120] Between 1992 and 2002, for example, only 35 percent of the CIA's clandestine case officers spent more than three years overseas recruiting assets.[121] Meanwhile, old Cold War spending patterns continued to favor technical intelligence, which was well suited for detecting the location of Soviet warheads, over human intelligence efforts better suited for penetrating terrorist groups on the ground.[122]

As for other personnel issues, the CIA failed to realign its personnel to meet the terrorist threat in large part because doing so would have violated the age-old expectation that those who volunteered their service to the intelligence community were guaranteed lifetime employment in return.[123] Decades of mistrust and compartmentalization between (and even within) intelligence agencies fed the widespread resistance to assuming temporary duty outside one's home agency.[124] And because a successful temporary rotation program required the cooperation of every agency in the community, it was especially difficult to implement. Director Tenet's rotation directive was easy to ignore.

In sum, despite a high degree of consensus and a range of potential fixes, critical deficiencies in the CIA's structure, prioritization process, human intelligence capabilities, and personnel systems were never remedied before the September 11 terrorist attacks. Reforms from within ran into resistance from entrenched routines and a firmly established culture. At the same time, external reforms generated opposition or indifference from key political players.

Conclusion

Since the September 11 attacks, members of Congress, the 9/11 commission, executive branch officials, and intelligence experts have offered numerous proposals for reform of the U.S. intelligence community. These efforts, and their limited success, underscore three implications of the preceding analysis. First, it appears that the nature of organizations, rational self-interest, and the fragmented federal government hinder adaptation even after catastrophic failure. Efforts to reform the U.S. intelligence community sputtered for nearly three years after the worst terrorist attacks in U.S. history, succeeded only after the harmonic convergence of an extraordinary set of factors, and then produced only modest changes.

On at least three occasions after September 11, opportunities for intelligence reform arose but did not produce results. The first came in early 2002, when Brent Scowcroft, chairman of the President's Foreign Intelligence Advisory Board, delivered a classified report to President George W. Bush urging a radical overhaul of the U.S. intelligence community. The proposal included transferring control over the three largest defense intelligence collection agencies to the director of central intelligence. Defense Department objections were so strong, however, that the president took no action.[125] Second, in November 2002, legislation established a new body, the Department of Homeland Security, but skirted the issue of intelligence reform.[126] The third opportunity came in December 2002, when the Congressional Joint Inquiry issued its final report investigating the September 11 attacks. The report's nineteen recommendations included establishing a powerful new director of national intelligence, revamping the intelligence priority process, and considering whether a new domestic intelligence agency should replace the FBI. But as Richard Falkenrath notes, the report's recommendations "were ignored."[127]

Only in July 2004 did three factors converge to make modest changes possible: CIA Director George Tenet resigned; the Senate Intelligence Committee issued a scathing report criticizing the U.S. intelligence community's prewar assessments of Iraqi biological, nuclear, and chemical weapons capabilities; and the 9/11 commission issued its final report. Tenet's resignation removed the U.S. intelligence community's staunchest defender and thus weakened bureaucratic resistance to reform. The Senate Intelligence Committee's Iraq report galvanized committee members and shifted the electoral incentives for all members of Congress.[128] Issued during the height of the congressional and presidential campaign season, the report linked intelligence problems to a powerful domestic political issue: whether legislators voted to authorize the Iraq war based on flawed intelligence assessments. Finally, the 9/11 commission created a media sensation when it released its report and launched a campaign, supported by several of the 9/11 victims' family groups, to have Congress enact its recommendations. Between July and passage of the Intelligence Reform and Prevention Act in December 2004, the commission received greater national television news coverage than the war in Iraq.[129] Even with all of these factors, however, the intelligence reform bill was nearly derailed and was ultimately diluted by vigorous opposition from House Armed Services Committee Chairman Duncan Hunter, House Judiciary Committee Chairman James Sensenbrenner, objections from the Defense Department, and tepid public support from President Bush.

Reform efforts since September 11 also suggest that changes to U.S. intelligence agencies are likely to continue lagging behind external environmental demands. The constraints that hinder adaptation in U.S. intelligence agencies can be mitigated by extraordinary events, but these constraints can never be eliminated entirely. Organizations, even those under duress like the CIA and FBI, often find it easier to resist change than embrace it. Conflict and self-interest are ever-present in politics. And the United States' separation of powers system will always provide opportunities for opponents of reform to water down legislative proposals.

All of these forces can be seen hindering intelligence reform efforts since the September 11 attacks. The FBI's aversion to technology is so deeply entrenched, for example—one veteran agent described the prevailing culture as "real men don't type"[130]—that the agency has failed to develop a functioning electronic database for its case files, even though FBI Director Robert Mueller declared the initiative a top priority after September 11 and spent $170 million on it.[131] As for legislative changes, the Intelligence Reform and Prevention Act created a new director of national intelligence, as the 9/11 commission recommended. To win passage of the bill, however, reformers had to dilute the DNI's budgetary, personnel, and management authorities, leaving many to wonder whether the position can function effectively. Moreover, the commission avoided recommending more radical changes—such as removing intelligence agencies completely from Pentagon control—that could have more comprehensively addressed the "deep institutional failings" that it found, but would have been harder to achieve.[132]

Finally, intelligence reform efforts since September 11 reveal a tendency to view organizational deficiencies as structural problems. The two core recommendations of the 9/11 commission and the Intelligence Reform and Prevention Act—creating a single head of the U.S. intelligence community and new centers to integrate collection, analysis, and operational planning on issues such as counterterrorism—focus entirely on structure. Although it is true that U.S. intelligence agencies have been hobbled for decades by a dysfunctional structure, this article suggests that the inability of U.S. intelligence agencies to adapt to the terrorist threat also stems from organizational routines and cultures that are highly resistant to change.

Successful reform must target these forces as well. Operating deep within U.S. intelligence agencies, they are the silent killers of innovation. No intelligence structure can dramatically improve U.S. intelligence capabilities so long as intelligence officials view the world through old lenses and cling to old ways. For example, the reluctance to share information across agency lines is deeply engrained, based more on the values and habits that have developed inside U.S. intelligence agencies and the policies that have reinforced them than on official organization charts. The fifteen agencies of the U.S. intelligence community have not functioned as a coherent whole mostly because their employees have never seen themselves as part of the same team. Current policies still provide weak incentives for intelligence officials to discard these traditional parochial perspectives; most intelligence professionals can spend twenty years or more cloistered in their home agencies without a single communitywide training experience or assignment to another intelligence organization.

Fixing these problems is difficult but not impossible. New legislation could provide incentives and opportunities to establish informal networks and build trust between intelligence officials across agencies in two ways: by requiring the establishment of communitywide training programs early in officials' careers, before they become attached to parochial views, and by requiring rotational assignments to other agencies for promotion to the senior ranks. Strangely, the 9/11 commission noted how a rotational requirement in the Defense Department "transformed the collective mind-set" of the military services and dramatically improved integration between them, but did not recommend such a requirement for U.S. intelligence officials.[133]

A few months after September 11, Richard Betts wrote, "The awful truth is that even the best intelligence systems will have big failures."[134] Evidence suggests, however, that the U.S. intelligence community was nowhere close to being the best before the September 11 attacks. Improving the future performance of U.S. intelligence agencies requires understanding better the sources of organizational weaknesses, the barriers to organizational adaptation, and ways to overcome them.

Questions for Further Discussion

1. Why did changes undertaken by the intelligence community in the aftermath of the Cold War leave it ill prepared to meet the terrorist challenge?

2. If implemented, do you think that the reforms recommended for the intelligence community by various commissions would have helped the government stop the Al Qaeda attacks on September 11, 2001?

3. What impediments do organizations face when it comes to change and reform?

4. Do you think that the new Director of National Intelligence can instigate reform of the intelligence community and bring about greater cohesion to the 16 secret agencies?

Endnotes

1. Eleanor Hill,"The Intelligence Community's Knowledge of the September 11 Hijackers Prior to September 11, 2001," testimony before the Senate Select Committee on Intelligence [SSCI] and House Permanent Select Committee on Intelligence [HPSCI], 107th Cong., 2nd sess., September 20, 2002, p. 6.
2. George Tenet, testimony before the SSCI and HPSCI, 107th Cong., 2nd sess., October17, 2002.
3. Tenet issued the memo on December 4, 1998. Excerpts can be found in Eleanor Hill, "Joint Inquiry Staff Statement, Part I," SSCI and HPSCI, 107th Cong., 2nd sess., September 18, 2002, p. 12. For threat reporting, see *The 9/11 Commission Report: Final Report of the National Commission on Terrorist Attacks Upon the United States* (New York: W.W. Norton, 2004), pp. 254–263.
4. In addition to the CIA, the intelligence community consists of the Federal Bureau of Investigation, the Defense Intelligence Agency, the National Geospatial-Intelligence Agency (formerly the National Imagery and Mapping Agency), the National Reconnaissance Office, the National Security Agency, and intelligence units in the Air Force, the Army, the Coast Guard, the Navy, the Marine Corps, the State Department, the Energy Department, and the Treasury Department. In 2003 the creation of the Department of Homeland Security added a fifteenth agency to the community.
5. Hill, "The Intelligence Community's Knowledge of the September 11 Hijackers Prior to September 11, 2001," pp. 7–8. The Joint Inquiry unearthed a December 1999 memo providing general guidance about placing terrorists on the State Department's watch list, but the investigation found no routine or formal programs in place to ensure that adding names to the watch list received regular attention. Nor were there any consistent guidelines about thresholds for placing suspected terrorists on the watch list. Tenet testimony before SSCI and HPSCI, October 17, 2002; *Joint Inquiry Into Intelligence Community Activities Before and After the Terrorist Attacks of September 11, 2001*, report of the U.S. Select Committee on Intelligence and U.S. House Permanent Select Committee on Intelligence, S. Report No. 107-351, H. Report No. 107-792, 107th Cong., 2d sess., December 2002 [hereafter *Joint Inquiry Final Report*], p. 147.
6. Hill, "The Intelligence Community's Knowledge of the September 11 Hijackers Prior to September 11, 2001," p. 8.
7. Samuel L. Berger, testimony before the National Commission on Terrorist Acts upon the United States, eighth public hearing, "Counterterrorism Policy," March 24, 2004, <http://www.9-11commission.gov/hearings/hearing8/berger_statement.pdf>.
8. Robert Gates, quoted in John H. Hedley, "The Intelligence Community: Is it Broken? How to Fix It?" *Studies in Intelligence*, Vol. 39, No. 5 (1996), p. 14.
9. National foreign intelligence program budgets declined every year between 1990 and 1996 and, with the exception of one large 1999 supplemental, remained basically flat between 1996 and 2000. *The 9/11 Commission Report*, p. 93.
10. *Joint Inquiry Final Report*, pp. 254, 257.
11. Ibid., p. 4.
12. *The 9/11 Commission Report*, p. 76.
13. This information was provided to the Joint Inquiry by former National Security Adviser Samuel Berger. See ibid., p. 12.
14. George Tenet, "Worldwide Threat—Converging Dangers in a Post 9/11 World," testimony before the SSCI, 107th Cong., 1st sess., February 6, 2002.
15. See in particular Thomas Powers, "The Trouble with the CIA," *New York Review of Books*, January 17, 2002, <http://www.nybooks.com/articles/15109>.
16. Interview, Washington, D.C., April 17, 2002.
17. James G. March, "Footnotes to Organizational Change," *Administrative Science Quarterly*, Vol. 26, No. 4 (December 1981), p. 563.
18. Michael T. Hannan and John Freeman, "Structural Inertia and Organizational Change," *American Sociological Review*, Vol. 49, No. 2 (April 1984), p. 151.
19. R. James Woolsey, "World Trouble Spots," testimony before the SSCI, 103d Cong., 2d sess., January 25, 1994; R. James Woolsey, "World Threat Assessment Brief," testimony before the SSCI, 104th Cong., 1st sess., January 10, 1995; John Deutch, "Worldwide Threats to U.S. National Security," testimony before the SSCI, 104th Cong., 2d sess., February 22, 1996; George Tenet, "Worldwide Threats to National Security," testimony before the Senate Armed Services Committee, 105th Cong., 1st sess., February 6, 1997; George Tenet, "Worldwide Threats to National Security," testimony before the SSCI, 105th Cong., 2d sess., January 28, 1998; George Tenet, "Worldwide Threats to U.S. National Security," testimony before the Senate Armed Services Committee, 106th Cong., 1st sess., February 2, 1999; George Tenet, "Annual Assessment of Security Threats against the United States," testimony before the SSCI, 106th Cong., 2d sess., February 2, 2000; and George Tenet, "Worldwide Threats to National Security," testimony before the SSCI, 107th Cong., 1st sess., February 7, 2001.
20. Hill, "Joint Inquiry Staff Statement, Part I."

21. Among these were the 1993 World Trade Center attack; the 1993 New York City landmarks plot; the 1995 Bojinka plot, in which plans were uncovered in the Philippines to assassinate Pope John Paul II, bomb the U.S. and Israeli embassies in Manila, blow up several American aircraft flying Asian routes, and crash an airplane into CIA headquarters; and the 1999 disruption of the millennium attack against Los Angeles International Airport.

22. For an English translation of the *fatwa*, see <http://www.fas.org/irp/world/para/docs/980223-fatwa. htm>.

23. Hill, "Joint Inquiry Staff Statement, Part I," p. 9.

24. *The 9/11 Commission Report*, p. 70.

25. Quotation from memo included in Hill, "Joint Inquiry Staff Statement, Part I," p. 12.

26. Hill, "Joint Inquiry Staff Statement, Part I," p. 12.

27. Tenet, "Worldwide Threats to U.S. National Security," testimony before the Senate Armed Services Committee, 106th Cong., 1st sess., February 2, 1999.

28. Tenet, "Annual Assessment of Security Threats against the United States."

29. Tenet, "Worldwide Threats to National Security," testimony before the Senate Select Committee on Intelligence, 107th Cong., 1st sess., February 7, 2001.

30. Interview, Washington, D.C., April 17, 2002.

31. R. James Woolsey, remarks to the American Bar Association, Washington, D.C., April 29, 1994.

32. John P. O'Neill, excerpts from a speech to the National Strategy Forum, Chicago, Illinois, June 11, 1997, <http://www.nationalstrategy.com/speakers/oneill.html>.

33. National Defense Panel, *Transforming Defense: National Security in the 21st Century*, December 1, 1997, <http://www.fas.org/man/docs/ndp>; and William S. Cohen, U.S. Department of Defense, *Report of the Quadrennial Defense Review*, May 1997, <http://www.defenselink.mil/pubs/qdr>.

34. President William Clinton, "Remarks to the Opening Session of the 53rd United Nations General Assembly, United Nations," New York, New York, September 21, 1998, <http://www.state.gov/www/global/terrorism/980921_ pres_terror.html>.

35. William S. Cohen, "Preparing for a Grave New World," *Washington Post*, July 26, 1999, p. A19.

36. Commission on the Roles and Capabilities of the United States Intelligence Community [Aspin-Brown commission], *Preparing for the 21st Century: An Appraisal of U.S. Intelligence* (Washington, D.C.: U.S. Government Printing Office [U.S. GPO], 1996); Commission to Assess the Organization of the Federal Government to Combat the Proliferation of Weapons of Mass Destruction [Deutch commission], *Combating Proliferation of Weapons of Mass Destruction* (Washington, D.C.: U.S. GPO, 1999); Advisory Panel to Assess Domestic Response Capabilities for Terrorism Involving Weapons of Mass Destruction [1999 Gilmore commission], *First Annual Report to the President and the Congress: Assessing the Threat* (Washington, D.C.: U.S. GPO, 1999); Advisory Panel to Assess Domestic Response Capabilities for Terrorism Involving Weapons of Mass Destruction [2000 Gilmore commission], *Second Annual Report to the President and the Congress: Toward a National Strategy for Combating Terrorism* (Washington, D.C.: U.S. GPO, 2000); National Commission on Terrorism [Bremer commission], *Countering the Changing Threat of International Terrorism* (Washington, D.C.: U.S. GPO, 2000); U.S. Commission on National Security/21st Century [Hart-Rudman commission], *Road Map for National Security: Imperative for Change* (Washington, D.C.: U.S. GPO, 2001); and Commission on the Advancement of Federal Law Enforcement [Webster commission], *Law Enforcement in a New Century and a Changing World: Improving the Administration of Federal Law Enforcement* (Washington, D.C.: U.S. GPO, 2000).

37. National Performance Review, "The Intelligence Community: Recommendations and Actions," in *From Red Tape to Results: Creating a Government That Works Better and Costs Less* (Washington, D.C.: U.S. GPO, September 1993); National Performance Review, *National Performance Review Phase II Initiatives: An Intelligence Community Report* (Washington, D.C.: U.S. GPO, 1995); House Permanent Select Committee on Intelligence, *IC21: The Intelligence Community in the 21st Century* (Washington, D.C.: U.S. GPO, 1996); and Federal Bureau of Investigation, *Draft FBI Strategic Plan: 1998–2003, Keeping Tomorrow Safe* (Washington, D.C.: U.S. GPO, 1998).

38. Council on Foreign Relations Independent Task Force, *Making Intelligence Smarter: The Future of U.S. Intelligence* (New York: Council on Foreign Relations, 1996); Twentieth Century Fund Task Force on the Future of U.S. Intelligence, *In From the Cold: The Report of the Twentieth Century Fund Task Force on the Future of U.S. Intelligence* (New York: Twentieth Century Fund Press, 1996); and National Institute for Public Policy, *Modernizing Intelligence: Structure and Change for the 21st Century* (Fairfax, Va.: National Institute for Public Policy, 2002).

39. Council on Foreign Relations Independent Task Force, *Making Intelligence Smarter*, p. 1.

40. House Permanent Select Committee on Intelligence, IC21, "Overview and Summary," p. 5.

41. Ibid., p. 7.

42. Ibid., p. 26.

43. Ibid., p. 28.

44. National Commission on Terrorism, *Countering the Changing Threat of International Terrorism*, p. iv.

45. Ibid., p. 13.

46. The Gilmore commission recommendations are from its 1999 and 2000 reports. The panel issued two other reports after September 11 that were not included.

47. Amy Zegart, "Blue Ribbons, Black Boxes: Toward a Better Understanding of Presidential Commissions," *Presidential Studies Quarterly*, Vol. 35, No. 2 (June 2004), pp. 366–393.

48. U.S. Commission on National Security/21st Century, *Road Map for National Security*, p. x.

49. U.S. Commission on National Security/21st Century, *New World Coming: American Security in the 21st Century: Major Themes and Implications*, September 15, 1999, p. 138.

50. Notable exceptions are Scott D. Sagan, *The Limits of Safety: Organizations, Accidents, and Nuclear Weapons* (Princeton, N.J.: Princeton University Press, 1993); and Lynn Eden, *Whole World on Fire: Organizations, Knowledge, and Nuclear Weapons Devastation* (Ithaca, N.Y.: Cornell University Press, 2003).

51. Glenn R. Carroll, "Organizational Ecology," *Annual Review of Sociology*, Vol. 10 (1984), pp. 71–93; Michael T. Hannan and John Henry Freeman, "The Population Ecology of Organizations," *American Journal of Sociology*, Vol. 82, No. 5 (March 1977), pp. 929–964; Michael T. Hannan and John Henry Freeman, "Structural Inertia and Organizational Change," *American Sociological Review*, Vol. 49, No. 2 (April 1984), pp. 149–164; and Michael T. Hannan and John Henry

Freeman, *Organizational Ecology* (Cambridge, Mass.: Harvard University Press, 1989).

52. Joel A. C. Baum and Jitendra V. Singh, *Evolutionary Dynamics of Organizations* (Oxford: Oxford University Press, 1994); and Howard Aldrich, *Organizations Evolving* (London: Sage, 1999).

53. Barbara Levitt and James G. March, "Organizational Learning," *Annual Review of Sociology*, Vol. 14 (1988), pp. 319–340; Richard M. Cyert and James G. March, *A Behavioral Theory of the Firm* (London: Blackwell, 1963); Mary Ann Glynn, Theresa K. Lant, and Frances J. Milliken, "Mapping Learning Processes in Organizations: A Multi-Level Framework Linking Learning and Organizing," in James R. Meindl, Joseph F. Porac, and Chuck Stubbart, eds., *Advances in Managerial Cognition and Organizational Information Processing*, Vol. 5 (Greenwich, Conn.: JAI Press, 1994), pp. 43–83; Anne S. Miner and Stephen J. Mezias, "Ugly Duckling No More: Pasts and Futures of Organizational Learning Research," *Organization Science*, Vol. 7, No. 1 (January-February 1996), pp. 88–99; and James G. March, "Exploration and Exploitation in Organizational Learning," *Organization Science*, Vol. 2, No. 1 (February 1991), pp. 71–87.

54. Cyert and March, *A Behavioral Theory of the Firm*, p. xi.

55. Aldrich's point should not be minimized. He notes that large, publicly traded corporations constitute less than 0.05 percent of all U.S. organizations using a corporate form. Aldrich, *Organizations Evolving*, p. 8.

56. For more on the difference between the private and public sectors, see James Q. Wilson, *Bureaucracy: What Government Agencies Do and Why They Do It* (New York: Basic Books, 2000); Terry M. Moe, "The Politics of Structural Choice: Toward a Theory of Public Bureaucracy," in Oliver E. Williamson, ed., *Organization Theory: From Chester Barnard to the Present and Beyond* (Oxford: Oxford University Press, 1990), pp. 116–153; and Terry M. Moe, "The New Economics of Organization," *American Journal of Political Science*, Vol. 28, No. 4 (November 1984), pp. 739–777.

57. For an overview of this approach, see Hannan and Freeman, "Structural Inertia and Organization Change"; and Hannan and Freeman, "The Population of Ecology Organizations."

58. Anthony Downs, *Inside Bureaucracy* (Boston: Little, Brown, 1967); Arthur Stinchcombe, "Social Structures and Organizations," in James G. March, ed., *Handbook of Organizations* (Chicago: Rand McNally, 1965), pp. 142–193; Herbert Kaufman, *Are Government Organizations Immortal?* (Washington, D.C.: Brookings, 1976); and Theodore J. Lowi, *The End of Liberalism: The Second Republic of the United States* (New York: W.W. Norton, 1979).

59. Kaufman, *Are Government Agencies Immortal?* p. 34. The durability of agencies has more recently come into question. See David E. Lewis, *Presidents and the Politics of Agency Design: Political Insulation in the United States Government Bureaucracy, 1946–1997* (Stanford, Calif.: Stanford University Press, 2003); and Daniel P. Carpenter, *The Forging of Bureaucratic Autonomy: Reputations, Networks, and Policy Innovation in Executive Agencies, 1862–1928* (Princeton, N.J.: Princeton University Press, 2000).

60. Howard E. Aldrich, *Organizations and Environments* (Englewood Cliffs, N.J.: Prentice Hall, 1979).

61. Aldrich, *Organizations Evolving*, p. 43.

62. Charles Perrow, *Complex Organizations: A Critical Essay*, 3d ed. (New York: McGraw-Hill, 1986), p. 213.

63. Mathew D. McCubbins, "The Legislative Design of Regulatory Structure," *American Journal of Political Science*, Vol. 29, No. 4 (November 1985), pp. 721–748; and Barry Weingast and Mark Moran, "Bureaucratic Discretion or Congressional Control? Regulatory Policymaking by the Federal Trade Commission," *Journal of Political Economy*, Vol. 91, No. 5 (October 1983), pp. 775–800.

64. David Epstein and Sharyn O'Halloran make the distinction between ex ante and ongoing oversight mechanisms. Epstein and O'Halloran, "Administrative Procedures, Information, and Agency Discretion," *American Journal of Political Science*, Vol. 38, No. 3 (August 1994), pp. 697–722. For ex ante controls, see Murray J. Horn, *The Political Economy of Public Administration: Institutional Choice in the Public Sector* (New York: Cambridge University Press, 1995); Mathew D. McCubbins and Thomas Schwartz, "Congressional Oversight Overlooked: Police Patrol versus Fire Alarm," *American Journal of Political Science*, Vol. 28, No. 1 (February 1984), pp. 165–179; and Mathew D. McCubbins, Roger Noll, and Barry Weingast, "Administrative Procedures as Instruments of Political Control," *Journal of Law, Economics, and Organization*, Vol. 3, No. 2 (Autumn 1987), pp. 243–277. For ongoing controls, see Randall Calvert, Mark Moran, and Barry Weingast, "Congressional Influence over Policy Making: The Case of the FTC," in Mathew D. McCubbins and Terry Sullivan, eds., *Congress: Structure and Policy* (Cambridge: Cambridge University Press, 1987); and Randall Calvert, Mathew D. McCubbins, and Barry Weingast, "A Theory of Political Control and Agency Discretion," *American Journal of Political Science*, Vol. 33, No. 3 (August 1989), pp. 588–611. For how legislators choose between options, see Kathleen Bawn, "Political Control versus Expertise: Congressional Choices about Administrative Procedures," *American Political Science Review*, Vol. 89, No. 1 (March 1995), pp. 62–73; and David Epstein and Sharyn O'Halloran, *Delegating Powers* (New York: Cambridge University Press, 1999).

65. Mathew D. McCubbins, "The Legislative Design of Regulatory Structure," *American Journal of Political Science*, Vol. 29, No. 4 (November 1985), p. 728.

66. Calvert, Moran, and Weingast, "Congressional Influence over Policy Making."

67. Terry M. Moe, "An Assessment of the Positive Theory of 'Congressional Dominance,'" *Legislative Studies Quarterly*, Vol. 12, No. 4 (November 1987), pp. 475–520.

68. Epstein and O'Halloran, *Delegating Powers*, p. 29.

69. I do not mean to suggest that all agency heads are so well intentioned and interested in maximizing organizational performance. Instead, the device is a heuristic used to tease out the ways in which agencies can be reformed and the forces that are likely to keep reforms from succeeding.

70. For an alternative view, see James G. March and Johan P. Olsen, *Ambiguity and Choice in Organizations* (Bergen, Norway: Universitetsforlaget, 1976).

71. Aldrich, *Organizations Evolving*, p. 262.

72. Proprietary data provided by *Zagat* to author, February 2, 2001.

73. Aldrich, *Organizations Evolving*, p. 257. See also Joseph W. Duncan and Douglas P. Handler, "The Misunderstood Role of Small Business," *Business Economics*, Vol. 29, No. 3 (July 1994), pp. 1–6.

74. Wilson, *Bureaucracy*.

75. *The Intelligence Reform and Terrorism Prevention Act of 2004*, Public Law 108-458, 108th Cong., 2d sess., December 17, 2004.

76. Wilson, *Bureaucracy*; and Joel Aberbach and Bert Rockman, *In the Web of Politics: Three Decades of the U.S. Federal Executive* (Washington, D.C.: Brookings, 2000).

77. Hannan and Freeman, "Structural Inertia and Organizational Change."

78. Barbara Levitt and James G. March, "Organizational Learning," *Annual Review of Sociology*, Vol. 14 (1988), pp. 322–323.

79. Hannan and Freeman, "Structural Inertia and Organizational Change," pp. 149–164.

80. Major works arguing that administrative agencies become more durable as they get older include Downs, *Inside Bureaucracy*; Kaufman, *Are Government Organizations Immortal?*; and Lowi, *The End of Liberalism*. A great deal of work suggests that government agencies are like firms and other organizations in this regard. See Stinchcombe, "Social Structures and Organizations."

81. Herbert Simon, "Public Administration in Today's World of Organizations and Markets," John Gaus lecture, annual meeting of the American Political Science Association, Washington, D.C., September 1, 2000, reprinted in *PS: Political Science and Politics*, Vol. 33, No. 4 (December 2000), pp. 752–754; and Charles Perrow, *Normal Accidents: Living With High-Risk Technologies* (Princeton, N.J.: Princeton University Press, 1999).

82. Terry M. Moe, "The Politicized Presidency," in John E. Chubb and Paul E. Peterson, eds., *The New Direction in American Politics* (Washington, D.C.: Brookings, 1985).

83. For a historical overview of intelligence reform efforts, see Richard A. Best Jr., *Proposals for Intelligence Reorganization, 1949–2004* (Washington, D.C.: Congressional Research Service, 2004).

84. David Mayhew, *Congress: The Electoral Connection* (New Haven, Conn.: Yale University Press, 1974).

85. Amy Zegart, *Flawed by Design: The Evolution of the CIA, JCS, and NSC* (Stanford, Calif.: Stanford University Press, 1999).

86. Terry M. Moe, "The Politics of Bureaucratic Structure," in John E. Chubb and Paul E. Peterson, eds., *Can the Government Govern?* (Washington, D.C.: Brookings, 1989), p. 326.

87. Zegart, *Flawed by Design*.

88. Ibid.

89. Interview, Los Angeles, California, October 18, 2004.

90. Council on Foreign Relations Independent Task Force, *Making Intelligence Smarter*, p. 25.

91. The two exceptions were the Webster and Bremer commissions.

92. National Performance Review, "The Intelligence Community."

93. House Permanent Select Committee on Intelligence, IC21, "Overview and Summary," p. 26.

94. U.S. Commission on National Security/21st Century, *Road Map for National Security*, p. 82.

95. These were the Webster and Deutch commissions.

96. The Bremer and Gilmore commissions recommended abolishing the guidelines. The Council on Foreign Relations task force and the Hart-Rudman commission urged the CIA to review the guidelines and make recruiting clandestine assets one of the intelligence community's top priorities. For effects of the "scrub order," see Seymour M. Hersh, "Annals of National Se-

97. curity: What Went Wrong," *New Yorker*, December 18, 2001, p. 40.

97. The National Performance Review, "The Intelligence Community."

98. In a 2004 report, the House Intelligence Committee revealed that it had repeatedly criticized the CIA's human intelligence efforts and recommended corrective action in classified annexes to its annual authorization bills years before September 11. The committee noted, "After years of trying to convince, suggest, urge, entice, cajole, and pressure CIA to make wide-reaching changes in the way it conducts its HUMINT [human intelligence] mission . . . CIA, in the committee's view, continues down a road leading over a proverbial cliff." House Permanent Select Committee on Intelligence, *Intelligence Authorization Act for FY 2005*, H. Report 108-558, 108th Cong., 2d sess., June 21, 2004, p. 24.

99. National Institute for Public Policy, *Modernizing Intelligence*, pp. 85–98.

100. House Permanent Select Committee on Intelligence, IC21, "Intelligence Community Management," p. 21.

101. The Hart-Rudman commission had a broader focus, advocating a massive new educational initiative to improve the scientific and mathematics base for future national security needs.

102. Commission on the Roles and Capabilities of the United States Intelligence Community, *Preparing for the 21st Century*, pp. 2–7.

103. The two exceptions were the Gilmore and Hart-Rudman commissions.

104. *Joint Inquiry Final Report*, p. 43.

105. The 9/11 Commission, "The Performance of the Intelligence Community," staff statement No. 11, April 14, 2004, p. 12.

106. *The 9/11 Commission Report*, p. 357; and *Joint Inquiry Final Report*, pp. 236–237.

107. *Joint Inquiry Final Report*, p. 49.

108. The 9/11 Commission, "The Performance of the Intelligence Community," p. 9.

109. *Joint Inquiry Final Report*, p. 49.

110. *The 9/11 Commission Report*, p. 90.

111. *Joint Inquiry Final Report*, p. 265.

112. Hersh, "Annals of National Security."

113. Telephone interview with senior intelligence official, June 15, 2004.

114. "Intelligence Gaps: America's Spy Network Needs a Quick Fix," editorial, *San Diego Union Tribune*, April 22, 2002, p. B6.

115. Powers, "The Trouble with the CIA."

116. *Joint Inquiry Final Report*, p. xvi.

117. Telephone interview with senior intelligence official, January 30, 2004.

118. Spencer Ackerman and John B. Judis, "The Operator," *New Republic Online*, September 22, 2003, <http://www.tnr.com>.

119. *Congress and the Nation*, Vol. 9 (*1993–1996*): *A Review of Government and Politics* (Washington, D.C.: Congressional Quarterly Press, 1998), pp. 242–246.

120. Robert Baer, *See No Evil: The True Story of a Ground Soldier in the CIA's War on Terrorism* (New York: Crown, 2002); and Powers, "The Trouble With the CIA."

121. Mike DeWine, "Additional Comments," *Joint Inquiry Final Report*, p. 11.

122. See, for example, Robert David Steele, *The New Craft of Intelligence: Personal, Public, and Political* (Oakton, Va.: OSS International Press, 2002).

123. John Gannon, a senior intelligence official who moved to the private sector after September 11, said that he had fired more people in eight months in the private sector than during his entire career in the intelligence community. "Special Report: Time for a Rethink—America's Intelligence Services," *Economist*, April 20, 2002, pp. 23–25.

124. Telephone interview with senior intelligence official, February 5, 2004.

125. Walter Pincus, "Rumsfeld Casts Doubt on Intelligence Reform; Changes Suggested by Presidential Panel," *Washington Post*, April 9, 2002, p. A17; and Spencer Ackerman, "Small Change," *New Republic*, December 13, 2004, p. 12.

126. *The Homeland Security Act of 2002*, Public Law 107-296, 107th Cong., 2d sess., November 25, 2002.

127. Richard A. Falkenrath, "*The 9/11 Commission Report*: A Review Essay," *International Security*, Vol. 29, No. 3 (Winter 2004/05), p. 172.

128. Senate Select Committee on Intelligence, *U.S. Intelligence Community's Prewar Intelligence Assessments on Iraq*, 108th Cong., 2d sess., July 9, 2004.

129. Analysis from LexisNexis using the search terms "9/11 Commission" and "Iraq War" between July 22, 2004, and December 10, 2004.

130. Quoted in Eric Lichtblau and Charles Piller, "Without a Clue: How the FBI Lost Its Way," *Milwaukee Journal Sentinel*, August 11, 2002, p. 01J.

131. Richard B. Schmitt and Charles Piller, "FBI Draws Heat Over Pricey Software Trouble," *Los Angeles Times*, January 14, 2005, p. A12; and Glenn A. Fine, "The Federal Bureau of Investigation's Trilogy Technology Modernization Project," testimony before the Senate Committee on Appropriations Subcommittee on Commerce, Justice, State, and the Judiciary, 109th Cong., 1st sess., February 3, 2005, <http://www.usdoj.gov/oig/testimony/0502/final.pdf>.

132. *The 9/11 Commission Report*, p. 265.

133. Ibid., p. 409.

134. Richard K. Betts, "Fixing Intelligence," *Foreign Affairs*, Vol. 81, No. 1 (January/February 2002), p. 44. ✦

Reprinted with permission from Amy B. Zegart, "September 11 and the Adaptation Failure of U.S. Intelligence Agencies," *International Security*, 29:4 (Spring, 2005): 78–111. © 2005 by the President and Fellows of Harvard College and the Massachusetts Institute of Technology.

35

The 9/11 Attacks and Iraqi WMD Failures

Loch K. Johnson

Both the 9/11 attacks and the faulty prediction about possible weapons of mass destruction in Iraq in 2002 revealed serious flaws in the U.S. intelligence process. In this chapter, Loch K. Johnson exams how these failures occurred and what might be done to avoid similar errors in the future.

The main purpose of intelligence is to provide accurate, timely, and comprehensive information to the president and other policymakers to inform decision making. The task of providing useful information to government officials is a complex matter with many opportunities for error. Uncertainty and ambiguity dominate the environment in which key decisions are made. Accordingly, the numerous pitfalls that exist in the conduct of intelligence make some degree of failure inevitable.[1] Despite the inherent impossibility of perfect intelligence, reforming U.S. intelligence agencies can improve their performance and reduce the frequency of failure.

The U.S. intelligence community faces new challenges as its most pressing targets—particularly terrorist organizations—are structured to elude many of the tools of information-gathering that have proven successful in the past. Weaknesses exist in each step of the intelligence cycle, from planning and direction to collection, processing, analysis, and dissemination.[2] The mobilization of U.S. intelligence against these new threats requires not only redirected resources toward increased human intelligence but also a realignment of attitudes within and among the intelligence bureaucracies. The U.S. intelligence apparatus is constrained by miscommunication between analysts and policymakers resulting from sourcing, packaging, and sometimes distorting information. The intelligence shortcomings in advance of the September 11 attacks and the war in Iraq offer lessons for reform. Investments in new sources of human intelligence and data-mining can help boost U.S. information-gathering capabilities, though genuine intelligence reform will only be possible if the national director of intelligence is invested with the authority to override the bureaucratic turf wars among U.S. intelligence agencies.

The Intelligence Cycle

The planning and direction phase must account for a world with 191 states and a plethora of groups, factions, and gangs—some of which have adversarial relationships with the United States. Speaking just after the end of the Cold War, R. James Woolsey, director of central intelligence (DCI) during the Clinton administration, observed that, "We live now in a jungle filled with a bewildering variety of poisonous snakes."[3] At some point the degree of danger posed by an adversary can become painfully evident, as in the case of al-Qaeda and its attacks against New York City and Washington, D.C., on September 11, 2001. Unfortunately, no one can predict exactly when and where danger will strike, in part because we live in a world filled with secrets and mysteries.

By secrets, intelligence experts refer to information the United States might be able to discern even though it is concealed by another nation or group. For example, the numbers of Chinese tanks and nuclear submarines are discoverable but concealed by the Chinese government. In contrast, mysteries are events no one can know about until they happen because they lie beyond the limited human capacity to foresee. For example, no one knows who will be the next president of Russia. As former Secretary of State Dean Rusk liked to say, "Fate has not given mankind the capacity to pierce the fog of the future."[4]

Within this environment, intelligence agencies are faced with the task of determining intelligence priorities, a process known as threat assessment. Experts and policymakers gather periodically to evaluate the perils that confront the United States and establish a ladder of priorities from the most dangerous (Tiers 1A and 1B) to the least (Tier 4). Bias and guesswork enter the picture, along with the limitations caused by the uncertainty that surrounds the future. Where should one place China in the threat assessment? What about Russia, or Cuba? The outcome of these debates shapes the priorities for some $44 billion worth of intelligence spending each year. It also determines the areas U.S. spies will infiltrate, sets the orbits for surveillance satellites, and establishes the flight patterns of reconnaissance aircraft.

To improve the threat assessment process, the United States has undertaken nine major inquiries into its intelligence apparatus since the end of the Cold War. Each has concluded that policymakers failed to clarify during the planning-and-direction phase of the intelligence cycle exactly what kinds of information they needed. Consequently, intelligence officers often remain ignorant of the data desired by policy officials, who in turn tend to assume that the intelligence agencies will divine the issues that await action at the White House, the State Department, and other important offices in Washington.

Among policy officials, the president and his top aides are the most important consumers of intelligence in the executive branch. These aides include members of the cabinet who deal with foreign and national security issues, along with the staff of the National Security Council (NSC). These men and women are pulled in many different directions by the demands of their daily schedules. As a result, they are reluctant to devote much time, if any, to updating their intelligence priorities.

Adding to this problem is spotty communication between analysts and decision makers. Sometimes NSC staffers, on the job for a year or more, have never spoken with experienced intelligence analysts on the National Intelligence Council who cover the same areas. This breakdown in communication stems from inadequate liaison relationships between the government's policy departments and the intelligence agencies. The lack of synchronization causes frustration on both sides. All too often policymakers scrawl "irrelevant" or "OBE" (overtaken by events) in ink across intelligence reports.

The collection phase, which follows planning and direction in the intelligence cycle, faces challenges as well. Even a superpower like the United States is unable to cover the globe with expensive surveillance platforms (hardware), such as reconnaissance aircraft, satellites, and ground-based listening posts. During the Cold War, satellite photography monitored the missiles and armies of opponents, rendering a surprise attack like Pearl Harbor unlikely. Today however, cameras on satellites and airplanes are unable to peer inside al-Qaeda tents or into the deep underground caverns where North Korea constructs nuclear weapons. Though they comprise a high percentage of the funds allocated in the annual intelligence budget, costly hardware is of questionable value in tracking many contemporary U.S. security concerns.

Many of the best contributions from spy machines come from relatively inexpensive unmanned aerial vehicles, notably the Predator, which has proven effective at scouring the Iraqi and Afghan countryside in search of insurgents. On occasion, the far more costly surveillance satellites have demonstrated their value by intercepting revealing telephone conversations among terrorists and other enemies (a method known as signals intelligence, the capture of communications from one person or group to another). Moreover, satellite images of Russian and Chinese missile sites, or North Korean troop movements, remain valuable to the security of the United States. Still, in the case of terrorism, it would be more advantageous to have a human agent well placed inside the upper reaches of al-Qaeda. Such an agent, or asset, would be worth a dozen multibillion-dollar satellites.

Yet human intelligence has its limitations as well. Against closed societies like North Korea, Iran, and Saddam Hussein's Iraq, local assets are difficult to recruit. This is especially so because the United States focused for decades on the communist world and largely ignored the study of the languages, history, and culture necessary to operate in such places as the Middle East and Asia. Few U.S. citizens have mastered the nuances of Pashto, Arabic, or Farsi; fewer still are willing to work in perilous locations overseas for government wages.

Even if successfully recruited, indigenous assets can be unreliable. They are known to fabricate reports, sell information to the highest bidder, and scheme as false defectors or double-agents. Intelligence assets are not boy scouts or nuns; they are often driven by avarice and travel without moral compasses. "Curveball," the prophetically codenamed German agent, provides a typical illustration of the risks involved in human intelligence. Spying inside Iraq in 2002, Curveball convinced the German intelligence service that weapons of mass destruction (WMD) existed in Saddam's regime. The Central Intelligence Agency, in turn, took the bait through its liaison with the Germans.

Not every human intelligence asset turns out to be as deceptive as Curveball. Now and then a foreign spy provides extraordinarily useful information to the United States, as did the Soviet military intelligence officer Oleg Penkosky during the Cold War. Information from Col. Penkosky, coupled with photographs taken by U-2 reconnaissance aircraft, helped the CIA identify the presence of Soviet nuclear missiles in Cuba in 1962. With occasional successes like Penkosky in mind, the United States and most other countries continue their search for reliable and productive assets, even if the cost-benefit ratio has been disappointing.

Whether collected by machines or human agents, intelligence must be converted into usable information. For example, intercepted telephone conversations in Farsi must be translated into English. Messages may have to be decoded. This is done during the processing phase of the intelligence cycle. Each day, over four hundred satellite images, along with thousands of telephone intercepts, some in difficult codes, are collected by intelligence agencies. Yet the United States lacks sufficient translators, photo-interpreters, and code-breakers. In response to a query about the major problems facing U.S. intelligence, a recent director of the National Security Agency (NSA), Vice Admiral J. M. McConnell, identified three: "processing, processing, and processing."[5]

As the public now knows, the day before the September 11 attacks the NSA intercepted a telephone message in Farsi from a suspected al-Qaeda operative. The message, translated on September 12, proclaimed, "Tomorrow is zero hour." As it stands, the vast majority of information gathered by the intelligence agencies is never examined. This is a supreme challenge for the government's information technology specialists—improving the capacity of the United States to mine intelligence data more rapidly, separating the noise from the vital signals that decision makers need to know.

The heart of the intelligence cycle is the analysis phase, where the task is to bring insight to the information that has been collected and processed. The method is straightforward: hire qualified people to sift through all the available information in an attempt to predict what events may happen next in the world. Given the limitations of human forecasting, Dean Rusk suggested that all intelligence reports ought to start off with the caveat: "Damned if I know, but if you want our best guess, well, here it is."[6]

The intelligence cycle concludes with the dissemination phase. Perhaps the greatest paradox of U.S. intelligence is that so much effort and funding go into gathering information for policymakers only for them to ignore it. Some of the best assistant secretaries of defense and state have conceded that they spent, at best, five minutes a day scanning intelligence reports; they were simply too overwhelmed with other obligations.[7] Officials even higher in the policy hierarchy have even less time to read intelligence reports. The first challenge of dissemination, then, is to catch the attention of busy leaders, which is why marketing is a critical part of the intelligence cycle.

In marketing their products to consumers, the intelligence agencies confront several potential obstacles. Policymakers may choose to manipulate intelligence to fit their own political views or ideological predispositions—distortion by politicization.[8] Intelligence officers themselves may succumb to the temptation to slant information to suit the needs of policymakers as a way of advancing their career, delivering "intelligence to please." Fortunately, analysts rarely succumb to this temptation, because most of them are imbued with a sense of profes-

sional ethics that shuns twisting information to please politicians.

More common is politicization on the consumer side, when policymakers bend the facts. Speaking truth to power is a notoriously difficult endeavor. Those in power often do not want to hear information that runs counter to their policy preferences; hence, they sometimes distort intelligence reports. Decision makers may cherry-pick snippets of information and analysis from intelligence reports that uphold their stated policy positions, ignoring contrary facts or conclusions. More blatant still, government officials have been known to discount entire intelligence reports, as President Lyndon B. Johnson did with CIA analyses that provided a dismal prognosis for U.S. military success in the Vietnam War, or as the second Bush administration did with CIA reports that found no connections between al-Qaeda and Saddam Hussein's regime in Iraq. In such instances, the unenviable but vital responsibility of intelligence managers is to call policy officials to account for their distortions, publicly if necessary.

As this examination of the intelligence cycle indicates, many opportunities for error and distortion present themselves as intelligence makes its way from the field into the hands of decision makers. Nonetheless, U.S. intelligence agencies have some advantages in their quest for information. Willing to spend vast sums of money on espionage, the United States enjoys the largest, most sophisticated information-gathering apparatus in the world. This bureaucracy brings in a torrent of information from across the globe, some of which has been invaluable for defending U.S. overseas interests and homeland security. The intelligence agencies are expert, as well, in packaging and delivering their assessments of international affairs to the right people in government in a timely manner. Even so, intelligence failures continue to happen. Perhaps nothing illustrates this reality so clearly as two recent cases: the attacks of September 11, 2001, and the misjudgment about the presence of weapons of mass destruction in Iraq.

The 9/11 Intelligence Failure

U.S. intelligence agencies performed in a more credible manner to warn the nation of the terrorist threat before September 11, 2001, than is usually acknowledged. As early as 1995, the CIA's Counterterrorism Center (CTC) cautioned the White House that "aerial terrorism seems likely at some point—filling an airplane with explosives and dive-bombing a target."[9] The warning erred only in its failure to comprehend that hijacked commercial aircraft with their highly volatile jet fuel, would be powerful missiles without added explosives. Analysts in the CTC had good reason to be concerned about aerial terrorism during the 1990s. Frequent reports had surfaced in the media about terrorist schemes to fly an airplane into the Eiffel Tower or into CIA head-quarters. The CTC's warnings on this topic appeared in high policy circles with regularity between 1995 and 2001.

Yet the CTC never provided officials with precise information about the timing or location of the anticipated hijackings, the kind of actionable intelligence that would have allowed U.S. authorities to intercept the terrorists before they boarded the airplanes. Moreover, the intelligence agencies flooded officials with dire warnings about other possible threats, from trucks filled with dynamite exploding in urban tunnels to attacks against the nation's railroad system, crops, livestock, computer infrastructure, and water supplies. Missing in these reports was a sense of priority or probability among the threats, as well as the degree of specificity necessary to take timely protective measures.

Moreover, government inquiries have discovered that the intelligence agencies failed to coordinate and act on the few shards of specific information they did have regarding the September 11 operatives.[10] For instance, the agencies proved unable to track two of the nineteen terrorists, despite warnings from the CIA to the Federal Bureau of Investigation about the terrorists' arrival in San Diego. Furthermore, the FBI failed to respond to warnings from its own agents in Phoenix and Minneapolis about suspicious flight training undertaken by foreigners in those cities. And the Department of Defense smothered warnings from the "Able Danger" group of military intelligence officers who had apparently discovered the presence of sixty foreign terrorists in the United States almost two years before the September 11 attacks.[11] Among the sixty were four of the September 11 hijackers, including their Egyptian-born leader, Mohamed Atta.

At a deeper level, September 11 was an intelligence failure because the CIA had no assets within al-Qaeda, because the National Security Agency (NSA) fell far behind on translating relevant signals intelligence intercepts involving suspected terrorists, and because all of the intelligence agencies lacked sufficient language skills and understanding about nations in the Middle East and South Asia and the objectives and likely motivations of al-Qaeda.

Yet September 11 was more than an intelligence failure; it was a policy failure too. Despite the CIA's warnings about aerial terrorism, for example, neither the Clinton nor the second Bush administrations took meaningful steps to tighten airport security, warn pilots, seal off cockpits, field air marshals, or even alert top officials in the Department of Transportation about the terrorist danger.

Iraqi Weapons of Mass Destruction

The intelligence failures regarding Iraqi weapons of mass destruction were in some ways even more troubling than those that preceded the September 11 attacks. The National Intelligence Estimate (NIE) of October 2002 concluded, as did most intelligence agencies and outside analysts, that unconventional weapons were most likely present in Iraq. This assessment was based on several inaccurate sources of information. First, since the intelligence community had no significant human assets in Iraq during the interwar years, analysts in the United States extrapolated from what they knew when the United States last had "boots on the ground"—after the first Persian Gulf War in 1991. At that time, the CIA learned that its pre-war estimates regarding Iraqi WMD were inaccurate; Iraq's weapons program had advanced far beyond what the CIA's analysts had projected. After U.S. troops departed Iraq in 1991, the CIA lacked reliable sources on the ground. Thus, in the run-up to the second Persian Gulf War, CIA analysts compensated for earlier underestimates by overestimating the probability of Iraqi WMD.

The available human intelligence proved problematic. Reports from the German asset Curveball, whose reliability was vouched for by the Germans, also factored into the CIA's miscalculations. Only recently have the Germans conceded that the Iraqi exile was in fact lying. Moreover, the confessions of a captured al-Qaeda member, Ibn al-Shaykh al-Libi, interrogated by the Defense Intelligence Agency (DIA), also proved to be fabrications.[12] In addition, the Iraqi National Congress, led by another Iraqi exile, Ahmed Chalabi, claimed knowledge of Iraq's activities and informed U.S. intelligence agencies and the second Bush administration that Saddam Hussein was pursuing nuclear weapons. Chalabi's reliability has since been called into question. Critics maintain that his purpose may have been chiefly to push for a U.S. invasion so that he might advance his personal political agenda and replace Hussein as president of Iraq.

CIA analysts were also aware that British intelligence was concerned about the existence of Iraqi WMD. Yet British government inquiries into this matter, notably the Butler Report, disclosed that the worries of British intelligence analysts focused on a possible Iraqi use of tactical chemical or biological weapons on the battlefield by Hussein if he faced an invasion, as opposed to strategic WMD that could directly strike the United Kingdom, the United

States, or even their military forces in the Middle East away from the battlefield.

It is often claimed that the second Bush Administration pressured intelligence analysts to write an NIE that emphasized the probability of weapons of mass destruction in Iraq. Such a finding would have supported a policy to invade Iraq and overthrow Hussein's regime, which some argue was the administration's desired course of action regardless of whether the Iraqi dictator had an unconventional weapons program. Vice President Dick Cheney visited CIA headquarters an unprecedented eight times prior to the publication of the 2002 NIE, pressing analysts on their conclusions whenever they strayed from his conviction that Iraq was pursuing capabilities in weapons of mass destruction. The CIA analysts whom Cheney visited assert, however, that they felt no sense of intimidation by his presence; on the contrary, they were pleased to have such unusual high-level attention paid to their work.[13]

Then-Secretary of State Colin Powell also visited with CIA officials to probe the strength of evidence concerning WMD in Iraq, especially on the eve of his appearance before the United Nations on February 3, 2003, to make the case that Saddam Hussein was a great danger. During his preparation, Powell encountered some disagreement among intelligence analysts, including dissent within his own intelligence organization, the Department of State's Bureau of Intelligence and Research (INR). He also learned of other pockets of dissent inside the Department of Energy's intelligence unit and the Air Force's intelligence service. Yet, the analytic behemoths of the intelligence community, most notably the CIA and the DIA, maintained that Iraq probably did possess weapons of mass destruction. Their reasoning pivoted on Iraq's purchase of 60,000 high-strength aluminum tubes, which, they argued, seemed designed for a uranium centrifuge and a nuclear weapons program.[14] Moreover, then-DCI George Tenet vigorously backed the majority opinion. Secretary Powell deferred to this powerful coalition, even though analysts in INR and the Department of Energy pointed out that the aluminum tubes were more likely combustion chambers for conventional rockets. For the most part, though, these were internal disputes that took place outside the hearing of the American public. The dissenting views of the smaller agencies were largely dismissed by the larger and more powerful agencies.

President George W. Bush himself questioned Tenet directly about his confidence in the October 2002 NIE. As reported by Bob Woodward of the *Washington Post*, the intelligence director assured the president that the presence of weapons of mass destruction in Iraq was a "slam dunk."[15] A careful reading of the NIE indicates, however, that the analysts who wrote the assessment hardly claimed perfect knowledge about the state of Saddam Hussein's unconventional weapons program. The odds favored finding WMD, but analysts inserted caveats into the estimate regarding the "softness" of the data.

This softness is precisely what Tenet should have underscored for the president. The DCI should have pointed out that the NIE was not a definitive report—indeed, it was a rushed job prepared in only three weeks—that additional on-the-ground fact-finding was sorely needed, and that the CIA felt uneasy about the human intelligence reporting provided by Curveball, al-Libi, and Chalabi. A briefing along these lines from Tenet to the president would have highlighted the need for a delay in the invasion plans until UN weapons inspectors had cleared up the intelligence ambiguities. Instead, the White House appears to have been all too ready to accept the convenient findings of some intelligence agencies that happened to run parallel to its own policy ambitions, namely, regime change in Iraq. As a result, Tenet evidently fell into a trap that awaits every U.S. spymaster: the snare of White House politics. Caught up in the administration's euphoria for war against Saddam Hussein, the pursuit of democracy in the Middle East, and a demonstration of U.S. military might as a warning to adversaries, Tenet's reassurance provided an intelligence linchpin for the president to confirm his argument in favor of an Iraqi invasion.

Earlier, Tenet had failed to set the record straight at another important moment in the WMD debate. Inserted into the State of the Union address in 2003 was an assertion that Iraq had attempted to purchase 500 tons of yellowcake uranium from Niger, indicating that Hussein was indeed pursuing a nuclear weapons program. The CIA looked into this allegation by sending former U.S. Ambassador to Niger Joseph C. Wilson IV to make direct inquiries. The ambassador, however, found no evidence to support the hypothesis and the CIA reported this conclusion to the deputy national security advisor, Steven H. Hadley, well in advance of the State of the Union address. Yet the speech included the yellowcake claim anyway, which was now cloaked with the legitimacy of the president's own word in a nationally televised address. Tenet later claimed that he had not seen an advance copy of the speech and was therefore unable to amend the text. The "eighteen words" regarding Nigerian yellowcake have since become a focus of war critics, as has the outing of Wilson's wife, Valerie Plame, as an undercover CIA operative.

The unwillingness of the CIA to confront policy officials who exaggerated intelligence reporting has been perhaps the most disquieting aspect of the WMD intelligence debates. Throughout these distortions, the CIA mostly stood mute. One exception occurred when analysts complained publicly, through anonymous media leaks, that Vice President Cheney was in error to insist that a significant tie existed between al-Qaeda and the Iraqi government. Intelligence reporting had concluded that no such connection existed, though CIA analysts warned that a bond might be forged between global jihadists and Baghdad—or insurgent remnants—if the West were to invade Iraq. Despite the CIA's findings to the contrary, Cheney continued to state publicly that al-Qaeda and the Hussein regime were secretly allied.

Proposals for Reform

The American public must come to understand that intelligence agencies, like any human enterprise, will always have their share of failures. Nevertheless, much can be done to reduce the chance of mistakes. At the planning and direction phase, policy officials must define information needs with greater precision. Collection has been too broad and requires a sharper focus. What exactly do decision makers need to know? On what specific topics should the intelligence agencies focus? The tasking of intelligence agencies is often vaguely spelled out, if at all, and the result is an overly diffuse global intelligence collection effort. The president should issue a quarterly National Security Council Intelligence Directive that updates the administration's threat assessment and current intelligence needs. The president should insist on specific directives—for example, "Track all uranium shipments from Niger, worldwide"—rather than vague orders like "Provide the Secretary of Defense with intelligence on Niger."

Within the collection phase, renewed concentration on human intelligence is critical. Since 1947, technical intelligence such as signals intelligence and satellite imagery has dominated the U.S. intelligence budget at the expense of human intelligence. The intelligence budget is just beginning to shift funds toward human intelligence. Funding, however, is only the first step. Spy rings are relatively inexpensive to set up; the more difficult challenge is to develop among intelligence officers the language skills and knowledge of foreign cultures necessary for the effective recruitment of assets abroad. This effort cannot succeed overnight; it is bound to take at least ten to fifteen years. The creation of government scholarships to attract top students into the intelligence agencies, such as the Pat Roberts Intelligence Scholars Program, is a step in the right direction. In return for service in an intelligence

agency for a period of time, usually two to three years, the government covers college tuition for students studying foreign languages and cultures.

The intelligence agencies must also do more to recruit U.S. citizens with ethnic heritages germane to strategic areas such as the Middle East, South Asia, and other regions largely ignored during the Cold War. For example, Arab-Americans, who face enhanced scrutiny, need to be recruited into the intelligence agencies in much larger numbers and should not be shunned as prima facie security risks. Once cleared through the normal background security checks, Arab-Americans who wish to work in the government should be actively recruited.

Successful recruitment will also require better salaries, since the private sector is also seeking workers with backgrounds in foreign languages and cultures. Although public sector positions pay less than private sector jobs, many top college students would rather serve the United States in the struggle against global terrorism and other threats than hunt down obscure cases in the library of a law firm. Reducing the financial tradeoffs necessary to making such a career choice would go a long way to ensuring that more talented young people are brought into government service.

Equally important will be efforts to expand the CIA's use of what are called NOCs—U.S. citizens under non-official cover—who operate within a local society, say, as an investment banker in Egypt, a hotel manager in Dubai, or an oil rigger in Bahrain. Moving intelligence officers out of embassies and into the field will make them more likely to meet potential assets and understand the undercurrents of foreign societies. In light of the added hardships and risks of a NOC career, salaries and bonuses should be considerably higher for those who select this path, and more effort will have to be put into crafting their covers, their methods of communication with CIA headquarters, and their rescue if they find themselves in jeopardy overseas.

Furthermore, the United States must examine anew the relationship between the FBI and the Foreign Intelligence Surveillance Court. Established by the Foreign Intelligence Surveillance Act (FISA) of 1978, this court reviews warrant requests for national security wiretaps and other forms of electronic surveillance, as well as physical searches. As a safeguard against intelligence agencies overstepping their powers, as occurred with the FBI in the 1960s and is a subject of current inquiry with the NSA, the FISA Court stands as a vital check on the merits of surveillance requests.[16] Yet steps must also be taken to ensure that warrants can be acquired with dispatch in properly documented cases of national security threats. This did not happen in the case of a suspected al-Qaeda member in Minneapolis prior to the September 11 attacks. When information is collected by the CIA or other intelligence agencies regarding terrorists traveling toward or operating within the United States, the FBI must be alerted quickly and clearly so that it can conduct follow-up surveillance.

At the processing phase, the intelligence agencies are behind the curve on data-mining. Here, too, the federal government must pay higher salaries and bonuses to attract top talent who can assist the intelligence agencies in overcoming information technology deficiencies. By setting up a quasi-government company in Silicon Valley called "In-Q-Tel," the CIA has already reached out to some of the nation's top computer talent. Further outreach and more money are critical. The intelligence agencies desperately need to bring in IT expertise to integrate their systems, while at the same time enhancing firewalls to protect sensitive intelligence from theft by outside hackers and foreign intelligence services. The FBI in particular has lost credibility among Capitol Hill appropriators, having spent over $580 billion on a nonfunctioning computer system.[17] A reputable outsider recruited into a senior intelligence management position might be able to restore congressional confidence and attract the necessary appropriations to achieve seamless integration among intelligence agencies. The central technological challenge has two elements. First, as information is gathered by the intelligence agencies from around the world, sophisticated machine-sorting techniques are necessary to separate key signals from the high percentage of surrounding "noise" that streams into the secret agencies. Second, useful intelligence must be rapidly shared among the intelligence agencies in Washington, as well as with law enforcement and intelligence officials at the state and local levels. This requires an effective integration of computer networks, both horizontally (in the nation's capital) and vertically (downward to state and local counterterrorism officials).

During the analytical phase, intelligence officers will need to be more careful about including caveats and nuances in their reporting, as well as making clear just how good—or bad—their sources are. For their part, the president and other policymakers must let it be known to intelligence managers and analysts that vague generalities will not be accepted in NIEs and other reports.

One high-level intelligence briefer told the Aspin-Brown Commission in 1996 that North Korea "might have one or two nuclear weapons or it might not have any."[18] Missing was a sense of what analysts believed were the probabilities of a North Korean nuclear weapon within the next year. When an analyst presents a list of threats without any sense

of which ones are most likely, the result is paralysis among policymakers.

Intelligence collectors and analysts must also be more thorough in vetting their sources. When the Germans balked at allowing the CIA to conduct its own interviews with the asset Curveball, the CIA's analysts should have downgraded the quality of this source to a low level or declined to use the source at all. Important, too, are efforts to ensure that policymakers understand the reasons behind dissents voiced by intelligence agencies or individual analysts. Their arguments must be showcased, along with the prevailing majority opinions, so that policymakers have a full understanding of the key points of contention. During the Iraqi WMD debate, the contrary views of the Department of Energy, the State Department's Bureau of Intelligence and Research, and the Air Force were insufficiently underscored.

At the dissemination phase, analysts and intelligence managers should be trained to resist more effectively pressures from policymakers to "cook" intelligence. A self-imposed wall must separate analysts from an administration's policy ambitions. Further, analysts must be determined to set the record straight for the public if intelligence reports are twisted for policy purposes by government officials. Intelligence officers, particularly the nation's intelligence director, must be brutally candid with respect to the limits of the reports they have prepared, warning the president and other officials about the extent to which conclusions are based on conjecture more than empirical indicators, such as unambiguous imagery. Those parts of reports that are largely speculative must be carefully delineated from the fact-based findings.

Fresh incentives can be established to encourage the maintenance of a wall between analysts and policymakers, one that will not prevent them from communicating with one another but that erects a barrier against the coloration of intelligence to suit policy objectives. One stick would be to fire analysts who violate the norms of objectivity. Carrots would include promotions, bonuses, and special recognition to those analysts who display exemplary professional conduct. Though rarely used, A-team, B-team exercises in competitive analysis are a useful means for validating objectivity, as long as the teams are staffed with unbiased experts. Above all, the integrity of the analytic process depends on the recruitment of honest men and women into the intelligence agencies.

Critical, too, is the need for constructing better bridges between policymakers and intelligence agencies. The best approach is for the agencies to gain permission to place liaison officers in policy departments so they can attend staff meetings, periodically discuss with decision makers their information needs, and learn from the inside how they can help with timely factual information and objective analysis. With this approach, intelligence is more likely to be relevant to the immediate agendas of government leaders.

No intelligence reform proposal is more important than putting in place a Director of National Intelligence (DNI) with full budget and appointment powers over all intelligence agencies, a true leader with a broad perspective on spending, planning, collection, processing, analysis, and dissemination—someone who could overcome the stovepiped autonomy of the individual intelligence agencies that has plagued them since 1947. The creation of a strong intelligence chief has been the core recommendation of major intelligence reform commissions since 1949, most recently of the 9/11 Commission in 2004.

Over the years, the Department of Defense (DoD) has skillfully resisted the idea of creating a DNI, jealously guarding its military intelligence prerogatives against the possible encroachment of a civilian intelligence chief. Finally, in 2004, with the passage by Congress of the Intelligence Reform and Terrorism Prevention Act, the 9/11 Commission seemed to have achieved the impossible: the establishment of a robust DNI. Yet a close look at the statute reveals that the DoD and its allies in Congress have managed to dilute and obfuscate the authority of the new intelligence director.[19] As a result, the inaugural DNI, Ambassador John D. Negroponte, faces an uphill bale to consolidate his control over the entire intelligence establishment. His most important challenge will be to persuade the intelligence agencies to pool their information more effectively. In light of the DoD's opposition to a strong DNI, the ambassador's chances for gathering together the reins of a set of agencies so obviously fissile appear slim—unless President Bush or his successor demands a genuine leader for U.S. intelligence, not just a figurehead.

Over the objections of the secretary of defense, a president would have to insist that the DNI be given the authority to hire and fire all intelligence personnel, as well as determine—in consultation with their senior management teams—the budgets of each agency. With these prerogatives, the DNI would finally serve as a hoop to bind together the fifteen staves of the intelligence "community."

President Bush is an unlikely candidate to force this issue given distractions from the wars in Iraq and Afghanistan, the campaign against global terrorism, and his dependence on Secretary of Defense Donald H. Rumsfeld. Furthermore, the president has never exhibited much interest in intelligence reform. His administration initially opposed a joint congressional investigation into the intelligence errors related to the attacks of September 11. Then, once the panel was formed, the administration stonewalled the inquiry. The White House also tried to block the creation of the 9/11 Commission, but finally acceded to pressures from the families of the September 11 victims and grudgingly cooperated with its investigation.

The absence of consistent presidential leadership to strengthen the U.S. intelligence shield is unfortunate. The need to bring unity and coordination to the nation's intelligence agencies is a matter of enormous importance. The security of the United States rides heavily on the outcome of this struggle now unfolding in Washington. If the government proves unwilling or unable to make the necessary improvements to protect the nation, citizens will have to demand change through public lobbying or, if necessary, the ballot box.

Questions for Further Discussion

1. What intelligence failures occurred in the lead-up to the 9/11 terrorist attacks in 2001, and why?

2. What intelligence failures occurred in the lead-up to the mistaken judgments about WMDs in Iraq in 2002, and why?

3. What policy failures occurred in both cases? Were members of Congress culpable, too?

4. What steps can be taken to avoid a repetition of the 9/11 and Iraqi WMD intelligence and policy failures?

Endnotes

1. See Williamson Murray and Mark Grimsley, "Introduction: On Strategy," *The Making of Strategy: Rulers, States, and War*, eds. Williamson Murray, Alvin Bernstein, and MacGregor Knox (New York: Cambridge University Press, 1994), 1–23; and Richard K. Betts, "Analysis, War and Decision: Why Intelligence Failures Are Inevitable," *World Politics* 31 (October 1978): 61–89.

2. On the intelligence cycle and the structure of the U.S. intelligence community, see Loch K. Johnson, *America's Secret Power* (New York: Oxford University Press, 1989); *Secret Agencies* (New Haven: Yale University Press, 1996); and Mark M. Lowenthal, *Intelligence: From Secrets to Policy*, 2nd edition (Washington, DC: CQ Press, 2003).

3. Quoted in "Indiana Jim and the Temple of Spooks," *The Economist*, 20 March 1993, 34.

4. Dean Rusk, interview with author, Athens, Georgia, 21 February 1988.

5. J. M. McConnell quoted by senior NSA official, interview with author, Washington, DC, 14 July 1994.

6. Dean Rusk, interview with author, Athens, Georgia, 21 February 1988).

7. See, for example, Loch K. Johnson, *Bombs, Bugs, Drugs, and Thugs: Intelligence and America's Quest for Security* (New York: New York University Press, 2000), 194.

8. See Loch K. Johnson and James J. Wirtz, eds., *Strategic Intelligence: Windows Into a Secret World* (Los Angeles: Roxbury, 2004), 167–218.

9. See Loch K. Johnson, "The Aspin-Brown Intelligence Inquiry: Behind the Closed Doors of a Blue Ribbon Commission," *Studies in Intelligence* 48 (Winter 2004): 12.

10. See National Commission on Terrorist Attacks Upon the United States, The 9/11 Commission Report, *Final Report of the National Commission on Terrorist Attacks Upon the United States* (New York: Norton, 2004).

11. Louis Freeh, "Why Did the 9/11 Commission Ignore 'Able Danger'?" *Wall Street Journal,* 17 November 2005, A16.

12. Douglas Jehl, "Report Warned Bush Team About Intelligence Doubts," *New York Times,* 6 November 2005, A14. The report in the title refers to a DIA analysis prepared and circulated to government officials in February 2002.

13. CIA analysts, interviews with author, Washington, DC, June 15, 2005.

14. See the account in David Barstow, William J. Broad, and Jeff Gerth, "How the White House Used Disputed Arms Intelligence," *New York Times,* 3 October 2004, A1, A16–18.

15. Bob Woodward, *Plan of Attack* (New York: Simon & Schuster, 2004), 249.

16. See Loch K. Johnson, "Congressional Supervision of America's Secret Agencies: The Experience and Legacy of the Church Committee," *Public Administration Review* 64 (January 2004): 3–14.

17. See Daniel Benjamin and Steven Simon, *The Next Attack: The Failure of the War on Terror and a Strategy for Getting It Right* (New York: Times Books/Henry Holt & Company, 2005).

18. Member of the Aspin-Brown Commission, interview with author, Washington, DC, 22 March 1997.

19. See, for example, the critique by John Brennan, "Is This Intelligence?" *Washington Post,* 20 November 2005, B1. ✦

Reprinted with permission from Loch K. Johnson, "A Framework for Strengthening U.S. Intelligence," *Yale Journal of International Affairs* 1 (Winter/Spring 2006): 116–131.

Part X

Intelligence in Other Lands

Hamlet: ". . . For every man hath business and
desire
Such as it is . . ."

—*Shakespeare*, Hamlet, *1.5.130–131*

Although most states, nonstate actors, and even corporations have organizations that collect, analyze, and disseminate information, intelligence organizations are not all cut from the same mold. They often undertake different missions, have different capabilities, and are subjected to different types of public or governmental oversight. The U.S. intelligence community is not a typical national intelligence organization. It specializes in technical intelligence collection (e.g., electronic and photographic space surveillance), and it takes a "social science" approach to intelligence analysis. It is also governed by a strict normative and legal code of conduct that is supposed to distance intelligence work from domestic politics.

The United States also is a relative newcomer when it comes to running large intelligence organizations, although at moments of crisis the nation has usually found a way to recruit spies and organize their "take" to meet military and diplomatic needs. Other great powers—France, Great Britain, China, Russia—have long maintained competent and sometimes quite extensive intelligence organizations and operations. Additionally, smaller states—Israel and interwar Poland, for example—have developed highly capable intelligence organizations to offset powerful and threatening neighbors. In fact, it was Polish intelligence that gave the Allies in World War II their greatest asset. Polish mathematicians reproduced a German code ma-

chine, known as "Enigma," and using outmoded code "keys" supplied to them by French intelligence were able to read encoded Nazi radio traffic. The intelligence produced by Enigma, known as "Ultra," was closely guarded and highly valued by the Allies because it literally gave them the capability to read Nazi war plans before they were received by frontline commanders.

Classification and Comparison of Organizations

There is no commonly accepted scheme for separating intelligence agencies into categories, but scholars have used several variables to facilitate the comparative study of intelligence organizations. First, scholars classify national intelligence organization in terms of whether they perform covert actions, paramilitary operations, espionage, technical collection, military intelligence, political intelligence, or internal security and surveillance. They are also interested in determining which of these operations tends to dominate a state's approach to intelligence and who or which agency actually runs the overall intelligence operation. Sometimes states maintain separate organizations to undertake each intelligence function, and sometimes several or all functions are lumped together in a single organization. National priorities and resource constraints can also limit the scope of intelligence activities: Few states have the capability to launch reconnaissance satellites to observe their opponents from space or to monitor events in more then a few areas of special interest. Additionally, culture, history, and tradition shape intelligence organizations and national outlooks about the proper role of intelli-

506

gence organizations in foreign, defense, and domestic policy.

Second, scholars often use an important distinguishing characteristic to classify national intelligence and security organizations. They look to see whether a division of responsibility exists between monitoring external threats and domestic security and surveillance. States that maintain this distinction between external and domestic activities have a greater likelihood of having professional intelligence organizations that are responsive to the rule of law and oversight by other government institutions and elected officials. By contrast, when domestic and external intelligence and security activities are undertaken by a single organization, most scholars believe that it is likely that intelligence will simply be used as an instrument of state terror to keep a ruling party, clique, or dictator in power. John Dziak (1988) has called this second type of intelligence institution the "counterintelligence state."

The counterintelligence state forms when the distinction between legitimate government and intelligence infrastructure vanishes and the resources of the state come to serve the interests of the ruling elite, which include intelligence functionaries. The counterintelligence state maintains a large intelligence-security force that is responsible for identifying and responding to both domestic and international threats to the regime. Left to its own devices, it often identifies broad and arbitrary domestic and foreign threats, placing virtually everyone not in the intelligence-security force under suspicion. These threats, in turn, justify calls for constant vigilance and the maintenance of a large surveillance and enforcement apparatus. The intelligence-security force is never accountable to the public. Instead, it protects the privileges of the members of the regime and security apparatus itself (Waller 1994). In the counterintelligence state, all political and social dissent is identified as a threat to national security and a crime against the state.

In the past, counterintelligence states have been linked to the influence of the "dead hand of ideology" on state security organizations. In other words, ideology itself predetermines domestic and international threats to the state or regime; the nature, source, or severity of the threats to the nation is not something open to discussion or analysis under these circumstances. Steven David (1999), however, has developed a theory of "omnibalancing" that can also account for the rise of the counterintelligence state. David stands traditional realist notions of security on their head by suggesting that for many states, internal threats—not the military threat posed by other states—preoccupy national leaders. In these situations, political dissidents, ri-

val ethnic or religious factions, or state institutions themselves (such as the military) pose the greatest threat to regime survival. The intelligence-security force thus becomes the premier government institution; senior intelligence officials often find themselves at the top of the ruling regime.

Third, scholars are interested in the degree to which intelligence organizations exist as independent institutions within a government and the degree to which they are held accountable by other bodies for their activities and performance. The counterintelligence state represents an extreme situation when intelligence work, national policy, and what amounts to "oversight" are fused into a single entity. Intelligence organizations, however, are subjected to different amounts of scrutiny and enjoy varying degrees of autonomy. Some intelligence agencies face judicial or legislative oversight that requires detailed and highly classified information about their activities. Others are subjected to less public oversight: Intelligence managers might simply have to offer general reports to some executive authority. Of related interest is the degree to which intelligence work emerges as a recognized profession within a state and the history and culture that shapes the way intelligence organizations operate.

Fourth, intelligence institutions vary in terms of the degree to which they conduct scientific and technical intelligence. Some maintain highly effective programs to reverse-engineer captured weapons or other items of military or industrial significance. Some intelligence organizations focus on economic espionage—gathering corporate secrets, product designs, and research results—to support domestic enterprises. Not all intelligence organizations apply traditional social science methodology in intelligence analysis. Some rely on espionage alone or on commercially or publicly available information to gain insights into their opponent's motivations and behavior. The *Komitet Gosudarstvennoy Bezopasnosti* (KGB), for example, maintained a minimum analytic capability and relied on espionage for insights into current events. The KGB often delivered this raw intelligence directly to senior Soviet officials. This lack of analytical capability sometimes led to bizarre activities. In the weeks leading up to the Cuban Missile Crisis, Soviet agents fanned out across Washington trying to pick up bits of information about the Kennedy Administration's response to the Soviet decision to deploy long-range nuclear-armed missiles to Cuba. It was unlikely, however, that officials would be discussing Soviet missile deployments to Cuba—especially if the missiles remained, as the Soviets intended, hidden from the prying eyes of U.S. reconnaissance capabilities. It is difficult to accept, but one of the world's largest intelligence organizations relied on overheard loose talk in D.C. bars and bistros as its primary mode of "analysis."

Fifth, scholars often classify intelligence organizations in terms of their collaborative activities—that is, the nature and intensity of their relationships with foreign intelligence agencies. Most intelligence organizations maintain formal and informal contacts with friendly and even rival intelligence agencies. These channels are used to backstop normal diplomatic communications by providing secure methods of transmitting sensitive information, to conform to or explain formal and public diplomatic positions, or to communicate when normal diplomatic relations have been severed. Among allied governments, collaboration among intelligence agencies can be highly extensive, and in some instances—such as the war on terrorism—it is actually crucial to success. Governments often decide to share classified information, and intelligence professionals are usually charged with delivering these materials. Sometimes personnel in friendly intelligence agencies cannot resist the opportunity to exploit existing lines of communication to penetrate other intelligence organizations. For instance, in the mid-1980s, Israeli intelligence officers used Jonathan Pollard, a U.S. intelligence analyst who volunteered to spy for Israel, to obtain classified U.S. information that was not granted through formal intelligence channels.

Some Examples of Foreign Intelligence Services

More information is publicly available about the U.S. intelligence community than about all other national intelligence agencies combined. It is difficult to say exactly what accounts for this state of affairs, but it can probably be attributed to American attitudes toward intelligence and government. Americans generally dislike secret organizations and secret government, while at the same time they are fascinated by the technical accomplishments and rumors of daring spies and covert operations undertaken by the intelligence community. All intelligence communities, however, are influenced by the specific history, culture, and legal setting in which they evolve. The three intelligence communities briefly described here—British, French, and Russian—are different, but each attempts to maintain internal security, foreign intelligence, and covert operations.

Great Britain

The responsibility for intelligence oversight in Great Britain resides with the Cabinet (which represents the dominant party or coalition in Parlia-

ment). The prime minister is responsible for all of the country's intelligence agencies and chairs the Ministerial Committee on Intelligence Services. A Parliamentary Intelligence and Security Committee provides additional intelligence oversight and reports to the prime minister about once a year. The difference between external and internal intelligence operations in Great Britain is less distinct than it is in the United States, although in the aftermath of September 11 the separation of foreign and domestic intelligence operations within the United States is also beginning to break down. The British government, unlike the U.S. government, can exercise prior restraint when it comes to publication of articles that reveal classified information. In other words, the British government can take legal action to stop "leaks" before they make it into the press. British and U.S. intelligence services routinely share classified information.

There are three major organizations within the British intelligence community. MI5, also known as the Security Service, is primarily responsible for domestic security and surveillance. Its activities are directed against criminals, espionage, and terrorists. MI6, also known as the Secret Intelligence Service, collects and analyzes information about external threats. The British government also maintains a service similar to the U.S. National Security Agency, called the GCHQ (Government Communication Headquarters), which collects and analyzes signals intelligence.

France

Although intelligence oversight in Great Britain resembles the system in the United States to the extent that both the executive and legislative branches of government monitor events within the intelligence community, oversight procedures in France are weak and ill-defined. In the aftermath of the 1995 *Rainbow Warrior* incident, when French intelligence operatives blew up a Greenpeace vessel, killing one crew member, there was a renewed interest in intelligence oversight. A *Comité Interministerielle de Renseignement* (the Interministry Committee on Intelligence) was formed. Made up mainly of civil servants, its goal is primarily to collate intelligence analysis rather than "control" intelligence operations. There also is a parliamentary committee intended to provide some oversight, but in a strong presidential system, parliamentary committees are relatively benign. Part of the intelligence community reports to the Defense Ministry, while other parts report to the Minister of the Interior.

The French intelligence community consists of several organizations. The DSGE (*Direction Generale de la Securite Exteriure*, or General Directorate for External Security) is responsible for producing strategic estimates to support the foreign ministry, humint, sigint, clandestine operations, and economic espionage. The DSGE reports to the Defense Ministry. The DRM (*Directoire du Renseignement Militaire,* or Directorate of Military Intelligence) is responsible for supporting the French military. It also is responsible for technical intelligence and for conducting imagery analysis. The DPSD (*Directorire de la Protection et e la Securite de la Defense,* or Directorate for Defense Protection and Security) is responsible for observing the French military, with an eye toward monitoring its political reliability. In addition, French presidents sometimes form their own ad hoc or "private" intelligence cells to deal with especially sensitive issues.

Russia

In the early 1990s, the KGB was divided into several agencies. The Federal Security Service (FSB—*Federal'naya Sluzba Besnopasnoti*) is responsible for domestic security and for counterintelligence. The Foreign Intelligence Service (SVR—*Sluzhba Vneshnei Razvedki*) is responsible for economic espionage, for humint, and for maintaining contacts with other foreign intelligence agencies. The SVR works with foreign intelligence organizations on halting black market trade in weapons of mass destruction and precursor materials, conducting the war on terrorism, stopping the drug trade, and combating organized crime and money laundering. The SVR also serves as a liaison with the intelligence services of several former Soviet republics, including Azerbaijan and Belarus. The Federal Border Service (FPS—*Federal'naya Pogranichnaya Sluzhba*) conducts security operations, intelligence gathering, and counterintelligence along Russia's borders. It also focuses on counter-drug operations to stop the movement of illicit drugs into and through Russia. In addition to these major intelligence services, about eight other agencies supply paramilitary, police, and special operations units to supplement intelligence and security operations.

The Soviet Union was the quintessential counterintelligence state, the merger of intelligence, security, and policymaking bodies that inspired John Dziak to coin the term in the 1980s. Given this history, it is not surprising that intelligence oversight has barely taken hold inside the emerging Russian democracy. According to Mark Kramer, the large Russian intelligence community is only partially accountable to elected officials:

> Most observers inside and outside Russia agree that democratic control of the intelligence/security complex is tenuous at best and, in some cases, nonexistent. Russia's intelligence and security forces enjoy extraordinary powers both formal and informal to act on their own. Although greater democratic oversight will not necessarily ensure that Russia's intelligence and security agencies are used for purposes conducive to democracy, the lack of democratic control all but guarantees that grave abuses will occur. (Kramer 2002, 1)

The path toward democratic oversight of intelligence services is even less clear-cut in other former Soviet Republics. Kramer (2002) notes that intelligence organizations have been used for partisan political purposes in Ukraine, Belarus, Georgia, Armenia, Azerbaijan, Central Asia, and Moldova.

The Readings

In the selections that follow, our authors provide some insights into the history, culture, and capabilities of the national intelligence communities that they survey. In Chapter 36, Robert Pringle describes how the legacy of the counterintelligence state still influences the organizations that were created from the remains of the KGB, which was dismantled with the demise of the Soviet Union. He suggests that the path to real intelligence reform requires not only the Russian people but the leaders of Russia's new intelligence community to recognize and rectify the sins of the past. Pringle suggests that Russia might be freed from the "dead hand of ideology" that stifled political discourse and creativity in the Soviet Union, but the intelligence community, staffed by veterans from the old system, might find that old habits die hard.

In Chapter 37, Thomas Bruneau tackles the problem of reforming the counterintelligence state in his essay, "Controlling Intelligence in New Democracies." Although much attention has been focused on how states make the transition to democracy, little of this literature addresses the unique issues involved in reforming intelligence agencies. No matter where democracy takes root, elected officials and civil servants have to reform the corrupt intelligence organizations maintained by the counterintelligence state. All fledgling democracies require security and intelligence services, if for no other reason than to protect them from the reactionary forces of some deposed dictator.

The final selection in this reader, Chapter 38, consists of excerpts from the Butler Commission Report, presenting an overview of the way British officials view the process of producing finished intelligence, as well as a look at the relationship between intelligence and foreign/defense policy in the United Kingdom. The Report also examines British intelligence analysis ("assessment") regarding the threat posed by weapons of mass destruction (WMDs) in Iraq prior to the Persian Gulf War that began in 2003. ✦

36

The Heritage and Future of the Russian Intelligence Community

Robert W. Pringle

In this postmortem on the *Komitet Gosudarstvennoy Bezopasnosti* (KGB), the Soviet State Security Service, Pringle describes how this Soviet intelligence apparatus kept the citizens of the U.S.S.R. in line and protected the regime from ideological and political threats, whether from inside or from abroad. He paints a compelling picture of an intelligence system where ideological purity, not analytical rigor, mattered most and where the distinction between intelligence analysis and policymaking simply did not exist. Pringle also describes the difficult task facing the government in Moscow as it attempted to create new intelligence organizations from the remnants of the KGB, by separating the new Russian intelligence agencies from the "dead hand of ideology" and Stalinist procedures that dominated its past.

In every medium in the new Russia, the old KGB is back. Bookstores are filled with memoirs and reminiscences by former KGB officers, bragging about their cold war exploits. A glorified version of the KGB's history has been released on CD-ROM. And a group of enterprising former spies has published a KGB guidebook to cities around the world.

This post-cold war propaganda offensive is more than an effort by KGB veterans to refight the cold war one more time. It seems designed to provide the service with political legitimacy in the post-Soviet, post-cold war world, and to distance the new Russian intelligence and security services from their Soviet heritage. Some Russian journalists have suggested that the new Russian Foreign Intelligence Service (SVR) and the Federal Security Service (FSB) distortion of their KGB past is designed to pave the way for a return to the centralized Soviet intelligence and security system.

Evaluating the Past

Every 20th of December, the SVR—like its predecessor, the KGB First Chief (Foreign Intelligence) Directorate—gathers to celebrate its birthday. Last December, President Boris Yeltsin rose from his sick bed to wish his secret servants well. On 20 December, Yeltsin—once a victim of KGB provocations—minimized the impact of the crimes of the Stalin era, stating "As I look back I realize that we nearly overdid it when we condemned the crimes committed by the security service."[1]

"Intelligence Glasnost" has taken off in the past few years. In 1996, the SVR began publishing a six-volume history of Russian foreign intelligence from Czar Ivan the Terrible to Mikhail Gorbachev. The service has also sponsored hundreds of semi-official books and the publication of journals on intelligence and counterintelligence.[2] The new in-house histories provide the equivalent of a PG film version of KGB foreign intelligence, rarely addressing its more nefarious operations such as the murder of Leon Trotsky in Mexico; the kidnaping of Soviet dissenters in Paris in the 1920s and Berlin in the 1950s; and KGB connivance with the Bulgarian government in the murder of a noted Bulgarian dissenter in London in 1978. Nor do they address how the KGB contributed to Moscow's defeat in the Cold War and the ultimate collapse of the Soviet Union itself.

Top-secret Communist Party and KGB documents from the Soviet period, as well as the memoirs of leaders of the former USSR, suggest that despite some stunningly successful operations and brilliant tradecraft, the KGB repeatedly failed to provide the Kremlin leadership with accurate intelligence on issues affecting the very survival of the Soviet state. A KGB history, which could be based on such documents and memoirs, would discuss a number of critical intelligence failures or miscalculations: intervention in Afghanistan; resurgent nationalism in Central Asia and the Baltics; and the impact of Moscow's mishandling of human rights issues, to name but a few. In addition, the information suggests that the other reasons for the KGB's failing was the service's hidebound Marxist ideology, overdependence on covert action, lack of analytical competence, and internal corruption.[3]

The Dead Hand of Ideology

The KGB of the cold war was an ideological service. Its last chairman, Vadim Bakatin, remembered in his memoirs that the only books in the bomb shelter built by the KGB 300 feet under the Kremlin in the 1980s for the Soviet leadership were the collected works of Lenin. Gorbachev observed in his memoirs that the foreign intelligence service was "at least as conservative and ideologically 'drilled' as most of the bureaucrats in our domestic administration."[4]

KGB documents repeatedly emphasized the role of the Communist Party. For example, the KGB's top-secret annual report for 1985 asserted in the lead paragraph that the service

> carried out all its activities under the direct control of the Central Committee and invariably acted in strict accord with the political line worked out by the Party. *Chekists* [intelligence and security officers] rigorously observed socialist legality and continually relied on the assistance of the broad masses of toilers.[5]

The ideological straitjacket distorted realities of developments both outside and within the crumbling Soviet Union:

- The head of the First Chief Directorate told his senior officers in 1983 that the threat of nuclear war was a result of "deepening economic and social crisis in the capitalist world . . . American monopolies would like to recover the positions they have lost in recent decades and conquer fresh ones."

- KGB Chairman Viktor Chebrikov stated in 1987 that Western intelligence services had crafted covert action concepts used against the Soviet Union "from the arsenal of Trotskyism and other opportunist currents." Chebrikov went on to assert that the CIA and other services had introduced the "virus of nationalism" into the Baltic where, he said, it was producing anti-Soviet sedition. A former KGB colonel commented dryly that "it was quite likely that Chebrikov believed much of this nonsense."[6]

At times the KGB's concern with the ideological threat reached ludicrous extremes. For example, then-KGB Chairman Vitali V. Fedorchuk warned the Politburo in 1982 that Russian artists were increasingly drawn into marriages with foreigners, and that at the July 1982 Tchaikovsky Competition in Moscow, British pianists had received greater ovations—"that at times clearly were meant to be provocative"—than Soviet artists.[7]

The Never-Ending Search for Enemies

Domestic security and counterintelligence, not foreign intelligence, were the priorities of the fathers of the Soviet state. For the first three years of its existence (1917–1920), the Cheka was primarily targeted against Russian counterrevolutionaries and their foreign supporters. In the first 20 years of the Soviet state, the Cheka's major foreign accomplishments included: Trotsky's murder, the penetration of the White Russian movement in Europe and Asia, and kidnappings and murders of leaders of the White Movement in Paris.[8]

Driven by a militant ideology and counterintelligence imperatives during the cold war, KGB residencies abroad expended almost as much effort thwarting imaginary perceived threats as they did chasing Western secrets. For example:

- Soviet intelligence messages from the New York residency in the 1940s indicated the services collected intelligence on Aleksandr Kerensky, the last head of the Provisional Government, who fled Russia in 1917.

- Other messages show that the residency directed the kidnappings of Soviet seamen who jumped ship in American ports and their forcible repatriation to the Soviet Union.[9]

Even after Stalin's death, the KGB refused to remove a critical mote from its eye—that dissent was not treason.

- In 1967, the top-secret annual KGB report to General Secretary Leonid Brezhnev emphasized in the lead paragraph that the KGB had created a "Fifth Directorate" to conduct ideological counterintelligence operations. "The Fifth," under its redoubtable chief, General Filip Bobkov, designed operations against a generation of dissenters and activists, including Nobel-laureates Andrei Sakharov and Aleksandr Solzhenitsyn. These operations, according to KGB documents, included the placement of hundreds of articles in the world press denouncing Solzhenitsyn as an anti-Semite and Sakharov as insane.[10]

- In the early 1980s, then KGB boss Yuri Andropov told an East German colleague that Jewish activist Anatoly Shcharanskiy could not be released from a forced labor camp because "He will carry the flag for all the Jews. Stalin's anti-Semitic excesses have left these people with a big grievance against the Soviet state and they have powerful friends abroad. We cannot allow this at the moment."[11]

- According to a noted British journalist, the KGB never stopped labeling Muslim religious activists in Central Asia as Saudi or American agents. As late as 1989, the KGB was trying to portray the Islamic Renaissance Party in Uzbekistan as an arm of Saudi intelligence.[12]

Covert Action, Collection, and Analysis

The most that ever came from the KGB were the cryptic reports about the exile of a spy or connections between dissidents and some 'imperialist intelligence service.'

—*Gorbachev*, Memoirs *(p. 204)*

While the KGB had a far larger presence overseas than other countries' intelligence services, its analytical component was far smaller and weaker than other major services. According to Soviet defectors, the Directorate of Intelligence Analysis (RI) had a staff of fewer than 250 people, and was primarily responsible for completing and editing intelligence reports from the field, rather than producing finished analysis. Important intelligence information was passed by KGB residencies directly to the Central Committee staff. These *Instantsiya*—Russian for "authority"—cables from the field were analyzed and consumed by the leadership without any input from intelligence professionals.

The KGB came by this institutional deformity historically. Stalin read agents' reports and told his intelligence chiefs not to bother him with analysis. According to one such report, Stalin said the price of wool in Germany would be the key indicator of Hitler's preparations for an invasion of the Soviet Union. Stalin argued that the German Army would begin buying wool for winter coats in the year before an invasion. Unfortunately for Stalin and millions of Red Army soldiers, Hitler believed Russia would be defeated before winter fell![13]

In the Gorbachev era, the KGB sent most of its sensitive intelligence reports directly to the Central Committee, without any leavening by analysts. According to the 1985 annual KGB Report, of 8,000 items of special political information (reports) sent to higher authorities, only 186 were analytical estimates of "special importance." The annual report noted that in the same period, the KGB provided the Soviet scientific establishment with 40,000 pieces of information and 12,000 model types for technical analysis. KGB Reports for the following years indicate a similar pattern.[14]

Some senior KGB analysts tended to Leninist positions, and flavored their finished intelligence analysis with paranoid comments on Western policies. Lieutenant General Nikolai Leonov, head of assessments for several years, described the West in the spring of 1991 as "vultures circling over the Soviet Union." America's avowed policy, the KGB general insisted, was to generate racial hatred and destroy the Soviet Union.[15]

Senior KGB officers valued active measures (covert action) over intelligence collection and analysis. According to a former KGB officer, the service's political intelligence officers were expected to spend 25 percent of their time on active measures.[16] Moreover, in the last years of the Cold War, covert actions were aimed at supporting fraternal Communist parties and slowing the democratization of Eastern Europe:

- The KGB continued to play 'postman' for the Soviet Communist Party into the 1990s, transmitting millions of dollars to foreign Communists. During the Gorbachev years, the service sent more than $10 million to the Communist Party of the United States.

- The most notorious Soviet active measure of the cold war was the effort to blame the United States for the development and spread of AIDS. This campaign, directed by Service A of the First Chief Directorate, received major coverage in some 40 Third World countries in 1987 alone. But in the West the AIDS covert action boomeranged to some extent against Moscow and Gorbachev; for example, it triggered a Congressional investigation into Soviet intelligence activities against the United States. In 1992, SVR Chief (now foreign minister) Yevgeniy Primakov apologized for the KGB's role in the campaign.

Treason and Corruption

The KGB was more immune than other Soviet institutions to corruption. A former KGB general noted in the last year of Soviet power, however, that the "moral sleaziness that is typical of our higher circles is reflected in the activities of the KGB as in a mirror." While bribetaking was not typical of the KGB, in the 1980s the KGB in the general's words produced "a whole constellation of traitors." Indeed, the KGB officer who ran American turncoat Aldrich Ames admitted in 1996, in his first interview by the Russian press, that the CIA "had dozens of agents inside the KGB and the GRU" and that the services were "shaken by periodic betrayals."[17]

An even better witness to KGB corruption was its former deputy director, Filip Bobkov. Bobkov, who completed 46 years of service in the KGB with the rank of Army General, admitted in his memoirs that the CIA had agents within the KGB's intelligence, counterintelligence, and communications directorates in the 1980s. Bobkov cited the case of a KGB counterintelligence officer working against the CIA station in Moscow who volunteered to work in place for the CIA despite the risk. It was, wrote Bobkov, "a bolt of lightning from the clear sky that one of our majors in counterintelligence was an agent of the CIA." (Major Sergei Vorontsov was betrayed by Ames and later executed.)[18]

In one of its final operations the KGB functioned not as intelligence service but rather as bank robbers: it was one of the main looters of the Communist Party's treasury. According to Central Committee documents published immediately after the abortive August 1991 putsch, the KGB helped the Central Committee export billions of dollars to the West to preclude possible seizure by a post-Communist Government. These documents show that in 1990 and 1991 the KGB established businesses in the West to hide money abroad for the party elite.[19]

Implications

The greatest threat to the KGB is its own past.

—*Christopher Andrew,* Inside the KGB

Russian reformers are haunted by the failure of the post-Stalinist reformers to liquidate the secret police. Following Stalin's death in 1953, fewer than a dozen KGB generals were shot for treason—not for maintaining the brutal system—while 38 other general officers were stripped of their rank. Russian historian Yevgeniya Albats, a specialist on the KGB, noted that "a Soviet Nuremberg was unthinkable, for like the German Nuremberg, it would have revealed the criminality of the ideology, the system in whose name these actions had been committed."[20]

Former components of the KGB—especially the SVR—have sought to preempt objective analyses of its history. A few KGB veterans have been selectively given access to relevant files from the 1930s and 1940s, but other scholars' efforts to obtain such access have been largely frustrated. The result has been—to quote a former KGB officer who was fired in 1990 for suggesting that his service be downsized—the prevalence of official histories in which "even the minutest successes used to become cast in solemn bronze."[21]

Back to the Future?

As God is my witness, we left worse Chekists in place.

—*Yevgeniya Albats,* The State Within a State

Some Russian reformers are concerned that their country has missed yet another opportunity

for a Russian Nuremberg. They note that although the Yeltsin administration has divided the Soviet KGB into several services (see Table 36.1), it has not reformed the component parts of this intelligence community.

Reformers such as Albats emphasize that leadership of the new intelligence and security services remains in the hands of KGB veterans—men molded in a "KGB mindset." Albats quotes a 1991 poll that found 77.6 percent of KGB were convinced that "saboteurs" were responsible for the collapse of the Soviet economy; 75 percent believed the CIA was responsible for ethnic unrest.[22] These men, she argued, are unlikely to initiate or welcome change in the structure of Russian intelligence. A number of factors support this assessment:

- The services report to the President and his entourage with little parliamentary oversight. The liberal civil servant appointed in 1994 by Presi-

---

Table 36.1

Plus CA Change: *The New Russian Intelligence Community*

In 1991, the KGB had a staff of 488,000, of whom 220,000 served in the Border Guards. The new Russian intelligence community was formed from various KGB components:

Foreign Intelligence:	The First Chief Directorate was transformed into the Foreign Intelligence Service (SVR).
Counterintelligence:	The Second and Third Chief Directorates (counterintelligence and military counterintelligence), along with surveillance and other anti-criminal elements of the KGB, became the Federal Security Service (FSB). In early 1998, they received authority to take control of the Chief Directorate of Border Guards.
Signals Intelligence:	The Eighth and Sixteenth Chief Directorates (Government Communications and SIGINT) were folded into the new Federal Agency for Government Communications and Information (FAPSI).
Leadership Protection:	The Ninth (Guards) Directorate became the Service for the Protection of the President (SBP) and the Government Protection Administration (GUO).

dent Yeltsin to oversee the SVR and FSB was recently fired quietly.

- The intelligence and counterintelligence services are approximately the same size as in 1991. The FSB, according to Russian news reports, has a staff of 80,000—four times that of the FBI.

- The KGB archives remain largely uninspected by historians; moreover, there has been no effort to reveal the names of informers.

- Not one former KGB officer has been convicted for crimes committed during the Soviet period. KGB officers who resigned in protest in the last years of the Gorbachev era have not been rehired and are still widely reviled as traitors.[23]

The reformers argue that without an accounting for the past, the security and intelligence establishment will recast itself in the model of Soviet intelligence. Actions by the new counterintelligence organization, the Federal Security Service (FSB) and the SVR seem to support this pessimistic assessment. For example:

- In December 1995, the FSB arrested a former Soviet naval officer on charges of treason and espionage for writing a history of military pollution in the Arctic. The officer was held for 13 months and was recently rearrested.

- On several other occasions over the past year, the FSB has detained and expelled American scientists accused of espionage against Russia. In every case, the U.S. scientist had been invited by a Russian institution.

- New legislation—strongly supported by the SVR and FSB—has tightly defined "state secrets" to include information about such critical issues as maps of the Moscow metro and water system.[24]

For Students of Russian Intelligence

Since 1990, reliable primary and memoir material on Soviet intelligence available to scholars has grown from a trickle to a flood. This information enables scholars, as well as intelligence professionals, to make more sophisticated judgments about the structure of the Russian intelligence community. It allows them to understand the political and intellectual baggage of the men who will conduct and direct Russian intelligence operations well into the next millennium. In a country where intelli-

gence and counterintelligence are far more a part of statecraft than in the West, this is critical. Five centuries before Soviet intelligence plotted the assassination of Trotsky and created an intelligence aparat to steal Western nuclear secrets, a Russian official told the British ambassador to the court of Ivan the Terrible: "Only spies come to Russia."

Questions for Further Discussion

1. Was the old KGB better at tradecraft or analysis?

2. Did the KGB substitute ideology for analytical capabilities?

3. Whatever happened to former KGB officers?

4. Do you agree with Pringle's idea that an accounting for past intelligence crimes will help prevent future abuses in newly emerging democracies?

Endnotes

1. *Rossiiskaya gazeta*, 20 December 1997, p. 1.
2. Two volumes of the history (*Ocherki Istorii Rossiskoi Veneshei Razvedki*) have been published, covering the period to 1931.
3. Yevgenia Albats, *The State Within a State: The KGB and Its Hold on Russia Past, Present and Future* (New York: Farrar, Straus and Giroux, 1994).
4. Vadim Bakatin, (*Farewell to the KGB*); Interview with Vadim Bakatin, *Isvestiya*, 2 January 1992; Mikhail Gorbachev, *Memoirs* (New York: Doubleday), 1996, pp. 401–402.
5. Top Secret KGB Annual Report for 1985, document No. 321-Ch/Ov dated 19 February 1986.
6. KGB World-wide Circular Cable 156/54, dated 1 February 1984, quoted in Christopher Andrew and Oleg Gordievsky, *Comrade Kryuchkov's Instructions* (Stanford: Stanford University Press, 1993), p. 6; Andrew and Gordievsky, *Inside the KGB* (New York: HarperCollins, 1990), p. 625; *Pravda*, 11 September 1987, p. 1.
7. KGB Memorandum 2278-f, 22 November 1982, and 1479-f, 19 July 1982, quoted in Albats, op. cit., pp. 180–181.
8. "Pervii rukovoditel Chekistkoi razvedki," ("First leaders of Cheka Intelligence") *Novosti Razvedki i Kontrrazyedki* 23 (1995), p. 3.
9. San Francisco 65 to Moscow, 10 February 1944 and 568 to Moscow, 7 November 1945. In *VENONA: Soviet Espionage and the American Response, 1939–1957* (Washington: U.S. Government Printing Office, 1996).
10. Filip Bobkov, *KGB i Vlast (The KGB and the Power)* (Moscow: Veteran MP, 1995), passim; Michael Scammell, ed., *The Solzhenitsyn Files* (Chicago: Edition q, 1995); KGB Annual Report of 1967.
11. Markus Wolf, *Man Without a Face* (New York: Random House, 1997), p. 219; Politburo Meeting of 22 June 1978, *Cold War International History Project* (Hereafter *CWIHP*) Vol. VIII, p. 119. Documents from the Communist Party archives indicate that Andropov in

1978 recommended to the Politburo that Shcharan-skiy receive a "stern sentence." A Soviet court gave the dissenter 15 years.

12. Dilip Hiro, *Between Marx and Mohammed* (London: HarperCollins, 1994), p. 173.
13. John Erickson, *The Road to Stalingrad* (London: Weidenfeld and Nicolson, 1975), p. 59. According to a Ministry of Foreign Affairs official, Stalin had George Kennan's "X" article in *Foreign Affairs* translated into Russian so that he could read it. *CWIHP*, Vol. VI–VII (Winter 1995–96), p. 272.
14. *KGB Annual Report for 1985*, No. 321-Ch/Ov, dated 19 February 1986.
15. *Sovetskaya Rossiya*, 26 April 1991, quoted in *Comrade Kryuchkov's Instructions*, op. cit., p. 219.
16. *Inside the KGB*, op. cit., p. 629.
17. Oleg Kalugin, "Confessions of a General Fallen from Grace," *Vechernaya Moskva*, 3 November 1990, pp. 3–4; Viktor Cherkashin, "Life Sentences and Executions," *Nezavisimoye Voennoye Obrozreniye*.
18. Bobkov, op. cit., p. 246.

19. "Partiya kommunistov na Puti Rynku" ("The Party of Communists on the Path to the Market" *Istoricheskii Arkhiv* No. 1 (1992), pp. 6–8; *Komsomolskya pravda*, 1 September 1991, p. 1. See also reporting by Jennifer Gould in the *Toronto Star*, 13 November 1993.
20. Albats, op. cit., pp. 114, 119.
21. Mikhail Lubimov, formerly KGB resident in Denmark, in *Moscow News*, No. 9.
22. Albats, op. cit., pp. 220–221. The survey was published following the August 1991 putsch in *Moskovskoi novosti*, 3 November 1991.
23. Alexander Rahr, "The Revival of a Strong KGB," *RFE/RL Research Report*, Vol. 11, 14 May 1993, pp. 74–79.
24. *Obshchaya gazeta*, 19 January 1998. ✦

Reprinted with permission from Robert W. Pringle, "The Heritage and Future of Russian Intelligence," *International Journal of Intelligence and Counterintelligence* 9 (January 1994): 12–21.

37

Controlling Intelligence in New Democracies

Thomas C. Bruneau

What happens to the internal security and intelligence apparatus when democratic forces overwhelm dictatorships? If one topples the police state, what does one do with the secret police? In this essay, Bruneau describes an issue that is often overlooked in the literature on transitions to democracy: the reform of intelligence organizations and their role in fledgling democracies.

Consolidation of the new democracies that have emerged worldwide during the last decade and a half is the main political challenge facing political leaders in these countries and world leaders at the beginning of the twenty-first century. Democratic consolidation requires restructuring the economy and bringing the armed forces under civilian control.

Probably the most problematic issue in civil-military relations is control of the intelligence apparatus. This is due not only to the legacies of the prior, non-democratic, regimes in which the intelligence or security apparatus was a key element of control, and in which human rights abuses often followed, but also to the inherent tension everywhere between intelligence and democracy. Admiral Stansfield Turner, a former United States Director of Central Intelligence, succinctly defines this tension: "Secret agencies within democratic governments are anachronisms, because popular controls break down when citizens cannot know everything their government is doing."[1]

Any discussion of control and intelligence is difficult, for several reasons. First, the terms and concepts associated with intelligence are not agreed upon and are ambiguous. Second, much about intelligence is secret; knowledge is power and those who hold it want to keep it secret. Intelligence professionals constitute a special club, even within their own militaries or civilian organizations. They

minimize the knowledge outsiders have about them and their activities. Third, little has been written about intelligence and democratization. Much of the good material on intelligence and democracy pertains to the established democracies, such as Great Britain, France, and the United States, where the goal is to reiterate the need to control the intelligence apparatus lest it undermine the democracy.[2] Consequently, the purpose here is to help demythologize intelligence in new democracies by introducing some key issues in the structures and processes of doing intelligence, and thereby provide a foundation for those who want to initiate firmer control of their intelligence apparatuses.

The Counterintelligence State

In virtually all authoritarian regimes (including the former Soviet bloc) the intelligence apparatus is a key element for maintaining power. These regimes are based on something other than democratic legitimacy exercised through free elections. They rely on organizations to identify domestic opponents, neutralize opposition to the government, and seek through a variety of means, including a controlled media, to generate at least domestic apathy. In most cases, these organizations are security services. Precisely because of this heavy reliance and its centrality to power, the intelligence apparatus grows in size and power, with the result that it is largely autonomous even within authoritarian regimes.[3] In these countries, intelligence means mainly counterintelligence, that is, protecting the state's secrets from outsiders, meaning anyone outside the central core of power. And, as almost anything can be defined as a state secret, the scope of that which is to be controlled is immense. While in most instances, the intelligence service rhetorically links internal opposition to putative foreign enemies, the overwhelming focus of the intelligence service in most countries is domestic opposition and not other states.[4]

Among the many negative legacies of the intelligence services in new democracies, probably the most negative is their involvement in human rights abuses. The information they gather on their own people is at times obtained through abusive methods and used in arbitrary and violent means to eliminate domestic opposition. They are, in short, integrally associated with the human rights abuses that characterize most authoritarian regimes most of the time. While the overall popular legacy is negative, there is little awareness of intelligence functions and organizations. Most civilian politicians, let alone the public at large, do not know enough about intelligence to be able to have an informed opinion about it. In some newly democratic countries there is real concern that the intelligence apparatus has accumulated, and is still collecting, information that could be used against average civilians and politicians. Thus, the lack of information about intelligence communities is often combined with fear, which perpetuates the lack of information.

The Challenge of Democratic Consolidation

Despite scholarly efforts to develop models of democratic transitions, these are largely sui generis and defy generalization. Studies have shown that authoritarian regimes have collapsed due to their successes as well as their failures, or the actions or inaction by domestic elites or foreigners. But, in any case, power finally passes on to more or less popularly elected civilians.[5] Transitions mainly allow new, democratic regimes to emerge, but they do not necessarily result in stable democratic regimes.

Today, the main focus is on democratic consolidation because it reflects the idea that a new regime's structures and processes are becoming stable. That is, a democratic regime is consolidated when the elites and the masses accept it as "the only game in town."[6] This acceptance is no easy task, especially when considering the basic characteristics for a regime to be termed democratic. A standard definition of contemporary democracy is:

> Modern political democracy is a system of governance in which rulers are held accountable for their actions in the public realm by citizens, acting indirectly through the competition and cooperation of their elected representatives.[7]

For accountability to function minimal conditions of procedure are necessary. These include the seven common fundamental factors ensuring free and fair elections such as freedom of speech, association, running for office, and the like, which constitute a corpus of guarantees requiring a supportive culture to survive. As more countries consolidate their new democracies, scholars have identified a further defining characteristic: the requirement that no unelected body, such as a council of mullahs or a military revolutionary council, has authority over the popularly elected officials.

A political situation in which these guarantees function is obviously very far from the structures and culture of the predecessor authoritarian regime. Major challenges are found in both the lack of recent governmental experience with democracy, and the general population's lacking a background in these new structures and processes. Also, in most cases, these countries are confronting economic problems, often accompanied by social disruption. Because democracy is a very demanding political system for elites and average citizens, both should be involved for it to function well. New democracies are very tentative. The issue is how to develop trust and transparency in the context of the legacy of authoritarianism. At times, the intelligence apparatus is not under government control, but instead has power over civilian officials. This seems to be the case in Russia today.[8] An elected government that does not control intelligence is, by definition, not a consolidated democracy.

The Meaning of Intelligence

The scope and diversity of intelligence leads to disagreement on its meaning.[9] Intelligence is defined mainly by process. That is, the process of gathering and using information for some purpose. Since processes are varied, as are the sources of information and their ends, much is of necessity left vague. Most discussions within the intelligence community center on tradecraft; the "how to" of sources, methods, and analysis rather than the "what is?" Further, the intelligence community, either by design or habit, is characterized by vagueness and ambiguity. This attitude or approach is probably intentional: to not convey information. An awareness of intelligence and its limits leads to an even greater appreciation that not everything is knowable, let alone known. Moreover, intelligence officers are trained to collect information and not to provide it, except to very few of their superiors with a need to know. This tendency pervades the whole field of intelligence: they are professionals in intelligence; information is their vocation. To give it away makes no sense, unless intended as disinformation.

In focusing on the new democracies, a broad definition of intelligence must be used in order to convey the scope of what it can include, which is extremely broad.[10] Glenn P. Hastedt in *Controlling Intelligence* states succinctly: "The four elements of intelligence are clandestine collection, analysis and estimates, covert action, and counterintelligence."[11] Loch K. Johnson elaborates this synthesis:

> Intelligence commonly encompasses two broad meanings. First, the secret agencies acquire and interpret information about threats and opportunities that confront the nation, in an imperfect attempt to reduce the gaps and ambiguities that plague open sources of knowledge about the world. A nation especially seeks secret information to help it prevail in times of war, with as few casualties as possible. Second, based on information derived from denied and open sources, policymakers call upon their intelligence agencies to shield the nation against harm (counterintelligence) while advancing its interests

through the secret manipulation of foreign events and personalities (covert action). Intelligence thus involves both information and response.[12]

Intelligence also refers to the organization collecting the information and the information collected. Because all individuals and organizations collect and process information, this information in itself is not the defining characteristic. Instead, the key characteristics are that these functions are centered in and intended for the state, and they are secret. This knowledge thus has a dual nature; it is information but it is secret information used by the state in potential or real conflicts.

Obviously not every country has robust capabilities in all four intelligence functions, but the fact that they exist, that any nation has these capabilities, means that intelligence must be understood within a global framework. Intelligence, created to defend the state must also take into consideration the instruments potential enemies have available, along with the fact that they will be involved in, or even the target of, collection and covert action.

Intelligence and Democracy

All countries have an intelligence apparatus of some scope and capability. The question for new democracies is: what kind of intelligence do they need and how can it be controlled? While the challenge is especially severe in the new democracies, democratic control of intelligence is a challenge everywhere for at least four reasons. First, as Pat Holt states, "Secrecy is the enemy of democracy."[13] Why? Because secrecy encourages abuse. If there is secrecy how can there be accountability, the operative mechanism of democracy? Because intelligence organizations are secret they themselves can avoid the checks and balances on which democracy is based. Second, intelligence agencies are not only secret but they also collect and analyze information, and information means power. Intelligence organizations take on agendas and purposes of their own. Secrecy limits public scrutiny. Peter Gill uses the analogy of the "Gore-Tex" state to illustrate the degree of domestic penetration by the security intelligence services. Information flows in one direction and not two directions: to the intelligence services and not from them to state and society.[14] Intelligence may be autonomous from state control and, through the use of information that others do not have, can determine policy. Two additional perceptual or behavioral elements, beyond secrecy and the unique control of information, hinder democratic control of intelligence organizations. Intelligence agents and organizations routinely break laws abroad. Indeed, in most cases they do not admit to who they are or for whom they work. Further, spying is illegal everywhere. Intelligence managers provide undeclared funds to foreign nationals as agents and authors of articles, tap phones, steal documents, and the like, all of which are illegal. There may be a problem in making the distinction breaking laws abroad and not breaking them at home. The self-justification is that intelligence is critical to defense of the nation. According to Peter Wright, "It [intelligence] is a constant war, and you face a constantly shifting target."[15] It is up to the intelligence organizations to root out spies, domestic and foreign, who are threats to the nation. They may easily perceive that they, more than anyone else, really know what is going on; how dangerous the threat really is.

In view of the difficulty everywhere to control intelligence, and considering the background in most new democracies, what are the choices to be made and what are the implications of different options for democratic control? Initially, and this is a requirement regarding the armed forces in general, democracies must establish a clear and comprehensive legal framework. Intelligence is "slippery." If the legal framework is not clear and explicit, intelligence agencies can never be brought under control. The legal framework must emerge from democratic structures and processes, and must seek to ensure continuation in the area of intelligence of the democratic values that they seek to promote. In South Africa, for example, soon after the transition to majority rule in 1994, the government initiated, through the legislative process, reform of the intelligence apparatus. This involved three major bills in parliament, which clearly defined and restructured the intelligence system.[16] In Brazil, it took considerably longer after the transition to civilian government in 1985; indeed, it was only in 1999 that the ABIN (Brazilian Intelligence Agency) was created to replace the authoritarian regime's National Intelligence Service (SIN). The Brazilian Congress played a central role in the creation of ABIN, and the legislation does provide a legal basis for civilian control of intelligence.[17] But in 2000, an upheaval took place after allegations of misuse of the Brazilian intelligence apparatus.

There are three general decisions to be made regarding intelligence, which should be stipulated, in this clear and explicit legal framework. The first choice is to determine which of the four intelligence functions will be implemented and how much of the country's resources will be allocated to them. The former part of the question can be answered only by assessing the global and regional situation, alliances, recent history, and available resources. The latter part of the question is a political decision.

How much is intelligence worth? Obviously it is worth a great deal if it provides the nation with the means to maintain its independence in the face of a hostile neighbor. Intelligence also can be valuable in lieu of larger forces. By allowing a country to focus its forces on the most serious threats, it thereby minimizes redundancy and higher operational costs. But assessing its real worth requires a political decision. The mere fact of having a certain level of intelligence capability may not avoid hostile intentions and actions. Its relationship with other, more powerful, countries that may share intelligence capabilities with it is also a factor. These decisions cannot be made in a vacuum; they should be integrated into an overall framework for defense decisionmaking. But the main determinant must be an analysis of what the nation requires and how much it is willing to pay for it. This is, of course, a general issue in civil-military relations.

Making these decisions and achieving coordination is consistently the task of the top level of the executive branch of government. In the United States, the National Security Council holds this responsibility. In Brazil, after the most recent reforms, it is the Secretariat of Institutional Security directly under the president. In South Africa, after the reforms in the mid-1990s, the National Intelligence Coordinating Committee reports directly to the president and the cabinet.

The second major choice concerns the intelligence balance between civilian and military organizations, both in terms of production (collection and analysis) and consumption. In most countries, intelligence has been a military monopoly. During democratic consolidation decisions must be made as to whether military intelligence should be replaced in whole or in part by new civilian organizations. In short, should the military have responsibilities only in military intelligence, and civilians assume responsibility in strategic intelligence and counterintelligence? Equally important is intelligence consumption. To whom is the intelligence product distributed? Only the president of the country, his director for intelligence, members of the cabinet such as Interior; the military, the congress, who else? Obviously, access to the information, and the form in which it is made available, has great implications for the potential power of those who receive it. The 1996 Guatemala peace agreement, the "Accord on Strengthening of Civil Power and the Function of the Army in a Democratic Society," stipulated that "a civil department of intelligence and analysis of information" would be created. By April 2000 the new structure, which included one military and two civilian intelligence organizations, had been defined, but implementa-tion was delayed due to the failure of the referendum on constitutional revisions later in the year.

A sub-theme of the balance between civilian and military institutions is the issue of internal and external intelligence. Does the same organization have responsibility for domestic (mainly counterintelligence) as well as foreign intelligence? If these functions are fused, what controls prevent their use for personal political purposes? In most democracies the functions are separate. In the United States, the Federal Bureau of Investigation (FBI) handles counterintelligence within the United States, while the Central Intelligence Agency (CIA) has performed both functions outside the country. In most European democracies the functions are divided between counterintelligence and foreign intelligence, the organizations doing their tasks wherever necessary, at home or abroad. Because they are focused mainly internally, this has not been much of an issue in most of the new democracies. Domestic intelligence is notably cheap in comparison to external intelligence, which most countries cannot afford to do professionally.

The third choice concerns the relationship between intelligence and policy. This also logically involves the issue of coordination among the intelligence organizations. Is all intelligence to be formally coordinated by a director of central intelligence, as in the United States, but, because the DCI is not in the cabinet, separate from policy? Or, is it separate, as with MI5 and MI6 in Great Britain? But, since both are located within the UK Foreign Office, intelligence is closely linked with policy.

The main issue here concerns an ongoing debate about the implications when objective intelligence analysis is closely linked to policy, versus the supposed loss of efficiency by having intelligence that is not linked. There are great variations in how democracies handle this issue,[18] depending on a country's political traditions and structures. But the underlying issue is whether intelligence is policy-relevant but not policy-driven. One critique of U.S. covert action is that these actions all fuse within the CIA. Rather than objectively providing intelligence, the Agency develops and conducts the policy, and largely evaluates its success. Glenn Hastedt, who has published one of the few books on controlling intelligence, makes his position explicit on this issue: "The purpose of intelligence is to inform and warn policy-makers. The choice of what to do lies with the policy-maker. If intelligence is brought into too close a contact with policy making it runs the risk of being corrupted."[19] It is too early to determine how the new democracies are dealing with this issue since they are still in the process of defining and implementing new structures and processes in the (often newly created) ministries of defense and the intelligence organizations. Argentina is probably the furthest along in the implementation of new structures in both areas, but even here the structures are still changing substantially and much remains personality-driven.[20]

All three decisions hold implications for democratic control over intelligence. The first choice, about intelligence functions, has obvious implications especially regarding counterintelligence: to include or exclude it. The second, civilian vs. military location of the intelligence function, has implications in terms of civilian control over the armed forces, and then civilian control over intelligence. Third, a very close link with policy can make intelligence less a function of information gathering and analysis, and more a tool used by political leaders to retain power. In the cases with which I am most familiar—Argentina, Brazil, Guatemala, and South Africa—the research suggests that they are dealing well with decisions one and two, but number three remains elusive.

Explicit Control Over Intelligence

A common mechanism of controlling intelligence is its separation into different agencies. Policymakers should prevent any single agency from having a monopoly on intelligence, as is done in the United States. A possible arrangement is the maintenance of separate intelligence organizations for each of the armed forces and the police, and separate organizations for domestic and foreign intelligence. This proliferation of organizations may or may not be efficient, because the different agencies are likely to battle among themselves, but it eliminates the chances of monopoly by any single organization or individual and creates opportunities for more democratic control. Most countries that are seeking to reform their intelligence structures have moved in this direction. The four cited previously, as well as others with which I am familiar in Europe and Central America, have created civilian intelligence organizations to complement (even compete with) the military intelligence organizations. In Brazil and Guatemala, for example, there are two civilian organizations.

A second mechanism for democratic control is oversight. Does anyone have oversight over intelligence, or does the apparatus alone have responsibility for monitoring its own performance? The latter option is extremely dangerous. In the United States oversight has expanded to the current situation where the intelligence agencies have inspectors general, the executive has oversight bodies, and the two houses of Congress have legislative oversight committees.[21] In Great Britain, oversight remains very limited, but democratic institutions are hallowed. In countries that are seeking to consolidate their democracies, if intelligence is to be under democratic civilian control, oversight is required. How far it extends, and under what terms it operates, will vary tremendously. Oversight has immediate implications for both control and popular support for intelligence.

Since knowledge equals power, specifying who has access to the intelligence and in what form is important. Is it limited to only the military or do civilians in the executive branch also have access? What about the legislature? Do any or all of them have access, even prior to operations such as covert actions? This issue concerns not just immediate distribution of intelligence (which here extends to covert actions as well) but the general availability of information after a certain period of time. The possibility of wider distribution also holds implications for control. If the agencies know that in the future the files will be opened for public scrutiny, they must be careful of their behavior.

An inherent dilemma is the trade-off between democratic control over intelligence and the effectiveness of an intelligence apparatus doing its job to defend the nation. This dilemma can be reduced to the tension between accountability, which requires transparency, and the intelligence function, which requires secrecy. For example, does legislative oversight result in officers or agents being uncovered? Democracies wrestle with this dilemma constantly and there is no easy or sure solution. Rather, constant attention and adjustment are required. In discussing legislative oversight, the issue of the reliability or sense of responsibility of legislators always comes up. Making an a priori judgment on this issue is very difficult, but it should be noted that since the imposition of legislative oversight in the United States in the 1970s, there have been far fewer cases of the releasing of classified information by members of Congress or their staffs than of leaks from the Executive branch. The issue is not just oversight, but its implementation, and by whom.

The possibility exists that democratically elected civilians may not in fact be interested in controlling the intelligence apparatus in new democracies. In virtually all of these countries, elections are a new and relatively fragile means of determining who has power. Even in old and stable democracies leaders often prefer "plausible deniability" rather than acknowledged access to the information required to control a potentially controversial or dangerous organization or operation.[22] Logically this would be even more the case in newer democracies. First, the politicians may be afraid of antagonizing the intelligence apparatus through efforts to control it because the security organization might have something embarrassing on them. Second, they may be afraid because the intelligence organization might have previously engaged in arbitrary and violent actions, and the politicians are not sure that a corner has been turned. Third, there are probably no votes to be won in attempting to control an organization that most people either don't know about or want to ignore.

Generally, the issue of democratic control of intelligence can be profitably discussed only in those countries that have already sorted out the more general issues of civilian control of the military, and have begun to institutionalize the structures and processes for this control. In the others, the environment remains too opaque or tense for open discussion of intelligence organizations and oversight. Intelligence is nowhere the first issue the new civilian leadership wants to confront.

Toward Democratic Control of Intelligence

For those countries that want to begin to exert democratic civilian control over the intelligence apparatus several tasks must be undertaken. These actions resemble those of asserting general civilian control over the military, but are more acute due to secrecy and the penetration of state and society through the counterintelligence function.[23] The tasks that follow are not prioritized, and should instead be pursued simultaneously. They concern civilian competence, public interest and then pressure, and the profession of intelligence.

A. The first task is to motivate civilians to learn about intelligence so they can control it. In most authoritarian regimes intelligence is monopolized by the military and civilians have little or no role whatsoever. These countries will be unable to control intelligence unless they prepare civilians to learn enough to both understand what intelligence is all about and to achieve some degree of cooperation, if not respect, from the intelligence professionals. This process is not easy, but it has to start somewhere. It should begin with the formal and public commitment by a government to reviewing intelligence toward the goal of establishing a new policy. In Argentina, Brazil, Guatemala, and South Africa, this happened, due mainly to political and institutional bargains resulting from democratic transitions. The commitment must also open the possibility for civilian positions in intelligence. Otherwise, as in general civil-military relations, civilians will not come forward if they cannot anticipate viable careers. Civilians can then begin to learn about intelligence by reading the unclassified literature from several countries, and taking advantage of co-operative training arrangements in intelligence with other nations. (For example, the Naval Postgraduate School in Monterey, California, offered a week-long seminar specifically on this topic in Argentina in September 1998, and corresponds regularly with civilian specialists in intelligence in the four countries just noted. The school also offers a semester-long course on the topic of "Intelligence and Democracy" in a masters' degree program.)

B. The second, broader task is to encourage a political culture which supports the legitimate role of intelligence in a democracy but does not allow it to run rampant. Former Defense Secretary James A. Schlesinger, also a former Director of Central Intelligence, has made this point: "[T]o preserve secrecy, especially in a democracy, security must be part of an accepted pattern of behavior outside of government and inside."[24] The responsibility must go in both directions: from control of intelligence by democratically-elected civilians but from them as well a pledge to not release classified information for personal or political reasons.

How can this culture be encouraged? As in the general case of democratic civil-military relations, by generating a public debate. The challenge is to break through the current public apathy toward or fear of intelligence by initiating the debate. In some older democracies, including Canada, France, Great Britain, and the United States, a fairly regular debate is stimulated by non-governmental organizations (NGOs) and the media, which are periodically galvanized by intelligence fiascoes that become public. The role of the media is crucial, and their awareness of intelligence can be encouraged in the same manner as the public. Again, the debate can be stimulated by the politicians' commitment to establish a policy on intelligence. Such a debate has been initiated in a few of the newer democracies. The Peace Accords in Guatemala between the government and the guerrillas signed in December 1996 stipulated, in several sections, that intelligence would be transformed and put under civilian oversight. These commitments led to public seminars on intelligence, publications by NGOs, and articles in the newspapers.[25] In Argentina, a debate was initiated by a small number of civilians realizing that democratic consolidation requires civilian control over intelligence.[26] And, more recently, the Brazilian government's commitment to revise the intelligence system has generated a public debate.[27] This debate serves numerous important functions: (a) It demythologizes intelligence, thereby allowing outsiders to more realistically assess its necessity and value to the country; (b) it creates legitimate positions for civilians who want to become intelligence specialists; and (c) it puts pressure on the government to be more transparent. International

NGOs are very willing to assist countries in generating this debate.[28]

C. The third task is not about civilians or the public in general, but concerns the selection, training, and overall preparation of intelligence professionals: those who specialize as intelligence officers working for the state. The focus on intelligence as a profession is particularly apt because, more than any other single profession, its practitioners are controlled, even in a democracy, by professional norms more than outside controls (such as oversight).[29] In contrast, in addition to their self-policing or ethic, doctors are regulated by the legal system and licensing boards, lawyers by the legal system and bar associations, politicians by the legal system and elections, and the armed forces by budgets, promotions, and myriad civilian control mechanisms. But, in the last analysis, intelligence professionals are controlled only by the external structures and processes noted above, if that. They are regularly granted the impunity to break laws abroad and have tremendous leeway within their own country and organization. Secrecy allows them to operate with an unusual amount of autonomy. They are also ensconced in a bureaucracy with other like-minded personnel, develop a closed-club mentality, and are usually very suspicious of outsiders, including at times their superiors.

Intelligence as a Profession

A profession can be defined in terms of three criteria: expertise, corporateness, and responsibility.[30] In the case of intelligence, the criteria are as follows:

First, "expertise," as defined in line with the four intelligence functions defined earlier: collection, analysis, counterintelligence, and covert action. The range of what intelligence professionals do is extremely diverse. What unifies them, or characterizes them as intelligence professionals, is secrecy. And, unlike other professions, which feature certain limited aspects of patient or client privacy or privilege, the intelligence professional is defined by secrecy. (The military profession also has elements of secrecy but these pertain mainly to intelligence.) In reference to covert action, one of America's foremost intelligence professionals, the late Richard M. Bissell Jr., stated:

> The professional competence of a clandestine service consists of, and is measured by, its ability to carry out operations secretly (or deniably), much as lawyers' competence consists in their ability to win cases, and doctors' in their ability to prevent or treat illness. The clandestine service may number among its members brilliant

journalists, able warriors, and superior political analysts, but the professional skill for which, presumably, they are hired is the ability to organize and conduct operations covertly. This is a rather specialized skill not widely found outside of intelligence and internal security services.[31]

And, in reference to counterintelligence, Peter Wright, one of Britain's foremost intelligence professionals, commented:

> The profession of intelligence is a solitary one. There is camaraderie, of course, but in the end you are alone with your secrets. You live and work at a feverish pitch of excitement, dependent always on the help of your colleagues. But you always move on, whether to a new branch or department, or to a new operation. And when you move on, you inherit new secrets which subtly divorce you from those you have worked with before. Contacts, especially with the outside world, are casual, since the largest part of yourself cannot be shared.[32]

Their expertise is thus diverse, as is intelligence itself, and the defining characteristic of the profession is secrecy.

Second, "corporateness," as defined by intelligence officers' access to secret systems, documents, information, sources, and operations. As doctors enter the profession through boards, internships, and residencies; professors by comprehensive examinations and Ph.D. dissertations; and lawyers by bar exams, intelligence professionals enter via security clearances. Clearances are the control mechanism for entry into and continuance in the profession. There are few common educational requirements for intelligence professionals, even among various intelligence organizations within one country, and little else defines corporate identity but access to classified information.[33] In intelligence everything is compartmented; different levels of clearances, plus the need to know, determine access. Even officers with similarly high clearances do not, and are not supposed to, discuss information unless they have "need to know," in terms of current projects and responsibilities. Security clearances and secretly working together on secret information and projects create identification as members of a unique club. A certain arrogance, or sense of impunity may also develop, since if nobody else knows, then how can those who don't know control those who do?

Third, the "responsibility" of the intelligence professional is to serve in defense of the state. But consideration of the first two criteria (expertise in secret matters and access via security clearances), leads inexorably to a profession which largely governs itself according to its own definition of responsibility. In new democracies, this situation is doubly serious, because the state was not previously accountable to the general population and the intelligence agents may not have been responsible even to the small group controlling the state. Who can know and who is to control? The sense of responsibility is incredibly important: even in stable democracies enough incidents come to light to cause concern that the officers are not serving the state. Or that they are serving it in limited organizational terms and not in accordance with those of the democratically-elected political leadership. This sense is captured in a quote from the CIA's former counterintelligence chief, James Angleton, when testifying before Congress on why the Agency had not destroyed stocks of a toxic poison: "It is inconceivable that a secret intelligence arm of the government has to comply with all the overt orders of the government."[34] Accommodating this attitude with the procedures and culture of democracy is difficult.

To Change a Profession

Major efforts must be made in the new democracies to promote and inculcate a sense of professional responsibility by making intelligence officers and agencies accountable to the state via the democratically elected leaders. How to do this? By committing great attention and resources to recruitment and training of professionals and requiring that they remain involved in the larger polity and society. The specifics of this prescription have to be defined separately for each nation. One of the biggest difficulties in achieving this result is that governments will most easily recruit retired military men and women into civilian intelligence positions. They may have taken off the uniform, but their service attitudes remain. But if new, non-military personnel cannot be found, then can the ethic of responsibility be changed? In most countries little explicit attention is given to promoting this ethic.[35] In the older democracies, the larger society supports responsibility to the democratic state, and political institutions are generally not under question, so there is less need to promote the responsibility ethic. In newer democracies, the need to promote it is clear, as is promoting an open debate on intelligence, interesting civilians in the field.[36] Apparently, none of the new democracies has yet focused on changing the profession. But much dealing with intelligence is secret, and outsiders would be unlikely to know about reforms in training. Or, better stated, those who know are not likely to divulge the information.

A Necessary Function

All nations engage in intelligence activities at one scale or another; they must as other countries do. No nation can afford to not know what is going on outside and inside its borders, and if necessary counter other countries' efforts to influence developments in that country. The intelligence services of most authoritarian regimes are central to their survival, usually in the most negative manner imaginable. In the midst of democratic consolidation, seeking to ensure democratic control over intelligence is both necessary and extremely difficult. Yet, in many countries there is still virtually no public recognition of this need. But, without decisive action an authoritarian intelligence apparatus will remain a state within a state and prevent democratic consolidation. Like all else in civil-military relations, the many challenges require continual efforts on the part of civilians and officers to achieve the most appropriate balance of efficiency and transparency for the country. Today, however, a small but significant group of countries have undertaken to reform their intelligence systems and generated a public debate on the matter. This is an area in which international assistance is and should remain available.

Questions for Further Discussion

1. What is a counterintelligence state?

2. What are the conditions necessary for democracies to control intelligence organizations?

3. What special challenges do new democracies face when it comes to intelligence oversight and control?

4. How might the creations of an "intelligence profession" help to protect emerging democracies?

Endnotes

1. Admiral Stansfield Turner, *Secrecy and Democracy: The CIA in Transition* (Boston: Houghton Mifflin, 1985), p. 3. I make a few references to this book for several reasons. Turner was Director of Central Intelligence from 1977 to 1981 and, as such, head of the largest intelligence community in the world. The period was characterized by the implementation of changes in the system due to the exposés after the Watergate scandal and the alleged assassination attempts of foreign leaders resulting in congressional hearings and the imposition of congressional oversight. And Turner, a complete outsider to the community himself working for an outsider President, is candid about the intelligence agents as professionals and the bureaucratic nature of the intelligence community. As an unabash-

edly critical manager of the intelligence community in a time of great turbulence, he conveys the sense of control that is the focus of this paper. It must be noted that he was very unpopular with large sectors of the community. My citing him does not mean I agree with everything he says in the book.

2. The literature on intelligence is routinely broken down into four categories: memoirs of retired intelligence professionals; exposés by disgruntled former professionals, journalists, and activists; government reports, studies, and documents; and academic studies. Of these four categories only the last is largely objective. The other three are motivated by personal, partisan, or national goals, and thus contain some kind of bias or "agenda." The literature in any one category is not so abundant that an interested student can dispense with material in any single category. Much material on the United States and Russia is available in books or journal articles, less on European democracies and South Africa, and very little on the new democracies. The Internet has made available sources of information on aspects of intelligence throughout the world. To the best of my knowledge, however, no literature provides the background and discussion of issues in which to locate this current Internet information on the new democracies. Further, its being found on the Internet does not guarantee that it is accurate. In sum, the available material remains sketchy and an overall conceptual framework has yet to be written.

3. For excellent insights into the scope and power of intelligence in a "typical" authoritarian regime see Alfred Stepan, *Rethinking Military Politics: Brazil and the Southern Cone* (Princeton, NJ: Princeton University Press, 1988), pp. 19–20, where he compares the prerogatives of the Brazilian National Security Service (SNI) to the intelligence organizations in several established democracies.

4. In the USSR, and now Russia, scholars have coined the term "counterintelligence state" to capture the sense of its pervasiveness. Waller defines it as follows: "The counterintelligence state is characterized by the presence of a large, elite force acting as the watchdog of a security defined so broadly and arbitrarily that the state must maintain an enormous vigilance and enforcement apparatus far out of proportion to the needs of a real democracy, even one as unstable as that of Russia. This apparatus is not accountable to the public and enjoys immense police powers with few checks against it. The powers are not designed to protect the rights of the individual, despite rhetoric to the contrary, but to protect the privileges of the ruling class and the Chekist organs themselves." J. Michael Waller, *Secret Empire: The KGB in Russia Today* (Boulder: Westview Press, 1994), p. 13. The original conceptualization was by John J. Dziak, *Chekisty: A History of the KGB* (Lexington: Lexington Books, 1988).

5. Thus, rather than explanation one of the most highly regarded students of Comparative Politics comes up with "factors" explaining transitions. See Samuel Huntington, *The Third Wave Democratization in the Late Twentieth Century* (Norman: University of Oklahoma Press, 1991).

6. Among other sources on this approach, see the following. John Higley and Richard Gunther, eds., *Elites and Democratic Consolidation in Latin America and Southern Europe* (Cambridge: Cambridge University Press, 1992), pp. 3–4, and Juan J. Linz and Alfred Stepan, *Problems of Democratic Transition and Consolidation: Southern Europe, South America, and Post-Commu-*

nist Europe (Baltimore: Johns Hopkins University Press, 1996), pp. 5–6.

7. Philippe C. Schmitter and Terry Lynn Karl, "What Democracy Is ... and Is Not," in Larry Diamond and Marc F. Plattner, eds., *The Global Resurgence of Democracy* (Baltimore: Johns Hopkins University Press, 1993), p. 40.

8. According to Waller, the KGB, or its successors, remain very powerful. "Indeed, given the lack of meaningful controls over them, the security organs may be considered Russia's fourth branch of government if not its core." Waller, 1994, p. 296. See also pp. 219–220. This seems to be the general consensus regarding Russia. For example, Knight states: "Real, lasting democracy is incompatible with a security apparatus wielding the power and influence that it still holds in Russia." Amy Knight, *Spies Without Cloaks: The KGB's Successors* (Princeton, NJ: Princeton University Press, 1996), p. 244. With Vladimir Putin now in power some analysts consider that the intelligence apparatus has captured the state. Author's discussions with informed Russians and experts on Russia.

9. For a discussion of different meanings, see Glenn Hastedt, "Controlling Intelligence: Defining the Problem," in Glenn Hastedt, ed., *Controlling Intelligence* (London: Frank Cass, 1991), p. 68.

10. For example, the CIA in its unclassified "A Consumer's Guide to Intelligence" describes only sources and analysis. It does not include the more controversial intelligence functions of counterintelligence and covert action, which, in contrast, are the focus of books in the memoir and exposé categories. This handbook, dated July 1995, was prepared by the Public Affairs Staff, and is coded PAS 95-00010.

11. Hastedt, 1991, p. 6.

12. Loch K. Johnson, *Secret Agencies: U.S. Intelligence in a Hostile World* (New Haven: Yale University Press, 1996), p. 119.

13. Pat M. Holt, *Secret Intelligence and Public Policy: A Dilemma of Democracy* (Washington: CQ Press, 1995), p. 3.

14. Gill 1993, pp. 79–82.

15. Peter Wright, *Spycatcher: The Candid Autobiography of a Senior Intelligence Officer* (New York: Viking, 1987), p. 169.

16. For details see Shaun McCarthy, "South Africa's Intelligence Reformation," in *International Journal of Intelligence and Counterintelligence*, Vol. 9, #1 (Spring 1996), pp. 63–71.

17. Author's interviews in Brasilia, including with deputies and senators, during the week of 8 August 1999. See also, Larry Rohter, "Spy Agency in Brazil Is Accused of Abuses," *New York Times*, 14 December 2000, p. A15.

18. The main options are nicely summarized in Johnson, 1996, pp. 129–131. The Director of Central Intelligence may not in fact be able to coordinate all intelligence since he does not control the budgets for the larger and more expensive collection and analysis assets.

19. Hastedt, 1991, p. 10. For the comments on covert action, see Admiral Stansfield Turner, 1985, p. 174.

20. This assertion is based on the author's interviews in Buenos Aires regarding both the Ministry of Defense and the intelligence systems during the week of 3 April 2000.

21. For very positive comments, see Stansfield Turner, 1985, especially p. 132 and pp. 269–271. For the background and details on congressional oversight, see L.

Britt Snider, *Sharing Secrets With Lawmakers: Congress as a User of Intelligence* (CIA: Center for the Study of Intelligence, February 1997.)

22. The most famous recent instance of this was the "Iran-Contra" scandal during the Reagan administration. See, for example, Christopher Andrew, *For the President's Eyes Only: Secret Intelligence and the American Presidency from Washington to Bush* (New York: HarperCollins, 1995), pp. 478–493.

23. It should be noted that the similarity between intelligence and civil-military relations has been touched upon in Uri Bar-Joseph, *Intelligence Intervention in the Politics of Democratic States The United States, Israel, and Britain* (University Park, Pa: Pennsylvania State University Press, 1995). However, Bar-Joseph deals only with established democracies and thus has a very restricted view of the problems of civil-military relations. He does not deal with the especially difficult problems of controlling intelligence in new democracies.

24. Quoted in Adda Bozeman, "Political Intelligence in Non-Western Societies: Suggestions for Comparative Research," in Roy Godson, ed., *Comparing Foreign Intelligence: The U.S., the USSR, the U.K. & the Third World* (Washington: Pergamon-Brassey's, 1988), p. 133.

25. For one example of a major contribution to the debate see Fundacion Myrna Mack, "Hacia un Paradigma Democratico del Sistema de Inteligencia en Guatemala," Guatemala, Octubre de 1997.

26. An example here is Eduardo E. Estevez, "La Reformulación de la Inteligencia Estratégica: Bases para su Comprensión," Departamento de Posgrado, Facultad e Derecho y Ciencias Sociales, Universidad de Buenos Aires, Septiembre de 1997.

27. Larry Rohter, "Spy Agency In Brazil Is Accused Of Abuses."

28. The Federation of American Scientists, for example, publishes a "Secrecy & Government Bulletin," and is active internationally. See <http://www.fas.org/sgp>.

29. Glenn Hastedt's argument is that formal-legalistic controls have limited value in controlling intelligence and informal norms and values are extremely important. I agree, but he studies only the U.S., and at that, only the Directors of Central Intelligence. See Glenn Hastedt, "Controlling Intelligence: The Values of Intelligence Professionals," in Hastedt, 1991, pp. 97–112.

30. While the sociological literature on professions is huge, going back at least to Max Weber, that which is most pertinent here is the literature on the military as a profession. The classic is Samuel P. Huntington, *The Soldier and the State* (Cambridge: Harvard University Press, 1957). The most useful additions and critiques include the following: Bengt Abrahamsson, *Military Professionalization and Political Power* (Beverly Hills: Sage Publications, 1972); Peter D. Feaver, "The Civil-Military Problematique: Huntington, Janowitz, and the Question of Civilian Control," *Armed Forces & Society*, Winter 1996, pp. 149–177; and Samuel E. Finer, *The Man on Horseback: The Role of the Military in Politics* (New York: Praeger Publishers, 1962).

31. Richard M. Bissell, Jr. (with Jonathan E. Lewis and Francis T. Pudlo), *Reflections of a Cold Warrior: From Yalta to the Bay of Pigs* (New Haven, CT: Yale University Press, 1996), p. 216.

32. Wright, 1987, p. 67.

33. Bar-Joseph, 1995, p. 49 notes the absence of formal educational requirements. The absence of educational elements leads him in large part to not consider intelligence as a profession with which I do totally disagree.

34. Quote in Stansfield Turner, 1985, p. 178.

35. This is precisely what Hastedt advocates: "Only by seeking to structure how intelligence professionals see their job can one hope to prevent abuses from occurring in the first place or ensure responsiveness." See Hastedt, 1991, p. 14.

36. The other side of the recruitment is retirement of intelligence professionals. It is important for governments to ensure that their intelligence organizations create stable career progression based on merit, including provisions for decent retirement after service. This ensures loyalty and gives them options to not stay on in intelligence functions, or even worse, to turn to illegal activities since their skills are not easily transferable to other occupations. ✦

Reprinted with permission from Thomas C. Bruneau, "Controlling Intelligence in New Democracies," *International Journal of Intelligence and Counterintelligence* 14 (Fall 2001): 323–341.

38

The British Experience With Intelligence Failure

Butler Panel of Inquiry

In this excerpt from their insightful report, the Butler Commission offers a snapshot of how British intelligence works its way through the intelligence cycle to produce finished intelligence for policymakers. It highlights the strengths and limitations of this process and provides a brief history of the way British intelligence assessed and responded to the threat posed by al-Qaeda. It is a classic statement of the challenge confronting intelligence analysis.

> "Much of the intelligence that we receive in war is contradictory, even more of it is plain wrong, and most of it is fairly dubious. What one can require of an officer, under these circumstances, is a certain degree of discrimination, which can only be gained from knowledge of men and affairs and from good judgement. The law of probability must be his guide."
>
> [*Clausewitz, On War, Vol I, Bk I, Ch VI*]

CHAPTER 1. THE NATURE AND USE OF INTELLIGENCE

1.1 Introduction

20. In view of the subject matter of our Review, and of what we have found in the course of it, we think that it may be helpful to the general reader to describe the nature of intelligence; the successive processes of validation, analysis and assessment which are necessary for using it properly; its limitations; and the risks which nevertheless remain.

21. Governmental decisions and actions, at home and abroad, are based on many types of information. Most is openly available or compiled, much is published, and some is consciously provided by individuals, organisations or other governments in confidence. A great deal of such information may be accurate, or accurate enough in its own terms. But equally much is at best uninformed, while some is positively intended to mislead. To supplement their knowledge in areas of concern where information is for one reason or another inadequate, governments turn to secret sources. Information acquired against the wishes and (generally) without the knowledge of its originators or possessors is processed by collation with other material, validation, analysis and assessment and finally disseminated as 'intelligence'. To emphasise the point, the term 'secret intelligence' is often used (as, for instance, enshrined in the title of the Secret Intelligence Service), but in this Review we shall use the simple word 'intelligence'.

22. The protective security barriers which intelligence collectors have to penetrate are usually formidable, and particularly so in the case of programmes which are the subject of this Review. Nuclear, biological and chemical programmes are amongst the ultimate state secrets, controlled by layers of security protection going beyond those applied to conventional weapons. Those of the greatest concern to governments are usually embedded within a strong apparatus of state control. Few of the many people who are necessarily involved in such programmes have a view of more than their own immediate working environment, and very few have comprehensive knowledge of the arrangements for the control, storage, release and use of the resulting weapons. At every stage from initial research and development to deployed forces, nuclear, biological and chemical weapons and their delivery systems are treated as being of particular sensitivity, often to the extent of the establishment of special command and control arrangements in parallel with, but separate from, normal state or military channels.

1.2 Collection

23. The UK has three intelligence and security agencies ('the agencies') responsible for the collection of intelligence[1]: the Secret Intelligence Service (SIS), the Security Service and Government Communications Headquarters (GCHQ). The Defence Intelligence Staff (DIS), part of the Ministry of Defence (MOD), also manages some intelligence collection, notably that of imagery, but its main function is all-source analysis and assessment and the production of collated results, primarily to serve MOD requirements.

24. There is a panoply of collection techniques to acquire intelligence which do not exactly correspond to inter-departmental organisational boundaries. The three main ones are signals intelligence (the product of interception, generally abbreviated

to 'Sigint'); information from human sources such as classical espionage agents (which is conveniently described, by extension from the previous category, as 'Humint'); and photography, or more generally imagery ('Imint'). Signals intelligence and human intelligence are of widespread and general applicability. They can produce intelligence on any topic (for example, the intentions, plans, negotiations, activities and achievements of people involved in the development, acquisition, deployment and use of unconventional weapons), since ultimately the data they acquire stem from the human beings involved. Imagery is more confined to the study of objects (buildings, aircraft, roads, topography), though modern techniques have extended its abilities (for example, infra-red photography can in some circumstances show where an object was, even though it may have gone by the time the photograph is taken).

25. There are also other, more specialised intelligence techniques, some of particular relevance to this Review[2]. For example, the development of nuclear explosives inevitably involves highly-radioactive materials, radiation from which may be detected. Leakage from facilities concerned with the development of chemical and biological agents, and deposits in testing areas, can provide characteristic indicators. Missile testing may involve the generation of considerable heat, which can be detected, and missiles may be tracked by radar.

26. In the case of the weapons covered by this Review, there is additionally another category of information which is frequently mentioned by the Joint Intelligence Committee (JIC) in its assessments. International inspection and enforcement bodies have been established, on a permanent basis (e.g. the International Atomic Energy Agency), or temporary basis (e.g. the United Nations Special Commission), to ensure compliance with international treaties or United Nations resolutions[3]. Some of the findings and reports of these bodies are published on an official basis to United Nations members and are of considerable importance. In Iraq between 1991 and 1998, in many ways they surpassed anything that national intelligence agencies could do, but since their work is carried out on behalf of the United Nations it can hardly be considered 'intelligence' by the definitions to which we are working. Data obtained in the course of work on export licensing can also be important.

1.3 Validation

27. Intelligence, though it may not differ in type or, often, reliability from other forms of information used by governments, operates in a field of particular difficulty. By definition the data it is trying to provide have been deliberately concealed. Before the actual content of an intelligence report can be considered, the validity of the process which has led to its production must be confirmed. For imagery and signals intelligence this is not usually an issue, although even here the danger of deception must be considered. But for human intelligence the validation process is vital.

28. Human intelligence reports are usually available only at second-hand (for example, when the original informant talks to a case officer[4] who interprets—often literally—his words to construct an intelligence report), and maybe third- or fourth-hand (the original informant talks to a friend, who more or less indirectly talks to a case officer). Documentary or other physical evidence is often more compelling than the best oral report[5], and has the advantage of being more accessible to specialised examination, but is usually more difficult to acquire. Conventional oral reporting can be difficult enough if all in the chain understand the subject under discussion. When the topic is unfamiliar to one or more of the people involved, as can be the case when details of (say) nuclear weapons design are at issue, there is always the chance of misunderstanding. There is in such cases a considerable load on the case officer to be familiar with the subject-matter and sufficiently expert in explaining it. It need only be added that often those involved in providing intelligence may for one reason or another have deliberately misrepresented (or at least concealed) their true identities, their country of origin or their employment to their interlocutors[6], to show how great is the need for careful evaluation of the validity of any information which eventually arrives.

29. The validation of a reporting chain requires both care and time, and can generally only be conducted by the agency responsible for collection. The process is informed by the operational side of the agency, but must include a separate auditing element, which can consider cases objectively and quite apart from their apparent intelligence value. Has the informant been properly quoted, all the way along the chain? Does he have credible access to the facts he claims to know? Does he have the right knowledge to understand what he claims to be reporting? Could he be under opposition control, or be being fed information? Is he fabricating? Can the *bona fides*, activities, movements or locations attributed to those involved in acquiring or transmitting a report be checked? Do we understand the motivations of those involved, their private agenda[7], and hence the way in which their reports may be influenced by a desire to please or impress? How powerful is a wish for (in particular) financial reward? What, if any, distorting effect might such factors exert? Is there—at any stage—a deliberate intention to deceive? Generally speaking, the extent and

depth of validation required will depend on the counter-intelligence sophistication of the target, although the complexity of the operational situation will affect the possibility of confusion, misrepresentation or deception.

1.4 Analysis

30. The validation process will often have involved consideration of the coherence and consistency of intelligence being provided by an informant, as one of the ways in which that source's reliability can be tested. But at the next stage, analysis, the factual material inside the intelligence report is examined in its own right. This stage may not be required where the material is self-explanatory, or it may be readily subsumed into assessment and conducted by the same people. But much intelligence is fragmentary or specialised and needs at least a conscious analytic stage. Analysis assembles individual intelligence reports into meaningful strands, whether weapons programmes, military operations or diplomatic policies. Intelligence reports take on meaning as they are put into context. Analysis is also the process required to convert complex technical evidence into descriptions of real-world objects or events.

31. The department which receives the largest quantity of intelligence is the MOD, where analysis is carried out by the DIS[8] whose reports are distributed not only internally in the MOD but also to other relevant departments. Although the DIS is a component of the MOD, funded from the Defence Account and managed in accordance with defence priorities, it is a vital component of and contributor to the national intelligence machinery, and its priorities and work programme are linked with those of the Cabinet Office.

32. Analysis can be conducted only by people expert in the subject matter—a severe limitation when the topic is as specialised as biological warfare or uranium enrichment, or the internal dynamics of terrorist cells or networks. A special danger here can be the failure to recognise just what particular expertise is required. The British intelligence assessment of the German V-2 rocket during the Second World War was hindered by the involvement of the main British rocket expert, who opined that the object visible on test-stands could not possibly be a rocket. The unrecognised problem was that he was an expert only on *solid powder* rockets, of the type that the UK had developed for short-range artillery. It was true that a solid firework of the size of the V-2 was, with the technology then available, impracticable. But the Germans had developed *liquid-propellant* rocket engines, with the combustion chamber fed by powerful turbo-pumps. On that subject, there were no British experts.

1.5 Assessment

33. Assessment may be conducted separately from analysis or as an almost parallel process in the mind of the analyst. Intelligence reports often do not immediately fit into an established pattern, or extend a picture in the expected way. Assessment has to make choices, but in so doing runs the risk of selection that reinforces earlier conclusions. The risk is that uneven standards of proof may be applied; reports that fit the previous model are readily accepted, while contrary reports have to reach a higher threshold. This is not only perfectly understandable, it is the way perception normally operates. But in the intelligence world in which data are scanty, may be deliberately intended to confuse and may sometimes be more inadequate than can be appreciated, normal rules do not apply.

34. In the UK, assessment is usually explicitly described as 'all-source'. Given the imperfections of intelligence, it is vital that every scrap of evidence be examined, from the most secret sources through confidential diplomatic reports to openly published data. Intelligence cannot be checked too often. Corroboration is always important but seldom simple, particularly in the case of intelligence on 'hard targets'[9] such as nuclear, biological or chemical weapons programmes or proliferation networks. The simple fact of having apparently coincident reports from multiple types of intelligence sources is not in itself enough. Although reports from different sources may say the same thing, they may not necessarily *confirm* one another. Is a human intelligence report that a factory has been put into operation confirmed by imagery showing trucks moving around it? Or are both merely based on the same thing—observation of physical external activity? Reporting of different but mutually consistent activities can be complementary. This can build up knowledge to produce a picture which is more than the simple sum of the parts. But it may be false, if there is no link between the pieces other than the attractiveness of the resulting picture. Complementary information is not necessarily confirmatory information.

35. Multiple sources may conflict, and common sense has to be used in evaluation. A dozen captured soldiers may have provided mutually consistent and supportive reports about the availability of chemical weapons to their neighbouring battalion. But if these were flatly contradicted by a single report from a senior member of that battalion, which should be believed?

36. It is incorrect to say, as some commentators have done, that 'single source' intelligence is always suspect. A single photograph showing missiles on launchers, supporting a division deployed in the

field, trumps any number of agent reports that missiles are not part of a division's order of battle. During the Second World War, innumerable Allied command decisions were taken on the basis of intelligence reports from a single **type** of source (signals intelligence, providing decrypts of high-level German and Japanese military plans and orders), and quite often (e.g. re-routing convoys in the middle of the Atlantic) important decisions had to be taken on the basis of a **single report**. As before, common sense and experience are the key.

37. Assessment must always be aware that there may be a deeper level of reality at which apparently independent sources have a common origin. Multiple sources may have been marshalled in a deception campaign, as the Allies did in Operation Fortitude before D-Day to mislead the German High Command about the location of the landings. Although deception on so grand a scale is rare, the chance of being deceived is in inverse proportion to the number of independent sources—which, for 'hard targets', are few.

38. Many of the manifestations of nuclear, biological or chemical weapons programmes can have innocuous, or at least non-proscribed, explanations—the 'dual-use' problem. Nuclear developments can be for peaceful purposes. Technologies for the production of chemical and biological agents seldom diverge from those employed in normal civilian chemical or bio-chemical industries. And, in the case of missile development, some procurement and development activities may be permissible.

39. Thus, the recipients of intelligence have normally to make decisions on the basis of the balance of probabilities. That requires, first, the most effective deployment of all possible sources and, secondly, the most objective assessment possible, as unaffected as may be by motives and pressures which may distort judgement.

40. In the UK, central intelligence assessment is the responsibility of the Assessments Staff. This comprises some 30 senior and middle-ranking officials on secondment from other departments, within the Cabinet Office, together with secretarial and administrative support.

1.6 The Joint Intelligence Committee

41. The agencies and the DIS are brought together with important policy departments in the JIC[10]. The JIC was established in 1936 as a sub-committee of the Committee of Imperial Defence. During the Second World War, it comprised the heads of the agencies and the three Services' Directors of Intelligence, under the chairmanship of a senior member of the Foreign Office and was joined by other relevant departments such as the Ministry of

Economic Warfare, responsible for the Special Operations Executive.

42. The JIC has evolved since 1945. It became part of the Cabinet Office rather than of the Chiefs of Staff organisation in 1957. To the original membership of the JIC (intelligence producers, with users from MOD and the FCO) were added the Intelligence Co-ordinator when that post was established in 1968, the Treasury (1968), the Department of Trade and Industry (1997) and the Home Office (2000). Other departments attend when papers of relevance to them are taken. Representatives of the Australian, Canadian and United States intelligence communities also attend as appropriate. In 1993, the post of Chairman of the JIC and that of the Head of the Cabinet Office's Defence and Overseas Secretariat[11] were combined, the two posts remaining so until 1999. From 1992 to 2002, the chairmanship was combined with the post of Intelligence Co-ordinator. A new post of Security and Intelligence Co-ordinator was created in 2002, taking on the responsibilities of the previous Intelligence Co-ordinator together with wider responsibilities in the field of counter-terrorism and crisis management. The holder became a member of the JIC.

43. The JIC's main function[12], on which its regular weekly meetings are centred, is to provide:

> Ministers and senior officials with co-ordinated intelligence assessments on a range of issues of immediate and long-term importance to national interests, primarily in the fields of security, defence and foreign affairs.

The Assessments Staff are central to this role, and the Chief of the Assessments Staff is a member of the JIC in his own right. With the assistance of other departments, the Assessments Staff draft the JIC assessments, which are usually debated at Current Intelligence Groups (CIGs) including experts in the subject before being submitted to the JIC. The JIC can itself ask the Assessments Staff to draft an assessment, but the process is usually triggered by a request from a policy department. The forward programme of assessments to be produced is issued three times a year, but is revised and, when necessary, overridden by matters of more immediate concern. The JIC thus brings together in regular meetings the most senior people responsible for intelligence collection, for intelligence assessment and for the use of intelligence in the main departments for which it is collected, in order to construct and issue assessments on the subjects of greatest current concern. The process is robust, and the assessments that result are respected and used at all levels of government.

44. Intelligence is disseminated at various levels and in different forms. The agencies send reports

direct to users in departments and military commands; these reports are used by civil and military officials in their daily business, and some of them are selected and brought to Ministers' attention. The JIC's co-ordinated intelligence assessments, formally agreed at their weekly meetings, are sent to Ministers and senior officials. In addition the JIC produces Intelligence Updates and Immediate Assessments whenever required, which are sent to a standard distribution throughout government.

45. A feature of JIC assessments is that they contain single statements of position; unlike the practice in the US, there are no minority reports or noted dissents. When the intelligence is unclear or otherwise inadequate and the JIC at the end of its debate is still uncertain, it may report alternative interpretations of the facts before it such as they are; but in such cases all the membership agrees that the interpretations they are proposing are viable alternatives. The JIC does not (and this is borne out by our examination of several hundred JIC assessments in the course of our Review) characterise such alternatives as championed by individual members who disagree with colleagues' points of view. While the JIC has at times been criticised for its choice of language and the subtlety of the linguistic nuances and caveats it applies[13], it has responded that when the intelligence is ambiguous it should not be artificially simplified.

46. In the sometimes lengthy line that leads to the production of the JIC's output, all the components of the system—from collection through analysis and assessment to a well-briefed and educated readership—must function successfully. Problems can arise if the JIC has to make bricks without (enough) straw. Collection agencies may produce too little intelligence, or too much intelligence about the wrong subjects, or the right intelligence but too late to be of value. Although assessments generated under such circumstances may have proper caveats, with attention drawn to important gaps in knowledge and with the dubious steps in an argument clearly identified, they may reach misleading conclusions. Or—which is equally destructive of their purpose—even if they are correct they may be mistrusted. In either case, the reputation of the JIC product is at risk, and the Committee has on occasion refused to issue drafted papers which it has felt are not sufficiently supported by new intelligence or add nothing to the information already publicly available.

1.7 The Limitations of Intelligence

47. Intelligence merely provides techniques for improving the basis of knowledge. As with other techniques, it can be a dangerous tool if its limitations are not recognised by those who seek to use it.

48. The intelligence processes described above (validation, analysis, assessment) are designed to transform the raw material of intelligence so that it can be assimilated in the same way as other information provided to decision-makers at all levels of government. Validation should remove information which is unreliable (including reporting which has been deliberately inserted to mislead). Analysis should assemble fragmentary intelligence into coherent meaningful accounts. Assessment should put intelligence into a sensible real-world context and identify how it can affect policy-making. But there are limitations, some inherent and some practical on the scope of intelligence, which have to be recognised by its ultimate recipients if it is to be used wisely.

49. The most important limitation on intelligence is its incompleteness. Much ingenuity and effort is spent on making secret information difficult to acquire and hard to analyse. Although the intelligence process may overcome such barriers, intelligence seldom acquires the full story. In fact, it is often, when first acquired, sporadic and patchy, and even after analysis may still be at best inferential.

50. The very way that intelligence is presented can contribute to this misperception. The necessary protective security procedures with which intelligence is handled can reinforce a mystique of omniscience. Intelligence is not only—like many other sources—incomplete, it can be incomplete in undetectable ways. There is always pressure, at the assessment stage if not before, to create an internally consistent and intellectually satisfying picture. When intelligence becomes the dominant, or even the only, source of government information, it can become very difficult for the assessment process to establish a context and to recognise that there may be gaps in that picture.

51. A hidden limitation of intelligence is its inability to transform a mystery into a secret. In principle, intelligence can be expected to uncover secrets. The enemy's order of battle may not be known, but it is knowable. The enemy's intentions may not be known, but they too are knowable. But mysteries are essentially unknowable: what a leader **truly** believes, or what his reaction would be in certain circumstances, cannot be known, but can only be judged. JIC judgements have to cover both secrets and mysteries. Judgement must still be informed by the best available information, which often means a contribution from intelligence. But it cannot import certainty.

52. These limitations are best offset by ensuring that the ultimate users of intelligence, the decision-makers at all levels, properly understand its strengths and limitations and have the opportunity to acquire experience in handling it. It is not easy to

do this while preserving the security of sensitive sources and methods. But unless intelligence is properly handled at this final stage, all preceding effort and expenditure is wasted.

1.8 Risks to Good Assessment

53. It is a well-known phenomenon within intelligence communities that memory of past failures can cause over-estimation next time around. It is equally possible to be misled by past success. For 45 years of Cold War, the intelligence community's major task was to assess the intentions and capabilities of the Soviet Union and its satellite states[14]. As the details which had been sought became more accessible, first through *glasnost* and explicit exchanges of data under international agreements and then fairly readily through open sources after the dissolution of the Soviet empire, most of the intelligence community's conclusions were vindicated—at least in the areas in which it had spent the largest part of its efforts, the Soviet bloc's military equipment, capabilities and order of battle.

54. But it is risky to transfer one model to cases where that model will only partially apply. Against dictatorships, dependent upon personal or tribal loyalties and insensitive to international politics, an approach that worked well for a highly-structured, relatively cohesive state target is not necessarily applicable even though many aspects of the work may appear to be identical. The targets which the UK intelligence community needs to study most carefully today are those that structurally and culturally look least like the Government and society it serves. We return to this when we consider terrorism, at Chapter 3.

55. Risks in intelligence assessment will arise if this limitation is not readily recognised. There may be no choice but to apply the same intelligence processes, methods and resources to one target as were developed for and applied to others. But it is important to recognise that the resulting intelligence may need to be analysed and assessed in different ways.

56. A further risk is that of 'mirror-imaging'—the belief that can permeate some intelligence analysts that the practices and values of their own cultures are universal. The more diffuse range of security challenges of the 21st century means that it will not be possible to accumulate the breadth and depth of understanding which intelligence collectors, analysts and users built up over the years about the single subject of the Soviet Union. But the more alien the target, the more important is the ability of intelligence analysts to appreciate that their own assumptions do not necessarily apply everywhere. The motives and methods of non-state organisations built on a special interest (whether criminal, religious or political) can be particularly hard for members of a stable society to assess.

57. There is also the risk of 'group think'—the development of a 'prevailing wisdom'. Well-developed imagination at all stages of the intelligence process is required to overcome preconceptions. There is a case for encouraging it by providing for structured challenge, with established methods and procedures, often described as a 'Devil's advocate' or a 'red teaming' approach. This may also assist in countering another danger: when problems are many and diverse, on any one of them the number of experts can be dangerously small, and individual, possibly idiosyncratic, views may pass unchallenged.

58. One final point should be mentioned here, to which we return in our Conclusions. The assessment process must be informed by an understanding of policy-makers' requirements for information, but must avoid being so captured by policy objectives that it reports the world as policy-makers would wish it to be rather than as it is. The JIC is part (and an important part) of the UK's governmental machinery or it is nothing; but to have any value its product must be objective. The JIC has always been very conscious of this.

1.9 The Use of Intelligence

59. In addition to the use of intelligence to inform government policy . . . there are important applications in the enforcement of compliance with national law or international treaties and other obligations, in warning of untoward events, in the support of military and law enforcement operations, and in long-term planning for future national security capabilities. . . .

CHAPTER 3. TERRORISM[1]

3.1 Scope

110. We have examined intelligence reports and assessments on the links between terrorism and chemical, biological, radiological and nuclear weapons, and the use made of that intelligence, from when it began in the early 1990s to emerge as a topic of interest to the Joint Intelligence Committee (JIC). For the purpose of illustrating the contribution made by intelligence to policy formulation by the Government and to actions taken on the basis of that policy, we have focussed on the scope and quality of intelligence reports and assessments on the use by terrorists and extremists of unconventional weapons, and the extent to which they were validated by subsequent discoveries in Afghanistan. To avoid prejudicing current operations, we do not

cover in this Report more recent intelligence assessments or findings.

3.2 The Period up to 1995

111. In the late 1980s, the possibility that terrorist groups might seek to use unconventional weapons was considered remote. In surveys of nuclear, biological and chemical weapons proliferation in 1989, the JIC dealt briefly with the possibility that such technology might be used by terrorists:

> We believe that even the most sophisticated and well-organised terrorist group is highly unlikely to be able to steal and then detonate a nuclear weapon within the foreseeable future. . . . At present the most feasible terrorist nuclear incident would probably be a credible hoax. A terrorist threat to detonate a nuclear device would be difficult to dismiss entirely in view of the increasing number of producers of fissile material in a variety of countries and the problems of accounting fully for all material produced. Terrorists might see a seemingly plausible and preferably well publicised warning of an imminent nuclear attack as potentially a very effective means of blackmailing governments. [JIC, 3 July 1989]

and:

> We have no intelligence that any terrorist group makes CBW agents, possesses any such agents or is currently contemplating attacks using CBW agents or other toxic chemicals. The use of CBW agents by terrorists would generate widespread fear and could cause large numbers of casualties. The mere threat of such use could be sufficient to cause panic.
>
> A terrorist would need only small quantities of CW agents. The simpler ones could in principle be made by anyone with a knowledge of A-level chemistry using readily obtainable materials. We believe that terrorist organisations could also readily obtain and handle without insurmountable difficulty, suitable bacteria, viruses and certain toxins.
>
> Although CBW proliferation undoubtedly increases the risk that CBW agents could be stolen by or even supplied to terrorists by state sponsors . . . this prospect must be viewed against a background where many suitable agents can be manufactured in small quantities using easily available materials. So as far as terrorism is concerned, proliferation (if it comes about) may not necessarily be much affected by the actions of States with the relevant capability. [JIC, 26 June 1989]

112. The main strands in this assessment set the standard for the next few years. There was no credible evidence of terrorist interest in nuclear, biologi-

cal or chemical weapons; hoaxes and threats might be more disruptive than actual use; terrorists were very unlikely to be able to acquire nuclear devices; and the fact that some states possessed nuclear, biological or chemical weapons was unlikely to affect the risk of their use by terrorists.

113. In April 1992[2], in its first assessment specifically on the threat of attacks by terrorists using chemical, biological, radiological or nuclear weapons, the JIC considered the technical options, but emphasised the difficulties which were thought likely to render such methods unattractive options for terrorist groups:

> They may be deterred by the danger to their own members, or by the risk of alienating the public and especially their own supporters. They may also fear that an attack would cause international outrage leading to determined efforts on an international scale to bring them to book. By contrast, conventional weapons are cheaper, easier to procure, and offer equal or greater effectiveness against traditional targets (such as prominent individuals, members of the security forces, government buildings). [JIC, 23 April 1992]

This, too, was to become a feature of JIC assessments: for most terrorist uses, conventional weapons were better.

114. By October 1994, there had been a number of media reports—some correct—of fissile material being available on the black market. In the first of several such studies, the JIC did not consider that these affected its overall assessment:

> Despite the possibility which now exists of obtaining fissile material, it is extremely unlikely that a terrorist group could produce even a crude nuclear device; nor is there any evidence that any group has contemplated the use of nuclear weapons. A more plausible scenario might be the dispersal of radioactive materials by conventional explosives or other means to achieve radiological contamination. The actual danger to the public from radioactivity would probably be small—smaller in some cases than to the terrorists. But such an attack (or its threat) could be highly effective in causing panic and public concern.
>
> We believe that terrorists would not be able to acquire or deploy a nuclear weapon; radiological attacks are possible but unlikely. Attacks involving chemical or biological agents are also unlikely, though use of toxic chemical substances (for which there are some limited precedents) remains a possibility. [JIC, 13–19 October 1994]

3.3 1995–1997

115. By June 1995, the JIC was assessing the threat posed by Islamist extremists; the terrorist

threat was spreading outside the Middle East. The JIC commented on the use of suicide tactics, a strand which was subsequently to become significant in such assessments:

> Selective interpretation of the Muslim faith enables such groups to justify terrorist violence and to recruit 'martyrs' for suicide attacks. [JIC, 8 June 1995]

116. However, the first serious use of chemicals by terrorists was not by Islamist extremists. The sarin gas attack in the Tokyo underground by the Aum Shinrikyo sect came in March 1995[3]. In a 1996 assessment of the nuclear, biological and chemical threat to the UK[4] (which responded to the G7 declaration at the Lyons summit in June that year that special attention should be paid to the threat of use of nuclear, biological and chemical materials for terrorist purposes) the JIC stuck to its previous line, though noting the Aum Shinrikyo attack:

> There is no indication of any terrorist or other group showing interest in the use of nuclear, biological or chemical (NBC) materials against the UK. For a number of reasons, conventional weapons are likely to remain more attractive for terrorist purposes. But last year's nerve agent attack in Tokyo will have heightened interest and, with ever more NBC information publicly available, hoaxes threatening NBC use are likely to become more difficult to assess. [JIC, 4 July 1996]

3.4 1998–1999

117. Usama bin Laden first became known as a high-profile supporter of Islamist extremism while fighting against Soviet forces in Afghanistan during the 1980s. Expelled from Saudi Arabia in 1991 and from Sudan in 1996, he returned to Afghanistan. Evidence of his interest in unconventional weapons accumulated, and was summarised by the JIC in November 1998:

> He has a long-standing interest in the potential terrorist use of CBR materials, and recent intelligence suggests his ideas about using toxic materials are maturing and being developed in more detail. . . . There is also secret reporting that he may have obtained some CB material—and that he is interested in nuclear materials. We assess that he lacks the expertise or facilities even to begin making a nuclear weapon, but he might seek to make a radiological device. [JIC, 25 November 1998]

118. Seven months later, in June 1999, the JIC had received more intelligence, and reassessed the threat from Usama bin Laden's organisation accordingly:

> Most of UBL's planned attacks would use conventional terrorist weapons. But he continues to seek chemical, biological, radiological and nuclear material and to develop a capability for its terrorist use. There is insufficient evidence to conclude that he has yet acquired radiological or nuclear material. In contrast, we now assess that his followers have access to some unspecified chemical or biological material. Some have received basic training in its use against individuals or in confined spaces.

> In April a leading Egyptian terrorist, apparently believing the information was already known to the authorities, told an Egyptian court that UBL had CB 'weapons' which he would use against US or Israeli targets. [JIC, 9 June 1999]

Intelligence reports of bin Laden's associates falling for nuclear materiel frauds suggested, however, that they were not well advised on nuclear matters.

119. A month later, in July 1999, the JIC explained an important change in one of the major assumptions underpinning its previous assessments—some terrorists were no longer reluctant to cause mass casualties, for example some Islamist extremist terrorists and Aum Shinrikyo:

> Over the 1990s there has been a significant increase in the quantity and quality of intelligence that some terrorists are interested in CBRN—and particularly in chemical and biological—materials as weapons. The risk of a CBRN terrorist incident has risen, albeit from a low base. In part this increase reflects the rise of Islamic extremism and ethnic hatred as terrorist motivations: some of the terrorists thus motivated are less constrained by considerations such as public support, casualties among innocent bystanders, or the prospect of retaliation. It may also reflect the increasing availability of information about making and using CB materials, and the publicity attracted by major incidents and hoaxes. Whether the attacker's aim is political or economic blackmail, or severe disruption, society's vulnerability to terrorist attack from CB or radiological materials is high, exacerbated by the lack of a tried and tested CB counter-terrorist response in some countries. [JIC, 15 July 1999]

120. In the same assessment, the JIC made its own judgement, in the absence of specific intelligence, that Usama bin Laden had after several years been successful in acquiring non-conventional weapons. That judgement was later shown to be correct:

> There have been important developments in [Islamist extremist] terrorism. It has become clear that Usama Bin Laden has been seeking CBRN materials. . . . His wealth permits him to fund procurement, training and experimentation to an extent unmatched by other terror-

ists. . . . Given the quality and quantity of intelligence about his interest in CB materials, the length of time he has sought them, and the relative ease with which they can be made, we assess that he has by now acquired or made at least modest quantities of CB materials—even if their exact nature and effectiveness are unclear. The significance of his possession of CB materials is that, in contrast to other terrorists interested in CB, he wishes to target US, British and other interests worldwide. There is also intelligence on training in the use of chemicals as weapons in a terrorist camp in Afghanistan, although it is not yet clear if this is under Bin Laden's auspices. The CB threat is likely to be higher abroad than in the UK, reflecting the location of Bin Laden and his allies, the vulnerability of potential targets, and the effectiveness of local security authorities. Targets may include British official sites or related facilities overseas. That said, Bin Laden's attacks remain more likely to employ conventional weapons than CB materials. [JIC, 15 July 1999]

121. However the JIC still retained its overall conclusion, that:

. . . the indications of terrorist interest in CBRN materials have yet to be matched by a comparable amount of evidence about possession and intent to use CBRN. Most terrorists continue to favour conventional weapons, as easier to use, more reliable, safer and more controllable than CBRN materials. [JIC, 15 July 1999]

3.5 2000–2001

122. By January 2000, in an assessment of conventional threats, the JIC summarised bin Laden's aspirations for non-conventional weapons:

UBL retains his interest in obtaining chemical, biological, radiological and nuclear (CBRN) materials and expertise. In autumn 1999 there was intelligence that he had recruited . . . chemicals specialists. . . . Our assessment remains that UBL has some toxic chemical or biological materials, and an understanding of their utility as terrorist weapons. But we have yet to see hard intelligence that he possesses genuine nuclear material. [JIC, 12 January 2000]

123. By August 2000, the JIC was clear that, although there were other Islamist extremist groups[5] with an interest in non-conventional weapons, Usama bin Laden posed the most severe threat:

Some [Islamist extremist groups] are interested in exploring the use of chemical or biological materials as weapons. In the forefront is UBL. . . . [JIC, 9 August 2000]

124. In January 2001, the JIC reported at length on the terrorist threat from unconventional weap-

ons and emphasised the unique nature of the threat from Usama bin Laden:

The actual threat does not match the media hype. Almost all the available intelligence refers to terrorist interest in CB materials, rather than to specific attack plans. There is no credible intelligence that any terrorist except UBL has the capability or serious intent to explore the use of weapons-grade nuclear materials—nor, except for Chechen extremists, radiological material. Terrorists interested in CB are generally those least constrained by public opinion or their members' or supporters' sensitivities. Their resources and targets tend to be abroad rather than in Britain, so the risk of attacks using toxic materials has always been greater overseas.

UBL has sought CBRN materials for use as terrorist weapons. . . . From his public statements and interviews it is clear that he believes it is legitimate to use them as weapons and his wealth has allowed him to fund procurement, experimentation and training. There is plentiful intelligence that this interest is sustained, mostly relating to toxic materials.

In 1999 he sought equipment for a chemical weapons lab in Afghanistan, and claimed already to have . . . experts working there. [JIC, 10 January 2001]

3.6 The Aftermath of 9/11

125. In an important paper shortly after the attacks of 11 September 2001, the JIC made clear the way in which Usama bin Laden's philosophy, combined with suicide attacks, had changed the calculus of threat. This assessment summarised the new security challenge which . . . was to become dominant in the thinking of British Ministers—the desire of terrorists and extremists to cause casualties on a massive scale, undeterred by the fear of alienating the public or their own supporters that had been noted as a constraining factor in JIC assessments in the early 1990s or by considerations of personal survival. To this fundamental shift in the JIC's judgement on the likely motivation and goals of terrorists and extremists was added a corresponding shift in its conclusions about the attractiveness of nuclear, biological or chemical weapons. Thus, in September 2001 the JIC noted that:

Many defensive and preventive measures taken against terrorism (such as ensuring that passenger and luggage travel together) still presuppose that the terrorist will want to survive the attack. But suicide attackers, especially those backed by sophisticated planning and pursuing non-negotiable objectives, negate many security measures and widen society's vulnerability. New strategies are required to counter the threat of terrorists willing, or even eager, to sacrifice their lives as martyrs in Islamic extremist or other causes—although there can be no complete protection against them.

In the context of UBL's jihad, casualties and destruction could be an end in themselves as much as a means to an end (Footnote: UBL's stated objective is to secure US withdrawal from the Middle East or, failing that, to provoke a reaction which would further demonise the US in the eyes of Muslims and destabilise moderate Arab states that he perceives as un-Islamic). He has no interest in negotiation and there is no indication that he can be deterred. [JIC, 18 September 2001]

126. The JIC also went on in this paper to note Usama bin Laden's interest in nuclear devices.

127. The British Government's dossier of 4 October 2001,[6] which attributed the attacks of 11 September 2001 to Usama bin Laden, also reflected the attractiveness to him of nuclear, biological and chemical weapons, saying that:

From the early 1990s Usama bin Laden has sought to obtain nuclear and chemical materials for use as weapons of terror.

and reminding its readership that:

When asked in 1998 about obtaining chemical or nuclear weapons he said "acquiring such weapons for the defence of Muslims (was) a religious duty". [Government's dossier, 4 October 2001]

3.7 Intelligence on UbL'S Capabilities and Its Validation

128. A considerable quantity of evidence of Usama bin Laden's capabilities in the nuclear, biological and chemical fields was uncovered after the US-led military action in Afghanistan in October 2001. This section compares these discoveries with JIC judgements beforehand.

Nuclear

129. In 1999, the JIC reported Usama bin Laden's claims to be setting up a laboratory in Afghanistan. Following the collapse of the Taliban regime, in January 2002 the United Nations Security Council listed a former Pakistani nuclear scientist Bashir Mahmoud as associated with the Taliban or Al Qaida.

Chemical

130. Intelligence reporting from 1999 onwards testified to the activities of Abu Khabbab, an explosives and chemicals expert who ran training courses which included information on how to make and use poisons. This was confirmed by discoveries in Afghanistan such as a video showing chemical experiments being carried out on ani-

mals, and by the finding of numerous training manuals.

Biological

131. In 1999, the JIC reported that:

In February 1999 one of his followers claimed that UBL intended to attack US and UK targets in India, Indonesia and the US, by using means which even the US could not counter, implying the use of chemical or biological material. [JIC, 9 June 1999]

132. Some work with biological agents was also attributed to Abu Khabbab, though the evidence was not detailed. However, the JIC's judgement that Al Qaida was developing biological weapons was confirmed by the discovery in Afghanistan of the Kandahar laboratory, and evidence that scientists had been recruited.

3.8 Intelligence Responses to International Terrorism

133. Few of the measures being taken by the Government to improve the response to the terrorist threat are unique to attacks using chemical, biological, radiological and nuclear materials. The threat is international, and has motivated intelligence organisations to intensify both national and international collaboration on an unprecedented scale. **All of the UK intelligence agencies are developing new techniques, and we have seen clear evidence that they are co-operating at all levels.**

134. The most obvious embodiment of enhanced inter-departmental co-operation in the UK is the Joint Terrorism Analysis Centre (JTAC). This is a multi-agency organisation, hosted by the Security Service but staffed by personnel seconded from all of the agencies, law enforcement organisations and relevant departments. Its staff retain links to their parent departments and, operating on a round-the-clock basis, pool information to produce continuous assessments of threats within the UK, to British interests abroad and of terrorist activities generally. **JTAC has now been operating for over a year and has proved a success.**

135. The Security Service and Home Office are improving public education, through web sites and by other means, for both long-term and immediate appreciation of terrorist threats.

136. **International counter-terrorism collaboration has also been significantly enhanced in the past six or seven years. Though we understand that other countries have not yet achieved the same level of inter-departmental synthesis, considerable developments have taken place. Staff of the UK intelligence and security agencies are today in much wider contact with their**

opposite numbers throughout the world. We have, for example, been briefed on a recent successful counter-terrorist operation which involved eight different countries working together. **We note these initiatives, but remain concerned that the procedures of the international community are still not sufficiently aligned to match the threat.**

Questions for Further Discussion

1. How would you contrast the investigative methods and the findings of this British inquiry into Iraqi WMDs compared to the Silberman-Robb Report?

2. What parallels and differences exist between the British and American recommendations that came out of the Iraqi WMD intelligence failures?

3. What does the Butler Report conclude about the role of the nation's intelligence chief—in this case, the chair of the Joint Intelligence Committee (JIC)?

4. What was the conclusion about "humint" reached by the Butler panel, and how does it compare with the Silberman-Robb conclusion on this topic?

Endnotes

Chapter 1

1. They also have other functions not relevant here.
2. The term 'Masint' (Measurement and Signature Intelligence) has been coined for at least some of these techniques, though they lack the unifying themes which characterise Sigint and Humint.
3. Such bodies often also have a wider operational role in the implementation of treaties or Security Council Resolutions.
4. An official responsible for handling and receiving reports from human intelligence sources.
5. Such evidence is no more immune to deception or fabrication than is oral testimony, though of a different type.
6. The ultimate in such deceptions is the classic 'double agent', who is infiltrated into an espionage network to discover, misinform, expose or pervert it.
7. We have been assured that SIS has for half a century been viscerally wary of emigre organisations. We return to this below in the context of Iraq.
8. The DIS also has other management and intelligence collection responsibilities.
9. In a sense, almost all intelligence is conducted against 'hard targets'. If the information were readily available, it would not be necessary to call on intelligence resources to acquire it. But within the hierarchy of in-

telligence activities it is inevitable, given the protection afforded to nuclear, biological and chemical weapons programmes, that they are among the hardest targets.
10. For a fuller description see *National Intelligence Machinery*, HMSO 2001, which puts the JIC into context within the structures of Parliamentary and Cabinet government.
11. From 1984 to the end of 1993 the Chairman of the JIC was also the Prime Minister's Foreign Policy Adviser. This title was revived in September 2001 and assumed by the Head of the Defence and Overseas Secretariat.
12. The JIC also has other responsibilities, for the establishment of intelligence collection priorities and monitoring of agency performance.
13. We have been told that some readers believe that important distinctions are intended between such phrases as "intelligence indicates . . .", "intelligence demonstrates . . ." and "intelligence shows . . .", or between "we assess that . . .", "we judge that . . ." and "we believe that . . .". We have also been told that there is in reality no established glossary, and that drafters and JIC members actually employ their natural language.
14. The intelligence community did, of course, have many other tasks during this period ranging from the consequences of the withdrawal from empire through the many facets of the conflicts and confrontations in the Middle East to the Falklands War.

Chapter 3

1. This section is limited to intelligence on the use by terrorists of chemical, biological, radiological and nuclear weapons. The large majority of terrorist actions employ conventional armaments and explosives, and are not relevant to this Review.
2. It was also in 1992 that a Kurdish terrorist group tried to poison the water supply of a Turkish airbase using cyanide.
3. The sect had carried out sporadic and unsuccessful open-air attacks using a range of agents since 1990. One attack (using sarin) in Matsumoto in June 1994 caused 7 deaths and 264 people were hospitalised. These earlier attacks were little noticed outside Japan.
4. Because of its limited ambit this paper did not take note of the then recent Chechen guerrilla operation to place minute quantities of caesium-137 in a Moscow park.
5. The JIC was a year later to comment that the word 'groups' can be misleading in the context of Islamist extremist terrorists. "There are established groups in different countries, usually working to a national agenda, but the networks associated with UBL are changeable ad hoc groupings of individuals who share his agenda, and who may come together only for a particular operation. Nevertheless, 'groups' is used as a short form for want of another available term."
6. *"Responsibility for the Terrorist Atrocities in the United States, 11 September 2001".* ✦

Reprinted from "Review of Intelligence on Weapons of Mass Destruction," *Report of a Committee of Privy Counsellors*, Chairman: Lord Butler, HC 898 (July 14, 2004): 7–16, 29–36.

U.S. Intelligence Leadership, 1947–2007

Director, National Intelligence
2005–2007   John D. Negroponte
2007–   J. M. ("Mike") McConnell

Directors, Central Intelligence
1947–1950   Rear Adm. Roscoe H. Hillenkoetter
1950–1953   Gen. Walter Bedell Smith
1953–1961   Allen W. Dulles
1961–1965   John A. McCone
1965–1966   Vice Adm. William F. Raborn, Jr.
1966–1973   Richard Helms
1973   James R. Schlesinger
1973–1976   William E. Colby
1976–1977   George H. W. Bush
1977–1981   Adm. Stansfield Turner
1981–1987   William J. Casey
1987–1991   William H. Webster
1991–1993   Robert M. Gates
1993–1995   R. James Woolsey
1995–1997   John M. Deutch
1997–2004   George J. Tenet
2004–2005   Porter J. Goss

Chairs, Senate Select Committee on Intelligence
1976–1977   Daniel K. Inouye, Democrat, Hawaii
1977–1981   Birch Bayh, Democrat, Indiana
1981–1985   Barry Goldwater, Republican, Arizona
1985–1987   David Durenberger, Republican, Minnesota
1987–1993   David L. Boren, Democrat, Oklahoma
1993–1995   Dennis DeConcini, Democrat, Arizona
1995–1997   Arlan Specter, Republican, Pennsylvania
1997–2001   Richard C. Shelby, Republican, Alabama
2001–2003   Bob Graham, Democrat, Florida
2003–2006   Pat Roberts, Republican, Kansas
2006–   John D. Rockefeller IV, Democrat, West Virginia

Chairs, House Permanent Select Committee on Intelligence
1977–1985   Edward P. Boland, Democrat, Massachusetts
1985–1987   Lee H. Hamilton, Democrat, Indiana
1987–1989   Louis Stokes, Democrat, Ohio
1989–1991   Anthony C. Beilenson, Democrat, California
1991–1993   Dave McCurdy, Democrat, Oklahoma
1993–1995   Dan Glickman, Democrat, Kansas
1995–1997   Larry Combest, Republican, Texas
1997–2004   Porter J. Goss, Republican, Florida
2004–2006   Peter Hoekstra, Republican, Michigan
2007–   Silvestre Reyes, Democrat, Texas ✦

The Organization of the U.S. Intelligence Community

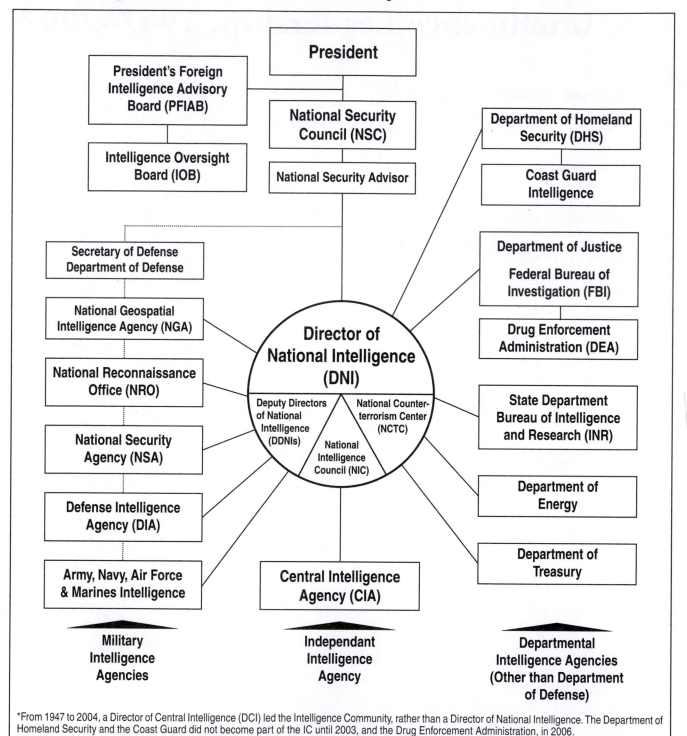

Intelligence Websites

This listing draws in part on helpful suggestions from Professor Frank Smist and the late John Macartney.

General

- http://www.columbia.edu/cu/lweb/indiv/lehman/guides/intell.html>
- http://www.loyola.edu/dept/politics/intel.html

National Security Act of 1947

- http://www.intelligence.gov/0-natsecact_1947.shtml>

Director of National Intelligence

- http://www.odni.gov

Center for the Study of Intelligence

- https://www.cia.gov/csi/

Intelligence Agencies

- https://www.cia.gov
- http://www.fbi.gov
- http://www.state.gov
- http://www.defenselink.mil
- http://www.usdoj.gov
- http://www.nsa.gov

National Security Archive

- http://www.gwu.edu/~nsarchiv/

Congressional Oversight Committees

- http://www.senate.gov
- http://intelligence.house.gov
- http://www.gpoaccess.gov/congress/house/permintel/index.html

Association of Former Intelligence Officers

- http://www.afio.com

National Military Intelligence Association

- http://www.nmia.org

Federation of American Scientists

- http://www.fas.org

Counterintelligence

- http://www.ncix.gov
- http://www.fbi.gov/hq/ci/cointell.htm

Intelligence Reports

- http://www.gpoaccess.gov/int/report.html (Aspin-Brown Commission, 1996)
- http://www.gpo.gov/congress/house/intel/ic21/ic21_toc.html (HPSCI Staff Report, 1996)
- http://www.fas.org/irp/congress/1998_cr/s980731-rumsfeld.htm (Rumsfeld Commission, 1998)
- http://www.fas.org/irp/cia/product/jeremiah.html (Jeremiah Report on Indian nuclear tests, 1998)
- https://www.cia.gov/csi/books/shermankent/toc.html (commentary on famed CIA analyst Sherman Kent)
- http://www.dni.gov/nic/foia_vietnam_content.html (Vietnam documents)

- https://www.cia.gov/csi/books/princeton/index
  .html (Soviet NIEs)

- http://www.fas.org/irp/congress/2004_rpt/h10-
  558.pdf (HPSCI Report on Humint)

- http://www.hanford.gov/oci/maindocs/ci_r_
  docs/amescase.pdf (SSCI Report on Ames)

- http://govinfo.library.unt.edu/nssg/Reports/re
  ports.htm (Hart-Rudman Commission, 2001)

- http://www.faqs.org/docs/911/911Report.html
  (Kean Commission, 2004)

- http://www.wmd.gov/report/ (Silberman-Robb
  Commission, 2005) ◆

Select Bibliography

Aldrich, Richard J. 2002. *The Hidden Hand: Britain, America, and Cold War Secret Intelligence.* Woodstock, NY: Overlook Press, 2002.

Anderson, Jack. 1973. "How the CIA Snooped Inside Russia,"*Washington Post* (December 10): B17.

Andrew, Christopher. 1995. *For the President's Eyes Only: Secret Intelligence and the American Presidency From Washington to Bush.* New York: HarperCollins.

Aspin-Brown Commission. 1996. *Preparing for the 21st Century: An Appraisal of U.S. Intelligence.* Report of the Commission on the Roles and Capabilities of the United States Intelligence Community. Washington, DC: Government Printing Office.

Bamford, James. 1984. *The Puzzle Palace.* Boston: Houghton Mifflin.

Berkowitz, Bruce, and Allen Goodman. 2000. *Best Truth: Intelligence in the Information Age.* New Haven, CT: Yale University Press.

Betts, Richard K. 2002. "Fixing Intelligence," *Foreign Affairs* 81 (January–February): 43–59.

Bissell, Richard M., Jr., with Jonathan E. Lewis and Frances T. Rudlo. 1996. *Reflections of a Cold War.* New Haven, CT: Yale University Press.

Born, Hans, Loch K. Johnson, and Ian Leigh. 2005. *Who's Watching the Spies? Establishing Intelligence Service Accountability.* Washington, DC: Potomac Books.

Brugioni, Dino A. 1969. "The Unidentifieds," *Studies in Intelligence* (Summer): 1–20.

Burrows, William E. 1986. *Deep Black: Space Espionage and National Security.* New York: Random House.

Campbell, Duncan. 2003. "Afghan Prisoners Beaten to Death," *The Guardian* (March 7): 1.

Central Intelligence Agency. 1983. *Fact Book on Intelligence.*

Church Committee (Select Committee to Study Governmental Operations with Respect to Intelligence Activities). 1975a. Declassified CIA memorandum, Committee files, U.S. Senate, 94th Cong., 2d Sess.

——. 1975b. "Alleged Assassination Plots Involving Foreign Leaders," *Interim Report. S. Rept. No. 94–465.* Washington, DC: U.S. Government Printing Office.

——. 1976. *Final Report, Sen. Rept. No. 94–755,* vol. 1. Washington, DC: U.S. Government Printing Office.

Cirincione, Joseph. 2000. "Assessing the Assessment: The 1999 National Intelligence Estimate of the Ballistic Missile Threat," *Nonproliferation Review* 7 (Spring): 125–137.

Cohen, William S., and George J. Mitchell. 1988. *Men of Zeal: A Candid Inside Story of the Iran-Contra Hearings.* New York: Viking.

Colby, William E., and Peter Forbath. 1978. *Honorable Men: My Life in the CIA.* New York: Simon & Schuster.

Commission on Government Security, Report. 1957. Washington, DC: U.S. Government Printing Office.

Cradock, Percy. 2002. *Know Your Enemy: How the Joint Intelligence Committee Saw the World.* London: John Murray.

Currie, James. 1998. "Iran-*Contra* and Congressional Oversight of the CIA," *International Journal of Intelligence and Counterintelligence* 11 (Summer): 185–210.

Gates, Robert M. 1996. *From the Shadows.* New York: Simon & Schuster.

Godson, Roy S. 1996. *Dirty Tricks or Trump Cards: U.S. Covert Action and Counterintelligence.* Washington, DC: Brassey's, 1996.

Graham, Bob, with Jeff Nussbaum. 2004. *Intelligence Matters.* New York: Random House.

Halpern, Samuel, and Hayden B. Peake, "Did Angleton Jail Nosenko?" *International Journal of Intelligence and Counterintelligence* 3 (Winter): 451–464.

Handel, Michael. 1977. "The Yom Kippur War and the Inevitability of Surprise," *International Studies Quarterly* 21, 3: 461–501.

Harden, Toby. 2003. "CIA 'Pressure' on Al Qaeda Chief," *Washington Post* (March 6): A1.

Hastedt, Glenn. 1986. "The Constitutional Control of Intelligence," *Intelligence and National Security* 1 (May): 255–271.

Hennessy, Peter. 2003. *The Secret State: Whitehall and the Cold War.* London: Penguin.

Herman, Michael. 1996. *Intelligence Power in Peace and War.* New York: Cambridge University Press.

Heuer, Richard J., Jr. 1999. *Psychology of Intelligence Analysis.* Washington, DC: Center for the Study of Intelligence.

——. 1981. "Strategic Deception and Counterdeception," *International Studies Quarterly* 25 (June): 294–327.

Hitz, Frederick P. 2004. *The Great Game: The Myth and Reality of Espionage.* New York: Knopf.

Hulnick, Arthur S. 1986. "The Intelligence Producer-Policy Consumer Linkage: A Theoretical Approach," *Intelligence and National Security* 1 (May): 212–233.

——. 1999. *Fixing the Spy Machine: Preparing American Intelligence for the Twenty-First Century.* Westport, CT: Praeger.

Jackson, William R. 1990. "Congressional Oversight of Intelligence: Search for a Framework," *Intelligence and National Security* 5 (July): 113–137.

Jeffreys-Jones, Rhodri. 1989. *The CIA and American Democracy.* New Haven, CT: Yale University Press.

Jervis, Robert. 1986–87. "Intelligence and Foreign Policy," *International Security* 11 (Winter): 141–161.

Johnson, Loch K. 1980. "The U.S. Congress and the CIA: Monitoring the Dark Side of Government," *Legislative Studies Quarterly* 5 (November): 477–99.

——. 1985. *A Season Inquiry: The Senate Intelligence Investigation.* Lexington: University Press of Kentucky.

——. 1989. *America's Secret Power: The CIA in a Democratic Society.* New York: Oxford University Press.

——. 1996. *Secret Agencies: U.S. Intelligence in a Hostile World.* New Haven, CT: Yale University Press.

——. 2000. *Bombs, Bugs, Drugs, and Thugs: Intelligence and America's Quest for Security,* p. 177. New York: New York University Press.

——. 2001. "The CIA's Weakest Link," *Washington Monthly* 33 (July/August): 9–14.

——. 2004. "The Aspin-Brown Intelligence Inquiry: Behind the Closed Doors of a Blue Ribbon Commission," *Studies in Intelligence* 48 (Winter), pp. 1-20.

——. 2007. *Seven Sins of American Foreign Policy.* New York: Longman.

——, (ed.). 2007a. *Strategic Intelligence,* 5 Vols. Westport, CT: Praeger.

——, (ed.). 2007b. *Handbook of Intelligence Studies.* London: Routledge.

Johnson, Paul. 1997. "No Cloak and Dagger Required: Intelligence Support to U.N. Peacekeeping," *Intelligence and National Security* 12 (October): 102–112.

Johnson, William R. 1987. *Thwarting Enemies at Home and Abroad: How to Be a Counterintelligence Office.* Bethesda, MD: Stone Trail Press.

Kaiser, Frederick M. 1992. "Congress and the Intelligence Community: Taking the Road Less Traveled," in Roger H. Davidson (ed.), *The Postreform Congress.* New York: St. Martin's Press: 279–300.

Kam, Ephraim. 1988. *Surprise Attack.* Cambridge: Harvard University Press.

Kent, Sherman. 1949. *Strategic Intelligence for American World Policy.* Princeton: Princeton University Press.

Knott, Stephen F. 1996. *Secret and Sanctioned: Covert Operations and the American Presidency.* New York: Oxford University Press.

Kramer, Mark. 2002. "Oversight of Russian's Intelligence and Security Agencies: The Need for and Prospects of Democratic Control," PONARS Policy Memo 281, <http://www.csis.org/ruseura/ponars/policymemos/pm_0281.pdf>.

Lowenthal, Mark M. 2005. *U.S. Intelligence: Evolution and Anatomy,* 3rd ed. Westport, CT: Praeger.

——. 2006. *Intelligence: From Secrets to Policy,* 3rd ed. Washington, DC: CQ Press.

Masterman, Sir John. 1972. *Double Cross System of the War of 1939–45.* New Haven, CT: Yale University Press.

May, Ernest R. 1992. "Intelligence: Backing Into the Future," *Foreign Affairs* 71 (Summer): 63–72.

Millis, John. 1998. Speech, Central Intelligence Retiree's Association, Langley, Virginia.

Naylor, Sean. 2003. "The Lessons of Anaconda," *New York Times* (March 2): A13.

9/11 Commission. 2004. *Report.* New York: Norton.

Odom, William. 2003. *Fixing Intelligence.* New Haven, CT: Yale University Press.

Omsted, Kathryn. 1996. *Challenging the Secret Government: The Post-Watergate Investigations of the CIA and FBI.* Chapel Hill: University of North Carolina Press.

——. 2002. *Red Spy Queen: A Biography of Elizabeth Bentley.* Chapel Hill: University of North Carolina Press.

Pelosi, Nancy (D, California). 2002. Remarks to Loch K. Johnson, Athens, Georgia (November 26).

Powers, Thomas. 1979. *The Man Who Kept the Secrets: Richard Helms and the CIA.* New York: Knopf.

Prados, John. 1986. *Presidents' Secret Wars: CIA and Pentagon Covert Operations Since World War II.* New York: Dial.

Ransom, Harry Howe. 1970. *The Intelligence Establishment.* Cambridge, MA: Harvard University Press.

Rashid, A. 1999. "The Taliban: Exporting Extremism," *Foreign Affairs* 78: 22–35.

Richelson, Jeffrey. 1999. *The U.S. Intelligence Community,* 4th ed. Cambridge, MA: Ballinger.

Rockefeller Commission. 1975. *Report.* Washington, DC: Government Printing Office.

Schelling, Thomas C. 1962. "Preface" to Roberta Wohlstetter, *Pearl Harbor: Warning and Decision.* Stanford, CA: Stanford University Press.

Schwarz, Frederick A. O., Jr. 1987. "Recalling Major Lessons of the Church Committee," *New York Times* (July 20): A25.

Scoville, Herbert. 1976. "Is Espionage Necessary for Our Security?" *Foreign Affairs* 54 (April): 482–495.

Senate Select Committee on Secret Military Assistance to Iran and the Nicaraguan Opposition and House Select Committee to Investigate Covert Arms Transactions with Iran. 1987. *Hearings and Final Report.* Washington, DC: Government Printing Office.

Shulsky, Abram N., and Gary J. Schmitt. 1993. *Silent Warfare: Understanding the World of Intelligence,* 2nd rev. ed. Washington, DC: Brassey's.

Sims, Jennifer E., and Burton Gerber (eds.). 2005. *Transforming U.S. Intelligence.* Washington, DC: Georgetown University Press.

Smist, Frank J., Jr. 1994. *Congress Oversees the United States Intelligence Community,* 2nd ed. Knoxville: University of Tennessee Press.

Snider, L. Britt. 1997. *Sharing Secrets With Lawmakers: Congress as a User of Intelligence.* Washington, DC: Central Intelligence Agency, Center for the Study of Intelligence.

Steele, Robert D. 1999. "Relevant Information and All-Source Analysis: The Emerging Revolution," *American Intelligence Journal* 19: 23–30.

Theoharis, Athan G. 1978. *Spying on Americans: Political Surveillance From Hoover to the Huston Plan.* Philadelphia: Temple University Press.

—— (ed.). 2006. *The Central Intelligence Agency: Security Under Scrutiny.* Westport, CT: Greenwood Press.

Treverton, Gregory F. 1987. *Covert Action: The Limits of Intervention in the Postwar World.* New York: Basic Books.

——. 2001. *Reshaping National Intelligence for an Age of Information.* New York: Cambridge University Press.

Troy, Thomas F. 1991–92. "The 'Correct' Definition of Intelligence," *International Journal of Intelligence and Counterintelligence* 5 (Winter): 433–454.

Turner, Michael A. 2005. *Why Secret Intelligence Fails.* Washington, DC: Potomac Books.

Turner, Stansfield. 1985. *Secrecy and Democracy: The CIA in Transition.* Boston: Houghton Mifflin.

——. 2005. *Burn Before Reading.* New York: Hyperion.

Usowski, Peter S. 1988. "John McCone and the Cuban Missile Crisis: A Persistent Approach to the Intelligence-Policy Relationship," *International Journal of Intelligence and Counterintelligence* 2 (Winter): 547–576.

Waller, Michael J. 1994. *Secret Empire: The KGB in Russia Today.* Boulder, CO: Westview.

Westerfield, H. Bradford. 1995. *Inside CIA's Private World: Declassified Articles From the Agency's Internal Journal, 1995–1992.* New Haven, CT: Yale University Press.

Wicker, Tom, et al. 1966. "CIA Operations: A Plot Scuttled." *New York Times,* April 25: A1.

Wirtz, James J. 1998. "Organizing for Crisis Intelligence: Lessons from the Cuban Missile Crisis," in James G. Blight and David A. Welch (eds.), *Intelligence and the Cuban Missile Crisis.* London: Frank Cass.

——. 1991. *Intelligence Failure in War: The American Military and the Tet Offensive.* Ithaca, NY: Cornell University Press.

Wise, David. 1976. *The American Police State: The Government Against the People.* New York: Random House.

Wohlstetter, Roberta. 1962. *Pearl Harbor: Warning and Decision.* Stanford: Stanford University Press.

Woolsey, R. James. 1993. Testimony, *Hearings,* U.S. Senate Select Committee on Intelligence, 103rd Cong., 2nd Sess.: March 6.

Zegart, Amy B. 2007. *Failure and Consequence: Understanding U.S. Intelligence and the Origins of 9/11.* Princeton, NJ: Princeton University Press.

Zuehlke, Arthur A. 1980. In Roy S. Godson (ed.), *Intelligence Requirements for the 1980s: Counterintelligence.* Washington, DC: National Strategy Information Center. ✦

Name Index

Subject Index